Bernard P Zeigler

POLYTECHNIC INSTITUTE OF BROOKLYN

MICROWAVE RESEARCH INSTITUTE

SYMPOSIA SERIES

I	Modern Network Synthesis	April 1952
II	Nonlinear Circuit Analysis	April 1953
III	Information Networks	April 1954
IV	Modern Advances in Microwave Techniques	November 1954
V	Modern Network Synthesis II	April 1955
VI	Nonlinear Circuit Analysis II	April 1956
VII	The Role of Solid State Phenomena in Electric Circuits	April 1957
VIII	Electronic Waveguides	April 1958
IX	Millimeter Waves	March–April 1959
X	Active Networks and Feedback Systems	April 1960
XI	Electromagnetics and Fluid Dynamics of Gaseous Plasma	April 1961
XII	Mathematical Theory of Automata	April 1962
XIII	Optical Masers	April 1963
XIV	Quasi-Optics	June 1964
XV	System Theory	April 1965
XVI	Generalized Networks	April 1966
XVII	Modern Optics	March 1967
XVIII	Turbulence of Fluids and Plasmas	April 1968
XIX	Computer Processing in Communications	April 1969
XX	Submillimeter Waves	March–April 1970
XXI	Computers and Automata	April 1971
XXII	Computer-Communications Networks and Teletraffic	April 1972

Sponsored by
The Polytechnic Institute of Brooklyn
Microwave Research Institute

In Cooperation with
The Institute of Electrical and Electronics Engineers
Computer Society
The Society for Industrial and Applied Mathematics

Cosponsored by
The Air Force Office of Scientific Research
The Office of Naval Research
The U.S. Army Research Office

Arrangements for this Symposium were sponsored in part by the Joint Services Electronics Program under Contract Number F44620-69-C-0047.

DISTRIBUTORS: WILEY-INTERSCIENCE, A DIVISION OF JOHN WILEY & SONS, INC. NEW YORK/LONDON/SYDNEY/TORONTO

PROCEEDINGS OF THE SYMPOSIUM ON

COMPUTERS AND AUTOMATA

New York, N.Y., April 13–15, 1971

Microwave Research Institute Symposia Series
JEROME FOX, Editor

Volume XXI

POLYTECHNIC PRESS
OF THE
POLYTECHNIC INSTITUTE OF BROOKLYN, BROOKLYN, N. Y.

Edited by
Jerome Fox

Associate Editor
Mark Howard Schlam

Library of Congress Catalog Card Number 70-185593

TABLE OF CONTENTS

FOREWORD

WELCOMING ADDRESS

DR. BENJAMIN ADLER
Acting President, Polytechnic Institute of Brooklyn

It is a privilege and pleasure for me to welcome this group to this MRI Symposium. Those of you who have attended previous symposia certainly remember that I was introduced as Acting President of Polytechnic Institute of Brooklyn on those occasions. I am getting to be known as the perennial Acting President, and this is one of the areas I want to discuss with you this morning.

The papers seem very interesting and I want to get down to being a listener. But I do want to point out to you that some of the problems that we have had for the past two years, are related to not having a permanent president. When President Weber reached retirement age and left us, I happened to be available and agreed to pitch in for a few months, and here I still am, two years later. I was very surprised when Jerry Fox showed me the preliminary copy of the prepared papers and the speeches from the last symposium on *Submillimeter Waves*. I remember making some remarks, and when I opened the page and looked at some of the things I said, I'm very much afraid that I am going to repeat the same things that I said at that time—but I think I can give you some encouragement towards some progress along the lines of solving our problems.

At that time, we had two problems: We needed a President; and we were trying to work out an arrangement with the State University. Right now, we have two problems, and yes, you guessed what they are. But I must say that we are very, very close to working out an arrangement with both the State University and the City University of New York. This has not yet been announced simply because we don't have all the details worked out, but one of the little details in connection with that move has to do with the banner you see right in front of the rostrum.

We haven't used (and I don't know where they dug this old banner up) *BPI* as our identification for quite a number of years. Right now, it is *PIB*, Polytechnic Institute of Brooklyn. Well, Brooklyn Polytechnic Institute may again be resurrected as we join one of the public institutions in New York State. Our identification as a Brooklyn-based Institution appears to be developing as an important ingredient in completing an arrangement with CUNY. So I want to tell Jerry Fox and those who run this meeting, "Wherever you found that banner, try to find some more because I think we may need them again." In any case, I think that things are looking up and we are moving rapidly toward an arrangement that will assure us of continuity. We have a President Designate who has not yet been announced simply because he will only come with us after we complete our arrangements with the State and the City, and I think we may have an announcement to make within a month.

Be that as it may, I just want to express my sincere thanks to those who are cooperating with us in making this symposium possible and mention in particular the value of the support that we continue to receive from the Joint Services. We call this our Base program which has been going on ever since Dr. Ernst Weber started MRI. It started with a different format in the beginning, but it's only through this continuous activity and support that the Polytechnic has been able to achieve its level of excellence in the areas covered by MRI: *electronics, electrophysics, electrical engineering,* and so forth.

Today our symposium is in the area of information science and you might ask, "Why information science with the Microwave Research Institute?" One good answer is that we happen to have the facilities, the backing, and the funding to put on a show like this and to attract the kind of speakers that we have with us today. The other is that information science is the kind of discipline that pervades all areas of activity and definitely involves communications. We're going to see a tremendous explosion in this area, which makes this symposium so important at this time. Again, let me thank you for coming. I want to wish you every success for a fine and beneficial meeting.

GREETINGS FROM THE COSPONSORING AGENCIES

MR. PETER R. MURRAY

Deputy Director of Laboratories for Technology, Air Force Systems Command

It gives me great pleasure to participate in this twenty-first annual symposium arranged by the Microwave Research Institute of the Polytechnic Institute of Brooklyn, and to represent the Departments of the Army, Navy, and Air Force in extending best wishes for a very successful meeting on computers and automata.

I must say that I think your forward planning committee did an excellent job of picking a proper subject—for it is timely, important, and the effects can be extremely far reaching. The occasion of this symposia is equally as important as the subject—since in this overall area we universally suffer from a very-large communications "gap."

If just one person in attendance goes away with something of importance that he or she didn't know before, and does something about it, then all your work, all the travel, everything will have been amply repaid over and over again, and the symposia will be a howling success. Yet how often can that success be so obscure that even the participants have difficulty on "hind-sighting" later on.

As you know, we in the DoD have been under some criticism as part of the MIC—the military industrial complex, that is. But welcome aboard my friends—because in the mind's eye of the public, that C in MIC can just as easily stand for COMPUTER! Ask the man who has been billed wrongly, or hasn't been paid on time, or didn't get his state car license forms, etc., etc., etc.!

Now the remarkable thing to me about all this computer business is how the word "large" has changed its meaning over the years. After all, I visited whirlwind in the basement of MIT when it was working out the fundamentals of sector air defense. How I remember the racks and racks of relays and hot cathodes—especially 6SN7 twin-triodes. They must have been made by the billions! And that was a large computer, but only physically by today's standards. Today with large-scale integrated microcircuits, computers with more capability can be misplaced!

To those of us involved in airborne applications this downward trend in size, weight, and power required is extremely important. It has added an element of information and signal processing on a scale we hadn't dreamed of twenty years ago! But with it has come a driving responsibility to do our homework in the information-handling "architecting"—so that software and hardware flow together easily, and swiftly, and efficiently in order to serve man—not deliver him to an early grave!

And automata to me seem to be a very logical extension and exploitation of our expanding capability to do both software and hardware for increasingly-complex situations. But I plead with you to occasionally take time to translate this potential into clear, ordinary English for those people who have to make pivotal decisions! Just remember that although very-logical processes carried on serially and in parallel at nearly the speed of light may remain totally logical to you, there are many to whom it remains "black magic"!

We badly need information processing "architects" and those who can describe such work clearly. Perhaps in the papers today, we shall have the very good fortune to spot some of each! Thank you!

MR. ROBERT H. TANNER

Vice President, The Institute of Electrical and Electronics Engineers

I am very pleased to bring you the greetings and good wishes of the Institute of Electrical and Electronics Engineers, one of the cosponsors of this annual symposium on Computers and Automata. This has been a long and happy association and I hope that it will last for many years, despite the changing pressures which beset our profession and industry. Over the past year, particularly in some segments, these pressures have largely been negative and have left in their path unpleasant vacuums in many job situations. Unfortunately, we have become so accustomed over many years to the full employment of engineers that the present unemployment has caught many of us unaware, and unprepared to deal with it, and much individual unhappiness has resulted.

Many people are asking, and rightly so, what IEEE is doing about the present situation, and though my time is short I would like to try and answer this question. Immediately the seriousness of the trend was recognized, the Executive Committee and Board of Directors began to study ways in which the Institute could help those of its members who had lost their jobs or were in danger of so doing. The results of these deliberations are now appearing in a series of interconnected actions which have been announced month by month in the "Inside IEEE" column in *Spectrum*. The agreement with NSPE to provide certain useful services to IEEE members for much less than full membership in NSPE; the halving of membership dues for unemployed members; cooperation with AIAA (whose membership is drawn from the hardest-hit sector of the industry) in seminars on unemployment; and lastly a positive drive, spearheaded by various U.S.-government departments, but with IEEE taking a lead among the technical and professional organizations, to set up action committees in the nine main centres of technological unemployment; these are the beginnings of a program which IEEE is undertaking, within the limits of its constitution, to improve conditions, and set the industry back on the track to renewed prosperity and full employment.

Should we stay within the limits of our constitution, or should we reorient the Institute along the lines of the American Medical or Bar Associations, so that we could carry out direct lobbying to influence U.S. governments? This is a big question which cannot be dealt with in the two minutes I have left. But we should remember that IEEE is, as were its predecessors before it, a technical rather than a professional organization, composed of only a portion of the whole engineering profession, yet covering this portion on an international basis. In my opinion, a viable professional society should embrace the whole of its profession, but on a national basis since the influencing of legislation in clearly a national affair. It would no doubt be possible to restructure IEEE into such a format, but in so doing it would lose almost all of its present characteristics, and would become in fact another NSPE limited to electrical engineering, and thus with less power behind its pronouncements. At the Monday night seminar at the recent New York convention, one speaker claimed that 50,000 of our members wanted IEEE to become a union. Assuming for a moment he is right, two points spring to the mind: firstly there must then be 120,000 who *don't* want it to become a union; and secondly, the 50,000 could form a much better organization from scratch, rather than trying to convert the IEEE. In my opinion, the Institute would not make a very good union: I know for certain that I wouldn't make a good union leader!

Well, as they say in the magazines, look for exciting new developments in forthcoming issues of "Inside IEEE." Meanwhile, I wish you an interesting and profitable symposium.

DR. DONALD L. THOMSEN, JR.

Chairman of the Board of Trustees, Society for Industrial and Applied Mathematics

On behalf of the Society for Industrial and Applied Mathematics (SIAM) I am very happy to greet you this morning on the occasion of the twenty-first Polytechnic Institute of Brooklyn Symposium, and at the same time express SIAM's appreciation for the invitation to participate formally as a cooperating professional society. In particular, I bring you greetings from SIAM's president, Dr. B. H. Colvin, Head of Mathematics and Information Science, the Boeing Company, who should be here speaking to you instead of myself. Dr. Colvin told me last evening that he deeply regretted he was unable to come East this week and attend these sessions; he commented specifically to me noting their high quality.

SIAM is particularly glad to cooperate in this symposium since the objectives as stated in your advance program parallel to a considerable degree those of SIAM. The idea of "bringing together workers in both the field of computers and of automata," if one extends in a perfectly-natural way the field of application and simultaneously places mathematics in juxtaposition with automata (which your advance program also shows), is in harmony with SIAM's stated objectives to "further the application of mathematics to industry and science and promote basic research in mathematics leading to new techniques useful to industry and science."

It was in an atmosphere of a widening gulf, especially between those in industry who had real problems requiring mathematical analysis and those who had become overly enamored with the beauties of mathematical abstractions, that SIAM came into existence in 1952. I hasten to add that the reappearance of such a gulf even within SIAM itself is an ever-present possibility, maybe I should even say threat. And I would like to tell in this connection a short one on ourselves.

Several years ago SIAM held a meeting whose principal theme was combinatorics. The comment reached me afterwards that it was an excellent meeting with regard to the papers presented but it might just as well have been sponsored by a pure-mathematics society! Particularly for a field of mathematics related to the development of digital computers, one would have thought SIAM would not have strayed in this manner from its fundamental objectives. Straying once in a while is, however, probably not all that bad—it can serve to reinforce one's fundamental objectives.

The most enduring mathematics seems to have its origin in man's attempts to understand some real-world phenomenon and also in some deep involvement as well in that same real-world phenomenon. The abstractions which come later on that base can also become useful in again solving real-world problems. In a similar way this symposium reflects the joining of "workers in both the field of computers and automata," which had its "origin in the computer field" and has subsequently "developed independently."

Such a symposium as this one should serve to bridge if not to narrow or even prevent the kind of gulf which might otherwise develop as in the referenced instance in mathematics. The potential is evidently there for this to happen for I have already heard a distinguished head of a computer-science department express concern over the tendency of some computer-science departments, including his own, to follow a history similar to that of many mathematics departments. In fact, it is this very attitude of unconcern toward the solution of real-world problems on the part of such a relatively-large number of mathematicians that has contributed to the ingrown atmosphere of these same departments and eventually, at least in part, to their economic plight today. And the same could happen to computer science. Symposia with an excellent-quality program such as this one provide a deterrent to such a course and also reflect a positive anticipation of the potential dangers to such a course in the future.

As you can see, we believe this symposium represents a major step in the right direction.

SIAM is very glad to have been invited once again (for the fourth time I believe) to cooperate in this outstanding annual event whose purpose and philosophy it enthusiastically applauds.

THE POTENTIAL OF THE COMPUTER IN EDUCATION

Dr. M. E. Van Valkenburg
Chairman, Department of Electrical Engineering, Princeton University

As you read the title, you must have sensed that the most important or significant word is *potential*. The use of the computer in education is generally accepted from the elementary to college levels, although there remain many problems of implementation. The word "potential" should imply something about the future, and to discuss the future, we should assess where we now stand.

In the long run, the kind of education we give must relate to the real world after graduation. We know that the time constant for this adjustment is sometimes long. My own view is that it won't be long until everyone working in technology or science will work with a computer terminal of one kind or another near at hand. The computer will permeate most of our human creative effort, as well as our accounting and record keeping. I do not believe that everyone who uses the computer will understand its workings anymore than I believe that all people using the automobile understand it. In other words, the computer will take its place as one of the fruits of technology that is accepted and utilized, but not worshipped. I am reminded of an article in a recent issue of *DAEDALUS* by H. J. Hanham. After describing the use of the computer by historians, he says: "For most working historians, the greatest innovation of recent times has been the *Xerox machine*, not the computer." I will resist the temptation to ask you whether, if you had to give up one or the other, the Xerox or the computer would go!

Returning to an assessment of the present of the use of the computer in education, let me describe my views in terms of various levels of instruction. I shall confine my comments to engineering and science, initially at least. My listing:

(1) A course in FORTRAN or equivalent. Such instruction is offered at all universities and many high schools. It is available in various forms of self instruction

(2) The use of simulation languages, such as, ECAP, SIMSCRIPT, STRESS and the like. This is widespread but not universal in engineering schools, and in other isolated disciplines

(3) The use of the minicomputer—for programming, hands-on experience or the control of experiments

(4) The foundations of computer science and engineering. Some canonical courses are developing at schools with computer-science programs

---

Address presented at the banquet following the opening day of the Symposium on Computers and Automata, Polytechnic Institute of Brooklyn, April 13–15, 1971.

(5) Digital systems in engineering. The engineer works with systems—more and more of these systems include a digital computer, or, at least, digital signals and processors. The analysis of such systems as well as their design is an important area of engineering education that we are just beginning to explore
(6) Finally, digital-computer engineering—both hardware and software.

Now let me work *backwards* and comment on each of the levels I have described.

The levels I have described as (5) and (6) reside primarily with the experts whose daily work consists of solving real-world computer problems. These experts are largely self educated, or educated by "on-the-job" training. The information is not yet codified for presentation to students in the classroom. And progress toward a set of canonical textbooks is painfully slow.

The areas represented by Levels (4), (5), and (6) is that which has received primary emphasis by the COSINE Committee. COSINE is an acronym for Computers in Electrical Engineering; this COSINE Committee is associated with the Commission on Education of the National Academy of Engineering, and operates through support by the National Science Foundation.

May I digress long enough to tell you something of this Committee of which I have served as Chairman since 1968, having recently been replaced by C. L. Coates. COSINE was formed in 1965 to suggest direction and encourage action in incorporating the computer in the electrical engineering curriculum. This has been done through meetings of department chairmen, meetings with representatives of industry and government, summer institutes, and issuing reports by the committee or prepared by appointed task forces. The titles of reports by these task forces indicate the thrust of committee efforts:

(1) "Some Specifications for a Computer-Oriented First Course in Electrical Engineering"
(2) "An Undergraduate Electrical-Engineering Course on Computer Organization"
(3) "Some Specifications for an Undergraduate Course in Digital Subsystems"
(4) "An Undergraduate Computer-Engineering Option for Electrical Engineering"
(5) "Impact of Computers on Electrical Engineering Education—A View from Industry"
(6) "Digital Systems Laboratories—Courses and Laboratory Development"
(7) "Computer-Aided Design"
(8) "An Undergraduate Course on Operating-Systems Principles"
(9) "Minicomputers".

There has been a strong organizational trend to provide computer engineering as an option or program within electrical engineering. In a survey I completed in February 1971, in which 203 departments responded, 87 indicated that they now offer an undergraduate option or program in electrical engineering. An additional 35 without such options now indicated new plans were in progress for their implementation within the next year.

Returning now to my level classifications, Level (3) is the minicomputer. As you all know, we are in the midst of a revolution in minicomputers. The cost is low and getting lower. The machine offers the advantages in education of hands-on kind of experience (which is certainly not practical in computer centers), and real-time control of experiments. It is possible to connect such machines to large computers such as are found in computer centers, as was recently done by a small group of undergraduates at Princeton. The potential of the minicomputer in engineering education is just beginning to be realized, and is certainly exciting for the future!

Level (2) was the use of a simulation language in instruction, such as ECAP, SIMSCRIPT, etc. One of the first experiences with the use of such a compiler in electrical engineering was by William H. Huggins and his associates at the Johns Hopkins University. Using a program known as JOBSHOP, students at the sophomore level designed electronic circuits and assessed the economic merit of their design. Conceptually, it was shown that the sophomores could do a respectable job of design of transistor circuits with little background and little instructions. The motivational factor was very large, of course, as others have shown since that time. The real barrier, one that comes up again and again, is the *cost* of instruction for a class. Now, we have been in an era when such costs were payed for using "funny money," funds allocated by the University for education, or the equivalent of money used to pay for time that the computer would otherwise not be operating. Alas, the days of funny money are also coming to an end. Faced with real money barriers, many universities have had to limit the educational use of the computer in spite of any advantages that may have been demonstrated. The real cost is likely \$5 per hour of \$65/student/subject, as computed by L. D. Smullin of M.I.T. It becomes clear that a limitation must be placed on the extent to which students use the computer, unless some breakthrough in financing is found.

It would be unfair not to mention that paralleling, or even ahead of the activities I have described and attributed to the influence of COSINE, have been the action of the C^3S group of the ACM (Curriculum Committee in Computer Science of the Association for Computing Machinery). Certainly their model curricula have had a profound influence on the development of computer science, especially within the liberal-arts environment.

Now we arrive at Level (1), the so-called FORTRAN course taken by all students who find the interest. With a few exceptions, these students are in engineering, science, and mathematics. Such courses are relatively easy to implement, there being no scarcity of textbooks, and relatively inexpensive in terms of computer time. There would be no problem here except for one fact: The course is taken primarily by students in engineering, science, and mathematics! What about the "Silent Majority"?

This fact has been recognized in many places. Courses have been organized with the informal title of "Computing for People Who Hate the Digital Computer." This is one of the problems that we face. This is not really Level (1), for reasons I will discuss. Perhaps we should call it Level (0).

The Level (0) course at Harvard is taught by Bossert and has an enrollment of about 600 students! A similar course is taught at Dartmouth by Kurtz and others with an enrollment as high as 400. At Princeton, we hope to enter this game next year, with a course offered by Hamming. In announcing his appointment at Yale, it was indicated that Perlis will stress "the use of the computer by the nonscientist."

There are several problems of Level (0) people, and these problems spill over into Level (1), (2), and (3) people, too. Perhaps I may use my son, David, to illustrate one of these. David was introduced to the computer by a friend, a member of his peer group—not by an instructor or his father. When he grasped the basic idea, he became totally immersed, and spent hours at all times of the day and night at the computer center, trying new ideas, solving problems, and exploring his new discovery. I remember that he tried to write a program to produce all of the verb forms in Latin, since he was taking Latin at that time. After this initial burst of enthusiasm, his use of the computer has dropped off, so that he seldom goes there any more. He can use the machine when he needs to. The problem is that he seldom has that need. And he has tired of inventing problems just to show that he can do it. Lesson: What good is a digital computer if you can solve all of your problems with the slide rule or on the back of an envelope?

David's problem was *not* that you communicate with a computer in a very unnatural way, with the annoying thought that the language is subject to almost constant change. Even FORTRAN was too complicated for many. Was not the breakthrough at Dartmouth produced by the implementation of a simple language, BASIC? The use of a mathematically- (or logically-) oriented language that is complex and, for most people, unnatural is too much of a barrier for many people—especially for "people who hate the computer."

It is not obvious that a better language will be the answer. The real boon for many people will be the development of a system of computer graphics, with ease in communication, and also ease in interaction. We are dealing with a generation of students who are chronic television viewers. It seems likely that they will learn better by an input that is neither the spoken word, the written word, nor the typewritten word. We have a long way to go before this is possible within our financial resources!

Let me turn next to an even more basic problem: The mathematical preparation of students for engineering and science has not yet entered the computer age!

It is nothing new to you that the computer operates in terms of discrete mathematics, that we never approach the limit so that $\Delta t \longrightarrow dt$ has meaning. You understood this at the beginning of your formal course in calculus, for example; the remainder of the course was devoted to the limit case of the integral rather than the summation derivative over a differential increment.

Even numerical methods were introduced early in your mathematical training, but then likely forgotten as analytical methods became established. You, in the audience have returned to learn the discrete case, algorithm, numerical methods, and the rest. What would happen if we stressed this kind of mathematics in the beginning, treating the limit case as a special case—if at all? We have not tried it, except for a few small experiments, and so it is not possible to say.

The experiments that should be done are those involved with introducing courses to stress discrete mathematics, the algorithmic approach, meaningful numerical methods. We need less stress on theorem proving, on special tricks that may be used for the evaluation of certain classes of integrals. Indeed, we might question whether a course in calculus which is not organized is needed at all. What we really need is to rethink the structure of the mathematical training of students of engineering, perhaps science, too. Everything should be questioned. This is no mean task, of course; nor is the task of preparing suitable textbook material after the basic decisions have been made. We are talking in terms of tens of man-years of effort.

What are the obstacles to progress? I have mentioned a real one previously: cost. Funds available are diminishing as we enter the period of the "Seven Lean Years." The budgets of computer centers are tightening, and funds from the traditional sources for educational experimentation are drying up. There is also the question of manpower, or better the product of energy and manpower. There is always the question of lethargy. The old methods have worked well, haven't they? After all, all those attending this symposium are largely products of the old methods! Yet in each of us there must be the suspicion that it could be done easier, that there must be a logical order more effective than the one used in the past.

Let me close by complimenting those at the symposium on your choice of a field in which to work. You might have chosen a field reaching maturity where only small refinements are needed. Instead you have chosen one where we know no answers for sure, and only some of the questions. We have unfortunate constraints. Most important, I think, we have opportunity, enough to last for a long time.

PROGRAM

TUESDAY—APRIL 13, 1971

OPENING SESSION—9:30 A.M.

Chairman: A. A. Oliner
Polytechnic Institute of Brooklyn

Welcome
Dr. Benjamin Adler, *Acting President, Polytechnic Institute of Brooklyn*

Opening Remarks
For the Sponsoring Agencies and the Cooperating Societies
Mr. Peter R. Murray, *Deputy Director of Laboratories for Technology, Air Force Systems Command*
Mr. Robert H. Tanner, *Vice President, Institute of Electrical and Electronics Engineers*
Dr. Donald L. Thomsen, Jr., *Chairman of The Board of Trustees, Society for Industrial and Applied Mathematics*

SESSION I—INTRODUCTION

Chairman: E. J. Smith
Polytechnic Institute of Brooklyn

Computation Speed of Fixed and Self-Modifying Programs
J. Hartmanis, *Cornell University, Ithaca, NY*

Toward a Mathematical Semantics for Computer Languages
D. Scott, *Princeton University, Princeton, NJ;* and C. Strachey, *University of Oxford, England*

On the Design and Specification of a Common Base Language
J. B. Dennis, *Massachusetts Institute of Technology, Cambridge, MA*

SESSION II—2:00 P.M.
PROGRAMMING LANGUAGES

Chairman: A. A. Grau
Northwestern University, Evanston, IL

An ALGOL Compiler, Designed Using Automata Theory
P. M. Lewis and D. J. Rosenkrantz, *G.E. Research and Development Center, Schenectady, NY*

NUCLEOL—A Minimal List Processor and Its Formal Definition
J. Nievergelt, *University of Illinois, Urbana, IL*

On the Definition of Higher Level Language Machines
D. Bjørner, *IBM Research Laboratory, San Jose, CA*

Computer Program Models
C. V. Ramamoorthy, *University of Texas, Austin, TX*
Fuzzy Programs—Theory and Applications
S. K. Chang, *Cornell University, Ithaca, NY*

WEDNESDAY—APRIL 14, 1971

SESSION III—9:00 A.M.
OPERATING SYSTEMS

Chairman: H. W. Lawson, Jr.
Polytechnic Institute of Brooklyn

Design Principles for a High Performance System
H. Schorr, *IBM Thomas J. Watson Research Center, Yorktown Heights, NY*
An Approach to Hardware/Software Architectural Trade-Off Decisions
J. E. Deans and C. V. Ramamoorthy, *University of Texas, Austin, TX*
The Dynamic Variation of Software, Firmware and Hardware
D. Pager, *University of Hawaii, Honolulu, HI*
A Formal Microprogram Model of Parallelism and Register-Sharing
E. G. Coffman, Jr., *Pennsylvania State University, University Park, PA*
Toward Optimal Paginations for Structured Programs
L. Yelowitz, *Johns Hopkins University, Baltimore, MD*
Minimizing Wasted Space in Partitioned Segmentation
S. E. Gelenbe, *University of Michigan, Ann Arbor, MI* and, J. L. W. Kessels and J. C. A. Boekhorst, *Philips Research Laboratories, Waalre, The Netherlands*
Probability Models for Computer Systems
T. Gergely, *Hungarian Academy of Science, Budapest, Hungary*
On Transferences and Priorities in Computer Systems and Networks
J. Santos and M. I. Otero, *Universidad Nacional del Sur, Bahia Blanca, Argentina*
A Simple Model for Multiple Resource Allocation in Operating Systems
D. L. Epley, *University of Iowa, Iowa City, IA* and D. L. Boyd, *University of Minnesota, Minneapolis, MN*
Scheduling of Real-Time Computer Systems (Title only)*
D. L. Epley, *University of Iowa, Iowa City, IA*

---

*Papers designated (Title only) will be included in the published Proceedings but will not be read at the symposium.

SESSION IV—2:00 P.M.
COMPUTATION COMPLEXITY

Chairman: J. D. Ullman
Princeton University, Princeton, NJ

The Complexity of Combinatorial Computations: A Survey
E. L. Lawler, *University of California, Berkeley, CA*

Minimal Growth Rate Merge-Sort
M. E. Arkun, *Polytechnic Institute of Brooklyn*

Are Humanly Recognizable Patterns Effective?
R. J. Nelson, *Case Western Reserve University, Cleveland, OH*

Similarities in Games and Their Use in Strategy Construction
R. B. Banerji, *Case Western Reserve University, Cleveland, OH*

An Automaton Theoretic Approach to the FFT
M. Depeyrot, J. Mondelli, and J. P. Marmorat, *Centre d'Automatique, Fontainebleau, France*

On the Automatic Proof of the Correctness of Program-Schemata
M. Somalvico (*visiting Stanford University*), *Laboratorio di Calcolatori, Politechnico di Milano, Milan, Italy*

An Interactive System for Program Verification
T. Lyons and J. Bruno, *Princeton University, Princeton, NJ*

Subrecursive Programming Languages for $\mathcal{R}^n$
R. L. Constable, *Cornell University, Ithaca, NY*

THURSDAY—APRIL 15, 1971

SESSION V—9:00 A.M.
LOGICAL DESIGN

Chairman: R. E. Miller
IBM Watson Research Center, Yorktown Heights, NY

Ring Sum Expansions of Boolean Functions
M. Davio, *MBLE Research Laboratory, Brussels, Belgium*

The Lattice Structure of Graph Partitions
E. A. Schroeppel, *Polytechnic Institute of Brooklyn;* and A. C. McKellar, *IBM Watson Research Center, Yorktown Heights, NY*

Logical Design of Sequential Machines
V. G. Lazarev, *The Institute of Information Transmission Problems, Moscow, U.S.S.R.*

Methods for Realizing Sequential Machines on Identical Integrated Circuits
S. P. Kartashev, *Johns Hopkins University, Baltimore, MD*

Implementation of Checkable Acyclic Automata by Morphic Boolean Functions
W. C. Carter, A. B. Wadia, and D. C. Jessep, Jr., *IBM Watson Research Center, Yorktown Heights, NY*

Fault Equivalence in Sequential Machines
E. J. McCluskey, *Stanford University, Stanford, CA*

Digital Computer Arithmetic: A Unified Algorithmic Specification
A. Avižienis, *University of California, Los Angeles, CA*
Cellular Arrays and Arithmetic Units—A Synthesis Procedure
R. G. Cornell and H. C. Torng, *Cornell University, Ithaca, NY*

SESSION VI—2:00 P.M.
COMPUTER MODELS

Chairman: T. H. Crowley
Bell Telephone Laboratories, Whippany, NJ

A Model of the Digital Computer
S. Amoroso, *U.S. Army Electronics Command, Fort Monmouth, NJ* and *Stevens Institute of Technology, Hoboken, NJ;* and S. Bloom, *Stevens Institute of Technology, Hoboken, NJ*
Modeling and Simulation: Structure Preserving Relations for Continuous and Discrete Time Systems
B. P. Zeigler, *University of Michigan, Ann Arbor, MI*
General Purpose Cellular Computers
A. E. Laemmel, *Polytechnic Institute of Brooklyn*
Use of the Golay Logic Processor in Pattern Recognition Studies Using Hexagonal Local Neighbor Logic
K. Preston, Jr., *Perkin-Elmer Corp., Norwalk, CT*
Implementation of a Cellular Computing Memory Array
E. Della Torre and F. K. W. Ho, *McMaster University, Hamilton, Ontario, Canada*
A Computer Modeled after an Automaton
M. R. Schaffner, *Smithsonian Astrophysical Observatory* and *Massachusetts Institute of Technology, Cambridge MA*

INTRODUCTION

A. E. Laemmel
Polytechnic Institute of Brooklyn, Farmingdale, NY

Although held at a time when the number of meetings and symposia dealing with virtually every aspect of computers, computation, and automata had grown to substantial numbers, the MRI Symposium on Computers and Automata was planned to achieve a special purpose: to bring together the theoretical and the practical, so that each might stimulate and lend perspective to the other. In order to dispel any possible misunderstanding, the automata referred to are neither the clockwork puppets of the Victorian era, nor the automated factories of today. Rather the title refers to the theories of abstract automata such as finite-state transducers and Turing machines. Automata theory seems to have started largely by the need to systematize the design of certain parts of electronic digital computers, but it has grown into an independent discipline whose connection with practical problems is at times quite tenuous. Of course, this process—a mathematical theory is suggested by a practical problem, it develops independently and abstractly, and then it is again applied to practical problems—has occurred many times in history.

Several examples of the interactions of abstract theory and practical application can be found in the precursors of the present subjects. Ancient architects had a need to perform many geometrical constructions with primitive instruments, for example, trisecting a given angle with compass and straightedge. The question of exactly which such constructions were possible lead to the study of algebraic equations and in particular, to the study of finite fields by Galois. Constructions with compass and straightedge had ceased to be of much practical interest, and Galois theory was taught only to pure mathematicians. However, when error correcting codes were desired for modern communication systems and computers, this abstract theory proved to be just what was needed, and it is now taught to engineers. The great success of mathematics in solving numerical problems prompted many mathematicians from Leibnitz to Boole to attempt to develop a similar facility for solving complicated logical problems. Boolean algebra never became an everyday tool for logical problems, although it did start a successful program to place most branches of mathematics on a more rigorous foundation. This application, as exemplified by the work of Whitehead and Russell [1], was quite abstract. Boolean algebra did return to more concrete application in the design of switching circuits. The hopes that Boolean algebra and more general systems of symbolic logic could decide all mathematical questions were shattered by among others, Turing and his famous machine [2]. This

Contributed to the Proceedings of the Symposium on Computers and Automata
Polytechnic Institute of Brooklyn, April 13–15, 1971.

machine was, and still is, only a paper machine; but when electronic digital computers began to be built a few years later, Turing himself took part in some of the early practical development. There are many other areas of mathematics where the emphasis has gone from an original practical need, through an abstract phase of pure mathematics, and back to concrete applications. Consider the sequences: Galois theory to group theory to quantum mechanics, group theory to semigroup theory to sequential machine decomposition, gambling to probability theory to statistical communication theory, physical optics to Maxwell theory to Hertz and Marconi, Euclidean geometry to nonEuclidean geometry to Einstein applications in physics, etc. In most cases the abstract and concrete aspects were studied by entirely different people, each with little or no knowledge of the other's needs and views. The application to practical devices is usually made when the appropriate technology made the construction of the device economical, not when an engineer suddenly discovers a useful mathematical theory. However, the whole process probably can be speeded up by encouraging an exchange of ideas between mathematicians and engineers.

AUTOMATA THEORY

The present meaning of *automaton* and *automata theory* can probably best be given by examples. There are now quite a few books on automata theory, including those by Arbib [3], Booth [4], Minsky [5], Nelson [6], and Shannon and McCarthy [7]. Several of the books mentioned do not even define automaton and some define it in a way which is unintelligible to someone not in the field. Finite state machines and Turing machines are examples of automata, as are almost all machines which process strings of information-bearing symbols, or which make decisions.

What can an automaton do? One quickly finds that there exist universal Turing machines which can do any computation that any other possible machine can do! Furthermore, as the example given by Minsky shows, such a universal machine need not be very complicated and can easily be described on a single page. The naive reader might expect to learn quite a bit by studying the structure of such a universal machine, and he might think himself very fortunate to possess such a machine. The reader would be quickly disillusioned when he finds that the universal machine U does what a special machine M does only after M is made a part of U; and that if he does not know how to make M, then he cannot use U to solve M's problem. Note that although M itself is not fed into U, just the description of M is, the essence of an information handling machine is its description and not its physical embodiment. This situation is familiar to almost everyone nowadays; the computer can do nothing without being properly programmed.

The next thing which might catch the eye of a browser in automata theory is that there are unsolvable problems. These are not merely difficult; it has been shown that no Turing machine can exist which can tell if another particular Turing machine will halt or run forever. Some demonstrations of this result very easily followed, e.g., Minsky's; and even a reader new to the subject can taste some of the difficulties in the related Tag [5, 8] and Busy Beaver [9] problems.

This halting problem for Turing machines has proved to be the basis for almost all unsolvable problems, including in particular the unsolvability of the Hilbert decision problem in the logic of mathematics mentioned above [2]. One of the applications of the halting problem is to show the impossibility of writing a computer program which analyzes other programs to see if it has any unending loops. A letter pointing this out by one of the present authors, C. Strachey, started an interesting and amusing controversy in a British journal [10].

Of course, automata theory has also produced many deep and meaningful positive results. In the future these will probably lead to a comprehensive mathematical theory of computers. The theory of computers should be analogous to the communication theory of Shannon [11]: It should show how to calculate quantitatively the capacity of a computer, the cost of a computer, and the difficulty of a problem. The germ of such a theory can be found in abstract automata theory. A heirarchy of machines is established such as Turing machine–pushdown automaton–finite-state machine. These are ordered in their computation capacity by showing that each can perform any calculation which can be done by a machine after it in the series, and by showing that each can perform at least one calculation which the next lower machine cannot perform. The theory as it stands is quite elegant in its own right, but as a practical theory of computers it might be criticized as follows:

(1) The examples of calculations tend to be in the field of formal language manipulations of little practical importance. Of course these problems are important to compiler designers, but they are not typical of the problems the compiled program works on
(2) The theory is qualitative, e.g., lumping together the largest electronic computer and the smallest sequential relay circuit. To take an extreme example, a digital computer is a finite-state machine, but it could hardly be designed using finite-state synthesis methods, and its practical computation power is not suggested by the position of finite-state machines in the automata heirarchy
(3) The time required for the calculation is usually not considered. There are papers on Turing machine time complexity, but many contain such things as the speed-up theorem: If a T.M. can perform a calculation in t sec, then a T.M. can perform it in t/k sec, where k is any real number. The term "real time" in practice means more than a linear increase in computation time; the constant involved is vital.

In spite of the fact that automata theory does not provide a comprehensive theory of computers, it is certainly true that many parts of automata theory are useful to a computer designer or user. As examples taken from the present symposium: Lewis and Rosenkrantz (p. 75) have used pushdown automata to design a compiler; Bjørner (p. 105) has used pushdown automata and regular expression in the design of a computer language; Gergely (p. 251) and Santos and Otero (p. 265) have found some of the mathematical formalisms of finite-state machine theory convenient to express their work on the statistics of information flow between parts of a computer; Nelson (p. 327) has examined the connection between Turing machine effectiveness of computation with that occurring in the human pattern recognizer; Depeyrot, Mondelli, and Marmorat (p. 359) have shown the connection between the fast Fourier transform in various guises and semigroups; Lyons and Bruno (p. 379) use some of the techniques of mechanical theorem-proving to allow a program to verify some properties of his program; and Constable (p. 393) describes the connection between recursive function classes and program complexity. Idealized models, similar to those used in automata theory, have been described by Amoroso and Bloom (p. 539) for the digital computer, and by Zeigler (p. 561) for certain biological systems. As can be seen from the contents, there are also several papers on the use in computers of arrays of finite-state machines, an idea which might be said to have originated in automata theory.

Several of the more computer-oriented papers at the symposium do not appear to directly use automata theory, but they do contribute to the theory and practice of computer design. The problem of getting more computation for a given cost is currently being attacked by improving the computer itself, and also by making it easier for a person with almost no programming experience to efficiently utilize the computer. The latter is done: (1) By designing better programming languages; and (2) By tying these languages more closely to the underlying mathematical and logical problem-solving processes. Generally speaking, computers are being improved. (3) In the small by faster, cheaper and more reliable circuits; and (4) In the large by modifying the architecture to conform to the modern programming languages and modes of computer use. The symposium had papers reporting on developments in the forefront of each of the four subdivisions just mentioned.

(1) The work of J. B. Dennis of MIT (p. 47) which was motivated by the Project MAC and the ARPA Network programs, described a means of creating a common-base language in terms of which more special computer languages may be referred or specified
(2) The results of collaboration by two pioneers in the field, D. Scott of Princeton and C. Strachey of Oxford, are described in a paper (p. 19) which deals with the problem of treating the semantics of computer languages by mathematical means
(3) E. J. McCluskey of Stanford University (p. 483) and others present new results on the subject of fault equivalence in sequential machines, an area of theoretical and practical interest which is concerned with the diagnosis of machine faults
(4) H. Schorr of the IBM, T. J. Watson Research Center (p. 165) describes the results of an advanced study of the IBM Group which examined a proposed computer designed to be ten times faster than the largest system 360 machine, thus providing a look into the future and exposing new problems to be dealt with.

The current trend toward large computers with multilevel memory systems which are time-shared by many users has generated considerable interest in a field called *operating systems*. There are several papers on a necessary part of such systems, the paging problem, which refers to the efficient transfer of blocks of data and program in and out of the fast memory. Finally, it is unfortunate that these proceedings cannot reproduce the interesting film of the Golay cellular picture processor which was shown by Preston, but his paper (p. 609) describes the very practical application of a cellular automaton to medical problems.

REFERENCES

[1] A. N. Whitehead and B. Russell, *Principia Mathematica* (Cambridge, 1913). Also paperback edition of first part: (Cambridge, 1962).

[2] A. M. Turing, "On Computable Numbers, with an Application to the Entscheidungsproblem," *Proc. London Math. Soc.*, Ser. 2, **42**, 230–265 (1936–7).

[3] M. A. Arbib, *Theories of Abstract Automata* (Prentice-Hall, 1969).

[4] T. L. Booth, *Sequential Machines and Automata Theory* (Wiley, 1967).

[5] M. L. Minsky, *Computation: Finite and Infinite Machines* (Prentice-Hall, 1967).

[6] R. J. Nelson, *Introduction to Automata* (Wiley, 1968).

[7] C. E. Shannon and J. McCarthy, *Automata Studies* (Princeton U. Press, 1956).

[8] S. Watanabe, "Periodicity of Post's Normal Process of Tag," *Mathematical Theory of Automata*, 83 (Polytechnic Institute of Brooklyn, 1963).

[9] T. Rado, "On a Simple Source for Noncomputable Functions," *Mathematical Theory of Automata*, 75 (Polytechnic Institute of Brooklyn, 1963).

[10] *Computer Journal*, **7**, 313; **8**, 72, 175–6, 215, 329–330, 1965.

[11] C. E. Shannon, "Mathematical Theory of Communication," *Bell Sys. Tech. J.*, **27**, 379–423, 623–656 (July and October 1948).

SIZE ARGUMENTS IN THE STUDY OF COMPUTATION SPEEDS

J. Hartmanis

Department of Computer Science, Cornell University, Ithaca, NY

and

Gesellschaft für Mathematik und Datenverarbeitung MBH, Bonn, West Germany

In this paper we use arguments about the size of the computed functions to investigate the computation speed of Turing machines. It turns out that the size arguments yield several new results which we have not been able to obtain previously by diagonalization. For example, we show that for arbitrarily large running times $T(n)$ there exist functions which can be computed on a one-tape Turing machine in time $T(n)$ but not in time $t(n)$ provided

$$\lim_{n\to\infty} \frac{t(n)}{T(n)} = 0 .$$

The same result is also shown to hold for many-tape machines. We show furthermore, that there exist arbitrarily complex computations for which one-tape machines are slower than two-tape machines by a factor equal to the logarithm of the computation time of the two-tape machine. We conclude by discussing several other computational complexity measures and compare results obtained by diagonalization and size arguments.

I. INTRODUCTION

In the study of computational complexity we have relied heavily on diagonalization arguments to exhibit functions with well-defined computation speeds. In general, these results prove for a given computational complexity measure the existence of a recursive function g, such that for arbitrarily large computation times $T(n)$ there exist functions computable in time $g \circ T(n)$ but not in time $T(n)$. Thus the function g tells us how well we can bound the computation speed for difficult computations in a given measure. For the computation speeds of one-tape as well as multitape Turing machines we have only been able to show by means of diagonal arguments that $g \circ T(n)$ does not have to be much larger than $T(n) \log T(n)$ [1, 2]. For one-tape Turing machines the result has the following form [1]: for arbitrarily large running times $T(n)$ there exist functions which can be computed on a one-tape Turing machine in time $T(n) \log T(n)$ but not in time $t(n)$, provided

$$\lim_{n\to\infty} \frac{t(n)}{T(n)} = 0 .$$

Presented at the Symposium on Computers and Automata
Polytechnic Institute of Brooklyn, April 13-15, 1971.

For many tape machines the corresponding result asserts [2]: if $T(n)$ is a running time then there exists a function which can be computed on a multitape Turing machine in time $T(n)$ but not in time $t(n)$, provided

$$\lim_{n\to\infty} \frac{t(n) \log t(n)}{T(n)} = 0 .$$

It should be recalled that for small running times $T(n) \leq n^2$, considerably stronger results have been obtained for one-tape machines by means of "information-transfer" or "crossing-sequence" arguments [1, 3, 4]. Unfortunately, these arguments could not be extended directly to arbitrarily large running times.*

In this paper we use arguments about the size of the computed functions to show that for arbitrarily large running times $T(n)$ of one-tape Turing machines we can exhibit functions which can be computed in time $T(n)$ but not in time $t(n)$, provided

$$\lim_{n\to\infty} \frac{t(n)}{T(n)} = 0 .$$

This result also holds for multitape Turing machines.

By the same reasoning it can also be shown that many-tape Turing machines are faster than one-tape Turing machines for arbitrarily long computations. We show that if $T(n)$ is the running time of a one-tape Turing machine then there exists a function which can be computed in time $T(n)$ on a two-tape Turing machine but cannot be computed in time $t(n)$ on any one-tape machine provided

$$\lim_{n\to\infty} \frac{t(n)}{T(n) \log T(n)} = 0 .$$

Thus the computation time on the one-tape Turing machine cannot grow more slowly than $T(n) \log T(n)$.

To further illustrate the power of size arguments we show that when we use a fixed-universal Turing machine, then for arbitrarily-large time bounds there exist functions whose computation time cannot be improved by an arbitrary-positive constant factor, as is the case for general Turing-machine computations [1, 5]. In conclusion we take a quick look at three other computational complexity measures and discuss why for two of them size arguments yield sharper results than diagonalization arguments. For the third measure, which is based on one-tape Turing machines with "jump" operations, we show that diagonalization yields, for complexity classes of zero-one functions, the same results as size arguments for complexity classes of unbounded functions.

II. SIZE ARGUMENTS

In the first part of this paper we are concerned with the computation speeds of one-tape Turing machines. We say that a function $f(n)$, mapping positive integers into positive integers, is *computable in time* $T(n)$ on a one-tape Turing machine iff there exists a one-tape Turing machine M which started with input n written (in binary notation) on its tape, halts in $T(n)$ or fewer operations with $f(n)$ printed (in binary notation) on its tape. Symbolically we write

*Note that in the above results n stands for the length of the input. In the following results n denotes the numerical value of the input.

$$f \in C^1_{T(n)} ,$$

where $C^1_{T(n)}$ denotes all functions computable in time $T(n)$ on a one-tape Turing machine. Without any loss of generality we assume that our one-tape Turing machine moves its head on each operation and that the tape is only unbounded to the right. The machine is started on the left-most tape square which contains the first digit on the input sequence.

The same definition of computation time holds for multitape machines with the provision that the input is written on the input tape and that the output must be printed on the output tape. We let $C_{T(n)}$ denote all functions computable in time $T(n)$ on multitape Turing machines and write $C^k_{T(n)}$ to denote the set of functions computable in time $T(n)$ on k-tape Turing machines. We will add $\{0, 1\}$ to the superscript of the complexity class to show that we are considering only zero-one functions.

For a one-tape Turing machine with input n we define on each boundary between two adjacent tape squares a *crossing sequence* [1, 3] as the sequence of states $s_1, s_2, s_3, \cdots$, the machine is in as it crosses this boundary during the computation when started on input n. Thus s_k is the state M is in on the kth crossing of this boundary. Note that if M halts on input n then only a finite number of its crossing sequences are non-null and the sum of the lengths of all crossing sequences gives the number of operations performed by the Turing machine on input n before halting.

Our first result simply points out that any one-tape Turing machine which halts must generate different crossing sequences on all boundaries between tape squares on the initially-blank part of the tape. For a detailed discussion of crossing-sequence arguments see [3, 1].

LEMMA. *If a one-tape Turing machine M halts on input n then all non-null crossing sequences which M generates on its initially blank part of the tape must be distinct.*

Proof. If the machine M ever generates two identical non-null crossing sequences on the initially blank part of the tape, then it must generate an unbounded number of such crossing sequences. To see this just observe that all the information carried across a boundary by M is contained in the crossing sequence. On the initially blank part of the tape there cannot be any information on the tape, as the machine generates the original duplication of the crossing sequence. Thus all the information carried across the first identical-crossing sequence C_1 which results in generation of $C_2, C_2 = C_1$, is also carried across C_2 and an identical crossing sequence C_3, etc., will be generated further to the right on the tape. Thus M generates an unbounded number of crossing sequences and does not halt. Q.E.D.

LEMMA. *Let M be an one-tape Turing machine with q $(q \geq 2)$ states, which for an input of length ℓ* writes on $L(\ell)$ *different tape squares* $L(\ell) > \ell$. *Then M performs at least*

$$\frac{1}{q^2}\,[L(\ell) - \ell]\,[\log_q [L(\ell) - \ell] - 2] ,$$

operations for this input before halting.

Proof. By the previous lemma M must generate at least $L(\ell) - \ell$ different crossing sequences before halting. Since M has q states it can generate q^k different crossing sequences of length k. If M does the most economical thing and generates the shortest possible crossing sequences, then it has to generate all crossing sequences up to length $d - 1$, where d is the smallest integer such that

$$\sum_{k=1}^{d} q^k \geq L(\ell) - \ell \ .$$

Note that any other pattern of generating the $L(\ell) - \ell$ different crossing sequences requires more operations. Thus

$$\frac{q^{d+1} - 1}{q - 1} \geq L(\ell) - \ell \ ,$$

and for $q \geq 2$

$$q^{d+1} \geq L(\ell) - \ell \ ,$$

or

$$d + 1 \geq \log_q [L(\ell) - \ell] \ .$$

Since M does not necessarily have to generate all crossing sequences of length d we now compute how many operations are needed to generate all crossing sequences up to and including length $d - 1$. Since there are q^k crossing sequences of length k the number of operations required is not less than

$$\sum_{k=1}^{\log_q[L(\ell)-\ell]-2} kq^k \geq [\log_q [L(\ell) - \ell] - 2]\, q^{\log_q[L(\ell)-\ell]-2}$$

$$\geq \frac{1}{q^2} [L(\ell) - \ell]\, [\log_q [L(\ell) - \ell] - 2] \ . \quad \text{Q.E.D.}$$

Note that for $L(\ell)$ which grow faster than linearly we can replace this formula by

$$\frac{1}{q^2} [L(\ell) - \ell]\, (\log_q [L(\ell) - \ell] - 2) \geq \frac{1}{2q^2} L(\ell) \log_q L(\ell)$$

$$= \frac{\log_2 q}{2q^2} L(\ell) \log_2 L(\ell) \ ,$$

for sufficiently large values of $L(\ell)$. From the previous lemma and observation we get the next result.

THEOREM. *Let M be a q state, one-tape Turing machine which computes a function $f(n) >> 2^n$. Then for large values of n the computation time $T(n)$ of $f(n)$ must satisfy the inequality*

$$T(n) \geq \frac{1}{2q^2} [\log_2 f(n)] \cdot [\log_q \log_2 f(n)] \ .$$

The above result relates the computation speed to the size of the function computed. Next we show that we can construct functions whose computation time is very nearly the predicted minimal time and thus show that their computation time cannot be improved by more than a constant factor.

THEOREM. *There exist arbitrarily large functions $f_i(n)$ such that $f_i(n)$ is computable in $T_i(n)$ operations on a one-tape Turing machine but not in $t(n)$ operations provided*

$$\lim_{n\to\infty} \frac{t(n)}{T_i(n)} = 0 \ .$$

In other words, there exist arbitrarily large $T_i(n)$ such that

$$\lim_{n\to\infty} \frac{t(n)}{T_i(n)} = 0 \ ,$$

implies that

$$C_t^1 \underset{\neq}{\subset} C_{T_i}^1 \ .$$

Proof. We first observe that there exist arbitrarily large running times $T'(n)$ in which a Turing machine can mark off at least $\log_2 T'(n)$ tape squares for large n. As a matter of fact for any large running time $T''(n)$ achieved by a two-symbol Turing machine the machine must use more than $\log_3 T''(n)$ tape squares. Since otherwise it must repeat some total-state, tape-head and tape-pattern configuration and therfore cannot halt. These Turing machines can easily be modified to yield at least $\log_2 T'(n)$ marked tape squares in $T'(n)$ operations.

Furthermore, we observe that there exists a one-tape Turing machine which for any input of length ℓ can mark off 2^ℓ tape squares in less that $c \cdot 2^\ell \ell$ operations. This can be done by just counting on the ℓ tape squares from 1 to 2^ℓ and after each counting move the ℓ tape squares over to the right by one tape square.

We now consider the Turing machine which first marks off

$$g(n) \geq \log_2 T'(n) \ ,$$

tape squares in $T'(n)$ operations and then marks off $2^{g(n)}$ tape squares by writing a one followed by $2^{g(n)}$ zeros in $c2^{g(n)} g(n)$ operations. Thus this machine computes

$$f(n) = 2^{2^{g(n)}} \ ,$$

in

$$T(n) \leq c \cdot 2^{g(n)} g(n) + T'(n) \leq c_1 2^{g(n)} g(n) \ ,$$

operations. On the other hand, our lemma asserts that any one-tape, q-state Turing machine which computes

$$f(n) = 2^{2^{g(n)}} \ ,$$

must have a running time $t(n)$ satisfying

$$t(n) \geq \frac{\log_q^2}{2q^2} \cdot g(n) \, 2^{g(n)} \ ,$$

for large n. This implies that $f(n)$ is computable in

$$T(n) \leq c_1 g(n) 2^{g(n)} \quad ,$$

but not computable in $t(n)$ such that

$$\lim_{n\to\infty} \frac{t(n)}{T(n)} = 0 \quad . \qquad \text{Q.E.D.}$$

It would be very interesting to find out whether the same result holds when we restrict ourselves to zero-one functions. So far we have not been able to make any improvement for zero-one functions of the Hennie-Stearns result [2] mentioned in the Introduction. Nevertheless, the above result shows that for arbitrarily large functions we can bound the computation times very tightly and obtain a much stronger result.

We now use the above result to show that for arbitrarily long computations two-tape machines are faster than one-tape machines.

THEOREM. *Let $T(n)$ be the running time of a one-tape Turing machine. Then there exists a function $f(n)$ which is computable in time $T(n)$ on a two-tape machine and the running time $t(n)$ of any one-tape Turing machine with q states computing $f(n)$ must satisfy the inequality*

$$t(n) \geq \frac{1}{4q^2} \cdot T(n) \cdot \log_q T(n) \quad ,$$

for large n.

Proof. Let the two-tape machine M operate on the input tape as a one-tape machine whose running time is $T(n)$ operates on its tape. On the output tape, M prints a sequence of ones. Thus M computes

$$f(n) = 2^{T(n)} - 1 \quad ,$$

in time $T(n)$.

On the other hand, by a previous lemma we know that a q-state, one-tape machine requires for large n, time

$$t(n) \geq \frac{1}{2q^2} (\log_2 f(n)) (\log_q \log_2 f(n)) \quad ,$$

to compute $f(n)$. From this it follows that

$$t(n) \geq \frac{1}{4q^2} T(n) \cdot \log_q T(n) \quad ,$$

for large n. Q.E.D.

We can express this result in a different way:

COROLLARY. *Let $T(n)$ be the running-time of a one-tape Turing machine. Then there exists a function $f(n)$ computable in $T(n)$ operations on a two-tape machine and not computable in time $t(n)$ on a one-tape machine provided*

$$\lim_{n\to\infty} \frac{t(n)}{T(n) \log_2 T(n)} = 0 \quad .$$

It would be very interesting to prove the same result without the use of the size argument. Unfortunately, we have no such proof and thus it is still an open problem to prove that the computation of zero-one functions on two-tape machines is faster than on one-tape machines for arbitrarily long computations. Recall that up till now it was only known that for real-time computations, two-tape machines were faster than one-tape machines [2, 4].

Furthermore, even using size arguments we have not been able to show for $k \geq 3$ that k-tape machines are faster than $(k - 1)$-tape machines for arbitrarily long computations.

The next result shows that size arguments can very simply yield new results for time bounds of multitape Turing machine computations.

THEOREM. *Let $T(n)$ be the running-time of a multitape Turing machine. Then there exists a function $f(n)$ which can be computed in time $T(n)$ but cannot be computed in time $t(n)$ by any multitape Turing machine provided*

$$\lim_{n\to\infty} \frac{t(n)}{T(n)} = 0 .$$

In other words, for running time $T(n)$

$$\lim_{n\to\infty} \frac{t(n)}{T(n)} ,$$

implies that

$$C_t \underset{\neq}{\subset} C_T .$$

Proof. Let $T(n)$ be the running time of a k-tape machine M. Construct a $(k+1)$-tape machine M' so that the first k tapes of M' are used as tapes of the machine M. The last tape is used as the output tape and M' prints a sequence of ones, one on each operation. Thus M' computes

$$f(n) = 2^{T(n)} - 1 .$$

Any other multitape Turing machine running in time $t(n)$ can compute at best a function of size

$$g(n) \leq q^{t(n)} .$$

If

$$\lim_{n\to\infty} \frac{t(n)}{T(n)} = 0 ,$$

then for large n

$$q^{t(n)} < 2^{T(n)} - 1 ,$$

and we see that

$$C_t \underset{\neq}{\subset} C_T . \quad \text{Q.E.D.}$$

Again the open problem is to determine whether this result holds for complexity classes of zero-one functions.

III. COMPLEXITY CLASSES DEFINED BY UNIVERSAL TURING MACHINES

We know that for larger computation times any multi-tape or one-tape Turing machine computation can be speeded up by any positive factor by selecting a larger Turing machine with more tape symbols [1, 5]. In this section we show that this is not the case when we use a fixed universal Turing machine as our computer.

Let M be a one-tape, universal Turing machine which interprets the first binary string up to the marker "#" on its tape as an algorithm (description of another one-tape Turing machine), and the second binary string as the input to which the algorithm is to be applied. The output is to be placed on the tape to the right of the input between appropriate markers.

Clearly this universal Turing machine with its algorithms defines a computational-complexity measure if we assign to each algorithm A_i the step-counting function $T_i(n)$ given by the number of operations performed by M with algorithm A_i on input n before halting. We let $C^M_{T(n)}$ denote the set of all functions computable almost everywhere in the bound $T(n)$.

THEOREM. *There exists a universal Turing machine M such that for any recursive $t(n)$ there exists a running time $T(n) \geq t(n)$ and a constant k such that*

$$C^M_{T(n)/k} \underset{\neq}{\subset} C^M_{T(n)} .$$

Proof. By a previous lemma we know that a q-state, one-tape machine requires $T_i(n)$ operations to compute a large $f_i(n)$, with

$$T_i(n) \geq \frac{\log_q^2}{2q^2} (\log_2 f_i(n)) (\log_2 \log_2 f_i(n)) ,$$

for large n. At the same time we can construct a universal Turing machine which can compute arbitrarily complex functions $f_i(n)$ in time

$$T_i(n) \leq c_i \cdot (\log_2 f_i(n)) (\log_2 \log_2 f_i(n)) ,$$

where the constant depends on the size of the algorithm for $f_i(n)$. This is achieved by first recalling (from one of our previous proofs) that there exist single-tape Turing machines which compute arbitrarily large functions within a constant times of the minimal time mentioned above; and secondly by observing that there exist universal Turing machines which for each algorithm can simulate the computation by not taking more than a constant times the number of operations performed by the original machine (the constant depends on the algorithm). This simulation is performed by always moving along a copy of the algorithm which is being executed and thus insuring that for each simulated operation no more than a fixed number of operations are required.

Combining the two inequalities we see that for

$$k > \frac{c_i 2q^2}{\log_q^2} ,$$

we cannot speed up the computation of $f_i(n)$ by a factor k and thus conclude that

$$C^M_{T_i/k} \underset{\neq}{\subset} C^M_{T_i} \quad . \quad \text{Q.E.D.}$$

Again the fascinating open problem is to determine whether the same result holds for complexity classes of zero-one functions. It would also be interesting to show that this result holds for all universal Turing machines. The best result we have been able to obtain for this computational complexity measure for zero-one function is stated below.

THEOREM. *There exists a universal Turing machine M and arbitrarily large running times $T_i(n)$ such that*

$$\lim_{n\to\infty} \frac{t(n)}{T_i(n)} = 0 \quad ,$$

implies that

$$C^{M\{0,1\}}_{t(n)} \underset{\neq}{\subset} C^{M\{0,1\}}_{T(n)\log T(n)} \quad .$$

Proof. The proof is obtained by an obvious modification of the proof for the corresponding result about one-tape machines in [1]. Q.E.D.

IV. OTHER TURING-MACHINE VARIANTS

To further illustrate the power of the size argument and its relation to diagonalization, we discuss three other computational-complexity measures based on modified one-tape Turing machines.

It should be recalled that our previous diagonalization arguments to prove that some function cannot be computed in time $t(n)$ have involved two different computations [1, 2, 5]. One computation just simulated all other Turing machines and changed the result to construct the desired (diagonalized) function; the other computation kept track of how many simulation operations had been performed and shut the computation off when it tried to exceed a given bound. For one-tape Turing machines the simulation part is quite easy but the running of two processes on one-tape is more difficult and this is reflected in the rather weak result we can get by means of simulation [1]. For multitape Turing machines the problem is reversed [2, 5]: running two processes in parallel is easy since we just add the necessary tapes and expand the machine to behave like the two desired machines. On the other hand, simulation is more difficult since we have to simulate machines with arbitrarily many tapes on a machine with a fixed number of tapes. Thus in this case the simulation causes the weakness in the corresponding result [2]. For a more detailed discussion of these observations see [6].

To gain further insight in these problems, we now define three new complexity measures. The first two models overcome the problem of running two processes simultaneously on a one-tape machine. Unfortunately, though they solve the parallelism problem, they complicate the simulation problem and we have not been able to exploit the additional power to prove as good results for zero-one functions as we can obtain by size arguments for unbounded functions.

The first computational-complexity measure is defined by using one-tape Turing machines and counting the number of symbols printed, rather than all operations performed. (With the agreement that if the machine does not halt, then the amount of ink used is undefined, even if the machine does not do any more printing. Note that this can be recursively determined and thus we have a valid computational-complexity measure.) This "ink-" based computational complexity measure has the advantage that a search for a symbol or moving the head from one computation to another does not cost anything. At the same time we have not been able to devise a way where we can simulate other Turing machines without using ink if they do not use ink. Thus it is still an open problem whether for arbitrarily-large ink bounds $I_i(n)$

$$\lim_{n\to\infty} \frac{I(n)}{I_i(n)} = 0 \; ,$$

implies that there exists a zero-one function which can be computed with $I_i(n)$ ink but not with $I(n)$ ink. On the other hand, by using size arguments we can easily show that such a result holds for unbounded functions.

A similar situation arises when we consider computational complexity measures based on the number of operations performed by one-tape Turing machines with the ability to jump to the nearest specified symbol in one operation. These machines operate as regular Turing machines until they enter a special state which transfers their heads in one operation to the nearest tape symbol specified by the state (if no such symbol is printed on the tape, the machine halts). Again these jump operations make the running of two simultaneous processes easy but the simulation becomes more difficult. The difficulty is very similar to the one arising for multitape Turing machines [2, 5]; that is, we must simulate machines with arbitrarily many symbols to which they can jump on a machine with a fixed number of jump symbols. Thus again, just as in the previous case, we have not been able to obtain as sharp a result for zero-one functions as we can obtain by size arguments for unbounded functions.

Finally, we discuss a complexity measure for which we can obtain the same result for complexity classes of zero-one functions by means of diagonalization, as for complexity classes of unbounded functions with size arguments.

Consider one-tape Turing machines with special marker "#" and a "jump" state which can be used to transfer the head in one operation to the nearest specified subsequence on the tape as follows: let x be any binary sequence placed between two markers, $\# x \#$, then by placing its head on the left marker and entering the jump state, the head is transferred in one operation to the nearest left marker bounding the sequence $\# x \#$, if such a second sequence exists, otherwise the machine halts. Again we obtain a computational-complexity measure by counting the number of operations performed by such a Turing machine with jump instructions. Fortunately, for this measure we get the following result.

THEOREM. *Let $T(n) \geq n$ be the running time of a Turing machine. Then there exists a zero-one function computable on a Turing machine with jump instructions in time $T(n)$ but not in time $t(n)$ provided*

$$\lim_{n\to\infty} \frac{t(n)}{T(n)} = 0 \; .$$

That is

$$C_t^{J\{0,1\}} \subsetneq C_T^{J\{0,1\}} ,$$

where J indicates that we are considering Turing machines with jump operations.

Proof. The proof is obtained by a standard diagonalization argument used in [1]. The only trick is that we reserve the shortest sequences # 0 #, # 1 # as markers to jump back and forth between the simulation and the computation counting up to $T(n)$. The longer sequences of symbols are used to encode the simulated computation. Since these encodings and jumps between the two computations can only increase the computation time by a constant factor, the result follows easily. Q.E.D.

V. CONCLUSION

In this paper we showed that size arguments can give very sharp results about complexity classes and solved some problems which we have not been able to resolve by means of diagonalization. At the same time we had to state these results for complexity classes consisting of all functions computable in a given bound, whereas diagonalization usually yields results about zero-one functions. This has left us with several tantalizing conjectures for complexity classes of zero-one functions which we know to be true for unrestricted complexity classes. It would be rather surprising if the results for complexity classes of zero-one functions would turn out to be different than those obtained in this paper for unrestricted complexity classes.

It should be pointed out that it is not difficult to construct computational-complexity measures for which the results for complexity classes of zero-one functions differ radically from those of unbounded functions. On the other hand, these computational complexity measures are quite artificially constructed and it would be surprising if such a situation would exist for any of the complexity measures discussed in this paper.

ACKNOWLEDGEMENTS

This research has been supported in part by National Science Foundation Grant No. GJ-155.

REFERENCES

[1] J. Hartmanis, "Computational Complexity of One-Tape Turing Machine Computations," *J. ACM*, **15**, 325–339 (1968).

[2] F. C. Hennie and R. E. Stearns, "Two-Tape Simulation of Multi-Tape Turing Machines," *J. ACM*, **13**, 533–546 (1966).

[3] F. C. Hennie, "One-Tape, Off-Line Turing Machine Computations," *Information & Control*, 8, 553–578 (1965).

[4] M. O. Rabin, "Real Time Computation," *Israel J. Math.*, 1, 203–211 (1964).

[5] J. Hartmanis and R. E. Stearns "On the Computational Complexity of Algorithms," *Trans. Am. Math. Soc.*, 117, 285–306 (1965).

[6] J. Hartmanis and J. E. Hopcroft, "An Overview of the Theory of Computational Complexity," *J. ACM* (to be published).

TOWARD A MATHEMATICAL SEMANTICS FOR COMPUTER LANGUAGES

Dana Scott

Department of Philosophy, Princeton University, Princeton, NJ

and

Christopher Strachey

Programming Research Group, Oxford University, Oxford, England

Compilers for high-level languages are generally constructed to give the complete translation of the programs into machine language. As machines merely juggle bit patterns, the concepts of the original language may be lost or at least obscured during this passage. The purpose of a mathematical semantics is to give a correct and meaningful correspondence between programs and mathematical entities in a way that is entirely independent of an implementation. This plan is illustrated in a very elementary way in the introduction. Section II connects the general method with the usual idea of state transformations. The next section shows why the mathematics of functions has to be modified to accommodate recursive commands. Section IV explains the modification. Section V introduces the environments for handling variables and identifiers, and shows how the semantical equations define equivalence of programs. Section VI gives an exposition of the new type of mathematical function spaces that are required for the semantics of procedures when these are allowed in assignment statements. The conclusion traces some of the background of the project and points the way to future work.

I. INTRODUCTION

The idea of a *mathematical* semantics for a language is perfectly well illustrated by the contrast between *numerals* on the one hand and *numbers* on the other. The numerals are *expressions* in a certain familiar language; while the numbers are mathematical *objects* (abstract objects) which provide the intended *interpretations* of the expressions. We need the expressions to be able to communicate the results of our theorizings about the numbers, but the symbols themselves should not be confused with the concepts they denote. For one thing, there are many *different* languages adequate for conveying the *same* concepts (e.g., binary, octal, or decimal numerals). For another, even in the *same* language many different expressions can denote the same concepts (e.g., $2 + 2$, 4, $1 + (1 + (1 + 1))$, etc.). The problem of explaining these *equivalences* of expressions (whether in the same or different languages) is one of the tasks of semantics and is much too important to be left to syntax alone. Besides, the mathematical concepts are required for the *proof* that the various equivalences have been *correctly* described.

Contributed to the Proceedings of the Symposium on Computers and Automata Polytechnic Institute of Brooklyn, April 13–15, 1971.

In more detail we may consider the following explicit syntax for binary numerals

NUMERALS

$$\nu ::= 0 \mid 1 \mid \nu 0 \mid \nu 1 \ .$$

Here we have used the Greek letter ν as a *metavariable* over the syntactical category of numerals, and the category itself is being given a *recursive definition* in the usual way. Thus, a numeral *is* either one of the digits 0 or 1 or is the result of suffixing one of these digits to a previously obtained numeral. Let the set of all numerals be called Nml for short.

Semantically speaking each of the numerals is meant to denote a unique number. Let N be the set of numbers. (The elements of Nml are expressions; while the elements of N are mathematical objects conceived in abstraction independently of notation.) The obvious principle of interpretation provides a function, the *evaluation mapping*, which we might call $\mathcal{V}$, and which has the functional character:

$$\mathcal{V} : \mathrm{Nml} \longrightarrow \mathrm{N} \ .$$

Thus for each $\nu \in \mathrm{Nml}$, the function value

$$\mathcal{V} [\![\nu]\!] \ ,$$

is the number denoted by ν.

How is the evaluation function $\mathcal{V}$ determined? Inasmuch as it is to be defined on a recursively defined set Nml, it is reasonable that $\mathcal{V}$ should itself be given a recursive definition. Indeed by following exactly the four clauses of the recursive definition Nml, we are motivated by our understanding of numerals to write

$$\begin{aligned} \mathcal{V} [\![0]\!] &= \mathit{0} \ , \\ \mathcal{V} [\![1]\!] &= \mathit{1} \ , \\ \mathcal{V} [\![\nu 0]\!] &= \mathit{2} \cdot \mathcal{V} [\![\nu]\!] \ , \\ \mathcal{V} [\![\nu 1]\!] &= \mathit{2} \cdot \mathcal{V} [\![\nu]\!] + \mathit{1} \ . \end{aligned}$$

Here on the left-hand side of the equations, $\mathcal{V}$ is being applied to expressions; while on the right-hand side the values are given. To borrow the relevant terminology from logic, the numerical expressions belong to the *object language*; whereas the definition of $\mathcal{V}$ is given in the *metalanguage*. To be able to write down explicitly the definition of $\mathcal{V}$, some metalinguistic symbolization is of course required. The metalinguistic expressions must at all cost be distinguished from those in the object language. (We have put the object language 0 and 1 in Roman typeface and the metalanguage *0, 1, 2* in italics. Logicians often take further precautions by enclosing the object language expressions in quotes; the quotation-expressions can then be regarded as part of the metalanguage, and thus the languages are "insulated" from one another. In this paper, however, our object languages are simple enough making the use of such devices less critical. The separation needs to be observed nevertheless, and in the semantic equations we have enclosed the object language expressions in the special brackets $[\![\ \ ]\!]$ merely as an aid to the eye.)

Granted that there is a distinction between symbol and object, it may still seem that the above equations for $\mathcal{V}$ are circular or nearly vacuous in content. Such a conclusion is wrong, however, because there is an easily appreciated point to the definition: namely, the explication of the *positional notation.* In our metalanguage we need never have heard of decimals or binaries. We do require, though, the concept of *number*, the concepts of *zero* and *one*, the concepts of *addition* and *multiplication*. (By definition $2 = 1 + 1$, say, and if we want, the whole *theory* of numbers could be conveyed in the metalanguage with the help of *Roman numerals* augmented with a few tricks from algebra such as the use of *operation symbols* and *variables*.) These concepts, fundamental as they are, cannot be strictly said to *imply* the positional notation. In fact, the clever use of 0 to help form strings of digits was a *discovery of language*. This discovery in no way changed the abstract nature of number, but it was a tremendous help in popularizing the use of arithmetic ideas—and there seems to be a perfectly good parallel here with computer languages many of which contain in their syntactical structures quite as clever discoveries of language.

One point that encourages confusion in thinking about numbers is the possibility of having a *complete* and *canonical* naming system for them. In the illustrative syntax for binary numerals we have been considering, such strings as 0 0 1 1 0 1 were allowed. As everyone knows the initial run of 0's is unnecessary for we can show that

$$\mathcal{V}[\![0\;0\;1\;1\;0\;1]\!] = \mathcal{V}[\![1\;1\;0\;1]\!] = \mathrm{XIII}.$$

This type of straight-forward deletion gives us the only possible equivalences in this very simple language. The *reduced* numerals (i.e., numerals of the forms 0 and 1ν, where $\nu \in \mathrm{Nml}$ is arbitrary) are then in a one-one correspondence with the numbers. We can then work exclusively with these normal forms, and it is so easy to think of these expressions as *being* the numbers—especially if one is familiar with only one notational system. The attitude is wrong-headed, however. But for many activities there may be no real harm, since the confused mind will give the *same answers* as the clear-headed person. The notationally bound thinker may often be distinguished by the way he feels that he has to specify all his operations by algorithmic symbol manipulations (as in digitwise addition of numerals). Again there may be no real harm in this—if the algorithms are correctly given. And in the case of numbers the two approaches can be brought together (the symbolic and the conceptual), for our system of reduced numerals can, by a slight amount of good will, be regarded as a *model* for number theory. Since we know that *all* such models are isomorphic, there is not much mathematical advantage in using one model over another. This is a sense in which numbers can be consistently confused with numerals. But the confusion does not really do us any good either.

The reasons why the number/numeral confusion should be avoided are many. For one reason, we may turn the isomorphism argument the other way round: If all models of number theory are isomorphic, you may *not* want to single out a particular one at all. Because the semantical ideas will equally well apply to all of them, you may want to leave open the possibility of *shifting* from one to another. This is somewhat analogous in computer language semantics to allowing different representations to be used in different machines to implement the same language (in hopefully isomorphic ways). In the case of numbers not much advantage is bought by this freedom, but any attitude of restricting generality is a bad habit which can be misleading in analogous but more complicated situations.

A more important reason for not getting into this habit comes to light when one realizes that for some systems of mathematical concepts no fully adequate notational system is possible: the real numbers are the prime example. Of course it will be objected that this realm of mathematics is much too abstract, much too infinitary, much too distant from real-life computation. This objection cannot stand careful conceptual investigation, but a full answer would take us too far from the topic of this paper. A quite adequate answer concerns not the mathematically very pure structures such as the real numbers, but rather our theories of *classes* of similar but different structures. That is to say, for the semantic investigation of certain language features it may not be appropriate to single out one (isomorphism type of) structure, but for many reasons—generality, lack of knowledge, for the sake of experiment—we may want the *same* semantical equations to be employed over the *whole class* of structures. Since the structures need no longer be isomorphic, different structures may lead to quite different normal forms for expressions. (The mathematical theory of groups, for instance, could provide us innumerable such examples.) Hence, no one system of "numerals" would any longer suffice. Even if the separate structures could somehow each be symbolically constructed, the effort would be beside the point: what we are trying to get at are the *common features* of the structures. The various *ad hoc* details would only detract from this higher purpose.

To bring this introductory sermon to a close: the point of our approach is to allow a proper balance between rigorous formulation, generality of application, and conceptual simplicity. One essential achievement of the method we shall wish to claim is that by insisting on a suitable level of abstraction and by emphasizing the right details we are going to hit squarely what can be called *the* mathematical meaning of a language. In the trivial example of the binary numerals discussed above everyone will agree that the evaluation function $\mathcal{V}$ is indeed correctly defined. That much is obvious. Note, however, that having accepted this fact, it is then possible to prove that certain numerical algorithms are *correct* (digitwise addition, say), and before we had the definition this question did not even make sense. (Specifically, digitwise addition is an operation $\nu_0 \oplus \nu_1$ defined on numerals ν_0, ν_1. What one needs to prove is that

$$\mathcal{V}[\![\nu_0 \oplus \nu_1]\!] = \mathcal{V}[\![\nu_0]\!] + \mathcal{V}[\![\nu_1]\!] \ ,$$

with symbolic addition on the left and conceptual addition on the right. It is not difficult to do this, but one needs an inductive argument.) These are simple points, but it is easy to lose sight of them when the languages get involved.

II. STATES AND COMMANDS

We begin by postulating that the interpretation of the language depends on the *states* of "the system." That is to say, computer oriented languages differ from their mathematical counterparts by virtue of their *dynamic* character. An expression does not generally possess *one* uniquely determined value of the expected sort, but rather the value depends upon the state of the system at the time of initialization of evaluation. What increases the dynamic character of the evaluation process is the fact that the act of evaluation may very well alter the initial state. Thus the working out of a compound expression can require several changes of state, and the treatment of a subexpression generally has to wait for the moment at which the state can be provided appropriate to its evaluation. Therefore the "algebra" of equivalences of such expressions need not be as "beautiful" as the well-known mathematical examples. This does not mean that the semantics of such languages will be *less* mathematical, only an order more complex.

Part of our assumption is that the states of the system form a *set* S, and the dynamic character of the language will require us to consider *transformations* of this S into itself: the state transformations. For the moment let us write (in our metalanguage)

$$[\mathrm{S} \longrightarrow \mathrm{S}] \ ,$$

for the set of *all* state transformations (this set may require restriction later). By a *transformation* $f \in [\mathrm{S} \longrightarrow \mathrm{S}]$ we understand the ordinary concept of a mathematical *function* defined on S with values in S. Functions in the mathematical sense are abstract objects—they can be *defined* in various linguistic forms, but after the definition is interpreted all that is left is the bare *correspondence* between *arguments* $\sigma \in \mathrm{S}$ and *values* $f(\sigma) \in \mathrm{S}$. In particular two functions which assume the same values for the same arguments are mathematically identical—even though they might have been defined in some object language in quite different ways.

The simplest way to regard the state transformations from σ to $f(\sigma)$ is that they give the results of executing a *command*. No explicit values are required; one is merely being asked to "move along." Of course certain "values" may be implicit in σ, and they may be changed in passing to $f(\sigma)$ (e.g., ones *position*). The command, however, is concerned more with the overall change; other kinds of expressions can be used to extract from a state $\sigma \in \mathrm{S}$ any relevant values. But one syntactic category in our language will be that of commands; let us call the set of these expressions Cmd. Given $\gamma \in \mathrm{Cmd}$, no matter how complex, the mathematical meaning of this expression is an associated state transformation $\mathcal{C}[\![\gamma]\!] \in [\mathrm{S} \longrightarrow \mathrm{S}]$. That is, the semantics of commands is to provide us with a mapping

$$\mathcal{C}\colon \mathrm{Cmd} \longrightarrow [\mathrm{S} \longrightarrow \mathrm{S}] \ ,$$

just as the semantics of numerals gave us

$$\mathcal{V}\colon \mathrm{Nml} \longrightarrow \mathrm{N} \ .$$

What is vague here is that we have no idea what commands are, whereas numerals were standard. That we have at this stage no idea what states $\sigma \in \mathrm{S}$ are is far less serious, because that is the part of the interpretation we are on purpose leaving open.

It is not difficult to be more explicit about the syntax of commands, however, because there are several quite natural ways of combining them. An initial syntax might look as follows

COMMANDS

$$\gamma ::= (\gamma) \mid \phi \mid \text{dummy} \mid$$
$$\varepsilon \longrightarrow \gamma_0, \gamma_1 \mid \gamma_0; \gamma_1 \ .$$

Here the Greek letter γ is a metavariable over the category (Cmd) which is being given a recursive definition. On the right-hand side of the definition the γ, γ_0, γ_1 can be regarded as *previously* obtained commands, where the subscripts are required in a binary composition to allow for *different* commands to be chosen. If in one clause of the definition the *same* γ appeared twice, we would intend that the same previously obtained expression be used in both positions. There is no implied connection between the γs in the separate clauses. The Greek letters ϕ and ε are meant to refer to other syntactic categories yet to be explained. The expression dummy is a *constant* command (an "atomic" command expression).

As anyone can see (assuming that the categories of ϕ and ε are simple) the set Cmd is going to be a context-free language. Also obvious is the fact that the language is *ambiguous*—thus $\gamma_0; \gamma_1; \gamma_2$ can be parsed in two different ways at least. Machines generally prefer their languages *unambiguous*; while humans enjoy a little uncertainty, or at least they find ways to overlook ambiguities by giving each other the benefit of the doubt. Sometimes ambiguities make no difference (as in $\gamma_0; \gamma_1; \gamma_2$), but at other times they are quite tiresome (as in $\varepsilon \longrightarrow \gamma_0, \gamma_1; \gamma_2$). We shall deal with this problem presently, but in the meantime note the clause (γ) in the definition. This clause allows us to form $(\varepsilon \longrightarrow \gamma_0, \gamma_1); \gamma_2$ or $\varepsilon \longrightarrow \gamma_0, (\gamma_1; \gamma_2)$ which are similar to the ambiguous expression but which have one chance less of being ambiguous. With a sufficient nesting of parentheses all ambiguity can be eliminated; or, speaking more precisely, there is a completely unambiguous sublanguage of Cmd. The only trouble with us humans is that the majority find writing in this sublanguage a terrific bore; hence the tendency to the more dangerous syntax.

Before we can be more precise about Cmd and the interpretation $\mathcal{C}$, we have to discuss the ε. For the time being $\varepsilon \in$ Exp, the class of *Boolean expressions* (we shall allow other types of expressions later). As a starter at a syntax we can write

EXPRESSIONS

$$\varepsilon ::= (\varepsilon) \mid \pi \mid \text{true} \mid \text{false} \mid \varepsilon_0 \longrightarrow \varepsilon_1, \varepsilon_2 \ .$$

The same remarks about ambiguity apply. The π are certain atomic expressions which we shall not stop to detail now. The Boolean expressions true and false are constants, and $\varepsilon_0 \longrightarrow \varepsilon_1, \varepsilon_2$ is the well-known conditional expression (short for: if ε_0 then ε_1 else ε_2, which some may prefer).

What of interpretation? In the first place we postulate the set T of *truth values* which contains the elements *true* and *false* corresponding to true and false. But the meaning $\mathcal{E}[\![\varepsilon]\!]$ is not going to be simply an element of T, for in general values must depend on states. Besides this evaluation may *cause* a change of state. Thus the correct functional character of $\mathcal{E}$ is

$$\mathcal{E}: \text{Exp} \longrightarrow [S \longrightarrow [T \times S]] \ .$$

This means that given $\varepsilon \in \text{Exp}$ and $\sigma \in S$, then

$$\mathcal{E}[\![\varepsilon]\!](\sigma) = \langle t, \sigma' \rangle \ ,$$

where $t \in T$ is the value of ε given σ, and σ' is the resultant state after the evaluation and may differ from σ as it may have been changed by the evaluation. (Here $T \times S$ is the usual *cartesian product* of sets and $\langle \cdot , \cdot \rangle$ is the *pairing* function.)

Before giving the clauses that define $\mathcal{C}$ and $\mathcal{E}$, it is useful to introduce several mathematical operations on functions. If $f: B \longrightarrow C$ and $g: A \longrightarrow B$, then as usual we write $f \circ g: A \longrightarrow C$ for the *composition*, where

$$(f \circ g)(\alpha) = f(g(\alpha)) \ ,$$

for all $\alpha \in A$. We have further

$$P: A \longrightarrow [B \longrightarrow [A \times B]] \ ,$$
$$M_0: A \times B \longrightarrow A \ ,$$
$$M_1: A \times B \longrightarrow B \ ,$$

where

$$P(\alpha)(\beta) = \langle \alpha, \beta \rangle \ ,$$
$$M_0(\langle \alpha, \beta \rangle) = \alpha \ ,$$
$$M_1(\langle \alpha, \beta \rangle) = \beta \ ,$$

for all $\alpha \in A$, $\beta \in B$. Finally, if $p: A' \longrightarrow [B \longrightarrow C]$ and $q: A \longrightarrow A' \times B$, then $p * q: A \longrightarrow C$, where

$$(p * q)(\alpha) = p\left(M_0(q(\alpha))\right)\left(M_1(q(\alpha))\right) \ ,$$

for all $\alpha \in A$. On all of these operations and special functions we ought to write some kind of ABC subscripts, because strictly speaking they depend on the choice of the various sets; we have omitted these subscripts as they can easily be deduced from the context. The same goes for the *identity* function

$$I: A \longrightarrow A \ ,$$

where

$$I(\alpha) = \alpha \ ,$$

for all $\alpha \in A$.

Turning now to the mapping $\mathcal{E}$ we have clause by clause

$$\mathcal{E}[\![(\varepsilon)]\!] = \mathcal{E}[\![\varepsilon]\!]$$

because parentheses add nothing to the meaning.

$$\mathcal{E}[\![\pi]\!] = (\text{some given } S \longrightarrow [T \times S]) \ ,$$

because each atomic expression π must have a given meaning. (Which meaning this is, need not concern us here, since at the moment all we consider is the *form* of the semantic definition.)

$$\mathcal{E}[\![\text{true}]\!] = P(\mathit{true}) \quad ,$$

and

$$\mathcal{E}[\![\text{false}]\!] = P(\mathit{false}) \quad ,$$

because true and false are constants which can be evaluated "instantaneously" without change of state. This means that for all σ

$$\mathcal{E}[\![\text{true}]\!](\sigma) = <\mathit{true}, \sigma> \quad ,$$

and

$$\mathcal{E}[\![\text{false}]\!](\sigma) = <\mathit{false}, \sigma> \quad .$$

$$\mathcal{E}[\![\varepsilon_0 \longrightarrow \varepsilon_1, \varepsilon_2]\!] = \mathit{Cond}(\mathcal{E}[\![\varepsilon_1]\!], \mathcal{E}[\![\varepsilon_2]\!]) * \mathcal{E}[\![\varepsilon_0]\!] \quad ,$$

where the function

$$\mathit{Cond}\colon [\mathrm{S} \longrightarrow \mathrm{T} \times \mathrm{S}] \times [\mathrm{S} \longrightarrow \mathrm{T} \times \mathrm{S}] \longrightarrow [\mathrm{T} \longrightarrow [\mathrm{S} \longrightarrow \mathrm{T} \times \mathrm{S}]] \quad ,$$

is such that

$$\mathit{Cond}(\mathrm{e}_1, \mathrm{e}_2)(t) = t \longrightarrow \mathrm{e}_1, \mathrm{e}_2 \quad ,$$

so that

$$\mathit{Cond}(\mathrm{e}_1, \mathrm{e}_2)(t)(\sigma) = \begin{cases} \mathrm{e}_1(\sigma), & \text{if } t = \mathit{true} \quad , \\ \mathrm{e}_2(\sigma), & \text{if } t = \mathit{false} \quad , \end{cases}$$

for all e_1, e_2, t, σ in appropriate sets.

It is now possible to give the clauses of the definition of $\mathcal{C}$

$$\mathcal{C}[\![(\gamma)]\!] = \mathcal{C}[\![\gamma]\!] \quad ,$$
$$\mathcal{C}[\![\phi]\!] = (\text{some given S} \longrightarrow \text{S}) \quad ,$$
$$\mathcal{C}[\![\text{dummy}]\!] = I \quad ,$$
$$\mathcal{C}[\![\varepsilon \longrightarrow \gamma_0, \gamma_1]\!] = \mathit{Cond}(\mathcal{C}[\![\gamma_0]\!], \mathcal{C}[\![\gamma_1]\!]) * \mathcal{E}[\![\varepsilon]\!] \quad ,$$
$$\mathcal{C}[\![\gamma_0; \gamma_1]\!] = \mathcal{C}[\![\gamma_1]\!] \circ \mathcal{C}[\![\gamma_0]\!] \quad .$$

These functional equations can all be read in words: $\mathcal{C}[\![(\gamma)]\!]$ is of course the same as $\mathcal{C}[\![\gamma]\!]$. Next $\mathcal{C}[\![\phi]\!]$ is a given state transformation, since ϕ is taken for the moment as a primitive (or atomic) command. (Later we could introduce some syntax for the category of ϕ if we wished, and this would require further semantic equations of a similar sort.) The dummy-*command* is next being interpreted as the "do nothing" transformation. The *conditional-command* on the other hand requires a conditional operator similar to the one used for expressions, except that the domain of definition is altered to make it appropriate to commands. Specifically we have

$$\mathit{Cond}\colon [\mathrm{S} \longrightarrow \mathrm{S}] \times [\mathrm{S} \longrightarrow \mathrm{S}] \longrightarrow [\mathrm{T} \longrightarrow [\mathrm{S} \longrightarrow \mathrm{S}]] \quad .$$

Some subscripts ought to be introduced to indicate the difference between the two kinds of *Cond*-functions, but we are relying on the context to make this clear. Finally $\gamma_0;\gamma_1$ is being interpreted as the *sequencing* operation on commands, which in terms of state transformations is simply the *composition of functions*. Note, however, the *order* of application. The "positional notation" of the command language conventionally places the first command to be executed on the left and the following one on the right. The convention with mathematical composition of functions is just the opposite. (The reason being the common use of $f(x)$ rather than xf for the function-value notation.)

In format these equations for $\mathcal{C}$ and $\mathcal{E}$ are not much different from those for $\mathcal{V}$ as applied to the numerals. In all cases there is a syntactical definition in several clauses. The semantical definition is "syntax-directed" in that it follows the same order of clauses and transforms each language construct into the intended operation on the meanings of the parts. In the case of numerals the meanings were familiar mathematical objects on which many familiar operations (addition, multiplication, etc.) were already defined. In the case of commands and Boolean expressions, the values were not so well known, nor were the operations (such as *Cond*) very common. Nevertheless, the domains $[S \longrightarrow S]$ and $[S \longrightarrow T \times S]$ are quite appropriate to the ideas that are being explained, and the various operations ($\circ$, $*$, P, M_0, M_1) are natural ones for these domains.

That it is necessary to construct meanings out of *functions* ($[S \longrightarrow S]$) may seem bothersome, but it should not be deplored. After all the idea of function is one of the greatest of our mathematical discoveries. The calculus would be impossible without functions, and the development of the subject would be unthinkable without the use of various operators (derivative, integral, etc.) and consideration of the equations involving them. Though formal languages are not generally made explicit, still there is constant translation from intuitive ideas to mathematical concepts (*velocity* means derivative, *area* means integral, *superposition* means addition of functions, and so on). In the case of computer languages we cannot say yet that we have introduced concepts anywhere near as important as those of the calculus, but the *spirit* of mathematizing ideas can and ought to be carried over. That the project is a useful activity remains to be demonstrated, but the treatment of *recursion* in the next section ought to indicate some of the advantages of the mathematical approach.

Before turning to more important concepts, the question of *ambiguity* must be faced again. We have allowed our grammars to be ambiguous, and so strictly speaking the semantical mappings $\mathcal{C}$ and $\mathcal{E}$ are not well defined. ($\mathcal{V}$ on Nml was well defined because that grammar was not ambiguous.) Is there a mistake here? We think not. Our attitude is that the meaning of an expression depends on the way it is parsed. From this point of view the mappings $\mathcal{C}$ and $\mathcal{E}$ are defined *not* on expressions *simpliciter* but rather on the annotated *deduction trees* for expressions based on rules of the grammar. (If one wishes a linear notation, a fully bracketed language could be introduced in the usual way, and then the expressions we have written above would result by deletion of the brackets and subscripts.) As emphasized above these brackets (or trees) are intolerable to write; hence, as long as we keep our semantic equations "in step" with the syntactical definitions and warn the reader of the oversimplification, it will be clear what is intended without the burden of any more notation. (In the terminology of Knuth [2, 3] we are still using only *synthesized* attributes in assigning meanings to expressions. Whether the *inherited-attribute* approach is convenient is something we must consider further, and there is no doubt that Knuth's way of introducing both bottom-up and top-down dependencies between semantic equations is an interesting notion. Be that as it may, the point of our paper is the study of *what* it is that semantic equations assign to expressions. The *path* by which the assignment is made is at the moment a secondary issue.)

III. RECURSION

The language of commands and expressions as introduced in the last section is at best of illustrative value. It was useful to see in not too horrible detail the connections between the syntactical and semantical equations. But the actual language used was of very limited expressive power. The command structure was of a very *direct* sort: the execution of such a command would proceed along a "branch" of a *tree*, the commands being composed in sequence and the choice of path at a branch point being decided by evaluation of a conditional expression. In Scott [6] the expressive power of such a language was expanded by the introduction of a certain kind of *infinite* tree, but the mathematics of this approach would take us too far afield here. And in any case, it is rather fully explained in that paper. Our interest here lies in more conventional language features; in particular those that can be written down in finite space. This does not mean that thinking of finite expressions as being "unrolled" into infinite trees might not be mathematically illuminating, rather we do not have the time to discuss it in this paper.

The question that leads to infinite trees is of course that of *recursively defined* commands. By way of example suppose that exit is a primitive command, as is fudge. Moreover, suppose that test is a primitive Boolean expression. One would wish then to introduce a command *loop* by the equation

$$loop = (\text{test} \longrightarrow \text{fudge};\ loop,\ \text{exit}) \ .$$

In other words, to loop means to alternate testing and fudging until a negative test is produced. At that moment a hasty exit is then required without further fudging. This is one of the simplest and most familiar examples. More generally it will be desired to introduce a whole *sequence* of interrelated commands $\xi_0, \xi_1, \xi_2, \cdots, \xi_{n-1}$ by a system of equations

$$\xi_0 = \gamma_0,\ \xi_1 = \gamma_1,\ \cdots,\ \xi_{n-1} = \gamma_{n-1} \ ,$$

where we may think of ξ_0 as the *principal* command to be executed and the remaining ξ_i as *auxiliary* commands introduced to aid the definition. Now the γ_j command expressions will involve reference to the ξ_i commands, just as in the *loop* example. Sometimes it is possible to eliminate the auxiliary commands at the expense of perspicuity by substitution of one equation in another. But at other times the elimination is not possible or not at all obvious. In any case it is a language feature of well-known convenience to allow simultaneous equations. All of this is very familiar ground.

Syntactically, to accommodate this recursive style of command definition, we must expand the language to allow for (temporary) *identifiers* which will refer to these auxiliary commands, the precise reference being controlled by a scheme of *declaration.* The exact style of identifiers need not concern us here; all we require is a syntactical category Id of expressions distinct from the other kinds of expressions mentioned so far. Besides this Id should be infinite to allow for as many auxiliaries as we please. We use the Greek ξ to range over Id.

Having provided identifiers, we then need to combine them with other command expressions. Of course an identifier standing alone will be allowed in the expanded Cmd. In this way identifiers can be included in the interiors of commands. Further the system of equations indicated above can be recorded in the following declaration scheme

$$\S\ \xi_0, \xi_1, \xi_2, \cdots, \xi_{n-1} : \gamma_0, \gamma_1, \gamma_2, \cdots, \gamma_{n-1}\ \$$$

where we have slightly torn apart the equations. The initial list of identifiers tells us to "watch out" because some auxiliaries are being introduced—in the order given. The following sequence of commands tells us how to use these auxiliaries with $\xi_i = \gamma_i$ intended—in the order as written. Recursion is permitted because the various ξ_i may occur within the γ_j. Having gone to the trouble of writing ξ_0 first, we may not only regard this expression as a scheme of declaration but also as an instruction to carry out ξ_0 *first*, thereby activating the other ξ_i as necessary under the control of the γ_j. (The brackets § and \$ are not strictly necessary, since we could regard : as the declaration operation and employ the colorless (and) to block ambiguity—but one can carry linguistic stinginess too far.)

This expansion of expression now requires a revision of the syntax for commands whereby the principal syntactical equation (for γ) is accompanied by some auxiliary equations for sequences (namely ξ^n and γ^n)

COMMANDS

$$\begin{aligned}
\gamma ::= &\ (\gamma) \mid \phi \mid \text{dummy} \mid \xi \mid \\
&\ \varepsilon \longrightarrow \gamma_0, \gamma_1 \mid \gamma_0 ; \gamma_1 \mid \\
&\ \S\ \xi^n : \gamma^n\ \$
\end{aligned}$$

$$\xi^n ::= \xi_0, \xi_1, \xi_2, \cdots, \xi_{n-1}\ (n > 0, \text{ the } \xi_i \text{ distinct}) \ ,$$

$$\gamma^n ::= \gamma_0, \gamma_1, \gamma_2, \cdots, \gamma_{n-1}\ (n > 0, \text{ the } \gamma_j \text{ arbitrary}) \ .$$

A word of explanation is in order here. Greek ξ is a metavariable over identifiers, while ξ^n by definition is a metavariable over n-tuples of *distinct* identifiers. (We keep $n > 0$, so the n-tuples are nonempty.) The metavariable γ^n ranges over n-tuples of commands (again, $n > 0$). In the last clause of the definition for γ note that the ξ^n and γ^n have the *same* n. Our language therefore is no longer context-free. But, if we may say so, who cares? Context-free languages have limited usefulness. Note, too, that we have not tried to torture ourselves with too rigorous a style of BNF syntactical definition. We deny that our syntax is not rigorous or even unaesthetic. On the other hand, if someone has a really neat language definition system that is as easy to comprehend at this level of discussion, we shall be glad to consider it. The last thing we want to be is dogmatic about *language*: it is in the mathematization of *concepts* that we have a certain amount of dogma to sell.

For the time being we introduce no revision in the definition of Boolean expressions $\mathcal{E}$. Note that the command construction

$$\S\ \xi^n : \gamma^n\ \$$$

is, logically speaking, a *variable-binding operator*. The identifiers ξ^n are the *bound* variables (and, since a matching with the γ^n is intended, they must be kept distinct); whereas other identifiers which occur may occur as *free variables* because the construction can be iterated. A certain semantical device will have to be introduced to handle this problem of scope of identifiers.

There are other problems, however, and the *loop*-example will suffice for illustration. In the official notation there are no equations for commands as such; rather our example above becomes

$$\S\ loop\text{: (test} \longrightarrow \text{fudge; } loop\text{, exit) } \$$$

which is a command with the understanding that $loop \in \text{Id}$. What is the exact meaning of this command? Whatever it is our dogma says it must be a state transformation in $[\text{S} \longrightarrow \text{S}]$. Let the command be called λ for short. We are asking what $\mathcal{C}[\![\lambda]\!]$ should be. Intuitively we want

$$\begin{aligned}\mathcal{C}[\![\lambda]\!] &= \mathcal{C}[\![\text{test} \longrightarrow \text{fudge; } \lambda\text{, exit}]\!] \ ,\\ &= Cond\,(\mathcal{C}[\![\lambda]\!] \circ \mathcal{C}[\![\text{fudge}]\!], \mathcal{C}[\![\text{exit}]\!]) * \mathcal{E}[\![\text{test}]\!] \ .\end{aligned}$$

To simplify our thinking here let

$$\begin{aligned}\ell &= \mathcal{C}[\![\lambda]\!] \ ,\\ f &= \mathcal{C}[\![\text{fudge}]\!] \ ,\\ \text{e} &= \mathcal{C}[\![\text{exit}]\!] \ ,\\ t &= \mathcal{E}[\![\text{test}]\!] \ ,\end{aligned}$$

where

$$\begin{aligned}\ell, f, \text{e} &\in [\text{S} \longrightarrow \text{S}] \ ,\\ t &\in [\text{S} \longrightarrow \text{T} \times \text{S}] \ .\end{aligned}$$

Of these f, e, and t are *known*, while ℓ is the *unknown* we seek. The functional equation for ℓ reads

$$\ell = Cond\,(\ell \circ f, \text{e}) * t \ .$$

Some solution or other to this equation—if any exists—has the right to be called $\mathcal{C}[\![\lambda]\!]$, the meaning of the *loop*-command as a state transformation.

Now comes the rub. So far we have not analyzed the nature of the set S at all, because we opted for extreme generality. If we stick to this generality and allow the functions f, e, and t to be *arbitrary* functions, then it is easy to construct an example where *no* solution for ℓ exists in the above equation at all. The reason is simple: f, e, and t are *total* functions so interrelated that any attempt to define ℓ as required sets up an *infinite loop*; so that *no* choice of values can be made to satisfy the equation as a functional equation between total functions.

The solution to this problem is easy enough and is well known: we modify our idea about the function space [S $\longrightarrow$ S]. We no longer demand that functions be total but understand the functions in [S $\longrightarrow$ S] to be partial functions. Thus for certain $\sigma \in S$ and certain $g \in$ [S $\longrightarrow$ S] we allow $g(\sigma)$ to be undefined. With this convention it can then be shown that the equation for ℓ does indeed have a solution in the partial function sense, and in fact it has a *least* solution. (By *least* we mean that the "graph" of the function is included in every other solution.) This approach is that of Park [4] and many others. (See references in Engeler [1].) Suitable as it is for many purposes and simple as it is, it is not quite the method we wish to adopt. Our method is related, but it is made a little more sophisticated in order to supply a closer analysis of the nature of the elements of S which is required for the explanation of other language features.

IV. LATTICES AND FIXED POINTS

In the last section we found it necessary to expand [S $\longrightarrow$ S] to allow for partial functions. The set of all partial functions is *partially ordered* by the relationship of one function's being *included* in the other. Under this partial ordering the set [S $\longrightarrow$ S] takes on a structure which has quite pleasant properties. These properties can be formulated in an abstract way, so that the proof of the existence of solutions to fixed-point equations can easily be given. In order to regularize and generalize this argument, it turns out to be natural to derive the structure on [S $\longrightarrow$ S] from structure on S. This is accomplished by *expanding* S until it becomes a partially ordered set itself—in fact, S will be made into a *complete lattice*. Just how this construction of an expanded S is to be done requires a closer examination of the kind of elements S should have. We will have to return to this question in more detail in Section VI. For the time being suppose that the expansion has been made.

Speaking a bit more generally for the moment, the structure of a complete lattice on a particular domain (set) D requires first a partial ordering which we write as

$$x \sqsubseteq y \ ,$$

for $x, y \in D$. This relationship is *reflexive*, *transitive*, and *anti-symmetric*. Next, if $X \subseteq D$ is a subset of D, we assume the existence of an element of D, called the *least upper bound* (*lub*) of the subset X, which we write as

$$\bigsqcup X \ .$$

We have for all $y \in D$

$$\bigsqcup X \sqsubseteq y \text{ iff } x \sqsubseteq y \text{ (for all } x \in X) \ ,$$

and this condition uniquely characterizes $\bigsqcup X \in D$. A complete lattice *is* a partially ordered set in which *lub*s always exist.

Among the *lub*s in a complete lattice there are two extreme ones: the *lub* of *nothing* and the *lub* of *everything*. That is to say, the empty subset $\emptyset$ and the full subset D will both have *lub*s to which we give special names

$$\bot = \bigsqcup \emptyset \text{ and } \top = \bigsqcup D \ .$$

Note that for all $x \in D$ it is the case that

$$\bot \sqsubseteq x \sqsubseteq \top .$$

We can think of $\bot$ as the *weakest* element and $\top$ as the *strongest element* of D. The *ordinary* elements are somewhere in between, and $\bot$ and $\top$ should be considered rather extraordinary. (We can call them *bottom* and *top.*)

An intuitive way of reading the relationship $x \sqsubseteq y$ is to say that x *approximates* y. Thus x is worse and y is better. But take care, the sense of approximation being used here is a *qualitative one* of what we might style *direct approximation.* The statement $x \sqsubseteq y$ does *not* mean that x is *very near* y, but rather that x is a *poorer version* of y, that x is only partially specified and that it can be *improved* to y without changing any of the definite features of x. For example in the case of partial functions, $\sqsubseteq$ means *inclusion* of graphs (the graph of a function is just the set of ordered pairs of arguments and function values); hence, *improvement* means *adding* new ordered pairs. The smaller set of ordered pairs can indeed be said to be an approximation to the larger one. (In the case of partial functions treated by graphs in the ordinary way, the structure becomes a lattice only when $\top$ is added in a somewhat artificial way as a *top* element which is not represented as a set of ordered pairs. We shall discuss partial functions in a slightly different way below.) Additional examples of approximations treated in this way can be found in Scott [5, 6].

If we take the notion of approximation seriously, then we have to rethink what we mean by *function.* Thus if

$$f: D \longrightarrow D ,$$

and

$$x \sqsubseteq y ,$$

then f should not juggle x and y around in too arbitrary a fashion. Indeed it ought to follow that

$$f(x) \sqsubseteq f(y) ,$$

because *if* we improve x to y, *then* in "calculating" $f(y)$ the calculation should be just an improvement over that for $f(x)$. Mathematically speaking the reasonable functions ought to be *monotonic* (i.e., $\sqsubseteq$ preserving).

Besides the intuitive motivation for monotonic functions, we have the well-known mathematical fact that *monotonic functions on complete lattices always have fixed points.* They even have *least* fixed points. This makes their use most convenient for our purposes.* Actually the functions we use—which are appropriate to computation theory—have an even stronger property: they are *continuous.* (See the discussion in Scott [5, 6].) We shall assume this stronger

*The argument for fixed points is as follows. Let $f: D \longrightarrow D$ be monotonic. Let $Y \subseteq D$ be the subset of all $y \in D$ such that $y \sqsubseteq z$ whenever $f(z) \sqsubseteq z \in D$. Let $x = \bigsqcup Y$. To show that $x = f(x)$, note first that $x \in Y$; because if $f(z) \sqsubseteq z$, then $y \sqsubseteq z$ for all $y \in Y$, so $x \sqsubseteq z$. Next note that $f(x) \in Y$; because if $f(z) \sqsubseteq z$, then $x \sqsubseteq z$, and so $f(x) \sqsubseteq f(z) \sqsubseteq z$ by monotonicity. Therefore $f(x) \sqsubseteq \bigsqcup Y = x$. But then $f(f(x)) \sqsubseteq f(x)$, again by monotonicity, so $x \sqsubseteq f(x)$ because $x \in Y$. Thus $x = f(x)$.

property but shall not go into the technical details in this paper. The reader should only be assured that normal functions are automatically continuous.

What does all this theory have to do with the subject of semantics? Step by step the relevance is this: Commands (programs) are naturally thought of as defining state transformations. Recursive commands require partial functions. Solving for these partial functions is just finding (minimal) fixed points in certain functional equations. In general the existence of fixed points is justified by a lattice-theoretic argument. Therefore, if we can see the connection between lattices and partial functions, the relevance of the theory will be established.

Returning to S, we promised to expand it to a lattice. This can be done in many ways, but for simplicity suppose that the initial version of S was just an abstract set, S_0, say. In S_0 we assume no particular connections between the elements for the sake of argument. The expanded S results merely by the adjunction of the two, new "fictitious" elements $\perp$ and $\top$. The partial ordering $\sqsubseteq$ aside from satisfying the usual axioms, provides in addition only the relationships

$$\perp \sqsubseteq x \sqsubseteq \top .$$

(For pictures of these and other partial orderings consult Scott [5, 6].) This expanded S becomes a complete lattice in a rather trivial way, and the construction should not be taken as being typical.

The function space $[S \longrightarrow S]$ is not regarded as being the set of *all monotonic functions* from S into S. (In more interesting lattices we shall restrict our function spaces to the continuous functions; in this example the restriction makes no difference.) For $\sigma \in S$ and $g \in [S \longrightarrow S]$ when we formerly wrote that

$$g(\sigma) \text{ is } \textit{undefined} \quad ,$$

we shall now write simply

$$g(\sigma) = \perp \ .$$

The new element $\perp$ can be regarded as an "embodiment" of the undefined. (The companion equation $g(\sigma) = \top$ could be read "$g(\sigma)$ is *overdefined,*" but the utility of this concept is not as obvious.) Now if f, $g \in [S \longrightarrow S]$ are any two functions, we can write

$$f \sqsubseteq g \quad ,$$

to mean that

$$f(\sigma) \sqsubseteq g(\sigma) \quad ,$$

for all $\sigma \in S$. This definition at once structures $[S \longrightarrow S]$ as a partially ordered set and indeed as a complete lattice. This is a natural definition for g's being an improvement over f, if one reads it in words, and it corresponds to our previous ideas about functions. Thus if $f(\sigma) = \perp$ (is undefined), then $g(\sigma)$ is *unrestricted* and can be any element of S. If $f(\sigma)$ is better defined (say, $f(\sigma) = \sigma'$, $\sigma' \in S$), then $g(\sigma)$ can only be σ' or $\top$ if the relationship $f \sqsubseteq g$ is going to hold. Hence $f \sqsubseteq g$ means just about what we intended when we said that the ordinary graph of f is included in that of g.

Note that by the embodiment of $\perp$, what used to be *partial* functions are now *total* functions in the expanded sense, because $g(\sigma) = \perp$ is an allowed "value." This may seem like a silly thing to do, but the main mathematical point is that the lattice structure on $[S \longrightarrow S]$ is now *derived,* by means of a simple definition, from the lattice structure on S. *And* by the very same regular process we can provide lattice structure on $[S \longrightarrow S] \longrightarrow [S \longrightarrow S]$, and in general on *any* $[D \longrightarrow D']$—always remembering to use the set of continuous functions for this construction.

We can now make more precise that we mean by T as a lattice; namely $T = \{\perp, \mathit{false}, \mathit{true}, \top\}$, where $\perp \sqsubseteq t \sqsubseteq \top$ holds for $t \in T$, but $\mathit{false} \not\sqsubseteq \mathit{true}$ and $\mathit{true} \not\sqsubseteq \mathit{false}$. We have used T in the context $T \times S$, and in general any $D \times D'$ can be construed as a lattice if D and D' are. One has only to define

$$<x, x'> \sqsubseteq <y, y'> \text{ iff } x \sqsubseteq y \text{ and } x' \sqsubseteq y' \quad ,$$

for all $x, y \in D$ and $x', y' \in D'$. In this way all of the domains $[T \longrightarrow [S \longrightarrow T \times S]]$, etc. can be regarded as lattices, and by the general method fixed points can be obtained when necessary. In particular in the equation

$$\ell = \mathit{Cond}\,(\ell \circ f, e) * t \quad ,$$

f, e, t were certain *constants* in their intended domains, and *Cond,* $\circ$, $*$ were certain functions (operators) on these domains. Under the present interpretation all these domains are lattices, and it can be checked that all these functions are indeed continuous. Therefore, the function

$$F: [S \longrightarrow S] \longrightarrow [S \longrightarrow S] \quad ,$$

where

$$F(\ell) = \mathit{Cond}\,(\ell \circ f, e) * t \quad ,$$

is itself a continuous function; and we know that such functions have fixed points. The price of generality is high, but eventually there are some returns on your investment.

Another kind of pay-off was discussed in some detail in Scott [6]. In that paper the *syntactical* domains were taken to be lattices also, and it was found that the mapping

$$\mathcal{C}: \text{Cmd} \longrightarrow [S \longrightarrow S] \quad ,$$

was not only continuous but its *existence* could be proved by the very same lattice-theoretical argument *via* fixed points. That is a rather fundamental point and unifies the theory considerably.

The whole process of forming fixed points can be given a functional formulation. Let D be any complete lattice and let $[D \longrightarrow D]$ be the lattice of continuous functions. Then there is a mapping

$$Y: [D \longrightarrow D] \longrightarrow D \quad ,$$

such that for each $f \in [D \longrightarrow D]$ the element $Y(f) \in D$ *is* the least fixed point of f. Hence

$$f(Y(f)) = Y(f) \quad ,$$

will be satisfied. What is remarkable and particularly useful is that Y itself is *continuous*. Thus if we employ Y in various equations along with other continuous functions we can rest assured that the compound functions obtained are also continuous. This makes the theory very *smooth*, if the reader will forgive the pun.

In making up these lattices it is sometimes useful to join two lattices together into one. We write $D + D'$ to mean the result of taking a copy of D and a disjoint copy of D' and forming the *union*. To make this union a lattice we *identify* the $\bot \in D$ with the $\bot' \in D'$ and similarly for $\top \in D$ and $\top' \in D'$ ($\bot = \bot'$ and $\top = \top'$). Thus, for "ordinary" elements of $D + D'$ we can say, roughly, that either they are elements of D or of D' but not both. The $\sqsubseteq$ relations are carried over directly with *no* connections imposed between the elements of the disjoint parts. We shall discuss in Section VI considerably more complex constructions of lattices of a "recursive" nature, but first it is necessary to explain the semantical treatment of identifiers.

V. IDENTIFIERS AND ENVIRONMENTS

In Section III we introduced into our syntax for commands the *identifiers* ($\xi \in \mathrm{Id}$). An identifier standing alone is an "unknown" having no predetermined meaning of its own—in contrast to the constants. The way one wishes to use identifiers, however, is to give them *temporary* meanings which can be altered within the differing scopes of different operators. The way to indicate a temporary assignment of meanings is by a function

$$\rho : \mathrm{Id} \longrightarrow [S \longrightarrow S] \ ,$$

which we call (the current) *environment* of the identifiers. We use $[S \longrightarrow S]$ here because in the elementary command language the values of the variables are to be command values. In other languages with other types of variables other types of values would have to be used.

Let us write for short

$$\mathrm{Env} = [\mathrm{Id} \longrightarrow [S \longrightarrow S]] \ .$$

Now it will no longer be true that a command has a "fixed" value, because our syntax allows $\gamma \in \mathrm{Cmd}$ to contain variables. What we have to do is to redefine $\mathcal{C}$ so that

$$\mathcal{C} : \mathrm{Cmd} \longrightarrow [\mathrm{Env} \longrightarrow [S \longrightarrow S]] \ .$$

That is to say, given $\gamma \in \mathrm{Cmd}$, we do not evaluate at once $\mathcal{C}[\![\gamma]\!]$ but rather have to provide the current $\rho \in \mathrm{Env}$ to find $\mathcal{C}[\![\gamma]\!](\rho)$ as a state transformation.

The details of this redefinition of $\mathcal{C}$ will require alterations of the environments. Our notation for this is the following. Suppose $\xi \in \mathrm{Id}$, $\theta \in [S \longrightarrow S]$, and $\rho \in \mathrm{Env}$. Then

$$\rho[\theta/\xi] \in \mathrm{Env} \ ,$$

is that environment ρ' which is just like ρ except for the one identifier ξ where we define

$$\rho'[\![\xi]\!] = \theta \ .$$

(Thus $\rho' = \rho[\theta/\xi]$ is the *modification* of the function ρ just at the argument ξ to have the prescribed value θ.) Generalizing this idea we can also write

$$\rho[\theta^n/\xi^n] \quad ,$$

where $\theta^n \in [S \longrightarrow S]^n$, the set of n-tuples of state transformations. Here ξ^n is a group of n distinct identifiers and the alteration changes all the n values of the original ρ. (These definitions require just a bit more rigor when Id is taken as a lattice in the more abstract version of syntax of Scott [6].)

We can now state the revised clauses of the semantical definition for $\mathcal{C}$. (The function $\mathcal{E}$ retains its former definition, because in this simple language Boolean expressions contain no identifiers.)

$$\begin{aligned}
&\mathcal{C}[\![(\gamma)]\!](\rho) = \mathcal{C}[\![\gamma]\!](\rho) \quad ,\\
&\mathcal{C}[\![\phi]\!](\rho) = (\text{some given } S \longrightarrow S) \quad ,\\
&\mathcal{C}[\![\text{dummy}]\!](\rho) = I \quad ,\\
&\mathcal{C}[\![\xi]\!](\rho) = \rho[\![\xi]\!] \quad ,\\
&\mathcal{C}[\![\varepsilon \longrightarrow \gamma_0, \gamma_1]\!](\rho) = \mathit{Cond}(\mathcal{C}[\![\gamma_0]\!](\rho), \mathcal{C}[\![\gamma_1]\!](\rho)) * \mathcal{E}[\![\varepsilon]\!] \quad ,\\
&\mathcal{C}[\![\gamma_0 ; \gamma_1]\!](\rho) = \mathcal{C}[\![\gamma_1]\!](\rho) \circ \mathcal{C}[\![\gamma_0]\!](\rho) \quad ,\\
&\mathcal{C}[\![\S\xi^n : \gamma^n \$]\!](\rho) = M_0^n\left(Y(\lambda\theta^n.\mathcal{C}[\![\gamma^n]\!](\rho[\theta^n/\xi^n]))\right) \quad .
\end{aligned}$$

These clauses are quite similar to the previous ones, except that the environment is dragged along into the interpretation of each compound command. It is invoked whenever an identifier stands in the place of a command (giving $\rho[\![\xi]\!]$ in the fourth clause). It is altered whenever identifiers are bound as formal parameters. This last clause requires a gloss.

First off if $\rho' \in \text{Env}$, then

$$\mathcal{C}[\![\gamma^n]\!](\rho') = \langle \mathcal{C}[\![\gamma_0]\!](\rho'), \mathcal{C}[\![\gamma_1]\!](\rho'), \cdots, \mathcal{C}[\![\gamma_{n-1}]\!](\rho') \rangle \quad ,$$

where $\gamma^n = \gamma_0, \gamma_1, \gamma_2, \cdots, \gamma_{n-1}$ is an n-tuple of commands. Therefore the metaexpression

$$\mathcal{C}[\![\gamma^n]\!](\rho[\theta^n/\xi^n]) \quad ,$$

can be regarded as a *function* of the n-tuple $\theta^n \in [S \longrightarrow S]^n$ whose values are also in $[S \longrightarrow S]^n$. The λ-expression

$$\lambda\theta^n.\mathcal{C}[\![\gamma^n]\!](\rho[\theta^n/\xi^n]) \quad ,$$

is just the name of that function in the domain

$$[S \longrightarrow S]^n \longrightarrow [S \longrightarrow S]^n \quad .$$

The Y-operator used in the equation above is then to have the logical type

$$[[S \longrightarrow S]^n \longrightarrow [S \longrightarrow S]^n] \longrightarrow [S \longrightarrow S]^n \quad .$$

(Cf. the end of the last section taking $D = [S \longrightarrow S]^n$.) The value of this Y-operator is an n-tuple, and M_0^n is the *selector* function such that

$$M_0^n(\langle \theta_0, \theta_1, \theta_2, \cdots, \theta_{n-1} \rangle) = \theta_0 \quad .$$

What we are doing here, then, is finding the least solution to the equation (really:

a *system* of n equations)

$$<\theta_0, \theta_1, \theta_2, \cdots, \theta_{n-1}> = \mathcal{C}[\![\gamma^n]\!](\rho[\theta^n/\xi^n]) ,$$

and setting

$$\mathcal{C}[\![\S\xi^n : \gamma^n \$]\!](\rho) = \theta_0 .$$

Our mathematical equations describe this process rather succinctly with the aid of the various functional operators. At first sight these operators seem horrendous, but actually they are not hard to read. Furthermore they *hide* just the right things leaving the structure and sequencing of the operations quite apparent. It would also seem to be an advantage to condense the various clauses to one or two lines: If one can actually write equations in detail, he may have a chance of proving a theorem. And his chances are improved if the equations are not too long. It remains to be seen, admittedly, whether the method is going to be really practical for more complex languages.

In the introduction we spoke of *models* for a theory, and it will be useful now to return to this discussion in the present context. The concepts of our language are separated into two kinds: the *primitive notions* and the *logical constructs* which are built on these. In the simple command language the primitive notions are the set of states S and the objects denoted by the π's and ϕ's. Let us introduce explicitly syntactical categories for these

$$\pi \in \mathrm{Pred} \quad \text{and} \quad \phi \in \mathrm{Op} ,$$

for the atomic predicates and operations. All the other concepts like the Boolean values, the conditional expressions, the sequencing and looping of commands are treated as logical notions with fixed meanings. The only chance for variation then lies in the primitive concepts. The interpretation of them would be established by giving mappings

$$\mathcal{P} : \mathrm{Pred} \longrightarrow [\mathrm{S} \longrightarrow \mathrm{T} \times \mathrm{S}] ,$$

and

$$\mathcal{O} : \mathrm{Op} \longrightarrow [\mathrm{S} \longrightarrow \mathrm{S}] ,$$

once S has been determined. We could then say that in broad outline models are given as

$$\mathrm{M} = <\mathrm{S}, \mathcal{P}, \mathcal{O}> ,$$

because once these features are specified the meanings of all expressions in the language are fixed. Of course all we have explained here is the *logical types* of $\mathcal{P}$ and $\mathcal{O}$, but that is all one needs to give the semantical definitions for

$$\mathcal{C}_\mathrm{M} : \mathrm{Cmd} \longrightarrow [\mathrm{S} \longrightarrow \mathrm{S}] ,$$

and

$$\mathcal{E}_\mathrm{M} : \mathrm{Exp} \longrightarrow [\mathrm{S} \longrightarrow \mathrm{T} \times \mathrm{S}] .$$

(That is, in the semantical definitions we should replace $\mathcal{C}$ by $\mathcal{C}_\mathrm{M}$ and $\mathcal{E}$ by $\mathcal{E}_\mathrm{M}$ and modify the atomic clauses to read

$$\mathcal{C}_\mathrm{M}[\![\phi]\!](\rho) = \mathcal{O}[\![\phi]\!], \quad \text{and} \quad \mathcal{E}_\mathrm{M}[\![\pi]\!] = \mathcal{P}[\![\pi]\!] .$$

By the way, in Scott [6] the $\mathcal{O}$ and the $\mathcal{P}$ were treated as parameters and it was noted that with S fixed both $\mathcal{C}_M$ and $\mathcal{E}_M$ are *continuous* in these parameters.)

With this point of view we can specialize and vary M in restricted classes that actually *are* models for some reasonable concept of computational structure —as we contemplated for various models of the theory of integers. Besides this we can *compare* two models. Thus if γ_0 and γ_1 are two commands, we say that they are *equivalent* in M iff

$$\mathcal{C}_M[\![\gamma_0]\!] = \mathcal{C}_M[\![\gamma_1]\!] \ .$$

It may very well be that γ_0 and γ_1 are equivalent in M but not in M′. That may be an interesting fact. Whether it is or not, we can at least say what we mean with the aid of our semantical definitions.

VI. PROCEDURES

The language features discussed up to this point have been of the most elementary sort and were kept simple just for the sake of illustration. Even so the mathematical entities associated with the commands and expressions were involved enough. Fortunately the level of complication that we have reached is a plateau on which a variety of other features can be accommodated without too much additional effort. Among the features pressing for recognition is of course the *assignment statement.* No programming language can be called practical if it does not include the assignment statement in some form. The issues surrounding the proper interpretation of the assignment statement, however, require a rather full treatment of their own, and this will have to be reserved for another publication [11]. In this section we select only one concept—that of a procedure—to discuss in any detail, mainly because it fits in well with our previous discussion of identifiers and function spaces. Even with this addition the language remains fragmentary. (In the syntax we shall make provision for an assignment statement, but the semantics of it and some other related ideas will only be briefly sketched. These inclusions are made so that the reader can grasp something of the style of the languages we are considering.)

In order to be able to include other concepts in our language a substantial extension of the repertoire of expressions beyond the Boolean level will be necessary. In some languages this is done through the introduction of a host of syntactical categories. This may be a practical idea to aid automatic syntax checking and error detection, but for understanding the language as a whole it is sometimes a formidable hurdle. For the sake of exposition we pretend that all the type checking is going to be done at *run time.* Thus all the expressions that have *values* will be massed together into one category. Before we start to define the category we should stop to consider what the values are going to be.

We always need *Boolean values* (T), and we may as well throw in at this point (integer) *arithmetic* values (N). If we will be getting into assignments, then some expressions will have *locations* (addresses) for values (L). In this paper we will not say too much about them, but we want to leave room for them. Next we bring up the suggestion that at some point one may want to store—or maybe pass as a parameter—a *command.* Hence we are going to allow elements of $C = [S \longrightarrow S]$ as values of expressions also. Finally we come to procedures (P).

A procedure is very much like a mathematical function. Now some functions have restricted domains, while others are more widely defined. We do not wish to consider here typed functions, so we shall attempt to permit our functions a free range of arguments and values. The different sorts of values were just described in the last paragraph. Let us put them together into one space, the *value space*

$$V = T + N + L + C + P \ .$$

Again for simplicity we restrict attention to *one-parameter* procedures; that is, the domain of a function will be V itself. The values will also turn up in V but the path cannot be so direct. Remember that every evaluation has to depend on the state of the system, and that any action generally has to effect a change of state. It will be just the same for procedures: evaluating a procedure at an argument may produce along with a value a change of state. This argument suggests that

$$P = [V \longrightarrow [S \longrightarrow V \times S]] \ .$$

Thus if $p \in P$ and $x \in V$, then we cannot find a value from $p(x)$ until we look at $\sigma \in S$. Then we get

$$p(x)(\sigma) = \langle y, \sigma' \rangle \ ,$$

where y is the value and σ' is the (possibly) altered state. That seems just fine.

Or does it? Suppose the state space were a one-element space which could be dropped from consideration. Suppose that we are in a dropping mood and that we forget about N, L, and C as well. Then the equation for V comes down to

$$V = T + P \ ,$$

which after substitution reads

$$V = T + [V \longrightarrow V] \ .$$

In words we can say that under the reduction every element of V is *either* a Boolean value *or* a function. It still sounds good, but there is trouble: in ordinary set theory there are *no such spaces*! Why? Because there is a cardinality question. V must have at least two elements; but if so, then by Cantor's Theorem the space of *all* functions $[V \longrightarrow V]$ always has *more* elements than V. Hence, the equation is impossible.

Here is the place where the lattice-theoretic pay-off is especially generous. By restricting $[V \longrightarrow V]$ to *continuous* functions the cardinality of the function space is considerably reduced. That is a help, but it is not enough just to have V and $T + [V \longrightarrow V]$ in any one-one correspondence. The correspondence must be *continuous*; then everything is fine, because we can rest assured that all our functional equations involve only continuous functions. (Remember, to be able to use a function as an argument of other operators, we must keep it *inside* the proper spaces.) The way to achieve a continuous isomorphism is not quite obvious and demands an inductive construction. Some remarks are given in Scott [5] and further hints are found in Scott [6]. The full details will be presented in papers under preparation (see references in the bibliography). In any case the outcome is that the construction of such self-referential spaces is not only possible, but they can be made to suit a variety of purposes—as long as one can be happy with continuous functions. Since we can argue that computability theory *is* happy with continuous functions, all is well, and the existence of the big value space V can be taken for granted.

All right, what then is the (a) language that might go along with V? (The authors have the peculiar idea that the domains of our concepts can be quite rigorously laid out *before* we make final the choice of the language in which we are going to describe these concepts. And it may turn out that the *same* domain is suitable for *several* languages. This is not to deny that there may be some vague ideas of language which influence our choice of domains. What we suggest is that, in order to sort out your ideas, you put your domains out on the table first. Then we can all start talking about them.) A possible format of the language would retain the distinction in category between Cmd and Exp. (This is a point one might wish to debate—but we do not have the space to do it here.) It is Exp that will undergo the major expansion over the earlier language, so we give Cmd first:

COMMANDS

$$\begin{aligned}\gamma ::= {} & (\gamma) \mid \phi \mid \text{dummy} \mid \xi \mid \\ & \varepsilon \longrightarrow \gamma_0, \gamma_1 \mid \gamma_0; \gamma_1 \mid \\ & \S \xi^n : \gamma^n \$ \mid \\ & \varepsilon! \mid \varepsilon_0 := \varepsilon_1 \ .\end{aligned}$$

This looks almost the same as before except for the last two clauses. Since we will convert commands into expressions, the $\varepsilon!$ is needed for the reverse process. The $\varepsilon_0 := \varepsilon_1$ is the assignment statement taken as a command to make the required assignment.

Turning now to expressions we must take note of the five parts of V:

EXPRESSIONS

$$\begin{aligned}\varepsilon ::= {} & (\varepsilon) \mid \pi \mid \xi \mid \\ & \varepsilon : \mathrm{T} \mid \text{true} \mid \text{false} \mid \varepsilon_0 \longrightarrow \varepsilon_1, \varepsilon_2 \mid \varepsilon_0 = \varepsilon_1 \mid \\ & \varepsilon : \mathrm{N} \mid \nu \mid \varepsilon_0 \,\omega\, \varepsilon_1 \mid \\ & \varepsilon : \mathrm{L} \mid \uparrow \varepsilon \mid \downarrow \varepsilon \mid \\ & \varepsilon : \mathrm{C} \mid : \gamma \mid \\ & \varepsilon : \mathrm{P} \mid \lambda \xi . \varepsilon \mid \varepsilon_0 \varepsilon_1 \mid \\ & \gamma \text{ resultis } \varepsilon \ .\end{aligned}$$

Note that identifiers occur in both Cmd and Exp. Some may wish to avoid the overlap, but it actually does not cause any difficulty, because we will separate values in a moment.

Before trying to understand the features of this language, it will be well to state the exact logical types of the semantical functions. An identifier will be assigned an element *either* from C *or* from V depending on how it is to be used. This means that now we shall have to set

$$\mathrm{Env} = [\mathrm{Id} \longrightarrow \mathrm{C} + \mathrm{V}] \ .$$

Strictly speaking C, V, and C + V are all different domains even though the first two are matched with *parts* of C + V. We shall require a more precise notation to indicate this matching. A completely precise symbolism would be cumbersome, so we write

$$(\theta \text{ in } [C + V]) \quad \text{and} \quad (\beta \text{ in } [C + V]) \ ,$$

where $\theta \in C$ and $\beta \in V$ to indicate the *corresponding* elements of C + V. For $\delta \in C + V$ we write

$$\delta | C \quad \text{and} \quad \delta | V \ ,$$

to indicate the "projection" from C + V onto its two parts. (In case δ corresponds to an element of C, then $\delta | V = \bot$; and if δ comes from V, then $\delta | C = \bot$. The lack of precision becomes clear for spaces such as C + C where one would have to distinguish between left- and right-hand parts.)

The logical types of the functions $\mathcal{C}$ and $\mathcal{E}$ now will be these

$$\mathcal{C} : \text{Cmd} \longrightarrow [\text{Env} \longrightarrow [S \longrightarrow S]] \ ,$$

and

$$\mathcal{E} : \text{Exp} \longrightarrow [\text{Env} \longrightarrow [S \longrightarrow V \times S]] \ .$$

We shall not state all the semantical equations, since either they have already been discussed enough for the simpler language, or they require too much additional development. But a few can be shown.

For the case of identifiers, we use

$$\mathcal{C} [\![\xi]\!] (\rho) = \rho [\![\xi]\!] | C \ ,$$

and

$$\mathcal{E} [\![\xi]\!] (\rho) = \lambda \sigma . \langle \rho [\![\xi]\!] | V, \sigma \rangle \ ,$$

which keep the types straight. Note that in the latter equation we had to make the right hand side a function of $\sigma \in S$ with values in $V \times S$. The point is that if we ask for the value of ξ as an expression relative to the environment and the state of the system, then the answer is to be just $\rho(\xi) | V$ *without* any change of state.

With the two new kinds of commands, we have in the first instance

$$\mathcal{C} [\![\varepsilon !]\!] (\rho) = Do * \mathcal{E} [\![\varepsilon]\!] (\rho) \ ,$$

where *Do* is a special operator defined as follows

$$Do : V \longrightarrow [S \longrightarrow S],$$

and

$$Do(\beta)(\sigma') = (\beta | C)(\sigma') \ .$$

By this we mean to indicate that $C = [S \longrightarrow S]$ is itself a part of V. Thus if

$$\mathcal{E} [\![\varepsilon]\!] (\rho)(\sigma) = \langle \beta, \sigma' \rangle \ ,$$

then we project β into $\beta | C$ and apply that to σ' obtaining

$$\sigma'' = (\beta | C)(\sigma') \ .$$

That is the resultant change of state in executing $\varepsilon!$ so that

$$\mathcal{C} [\![\varepsilon !]\!] (\rho)(\sigma) = \sigma'' \ .$$

In the second instance, the assignment command, the sequence of events is more complicated.

In this paper we shall not try to write the equation for

$$\mathcal{C}[\![\varepsilon_0 := \varepsilon_1]\!] (\rho)(\sigma) \ ,$$

but we can say in words more or less what happens. We first evaluate

$$\mathcal{E}[\![\varepsilon_0]\!] (\rho)(\sigma) = \langle \beta, \sigma' \rangle \ ,$$

and project β to $\alpha = \beta \mid L$, a location. Next we evaluate

$$\mathcal{E}[\![\varepsilon_1]\!] (\rho)(\sigma') = \langle \beta', \sigma'' \rangle \ .$$

Now comes the scuffle. If β' is not in the part of V which comes from L, we set $\beta'' = \beta'$. However, if β' *does* correspond to a location, then we consider $\alpha' = \beta' \mid L$. At this point we reveal that these mysterious "states of the system" are the internal states of our hypothetical machine. That is to say, σ'' represents (among other things) the current state of the *memory* of the machine—a memory which provides *contents* for *locations*. Thus there is a function to be applied to extract the desired contents, and we can write

$$\beta'' = \mathit{Contents}(\alpha')(\sigma'') \ .$$

In any case we have $\beta'' \in V$. Finally there is one last transformation to be made: we have a location α and a value β'' and the current state σ''. All that remains is to *assign* β'' to α in σ'' obtaining

$$\sigma''' = \mathit{Assign}(\alpha, \beta'')(\sigma'') \ .$$

We then assert that the equation

$$\mathcal{C}[\![\varepsilon_0 := \varepsilon_1]\!] (\rho)(\sigma) = \sigma''' \ ,$$

makes the interpretation of the command what is usually intended. Well, that is reasonably precise, but it only becomes completely rigorous when we give an explicit *construction* of S as a domain of internal states along with the concomitant functions *Contents* and *Assign*. The exposition of these ideas is the task of Strachey [11].

Shifting now to the semantics of expressions, the compounds of the sort $\varepsilon : D$ are meant as Boolean-valued predicates which distinguish between the various parts of V; namely, D = T, N, L, C, or P. Take note of the fact that T has been made a part of V so that after a Boolean value $t \in T$ has been found, it will have to be injected into V. For example, to find the value of

$$\mathcal{E}[\![\varepsilon_0 = \varepsilon_1]\!] (\rho)(\sigma) \ ,$$

we have to evaluate ε_0, then ε_1, then see if they belong to the same part of V. If they do and the part is T, N, or L, then a test for *equality* is meaningful. We carry the test out, get a truth value, and then wrap it up into V. Remember too that the state of the system will have been changing.

We need not discuss here the evaluation of numerals (ν) or arithmetic operations (ω). The mysterious operators $\uparrow$ and $\downarrow$ are for *referencing* and *dereferencing*—operations involving locations. Thus to evaluate

$$\mathcal{E}[\![\uparrow \varepsilon]\!] (\rho)(\sigma) \ ,$$

we have to find first

$$\mathcal{E}[\![\, \varepsilon \,]\!](\rho)(\sigma) = \langle \beta, \sigma' \rangle \;.$$

Then we have to find a *new* (unused) location α in σ and take

$$\sigma'' = \mathit{Assign}(\alpha, \beta)(\sigma') \;,$$

making

$$\mathcal{E}[\![\, \uparrow \varepsilon \,]\!](\rho)(\sigma) = \langle \alpha, \sigma'' \rangle \;.$$

In other words $\uparrow\varepsilon$ gives a *reference* to the value of ε. Obviously we want $\downarrow\varepsilon$ to be the opposite: ε is evaluated as having a value in L and then the *contents* of the current state of the system provide the value for $\downarrow\varepsilon$.

In the case of commands as expressions we take

$$\mathcal{E}[\![\, : \gamma \,]\!](\rho)(\sigma) = \langle \mathcal{C}[\![\, \gamma \,]\!](\rho) \text{ in } \mathrm{V}, \sigma \rangle \;.$$

Note especially that *no* change of state has taken place and that $\mathcal{C}[\![\, \gamma \,]\!](\rho)$ has not been activated. The command has been "read," so to speak, but it has not been executed. Why do we do this? Because one may wish to store a command or pass it as a parameter *without* executing it. In that way it can be set up and then set aside for later use.

Before we finish our survey of the semantics with a look at procedures, the resultis-construct can be given a quick explanation

$$\mathcal{E}[\![\, \gamma \text{ resultis } \varepsilon \,]\!](\rho) = \mathcal{E}[\![\, \varepsilon \,]\!](\rho) \circ \mathcal{C}[\![\, \gamma \,]\!](\rho) \;.$$

That is to say, do γ first, *then* evaluate ε. This combination is very similar to $\gamma_0;\gamma_1$ but is of a different syntactical category.

Finally, we come to procedures where the notation used in the language is just that of the functional abstraction/functional application sort. Abstraction is easy

$$\mathcal{E}[\![\, \lambda\xi . \varepsilon \,]\!](\rho)(\sigma) = \langle f \text{ in } V, \sigma \rangle \;,$$

where $f \in \mathrm{P}$ is defined by

$$f = \lambda\beta . \mathcal{E}[\![\, \varepsilon \,]\!](\rho[\beta \text{ in } \mathrm{C} + \mathrm{V}/\xi]) \;.$$

Here $\beta \in \mathrm{V}$ and

$$f : \mathrm{V} \longrightarrow [\mathrm{S} \longrightarrow \mathrm{V} \times \mathrm{S}] \;,$$

comes out correctly by reference to the logical type of $\mathcal{E}$. Note that the evaluation of a functional abstraction requires no change of state. This is reasonable because none of the state transformations that may be lurking in ε can come out in the open until we know the value of σ. This cannot be known at the time the function is defined; we have to wait until it is applied to an argument.

Application can be interpreted in at least two ways. We take a more direct path—which might not be the most flexible. Thus to evaluate

$$\mathcal{E}[\![\, \varepsilon_0 \varepsilon_1 \,]\!](\rho)(\sigma) \;,$$

first find

$$\mathcal{E}[\![\, \varepsilon_0 \,]\!](\rho)(\sigma) = \langle \beta, \sigma' \rangle \;,$$

and set $f = \beta \mid P$. Then find

$$\mathcal{E}[\![\varepsilon_1]\!] (\rho)(\sigma') = \langle \beta', \sigma'' \rangle \quad ,$$

and set

$$\mathcal{E}[\![\varepsilon_0 \varepsilon_1]\!] (\rho)(\sigma) = f(\beta')(\sigma'') \quad .$$

(The "indirect" route would test β to see if it were an L, if so all it would require is to look up the contents of that location and try to use that value. If β were not in the L part of V, then we would proceed as above.)

By the time we got around to the procedures there was not so very much to say. The point is of course that

$$\lambda\xi.\varepsilon \quad ,$$

is but one clause of a highly recursive definition. The ε can be any compound expression. Thus the value of $\lambda\xi.\varepsilon$ is a complicated function. The construction of our value space allows us to treat this function (a mathematical object) just like any other value. It can be used as an argument of another function, it can be stored, it can be thought about in a mathematical way.

VII. CONCLUSION

There are many features missing from the language of the last section; to name a few: lists, structured values, initialization of parameters, more flexible parameter passing, recursive procedure definitions. This last is very important. Even though the space

$$[V \longrightarrow [S \longrightarrow V \times S]] \quad ,$$

contains all the values of procedures, we gave no notation for recursively defined procedures the way we did for recursively defined commands. The reason for passing over that topic is the difficulty in keeping track of the state transformations involved in such definitions. This will have to be a topic for another essay.

Despite the shortcomings of the present exposition, we do feel, however, that we have demonstrated the possibility of a mathematical semantics for sophisticated languages. And we hope by now the reader understands what we mean by "mathematical semantics." In this approach the semantical functions give mathematical values to expressions—values related to some given model. The values of expressions are determined in such a way that the value of a whole expression depends functionally on the values of its parts—the exact connection being found through the clauses of the syntactical definition of the language. In this way the syntax is kept to a minimum so one can concentrate on the semantical interpretation.

The advantages of the method are many. In the first place we feel that it gets at the essence of meaning without having to formalize any bookkeeping, symbol tables, identifier lists, road maps or what have you—as is necessary in some language definitions. Furthermore, the method is conceptual and is not just a formal translation from one language into another. Sometimes the translation scheme is useful, but usually a full translation, say into the language of an "abstract" machine, makes it hard to discuss the features of the original language in isolation. As we have shown above we can move through the language one clause at a time, stopping to get a clear understanding of each construct by itself.

The present paper is one of a series that is the outcome of a collaboration which the authors started in the fall of 1969; further papers are mentioned in the references. As it now stands this theory falls into two rather distinct parts: the development of the appropriate mathematical apparatus, and its application to the application of programming languages. From a logical point of view the development of the mathematical foundations should obviously precede their application, but as often happens it is difficult to know exactly what mathematical apparatus is needed until some applications have been attempted.

The genesis of this approach is a paper given at a Working Conference on Formal Language Description Languages sponsored by IFIP in September 1964 (Strachey [10]). Although that paper contained the beginnings of the semantical ideas described here, it was quite unsatisfactory from a mathematical point of view. Not only was there no attempt at mathematical rigor, but the very existence of some of the objects used was not certain. For example, referring again to the domain mentioned in Section VI which is quite naturally associated with interpretations of reasonable languages

$$V = T + N + L + [S \longrightarrow S] + [V \longrightarrow [S \longrightarrow V \times S]] \quad ,$$

it is particularly important to note that such a domain *cannot* be constructed by ordinary set-theoretical means. Hence, the need for some such mathematical apparatus as we have presented here was forced on us. The present paper covers much the same ground as Strachey [10], but this time the mathematical foundations are secure. It is also intended to act as a bridge between the formal mathematical foundations and their applications to programming languages by explaining in some detail the notation and techniques we have found to be most useful.

Very much work remains to be done. An essential topic will be the discussion of the relation between the mathematical semantics for a language and the implementation of the language. What we claim the mathematics will have provided is the standard against which to judge an implementation. Thus if $\lambda\xi.\varepsilon$ is a function definition, then our semantics tells us which function—as a mathematical object—was intended. Any implementation must provide us with answers that are in complete harmony with this function in the same way we expect even the simplest desk calculator to be able to add. An interesting question here is whether the function defined by $\lambda\xi.\varepsilon$ is calculable at all—in any sense. All of these questions are basic and do not even make sense without the proper mathematical foundation, which is just what we think our theory provides.

REFERENCES

[1] "Semantics of Algorithmic Languages," *Springer Lecture Notes in Mathematics*, **188**, (E. Engeler, Ed., 1971).

[2] D. E. Knuth, "Semantics of Context-Free Languages," *Mathematical Systems Theory*, **2**, 127–145 (1968).

[3] ———, "Examples of Formal Semantics," *Springer Lecture Notes in Mathematics*, **188**, 212–235 (E. Engeler, Ed., 1971).

[4] D. Park, "Fixpoint Induction and Proofs of Program Properties," *Machine Intelligence*, **5**, 59–78 (1969).

[5] D. Scott, "Outline of a Mathematical Theory of Computation," *Proc. 4th Ann. Princeton Conf. Information Sciences and Systems*, 169–176 (1970).

[6] ———, "The Lattice of Flow Diagrams," *Springer Lecture Notes in Mathematics*, **188**, 311–366 (E. Engeler, Ed., 1971).

[7] ———, "Continuous Lattices," *Proc. Dalhousie Conf.*, Springer Lecture Notes (to be published).

[8] ———, "Lattice-theoretic Models for Various Type-Free Calculi" (to be published).

[9] ———, "Data Types as Lattices" (to be published).

[10] C. Strachey, "Towards a Formal Semantics," *Formal Language Description Languages*, 198–220 (T. B. Steel, Ed., North Holland, 1966).

[11] ———, "An Abstract Model for Storage" (to be published).

ON THE DESIGN AND SPECIFICATION OF A COMMON BASE LANGUAGE

Jack B. Dennis[†]
Massachusetts Institute of Technology, Cambridge, MA

This is a report on the work of the Computation Structures Group of Project MAC toward the design and specification of a common base language for programs and information structures. We envision that the meanings of programs expressed in practical source languages will be defined by rules of translation into the base language. The meanings of programs in the base language is fixed by rules of interpretation which constitute a transition system called the interpreter for the base language. We view the base-language interpreter as the functional specification of a computer system in which emphasis is placed on programming generality—the ability of users to build complex programs by combining independently-written program modules.

Our concept of a common base language is similar to the abstract programs of the Vienna definition method—but a single class of abstract programs applies to all source languages to be encompassed. The semantic constructs of the base language must be just those fundamental constructs necessary for the effective realization of the desired range of source languages. Thus we seek simplicity in the design of the interpreter at the expense of increased complexity of the translator from a source language to the base language. As an illustration of this philosophy, we present a rudimentary form of the base language in which nonlocal references are not permitted, and show how programs expressed in a simple block-structured language may be translated into this base language.

The importance of representing concurrency within and among computations executed by the interpreter is discussed, and our approach toward incorporating concurrency of action in the base language is outlined.

INTRODUCTION

The Computation Structures Group of Project MAC is working toward the design and specification of a base language for programs and information structures. The base language is intended to serve as a common intermediate representation for programs expressed in a variety of source programming languages.

The motivation for this work is the design of computer systems in which the creation of correct programs is as convenient and easy as possible. A major ingredient in the convenient synthesis of programs is the ability to build large programs by combining simpler procedures or program modules, written independently, and perhaps by different individuals using different source languages.

[†]Computation Structures Group, Project MAC, MIT.

Presented at the Symposium on Computers and Automata
Polytechnic Institute of Brooklyn, April 13-15, 1971.

This ability of a computer system to support modular programming we have called *programming generality* [3, 4]. Programming generality requires the communication of data among independently-specified procedures, and thus that the semantics of the languages in which these procedures are expressed must be defined in terms of a common collection of data types and a common concept of data structure.

We have observed that the achievement of programming generality is very difficult in conventional computer systems, primarily because of the variety of data reference and access methods that must be used for the implementation of large programs with acceptable efficiency. For example, data structures that vary in size and form during a computation are given different representations from those that are static; data that reside in different storage media are accessed by different means of reference; clashes of identifiers appearing in different blocks or procedures are prevented by design in some source languages but similar consideration has not been given to the naming and referencing of cataloged files and procedures in the operating environment of programs. These limitations on the degree of generality possible in computer systems of conventional architecture have led us to study new concepts of computer-system organization through which these limitations on programming generality might be overcome.

In this effort we are working at the same time on developing the base language and on concepts of computer architecture suited to the execution of computations specified by base-language programs. That is, we regard the base language we seek to define as a specification of the functional operation of a computer system. Thus our work on the base language is strongly influenced by hardware concepts derived from the requirements of programming generality [3].

In particular, the choice of trees with shared substructures as our universal representation for information structures is based in part on a conviction that there are attractive hardware realizations of memory systems for tree-structured data. For example, Gertz [8] considers how such a memory system might be designed as a hierarchy of associative memories. Also, the base language is intended to represent the concurrency of parts of computations in a way that permits their execution in parallel. One reason for emphasizing concurrency is that it is essential to the description of certain computations—in particular, when a response is required to whichever one of several independent events is first to occur. An example is a program that must react to the first message received from either of two remote terminals. Furthermore, we believe that exploiting the potential concurrency in programs will be important in realizing efficient computer systems that offer programming generality. This is because concurrent execution of program parts increases the utilization of processing hardware by providing many activities that can be carried forward while other activities are blocked pending retrieval of information from slower parts of the computer-system memory.

Our proposal for the definition of a common base language may seem like a rebirth of the proposal to develop a Universal Computer-Oriented Language [24]. Thus it is reasonable to inquire whether there is any better chance that the development suggested here will succeed whereas this earlier work did not result in a useful contribution to the art. Our confidence in eventual success rests on important trends in the computer field during the past ten years and fundamental differences in philosophy. The most important change is the increased importance of achieving greater programming generality in future computer systems. The cost of acquiring and operating the hardware portion of computer systems has become dominated by the expense of creating and maintaining the system and application software. At present, there is great interest in the exchange of programs and data among computer installations, and in building complex procedures from components through the facilities of time-shared computers. Computer users are often prepared to forsake efficiency of programs to gain the ability to operate them in different environments, and the ability to use the program in conjunction with other programs to accomplish a desired objective.

Furthermore, the pace of programming-language evolution has slowed. It is rare that a fundamentally new concept for representing algorithms is introduced. Workers on programming-language design have turned to refining the conceptual basis of program representation, providing more natural modes of expressing algorithms in different fields, and consolidating diverse ways of representing similar actions. Today, there is good reason to expect that a basic set of notions about data and control structures will be sufficient to encompass a usefully large class of practical programming languages and applications. In particular, the set of elementary data types used in computation has not changed significantly since the first years of the stored program computer—they are the integers, representations for real numbers, the truth values **true** and **false**, strings of bits, and strings of symbols from an alphabet. Also, considerable attention is currently devoted to the development of useful abstract models for information structures, and the prospects are good that these efforts will converge on a satisfactory general model.

We are also encouraged by others who are striving toward similar goals. Andrei Ershov is directing a group at the Novosibirsk Computing Center of the Soviet Union in the development of a common "internal language" for use in an optimizing compiler for three different languages: PL/I; Algol 68; and Simula 67 [7]. The internal language would be a representation common to the three source languages and is to serve as the representation in which transformations are performed for machine-independent optimization.

The "contour model" for program execution, as explained by Johnston [10] and Berry [1] provides a readily understood vehicle for explaining the semantics of programming languages such as Algol 60, PL/I, and Algol 68 in which programs have a nested-block structure. It is easy to imagine how the contour model could be formalized and thus serve as a basis for specifying the formal semantics of programming languages. The contour model may be considered as a proposal for a common base language and as a guide for the design of computer systems that implement block-structured languages.

John Iliffe has for some time recognized some of the fundamental implications of programming generality with respect to computer organization. His book, *Basic Machine Principles* [9] is a good exposition of his ideas which are argued from the limitations of conventional computer hardware in executing general algorithms. Again, Iliffe's machine defines a scheme of program representation that could be thought of as a common base language. However, Iliffe has not discussed his ideas from this viewpoint.

FORMAL SEMANTICS

When the meaning of algorithms expressed in some programming language has been specified in precise terms, we say that a *formal semantics* for the language has been given. A formal semantics for a programming language generally takes the form of two sets of rules: one set being a *translator*; and the second set being an *interpreter*. The translator specifies a transformation of any well-formed program expressed in the source language (the *concrete language*) into an equivalent program expressed in a second language—the *abstract language* of the definition. The interpreter expresses the meaning of programs in the abstract language by giving explicit directions for carrying out the computation of any well-formed abstract program as a countable set of primitive steps.

It would be possible to specify the formal semantics of a programming language by giving an interpreter for the concrete programs of the source language. The translator is then the identity transformation. Yet the inclusion of a translator in the definition scheme has important advantages. For one, the phrase structure of a programming language viewed as a set of strings on some alphabet usually does not correspond well with the semantic structure of programs. Thus it is desirable to give the semantic rules of interpretation for a representation of the program that more naturally represents its semantic structure. Furthermore, many constructs present in source languages are provided for convenience rather than as fundamental linguistic features. By arranging the translator to replace occurrences of these constructs with more-basic constructs, a simpler abstract language is possible, and its interpreter can be made more-readily understandable and therefore more useful as a tool for the design and specification of computer languages and systems.

The abstract language that has received the most attention as a base for the formal semantics of programming languages is the lambda calculus of Church. For several reasons we have found the lambda calculus unsuited to our work. The most serious problem is that the lambda calculus does not deal directly with structured data. Thus it is inconvenient to use the lambda calculus as a common target language for programs that make use of selection to reference components of information structures. It also rules out modeling of sharing in the form of two or more structures having the same substructure as a component.

A second defect in terms of our goals is that the lambda calculus incorporates the concept of free and bound variables characteristic of block-structured programming languages. We prefer to exclude these concepts so the base language and its interpreter are simpler and more readily applied to the study of computer organization. Later in the paper we show how block-structured programs may be translated into base-language programs using the rudimentary version of the base language introduced below. This translation of block-structured programs into programs that are not block structured is an important example of how simplicity in the interpreter may be obtained by translating source-language constructs into more-primitive constructs.

Our thoughts on the definition of programming languages in terms of a base language are closely related to the formal methods developed at the IBM Vienna Laboratory [17, 18], and which derive from the ideas of McCarthy [19, 20] and Landin [13, 14]. For the formal semantics of programming languages, a general model is required for the data on which programs act. We regard data as consisting of *elementary objects* and *compound objects* formed by combining elementary objects into data structures.

Elementary objects are data items whose structure in terms of simpler objects is not relevant to the description of algorithms. For the purposes of this paper, the class E of elementary objects is

$$E = Z \cup R \cup W ,$$

where: Z = the class of integers; R = a set of representations for real numbers; and W = the set of all strings on some alphabet.

Data structures are often represented by directed graphs in which elementary objects are associated with nodes, and each arc is labeled by a member of a set S of *selectors*. In the case of objects used by the Vienna group, the graphs are restricted to be trees, and elementary objects are associated only with leaf nodes. We prefer a less restricted class so an object may have distinct component objects that share some third object as a common component. The reader will see that this possibility of sharing is essential to the formulation of the base language and interpreter presented here. Our class of objects is defined as follows.

DEFINITION. *Let* E *be a class of* elementary objects, *and let* S *be a class of* selectors. *An* object *is a directed acyclic graph having a single root node from which all other nodes may be reached over directed paths. Each arc is labeled with one selector in* S, *and an elementary object in* E *may be associated with each leaf node.*

We use integers and strings as selectors

$$S = Z \cup W .$$

Figure 1 gives an example of an object. Leaf nodes having associated elementary objects are represented by circles with the element of E written inside; integers are represented by numerals, strings are enclosed in single quotes, and reals have decimal points. Other nodes are represented by solid dots, with a horizontal bar if there is more than one emanating arc.

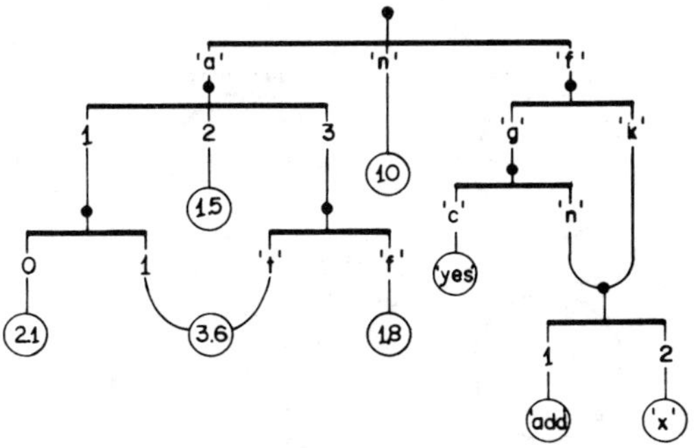

Fig. 1. An example of an object.

The node of an object reached by traversing an arc emanating from its root node is itself the root node of an object called a *component* of the original object. The component object consists of all nodes and arcs that can be reached by directed paths from its root node.

At present, we rule out directed cycles in the graphs of objects for several reasons: In the first place, the data structures of the most important source languages are readily modelled as objects according to our definition. Also, it seems that realizing the maximal concurrency of computations on data structures will be difficult to do with a guarantee of determinism if objects are permitted to contain cycles. Finally, the possibility of cycles invalidates the reference-count technique of freeing storage for data items no longer accessible to computations, and some more-general garbage-collection scheme must be used. The general techniques do not seem attractive with regard to the concepts of computer organization we have been studying—especially when data items are distributed among several physical levels of memory.

It is convenient to introduce our concept of a base language and its interpreter by comparison with the Vienna definition method as represented by the formal definitions of Algol 60 [15] and PL/I [18]. The Vienna method is outlined in Figure 2. The concrete programs of the programming language being defined are mapped into abstract programs by the translator. A concrete program is a string of symbols that satisfies a concrete syntax usually expressed as a form of context-free grammar. The interpreter is a nondeterministic state-transition system defined by a relation that specifies all possible next states for any state of the interpreter. Abstract programs and the states of the interpreter are represented by objects (trees). Figure 2 shows the three major components of interpreter states. The 'text'-component is the abstract program being interpreted. The 'mem'-component is an object that contains the values of variables in the abstract program, thus serving as a model of memory. The 'cont'-component of the state contains information about statements of the abstract program whose execution is in progress. The interpreter is specified as a nondeterministic system so activities may be carried out concurrently where permitted by the language being defined.

For comparison, note that a separate class of abstract programs and interpreter are specified for each formal definition of a source language; that states of the interpreter model only the information structures related to execution of

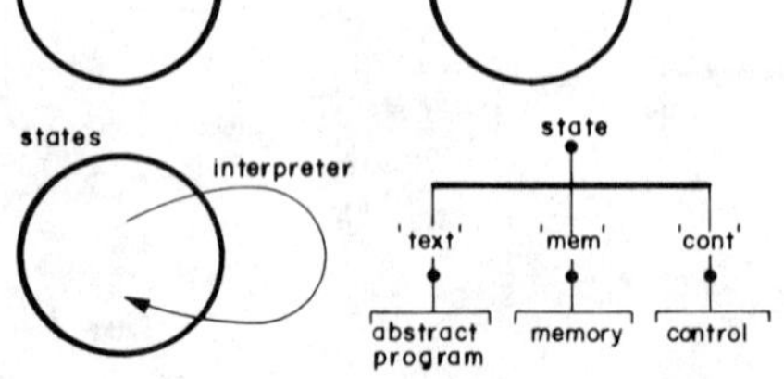

Fig. 2. Language definition by the Vienna method.

one abstract program; and that statements in the concrete program retain their identity as distinct parts of the corresponding abstract program.

Figure 3 is the corresponding outline showing how source languages would be defined in terms of a common base language. A single class of abstract programs constitutes the base language. Concrete programs in source languages (*L*1 and *L*2 in the figure) are defined by translators into the base language—the class of abstract programs serves as the common target representation for several source languages. For this to be effectively possible, the base language should be the "least common denominator" of the set of source languages to be accommodated. The structure of abstract programs cannot reflect the peculiarities of any particular source language, but must provide a set of fundamental linguistic constructs in terms of which the features of these source languages may be realized. The translators themselves should be specified in terms of the base language, probably by means of a specialized source language. Formally, abstract programs in the base language, and states of the interpreter are elements of our class of objects defined above.

The structure of states of the interpreter for the base language is shown in Figure 4. Since we regard the interpreter for the base language as a complete specification for the functional operation of a computer system, a state of the interpreter represents the totality of programs, data, and control information present in a computer system. In Figure 4 the *universe* is an object that represents all information present in the computer system when the system is idle—that is, when no computation is in progress. The universe has *data structures*

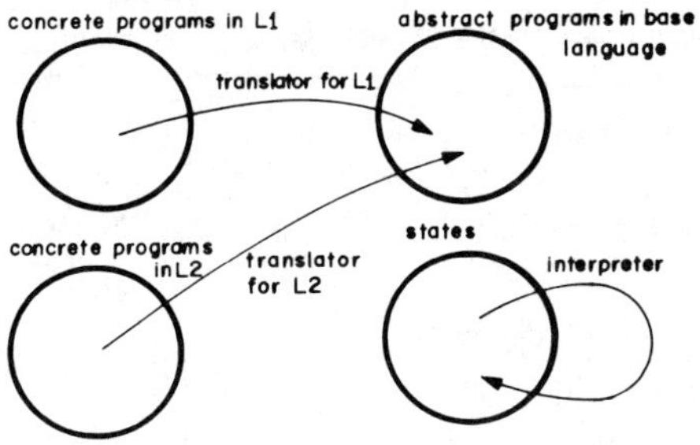

Fig. 3. Language definition in terms of a common base language.

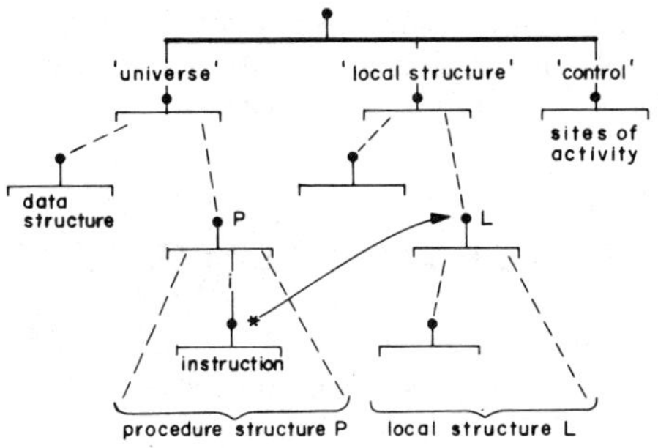

Fig. 4. Structure of objects representing states of the base-language interpreter.

and *procedure structures* as constituent objects. Any object is a legitimate data structure; for example, a data structure may have components that are procedure structures. A procedure structure is an object that represents a procedure expressed in the base language. It has components which are *instructions* of the base language, data structures, or other procedure structures. So that multiple activations of procedures may be accommodated, a procedure structure remains unaltered during its interpretation.

The *local structure* of an interpreter state contains a local structure for each current activation of each base-language procedure. Each local structure has as components the local structures of all procedure activations initiated within it. Thus the hierarchy of local structures represents the dynamic relationship of procedure activations. One may think of the root local structure as the nucleus of an operating system that initiates independent, concurrent computations on behalf of system users as they request activation of procedures from the system files (the universe).

The local structure of a procedure activation has a component object for each variable of the base-language procedure. The selector of each component is its identifier in the instructions of the procedure. These objects may be elementary or compound objects and may be common with objects within the universe or within local structures of other procedure activations.

The *control* component of an interpreter state is an unordered set of *sites of activity*. A typical site of activity is represented in Fig. 4 by an asterisk at an instruction of procedure P and an arrow to the local structure L for some activation of P. This is analogous to the "instruction pointer/environment pointer" combination that represents a site of activity in Johnston's contour model [10]. Since several activations of a procedure may exist concurrently, there may be two or more sites of activity involving the same instruction of some procedure, but designating different local structures. Also, within one activation of a procedure, several instructions may be active concurrently; thus asterisks on different instructions of a procedure may have arrows to the same local structure.

Each state transition of the interpreter executes one instruction for some procedure activation, at a site of activity selected arbitrarily from the control of the current state. Thus the interpreter is a nondeterministic transition system. In the state resulting from a transition, the chosen site of activity is replaced according to the sequencing rules of the base language. Replacement with two sites of activity designating two successor instructions would occur in interpretation of a *fork* instruction; deletion of the site of activity without replacement would occur in execution of a *quit* or *join* instruction.

INTERPRETATION OF A RUDIMENTARY BASE LANGUAGE

Next we show how typical instructions of a rudimentary base language would be implemented by state transitions of an interpreter. This will put the concepts expressed above into more concrete form, and provide a basis for understanding the translation of block-structured languages into the base language. Because consideration of concurrency in programs has led to concepts of program representation unfamiliar to most readers, and because these concepts are not sufficiently advanced, we will use for illustration a base language employing conventional instruction sequencing. The instructions of a procedure are objects selected by successive integers, with 0 being the selector of the initial instruction.

The effect of representative instructions on the interpreter state is shown in Figs. 5 through 11 in the form of before/after pictures of relevant state components. In these figures, P marks the root of the procedure structure containing an instruction under consideration as its i component, and $L(P)$ is the root of the local structure for the relevant activation of P.

The add instruction is typical of instructions that apply binary operations to elementary objects. The instruction

add '*u*', '*v*', '*w*'

is an object having as components the four elementary objects 'add', '*u*', '*v*', and '*w*'. These are interpreted as an operation code and three *address fields* used as selectors for operands and result in the local structure $L(P)$. The state transition is shown in Figure 5. Note that the site of activity advances sequentially to the $(i + 1)$-component of P.

Let us say that a procedure activation has *direct access* to a data structure if the data structure is the s-component of the local structure for some selector s. The instruction

select '*p*', '*n*', '*q*'

is used to gain direct access to the '*n*'-component of a data structure to which direct access exists. This instruction makes the object that is the ('*p*'·'*n*')-component of $L(P)$ also the '*q*'-component of $L(P)$ as shown by Figure 6.

Literal values are retrieved from the procedure structure by const instructions such as

const 1.5, '*x*'

which makes the elementary object 1.5 the '*x*'-component of $L(P)$. Select and const instructions may be used to build arbitrary data structures as illustrated in Figure 7. Note that execution of select '*p*', '*n*', '*x*' implies creation of an '*n*'-component of the object selected by '*p*' if none already exists.

Figure 8 shows how the instruction

link '*p*', '*n*', '*q*'

establishes an arc between two objects (the '*p*'- and '*q*'-components of $L(P)$)

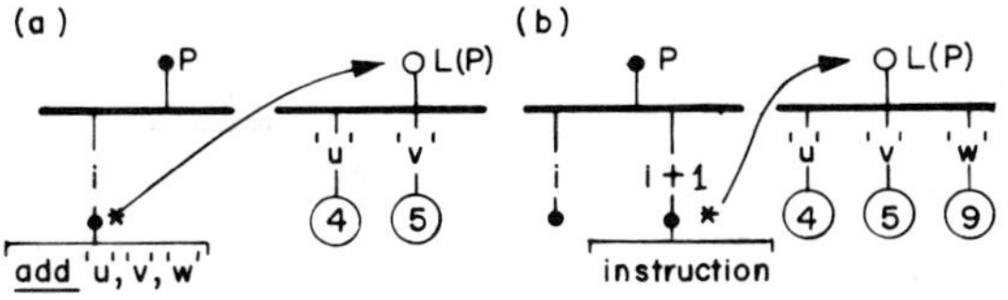

Fig. 5. Interpretation of an instruction specifying a binary operation.

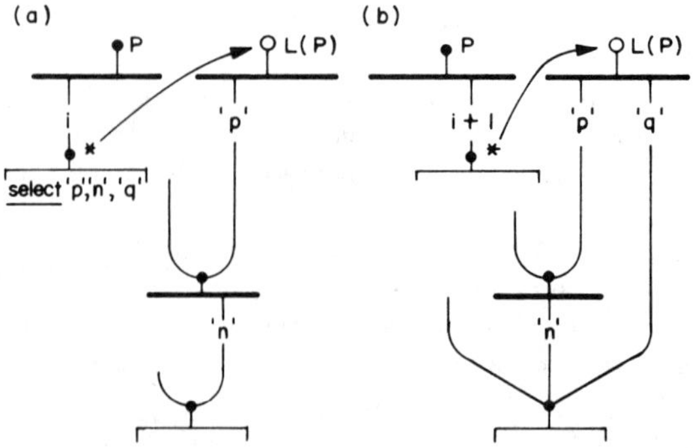

Fig. 6. Interpretation of a select instruction.

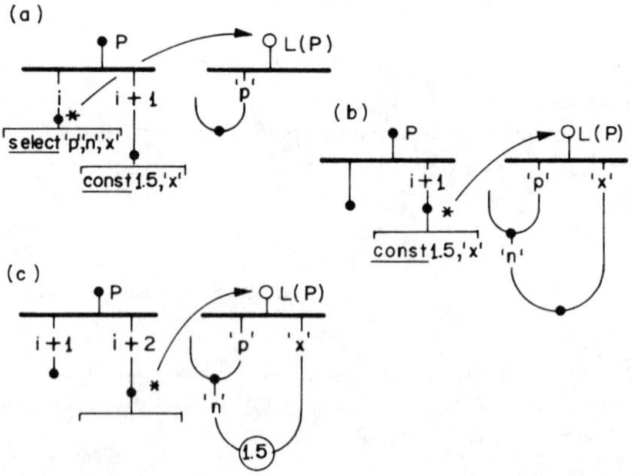

Fig. 7. Structure building using select and const instructions.

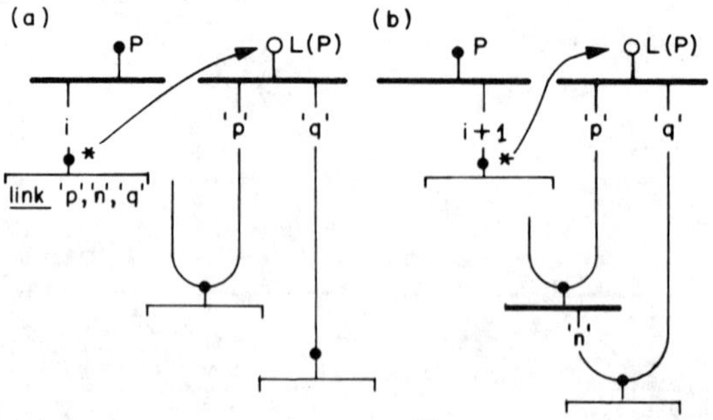

Fig. 8. Insertion of an arc by a link instruction.

to which direct access exists. Execution of this instruction makes the 'q'-component of $L(P)$ also the ('p' • 'n')-component of $L(P)$.

The link instruction is the means for establishing sharing—making one object a common component of two distinct objects. Unless some restriction is built into the base language or its interpreter, use of link instructions can introduce cycles into the interpreter state. At present we do not know how use of link instructions should be limited so introduction of cycles cannot occur. One way in which cycles can arise occurs in the interpretation of block structured programs by the scheme given in the next section of the paper.

The instruction

delete 'p', 'n'

erases the arc labelled 'n' emanating from the root of the 'p'-component of $L(P)$. Any nodes and arcs that are unrooted after the erasure cease to be part of the interpreter state, as shown in Figure 9.

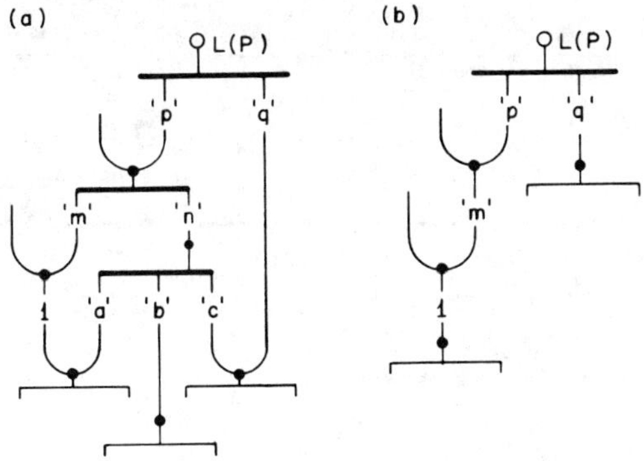

Fig. 9. The effect of executing a delete instruction.

Activation of a new procedure is accomplished by the instruction

apply 'f', 'a'

where the 'f'-component of $L(P)$ is the procedure structure F of the procedure to be activated, and the 'a'-component of $L(P)$ is an object (an *argument structure*) that contains as components all data required by the procedure (e.g., actual parameter values) to perform its function. Execution of the apply instruction causes the state transition illustrated in Fig. 10: A root node $L(F)$ is created for the local structure of the new activation; the argument structure is made the A-component of $L(F)$; a new site of activity is denoted by an asterisk on the 0-component of F and an arrow to $L(F)$; and the original site of activity is advanced to the $(i + 1)$-instruction of P and made dormant as indicated by the parentheses.

A procedure activation is terminated by the instruction

return

which causes the state transition displayed in Figure 11. The root node $L(F)$ is

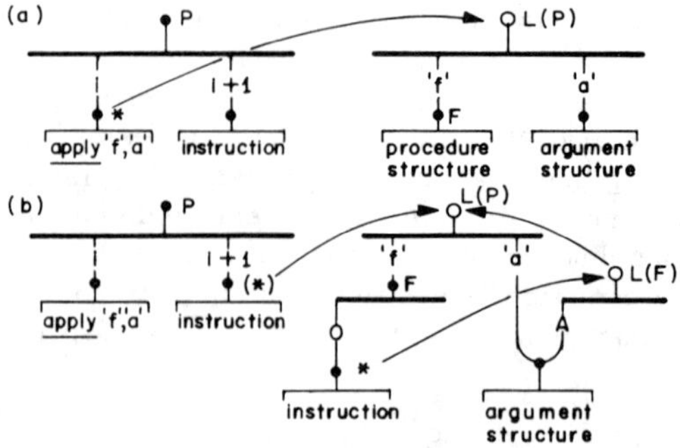

Fig. 10. Initiation of a procedure activation by an apply instruction.

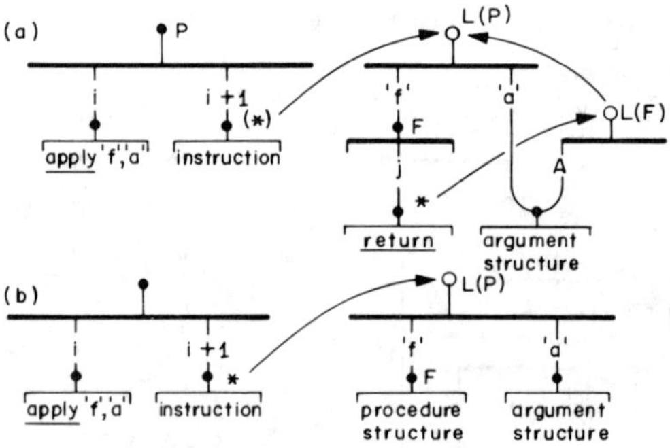

Fig. 11. Termination of a procedure activation by a return instruction.

erased, deleting all parts of the local structure of F that are not linked to the argument structure; the site of activity at the return instruction disappears; and the dormant site of activity in the activating procedure is activated. Note that the entire effect of executing procedure F is conveyed to the activation of P by way of the argument structure.

To apply a procedure, its procedure structure must be a component of the local structure of the current procedure activation. If the procedure to be activated is the 'g'-component of the procedure structure P in execution, execution of the instruction

move 'g', 'f'

will make it directly accessible by identifying the 'f'-component of $L(P)$ with the 'g'-component of P.

TRANSLATION OF BLOCK-STRUCTURED LANGUAGES

Many important programming languages for practical computation are block structured; the texts of blocks and procedures are nested, and identifiers in one text may refer to variables defined in other texts. Since we do not plan to include in the base language provision for directly representing references by a procedure to external objects, we must show how the execution of block-structured programs may be simulated through translation into the base language and execution by the base-language interpreter. The following discussion gives one way in which this may be accomplished—a way that seems attractive in relation to the concepts of computer organization we are investigating. This discussion also serves as a good example of how complexity in a source language may be represented in the rules of translation rather than in the rules of interpretation of a formal definition.

For this discussion we will use an elementary block structured language. Identifiers are declared by the lines

<u>integer</u> x or <u>proced</u> x

to denote simple variables or procedures. Basic statement types include: Assignment statements such as

$$x := g(u, v)$$

where: x, u, and v are simple variable identifiers; and g denotes an unspecified function. Procedure applications of the form

<u>apply</u> $f(x, y)$ or $z :=$ <u>apply</u> $f(x, y)$

where f is a procedure identifier, the second form being used for a value returning procedure. Conditional statements like

<u>if</u> $p(x)$ <u>then</u> $S1$ <u>else</u> $S2$

And iteration statements like

<u>while</u> $p(x)$ <u>do</u> $S1$

where p denotes an unspecified predicate and $S1$ and $S2$ are basic statements or a sequence of statements delimited by <u>begin</u>, <u>end</u>

A procedure variable f may be assigned a value by a declaration statement having the form

```
f := procedure (x, ··· , y)
     begin
       .
       .
       .
     end
```

where $x, \cdots, y$ are the formal parameters. A statement

<u>return</u> z

specifies the result of a value-returning procedure. The lines between <u>begin</u> and <u>end</u>, together with the list of formal parameters, make up the <u>text</u> of the procedure.

A program in this language has the form of a nested set of procedure declarations. Except for the text of the outermost declaration, each text is <u>*enclosed*</u> by the text within which its declaration appears. As in Algol 60, each identifier is local to the text in which it is declared, and the meaning of a nonlocal appearance of an identifier is defined to be the same as its meaning in the enclosing text. The formal parameters of a procedure are local identifiers of the text being declared.

The meaning of block-structured programs can be expressed in terms of a tree of symbol tables as has been explained by Weizenbaum [26], or in terms of the contour model. The interested reader should study the work of Berry [2] and Lucas [16] for other discussions of formal implementations of block-structured programs and their equivalence.

To simulate the execution of a block-structured program by a base-language program, we need a scheme for implementing the nonlocal references of the source program. Our method is to augment the argument structure associated with a procedure activation in the base-language interpreter so that all external objects to which reference is required by the block-structured procedure are accessed as components of the argument structure.

To make matters precise, it is convenient to adopt some notation. Suppose T is the text of a procedure declaration. We write $B(T)$ to denote the set of identifiers declared within T (local to T). The set $X(T)$ of *external identifiers* associated with text T is defined as follows: We write $T' < T$ if text T' is nested within text T, that is, if there is a sequence of texts $T_0, T_1, T_2, \cdots, T_k$ such that $T = T_0$, $T' = T_k$, and T_i encloses T_{i+1} for $i = 0, 1, 2, \cdots, k-1$. Then $X(T)$ contains each identifier x that has a nonlocal appearance in some text T', $T' \leq T$, and is not local to any text T'', $T' < T'' \leq T$.

In these terms we can describe the formats of the local structures and argument structures to be used in simulation of block structure in the base language. Corresponding to the activation record for an activation of procedure text T, a local structure (L-structure) is formed by the base language program. The L-structure has the format shown in Figure 12(a). It has an E-component in which

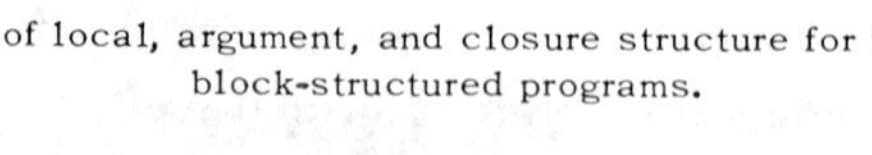

Fig. 12. Formats of local, argument, and closure structure for the interpretation of block-structured programs.

a value is associated with each identifier in $B(T) \cup X(T)$, that is, each local and each external identifier of T. The L-structure also includes components for temporary values required by the base language instructions that interpret the text T.

The argument structure (A-structure) for an activation of procedure text T will have one component for each formal parameter of the text T, and in addition, an E-component that conveys access to objects referenced by the external identifiers of T, as shown in Figure 12(b).

A procedure identifier is given a value by a procedure-declaration statement including a text T. Because procedure values may be assigned to nonlocal identifiers, and may be passed to the calling activation by a value-returning procedure, activations of the text T may occur in situations where there is no clear meaning for the external identifiers of T. The usual solution to this problem is to let a procedure value be an object called a *closure* of the text T (a *C-structure*) having two components as in Figure 12(c). The T-component of a closure is the text itself. The E-component (environment) includes an x-component for each x in $X(T)$, and gives an activation of the text access to objects referenced by its external identifiers.

Usually, the meaning of the external identifiers of a closure of T is fixed at the time the closure is created by execution of the declaration of T. Each $x \in X(T)$ is given the same meaning as the current meaning of x in the text T' that encloses the declaration statement.

The way in which block structured programs may be simulated by the base language interpreter is best introduced by an example. The following program is adapted from Weizenbaum's paper [26]

PROGRAM 1.

```
      ┌ p := procedure
      │ begin proced f, q, r; integer u, v, z
      │
      │      ┌ f := procedure (x); integer x
P ────┤      │ begin proced g
      │      │
      │ F ───┤        ┌ g := procedure (y); integer y
      │      │   G ───┤ begin integer t
      │      │        │      t := (x + y) ↑ 2
      │      │        │      return t
      │      │        └ end
      │      │
      │      │          return g
      │      └ end
      │
      │        q := apply f(1)
      │        r := apply f(2)
      │        u := apply q(3)
      │        v := apply r (5)
      │        z := u + v
      └ end
```

The program consists of three procedure texts P, F and G having local and external identifiers as follows

$B(P) = \{f, q, r, u, v, z\}$ $\qquad B(F) = \{x, g\}$ $\qquad B(G) = \{t, y\}$

$X(P) = \phi$ $\qquad X(F) = \phi$ $\qquad X(G) = \{x\}$

Following Weizenbaum and Johnston, we display the progress of a computation by giving a series of *snapshots* of the interpreter state, chosen to illustrate points about the execution mechanism. For procedure P, the initial state of the interpreter (Snapshot 1, Fig. 13) includes the text of P in the form of a procedure

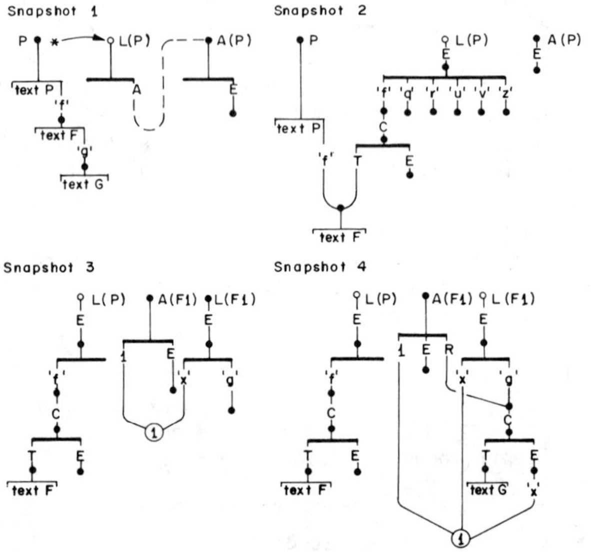

Fig. 13. Interpretation of a block-structured program—formation of a closure of text G.

structure. This procedure structure is in fact a tree of procedure structures; for each text $T \leq P$, the procedure structure for T has as a component a procedure structure for each text enclosed by T. We will not describe further the coding of procedure texts as sets of instructions, as the required instruction sequences will be clear from the discussion of the state transitions seen in the series of snapshots. The initial state also includes a local structure $L(P)$ that will serve as the activation record for procedure P; it is empty except for the argument structure $A(P)$, which consists of an empty E-component.

For clarity, the arcs that make each argument structure a component of the local structures of the calling and called procedures are omitted from the snapshots. Also, we will not include the procedure structure for P in subsequent snapshots, its presence being understood throughout the computation.

The first step performed by instructions of the base language representation of P is to create an E-component of its L-structure, and an $(E \cdot \text{'x'})$-component for each identifier x in $B(P) \cup X(P) = \{f, q, r, u, v, z\}$. Execution of the declaration of text F yields Snapshot 2. The $(E \cdot \text{'}f\text{'} \cdot C)$-component of $L(P)$ is now a closure of F represented by a C-structure. Its T-component is the text of F and is shared with the text of P, its E-component is empty because $X(F) = \phi$.

The first step in the execution of

$$q := \underline{\text{apply}}\ f(1)$$

is to form an appropriate argument structure $A(F1)$. Its 1-component is the actual parameter value, and its E-component is empty, again because $X(F) = \phi$. Activation of the procedure structure for F creates an L-structure $L(F1)$. The first action by instructions of F is to associate actual parameters with identifiers in $B(F)$. Thus the ($E\cdot$ 'x')-component of $L(F1)$ is linked to the 1-component of $A(F1)$, as in Snapshot 3.

Snapshot 4 shows the effect of interpreting the declaration of G. This adds a closure of G as the ($E\cdot$ 'g' $\cdot C$)-component of $L(F1)$. The meaning of identifier x, which is an external identifier of G, is fixed in the closure by making the ($E\cdot$ 'x')-component of the closure identical with the ($E\cdot$ 'x')-component of the current L-structure. Snapshot 4 also shows the effect of the statement return g which links the ($E\cdot$ 'g')-component of $L(F1)$ as the R-component (result value) of the argument structure $A(F1)$. This action completes execution of the instructions of F, hence $L(F1)$ is deleted and execution of instructions of P is resumed. To complete interpretation of the statement $q :=$ apply $f(1)$, the R-component of $A(F1)$ is made the ($E\cdot$ 'q')-component of $L(P)$, and $A(F1)$ is deleted. The result is shown in Snapshot 5 (Fig. 14), which also shows the effect of interpreting $r :=$ apply $f(2)$ by a similar sequence of events.

The progress of this computation through Snapshot 5 illustrates how values required to interpret external references may be conveyed to a procedure activation via the argument structure, and how closures of text may be formed to fix the meaning of the external (free) identifiers in a procedure declaration—all

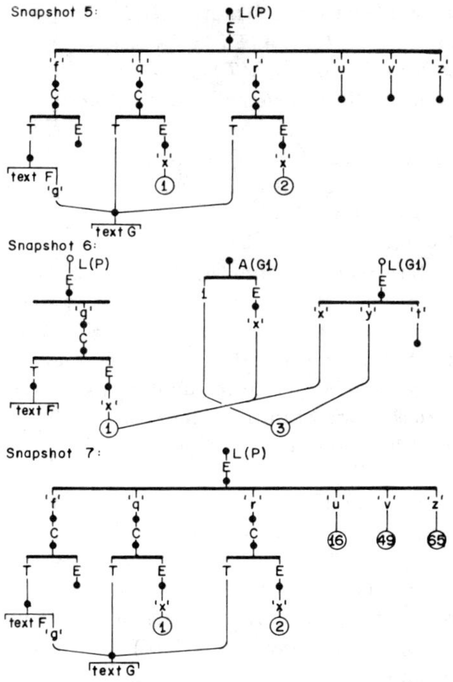

Fig. 14. Interpretation of a block-structured program—application of closures.

without going outside the base language features we have introduced. The remaining snapshots show what is involved in applying a closure with a nonempty E-component.

Interpretation of the statement $u :=$ apply $q(3)$ begins with formation of an argument structure $A(G1)$ as in Snapshot 6, Figure 14. Here, since $X(G) = \{x\}$, an $(E \cdot 'x')$-component of $A(G1)$ is created and made identical with the $(E \cdot 'x')$-component of the closure value of q in $L(P)$. Then the initial instructions of G identify the $(E \cdot 'y')$-component of $L(G1)$ with the 1-component of $A(G1)$, and, since $x \in X(G)$, identify the $(E \cdot 'x')$-component of $L(G1)$ with the $(E \cdot 'x')$-component of $A(G1)$. Instructions corresponding to the body of G compute the value $t = (1 + 3) \uparrow 2 = 16$ which is returned as the R-component of $A(G1)$. The result is Snapshot 7 which includes the effect of interpreting the statements $v :=$ apply $r(5)$ and $z := u + v$.

With the above example as a guide, we can formulate a general set of rules governing the simulation of block structured programs by the base-language interpreter.

(1) Formation of an argument structure for application of a closure of text T
   - (a) The ith actual parameter for application of text T is made the i-component of $A(T)$
   - (b) For each identifier x in $X(T)$, the $(E \cdot 'x')$-component of the closure of T to be applied is made the $(E \cdot 'x')$-component of $A(T)$

(2) Initialization of the local structure $L(T)$
   - (a) For each $x \in X(T)$, the $(E \cdot 'x')$-component of $A(T)$ is made the $(E \cdot 'x')$-component of $L(T)$
   - (b) For each $x \in B(T)$, an empty $(E \cdot 'x')$-component is appended to $L(T)$
   - (c) Each actual parameter value (i-component of $A(T)$) is made the $(E \cdot 'x')$-component of $L(T)$, where x is the identifier of the ith formal parameter

(3) Return of value
   - (a) Interpretation of the statement return x makes the R-component of $A(T)$ identical with the $(E \cdot 'x')$-component of $L(T)$
   - (b) Interpretation of $z :=$ apply $f(\cdots)$ in text T is completed by making the $(E \cdot 'z')$-component of $L(T)$ identical with the R-component of the argument structure for application of the closure f
   - (c) The argument structure is deleted from $L(T)$

(4) Formation of a closure of text T as the value of identifier f in an activation of text T'
   - (a) The new C-structure is the $(E \cdot 'f' \cdot C)$-component of $L(T')$
   - (b) The text T is made the T-component of the C-structure
   - (c) For each $x \in X(T)$, the $(E \cdot 'x')$-component of $L(T')$ is made the $(E \cdot 'x')$-component of the C-structure

(5) Interpretation of a procedure assignment statement $f := g$ in text T
   - (a) The $(E \cdot 'g' \cdot C)$-component of $L(T)$ is made the $(E \cdot 'f' \cdot C)$-component of $L(T)$, a previously-existing C-arc from procedure node $E \cdot 'f'$ being deleted.

CYCLES AND THEIR PREVENTION

The method of simulating block-structured programs presented above has a major defect in terms of our objectives for the base language: Interpretation of programs can lead to interpreter states for which the graph of the state has directed cycles and is not an object according to our definition. The simplest case is the following program

PROGRAM 2.

```
p := procedure (u)
begin
        f := procedure (x); integer x
        begin
                if x = 0 then return 1
                x := g(x)
                z := apply f(x)
                return z
        end
        apply f(u)
end
```

The snapshot in Fig. 15(a) shows the situation just after interpretation of the declaration of text *F*. The cycle arises because of the free occurrence of *f* within text *F*, where the value of *f* is a closure of *F*.

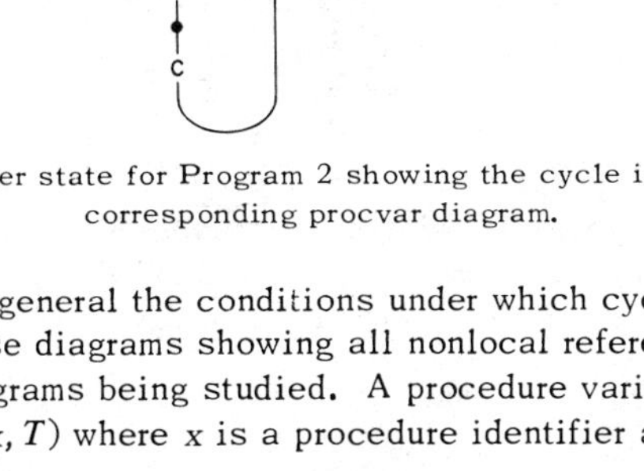

Fig. 15. Interpreter state for Program 2 showing the cycle introduced, and the corresponding procvar diagram.

To understand in general the conditions under which cycles are introduced, it is instructive to use diagrams showing all nonlocal references to the procedure variables of programs being studied. A procedure variable is uniquely specified by a pair (x, T) where x is a procedure identifier and T is a text in which x is declared, that is, $x \in B(T)$. We write $R(x, T)$ to represent the *range* of a procedure variable; $R(x, T)$ is a set containing each text T' such that the variable (x, T) could be assigned a closure of T' as its value during program execution. The range of a procedure variable may be determined by tracing references to, and assignments of, the closures defined by procedure declarations. We suspect that, unless a program has redundant or unproductive statements, there will be some interpretation for its function and predicate symbols such that each element of the range of a procedure variable occurs as its value in some computation by the program.

To construct the procedure variable diagram (*procvar* diagram for short) of a block structured program, represent the texts of the program by closed contours nested in the same way as the texts. The area inside the contour for T but outside contours for texts enclosed by T is the *locality* of T. Let (x, T) be a procedure variable of the program, and represent it by a solid dot labeled x and placed in the locality of T. Place a small open circle in the locality of T' for each text T' with $T' < T$ in which identifier x refers to the procedure variable (x, T). Join each of these circles to the solid dot denoting (x, T) by arcs without arrows. For each text T' in the range of variable (x, T), draw an arrow from the solid dot representing (x, T) to the contour for T'. Repeat these steps for each procedure variable of the program.

The procvar diagram for Program 2 is shown in Fig. 15(b), and the diagram for Program 1 appears in Figure 16.

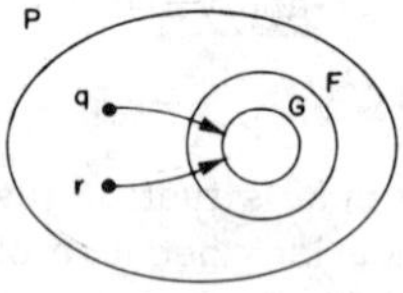

Fig. 16. Procvar diagram for Program 1 showing absence of necessary conditions for the occurrence of cycles.

Next we formulate a necessary condition for a block-structured program to generate cycles when interpreted according to our rules of simulation. First consider the forms a cycle must have in an interpreter state. There are nine kinds of nodes involved in the interpretation of block structured programs:

L:	Root nodes of L-structures
$L \cdot E$:	Environment nodes of L-structures
A:	Root nodes of A-structures
$A \cdot E$:	Environment nodes of A-structures
S:	Simple variable nodes
P:	Procedure variable nodes
C:	Root nodes of C-structures
$C \cdot T$:	Text nodes of C-structures
$C \cdot E$:	Environment nodes of C-structures

Of these, types L and A cannot occur in cycles because no action by the interpreter creates any arcs terminating on L-nodes or A-nodes (aside from the implicit links we have omitted from the diagrams). Further, arcs terminating on $(L \cdot E)$- or $(A \cdot E)$-nodes can only emanate from L- and A-nodes, respectively. Hence these node types cannot occur in cycles. No arcs emanate from S-nodes, and no arcs from procedure structures terminate on nodes of L-structures; therefore S-nodes and T-nodes cannot occur in cycles. These considerations leave just three kinds of arcs that can be members of any cycle (x is some procedure identifier)

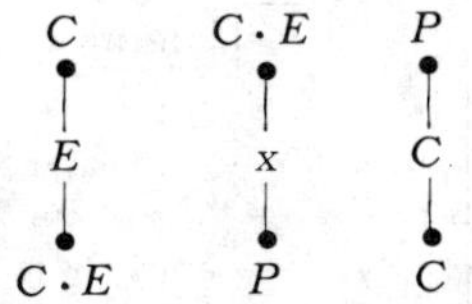

Thus a cycle in an interpreter state consists of a series of triplets, each triplet having one of each kind of arc, in the order shown above. From this reasoning, we deduce that a cycle arises from interpretation of a block structured program only if there is a finite sequence of texts $T_1, T_2, T_3, \cdots, T_k$, and a corresponding sequence of identifiers $x_1, x_2, \cdots, x_k$ that meet these conditions:

(1) Each x_i is an external procedure identifier of T_i: $x_i \in X(T_i)$. Let (x_i, T_i') be the procedure variable denoted by x_i in text T_i. Note that $T_i < T_i'$

(2) For each i and with $j = (i \bmod k) + 1$, T_j is in the range of (x_i, T_i').

These conditions imply that the procvar diagram of a program has a cycle of arrows such that each arrow terminates on the contour of a text that contains an external reference to the procedure variable from which the next arrow emanates. For Program 2, Fig. 15(b) shows a cycle that involves just one procedure variable (f, F).

Program 3 is a nest of procedures activated recursively. The procvar diagram for this program is shown in Fig. 17(a), and Fig. 17(b) illustrates the interpreter state resulting from simulation through the first activation of text G. Still the cycle only involves procedure variable (f, P) because the only external reference is the appearance of f in test G.

Program 4 illustrates how more complex cycles may be created.

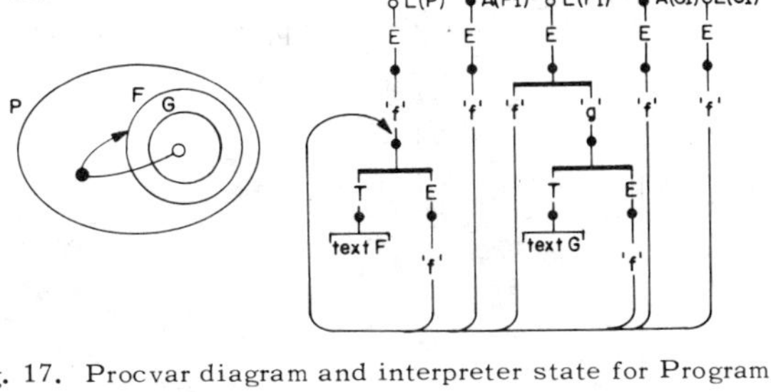

Fig. 17. Procvar diagram and interpreter state for Program 3.

PROGRAM 3.

```
     ┌ p := procedure ( )
     │ begin
P ───┤          ┌ f := procedure ( )
     │     F ───┤ begin
     │          │          ┌ g := procedure ( )
     │          │     G ───┤
     │          │          └ begin ··· apply f( ) ··· end
     │          │                .
     │          │                .
     │          │                .
     │          │            apply g ( )
     │          │                .
     │          │                .
     │          │                .
     │          └ end
     │             .
     │             .
     │             .
     │          apply f( )
     │             .
     │             .
     │             .
     └ end
```

PROGRAM 4.

```
     ┌ p := procedure ( )
P ───┤ begin
     │          ┌ f := procedure ( )
     │     F ───┤
     │          └ begin ··· apply g( ) ··· end
     │
     │          ┌ g := procedure ( )
     │     G ───┤
     │          └ begin ··· apply f( ) ··· end
     │                .
     │                .
     │                .
     │            apply f( )
     │                .
     │                .
     │                .
     └ end
```

Figure 18 gives the procvar diagram for Program 4 and shows the state of the interpreter after the declarations of F and G have been executed. The cycle involves procedure variables (f, P) and (g, P).

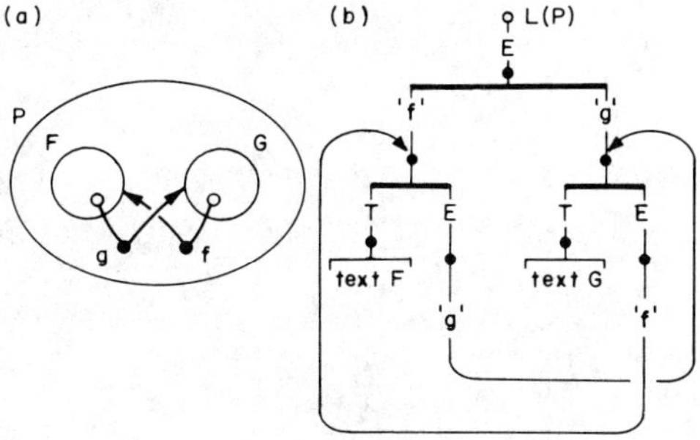

Fig. 18. Procvar diagram and interpreter state for Program 4.

We have found that many block structured programs can be rewritten so they accomplish the original computation but no longer satisfy the necessary condition for the creation of cycles. The principle is to convey closures to and from a procedure activation by passing them as parameters or results rather than by external references. In this way, the three example programs may be rewritten as the three transformed programs given below. In each case the texts of the transformed programs do not contain any external references to procedure variables and therefore cannot lead to cycles when performed by the interpreter we have described.

PROGRAM 2′.

```
     ┌ p := procedure (u)
     │ begin
     │        ┌ f := procedure (h, x) proced h, integer x
P ───┤        │ begin
     │   F ───┤          if x = 0 then return 1
     │        │          x := g(x)
     │        │          z := apply h(h, x)
     │        │          return z
     │        └ end
     │
     │          apply f(f, u)
     └ end
```

Several interesting questions are unresolved at this writing. We do not know in what sense, if any, the necessary condition formulated above is a sufficient condition for the formation of cycles during interpretation according to the

PROGRAM 3′.

```
P —┌ p := procedure ( )
   │ begin
   │        F —┌ f := procedure (h,   ); proced h
   │           │ begin
   │           │        G —┌ g := procedure (k,   ); proced k
   │           │           └ begin ··· apply k(k,   ) ··· end
   │           │                  .
   │           │                  .
   │           │                  .
   │           │             apply g(h,   )
   │           │                  .
   │           │                  .
   │           │                  .
   │           └ end
   │                .
   │                .
   │                .
   │             apply f(f,   )
   │                .
   │                .
   │                .
   └ end
```

PROGRAM 4′.

```
P —┌ p := procedure ( )
   │ begin
   │        F —┌ f := procedure (h, k,   )
   │           └ begin ··· apply k(h, k,   ) ··· end
   │
   │        G —┌ g := procedure (h, k,   )
   │           └ begin ··· apply h(h, k,   ) ··· end
   │                .
   │                .
   │                .
   │             apply f(f, g,   )
   │                .
   │                .
   │                .
   └ end
```

scheme outlined. Also, we do not know a general method for rewriting block structured programs so that cycles will not arise during execution.

REPRESENTATION OF CONCURRENCY IN THE BASE LANGUAGE

A subject of major importance in the design of the base language is the representation of concurrent activities. In the introduction we noted that some computations inherently involve concurrent processes and cannot be simulated by sequential programs—also, that a high degree of concurrency within computations may prove essential to the practical realization of computer systems with programming generality. To these motivations we may add that some contemporary source languages, notably PL/I, have explicit provision for programming concurrent processes.

We regard the state transitions of the interpreter as representing the progress of all activities in a computer system that is executing many programs simultaneously. The basic requirements for representing concurrent actions in the interpreter are met by providing for many sites of activity in the control component of the state (Fig. 3), and by organizing the local structures of procedure activations as a tree so a procedure may spawn independent, concurrent activations of component procedures. Multiple sites of activity may represent many actions required to accomplish different parts of one computation as well as parallel execution of many independent computations.

Consideration of concurrent computation brings in the issue of nondeterminacy—the possibility that computed results will depend on the relative timing with which the concurrent activities are carried forward. The work of Van Horn [27], Rodriguez [22] and others has shown that computer systems can be designed so that parallelism in computations may be realized while determinacy is guaranteed for any program written for the system. The ability of a computer user to direct the system to carry out computations with a guarantee of determinacy is very important. Most programs are intended to implement a functional dependence of results on inputs, and determinism is essential to the verification of their correctness.

There are two ways of providing a guarantee of determinacy to the user of a computer system. The distinction is whether the class of abstract or base language programs is constrained by the design of the interpreter to describe only determinate computations. If this is the case, then any abstract program resulting from compilation will be determinate in execution. Furthermore, if the compiler is itself a determinate procedure, then each translatable source program represents a determinate procedure. On the other hand, if the design of the interpreter does not guarantee determinacy of abstract programs, determinacy of source programs, when desired, must be ensured by the translator.

In the base language, it is necessary to provide for computations that are inherently nondeterminate, such as the example of a process awaiting the first response from either of two terminals. We want to include in the base language primitive features for representing essential forms of nondeterminacy. In principle, we wish to guarantee that any (base-language) procedure that does not use these features will be determinate in its operation. Furthermore, use of base-language primitives for the construction of nondeterminate procedures is intended to be such that the choice among alternative outcomes always originates from the source intended by the program author, and never from timing relationships unrelated to his computation.

Our current thoughts regarding representation of base-language procedures so as to guarantee determinacy are based on *data-flow* representations for programs in which each operation is activated by the arrival of its operands, and each result is transmitted, as soon as it is ready, to those operations requiring its use. Rodriguez [22] has formulated a data-flow model that applies to programs involving assignment, conditional, and iteration statements, and data represented by simple variables. Procedures represented by Rodriguez program graphs are naturally parallel and the rules for their execution guarantee determinacy. In [3], Dennis has given a similar program graph model for procedures that transform data structures, but do not involve conditional or iteration steps. Determinacy is guaranteed for these program graphs if they satisfy a readily-testable condition.

We hope to be successful in combining and extending these two models to obtain a satisfactory data-flow model for all determinate procedures. If this objective can be achieved, we expect to use program graphs as the nucleus of the base language. On the basis of improved understanding of parallel programs obtained by recent research on program schemes by Karp and Miller [11], Paterson [21], Slutz [23], and Keller [12], we are optimistic about finding an inherently determinate scheme for representing the concurrency present in most algorithms.

CONCLUSION

This article has been an introduction to the goals, philosophy and methods of our current work on the design of a base language. The material presented is an "instantaneous description" of an activity that still has far to go—many issues need to be satisfactorily resolved before we will be pleased with our effort. In addition to the representation of concurrency, the base language must encompass certain concepts and capabilities beyond those normally provided in contemporary source languages. Four aspects of this kind are:

(1) Generation and transformation of information structures that share component structures
(2) Concurrent processes that, in pairs, have producer-consumer relationships
(3) Programming systems that are able to generate base language programs and monitor their execution
(4) Provision for controlling and sharing access to procedures and data structures among users of a computer system.

We are continuing investigation of how these capabilities should be incorporated in the base language. Some ideas on intercommunicating processes have been reported briefly [5]. Some thoughts on program monitoring and controlled sharing of information are given by Dennis and Van Horn [6], and by Vanderbilt [25].

ACKNOWLEDGEMENT

The work discussed in this article was done at Project MAC, MIT, and was supported in part by the National Science Foundation under Research Grant GJ-432, and in part by the Advanced Research Projects Agency, Department of Defense, under Naval Research Contract N00014-70-A-0362-0001.

REFERENCES

[1] D. M. Berry, "Introduction to Oregano," *Proc. Symp. Data Structures in Programming Languages, SIGPLAN Notices, ACM,* **6**, No. 2, 171–190 (February 1971).

[2] D. M. Berry, "Block Structure: Retention or Deletion?, *Proc. Third Annual ACM Symp. Theory of Computing,* 86–100 (May 1971).

[3] J. B. Dennis, "Programming Generality, Parallelism, and Computer Architecture," *Information Processing 68,* North-Holland, Amsterdam, 484–492 (1969).

[4] J. B. Dennis, Future Trends in Time-Sharing Systems; *Time-Sharing Innovation for Operations Research and Decision-Making,* Washington Operations Research Council, 229–235 (1969).

[5] J. B. Dennis, "Coroutines and Parallel Computation," *Princeton Conference on Information Sciences and Systems,* Princeton, New Jersey (March 1971).

[6] J. B. Dennis and E. C. Van Horn, "Programming Semantics for Multiprogrammed Computations," *Comm. ACM,* **9**, No. 3, 143–155 (March 1966).

[7] A. P. Ershov (lecture at M.I.T., November 1970).

[8] J. L. Gertz, "Hierarchical Associative Memories for Parallel Computation," Report MAC-TR-69, Project MAC, M.I.T., Cambridge, Mass. (June 1970).

[9] J. K. Iliffe, *Basic Machine Principles* (New York: American Elsevier, 1968).

[10] J. B. Johnston, "The Contour Model of Block-Structured Processes," *Proc. Symp. Data Structures in Programming Languages, SIGPLAN Notices, ACM,* **6**, No. 2, 55–82 (February 1971).

[11] R. M. Karp and R. E. Miller, "Parallel Program Schemata," *J. Comput. Sys. Sci.,* **3**, No. 2, 147–195 (May 1969).

[12] R. M. Keller, "On Maximally Parallel Schemata," *IEEE Conf. Rec. Eleventh Annual Symp. Switching and Automata Theory,* 32–50 (October 1970).

[13] P. J. Landin, "The Mechanical Evaluation of Expressions," *Comput. J.,* **6**, No. 4, 308–320 (January 1964).

[14] P. J. Landin, "Correspondence Between Algol 60 and Church's Lambda Notation (Parts I and II)," Part I: *Comm. ACM,* **8**, No. 2, 89–101 (February 1965), Part II: *Comm. ACM,* **8**, No. 3, 158–165 (March 1965).

[15] P. Lauer, "Formal Definition of Algol 60," Technical Report TR 25.088, IBM Laboratory, Vienna (December 1968).

[16] P. Lucas, "Two Constructive Realizations of the Block Concept and Their Equivalence," Technical Report TR 25.085, IBM Laboratory, Vienna (June 1968).

[17] P. Lucas, P. Lauer, and H. Stigleitner, "Method and Notation for the Formal Definition of Programming Languages," Technical Report TR 25.087, IBM Laboratory, Vienna (June 1968).

[18] P. Lucas and K. Walk, "On the Formal Description of PL/I," *Annual Rev. Automatic Programming,* **6**, Part 3, 105–182, Pergamon Press (1969).

[19] J. McCarthy, "Towards a Mathematical Science of Computation," *Information Processing,* **62**, North-Holland, Amsterdam, 21–28 (1963).

[20] J. McCarthy, "A Formal Description of a Subset of Algol," *Formal Language Description Languages for Computer Programming*, 1–12 (North-Holland, Amsterdam 1966).

[21] M. S. Paterson, "Program Schemata," *Machine Intelligence*, **3**, 19–31 (New York: American Elsevier, 1968).

[22] J. E. Rodriguez, "A Graph Model for Parallel Computations, Report MAC-TR-64, Project MAC, M.I.T., Cambridge, Mass. (September 1969).

[23] D. R. Slutz, "The Flow Graph Schemata Model of Parallel Computation," Report MAC-TR-53, Project MAC, M.I.T., Cambridge, Mass. (September 1968).

[24] T. B. Steel, Jr., "UNCOL: The Myth and the Fact," *Annual Review in Automatic Programming*, **2**, 325–344 (Pergamon Press 1961).

[25] D. H. Vanderbilt, "Controlled Information Sharing in a Computer Utility," Report MAC-TR-67, Project MAC, M.I.T., Cambridge, Mass. (October 1969).

[26] J. Weizenbaum, "The Funarg Problem Explained" (March 1968) (unpublished memorandum).

[27] E. C. Van Horn, "Computer Design for Asynchronously Reproducible Multiprocessing," Report MAC-TR-34, Project MAC, M.I.T., Cambridge, Mass. (November 1966).

AN ALGOL COMPILER DESIGNED USING AUTOMATA THEORY

P. M. Lewis II and D. J. Rosenkrantz
General Electric Research & Development Center, Schenectady, NY

An ALGOL compiler was designed and built using recently-developed concepts in automata theory. Its compile speed is in excess of 10,000 line/min on a 1 μsec computer.

Automaton models such as finite-state machines and pushdown machines were used as the basic building blocks of the compiler. The main theorem used in the design is: a simple syntax directed translation on an $LL(k)$ grammar can be performed by a one-state pushdown machine. In order to use this theorem, an $LL(1)$ grammar was developed for the part of ALGOL to be processed by the syntax box of the compiler; this grammar is given in the Appendix.

I. INTRODUCTION

Recent developments in automata theory have suggested a framework for a theory of compiler design based on using automaton models, such as finite-state machines and pushdown machines, as the basic building blocks. In order to demonstrate the validity of this approach, an ALGOL 60 compiler [1] was designed and constructed, based on various automata-theory concepts. The compiler was designed to achieve rapid compilation consistent with the execution speed and memory requirements of current ALGOL compilers. The resulting compiler has a compile speed in excess of 10,000 line/min on a 1 μsec GE600 computer (based on an average of 45 characters per line).

The compiler consists of two passes: The first pass contains a lexical box and a syntax box. It translates the source string into an intermediate string, while producing a symbol table; The second pass contains a semantic box and a code generator. It converts the intermediate string into object code.

The lexical box is based on a finite state machine, and occupies 2,000 36-bit words. The syntax box is based on a deterministic pushdown machine, and occupies 8,000 words. The second pass occupies 13,000 words.

II. THE LEXICAL BOX

The lexical box inputs the character string that represents the source program and converts it into a string of lexical tokens. Each time a token is constructed, it is passed on to the syntax box. There are 29 such tokens, and they are

Presented at the Symposium on Computers and Automata
Polytechnic Institute of Brooklyn, April 13-15, 1971.

represented internally as consecutive integers. The names of the tokens are:

ARRAY	PROCEDURE	OPERATOR
BEGIN	STEP	,
DO	SWITCH	:
ELSE	THEN	;
END	TYPE	:=
FOR	UNTIL	(
GO TO	VALUE	)
IF	WHILE	[
LABEL	IDENTIFIER	]
OWN	CONSTANT	

Several of these tokens have an associated value that is passed to the syntax box along with the token.

The value of the token OPERATOR is an indication as to which of the 17 operators it is.

The value of the token TYPE is an indication as to which of the five types (integer, real, extended real, Boolean, or string) it is.

The value of the token CONSTANT is a pointer to the symbol table entry for the constant. The lexical box processes the constant, producing an error message if it has an improper format, and creates a symbol-table entry that contains the value of the constant and other information about it.

The value of the token IDENTIFIER is an identification number. These identification numbers are consecutive integers that the lexical box assigns to the identifier names. Each occurrence in the source program of a particular identifier is replaced by a token whose value is the identification number for that identifier. (The association of identifiers with their declarations is done later, in the semantic box.) The lexical box also produces a name table, which is an indexed table whose i^{th} entry is the symbolic name for the identifier with value i. Incidentally, the first few identifier numbers are used for the built in procedures, such as SIN and PRINT.

The lexical box contains lexical tables that build up the identifiers and reserved words from their component characters. The lexical tables initially contain the reserved words and the names of the procedures. As new identifiers' names are encountered they are added to the appropriate tables.

The operation of the lexical box is based on a finite-state transducer that was designed and built using conventional techniques.

III. THE SYNTAX BOX

The syntax box is a one-state pushdown translator which was designed using the following steps:

(1) An *LL* (1) grammar [2, 3] was written for the language the syntax box was to process. Because of the *LL* (1) property, this grammar can be parsed top down without backtrack since the next input symbol uniquely determines which production must be applied to the top stack symbol

(2) The input-output relation of the box was written as a simple syntax-directed translation [2] on the LL (1) grammar
(3) The pushdown machine was designed using the theorem [2] that a simple syntax-directed translation on an LL (k) grammar can be performed by a deterministic one-state pushdown transducer.

A. Underlying Grammar

The underlying context-free grammar on which the syntax box is based generates a different language than the grammar given in the ALGOL report [4]. The differences occur for two reasons:

(1) The input string to the syntax box is not the characters of the ALGOL source program, but the tokens outputed by the lexical box. Thus the terminal set for the underlying grammar is different then that for the grammar in the ALGOL report. This implies that the languages generated by the grammars are different, as well as the grammars themselves
(2) Since the principle objective of the design was to use the theorem described in step (3) above, it was necessary for the underlying grammar to be LL (1). Actually to simplify matters even further, the grammar was specified to be LL (1) with the additional property that each non-null production begins with a terminal symbol.* Since the grammar given in the ALGOL report, even with the appropriate changes in the terminal vocabulary, is not LL (1), an attempt was made to transform this grammar into a new LL (1) grammar for the same language.

This was found to be impossible. There is no LL (1) grammar that generates the same language as the grammar in the ALGOL report (with or without the changes in terminal symbols as described above). However, there are only a small number of places in the grammar where the LL (1) condition cannot be satisfied. These are mainly places where the types of expressions (INTEGER, BOOLEAN, etc.) are specified by the grammar instead of by the semantics as in most other parts of the language.

Therefore a decision was made to treat all type checking as a semantic operation to be done by the semantic box. Then the type-checking considerations can be omitted from the grammar and an LL (1) grammar can be written for the syntax box. However, the language generated by this grammar contains some strings that are not generated by the grammar of the ALGOL report; these strings are rejected by the semantic box. For instance, the expression

$$A + (B = C) \quad ,$$

is accepted by the syntax box. However, the semantic box will realize that $(B = C)$ is a Boolean result that cannot be an operand of $+$. Note that the second

*This property, together with the definition of LL (1) grammars, implies that each non-null production for a nonterminal begins with a distinct terminal, and, if a nonterminal A has a production $A \longrightarrow \varepsilon$, then none of the terminals that can begin the other productions for A can also follow A in a sentential form.

pass needs machinery for type checking anyway since the first pass cannot in general do type checking when identifiers are involved. For instance consider the following program:

```
BEGIN PROCEDURE F;
                                        X: = Y + Z;
          REAL X, Y;
          BOOLEAN Z;
END
```

While processing the statement $X := Y + Z$, the syntax box has not yet encountered the declaration for Z and therefore does not know that it is a Boolean variable.

This deferring of all type checking to the second pass, which must contain code for type checking anyway, permits the underlying grammar for the syntax box to be LL (1). A more efficient syntax box is thus obtained without adversely affecting the performance of the rest of the compiler. The language accepted by the compiler as a whole is unchanged; the only effect is that certain features of the language that are considered to be syntactic in the ALGOL report are considered semantic in this compiler.

B. The Intermediate String

The syntax box produces an intermediate string and a symbol table. The intermediate string is a syntax directed translation of the input program. For instance the statement

$$X := A + B * C \quad ,$$

might be translated into

$$\text{MULT } j_B j_C r_1 \text{ ADD } j_A r_1 r_2 \text{ ASSIGN } r_2 j_X \quad ,$$

where: j_A, j_B, j_C, and j_X are the identifier numbers for A, B, C, and X, respectively; and r_1 and r_2 are partial-result pointers.

The partial-result cells are used by the code generator to keep track of the type and run time location of partial results. The first pass produces an intermediate string which contains pointers to the partial-result cells; but no storage is used for these cells during the first pass because nothing is written into these cells until the second pass. However, the first pass keeps track of the maximum number of such cells which will be needed at one time and has space reserved for them during the second pass. The cells are dynamically allocated by the syntax box so that at the end of most statements the partial result cells for the statement can be reused.

Each component of the output string, such as MULT j_B j_C r_1 is called an atom. Each atom consists of a basic output symbol, such as MULT and a list of parameters, such as j_B, j_C, and r_1. The interpretation of MULT j_B j_C r_1 is "multiply B by C and call the result r_1." Each atom must be expanded into the appropriate machine instructions by the second pass.

The translation of the source string into the intermediate string was specified as a syntax-directed translation. Such a translation is described by associating with each production in the grammar a translation element that specifies the translation of the production in terms of the translation of its components. For instance, if the grammar had the production

<statement> ⟶ IF <expression> THEN <simple statement> ,

then the translation element for this production might be

<expression>$_r$ JUMPF $r\,L\,1$ <simple statement> LABEL $L\,1$,

where: JUMPF and LABEL are atoms; r is a pointer to the symbol table entry for the result of the expression; and $L1$ is a symbol-table entry for a specially-created label. This translation element says that the translation of the statement is the translation of the expression (whatever that turns out to be), followed by JUMPF $r\,L\,1$, followed by the translation of the simple statement, followed by LABEL $L1$.

The interpretation of the atom JUMPF $r\,L\,1$ is "if the Boolean value specified by r is FALSE, jump to the label specified by $L\,1$."

C. The Pushdown Machine

The grammar is implicitly incorporated into the fixed-control unit of the one-state pushdown machine that is used to implement the syntax box. Since the underlying grammar is LL (1), the top symbol on the pushdown stack and the next input symbol specify the next production (for the top symbol on the stack). This specification is described by the *transition table*. The transition table is a two-dimensional table which has a row for each possible input symbol and a column for each symbol which can appear on top of the stack. Each entry in the table is a pointer to a routine which performs the necessary processing.

As an example of one of these routines, suppose that the grammar contained the production and translation element given in the previous section for the conditional statement. Then the transition table entry for <statement> as the top stack symbol and *IF* as the input symbol would point to a routine which would perform the following operations:

(1) Get a pointer to a new symbol table entry for the newly created label $L1$
(2) Replace the top stack symbol <statement> with the following sequence of stack symbols:

<expression>

JUMPF – $L\,1$

THEN

<simple statement>

LABEL $L1$

Subsequently, when the output symbols such as JUMPF appear on top of the stack, they are immediately added to the intermediate string. Note that the first parameter of the JUMPF atom is not filled in at this time; instead a pointer is placed to a cell in which a pointer to the symbol-table entry for the result of the expression will subsequently be placed.

There are three types of routines:

(1) If the combination of top symbol and input symbol indicates an error, then a pointer to an error routine is placed in the entry. Each entry can have its own error routine; and the compiler in fact has a large number of routines which are tailored to specific errors.
(2) If the top symbol is a terminal and the input symbol is the same terminal, then a routine is called which pops the terminal off the stack, moves down the stack to the next symbol, and calls for the next input symbol.
(3) If the top symbol is a nonterminal and the input symbol indicates that a production is applicable, then the table entry contains a pointer to a routine for that production. This routine will replace the nonterminal on top of the stack with the right side of the production, insert atoms from the translation element where appropriate, perform any associated updating of tags and counters, and do any necessary processing of the symbol table. The terminal symbols that occur prior to the first nonterminal in the production are processed by the routine, instead of being pushed on the stack.

Note that the parsing is done very quickly since each entry of the transition table points to the correct production. Note also that the errors are treated like the productions, in that their routines can also describe how to process the stack and tables.

A technique used to reduce the number of productions and the size of the transition table is the combination of several nonterminals into a single nonterminal with a tag which tells which nonterminal it represents. For example there is only one nonterminal for <expression> with a tag to denote whether or not it can be a conditional expression, i.e., $\langle\text{expression}\rangle_{\text{UNCOND}}$ or $\langle\text{expression}\rangle_{\text{COND}}$. Any appropriate checking of the tag is done by the routine pointed to by the transition-table entry for the combined nonterminal. This technique is similar to the way in which several terminal symbols were combined into a single lexical token with an associated value indicator.

The grammar has 30 of these combined, or basic, nonterminals. In addition, 7 of the 29 tokens can appear as top-stack symbols. As a result, the transition table is a 29×37 array. The Appendix contains a somewhat improved version of the grammar used for the syntax box. It contains 112 productions, although for reasons discussed in the Appendix, the actual grammar used in the compiler had only 101 productions.

The entire syntax box occupies about 8K of storage which is organized approximately as follows

1K – Transition table

3K – Error routines, including storage of error messages

4K – Routines for individual productions.

Thus the 101 production routines require on the average fewer than 40 machine instructions each. This gives some measure of their simplicity and their speed of operation since they contain no loops or subroutine calls.

IV. SEMANTIC BOX

The behavior of the semantic box was described by augmenting the underlying context-free grammar to obtain a property grammar [5] that specifies the semantics. However, the processing technique that was used is different than the general ones for property grammars [5, 6], and will be published elsewhere.

V. CODE GENERATOR

The code generator is of an advanced type, but was not designed using automata theory concepts directly.

APPENDIX—THE GRAMMAR USED IN THE SYNTAX BOX

Section A-5 of this appendix contains a somewhat improved version of the grammar used in the syntax box of the ALGOL compiler. It differs from that actually used in the compiler in the handling of expressions and conditional statements.

A-1. Expressions

In contrast to the grammar given by the ALGOL report which distinguishes between Boolean, arithmetic, and designational expressions, the grammar used in the compiler has only one kind of expression, which includes Boolean, arithmetic, designational, and even string expressions. As explained in Section III.A of the text, this was required to allow the grammar to be $LL(1)$. The new grammar generates certain expressions that are not legal ALGOL expressions, but these are detected in the semantic box as is also discussed in Section III.A.

The portion of the grammar that deals with expressions, e.g., Production 106–112, was developed in collaboration with R. E. Stearns. It uses two basic nonterminals <expression> and <remainder>, each of which has two tags. Also the terminal symbol OPERATOR has a tag that is the precedence number of the particular operator involved. The operators corresponding to each precedence number are:

1	EQUIV
2	IMPLY
3	OR
4	AND
5	NOT
6	$>, \geq, =, \neq, <, \leq$
7	$+, -$
8	$*, /, \div$
9	$\uparrow$

For the nonterminal <expression>, the first tag is an integer between 1 and 10 that restricts the operators that can appear in the expression to those with precedence numbers greater or equal to the tag (except for operators enclosed in parentheses). The second tag is an indicator that can have either the value COND, if the expression can be conditional, or UNCOND, if it cannot be conditional.

The nonterminal <remainder> has two tags, of which the first is an integer between 1 and 10, and the second is an integer between 1 and 9. The tags restrict the first operator in the derivation of <remainder> to have a precedence number between these two integers.

Although the nonterminal <remainder> requires two tags in the grammar, only the first tag is needed when an input string is processed by the top-down pushdown machine. To see that the second tag can be ignored, observe that the only time when the tag would be checked by the machine is when a choice must be made between productions 111 and 112 because $\langle\text{remainder}\rangle_{i,j}$ is the top-stack symbol and OPERATOR_n is the input symbol. In this situation, a comparison of j and n may influence the choice of which production to use. But first observe that if $j = 9$, it will never be true that $j < n$. Secondly, if j is <9, then $\langle\text{remainder}\rangle_{i,j}$ was first pushed on the stack because of its occurrence in production 100, 110, or 111. Therefore at the time it was first pushed on the stack, $\langle\text{expression}\rangle_{j+1}$ was pushed above it. However $\langle\text{expression}\rangle_{j+1}$ and its descendants cannot be popped off the stack with OPERATOR_n as the next input symbol unless $n < j + 1$. Furthermore, the only way in which $\langle\text{remainder}\rangle_{i,j}$ can be the top stack symbol with OPERATOR_n as the next input symbol is for OPERATOR_n to have popped off the last descendant of $\langle\text{expression}\rangle_{j+1}$, thereby exposing $\langle\text{remainder}\rangle_{i,j}$ as the top-stack symbol, with $n \leq j$. Therefore n does not have to be compared with j and the second tag can be omitted from the operation of the pushdown machine.

A-2. Tags on ⟨procedure tail⟩

The nonterminal <procedure tail> has a tag that can be either VALUE or NOVALUE. This tag is used to ensure that a procedure declaration contains at most one value part, and that it precedes the specification part.

A-3. Comments Within Parameter Lists

The nonterminals <unfinished actuals list> and <unfinished comment> do not appear in the transition table and productions 34, 35, 94, and 95 do not appear explicitly in the compiler. These productions are instead implicitly handled by the routines for productions 32 and 93, which handle this kind of comment without recourse to the transition table.

A-4. Conditional Statements

In the compiler conditional statements are handled somewhat differently than in the grammar given here. The nonterminals <then stat> and <then ident rem>, as well as productions 73–84 are eliminated. Production 61 is replaced by the production

<statement> ⟶ IF <expression>$_{1,COND}$ THEN <statement> <if rem>

with corresponding changes in productions 13 and 46. Tags on <statement> and <if rem> then check that the <statement> after the THEN is not a conditional statement, and if it is a conditional statement, then production 85 cannot be used for <if rem>. These tags provide no difficulty in practice, although technically the tagged grammar is not *LL* (1) since the tag on <if rem> cannot be determined until the statement after the THEN is encountered.

A-5. LL(1) Grammar for ALGOL

1. <program> ⟶ IDENTIFIER: <program>
2. <program> ⟶ BEGIN <program body>
3. <program body> ⟶ ARRAY IDENTIFIER <array list> <array tail>
4. <program body> ⟶ OWN TYPE <own list>
5. <program body> ⟶ TYPE <type rem>
6. <program body> ⟶ PROCEDURE IDENTIFIER <procedure rem> <program body>
7. <program body> ⟶ SWITCH IDENTIFIER: = <expression>$_{1,COND}$ <switch rem> <program body>
8. <program body> ⟶ BEGIN <program body> <punct stat list>
9. <program body> ⟶ END
10. <program body> ⟶ FOR IDENTIFIER <subscript part> <expression>$_{1,COND}$ <for rem> <punct stat list>
11. <program body> ⟶ GOTO <expression>$_{1,COND}$ <punct stat list>
12. <program body> ⟶ IDENTIFIER <ident rem> <punct state list>
13. <program body> ⟶ IF <expression>$_{1,COND}$ THEN <then stat><punct stat list>
14. <program body> ⟶ ; <statement> <punct stat list>
15. <array list> ⟶ , IDENTIFIER <array list>
16. <array list> ⟶ [<expression>$_{1,COND}$: <expression>$_{1,COND}$ <bound pairs>
17. <array tail> ⟶ , IDENTIFIER <array list> <array tail>
18. <array tail> ⟶ ; <program body>
19. <bound pairs> ⟶ , <expression>$_{1,COND}$: <expression>$_{1,COND}$ <bound pairs>
20. <bound pairs> ⟶]
21. <own list> ⟶ ARRAY IDENTIFIER <array list> <array tail>
22. <own list> ⟶ IDENTIFIER <declared variable list>
23. <declared variable list> ⟶ , IDENTIFIER <declared variable list>
24. <declared variable list> ⟶ ; <program body>
25. <type rem> ⟶ ARRAY IDENTIFIER <array list> <array tail>
26. <type rem> ⟶ IDENTIFIER <declared variable list>
27. <type rem> ⟶ PROCEDURE IDENTIFIER <procedure rem> <program body>
28. <procedure rem> ⟶ (IDENTIFIER <formals list>

29. <procedure rem> ⟶ ; <statement>;
30. <formals list> ⟶ , IDENTIFIER <formals list>
31. <formals list> ⟶) <formals rem>
32. <formals rem> ⟶ IDENTIFIER <unfinished comment>: (identifier <formals list>
33. <formals rem> ⟶ ; <procedure tail>$_{\text{VALUE}}$
34. <unfinished comment> ⟶ IDENTIFIER <unfinished comment>
35. <unfinished comment> ⟶ ε
36. <procedure tail>$_{\text{VALUE}}$ ⟶ VALUE IDENTIFIER <formals description>
37. <procedure tail>$_{\text{VALUE or NOVALUE}}$ ⟶ ARRAY IDENTIFIER <formals description>
38. <procedure tail>$_{\text{VALUE or NOVALUE}}$ ⟶ LABEL IDENTIFIER <formals description>
39. <procedure tail>$_{\text{VALUE or NOVALUE}}$ ⟶ PROCEDURE IDENTIFIER <formals description>
40. <procedure tail>$_{\text{VALUE or NOVALUE}}$ ⟶ SWITCH IDENTIFIER <formals description>
41. <procedure tail>$_{\text{VALUE or NOVALUE}}$ ⟶ TYPE <formals type>
42. <procedure tail>$_{\text{VALUE or NOVALUE}}$ ⟶ BEGIN <program body>;
43. <procedure tail>$_{\text{VALUE or NOVALUE}}$ ⟶ FOR IDENTIFIER <subscript part> <expression>$_{\text{1,COND}}$ <for rem>;
44. <procedure tail>$_{\text{VALUE or NOVALUE}}$ ⟶ IDENTIFIER <ident rem>;
45. <procedure tail>$_{\text{VALUE or NOVALUE}}$ ⟶ GOTO <expression>$_{\text{1,COND}}$;
46. <procedure tail>$_{\text{VALUE or NOVALUE}}$ ⟶ IF <expression>$_{\text{1,COND}}$ THEN <then stat>;
47. <procedure tail>$_{\text{VALUE or NOVALUE}}$ ⟶ ;
48. <formals description> ⟶ , IDENTIFIER <formals description>
49. <formals description> ⟶ ; <procedure tail>$_{\text{NOVALUE}}$
50. <formals type> ⟶ ARRAY IDENTIFIER <formals description>
51. <formals type> ⟶ IDENTIFIER <formals description>
52. <formals type> ⟶ PROCEDURE IDENTIFIER <formals description>
53. <switch rem> ⟶ , <expression>$_{\text{1,COND}}$ <switch rem>
54. <switch rem> ⟶ ;
55. <punct stat list> ⟶ END
56. <punct stat list> ⟶ ; <statement> <punct stat list>
57. <statement> ⟶ BEGIN <program body>
58. <statement> ⟶ FOR IDENTIFIER <subscript part> <expression>$_{\text{1,COND}}$ <for rem>
59. <statement> ⟶ GOTO <expression>$_{\text{1,COND}}$
60. <statement> ⟶ IDENTIFIER <ident rem>
61. <statement> ⟶ IF <expression>$_{\text{1,COND}}$ THEN <then stat>

62. <statement> ⟶ ε
63. <subscript part> ⟶ : =
64. <subscript part> ⟶ [<expression>$_{1,\mathrm{COND}}$ <punct subscript list>: =
65. <punct subscript list> ⟶]
66. <punct subscript list> ⟶ , <expression>$_{1,\mathrm{COND}}$ <punct subscript list>
67. <for rem> ⟶ DO <statement>
68. <for rem> ⟶ STEP <expression>$_{1,\mathrm{COND}}$ UNTIL <expression>$_{1,\mathrm{COND}}$ <punct for rem>
69. <for rem> ⟶ WHILE <expression>$_{1,\mathrm{COND}}$ <punct for rem>
70. <for rem> ⟶ , <expression>$_{1,\mathrm{COND}}$ <for rem>
71. <punct for rem> ⟶ DO <statement>
72. <punct for rem> ⟶ , <expression>$_{1,\mathrm{COND}}$ <for rem>
73. <then stat> ⟶ BEGIN <program body> <if rem>
74. <then stat> ⟶ FOR IDENTIFIER <subscript part> <expression>$_{1,\mathrm{COND}}$ <for rem>
75. <then stat> ⟶ GOTO <expression>$_{1,\mathrm{COND}}$ <if rem>
76. <then stat> ⟶ IDENTIFIER <then ident rem>
77. <then stat> ⟶ ELSE <statement>
78. <then stat> ⟶ ε
79. <then ident rem> ⟶ : <then stat>
80. <then ident rem> ⟶ (<expression>$_{1,\mathrm{COND}}$ <actuals list> <if rem>
81. <then ident rem> ⟶ [<expression>$_{1,\mathrm{COND}}$ <punct subsc list>: = <assign rem> <if rem>
82. <then ident rem> ⟶ : = <assign rem> <if rem>
83. <then ident rem> ⟶ ELSE <statement>
84. <then ident rem> ⟶ ε
85. <if rem> ⟶ ELSE <statement>
86. <if rem> ⟶ ε
87. <ident rem> ⟶ : <statement>
88. <ident rem> ⟶ (<expression>$_{1,\mathrm{COND}}$ <actuals list>
89. <ident rem> ⟶ [<expression>$_{1,\mathrm{COND}}$ <punct subsc list>: = <assign rem>
90. <ident rem> ⟶ : = <assign rem>
91. <ident rem> ⟶ ε
92. <actuals list> ⟶ , <expression>$_{1,\mathrm{COND}}$ <actuals list>
93. <actuals list> ⟶) <unfinished actuals list>
94. <unfinished actuals list> ⟶ ε
95. <unfinished actuals list> ⟶ IDENTIFIER <unfinished comment>: (<expression>$_{1,\mathrm{COND}}$ <actuals list>
96. <assign rem> ⟶ (<expression>$_{1,\mathrm{COND}}$) <remainder>$_{1,9}$

97. $\langle\text{assign rem}\rangle \longrightarrow \text{CONSTANT}\ \langle\text{remainder}\rangle_{1,9}$

98. $\langle\text{assign rem}\rangle \longrightarrow \text{IF}\ \langle\text{expression}\rangle_{1,\text{COND}}\ \text{THEN}\ \langle\text{expression}\rangle_{1,\text{COND}}\ \text{ELSE}\ \langle\text{expression}\rangle_{1,\text{COND}}$

99. $\langle\text{assign rem}\rangle \longrightarrow \text{IDENTIFIER}\ \langle\text{ident cont}\rangle\ \langle\text{remainder}\rangle_{1,9}\ \langle\text{assign continue}\rangle$

100. $\langle\text{assign rem}\rangle \longrightarrow \text{OPERATOR}_{m}\ \langle\text{expression}\rangle_{m+1,\text{UNCOND}}\ \langle\text{remainder}\rangle_{1,m}$ for $m = 5$ or 7

101. $\langle\text{assign continue}\rangle \longrightarrow\ :=\ \langle\text{assign rem}\rangle$

102. $\langle\text{assign continue}\rangle \longrightarrow \varepsilon$

103. $\langle\text{ident cont}\rangle \longrightarrow (\langle\text{expression}\rangle_{1,\text{COND}}\ \langle\text{actuals list}\rangle$

104. $\langle\text{ident cont}\rangle \longrightarrow [\langle\text{expression}\rangle_{1,\text{COND}}\ \langle\text{punct subscript list}\rangle$

105. $\langle\text{ident cont}\rangle \longrightarrow \varepsilon$

106. $\langle\text{expression}\rangle_{i,\text{COND or UNCOND}} \longrightarrow \text{CONSTANT}\ \langle\text{remainder}\rangle_{i,9}$

107. $\langle\text{expression}\rangle_{i,\text{COND or UNCOND}} \longrightarrow \text{IDENTIFIER}\ \langle\text{ident cont}\rangle\ \langle\text{remainder}\rangle_{i,9}$

108. $\langle\text{expression}\rangle_{i,\text{COND or UNCOND}} \longrightarrow (\langle\text{expression}\rangle_{1,\text{COND}})\ \langle\text{remainder}\rangle_{i,9}$

109. $\langle\text{expression}\rangle_{1,\text{COND}} \longrightarrow \text{IF}\ \langle\text{expression}\rangle_{1,\text{COND}}\ \text{THEN}\ \langle\text{expression}\rangle_{1,\text{UNCOND}}\ \text{ELSE}\ \langle\text{expression}\rangle_{1,\text{COND}}$

110. $\langle\text{expression}\rangle_{i,\text{COND or UNCOND}} \longrightarrow \text{OPERATOR}_{m}\ \langle\text{expression}\rangle_{m+1,\text{UNCOND}}\ \langle\text{remainder}\rangle_{i,m}$ for $i \leq m$; $m = 5$ or 7

111. $\langle\text{remainder}\rangle_{i,j} \longrightarrow \text{OPERATOR}_{m}\ \langle\text{expression}\rangle_{m+1,\text{UNCOND}}\ \langle\text{remainder}\rangle_{i,m}$ for $i \leq m \leq j$; $m \neq 5$

112. $\langle\text{remainder}\rangle_{i,j} \longrightarrow \varepsilon$

ACKNOWLEDGEMENT

The following people made significant contributions to the design and coding of the compiler: Gary J. Fisher, Jack P. Gelb, John S. Hutchison, Alyce W. Orne, Melvin Sabel, and Walter W. Stone.

In particular, the implementation and coding of the finite-state machine for the lexical box was done by John S. Hutchison; the implementation and coding of the pushdown translator for the syntax box was done by Jack P. Gelb; the concept and design of the code generator was done by Walter W. Stone; and the design and coding of the system interface was done by Gary J. Fisher.

Richard E. Stearns acted as a consultant for the entire project, particularly the semantic box.

REFERENCES

[1] *R&DC ALGOL Programming Manual—Preliminary Version*, General Electric Research and Development Center Report 70-G-006, Schenectady, New York (1970).

[2] P. M. Lewis II and R. E. Stearns, "Syntax-Directed Translation," *J. ACM*, 15, 465–488 (July 1968).

[3] D. J. Rosenkrantz and R. E. Stearns, "Properties of Deterministic Top-Down Grammars," *Information & Control*, 17, 226–256 (October 1970).

[4] P. Naur et. al., "Revised Report on the Algorithmic Language ALGOL 60," *Comm. ACM*, 6, 1–17 (January 1963).

[5] R. E. Stearns and P. M. Lewis II, "Property Grammars and Table Machines," *Information & Control*, 14, 524–549 (June 1967).

[6] R. E. Stearns and D. J. Rosenkrantz, "Table Machine Simulation," *IEEE Conf. Record of 1969 Tenth Annual Symp. on Switching and Automata Theory*, 118–128 (1969).

NUCLEOL—
A TREE-PROCESSING LANGUAGE

J. Nievergelt and L. Lukaszewicz*
Department of Computer Science, University of Illinois at Urbana-Champaign, Urbana, IL

NUCLEOL is a small programming language designed for processing tree-structured data, and intended as a basis in terms of which higher-level tree-processing languages could be implemented easily and efficiently. Hence, its design aims at:

(a) Simplicity
(b) General data structures and a small, well-chosen set of primitive operations
(c) Complete and rigorous definition.

I. BACKGROUND AND PURPOSE OF NUCLEOL

The programming language NUCLEOL is the focal point of a project which has the following major goals:

(1) To develop and study language features which are particularly well suited to processing tree-structured data
(2) To develop a system which is as simple as possible; yet is sufficient, in a practical sense, to serve as a basis for convenient implementation of any list-processing language which operates on tree-structured data
(3) To experiment with techniques of formal definition of programming languages which allow the definition to be a major component of the implementation of the language.

Because NUCLEOL is mainly a tool for developing and testing novel ideas, rather than a software package for public use, it has evolved a fair deal over the past few years. This paper is to be regarded as a progress report on a continuing project rather than a final description of the language. We begin by giving a brief account of the development of NUCLEOL since its conception in 1968.

The NUCLEOL project had its origin in our experiences with transferring a symbol-manipulation language from one computer to others. The language in question is EOL [1, 2], which was first implemented on the Polish computer ZAM at the Institute for Mathematical Machines in Warsaw and later on an IBM 7094 and an IBM 360 at the University of Illinois.

*On leave from the Polish Academy of Sciences, Warsaw.

Presented at the Symposium on Computers and Automata
Polytechnic Institute of Brooklyn, April 13–15, 1971.

The idea was to facilitate future implementations of EOL or other higher-level list-processing languages by designing a simple list processor based on rather general data structures, but with only a small, well-chosen set of primitive operations; i.e., to simulate a computer specifically adapted to list processing. The design which resulted has been described in [3, 4]. It had been quite strongly influenced by EOL, and hence was appropriately named NUCLEOL. This first version of NUCLEOL was implemented as a PL/1 program in 1969. A notable feature was a formal definition of the language which was used directly in the implementation [5]. The adequacy of NUCLEOL for its intended purpose of tree processing was tested by using it as a basis for a transformational-grammar system [6, 7], in which tree transformations could be described by pattern-replacement rules of the generality commonly used in specifying transformational grammars.

Beginning in 1970, M. Iglewski wrote a formal definition of NUCLEOL, using the Vienna definition method, at the Polish Academy of Sciences in Warsaw. Current efforts of this group are directed towards automatically interpreting this formal definition so it can serve as a standard implementation of NUCLEOL.

The main part of this paper, Section II, is an informal introduction to a revised version of NUCLEOL, which differs from the earlier one primarily by having a much more powerful scheme for addressing nodes and subtrees of trees. Section III describes our experiences with two approaches to the formal definition of NUCLEOL.

II. THE MAIN FEATURES OF NUCLEOL

NUCLEOL is intended to be a small system for processing tree-structured data, which can serve as a basis for implementing higher level tree-processing languages conveniently. It can also be regarded as a proposed organization of a computer specifically designed for tree-processing. Because of this goal, NUCLEOL contains notions of two different kinds: high level notions, which involve trees and their structure (see Section II.A), and low level notions, which allow the user access to the building blocks in terms of which trees are represented (see Section II.B).

A. Trees and Their Linear Representation

NUCLEOL programs as well as data can be regarded as rooted ordered trees (in the sense that a left-to-right order is imposed on the sons of every node). An example of the tree aspects is shown in Figure 1.

Internal nodes of a tree are represented by a pair of *parentheses* ⟬ ⟭. Terminal nodes, or leaves, are represented by a circle ○, except for precisely one leaf, called the *scanner*, which is represented by ⤊.

Subtrees rooted at an internal node (a pair of matching parentheses) are called *blocks* (there are two of these in Fig. 1, where they are enclosed by dashed lines). Leaves are considered to be blocks also, except for the scanner.

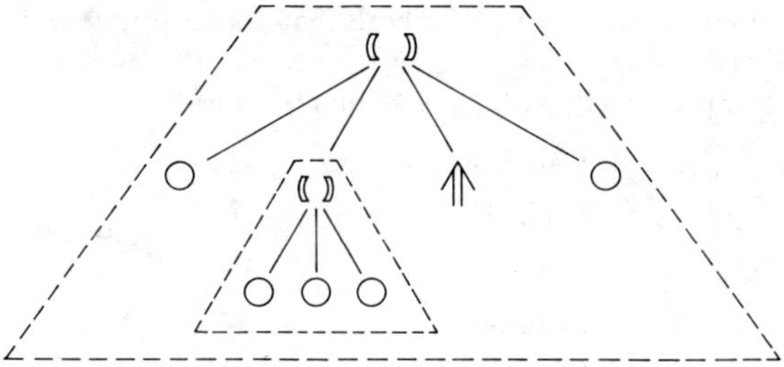

Fig. 1. Tree diagram. Blocks are enclosed by dashed lines.

A tree may be interpreted by NUCLEOL either as a program or as data. In the first case, the tree represents the block structure of the program, and the motion of the scanner represents the flow of control through the program. In the second case, the scanner simply provides access to the tree and its parts. In the case of both data trees and programs, a circled leaf may be either an instruction or a data block.

Trees are represented in NUCLEOL as *well-formed strings* (WFS) of units called *constituents*. Constituents will be discussed in the next section, but the syntax of WFS can still be presented here in terms of the higher syntactic categories <data block> and <instruction> (which, in turn, are represented by sequences of constituents as is discussed in later sections).

The syntax of a WFS is best described by a few productions in (a slightly-modified) Backus-Naur form. The notation <something*> means "zero or more occurrences of <something>."

<WFS> : = <LXP> <block*> <sblock> <block*> <RXP> ,

<sblock> : = <scanner> | <LP> <block*> <sblock> <block*> <RP> ,

<block> : = <data block> | <instruction> | <LP> <block*> <RP> .

If we replace the syntactic categories <scanner> by ⇑, <LXP> (left exterternal parenthesis) and <LP> (left parenthesis) by ⟪, similarly <RXP> and <RP> by ⟫, and <data block> and <instruction> by a circle ○, these productions allow one to generate the WFS

⟪○⟪○○○⟫⇑○⟫ ,

which is the linear representation of the tree of Figure 1.

B. Constituents—The Building Blocks of the Representation

Constituents are the building blocks in terms of which trees are represented in NUCLEOL. A constituent consists of the following three fields: its *type*, an *attribute*, and a *value*. We will write constituents as follows

$$T_{A\ v} \ ,$$

where: T denotes the type; A the attribute; and v the value. Where the attribute and/or the value are unimportant, or where they assume a default value ("null"), A and v may be omitted.

There are six different types of constituents, namely:

Left Parenthesis	⦅
Right Parenthesis	⦆
Scanner	⇑
Reference	ℝ
Keyword	𝕂
Data Constituent	𝔻

Parentheses, which must occur in a WFS in a balanced way, allow a WFS to be interpreted as a tree, with a pair of matching parenthesis corresponding to an internal node. In a program, left and right parentheses serve the function of the *begin* and *end* of a program block. In this case, the attribute of the parenthesis, called the *protection attribute*, determines whether control may enter into or exit from the program block, in a way to be described later (see Section II.H).

The value of *external* (outermost) parentheses is a *name*, which is the name of the WFS enclosed by these parentheses.

There is a unique *scanner* in every WFS. It provides access to a data WFS, and represents the flow of control in a program WFS. Its attribute distinguishes data WFSs from the WFS currently being executed, and in the latter case, serves an important function as the *mode* (to be described in Sections II.E and II.H). The scanner can be moved around in a manner convenient for both the interpretations of a WFS as a tree or as a linear sequence (see Section II.G).

Reference constituents perform the function of addressing, either an entire WFS or its parts, such as blocks, constituents, and even the gaps between adjacent blocks (for the purpose of inserting new blocks). This addressing scheme is one of the most powerful features of NUCLEOL and will be discussed in detail in Section II.F.

Keywords, in conjunction with references, are the building blocks from which NUCLEOL instructions are composed. There are only four keywords for primitive instructions, but an unspecified number of keywords for user-defined instructions.

Data constituents are used to represent data items such as integers, character strings, or bit strings. The attribute of a data constituent identifies the type of data it holds, and its value is the data item to be held. Data constituents can be combined to form data blocks.

C. Some Features NUCLEOL Leaves Unspecified

NUCLEOL leaves many important features of a programming language unspecified, such as: what data types there are, and what operations on these data types are provided. The reason for this omission is the following.

NUCLEOL does not aim at being a complete programming language, but only the core, or "nucleus" of a language for processing tree-structured data. As such, it incorporates only those concepts and operations as primitive which can be expected to be common to all tree-processing systems; namely, the structural operations on trees. All operations on data which may be associated with nodes in trees are considered to exist only in particular *extensions* of NUCLEOL.

Thus, all that NUCLEOL says about data is that there are data blocks, that each block consists of a sequence of data constituents, and that each data constituent has an attribute and a value. And it provides means for addressing such a data block as a whole (and maybe move it around in the tree), for addressing each of its constituents, and for addressing the attribute—and the value fields of this constituent.

For purposes of illustration and in later examples, we will assume an extension of NUCLEOL (the one implemented in our first version of the system) which has the following kinds of data blocks:

(a) Integer, represented by a single data constituent with attribute *I*; e.g., $\mathbb{D}_I$ – 17

(b) Bitstring of fixed length, represented by a single constituent with attribute *B*; e.g., $\mathbb{D}_B$ '01101010'

(c) Character strings of arbitrary length represented by a sequence of as many constituents as needed, assuming that one constituent can hold up to four characters. All the constituents have attribute *A* except the last one which has attribute *C*.

CHARACTER STRING	REPRESENTATION AS A DATA BLOCK
'*WXYZ*'	$\mathbb{D}_C$ '*WXYZ*'
'*ABCDEFGHI*'	$\mathbb{D}_A$ '*ABCD*' $\mathbb{D}_A$ '*EFGH*' $\mathbb{D}_C$ '*I*'

With these data types one might then have instructions for arithmetic operations on integers, Boolean operations on bitstrings, and operations for concatenating and splitting character strings. These instructions are considered to be *defined* instructions, as opposed to the *primitive* instructions which will be described in Section II.G.

D. NUCLEOL States

A NUCLEOL *state* is a set of WFSs no two of which have the same name, and exactly one of which has a scanner whose attribute characterizes it as the execution scanner. The following three WFSs serve as an example of a NUCLEOL state.

⟦ SINK ⇑ ⟧

⟦ SOURCE $\mathbb{D}_I$ 17 ⟦ $\mathbb{D}_B$ '0110101' $\mathbb{D}_C$ '*ABC*' ⟧ ⇑ ⟧

⟦ PROG ⇑$_N$ ⟦$_N$ $\mathbb{K}_P$ MOVE $\mathbb{R}_D$ SOURCE. ⟵ $\mathbb{R}_G$ SINK. *L* ⟧$_B$ ⟧

The WFS called SINK is as small as it can be, since every WFS must contain at least a scanner and a pair of external parentheses. The scanner of WFS SOURCE has a block to its left but none to its right. The WFS called PROG is a program. Its scanner, which is placed in the leftmost position available to it, is characterized by its attribute *N* (for *neutral*) to be the *execution scanner*. Its motion will represent the flow of control through the program.

E. Example of a NUCLEOL Computation

A NUCLEOL state contains all the information required for executing a program. The semantics of NUCLEOL is defined by a function NUCSTEP, which assigns to *some* of the states a next state. A NUCLEOL computation is a sequence of states, each one of which gets transformed by NUCSTEP into its successor. If there is a last state, then NUCSTEP is undefined on it. The set of states on which NUCSTEP is undefined is partitioned into two classes. *Final states,* characterized by the fact that the execution scanner is in its right most position, just in front of the right external parenthesis; and *error states,* all other states on which NUCSTEP is undefined.

Let us now trace the sequence of successive states generated by repeated application of the function NUCSTEP on the state described above.

First step. The attribute (N) of the execution scanner is matched against the protection attribute (N) of the $(\!($ constituent to its right. Because they match, the scanner *enters* the block, i.e., is shifted past the constituent to its right (if the attributes do not match, the execution scanner *skips* around the block to its right).

Second step. The $\mathbb{K}$-constituent to the right of the execution scanner is the first constituent of an instruction, which consists in this case of the keyword $\mathbb{K}_P$ MOVE (where the attribute P indicates that this is a primitive instruction rather than a defined one) and of two references. The constituent $\mathbb{R}_D$ SOURCE. $\leftarrow$ refers to the block immediately to the left of the scanner of WFS SOURCE. Its attribute D indicates that this is a *destructive* block reference, which means that after this reference has been executed, the referenced block is deleted from its WFS. The second reference constituent $\mathbb{R}_G$ SINK. L indicates that the block which has just been deleted is to be inserted in the gap immediately to the left of scanner SINK. Thereafter, the execution scanner is placed to the right of the instruction just executed.

Third step. The execution scanner, which still has an attribute N, cannot pass through the $)\!)_B$ constituent with attribute B. This causes the scanner to *bounce* to the corresponding left parenthesis, where it finds itself again in front of the MOVE instruction.

Fourth step. The MOVE instruction is executed again, and this time the data block consisting of the single constituent $\mathbb{D}_I$ 17 is deleted from WFS SOURCE and inserted in the gap to the left of the scanner of WFS SINK. Then the execution scanner moves past the instruction.

Fifth step. Execution scanner bounces again.

Sixth step. The execution scanner attempts to execute the MOVE instruction a third time. During evaluation of its first reference $\mathbb{R}_D$ SOURCE. $\leftarrow$, however, it is found that now there is no block to the left of the scanner SOURCE. This causes the execution scanner to skip the MOVE instruction as before, but now its attribute changes from N to B, which is a mnemonic for "block fault."

Seventh step. Now that the attribute of the execution scanner matches the attribute of the parenthesis, the scanner passes through the $)\!)_B$, instead of bouncing, and places itself in its rightmost position. Since this results in a final state, the computation ends.

Hence, the one-instruction program above has the effect of deleting all the blocks (at a given level of nesting—in this case all first-level blocks) from WFS SOURCE and inserting them in *reversed* order in WFS SINK.

F. The Tree Addressing Scheme

One of the most powerful features of NUCLEOL is its scheme for addressing the various parts of a WFS, such as blocks, constituents, and gaps between adjacent blocks.

Addresses, or references, are represented by $\mathbb{R}$ constituents in the following way. The attribute of an $\mathbb{R}$ constituent indicates what kind of object is being addressed, and the value part of this $\mathbb{R}$ constituent contains an address sequence which identifies this object.

The possible values of the attribute of $\mathbb{R}$ constituents, and the corresponding kinds of references are:

W	WFS reference
S	Scanner reference
B	Nondestructive block reference
D	Destructive block reference
G	Gap reference
C	Constituent reference
F	Field reference.

The address sequences corresponding to these kinds of references are strings generated by the finite-state diagram of Fig. 2 (by beginning at the node labeled START and ending at any other node).

The following examples of reference constituents explain the meaning of such address sequences.

$\mathbb{R}_W X$ A WFS reference. If there is a WFS called *X*, this reference succeeds; if not, the reference fails, and this fact is recorded

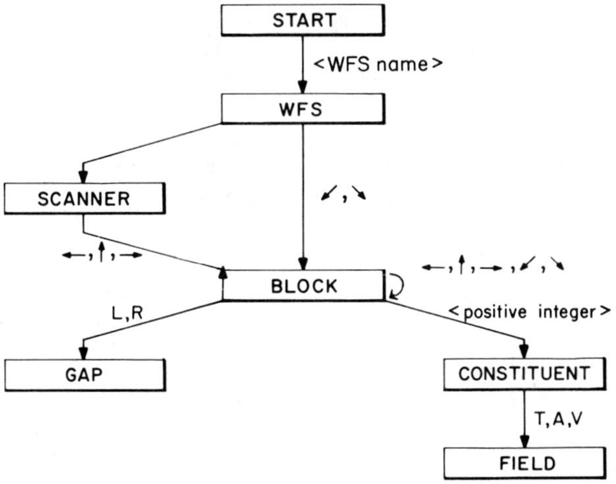

Fig. 2. Finite-state diagram.

by setting the *mode* of NUCLEOL, i.e., the attribute of the execution scanner, to W (mnemonic for "WFS fault")

$\mathbb{R}_S\, X.$ Reference to the scanner of WFS X

$\mathbb{R}_B\, X. \uparrow$ Reference to the block which immediately surrounds the scanner of WFS X

$\mathbb{R}_D\, X \swarrow$ Destructive block reference to the leftmost immediate subblock of WFS X. Causes this block to be deleted from WFS X.

Each of the five arrow operators leads from a block to:

$\uparrow$ The immediately-surrounding block

$\leftarrow$ The left-adjacent block

$\rightarrow$ The right-adjacent block

$\swarrow$ The leftmost-immediate subblock

$\searrow$ The rightmost-immediate subblock.

This is illustrated in Figure 3.

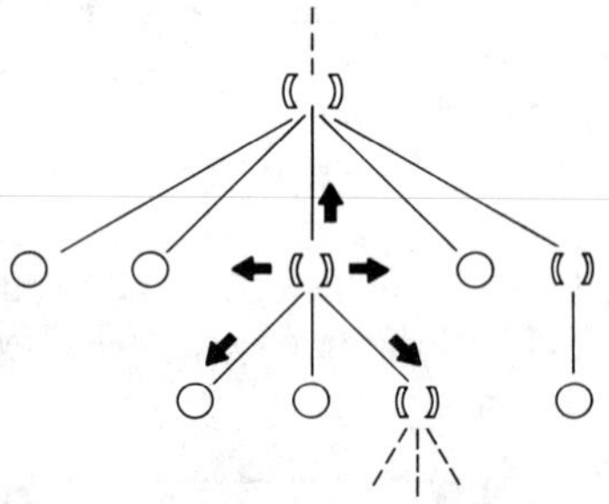

Fig. 3. Blocks addressed by the arrow operators.

Initial access to a block is either from the entire WFS (the root of the tree) to its leftmost- and rightmost-immediate subblocks, or from the scanner to its left-adjacent, right-adjacent, or immediately-surrounding block, as shown in Figure 4.

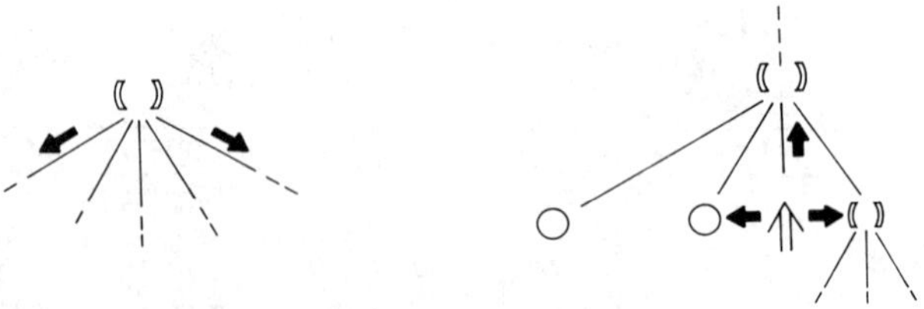

Fig. 4. Initial access to a block.

Since these arrow operators can be catenated in an address sequence, it is possible to address in one reference the subtree (block) whose root is in a fixed position relative to either the root of the entire tree, or the current scanner position.

To continue with our examples:

$\mathbb{R}_G\ X. \longrightarrow R$ Reference to the gap which is immediately to the right of the right neighbor block of the scanner of WFS X (Gap 1 in Figure 5)

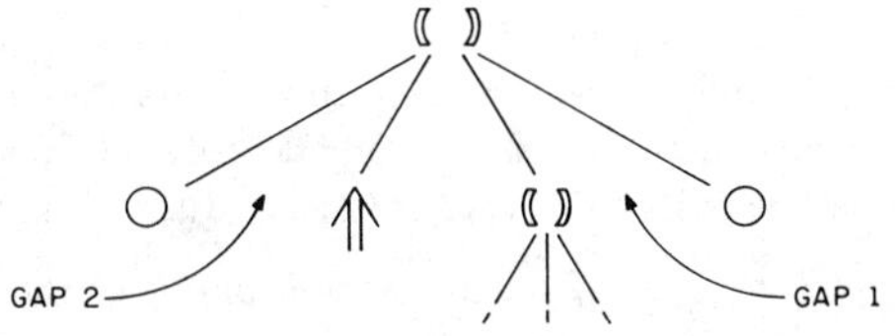

Figure 5.

$\mathbb{R}_G\ X.R$ and $\mathbb{R}_G\ X. \longrightarrow L$ Both are references to the gap immediately to the right of Scanner X (Gap 2 in Figure 5).

Since a data block or an instruction in NUCLEOL consists of a sequence of constituents, one can address a constituent within such a block by its sequence number. Thus, if PROG is the WFS shown in Section II.D.

$\mathbb{R}_C$ PROG $\swarrow\swarrow 3$ Reference to the third constituent of the MOVE instruction, namely to the reference constituent $\mathbb{R}_G$ SINK.L.

For a parenthesized block, its left parenthesis is its first constituent, and its right parenthesis is its second constituent. Thus, if $\mathbb{R}_B\ X \swarrow\longrightarrow\ \longrightarrow$ refers to a parenthesized block in WFS X, then $\mathbb{R}_C\ X \swarrow\longrightarrow\ \longrightarrow 1$ and $\mathbb{R}_C\ X \swarrow\longrightarrow\ \longrightarrow 2$ refer to its left-and-right parentheses, respectively.

Finally, the operators T, A, V, when appended to a constituent reference, provide a reference to any of the three fields of a constituent: its type, attribute, and value. Thus, if WFS SOURCE is as shown in II.D, then

$\mathbb{R}_F$ SOURCE. $\longleftarrow \searrow 1V$ Reference to the value of the constituent $\mathbb{D}_C$ 'ABC', namely the character string 'ABC'.

$\mathbb{R}_F$ SOURCE. $\longleftarrow\ \longleftarrow\ 1A$
and
$\mathbb{R}_F$ SOURCE $\swarrow 1A$

References to the attribute I of the constituent $\mathbb{D}_I$ 17.

When a reference is evaluated, the address sequence is interpreted from left to right. At any step in this process, a reference can fail if a WFS, a block, or a constituent does not exist at the indicated place. If so, the attempted evaluation of the reference terminates, and the mode (attribute of execution scanner) assumes the value W, B, or C, to indicate that a WFS fault, a block fault, or a constituent fault has occurred.

G. The Primitive Instructions

The primitive instructions of NUCLEOL aim at being a small but sufficient set in terms of which operations on rooted trees can be expressed conveniently and efficiently.

Operations on data values are not among them. As was mentioned in II.C, these are considered to exist in particular extensions of NUCLEOL. It is clear that, since NUCLEOL provides references to the value field of constituents, operations on these values can easily be introduced in the framework provided by NUCLEOL.

It is notable that the apparently-limited primitive instructions of NUCLEOL, in conjunction with the bounce-and-skip technique to be discussed in the next section, provide sufficient means for directing the flow of control in programs.

NUCLEOL provides the following four primitive instructions with keywords:

$\mathbb{K}_P$ POSCAN $\mathbb{R}_G$	Position the scanner of the WFS named in the address sequence of R_G in the gap referenced by R_G. If this WFS is the one currently being executed, this results in a jump
$\mathbb{K}_P$ MOVE ($\mathbb{R}_D$ or $\mathbb{R}_B$) $\mathbb{R}_G$	Either delete or make a copy of the block referenced by the first R constituent of the instruction, and insert this block into the gap referenced by $\mathbb{R}_G$
$\mathbb{K}_P$ BLOCK $\mathbb{R}_G$ $\mathbb{R}_G$	If the gaps g_1 and g_2 referenced by the two reference constituents are in such a position that inserting a ⦅ at g_1 and a ⦆ at g_2 results in these two parentheses forming a matched pair, insert them; thus replacing a forest of subtrees by a single subtree. (The matching property can be determined by inspecting the two address sequences.) If not, set the mode to I (for "instruction fault")
$\mathbb{K}_P$ DEBLOCK $\mathbb{R}_B$	If the block referenced by $\mathbb{R}_B$ is a parenthesized block, delete its two parentheses, thus replacing a subtree, T, by the forest of the subtrees of T. If the referenced block is not a parenthesized block, set the mode to I (for "instruction fault").

In addition to these four, a single reference is also considered to be a primitive instruction. Executing a scanner reference makes the scanner being referenced the execution scanner, thus transferring control to another WFS at whatever point its scanner is positioned. Thus, this mechanism can be used to provide subroutine calls and coroutine jumps.

Executing any other reference constituent serves the purpose of testing whether the referenced object exists, the result being recorded by setting the mode to W, B, or C if a WFS fault, block fault, or constituent fault occurred, respectively. Executing a destructive block reference $\mathbb{R}_D$ may serve the additional purpose of deleting a block.

H. Bounce-and-Skip

In addition to the instruction POSCAN (as applied to the execution scanner) and to executing a scanner reference, NUCLEOL provides yet another technique for directing the flow of control in programs, which is implicit in the way the execution scanner interacts with parentheses.

It operates as follows: each ⦅ and ⦆ has a "protection" attribute, which is a list of all the values of the mode, (i.e., the attribute of the execution scanner), under which the execution scanner can pass through the parenthesis (i.e., enter a block through a ⦅ or exit from a block through a ⦆).

Since the mode is set to different values when executing instructions (including single references), parentheses provide a means of testing whether an instruction was carried out to its completion, and if not, at what stage during its execution a fault occurred.

The rules which govern this motion of the execution scanner are as follows: If the execution scanner enters a block or leaves a block, then the mode variable is reset to N ("neutral"). If it cannot enter through a ⦅ , it *skips* the block, and if it cannot exit through a ⦆, it *bounces* and positions itself just inside the matching ⦅ .

This technique, called bounce-and-skip, has been described in [8]. One might add that the large number of possible mode values in NUCLEOL makes bounce-and-skip here more useful than in the case described in [8].

III. EXPERIMENTS WITH TECHNIQUES OF FORMAL DEFINITION

Describing a programming language and *defining* it are two very different things. In a description to someone unfamiliar with a language one wants to stress a few highlights and avoid burdening his memory with details. This is what we have attempted to do in the previous section. In a definition, on the other hand, one has to say everything there is to say. Because of the intended use of NUCLEOL as a basis in terms of which other languages may be implemented, there is a definite need for a complete rigorous definition.

While there are well-established tools for the definition of the syntax of programming languages, the situation is completely different with respect to semantics. Hence, we have been experimenting with various techniques of formal definition of programming languages.

We insisted that the definition should serve the dual purpose of defining NUCLEOL both to humans and to machines. This principle has not been implemented in practice in other formal definitions of actual programming languages (e.g., ALGOL [9], PL/1 [10]). However, we consider it to be a principle of great importance, and we expect that in the future one will insist that a formal definition be used as (or at least *in*) the standard implementation of a particular language.

Approaches to the formal definition of the semantics of programming languages used in the past fall into two major categories:

(a) To specify rules which assign to an arbitrary program in the language to be defined a function which performs the same transformation on the data as the program. Landin's definition of ALGOL [9] is an example of this approach.

(b) To specify an interpreter for the language, in terms of a well-chosen, machine-independent set of basic operations. This approach has been proposed by McCarthy [11], and forms the basis for the formal definition of PL/1 [10], and has been used to prove the correctness of a miniature compiler [12].

It appears obvious that, for most of today's programming languages, the second approach lends itself better to using the definition as part of the implementation than the first one does. (An exception to this might be a language like "pure" LISP, where "programming" naturally means "defining functions".) For NUCLEOL, a language whose programs are sequences of instructions, a model which emphasizes the dynamic aspects of program execution, rather than a static function definition, clearly seemed appropriate, and hence we chose the second approach.

A. A Formal Definition Which is Used in the Implementation

Our first formal definition of NUCLEOL was written along lines proposed by McCarthy [11].

This definition consisted of the following four parts:

(1) A list of basic predicates and functions which are part of the abstract syntax of the language

(2) An interpreter which defines the transition function NUCSTEP in terms of the basic predicates and functions

(3) Axioms which relate the basic functions and predicates to each other

(4) The concrete syntax which defines a particular representation (the "reference language") for NUCLEOL.

A brief description of the first three parts follows. The concrete syntax is conventional and will not be mentioned.

(1) NUCLEOL required about a dozen basic predicates, and about forty basic functions. Most basic predicates identify a syntactic category which one wants to introduce in the language. Since NUCLEOL uses the concepts "state", "WFS", "block", "constituent", among others, one has the predicates IS_STATE, IS_WFS, IS_BLOCK, IS_CONSTITUENT.

With each predicate which identifies a syntactic category, a sufficient number of basic functions are introduced to perform all the operations which one needs to do on elements of this type. E.g., with the predicate IS_STATE we have the functions:

EXEC (STATE)	Gives the name of the WFS currently being executed

WFS_NAMED (WFS_NAME)	Returns the WFS with a given name (a table look-up procedure)
KILL (WFS_NAME)	Delete the WFS with a given name from the state
CREATE (WFS_NAME, WFS)	Add a WFS to the state and name it.

Similarly, the following functions are associated with the predicate IS_BLOCK:

BLOCK_AT	(BLOCKREFERENCE)
DELETE	(BLOCKREFERENCE)
INSERT	(BLOCK, GAPREFERENCE)

(2) The interpreter defines the transition function NUCSTEP in terms of the basic predicates and functions of the abstract syntax. It is at the same time a 400-statement PL/1 program. PL/1 was chosen because, among well-known high-level languages, it offers the greatest flexibility of notation, which is an important point if a program is to be its own documentation.

This interpreter constituted about one third of the entire implementation of NUCLEOL. But it was undoubtedly the most important and illuminating part of the implementation. The routines which implemented the basic functions and predicates were often conceptually simple, but tricky in detail, and certainly too machine-dependent (in this case, PL/1-dependent) to be very enlightening.

Hence, these routines were rightly excluded from the formal definition of NUCLEOL.

(3) Axioms are relations between the basic predicates and functions which must hold in any concrete realization of NUCLEOL. They define these functions and predicates without assuming any particular machine representation of WFSs and constituents. There are about 60 axioms. A typical axiom states that the basic functions DELETE and INSERT are inverse operations; i.e., if a block is deleted from a WFS and then is inserted in the gap created by its deletion, the WFS remains unchanged.

The relationship between this formal definition and the implementation is summarized in Figure 6.

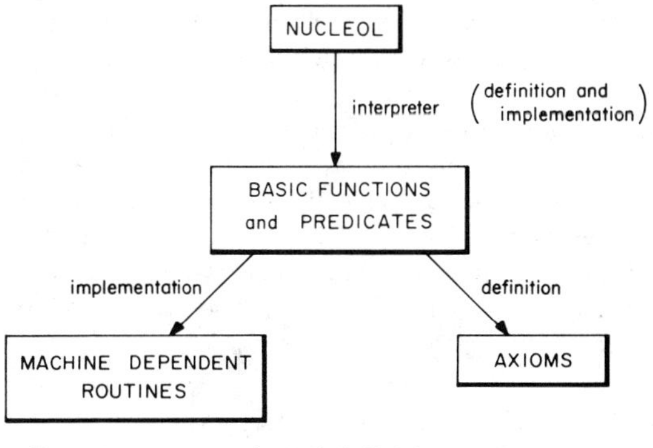

Fig. 6. Relation between formal definition and implementation.

We concluded from this experiment that it is both feasible and useful to combine the formal definition of a programming language with its implementation. However, many problems of a practical nature were encountered, and they usually resulted in some compromise between theoretical elegance and efficient programming. The following is a case in point.

From a theoretical point of view, one would like to introduce as few basic predicates and functions as possible, but from the point of view of efficiency of the program the situation is different: a function which is a special case of another one can often be implemented much more efficiently than the general one, and hence one may want to have both.

Another source of differences between what one likes to have in a definition and in an implementation has to do with system functions like error handling, diagnostics, listing, bounds on time and memory, etc. In a first approach to the definition of a language, one likes to ignore these aspects (our definition, e.g., does not mention I/O: It is assumed to happen through the initial and final state of the execution sequence), but no implementation can exist without them. Initially, we thought these system functions should remain "implementation features" which are not part of the formal definition. This might be reasonable if these functions could be neatly separated (logically and physically) from the rest, but such is not our experience. We conclude that future formal definitions will have to face the problem of describing system functions, since the latter are too significant an aspect to be ignored.

The statements which implement system functions are relatively few (of the order of two hundred), but they are logically important and physically interspersed throughout the rest of the interpreter. In contrast to this, the implementation of the basic predicates and functions is voluminous (1,000 statements, as opposed to 400 for the top part of the interpreter). Yet we feel that these programs are rightly omitted from the formal definition, and that it would be a mistake to choose basic predicates and functions at a lower level than we did. These programs are much too machine- (in this case, PL/1-) dependent to be enlightening.

We consider that defining the semantics of the basic predicates and functions by means of axioms (rather than a particular implementation) is the correct approach. However, these axioms should also be used in the implementation: ideally by having a processor which generates code for the basic functions and predicates given the axioms and a description of the target machine, or, more realistically, by having a processor which checks that a given implementation satisfies the axioms.

It is a regrettable shortcoming that our implementation did not use the axioms at all. The explanation is simply that we considered either of the two schemes mentioned above to be a research project in its own right, which could not reasonably be attacked as part of the NUCLEOL effort. We consider the use of the axioms to automatically verify or possibly generate code for the basic predicates and functions to be the major unsolved problem we have encountered in this project.

B. Formal Definition Using the Vienna Method

The second formal definition of NUCLEOL was written using the techniques and notation developed by the IBM Laboratory in Vienna for the formal definition of PL/1 [10]. The Vienna method appears to be well suited even for the definition of languages which are very different from PL/1.

The abstract syntax of NUCLEOL turned out to be extremely simple, but some of this simplicity was bought at the cost of a more complex interpreter. The experience gained in writing this formal definition had a significant influence on the design of the new version of NUCLEOL, which is both more general and simpler than the first one. Current efforts are focused on using this definition directly in an implementation of NUCLEOL, but it is too early to assess this project.

IV. CONCLUSIONS

We believe that NUCLEOL has certain unique features related to the processing of tree-structured data which are worth serious consideration, particularly since existing high-level languages tend to have only very rudimentary operations for this purpose. Some of the features present in NUCLEOL, such as the scheme used for addressing blocks (subtrees), constituents (nodes), and gaps, appear to be of general applicability in processing tree-structured data.

ACKNOWLEDGEMENT

Many people have cooperated and given valuable advice in various phases of the NUCLEOL project. In particular, we would like to acknowledge the contributions of: Freda Fischer, M. I. Irland, and J. R. Sidlo in the design of the first version of NUCLEOL; K. Maruyama in the implementation of NUCLEOL; M. I. Irland in the formal definition of NUCLEOL and discussions on the present version; M. Iglewski in the formal definition of NUCLEOL using the Vienna method.

Our work has been supported by the Department of Computer Science at the University of Illinois, Urbana, Illinois, the National Science Foundation under Grants GJ 217 and GJ 328, and the Polish Academy of Sciences.

REFERENCES

[1] L. Lukaszewicz, "EOL—A Symbol-Manipulation Language," *Comput. J.*, **10**, No. 1 (May 1967).

[2] L. Lukaszewicz and J. Nievergelt, "EOL Report," and "EOL Programming Examples," University of Illinois, Department of Computer Science, Urbana, Illinois, Report Nos. 241, 242 (September 1967).

[3] J. R. Sidlo, "NUCLEOL—The Basis for the List-Processing Language EOL-4," MSc. Thesis, University of Illinois, Urbana, Illinois (August 1968).

[4] J. Nievergelt et al., "NUCLEOL—A Minimal List Processor," *Proc. Purdue Centennial Year Symp. on Information Processing*, 92–103 (1969). Also: University of Illinois, Department of Computer Science, Urbana, Illinois, Report No. 324 (April 1969).

[5] Irwin-Zarecki and M. I. Irland, "NUCLEOL as a Formal System," University of Illinois, Department of Computer Science, Urbana, Illinois, Report No. 310 (February 1969) (MSc. Thesis).

[6] K. Maruyama, "A Tree Transformation System Based on NUCLEOL," University of Illinois, Department of Computer Science, Urbana, Illinois, Report No. 376 (February 1970) (MSc. Thesis).

[7] N. Bracha, "A Computer System for Grammatical Transformations," University of Illinois, Department of Computer Science, Urbana, Illinois, Report No. 387 (February 1970) (MSc. Thesis).

[8] J. Nievergelt and M. I. Irland, "Bounce-and-Skip—A Technique for Directing the Flow of Control in Programs," *Comput. J.*, **13**, No. 3, 261-262 (August 1970).

[9] P. J. Landin, "A Correspondence Between ALGOL 60 and Church's Lambda Notation," *Comm. ACM*, **8**, No. 2, 89–101 (February 1965). Also No. 3, 158–165 (March 1965).

[10] P. Lucas and K. Walk, "On the Formal Description of PL/1," *Annual Review in Automatic Programming*, **6**, Part 3, 105–182 (1969).

[11] J. McCarthy, "A Formal Description of a Subset of ALGOL," *Formal Language Description Languages for Computer Programming*, 1–12 (T. B. Steel, Ed., North Holland, 1966).

[12] J. McCarthy, and J. A. Painter, "Correctness of a Compiler for Arithmetic Expressions," *Mathematical Aspects of Computer Science*, **19**, 33–41 (J. T. Schwartz, Ed., American Math Society, 1967).

ON THE DEFINITION OF HIGHER-LEVEL-LANGUAGE MACHINES

Dines Bjørner
IBM Research Laboratory, San Jose, CA

In this note we show an example of a systematic approach to computer architecture and machine language design. The advocated systematicity is based on the use of finite-state machines, regular expressions, push-down translators and context-free grammars. We show how to relate formal syntax and formal semantics to the conceptual data flow in the underlying machine organization. Our example demonstrates a novel addressing scheme and builds on a hierarchy of schemes whereby the machine instruction scheme is composed from a string or syllable scheme and contains an operator scheme and a name scheme. It is believed that this approach, when used, will lead to clean, well-structured and extensible computer architectures, specifically such oriented towards higher-level languages.

The style of this note is tutorial. We are, however, not surveying the relevant literature and presenting a consensus of what it contains. Instead, we are giving a number of novel design techniques, not in the most general of settings, but through a specific example. The tutorial approach has been selected because it allows us to develop a controlled, step-by-step, unravelling of various design aspects with increasingly more complex designs. This is in contrast to the presentation of an already completed design.

I. INTRODUCTION

In this introduction, we shall outline first the general subject, then the conceptual and historical framework, and finally the specific approach.

1.1 General Subject

The subject of this note is the design of a computer architecture from the point of view of designing the machine language. This has been the traditional approach—and could possibly be shown inadequate and, thus, a dangerous method. We will not philosophize on these dangers further—rather our short-range aim is to clean up exactly that methodology, so to speak, give it a structure, and provide design tools.

1.2 Conceptual Framework

We shall tentatively make a distinction between the meanings of "machine organization" and "computer architecture."

Presented at the Symposium on Computers and Automata
Polytechnic Institute of Brooklyn, April 13–15, 1971.

The latter is, roughly speaking, what the assembler or machine language programmer sees; the lowest level on which a user can exploit the individual system resources.

Generally speaking, machine organization is the particular combination of hardware registers, busses, transformational networks, and controls, whether by means of microprogramming or active sequencers.

Conventionally, architectures have been specified in terms of machine instruction sets, their format and repertoire, the admissible data or operand structures, storage and addressing, and rules for instruction sequencing. Additionally, architectures seem to have been conceived in a stepwise manner in which the design of data formats and instruction sets (formats and repertoire) preceded the design of input/output commands and the channel and interface structure. This latter design phase was then followed by the specification of status switching and interrupt structures.

Conceptually, the architectural design process precedes the machine organization design, and within the latter, the data-flow layout precedes the design of controls for the data flow, but not the means of control. Thus, it is no wonder that the machine organization most often mirrors the architecture, and, conversely, perhaps for reasons of technology constraints, that the architecture specifications have been heavily influenced by machine organization details and restrictions.

We now see emerging, better understanding of the relation between computer architecture and machine organization. It is common knowledge that a given computer architecture admits a whole range of compatible machine organizations, *and* that a given machine organization admits more distinct computer architectures than the one it was originally designed to fit.

We can therefore, introduce "layers of abstraction" into the architectural design-specification process. The outermost layer reflects the inherent primitives of the class of algorithmic processes to be carried out by our system. Within this layer we resolve three apparently distinct programming problems:

(a) The data structure specification
(b) The data transformation-oriented which is concerned with operations on data performing the "actual" calculations
(c) The programmer-oriented, which is concerned with the flow of evaluation, i.e., control, organizing the pattern of computation.

The inner layers bridge the gap between the idealized outer layer and the feasible and desirable machine organizations.

However, the conventional lowest-level computer architecture is no longer what the user primarily sees. Rather, it is a set of higher-level languages and an operating environment (a monitor system). The set of machine instructions and allowable data types (often "typeless") can be said to form a basis for a language, only there is no restrictive rule built into the machine as to how these instructions may be combined—any combination goes! The structure of the machine language and the structure of any of the higher-level languages do not map easily into one another.

1.3 Historical Background

Postulating the desirability of higher-level languages, there has been a number of attempts [1–15] to architecturally design computers that fit a given higher-level language (dialect) more directly. At least one design [16] takes an existing machine organization and—through microprogramming—lets it accept a new, language-directed architecture. Two proprosals [17–19] take the view of creating a language "friendly" computer; [17, 18] being centered around a symbolic design rather than an absolute bit-oriented specification. [20] contains an analysis of the applicability of various instruction schemes to language processes. McKeeman [21] is now attempting the design of a language "sensitive" computer—one that, so to speak, has the compiler-compiler built into its hardware.

1.4 Outline of Approaches

In order to design an architecture properly, and in order to insure an orderly implementation, the following approach to the first step, the design, therefore seems, at least aesthetically, desirable.

First one must *choose* a definition scheme from within a class of such schemes. A definition scheme is a methodology for specifying:

(a) The data structures capable of being handled by the machine data flow
(b) The conceptual data flow and transformation
(c) The control of the flow.

A specific instance of an architecture can, e.g., use the conventional definition scheme of an exhaustive enumeration and explication of binary-coded machine instruction, etc. Or, it could use the scheme of syntactical definition as used in a higher-level language—coupled with some formal approach to the definition of semantics. We shall choose the latter approach.

We shall therefore not, in this report at least, investigate the class of well-structured definition schemes. Such an investigation is desirable. It could, maybe should, lead to a method by which one can compare various instances of schemes in order to derive their relative merits and disadvantages. In [22] we have outlined one approach for such an undertaking. Work in this area is being continued.

Second, once a definition scheme has been chosen within which (a–c) are being pursued, one must *decide* to which level of sophistication one wishes to bind the architecture to the specific characteristics of a class of machine organizations. The microprogrammable level, and the procedure problem oriented higher-level-language level, denote two apparent extremes. We choose some level in between, at a level of sophistication somewhat higher than that of a machine-instruction-oriented architecture.

Third, within the particular level of sophistication, one must *delineate* the variety of different constructs available for expressing individual tokens in the chosen language. A token in a conventional computer, e.g., System/370 is an instruction, a data item or addresses of instruction and data. A token in a higher-level language, such as ALGOL, is often recursively defined. It may be a statement, a block, or it may be a token of a data type. Corresponding to addresses in machine language oriented architectures, we here have labels and names. The contextual rules for what they point to are quite complex. A token in our example is an instruction—but this instruction resembles more a statement of a higher-level language than a conventional machine instruction. At this level, we make no choice as to the set of operators and the makeup of data types. We do, however, show a particular instance of a naming scheme.

Finally, at the lowest level one must *select* the concrete representation of the individual elements (or syllables), the composition of which leads to tokens. Here we present a syllable scheme that amounts to self-described strings.

Sections 2 and 4 treat the basis for operator schemes (a), Section 5 the sequencing scheme (b) and Section 3 the operand and data-structures scheme (c).

2. SIMPLE INSTRUCTIONS

For the purpose of the present exposition we shall only cover *value-returning instructions*. First we shall, however, give a brief survey of these and of conventional assignment statements as known in conventional higher-level programming languages such as FORTRAN, ALGOL 60, PL/I and the like.

The format (or *syntax*) of conventional value-returning instructions is built up from one operator field and zero, one, two; but normally no more than three operand fields. An operand field usually contains the address (components) locating the operand; or it is an immediate operand, i.e., contains the operand itself. In the latter case there is, usually, at most one such immediate operand field. See examples Figure 1.

The *syntax* of *assignment statements* provide for a left part and a right part. The left part usually is a variable name followed by the assignment operator.

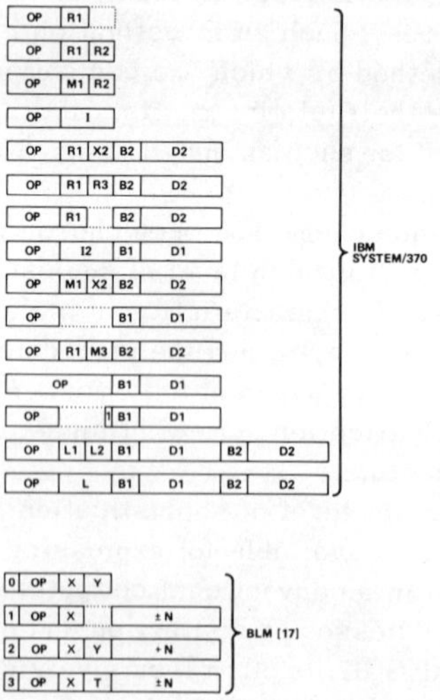

Fig. 1. Sample instruction formats.

Grammar:

$W \longrightarrow A;$

$A \longrightarrow LE$

$L \longrightarrow I \longleftarrow$

$E \longrightarrow E + T \mid E - T \mid T \mid - T$

$T \longrightarrow T * P \mid T/P \mid P$

$P \longrightarrow I \uparrow P \mid (E) \mid I$

$I \longrightarrow a \mid b \mid c \mid \ldots \mid z$

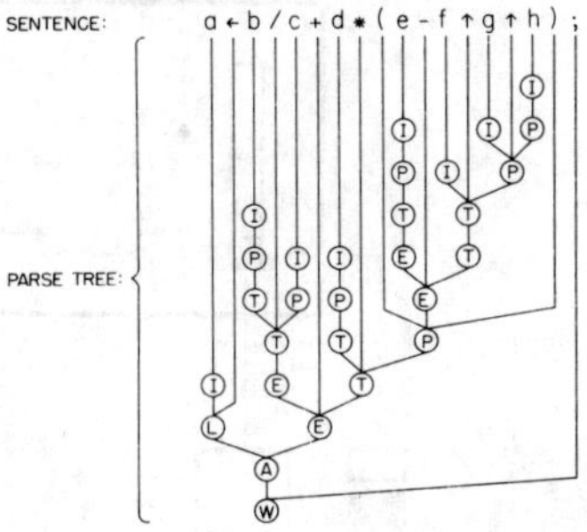

Fig. 2. Assignment statement, example syntax, parse, and sentence.

The right part is an expression. It is built up from constants, variables and function designators. These are operated upon by operators. See example Figure 2.

Addresses and names denote cells in the usual sense. *Execution* of an assignment statement first proceeds through an evaluation of the right-part expression. Then the resulting value is assigned (or returned) to the cell denoted by the left-part name.

The execution of a value-returning instruction proceeds somewhat like that of an assignment statement. Some or all of the addresses may be implicit. The operator, e.g., applies to values out of a stack, returning a result to the same stack; or the assignment by convention occurs to a fixed cell or to a cell that was also used as a source location.

Most value-returning instruction operators are usually either unary or binary. Thus, there is no need for explicitly stating where intermediate results are to be temporarily stored for the simple reason that there are no intermediate results. In the evaluation, however, of the higher-level-language assignment statement, intermediate results do develop. Most machine implementations of compilers for such languages require that the compiler generate explicit references to such temporary cells. Some machines, however, always leave intermediate results on a stack which is therefore implicitly referenced. Our specific instruction scheme borrows from both of the above related mechanisms, the instruction and the assignment statement.

The abstract scheme is shown through a concrete example. The example illustrates two concepts.

On a higher level it serves to illuminate how context-free grammars, finite-state machines, and push-down machines can be used to define instructions themselves. This is not related to stack-oriented machines in the sense of [5, 10, 12].

On a lower level the example points out specific techniques and problems relevant to processor architecture. We are here concerned with the formal means for defining the semantics of instructions and of the environment upon which instructions work.

2.1 Instruction Environment

The environment upon which value returning instructions act basically has four elements: storage, decoder, queue and functional unit(s). See Figure 3. This is also the environment within which these instructions exist.

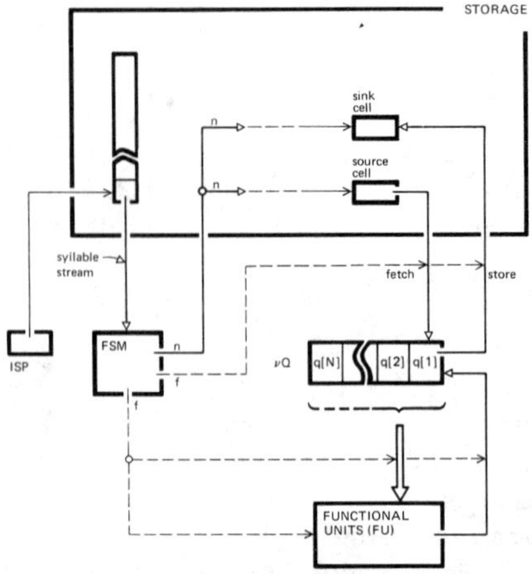

Fig. 3. Instruction environment.

Instructions are fetched from *storage* and decoded or *translated* by a *finite-state machine* (FSM). This translator directs that operands (names or values) be fetched from storage and temporarily stored in a finite-length *queue*. The FSM also directs a *functional unit* to empty the queue, act upon all its members and return a single value to the queue. Finally, the FSM directs the single-value result in the queue to be stored in storage. The span of actions between initial machine start-up and the storage of a result or between two successive result storages constitutes the execution of one instruction.

2.2 Instruction Translator and Syntax

An instruction is a finite-length string of *syllables*. These syllables are thought of as streaming out of storage into the FSM. The FSM makes one *state transition* per *input syllable*. It outputs one *output-control symbol* per input syllable. Initially, the FSM is started up in state 1. The string of syllables received between successive state 1 transitions constitutes one instruction.

The set Σ, of all syllables can be grouped in two subsets

$$\Sigma = \Sigma_f \cup \Sigma_n \ , \tag{1}$$

where: Σ_f is the finite set of all (functional) operators; and Σ_n is the (potentially infinite) set of all names (or addresses) of cells.

$$\Sigma_f = \{f_1', f_1'', f_1, f_2, \cdots, f_N\} \qquad (n \in \Sigma_n) \ . \tag{2}$$

f_i, for $1 \leq i \leq N$, denotes a finite set of operators each of which applies to i operands. f_1' and f_1'' are essentially delimiters; as such they have been classified as unary operators.

The finite-state machine is defined by Fig. 4 or by the equivalent finite state grammar G on Figure 5.

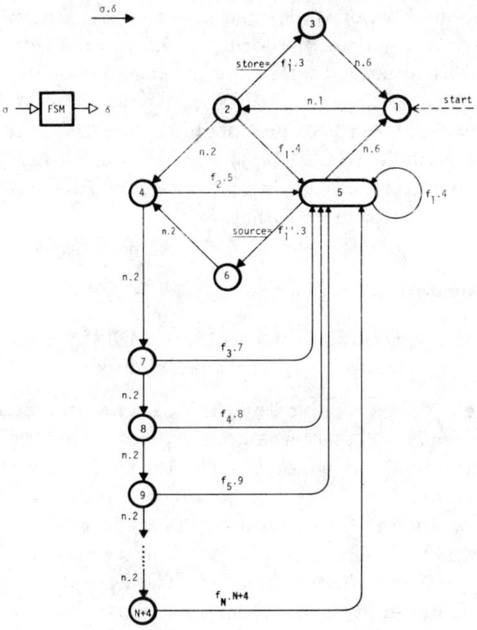

Fig. 4. Instruction translator.

s	BNF Productions		
1	<instruction>	: : =	<right part> <left part>
3|5	<left part>	: : =	<name>
1	<right part>	: : =	<name> <list>
2	<list>	: : =	destination
		: : =	unary operator <value>
		: : =	<name> <list 1>
5	<value>	: : =	unary operator <value>
		: : =	source <source>
		: : =	
6	<source>	: : =	<name> <list 1>
4 7 N+3	{ <list i>	: : =	<name> <list i+1> } 1≤i≤N-2
		: : =	i+1'ary operator <value> }
N+4	<list N-1>	: : =	N-ary operator <value>
	<name>	: : =	n

INSTRUCTION SYNTAX G

Productions in curly brackets denote a set of N-2 pairs of productions.
s the FSM state corresponding to nonterminal left symbols.

FSM Output	Action upon Environment	
.0	i ← 1;	(3)
.1	q[i] ← n;*	(4)
.2	i ← i+1; q[i] ← n;*	(5)
.3	;	(6)
.4	q[1] ← f_1(q[1]);	(7)
.5	q[1] ← f_2(q[1], q[2]); i ← 1;	(8)
.6	n ← q[1];	(9)
.i+4	q[1] ← f_i(q[1], ..., q[i]); i ← 1; for 3 ≤ i ≤ N.	(10)

INSTRUCTION SEMANTICS

The semantics defined by (6) amounts to a void statement
(* See comments in Section 2.4.2.)

Fig. 5. Instruction syntax and semantics.

Either of these, the FSM or G, defines all correct instruction strings of syllables. The FSM has "recognized" a complete instruction from whence it leaves state 1 until it returns to state 1. During that same sequence the FSM also "transduces" the syllable string. That is, maps the input string into an output-control string. Transitions in FSM are labeled σ, δ where σ is the input syllable and δ is the output symbol. Not all input syllables are allowed in any one state. Those not shown would, if received in that state, lead the FSM to an error state. We have not shown that error state either.

2.3 Instruction Semantics

We now define the semantics of instructions. First, we give an informal description. In this way we informally cover the syntax of instructions too.

n: Denotes a name. Names received by the FSM in states other than 3 and 5 denote *source operands*. These names are evaluated and the operands themselves moved into a value queue νQ. The length of νQ is N. Names received by the FSM in states 3 and 5 denote *destination locations*. They result in the single value now left in νQ to be stored in that location

f_i: Denotes an operator. i indicates whether f_i is a unary- ($i = 1$), a binary- ($i = 2$), $\cdots$, or an Nary- ($i = N$) operator. The definition of the FSM guarantees that when f_i is received, then there are exactly i values in νQ.

All f_i operators act on all elements $(n_{j1}, n_{j2}, n_{j3}, \cdots, n_{ji})$ in νQ by moving them to some functional unit in which the function f_i is applied and from which the single value result $f_i(n_{j1}, n_{j2}, n_{j3}, \cdots, n_{ji})$, is returned to νQ. In the meantime νQ has been emptied and the returned result is thus the only value (or operand) now in νQ.

Two "operators" play a special role:

f_1': Denotes a *store* operator. It essentially serves as a delimiter. The delimiter prepares for the next received name to denote a *destination* location

f_1'': Denotes a *source* operator. It, again, serves as a delimiter. The delimiter prepares for the next received name to denote a source operand to be joined to νQ.

Next we give a more formal definition of the semantics. It is listed on Fig. 5 relative to the individual output symbols. The meta language used in the definition itself is, however, only informally defined.

The queue νQ is treated as an N cell vector $\nu Q = q[1], q[2], q[3], \cdots, q[N]$. With the vector we associate a pointer cell i. By $f(Q)$ we mean functional application of the operator **f** to values of elements of the vector νQ, even if νQ contains only one element. By $\ell \longleftarrow r$ we mean that an evaluation of the right-part r is to replace the content of the cell denoted by the label ℓ.

2.4 Comments

(1) It is easily seen, now, how simple assignment statements map into instructions. For example:

	ASSIGNMENT STATEMENT	INSTRUCTION	
(11a)	$a: = b$	$b \longrightarrow a$	(11i)
(12a)	$a: = b + c$	$cb + a$	(12i)
(13a)	$a: = b + c*d$	$dc* \longleftarrow b + a$	(13i)

where: a, b, c, d are names; "$\longrightarrow$" is the destination operator, "$\longleftarrow$" is the source operator; and +, * are examples of binary operators.

It is likewise seen that the following instructions map into less obvious assignment statements:

	INSTRUCTION	ASSIGNMENT STATEMENT	
(14i)	$dc + \longleftarrow b*a$	$a: = b*(c + d)$	(14a)
(15i)	$hg + \longleftarrow f* \longleftarrow e + \longleftarrow d* \longleftarrow c + \longleftarrow b*a$	$a: = b*\big(c + d*(e + f*(g + h))\big)$	(15a)

This latter mapping amounts to rewriting assignment statements, e.g.

$$a: = b*c + d*e + f*g + h \quad . \tag{16}$$

If we mean

$$a: = b*\big(c + d*(e + f*(g + h))\big) \quad . \tag{17}$$

That is, we evaluate Eq. (16) right to left with no rules of precedence among operators. With this interpretation Eq. (16) is an example of a language statement which is not found in FORTRAN, ALGOL, or PL/I, but is used extensively in PL360 [23] and APL [24]. We shall, therefore, not elaborate on such languages here, but only make the comment that the suggested instruction scheme fits very nicely to languages of the structure of PL360 and APL.

(2) We can easily augment the definition to include constants wherever source operand names are allowed. That is, wherever we have a transition labeled $n.1$ or $n.2$ we add a new transition labeled $c.N + 5$, respectively $c.N + 6$. These transitions are "parallel" to the above transitions in that they go from and to the same pair of states. c denotes a constant, i.e., an immediate operand. The extended semantics become

FSM OUTPUT	ACTION UPON ENVIRONMENT	
$.N + 5$	$q[i] \longleftarrow$ 'c'	(18)
$.N + 6$	$i \longleftarrow i + 1;\ q[i] \longleftarrow$ 'c'	(19)

where 'c' indicates that no evaluation of c takes place, that in other words c itself is put into Q.

(3) We have shown states 7 through $N + 4$ ($N > 2$) only to indicate how the FSM definition provides for simple extensions. In fact, one could fold states 7 through $N + 4$ into state 4. Then state 4 would contain a loop transition labeled $n.2'$ and transition f_2 to state 5 should be relabeled $f_j.5'$, see Figure 6. The "folded" semantics would then become

FSM OUTPUT	ACTION UPON ENVIRONMENT	

.5′	*if* $i = j$ *then*
	begin
	$q[1] \leftarrow f_j(q[1], \cdots, q[i])$;
	$i \leftarrow 1$
	end
	else
	go to error state ;
		(20)

(4) In the original scheme we had some redundancy. In fact, we did not need the vector counter i. Instead we could extract μ, the current value of index i from the present state, s. The changed semantics would then amount to

FSM OUTPUT	ACTION UPON ENVIRONMENT	
.1 .2	$q[\mu(s)] \leftarrow n$,	(21)
.5	$q[1] \leftarrow f_2(q[1], q[2])$,	(22)
$.i + 4$	$q[1] \leftarrow f_i(q[1], q[2], q[3], \cdots, q[\mu(i)])$ $(3 \le i \le n)$.	(23)

where we list μ: $\mu(1) = 1$, $\mu(2) = 2$, $\mu(6) = 2$, $\mu(i + 4) = 1$ $(3 \le i \le N)$. That is, part of the state machine itself is the counter.

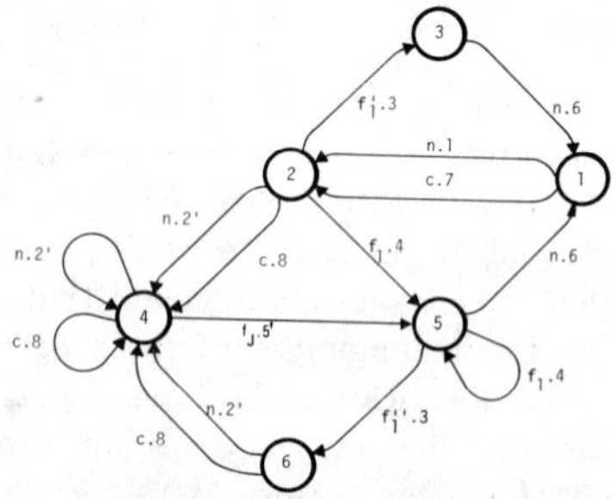

Fig. 6. Folded-instruction translator.

3. NAMES AND ADDRESSES

We now address ourselves to an increasingly more-precise definition of names —such as we use them in connection with storage cells. Like when we were concerned with the formal definition of instructions and had to specify their environment so we must now specify the *storage* and *name* environments.

3.1 Storage Environment

By the storage—or storage system—we mean the ensemble of programmer-(addressable or) accessible machine registers, high-speed buffers, main core storage, drum, disk, tape, and archival storage.

We shall view this storage system as providing a potentially-infinite, symbolically-addressed, multilinear name space. The combined use of the two, apparently conflicting words, "address" and "name" will be resolved in the following. For an introduction to ideas on symbolically-addressed storage we refer to [17, 25].

For the purpose of the present section we may think of information in storage as representing two classes of information: *data* such as numerical data (integer and real), character strings, logical bit strings, etc., and *descriptors.* A descriptor is essentially a *pointer.* It defines a *linear segment* of either data or descriptors. Segments are usually of finite extent E. Descriptors may be manipulated dynamically thus possibly changing the type of what they point to, i.e., define. *Segments are named.* To gain access to some element in a segment one provides the storage system with:

(1) The name s of the segment
(2) A non-negative displacement α from the zeroth element in that segment
(3) A possibly-empty set X of negative or positive-valued indices I, to be added to the displacement, see Figure 7.

The proper combination of s, α, and elements of X constitute a name. The arithmetic sum of α and all indices are checked against E, i.e., to lie within the named segment.

The execution time profile of accessible data is defined by a *data-process descriptor base* (DPB) which itself defines a *base descriptor* segment of extent 2. Base descriptor 1 (BD1) by convention defines a potentially-infinite linear data segment. We call this the *scratch segment.* The recursive definition of descriptors and segments applies to base descriptor 0 (BD0). See Figure 12.

From the definition it follows that parts of storage will be logically structured as a finite-directed graph. The nodes of the graph denote storage cells of type: data or descriptor. Nodes of type data are terminal nodes. They do not point to any other node, but stand for themselves. We restrict the pointer capability of descriptor nodes such that the graphs contain no cycles. If furthermore, no two descriptors point to overlapping segments, then the graph is a finite rooted tree. BD0 is then the root of the tree. If we relax the last restriction, we will still get a rooted graph, but it will resemble a partially collapsed tree. We shall assume the latter to be the general case.

We call the tree emanating from BD0 a *structured segment.*

From the recursive definition of descriptors and segments, it also follows that segment names, s, are themselves names composed by recursive composition of names.

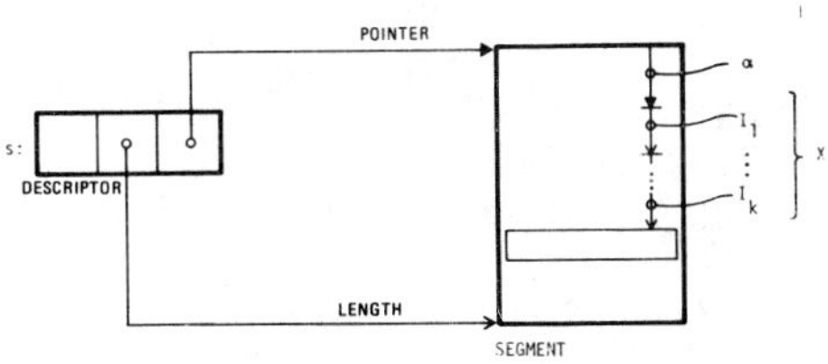

Fig. 7. Descriptor and segment structure.

3.2 Name Syntax

We now define a name n by a recursive regular-expression equation

$$n = (\underline{i}n)^* \alpha \mid (\cdot (\underline{i}n)^* \alpha)^+ \ , \tag{24}$$

α is a literal denoting itself. The asterisk "*" allows for *zero, one,* or *more* repetitions of indices $\underline{i}n$. The plus "+" allows for *one* or *more* repetitions of relative segment identifiers $\cdot (\underline{i}n)^*\alpha$.

Cells in the structured segment are accessed by names of the format defined to the right of the vertical bar, whereas names in the scratch segment have the format defined between = and |.

A single application of $\cdot (\underline{i}n)^* \alpha_1$ to DPB provides access to some element S_1 in the segment reached from BD0. A "double" occurrence $\cdot (\underline{i}n)^* \alpha_1 \cdot (\underline{i}n)^* \alpha_2$ provides access to some element in the segment defined by S_1 provided BD0 defines a descriptor segment, otherwise the name $\cdot (\underline{i}n)^* \alpha_1 \cdot (\underline{i}n)^* \alpha_2$ is erroneous, and so forth. The name of a cell in the structured segment therefore identifies the path from BD0 through a succession of descriptor segments.

If all but the first set of indices in the relative-segment identifiers were omitted, and if the corresponding displacements α were 0 then successive application of k dots ($\cdot$) would correspond to a k-level indirect "addressing."

The fact that the segment identifier $\cdot (\underline{i}n)^* \alpha$ in a string $u \cdot (\underline{i}n)^* \alpha v$, where $u, v \in (\cdot (\underline{i}n)^* \alpha)^*$, is "relative" or "local" to whatever descriptor was selected by u, accounts for our use of the word naming—rather than addressing scheme. This coincides with similar terminology used in higher-level programming languages.

The naming scheme then, in a sense, embodies three well-known techniques used in addressing: *indexing, indirectness,* and *relativity*.

We now give two grammars, G1 and G2, both of which generate the set of names defined by the recursive regular expression, see Figure 8.

3.3 Name Translators

From the grammars we can construct the parsers which output the syntactic structure of any sentence (i.e., name) in the language $L(G)$, generated by G = G1 or G = G2. We choose to come up with parsers of the deterministic push-down machine type and have accordingly given our grammars such a form that

Example G1	Example G2
[0] $n \to \bar{N} \dashv$	[0] $n \to \bar{N}\ D$
[1] $\bar{N} \to X\alpha$	[1] $\bar{N} \to X\alpha$
[2] $\bar{N} \to L$	[2] $\bar{N} \to SL$
[3] $L \to LS$	[3] $L \to SL$
[4] $L \to S$	[4] $L \to$
[5] $S \to \cdot X\alpha$	[5] $S \to \cdot X\alpha$
[6] $X \to XI$	[6] $X \to IX$
[7] $X \to$	[7] $X \to$
[8] $I \to \underline{i}\bar{N}$	[8] $I \to \underline{i}\bar{N}$
	[9] $D \to \dashv$

Fig. 8. Name grammars 1 and 2.

they are respectively bottom-up and top-down translatable with bound 1, i.e., LR(0 | 1)† and LL(1). For the theory behind LR(K) and LL(1) grammars see [26, 27, 28, 29]. The specific algorithms used in constructing the translators are found in [28]. The resulting bottom-up and top-down translators are shown in Figures 9 and 10.

The structure of the LR(0 | 1) and the LL(1) pushdown translator is shown in Figure 11. Upon each state transition the translator may be thought of as first outputting the list x between enclosed brackets '[x]', then, if so defined by '$\underline{s}_j$', to push state j onto the stack PS, in parallel with some possible later output list y defined by '(y)'. The machine finally pushes the next state, s', to the stack top "state register" SR. A transition is the result of reading the next input syllable in conjunction with popping the value of the SR into the combinational logic CL. Whether PS is empty ε, or not $\bar{\varepsilon}$, can be tested by sensing only SR. If a transition defines the next state to be popped $\underline{u}$, from PS, then no state label s', is pushed but instead the current content of SR is popped into CL. If the external output is defined $[x, ^\circ]$ then the list x is output first and then followed by some stacked output list y emanating from SR. This latter remark applies in general to LR translators only.

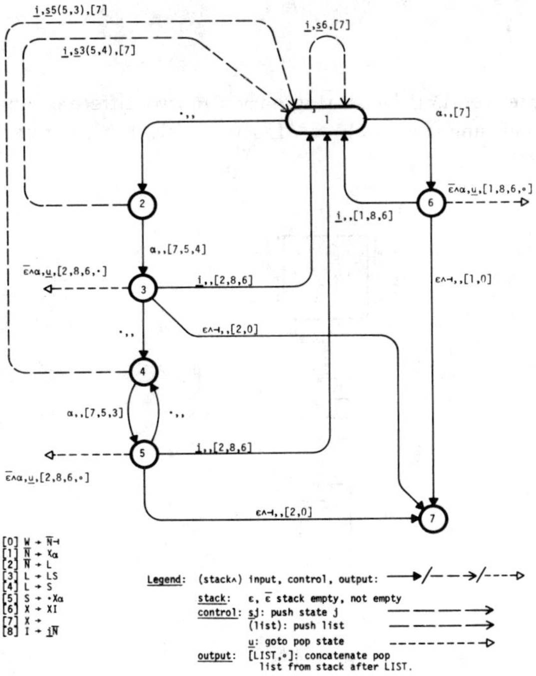

Fig. 9. Bottom-up PLR(0 | 1) translator.

†An LR(P | Q) translator has outputs delayed anywhere from P to Q symbols from the corresponding input symbol ($0 \leq P \leq Q = K$).

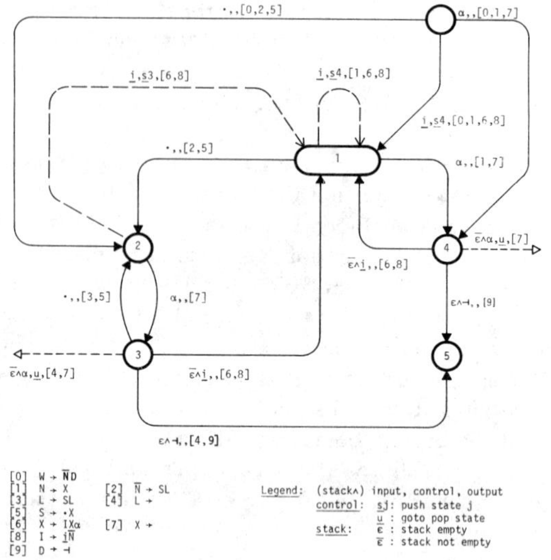

Fig. 10. Top-down PLL (1) translator.

3.4 Example

In the example we shall be stating names in two different languages. A more readily understood language such as ALGOL or PL/I and our example machine language.

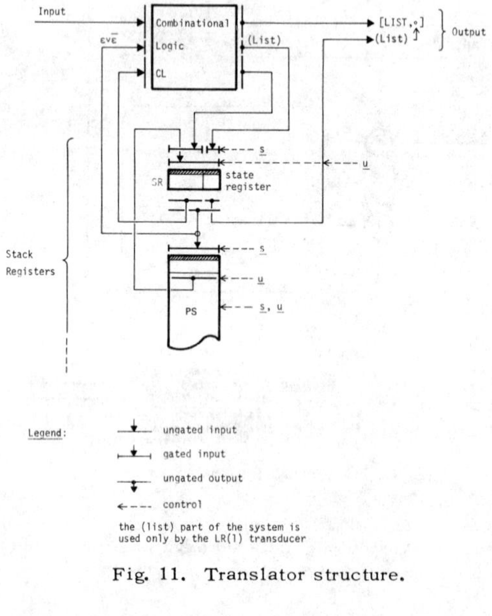

Fig. 11. Translator structure.

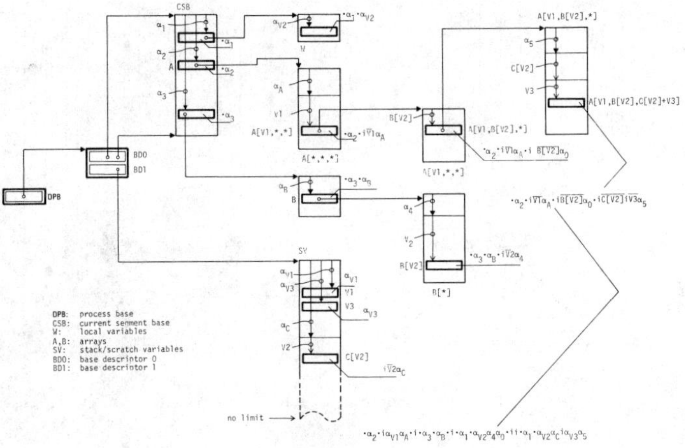

Fig. 12. Data-structure example.

In Fig. 12 we show a particular instance of a process-data structure as it is reflected back into the storage hierarchy. Segments identified by W, $A[V1, B[V2], *]$, $B[*]$ and SV are data segments. The rest are descriptor segments, some of which define code segments. $V1$, $V2$, $V3$, $C[V2]$ and $A[V1, B[V2], C[V2] + V3]$ are data cell identifiers. A, $A[V1, *, *]$, $A[V1, B[V2], *]$ and B are descriptor cell identifiers. The corresponding names are α_{V1}, $\cdot\alpha_1\cdot\alpha_{V2}$, α_{V3}, $i\overline{V2}\alpha_c$, etc.—as shown underlined and next to corresponding cells. By placing a bar over some identifier term in the name, we mean to indicate that one should perform a substitution of the proper name in its place. α_0 denotes a zero displacement. The name

$$.\alpha_2.i\alpha_{V1}\,\alpha_A.i.\alpha_3.\alpha_B.i.\alpha_1.\alpha_{V2}\,\alpha_4\,\alpha_0.ii.\alpha_1.\alpha_{V2}\,\alpha_c\,i\alpha_{V3}\,\alpha_5 \quad , \tag{25}$$

corresponds to the identifier

$$A[V1, B[V2], C[V2] + V3] \quad . \tag{26}$$

This example was contrived in order to reflect some block structure in the higher-level language. This block structure is not readily apparent from the identifier (26). The conversion from (26) to (25) is therefore based on knowledge of the block structure.

3.5 Parsing Trees

The parse structures of the example name as imposed by the two grammars are shown in Figures 13 and 14. Names are input, left to right to either push-down transducer. The resulting state sequencing, intermediate stacking and output sequence is shown in Figure 15.

The top-down grammar specifies the ordered sequence of segment names as having their root in the root segment BD0, whereas the bottom-up grammar specifies that sequence to have its root (or call it goal) in the leaf segment. In both

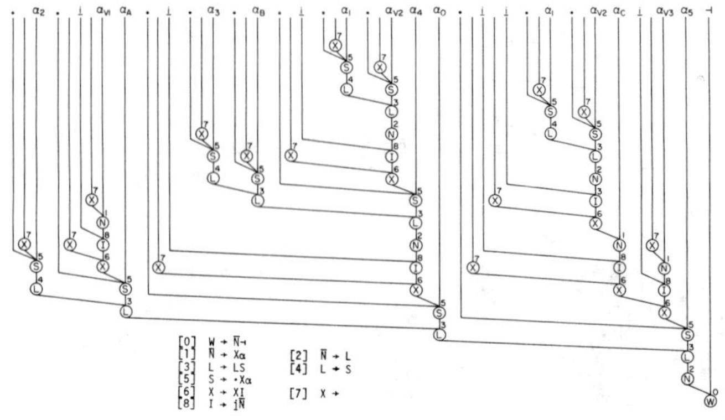

Fig. 13. Bottom-up LR parse tree.

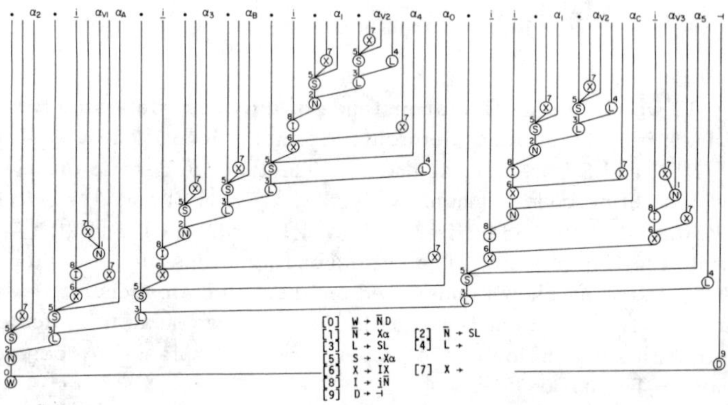

Fig. 14. Top-down LL parse tree.

cases however, the name itself, when read left to right, specifies (or assumes) first the root segment and last the leaf segment. This is in accordance with the fact, or restriction, that when starting out we only know, or assume, the whereabouts of the root segment.

3.6 Name Environment

The environment, Fig. 16, in which names are translated and the one on which the translator output is brought to act, is dependent somewhat on whether the name translator is parsing bottom up or top down. We first take the PLR(0 | 1) translators.

3.6.1 LR Environment

The bottom-up translated name environment adds essentially two new elements to our storage system: (1) An *address queue* αQ, into which all α's in the name string are routed. (A reference to αQ always returns and removes the oldest member of αQ); and (2) A *descriptor stack* DS on which temporary-index,

input	PLL(1) state	output	stack	PLR(0|1) state	output	stack
	1			1		
.	2	[0,2,5]		2		
α_2	3	[7]		3	[7,5,4]	
.	2	[3,5]		4		
$\underline{i}$	1	[6,8]	3	1	[7]	5(5,3)
α_{VI}	4	[1,7]	3	6	[7]	5(5,3)
α_A	3	[7]		5	[1,8,6,5,3]	
.	2	[3,5]		4		
$\underline{i}$	1	[6,8]	3	1	[7]	5(5,3)
.	2	[2,5]	3	2		5(5,3)
α_3	3	[7]	3	3	[7,5,4]	5(5,3)
.	2	[3,5]	3	4		5(5,3)
α_B	3	[7]	3	5	[7,5,3]	5(5,3)
.	2	[3,5]	3	4		5(5,3)
$\underline{i}$	1	[6,8]	3,3	1	[7]	5(5,3),5(5,3)
.	2	[2,5]	3,3	2		5(5,3),5(5,3)
α_1	3	[7]	3,3	3	[7,5,4]	5(5,3),5(5,3)
.	2	[3,5]	3,3	4		5(5,3),5(5,3)
α_{V2}	3	[7]	3,3	5	[7,5,3]	5(5,3),5(5,3)
α_4	3	[4,7]	3	5	[2,8,6,5,3]	5(5,3)
α_D	3	[4,7]		5	[2,8,6,5,3]	
.	2	[3,5]		4		
$\underline{i}$	1	[6,8]	3	1	[7]	5(5,3)
$\underline{i}$	1	[1,6,8]	4,3	1	[7]	6,5(5,3)
.	2	[2,5]	4,3	1	[7]	6,5(5,3)
α_1	3	[7]	4,3	3	[7,5,4]	6,5(5,3)
.	2	[3,5]	4,3	4		6,5(5,3)
α_{V2}	3	[7]	4,3	5	[7,5,3]	6,5(5,3)
α_C	4	[4,7]	3	6	[2,8,6]	5(5,3)
$\underline{i}$	1	[6,8]	3	1	[1,8,6]	5(5,3)
α_{V3}	4	[1,7]	3	6	[7]	5(5,3)
α_5	3	[7]		5	[1,8,6,5,3]	
⊣	5	[4,9]		7	[2,0]	

PLL(1):
[0] W → ND
[1] N → X
[2] N → SL
[3] L → SL
[4] L →
[5] S → .X
[6] X → IX
[7] X →
[8] I → $\underline{i}$N
[9] D → ⊣

PLR(0|1):
[0] W → N
[1] N → X
[2] N → L
[3] L → LS
[4] L → S
[5] S → .X
[6] X → XI
[7] X →
[8] I → $\underline{i}$N

Fig. 15. Name input, state transition, and output.

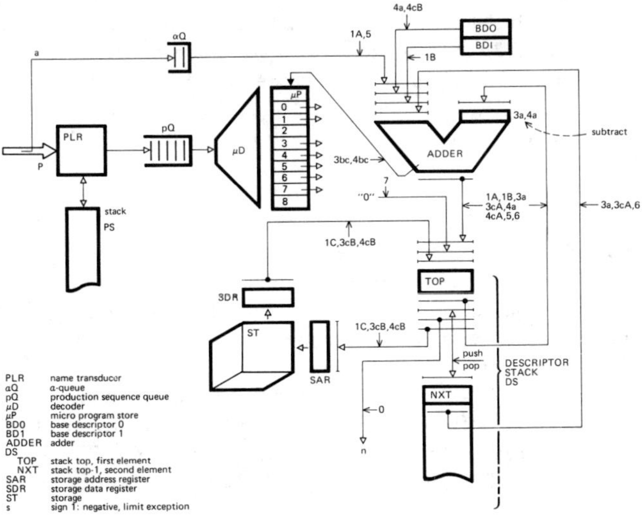

Fig. 16. PLR name-evaluation machine (environment).

Production	PLL/Output	Actions upon Environment	Comment
$W \to \overline{N}\dashv$	0:	DS[j] → n;	Deliver Value at Name Location
$\overline{N} \to X\alpha$	1:	M(DS[j]+αQ+BD1) → DS[j];	Fetch Value
$\overline{N} \to L$	2:	;	Void Statement
L → LS	3 a: b: c:	<u>if</u> DS[j] > L(DS[j-1]) <u>then</u> LIMITERROR <u>else</u> <u>begin</u> M(DS[j]+P(DS[j-1]))→DS[j-1]; j ← j-1 <u>end</u>;	Check Limit Fetch Value or Descriptor (Pop)
L → S	4 a: b: c:	<u>if</u> DS[j] > L(BDO) <u>then</u> LIMITERROR <u>else</u> M(DS[j]+P(BDO))→DS[j];	Check Limit Fetch Value or Descriptor
$S \to \cdot X\alpha$	5:	αQ+DS[j]→DS[j];	Add Displacement
X → XI	6:	DS[j-1]+DS[j] → DS[j-1]; j ← j-1;	Sum Indices (Pop)
X →	7:	'0' → DS[j+1]; j ← j+1;	Initial Index = 0 (Push)
$I \to \underline{i}\overline{N}$	8:	;	Void Statement

Fig. 17. PLR semantics.

pointer, and limit values are stored. In the semantic specification, Fig. 17, we shall treat DS as an infinite vector DS[*]. We need make no assumption about the initial value of the descriptor stack pointer index j. This enables us to use the stack for other than name evaluation purposes. We omit specification of the LIMITERROR error exit or recovery procedure.

There are three simple procedures

$$M(A) \text{ returns the value at storage location } A \quad ,$$
$$L(R) \text{ returns the limit value in register } R \quad ,$$
$$P(R) \text{ returns the pointer value in register } R \quad .$$

Left pointing arrows "←" are used here to indicate simple stack-pointer adjustments; right pointing arrows "→" to indicate data transfers. The limit check is accomplished by subtraction of two stack-top elements without popping the stack. Statements 1, 3c and 4c, if executed on the example data flow Fig. 16, require respectively, 2, 3, and 3 phases. These are indicated by suffixing A, B, or C to statement labels. We have indicated on the data flow which paths are controlled when.

3.6.2 LL Environment

We again require the addition of the *address queue* αQ, and the temporary *descriptor stack* DS, to our storage system environment. In that environment we, however, change the output of the PLL translator from being queued to being stacked. That is, pQ is replaced by an intermediate output stack μS. Figure 18 illustrates the replacement.

The output from the PLL is partitioned in the following way. The translator is in a wait state, to be defined. When signaled to output, it keeps pushing output onto μS until it attempts to place a number different from 7 at a time the μS stacktop contains a 7. Then it goes to a wait state, temporarily storing the attempted output in a *wait cell C*.

The content of μS is popped by the remainder of the environment, specifically

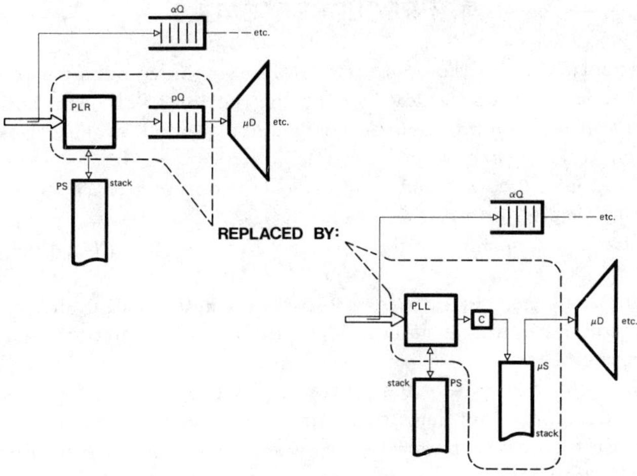

Fig. 18. Conversion from PLR to PLL name-evaluation machine.

the decoder μD, in the following way. Only when PLL is in a wait state can μD pop μS. μD starts popping μS immediately after PLL has entered a wait state. μD keeps popping μS until it has popped a 2 or 3 *or* until it attempts to pop a second 8 after a 1.

The function of the μS stack and the reasoning behind the peculiar rules for pushing and in particular popping the content of μS, essentially amounts to changing the top-down output to a partial- or pseudo-bottom-up output. Recall the remark in Section 3.5.

With these rules the semantics for the top-down mapping of *n* into the computation of the address proper can be stated in terms very similar to those of the "bottom-up semantics." See Figure 19.

Production	PLL/Output	Actions upon Environment	Same as PLR/
$W \to \bar{N}D$	0:	DS[j] → n;	0
$\bar{N} \to X\alpha$	1:	M(DS[j] + αQ + BD1) → DS[j];	1
$\bar{N} \to SL$	2:	<u>if</u> DS[j] > L(BDO) <u>then</u> LIMITERROR <u>else</u> M(DS[j] + P(BDO)) → DS[j];	4
$L \to SL$	3:	<u>if</u> DS[j] > L(DS[j-1]) <u>then</u> LIMITERROR <u>else</u> <u>begin</u> M(DS[j] + P(DS[j-1])) → DS[j]; j ← j-1 <u>end</u>;	3
$L \to$	4:	;	2
$S \to \cdot X\alpha$	5:	αQ + DS[j] → DS[j];	5
$X \to IX$	6:	DS[j-1] + DS[j] → DS[j-1]; j ← j-1;	6
$X \to$	7:	'0' → DS[j+1]; j ← j+1;	7
$I \to \underline{i}\bar{N}$	8:	;	8
$D \to \dashv$	9:	;	(8)

Fig. 19. PLL semantics.

4. PROCEDURE CALLS

In an instruction string the operator syllables (f) have been treated differently from names (n), at least on the level of the instruction itself. On the level of the microprogram (or other control sequence) f may be treated as the name of a microprogram (or control sequence).

We now introduce *function names* into the instruction stream. Specifically we provide for the simple call of *procedures*.

The syntactic and semantic rules governing procedure *call* and *return* are the following.

A procedure call must involve from 0 to N parameters, all called by value. A procedure returns but a single value. The called routine must store all passed arguments immediately.

A procedure call consists of the prefix λ, denoting: 'call', followed by the name of the procedure—that name essentially maps into the address of the routine. A procedure call with parameters may appear whenever a simple (functional) operator may appear. A procedure call without parameters can occur only from state 1. No parameters are then being passed. See Figure 20. The semantics of the procedure name transduction are such that the next-syllable input to FSM now comes from the procedure code rather than from the calling code. The procedure code (normally) terminates with a *return* to the calling code, that is to the syllable immediately following the procedure name after λ. The procedure code is, therefore, to be viewed as being nested within the calling code. This nesting may occur recursively, i.e., to any depth.

The return from a procedure results in a single value, 'status', being left in νQ. The question is, therefore, should the FSM or should some other device take

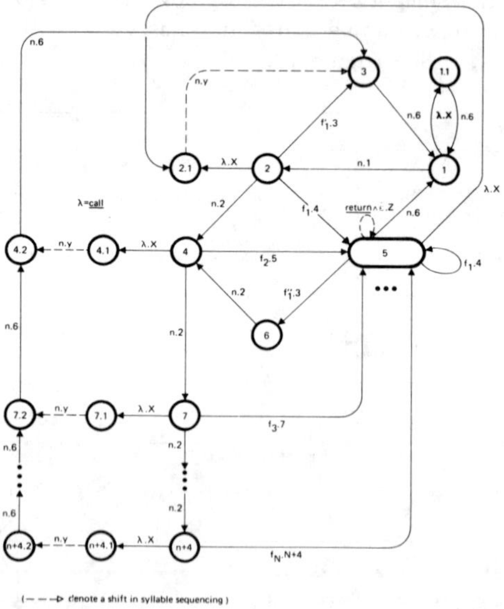

Fig. 20. Instruction translator showing procedure-call transitions.

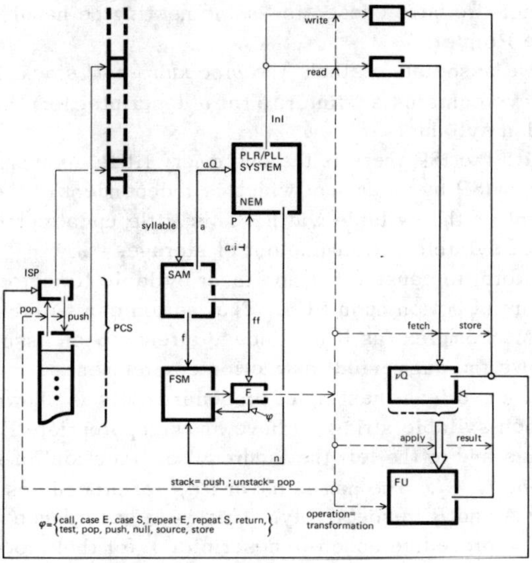

Fig. 21. Language machine.

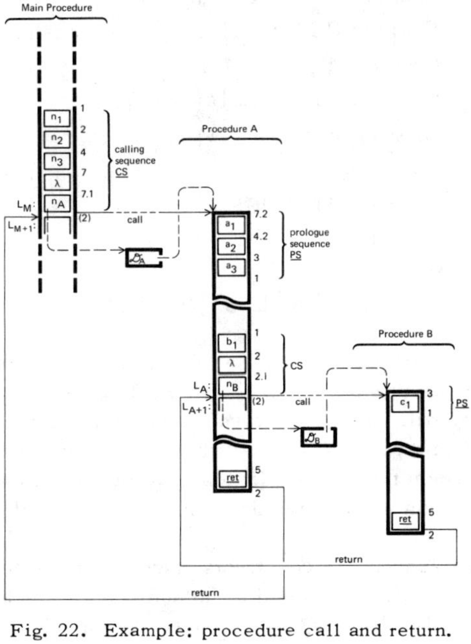

Fig. 22. Example: procedure call and return.

care of the nesting. We have chosen to let the nesting be handled by the "Instruction Syllable Pointer."

With the ISP we associate a stack, the *procedure-call stack* (PCS). The top (ISP) of PCS always contains a pointer to (or a descriptor for) the currently-scanned instruction syllable.

Associated with the ISP there is the customary little autonomous robot process which updates ISP by an amount which is independent of the syllable content, but dependent on the syllable width. This little update process effects a linear trajectory of syllables streaming out of storage.

In order, therefore, to cause other nonlinear syllable trajectories, we must establish some means of action upon PCS. That action can suitably be directed from the $\langle \nu Q, \mathrm{FSM} \rangle$ complex (as it has indeed already been assumed).

Figure 21 shows the augmented instruction environment.

An example of a two-level nesting of procedure calls is shown in Figure 22. To the right of each syllable string we have shown appropriate FSM states between the syllables and to the left the 'address' or 'location' of some syllables: L_M, L_{M+1}, L_A, and L_{A+1}. The names n_A and n_B, of procedures A and B are evaluated to give A and B, respectively. This is in accordance with our desire to let the name of a procedure denote a descriptor $\mathfrak{D}$ for that procedure. The semantics then evaluate $\mathfrak{D}$.

The semantics are now given.

FSM OUTPUT	ACTION UPON ENVIRONMENT	ABBREVIATED FORM (where ISP $\notin$ PCS)	
$.x$	;		(27)
$.y$	*comment* ISP = PCS[k] ;		
	$P(n) \longrightarrow$ PCS[$k+1$] ;	push (PCS, ISP) ;	(28)
	$k \longleftarrow k+1$;	$P(n) \longrightarrow$ ISP ;	
	comment ISP = PCS[k] ;		
$.z$	*comment* ISP = PCS[k] ;		
	$k \longleftarrow k-1$;	pop (PCS) ;	(29)
	comment ISP = PCS[k] ;		

5. CONTROL STRUCTURES

In this section we formalize the notion of descriptor structures. These were first introduced informally in Section 3.1. There they were applied only to data structures. Now they will be applied to code or syllable structures as well. It is outside the scope of this paper to give a "theory of descriptor structures" and an investigation of their potential uses. Instead, we settle for two particular instances of its application to the formalization of various nonlinear syllable-flow sequencing schemes.

The two examples assume the constructs made available for the purpose of procedure calling [30, 31, 32], and require the addition of stacks fsmS and νQS, respectively to the FSM and the νQ; see Figures 23 and 24. Alternatively one

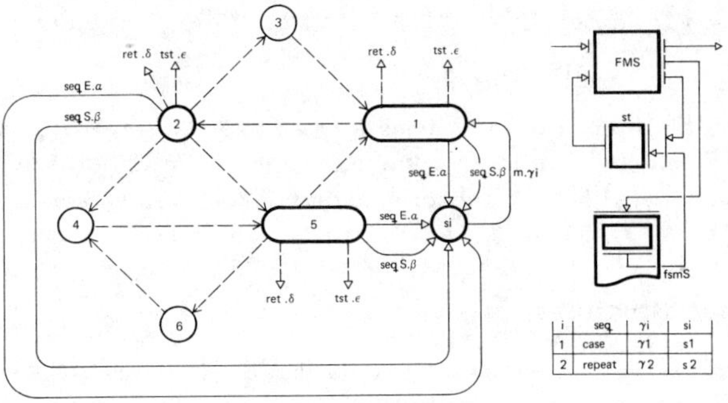

Fig. 23. Instruction translator showing sequencing transitions.

could do without at least the fsmS—or one could merge all stacks involved in our machine. Again we feel this to be outside the scope of this paper; its primary objective not being any particular, nor necessarily optimal, design, but rather the presentation of various formal schemes applicable to the architectural design of computers.

In bringing forth the examples, we shall be quoting instances of programming constructs in two languages: a concrete language $\mathcal{L}_\mathcal{C}$, and an abstract language $\mathcal{L}_\mathcal{A}$. The latter is the one to be defined formally as part of the sample architecture. Problems of converting programs in $\mathcal{L}_\mathcal{C}$ to programs in $\mathcal{L}_\mathcal{A}$ have been treated conceptually in [37].

The system produced so far is centered around $\mathcal{L}_\mathcal{A}$ *instructions* corresponding to $\mathcal{L}_\mathcal{C}$ *statements*. We shall henceforth blur the distinction between statements and expressions—without giving a completely satisfactory and exhaustive formal treatment of these two notions. An FSM state transition from state 5 to state 1 shall have the value of νQ unchanged, as was already specified by Equation (9). A syllable sequence leading the FSM from state 1 to 2 or 5 corresponds to an $\mathcal{L}_\mathcal{A}$ *value*, respectively an $\mathcal{L}_\mathcal{C}$ *expression*.

5.1 Two General Sequencing Constructs in $\mathcal{L}_\mathcal{C}$

It can be shown that one does not need the goto construct in an $\mathcal{L}_\mathcal{C}$ provided some other, less harmful [33], constructs are available. For example [34, 35]

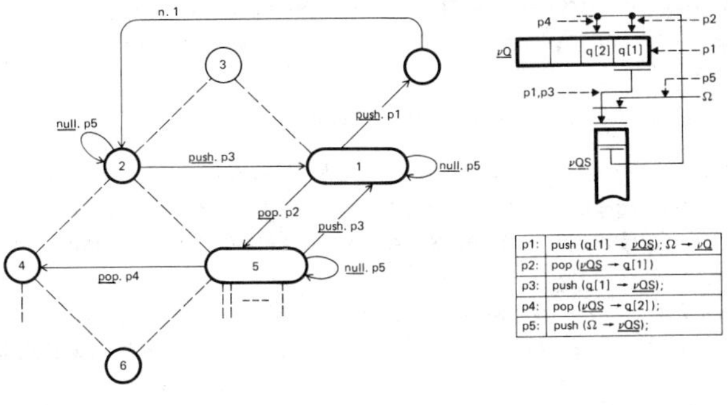

Fig. 24. Instruction translator showing value-stack operations.

$$\textit{form 1:}\quad \underline{\text{case}}\ \langle\mathcal{F}_i\rangle\ \underline{\text{of}}\ \left(\langle\mathcal{F}\rangle_1,\ \langle\mathcal{F}\rangle_2,\ \langle\mathcal{F}\rangle_3, \cdots,\ \langle\mathcal{F}\rangle_M\right), \tag{30}$$

$$\textit{form 2:}\quad \underline{\text{while}}\ \langle\mathcal{F}_b\rangle\ \underline{\text{do}}\ \langle\mathcal{F}\rangle\ . \tag{31}$$

$\langle\mathcal{F}\rangle$ denotes a form, i.e., a statement or an expression. With subscript i specifically one that leaves an integer value, preferably in the closed interval 1 through M, in νQ ($q[1]$). With subscript b one that leaves either 'truth' or 'falsity' in νQ. $\langle\mathcal{F}\rangle_j$, where $1 \leq j \leq M$, denotes any form $\langle\mathcal{F}\rangle$.

5.2 Descriptor Structures

We now define the corresponding tokens in $\mathcal{L}_{\mathcal{A}}$. In doing so, we will be introducing a "two-dimensional" definitional scheme. The first "dimension" is the conventional BNF syntax. The second "dimension" is a *descriptor generator scheme* ψ, of which we now give an example. ψ essentially allows for four types of generators

$$[n] \longrightarrow [d]\ , \tag{32}$$

$$[n] \longrightarrow [\mathfrak{D}]\ , \tag{33}$$

$$[p] \longrightarrow [\mathfrak{D}]^{0m}\ , \tag{34}$$

$$[p] \longrightarrow [\mathcal{C}]^{0m}\ , \tag{35}$$

where: $\langle n\rangle$ is a name whose syntactic form has previously been defined; $\langle p\rangle$ is a pointer; $\langle d\rangle$ is a single data item; $\langle\mathfrak{D}\rangle$ is a descriptor; and $\langle\mathcal{C}\rangle$ is a cell. The superscript $0m$ denotes 0, 1 or more (up to m) concatenated instances of the superscripted metavariable.

The syntax of $\langle p\rangle$, and later $\langle\ell\rangle$, amounts to $\langle$unsigned integer$\rangle$'s. In general $\langle\mathfrak{D}\rangle$ fits the syntactic template

$$\langle t\rangle\ \langle\ell\rangle\ \langle p\rangle\ , \tag{36}$$

where: $\langle t\rangle$ denotes '*type*'; $\langle\ell\rangle$ '*length*'; and $\langle p\rangle$ '*pointer*'. $\langle\mathcal{C}\rangle$ is either a self-described sequence of data syllables making up one data item, or a likewise sequence of instruction syllables. The reader will soon be capable of filling in the omitted details on these and other trivial concepts.

The semantics of ψ say: $\longrightarrow$ denotes that the left part is reducible to a terminal object which points to a segment of $0m$ descriptors or $0m$ cells. $\langle\ell\rangle$ accordingly denotes the specific value of $0m$. We now detail the exact relationship between type, length, and pointer, and detail what pointer points to.

5.3 Statement and Expression Forms

But first we allow ourselves the last bit of generalization. Each form may occur either as a statement or as an expression, that is: in $\mathcal{L}_{\mathcal{A}}$ as an instruction or as a value. Instructions are values having a side-effect, namely the storing of the value in νQ.

Whether the form $\langle\mathcal{F}\rangle$ occurs as a statement or as an expression can in $\mathcal{L}_{\mathcal{C}}$ be seen from the context. But usually computer architectures are not based on looking around in the syllable stream in order to detect contexts. Instead the machines act solely predictably, top down, on each syllable as it arrives. We choose to follow convention and must therefore indicate the proper context explicitly to the system. We select to do so by keeping separate operators for the expression (E) and statement (S) cases. Through these operators the machine then specifies the stacking of a return FSM state, either 1 if E, or 5 if S, on the statestack. Other cheaper solutions, not including stacks, exist; but these result in a loss of control over well-formed instruction syllable sequences.

5.4 $\mathcal{L}_{\mathfrak{A}}$ Sequencing Constructs

We now define the $\mathcal{L}_{\mathfrak{A}}$ equivalents of *form* 1 and *form* 2 using the two-dimensional scheme

$$f1\text{E:}\quad \langle \mathcal{F}_I \rangle\ \underline{\text{case E}}\ \langle n_{\text{case}} \rangle\ , \tag{37}$$

$$f1\text{S:}\quad \langle \mathcal{F}_I \rangle\ \underline{\text{case S}}\ \langle n_{\text{case}} \rangle\ , \tag{38}$$

$$f2\text{E:}\quad \underline{\text{null}}\ \underline{\text{repeat E}}\ \langle n_{\text{repeatE}} \rangle\ \underline{\text{pop}} \tag{39}$$

$$f2\text{S:}\quad \underline{\text{repeat S}}\ \langle n_{\text{repeatS}} \rangle\ . \tag{40}$$

$\langle \mathcal{F}_I \rangle$ is any syllable sequence leading to either of states 1, 2 or 5, i.e., leaving a single value in νQ.

$$[n_{\text{case}}] \longrightarrow [D_{\text{case}}]\ , \tag{41}$$

$$\langle n_{\text{case}} \rangle ::= \langle \text{name} \rangle\ , \tag{42}$$

$$\langle D_{\text{case}} \rangle ::= \underline{\text{case}}\ \langle M \rangle\ \langle \text{ptrCASE} \rangle\ , \tag{43}$$

where the value of the terminal object $\langle M \rangle$ is M $(M \geq 0)$.

$$[\text{ptrCASE}] \longrightarrow [D]^M\ (\equiv [D_1][D_2][D_3] \cdots [D_M])\ , \tag{44}$$

$$\langle D_j \rangle ::= \langle D_{\text{code}} \rangle \mid \langle D_{\text{block}} \rangle\ (1 \leq j \leq M)\ . \tag{45}$$

And

$$[n_{\text{repeat(E/S)}}] \longrightarrow [D_{\text{repeat(E/S)}}]\ , \tag{46}$$

$$\langle D_{\text{repeat(E/S)}} \rangle ::= \underline{\text{repeat}}\ 2\ \langle \text{ptrREPEAT(E/S)} \rangle\ , \tag{47}$$

$$[\text{ptrREPEAT(E/S)}] \longrightarrow [D_{\text{tst}}][D_{\text{ret(E/S)}}]\ , \tag{48}$$

$$\langle D_{\text{tst}} \rangle ::= \langle D_{\text{tstcode}} \rangle \mid \langle D_{\text{tstblock}} \rangle\ , \tag{49}$$

$$\langle D_{\text{retE}} \rangle ::= \langle D_{\text{codeE}} \rangle \mid \langle D_{\text{blockE}} \rangle\ , \tag{50}$$

$$\langle D_{\text{retS}} \rangle ::= \langle D_{\text{codeS}} \rangle \mid \langle D_{\text{blockS}} \rangle\ , \tag{51}$$

$$\langle D_{\text{tstcode}} \rangle ::= \underline{\text{code}}\ \langle L_B \rangle\ \langle \text{ptrTST} \rangle\ , \tag{52}$$

where value of terminal object $\langle L_B \rangle$ is L_B, $L_B > 1$.

$$[\text{ptrTST}] \longrightarrow \{[\text{is}]^{L_B-1}[\nu\text{s}][\underline{\text{tst}}] \mid [\text{is}]^{L_B-1}[\underline{\text{tst}}]\}\ , \tag{53}$$

where [is] and [νs] denote respectively instructions and values, syllable sequence $\{X \mid Y\}$ denotes either X or Y, but not both.

$$\langle D_{\text{tstblock}} \rangle ::= \underline{\text{block}}\ 2\ \langle \text{ptrTSTblock} \rangle\ , \tag{54}$$

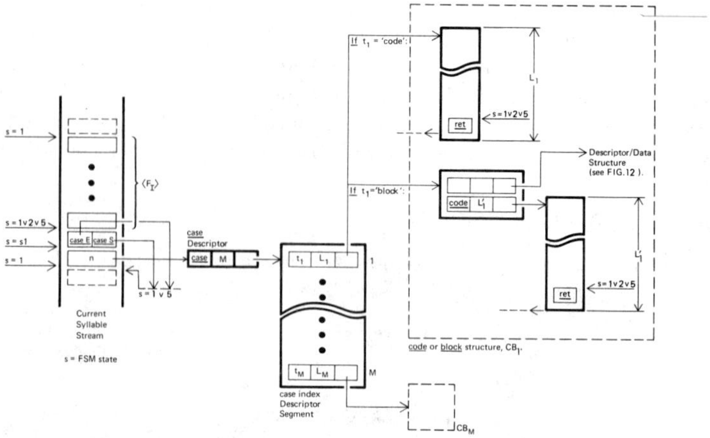

Fig. 25. case control structure.

$$[\text{ptrTSTblock}] \longrightarrow [D_v][D_{\text{tstcode}}] \ , \tag{55}$$

where $\langle D_v \rangle$ reduces to and generates a data structure, see below.

Sacrificing completeness in exposition, we now conclude by finalizing only $\langle D_{\text{codeE}} \rangle$ and $\langle D_{\text{codeS}} \rangle$. The reader will then be able to fill in what is being left unspecified.

$$\langle D_{\text{codeE}} \rangle ::= \underline{\text{code}} \ \langle J \rangle \ \langle \text{ptrE} \rangle \ , \tag{56}$$

$$[\text{ptrE}] \longrightarrow [\underline{\text{pop}}] \{[\text{is}]^{J-3} \mid [\text{is}]^{J-3}[\nu\text{s}]\} [\underline{\text{push}}][\underline{\text{ret}}], \text{ etc.} \ , \tag{57}$$

$$[\text{ptrS}] \longrightarrow \{[\text{is}]^{J-1}[\nu\text{s}][\underline{\text{ret}}] \mid [\text{is}]^{J-1}[\underline{\text{ret}}]\} \ . \tag{58}$$

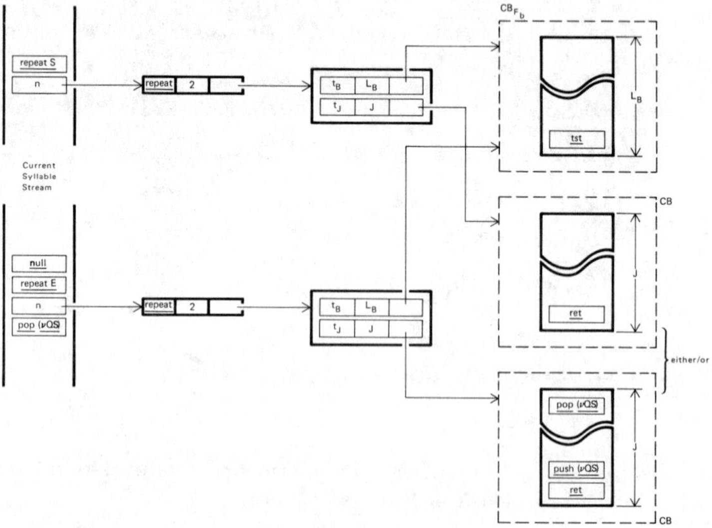

Fig. 26. repeat control structure.

α	push (fsmS ← 5);
β	push (fsmS ← 1);
γ1	push (PCS ← ISP); ISP ← (if (νQ < 1) v(νQ > L[n]) then systemcall(1) else if T[P[n] + (νQ -1)D] = "code" then P[P[n] + (νQ - 1)D] else if T[P[n] + (νQ - 1)D] = "block" then P[P[P[n] + (νQ - 1)D] + 1D] else systemcall(2)); νQ ← Ω;
γ2	push (PCS ← ISP); push (PCS ← (if T[P[n]] = "code" then P[P[n]] else if T[P[n]] = "block" then P[P[P[n]] + 1D] else Ω)); push (PCS ← (if T[P[n] + 1D] = "code" then P[P[n] + 1D] else if T[P[n] + 1D] = "block" then P[P[P[n] + 1D] + 1D] else Ω)); ISP ← (if PCS[2] = Ω v PCS[1] = Ω then (pop(PCS); pop(PCS); systemcall(3)) else PCS[2]); νQ ← Ω;
δ	pop (fsmS → st); pop (PCS → ISP);

ε	if νQ = "false"
	then (pop (PCS); pop (PCS); pop (PCS → ISP); pop (fsmS → st))
	else
	if νQ = "true"
	then (push (PCS ← PCS[2]; ISP ← PCS[2]; st ← 1)
	else (pop(PCS); pop (PCS); pop (fsmS); st ← 1
	systemcall(4));

Fig. 27. Control-structure semantics.

Figures 25 and 26 reflect the above schemes. The possible states from which the new sequencing constructs can occur are shown in Figure 23. The semantics referred to on that figure are defined in the table of Figure 27.

The combined semantics of null, pop, push, and α, β, γ, δ, ε result in the value of the last evaluation of $\langle \mathcal{F} \rangle$ in *form* 2 occurring as an expression being left on top of νQS when control is given back to the syllable string in which the call occurred. In case $\langle \mathcal{F}_b \rangle$ initially was *false* then the popped value corresponds to the null value. If (31) occurs as a statement, then the value of νQ upon return is always either *falsity* or *truth*. That is: (31) occurring as S leads to the value of $\langle \mathcal{F}_b \rangle$, whereas (31) occurring as E results in either null value or the value of the last expression of $\langle \mathcal{F} \rangle$.

We need explain four notational symbols. $\mathcal{T}[x]$ extracts the type descriptor from the descriptor pointed to by x which is either a name or a pointer. $\mathcal{P}[x]$ then extracts the corresponding pointer. $\mathcal{L}[x]$, the number of items pointed to by $\mathcal{P}[x]$. $\nu Q\mathcal{D}$ and $1\mathcal{D}$ denote an increment in the number of descriptors, $\nu Q\mathcal{D}$ as many descriptor widths as denoted by the integer value of νQ, $1\mathcal{D}$ one. We refer to [32] for further treatment of the interaction between (b) data transformations and (c) control structures.

6. SYLLABLE SCHEME

Recall at this time that instructions were built up from sequences ss, of syllables {*f*, *n*, call, caseE, caseS, repeatE, repeatS, return, test, pop, push, null, source, store}, that *f* ranges over a finite set and that *n* is a string embedded in ss. The structure of ss was given by either the finite-state machine of Fig. 4 or the grammar of Figure 5. The structure of *n* was given by the recursive regular expression Eq. (24), to which corresponds the grammars of Fig. 8 and the push-down translators of Figures 9 and 10. Within n we operate with the following set of syllables $\{\alpha, ., \underline{i}, \dashv\}$ where α ranges over an essentially infinite set of syllables.

In conventional instruction schemes the explicit position or even the implicit presence of the above operators is either fixed for all instructions or is given by some coding of the instruction itself, usually embedded in the single operator, that is: is recovered through an interpretation (decoding) of the operator, and the conventional instructions allow only a finite set of α's.

We shall allow not only α but also f to range arbitrarily—and we have throughout assumed that the interpretation of the operators is not the basis for discovering the position of α's, f's and other operators.

One solution to the implementation of such a scheme is to let the syllable stream itself, exclusive of the actual "meaning" of syllables, identify the break between operators and α's—and between f operators and other operators. We shall base our example on such an *internal-formatting* implementation.

6.1 Internal-Format Scheme

In the internal, self-described, format scheme we let a syllable consist of one or more grains, and prefix each grain with a grain descriptor ∂ giving the type of the syllable. The type ∂ and not the value ν of the grain is then passed on to either the FSM or the PLR/PLL translators. One could let the descriptor be followed by a length indicator for the syllable—or one could let all syllables be some variable multiple of some smallest grain (byte), with each grain (∂, ν) itself carrying a descriptor ∂. We have chosen to illustrate the latter scheme only. The specific solution is given in Figure 28. The resulting syllable attribute machine, SAM, has three states. State 1 corresponds to the receipt of name operator symbols ($\underline{i}$, ., $\dashv$), state 2 to the receipt of the variable length α syllables and state 3 to the receipt of the variable length f syllables.

Note that $\partial = 00$ ($\partial = 01$, $\partial = 10$) always signal the arrival of an α-grain (respectively name operator or f-grain), but that $\partial = 11$ in states 2 and 3 signal the

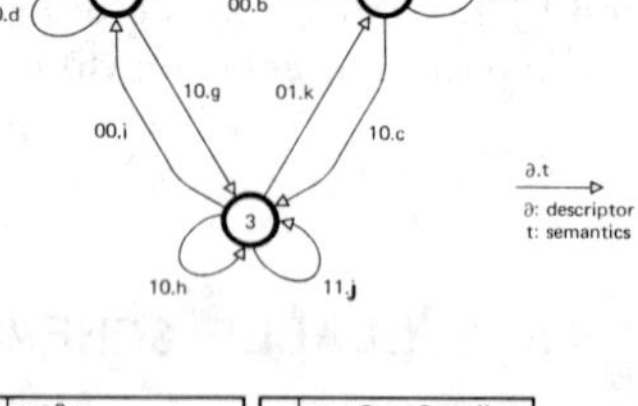

t	action
.a	v→P;
.b	v→a;
.c	v→ff;
.d	v ∥ a→a;
.e	a→αQ; α→P; v→a;
.f	a→αQ; α→P; v→P;

t	action
.g	a→αQ; α→P; v→ff;
.h	ff→F; f→FSM; v→ff;
.i	ff→F; f→FSM; v→a;
.j	v ∥ ff→ff;
.k	ff→F; f→FSM; v→P;
.l	ERROR;

state 1: n-operator, state 2: α-grain, state 3: f-grain

Fig. 28. Syllable-attribute machine.

shift from one α-, respectively one f-, syllable to the next. The 3 state SAM thus enables the proper distinction between appropriate different semantic courses of action (.t).

P denotes the input to the PLR or PLL translator, FSM that of the finite-state machine input. These inputs require only the input-class identification (the type) not the actual value of α and f, the only variables. These are input to αQ respectively F after first having been properly assembled (concatenated: $\|$) from segments of grains on respectively the a and the ff bus. The loading of F and αQ results in the input of type indicators φ, respectively α, to FSM, respectively PRL or PLL. The 'f' input to FSM signals class input from F rather than P. Note that further input-class determination for FSM and P is carried out by these devices themselves and not by SAM.

Figure 21 shows the proper interconnection of SAM, FSM, and NEM. When the NEM complex has recognized a complete name n, NEM sends a name indicator n to FSM.

The Huffman code-like decomposition of syllables into grains provide for an open-ended or extendable design while at the same time preserving storage space.

7. CONCLUSION

We have advocated a specific approach to the design of computer architectures, and within the approach identified layers of abstraction [36]. Within each of these we have discussed several alternative solutions and chosen to illustrate one. The particular examples must therefore not be construed as our main contribution. We have, for example, not at all been concerned with the "efficiency" of the specific solutions. We find the cost/performance issue entirely a separate one that should be pursued independently of the methodology of specification, but one that can only be evaluated meaningfully once such a complete and mechanizable methodology exists.

Our methodology involved not only the use of finite-state machines, context-free grammars, regular expressions and push-down translators, but also the proper identification of the environment upon which the machines and translators could act. This environment consisted of a conceptual, abstract machine, data flow, a scheme of storage referencing and a rather sketched scheme of control flow sequencing. With the machines we associated outputs, with these outputs and the syntactic productions of the grammars we associated semantic rules of action upon the data flow and storage structure.

We believe that the present paper justifies four theses that we find important in the pursuit of good computer architectures:

THESIS 1. It is often better to design by directly thinking and constructing in terms of *finite-state controls* (automata) rather than some more *abstract grammar*. In the paper we see the repeated use of basically the same frame of an automaton for various uses; these uses are then best understood and related to another through exactly that automaton! Figures 6, 20, 25 and 26 all evolve from Figure 4. It is then easy to see immediately the implemental implications brought about by the proposal of new features. Some such features suggest themselves more readily when the basic design follows the above pattern. Also, one can understand better, we think, the differences between *instructions* and *values* (*statements* and *expressions*) by relating to automaton states 1, 2, and 5.

THESIS 2. Conventional machine-instruction *addressing schemes* have all been unified in one *naming scheme*. This scheme reflects the basic aspects of *absolute, relative, indirect,* and *indexed,* addressing. It is important to provide a common framework for all these addressing mechanisms, e.g., by relating them to the same syntax, translator, semantics, and environments.

THESIS 3. Conventional machine-instruction status switching, subroutine linkage, conditional and direct branching should all be presented—and thus also evolve—on the basis of a common underlying control structure rather than by exhaustive enumeration of all cases. We have sketched such a control structure in Fig. 26, Eqs. (32)-(35), in semantics (α, β, δ) of Fig. 27 and in the environment of Figure 21. We have further detailed some applications in Figs. 23 and 24, Eqs. (41)-(58) and semantics ($\gamma 1, \gamma 2, \varepsilon$) of Figure 27.

THESIS 4. The concurrent specification of a computing system in terms of syntax, finite-state controls, stacks, semantics, and environments all amount to a *model* for a *class of computations*. We believe it important to pursue all these model parts simultaneously. We believe it important to provide simple definitional tools, not just one, but a consistent and complementing variety. These may have to fit together in a hierarchical fashion—or may cascade into one another. We find that we are then able to provide for uncluttered, complete and unambiguous designs.

REFERENCES

[1] J. P. Anderson, "A Computer for Direct Execution of Algorithmic Languages," *Proc. Eastern Joint Comp. Conf.*, **20**, 184–193 (ALGOL-60) (1961).

[2] W. Lonergan and P. King, "Design of the B-5000 System," *Datamation*, **7**.

[3] A. C. Haley, "The KDF-9 Computer System," *FJCC*, **22** (1962).

[4] N. H. Takahashi, K. Yoshiro, and K. Fuchi, "System Design of the ETL MK-6 Computer," *Proc. IFIP Cong. 62*.

[5] R. H. Allmark and J. R. Lucking, "Design of an Arithmetic Unit Incorporating a Nesting Store," *Proc. IFIP Cong. 62*, 694–697 (1962).

[6] J. E. Meggitt, "A Character Computer for High-Level Language Interpretation," *IBM Sys. J.*, **3**, 68–78 (1964).

[7] A. J. Melbourne and J. M. Pugmire, "A Small Computer for the Direct Processing of FORTRAN Statement," *Comput. J.*, **8**, 24–27 (April 1965).

[8] T. R. Bashkow, A. Sasson, and A. Kronfeld, "Systems Design of a FORTRAN Machine," *IEEE Trans. Electr. Comput.*, **EC-16**, 485–499 (August 1967).

[9] W. M. McKeeman, "Language-Directed Computer Design," *Proc. FJCC*, 413–417 (1967).

[10] E. A. Hauck and B. A. Dent, "Burroughs B6500/B7500 Stack Mechanism," *Proc. SJCC*, 245–251 (1968).

[11] S. C. Wang, "On the Direct Implementation of Algorithmic Scientific Computer Languages," PhD. Thesis, University of Minnesota (June 1968).

[12] A. N. Myamlin and V. K. Smirnov, "Computer with Stack Memory," *Proc. IFIP 68*, **D**, D91–D96, Edinburgh (August 1968).

[13] M. Sugimoto, "PL/I Reducer and Direct Processor," *Proc. 24th National Conf. ACM*, San Francisco, 519–538 (August 1969).

[14] P. S. Abrams, "An APL Machine," PhD. Thesis, Stanford University (Stanford Linear Accelerator Center) SLAC Report No. 114 (February 1964).

[15] K. J. Thurber and J. W. Myrna, "System Design of a Cellular APL Computer," *IEEE Trans. Comput.*, **C-19**, No. 4, 291–303 (April 1970).

[16] H. Weber, "A Microprogrammed Implementation of EULER on IBM System/360 Model 30," *Comm. ACM*, **10**, 549–558 (1967).

[17] J. K. Iliffe, "Basic Machine Principles" (American Elsevier Publishing Co. (in Europe, London: MacDonald, 1968).

[18] J. K. Iliffe, "Elements of BLM," *Comput. J.*, **12**, 251–258 (September 1969).

[19] T. Kilburn, D. Morris, J. S. Rohl, and F. H. Sumner, "A System Design Proposal," *Proc. IFIP 68*, **D**, D76–D80, Edinburgh (August 1968).

[20] H. W. Lawson, "Programming-Language-Oriented Instruction Streams," *IEEE Trans. Comput.*, **C-17**, No. 5, 476–485 (May 1962).

[21] W. McKeeman (University of California, Santa Cruz), Stanford University Colloquium Notes.

[22] D. Bjørner, "Register Transfer and Transformation Machines," Towards a Theory of Machine Organization," *Proc. 3rd Hawaii Int. Conf. Systems Sci.*, 461–467 (January 1970).

[23] N. Wirth, "PL360—A Programming Language for the 360 Computers," *J. ACM*, **15**, No. 1, 37–74 (January 1968).

[24] A. D. Falkoff and K. E. Iverson, "The APL/360 Terminal System," *Proc. ACM Symp. Experimental Systems Applied Math.* (Academic Press, 1968).

[25] M. V. Wilkes, "Time-Sharing Computer Systems" (American Elsevier, 1969).

[26] D. E. Knuth, "On the Translation of Languages from Left to Right," *Information & Control*, **8**, 607–639 (December 1965).

[27] D. E. Knuth, "Top-Down Syntax Analysis," notes, 1967 International Summer School on Computer Programming, Copenhagen, Denmark (August 1967).

[28] D. Bjørner, "The Theory of Finite-State Syntax-Directed Translations," PhD. Thesis, Lab. for Pulse and Digital Techniques, Technical Univ. of Denmark (January 1969).

[29] D. Bjørner, "The Synthesis of Finite-State Top-Down and Bottom-Up Transducers," *Proc. 11th Ann. IEEE Symp. Switching and Automata Theory*, Santa Monica, 122–000 (October 28–30, 1970).

[30] P. J. Landin, "The Mechanical Evaluation of Expressions," *Comput. J.*, **6**, No. 4, 308–320 (January 1964).

[31] D. E. Knuth and R. W. Floyd, "Notes on Avoiding go to Statements," Stanford University Comp. Science Dept., Report CS148 (January 1970).

[32] D. Bjørner, "Flowchart Machines," *BIT*, **10**, No. 4, 415–442 (1970).

[33] E. W. Dijkstra, "Go To Statement Considered Harmful," Letter to Editor, *Comm. ACM*, **11**, No. 3, 147–148 (March 1968).

[34] N. Wirth and C. A. R. Hoare, "A Contribution to the Development of ALGOL," *Comm. ACM*, **9**, No. 6, 413–432 (June 1966).

[35] Strachey et al., "The Main Features of CPL," *Comput. J.*, **6**, 134–143 (1963).

[36] E. W. Dijkstra, "Complexity Controlled by Hierarchical Ordering of Function and Variability," in *Software Engineering*, 181–185 (Naur and Randell, Eds., NATO Sci. Comm. Report, 1969).

[37] P. Lucas, P. Laver, and H. Stigleitner, "Method and Notation for the Formal Definition of Programming Languages," *IBM Vienna Lab Technical Report*, TR 25.087 (June 1968).

COMPUTER PROGRAM MODELS

C. V. Ramamoorthy

Department of Electrical Engineering, The University of Texas at Austin, Austin, TX

Proper representation and modeling are important ingredients for the analysis of computer programs. The purpose of this paper is to survey and comment on various models of computer programs, primarily from the standpoint of their practical usefulness.

Three models: the graph model; the sequential machine model; and the decision table model are discussed. The suitability of the models are explored with the following considerations in mind:

(a) *Program Analysis for Testing and Debugging.* The models must provide aid for detecting structural and logical flaws, for locating redundant code, and for determining test points and break points for checking out subsets of the program

(b) *Execution-Time Determination.* The models must provide mathematical tractability to determine exact or good estimates of execution times of the whole program from the knowledge of certain activity statistics gathered during previous executions. This helps to locate strategic portions of the program which if improved could reduce total running time, etc.

(c) *Segmentation.* The model must be able to help in segmenting the program into coherent subsets for purposes of fitting it into physical-memory pages during execution. Proper segmenting would prevent a loss of wasteful transfers between main memory and the auxiliary mass memory. Segmentation is also helpful during program testing

(d) *Program Optimization.* Once a program is written and checked out, it is desirable to "optimize" the code by removing redundant or unused parts in it and generate an equivalent program that reduces the overall execution time. Thus program "optimization" could reduce the memory requirements of an object program and/or reduce its execution time. Proper program models and analysis based on it should provide techniques for optimization

(e) *Recognition and Use of Parallelism.* Programs can be analyzed for inherent parallelism of execution of their subsets. The program modeling influences the nature of recognition process as well as the proper use of parallelism in the execution process. The latter includes the assignment of proper program subsets to processors so that the program can be executed in less time with less utilization of resources

(f) *Activity Measurement.* Program models should enable us to develop optimum location of activity-measuring devices within a program so that statistics can be derived on the use of program subsets and various system resources

(g) *Roll-Back and Recovery Points.* Safeguards must be instituted into a program so that temporary setbacks (system malfunctions) can be overcome by rolling back and restarting the program at a previous state guaranteed to be correct. Program modeling could help develop the theory and location of optimum roll-back points.

Presented at the Symposium on Computers and Automata
Polytechnic Institute of Brooklyn, April 13–15, 1971.

I. INTRODUCTION

In this paper we shall consider some models of computer programs primarily for simulation, analysis, and optimization. Flow charts and flow-chart-type representations often are used as models during program generation and documentation.

The analyses we shall consider are both qualitative and quantitative. Qualitative parameters of the program models are useful in program analysis during debugging, such as detection and location of structural flaws, redundant and unreachable code. Qualitative models also help in developing methods of program optimization as well as in computational parallelism detection and location.

Quantitatively, program models could provide estimates of execution times of programs from their constituent instruction execution times and the branching probabilities. Also such models provide methods of placing activity monitors at various strategic locations of the programs for purposes of metering and measuring the execution traffic in various parts of a program. Another important use of the quantitative models is to locate optimally (for certain, specified cost functions) rollback points within a program such that if for any reason the execution process is scuttled, the computation can be restarted at the nearest rollback point. The assumption here is that the computer stores the status information (for possible restart) at each rollback point. Since programs can be segmented into parallel-processable tasks, then the problem arises how to schedule these tasks for a multiprocessor with a fixed number of processors so that the total program can be executed in a minimum time using a minimum number of processors. The model and its analysis are important in answering these questions.

II. MODELS

We shall next consider some important characteristics of the models. The models must be appropriate and conceptually simple. They must be easily represented and manipulated in a computer. The representation of the process must be homogeneous such that the same analytical tools can be used at any level. This implies that by choosing the proper level of representation, details not useful for the problem at hand must be masked out. Another important requirement is that the modifications on the program being modeled should not be cumbersome in simulation. The model of the program should be useful in documentation. Finally, the model and the modeling process must be capable of validation.

In considering possible models for qualitative and quantitative analysis we shall briefly describe three specific models, viz., the sequential-machine model, the decision-table model and the simple-graph model. Our emphasis will be on the graph model. The models must portray both the structure as well as the behavior of the programs. In the case of the directed-graph model, one could derive quantitative information about its structure by simple manipulations of its matrix representation. By adding or including certain behavioral characteristics (parallelism, execution times, etc.) one can analyze the model to provide efficient utilization of the available computing resources.

A. Sequential-Machine Model

In the sequential-machine model, the computer (the sequential machine) is taken from state to state by a transition table (procedure) and a set of inputs (data). While such a model is useful to study the behavior of very simple (trivial) computer programs, the inability of the model to contend with a large number of states is evident. However, certain program-verification procedures [5] benefit from this type of modeling.

B. Decision-Table Model

Suggestions have been made to use decision tables as execution sequences (programs) for purposes of ease of comprehension and verification [1]. A program can thus be modeled and mapped into a decision table. A rudimentary decision table is illustrated in Table I. The vertical coordinate lists a set of conditions that may or may not occur in all possible combinations. The horizontal coordinate lists a set of actions to be taken by the program. These could be different procedures to execute or merely GO TO statements. Each column of the table indicates the subset of conditions that must be satisfied if the action listed under that column is to be carried out. *Y* stands for yes and *N* stands for no, and a dash (don't-care symbol) signifies that the particular condition involved is irrelevant to the action in the corresponding column. A decision table contains less information than a corresponding flow chart for the same logical process. A flow chart of a conditional phrase contains the logical rules of the problem and also specifies the order in which various tests will be carried out. The decision table does not indicate how the logic should be structured in terms of program steps. However, it provides a partial verification of the logical correctness of the program. Also, all assumptions made by the programmer are displayed as possible input conditions. Since more than one action could be initiated under each condition, opportunities for parallel processing are explicitly indicated.

TABLE I. Example of a decision table.

	Action 1	Action 2
Condition 1	Y	N
Condition 2	Y	-
Condition 3	N	-

C. Directed-Graph Model

As will be shown, this model of the computer program is useful for both qualitative and quantitative studies. It really originated from the flow chart. This representation is conceptually simple and natural. In a computer, the graph can be represented either as a matrix array [2] or as a list [3]. The matrix representation is especially useful in structure analysis which also allows quantitative problems to be easily formulated. However, analysis computations can be quite complex [4]. Given the graph model of the program, we can study the qualitative characteristics some of which are:

(1) Logical structure analysis, e.g., loops, entrances, and exits of programs and their components
(2) Structural flaws, e.g., illegal entrances and exits, hidden loops, redundant code
(3) One could develop better ways of segmenting programs to reduce frequency of overlays and swaps
(4) The graph model helps code optimization by providing better execution properties by certain rearrangement of code
(5) The model can be used to locate the activity probes to monitor significant events taking place in the program
(6) The model can be used to detect parallel-processable segments in sequentially-organized programs.

Quantitative aspects of the graph model of programs can tell us about:

(1) Activity within subsets of a program
(2) Expected execution times
(3) Code-optimization-knowing activities
(4) Rollback points for recovery
(5) Scheduling of parallel-processable segments in a multiprocessor.

In this paper we shall focus only on: (a) program-code optimization; and (b) the detection of parallelism in a sequentially-organized program. Our purpose is to show the appropriateness of the model and its representation from a practical point of view.

III. ELEMENTS OF THE MODEL

For our discussion we shall define a program as consisting of a set of instructions with a specified sequence of execution on a given data. The program can be represented by a directed graph consisting of a set of nodes and a set of directed edges. A node can be defined as a computational task which consists of a sequence of instructions (and data) that must be executed consecutively with the following format: The first instruction in a node either initiates the program or is a target of a jump instruction, and the last instruction in a node either is the last (terminal) instruction of the program or a branch instruction. A branch can include more than one target. The directed edges represent allowed transitions between nodes.

IV. DETECTION OF PARALLELISM IN A SEQUENTIALLY-ORGANIZED PROGRAM GIVEN ITS PROGRAM GRAPH

The directed-graph representation of a program can be used to do more than simply represent the permissible flow of execution in the program as originally coded. An important extension of the program graph is the parallel-task graph which indicates the parallel processability of independent segments in the sequentially-organized program [6]. These segments, often referred to as tasks, represent portions of the source code which can be executed as separate entities once the values for the input variables in the task have been established. If the completion of a task generates values which are utilized by more than one task in the original sequential stream, then the tasks can be executed simultaneously, that is, in parallel.

Consider, for example, the directed-graph representation of a sequentially-coded program as shown in Figure 1. In this graph each node represents one or more lines of code in the original program. A branch from one node to another represents a permissible program transition. A node from which more than one branch emanates represents a conditional task whose outcome is not known until the task is completed at execution time.

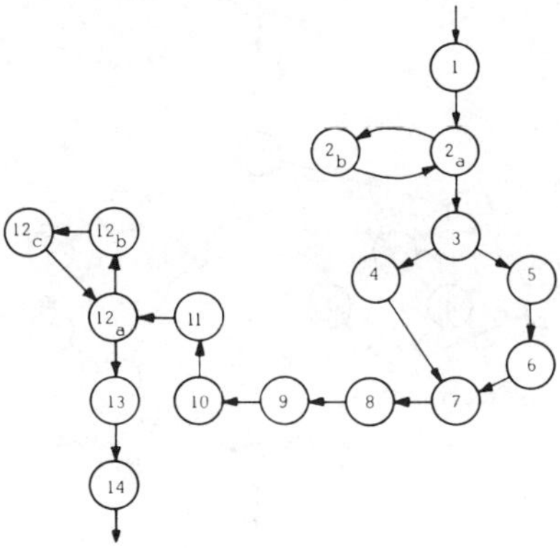

Fig. 1. Program graph of a serially-coded program.

Since the determination of parallel-processable tasks really implies an ordering in time, it is necessary to eliminate those conditions which would preclude such an ordering. The loop represented by tasks 2_a and 2_b, for example, suggests that task 2_a follows 2_b and 2_b follows 2_a; this apparent inconsistency is resolved by labeling the entire loop with a single task name. The loop-free or reduced graph for the original program graph is shown in Figure 2. If necessary, during this reduction the original graph is converted to a single-entry single-exit (SEC) graph by the addition of a single pseudonode which precedes all original-entry nodes and one which follows all original-exit nodes.

In order to schedule tasks for parallel execution, it is necessary to investigate the input-output requirements of each individual task. The parallel-task graph for the example program is shown in Figure 3. This graph indicates that Task 2 depends on an output generated by Task 1; thus Task 2 cannot be initiated until Task 1 is completed. Similarly, the input requirements of Tasks 3 and 8 are limited to outputs generated by Task 2. Upon completion of Task 2, Tasks 3 and 8 can be initiated *simultaneously*. This process is continued until the entire graph is analyzed.

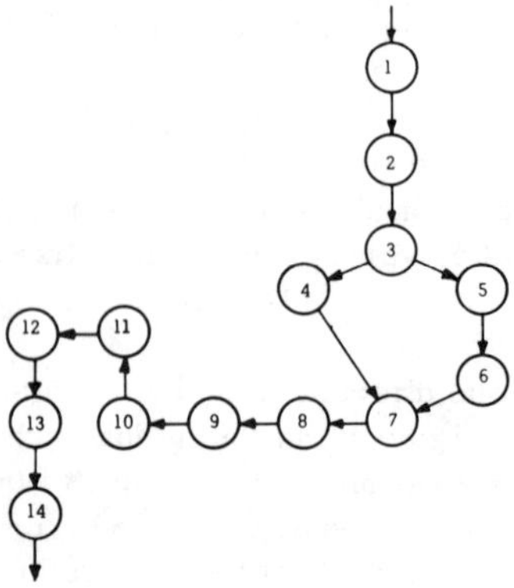

Fig. 2. Reduced program graph of the serially-coded program.

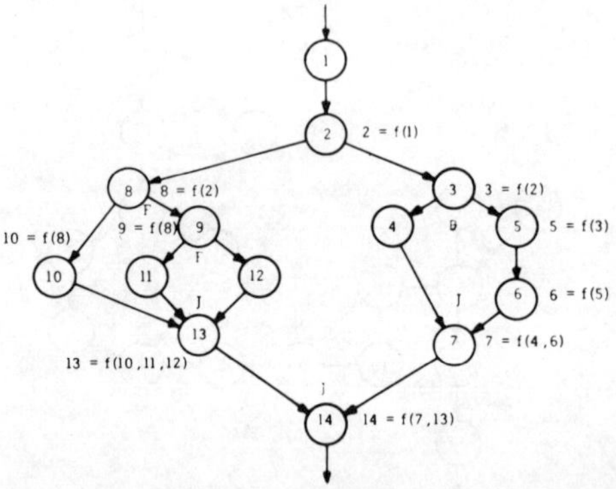

Fig. 3. Final program graph of the parallel-processable program.

The results of this analysis must still be communicated to the operating system in some convenient manner. This information is contained in the form of two tables shown below as Tables II and Table III. In Table II, the earliest time period during which a task can be initiated is indicated, and tasks possessing special characteristics are identified. All the successors of a FORK node can be initiated simultaneously, whereas only one of the potential successors of a BRANCH task will be executed. A JOIN task is one in which all of its predecessors must be completed before execution can continue beyond the JOIN. In addition, the input requirements of each task are identified.

Table III lists not only the earliest but also the latest time period during which a task can be executed. This is especially important when insufficient resources are available for processing all candidate tasks and the execution of some of the tasks must be postponed.

The analysis outlined above involves a considerable investment of time and system resources. Thus the matter of the suitability of a program for execution in a multiprocessor environment becomes very important. If a program has little inherent parallelism or is to be run only a few times, little benefit will be gained

TABLE II. Task-scheduling table.

TIME	INPUTS TO TASKS	TASK NUMBER	TASK TYPE
t_1	-	1	
t_2	1	2	FORK
t_3	2	3	BRANCH
t_3	2	8	FORK
t_4	3	4	
t_4	3	5	
t_4	8	9	FORK
t_4	8	10	
t_5	5	6	
t_5	9	11	
t_5	9	12	
t_6	4,6	7	JOIN
t_6	10,11,12	13	JOIN
t_7	7,13	14	JOIN

TABLE III. Permissible task-initiation time.

COLUMN PARTITIONS		PERMISSIBLE TASK INITIATION PERIODS	
TIME	TASK		
t_1	1	TASK	TIME
t_2	2	1	t_1
t_3	3,8	2	t_2
t_4	4,5,9,10	3	t_3
t_5	6,11,12	4	t_4,t_5
t_6	7,13	5	t_4
t_7	14	6	t_5
ROW PARTITIONS		7	t_6
t_1	1	8	t_3
t_2	2	9	t_4
t_3	3,8	10	t_4,t_5
t_4	5,9	11	t_5
t_5	4,6,10,11,12	12	t_5
t_6	7,13	13	t_6
t_7	14	14	t_7

from the information generated by the program-graph analysis. In addition, it would be highly desirable if the suitability question could be answered without performing the actual parallel-task analysis. The general subject of program suitability is discussed and the questions posed above are examined in detail in [4].

In a previous paragraph it was mentioned that a situation may exist in which the number of available processors may be less than the number of tasks which are ready for execution. Therefore, in order to achieve the desired objective—

the minimization of the total program-execution time—a task schedule which considers the requirements of the problem at hand, the hardware characteristics of the host environment, must be generated. Examples of task schedules for the program graph used throughout this discussion are shown in Figure 4. In the first schedule it is assumed that all tasks require equal processing time, while in the second schedule processing times are unequal. In both schedules it is assumed that three identical processors (P_1, P_2, P_3) are available and that once a task is begun by a processor it will remain assigned to that processor until the task is completed.

Throughout this discussion, parallelism and scheduling have been discussed in the context of tasks at the level of individual statements of a higher-level programming language. Parallelism (and the need for scheduling) can exist, however, at a lower level, e.g., independent subexpressions in a compound-arithmetic expression. Although in this situation the set of tasks constitutes a single statement in the higher-level language, the graph model described above can be used to find concurrently-executable subexpressions in an attempt to minimize execution time for the entire subexpression. This subject is discussed in detail in [7].

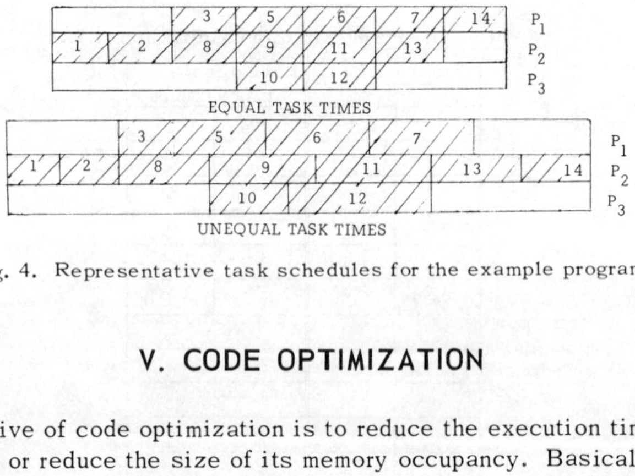

Fig. 4. Representative task schedules for the example program.

V. CODE OPTIMIZATION

The objective of code optimization is to reduce the execution time of the target program or reduce the size of its memory occupancy. Basically, code optimization involves the following essential steps:

(1) Recognition and deletion of both repeated and/or unused computations
(2) Moving instructions to less frequently executed areas by loop and activity analysis
(3) Recognition and coordination of parallel operations such that parallelism can be utilized effectively without creating resource conflicts. This is important in a multiprocessor environment
(4) Locating strategic parts in the program where slight improvements could result in substantial gain in the overall program execution.

The principles applicable to both programs and microprograms are given in [8]. It must be noted here that the programs are assumed to be operating correctly before analysis for code optimization can be begun.

In Figs. 5(a) and 5(b) we have portrayed an example in code optimization.

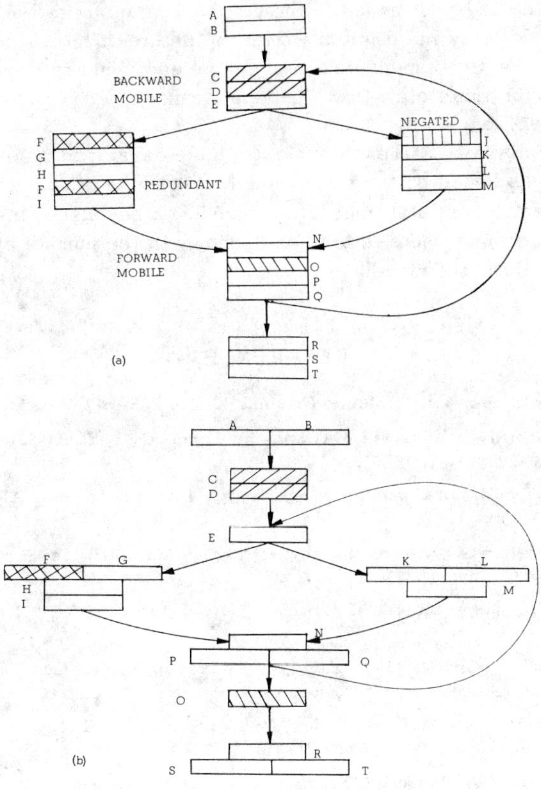

Fig. 5. Example of code optimization. (a) Before optimization. (b) After optimization.

The preliminary unoptimized version of the program graph is given in Figure 5(a). A possible optimized version of the program graph is given in Figure 5(b). The operations highlighted in the example are:

(1) *A* & *B* were recognized as parallel-processable operations and hence could be executed together
(2) Instructions *C* & *D* are moved out of the loop
(3) One of the two repeated operations (*F*) is removed. *J* was recognized as a negated (unused) operation and it was deleted. *F* & *G* are parallel-processable operations and therefore can be performed currently
(4) Operation *O* can be moved forwards from the loop.

Other operations in Fig. 5(b) can be likewise analyzed.

VI. CONCLUSIONS

The cost of qualitative analysis is high in terms of the number of computations (execution time) and memory. Loop analysis for example increases with the square of the number of nodes in the graph. The quantitative analyses based on the graph model vary in complexity with the nature of the objectives. Location of probes for activity measurements may be easy but the computation of expected-execution time, etc., from the measurements derived from simulation may be quite involved.

We at The University of Texas at Austin have developed a set of software-analysis packages based on the graph model. Since these analyses are based on one model, the total computational effort is reduced because many analyses use common computations. There is also an economy in the number of measurements needed for describing the model.

REFERENCES

[1] P. J. H. King, "Decision Tables," *Comput. J.*, **10**, 135–142 (August 1967).

[2] C. V. Ramamoorthy, "Analysis of Graphs by Connectivity Considerations," *J. ACM*, **13**, No. 2, 211–222 (April 1966).

[3] D. R. Knuth, *The Art of Computer Programming*, **1**, "Fundamental Algorithms" (Addison-Wesley).

[4] M. J. Gonzalez and C. V. Ramamoorthy, "Program Suitability for Parallel Processing," *IEEE-TEC* (June 1971).

[5] Z. Manna, "The Correctness of Programs," *J. Comput. Sys. Sci.*, **3**, No. 2, 119–127 (May 1969).

[6] C. V. Ramamoorthy and M. J. Gonzalez, "A Survey of Techniques for Recognition of Parallel-Processable Streams in Computer Programs," *Proc. FJCC*, 1–15 (1969).

[7] C. V. Ramamoorthy and M. J. Gonzales, "Subexpression Ordering in the Execution of Arithmetic Expressions," *Comm. ACM* (July 1971).

[8] R. L. Kleir and C. V. Ramamoorthy, "Optimization Strategies for Microprograms," *IEEE-TEC* (July 1971).

FUZZY PROGRAMS—THEORY AND APPLICATIONS

Shi-Kuo Chang†

School of Electrical Engineering, Cornell University, Ithaca, NY

An abstract model for the execution of fuzzy programs using finite-state machines is formulated. A modified simple-execution procedure is described. It is shown that the performance function of a fuzzy machine can be effectively constructed so that the program-execution (-searching) cost of a regular fuzzy program is minimized. Several application examples are discussed.

I. INTRODUCTION

A fuzzy program is a way of imprecisely specifying a course of action. In our daily life we encounter many situations in which the course of action cannot or need not be precisely specified. We human beings seem to have no great difficulty in understanding and executing fuzzy programs. Therefore, it is of interest to investigate whether machines can be designed or programmed to do the same.

Many problems in artificial intelligence, pattern recognition and information retrieval can be formulated as problems of finding efficient execution of fuzzy programs. For example, the problem solver may be instructed to "find the thief who is a tall and skinny man carrying a black suitcase" or to "pick up the book on the desk." In order to solve such problems (to find the thief, to pick up the book, etc.), the problem solver must first translate the given sequence of fuzzy, or imprecise, instructions into another sequence of more precise instructions. For example, the first fuzzy instruction can be translated into "find the man who is more than six feet tall and weighs less than 160 pounds and carries a black suitcase" and the second one into "go to the desk, search for the book on the desk and pick it up." It may be possible to translate the new instructions into even more precise instructions. For example, the instruction "go to the desk" can be further translated into the following sequence of instructions: "go one step forward. If the desk is within two feet then stop, otherwise go another step forward. If the desk is within two feet then stop, otherwise go another step forward···." Therefore, a given sequence of fuzzy instructions may finally be translated into another sequence of precise instructions which is not necessarily of the same length as the original one. The problem solver can now proceed to execute this sequence of translated instructions. If the translated instructions cannot be executed for one reason or another (there is no man more than six feet

† Present address: IBM Watson Research Center, Yorktown Heights, NY.

Presented at the Symposium on Computers and Automata
Polytechnic Institute of Brooklyn, April 13–15, 1971.

tall, there is no book on the desk, etc.), then the problem solver must try to find another translation for the fuzzy program. When all the alternatives have been tried without success, the problem solver will be forced to declare failure.

In this paper we will give precise definitions to the concepts described in the preceding paragraph. The problem solver will be taken to be a *finite-state machine*. The original sequence of fuzzy instructions will be called a *fuzzy program*. The translated sequence of precise instructions will be called a *machine program* because it serves as the actual input to the finite-state machine. The machine program which is the translation of a given fuzzy program is called its *execution* and a fuzzy program is called *executable* if it has such an execution. The system, taken as a whole, is regarded as a *fuzzy machine*.

The translation process is controlled by the *feasibility function* and the *performance function*. Suppose the machine is in a certain state and a certain fuzzy instruction is received. The feasibility function specifies all the possible translations for this fuzzy instruction, and the performance function assigns ratings to these possible translations. Thus we can use this information to find the execution with the highest rating, or the *optimal execution* of a given fuzzy program [5]. On the other hand, we can also use this information to guide us so that an efficient execution can be found. In this case, we aim at minimizing the *program-execution (-searching) cost*.

The main result of this paper is that the performance function can be constructed in such a way that the program-execution cost for a given fuzzy program can be minimized. The practical usefulness of the concepts described above will be demonstrated by several examples. The reader who is mainly interested in applications may proceed directly to Section V.

II. FORMULATION OF THE MODEL

An abstract model for the execution of fuzzy programs using finite-state machines will now be given. The model consists of three parts:

(1) The machine which performs the actual computation
(2) The fuzzy programs which control the action of the machine
(3) The relationship between the machine and the fuzzy programs.

The machine is assumed to be a finite-state machine and the fuzzy programs are assumed to be regular expressions. The relationship between the machine and the fuzzy programs is determined by the *feasibility function* f and the *performance function* λ.

DEFINITION 1. *A* finite-state machine *is a system*

$$M = (K, X, \Psi, x_0, T) \ ,$$

where: K *is a finite nonempty set (machine instructions)*; X *is a finite nonempty set (internal states)*; x_0 *is an element of* X *(the initial state)*; T *is a subset of* X *(final states)*; *and* Ψ *is a function from* $X \times K$ *into* X *(the transition function)*.

The transition function Ψ is extended to be a function from $X \times K^*$ into X in the usual manner

$$\Psi(x, e) = x \qquad \text{(for } x \in X) \ ,$$

$$\Psi(x, \bar{\mu} \cdot \mu) = \Psi(\Psi(x, \bar{\mu}), \mu) \qquad \text{(for } x \in X,\ \mu \in K,\ \bar{\mu} \in K^*) \ ,$$

where e denotes the null string.

An instruction string $\bar{\mu} = \mu_1 \mu_2 \mu_3 \cdots \mu_n$ in K^* is a *machine program* of M if

$$\Psi(x_0, \bar{\mu}) = \Psi\big(\cdots, \Psi(\Psi(x_0, \mu_1), \mu_2), \cdots, \mu_n\big) \in T \ .$$

DEFINITION 2. *A* fuzzy machine *is a system*

$$\hat{M} = (\Sigma, M, f, \lambda) \ ,$$

where: Σ *is a finite nonempty set (fuzzy instructions);* M *is a finite-state machine as defined in Definition 1;* f *is a function from* $X \times \Sigma \times K$ *into* $\{0, 1\}$ *(the feasibility function); and* λ *is a function from* $X \times \Sigma \times K$ *into* $[0, 1]$ *(the performance function).*

Intuitively, the feasibility function f gives the objective constraints for the machine to execute certain machine instructions in a particular situation. For example, if $f(x, \alpha, \mu) = 1$, then when M is in state x and the fuzzy instruction α is received, the machine instruction μ can be executed. Similarly, if $f(x, \alpha, \mu) = 0$, then the instruction μ cannot be executed in that situation.

On the other hand, the performance function λ gives a subjective performance evaluation for the machine to execute certain machine instructions in a particular situation. For example, if $\lambda(x, \alpha, \mu_1) = 0.9$, and $\lambda(x, \alpha, \mu_2) = 0.5$, then when M is in state x and the fuzzy instruction α is received, subjectively the machine instruction μ_1 gives a better performance than the machine instruction μ_2.

In the usual definition of fuzzy machines [15, 19] the two functions are combined into one. However, in order to keep objective constraints and subjective performance evaluation separate, the definition given above is preferable.

DEFINITION 3. *An* elementary fuzzy program $\bar{\alpha}$ *is a string in* Σ^*. *A* fuzzy program R *is a regular expression over* Σ. *Let* $\bar{\mu} = \mu_1 \mu_2 \mu_3 \cdots \mu_n$, *be a machine program of* M *and let* $x_0, x_1, x_2, \cdots, x_n$ *be the successive states of* M *when* M *executes* $\bar{\mu}$ *(i.e.,* $x_i = \Psi(x_{i-1}, \mu_i)$ $(1 \le i \le n)$*). The machine program* $\bar{\mu}$ *is said to be* an execution *of the elementary fuzzy program* $\bar{\alpha} = \alpha_1 \alpha_2 \alpha_3 \cdots \alpha_n$ *if* $f(x_{i-1}, \alpha_i, \mu_i) = 1$ $(1 \le i \le n)$. *A fuzzy program* R *is* executable *with respect to the fuzzy machine* $\hat{M}$ *if there is an elementary fuzzy program* $\bar{\alpha}$ *in* R *and a machine program* $\bar{\mu}$ *such that* $\bar{\mu}$ *is an execution of* $\bar{\alpha}$.

NOTATION. The state sequence $x_0, x_1, x_2, \cdots, x_n$ will sometimes be written in the form ${}_{x_0}(\alpha_1, \mu_1)\, {}_{x_1}(\alpha_2, \mu_2)_{x_2}, \cdots, {}_{x_{n-1}}(\alpha_n, \mu_n)_{x_n}$ to show its dependence on $\alpha_1 \alpha_2 \alpha_3 \cdots \alpha_n$ and $\mu_1 \mu_2 \mu_3 \cdots \mu_n$. Also, for notational convenience, $(\alpha_1 \alpha_2 \alpha_3 \cdots \alpha_k, \mu_1 \mu_2 \mu_3 \cdots \mu_k)$ and $(\alpha_1, \mu_1)(\alpha_2, \mu_2) \cdots (\alpha_k, \mu_k)$ will be used interchangeably.

Definition 3 says that a machine program $\bar{\mu}$ can be regarded to be an execution of an elementary fuzzy program $\bar{\alpha}$ if every machine instruction μ_i is feasible with respect to the situation in question or, in other words, $f(x_{i-1}, \alpha_i, \mu_i) = 1$ (for $1 \le i \le n$). A fuzzy program is simply a collection of elementary fuzzy programs. Therefore, if one of the elementary fuzzy programs has an execution, then the fuzzy program can be said to be executable.

An executable fuzzy program may have more than one execution. If an execution is thought of as one translation of the original fuzzy program, then the number of different executions is also the number of different translations for the fuzzy program. Therefore it is meaningful to define the degree of fuzziness of a fuzzy program as the number of different executions it possesses.

DEFINITION 4. *Given a fuzzy program R with respect to a fuzzy machine $\hat{M}$, let D_R denote the set of machine programs of $\hat{M}$ which are executions of elementary fuzzy programs in R.* The degree of fuzziness *of R, denoted by $d(R)$, is defined to be*

$$d(R) = \begin{cases} |D_R|, & \text{if } |D_R| \text{ is finite} , \\ \infty, & \text{otherwise} . \end{cases}$$

THEOREM 1. *For any regular fuzzy program R with respect to a fuzzy machine $\hat{M}$, D_R is regular.*

Proof. Construct a new finite-state machine M' as follows

$$M' = (\Sigma \times K, X \cup \{s\}, \psi', x_0, T) \ ,$$

where: $\Sigma \times K$ is the product of Σ and K (input symbols); s is a new symbol (sink state); and ψ' is a function from $(X \cup \{s\}) \times \Sigma \times K$ into $X \cup \{s\}$ (transition function) defined as

$$\psi'(x, (\alpha, \mu)) = \begin{cases} \psi(x, \mu), & \text{if } x \in X \text{ and } f(x, \alpha, \mu) = 1 , \\ s, & \text{if } x \in X \text{ and } f(x, \alpha, \mu) = 0 , \end{cases}$$

$$\psi'(s, (\alpha, \mu)) = s \ .$$

The set of strings accepted by M' is regular and is given by

$$Q = \{(\alpha_1, \mu_1)(\alpha_2, \mu_2)(\alpha_3, \mu_3) \cdots (\alpha_k, \mu_k); \quad \psi(x_0, \mu_1 \mu_2 \mu_3 \cdots \mu_k) \in T , \quad f(x_{i-1}, \alpha_i, \mu_i) = 1 \quad (1 \le i \le k)\} \ .$$

Define R'' as

$$R'' = \{(\alpha_1, \mu_1)(\alpha_2, \mu_2)(\alpha_3, \mu_3) \cdots (\alpha_k, \mu_k); \quad \alpha_1 \alpha_2 \alpha_3 \cdots \alpha_k \in R \quad (\mu_1 \mu_2 \mu_3 \cdots \mu_k \in K^*)\} \ .$$

Since R is regular, R'' is also regular. The intersection of Q and R'', denoted by R', is also regular.

$$R' = \{(\alpha_1, \mu_1)(\alpha_2, \mu_2)(\alpha_3, \mu_3) \cdots (\alpha_k, \mu_k); \quad \alpha_1 \alpha_2 \alpha_3 \cdots \alpha_k \in R , \quad \psi(x_0, \mu_1 \mu_2 \mu_3 \cdots \mu_k) \in T, \quad f(x_{i-1}, \alpha_i, \mu_i) = 1 \quad (1 \le i \le k)\} \ .$$

R' is the set of all $(\bar{\alpha}, \bar{\mu})$ such that $\bar{\alpha} \in R$ and $\bar{\mu}$ is an execution of $\bar{\alpha}$. Define a homomorphism τ from $\Sigma \times K$ into K as

$$\tau((\alpha, \mu)) = \mu \quad ((\alpha, \mu) \in \Sigma \times K) \ ,$$

and extend the homomorphism in the usual manner

$$\tau(e) = e \ ,$$

$$\tau((\bar{\beta}, \bar{\nu})(\alpha, \mu)) = \tau((\bar{\beta}, \bar{\nu}))\, \tau((\alpha, \mu)) \qquad ((\bar{\beta}, \bar{\nu}) \in (\Sigma \times K)^*, (\alpha, \mu) \in \Sigma \times K) \ .$$

The homomorphic image of a regular set is regular. Therefore, $D_R = \tau(R')$ is regular. Q.E.D.

COROLLARY. *For any regular fuzzy program R with respect to a fuzzy machine $\hat{M}$, $d(R)$ can be effectively computed.*

COROLLARY. *Let E_R denote the set of executable elementary fuzzy programs of a regular fuzzy program R. E_R is regular.*

COROLLARY. *The set of all elementary fuzzy programs executable on $\hat{M}$ and the set of all executions of elementary fuzzy programs in Σ^* are both regular.*

Since $R_1 \supseteq R_2$ implies $D_{R_1} \supseteq D_{R_2}$ and therefore $d(R_1) \geq d(R_2)$, it is clear that $d(\Sigma^*) \geq d(R)$ for any regular fuzzy program R. Σ^* can be regarded to be the fuzziest program. When the fuzzy program is Σ^*, the machine M is subject to no external control, and the experiment of finding an execution for Σ^* reduces to the *homing experiment* [10].

The fuzzy machine M can be modified so that the set of final states T coincides with X. The modification is as follows. Replace M by a new finite-state machine M''

$$M'' = (K \cup \{\mu_T\}, X, \Psi'', x_0, X) \quad ,$$

where: μ_T is a new symbol; and the new transition function Ψ'' is given by

$$\Psi''(x, \mu) = \Psi(x, \mu) \qquad (\mu \in K) \quad ,$$

$$\Psi''(x, \mu_T) = x \quad .$$

Replace the fuzzy machine $\hat{M}$ by $\hat{M}'' = (\Sigma \cup \{\alpha_T\}, M'', f'', \lambda'')$ where f'' and λ'' are given by

$$f''(x, \alpha, \mu) = \begin{cases} f(x, \alpha, \mu), & \text{if } \alpha \in \Sigma \ , \\ 1, & \text{if } \alpha = \alpha_T \ , \ x \in T \ , \text{ and } \mu = \mu_T \ , \\ 0, & \text{otherwise} \ . \end{cases}$$

$$\lambda''(x, \alpha, \mu) = \begin{cases} \lambda(x, \alpha, \mu), & \text{if } \alpha \in \Sigma \ , \\ 1, & \text{otherwise.} \end{cases}$$

The new fuzzy machine $\hat{M}''$ has a new fuzzy instruction α_T which is executable only when M'' is in a state $x \in T$. Its execution is the "dummy" machine instruction μ_T. Hence if we replace a fuzzy program R by $R\alpha_T$, the new fuzzy machine $\hat{M}''$ behaves exactly the same as the old machine.

The discussion above suggests that other *state-testing instructions* $\alpha_A, \alpha_B, \alpha_C, \cdots$, etc. can also be included into the set of fuzzy instructions for the (modified) fuzzy machine $\hat{M}$, where $A, B, C, \cdots$, etc. are subsets of X. The inclusion of such state-testing fuzzy instructions facilitates the writing of fuzzy programs.

For example, the fuzzy program $\alpha_1^* \alpha_{\{x\}} \alpha_2$ can be interpreted as follows: "Execute fuzzy instruction α_1 *several* times until the machine is in state x. Then execute fuzzy instruction α_2." As another example, the fuzzy program $\alpha_1(\alpha_T \alpha_1)^* \alpha_{X-T} \alpha_3$ can be interpreted as "Execute fuzzy instruction α_1; execute α_1 several times when M remains in a state of T; as soon as M enters a state of $X - T$, execute α_3." More concisely, the program can be rewritten as: "label: α_1; *if* $x \in T$ *then go to* label else α_3."

In [13] a systematic technique for translating flowchart programs into regular expressions has been developed. In the present case the flowchart programs can be regarded to be fuzzy flowchart programs. Similar translation technique can be used to obtain the regular expression corresponding to the fuzzy flowchart program.

III. EXECUTION OF FUZZY PROGRAMS

In this section we will describe a procedure for the execution of fuzzy programs. We will then prove that the performance function can be constructed so that the program-execution cost—to be defined below—is minimized.

The natural way to execute a fuzzy program is to select the *most-preferable instruction* at each step of program execution. For example, when $\hat{M}$ is in state x and the instruction α is received, and $f(x, \alpha, \mu_1) = f(x, \alpha, \mu_2) = 1$, $\lambda(x, \alpha, \mu_1) = 0.3$, $\lambda(x, \alpha, \mu_2) = 0.9$, then the machine instruction μ_2 will be selected. If this instruction turns out to be one which does not lead to any execution of the original fuzzy program, then the next-preferable machine instruction μ_1, will be selected, and so on. When all the alternatives have been tried without success, the fuzzy program is declared to be not executable. Therefore, this procedure is an exhaustive search for the execution of a given program. It will be called the *modified simple-execution procedure.* (The *simple-execution procedure* is one which tries *only* the most-preferable instructions [5]).

The modified simple-execution procedure is required to be *consistent* in the following sense: When there are several equally preferable instructions in a given situation, they will be selected in some predetermined order. If the same situation is encountered again, these instructions will again be selected in that predetermined order. In other words, no random selection of equally preferable instructions is allowed.

EXAMPLE 1. The finite-state machine is $M = (\{\mu_1, \mu_2\}, \{x_0, x_1\}, \Psi, x_0, \{x_1\})$ and the transition function Ψ is

Ψ	μ_1	μ_2
x_0	x_1	x_0
x_1	x_0	x_1

The fuzzy machine is $\hat{M} = (\{\alpha_1, \alpha_2\}, M, f, \lambda)$ whose feasibility function f is

f	μ_1	μ_2
(x_0, α_1)	1	1
(x_0, α_2)	0	0
(x_1, α_1)	1	1
(x_1, α_2)	1	1

and the performance function is either λ_1 or λ_2

λ_1	μ_1	μ_2
(x_0, α_1)	1	0
(x_0, α_2)	1	0
(x_1, α_1)	1	0
(x_1, α_2)	1	0

λ_2	μ_1	μ_2
(x_0, α_1)	1	0
(x_0, α_2)	1	0
(x_1, α_1)	0	1
(x_1, α_2)	0	1

Let the fuzzy program be $\overline{\alpha} = \alpha_1 \alpha_2$. The complete search tree is shown in Figure 1. If λ_1 is used, then the sequence of nodes visited by the modified sim-

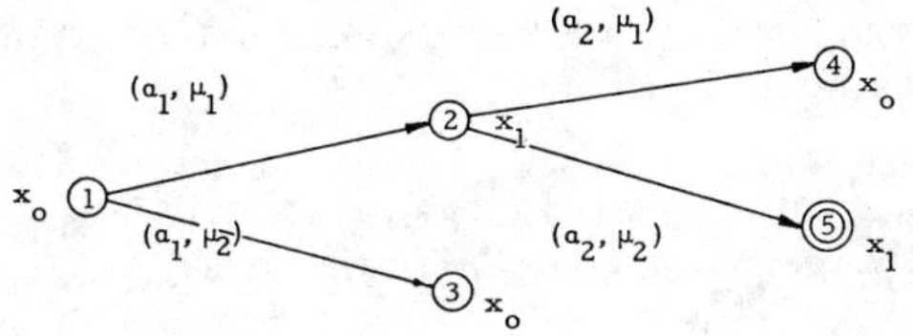

Figure 1.

ple execution procedure is 1245. On the other hand, if λ_2 is used, then the sequence of nodes visited is 125. In the first case three instructions are executed, namely μ_1, μ_1, μ_2. In the second case two instructions are executed and $\overline{\mu} = \mu_1 \mu_2$ is the execution of $\overline{\alpha}$.

The example suggests that the *program-execution cost* may be defined to be *the total cost of executing the instructions being tried in the search process.* The program-execution cost is minimized by selecting a *good* performance function.

DEFINITION 5. *The* modified simple execution procedure *for a fuzzy program R is as follows:*

(1) *If R contains the null string* e *and* $x_0 \in T$, *success exit. Otherwise go to Step 2*
(2) $i \longleftarrow 1$, $x(0) \longleftarrow x_0$, $R(0) \longleftarrow R$ (*the* $R(i)$ *are sets*)
(3) $P(i) \longleftarrow \{(\alpha, \mu)$: $\alpha\overline{\alpha}$ *in* $R(i-1)$ *for some* $\overline{\alpha}$ *in* Σ^*, μ *in* $K\}$ (*the* $P(i)$ *are sets*)
(4) *Select* (α, μ) *in* $P(i)$ *such that* $f(x(i-1), \alpha, \mu) = 1$ *and* $\lambda(x(i-1), \alpha, \mu) \geq \lambda(x(i-1), \alpha', \mu') \times f(x(i-1), \alpha', \mu')$ *for all other* (α', μ') *in* $P(i)$. *If there is such* (α, μ), *go to Step 5. Otherwise go to Step 8*
(5) $\mu(i) \longleftarrow \mu$, $x(i) \longleftarrow \psi(x(i-1), \mu)$, $P(i) \longleftarrow P(i) - \{(\alpha, \mu)\}$, $R(i) \longleftarrow \{\overline{\alpha}$: $\alpha\overline{\alpha}$ *in* $R(i-1)$ *and* $\overline{\alpha}$ *in* $\Sigma^*\}$
(6) *If* $R(i)$ *contains the null string* e *and* $x(i) \in T$, *go to Step 7. If* $R(i)$ *contains the null string* e *and* $x(i) \notin T$, *go to Step 4. Otherwise,* $i \longleftarrow i + 1$ *and go to Step 3*
(7) *Success exit. The execution is* $\mu(1)\mu(2)\mu(3) \cdots \mu(i)$
(8) $i \longleftarrow i - 1$. *If* $i = 0$, *failure exit. Otherwise, go to Step 4.*

In order to define the complete search tree formally, the nodes of the tree will be represented by $(\overline{\alpha}, \overline{\mu})$ pairs, and the branches by (α, μ) pairs, as shown in Figure 2.

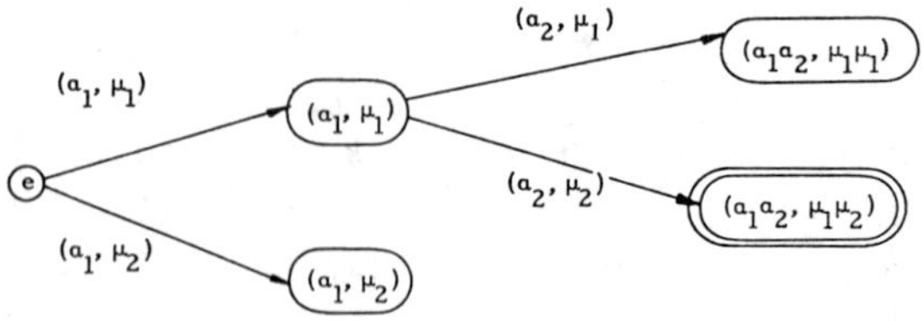

Figure 2.

DEFINITION 6. *Let $\hat{M}$ be the fuzzy machine and let R be a fuzzy program for $\hat{M}$. The* complete search tree Γ_R *for R is a rooted tree (V, E), where V is the set of nodes and E is the set of branches*

$$V = \{(\alpha_1, \mu_1)(\alpha_2, \mu_2)(\alpha_3, \mu_3) \cdots (\alpha_k, \mu_k): \alpha_1 \alpha_2 \alpha_3 \cdots \alpha_k \text{ in } R, \\ \mu_1 \mu_2 \mu_3 \cdots \mu_k \text{ in } K^* \text{ and for all } i \ (1 \le i \le k),\ f(x_{i-1}, \alpha_i, \mu_i) = 1, \\ x_i = \psi(x_{i-1}, \mu_i)\} \ ,$$

$$B = \{((\alpha_1, \mu_1)(\alpha_2, \mu_2)(\alpha_3, \mu_3) \cdots (\alpha_{k-1}, \mu_{k-1}), (\alpha_1, \mu_1)(\alpha_2, \mu_2)(\alpha_3, \mu_3) \\ \cdots (\alpha_k, \mu_k)): (\alpha_1, \mu_1)(\alpha_2, \mu_2)(\alpha_3, \mu_3) \cdots (\alpha_{k-1}, \mu_{k-1}) \text{ and } (\alpha_1, \mu_1) \\ (\alpha_2, \mu_2)(\alpha_3, \mu_3) \cdots (\alpha_k, \mu_k) \text{ are in } V \text{ and } f(\psi(x_0, \mu_1 \mu_2 \mu_3 \cdots \mu_{k-1}), \\ \alpha_k, \mu_k) = 1\} \ .$$

The node $((\alpha_1, \mu_1)(\alpha_2, \mu_2)(\alpha_3, \mu_3) \cdots (\alpha_k, \mu_k))$ is associated with the state $\Psi(x_0, \mu_1 \mu_2 \mu_3 \cdots \mu_k)$, and the branch $((\alpha_1, \mu_1)(\alpha_2, \mu_2)(\alpha_3, \mu_3) \cdots (\alpha_{k-1}, \mu_{k-1}),$ $(\alpha_1, \mu_1)(\alpha_2, \mu_2)(\alpha_3, \mu_3) \cdots (\alpha_k, \mu_k))$ is associated with the pair (α_k, μ_k).

DEFINITION 7. *Let c_{μ_i} be the cost of execution for μ_i in K ($c_{\mu_i} \ge 0$). The* program execution cost C_{pec} *of the executable fuzzy program R with respect to a fuzzy machine $\hat{M}$ using the modified simple-execution procedure is*

$$C_{\text{pec}} = \sum_{\substack{((\alpha_1, \mu_1) \cdots (\alpha_{k-1}, \mu_{k-1}), (\alpha_1, \mu_1) \cdots (\alpha_k, \mu_k)) \\ \text{in } B'}} c_{\mu_k} \ , \tag{3.1}$$

where B' is the set of branches in the complete search tree Γ_R which are visited by the procedure before it terminates and finds an execution for R.

Equation (3.1) can be rewritten as follows. Define a cost matrix $\mathbf{c}$ for the pair $(\overline{\alpha}, \overline{\mu})$ as

$$\mathbf{c} = \begin{array}{c} \\ (\alpha_{j_1}, \mu_{j_1}) \\ (\alpha_{j_2}, \mu_{j_2}) \\ \cdot \\ \cdot \\ \cdot \\ (\alpha_{j_m}, \mu_{j_m}) \end{array} \begin{array}{c} (x_0, \alpha_1, \mu_1) \quad (x_1, \alpha_2, \mu_2) \quad \cdots \quad (x_{n-1}, \alpha_n, \mu_n) \\ \begin{bmatrix} C_{1j_1} & C_{2j_1} & \cdots & C_{nj_1} \\ C_{1j_2} & C_{2j_2} & \cdots & C_{nj_2} \\ \cdot & \cdot & \cdot & \cdot \\ \cdot & \cdot & \cdot & \cdot \\ \cdot & \cdot & \cdot & \cdot \\ C_{1j_m} & C_{2j_m} & \cdots & C_{nj_m} \end{bmatrix} \end{array} , \tag{3.2}$$

where

$$C_{ijk} = \begin{cases} \text{cost of executing all instructions in the subtree starting from node } ((\alpha_1, \mu_1) \cdots (\alpha_{i-1}, \mu_{i-1})) \text{ and the first branch in the subtree is } (\alpha_{jk}, \mu_{jk}), & \text{if } \alpha_i = \alpha_{jk},\ \mu_i \neq \mu_{jk},\ f(x_{i-1}, \alpha_i, \mu_{jk}) = 1, \\ c_{\mu_{jk}}, & \text{if } \alpha_i = \alpha_{jk} \text{ and } \mu_i = \mu_{jk}, \\ 0, & \text{otherwise}, \end{cases} \tag{3.3}$$

and $(\alpha_{j_1}, \mu_{j_1}), (\alpha_{j_2}, \mu_{j_2}), (\alpha_{j_3}, \mu_{j_3}), \cdots (\alpha_{j_m}, \mu_{j_m})$ are all the possible pairs from $\Sigma \times K$.

Suppose $(\bar{\alpha}, \bar{\mu})$ is the pair of fuzzy program and machine program selected by the modified simple-execution procedure, then the program execution cost is

$$C_{\text{pec}} = \sum_{i=1}^{n} \sum_{k=1}^{m} C_{ijk}\, a_{ijk}, \tag{3.4}$$

where

$$a_{ijk} = \begin{cases} 1, & \text{if } \lambda(x_{i-1}, \alpha_i, \mu_i) \leq \lambda(x_{i-1}, \alpha_i, \mu_{jk}), \\ 0, & \text{otherwise}. \end{cases} \tag{3.5}$$

EXAMPLE 2. The cost matrix for $\bar{\alpha} = \alpha_1 \alpha_2$ and the fuzzy machine $\hat{M}$ defined in Example 1 is

$$\mathbf{c} = \begin{array}{c} \\ (\alpha_1, \mu_1) \\ (\alpha_1, \mu_2) \\ (\alpha_2, \mu_1) \\ (\alpha_2, \mu_2) \end{array} \begin{array}{c} (x_0, \alpha_1, \mu_1) \quad (x_1, \alpha_2, \mu_2) \\ \begin{bmatrix} c_{\mu_1} & 0 \\ c_{\mu_2} & 0 \\ 0 & c_{\mu_1} \\ 0 & c_{\mu_2} \end{bmatrix} \end{array}.$$

When λ_1 is used, since $\lambda_1(x_0, \alpha_1, \mu_1) > \lambda_1(x_0, \alpha_1, \mu_2)$ and $\lambda_1(x_1, \alpha_2, \mu_1) > \lambda_1(x_1, \alpha_2, \mu_2)$, the program-execution cost is

$$C_{\text{pec}} = c_{\mu_1} + c_{\mu_1} + c_{\mu_2}.$$

When λ_2 is used, since $\lambda_2(x_0, \alpha_1, \mu_1) > \lambda_2(x_0, \alpha_1, \mu_2)$ and $\lambda_2(x_1, \alpha_2, \mu_1) < \lambda_2(x_1, \alpha_2, \mu_2)$, the program-execution cost is

$$C_{\text{pec}} = c_{\mu_1} + c_{\mu_2}.$$

DEFINITION 8. *For a given fuzzy machine $\hat{M}$ and a given executable fuzzy program R, the performance function which yields the minimum program execution cost C_{pec} is called the* optimum-performance function, *denoted by λ_{op}.*

Given a cost matrix, we can construct a performance function so that the program-execution cost is minimized. The technique is described in [5]. There is a cost matrix $\mathbf{c}$ for each pair $(\bar{\alpha}, \bar{\mu})$ in R', where R' is defined as

$$R' = \{(\bar{\alpha}, \bar{\mu}) \colon \bar{\alpha} \in R \text{ and } \bar{\mu} \text{ is an execution of } \bar{\alpha}\}. \tag{3.6}$$

If R is finite, then R' is finite and the number of cost matrices is finite. Now some $(\bar{\alpha}, \bar{\mu}) \in R'$ may never be selected by the modified simple-execution procedure. Such nonexecutable $(\bar{\alpha}, \bar{\mu})$ should be disregarded.

DEFINITION 9. *If* $(\bar{\alpha}, \bar{\mu}) \in R'$ *can never be selected by the modified simple-execution procedure no matter what* λ *is used, then it is called* nonexecutable.

DEFINITION 10. *The* modified-cost matrix $\mathbf{c}'$ *is obtained from* $\mathbf{c}$ *as follows*

$$C'_{ij_k} = \begin{cases} \infty \, , & \text{if } (\alpha_{j_k}, \mu_{j_k}) \neq (\alpha_i, \mu_i) \text{ and } (\alpha_1, \mu_1) \cdots (\alpha_{i-1}, \mu_{i-1}) \\ & (\alpha_{j_k}, \mu_{j_k}) \text{ is prefix of another } (\bar{\alpha}', \bar{\mu}') \text{ in } R' \, , \\ C_{ij_k} \, , & \text{otherwise} \, . \end{cases} \tag{3.7}$$

LEMMA 2. $(\bar{\alpha}, \bar{\mu}) \in R'$ *is nonexecutable, iff either*: (*a*) *The minimum cost* C_{pec} *for the modified cost matrix* $\mathbf{c}'$ *is infinite; or* (*b*) *there is* $(\bar{\alpha}'', \bar{\mu}'')$ *in* R' *such that* $(\bar{\alpha}'', \bar{\mu}'')$ *is a prefix of* $(\bar{\alpha}, \bar{\mu})$.

Proof. If C_{pec} is infinite, then some term C_{ij_k} which is included in the sum Eq. (3.4) with nonzero a_{ij_k} is infinite. This implies that at the ith stage, the pair $(\alpha_{j_k}, \mu_{j_k})$ is selected before the pair (α_i, μ_i) is selected, and $(\alpha_1, \mu_1)(\alpha_2, \mu_2)(\alpha_3, \mu_3) \cdots (\alpha_{i-1}, \mu_{i-1})(\alpha_{j_k}, \mu_{j_k})$ is the prefix of another $(\bar{\alpha}', \bar{\mu}')$ in R'. Hence $(\bar{\alpha}', \bar{\mu}')$ instead of $(\bar{\alpha}, \bar{\mu})$ will be selected by the modified simple-execution procedure. Since C_{pec} is infinite for all λ, $(\bar{\alpha}, \bar{\mu})$ can never be selected and is nonexecutable.

If $(\bar{\alpha}'', \bar{\mu}'')$ is in R' and is the prefix of $(\bar{\alpha}, \bar{\mu})$, then in the complete search tree Γ_R, the node $(\bar{\alpha}'', \bar{\mu}'')$ is a predecessor of the node $(\bar{\alpha}, \bar{\mu})$. If node $(\bar{\alpha}'', \bar{\mu}'')$ is never selected, then $(\bar{\alpha}, \bar{\mu})$ will also never be selected. If $(\bar{\alpha}'', \bar{\mu}'')$ is selected, then since $(\bar{\alpha}'', \bar{\mu}'')$ is in R', the procedure should terminate and select $(\bar{\alpha}'', \bar{\mu}'')$. In either case $(\bar{\alpha}, \bar{\mu})$ is not selected. Hence it is nonexecutable.

Conversely, if the minimum cost C_{pec} is finite for some $\mathbf{c}'$ and $(\bar{\alpha}, \bar{\mu})$ has no prefix $(\bar{\alpha}'', \bar{\mu}'')$ in R', then for some performance function λ, the procedure will be able to select $(\bar{\alpha}, \bar{\mu})$ without being misled to select another $(\bar{\alpha}', \bar{\mu}')$. Therefore, $(\bar{\alpha}, \bar{\mu})$ is not nonexecutable. Q.E.D.

LEMMA 3. *If* R' *is finite and nonempty, then not all* $(\bar{\alpha}, \bar{\mu})$ *in* R' *are nonexecutable.*

Proof. Assume that all $(\bar{\alpha}, \bar{\mu})$ in R' are nonexecutable. By Lemma 2, either $(\bar{\alpha}, \bar{\mu})$ has a prefix $(\bar{\alpha}'', \bar{\mu}'')$ in R', or the minimum cost C_{pec} for $(\bar{\alpha}, \bar{\mu})$ is infinite. If every $(\bar{\alpha}, \bar{\mu})$ has a prefix in R', then the null string e must be in R'. But then the procedure can always select e as a trivial execution, a contradiction. Therefore, there exists $(\bar{\alpha}, \bar{\mu})$ in R' with no prefix $(\bar{\alpha}'', \bar{\mu}'')$ in R'. Denote the set of such $(\bar{\alpha}, \bar{\mu})$ by G. G is nonempty, and finite because R' is finite. Those $(\bar{\alpha}, \bar{\mu})$ with prefix in R' are clearly nonexecutable. Hence we may focus our attention on G. Since R is executable and since G is finite, some $(\bar{\alpha}, \bar{\mu})$ in G must be selected by the modified simple execution procedure. (Suppose not. The procedure will finally encounter some $(\bar{\alpha}', \bar{\mu}')$ not in G. By definition, $(\bar{\alpha}', \bar{\mu}')$ must have a prefix $(\bar{\alpha}, \bar{\mu})$ in G. That $(\bar{\alpha}, \bar{\mu})$ will be selected by the procedure.) Thus $(\bar{\alpha}, \bar{\mu})$ is not nonexecutable. A contradiction. Q.E.D.

By Lemma 2, the nonexecutable $(\bar{\alpha}, \bar{\mu})$ in R' can be found effectively. They may be disregarded. For the remaining $(\bar{\alpha}, \bar{\mu})$ in R', we can first construct a modified-cost matrix for each $(\bar{\alpha}, \bar{\mu})$, then find the performance function $\lambda_{\text{op}}^{(\bar{\alpha}, \bar{\mu})}$ for this $(\bar{\alpha}, \bar{\mu})$ which yields minimum cost $C_{\text{pec}}^{(\bar{\alpha}, \bar{\mu})}$. The optimum-performance function λ_{op} is the $\lambda_{\text{op}}^{(\bar{\alpha}, \bar{\mu})}$ which yields the smallest $C_{\text{pec}}^{(\bar{\alpha}, \bar{\mu})}$ of all $(\bar{\alpha}, \bar{\mu}) \in R'$. When R is finite, R' is finite and by Lemma 3, the optimum λ_{op} exists.

Thus we have proved that:

THEOREM 4. *For any finite executable regular fuzzy program* R, λ_{op} *can be constructed effectively.*

When R is infinite, the modified simple execution procedure may not terminate.

EXAMPLE 3. The machine is $M = (\{\mu_1, \mu_2\}, \{x_0, x_1\}, \psi, x_0, \{x_1\})$, and the fuzzy machine is $\hat{M} = (\{\alpha_1, \alpha_2\}, M, f, \lambda)$ where ψ, f, λ are

ψ	μ_1	μ_2
x_0	x_0	x_1
x_1	x_1	x_1

f	μ_1	μ_2
(x_0, α_1)	1	0
(x_0, α_2)	0	1
(x_1, α_1)	0	0
(x_1, α_2)	0	0

λ	μ_1	μ_2
(x_0, α_1)	1.0	0.5
(x_0, α_2)	0	0
(x_1, α_1)	0	0
(x_1, α_2)	0	0

If $R = (\alpha_1)^* \alpha_2$, then $D_R = (\mu_1)^* \mu_2$ and $E_R = R$. The search tree is as shown in Figure 3. Since $\lambda(x_0, \alpha_1, \mu_1) > \lambda(x_0, \alpha_2, \mu_2)$, (α_1, μ_1) will always be selected

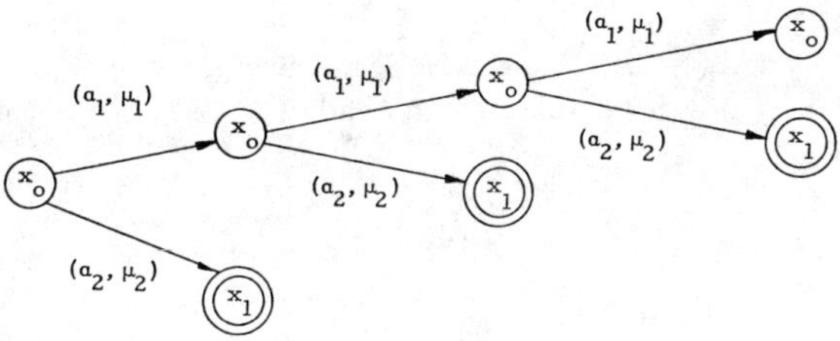

Figure 3.

and the procedure never terminates. However, if we choose $\lambda(x_0, \alpha_1, \mu_1) = 0.5$ and $\lambda(x_0, \alpha_2, \mu_2) = 1.0$, then the procedure terminates with the execution $\bar{\mu} = \mu_2$ and the program execution cost is $C_{pec} = c_{\mu_2}$.

The above example shows that the program execution cost may be undefined if the procedure fails to terminate. In this case an infinite number of instructions will be executed, and B' of Definition 7 is infinite. Therefore, Definition 7 should be modified as follows

$$C_{pec} = \begin{cases} \displaystyle\sum_{\substack{((\alpha_1,\mu_1)\cdots(\alpha_{k-1},\mu_{k-1}),(\alpha_1,\mu_1)\cdots(\alpha_k,\mu_k)) \\ \text{in } B'}} c_{\mu_k}, & \text{if } B' \text{ is finite} , \\ \infty, & \text{otherwise} . \end{cases} \tag{3.8}$$

Note that if $c_{\mu_j} > 0$ for all $\mu_j \in K$, then Eq. (3.8) is the same as Equation (3.1).

We now prove that except for a finite subset of R', $(\bar{\alpha}, \bar{\mu}) \in R'$ is always nonexecutable.

NOTATION. Let A^n be the finite regular set obtained from R' by replacing all the closure operators by positive integers less than or equal to n. For example, if $R' = (a^* + b)^*$, then $A^2 = \{e, (a + b), (a + b)^2, (a^2 + b), (a^2 + b)^2\}$. Clearly $A^n \subseteq R'$. In what follows, $n = |X|$.

LEMMA 5. *If $(\bar{\alpha}, \bar{\mu})$ is in $R' - A^n$, then $(\bar{\alpha}, \bar{\mu})$ is nonexecutable.*

Proof. Since $(\bar{\alpha}, \bar{\mu})$ is not in A^n, it is in A^ℓ for some $\ell > n$. Let ℓ be the smallest such integer. $(\bar{\alpha}, \bar{\mu})$ is, therefore, contained in an expression of the form

$$(\bar{\alpha}', \bar{\mu}')((\bar{\alpha}^1, \bar{\mu}^1) + (\bar{\alpha}^2, \bar{\mu}^2) + (\bar{\alpha}^3, \bar{\mu}^3) + \cdots + (\bar{\alpha}^k, \bar{\mu}^k))^\ell (\bar{\alpha}'', \bar{\mu}'') .$$

The pair $(\bar{\alpha}, \bar{\mu})$ is of the following form

$$(\bar{\alpha}, \bar{\mu}) = x_0(\bar{\alpha}', \bar{\mu}')_{x_1}(\bar{\alpha}_1, \bar{\mu}_1)_{x_2} \cdots {}_{x_i}(\bar{\alpha}_i, \bar{\mu}_i) \cdots {}_{x_j}(\bar{\alpha}_j, \bar{\mu}_j) \cdots$$

$$_{x_\ell}(\bar{\alpha}_\ell, \bar{\mu}_\ell)_{x_{\ell+1}}(\bar{\alpha}'', \bar{\mu}'') ,$$

where $(\bar{\alpha}_1, \bar{\mu}_1), (\bar{\alpha}_2, \bar{\mu}_2), (\bar{\alpha}_3, \bar{\mu}_3), \cdots, (\bar{\alpha}_\ell, \bar{\mu}_\ell)$ are in $\{(\bar{\alpha}^1, \bar{\mu}^1), (\bar{\alpha}^2, \bar{\mu}^2), (\bar{\alpha}^3, \bar{\mu}^3), \cdots, (\bar{\alpha}^k, \bar{\mu}^k)\}$. Since $\ell > n$, the number of states of M, there are indices i and j, $1 \leq i < j \leq \ell + 1$ such that $x_i = x_j$. We can form two new pairs $(\bar{\alpha}''', \bar{\mu}''')$ and $(\bar{\alpha}^{iv}, \bar{\mu}^{iv})$ as

$$(\bar{\alpha}''', \bar{\mu}''') = {}_{x_0}(\bar{\alpha}', \bar{\mu}')_{x_1}(\bar{\alpha}_1, \bar{\mu}_1) \cdots {}_{x_i}(\bar{\alpha}_j, \bar{\mu}_j)_{x_{j+1}} \cdots {}_{x_\ell}(\bar{\alpha}_\ell, \bar{\mu}_\ell)_{x_{\ell+1}}(\bar{\alpha}'', \bar{\mu}'') ,$$

$$(\bar{\alpha}^{iv}, \bar{\mu}^{iv}) = {}_{x_0}(\bar{\alpha}', \bar{\mu}')_{x_1}(\bar{\alpha}_1, \bar{\mu}_1) \cdots {}_{x_i}(\bar{\alpha}_i, \bar{\mu}_i)_{x_{i+1}} \cdots {}_{x_j}(\bar{\alpha}_i, \bar{\mu}_i)_{x_{i+1}} \cdots$$

$$_{x_j}(\bar{\alpha}_j, \bar{\mu}_j) \cdots {}_{x_\ell}(\bar{\alpha}_\ell, \bar{\mu}_\ell)_{x_{\ell+1}}(\bar{\alpha}'', \bar{\mu}'') ,$$

Both $(\bar{\alpha}''', \bar{\mu}''')$ and $(\bar{\alpha}^{iv}, \bar{\mu}^{iv})$ are in R'. We now proceed to show that either $(\bar{\alpha}''', \bar{\mu}''')$ or $(\bar{\alpha}^{iv}, \bar{\mu}^{iv})$ will be selected instead of $(\bar{\alpha}, \bar{\mu})$. We compare the string

$$(\bar{\alpha}_i, \bar{\mu}_i)(\bar{\alpha}_{i+1}, \bar{\mu}_{i+1}) \cdots (\bar{\alpha}'', \bar{\mu}'') ,$$

with the string

$$(\bar{\alpha}_j, \bar{\mu}_j)(\bar{\alpha}_{j+1}, \bar{\mu}_{j+1}) \cdots (\bar{\alpha}'', \bar{\mu}'') ,$$

and two cases are possible:

CASE 1: $(\bar{\alpha}_j, \bar{\mu}_j) \cdots (\bar{\alpha}'', \bar{\mu}'')$ is prefix of $(\bar{\alpha}_i, \bar{\mu}_i) \cdots (\bar{\alpha}'', \bar{\mu}'')$. In this case, $(\bar{\alpha}''', \bar{\mu}''')$ is the prefix of $(\bar{\alpha}, \bar{\mu})$ and both are in R'. Clearly, $(\bar{\alpha}''', \bar{\mu}''')$ will be selected instead of $(\bar{\alpha}, \bar{\mu})$.

CASE 2: $(\bar{\alpha}_j, \bar{\mu}_j) \cdots (\bar{\alpha}'', \bar{\mu}'')$ is not the prefix of $(\bar{\alpha}_i, \bar{\mu}_i) \cdots (\bar{\alpha}'', \bar{\mu}'')$. In this case, they must differ at some (α, μ). We can assume $(\bar{\alpha}_j, \bar{\mu}_j) \cdots (\bar{\alpha}'', \bar{\mu}'')$ to be of the form $(\bar{\beta}, \bar{v})(\alpha, \mu)(\bar{\beta}', \bar{v}')$ and $(\bar{\alpha}_i, \bar{\mu}_i) \cdots (\bar{\alpha}'', \bar{\mu}'')$ to be of the form $(\bar{\beta}, \bar{v})(\alpha', \mu')(\bar{\beta}'', \bar{v}'')$, with $(\alpha, \mu) \neq (\alpha', \mu')$. Therefore, we can compare $(\bar{\alpha}, \bar{\mu})$ and $(\bar{\alpha}''', \bar{\mu}''')$, or $(\bar{\alpha}, \bar{\mu})$ and $(\bar{\alpha}^{iv}, \bar{\mu}^{iv})$

$$(\bar{\alpha}, \bar{\mu}) = {}_{x_0}(\bar{\alpha}', \bar{\mu}')_{x_1}(\bar{\alpha}_1, \bar{\mu}_1) \cdots {}_{x_i}(\bar{\beta}, \bar{v})_x \underline{(\alpha, \mu)}_{x'}(\bar{\beta}'', \bar{v}'') ,$$

$$(\bar{\alpha}''', \bar{\mu}''') = {}_{x_0}(\bar{\alpha}', \bar{\mu}')_{x_1}(\bar{\alpha}_1, \bar{\mu}_1) \cdots {}_{x_i}(\bar{\beta}, \bar{v})_x \underline{(\alpha', \mu')}_{x''}(\bar{\beta}', \bar{v}') ,$$

$$(\bar{\alpha}, \bar{\mu}) = {}_{x_0}(\bar{\alpha}', \bar{\mu}')_{x_1}(\bar{\alpha}_1, \bar{\mu}_1) \cdots {}_{x_j}(\bar{\beta}, \bar{v})_x \underline{(\alpha', \mu')}_{x''}(\bar{\beta}', \bar{v}') ,$$

$$(\bar{\alpha}^{iv}, \bar{\mu}^{iv}) = {}_{x_0}(\bar{\alpha}', \bar{\mu}')_{x_1}(\bar{\alpha}_1, \bar{\mu}_1) \cdots {}_{x_j}(\bar{\beta}, \bar{v})_x \underline{(\alpha, \mu)}_{x'}(\bar{\beta}'', \bar{v}'') .$$

Since the procedure is consistent, when M is in state x, either (α, μ) is always selected or (α', μ') is always selected. But this implies that either $(\bar{\alpha}''', \bar{\mu}''')$ is selected or $(\bar{\alpha}^{iv}, \bar{\mu}^{iv})$ is selected instead of $(\bar{\alpha}, \bar{\mu})$. So $(\bar{\alpha}, \bar{\mu})$ is nonexecutable. Q.E.D.

Lemma 5 says that no $(\bar{\alpha}, \bar{\mu})$ in $R' - A^n$ can ever be selected by the modified simple-execution procedure, no matter what λ is used. Therefore, the procedure either terminates and selects some $(\bar{\alpha}, \bar{\mu})$ in the finite set A^n, or enters an endless loop. Whenever the procedure encounters an $(\bar{\alpha}, \bar{\mu})$ in $R' - A^n$, it has entered an endless loop.

Therefore:

THEOREM 6. *For a given fuzzy machine $\hat{M}$ and a given fuzzy program R, it is decidable whether the modified simple-execution procedure will terminate or not.*

By Lemma 5, only $(\overline{\alpha}, \overline{\mu})$ in A^n can possibly be selected. Since this set A^n is finite, by Theorem 4, λ_{op} can be effectively constructed. Thus we have the following theorem.

THEOREM 7. *For any executable regular fuzzy program R, λ_{op} can be effectively constructed.*

IV. EXECUTION OF ELEMENTARY FUZZY PROGRAMS

If the fuzzy program is an elementary fuzzy program of the form $\overline{\alpha} = \alpha_1 \alpha_2 \alpha_3 \cdots \alpha_n$, then there is a simple procedure to construct the optimum performance function from the cost matrix. The details are described in [5]. Moreover, the performance function can be constructed by updating a *learning matrix*. The updating procedure amounts to adding *correction vectors* to columns of the learning matrix. It resembles the learning procedure of a linear learning machine [17]. In [5] it is proved that, if every elementary fuzzy program in a *training set* has at most one execution, then the optimum-performance function is the one constructed by updating the learning matrix. Therefore, we can construct an *adaptive fuzzy machine* which can adjust its behavior by updating its learning matrix as it executes new fuzzy programs. Such notions are quite interesting, because the problem solver can not only execute fuzzy programs, but also learn from its experience in executing fuzzy programs.

Even when the fuzzy programs are not elementary, we still can include the learning matrix into an experimental problem-solving system so that it has an adaptable performance function. In Section V, several experimental problem-solving systems using the concepts described above will be discussed.

V. APPLICATIONS

A. Interpretation of Fuzzy Line Drawings

One of the problems in automated line-drawing analysis is to construct a cleaner drawing from the original drawing. For example, a chemist using an interactive chemical structure-analysis system will usually draw a rough sketch of the chemical structure on a tablet or a display device. It is desirable to obtain a cleaner version of the rough sketch so that the cleaner drawing can be redisplayed. The cleaner drawing can also be output through a plotter, a magnetic-film recorder, or a photocomposer. In this way clean copies are obtained.

A line drawing is just a collection of line segments. Therefore, it can be coded into a sequence of elementary line strokes [9]. In other words, it can be regarded to be an ''elementary fuzzy program.'' The problem of obtaining a clean drawing from the fuzzy drawing can then be thought of as one of finding an execution of the encoded elementary fuzzy program. In this case the execution is just another sequence of elementary line strokes. The ''context'' of a fuzzy line stroke determines the "state" of the machine. Given the "context" (the state") and the fuzzy line stroke (the "fuzzy instruction"), the best interpretation (the "machine instruction" with the highest rating) can be found. The validity of this interpretation is tested by prototype matching and structure analysis of the line drawing. Those interpretations that are invalid are rejected, and another interpretation must be found. The failure exit is taken when all the interpretations have been tried without success. It is clear that the system is a specific example of the "modified simple-execution procedure." The "prototypes" and "structures" must first be specified. For the interpretation of chemical structure diagrams, the "prototypes" are all kinds of polygons and the "structures" are all kinds of diagrams generated by interconnecting those polygons. For different kinds of drawings the specification may be different. Thus the system is quite general and can interpret different kinds of drawings.

An experimental program for fuzzy line-drawing interpretation has been written and some examples for the interpretation of interconnected polygons are shown in Figure 4. The program is described in detail in [6] and the structure-analysis

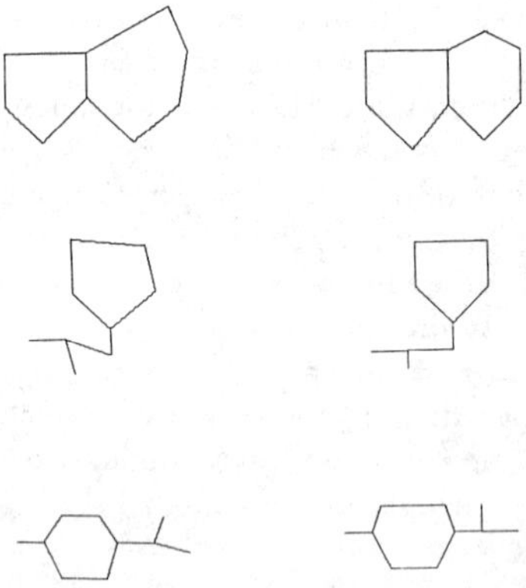

Figure 4.

method is described in [4]. The program is able to construct its own performance function through updating the learning matrix using the method described in [5]. It is hoped that this will enable the program to cope with the idiosyncrasy of the individual user of the system and will also reduce the program-execution time.

B. Simulation of Human Drivers

A FORTRAN program was written to simulate the behavior of a driver. A typical set of driving instructions is shown in Figure 5. The initial position is given (the last parameter being the initial direction of the driver) and a typical map is shown in Figure 6. It is easy to see that the program is indeed a fuzzy program. Let the fuzzy instructions be

α_{go}: Go straight one mile

α_R: Turn right

α_L: Turn right

```
THE INSTRUCTIONS

   1      GO STRAIGHT
   2      TURN RIGHT
   3      GO STRAIGHT
   4      TURN RIGHT
   5      GO 20 MILES UNTIL (AHEAD LIGHT)
   6      TURN LEFT
   7      GO STRAIGHT
   8      TURN RIGHT
   9      GO STRAIGHT UNTIL (RIGHT RESTAURANT)
  10      STOP

INITIAL POSITION

( 13 , 36 ,  3 )
```

Figure 5.

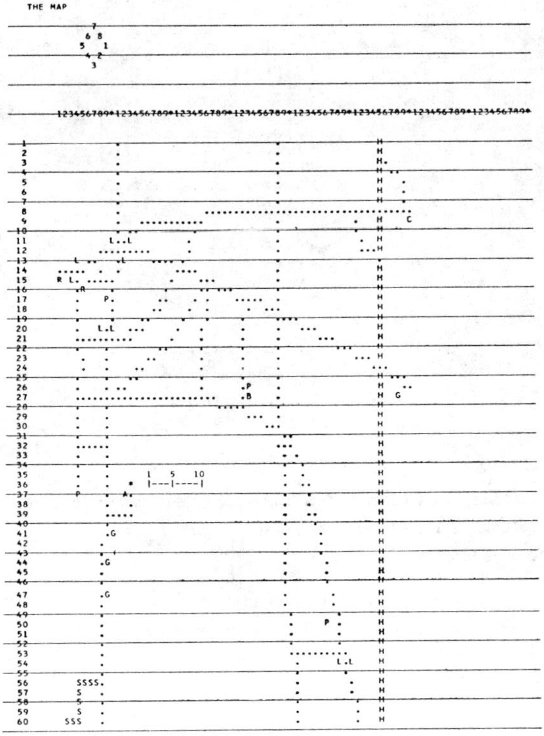

Figure 6.

a_S: Stop the car

a_{LIGHT} : State-testing instruction; there is traffic light ahead

a_{R-R} : State-testing instruction; there is restaurant at right,

then the fuzzy program for the set of driving instructions given in Fig. 5 is

$$\overline{a} = a_{\text{go}}^* \, a_R \, a_{\text{go}}^* \, a_R \, a_{\text{go}}^{17} \, a_{\text{go}}^* \, a_{\text{LIGHT}} \, a_L \, a_{\text{go}}^* \, a_R \, a_{\text{go}}^* \, a_{R-R} \, a_S \; .$$

Again, a modified simple execution procedure is used. In Fig. 7 the wandering path of the driver is shown, where "FUZZY" indicates that several alternatives exist, and "BACK UP" indicates that the driver is forced to turn back for

ACTION	INSTRUCTION	POSITION	LAMBDA
	~~(1) TIME= 0~~	~~(13 , 36 , 3)~~	~~S= 6~~
BACK UP	(2) TIME= 0	(13 , 37 , 3)	S=-1
	(1) TIME= 1	(13 , 37 , 3)	S= 6
~~BACK UP~~	~~(2) TIME= 0~~	~~(13 , 38 , 3)~~	~~S=-1~~
FUZZY	(1) TIME= 1	(13 , 38 , 3)	S= 6
	(2) TIME= 0	(13 , 39 , 3)	S= 4
	~~(3) TIME= 0~~	~~(12 , 39 , 5)~~	~~S= 6~~
BACK UP	(4) TIME= 0	(11 , 39 , 5)	S=-1
	(3) TIME= 1	(11 , 39 , 5)	S= 6
~~BACK UP~~	~~(4) TIME= 0~~	~~(10 , 39 , 5)~~	~~S=-1~~
FUZZY	(3) TIME= 1	(10 , 39 , 5)	S= 6
	(4) TIME= 0	(9 , 39 , 5)	S= 4
	~~(5) TIME= 0~~	~~(9 , 38 , 7)~~	~~S= 3~~
	(5) TIME= 1	(9 , 37 , 7)	S= 3
	(5) TIME= 1	(9 , 36 , 7)	S= 3
	~~(5) TIME= 1~~	~~(9 , 35 , 7)~~	~~S= 3~~
	(5) TIME= 1	(9 , 34 , 7)	S= 3
FUZZY	(5) TIME= 1	(9 , 33 , 7)	S= 3
~~FUZZY~~	~~(5) TIME= 1~~	~~(9 , 32 , 7)~~	~~S= 3~~
	(5) TIME= 1	(9 , 31 , 7)	S= 3
	(5) TIMF= 1	(9 , 30 , 7)	S= 3
	~~(5) TIME= 1~~	~~(9 , 29 , 7)~~	~~S= 3~~
FUZZY	(5) TIME= 1	(9 , 28 , 7)	S= 3
FUZZY	(5) TIME= 1	(9 , 27 , 7)	S= 3
	~~(5) TIME= 1~~	~~(9 , 26 , 7)~~	~~S= 3~~
	(5) TIME= 1	(9 , 25 , 7)	S= 3
	(5) TIME= 1	(9 , 24 , 7)	S= 3
	~~(5) TIME= 1~~	~~(9 , 23 , 7)~~	~~S= 3~~
FUZZY	(5) TIME= 1	(9 , 22 , 7)	S= 9
	(6) TIME= 0	(9 , 21 , 7)	S= 4
	~~(7) TIME= 0~~	~~(8 , 21 , 5)~~	~~S= 6~~
BACK UP	(8) TIME= 0	(7 , 21 , 5)	S=-1
	(7) TIME= 1	(7 , 21 , 5)	S= 6
~~BACK UP~~	~~(8) TIME= 0~~	~~(6 , 21 , 5)~~	~~S=-1~~
	(7) TIME= 1	(6 , 21 , 5)	S= 6
BACK UP	(8) TIME= 0	(5 , 21 , 5)	S=-1
~~FUZZY~~	~~(7) TIME= 1~~	~~(5 , 21 , 5)~~	~~S= 6~~
	(8) TIME= 0.	(4 , 21 , 5)	S= 4
	(9) TIME= 0	(4 , 20 , 7)	S= 3
	~~(9) TIME= 1~~	~~(4 , 19 , 7)~~	~~S= 3~~
	(9) TIME= 1	(4 , 18 , 7)	S= 6

Figure 7.

another try. The final path to the destination is shown in Figure 8. This program is also adaptive and can adjust its own performance function after fuzzy programs have been executed.

INSTRUCTION	POSITION
1	(13 , 39 , 3)
2	(12 , 39 , 5)
~~3~~	~~(9 , 39 , 5)~~
4	(9 , 38 , 7)
5	(9 , 21 , 7)
~~6~~	~~(8 , 21 , 5)~~
7	(4 , 21 , 5)
8	(4 , 20 , 7)
~~9~~	~~(4 , 17 , 7)~~

Figure 8.

Although the problem discussed here is a very specific one, it should be clear that other tree-searching problems and problems in information retrieval can possibly be treated in the same way. For such problems, perhaps only elementary fuzzy programs need to be considered.

C. Pattern Recognition

For on-line character recognition, one may also regard the problem as one of finding the execution of fuzzy programs. For example, in the training phase, one first draws the character *A* and then types in the character "*A*". This information may be regarded as a fuzzy program

$$\bar{a} = a_{\swarrow} a_{\searrow} a_{\rightarrow} a_{\{A\}},$$

where $a_{\{A\}}$ says that the machine should terminate in a state called "A". When the learning phase is over, one simply draws the character A and asks the machine to identify the character. The fuzzy program now is

$$\bar{a} = a_{\swarrow} a_{\searrow} a_{\rightarrow},$$

The state that the execution of the fuzzy program leads into then decides the identity of the character.

In the training phase the learning matrix is first constructed. The performance function can then be constructed which can be used subsequently. On the other hand, the performance function may be constructed using some other ad hoc method. One can then use the final state for the optimal execution of the fuzzy program to identify the character.

REFERENCES

[1] R. E. Bellman and L. A. Zadeh, "Decision-Making in a Fuzzy Environment," Report No. ERL-69-8, Electronics Research Laboratory, University of California, Berkeley (November 1969).

[2] R. E. Bellman, R. Kalaba, and L. A. Zadeh, "Abstraction and Pattern Classification," *J. Math. Anal. Appl.*, **13**, 1–7 (January 1966).

[3] C. L. Chang, "Fuzzy Topological Spaces," *J. Math. Anal. Appl.*, **24**, 182–190 (1968).

[4] S. K. Chang, "Picture-Processing Grammars and its Applications," *Information Sci.*, **3**, 121–148 (April 1971).

[5] S. K. Chang, "On the Execution of Fuzzy Programs Using Finite-State Machines" (to be published in *IEEE Trans. Comput.*).

[6] S. K. Chang, "Automated Interpretation and Editing of Fuzzy Line Drawings," *AFIPS Conf. Proc.*, *SJCC*, 393–399 (1971).

[7] S. S. L. Chang, "Fuzzy Dynamic Programming and the Decision Making Process," *Proc. 3rd Princeton Conf. Information Sci. and Systems*, 200–203 (1969).

[8] E. Feigenbaum, and J. Feldman, Eds., *Computers and Thought* (New York: McGraw-Hill, 1963).

[9] Freeman and Glass, "On the Quantization of Line-Drawing Data," *IEEE Trans. Sys. Sci. Cyber.*, **SSC-5**, No. 1 (January 1969).

[10] A. Gill, "Introduction to the Theory of Finite-State Machines," Ch. 4 (McGraw-Hill, 1962).

[11] J. Goguen, "*L*-fuzzy Sets," *J. Math. Anal. Appl.*, **18**, 145–174 (April 1967).

[12] P. E. Hart, N. J. Nilsson, and B. Raphael, "A Formal Basis for the Determination of Minimum-Cost Paths," *IEEE Trans. Sys. Sci. Cyber.*, **2**, 100–107 (July 1968).

[13] D. M. Kaplan, "Regular Expressions and the Equivalence of Programs," *J. Comput. Sys. Sci.*, **3**, 361–386 (1969).

[14] R. C. T. Lee, "Fuzzy Logic and Resolution Principle," *Proc. 2nd International Joint Artificial Intelligence Conf.*, London (1971).

[15] M. Mizumoto, J. Toyoda, and K. Tanaka, "Some Considerations on Fuzzy Automata," *J. Comput. Sys. Sci.*, **3**, 409–422 (1969).

[16] M. Nasu and N. Honda, "Fuzzy Events Realized by Finite Probabilistic Automata," Information & Control, **12**, 284–303 (1968).

[17] N. Nilson, "Learning Machines" (McGraw-Hill, 1965).

[18] Samuel, A. L., "Some Studies in Machine Learning Using the Game of Checkers, II—Recent Progress," *IBM J. Res. Dev.*, **11**. **6**, 601–617 (November 1967).

[19] E. S. Santos, "Maximum Automata," *Information & Control*, **13**, 363–377 (1968).

[20] E. S. Santos, "Fuzzy Algorithms," *Information & Control*, **17**, 326–339 (1970).

[21] J. R. Slagle and J. K. Dixon, "Experiments with Some Programs that Search Game Trees," *J. ACM*, **16**, No. 2, 189–207 (April 1969).

[22] J. R. Slagle, "Heuristic Search Programs," in *Theoretical Approaches to Non-numerical Problem Solving*, 246–273 (R. Banerji and M. Mesarovic, Eds., New York: Springer-Verlag, 1970).

[23] W. G. Wee, "On Generalization of Adaptive Algorithms and Application of the Fuzzy-Set Concept to Pattern Classification," Technical Report TR-EE-67-7, Purdue University (July 1967).

[24] L. A. Zadeh, "Fuzzy Sets," *Information & Control*, **8**, 338–353 (1965).

[25] L. A. Zadeh, "Fuzzy Algorithms," *Information & Control*, **12**, 94–102 (1968).

[26] L. A. Zadeh, "Probability Measures of Fuzzy Events," *J. Math. Anal. Appl.*, **23**, 421–427 (August 1968).

DESIGN PRINCIPLES FOR A HIGH-PERFORMANCE SYSTEM

H. Schorr

IBM Thomas J. Watson Research Center, Yorktown Heights, NY

An exploration was made of the essential principles of a system design for executing large scientific programs. The design included a powerful highly-concurrent CPU, new channels, a storage hierarchy with relocation and overlay hardware, a new maintenance architecture and new software. The software included a global-optimizing compiler designed to produce code which realized the full potential of the machine. The operating system was split into two parts: the nucleus which contains all of the privileged code; and the peripheral service part. The objective of the nucleus was to provide primitive multiprogramming capability for an on-line data-base environment with performance comparable to ad-hoc user coding.

INTRODUCTION

This paper describes the results of an exploratory design effort which was carried out in order to develop new methods of radically improving system performance especially on large scientific calculations. Heavy emphasis was placed on simultaneously addressing software and hardware problems both at the system and logic-design levels.

In addition to high performance on scientific problems, it was assumed that good performance was also required in batch, time-sharing, and on-line data-base environments. Moreover this level of performance must be directly realizable through the use of higher-level languages. The ability to modify the operating system and, in particular, to add varied and different I/O devices was felt to be important. Accordingly, the group set out to discover the design principles of a total system centered around a powerful CPU which was to be programmed mainly in higher-level languages. The system design turned out to include:

- A CPU with a high degree of parallelism
- An advanced memory system
- Auxiliary storage devices integrated into the system
- A maintenance architecture and availability strategy
- An extensible multiprogramming control program
- A language processing system featuring an optimizing compiler.

Presented at the Symposium on Computers and Automata
Polytechnic Institute of Brooklyn, April 13-15, 1971.

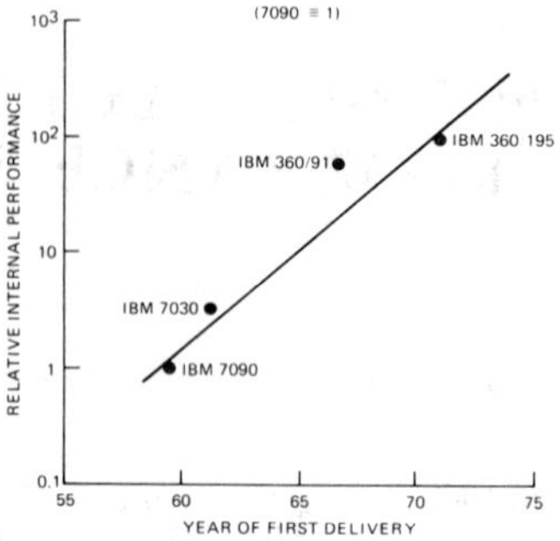

Fig. 1. Performance vs time of delivery.

II. THE CPU

If the average CPU performance is plotted as a function of time of first delivery, Fig. 1 results. For the mid 70s, then, it appeared appropriate to seek design principles that could achieve a CPU performance of 1,000 × IBM 7090 performance. CPU performance can be characterized as a function of circuit speed × number of circuits × architecture factor (Table I). It was assumed that

TABLE I. Architectural factor.

	RELATIVE PERFORMANCE	NUMBER OF CIRCUITS	CIRCUIT SPEED	ARCHITECTURAL FACTOR
IBM 7090	1	1	1	1
IBM 7030	3.5	3	1	1.2
IBM 360/91	60	13	4.2	1.1
IBM 360/195	96	13	4.2	1.7

circuit speed would improve by an order to magnitude over the 7090 so that the problem faced was to increase the number of circuits × architecture factor by two orders of magnitude over the 7090. This can only be obtained by employing some form of parallel execution—either: (1) extensions of the look-ahead principles of the IBM 7030 (Stretch) 360/91, 360/195; (2) vector or array processors; or (3) multiple instruction counters of some type. Use of the last type of parallelism *on a single* problem involved the solution of very difficult software problems. Vector and array processors were thought to be too specialized for effective use in general purpose areas. Therefore, attention quickly focused upon a single instruction counter machine with hardware controlled parallelism and an unconventional memory organization.

CPU Concurrency

The CPU was designed to achieve performance via concurrency in the operation of the following functions: instruction fetch, instruction decode, data fetch and index operations, arithmetic operators, as illustrated by Figure 2.

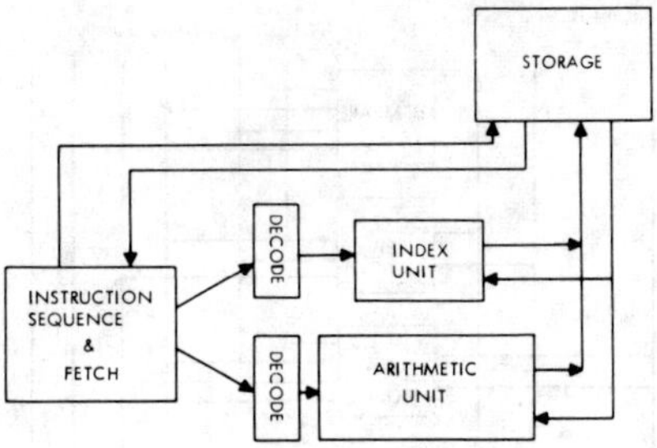

Fig. 2. CPU.

Each of the above operations themselves involved a high degree of concurrency: fetch multiple instructions—up to eight per cycle, decode multiple instructions—up to 16 per cycle, multiple load-store, index operations—up to three started per cycle, arithmetic operations—up to three started per cycle, process one branch instruction per cycle.

In the exploratory design, up to 50 different instructions could be decoded and in process concurrently (not counting storage). Multiple decoding was a new function examined by this project. By multiple decoding it is possible to initiate the execution of three index-type operations and three of the next eight arithmetic or logical-type instructions in every cycle. Eight arithmetic-type instructions are examined in each cycle to determine three executable instructions so that an instruction held up due to logical dependencies, register conflicts, memory interference, etc., does not impede the execution of any logically-independent instructions that follow it. This is especially useful in loops where the last instructions of the loop are usually dependent upon previous instructions, but where the instructions at the beginning of the loop are usually independent of those at the end.

High levels of arithmetic performance were obtained by having seven independent functional units which permitted different operations to be performed in parallel. Similarily, pipelining within the adders and multiplier [1] permitted three operations of the same kind to be in process concurrently by each one of these functional units; the arithmetic performance is summarized in Table II and the bussing given in Figure 3. For scientific calculations, double precision, in particular double precision inner product, was designed to be executed as fast as possible. Thus the bussing permits a single-precision multiply with double-precision product and a double-precision addition to be started on every cycle.

TABLE II. Summary of arithmetic performance.

	10^6 operations per second.		
FUNCTION	IBM 7090	IBM 360/91	EXPLORATORY DESIGN
Floating-Point Add	0.07	15	160
Floating-Point Multiply	0.04	6	80
Floating-Point Divide	0.03	2	12
Arithmetic Rate	0.046	11	240

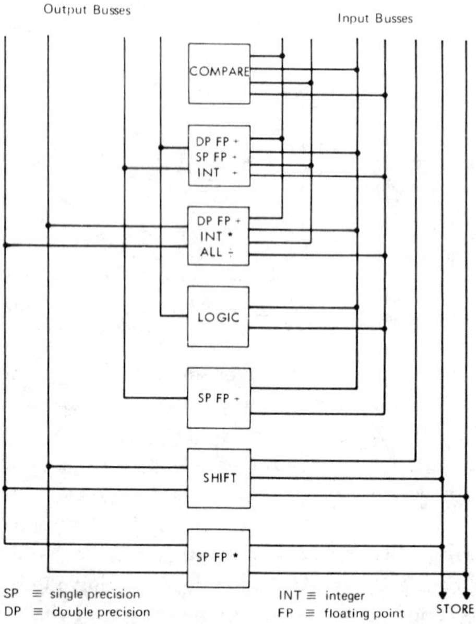

Fig. 3. *A*-unit bussing.

In addition, an attempt was made to design the bussing to minimize interference between instructions.

To supply the arithmetic unit with operands and to do the address arithmetic, a powerful index unit was designed. This unit consists of the functional units shown in Fig. 4, all of which can be pipelined.

Since a total of three index arithmetic and three floating/fixed-point operations can be initiated per cycle, a peak rate of six per cycle results.

Registers

To maintain an adequate supply of operands to sustain parallelism, the design included 31 arithmetic registers and 31 index registers. These arithmetic registers:

(1) Permit overlap of memory access with execution
(2) Hold data for multiple use
(3) Hold temporary results, constants, etc.
(4) Permit the compiler to schedule for maximum concurrency.

In addition 31 arithmetic backup registers provide further nonprogrammable operand buffers.

The number of indexed registers was chosen to permit:

(1) Permanent assignment to be made over an entire (sub) program
(2) Parameters to be left in registers to provide efficient subroutine and operating-system linkage
(3) Liberal use for basing purposes.

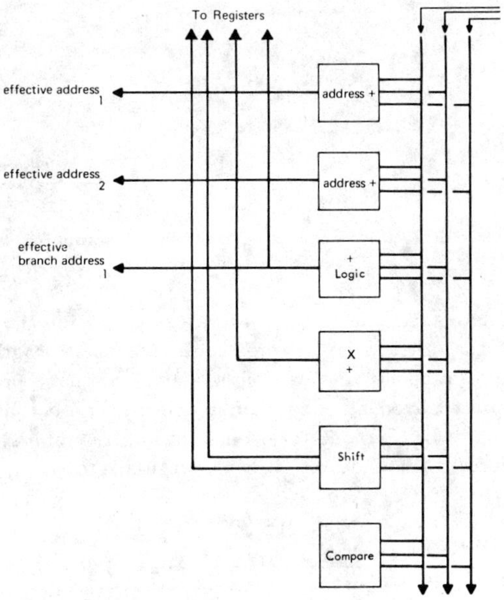

Fig. 4. *X*-unit bussing.

Branch Problem

In a highly-parallel machine, a branch instruction can cause a major loss of performance if the instruction-sequencing mechanism does not know which stream of instructions to prepare. This design proposed to overlap most branches via a combination of hardware and compiler by:

(1) Branch anticipation in which a conventional branch is replaced by a prepare-to-branch instruction and an exit instruction as in Figure 5
(2) Reduction of branches and exits
  (a) Branch instructions which test any function of any two condition registers
  (b) A skip instruction which causes programmer-marked instructions to be skipped at the arithmetic and index units rather than at the instruction-sequencing unit (which usually results in not delaying instruction fetching and processing)
(3) Reduction of the average branch delay via
  (a) Instruction-buffer registers which hold up to 96 instructions and which are associatively searched for a branch target
  (b) Instruction look-ahead on branches (prefetching of instructions on branch paths controlled by the history of previously-taken branches)
  (c) Index-unit instruction of a program being executed ahead of the arithmetic instructions (so that index-conditional branches can be executed in advance)
(4) Multiple-condition registers (24) which allow many tests to be made out of order with results prestored. Condition registers can be manipulated and combined by instructions.

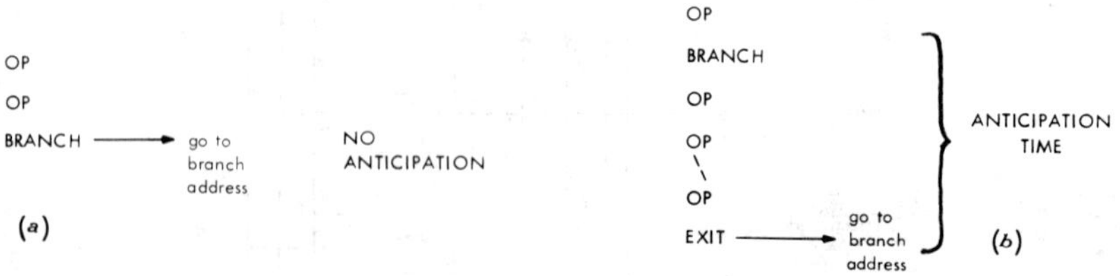

Fig. 5. Software-branch anticipation. (a) Conventional branching structure. (b) New branching structure.

Item (3) above discusses purely-hardware aids to solving the branching problem: utilization of the other three features required adroit programming or a compiler which could properly analyze higher-level-language programs. Indeed, the proposed compiler moved branches backwards in the code as far as possible, combined logical parts of IF-type statements into as few branches as possible, pushed tests forward in the code for early execution, etc.

INSTRUCTION SET (225 INSTRUCTIONS)

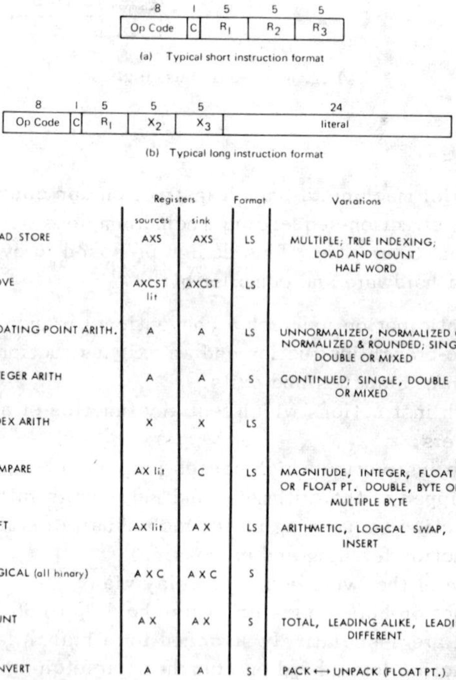

(a) Typical short instruction format

(b) Typical long instruction format

	Registers: sources	Registers: sink	Format	Variations
LOAD STORE	AXS	AXS	LS	MULTIPLE; TRUE INDEXING; LOAD AND COUNT HALF WORD
MOVE	AXCST lit	AXCST	LS	
FLOATING POINT ARITH.	A	A	LS	UNNORMALIZED, NORMALIZED OR NORMALIZED & ROUNDED; SINGLE DOUBLE OR MIXED
INTEGER ARITH	A	A	S	CONTINUED; SINGLE, DOUBLE OR MIXED
INDEX ARITH	X	X	LS	
COMPARE	AX lit	C	LS	MAGNITUDE, INTEGER, FLOAT PT., OR FLOAT PT. DOUBLE, BYTE OR MULTIPLE BYTE
SHIFT	AX lit	A X	LS	ARITHMETIC, LOGICAL SWAP, INSERT
LOGICAL (all binary)	A X C	A X C	S	
COUNT	A X	A X	S	TOTAL, LEADING ALIKE, LEADING DIFFERENT
CONVERT	A	A	S	PACK ⟷ UNPACK (FLOAT PT.) FLOAT PT. ⟷ INTEGER

CODE
A - Arithmetic
S - Special
T - IO Transmission

FORMAT
L - 48 bit instruction
S - 24 bit instruction

lit - 24 bit address part of instruction

(c) Instruction types

Fig. 6. Instruction set.

Instruction Set

The word size was set at 48 bits. Two interaction formats were used: halfword and fullword. The proposed instruction set featured a 24-bit address literal, double indexing, index-literal loads, three-address register-to-register instructions and a skip bit. Both the index and arithmetic operations include a complete set of logical and shift operations along with operations for direct communication between the units. Double and extended-precision (via hardware and programming) integer operations were included as well as halfword floating-point loads and stores. Execute, RX, VFL and decimal instructions were not included due to the implementation difficulties; the instruction set is summarized in Figure 6.

Performance

CPU performance was simulated on two problem kernels, one a straight arithmetic-limited problem, and the second a problem which was previously branch limited are shown in Figures 7 and 8. An average performance of two instructions per cycle achieves the goal of 1,000 × 7090 average. This was usually the minimum achieved on all kernels. Note that higher peak capabilities are needed to achieve this average.

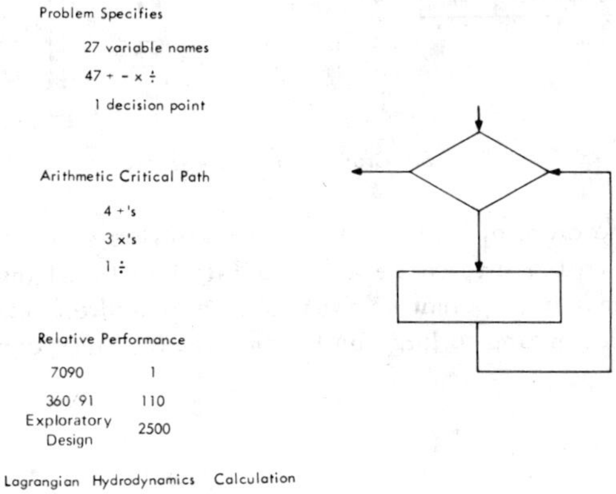

Fig. 7. Arithmetic kernel.

Interrupt

An interrupt can be considered as an asychronous branch, and thus it cannot be anticipated. It requires the current program to be stopped such that it can be restarted and the new program initiated. The system described above has as many as 50 instructions in process; an immediate stop requires a large amount of status to be saved. Rather than do this it was proposed that the hardware convert an interrupt to a branch, thus allowing instructions in process to be completed while the first instructions of the interrupt program are fetched. The cost in lost CPU processing was only on the average ten instructions while response

Problem Specifies

23 variable names

22 + - x ÷

11 decision points

Arithmetic Critical Path

8 +'s

4 x's

1 ÷

PERFORMANCE COMPARISON

	7090	360/91	Explor. Design
Total Storage Ref.	139	57	14
Instructions/cycle	.26	.4	1.8
Time (μ sec)	643	9	.4
7090 Improvement	1	72	1608

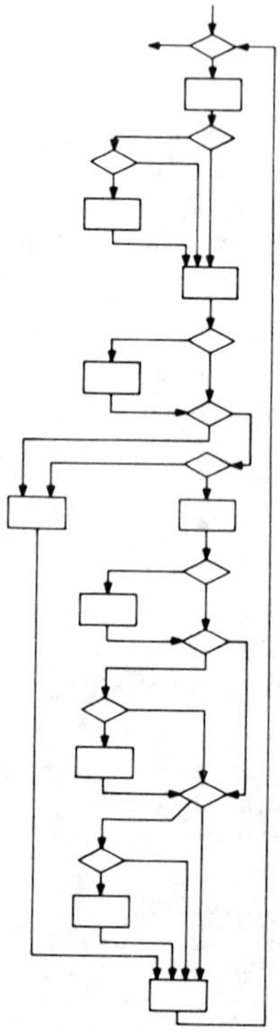

Fig. 8. Branch-limited kernel.

time could be of the order of ¼ μsec. In addition to this soft-interrupt facility a hard interrupt was included to cause an immediate halt to all instructions. This was necessary primarily to permit software action on address exceptions, etc., so that, for example, paging to large bulk memories or drums could be implemented.

Special Registers

To further aid the handling of interrupts and also for supervisor calls, the set of status and control bits that define the state of the machine were to be held in twenty 24-bit registers called special registers. Their function is given in Table III. Most of these could only be accessed while in privileged mode. The special registers permit fast switching between a problem program and the supervisor. By means of the alternate keys, programs could share storage-protected files.

I/O Module

The system was designed to work with standard System/360 I/O devices. A channel response to an initiation/termination sequence can take up to 32 μsec

TABLE III. Special registers.

NUMBER	NAME	LENGTH IN BITS	PRIVILEGED
0	Condition	24	no
1	Problem Exception	21	no
2	Problem Mask	21	no
3	Supervisory Exception	11	yes
4	Supervisory Mask	11	yes
5	Problem Normal Key	12	yes
6	Problem Alternate Key	12	yes
7	Supervisory Normal Key	12	yes
8	Supervisory Alternate Key	12	yes
9	Interruption Return Address	24	yes
10	Effective Branch Address	24	yes
11	Machine State	16	yes
12	Cycle Count	24	yes
13	Instruction Count	24	yes
14	Timer	24	yes
15	External Signal	24	yes
16	General Purpose	24	yes
17	General Purpose	24	yes
18	General Purpose	24	yes
19	General Purpose	24	yes

and it was decided not to have the CPU idle during such a sequence. The proposed solution was to add an I/O module which buffers initiation/termination sequences and thereby execute them concurrently with CPU computation as shown in Figure 9. This required the operating system to keep track of the fact that, for example, a Start I/O has been issued to a channel, but that it has not yet been accepted by the channel. Data was communicated to or from storage

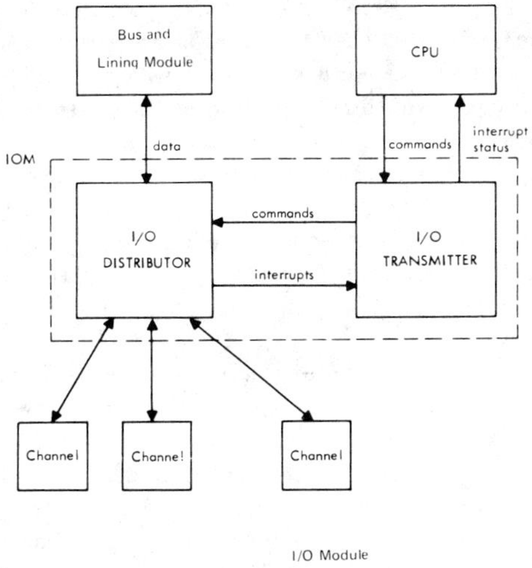

Fig. 9. I/O module.

without either CPU or I/O-transmitter (IOT) action so that both were free. On termination, the channel signalled the IOT which collects channel status before interrupting the CPU.

III. COMPILER

The CPU was a highly-concurrent CPU and its proper programming was ensured only if all of its features—multiple registers, arithmetic-functional units, condition registers, etc., were used properly. While this can be done by the assembly-language programmer, it was felt that the major amount of both the systems and application programming would be done in higher-level languages. At the start of the project, an effort was mounted to provide an optimizing compiler that would realize the full potential of the machine design. Such a compiler should also reduce global-execution redundancies and produce code comparable in size and execution time with hand-written code while producing correct answers of the same accuracy with no new side effects. It was also realized that a quick compiler was needed for debug runs, one-shot problems, etc.

Compiler Structure

It was readily apparent that an optimizing compiler for this machine was a major undertaking and that it should not be duplicated in full for every high-level language. It was therefore decided that the optimizer should work from a common internal language (IL) and that a front-end translator be added to the system for each language as required (see Figure 10). The proposed internal language was very machine dependent—its operators and operands were equivalent to machine operations, but there were no restrictions as to the number of registers that may be used. In addition, the IL was convenient for processing and contained: (1) information to make it traceable; (2) Relative data locations and extents; and (3) Any optimization directives that were included by the programmer. By having an IL it was felt that good code for many languages could be obtained by the relatively-easy process of adding a translator; this made the overall system more efficient. Moreover, it might be possible to combine programs (perhaps originating from different source languages) at the IL level. It also provided a standard base for other tools such as debugging statements, flow diagramming, etc.

It soon became apparent that for efficiency reasons, instructions should be rearranged to avoid bottlenecks and not presented in the unaltered order given by the output of, for example, a right-to-left scan. It was also observed that many of the optimizations in compilers, e.g., common-expression elimination, are basically independent of the target machine. Thus the optimizer was divided into two parts: one machine independent, and one machine dependent, as depicted in Figure 10. To minimize the interaction between parts, it was soon found that an adequate supply of registers was needed.

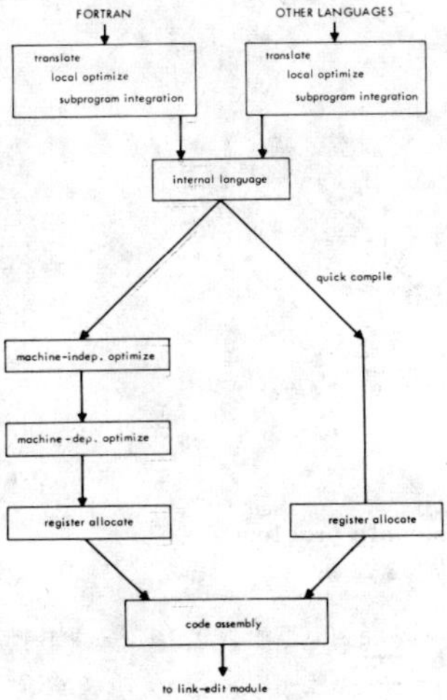

Fig. 10. Compiler.

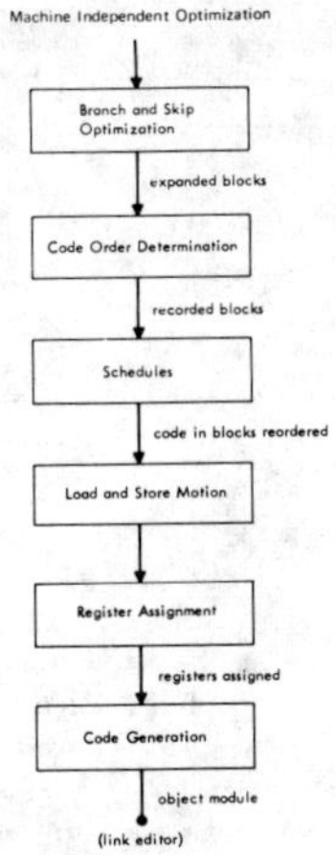

Fig. 11. Machine-dependent optimizer.

Machine-Independent Optimization

The major goal of the machine-independent part was to apply all optimizations to an entire program and not only to an inner loop [2, 3]. The first part of the machine-independent optimization was to determine the basic topology of a program in terms of basic blocks of code (one input point and one exit point). Optimization then proceeds from the innermost block outwards. Optimization utilized include global common-subexpression elimination, code motion, strength reduction (e.g., changing subscript-expression calculations to index-register increments in loops), constant propagation (index variables replaced by constants wherever possible), and dead-variable elimination (the deletion of unused definitions and instructions). The sequence of machine-independent optimize operations was as follows:

(1) Basic block finder
(2) Eliminate common subexpressions in basic blocks
(3) Propagate constants of singly-defined variables
(4) Control flow analysis
(5) Global common-subexpression elimination and code motion
(6) Chain uses and definitions globally
(7) Reduction in strength process
(8) Global-constant propagation
(9) Dead-variable and expression elimination.

Machine-Dependent Optimizations

Machine-dependent optimizations included:

(1) Skip and branch analysis
(2) Scheduling
(3) Register allocation.

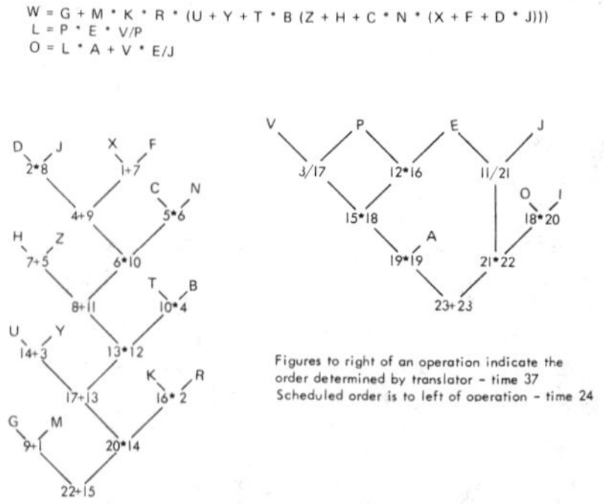

Fig. 12(a). Dependency tree of a sample problem.

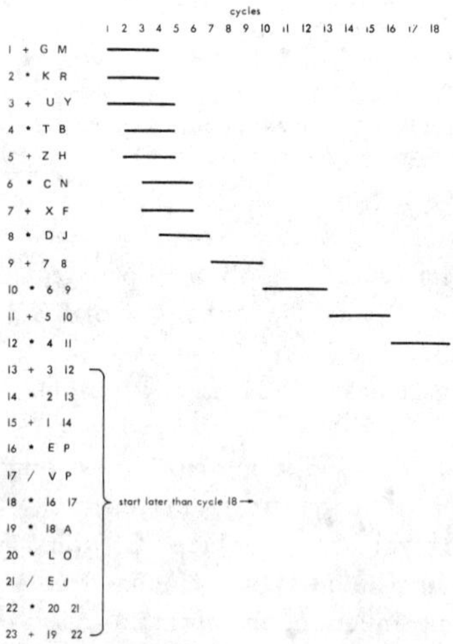

Fig. 12(b). Unscheduled sequence

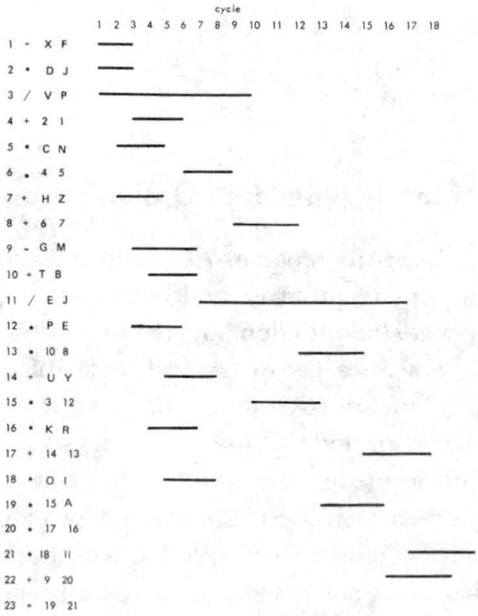

Fig. 12(c). Scheduled sequence.

In skip and branch analysis, basic blocks are merged to improve the schedule and eliminate transfers, and blocks are reordered to reduce transfer frequency. In scheduling, code sequences are ordered to minimize execution time. Finally, register limitations are considered and the necessary loads and stores introduced. A flowchart is given in Fig. 11 and the result of scheduling a problem shown in Figure 12. Other optimizations, especially those to smooth subroutine linkages, will be included.

FORTRAN Language Extensions for Systems Programming

Early in the study the question of a possible implementation langage for programs was considered. At the time this decision was made, code produced by PL/I compilers was not suitable. The decision was made to use an ASA FORTRAN which: gave access to most machine facilities; permitted more-complex data structures and part-word variables to be handled; and, interfaced with many primitive operation-system services. Specific features included: machine operations using symbolic variables (not registers), partial-word variables, storage allocation and hierarchy-level control, memory-mapping control, (e.g., interleaving, overlay, boundary alignment, partial-word packing), macros, new I/O, based variables, optimization directives, subroutine-interface control, recursive subroutines, debugging statements, and expanded definitions of expressions (if, then, else, ···).

IV. STORAGE HIERARCHY

As the proposed CPU was to operate in a general-purpose environment, it required support by a large auxiliary storage with an adequate data-transfer rate. Based on a study of time-sharing installations, 7090 job shops, and 7030 scientific usage, an average of one bit of I/O is required for each CPU instruction executed. Assuming that the goal of 1,000 times the 7090 was achieved, and assuming that the 7090 executed up to 160,000 instructions per second [4], then the system would require 160×10^6 bit/sec on the average. This represents the total average I/O required by the system, and consists of: (1) System programs; (2) Temporary storage (intermediate results); and (3) The jobs themselves (procedures and data).

In modern systems the first two components of the I/O can be supplied from drums or local core storage (LCS) in which the systems programs and intermediate results are stored. It remains, therefore, to introduce the job I/O from lower-level storage. How large is this component? This is unclear at this time, but it was estimated that about $\frac{1}{4}$ of the total average I/O, 40×10^6 bit/sec, should be an upper bound in scientific installations. If tapes alone are used to supply the job I/O, then a total of 80 units in continuous usage (mount, read, demount at top speed) would be required. The operators' problems in an installation such as the above would be immense. More importantly, conversational and real-time jobs require a response time better than that provided by an operator-serviced library. Reduction of operator intervention requires an increase in the size of on-line auxiliary storage. The required capacity of this on-line storage was estimated to be 10^9 words.

Staging

Storages capable of economically providing this capacity are characterized by low data rates (400K byte/sec) and slow access time ($\frac{1}{20}$ to 5 sec). If the CPU is directly multiprogrammed from such storage devices, a large number of jobs and care are involved. For example, consider a simple model involving identical jobs each of which executes 250,000 instructions between I/O requests for 25K bytes of data. As the CPU was assumed to perform 160×10^6 instruction/sec, it would have required the multiprogramming of at least

$$\left(\frac{1}{20} + \frac{25{,}000}{400{,}000}\right) \div \left(\frac{250{,}000}{160{,}000{,}000}\right) = 72 \quad ,$$

jobs to keep the CPU fully utilized even if no allowance is made for I/O interference. Assuming each job to require 200K bytes of electronic storage for program and data, this implies a core storage requirement in excess of

$$72 \times 200{,}000 = 14.4 \times 10^6 \text{ [bytes]} \ .$$

Appreciable reductions in this excessive core-storage requirement could be achieved only by significant improvements in I/O-access times and transfer rates. Devices with these improved characteristics such as fixed-head files (FHF) were far too expensive to use for the entire on-line storage of 10^9 words, however. This led to a multilevel on-line storage design in which jobs were *staged* from lower-cost devices to fixed-head files such as the IBM 2305 before moving to core.

Note that it is necessary to use much-larger blocking factors when moving data from lower levels to the FHF then when moving from the FHF to core. This is easily seen if we again use the simple model of 25,000 bytes per I/O request after the execution of each 250,000 instructions. If data are moved to the FHF in blocks of 25,000 bytes and used only once, then the number of accesses to lower-cost online storage is required to be at least

$$\frac{160{,}000{,}000}{250{,}000} = 640 \text{ per second} \ .$$

This access rate could not be economically satisfied by devices with access time in excess of $\frac{1}{20}$ second and larger blocking factors were thus required.

Core storage is required to buffer transfers from lower levels of on-line storage to the FHFs. The costs of staging, therefore, include:

(1) Core storage capacity for buffering
(2) Increased data flowing to and from core storage.

In general, the design of a multilevel-storage hierarchy is a complex multiparameter-optimization problem involving the following: number of levels, capacity (and therefore cost) of each level, data transfer rates between levels, blocking factors, access rates, organization of hardware and software to control transfers between levels.

The storage hierarchy which was settled upon as a design goal is given in Figure 13. Note that two levels of electronic storage were specified: a small high speed storage (HSS); and a larger, slower, main storage (MS). This decision was made for reasons analogous to those which led to the use of multiple levels of on-line storage. The following comments all apply to the hypothetical hierarchy of Figure 13.

(1) Use of FHFs reduces the level of multiprogramming (and hence the electronic storage required for job buffering) by a factor of three approximately
(2) System programs are specified to be core resident
(3) The FHF should be used in a sector-queuing mode with fixed-length

sector sizes. That is, accesses must be sorted by rotational position as in Figure 14 and multisector requests made. If this is done, a queuing delay (including rotational delay) of

$$\frac{1}{2} + \frac{\lambda}{2(1-\lambda)} = \frac{1}{2(1-\lambda)} \text{ revolutions },$$

is introduced where λ is the request rate specified as a fraction of the maximum data rate of a FHF reading continuously.

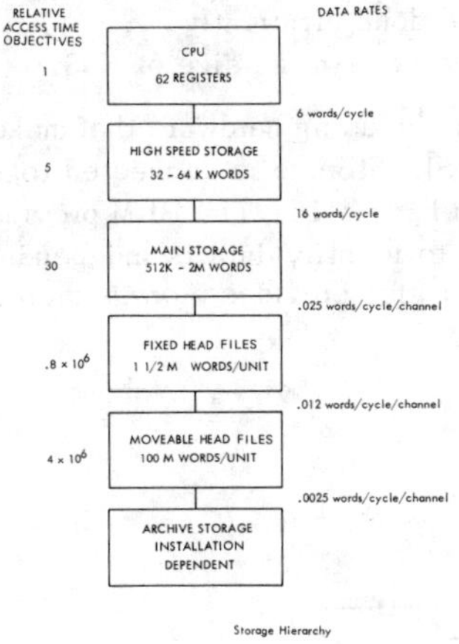

Fig. 13. Storage hierarchy.

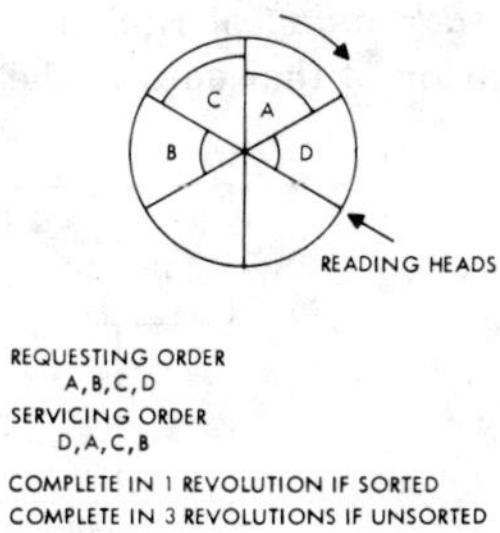

Fig. 14. Queue sorting.

Thus for $\lambda = 0.5$, to obtain a page, a delay of one revolution results. A plot of delay vs data rate is given in Figure 15. The same curve for FIFO-access method is also plotted and shows the much-greater data rates obtained by sorting requests. To benefit from such a strategy requires the operating system and problem programs to issue multiple-sector requests. Three fixed-length sector sizes were to be accommodated by the proposed operating system: they are 256, 1024, and 4096 words.

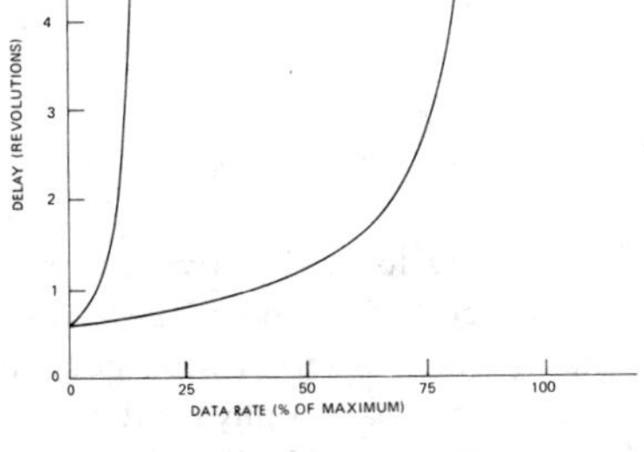

Fig. 15. Fixed-head file (FHF) queuing.

HSS-MS Storage Allocation and Addressing

The HSS was to have been relatively small but would have had the best access time of any storage; for efficiency the CPU must execute problems primarily out of HSS. The number of programs that have to be multiprogrammed requires a large amount of storage that can be economically supplied by using MS. The use of a two-level storage introduces several problems:

(1) Two addressing structures
(2) Two memories to allocate
(3) Transfer between HSS and MS must be done efficiently
(4) The overlay problem for programs greater than the size of HSS.

The system proposed to avoid these problems by using hardware that makes the two-level system look like a one-level system [5]. Storage is connected together by a buss and lining module (BLM) as shown in Figure 16. The BLM provides *virtual addressing* of HSS-MS: the address used to identify data is independent of the location of that data in the storage system; it also provides *storage protection.*

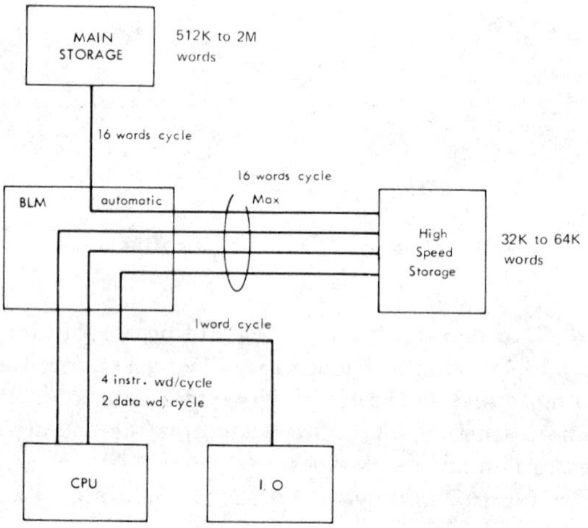

Fig. 16. Bus and lining module (BLM).

The addressing structure is shown in Fig. 17 and it should be noted to both CPU and channels.

Virtual Addressing

The set of virtual addresses is logically divided into 64-word pages. Any page may occupy *any* 64-word segment of MS. Pages are allocated in MS under the control of the operating system. Another storage, located in the BLM and called the directory, associates virtual to physical addresses. The directory works in units of 1, 4, 16, or 64 pages (64, 256, 1024, or 4096 words).

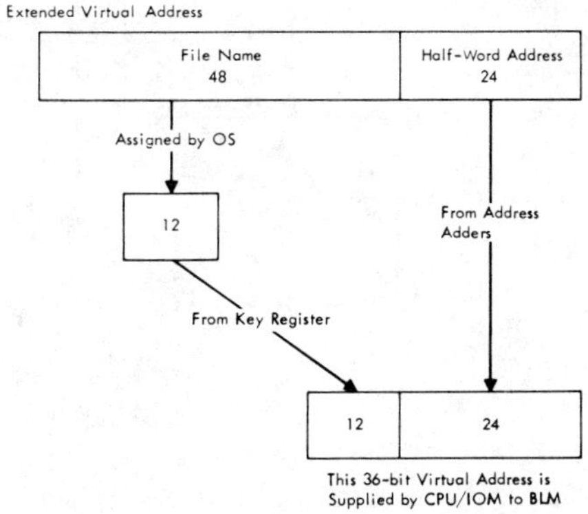

Fig. 17. Addressing structure.

Lining

The unit of transfer between HSS and MS is not a whole page but part of a page called a *line*. Since only part of a program is required at a given execution of a task, transferring only this required part of a program cuts down on the amount that must be transferred between HSS and MS. If the line size is one word then only what is needed is transferred and the effective program size is at a minimum. Unfortunately, hardware and programming constraints tend to require a larger line size. To reduce interference and utilize bandwidth the line size should be a multiple of the physical word size of MS. Similarly, it seems desirable to be able to utilize sequential data from MS. If the data is being processed at one word per cycle and the net access time to MS is c CPU cycles, then c words should be fetched from MS at a time. To minimize hardware, the line size should be large, i.e., the amount of control, and the size of the table which identifies the line in HSS is inversely proportional to line size. A line size of 16 or 32 words seemed to achieve the right balance; 32 words was chosen.

Assignment of Lines to HSS

The two extreme ways of assigning lines to HSS are: (1) Restricting a line to one fixed 32-word slot; or (2) Allowing it to occupy any available 32-word slot. The former results in too many conflicts due to lines competing for the same slot while the latter requires either an associative memory or the search of a large association table before accessing data. These solutions are too slow and expensive. The proposed choice was to allow a line to reside in either of two fixed 32-word slots; the storage utilization closely approaches that of an associative memory. This permits *simultaneous* access of both the data and the association table without excessive conflicts; raw HSS and bussing performance is degraded by no more than 20%. However, the HSS bandwidth required is doubled. The lining and MS to HSS transfer (swap) mechanisms are illustrated in Figures 18 and 19. The choice of which line to be swapped is based on a hot/cold replacement algorithm.

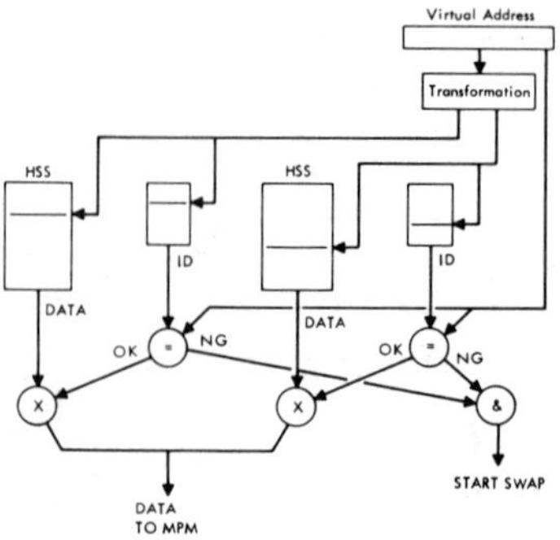

Fig. 18. Lining mechanism. Four accessing mechanisms operate concurrently: 2 for data fetch or store; 1 for I/O fetch or store; and 1 for instruction fetch.

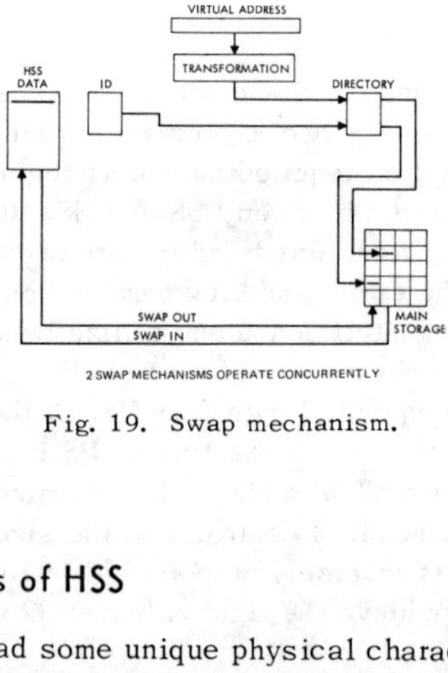

Fig. 19. Swap mechanism.

Size and Characteristics of HSS

The HSS would have had some unique physical characteristics; among them were that the cycle time is the same as the CPU cycle time. This permits a storage request to be made to a module on every CPU cycle and thus a 16-module system permits 16 requests per cycle to be serviced if there are no conflicts. The proposed system could make 14 requests per cycle (7 logical requests). At this rate, a queuing delay of less than ½ cycle results.

The size of the HSS was larger than the buffer stores provided in other systems. This is due primarily to two factors:

(1) Almost all the time (better than 99%) accesses must be made to lines already present in HSS or else performance falls off drastically. The attempt of the system is to have memory look like it has the capacity of MS with the access time of HSS

(2) I/O and its control resides in HSS and requires considerable space, approximately 10K. Thus HSS should be available in 32K and 64K word sizes.

V. I/O CONTROL AND CHANNELS

The efficient processing of I/O requires handling periodic arrivals of partial words, buffering them to some multiple of MS word size and then transferring them into MS. Rather than provide separate assembly registers for a large number of channels, it was better to add HSS capacity and let it be shared between I/O and programs; a line was selected as the I/O-buffer size. The transfer of data from buffers would then be carried out automatically by the BLM hardware via the line-replacement algorithm. The strategy of always accessing I/O through HSS also eliminates any copying back from HSS to MS before carrying out an I/O operation. I/O and its control is a very important operation in any system; the lines in HSS allocated to I/O are accessed with greater frequency by I/O than those accessed by other programs. This results in low probability of being swapped out and consequently I/O overruns were held to acceptable levels.

Channels

The proposed channels were to be more-directly controlled by program than in most IBM systems. That is, there is no hardware realization of software-implementable features such as chaining, queuing, or searching. Implementation of these features via program is facilitated by the availability of HSS and a very-powerful CPU. This means was chosen in order to reduce the channel cost. For example, if a large average data rate of between $\frac{1}{2}$ to 2 bits (depending upon the job mix) of I/O per instruction executed is to be accommodated, then for $1,000 \times$ 7090 and the higher I/O average-data rate, $1,000 \times 160,000 \times 2 = 320 \times 10^6$ bit/sec must be concurrently handled by the channels. The instantaneous rates would be higher. A factor of two in excess channel capacity is needed for staging and another factor of two is needed to limit queuing delay. Thus a total channel rate of 1280×10^6 bit/sec would be needed. Typical channels were limited to 10×10^6 bit/sec so that 128 channels would be needed. A high speed channel was designed which by transmitting a 48-bit word could achieve a maximum data rate of 400×10^6 bit/sec. Up to 64 standard and up to 32 of the above high-speed channels were allowed.

Greater use of program control permits a channel design utilizing minimal hardware; every four channels would share adders and control circuitry. In operation, each channel executes only a single command and then interrupts the CPU; chaining and queuing were to be provided in software. It should be mentioned that the study examined several alternate paths, including an I/O processor and high-speed channels which automatically handled queuing. These were rejected because of cost considerations and because they would have resulted in several other problems such as higher I/O overruns, storage allocation, cooperation in the use of commonly-accessed queues, the need for a separate I/O processor having its own HSS and operating system, etc. Analysis also showed that neither of these two approaches saved a great deal of CPU time, and in any case CPU time did not appear to be a limiting factor.

VI. OPERATING SYSTEM

Control over the I/O and the storage hierarchy in a multiprogramming environment were the key problems to be faced by the operating system. Also, the operating system would support terminal job entry, remote entry, real-time applications, new installation specified I/O devices and the ability for an installation to replace IBM-supplied systems programs by their own. It was felt that the best way to provide these features was to divide the operating system into two parts: a nucleus and peripheral services. The nucleus would consist of those services essential to the entire community of users, that is, the intersection of all their needs. This nucleus interfaced directly with the hardware and converted it into an extended machine in which users were isolated from one another but still retained sufficient control over the hardware so that they could maximize its use for the solution of their particular problems. The user, for example, was allowed to control the type of storage he would like to have pages of his file in and also control their transfer up and down the storage hierarchy with predictable response time.

The peripheral service routines were a user of nucleus services (and are no different from any other user) usually oriented towards providing maximum user convenience. For example, compilers, job-control-language interpreters, peripheral I/O, sequential and partitioned-access methods, etc., are peripheral service routines. These routines can be added to, replaced, etc., but any such changes are written in nonprivileged code and must obey the nucleus-interface conventions (as well as any peripheral-service conventions).

This rigid division of the operating system, as characterized in Fig. 20, provides for the separation of the users into two classes: those who are principally concerned with response and efficiency; and those concerned with convenience, adaptability, and versatility. The nucleus thus incorporated a strict set of rules and provided a set of services each of which had a predictable response time. Automatic-allocation schemes such as demand paging or data look-ahead buffering (as provided in sequential-access methods) would not be provided.

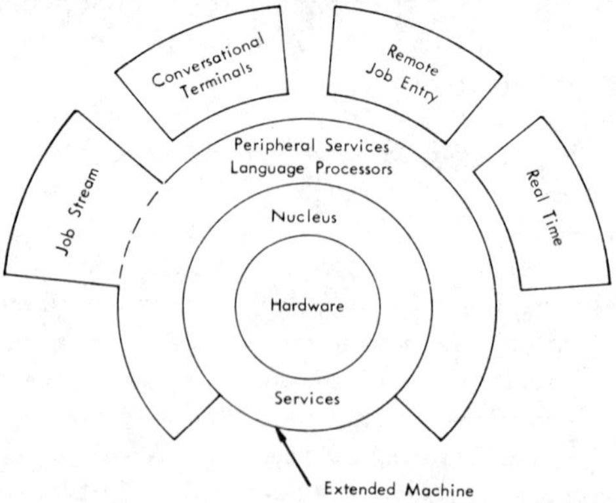

Fig. 20. Conceptual view of operating system.

Nucleus Services

The nucleus can be characterized as consisting of interrupt handling, task management, basic data management of the storage hierarchy and an I/O interface, and can be depicted pictorially as in Figure 21. The nucleus is entered only via SVCs and interrupts. The SVCs and interrupts are routed by the process dispatcher to the appropriate nucleus component (or to a task). The basic part of the operating system is the process dispatcher which has to operate disabled and was designed to operate with a minimum number of instruction executions. The logical consistency of the rest of nucleus is maintained by means of a set of locks on important facilities and nonreentrant pieces of code. An important part of the nucleus is the basic data management which catalogs, creates, destroys, and moves files within the storage hierarchy. A file was identified by a 48-bit file name. This file name was permanently associated with the file and was the only means by which a nucleus user could address it. The file name identified the file but did not refer *at any time* to the physical locations occupied by the file. The physical locations were specified in a *file index* which was maintained by the nucleus. Thus the name by which the programmer addressed a file did not have to be changed when movement between levels of storage hierarchy occurred and when a physical assignment was made within a level; this was also true for both MS and HSS. The use throughout the system of virtual addresses resulted in a simplification of the addressing structure since it did not reflect the levels of the hierarchy and it also provided for relocation throughout the system.

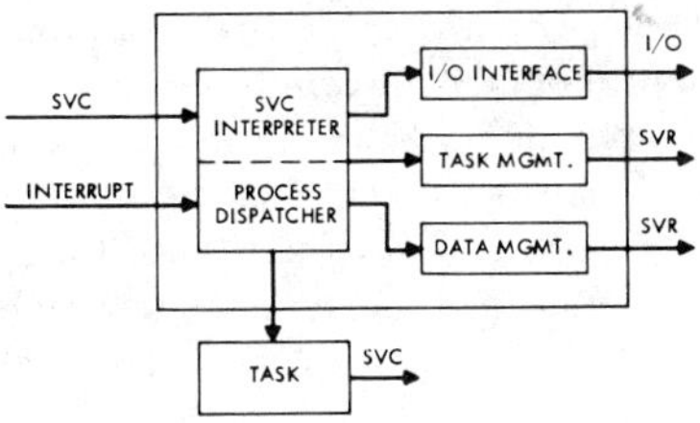

Fig. 21. Conceptual view of nucleus.

A file had as *attributes*:

(1) Its storage level within the hierarchy
(2) Its accessibility—whether it is read only or read/write.

These attributes could be assigned to *pages* or blocks of pages within a file.

In addition to a file with its physical addresses, the file index also specified other attributes of the file. The file index could be physically separate from the file itself. In general when active it should be on a faster device than the file itself so that a file access appears to be only slightly longer than the access time of the slower device. The collection of all file indexes constitutes the internal catalog which can be accessed *only by nucleus routines*. The basic nucleus data management services were: create file, move file index to storage level X, move data block to storage level X, copy data block X into data block Y.

Tasks

A task was considered to be an independent entity for the purposes of accounting and servicing requests. Tasks were created by other tasks *only* with no mother-daughter relationship as in OS/360. However, it was possible to have SVCs routed to another task rather than the nucleus. A task could communicate with another task via explicit commands and this same mechanism was used by the nucleus to communicate with a task. Each task is assigned to a *partition* which was assigned a certain percentage of the systems resources. This percentage was usually guaranteed to a partition and was not a static assignment, i.e., at any given instant a partition may have no resources assigned to it. A partition which at a given time has received less than its allotted amount of resources has priority over other partitions that have full allotments. Tasks were assigned priorities within partitions and were assigned resources on the basis of their previous utilization of those resources (a variation of exponential scheduling).

I/O Interface

The I/O interface includes the I/O drivers for members of the storage hierarchy, i.e., FHF, MHF, and archives. These devices are completely under the control of the nucleus, have fixed formats, and constitute the on-line data base. Other devices such as tapes, unit-record equipment, removable MHF disk packs, terminals, etc., cannot be completely under the nucleus' control because of the nature of the devices, data formats and their use which are usually unpredictable. These *external* I/O devices are controlled and protected by using the nucleus to interpret channel programs generated by the user. The nucleus replaced logical channels by physical channel numbers, translated data identifiers into MS virtual addresses, implemented System/360-like chaining and collected channel, control unit, and device status for return to the user. The nucleus did not take responsibility for correct use of the channel or error recovery.

TABLE IV.

MACHINE	EXTENDED MACHINE
Data Identification	*X*-Data Identification
12-Bit Keys	48-Bit File Name
24-Bit Logical Address	24-Bit Logical Address
Operations	*X*-Operations (SVCs)
Branch	(a) Direct *X*-Branch
	(b) Indirect *X*-Branch for Protection of ● Entry Points ● Reading ● Modification
Load } MS to Reg. Store }	Move } MS to Aux. Storage Copy }
I/O OPS (Privileged)	Symbolic Channel Programs

Extended Machine

The user of the nucleus would see an extended machine (Table IV) consisting of: files, tasks, unprivileged machine operations, extended machine operations (nucleus service requests) implemented through SVC instruction, and symbolic I/O channels. This gave the user effective access to all system resources without using privileged code. All other systems programs and all user programs operated in this environment.

Peripheral Services

These programs were designed to support large production jobs concurrently with small foreground jobs. Jobs could be entered into the job stream via spooled I/O with multiple entry (card readers, terminals, tape). Peripheral service routines were categorized as extended-data management, extended-task management, and external-device support. The main emphasis of extended-data management was the support of higher-level languages; it contained routines to provide basic and queued sequential-access methods. It was planned that each user would have his libraries whose main purpose would be to identify his files and to perform translation of alphanumeric file-editing facilities. Extendedtask management included routines for user command-language interpretation, standard-error recovery and debugging procedures, and operating-environment supervision. The latter included gross-scheduling, accounting, operator, and job-stream supervision routines. External-device support routines included spooling, tape-handling, and terminal-support routines.

Additions to the peripheral service routines to support conversational terminals and remote job entry, would have consisted of additional language facilities, interactive-terminal control, peripheral-processor support, and telecommunication support.

VII. MAINTENANCE ARCHITECTURE

There are several areas of maintenance that were addressed as part of the architectural design of the system. These were:

(1) Error control—the determination that an error has occurred, how it has propagated, and prescription for its repair
(2) Protection of the operating system—protect essential parts of the operating system against error and, attempt to insure the integrity of the files; facilitate fast re-IPL
(3) Checkpoint/restart—provide user function so that the user can use additional measures for maintaining the integrity of his data beyond those that the system provided
(4) Availability—reconfiguration of the system when a hardware failure occurs to provide a lesser amount of computing capacity
(5) Repair—discovery and location of a faulty, replaceable part.

It was felt that because these areas strongly interacted with other system-architecture areas they must be included in the initial overall design.

Error Control

Hardware error control for I/O consisted of specifying burst-error correction for FHF and standard byte parity for System/360 I/O devices. For HSS and MS, byte parity was also specified rather than the single-error correction possible with extra memory bits. The latter was eliminated because it did not appreciably increase availability, it did increase cost, and it affected the design and performance of the CPU; furthermore it causes some errors to be miscorrected.

For the CPU it was felt that parity did not provide a complete solution to error control; parity could provide detection on the data paths but not elsewhere and at great cost in both circuits and performance. Other hardware devices were similarily rejected. It was decided instead to propose running periodic diagnostic tests under the operating system. However, byte parity was maintained from the I/O devices through the channels, I/O module, and BLM since both ends, storage and devices, maintained parity.

Some error control is obtained via the nucleus. When an error occurs the nucleus can replace a file by a copy of it which has been maintained lower in the storage hierarchy. In general such copies should be maintained until the CPU has finished processing the MS copy. At this point the space occupied by the lower-level copy is returned to the free list. Of course, if the file has been changed in MS then there is nothing the nucleus could do but notify the user. The user of course can increase the likelihood of correctability by explicit update of lower-level copies. Work on providing user checkpointing did not proceed past this point.

The protection afforded to user data also aids in the preparation of the operating system since most operating-system tables are cataloged as part of the user data. The nucleus was protected against catalog loss by keeping a transaction log and by providing (redundant) identification of the file with the file. Re-IPL is facilitated by keeping a copy of nucleus on FHF to ensure quick reinitialization. Most of the effects of system software bugs were isolated by the separation of the nucleus from the peripheral services.

Availability

Failure of the CPU, BLM, or I/O transmitter would have caused the system to go down. In a system with 64K of HSS and more than 256K of MS a storage failure would not have caused unavailability. The system operated with half of a 64K HSS disabled with no software adjustments required. Similarly a system can function with all but one 256K block of MS disabled. System transition to these states is facilitated by the use of virtual addressing. All FHF and other I/O devices should be accessible by alternate paths.

A duplex system in which CPU, IOM, BLM, and HSS were duplicated was studied in a preliminary way. This augmented system would have been designed to operate in a reconfigured mode less than 200 hours a year and would be unavailable about one hour a year based on typical hardware-failure projections.

Repair

High availability can be achieved partly through rapid and semiautomatic repair. A failed, replaceable part could be automatically found by using a maintenance computer to compare all the triggers of the machine with simulated values of these triggers. The maintenance computer would either run the simulation or communicate with a remote computer running the simulator (which could be an identical system). The isolation strategy is flowcharted in Figure 22. It was our judgment that this technique will isolate 93% of the hardware failures thereby reducing manual intervention and keeping the duration of unscheduled interruption (DUI) to approximately two hours as shown in Figure 23. The hardcore required to run diagnostics consists mainly of logout of all control triggers, input to the instruction buffer and I/O-module register, and the maintenance register as shown in Figure 24. It is the ability to keep this hardcore to a minimum which allows the failure-detection program to proceed without manual intervention and this, in turn, helps keep the DUI to two hours. The time to physically replace a failed component is in the order of ½ hr. The replaceable part would generally be large and complex, e.g., a BSM of storage or a board of logic.

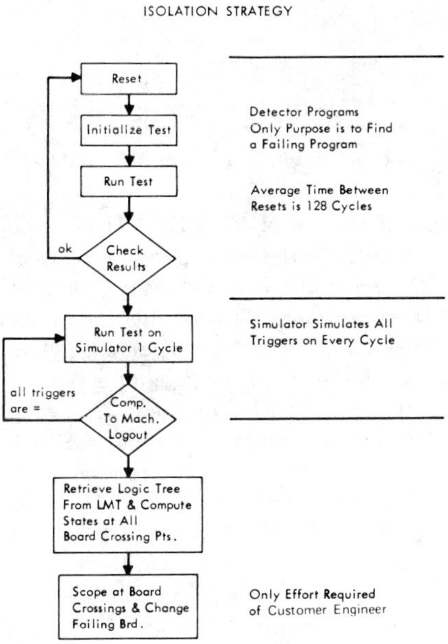

Fig. 22. Isolation strategy.

VIII. SIMULATION AND CHECKOUT SYSTEM

To aid in the design of this new system and the checkout of the software, various simulators were needed. Those used in the hardware design included an instruction simulator [6], a cycle-by-cycle CPU simulator, and BLM and storage

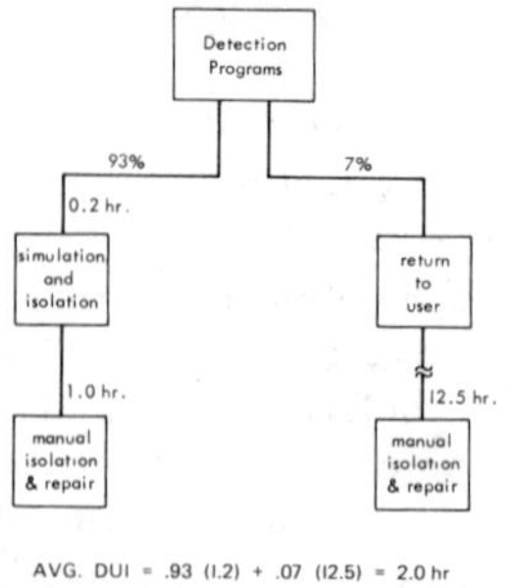

Fig. 23. Duration of unscheduled interrupt obtained by reducing hard-core and isolation strategy of Figure 22.

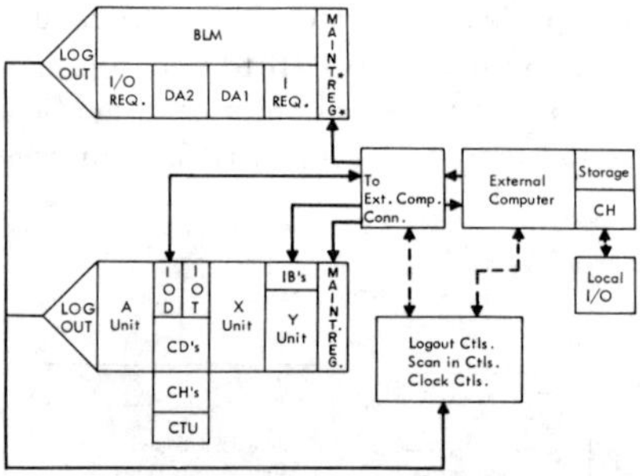

Fig. 24. Maintenance and data paths.

simulators. In addition, simulation of the FHF and of the storage hierarchy was performed at the system level. In the storage hierarchy simulation, a simple language was developed to describe job profiles in terms of storage requirements, I/O requests, and CPU instructions to be executed. These jobs were then processed by the system and various activities such as I/O and CPU busyness and storage requirements were plotted as a function of a time; in this manner both steady-state and transient behavior were studied. One result was that the scheduler should give I/O-limited jobs priority over CPU-limited jobs. That is, whenever an I/O request for an I/O-limited job is completed, the CPU should be switched to that job. Otherwise, it was found that I/O-limited jobs bunched up and eventually the system had no other jobs to work on. This resulted in the CPU becoming idle for long periods of time.

As software and hardware were being designed simultaneously, the only way to check out the software was to extensively debug and integrate it on a simulator, in this case on the System/360 under OS. Since the software itself (except for parts of the nucleus) was to be written entirely in Extended FORTRAN, the simulator had to include a compiler for this language. This compiler, called A360 FORTRAN, generated CPU code which served as input to a link editor, loader, library, etc., and finally the simulator itself. These were written in System/360 assembler and FORTRAN languages. The flowchart of the simulator is shown in Figure 25. The simulator control could interpret an elementary Job

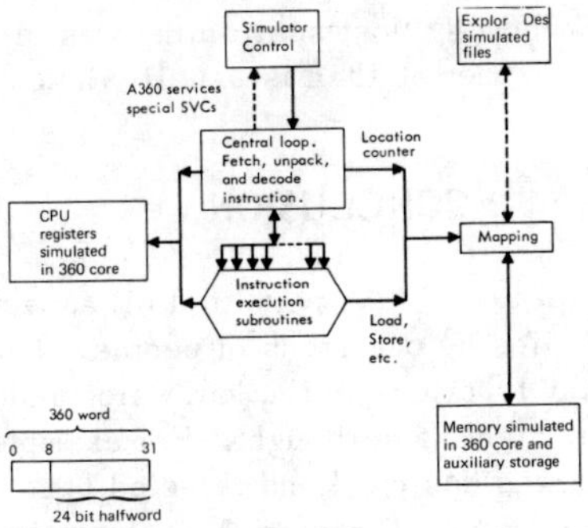

Fig. 25. Simulator flowchart.

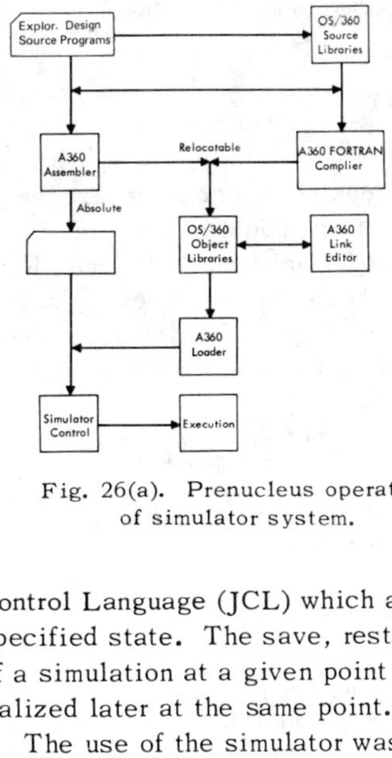

Fig. 26(a). Prenucleus operation of simulator system.

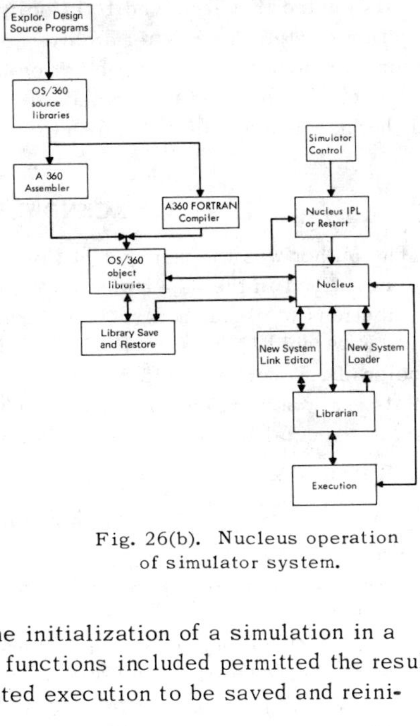

Fig. 26(b). Nucleus operation of simulator system.

Control Language (JCL) which allowed the initialization of a simulation in a specified state. The save, restore, etc., functions included permitted the results of a simulation at a given point of simulated execution to be saved and reinitialized later at the same point.

The use of the simulator was to proceed in an orderly manner; first the nucleus, the A360 FORTRAN compiler, and assembler were to be debugged. The entire system was to operate as shown in Figure 26(a). Rather than employ extensive scaffolding, it was decided to debug peripheral-service routines under the actual nucleus itself as depicted in Figure 26(b). This, while perhaps slower, would insure correctness of all interfaces and nucleus functions. The debugging of an extensive software package under simulation was felt to be feasible only when: (1) A higher-level language was used to write the software; (2) The simulator used was quite extensive; (3) The simulator would run under a modern system such as OS/360; (4) Most scaffolding was eliminated; and (5) There was more time to do the job than is usually the case.

CONCLUSION

The exploratory design of the system permitted all aspects of hardware and software tradeoffs to be studied by one group of people. This flexibility did not result in identifying as many functions in the hardware to aid the software as one's preconceived notions might have thought. For example, a machine to compile, simulate, and emulate was designed and rejected because of cost/performance and system-balance reasons. However, MS relocations, HSS lining, a large bulk memory (MS) and FHF record-ready features were considered essential hardware aids if a successful modern multiprogramming monitor was to be written. It was also noted that improved I/O (including an IBM 3330 with higher data rates) microfilm printers, and better archive devices would be needed to balance the system, particularly in noncomputation-bound environments.

The experiment was terminated after the major ideas had been fully explored and the knowledge obtained transmitted to product-development groups.

ACKNOWLEDGEMENT

The author was the manager of the group in which the major portion of the work described in the paper was performed. The ideas presented represent the contributions of all of these people. Particular mention should be made of F. Allen, R. Arnold, J. Beatty, P. Dauber, C. Freiman, C. Galtieri, D. Helman, R. Robelen, D. Rozenberg, and E. Sussenguth. J. Cocke, while not a member of the department, was a major contributor. The author's manager, J. E. Bertram, also deserves special thanks for his guidance and his technical contributions.

REFERENCES

[1] S. F. Anderson, J. G. Earle, R. E. Goldschmidt, D. M. Powers, "The IBM System/360 Model 91: Floating-Point Execution Unit," *IBM J. Res. Devel.*, **11**, No. 1, 34–53 (January 1967).

[2] F. Allen, "Program Optimization," *Ann. Rev. in Automatic Programming*, **5**, 239–307 (Oxford, England: Pergamon Press, 1969).

[3] J. Cocke and J. Schwartz, "Programming Languages and Their Compilers," 2nd Edition, Courant Institute of Mathematical Science, New York University (1970).

[4] K. E. Knight, "Changes in Computer Performance," *Datamation*, 40–54 (September 1968).

[5] J. S. Liptay, "Structural Aspects of the System/360 Model 85 II—The Cache," *IBM Sys. J.*, 7, No. 1, 15–21 (1968).

[6] D. P. Rozenberg and R. F. Savage, "A Proposal for the Computer-Design Process Based on Multilevel Simulation," IBM T. J. Watson Research Center, Yorktown Heights, New York, Report RC-3167 (December 2, 1970).

AN APPROACH TO HARDWARE/SOFTWARE ARCHITECTURAL TRADE-OFF DECISIONS

J. E. Deans
Texas Instruments Inc., Austin, TX
and
C. V. Ramamoorthy
University of Texas at Austin, Austin, TX

One of the more intriguing problems of computer architecture is the assignment of computational responsibility among the hierarchical processing potentials of hardware, firmware, and software. This paper presents an approach to this trade-off problem in which certain characteristics of the application area can be estimated or are known. The basic procedure is a type of alternative selection in which implementations from these hierarchical areas are available and a choice must be made among a collection of these in order to determine the system structure. A method for making these choices in an optimal sense is the main subject of the paper. Primary consideration is given to throughput/cost trade-offs with cost possibly referring to such resources as dollars, memory, power, weight, etc.

INTRODUCTION

Present-day technology is characterized by increasingly-complex systems consisting of a variety of different components operating as a unit to satisfy some processing requirement. Due to this very complexity, design of these systems is often an exceedingly-difficult problem. Typically the system is broken down into simpler subtasks each of which can then be implemented more or less independently of the others. Simulation of both the subtask implementations and that of the overall system can also be a considerable aid in the design process. Quite often however, even with the aid of simulation, the breakdown of the system into smaller parts results in some desirable characteristics of the total system being ignored or difficult to obtain. Characteristics of this type that usually trade off among one another might be cost, both recurring and nonrecurring, weight, power consumption and, where meaningful, execution time as in a primarily serial system based on or consisting of a digital computer for example. The techniques described in this report are intended to be applied to this type of problem. They are envisioned as applicable design aids in decisions concerning hardware, firmware, and software synthesis of special-purpose computers.

In order to accomplish this goal some interesting analytical methods will be called into play. However the general field of computer design is notoriously unamenable to analytic approaches and even in the narrow area of special-purpose

Presented at the Symposium on Computers and Automata
Polytechnic Institute of Brooklyn, April 13–15, 1971

computing the approaches to be described must be considered only as aids to the art of design and not as an entire design procedure.

BASIC APPROACH AND RESTRICTIONS

Essentially the approach used is to break the total task into a collection of subtasks such as instructions or subroutines so that the objective function relative to the performance of the total task can be defined over the subtask performances. Then the assumption is made that there are several alternative implementations possible for all or some of the subtasks and the idea is to (in some sense) optimize the objective function while simultaneously satisfying certain constraints on resource usage derivable from the proposed operating environment. This is to be done by "wisely" choosing among the subtask implementations. Note carefully that the use of the word optimal here can only have meaning among the known implementation selection. If one more of the subtasks has a poor selection of implementations to choose from, this approach can only hope to choose the "least poorest." Note further that if certain vital subtasks are not identified properly (i.e., a certain useful instruction is lacking) in the first step, then the application of the techniques to be described will in effect compound the error and again the best to hope for is a "good" inefficient design.

Finally our trade-off model will only deal directly with characteristics that are approximately additive over the subtasks. While important features such as execution time, cost, weight, certain types of power usage, etc., can be considered additive in nature, many others are definitely not. Examples of the latter are maintainability, diagnostic capability, reliability, and flexibility to name a few. To some degree the additive restriction can be alleviated by producing a series of suggested configurations that are "optimal" within a desired range of constraint bounds and then make narrower selections on other features.

FORMULATION

The initial mathematical formulation as a constrained optimization problem is now introduced. Define a variable x_{ij} having one of two integer values (1 or 0) to be the following

$$x_{ij} = \begin{cases} 1, \text{ if implementation alternative } j \text{ for subtask } i \text{ is selected} & , \\ 0, \text{ otherwise} & , \end{cases}$$

where $1 \leq i \leq n$ the total number of subtasks, and $1 \leq j \leq m_i$ the number of implementations proposed per i^{th} subtask. Using this variable a simple, but as shall be seen rather restricted, first-cut formulation of an execution-time minimizing problem can be stated as

minimize

$$\sum_{i=1}^{n} \sum_{j=1}^{m_i} x_{ij} t_{ij} f_i \quad ,$$

subject to resource constraints

$$\sum_{i=1}^{n} \sum_{j=1}^{m_i} x_{ij} r_{ij1} \le R_1, \cdots, \sum_{i=1}^{n} \sum_{j=1}^{m_i} x_{ij} r_{ijp} \le R_p \; ,$$

multiple-choice constraints force choice of one and only one implementation per subtask.

$$\sum_{j=1}^{m_1} x_{1j} = 1, \cdots, \sum_{j=1}^{m_n} x_{nj} = 1 \; .$$

In the preceding: f_i is the average usage frequency per subtask i for the problem solution; t_{ij} is the execution time possible using implementation j for the ith subtask; r_{ijk} is the resource usage of type k for the jth implementation of the ith subtask; and R_k is the maximum bound on usage of resource type k.

Similarly for a real-time application where execution time is a resource and it is preferred to minimize some type of cost objective then

minimize

$$\sum_{i \in G^1 \cup G^2} \sum_{j=1}^{m_i} x_{ij} c_{ij} \; ,$$

subject to

$$\sum_{i \in G^1} \sum_{j=1}^{m_i} x_{ij} t_{ij} g_i^1 \le T_1 \; ,$$

$$\sum_{i \in G^1} \sum_{j=1}^{m_i} x_{ij} t_{ij} g_i^1 + \sum_{i \in G^2} \sum_{j=1}^{m_i} x_{ij} t_{ij} g_i^2 \le T_2 \; ,$$

$$\sum_{j=1}^{m_i} x_{ij} = 1 \qquad (i \notin G^1 \cup G^2) \; .$$

Here G^1 and G^2 represent real time interrupt processing routines such that interrupt 1) has priority over 2) with time bounds of T_1 and T_2. The preceding formulations represent examples of compute and I/O bound objectives respectively. Intermingling of the two is also treatable in which case there are also some execution-time constraints in addition to the cost-type resources or the reverse in the second example.

CLASSIFICATION

Requirements on the x_{ij} variable to be 1 or 0 places the constrained-optimization formulation shown in the integer-programming class. Furthermore the specification placed on the x_{ij}'s; that they are disjointly partitioned by the unit-sum constraints mark these formulations as a special case of the general integer-programming problem called the multiple-choice problem [3, 6]. The larger general-integer problems can be quite difficult to solve and, so far as a guaranteed globally-optimal solution, this is also true of the multiple-choice subclass. There is a near-optimal procedure developed by Balintfy [1, 2, 5] available and this will be discussed in more detail shortly. However, at this point it is necessary to step back and take stock of some of the ramifications of the stated formulations. The blunt fact is that as previously phrased these formulations are practically useless in most any engineering sense due to several deficiencies in their implied assumptions.

DEFICIENCIES

The major deficiencies appear to be the following:

(1) Implementations are rarely "dedicated" as such to a single subtask. More likely there may be portions of the total system that are utilized by several subtasks. This is clearly the case with microprogramming. Subsystems such as this must be directly considered in any trade-off decision method purporting to be realistic

(2) While providing some treatment of hardware or software trade offs, the formulation as stated does not properly deal with the case in which certain values are actually dependent on others as with software execution time being dependent upon certain hardware execution times for example

(3) Interconnection costs between all combinations of implementations are assumed to be grouped with the individual implementation, negligible or constant

(4) Software-resource usage is poorly stated. In particular the modular properties of memory are not taken into account

(5) No allowance for optional subtasks. The formulations as previously phrased require at least and select at most one implementation per subtask

(6) A large amount of data are required, of which a considerable portion may be at best only an estimate.

In view of all this it almost seems that the best course of action would be to abandon this approach immediately. However, as shall be shown in the later sections, most of these deficiencies can apparently be alleviated to a satisfactory degree.

SOLUTION TECHNIQUES

As mentioned, perfectly-optimal solutions are usually not computationally feasible. However there does exist the excellent near-optimal heuristic of Balintfy that produces good solutions that are quite often optimal (Balintfy reports 10 out of 14 relatively complex problems optimally solved [1] and our experience tends to confirm this). This heuristic (termed a heuristic because it might not obtain a feasible solution when one exists) consists of choosing the best-performing implementation in each objective-function multiple-choice group as an initial trail solution and then applying two distinct types of iterations according to the following rules (if initially feasible the trail solution is of course optimal):

(a) Label the current-trial solution $x_{ij} = 1$ as x_{iB}
(b) Determine the most violated resource constraint $= k_0$
(c) (Forward iteration) Select a new implementation in one of the multiple choice groups to become part of the next-trial solution via

$$\min_{i,j} \{(p_{ij} - p_{iB})/(r_{iBk_0} - r_{ijk_0}) \mid r_{ijk_0} < r_{iBk_0};\ p_{ij} \geq p_{iB}\}$$

(d) If the resulting trail solution is not feasible go to (a), else
(e) (Reverse iteration) Improve the objective function via

$$\max_{i,j} \{(p_{ij} - p_{iB}) \mid p_{ij} > p_{iB}$$

(f) If feasible, relabel the trial solution and go to (e), else
(g) The last feasible solution is the desired near-optimal solution.

In the preceding: p_{ij} denotes objective performance; and r_{ijk} resource usage.

A forward iteration is similar to the dual-simplex procedure and is effected simply by bringing in a new implementation on the best improvement in performance/usage ratio. In practice the heuristic is rapid and the resulting solution is quite often optimal as mentioned. In the remainder of this paper, prime consideration will be to modify only within the multiple-choice structure allowing use of the basic Balintfy heuristic.

SUBSYSTEMS

Two approaches are presented for treating the subsystem problem. The first is somewhat similar to the set-up cost problem of operations research. Let s^q represent the ℓth cost type used by the qth subsystem and let

$$S^q = \{(i_1^q, j_1^q), \cdots, (i_{t_q}^q, j_{t_q}^q)\},$$

denote its membership (i.e., those implementations that use it). Introduce variables y_q such that

$$y_q = \begin{cases} 1, & \text{if subsystem } q \text{ chosen}, \\ 0, & \text{if not}, \end{cases}$$

then consider the following cost minimization problem statement with Q subsystems:

objective

$$\min \left\{ \sum_{i=1}^{n} \sum_{j=1}^{m_i} r_{ijo}\, x_{ij} + \sum_{q=1}^{Q} s_o^q\, y_{q1} \right\},$$

subject to resource constraints

$$\sum_{i=1}^{n} \sum_{j=1}^{m_i} r_{ij} \quad x_{ij} + \sum_{q=1}^{Q} s^q \; y_{q1} \leq R \quad \text{(for appropriate values of } \ell) \ ,$$

execution-time constraints

$$\sum_{i \in G^p} \sum_{j=1}^{m_i} g^p \, t_{ij} \, x_{ij} \leq T_p \quad \text{(for appropriate values of } p) \ ,$$

subsystem structure constraints with M_q an arbitrary integer constant $> S^q$

$$\sum_{(i,j) \in S^1} x_{ij} - M_1 \, y_{11} \leq 0, \cdots, \sum_{(i,j) \in S^Q} x_{ij} - M_Q \, y_{Q1} \leq 0 \ ,$$

multiple-choice structure constraints

$$\sum_{j=1}^{m_1} x_{1j} = 1, \cdots, \sum_{j=1}^{m_n} x_{nj} = 1 \ ,$$

$$y_{11} + y_{12} = 1, \cdots, y_{Q1} + y_{Q2} = 1 \ .$$

The subsystem structure constraints force the appropriate $y_{q1} = 1$ if any $(i, j) \in S^q$ are such that $x_{ij} = 1$. If all S^q members are zero the minimization operation forces y_{q1} to zero as desired. The y_{q2} are inserted to preserve the multiple-choice structure.

This approach has at least two disadvantages, the main one being the extra constraints required and the other is that use of a near-optimal technique instead of an optimal one may not force y_{q1} to zero when needed.

The second approach and the one that is eventually made use of involves alteration of implementation resource usage at each iteration, if needed, to reflect subsystem resource usage directly.

(1) If a particular subsystem is not used by any implementation now in the current solution, let all implementations using the subsystem reflect its total cost plus their own

(2) When a subsystem is used by a single implementation in the current solution, let the total cost of the subsystem be reflected in that implementation alone. There is one exception to this rule, namely, those implementations also using the subsystem and in the subtask group of the single implementation in the solution should also reflect the total cost of the subsystem plus their own

(3) If more than one of the current-solution implementations use the same subsystem, then do not reflect the subsystem cost in any implementation (still deducted from total cost).

With regard to multiple subsystem usage by one implementation clearly the superposition principle is obeyed.

While the second method may sound even more complex than the first, programming it is simpler and execution is apparently faster.

DEPENDENT VALUES

As far as our computational model is concerned, the concept of a software implementation is simply a collection of subtasks (and thus eventually a collection of implementations) that acts like a single subtask implementation. In general of course some of the utilized subtasks can also be software thus introducing the subroutine concept.

Now as a subtask implementation, resource usage and performance data are necessary and this requirement can lead to an amazingly complex problem. Performance data for software are derived from performance of the instructions (subtasks) that (eventually) make up a routine and typically some of these are not known prior to the problem solution. On the other side, resource usage for software is also a subtle concept. Usage on a per-word-of-memory-used basis might be applicable for some uses, but more realistically, modular characteristics should be reflected. This section deals only with performance (execution time is arbitrarily selected for the moment), modularity will be addressed later.

Again as with subsystems, two approaches are discussed: one utilizing additional constraints and artificial variables; and the other, iterative modification of the performance data.

For the first method the execution time t_k of the kth instruction is given by

$$t_k = \sum_{j=1}^{m_k} t_{kj} x_{kj} \ .$$

Denoting a software implementation $(i, j)^{\omega}$ and the total collection of software implementation index pairs by W^t, the execution time of a routine $(i, j)^{\omega}$ becomes

$$t_{ij}^{\omega} = \sum g_k t_k = \sum g_k \sum_{j=1}^{m_k} t_{kj} x_{kj} \qquad (k \in (i, j)^{\omega}) \ ,$$

with g_k the average usage of instruction (or subroutine) k in the ω software routine. Here $k \in (i, j)^{\omega}$ means that $k = i^{\omega}$ for some $(i^{\omega}, j^{\omega}) \in (i, j)^{\omega}$. Thus the objective function becomes

$$\min \left\{ \sum_{i=1}^{n} \sum_{\substack{j=1 \\ ((i,j) \notin W^t)}}^{m_i} f_i t_{ij} x_{ij} + \sum_{((i,j)^{\omega} \in W^t)} f_i x_{ij} \left[\sum_{(k \in (i,j)^{\omega})} g_k \sum_{j=1}^{m_k} t_{kj} x_{kj} \right] \right\}.$$

This alone should be enough to strike fear in the hearts of most veteran operations researchers but the actual situation can be even worse since it is possible for $(k, j) \in W^t$, as a subroutine, thus introducing more levels for certain t_{kj}'s although hopefully not ad infinitum since infinite recursion is not especially productive in usual systems.

The mathematical effect is to add variable product terms to the objective function. Thus the question is: How do we handle product terms? And the answer, or an answer, as usual is to torture the problem with more artificial variables and constraints. In particular for each $\prod_{j \in T} x_j$ with T containing only distinct indices (clearly $x^n = x$ for $x = (1, 0)$), replace with a new $(1, 0)$ variable

x_T and append two new constraints of the form:

(1) $x_T \geq \sum_{j \in T} x_j - |T| + 1$; redundant until all $x_{j \in T} = 1$, then $= x_T \geq 1$

(2) $x \leq [1/|T|] \cdot \left[\sum_{j \in T} x_j \right]$; forces $x_T < 1$ if any $x_{j \in T} = 0$ and when all

$x_{j \in T} = 1$, $x_T \leq 1$ as desired.

Occasionally several different product-term variables can combine constraints (1) or (2) into a single constraint or use the min operation. It is possible to, with a few more artificial variables, force the preceding to fit the multiple choice structure and thus use the Balintfy heuristic. But at the same time, the number of additional constraints needed can increase massively as the number of subroutine call levels increase. Fortunately there is another way.

The second method of solution to the dependent-value problem is to, at each iteration, update the execution time of each software implementation according to the instruction times given in the current-trial solution. In addition some changes in the average-usage figures are usually required since in effect more software is being considered for use by the system. Accomplishing this is a trifle more difficult than it might seem, although not as bad as the extra-constraint method, because of the linked-list-structure subroutine calls can imply. These structures necessitate possible movement up and/or down the calling list to calculate the effect of moving a software implementation into or out of the trial solution. Appropriate use of LIFO stacks however makes the problem tractable.

SOFTWARE RESOURCE USAGE

The resource usage of software occasionally can be approximated and treated as a set of numbers as with hardware via a resource usage per word of memory used maneuver. However, especially for small memories or situations where the use of additional software could require another module, continuous memory assumptions are seriously at fault. In general it is not even true that the cost of n modules is the same as n times the cost of one module. This also must be accounted for in any method used for treating modularity. And, for treating modularity, again two approaches seem possible. This time however, only one additional constraint is required for artificial variable and constraint method. Let

$$z_\ell \begin{cases} = 1, \text{ if } \ell \text{ modules of memory are used} , \\ = 0, \text{ if not} . \end{cases}$$

Clearly $\sum_{\ell=1}^{U} z_\ell = 1$ where U is an upper bound on the number of modules possible.

Now append one new constraint of the form

(1) $\sum_{(i,j) \in Wt} m_{ij} x_{ij} - \sum_{\ell=1}^{U} m_\ell z_\ell \leq 0$, here: m_{ij} is the amount of memory

needed for the $(i, j)^{\omega}$ software implementation; and m_{ℓ} is the amount of memory available in ℓ modules. Note that any predetermined memory needs, for required software for example, must be initially deducted from the m_{ℓ}

(2) Set to zero the resource-usage coefficients of $(i, j)^{\omega}$ or to an appropriate value if such is known

(3) Add to each resource constraint $\sum_{\ell=1}^{U} r_p z_{\ell}$ with r_p the amount of this type of resource used by ℓ modules of memory

(4) Append $\sum_{\ell=1}^{U} r_0 z_{\ell}$ on the objective function (for a cost-type 0 objective).

Items (1) and (4) cause $z_{\ell} = 1$ when ℓ modules are required if the solution is optimal. Theoretically at least a near-optimal approach might result in an improper assignment for z_{ℓ}. The Balintfy technique's reverse iteration seems, however, to guarantee a proper value for z_{ℓ} if an initial-feasible solution is found.

The other approach to memory modularity is to again iteratively modify data, this time the software-resource-usage values, and is the one used in the programmed-solution technique. Essentially this involves dynamically assigning resource usage to software implementations according to whether their memory needs will require more or less modules of memory given the implementation configuration, with associated total-memory-usage figure, selected by the current-solution iteration.

INTERCONNECTION COSTS

In theory interconnection costs can be handled by including the appropriate variable-product terms with associated resource usage in the resource constraints. For example the term $C_{\ell}^{IC} x_{12} x_{23} x_{45}$ would cause cost C_{ℓ}^{IC} to be applied to resource type ℓ whenever x_{12}, x_{23}, and x_{45} were chosen implementations.

These product terms could then be handled as previously mentioned or an iterative-modification attack used. Practically however there are usually too many different configurations to include, although a few may be treated in this manner. Quite often interconnection costs can be included directly with the appropriate implementation, specified as a subsystem, ignored or if relatively constant deducted from the original constraint bounds. If there are a considerable number of different configurations requiring widely varying and significant interconnection costs, the multiple-choice approach should not be used.

OPTIONAL SUBTASKS

By definition, an optional subtask cannot be used by the fixed software otherwise it would not be optional but required. Consequently the only time an optional subtask is required when a software implementation using this optional subtask is part of a solution. Thus the optional subtask acts like a subsystem. There is however one difference. Since it is optional, provision must be made for its *non* use which requires an artificial variable be appended to the subtask implementation set to allow selection of "no" implementation.

IMPERFECT DATA

The major practical limitation of the multiple-choice technique is usually the difficulty of obtaining the data. Quite probably implementations would have to be designed down to at least the logic-equation level for hardware and the assembly or machine-language level for software before truly accurate data are possible. Even then unforseen occurrences that might not show up until the actual application puts a question mark on the validity of some of the data values.

It can also be argued that possibly-excessive nonrecurring cost will be incurred in the design phase itself especially if, as the multiple-choice approach seems to require, the way to proceed is to crank out as many implementations per subtask as possible. A little insight quickly shows that this is not the method to use, rather judgement on the part of the designers should quickly eliminate a large portion of the implementation choices even before initial design work begins. The multiple-choice approach should come into use when remaining implementation choices have possible features that might cause them to be used in certain situations. These "certain situations" being specified by appropriate operating constraints. However, information on such constraints is likely to be even more difficult to obtain than implementation data. It is almost absurd to expect existence of an absolute bound on some resources, especially cost. Instead acceptable ranges are more likely. It is here that information obtained from varying the constraint bounds through these ranges is quite valuable. This is a type of parametric programming on the constraint bounds. For a single-resource constraint the bound itself can be the parameter. However, for the case of multiple-resource constraints a more involved relationship is usually necessary where all resource bounds are expressed as a function of a single parameter and the desired information is the objective function value with its solutions as this parameter is varied. This is typically represented in the form

$$\text{constraints}\begin{cases} \cdots \leq \alpha_1 + \beta_1 \theta \ , \\ \qquad\qquad \vdots \\ \cdots \leq \alpha_M + \beta_M \theta \ , \end{cases}$$

with: $\alpha_k + \beta_k \theta$ the constraint bound for the kth constraint; and θ the parameter of interest. A collection of solutions can then be determined as θ is varied through some predetermined range such as $[\theta_L, \theta_H]$. An example of this, for the simple case of one-cost constraint, is shown in Figure 1. A method has been developed by the authors to determine such solution collections for the general $\alpha_k + \beta_k \theta \geq 0$, for $\theta_L \leq \theta \leq \theta_H$. This method essentially involves assuming a value

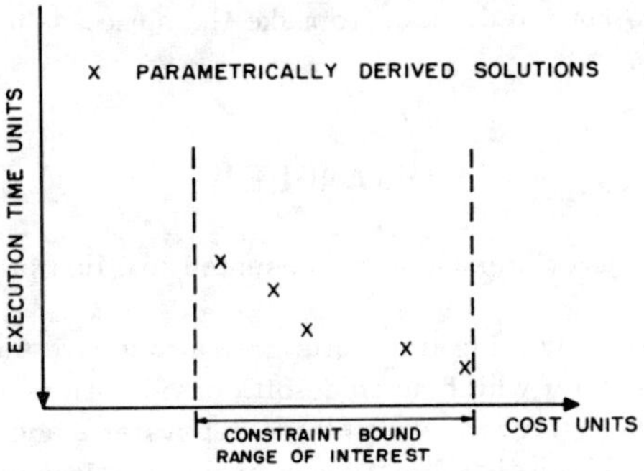

Fig. 1. Parametric-solution collections.

of θ, say θ_H, solving for a solution with the constraint bounds so defined, determining a new value of θ that first causes a constraint violation, resolving with this value and continuing until θ_L is reached. Similar approaches of this type are used in linear programming, see for example [4].

Parametric studies of other quantities in addition to constraint bounds are also of interest but are, in general, quite a difficult problem in integer programming and that also apparently holds true for the multiple-choice case. Consequently little effort has been expended in this area.

FINITENESS

One of the more desirable attributes of the Balintfy heuristic is that it will always terminate even if no solution is found. This is due to the restrictions placed on implementation entry/exit namely

$$r_{ijk_o} < r_{iBk_o}; \qquad p_{ij} \geq p_{iB} \quad ,$$

for forward iterations and

$$p_{ij} > p_{iB} \quad ,$$

for feasible changes in reverse iterations. Termination is thus assured since there is only a finite collection of implementations to choose from and satisfaction of these relations prevents cycling.

However, the solution techniques have now been changed to modify some of the quantities defining the problem during the iterations. Consequently the effect of this alteration on termination is now of interest. It is relatively easy to see that modification of r_{ijk} or p_{ij} terms (but not both) alone need not cause cycling so long as the quantities remain positive. This is not so apparent when both r_{ijk} and p_{ij} are subject to change as with the approaches described that are applicable to software performance/resource usage. Essentially however, even in the latter case, all that is needed is some mechanism to assure that no implementation is considered more than once during the forward-iteration phase or again no more than once during reverse iterations. The Balintfy inequality restrictions on entry/exit performed this for the simple case of no-data modification and it is not too difficult to make the same assurance for the modified-data case.

EXAMPLE

In this section a numeric example is presented to illustrate some of the concepts discussed.

Consider a problem involving trade offs only among five subtasks (there could be many other subtasks for which no trade-off considerations were necessary) each having unity usage frequency with three subsystems and two cost-type resource constraints in which the objective is execution-time minimization. Pertinent execution and cost data are presented in Table I.

TABLE I. Example performance/resource data.

SUBTASK	TIME				RESOURCE TYPE 1)				RESOURCE TYPE 2)			
IMPLEMENTATION	1	2	3	4	1	2	3	4	1	2	3	4
(1)	5.	13.	18.	SW	20.	13.	9.	3.	35.	19.	9.	5.
(2)	4.	5.	16.	—	20.	18.	11.	—	23.	25.	7.	—
(3)	10.	17.	20.	SW	52.	40.	35.	14.	63.	55.	30.	10.
(4)	8.	12.	—	—	14.	7.	—	—	21.	9.	—	—
(5)	9.	12.	16.	—	15.	13.	9.	—	23.	17.	8.	—

Implementations (1,4) and (3,4) are software and their descriptors are presented next.

TABLE II. Software-implementation descriptors.

IMPLEMENTATION	MEMORY	SUB-TASK —	USAGE	SUB-TASK	USAGE	SUB-TASK	USAGE
(1,4)	3K	2	7.	3	2.	—	—
(3,4)	4K	2	8.	4	10.	5	4.

Note that subroutine nesting is possible as (1,4) uses subtask (3) and thus possibly implementation (3,4). Two memory modules are available to contain predetermined software storage of 22K plus any optional software needs.

Table III. Memory-module definitions.

NUMBER	SIZE	RESOURCE TYPE 1)	RESOURCE TYPE 2
(1)	24K	8.	11.
(2)	30K	12.	15.

Module (2) includes (1) in our nomenclature.

Rounding out the example data are the subsystem descriptors in Table IV.

TABLE IV. Subsystem descriptor.

SUBSYSTEM	RESOURCE TYPE 1)	RESOURCE TYPE 2)	IMPLEMENTATIONS USING
(1)	18.	16.	(1, 2); (1, 3); (5, 1); (5, 2)
(2)	7.	8.	(2, 2); (3, 3)
(3)	9.	12.	(1, 3); (4, 2)

With bounds of

resource Type 1) = 68 ,
resource Type 2) = 110 .

The solution is

(1, 4); (2, 3); (3, 4); (4, 1); (5, 3) ,

with

objective function value of 968 ,
resource Type 1) usage of 62 ,
resource Type 2) usage of 66 ,

requiring the (2) memory module. Solution time for this problem was about 25 msec for a CDC 6600, FORTRAN code. Solution-memory requirements generally would be five to six times the space necessary to store the performance and resource data of the implementations. The extra space is needed to hold inverted files and incremental tables used during the solution. Even then memory needs are not especially horrendous as for example a problem having seventy-five subtasks and up to ten implementations per subtask requires about the same room as does the 6600 FORTRAN compiler.

CONCLUSION

This paper has concentrated on presenting some solution techniques applicable to certain types of computer-design problems; in particular those for which appropriate problem-application information is available. These techniques have their advantages in that being based on alternative selection they resemble a design approach commonly in use, they are applicable to relatively large problems and they can be used to select actual system components unlike more general tenets. As noted also, several deficiencies are present, most of which could be avoided, some of which could not. In addition the inner-product form of the objective function or constraints implies a serial time structure. In some cases, critical path treatment would be useful but this awaits future effort. Effort lately has been on developing example applications with concentration on extraction of the necessary numbers. Perhaps this can be presented in the form of a future paper.

In any event it is possible that the methods discussed could, in appropriate situations, free the designer's mind from worrying quite so much about feasibility details among the treatable quantities and concentrate more on other aspects such as ease of use, repairs, and diagnosis. If that is the case then the effort expended will have served some purpose.

ACKNOWLEDGEMENTS

The authors would like to express their appreciation to Drs. F. Glover and K. M. Chandy for their assistance in the integer-programming phases of the study.

REFERENCES

[1] J. L. Balintfy, "Menu Planning by Computer," *Comm. ACM* (April 1964).

[2] R. L. Gue, "A Decomposition Principle for the Zero-One Programming Problem," Technical Report CP-67102, Computer Science Center, SMU.

[3] W. C. Healy, Jr., "Multiple-Choice-Programming," *Operations Res.*, **12** (1964).

[4] F. S. Hillier and G. J. Liberman, *Introduction to Operations Res.* (Holden-Day, 1968).

[5] J. C. Liggett, "A General Multiple-Choice Formulation of an Algorithm by Balintfy," Technical Report CP-68004, Computer Sciences Center, SMU.

SOME NOTES ON SPEEDING UP CERTAIN LOOPS BY SOFTWARE, FIRMWARE, AND HARDWARE MEANS

David Pager

Information Sciences Program, University of Hawaii, Honolulu, HI

In this paper we discuss some ways of speeding up certain loops by software, firmware, and hardware means. The importance of the inner-loop calculation is emphasized and a simple, though as yet unused, programming technique is presented whereby the inner-loop time may be reduced by approximately 20%. The general problem of a program with many loops is then considered and a method is indicated for obtaining the maximum speed-up by means of the technique described earlier. Turning to firmware, we show how, by altering the normal algorithm used for the inner-loop calculation, a very substantial speed-up can be achieved with the use of microprogramming (above and beyond the savings in instruction decoding time). Finally we consider a means whereby a computer can alter its own hardware so as to achieve a speed-up of several orders for loops in which the resolution of decision tables accounts for a significant portion of the iteration time.

A large proportion of the computer time used by scientific programs is devoted to the manipulation of matrices; and about 95% of the work involved in the latter consists simply of repeated iterations of the inner loop

$$x_i' = x_i + ky_i \quad (\text{for } 1 \leq i \leq n) \quad (\text{or } \sum_{i=1}^{n} x_i y_i, \text{ the inner product*}) \; .$$

In fact the overall throughput of many scientific-computer establishments (particularly those involved in linear programming or the solution of large systems of linear equations) is closely related to the inner-loop time of their machines**. The annual dollar savings to be obtained through improving the efficiency of the inner loop by as much as 1% must be measured in the millions.

Our first note concerns a method for improving the inner loop by about 20%. It is both simple and obvious, and yet the idea has never been implemented in any of the standard matrix or linear-programming packages.

The usual coding employed for the inner-loop calculation may be expressed as

```
LOOP    Load k into a register
        Multiply from y indexed by j
        Add from x indexed by i
```

*or Winograd's formulation [14].

**For instance, a survey at the University of Hawaii showed that of the fourteen main users of its 360/65, thirteen were engaged in matrix calculations which consisted almost entirely of iterations of the inner loop.

Presented at the Symposium on Computers and Automata
Polytechnic Institute of Brooklyn, April 13–15, 1971.

Store in x indexed by i
Increment i and j. If $i \leq n$, go to LOOP otherwise go on to the next instruction.

A method for increasing the speed of the loop is to code a number of repetitions of the first four instructions with suitably-modified displacements to produce for some divisor m of n, an expansion of the form*

LOOP Load k into a register
Multiply from y indexed by j
Add from x indexed by i
Store in x indexed by i
Load k into a register
Multiply from $y + t$ indexed by j, where $y + t$ is the next-highest word address following y
Add from $x + t$ indexed by i
Store in $x + t$ indexed by i

.

.

.

Load k into a register
Multiply from $y + mt$ indexed by j
Add from $x + mt$ indexed by i
Store in $x + mt$ indexed by i
Increment i and j by mt. If $i \leq n$, go to LOOP otherwise go on to the next instruction.

On, for example, the IBM 360/75 the inner loop calculation in the first form (as used by the IBM 360 linear-programming and scientific-programming packages) takes 5.32 μsec. Of this, the housekeeping and branch, which in this case is one instruction, accounts for 1.2 μsec and thus forms 23% of the computer's inner-loop time. In the second version given above, the housekeeping and branch is executed less frequently, thus producing an effective inner-loop time which is $23\left(1 - \frac{1}{m}\right)$% shorter than that of the first version. For smaller machines the savings are not as great, but are usually in excess of 16%.

The above approach is of course not limited to the inner-loop calculation, but is applicable to any loop in which the housekeeping time is a significant portion of the loop time.

Most programs do not contain a sufficiently large number of frequently-iterated loops for there to be a problem in deciding which loops to expand by how much within the free space available. However programs of this kind *do* exist, and for these we provide the following observation.

Assume that there are n frequently-iterated loops under consideration. Let the storage required for the parts of the loops we are considering "repeating" be $a_1, a_2, a_3, \cdots, a_n$, let $t_1, t_2, t_3, \cdots, t_n$, respectively, be the total time spent

*If m does not divide n, then a small extra block of coding must be added to cater for the final r iterations, where r is the remainder of n divided by m. The code required can be generated automatically by supplying the parameters n and m to an appropriate macro.

in housekeeping for these loops (i.e., the number of times a loop is iterated times its associated housekeeping time) and let S be the available free storage. In these circumstances, to produce the fastest program, the number of times $x_1, x_2, x_3, \cdots, x_n$, respectively, which the loops are repeated must clearly be chosen so as to minimize

$$\sum_{i=1}^{n} \frac{t_i}{x_i}, \quad \text{subject to} \sum_{i=1}^{n} a_i x_i \leq S, \tag{1}$$

and the time saved in this case will be

$$\sum_{i=1}^{n} t_i - \sum_{i=1}^{n} \frac{t_i}{x_i}. \tag{2}$$

With a certain amount of manipulation, a method for finding an optimum solution (i.e., one producing the fastest program) in positive (but not necessarily integer) x_i to Eq. (1) can be used to obtain a solution in positive integers sufficiently close to the optimum one for the present purposes. Hence the theorem which follows provides a means for producing the program design required.

THEOREM. *Let n be an integer* ≥ 1 *and let S and, for* $1 \leq i \leq n$, a_i *and* t_i *be positive numbers. Then the values of* $x_1, x_2, x_3, \cdots, x_n$ *for which* $\sum_{i=1}^{n} \frac{t_i}{x_i}$ *is a minimum, subject to* $\sum_{i=1}^{n} a_i x_i \leq S$ *and the* x_i*'s being positive, are given by*

$$x_j = \frac{S\sqrt{\dfrac{t_j}{a_j}}}{\sum_{i=1}^{n} \sqrt{a_i t_i}} \quad (\text{for } 1 \leq j \leq n),$$

and in this case

$$\sum_{i=1}^{n} \frac{t_i}{x_i} = \frac{\left(\sum_{i=1}^{n} \sqrt{a_i t_i}\right)^2}{S},$$

(giving the savings in time by substitution in Equation (2)).

Proof. Clearly $\sum_{i=1}^{n} a_i x_i = S$ in the optimum case. Hence the expression to be minimized can be expressed as

$$\frac{a_1 t_1}{S - \sum_{i=2}^{n} a_i x_i} + \sum_{i=2}^{n} \frac{t_i}{x_i}.$$

For $2 \leq j \leq n$, the derivative with respect to x_j is zero when

$$\frac{a_1 t_1 a_j}{\left(S - \sum_{i=2}^{n} a_i x_i\right)^2} = \frac{t_j}{x_j^2} .$$

We thus obtain a set of linear equations in $x_2, x_3, x_4, \cdots, x_n$, whose solution yields the theorem's results. Q.E.D.

A number of people have experimented with producing microprograms for the inner-loop calculation [3]. As far as we know, none of these have involved radical departures from the first form we described, and the savings produced as compared with the machine instruction versions have been mainly due to obviating the need to repetitively retrieve and decode the instructions which the loop contains.* If one *excludes* instruction decoding time, the time taken to multiply two t-bit numbers in a computer is significantly greater than the time required for t additions. Thus, if one is going to be multiplying by the same constant k at each iteration, it pays to work out and store in local or control store in advance an appropriate set of multiples of k, and then using, if necessary, the hardware shift instructions available,** perform the multiplication concerned by means of suitable additions of these multiples. We have carried out this exercise on the IBM 360/30. The time taken to work out and store the 30 multiples of the fractional part of k required in this case ($\times i$ and $\times 16i$ (for $1 \leq i \leq 15$)) is 343 μsec. But the floating-point multiplication ky_i of the inner loop can now be effected by a microprogram routine which takes $71\frac{1}{4}$ μsec as opposed to the $194\frac{1}{4}$ μsec (excluding instruction decoding time) required by the standard floating-point-multiplication microprogram, a speed up which reduces the model 30's inner-loop time to $\frac{1}{3}$.

From firmware, we pass to hardware. A few automata theorists have speculated about computers which can alter their own circuitry. The technical means for doing so are available. What is lacking is not ability but motivation. What purpose would such a facility serve? How could the changes in circuitry required be determined? Would the benefits justify the costs? We describe here a purpose and a means for achieving it. By itself we do not believe the benefits would justify the costs. However the general-purpose manipulatory automata being developed at MIT and Stanford, the advent of computer-controlled wirewrap machines, and the degree of automation which already exists for the fabrication of circuits indicate, in our opinion, that the means required for the device which we describe below, will soon independently be made economically available.

The loops that we raise for consideration here, are highly iterated ones, in which multiway branches based upon Boolean decisions account for a significant portion of the iteration time. Such decisions, often expressed by means of decision tables, occur frequently, particularly in commercial and control programming. A simple example is where records representing a variety of transactions

*Husson [3] quotes a study by Hans Jeans for IBM as concluding that: "The mathematical inner-loop subroutines such as polynomial evaluation and vector-scalar multiplication will not be greatly improved by microprogramming. The inherently-slow arithmetic operations are not appreciably expedited by the microprogrammed composite operations, since the instruction fetch time saved remains a small fraction of the overall execution time."

**A shift and add microorder usually requires no more time than an add by itself.

are intermixed, and the action to be taken in each case depends on various fields within the record. There has been a lot of work [4, 5, 7, 9, 11–13] on the question of designing short* and fast programs for decision tables. The gains in speed for such programs which can be obtained by recourse to microprogramming are severely limited, because the degree of parallelism available from a given microinstruction is limited by the fixed structure of the CPU, and the microinstructions themselves can only be executed one at a time. In constrast the means for designing combinational circuits in which the various propositions making up a Boolean decision, such as comparisons between variables and constants, are all tested in parallel has been well worked out, and is capable of being automated [1, 2, 6]. Experience has shown that a special purpose circuit of this kind can be expected to operate over a thousand times faster than a comparable general-purpose computer.

Consider for example a decision such as "A is even, or if not, it is such that $A = 3$ or $A > 9$ but $A \neq 21$," where a branch depends upon the result. To resolve a question such as this, a general-purpose computer would have to execute a sequence of tests, compares, and conditional branches. However, the combinational circuit in Fig. 1, made up of a few dollars worth of components,

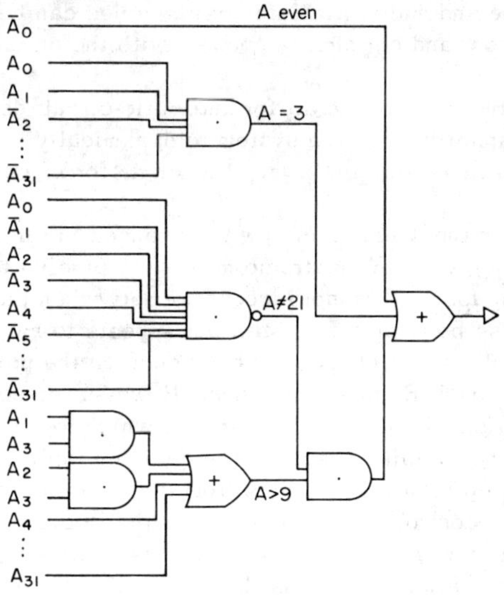

Fig. 1. Combinational circuit to decide whether A is even or, if not, is such that $A = 3$, or $A > 9$ but $A \neq 21$.

performs all the tests and comparisons in parallel. It would operate well within the minor-cycle time of a computer of comparable circuitry speed, and hence could be used to effect a special-purpose branch on Boolean decision in about the same time as a single conditional-branch instruction.

To take advantage of a speed-up of this kind, we propose that a data path be

*Though, according to Pager [8], the problem of finding the shortest program for a decision table is not solvable.

incorporated leading from the main-storage data-output bus of a computer to a special circuit board for integrated circuits. The computer would control the insertion and connection of the ICs required for the combinational circuit involved, and the output of this circuit would set a status bit or control a microprogram branch.

At the software level the user would issue a call to an appropriate supervisor routine, passing as parameter the Boolean decision to be tested by hardware. The supervisor routine would then set into motion the circuit building process and signal by an interruption or the setting of a flag when it was complete. A special built-in instruction "Branch on Boolean decision" would then be made use of in the subsequent program. At termination the user would specify to the supervisor whether to store or dispose of the circuit constructed. In the latter case the whole circuit could either be discarded, or else dismantled with the ICs returned to their hoppers for reuse.

A range of compromises exists between implementing complete automation in the above processes, and making use of operator assistance under computer direction and verification.

In the example given above we considered, in effect, a single-variable single-rule decision table. This by itself is sufficiently common to consider implementing alone. Multirule and multivariable decision tables can be tackled in a similar way. The cost and complexity goes up with the number of rules and variables.

Eventually, as the state of the art for automatic-circuit design advances, one could extend the capabilities of the system to dynamically implement various kinds of noncombinational circuits as well, such as for x^2 or the inner-loop calculation.

We have left open the question of how the changes in circuitry should be effected, whether by physical or electronic means. A purely electronic solution (including one using fast LSI random-access memory when these become available) would of course be most convenient, but appears to have a restricted application. Work such as that of [10] has been done on the problem of electronically synthesizing small Boolean functions. However, an approach of this kind can only cater for a small subset of the circuits which we are concerned with here, where each (say) 32-bit variable in the decision table gives rise to 32 inputs. If n is the total number of inputs from the decision table, k the number of independent input control lines which control the Boolean decision synthesized, and s the number of stages, then to synthesize an arbitrary Boolean decision of the input variables we must have $ks \geq 2^n$, which is a very large number for $n \geq 32$. Furthermore, the effect of the simplification obtained by considering the usual equivalence classes of Boolean functions is relatively minor to this case. Making use of physical manipulation to construct the circuits, on the other hand, provides much more generality in the decisions which are realizable, and would permit the implementation of almost all decision tables encountered in practice.

ACKNOWLEDGEMENT

This work was supported by the National Science Foundation under Grant GJ-596.

REFERENCES

[1] M. A. Breuer, "General Survey of Design Automation of Digital Computers," *Proc. IEEE*, **54**, 1708–1721 (1966).

[2] D. L. Dietmeyer, "Automated NAND Network Synthesis," *Comput. Des.*, **10**, 53–58 (1971).

[3] S. S. Husson, *Microprogramming: Principles and Practice*, 85 (New Jersey: Prentice-Hall, 1970).

[4] P. J. H. King, "Conversion of Decision Tables to Computer Programs by Rule-Mask Techniques," *Comm. ACM*, **9**, 796–801 (1966).

[5] H. W. Kirk, "Use of Decision Tables in Computer Programming," *Comm. ACM*, **8**, 41–43 (1965).

[6] M. A. Lettinger and G. W. Jacob, "An Algorithm for Sequential-Circuit Design," *Comput. Design*, **7**, 46–53 (1968).

[7] C. R. Muthukrishnan and V. Rajaraman, "On the Conversion of Decision Tables to Computer Programs," *Comm. ACM*, **13**, 347–351 (1970).

[8] D. Pager, "On the Problem of Finding Minimal Programs for Tables," *Information & Control*, **14**, 550–554 (1969).

[9] S. L. Pollack, "Conversion of Limited-Entry Decision Tables to Computer Programs," *Comm. ACM*, **8**, 677–682 (1965).

[10] F. P. Preparata and D. E. Muller, "On the Delay Required to Realize Boolean Functions," *IEEE Trans. Comput.*, **C20**, 459–461 (1971).

[11] L. I. Press, "Conversion of Decision Tables to Computer Programs," *Comm. ACM*, **8**, 385–390 (1965).

[12] L. T. Reinwald and R. M. Soland, "Conversion of Limited-Entry Decision Tables to Optimal Computer Programs I: Minimum Average Processing Time," *J. ACM*, **13**, 339–358 (1966).

[13] K. Shwayder, "Conversion of Limited-Entry Decision Tables to Computer Programs—a Proposed Modification to Pollack's Algorithm," *Comm. ACM*, **14**, 69–73 (1971).

[14] S. Winograd, "A New Algorithm for the Inner Product," *IEEE Trans. Comput.*, **C17**, 693–694 (1968).

A FORMAL MICROPROGRAM MODEL OF PARALLELISM AND REGISTER SHARING

E. G. Coffman, Jr.
Pennsylvania State University, University Park, PA

A simple combinatorial model of microprogram structure is proposed in order to provide a framework for the study of timing and sequencing-control problems arising in complex control units. The application of the model to determinacy and deadlock problems is illustrated.

I. INTRODUCTION

In the design of highly-parallel instruction control and execution units in very high performance systems the sequencing of primitive machine operations can be subject to subtle timing problems. The structure and sequencing within such machines as the System 360/Model 91 is a case in point [11]. The types of problems that arise have become well-known under the names of determinacy, deadlocks, synchronization, and mutual exclusion. In this paper our object is the formulation of a model which is based directly on internal machine structure and from which the above problems can be rigorously examined as they concern detailed machine design. In particular, the application of the model is developed in detail for the determinacy and deadlock problems [1-10].

To a large extent our formulation will amount to an *interpretation* of earlier work, but the special properties of this interpretation enable one to strengthen certain results and to provide others not possible in a general abstraction. Moreover, our approach is concerned with a model for the analysis of machine design rather than with a mechanism for conceiving or synthesizing new computation structures. Thus, we provide a mechanism for partial proofs of the correctness of design [1-7].

The specific goal will be the modeling of control and instruction-execution units. As a consequence, a second, and in our view an equally-important goal of the following development is the definition of a simple logical framework on which to base the teaching of computer architecture at the university level. With the type of model we suggest it is possible to describe systematically important principles of machine structure without the necessity for delving into the vast amount of (quickly antiquated) detail connected with specific systems.

In the model presented a machine instruction is viewed as a microprogram

Presented at the Symposium on Computers and Automata
Polytechnic Institute of Brooklyn, April 13-15, 1971

consisting of a set of micro-operations and a partial order that determines operational precedence. Programs are defined as sequences of instructions and program sequences are defined as sequences of micro-operations taken from the constituent instructions. In terms of these sequences the notions of determinacy and deadlocks are defined, after which certain properties of program sequences are proposed and shown to be necessary and sufficient to ensure a determinate and deadlock-free system.

II. DEFINITIONS AND NOTATION

Let $R = \{R_1, R_2, R_3, \cdots, R_r\}$ denote a set of addressable machine registers (e.g., general purpose registers, etc.) and $B = \{B_1, B_2, B_3, \cdots, B_b\}$ a set of non-addressable buffer machine registers. For example,in the Model 91 Floating Point Unit the registers in B would correspond to operand buffers, instruction buffers, output buffers, etc. The symbols in $R \cup B$ are to be regarded as register names, and informally, each register of each type is assumed to contain a sequence of w bits. We let W denote the set of (2^w) words corresponding to all possible register contents.

Let $t_1, t_2, t_3, \cdots, t_n$ be an increasing sequence of epochs corresponding to the times of occurrence of a series of events. We use the notation $\mathbf{R}(j) = [R_1(j), R_2(j), R_3(j), \cdots, R_r(j)]$ $(1 \leq j \leq n)$ to represent the *storage-state* (vector) just after t_j; i.e., just after the jth event. Thus, $R_i(j)$ denotes the *contents* $c(R_i)$, of register R_i just after t_j. Similarly, we define the state vector $\mathbf{B}(j)$ $(1 \leq j \leq n)$. We introduce the notation $f\colon W \times W \rightarrow W$ and let F denote the (finite) set of all such mappings f.

DEFINITION 1. *A micro-operation* $x = (f; a_0, a_1, a_2)$ *consists of a function* $f \in F$ *and the three addresses* a_0, a_1, a_2 *each taken from the set of symbols* $R \cup B$.

Informally, the interpretation of the event corresponding to the execution of a micro-operation is the assignment $a_0 \leftarrow f(a_1, a_2)$; i.e., just following the event we have $c(a_0) = f(c(a_1), c(a_2))$. Normally, f corresponds to a simple addition or logical operation. Also, by introducing "constant" registers, f may effectively denote unary operations such as register transfers, etc. For the purposes of this paper we do not include micro-operations which influence the sequence of micro-program control. Hereafter, $a_k(x)$ will denote the address $a_k (k = 0, 1, \text{ or } 2)$ of the micro-operation x.

DEFINITION 2. *Let* Y *denote a finite set of* instructions *where each* $y = (X, P)$ *in* Y *consists of a finite set* X *of micro-operations and a partial order* P *defined on* X.

The interpretation of the ordering relation is that of operational precedence. Thus, if (x, x') is in P then we say that the execution of x must precede that of x' and write $x < x'$. Moreover, we shall write $x <\cdot\, x'$ and say that x is a predecessor of x' whenever there exists a sequence $x = x_1, x_2, x_3, \cdots, x_k = x'$ such that $x_i < x_{i+1}$ $(1 \leq i \leq k-1)$. Any sequence $u_1, u_2, u_3, \cdots, u_{n(X)} = \langle u_j \rangle_{j=1}^{n(X)}$ where each u_j is a distinct element from X, $n(X) = |X|$, and where $u_j <\cdot\, u_{j'}$ implies $j < j'$ is called an *execution sequence* for y. Proper prefixes of execution sequences will be called *partial* execution sequences.

A *program* $p = <p(i)>_{i=1}^{s}$ is defined as a finite sequence of instructions; i.e., for each i $(1 \leq i \leq s)$ $p(i) \in Y$. With respect to p the instruction represented by $p(i)$ will be denoted $(X(i), P(i))$ and $n(i)$ will denote $|X(i)|$. Let $E_i = x_{i1}, x_{i2}, x_{i3}, \cdots, x_{in(i)}$ $(1 \leq i \leq s)$ denote execution sequences for the $p(i)$. A *program sequence* for p is defined as a merge of execution sequences $E_1, E_2, E_3, \cdots, E_s$ into a single sequence $E = u_1, u_2, u_3, \cdots, u_m$ where $m = \sum_{i=1}^{s} n(i)$. As usual the word "merge" implies that if $u_{j_1} = x_{ik_1}$, $u_{j_2} = x_{ik_2}$, and $k_1 < k_2$ then $j_1 < j_2$.

A simple example is shown in Fig. 1 for a program of four instructions. Ex-

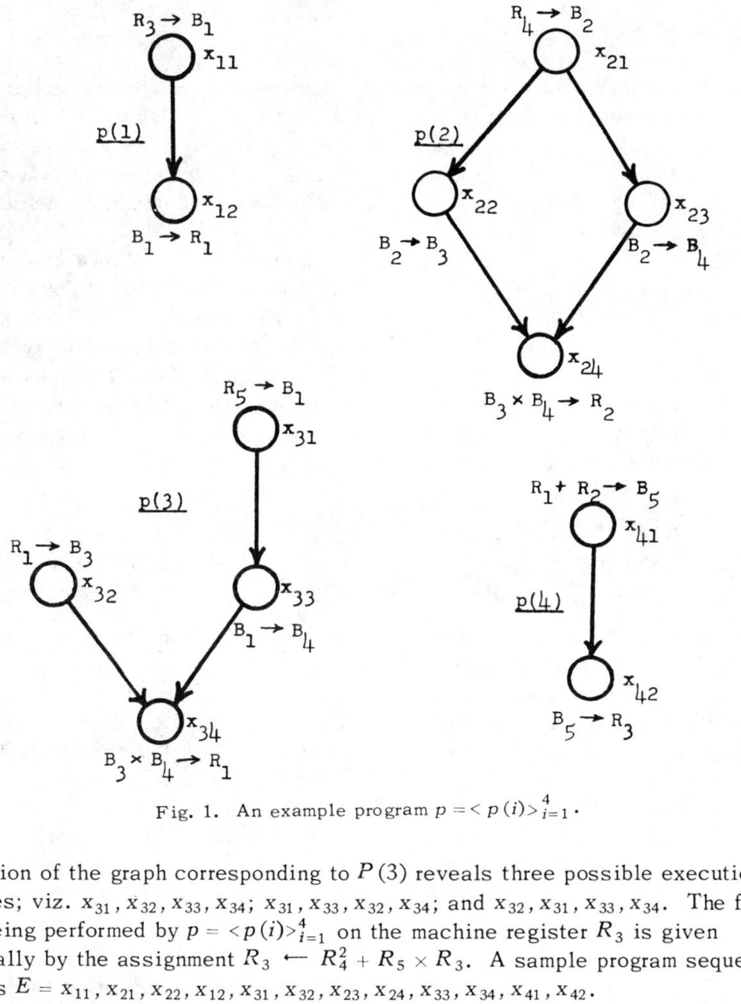

Fig. 1. An example program $p = <p(i)>_{i=1}^{4}$.

amination of the graph corresponding to $P(3)$ reveals three possible execution sequences; viz. $x_{31}, x_{32}, x_{33}, x_{34}$; $x_{31}, x_{33}, x_{32}, x_{34}$; and $x_{32}, x_{31}, x_{33}, x_{34}$. The function being performed by $p = <p(i)>_{i=1}^{4}$ on the machine register R_3 is given informally by the assignment $R_3 \leftarrow R_4^2 + R_5 \times R_3$. A sample program sequence for p is $E = x_{11}, x_{21}, x_{22}, x_{12}, x_{31}, x_{32}, x_{23}, x_{24}, x_{33}, x_{34}, x_{41}, x_{42}$.

To this point we have formalized the basic structure of the system whose timing problems are to be characterized and analyzed. The definition of these problems requires an association of state sequences with execution sequences. We do this next.

III. STATE SEQUENCES

The notion of determinacy (or functionality) is defined on the basis of the storage-state sequences whose transition rules we now define. Let $<\mathbf{R}(j)>_{j=0}^{m}$ be the storage-state sequence corresponding to the program sequence $<u_j>_{j=1}^{m}$ and let $\mathbf{R}(0)$ be a given initial state. For the jth transition $(1 \leq j \leq m)$ let $u_j = (f;\ a_0, a_1, a_2)$. Then for all i $(1 \leq i \leq r = |R|)$

$$R_i(j) = \begin{cases} f(a_1, a_2),\ a_0 = R_i\ , \\ R_i(j-1),\ a_0 \neq R_i\ . \end{cases}$$

Thus, at each transition the storage-state changes in at most one register and only by the assignment implied in a micro-operation for which a_0 is in R.

With respect to other timing problems the realizability of program sequences will be made to depend on the nonconflicting use of buffer registers by instructions. Buffer register usage will be modeled by so-called control-state sequences which we now define.

With each program sequence $E = <u_j>_{j=1}^{m}$ we associate a *control-state* sequence $<\mathbf{C}(j)>_{j=0}^{m}$ where $\mathbf{C}(0)$ is a given initial state. The control-state is given by a vector $\mathbf{C}(j) = (C_1(j), C_2(j), \cdots, C_b(j))$ where each $C_i(j)$ $(1 \leq i \leq b = |B|)$ is an integer in the set $\{0, 1, 2, \cdots, s\}$ and where s is the number of instructions represented in E. Just after the jth event $C_i(j) = 0$ means that B_i is not assigned to any instruction and $C_i(j) = k$ $(1 \leq k \leq s)$ signifies that B_i is assigned to $p(k)$. More specifically, for the jth transition $(1 \leq j \leq m)$ let u_j be a micro-operation in $X(\ell)$. Then for all i $(1 \leq i \leq b)$:

(1) If for all k $(k = 0, 1, \text{and } 2)$ $a_k(u_j) \neq B_i$ then $C_i(j) = C_i(j-1)$
(2) If there exists a k such that $a_k(u_j) = B_i$ *and* there exists a $j' > j$ for which $u_{j'}$ is also in $X(\ell)$ and $a_{k'}(u_{j'}) = B_i$ for some k' then $C_i(j) = \ell$
(3) $C_i(j) = 0$ in all other cases.

According to these rules all buffer registers used by a micro-operation are left available $(C_i(j) = 0)$ after execution, except in those cases when a later micro-operation in the same instruction requires one or more of the same registers. These rules reflect the requirement that once buffer registers are allocated to an instruction they are private to that instruction until it is finished with them.

In order to exhibit certain properties of control-state sequences it is convenient to introduce the relation $\mathbf{C}(j) \subseteq \mathbf{C}(k)$ which is defined to hold iff for all i, $C_i(j) \neq 0$ implies $C_i(j) = C_i(k)$. The results below follow from our definitions in a routine fashion.

LEMMA 1. *Let* $<\mathbf{C}(j)>_{j=0}^{m}$ *be a control-state sequence for the program sequence* $E = <u_j>_{j=1}^{m}$. *Then:*

(1) $\mathbf{C}(m) \subseteq \mathbf{C}(0)$
(2) *If* $<\mathbf{C}'(j)>_{j=0}^{m}$ *is another control-state sequence for* E *then* $\mathbf{C}(0) \subseteq \mathbf{C}'(0)$ *implies* $\mathbf{C}(j) \subseteq \mathbf{C}'(j)$ *for all* j $(0 \leq j \leq m)$.

A state $\mathbf{C}(j)$ will be termed *allowable* with respect to a micro-operation x in $X(\ell)$ iff $a_k(x) = B_i$ for some i, and k implies that $C_i(j) = 0$ or $C_i(j) = \ell$. Our subsequent interest will be concerned with *proper* program sequences $<u_j>_{j=1}^m$ for which there exist corresponding control-state sequences $<\mathbf{C}(j)>_{j=0}^m$ such that $\mathbf{C}(j-1)$ is allowable with respect to u_j for all j $(1 \leq j \leq m)$. We have the following properties of allowable states and proper sequences.

LEMMA 2.

(1) *If a program sequence E is proper with the initial state $\mathbf{C}(0)$ then E is proper with any initial state $\mathbf{C}'(0) \subseteq \mathbf{C}(0)$*

(2) *For each program there exists at least one proper sequence.*

Proof. The first property follows from Lemma 1 and the fact that if $\mathbf{C}'(j) \subseteq \mathbf{C}(j)$ and $\mathbf{C}(j)$ is allowable with respect to x then so is $\mathbf{C}'(j)$ allowable with respect to x. To verify the second property consider the program $p = <p(i)>_{i=1}^s$ and let $\{E_i\}_{i=1}^s$ be a set of execution sequences for the $p(i)$. Now form the sequence $E = <u_j>_{j=1}^m$ in such a way that the first $n(1)$ elements consist of E_1, the following $n(2)$ elements consist of E_2, and so on until E_s makes up the last $n(s)$ elements. Choosing the initial state $\mathbf{C}(0) = [0, 0, 0, \cdots, 0]$ we have $\mathbf{C}(0) = \mathbf{C}(n(1)) = \mathbf{C}(n(1) + n(2)) = \cdots = \mathbf{C}(m)$, and it follows that E is proper. Q.E.D.

At this point we have completed the formulation of a micro-program model on which to base the study of timing problems. In terms of this model the timing problems mentioned earlier can be modeled as follows.

DEFINITION 3. *For a given instruction $y = p(i)$ let E_i' and E_i'' be two proper execution sequences and let $<\mathbf{R}'(j)>_{j=0}^{n(i)}$ and $<\mathbf{R}''(j)>_{j=0}^{n(i)}$ be the corresponding storage-state sequences. If for every choice of E_i' and E_i'', $\mathbf{R}'(0) = \mathbf{R}''(0)$ implies $\mathbf{R}'(n(i)) = \mathbf{R}''(n(i))$ then y is said to be* determinate. *For a program $p = <p(i)>_{i=1}^s$ of determinate instructions let $E_1, E_2, E_3, \cdots, E_s$ be execution sequences for the $p(i)$ and let $E^* = E_1, E_2, E_3, \cdots, E_s$; i.e., the concatenation of the E_i. Let $<\mathbf{R}^*(j)>_{j=0}^m$ denote the corresponding storage-state sequence. If for every proper sequence E of p we have $\mathbf{R}(0) = \mathbf{R}^*(0)$ implies $\mathbf{R}(m) = \mathbf{R}^*(m)$ then p is* determinate.

As indicated in the above definition determinacy is of concern at both the program and instruction levels. This follows from the fact that a micro-operation can generally be sequenced in more than one way relative to micro-operations in other instructions as well as micro-operations in the same instruction. Clearly, a general object of microprogram design is to avoid entirely nondeterminate programs for which different execution sequences may lead to different final states even though the initial states are the same. Note that determinacy for programs is based on the requirement that execution sequences produce the same final state as that produced by the execution sequence (E^*) corresponding to the serial execution of the instructions.

Deadlocks can be modeled as follows. A *partial* (program) *sequence* is one formed from partial-execution sequences in such a way that there exists a corresponding (partial) control-state sequence consisting only of allowable states.

DEFINITION 4. *A program p is said to be subject to* register deadlocks *if there exists for some initial state at least one partial sequence which is the prefix of no (complete) proper sequence. Also, such a partial sequence is said to contain a register deadlock.*

As shown in Section V a partial sequence containing deadlocks occurs only when there is a circular chain of instructions each requiring a register allocated to another instruction in the chain. Normally, the design of control units must be such as to insure that programs are prevented from being subject to register deadlocks.

We have formalized the notions of determinacy and deadlocks because we shall illustrate these applications of the basic model in the next two sections. However, other timing problems can also be modeled. As an informal example we can represent the mutual-exclusion problem by simply defining two instructions to be mutually excluded in an execution sequence whenever they are executed serially in that sequence.

IV. DETERMINATE PROGRAMS

To illustrate the applicability of the basic model we now investigate necessary and sufficient conditions on the structure of proper sequences in order for an arbitrary program to be determinate. Define $A(x) = \{a_0(x), a_1(x), a_2(x)\}$. Let $E = \langle u_j \rangle_{j=1}^m$ be a proper sequence for the program $p = \langle p(\ell) \rangle_{\ell=1}^s$, and let $u_j = x \in X(\ell)$ and $u_{j'} = x' \in X(\ell')$ where $\ell < \ell'$. We shall say that x and x′ are *properly sequenced* with respect to register usage if $a_0(x) \in A(x') \cap R$ or $a_0(x') \in A(x) \cap R$ implies $j < j'$. Also, $p(\ell)$ and $p(\ell')$ are said to be properly sequenced in E if every pair of micro-operations $x \in X(\ell)$ and $x' \in X(\ell')$ is properly sequenced.

This proper-sequencing constraint simply requires that a micro-operation for $p(\ell)$ must appear before a micro-operation for $p(\ell')$, $\ell < \ell'$, if their result registers are the same or if the result register of one is the same as an operand register of the other, where the constraint applies only to the addressable registers R. Note that since the sequence formed in the proof of Lemma 2(b) clearly satisfies this sequencing constraint, Lemma 2 can be extended to state that there exists at least one such proper sequence for each program.

A given micro-operation $x = (f, a_0, a_1, a_2)$ is said to be unspecified if only the addresses a_0, a_1, and a_2 are assumed given. The mapping f constitutes a *specification* of x if it is assumed given along with a_0, a_1, and a_2. An instruction (program) is unspecified if any one of its constituent micro-operations (instructions) is unspecified. Of course, an unspecified instruction is determinate iff it is determinate for all specifications of its constituent micro-operations.

For the present purposes we shall assume that every instruction contains at least one micro-operation x such that $a_0(x) \in R$. (In view of the systems being modeled an instruction would otherwise be vacuous or null.)

THEOREM 1. *Let p denote an arbitrary program of determinate instructions. Then p is determinate for all specifications of its constituent micro-operations if every pair of instructions is properly sequenced with respect to register usage.*

Proof. Let $p = \langle p(i) \rangle_{i=1}^s$ denote the given program and consider an arbitrary proper sequence $E = \langle u_j \rangle_{j=1}^m$ in which the execution sequences for the $p(i)$ are denoted $E_i (1 \leq i \leq s)$. From E form the sequence $E' = \langle u'_j \rangle_{j=1}^m$ having the properties:

(1) $u'_{m'+1}, u'_{m'+2}, u'_{m'+3}, \cdots, u'_m = E_s$, where $m' = m - n(s)$

(2) If $u_{i_1} = u'_{j_1} \notin X(s)$, and $u_{i_2} = u'_{j_2} \notin X(s)$, then $i_1 < i_2$ implies $j_1 < j_2$.

That is, E' is formed by moving the micro-operations in E_s to the end of the sequence E. It is readily verified that if instructions are properly sequenced in E then they are also properly sequenced in E'. Moreover, the same final state is attained from identical initial states. Iterating this transformation to produce $E^* = E_1, E_2, E_3, \cdots, E_s$ and using an induction argument establishes the "if" part of the theorem. The "only if" part of the theorem follows from the requirements that instructions not be vacuous and that determinacy must hold for all specifications of the micro-operations. Q.E.D.

Similar to the program requirement, an individual instruction $p(i)$ will be determinate under the proper-sequencing constraint applied to $X(i)$. Note that determinacy of instructions is normally implemented in microprogram design; i.e., the appropriate partial order is "wired-in" for each instruction. On the other hand, the determinacy of programs is effected by dynamically checking the condition for proper sequencing. An ingenious technique for implementing this check implicitly is given by the "tagging" or chaining method described for the Model 91 Floating-Point Unit.

V. REGISTER DEADLOCKS

Register deadlocks are logical failures that can occur in programs whether or not they are determinate. Results concerning register deadlocks are most easily expressed in terms of directed graphs. Let $E = \langle u_j \rangle_{j=1}^{h}$ denote a partial sequence for $p = \langle p(i) \rangle_{i=1}^{s}$. Let D_h denote the set of all micro-operations in the sets $X(i)$ $(1 \leq i \leq s)$ not appearing in E but whose predecessors (if any) are all in E. Corresponding to E and an initial state $\mathbf{C}(0)$ we define a directed graph G_h consisting of the set of vertices $\{B_1, B_2, B_3 \cdots, B_b\}$ and a set Q of arcs defined as follows. The arc (B_i, B_j) from B_i to B_j is in Q if and only if there exist ℓ and ℓ' $(\ell \neq \ell')$ such that $C_i(h) = \ell$, $C_j(h) = \ell'$, and $a_k(x) = B_j$ for some k and $x \in D_h \cap X(\ell)$.

THEOREM 2. *A program p is subject to deadlocks iff there exist a partial sequence* $E = \langle u_j \rangle_{j=1}^{h}$ *and an initial state* $\mathbf{C}(0)$ *for which* G_h *contains a circuit.*

Proof. The "if" part is immediate since the instructions represented in the circuit of G_h can not proceed. If a program is subject to deadlocks there must exist a maximal-length partial sequence which is the prefix of no (complete) proper sequence. It follows that there must exist a set of the incomplete instructions at the end of such a sequence which must be unable to proceed only because they require registers held by others in the set. The "only if" part of the theorem follows directly. Q.E.D.

The threat of deadlocks can be removed completely in a number of ways. For example, if the execution of the first micro-operation of an instruction is delayed until all registers for all its micro-operations have been assigned (or reserved) then deadlocks can never occur. More formally, let A_i denote the set of buffer registers required by one or more micro-operations in $p(i)$; i.e.

$$A_i = B \cap \bigcup_{x \in X(i)} \{a_0(x), a_1(x), a_2(x)\} \ .$$

COROLLARY 1. *Consider the partial sequence* $E = \langle u_j \rangle_{j=1}^{h}$ *and let* $A_i(j)$ *denote the set of buffer registers assigned to* $p(i)$ *following the* j^{th} *event. If for all* j *and* $i_1 \neq i_2$ *we have* $(A_{i_1}(j) \neq \phi$ and $A_{i_2}(j) \neq \phi)$ *implies* $A_{i_1} \cap A_{i_2} = \phi$ *then* E *is the prefix of a (complete) proper sequence.*

Although with control units the conditions of Corollary 1 generally apply they preclude the flexibility and potential register utilization implicit in the basic model. A somewhat weaker sufficient condition for the complete avoidance of deadlock can be described as follows.

In the proper sequence E let $u_j = x \in X(\ell)$. If corresponding to E we have $C_i(j-1) \neq \ell$ and for some k $a_k(x) = B_i$, we say that B_i was *requested* by $u_j = x$. Now suppose the buffer registers can be partitioned into blocks $Z_i = \{B_{ij}\}_{j=1}^{b_i}$ $(i = 1, 2, 3, \cdots, z)$, such that if $B_{i_1 j_1}$ is requested by $u_j = x \in X(\ell)$ and $B_{i_2 j_2}$ is some register already assigned to $p(\ell)$ (because of an earlier micro-operation in $X(\ell)$) then it is always true that $z \geq i_1 \geq i_2$. We assume that once a register in Z_z has been assigned to $p(\ell)$ no new registers will be requested by subsequent micro-operations in $X(\ell)$. The above constraint on instruction execution sequences will be called *ordered-register usage.*

COROLLARY 2. *Programs whose instructions satisfy the constraint of ordered-register usage are deadlock-free.*

A typical example in which ordered register usage is observed occurs in those execution units where instructions first require an input buffer(s), then buffers for some functional unit, and then an output buffer. It is a simple matter to show that the set of deadlocked instructions whose existence was adduced in Theorem 2 must violate the constraint of ordered-register usage.

The above treatment of deadlocks has been simplified by the assumption that the buffer registers are individually addressed. In general, there may exist a number of buffer-register *types*, each type containing a number of identical and indistinguishable registers. Assuming that buffer types (rather than individual registers) are addressed we have a more general model. On the other hand, results similar to those given above are also possible for this more-general case.

VI. SUMMARY

We have proposed a simple combinatorial model of microprogram structure in order to provide a framework for the study of timing and sequencing problems arising in complex control units. The application of the model to determinacy and deadlock problems was illustrated. The unification represented by the basic model possesses not only a pedagogic value but it also provides the insight and perspective that stem from coherent treatments of classes of problems.

Certain weaknesses (causing lack of generality) have been accepted in order to maintain simplicity. For example, events correspond to (implicitly) indivisible micro-operations rather than micro-operation initiation and termination epochs. Also, microprograms (instructions) contain only the structure representable by partial orders. At the expense of greater detail more elaborate models can be devised, based on the present model, which remove these limitations. Of course, the results become more difficult to state (if in fact they can be generalized at all).

REFERENCES

[1] D. E. Muller and W. S. Bartley, "A Theory of Asynchronous Circuits," *Proc. of an International Symp. on the Theory of Switching*, 204–243 (Harvard University Press: Annals of the Computation Laboratory, 1959).

[2] R. M. Karp and R. E. Miller, "Properties of a Model for Parallel Computations: Determinacy, Termination, Queueing," *SIAM J. Appl. Math.*, **14**, No. 6, 1390–1411 (Nov. 1966).

[3] F. L. Luconi, "Completely-Functional Asynchronous Computational Structures," *IEEE Conference Record of 1967 Eighth Annual Symp. on Switching and Automata Theory*, 62–70 (October 18–20, 1967).

[4] A. J. Bernstein, "Analysis of Programs for Parallel Processing," *IEEE Trans. Electr. Comput.*, **EC-15**, No. 5, 757–763 (October 1966).

[5] J. E. Rodriguez, "A Graph Model for Parallel Computation," Ph.D. Thesis, Massachusetts Institute of Technology (September 1967).

[6] D. R. Slutz, "A Flow-Graph Schemata Model of Parallel Computation," PhD. Thesis, Massachusetts Institute of Technology (September 1968).

[7] J. Bruno, and S. M. Altman, "Asynchronous Control Networks," *IEEE Convention Record of 1969 Tenth Annual Symp. on Switching and Automata Theory*, 61–73 (October 1969).

[8] E. W. Dijkstra, "Cooperating Sequential Processes," *Programming Languages: NATO Advanced Study Institute*, Villard de Lans (1966), (F. Genuys, Ed., London: Academic Press, 1968).

[9] A. N. Habermann, "Prevention of System Deadlocks," *Comm. ACM*, **12**, 373–377, 385, (July 1969).

[10] A. Shoshani and E. G. Coffman, "Sequencing Tasks in Multiprocess Systems to Avoid Deadlocks," *IEEE Conference Record of 1970 Eleventh Annual Symp. on Switching and Automata Theory*, 225–233, October 1970.

[11] "The IBM System/360 Model 91," *IBM J. Res. and Dev.*, **11**, No. 1 (January 1967).

TOWARD OPTIMAL PAGINATIONS FOR STRUCTURED PROGRAMS

Lawrence Yelowitz

Department of Computer Science, The Johns Hopkins University, Baltimore, MD

A type of programming known as *structured* is described and illustrated. A model for paginations is then presented for structured programs which bases its decisions for the locations of page breaks upon the syntactic structure of the program. This represents a departure from previous research efforts. A simple algorithm is given to solve the paginating model.

I. INTRODUCTION

An open problem recently posed by Denning [1] concerns the effective utilization of certain properties of a program, such as its structure and looping properties, to improve performance in a paging environment. In the present paper we define a type of program called *structured program*, and report some progress toward the solution of the problem with respect to structured programming.

To help model the situation, we deal with the problem of paginations rather than paging, and we examine the instruction stream rather than the combined instruction-data stream. The paginating problem involves deciding where to make page breaks in the sequence of machine-instruction words. More formally, if Z is some given parameter (page size), the paginating problem concerns the partioning of the sequence of machine-instruction words into disjoint subsequences such that each subsequence contains at most Z words. In addition, if w_1 and w_2 are adjacent words in some subsequence, then they must be adjacent in the original sequence in the same order. The instruction stream with respect to an execution of some program P is the sequence of machine instructions of P handled by the control portion of a computer during that execution of P.

It is clear that pagination is a more static process than paging. Once the page breaks have been made they will not change during execution of the program; quite possibly, the same page breaks will be used in subsequent runs. Paging is a dynamic process, involving such things as placement policies, replacement policies, and fetching policies [1].

Previous research in paginations [2, 3] has focused on trying to paginate so as to minimize the sum of the probabilities of interpage branches. The present model departs from this view; paginations will be made based on the syntactic structure of the program. In particular, we give a quantitative measure to the somewhat vague notion of *preserving the structural units* of a program within the pages in which the machine code resides. Also, the trade-off between minimizing

Presented at the Symposium on Computers and Automata
Polytechnic Institute of Brooklyn, April 13–15, 1971.

the number of pages for a nested DO loop vs wasting words so as to achieve this minimization is made explicit. This trade-off is interpreted in the following sense: The model does not isolate the most deeply-nested DO loop and then paginate it. Rather, the code surrounding the most deeply-nested loop might itself be part of a deeply-nested loop, and so on with *its* surrounding code, etc., and this is taken into account. Sensitivity to the depth level of a loop is nevertheless present in the model.

It is felt that the present approach to paginations offers two advantages over the previous approach:

(i) Trying to minimize the sum of probabilities of interpage branches requires knowledge of the probabilities of each branch in the program. It may be difficult or impossible to supply them accurately. The present approach does not utilize probabilities

(ii) The present model is simpler to implement.

II. SOME FORMULAS FOR THE TOTAL NUMBER OF PAGINATIONS

We now give some recursive formulas to calculate the total number of possible paginations under various constraints; the formulas can also be used to systematically enumerate all the paginations. The theoretical results of this section will not be used explicitly in the model presented below:

A. *No restraints on the paginations.* This formula yields the number of paginations of N words of code, with page size = Z, such that each page has at least one word of code. Let $f(N, Z)$ represent this quantity where N and Z are each positive integers.

$$
\begin{aligned}
f(0,Z) &= f(1,Z) = 1 \ , \\
f(M,Z) &= 0 \qquad\qquad\qquad\qquad\qquad\qquad\qquad\qquad \text{(for } M < 0) \ , \\
f(N,Z) &= f(N-1,Z) + f(N-2,Z) + \cdots + f(N-Z,Z) \qquad \text{(for } N > 1) \ , \\
&= 2f(N-1,Z) - f(N-Z-1,Z) \ .
\end{aligned}
$$

B. *Each page (except possibly the last) must contain at least k words,* $1 \leq k \leq Z$. Let $g(N, k, Z)$ = the number of paginations of N words of code with page size Z, such that each page (except the last, possibly) contains at least k words.

$$
\begin{aligned}
g(X,k,Z) &= 1 \qquad \text{(for } X = 0, 1, 2, \cdots, k) \ , \\
g(M,k,Z) &= 0 \qquad \text{(for } M < 0) \ ,
\end{aligned}
$$

$$
g(N,k,Z) = g(N-k,k,Z) + g(N-k-1,k,Z) + \cdots + g(N-Z,k,Z) \qquad \text{(for } N > k) \ .
$$

C. *Every pair of adjacent pages must contain more than Z words,* where Z is the page size. We introduce some auxilliary notation to develop the required formula; define the formal symbol R as follows

$$
\begin{aligned}
R(X,k,Z) &= 1 \qquad\qquad\qquad \text{(for } X = 0, 1, 2, \cdots, Z) \ , \\
R(M,k,Z) &= 0 \qquad\qquad\qquad \text{(for } M < 0) \ ,
\end{aligned}
$$

$$R(X, k, Z) = \sum_{i=0}^{Z-k} R(X - Z + i, i + 1, Z) \qquad (\text{for } X > Z) \ .$$

Letting $h(N, Z)$ represent the number of paginations such that every pair of adjacent pages contains more than Z words, we have

$$h(N, Z) = R(N, 1, Z) \ .$$

III. STRUCTURED PROGRAMMING

The flow of control in a computer program is specified by its branching and looping properties. Structured programming is a disciplined way of developing a program so that these properties are implemented in terms of a small number of control structures. Notably absent from a structured-programming language is the arbitrary "GOTO" statement. The control structures utilized might vary from one language to another, but the three structures shown in Fig. 1 are typical.

It will be noticed (in terms of the flowchart form) that each structure as a single syntactic entity contains one input arrow and one output arrow. The same is true for the rectangular boxes appearing within each structure. Thus, it is possible topologically to replace a rectangular box by one of the three control structures. By doing so (recursively) an arbitrary number of times, it is possible to build up a structure of arbitrary complexity. By interpreting each predicate node

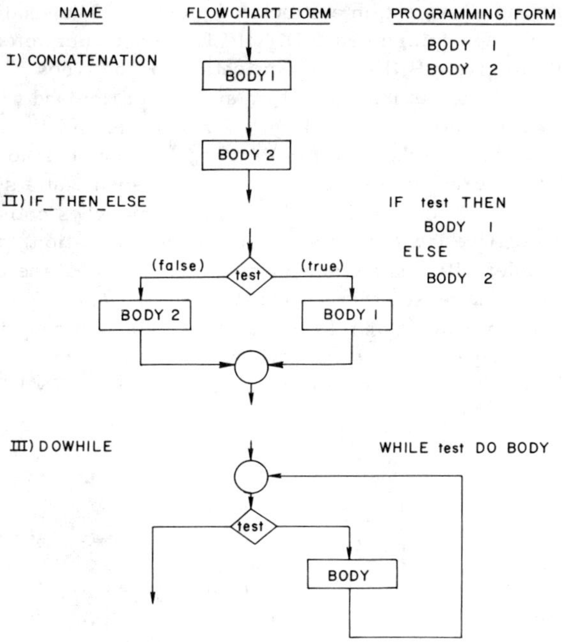

Fig. 1. Three typical control structures.

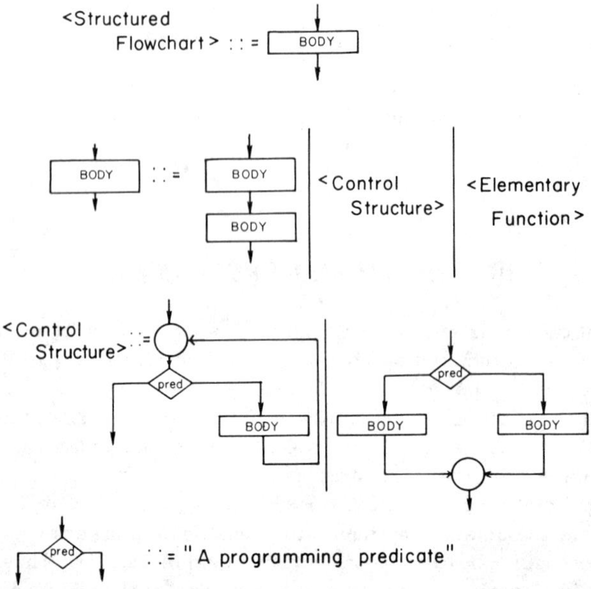

Fig. 2. BNF-like specification.

(diamond-shaped box) by a predicate in some language and each function node (rectangular box) by a nonbranching, nontesting statement in the language (e.g., assignment, shift, load) we obtain a structured program. The small circular "collecting nodes" appearing in each DOWHILE are not interpreted.

It is possible to give a BNF-like specification for the types of flowcharts we allow. This specification is intended as an aid to intuition and will not be used in a formal way in the current paper. Figure 2 gives this specification.

We note an ambiguity in the *flowchart language*, which does no real damage. Corresponding to the expansion shown in Fig. 3 it is seen that a sequence of M control structures, $M \geq 3$, can be derived in all possible ways corresponding to applying the associative law (with respect to a binary operation) to M elements. The interested reader will find a discussion and derivation of the appropriate formula in Niven [4]. The reason this ambiguity is not damaging is that in order to even talk of a sequence of M control structures, it is understood that the structures are executed sequentially if the first one is reached. In other words, no structure is subordinate to another with respect to the IF_THEN_ELSE or DOWHILE.

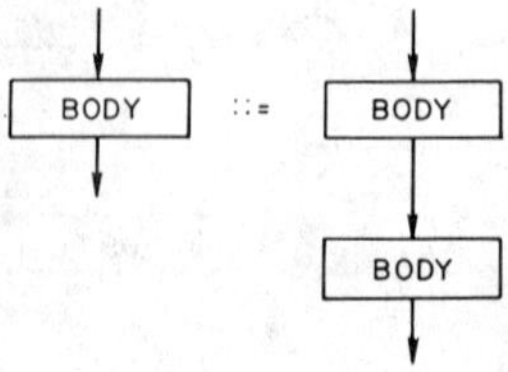

Fig. 3. Flowchart-language ambiguity.

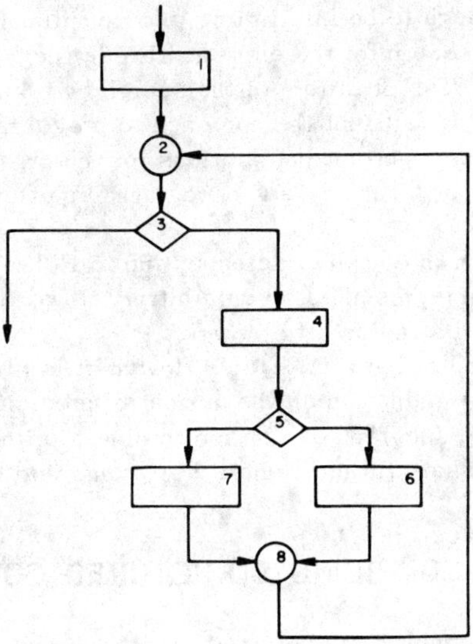

Fig. 4. Binary search for the element KEY in the N-dimensional array A. KEY: 1. $L = 1$; $H = N$; MORE $= T$; 3. MORE $= T$; 4. $M = L + (H - L + 1) \div 2$; 5. $A(M) =$ KEY; 6. INDEX $= M$; MORE $= F$; 7. "Reduce Interval."

We deliberately refrain from giving a formal definition for <pred> and <Elementary Function> to allow interpretation of a flowchart for different types of programming languages. As an example, Fig. 4 shows a structured flowchart and an interpretation of all its function and predicate boxes. The interpretation of Box 7 is not at a sufficiently elementary level to be considered a statement in a programming language. In Fig. 5, we further expand Box 7 and interpret the newly-formed nodes. Note the numbering of all the nodes (including collecting nodes) in a Dewey-decimal fashion. The interpretations of Figs. 4 and 5 together

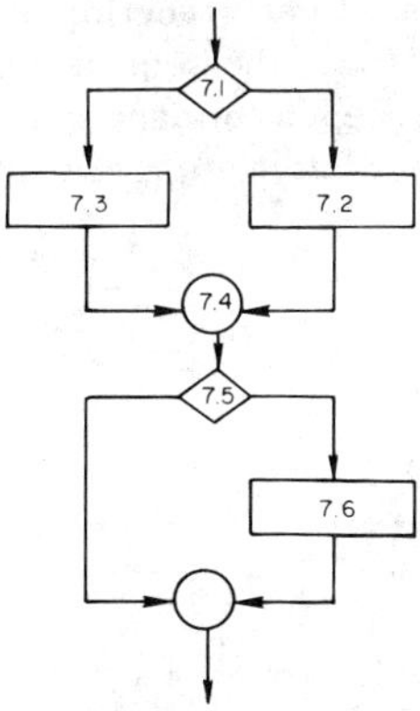

Fig. 5. Binary search for the element KEY in the N-dimensional array A. KEY: 7.1. $A(M) >$ KEY; 7.2. $H = M - 1$; 7.3. $L = M + 1$; 7.5. $L > H$; 7.6. MORE $= F$; INDEX $= 0$.

are now elementary enough to be intelligible to a compiler language. Figures 4 and 5 specify a binary search for the element KEY in the N-dimensional array A; INDEX denotes the success or failure of the search by taking a nonzero or zero value, respectively. It is felt that the approach to programming alluded to in this very simple example has important implications for the organization, documentation, and division of labor for much larger programming efforts; see, for example, Mills [5].

An important theorem in computer science, due to Bohm and Jacopini [6], proves that any program represented by an arbitrary flowchart can also be represented (effectively) by a structured flowchart.

It is interesting to note that a structured flowchart is always a planar graph. This is easily proved by induction on the number of predicate nodes. A more elegant proof notes that no subgraph can be isomorphic to either of the two Kuratowski subgraphs necessary for nonplanarity by examining max [in-degree, out-degree] for each node [7].

IV. COMPILING STRUCTURED CODE

It is a machine code which is paginated, but the discussion so far has been on higher-level structured flowcharts. It is pretty straight-forward to compile a structured program, at least with respect to implementing the control structure. The difficulty in compiling the nonbranching, nontesting statements depends, of course, on what sort of statements in this category are allowable in the language. We shall not deal with this topic here; for purpose of examples, we shall indicate how many words of machine code are used to compile a given function node. The schematics in Fig. 6 are illustrative of compiling-structured programs; $\{X\}$ represents the compiled code for X.

Of course it is possible for BODY 1 or BODY 2 to contain further instances of <CONTROL STRUCTURE>. In this case, some elementary stack operations are sufficient to completely implement the control logic. Figure 7 shows an uninterpreted-structured flowchart; its compiled code is given in Figure 8. The compiled code completely expands each function node into machine code; for example, function node A expands into the sequence of machine code $A1$, $A2$, $A3$, $A4$, $A5$. The number of words needed for each function node was decided arbitrarily by the author. Additional information in Figs. 7 and 8 will be used below.

```
IF test THEN                WHILE test DO
   BODY 1                      BODY
ELSE
   BODY 2


    IF not test GO TO L1    L1  IF not test GO TO L2
       {BODY 1}                    {BODY}
       GO TO L 2                   GO TO L1
L1     {BODY 2}             L2
L2     CONTINUE
```

Fig. 6. Examples of compiling-structured programs. $\{X\}$ represents the compiled code for X.

```
PROGRAM SCHEMATIC                          DEPTH

WHILE a Do                                   1
  A                                          1
  IF b THEN                                  1
    B                                        1
  ELSE                                       1
    WHILE c DO                               2
      C                                      2
      WHILE d DO                             3
        IF e THEN                            3
          D                                  3
        ELSE                                 3
          E                                  3
        F                                    3
    G                                        1
    WHILE f DO                               2
      H                                      2
  I                                          1
J                                            0
```

Fig. 7. Uninterpreted-structured flowchart.

WORD #	DEPTH	CODE		PAGE SIZE (Underlined word is last on page) 5	6	7	8	9	10	11	12
1	1	L1	if not-a GO TO L2								
2	1		A1	_							
3	1		A2								
4	1		A3								
5	1		A4								
6	1		A5		_	_	_			_	_
7	1		if not-b GO TO L3	_	_				_		
8	1		B1								
9	1		B2					_			
10	1		B3								
11	1		B4				_				
12	1		GO TO L9	_		_					
13	2	L3	if not-c GO TO L4		_						
14	2		C1								
15	2		C2								_
16	2		C3							_	
17	2		C4	_					_		
18	2		C5					_			
19	2		C6		_	_	_				
20	3	L5	if not-d GO TO L3								
21	3		if not-e GO TO L6								
22	3		D1	_							
23	3		D2								
24	3		D3								
25	3		D4		_						
26	3		D5			_					
27	3		GO TO L7	_			_	_	_	_	_
28	3	L6	E1								
29	3		E2								
30	3		E3	_							
31	3		E4		_						
32	3		E5								
33	3		E6			_					
34	3		E7								
35	3		E8	_			_	_	_	_	_
36	3	L7	F1								
37	3		F2		_						
38	3		F3								
39	3		F4	_							
40	3		F5			_					
41	3		F6								
42	3		F7								
43	3		GO TO L5		_		_	_	_	_	_
44	1	L4	G1	_							
45	1		G2					_			
46	1		G3				_				
47	1		G4			_					
48	1		G5		_						
49	1		G6	_					_		
50	2	L8	if not-f GO TO L9								
51	2		H1								
52	2		H2								
53	2		H3								
54	2		GO TO L8	_	_	_	_	_		_	_
55	1	L9	I1								
56	1		I2								
57	1		I3								
58	1		I4								
59	1		GO TO L1	_	_	_	_	_	_		
60	0	L2	J1	_							
61	0		J2								
62	0		J3								
63	0		J4								
64	0		J5								
65	0		RETURN	_	_	_	_	_	_	_	_

Fig. 8. Compiled code of flowchart in Figure 7.

V. A MODEL FOR PAGINATIONS

A. Depth Level in a Flowchart

To each node in the flowchart we associate a non-negative integer which specifies how deeply nested that node occurs with respect to the DOWHILE construct. A node not contained in any DOWHILE is specified as being at level 0. Note that depth level in this sense is not the same as the number of predicate nodes traversed in reaching a given node starting from the input edge to the graph. In Fig. 7, the depth level of each node is specified beneath each node.

The compiled code contains some unconditional GOTO statements that arise from implementing the DOWHILE and IF_THEN_ELSE. Each such GOTO may be thought of as the final statement of the preceding function node. For the moment, let us agree to assign the same depth level to these GOTOs as we assign to the other statements of the corresponding function node; later we will revise this view. Figure 8 indicates the depth level of each word of compiled code.

Starting from a structured flowchart, we have obtained the compiled code, and to each word in the compiled code we associate the integer that specifies its depth level. This is the starting point for our "string model," which we now discuss.

B. The String Model

Suppose the instruction code consists of:

$$\begin{gathered} a_1 \text{ words at depth level } d_1 \ , \\ a_2 \text{ words at depth level } d_2 \ , \\ \vdots \\ a_p \text{ words at depth level } d_p \ . \end{gathered}$$

Let X be some parameter > 1 and form the linear string of numerals:

$$0\, \underbrace{X^{d_1}\, X^{d_1} \ldots X^{d_1}}_{a_1 \text{ times}} \quad \underbrace{X^{d_2}\, X^{d_2} \ldots X^{d_2}}_{a_2 \text{ times}} \ldots \underbrace{X^{d_p}\, X^{d_p} \ldots X^{d_p}}_{a_p \text{ times.}}\, 0 \ .$$

We speak of *marking the string* by associating a special mark symbol with a subset of the numerals in the string. We also refer to individually-marked numerals. A string marking is *feasible* if the maximum number of symbols between 2 marked symbols (including exactly one of the marked symbols) is $\leq$ some parameter Z. A feasible marking is *optimal* if the sum corresponding to the individually-marked numerals is a minimum. The two zeros delimiting the string are always assumed marked. The problem is to find an optimal marking.

Intuitively the markings correspond to page breaks, with each marked symbol denoting the last word on its page.

The string model can be solved directly in a very simple fashion, which will be described below. First, however, it may be of some interest to observe a connection between the string model and a shortest-path problem.

C. A Shortest-Path Model for Optimal Markings

Represent each symbol in the string by a node. Corresponding to the left-hand 0 is a special node S, and to the right-hand 0 a special node T. Draw directed edges from S to each of the first Z nodes. For each node n which has an input edge, continually apply the following rule until it is no longer possible to draw any more edges:

> If n is a node other than the last Z nodes, draw a directed edge from node n to each of the following Z nodes. If n is one of the final Z nodes, draw a directed edge from n to all subsequent nodes, including node T.

Once all directed edges have been drawn, associate a distance with each edge as follows:

(i) All edges which are input to T have distance 0
(ii) Let VAL(N) be the number represented by the Nth symbol in the linear string (excluding the end zeros). For each edge e which is input to some node I, associate the distance VAL(I).

The solution to the optimal marking problem is now modeled in the following problem: Find the shortest path from S to T.

D. Solution of the String Model

The total number of words of machine code is given by $N = \sum_{i=1}^{P} a_i$. Let us allocate two one-dimensional arrays of length N, say A and B. We initialize A to contain the N numbers of the string model, excluding the end zeros. The elements of the B array are computed sequentially from $B[1]$ to $B[N]$ as follows (recall that Z is the page size):

(i) $B[i] = A[i] \qquad (i = 1, 2, 3, \cdots, Z)$
(ii) $B[i] = A[i] + \min_{i-Z \le j \le i-1} B[j] \qquad (i = Z+1, Z+2, Z+3, \cdots, N).$

We specify a pagination by specifying which words of machine code are to be the last words on a page. Having computed the B array, we specify these words as follows:

(1) Let j be the smallest index such that $B[j]$ is a minimum, $N - Z \le j \le N$
(2) Let j_1 represent the most-recently-chosen index. If $j_1 \le Z$ go to Step (3). Otherwise choose the next j to be the smallest index such that $B[j]$ is a minimum, $j_1 - Z \le j \le j_1$. Go to Step (2)
(3) The words of machine code corresponding to the indices j selected at Steps (1) and (2) define the set of last words on a page.

In the solution of the string model, an alternative approach is to allocate another one-dimensional array of length N, say C. As the B array is being computed, the corresponding entry in the C array is assigned the lowest index j which yields $\min B[j]$, $i - Z \le j \le i - 1$. Then instead of rescanning the B array to specify the pagination, we can use the C array as a chain of pointers to compute the indices j.

E. Proof of Optimality

Assume some other selection of indices j' yields a lower cost. Let the B' array reflect the cumulative cost of paginating up to and including word j, $1 \leq j \leq N$. Let k be the first index from the j' such that $B'[k] < B[k]$. From Rule (i) of calculating the B array, $k > Z$. Thus there must be some index ℓ among the j' such that $\ell < k$. Let ℓ_1 be the largest such index. $B'[\ell_1] \geq B[\ell_1]$ by the assumptions on k. But then Rule (ii) for calculating the B array implies that $B[k] \leq B'[k]$. Thus, no other selection of indices can yield a lower cost. An alternative proof utilizes the relationship between the string model and the shortest-path model and notes that in this context our algorithm is Dijkstra's permanent-labeling algorithm for shortest paths [8].

F. The "Last-Word-on-the-Page" Convention

In actuality, page breaks are made "between" the words, rather than "at" the words of machine code. Thus our convention of letting marked words be last on the page was somewhat arbitrary; they could just as readily have been first. One way of binding the model to our convention is to derive a new string model from the current one, using some suitable interpolating function to reflect the cost of making a page break between the words, then solve as before. To illustrate the flexibility of the model two other solutions are proposed.

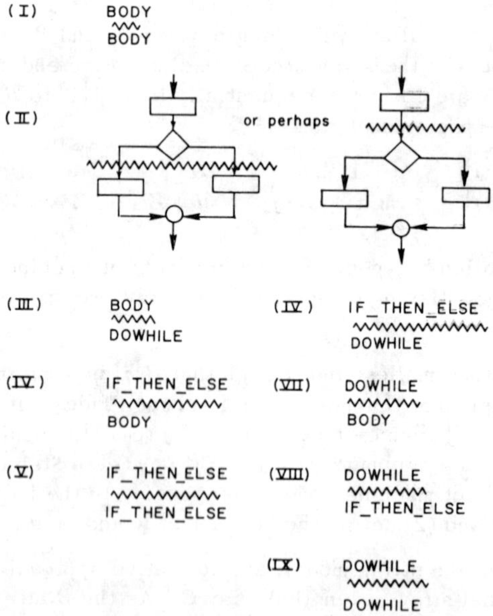

Fig. 9. Nine possible combinations of three control structures. Wavy line indicates appropriate place to make page break.

(1) Make a case analysis of all the possible combinations of two sequential-control structures. Since there are 3 control structures, there are 9 such combinations. Figure 9 indicates by a wavy line in the flowchart an appropriate place to make a page break, based on syntactic structure.

Having indicated by these wavy lines a place to make a page break that preserves syntactic structure, let *x* be the word of machine code immediately preceding the line, and *y* the word immediately following. For example, in Cases (VII), (VIII), and (IX), word *x* always corresponds to a GOTO instruction. We now modify the depth level of word *x* to be 1 less than that of word *y*. Then proceed with setting up the string model and solve as before.

(2) The second solution is similar to the first and presupposes the same sort of case analysis. Instead of actually changing the depth level, simply remember which words would have been changed. Solve as before, but in the event of a *tie* between two nodes that each lie on a shortest path, give preference to a *remembered* word.

G. Discussion of the Model and an Example

By exponentiating to the depth level with respect to DOWHILE, the model incorporates a higher cost for making a page break in a more-deeply-nested loop than a less-deeply-nested one. The case analysis above has singled out certain words as having more of a structure-preserving property than others and has manipulated the model appropriately. We feel that the model can accommodate experimentation with a variety of other cost functions and case analyses; for example, if probabilities are known at some predicate nodes, perhaps the sequence of machine instructions along the appropriate paths can be multiplied by the respective probabilities. Structured programming is helpful in this case by making completely visible the appropriate paths.

Figure 8 shows the paginations that resulted from applying the model (for a variety of page sizes) to the program whose flowchart and compiled code are represented in Figures 7 and 8. We manipulated the model by reducing the depth level of words 6, 27, 35, 43, 54, and 59 as described above. The parameter X of the string model took the value 2; interestingly, the identical paginations resulted for $X = 3$.

H. Why Structured Programming?

It appears that the model we have developed would be equally applicable to nonstructured programming. With arbitrary branching it would no doubt be more difficult to *establish* the level of nesting for each line of code (and perhaps the level of nesting would be ambiguous, varying with different execution paths all including some given line of code). Assuming we could get around these problems, the following significant problem still remains: our model in a certain sense reflects the *urgency* of including adjacent lines of code on the same page. If there were, for example, a conditional branch from within some function node to somewhere outside the node, then the words following the branch within the node would have a different level of urgency for inclusion on the same page as the words preceding the branch. Thus we restrict our model to structured programs.

ACKNOWLEDGEMENTS

The author would like to thank Dr. M. J. Flynn for his encouragement during the early stages of this research. As the research progressed, helpful comments were provided by J. Misra, Drs. R. Kosaraju, R. P. Rich, and M. Bellmore. Finally, a large debt of thanks is owed to Dr. H. D. Mills for many hours of enlightening discussion on the theoretical and practical implications of structured programming.

Work supported in part by the United States Atomic Energy Commission under Contract AT (30-1)-4209.

REFERENCES

[1] P. J. Denning, "Virtual Memory," *Comput. Surv.*, **2**, 153–189 (1970).

[2] B. W. Kernighan, "Optimal Sequential Partitions of Graphs," *J. ACM*, **18**, 33–40 (1971).

[3] T. C. Lowe, "Automatic Segmentation of Cyclic Program Structures Based on Connectivity and Processor Timing," *Comm. ACM*, **13**, 3–6, 9 (1970).

[4] I. Niven, *Mathematics of Choice* (New York: Random House, 1965).

[5] H. D. Mills, "Structured Programming in Large Systems" (unpublished).

[6] C. Bohm and G. Jacopini, "Flow Diagrams, Turing Machines, and Languages With Only Two Formation Rules," *Comm. ACM*, **9**, 366–371 (1966).

[7] R. G. Busaaker, and T. L. Saaty, *Finite Graphs and Networks: An Introduction With Applications* (New York: McGraw Hill, 1965).

[8] S. E. Dreyfus, "An Appraisal of Some Shortest-Path Algorithms," *Oper. Res.*, **17**, 395–412 (1969).

[9] E. W. Dijkstra, "GOTO Statement Considered Harmful," Letter to Editor, *Comm. ACM*, **1**, 538, 541 (1968).

MINIMIZING WASTED SPACE IN PARTITIONED SEGMENTATION

Erol Gelenbe
The University of Michigan, Department of Electrical and Computer Engineering, Ann Arbor, MI
and
J. C. A. Boekhorst and J. L. W. Kessels
Philips Research Laboratories, Waalre, The Netherlands

A paged virtual-memory system using a finite number of page sizes is considered. Two algorithms for assigning pages to segments are discussed. Both of these algorithms are simple to implement. The problem of choosing the page sizes so as to minimize the expected value of total wasted space in internal fragmentation and in a page table, per segment, is then solved for a probability-density function of segment size which may be expressed as a convex combination of Erlang densities.

I. INTRODUCTION

Virtual memory [1] utilizes an assortment of auxilliary-memory devices in conjunction with a primary-storage facility accessed directly by the central-processing units of a computer system to give the programmer the illusion that an extremely-large primary memory is available to him. Many systems incorporating a virtual memory allocate storage to a user's segments [2], where a segment is a logically self-contained unit of a program's storage requirements. The size of these segments will vary widely within a given computing system, and also among different computer systems. To alleviate the problems inherent in the management of blocks of storage of widely-varying length, a technique known as paging has been developed and implemented on many multiprogrammed computer systems equipped with a virtual memory [2, 3]. A page is a block of storage of fixed size in terms of which all storage requirements are allocated. Primary- and secondary-memory space is partitioned into pages and a page table (PT) [2], whose entries indicate the physical whereabouts of each page of the segment, is stored for each segment.

As a consequence of assigning an integral number of pages to a segment, storage space is wasted. This effect is known as internal fragmentation. The necessity of storing a PT is an additional source of wasted space known as external fragmentation*. These effects have been studied in detail by Randell [2] using descriptive and simulation methods, and he suggested a scheme using two page sizes to reduce total (internal-plus-external) fragmentation.

*This term is also used for the fragmentation of primary memory into a large number of unequal-sized blocks.

Presented at the Symposium on Computers and Automata
Polytechnic Institute of Brooklyn, April 13-15, 1971.

The usefulness of schemes utilizing multiple-page sizes in a given storage allocation system will depend on the following factors:

(1) The distribution of segment size in the system. This depends on the languages used in the system, the system managing programs and the frequency with which they appear, the sizes of programs run in the system, etc.
(2) The complexity of the algorithm assigning a set of "virtual" pages to each segment
(3) The page sizes chosen, and the number of distinct page sizes
(4) The nature and organization of storage devices in the system.

In systems in which rotating-mass memories are the main secondary-storage units, (4) may be the main drawback to the implementation of multiple-page sizes since techniques for reducing access time (such as sectoring and drum scheduling) are complicated by multiple-page sizes. The advent of rapid-access secondary-storage devices such as extended-core storage may eliminate this problem.

It is important that the automatic management of a computer system be effected without excessive overhead in storage and time requirements, therefore the page-assignment algorithms considered in this paper are relatively simple.

In this paper we bring analytical tools to bear upon the problem of determining an "optimum" set of page sizes with the objective of minimizing total fragmentation in a system similar to the one suggested by Randell [2].

The virtual memory system we consider is segmented and paged [3]. A finite number of page sizes denoted by

$$1 \leq C_1 < C_2 < \cdots < C_n \quad , \tag{1}$$

where n is fixed is available. We assume that $\dfrac{C_k}{C_{k-1}}$ $(2 \leq k \leq n)$, is an integer.

We consider two algorithms for assigning virtual pages to segments. Both of these algorithms, which we call A-1 and A-2 for convenience, are simple and do not need much storage. A-1 is a generalization of Randell's [2] algorithm as modified by Denning [1]. We use x to denote segment size.

Algorithm A-1

Let $N(k,x)$ $(1 \leq k \leq n)$, denote the number of pages of size C_k assigned to a segment of size x. Then

$$N(n,x) = \left\lfloor \frac{x}{C_n} \right\rfloor ,$$

$$N(k,x) = \left\lfloor \frac{x - \sum_{j=k+1}^{n} N(j,x) \cdot C_j}{C_k} \right\rfloor \qquad (2 \leq k \leq n-1) ,$$

$$N(1,x) = \left\lceil \frac{x - \sum_{j=2}^{n} N(j,x) \cdot C_j}{C_1} \right\rceil .$$

Algorithm A-2

Let $M(k,x)$ $(1 \leq k \leq n)$, denote the number of pages of size C_k assigned to a segment of size x. For $n = 1$

$$M(1,x) = \left\lceil \frac{x}{C_1} \right\rceil .$$

When $n > 1$

$$M(n,x) = \left\lfloor \frac{x + C_1 - 1}{C_n} \right\rfloor ,$$

$$M(k,x) = \left\lfloor \frac{x + C_1 - 1}{C_k} \right\rfloor - \left\lfloor \frac{x + C_1 - 1}{C_{k+1}} \right\rfloor \cdot \frac{C_{k+1}}{C_k} \quad (1 < k \leq n - 1) ,$$

$$M(1,x) = \left\lceil \frac{x}{C_1} \right\rceil - \left\lfloor \frac{x + C_1 - 1}{C_2} \right\rfloor \cdot \frac{C_2}{C_1} .$$

We first have to establish that A-1 and A-2 allocate enough virtual pages to a segment to contain all of it.

LEMMA 1.

$$\sum_{j=1}^{n} N(j,x) \cdot C_j \geq x ,$$

and

$$\sum_{j=1}^{n} M(j,x) \cdot C_j \geq x .$$

Proof. The statement for A-1 is obvious, as is that for A-2 when $n = 1$. Therefore consider A-2 with $n > 1$. We then have that

$$\sum_{j=1}^{n} M(j,x) \cdot C_j = \sum_{j=2}^{n} \left\lfloor \frac{x + C_1 - 1}{C_j} \right\rfloor \cdot C_j - \sum_{j=2}^{n} \left\lfloor \frac{x + C_1 - 1}{C_j} \right\rfloor \cdot C_j + \left\lceil \frac{x}{C_1} \right\rceil \cdot C_1 ,$$

completing the proof. Q.E.D.

Another point to be verified is that A-1 and A-2 assign a non-negative number of pages of each size.

LEMMA 2. *For* A-1 *and* A-2

$$N(j,x) \geq 0 ,$$

and

$$M(j,x) \geq 0 \ ,$$

for all $1 \leq j \leq n$ *and all* $x \geq 0$.

Proof. The statement is obvious for A-1 and for A-2 with $n = 1$. Therefore consider A-2 with $n > 1$. For any $a > 0$, $y \geq 0$

$$a \left\lfloor \frac{y}{a} \right\rfloor \leq y \ .$$

Therefore the statement is true for $1 \leq j \leq n$, since $C_1 \geq 1$ is also assumed. By the same token

$$\left\lfloor \frac{x + C_1 - 1}{C_2} \right\rfloor \frac{C_2}{C_1} \leq \left\lfloor \frac{x + C_1 - 1}{C_1} \right\rfloor \ .$$

With no loss of generality, we may express

$$x = a_1 C_1 + d_1 \ , \quad 0 \leq d_1 < C_1 \quad (a_1 \text{ an integer}) \ ,$$

so that

$$\left\lfloor \frac{x + C_1 - 1}{C_1} \right\rfloor = \left\lfloor a_1 + 1 + \left(\frac{d_1 - 1}{C_1}\right) \right\rfloor \leq \left\lceil \frac{x}{C_1} \right\rceil \ .$$

Q.E.D.

A-1 and A-2 do indeed assign different numbers of page for certain values of x and of page sizes. For instance, let $n = 2$ with $C_1 = 3$, $C_2 = 6$ and $x = 11$. Then $N(2,11) = 1$, $N(1,11) = 2$, so that 3 pages have been assigned by A-1. However A-2 will assign 2 pages since $M(2,11) = 2$ and $M(1,11) = 0$. Internal fragmentation will be the same for both algorithms. It is seen that A-2 is no more difficult than A-1 to implement. Furthermore, it will be shown that A-2 will never assign more pages to a segment than A-1, and that for most values of x it will assign fewer pages. Therefore we recommend A-2 over A-1, the latter having been suggested by Denning [1] as a minor modification of Randell's [2] partitioned segmentation.

In the sequel, we shall analize the average behavior of A-2 and A-1 (in the probabilistic sense) assuming that the distribution of segment size x is known, and the values of $C_1, C_2, C_3 \cdots, C_n$ minimizing total fragmentation on the average will be determined for certain distributions.

The problem studied here is a generalization of the "optimum page size" problem studied in detail by Gelenbe [4] and in a slightly-different context by Wolman [5].

II. PRELIMINARY ANALYSIS OF THE ALGORITHMS

For convenience, denote the expected value of segment size by λ, and let

$$N(x) = \sum_{j=1}^{n} N(j,x) \ ,$$

and

$$M(x) = \sum_{j=1}^{n} M(j, x) ,$$

while N and M are the expected values of $N(x)$ and $M(x)$, respectively. Total wasted space in internal fragmentation and in external fragmentation is then

$$F_1(x) = b\,N(x) + \sum_{j=1}^{n} N(j, x) \cdot C_j - x , \tag{1}$$

for A-1, b being the number of words per page in the PT, and

$$F_2(x) = b\,M(x) + \sum_{j=1}^{n} M(j, x) \cdot C_j - x , \tag{2}$$

for A-2, per segment. The expected value of total wasted space denoted by F_1, F_2 for A-1, A-2, respectively, is obtained by taking the expected value of $F_1(x)$, $F_2(x)$ with respect to the probability-density $p(x)$.

Our assumption that

$$\frac{C_{j+1}}{C_j} \quad (1 \leq j \leq n-1) , \tag{3}$$

is integer valued, which is quite reasonable in view of the fact that in any implementation the page sizes would be powers of two, allows us to make certain simplifications in A-1. These are summarized in the next lemma.

LEMMA 3. *With the assumption made in Eq. (3), the algorithm* A-1 *becomes*

$$N(k, x) = \left\lfloor \frac{x}{C_k} \right\rfloor - \left\lfloor \frac{x}{C_{k+1}} \right\rfloor \cdot \frac{C_{k+1}}{C_k} \quad (2 \leq k \leq n-1) ,$$

and

$$N(1, x) = \left\lceil \frac{x}{C_1} \right\rceil - \left\lfloor \frac{x}{C_2} \right\rfloor \frac{C_2}{C_1} ,$$

while $N(n, x)$ *remains unchanged.*

Proof. Let e be an integer and r a real number. Evidently

$$\lfloor r - e \rfloor = \lfloor r \rfloor - e .$$

Therefore

$$N(k, x) = \left\lfloor \frac{x}{C_k} \right\rfloor - \sum_{j=k+1}^{n} N(j, x) \left(\frac{C_j}{C_k} \right) \quad (2 \leq k \leq n-1) ,$$

and substituting for $k = n - 1$ proves the assertion for this case. This establishes the basis for an inductive argument, which we continue by hypothesizing that the assertion is true for all $N(k, x)$ $(j < k \leq n-1)$, where $j \geq 2$. Then

$$N(j, x) = \left\lfloor \frac{x}{C_j} \right\rfloor - \sum_{i=j+1}^{n} \left(\left\lfloor \frac{x}{C_i} \right\rfloor \frac{C_i}{C_j} - \left\lfloor \frac{x}{C_{i+1}} \right\rfloor \frac{C_{i+1}}{C_i} \frac{C_i}{C_j} \right) - \left\lfloor \frac{x}{C_n} \right\rfloor \frac{C_n}{C_j}$$

$$= \left\lfloor \frac{x}{C_j} \right\rfloor - \left\lfloor \frac{x}{C_{j+1}} \right\rfloor \frac{C_{j+1}}{C_j} .$$

The case for $j = 1$ is proved in similar fashion. Q.E.D.

Lemma 3 simplifies the analysis of A-1 considerably. We shall make frequent use of one more lemma.

LEMMA 4. *Let $T > 0$ be a constant and let $p(x) = 0$ for $x < 0$.*

$$E\left\{\left\lfloor \frac{x}{T} \right\rfloor\right\} = \sum_{i=0}^{\infty} i \int_{iT}^{(i+1)T} p(x)\, dx ,$$

and

$$E\left\{\left\lceil \frac{x}{T} \right\rceil\right\} = \sum_{i=1}^{\infty} i \int_{(i=1)T}^{iT} p(x)\, dx .$$

We can now compare $F_1(x)$ and $F_2(x)$ to determine which of the two page-assignment algorithms is more economical.

LEMMA 5. *For any x and assuming that C_k is divisible by C_{k-1} for 2 kn, we observe that*

$$N(x) - M(x) = \sum_{j=1}^{n-1} \left(\frac{C_{j+1}}{C_j} - 1 \right) \left(\left\lfloor \frac{x + C_1 - 1}{C_{j+1}} \right\rfloor - \left\lfloor \frac{x}{C_{j+1}} \right\rfloor \right) \geq 0 ,$$

and

$$F_1(x) - F_2(x) = b(N(x) - M(x)) \geq 0 .$$

Lemma 5 can be easily proved by using Lemma 3. We see that A-2 will give rise to no more table fragmentation than A-1, while A-1 may have greater table fragmentation for some values of x. On the other hand, internal fragmentation is identical for A-1 and A-2 for any x. Although A-2 is clearly superior to A-1, we shall proceed with the analysis of both algorithms for the sake of completeness.

The analysis presented here is restricted to the Erlang-k densities and their convex combinations as probability-density functions of segment size so that we are making the assumption that x is real valued rather than integer valued; this allows us to avoid combinatorial difficulties. The Erlang-k densities are chosen because of their mathematical tractability and the possibility of expressing many densities encountered in practice as their convex combinations. We will have need of some preliminary results which we now develop.

The Erlang-k density is defined as

$$p_k(x) = \begin{cases} \dfrac{x^k a^{k+1}}{k!} \exp(-xa), & \text{for } x \geq 0 , \\ 0, & \text{for } x < 0 , \end{cases}$$

where: k is a non-negative integer and a is a positive constant. The mean of the density, denoted by λ_k, is given by

$$\lambda_k = \frac{k+1}{a} .$$

LEMMA 6. *Let T be a positive constant and x a random variable with probability-density function $p_k(x)$. Then for $Ta < 1$,*

$$E_k^+ = E\left\{\left\lceil \frac{x}{T} \right\rceil\right\} = \frac{\lambda_k}{T} + \frac{1}{2} + \mathcal{O}(Ta) ,$$

and

$$E_k^- = E\left\{\left\lfloor \frac{x}{T} \right\rfloor\right\} = \frac{\lambda_k}{T} - \frac{1}{2} + \mathcal{O}(Ta) ,$$

for any natural number k.

Proof. We proceed by induction on k. As the basis consider the case of $k = 0$. Using Lemma 4 we easily obtain that

$$E_0^- = \frac{\exp(-Ta)}{1 - \exp(-Ta)} ,$$

which for $Ta < 1$ becomes

$$E_0^- = \frac{1 - Ta + \mathcal{O}(T^2 a^2)}{Ta\left(1 - \frac{1}{2} Ta\right) + \mathcal{O}(T^3 a^3)} ,$$

$$= \frac{1}{aT} - \frac{1}{2} + \mathcal{O}(Ta) ,$$

which establishes the basis for an inductive argument since $\lambda_0 = (1/a)$. Now assume that the formula for E_k^- holds for some k. For $k+1$ it becomes

$$E_{k+1}^- = \sum_{i=0}^{\infty} i \int_{iT}^{(i+1)T} \frac{x^{k+1} a^{k+2}}{(k+1)!} \exp(-xa)\, dx ,$$

$$= E_k^- - \sum_{i=0}^{\infty} i \left[\frac{x^{k+1} a^{k+1}}{(k+1)!} \exp(-xa) \right]_{iT}^{(i+1)T} ,$$

after applying the formula for integration by parts. It will be shown in Lemma 7 that for $Ta < 1$

$$-\sum_{i=0}^{\infty} i \left[\frac{x^{k+1} a^{k+1}}{(k+1)!} \exp(-xa) \right]_{iT}^{(i+1)T} = \frac{1}{Ta} + \mathcal{O}(Ta) .$$

Therefore

$$E_{k+1}^{-} = \frac{\lambda_k}{T} + \frac{1}{Ta} + \mathcal{O}(Ta) - \frac{1}{2} ,$$

$$= \frac{k+2}{Ta} + \mathcal{O}(Ta) - \frac{1}{2} ,$$

$$= \frac{\lambda_{k+1}}{T} - \frac{1}{2} + \mathcal{O}(Ta) ,$$

which completes the proof for E_k^-. We proceed in a similar way with E_k^+. We first establish the assertion for $k = 0$. This is achieved by observing that

$$E_0^+ = \frac{1}{(1 - \exp(-Ta))} ,$$

which for $Ta < 1$ becomes

$$E_0^+ = \frac{1}{Ta} + \frac{1}{2} + \mathcal{O}(Ta) ,$$

Assuming that the assertion is true for some k, we write

$$E_{k+1}^+ = E_k^+ - \sum_{i=1}^{\infty} i \left[\frac{x^{k+1}\, a^{k+1}}{(k+1)!} \exp(-xa) \right]_{(i-1)T}^{iT} ,$$

and complete the proof by stating that in Lemma 7 it will be shown that the summation in the above expression for E_{k+1}^+ reduces to $(1/Ta) + \mathcal{O}(Ta)$ when $Ta < 1$. Q.E.D.

LEMMA 7. *For* $Ta < 1$

$$-\sum_{i=0}^{\infty} i \left[\frac{x^{k+1}\, a^{k+1}}{(k+1)!} \exp(-xa) \right]_{iT}^{(i+1)T} = \frac{1}{Ta} + \mathcal{O}(Ta) ,$$

$$= -\sum_{i=1}^{\infty} i \left[\frac{x^{k+1}\, a^{k+1}}{(k+1)!} \exp(-xa) \right]_{(i-1)T}^{iT} ,$$

Proof. The proof is again by induction on k. The basis is the case with $k = 0$. After some algebra, it is seen that

$$-\sum_{i=0}^{\infty} i \left[xa \exp(-xa) \right]_{iT}^{(i+1)T} = aT \left[\frac{\exp(-Ta)}{(1 - \exp(-Ta))^2} \right] .$$

For $Ta \ll 1$, this becomes

$$aT \left[\frac{1 - Ta + (Ta)^2/2}{(Ta)^2 (1 - (Ta)/2)^2} \right] ,$$

which after some simplification reduces to

$$\frac{1}{Ta} + \mathcal{O}(Ta) ,$$

establishing the basis for the inductive argument for one of the expressions. We now assume that

$$\alpha_k = -\sum_{i=0}^{\infty} i \left[\frac{x^{k+1}\ a^{k+1}}{(k+1)!} \exp(-xa) \right]_{iT}^{(i+1)T} = \frac{1}{Ta} + \mathcal{O}(Ta) ,$$

for some k. Using the notation $\xi = Ta$, and writing

$$\alpha_k = \frac{1}{\xi} + \mathcal{O}(\xi) = \frac{1}{\xi} + u_1 \xi + u_2 \xi^2 + \cdots ,$$

where $u_1, u_2, u_3 \cdots$, are constants, without loss of generality, we see that

$$\frac{\partial}{\partial \xi} \alpha_k = \frac{k+1}{\xi} \alpha_k - \frac{k+2}{\xi} \alpha_{k+1} ,$$

which after some algebra gives

$$\alpha_{k+1} = \frac{1}{Ta} + \mathcal{O}(Ta) ,$$

completing the proof by induction for one of the terms. The proof for the other is ommitted since it follows identical lines. Q.E.D.

We can make similar statements concerning densities which are convex combinations of the Erlang densities. This is an obvious result and is stated without proof in the following lemma.

LEMMA 8. *Let* $c_1, c_2, c_3, \cdots, c_n$ *be positive constants whose sum is unity. Let* $q_1(x), q_2(x), q_3(x) \cdots, q_n(x)$ *be probability-density functions such that* $q_j(x) = p_{k_j}(x)$, *one of the Erlang densities for* $1 \le j \le n$. *Let* $q(x)$ *be the density with mean* λ *given by*

$$q(x) = \sum_{i=1}^{n} c_i \cdot q_i(x) .$$

Then

$$E\left\{\left\lceil \frac{x}{T} \right\rceil\right\} = \frac{\lambda}{T} + \frac{1}{2} + \mathcal{O}\left(\frac{T}{\lambda}\right) ,$$

and

$$E\left\{\left\lfloor \frac{x}{T} \right\rfloor\right\} = \frac{\lambda}{T} - \frac{1}{2} + \mathcal{O}\left(\frac{T}{\lambda}\right) ,$$

for $Ta < 1$ *in each* $q_j(x)$.

III. OPTIMUM CHOICE OF PAGE SIZES FOR A-1

In the sequel, we assume that segment size is a random variable with probability-density function $q(x)$, a convex combination of Erlang densities as in Lemma 8, with mean λ. Let N denote the expected value of $N(x)$, and F_1 the expected value of $F_1(x)$. Our concern will be with properties of A-1 when λ is very large. That is, we will determine values of $C_1, C_2, C_3, \cdots, C_n$ which will minimize F_1 asymptotically (as $\lambda \to \infty$). Therefore our values for $C_1, C_2, C_3, \cdots, C_n$ will be correct to first order, meaning that they will be arbitrarily close to the optimum values as λ becomes arbitrarily large.

Let us turn our attention to the formula for $F_1(x)$ given in Equation (1). Using Lemma 3, this may be expressed as

$$F_1(x) = C_1 \left\lceil \frac{x}{C_1} \right\rceil - x + b \left\{ \left\lceil \frac{x}{C_1} \right\rceil - \sum_{j=1}^{n-1} \left\lfloor \frac{x}{C_{j+1}} \right\rfloor \left(\frac{C_{j+1}}{C_j} - 1 \right) \right\} .$$

Since

$$\frac{\lambda}{T} \le E \left\{ \left\lceil \frac{x}{T} \right\rceil \right\} \le \frac{\lambda}{T} + 1 ,$$

and

$$\frac{\lambda}{T} - 1 \le E \left\{ \left\lfloor \frac{x}{T} \right\rfloor \right\} \le \frac{\lambda}{T} ,$$

we see that

$$b \frac{\lambda}{C_n} \le F_1 \le C_1 + b \left(\frac{\lambda}{C_n} + \sum_{j=1}^{n-1} \frac{C_{j+1}}{C_j} - (n-2) \right) , \qquad (4)$$

and depending on the value of λ, F_1 can be arbitrarily close to both bounds. Clearly, if F_1 is to be minimized asymptotically, the best one may do is to have that

$$\lim_{\lambda \to \infty} \frac{F_1}{\lambda} = 0 . \qquad (5)$$

This does not say much about the specific form of the optimum value of F_1; it does say certain things about $C_1, C_2, C_3, \cdots, C_n$ which optimize F_1 if Eq. (5) can be achieved. Namely, from Eq. (4) we see that we should examine values of $C_1, C_2, C_3, \cdots, C_n$ with the following property

$$\lim_{\lambda \to \infty} \frac{C_j}{\lambda} = 0 \quad (1 \le j \le n) ,$$

and

$$\lim_{\lambda \to \infty} C_n = \infty .$$

This allows us to make use of Lemma 8. We should turn to $C_1, C_2, C_3, \cdots, C_n$ without this property only if we discover that Eq. (5) cannot be achieved, which luckily will not happen. At this point the bulk of the work is done. Using Lemma 8, we write

$$F_1 = \frac{1}{2} C_1 + b \left(\frac{\lambda}{C_n} + \frac{1}{2} \sum_{j=1}^{n-1} \frac{C_{j+1}}{C_j} \frac{1}{2} (n-1) \right) ,$$

neglecting first-order terms. The set of equations

$$\frac{\partial}{\partial C_j} F_1 = 0 ,$$

have the unique solution

$$C_j^0 = b \left(\frac{2\lambda}{b} \right)^{\frac{j}{n+1}} \qquad (1 \leq j \leq n) ,$$

which minimizes F_1 since

$$\frac{\partial^2}{\partial^2 C_j} F_1 > 0; \; C_j > 0 \quad (1 \leq j \leq n) ,$$

The minimum value of F_1, F_1^0, is now obtained as

$$F_1^0 = (n+1) \left(\lambda \frac{b^n}{2^n} \right)^{\frac{1}{n+1}} - \frac{1}{2} (n-2) b ,$$

satisfying Equation (5).

IV. OPTIMUM CHOICE OF PAGE SIZES FOR A-2

We continue with a density of segment size given in Lemma 8. From the definition of algorithm A-2 we may write

$$F_2(x) = C_1 \left\lceil \frac{x}{C_1} \right\rceil - x + b \left[- \sum_{j=1}^{n-1} \left\lfloor \frac{x + C_1 - 1}{C_{j+1}} \right\rfloor \left(\frac{C_{j+1}}{C_j} - 1 \right) + \left\lceil \frac{x}{C_1} \right\rceil \right] ,$$

and its expected value will be denoted by F_2. Following the same arguments as in the previous section, we consider page sizes satisfying for $1 \leq j \leq n$

$$\lim_{\lambda \to \infty} \frac{C_j}{\lambda} = 0; \quad \lim_{\lambda \to \infty} C_n = \infty ,$$

so that we are able to make use of Lemma 8. We then obtain

$$F_2 = \frac{1}{2} C_1 + b \left(\frac{\lambda + C_1 - 1}{C_n} + \sum_{j=1}^{n-1} \frac{1}{2} \frac{C_{j+1}}{C_j} - \frac{1}{2} n + \frac{1}{C_1} \right) ,$$

omitting first-order terms.

To obtain the page sizes which minimize F_2 for large λ, we solve the equations

$$\frac{\partial}{\partial C_i} F_2 = 0 \ ,$$

which can be written as

$$C_1^2 = \frac{C_n}{C_n + 2b} (C_2 + 2) \ ,$$

$$C_i^2 = C_{i-1} C_{i+1} \quad (2 \leq i \leq n - 1) \ ,$$

$$C_n^2 = 2bC_{n-1} (\lambda + C_1 - 1) \ ,$$

and are satisfied (asymptotically as $\lambda \longrightarrow \infty$) by the page sizes $C_1^0, C_2^0, C_3^0, \cdots, C_n^0$ given in the previous section. The minimum value of F_2 for large λ is then

$$F_2^0 = F_1^0 - b \left[1 - \frac{C_1^0}{C_n^0} + \frac{1}{C_1^0} - \frac{1}{C_n^0} \right],$$

which, after neglecting terms which tend to zero as λ tends to infinity, becomes

$$F_2^0 = F_1^0 - b \ .$$

Since many multiprogrammed computer systems have a single page size, it is natural to compare the reduction in wasted space when multiple-page sizes are used with the single-page-size case.

Modifying slightly our notation, let us use $F_2(n)$ to denote the average wasted space for a system using A-2 with n pages. That is, $F_2(n) = F_2$. It is natural to be concerned about the percentage improvement in wasted space over the single page size ($n = 1$) case given by

$$I(n) = \frac{F_2(1) - F_2(n)}{F_2(1)} \times 100\% \ .$$

It is easily seen that for any fixed $n > 1$, $I(n)$ approaches 100% as λ approaches infinity. Even for small values of λ however, the gain can be considerable. With $n = 2$ and $b = 1$, $I(2)$ is close to 40% with $\lambda = 128$. If one attempts to determine the n which minimizes $F_2(n)$ for a fixed λ, one sees that it is proportional to the natural logarithm of λ. This value appears too large to be practical. Another approach to the problem considered here, which was suggested to the first author by Dr. Ugo Gagliardi, is to approach the minimization of F_1 or F_2 with respect to the page sizes and n simultaneously using a Lagrange-multiplier technique. We have not attempted this.

V. COMMENTS AND CONCLUSIONS

In this paper, two methods for assigning pages to segments using multiple-page sizes have been studied. Both methods have the property that the number of pages of size C_k assigned to any segment is bounded by C_{k+1}/C_k, $k = 1, 2, 3, \cdots, n - 1$, so that if if an upper bound to the number of segments resident in the primary memory is known, it is possible to reserve enough space to accomodate all pages except for the largest one (of size C_n) beforehand. A single-page table for all of the pages of a segment can be kept as in the single-page-size case. It is also possible to imagine systems which would vary a set of page sizes adaptively with variations in the distribution of segment size, and which use other schemes for assigning pages to segments. One approach which might be worth investigating is the assignment of a single-page size to segments, with the page size varying with the segment size.

Paging is a technique which simplifies the automatic storage-allocation problem in computer systems considerably. It brings with it the wastage of space in bookkeeping space and in the roundoff effect. The techniques we have studied here complicate the storage-allocation problem with respect to paging with a single-page size but allow a considerable reduction in wasted space.

Another storage-allocation technique which assigns blocks of fixed size, though in a different manner, is the buddy system. It may be interesting to compare the multiple-page-size schemes of this paper with the buddy system which assigns 2^k words to a request for x, if $2^k \geq x > 2^{k-1}$.

ACKNOWLEDGEMENTS

The authors are indebted to J. Klinkhamer and W. Euwe of the Philips Research Laboratories for numerous discussions and their encouragement. The work of E. Gelenbe was initiated at the Philips Research Laboratories and later continued at The University of Michigan with partial support from a Rackham Research Grant; he is grateful for the encouragement given him by Bernie Galler and Gene Lawler at Michigan.

REFERENCES

[1] P. J. Denning, "Virtual Memory," *Comput. Surv.*, **2**, (September 1970), 153–189.

[2] B. Randell, "A Note on Storage Fragmentation and Program Segmentation," *Comm. ACM*, **12**, 365–369, (July 1969).

[3] B. Arden et al., "Program and Addressing Structure in a Time-Sharing Environment," *J. ACM*, **13**, 1–16 (January 1966).

[4] E. Gelenbe, "A Note on Optimum Cell Size" (to be published).

[5] E. Wolman, "A Fixed Optimum Cell Size for Records of Various Lengths," *J. ACM*, **12**, 53–70 (January 1965).

PROBABILITY MODELS FOR COMPUTER SYSTEMS

T. Gergely
Central Research Institute for Physics of the Hungarian Academy of Sciences, Budapest, Hungary

For the execution of the synthesis of complicated computers and systems according to requirements, we have to possess a mathematical apparatus that can provide an adequate analysis of these systems. Recently, analytical or the computer imitation modeling or both together are used for the analysis of complicated systems. Currently, imitation modeling can produce better results. At the same time we need an adequate mathematical apparatus for the automatization of complicated computer planning. It can be in close connection with imitation models but meanwhile it must keep its precedence. Also the development of optional algorithms of computer operation units requires an analytical investigation. Further we shall speak about Idealized Computers (ICs) and they will mean the totality of computer hardware and software.

The description of a complicated system can be either a macro- or a microdescription depending on the aim of analysis. Furthermore, we distinguish the structural and the behavioral description. Considering the functioning and the application field of the system we obviously develop the analytic approach on a probability base. The structural macrodescription uses the theory of automata. Evidently, with the system becoming more and more complicated, and with taking its reliability into consideration only the probabilistic description is adequate. This leads to applications of the theory of probability automata. To make the synthesis theory of probability automata suitable for the synthesis of the IC, it is necessary to work out the examination methods of the behavior of the probability automata. We speak about the behavior of the IC when it is in connection with a given informational environment.

The following most important problems are to be solved by this new mathematical approach:

(1) Description of the incoming-information stream
(2) Mathematical models of the problems to be solved
(3) Description of the working processes of the IC (this must contain the hardware as well as the software problems)
(4) Functional description of the IC with operational control
(5) Description of the interaction of ICs belonging to the computer system
(6) Computer-man connection as the interaction of two complicated systems.

We can interpret the incoming information stream as the sequence of nonhomogeneous demands characterized by the time of inputs and a set of parameters. These demands can be described by stochastic vectors. The set of parameters is defined by the incoming tasks. The IC can be characterized by the definite set of its internal states, such that the IC can be described by a model assigning a set of variables to each time. The working processes of the IC can be described as the transitions of states. If we call the set of state transitions at a given time, an event, then the working of the IC can be represented by sequential-event set related to discrete times.

The solution is a multiphase-servicing process, where the transition of phases is random like, and the appearing times of the demands are dependent-probability variables.

Presented at the Symposium on Computers and Automata
Polytechnic Institute of Brooklyn, April 13-15, 1971.

It is the operating system which distributes the incoming information and determines the priority of demands. In several cases the macrodescription of the operating system can be done with the aid of probability automata.

Consequently the probability apparatus, used for the analysis of the IC must possess the following properties:

(a) It has to describe the evolutional process in the case when the probability variables are nonindependent and when the number of dependence is not constant

(b) It must be suitable for description of discrete-timed systems.

I. INTRODUCTION

The ever-wider applications of increasingly-complex computers and the appearance of new computer systems are continually confronting experts with new problems. In my opinion the most important of these are the following:

(1) The most effective utilization of the existing computer park. (In this context I would mention the results achieved in the field of economic distribution of incoming information streams, optimal control of computation processes, etc.)

(2) The extension of the information environment of the already-developed computer park, in other words the application of computers for the solution of new tasks arising in technical, scientific, and economic life (e.g., in research and designing work). In this respect simplification of the man-machine dialogue is of great importance

(3) Development of the computer park in accordance with new requirements. New computers have to possess, for example, a certain adaptiveness and learning abilities to be able to operate as well as possible in new information environments.

The solution of these problems requires, on one hand, the approach of the users' and the machine languages, and on the other, automatic control and optimization of computation processes and of the "user-machine" system.

In the following I shall deal with the second group of questions. Automatic control of computer systems and computation processes can be provided by the computer itself. The requisite hardware for automation has already been created by the rapidly-growing and outstandingly-successful electronics industry, and thus the task is now to develop control systems and to elaborate a general method for the synthesis of computers with automatic control.

II. THE AUTOMATIZATION OF COMPUTATION PROCESSES

By optimal control of computation processes we mean that the dead time of a computer or the units of a system is minimal, i.e., the system is balanced and at the same time the execution time of a task meets a given time criterion. A computer is balanced when, provided the task load is not zero, all the functional units of the computer are uniformly loaded and in no unit does dead time appear owing to unsuitable parameters in the burdening of another unit.

The appearance of Operating Systems (OSs) has represented the first step towards automation. An OS is defined as a program complex containing the well-ordered totality of procedures and routines involved in organizing the solution processes in the computer.

Among its other duties an OS must determine the solution sequence of incoming comands and diminish the total dead time of the computer, i.e., increase computation effectivity. The connections between a computer and its information environment* may be on line or off line; both connections can profitably use an OS. Automation of computation by an OS is, in effect, the control of the simultaneous solution of more than one program within a processor.

Nowadays we are witnessing a large-scale development of OSs as well as the inevitable accompanying growth of the related specialist literature. Without making any specific references to this literature I would like to mention three groups of OS realizations:

(1) Queue-up (q-) systems, in which the tasks wait in an ordered sequence for the processor to become free; the queue being established by the OS itself
(2) Time-sharing (TS) systems, in which each task in a queue is cyclically given a time quant of determined size by the processor
(3) Real-time (RT) systems, in which the tasks enter the processor in a priority sequence and according to some time criterion.

A common property of all three systems is the ability to interrupt the solution of a task and take another task in its place. With q-systems, the change of tasks in the processor ensues when the existing task turns to some peripheral unit and waits there for the answer; in TS systems the change occurs at the end of the quant; and in RT systems at the appearance of a higher-priority task. The sequence in which the tasks of a given requirement are executed is determined by the OS itself. In RT systems this raises the following problem: RT-type operation systems, as it is well known, are in use with computers employed in the on-line mode for the control of technological processes. The tasks which have to be solved arrive randomly and generally must be solved till a given moment to ensure the dynamics of the control. These tasks contain several common partial tasks in consequence of the closeness of the automatic-control system. The duty of an OS is the ordering of requirements in such a way that the number of such partial tasks requiring multiple solution is kept minimal. In this manner the processing time of the tasks can be shortened and the computer effectivity improved. Thus it is necessary to construct an algorithm which can analyze the incoming tasks and queue them up according to priority and logical requirements so that the desired time criterion can be realized during the solution of a task set.

The following step in the automation of computation processes is the development of the balanced, operation-controlled computers. It calls for structural as well as functional optimization in the automation of the computation processes. For instance in q-systems, complex-automatic control presumes the optimal determination of the memory capacities (core, secondary, disk, etc.), the division of

*The information environment of a computer can be defined as the set of tasks requiring solution and the users presenting these tasks. (The concept of a user in the context of computer control contains, for instance, the technological processes.)

paged programs between memories, and the dimensionality of the simultaneously-stored task set, as well as optimization of the operational speeds of the different units.

A further step in automation is the creation of adaptive systems which can modify their parameters according to changing requirements in such a manner that the operational criteria of the system remain optimal.

The balance of computers can be achieved only for a given task set, and thus a demand is rising for the creation of self-organizing operational systems. These systems vary their structure according to changes in the information environment in such a manner that the system remains balanced.

III. THE MATHEMATICAL BASIS OF SYNTHESIS AND ANALYSIS OF COMPUTERS

To achieve optimal control of computation processes we must first of all create an adequate mathematical description (model) of automatically-controlled computers.

There is a need for mathematical methods which can serve as a basis for the analysis and synthesis of computers and computer systems.

My aim here is to investigate what sort of properties are demanded of a mathematical apparatus that will be of use in the creation of a more-or-less general method for the description and synthesis of computers. In the following I shall mean by a computer the totality of hardware and software, and for this I shall use the concept of an Idealized Computer (IC).

In the analysis of a system, structural or behavioral micro- or macrodescriptions can be used. By the behavior of an IC I mean the activity (functioning) produced by the information environment. For example, during the execution of the program of a task the units taking part in an interaction and their parameters characterize the behavior of the IC. A macrodescription supposes the analysis of a system to the component parts of the structural or behavioral unit and the description of the interaction of these units. A microdescription, on the other hand, analyzes the system on the level of its building elements.

Synthesis of computers can proceed either: (a) from above downwards; or (b) from below upwards. The first method supposes a macrosynthesis on the level of the functional components of the system, with synthesis of the individual components following in increasingly greater detail. The second method proceeds in the reverse direction. In the design of complicated computer systems the first method has proved to be more effective.

From the above it is apparent that the problem in synthesis of automatically-controlled ICs lies in the determination of the parameters of the units and the structure of the computer, i.e., in the macrosynthesis of the IC. The design of units displaying the desired parameters is no problem, and thus during the analysis of the IC we must aim at giving a functional description (called *analysis* in the following) based on the macrostructural units.

The two main methods of analysis are the analytic and the imitation methods.

The first method uses a mathematical discipline apparatus for the functioning description of the IC which by its regularity is able to give adequate analytical relations for the characteristic features of the operational processes taking the parameters of the structural macrounits into account as well.

The second method imitates the functioning of the IC by a computer realization of the suitable algorithms given for the single operational processes and modeling programs. For the complete functional description of ICs it is often necessary to combine the two methods, and in these cases we speak about combined descriptive methods.

At present the imitative-descriptive method is the more frequently employed. It can be explained with the information of its comparatively-general apparatus. Special algorithmic languages suitable for system modeling which for the most part eliminate the inadequacies of traditional languages (complicated and hard to survey programs, long solution time, little effectivity) are now available. Modeling languages (e.g., GPSS III [1], SOL [2], SIMULA 67 [3], SLANG [4], etc.) give experts a manageable apparatus which makes the description of an IC easy. It is rather important from the users' viewpoint that the modern modeling languages generally are the basis for a quite-effective method for the collection and evaluation of statistical-functioning data which gives considerable information about the synthesis of ICs. In modeling it is important to distinguish the fundamental elements from the nonessential ones. It should be noted that a complete imitation model of a complicated IC is itself intricate.

The reason for the slow extension of analytically-descriptive methods is the lack of a general-mathematic apparatus. The analytical models that have so far been worked out have generally been intended to describe actual systems, and as they mostly use the properties of particular computers they lose all meaning when considered out of the given context. Clearly, the apparatus employed in these cases cannot be used as the basis of a general method. Models describing only one category of operation are suitable for the description of a wider class of computers, because they generally behave independently of the properties of those computers on which the category is composed. Models for the description of OSs are of this kind, and among these the analytical models of TS systems work best, giving fairly-exact descriptions of system operation under certain conditions [5, 6].

The results already realized allow us to conclude that they can give a more-flexible description of a system than the imitation models, which are only able to examine the effects of small changes on operation. Since mathematical methods of analysis serve as the basis for the synthesis of ICs, the above classification is valid for the mathematical methods of synthesis as well.

The mathematical apparatus of the synthesis should display the following properties:

(a) It must contain an effective method for statistical and dynamic description of the information environment
(b) It must give a flexible method for the description of the functioning of ICs
(c) It must be able to describe processes taking place parallely (e.g.,

when there are many processor ICs, or when there are several connected ICs)

(d) The functional description must take the hardware components and their parameters into account

(e) It must be suitable for the description of control processes

(f) It must give a method for the simultaneous description of the IC and its information environment (e.g., for the description of the man-machine relation as a unified system)

(g) It must give a method for the optimization of the IC parameters and for the selection of the optimum-control algorithms

(h) It must be relatively easy to operate and in a certain measure algorithmizable.

At present, sequential-imitation modeling is used for the synthesis of ICs. The imitation model varies in conformity with the plan of the IC, and the solutions selected in the course of the latter serve, e.g., for the analysis of the algorithms of the operational system. In this way the applied models are first of a partial character, giving the description of only one unit at a time, and only later do they become more generalized. Thus, as the planning of a complex IC proceeds, the imitation model, too, grows in complexity. As a consequence of this and a certain rigidity of the imitation models, it is plain that such a modeling apparatus cannot provide a suitable method for solving optimization tasks.

Considering that alongside this synthesis method a main role is played by the constructor, such imitation methods provide for quality control of the developed system and therefore cannot serve as bases for automizing the process of the synthesis. For this purpose and for the elimination of the above deficiencies, it is necessary to develop the general bases of the analytical method. The preliminary conditions already exist for applying a combined method in the synthesis of ICs, which while preserving the imitation models, shift the leading role to the analytical methods. Such a combined method presupposes the total synthesis of the IC and execution of the optimization tasks by the more-flexible analytical method.

If the mathematical analysis of the units of defined parameters is met with difficulties, they can be investigated with the help of partial-imitation methods. Further, with the analytical model from the results of partial modeling, the architecture and control unit of the IC (more exactly the parameters of both) are determined, and further the functional construction of the system. The task of synthesis is then the development of hardware (the connection tables of the IC, the complete technical documentation, etc.) and of software (instruction system, microprograms, internal and external languages, etc.). The software may be developed in part by using conventional methods, but problems arise which demand new methods as well, e.g., for minimizing the instructional microprograms [7].

IV. THE ANALYTICAL APPARATUS OF THE ANALYSIS

Let us examine in more detail the factors which the analytical apparatus must be able to describe. Firstly there is the description of the information environment of the IC, i.e., of the incoming-task stream. The tasks may be described by a parameter vector whose components are, e.g., the page number, the primary- and secondary-memory demand, the number of operations necessary, priority, etc. In this way the set of tasks of the IC information environment may be analyzed into certain types of tasks having parameter vectors of different values. The stream of tasks, i.e., the task sequence, is characterized by the frequency of the appearance or the intensity of a certain type of task, by the distribution of the time interval between the appearance of tasks, etc. The actual parameters essential for the analysis depend on the IC-control unit and its connection with the external environment (on line or off line). If a q-system IC can operate N tasks at a time and if any task leaving the system is replaced immediately by a new task, then only the parameter vector of N tasks contains useful information for the analysis (for synthesis), and not the moments of the appearance of the tasks.

The further investigation of the tasks may be statistical or dynamic. Statistical investigations deal with the construction of task programs (e.g., distribution of individual subroutine applications into the various types of tasks). Dynamic investigations follow the realization of the programs by the machine. This brings us to an examination of the interactions between the information environment and the ICs. In studies of tasks and task sets there are often cases where the individual components of a task are dependent probability variables in their realization. Similarly it occurs that the moments of the appearance of the individual tasks are not independent either, e.g., in the case of ICs used for process control. The tasks arrive at the IC through one or several channels. One of the most important parameters for the users is the transit time of a task through the IC, in other words the transmission capacity of the IC. This parameter determines how the IC will tackle the set of tasks appearing for solution. As far as the user is concerned this means that the presented task is solved either immediately, or it is accommodated in the queue of tasks waiting for solution, or it gets *lost* if the IC is busy. The units of the IC through which the task is realized are characterized by certain parameter (variable) sets. These parameters are, e.g., the number of places in the queues waiting for processor time or for secondary storage, transmission speed of the processor, the capacity of the individual information channels, etc. Some of these parameters are constant, others vary with the tasks and with the control.

Thus the transmission of task realizations through the IC, i.e., the operation of the IC, may be characterized by a process of sequential variation of parameter vectors, i.e., by the parameter time functions. These variations depend on the control system, the influence of the information environment, etc. The variations of the parameter vectors are of a random type and may occur at discrete moments (when the greatest common divisor of the moments of variation occurrences equals a number $k > 0$), or they may occur in any arbitrary moments (depending on the IC). In the latter case we speak of a continuous time. It sometimes occurs, that the moments of the parameter-vector variations are not independent. By considering the values assumed by the parameter vector as states, we arrive at the interpretation of the IC automaton theory. In view of the stochastic character of the state transition of the IC, a macrodescription is possible only by applying probability-automaton theory.

In the course of the analysis, the apparatus being developed must be able to describe the relationships between the parameters of the task stream and of the

IC, and the solution efficiency. The problem is thus similar to that with the mathematical apparatus used for the investigation of mass-service systems. This means that the IC may be regarded as a servicing apparatus (or apparatuses) of a mass-service system and the task stream as a stream of demands. An IC is the totality of the servicing apparatuses. The operation of these apparatuses may be parallel or sequential. Since ICs are probability automatons with no empty-state sets, we have to deal with a multiphase-servicing system in which there occur random phase transitions. This may be true for all parallelly-operating service units of the IC. In this way the solution (servicing) of a task (demand) occurs through several servicing units, or phases, e.g., an incoming task is first fixed by the IC in the memories. For this phase the servicing unit disposes of some s_1 parameter. This phase is followed by the solution in a unit with a parameter $s_2 \neq s_1$. This unit may be one and the same processor with different parameters for the various servicings. The operation of the secondary memories is characterized again by another parameter. The efficiency of servicing, or task solution, and of the servicing unit itself may be characterized by various quantities and functions, depending on the aims of the investigation: such are for example: the expected value of the dead time in the individual units, the average waiting time before solution starts, the average number of unsolved, outgoing tasks (lost tasks), the probability of a task being lost, the average length of the individual queue in the IC, and the average waiting time of the tasks in the individual queues. In some form these characterize the degree of suitability of the IC for the solution of a given set of tasks. Thus an analysis of this type supplies a good basis for the synthesis of the optimum IC and its control system. Considering the indeterministic character of the servicing system (IC) due to the reasons partly described above, an apparatus for the description of IC functioning must be based on the theory of stochastic processes.

V. THE MATHEMATICAL BASIS OF PROBABILITY MODELS

As is well known, the principal role in mass servicing or queue theory is played by stochastic processes, particularly by Markov processes and their extension (e.g., semiMarkov processes).

The application of such processes to the investigation of complex servicing systems like ICs presupposes a high degree of idealization and simplification. In certain cases this can be sufficiently accurate, but in the majority of the cases the significance of the probability models is highly diminished. Therefore more general-stochastic processes are needed which are capable of supplying an adequate model for the description and an analytically-mathematical apparatus for their analysis and synthesis. Such properties are displayed by the quasiMarkovian series [8] and Markov chains governed by a complicated-renewal process [9].

Let $\{\xi_n\}_0^\infty$ be a series of random variables with a state space $S = \{S_0, S_1, S_2, \cdots\}$ $(P\{\xi_n \in S, n = 0, 1, 2, \cdots\} = 1)$. The state $S_i \in S$ is called a Markov state if it follows from $\xi_n = S_i$ that $\{\xi_k\}_{n+1}^\infty$ is independent of $\{\xi_k\}_0^{n-1}$ for any arbitrary n $(n \geq 0)$. Let us denote the set of the Markov states by D $(D \subset S)$ and that of the nonMarkov states by D' $(D' = S \setminus D)$. The time moments when the random variable ξ_n attains the Markov state are called Markov moments. The stochastic series $\{\xi_n\}_0^\infty$ is called a quasiMarkovian series if D is not an empty set. We shall suppose, that $\{\xi_n\}_0^\infty$ will get into D an infinite number of times with one probability if D is not an empty set. It is obvious that if $D = S$ then the quasi-Markovian series $\{\xi_n\}_0^\infty$ (QMS) will be a Markov chain. Let us examine the evolution of a QMS. By the above definition the state assumed by the realization in some moment k ($k = 0, 1, 2, \cdots$) during the evolution of QMS depends on the states belonging to all preceding moments up to the last Markov moment, or in the absence of the latter up to the initial moment. So the states assumed by a QMS between two Markov moments are interdependent. If D is now a single-element set $D = \{\hat{S}\}$, then according to the above definition the further evolution of the QMS when $\xi_n = \hat{S}$ ($n = 0, 1, 2, \cdots$) will not depend on how state $\hat{S}$ was attained. It is easy to see that the QMS in this case is a renewal process.

The evolution of a QMS can be unequivocally represented by embedded and pulled-on Markov chains. The state space and the embedded Markov chain comprise the set D, and that of the pulled-on Markov chain is the set of vectors consisting of interdependent states, that is the sets of the vectors

$$(\mathbf{S}_{j_0}, \mathbf{S}_{j_1}, \mathbf{S}_{j_2}, \cdots, \mathbf{S}_{j_k}) \; (\mathbf{S}_{j_k} \in \mathbf{D}'; \; k = 0, 1, 2, \cdots)$$

and

$$[\mathbf{S}_i; \mathbf{S}_{j_1}, \mathbf{S}_{j_2}, \mathbf{S}_{j_3}, \cdots, \mathbf{S}_{j_k}] \; (\mathbf{S}_i \in D, \mathbf{S}_{j_k} \in D'; \; k = 1, 2, 3, \cdots) \; .$$

This method permits the determination of the stationary distribution of the QMS, that of the sojourn time in a given range of states, etc. It can be seen from the above discussion, that the QMSs supply a tool for the investigation of systems in which the beginning and end of the various events occur at moments which are integer multiples of some number $k > 0$. This method allows us to construct an adequate stochastic model, e.g., for task programs. We shall examine the programs at the level of the constructional units, e.g., at the microprogram level. In these cases the program can be described as a stochastic series evolving over the set of the constructional units.

From the state space determined by the set of the constructional units, a subset of states which will be Markovian can be easily selected. In this way the state space can be decomposed into two nonintersecting sets, i.e., into the sets of Markov and nonMarkov states. Thus if the program calls down a subroutine, then the first constructional unit of the source will always be a Markov state where as the other units will follow in a sequence depending on each other, i.e., they will belong to the set of nonMarkov states. In the case when the transition between the nonMarkov states appears with a probability of 1, the Markov chain model described in [7] is obtained; this corresponds to the embedded Markov chain of the QMS.

For the investigation of continuous-time systems, a Markov chain governed by a complicated-renewal process (in the following RPGMC) can be used. This is a homogeneous $(r + 2)$-dimensional Markov process $\{\xi(t); \eta_0(t), \eta_1(t), \eta_2(t), \cdots, n_r(t)\}$ in which the components are non-negative and assumed to be only integer values. The parameter r permits the real interdependences observable in a functioning system to be taken into consideration.

Let $\theta_1, \theta_2, \theta_3, \cdots, \theta_n$ $(n \geq 1)$ be a series of non-negative probability variables forming a Markov chain of rth order, for which

$$P\{\theta_n < x \mid \theta_{n-1} = y_1, \theta_{n-2} = y_2, \theta_{n-3} = y_3, \cdots, \theta_{n-r} = y_r\} = F(x \mid y_1, y_2, y_3, \cdots, y_r)(y_i \geq 0;\ i = 1, 2, 3, \cdots, r) \ .$$

Let us form the summation series of the random variables $\theta_1, \theta_2, \theta_3, \cdots, \theta_n$, $\tau_n = \theta_1 + \theta_2 + \theta_3 + \cdots + \theta_n$ $(n = 1, 2, 3, \cdots)$. The series consisting of components with the conditional-distribution function $F(x \mid y_1, y_2, y_3, \cdots, y_r)$ is called a complicated renewal process.

We can now examine the evolution of the process $\xi(t)$. Let $\xi(t \mid y_1, y_2, y_3, \cdots, y_r)(y_i \geq 0;\ i = 1, 2, 3, \cdots, r)$ be a family of homogeneous Markov chains assuming non-negative integer values. Over each interval (τ_n, τ_{n+1}) $(n \geq 1)$ the evolution of $\xi(t)$ corresponds with that of the Markov chain $\xi(t \mid \theta_n, \theta_{n-1}, \theta_{n-2}, \cdots, \theta_{n-r+1})$ in such a way that when $\xi(\tau_{n+1} - 0) = k$ then $\xi(t)$ goes into the state i at the time moment $\tau_{n+1} = \tau_n + \theta_{n+1}$ under the influence of the renewal process, i.e., this transition probability (denoted by b_{ki}) will depend on $\theta_{n-r+1}, \cdots, \theta_{n-1}, \theta_n, \theta_{n+1}$ so that $b_{ki} = b_{ki}(\theta_{n+1} \mid \theta_n, \theta_{n-1}, \theta_{n-2}, \cdots, \theta_{n-r+1})$. The evolution of $\xi(t)$ over the interval (τ_{n+1}, τ_{n+2}) will correspond to that of the Markov chain $\xi(t \mid \theta_{n+1}, \theta_n, \theta_{n-1}, \cdots, \theta_{n-r+2})$, etc. Now if $\xi(\tau_n + 0) = \xi_n$, $\eta_i(\tau_n + 0) = \eta_{in}$ $(i = 1, 2, 3, \cdots, r)$ then $\{\xi_n; \eta_{1n}, \eta_{2n}, \eta_{3n}, \cdots, \eta_{rn}\}$ will be the embedded Markov chain of the RPGMC. Such a chain allows us to determine the stationary distributions of the latter. The sojourn-time distribution of the RPGMC in a given range of the phase space, as well as other characteristic of the process, can be determined by the methods developed for the examination of the RPGMC. The apparatus of the RPGWC makes it possible to construct, e.g., an adequate stochastic model of operational systems whose control algorithms rely on the variations of stochastically-interdependent parameters for governing the computation processes and for task processing.

The analytical relationships obtained during the analysis (which will be based on the set of parameters considered) can be utilized for the synthesis of ICs. During the synthesis the parameters are selected with the help of these relationships in such a way that the criteria contained in the relationships can be met by the IC. Generally the values of some of the parameters are defined by conditions given a priori and the required criterion is satisfied by selection of the other parameter values on the basis of the above relationships. Since the ICs are very complicated, the analytical relationships given by their stochastic models are also complex and difficult to organize. In order to obtain the apparatus for an easily-manipulated synthesis, the relationships must first be modeled by computer. During the modeling, tables or nomograms can be constructed by varying the variables appearing in the relationships and the appropriate parameter values can be selected without any difficulty.

VI. A SIMPLE PROBABILITY MODEL

To illustrate the above, let us examine the analysis and synthesis of a computer-processing unit serving for the solution of a given task.

The probabilities of the arrival and nonarrival of a task at the time moments $\tau = 1, 2, 3, \cdots$, are p and q, respectively $(p + q = 1)$. One task is solved by the

$$p_{\ell} = \frac{\alpha(1-q^{\alpha+1}) + \alpha p \sum_{k=\alpha+2}^{N-\alpha} \sum_{n=0}^{\left[\frac{k-2}{\alpha+1}\right]} C^n_{k-2-\alpha n} p^n q^{k-2-(\alpha+1)n} + \sum_{m=\alpha-1}^{1} mp \sum_{n=0}^{\left[\frac{N-m-2}{\alpha+1}\right]} C^n_{N-m-2-\alpha n} p^n q^{N-m-2-(\alpha+1)n}}{(1-\alpha p)\dfrac{1-q^{\alpha+1}}{p} + (1+\alpha p) \sum_{k=\alpha+2}^{N-\alpha} \sum_{n=0}^{\left[\frac{k-2}{\alpha+1}\right]} C^n_{k-2-\alpha n} p^n q^{k-2-(\alpha+1)n} + \sum_{m=\alpha-1}^{1} (1+mp) \sum_{n=0}^{\left[\frac{N-m-2}{\alpha+1}\right]} C^n_{N-m-2-\alpha n} p^n q^{N-m-2} + \dfrac{1}{p} \sum_{n=0}^{\left[\frac{N-2}{\alpha+1}\right]} C^n_{N-2-\alpha n} p^n q^{N-2-(\alpha+1)n}}, \quad (1)$$

Fig. 1. Stationary task-loss probability. Here: $[X]$ is the integer part of X and $C^m_n = \dfrac{n!}{m!\,(n-m)!}$.

unit within N time units. Only one task at a time is solved by the unit and one is stored in its memory, where it may stay for α time units. The parameters N and α are characteristic constants of the unit. Tasks arriving when the unit is functioning and the memory also occupied will be lost. The purpose of the synthesis of such units is to select the above parameters in a way that the probability of

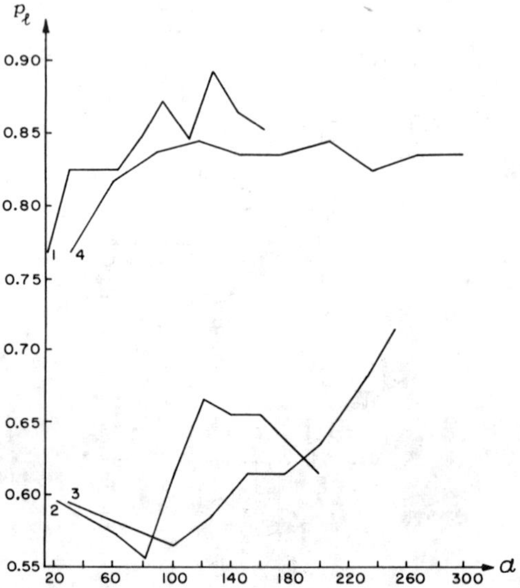

Fig. 2. Some functions $p_\ell = p_\ell(\alpha)$. $p = 10^{-2}$, $N_1 = 250$, $N_2 = 350$, $N_3 = 450$, and $N_4 = 550$.

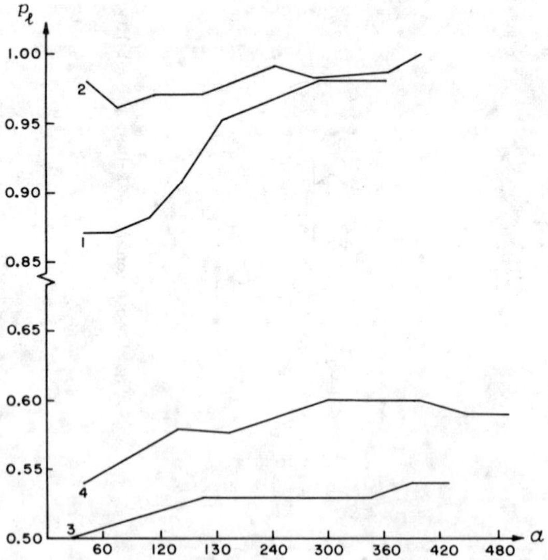

Fig. 3. Some functions $p_\ell = p_\ell(\alpha)$. $p = 5 \times 10^{-3}$, $N_1 = 650$, $N_2 = 750$, $N_3 = 850$, and $N_4 = 950$.

task losses should be minimum with a given p. The purpose of the analysis is to supply an adequate relationship between the stationary task-loss parobability (p_ℓ), N, α, and p. By carrying out the analysis with the help of the QMS we obtain* Eq. (1), see Figure 1 [10].

Because of its complexity, this relationship cannot be utilized directly for the synthesis and must first be modeled on the computer. In the course of modeling, the curves (function $p_\ell = p_\ell(\alpha)$) shown in Figs. 2 and 3 are obtained for the various N, α, and p values.

In the synthesis the α and N values may be selected in such a way that the value of p_ℓ is minimum with a given p. If N is given a priori by the functional requirements of the computer system, then the value of p_ℓ may be minimized by selecting α.

VII. CONCLUSIONS

In summary the following conclusions may be drawn:

(1) Optimization of computers and systems by automation of their functions is a practicable goal

(2) The synthesis of automatically-controlled computers and systems can be based on the results of analysis with an analytical-mathematical apparatus as parameters obtained from analysis based on imitation models are very hard if not impossible, to optimize

(3) The computer and the task to be solved form a complex mass-service system. Therefore in queuing theory the mathematical apparatus of the computer analysis is given by specific stochastic processes that take into account the properties the given task and the methods defined by them. These make it possible to construct adequate probability models of computer functioning

(4) The computer synthesis is based on the organical unit of probability models constructed by analytical methods and of imitation models of a unit not examinable analytically.

REFERENCES

[1] H. Herscovitch and T. H. Schneider, "GPSS III—An Expanded General-Purpose Simulator," *IBM Sys. J.*, **4**, No. 3 (1965).

[2] D. E. Knuth and I. L. McNeley, "A Formal Definition of SOL," *IEEE Trans. Electr. Comput.*, **EC-13** (1964).

[3] O-J Drahl, B. Myhrhaug, and K. Nygaard, "SIMULA 67 Common Base Language," Norwegian Computing Center (May, 1968).

[4] V. M. Glushkow et al., *Slang-Programing System for Digital-System Modeling, Ed. Institut of Cybernetic* (Kiev: 1969) (in Russian).

[5] A. L. Sherr, "An Analysis of Time-Shared Computer Systems," (Massachusetts: MIT Press, 1967).

[6] E. G. Coffman and L. K. Kleinlock, "Feedback Queuing Models for Time-Shared Systems," *J. Assoc. Comput. Mach.*, **15**, No. 4 (1968).

*During the analysis it was sufficient to work with a partial case of the QMS.

[7] V. M. Glushkow et al., "Computers With Advanced System Interpretation," *Ed. Naukova Dumka* (1970) (in Russian).

[8] T. Gergely and J. J. Yezhow, "QuasiMarkovian Series," *Sciantiarum Mathematicarum Hungarica*, No. 2 (1971) (in Russian).

[9] T. Gergely, J. J. Yezhow, and I. N. Tsukanow, "Markov Chain Governed by Complicated Renewal Processes," *Adv. Appl. Prob.*, No. 2 (1970).

[10] T. Gergely and V. P. Medvedew, "Investigation of the Ergodic Properties of a Digital Mass-Service System," *Theoretical Cybernetic*, No. 3 (Kiev: Institute of Cybernetics, 1971) (in Russian).

ON TRANSFERENCES AND PRIORITIES IN COMPUTER SYSTEMS AND NETWORKS

J. Santos and M. I. Otero
Universidad Nacional del Sur, Bahía Blanca, Argentina

The problem of organizing the flow of information between the units of a computer system or network is studied from the point of view of automata theory. The characteristics of the interconnecting graph are first considered and the advantages of minimizing the number of vertices with incoming local degree ≥ 2 are shown. The transferences are made through a channel controlled by a Transferences-and-Priorities processor. This is composed of two subautomata, both Moore machines, connected in cascade with feedback. The first one associates requests for transferences and availability signals issued by the units. From this association a request is made to the second subautomaton for the use of the channel. This is allocated according to a certain priority discipline which in turn depends on the number of critical units, their crisis times, and the bandwidth of the channel and its associated processor. Finally it is shown that the automata admit a finer decomposition in a rather large number of isomorphic, small submachines presenting a good case for LSI.

I. INTRODUCTION

In a very general sense a computer system or a computer network are formed by a certain number of units with a certain pattern of interconnections. The total throughput is highly dependent on the flow of information between units and the fact that in general they will be time shared makes possible the occurrence of simultaneous, conflicting requests for their use [1].

The space allocation of shared units (e.g., mass-storage media) is normally done by software (e.g., operating-system supervisor). Its time allocation falls generally within the strategy of the supervisor, although at the tactical level the use of a unit is normally controlled by hardware.

In what follows, a general design of this hardware will be presented from the point of view of automata theory, together with some particular solutions that take into consideration certain relationships between the numbers of units, the crisis times, and the bandwidth of the controller.

II. THE INTERCONNECTING GRAPH

The most general graph of interconnections between units is the directed complete graph with loops U_0. It is obvious that this structure is expensive and

Contributed to the Proceedings of the Symposium on Computers and Automata
Polytechnic Institute of Brooklyn, April 13–15, 1971.

has an unnecessary complexity. Because of that, the actual graph will be a subgraph $H \subset U_0$. In each vertex of incoming local degree ≥ 2, the possibility of simultaneous requests exists. Because of the short response time necessary for an efficient organization of transferences some form of hardware must normally be used there. Therefore, in order to save hardware, the designer should try to minimize the number of such vertices. This can be done by associating a device, not with a particular unit, but with groups of units (eventually all the units of the system in one group). The device controls a channel formed by a set of units-output gates going into an OR gate with multiple outputs directed back to the units. The channel and its associated control device is then another vertex in the graph.

III. THE TRANSFERENCES

Every transference of information between two units may be thought of as belonging to one of the followings two classes:

(i) A unit wants to retrieve some information from another unit
(ii) A unit wants to force information into another unit.

In the first case an address will be sent through the channel from the requesting unit to the data-giving unit when this is ready to make a readout. When the requested data is available and the requesting unit is ready to accept (write in) it, the data will be transferred from the second to the first unit.

In the second class of transferences, the data together with their associated addresses, will be transferred when the receiving unit is ready to accept them. In cases of conflicting requests for its use, the channel will be allocated according to a suitable discipline of priorities. This is essentially the job of the device controlling the channel. The device will be called the Transferences-and-Priorities Processor (TPP).

IV. THE TRANSFERENCES-AND-PRIORITIES PROCESSOR

The units will present their requests to the processor by means of a set of inputs Σ_u. The availability of the units (to read, to write, or to transfer requested data) will be made known to the automaton by means of another set of inputs Σ_a. The language the automaton will accept is a subset of the free monoid $\{(\Sigma_u + \Sigma_a), \cdot\}$, precluding words with repeated letters. The symbols + and $\cdot$ denote set-theoretical union and concatenation, respectively. Both types of signals

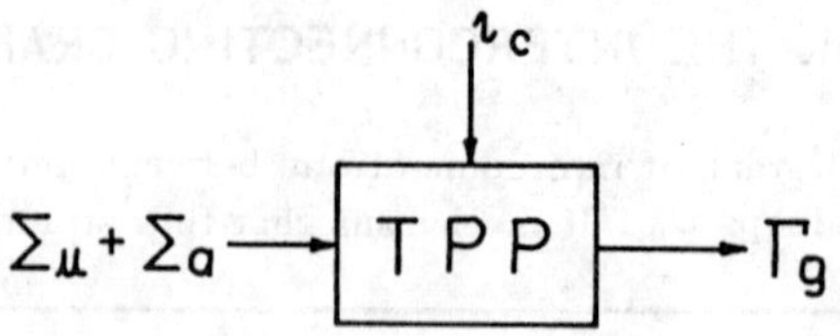

Fig. 1. Block diagram of the TPP.

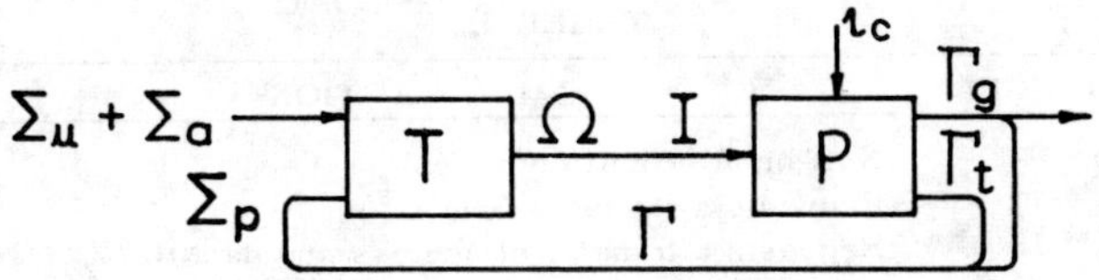

Fig. 2. The T and P automatons.

are associated and produce transitions towards a set of final states. The set of outputs Γ_g associated to certain final states of the processor will control the gates to perform the transference. The block diagram of the TPP is shown in Figure 1. The clock input ι_c is included to introduce synchronism.

From the above it is clear that the TPP can be thought of as being composed of two subautomata T and P: the first one associating requests and availabilities; and the second one applying a certain priority discipline to the associated signals. P, in turn, must let T and the units know that the channel has been allowed to perform a certain transference. To fulfill both requirements, T and P must be connected in cascade with feedback. Figure 2 shows the block diagram of the connection.

Let us now make a more detailed description of T and P.

V. THE *T* AUTOMATON

The finite set of units will be denoted $\mathfrak{N} = \{A, B, C, \cdots, N\}$. T is a Moore machine $\{S, \Sigma, \Omega, \rho, \mu\}$, where: S is the set of internal states; and $\Sigma = \Sigma_u + \Sigma_a + \Sigma_p$ is the set of inputs.

$$\Sigma_u = \{\{\Lambda\} + \{\sigma_{u\beta IJ}\}\} ,$$

$$\Sigma_a = \{\{\Lambda\} + \{\sigma_{a\alpha J}\}\} ,$$

$$\Sigma_p = \{\{\Lambda\} + \{\sigma_{p\alpha IJ}\} + \{\sigma_{p\beta J}\}\} .$$

Where: $\Omega = \{\{\Lambda\} + \{\omega_{\alpha IJ}\}\}$, the set of outputs; ρ is a transition function; and μ is an output function. In every case: $I, J \in \mathfrak{N}$; $\alpha \in \{r, v, w\}$; and $\beta \in \{r, w\}$. The meanings of Λ and each σ and ω are made clear in Table I.

The subscripts belong to three sets. The set $\{u, a, p\}$ identifies the type of signal (u: request; a: availability; and p: channel allocated). The set $\{r, v, w\}$ identifies the class and/or phase of transference (r: transference of address in retrieval; v; transference of data in retrieval; and w: transference of address and data when writing into). The set $\mathfrak{N}$ identifies the units involved in the transference.

In order to produce the availability signals, certain conditions must be fulfilled at the units. To produce an *available to read signal* the unit must be *not*

TABLE I.

SIGNAL	ORIGIN	ACTION
Λ	—	Null input or null output
σ_{urIJ}	I	Requests a retrieval from J
σ_{uwIJ}	I	Requests a transfer of address and data to J
σ_{arJ}	J	Indicates that J is available to read
σ_{avJ}	J	Indicates that J has available the requested data
σ_{awJ}	J	Indicates that J is available to write
σ_{prIJ}	P	Indicates channel allocated to transfer an address from I to J. It opens the OP gates of I's OP-address register, the IP gates of J's IP-address register, and it strobes the address from I to J.
σ_{prJ}	P	Indicates that J has been engaged in a reading cycle
σ_{pvJI}	P	Indicates channel allocated to transfer retrieved data from J to I. It opens the OP gates of J's OP-data register, the IP gates of I's input-data register and strobes data from J to I
σ_{pwIJ}	P	Indicates channel allocated to transfer address and data from I to J. It opens OP gates of I's OP-address and data registers, IP gates of J's IP-address and data registers, and strobes address and data from I to J
σ_{pwJ}	P	Indicates that J has been engaged in a writing cycle
ω_{rIJ}	T	Requests to P the use of the channel to transfer an address from I to J
ω_{vJI}	T	Requests to P the use of the channel to transfer retrieved data from J to I
ω_{wIJ}	T	Requests to P the use of the channel to transfer address and data from I to J

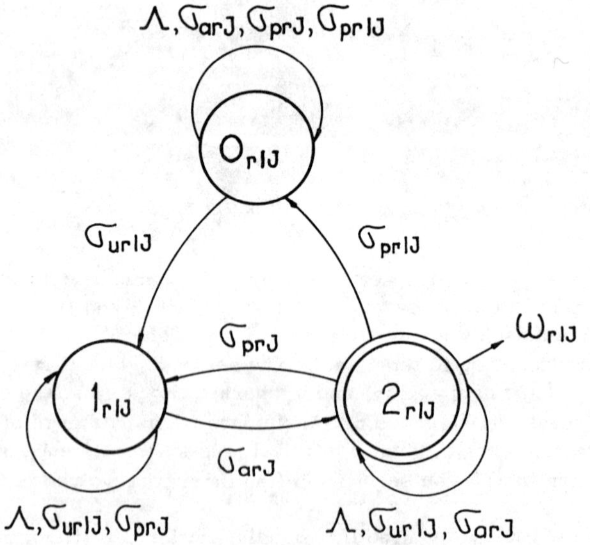

Fig. 3. The T_{rIJ} submachine.

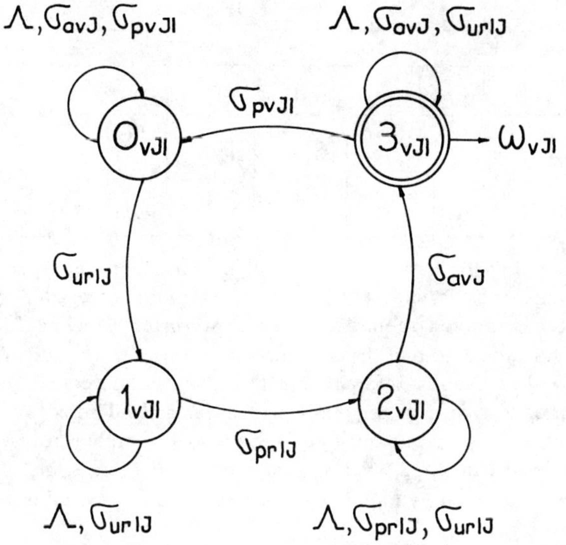

Fig. 4. The T_{aJI} submachine.

busy and have at least one output register clear or be in a writing cycle and have at least one input register clear.

In order to produce an *available to write* signal, the unit must be *not busy* or be engaged in a reading or writing cycle but with at least one input register clear.

The availability signals are defined keeping in mind the standard-output signals of most present-day, commercial, random-access memories. The signals of CPUs, direct-access memories, and peripheral equipment can be easily transformed into signals belonging to the previous set.

T is not strongly connected and admits parallel decomposition. There are only two basic types of submachines having three and four internal states. Figures 3 and 4 illustrate the basic submachines, respectively. Their transition and output functions are defined in Tables II and III. The first submachine handles the transference of an address from I to J when the first unit wants to retrieve information from the second one. The request is presented to the TPP by I, by means of σ_{urIJ} which produces the transition towards the 1_{rIJ} state. When J is available to read, σ_{arJ} is produced. With this input the submachine goes to the final

TABLE II.

S_{rIJ}	ρ_r					μ_r
	Λ	σ_{urIJ}	σ_{arJ}	σ_{prIJ}	σ_{prJ}	
0_{rIJ}	0_{rIJ}	1_{rIJ}	0_{rIJ}	0_{rIJ}	0_{rIJ}	Λ
1_{rIJ}	1_{rIJ}	1_{rIJ}	2_{rIJ}	—	1_{rIJ}	Λ
2_{rIJ}	2_{rIJ}	2_{rIJ}	2_{rIJ}	0_{rIJ}	1_{rIJ}	ω_{rIJ}

TABLE III.

S_{vJI}	ρ_v					μ_v
	Λ	σ_{urIJ}	σ_{prIJ}	σ_{avJ}	σ_{pvJI}	
0_{vJI}	0_{vJI}	1_{vJI}	—	0_{vJI}	0_{vJI}	Λ
1_{vJI}	1_{vJI}	1_{vJI}	2_{vJI}	1_{vJI}	—	Λ
2_{vJI}	2_{vJI}	2_{vJI}	2_{vJI}	3_{vJI}	—	Λ
3_{vJI}	3_{vJI}	3_{vJI}	—	3_{vJI}	0_{vJI}	ω_{vJI}

state 2_{rIJ} producing the output ω_{rIJ}, which, in turn, acts as input to the P subautomaton requesting the use of the channel to transfer the address. This request will later be served according to a certain priority schedule. When it is served, σ_{prIJ} is produced and the submachine returns to the initial state 0_{rIJ}. The same signal is used to inform I that the address has been accepted and σ_{urIJ} must stop. In case a similar request (to transfer and address towards J) is presented simultaneously by another submachine with a higher priority, the last one will be served first, σ_{prJ} will be produced a little later, and a return to the 1_{rIJ} will take place. There unit I will wait for J to be available to read, in order to present ω_{rIJ} again.

The functioning of the subautomaton in Fig. 4 is similar. It handles the transference of the requested information from J to I. With σ_{urIJ} the submachine makes a transition to state 1_{vJI}. When the channel is allocated, it goes to 2_{vJI}. When the information is available, it goes to 3_{vJI} and requests of P the use of the channel to transfer the data. When the transference is made, σ_{pvJI} is produced and the submachine goes back to the initial state 0_{vJI}. With the same signal, J is informed that data has been accepted.

The submachine handling the transference when I wants to write some information into J is isomorphic with the described in the first place, and it is illustrated in Figure 5.

The table for ρ_w and μ_w is similar to the first one, the only change being the substitution of the subscript w for r. If any unit can talk with any other, even with itself (e.g. relocation of data in mass stores), there will be n submachines of the type illustrated in each figure per unit. This gives a total of $3n^2$ submachines with a total of $10n^2$ internal states. In real practice however both figures will be considerably lower.

The T Automaton may be expressed as the parallel composition [2] of the $3n^2$ submachines. S however will only be a subset of the Cartesian product of the sets of internal states, because certain elements containing forbidden combinations are precluded. No element of S may contain, for instance, 0_{rIJ} and 1_{vJI}, because the input σ_{urIJ} producing the transition 0_{vJI} to 1_{vJI} will produce also 0_{rIJ} to 1_{rIJ}. For similar reasons the pairs $(1_{rIJ}, 0_{vJI})$, $(2_{rIJ}, 0_{vJI})$, $(2_{rIJ}, 2_{vJI})$ and $(2_{rIJ}, 3_{vJI})$ are also forbidden.

Σ is also a subset of the Cartesian product of the sets of inputs, precluding certain elements containing pairs of inputs that cannot be present simultaneously. For instance, the pair $(\sigma_{prIJ}, \sigma_{prJ})$ is excluded because σ_{prJ} always follows σ_{prIJ} with a certain delay. Ω is the Cartesian product of the outputs. ρ and μ are defined in the usual sense.

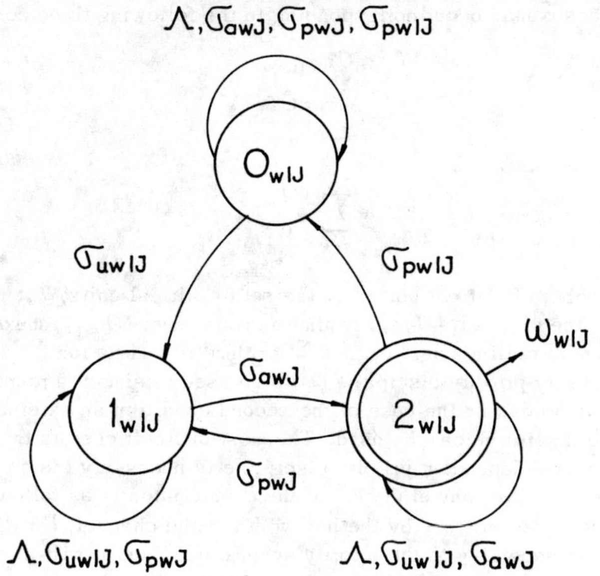

Fig. 5. The T_{wIJ} submachine.

Since an output ω results essentially from an association between a signal belonging to Σ_u and a signal belonging to Σ_a, the submachines can be implemented with associative electronic components [3]. Because T can be constructed with only two basic submachines highly repeated, a good case for LSI seems to exist.

VI. THE *P* AUTOMATON

P is also a Moore machine $\{Q, \mathrm{I}, \Gamma, \varepsilon, \theta\}$, where: Q is the set of internal states; $\mathrm{I} = \{\{\iota_c\} + \{\iota_{\alpha IJ}\}\}$, the set of inputs; ι_c is a synchronous input; and $\iota_{\alpha IJ} = \omega_{\alpha IJ}$; $\Gamma = \{\{\gamma_{\alpha IJ}\} + \{\gamma_{\beta J}\}\}$, the set of outputs; $\gamma_{\alpha IJ} = \sigma_{p\,\alpha IJ}$; and $\gamma_{\beta J} = \sigma_{p\,\beta J}$. In both cases $\alpha \in \{r, v, w\}$, $\beta \in \{r, w\}$, I, $J \in \mathfrak{N}$. ε and θ have the usual meaning of transition and output functions, respectively.

Except for the synchronous input ι_c, it may be said that $\mathrm{I} = \Omega$. T and P are therefore cascade connected. Since $\Sigma_p = \Gamma$, a feedback exists from P to T.

The design of the P automaton depends on the number of critical units, their crisis times, and the bandwidth of the channel and its associated processor.

Let's assume that the system has k units with a strict time constraint on the interval between a request to make a transference and the allocation of the channel to do it. Such units are critical in the sense that if the request is not served within that interval, the transference is disrupted by overwriting an output register or underwriting an input register.

Three main cases may occur corresponding to the following three conditions:

$$(1) \qquad kT_s \leq CT_{\min} \ ,$$

$$(2) \qquad \frac{CT_{\max}}{T_s} \geq \sum_{I \in \mathcal{K}} \left\lceil \frac{CT_{\max}}{CT_I} \right. ,$$

$$(3) \qquad \frac{CT_{\max}}{T_s} \geq \sum_{I \in \mathcal{K}} \frac{CT_{\max}}{CT_I} ,$$

where: k: number of critical units; $\mathcal{K}$: the set of critical units; T_s: inverse of the bandwidth of the channel; $CT_{\min}$: minimum crisis time; $CT_{\max}$: maximum crisis time; $\lceil$: monadic ceiling operator; and Σ: arithmetic summation.

The necessary-priority discipline [1] to be used is simply a round robin if the first condition holds. In the case of the second condition an externally-fixed nonpreemtive discipline can be used. The most difficult case is the third one: A dynamic or time-dependent priority discipline is necessary there [4].

The general philosophy of design of the P automaton is as follows: At a certain frequency determined by the bandwidth of the channel, P will select a certain request according to the priority scheme used and it will allocate the channel for the corresponding transference. Its output will open a set of output gates and a set of input gates, it will strobe information from one place to the other and it will generate feedback signals letting T and the units know the channel allocation. The periodicity of the process introduces an element of synchronism in the design. P can be thought of as being composed of two sub-automata P_1 and P_2. P_1 is a clock automaton [2] and P_2 is the priorities processor itself. Figure 6 represents the decomposition of P into P_1 and P_2.

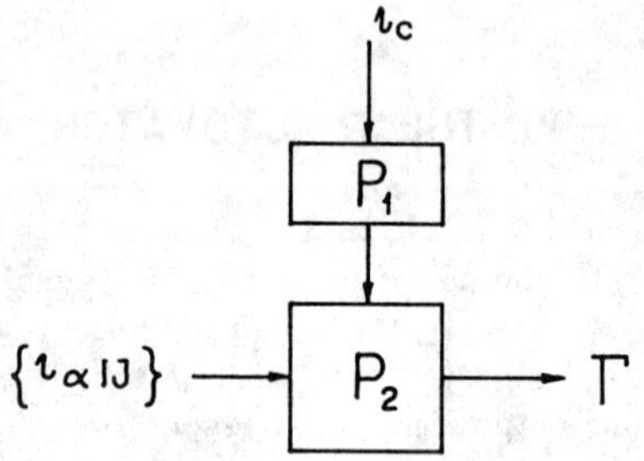

Fig. 6. The P automaton.

A. Round-Robin Discipline

The P Automaton has two round robins, one for critical and another one for noncritical units. The noncritical round robin is entered whenever there is no critical request. The mere presence of a critical request will have the effect of moving P into the critical round robin. The case is very simple and it will not be discussed further.

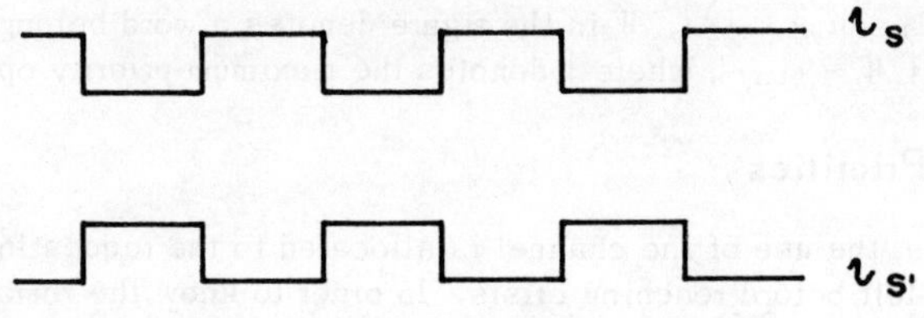

Fig. 7. Outputs of the clock automaton.

B. Externally-fixed nonpreemtive discipline

Figure 7 illustrates the waveforms generated on the outputs of the clock automaton.

The following notation will be used

$$I_1 = \{\iota_s, \iota_{s'}\} ,$$
$$I_2 = \{\{\Lambda\} + \{\iota_{\alpha IJ}\}\} .$$

On the elements of I_2 it is possible to define the operation priority such that it is closed, associative, and has an identity element (the ι of lowest priority). The set I_2 and the operation priority constitute therefore a monoid. I_2^Δ is subset of I_2^* precluding the words with repeated letters (no ι can be present twice simultaneously).

P_2 is illustrated in Figure 8. As can be seen, it admits a decomposition in two submachines generating respectively the set of signals $\{\gamma_{\alpha IJ}\}$ and $\{\gamma_{\beta J}\}$. Its

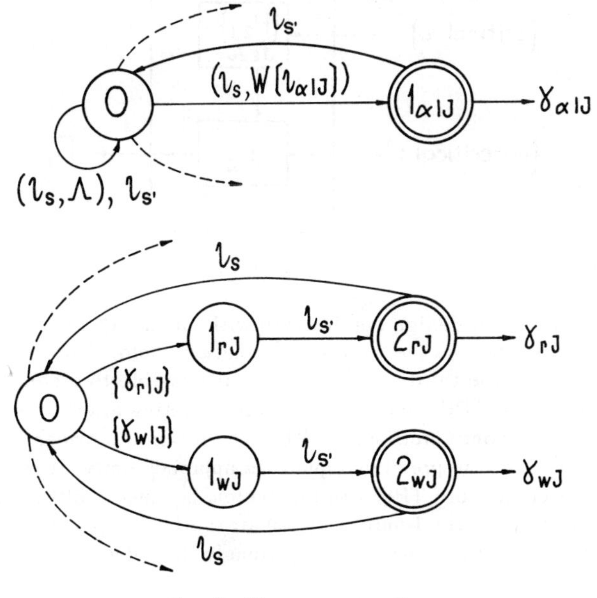

Fig. 8. Nonpreemptive P_2.

input set is $\{\mathrm{I}_1 + \{\iota_s\} \times \mathrm{I}_2^{\Delta}\}$. W in the figure denotes a word belonging to I_2 and $W[\iota_{\alpha IJ}] \in \{W \mid \lceil/W = \iota_{\alpha IJ}\}$, where $\lceil$ denotes the maximum-priority operator.

C. Dynamic Priorities

In this case, the use of the channel is allocated to the requesting unit with the least time left before reaching crisis. In order to know the remaining time before crisis occurs, P will have between P_1 and P_2 a set of subautomata P_{2J} $(J \in \mathcal{K})$ associated to critical units. The set of internal states of P_{2J} will have cardinality $(\mathrm{CT}_J \cdot f_s + 1)$, where: CT_J denotes the crisis time of unit J and f_s denotes the frequency of sampling. When a request involving unit J is presented, a transition occurs in the subautomaton P_2 from its initial state to a first state with output.

This state is final and its output is an input of relatively low priority to P_2. If the request is not served, P_{2J} will progress through different states with each sampling pulse and the priority of the request produced as output from each state will increase until reaching top priority when only one sampling pulse is available to strobe the transference. The design of P_{2J} is basically similar to the second case.

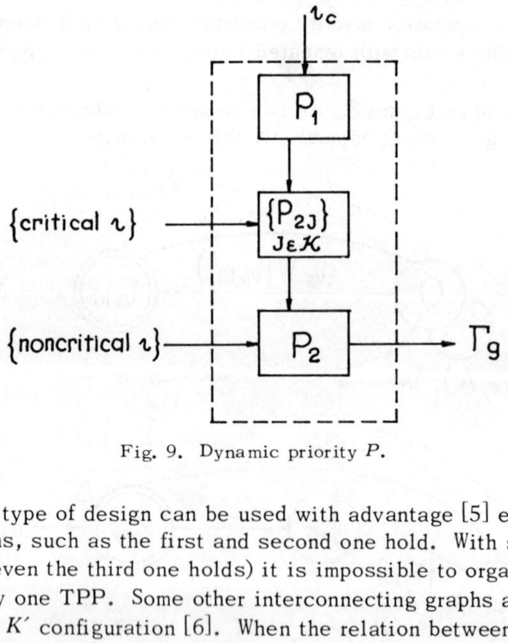

Fig. 9. Dynamic priority P.

This general type of design can be used with advantage [5] even if some weaker conditions, such as the first and second one hold. With stronger conditions (e.g., not even the third one holds) it is impossible to organize the transference with only one TPP. Some other interconnecting graphs are then used, for instance the $K - K'$ configuration [6]. When the relation between the left- and right-hand members of the previous equations approach unity, it may also be necessary to resort to more TPP's in the system because—although not reaching crisis—the traffic of critical units may impair the traffic of noncritical units so much that the total performance may be seriously degraded.

ACKNOWLEDGEMENT

This paper stems out of practical design made by the senior author during his stay as a Research Fellow at the Department of Computer Sciences, The University of Manchester, in 1969. The guidance and help of Prof. T. Kilburn is greatly appreciated.

REFERENCES

[1] E. Coffman and L. Kleinrock, "Feedback Queuing Models for Time-Sharing Systems," *J. ACC,* **15**, No. 4, 549–576 (October 1968).

[2] J. Hartmanis and R. Stearns, "Algebraic-Structure Theory of Sequential Machines" (New York: Prentice Hall, 1966).

[3] D. Aspinall et al., "An Integrated Associative-Memory Matrix," *Proc. IFIP Congress* 1968, D86–D90.

[4] H. Hellerman, "Digital-Computer-Systems Principles" (New York: McGraw Hill, 1967).

[5] M. Pirtle, "Intercommunications of Processors and Memory," *Proc. FJCC* 1967, **31**, 621–633 (November 1967).

[6] L. J. Boland et al., "The IBM System 360 Model 91 Storage System," IBM J. Res. Dev., **11**, No. 1, 54–68 (January 1967).

A SIMPLE MODEL FOR MULTIPLE-RESOURCE ALLOCATION IN OPERATING SYSTEMS

D. L. Boyd
Department of Computer Science, University of Minnesota, Minneapolis, MN
and
D. L. Epley
Department of Computer Science, University of Iowa, Iowa City, IA

A batch-processing multiprogramming system is modeled as a multiple-resource system. The interactions and relationships among the methods of allocating individual resources are examined. The model has three stages defined in terms of the system resources: a permanent resource allocation stage, a CPU stage, and an I/O stage. The model is a network queuing model under steady-state or equilibrium conditions. Principal results of the analysis are several interesting relationships between total system performance as indicated by job flow rate or throughput and the performance of individual stages. The relationships found may be used to define a set of measurements which may be used to evaluate an actual system.

I. INTRODUCTION

Allocating system resources among several concurrent users of the system is one of the major functions of multiprogramming computer systems. System resources include memory, input-output devices, data files, central processing units (CPU), and input-output channels (I/O). Certain resources such as the CPU and I/O channels may operate independently. However, resources such as memory, certain data files, and certain I/O devices must be distributed among the users in the system. This division must be made in accordance with the user's request for these resources.

It is the function of the operating system to allocate system resources to the users when requests are made. This allocation is made by choosing from the set of jobs competing for the use of a resource, the job or jobs which will provide good service to users, but yet maintain high resource utilization and hence a high job throughput rate.

Attention in this study was on basic batch-processing systems only. The objective was to model the multiple-resource allocation problem in these systems. In particular, a general model which would display the interaction of the methods of allocating individual resources was desired. Almost all previous work has dealt only with single-resource allocation problems.

The individual resource problem which has received the most attention is that of allocation of CPU time. Considerable empirical work has been done on

Presented at the Symposium on Computers and Automata
Polytechnic Institute of Brooklyn, April 13-15, 1971.

task dispatching and several good workable techniques are known [1, 10]. A great deal of analysis of various CPU scheduling disciplines or of time-shared system models has been done [8]. Multiple-resource models for time-shared systems have obtained some attention in [3, 4] and for batch-processing systems in [5].

II. FUNCTIONAL MODEL AND ASSUMPTIONS

A general description of a typical multiprogramming operating system is given in this section with emphasis on job flow through the system and on the allocation of individual resources as a job flows through the system. Other aspects of operating system functions are ignored since they are not important to this study.

The term *job* is used to indicate the basic unit of work submitted to the system facility. Because of the widespread usage of higher-level programming languages, a job is viewed as a collection of *steps* by many operating systems, for example, compile-load-execute.

The operating system identifies a job from the job queue. Either jobs or steps may be selected from this queue. The system resources are classified into two types, *permanent* and *demand* resources. After scheduling, the first operating system act upon the job or step is the allocation of permanent resources. In the multiple-resource model to be described, the basic unit of work is the step; that is, the step is the entity to which permanent resources are assigned.

The concept of permanent resources is introduced to describe those resources required by a job step before its "execution" can begin. Thus memory, input-output devices which cannot be shared by several job steps, and data files owned exclusively by the job step may be considered to be the basic permanent resources. Upon receipt of all required permanent resources, a job step then enters execution, which in the terminology adopted here, is the servicing of the job step by the two basic demand resources, CPU units and I/O channels. A basic assumption is needed to make the multiple-resource model reflect actual job processing by the system: the assigned permanent resources are retained by the job step throughout execution until the job step departs from the system. If both scheduling and permanent resource allocation are performed on job steps, this assumption is clearly satisfied. In operating systems, such as IBM/360, OS/MVT, where jobs are scheduled, but permanent resources are assigned to steps, the assumption is still valid, if the demand resource requests of different steps within a job are statistically the same. The effect of this assumption is that no distinction will be made between the units of job and step. Later, these two terms will be used interchangeably.

The demand resource requirements of a job step reflect the gross structure of programs: an alternating series of CPU requests and I/O service requests. The collection of events over time of scheduling these requests and servicing them is called the *execution* of the job step. For the purpose of describing CPU scheduling or dispatching, an individual CPU request is called a "task".

A block diagram showing job flow through the system is given in Figure 1.

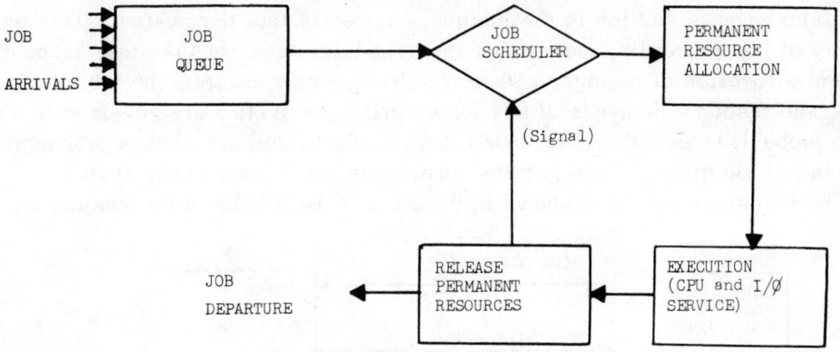

Fig. 1. Job flow through a batch-processing multiprogramming system.

The basic features of this flow have been outlined above but a few other features should be mentioned:

(1) When a user submits a job to the computer facility, the job is placed in a job queue on secondary memory where it awaits scheduling by the job scheduler. No attempt is made here to model the delays experienced by a job before it is scheduled by the job scheduler
(2) A new job cannot be selected for scheduling by the job scheduler until an old job completes execution and departs from the system; hence at any time a fixed number of jobs is always in the system. Each of these jobs is either waiting for permanent resources or is in execution. As indicated in Fig. 1, when a job completes execution, it releases permanent resources for possible allocation to jobs waiting for permanent resources or to the new job scheduled by the job scheduler
(3) The operation of the permanent resource allocation stage involves the problem of prevention of system deadlocks [6]. Several methods are known for solving this problem. Here, it shall be assumed that deadlocks never occur and that all permanent resources are allocated to a job before it enters execution. This means that a job never has to wait indefinitely for permanent resources.

III. TWO-STAGE MODEL AND THE TRANSITION PROBABILITIES $q(I|J)$

The multiple-resource model is first described by a two-stage model. The two stages are the *permanent resource subsystem* (PRS) and the *demand resource subsystem* (DRS). This model is used to define a set of transition probabilities which describe the movement of jobs from the PRS to the DRS. The effects which these transition probabilities have on the operation of the entire system are then explored.

Let the fixed number of jobs in the system be denoted by N. Assume that the job scheduler rule is uniform; that is, when a job completes execution, the job scheduler selects any job in the job queue for entry into the system. This uniformity of job scheduling means that the scheduler does not take into account the present allocation of resources when it selects a new job from the job queue. Thus, the resource demands of any job entering the system are governed by the same probability distributions. Also, assume that there are always jobs available in the job queue. Thus, at any time, there are N jobs in the system.

The two-stage model is shown in Figure 2. The N jobs of the system are

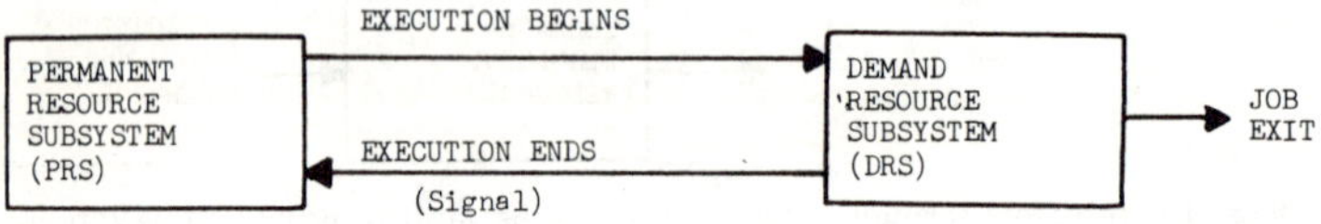

Fig. 2. Two-stage multiple-resource model.

divided between the PRS and the DRS. The jobs in the DRS are in execution and are competing for CPU and I/O services. The jobs in the PRS are waiting for permanent resources to be released in order that they may obtain sufficient resources for execution. A possible interpretation is that the jobs in execution are "blocking" the jobs waiting in the PRS.

When jobs cannot obtain permanent resources, a queue of jobs forms in the PRS. As described earlier, it is assumed that jobs are not blocked in the PRS indefinitely. Secondly, it is assumed that it is possible to allocate permanent resources to several jobs at one time. For example, suppose that a job in execution utilizes a large amount of memory and execution time. Several jobs may be queued in the PRS waiting for memory. When the large job completes execution, its memory is released and may be allocated to more than one job.

The time required to do the necessary steps of resource release by an old job, selection of a new job, and assignment of newly available resources to job(s) in PRS is negligibly small compared to the demand resource service time requests.* Thus, several jobs may exit from the PRS at the same time. Further, the frequency of service at the PRS is entirely dependent upon the rate at which jobs complete execution in the DRS system.

Let the pair $(k, N - k)$ denote a state of the system where k denotes the number of jobs in the DRS and $N - k$ denotes the number of jobs in the PRS for $k = 1, 2, 3, \cdots, N$. Let P_k denote the equilibrium probability that the system is in state $(k, N - k)$. Let R denote the expected rate at which jobs complete execution. Hence after a random interval of average length $1/R$, the system makes a transition to a new state.

Suppose that the system is in the state $(k, N - k)$ at the moment just prior to a job's completing execution. When the job completes, there will be a momentary transition to the state $(k - 1, N - k + 1)$. Depending on the requests for permanent resources and the resources left available by the $k - 1$ jobs in execution, there is a transition to one of the states $(k - 1 + x, N - k + 1 - x)$ where $x = 0, 1, 2, \cdots, N - k + 1$. Let $q(x|k - 1)$ denote the probability that this transition is

*The main implication of this assumption is that the service time of the PRS stage is independent of job-service requests; an alternative approach would be to use a constant for this service time, but this would add little to the realism of the model.

to state $(k - 1 + x, N - k + 1 - x)$, for $x = 0, 1, \cdots, N - k + 1$. Thus, $q(I \mid J)$ is the transition probability of entering the system state with $I + J$ jobs in execution, given that it was previously in the system state with $J + 1$ jobs in execution and that one job completes execution.

The transition probability $q(I|J)$ may be interpreted as the probability that exactly I jobs enter execution, given that a job has just completed execution, and that J jobs remain in the DRS. Alternatively, $q(I|J)$ is the probability that $N - (I + J)$ jobs must wait in the PRS until another job completes execution and releases its resources. The limits on the transition probabilities $q(I|J)$ are as follows: for each $J = 0, 1, 2, \cdots, N$ and $I = 0, 1, \cdots, N - J$ $(0 \leq q(I|J) \leq 1)$; secondly, $q(0|0) = 0$ which implies that at least one job is in execution at all times; thirdly, $q(0|N) = 1$ to insure that never more than N jobs are in execution; lastly, for each $J = 0, 1, 2, \cdots, N$, $\sum_{I=0}^{N-J} q(I|J) = 1$, implying at any time with J jobs in execution, a transition must occur if a job has just completed execution. Observe that the transition probabilities are a function *only* of the distribution of permanent-resource requests and of the number of resources available.

A. Determination of Transition Probabilities $q(I|J)$

The problem of determination of the transition probabilities $q(I|J)$ from distributions of individual permanent resource demands is now examined.* Assume that there are n_0 distinct permanent resources to be allocated at the PRS. Let C_i $(i = 1, 2, 3, \cdots, n_0)$ denote the total number of resources of type i which may be allocated. Let y_{iv} be random variables denoting the requirement of v jobs for the type-i permanent resource where $i = 1, 2, 3, \cdots, n_0$ and $v = 1, 2, 3, \cdots, N$. Note that by independence y_{iv} is the sum of v requests for the type-i permanent resource.

At this point an assumption must be made about the way in which permanent resources are allocated. It is assumed that all available permanent resources may be allocated to requesting jobs. This assumption may not be valid in the case of memory fragmentation at allocation time, and hence the memory allocator may not be free to use all available memory. This problem is not present in systems where jobs are dynamically relocated and free memory put into continuous blocks.

Let $G_v(Y_1, Y_2, Y_3, \cdots, Y_{n_0})$ $(Y_i = 0, 1, 2, \cdots, C_i)$ denote a family of distribution functions of the random variables $y_{1v}, y_{2v}, y_{3v}, \cdots, y_{n_0 v}$, for $v = 1, 2, 3, \cdots, n_0$. Let $G_0(C_1, C_2, C_3, \cdots, C_{n_0}) = 1$ and $G_I(C_1, C_2, C_3, \cdots, C_{n_0}) = 0$ for $I > N$. Then using the above resource allocation assumption, it can easily be seen that

$$q(I|J) = \frac{G_{I+J}(C_1, C_2, C_3, \cdots, C_{n_0}) - G_{I+J+1}(C_1, C_2, C_3, \cdots, C_{n_0})}{G_J(C_1, C_2, C_3, \cdots, C_{n_0})} \tag{3.1}$$

*The transition probabilities $q(I|J)$ may be determined directly through system measurements. However, since permanent resource requests are generally made explicitly by the jobs, it is felt that measuring their distributions will simplify the measurement problems.

for $J = 0, 1, 2, \cdots, N$ and $I = 0, 1, 2, \cdots, N - J$. Thus, the transition probabilities $q(I|J)$ may be used as a measure of the permanent resource requests made, as well as a measure of the system's ability to meet these requests.

B. Analysis of Two-Stage Model

Recall that P_k was defined to be the equilibrium probability that the system is in state $(k, N - k)$. It will now be shown that under certain conditions the equilibrium probabilities P_k may be derived from the transition probabilities. Hence, the distribution of the number of jobs in execution is determined solely by the distribution of permanent resources.

Define $A(t, t + \Delta t)$ to be the probability that a job departs from the DRS during the time interval t to $t + \Delta t$. Let $P_k(t)$ denote the probability that the system is in the state $(k, N - k)$ at time t. Then for an arbitrary state $(k, N - k)$, the probability $P_k(t + \Delta t)$ may be found by summing the adjacent state probabilities at time t multiplied by their respective transition probabilities [9]. Hence

$$P_k(t + \Delta t) = P_k(t)[1 - A(t, t + \Delta t)] + \sum_{i=0}^{k} P_{i+1}(t) A(t, t + t) q(k - i|i) \;, \qquad (3.2)$$

and

$$\frac{P_k(t + \Delta t) - P_k(t)}{\Delta t} = \left[\frac{A(t, t + \Delta t)}{\Delta t}\right] \left[P_k(t) - \sum_{i=0}^{k} P_{i+1}(t)\, q(k - i|i)\right] \;. \qquad (3.3)$$

By taking the limit as Δt goes to zero, we obtain

$$\frac{dP_k(t)}{dt} = -\left[\lim_{\Delta t \to 0} \frac{A(t, t + \Delta t)}{\Delta t}\right] \left[P_k(t) - \sum_{i=0}^{k} P_{i+1}(t)\, q(k - i|i)\right] \;. \qquad (3.4)$$

Under equilibrium conditions $dP_k(t)/dt = 0$, hence $\lim\limits_{\Delta t \to 0} \dfrac{A(t, t + \Delta t)}{\Delta t}$ must be nonzero in order to solve for the equilibrium probabilities P_k. Note that $\lim\limits_{\Delta t \to 0} \dfrac{A(t, t + \Delta t)}{\Delta t}$ can be interpreted as the departure rate from the DRS [11]. Hence, if the probability of a departure from the DRS is independent of the time which has elapsed since the last departure, then the equilibrium probability P_k may be determined. Note that this is a property of the exponential distribution and thus of each phase of the hyperexponential.

Under the above cases, the equilibrium state probabilities may be found from the following equations

$$P_0 = P_1\, q(0|0) = 0 \;,$$

$$P_x = \sum_{i=0}^{x} P_{i+1}\, q(x - i|i) \quad (x = 1, 2, 3, \cdots, N - 1) \;,$$

$$P_N = \sum_{i=0}^{N-1} P_{i+1}\, q(N-i|i) \ . \tag{3.5}$$

It can be shown that for $x = 1, 2, 3, \cdots, N-1$

$$P_{x+1} = \frac{\sum_{i=x+1}^{N} q(i|0)}{q(x|0)} P_x \ ,$$

$$= \prod_{y=1}^{x} \frac{\sum_{i=y+1}^{N} q(i|0)}{q(y|0)} P_1 \ . \tag{3.6}$$

By normalizing the probability distribution P_x ($x = 1, 2, 3, \cdots, N$), the value for P_1 can be solved. Hence the equilibrium probabilities are determined by the transition probabilities $q(I|J)$.

Let $P^R(k)$ denote the equilibrium distribution of jobs in the PRS. The values for $P^R(k)$ are determined from the equilibrium state distribution ($P_0, P_1, P_2, \cdots, P_N$) by the following relationship

$$P^R(k) = P_{N-k} \quad (k = 0, 1, 2, \cdots, N) \ . \tag{3.7}$$

The mean value of many system parameters may be found from this distribution. Let N_R denote the mean number of jobs waiting for permanent resources in the PRS and let N_S denote the mean number of jobs in execution. N_R and N_S are given by

$$N_R = \sum_{i=1}^{N} i P^R(i) \ , \tag{3.8}$$

and

$$N_S = N - N_R \ . \tag{3.9}$$

Assume that the mean departure rate from the DRS is R, then by using Little's Theorem [7]*, the mean length of time that a job must wait for permanent resources W_R in the PRS is

$$W_R = \frac{N_R}{R} \ . \tag{3.10}$$

If R is the arrival rate at the PRS and the system is in equilibrium, then R is also the PRS departure rate and the DRS arrival rate. This must be the case, for if over a long period of time the mean arrival rate at the PRS, for instance, is greater than the PRS departure rate, then an indefinitely large number of jobs

*In the system of interest, the rate is usually a departure rate rather than an arrival rate. Since the models used here have a fixed number in the system, i.e., the system is closed—the notion of arrival in the queuing sense is not applicable.

would wait at the PRS stage. Clearly, this is inconsistent with the equilibrium assumption. Consequently, the mean time required for a job to complete execution in the DRS is

$$F_S = \frac{N_S}{R} \; . \tag{3.11}$$

By adding Equations (3.10) and (3.11), the mean total system flow time is

$$F = F_S + W_S = \frac{N_S}{R} + \frac{N_R}{R} = \frac{N}{R} \; . \tag{3.12}$$

For a given N, it has been shown that the parameters N_R and N_S are determined completely by the PRS. However, the job throughput rate R is dependent upon the operation of the DRS as well as upon N_S. The two-stage model will now be expanded to three stages to study the operation of the DRS.

IV. THREE-STAGE MODEL

The DRS is now decomposed into its two types of service, CPU and I/O channel. The multiple-resource system is thus described by a three-stage model shown in Figure 3.

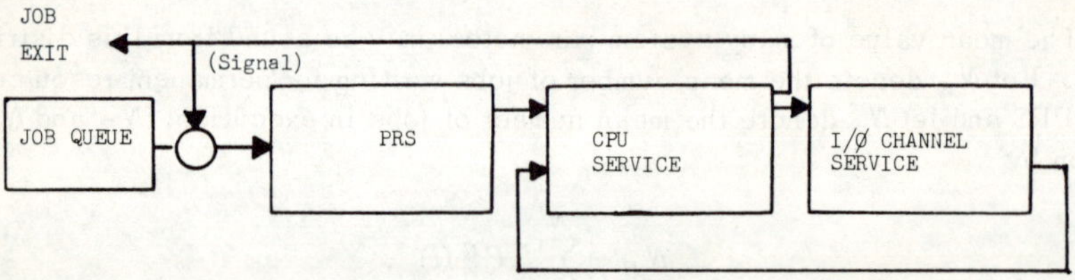

Fig. 3. Three-stage multiple-resource model.

The flow of a job through the system leads first through the PRS stage where permanent resources are allocated. It then makes a series of passes through the CPU and I/O stages, alternating between them.* Finally, it returns to the PRS stage where its resources are released and it is replaced by another job from the job queue, with jobs being selected randomly from the job queue. One complete *system cycle* is defined from the time a job first enters the PRS stage until it returns to the PRS state, releases its resources, and exits. Hence, the model as depicted in Fig. 3 is a closed, cyclic network of queues and servers with a finite number N always in the system.

The assumptions for the PRS stage are identical to the assumptions described previously for the PRS. The assumptions made for the CPU and I/O stages are as follows: when a job arrives at the DRS for execution, the CPU stage is the first and last stage utilized during the job's execution such that every job makes

*Some operating systems do allow users to overlap CPU execution and I/O service through special control instructions. However, this facility is usually used only by sophisticated users and is therefore not considered in this model.

exactly one more CPU request than I/O request during execution; no job is allowed to receive simultaneously both CPU and I/O service; finally, all overhead in both the CPU and I/O stages, as well as the transition time between stages, is negligibly small compared to service time or is included as part of service time.

The CPU and I/O stages of the DRS are modeled as queues and servers. When a job requests service, it is placed in a queue where it remains until selected for service. The possibility of multiple servers is allowed; i.e., the system may contain multiple CPUs and several I/O channels. Let S_C denote the number of identical CPUs and S_I, the number of identical I/O channels.

The CPU and I/O service times for job tasks are governed by probability distributions. No attempt is made to distinguish between the individual CPU tasks and the I/O requests of a job or between tasks and requests of different jobs. Thus, the service time requirements of each CPU task are taken from the same probability distribution $H(C)$; similarly, the service time requirement of each I/O request is taken from the same probability distribution $W(I)$.

$H(C)$ and $W(I)$ are treated as general distributions which can be determined by measurements of the job characteristics at a particular system. Further, the CPU dispatching rule which selects CPU tasks from the CPU queue and the I/O scheduling rule which schedules I/O requests from the I/O queue remain arbitrary, but fixed.

The expectation or mean value of the service time of a CPU task is

$$\overline{C} = E[C] = \int_0^\infty C\,dH(C) \ . \tag{4.1}$$

Let r be a discrete random variable denoting the number of CPU tasks requested by a job during execution. Since the CPU task times are independent and identically distributed, the total amount of CPU service time for a job requiring r services is

$$\hat{C}(r) = E[C_1 + C_2 + C_3 + \cdots + C_r] = r\overline{C} \ . \tag{4.2}$$

By averaging over jobs the distribution of r is found; hence, the mean total CPU service time of a job is

$$\hat{C} = E[C] \sum_{r=1}^{\infty} rP[r = R] = \overline{r}\overline{C} \ , \tag{4.3}$$

where $\overline{r} = E[r]$. Since $\overline{r}$ is the mean number of CPU services required by a job, $\overline{r} - 1$ is the mean number of I/O requests of a job.

Let I be a random variable denoting the I/O service time required to service one I/O request. As in the CPU case, the expectation of I is

$$\overline{I} = E[I] = \int_0^\infty I\,dW(I) \ , \tag{4.4}$$

and the mean total I/O service time required by a job is

$$\hat{I} = (\overline{r} - 1)\overline{I} \ . \tag{4.5}$$

From Equations (4.3) and (4.5), the mean total service time required by a job is

$$T = \hat{C} + \hat{I} = \bar{r}\bar{C} + (\bar{r} - 1)\bar{I} \ . \tag{4.6}$$

A system state is now defined in terms of the three-stage model. Let $(N - k_1 - k_2, k_1, k_2)$ denote a state of the system, where k_1 denotes the total number of jobs in the CPU state, in the queue or in service, k_2 denotes the total number of jobs in the I/O stage, in the queue or in service, and $N - k_1 - k_2$ denotes the number of jobs waiting for permanent resources in the PRS stage. Then $P(k_1, k_2)$ denotes the equilibrium probability that the system is in the state $(N - k_1 - k_2, k_1, k_2)$.

The problem of computing these equilibrium probabilities from a knowledge of the service time distribution has been considered in [2]. A general mean-value analysis of the three-stage model, requiring only knowledge of mean values of the various distributions, is now made.

A. Parameters of the Three-Stage Model

The following general problem is considered in this section: given mean values of the service distributions of jobs and mean values of the number of jobs in the various stages, what can be deduced about system performance? More important, what is the interaction of the stages under equilibrium conditions in terms of mean values of system parameters? As will be shown, a surprising amount of insight into system behavior is obtained from this simplified approach.

The following mean values are assumed to be known through, for example, measurement of the system:

(1) $\bar{C}, \bar{I}, \bar{r}$ as defined above

(2) Any two of the three descriptors, N_R, N_C, N_I, for the number in the stages; N_R is the mean number in the PRS stage; N_C in the CPU stage; and N_I in the I/O stage. N_R, N_C, and N_I are the mean values of the marginal distribution $P(k_1, k_2)$ defined previously.

$$P^C(k_1) = \sum_{k_2=0}^{N-k_1} P(k_1, k_2) \quad (k_1 = 0, 1, 2, \cdots, N) \ , \tag{4.7}$$

$$P^I(k_2) = \sum_{k_1=0}^{N-k_2} P(k_1, k_2) \quad (k_2 = 0, 1, 2, \cdots, N) \ , \tag{4.8}$$

$$P^R(k_3) = \sum_{k_1=0}^{N-k_3} P(k_1, N - k_3 - k_1) \quad (k_3 = 0, 1, 2, \cdots, N) \ . \tag{4.9}$$

Thus

$$N_C = \sum_{k_1=1}^{N} k_1 P^C(k_1) \ , \tag{4.10}$$

$$N_I = \sum_{k_2=1}^{N} k_2 P^I(k_2) \; , \tag{4.11}$$

$$N_R = \sum_{k_3=1}^{N} k_3 P^R(k_3) \; . \tag{4.12}$$

Of course by the closed nature of the model, the following relationship holds and implies that only two of the mean values need be measured

$$N = N_R + N_C + N_I \; . \tag{4.13}$$

Various types of system descriptors or performance criteria are now defined and formulas which allow their determination from the above known average values are derived.

B. Number of Jobs in Queues; Utilization Factors

For the PRS stage, service time is zero and the length of the queue is given by N_R. In the CPU and I/O stages, some jobs will be found in service and some jobs will be found in the queue. Suppose there are S servers in a stage and that k jobs are found in the stage; then, for $k \geq S$, S of those jobs are in service and $k - S$ jobs are waiting in the queue. The mean length of the queue is given by the sum

$$\sum_{k=1}^{N-S} kP(k+S) \; . \tag{4.14}$$

Thus, with S_C identical CPUs and S_I identical I/O channels, the length of the CPU queue L_C and the length of the I/O queue L_I are

$$L_C = \sum_{k_1=1}^{N-S_C} k_1 P^C(k_1 + S_C) \; , \tag{4.15}$$

and

$$L_I = \sum_{k_2=1}^{N-S_I} k_2 P^I(k_2 + S_I) \; . \tag{4.16}$$

Note the relationship between the mean number of jobs in a stage and the length of its queue. Consider the CPU stage, the following can be written

$$N_C - L_C = \sum_{k_1=1}^{N} k_1 P^C(k_1) - \sum_{k_1=1}^{N-S_C} k_1 P^C(k_1 + S_C)$$

$$= S_C \left[1 - \sum_{k_1=0}^{S_C} \left(\frac{S_C - k_1}{S_C} \right) P^C(k_1) \right] . \tag{4.17}$$

Consider the sum $\sum_{k_1=0}^{S_C} \left(\frac{S_C - k_1}{S_C}\right) P^C(k_1)$. This is the mean amount of time that all S_C servers are not busy. If there are $k' < S_C$ job tasks in the CPU stage, then k' servers are busy and $S_C - k'$ servers are idle, where $\frac{S_C - k'}{S_C}$ is the fraction of the S_C servers which are idle. Hence

$$\rho_C = 1 - \sum_{k_1=0}^{S_C} \left(\frac{S_C - k_1}{S_C}\right) P^C(k_1) \ , \tag{4.18}$$

is a measure of the portion of time, on the average, that the CPU stage is busy; ρ_C is termed the CPU-stage *utilization factor.* By Equation (4.17)

$$N_C - L_C = S_C \rho_C \ . \tag{4.19}$$

Similarly, the I/O stage with S_I identical channels yields

$$N_I - L_I = S_I \rho_I \ , \tag{4.20}$$

where

$$\rho_I = 1 - \sum_{k_2=0}^{S_I} \left(\frac{S_I - k_2}{S_I}\right) P^I(k_2) \ , \tag{4.21}$$

is the I/O-stage utilization factor.

C. Stage-Departure Rates and Flow Times

A convenient method of further analysis is to define the rate at which jobs depart from the CPU and I/O stages. A definition of rate for the CPU stage is made first and an analogous definition can be made for the I/O stage.

An intuitive argument for the definition is as follows. Suppose that $\rho_C = 1$; that is, all S_C processors at the CPU stage are busy 100% of the time. The average CPU service time for one CPU task is $\overline{C}$; hence on the average, after every $\overline{C}$ time units, a given processor completes one request. In terms of rate, jobs depart from the processor at the rate of $1/\overline{C}$. With S_C processors, the rate of job departure from the CPU stage is $S_C/\overline{C}$. If $\rho_C < 1$, this rate is decreased by the percentage of time that the processors are idle, and the job-departure rate from the CPU stage is

$$R_C = \rho_C \left(\frac{S_C}{\overline{C}}\right) \ . \tag{4.22}$$

This definition of departure rate may be verified as follows. Recall that it was argued previously in terms of the PRS stage that the job departure rate must equal the job arrival rate at that stage when the system is in equilibrium. Let the CPU stage arrival rate be denoted by R_C. By Little's formula applied to the

CPU stage, the mean *flow time* for a job to complete one CPU service is

$$F_C = \frac{N_C}{R_C} . \tag{4.23}$$

Applying Little's formula to the CPU queue only, the mean time that a job must wait in the queue before obtaining a processor is

$$W_C = \frac{L_C}{R_C} . \tag{4.24}$$

However, the mean flow time for a job at the CPU stage is the mean *wait time* plus the mean service time

$$F_C = W_C + \overline{C} . \tag{4.25}$$

By substituting Eqs. (4.23) and (4.24) into Eq. (4.25) and solving for R_C

$$R_C = \frac{N_C - L_C}{\overline{C}} . \tag{4.26}$$

Finally by Equation (4.19), the mean job departure rate for the CPU stage, under equilibrium, is

$$R_C = \rho_C \left(\frac{S_C}{\overline{C}}\right) . \tag{4.27}$$

Analogous equations can be found for the I/O stage.

$$R_I = \rho_I \left(\frac{S_I}{\overline{I}}\right) . \tag{4.28}$$

The mean wait time for one I/O service is

$$W_I = \frac{L_I}{R_I} . \tag{4.29}$$

The mean flow time for one I/O service is

$$F_I = W_I + \overline{I} = \frac{N_I}{R_I} . \tag{4.30}$$

D. System-Throughput Rate and Flow Time

Since the system is assumed to be in equilibrium, it has been shown that the arrival rate must equal the departure rate at that stage. Since the system is closed, the structure of the model, given in Fig. 3, implies that the arrival rate at the CPU stage R_C is the sum of the departure rate from the I/O stage R_I, and the departure rate from the PRS stage R. Or, equivalently

$$R = R_C - R_I . \tag{4.31}$$

Further, the rate of flow through the system is R since arrival rate equals departure rate at the PRS stage and thus R is the usual notion of *job throughput rate* in terms of these multiple resource models. A variety of other system descriptors are summarized below

$$N_S = N_C + N_I \text{ (mean number of jobs in execution)} \ , \tag{4.32}$$

$$F_S = \frac{N_S}{R} \text{ (mean flow time in execution stage)} \ , \tag{4.33}$$

$$W_R = \frac{N_R}{R} \text{ (mean flow or wait time in PRS stage)} \ , \tag{4.34}$$

$$F = W_R + F_S = N/R \text{ (mean flow time in system)} \ . \tag{4.35}$$

The last descriptor could be interpreted as job "turnaround time", but since the system models do not include the delays experienced by a job before it enters the system job queue nor is the wait time in the queue considered, F is not really consistent with this notion of turnaround time.

E. Relationship Between R_C and R_I

Equation (4.31) expresses the job throughput rate of the system in terms of the CPU and I/O stage departure rates R_C and R_I. The structure of the DRS system clearly indicates that these two rates are dependent upon each another. This interrelationship is now explored.

Observe that the mean flow time may be written as the sum of the mean flow times for each stage multiplied by the mean number of passes through that stage

$$F = W_R + \overline{r} F_C + (\overline{r} - 1) F_I \ . \tag{4.36}$$

Substituting from Equations (4.23), (4.30), (4.34), and (4.35)

$$\frac{N_C + N_I + N_R}{R_C - R_I} = \frac{N_R}{R_C - R_I} + \overline{r} \frac{N_C}{R_C} + (\overline{r} - 1) \frac{N_I}{R_I} \ ,$$

is found. Solving algebraically for R_I

$$R_I = \frac{\overline{r} - 1}{\overline{r}} R_C \ . \tag{4.37}$$

Substituting for R_I and R_C from Equations (4.27) and (4.28)

$$\frac{S_C \rho_C}{\overline{r} \overline{C}} = \frac{S_I \rho_I}{(\overline{r} - 1)\overline{I}} \quad \text{or} \quad \frac{S_C \rho_C}{\hat{C}} = \frac{S_I \rho_I}{\hat{I}} \ . \tag{4.38}$$

Hence, the mean job throughput rate is given in terms of either the mean CPU stage utilization or the mean I/O stage utilization

$$R = \frac{S_C \rho_C}{\hat{C}} = \frac{S_I \rho_I}{\hat{I}} \ . \tag{4.39}$$

From Equations (4.38) and (4.39), it is seen that the operation of one stage in the DRS system directly determines the operation of the other, under average value, equilibrium conditions. To summarize, the following ratios are of interest

$$\frac{R_C}{R_I} = \frac{\bar{r}}{\bar{r} - 1} ;$$

$$\frac{\rho_C}{\rho_I} = \frac{\hat{C}\ S_I}{\hat{I}\ S_C} . \qquad (4.40)$$

An interesting interpretation of this property is possible. Given CPU and I/O service demands expressed in terms of service rates or times whose units depend upon the hardware capabilities of the system, the operation of the DRS is determined by the slower stage. That is, any particular system is either "CPU-bound" or "I/O-bound". The bounding stage determines the rate at which demands are made upon the faster stage and directly determines the realized utilization of that stage.

For example, consider an I/O-bound system: $\rho_I = 1$. Then $R_I = S_I/\bar{I}$ and the realized operation of the CPU stage is

$$R_C^0 = \frac{\bar{r}}{\bar{r} - 1} \left(\frac{S_I}{\bar{I}}\right) ,$$

$$\rho_C^0 = \frac{\hat{C}}{\hat{I}} \left(\frac{S_I}{S_C}\right) . \qquad (4.41)$$

The condition $\rho_C = 1$ indicates the maximum potential operation of the CPU stage and corresponds to $R_C = S_C/\bar{C}$. The underutilization of the CPU stage, because of the I/O-bounded operation, is measured by the differences

$$\frac{S_C}{\bar{C}} - R_C^0 \text{ and } 1 - \rho_C^0 . \qquad (4.42)$$

V. CONCLUSION

The purpose of this study was to gain insight into some of the problem areas of batch-processing multiprogramming systems. In particular, the problem of greatest interest was the multiple-resource allocation problem.

Since improved system throughput rate is a performance goal of batch-processing multiprogramming systems, the mean-value equilibrium-rate analysis was a natural approach to use when studying these systems. This approach has revealed a set of relationships among the resource allocation stages of the system. From the relationships found, many of the intuitive notions about batch-processing multiprogramming systems have been validated.

These relationships have provided knowledge about the decomposition of the model. It has been shown that the interaction between the allocation of CPU service and the allocation of I/O service is important to the operation of these two stages. Conditions have been given for the decomposition of the PRS and DRS; i.e., it has been shown that the allocation of permanent resources determines completely the mean number of jobs in the DRS.

Finally, these relationships may be used to suggest a set of measurements to be used to evaluate system performance. For example, the following system measurements may be used as elements of a minimal set of measurements that may be used, with the relationships developed above, to find other system descriptors:

(1) F: mean system flow time per step
(2) $\hat{C}$: mean total CPU service time per step
(3) $\hat{I}$: mean total I/O service time per step
(4) $(\bar{r}-1)$: mean number of I/O requests per step
(5) F_S: mean total flow time in DRS per step
(6) $(\bar{r}-1)F_I$: mean total flow time in I/O stage per step.

Assuming that values are known for these measurements, and given the number of jobs N in the system, the number of I/O channels S_I, and the number of processors S_C, then many system descriptors may be calculated through algebraic manipulation of the above relationships. For example, the mean departure rates, the mean wait times, the mean number of jobs in stages and in queues, and the mean stage utilization factors may be calculated from these six measurements.

REFERENCES

[1] F. Baskett, J. C. Browne, and W. M. Raike, "The Management of a Multilevel Non-paged Memory System." *Proc. AFIPS 1970 Spring Joint Computer Conf.*, 459–465 (1970).

[2] D. L. Boyd and D. L. Epley, "Analysis of CPU Dispatching Rules for Batch-Multiprogramming Computer Systems," presented at the 39th National ORSA meeting (May 1971).

[3] F. J. Corbató et al., "An Experimental Time-Sharing System," *Proc. AFIPS 1962 Spring Joint Computer Conf.*, 21 335–344 (New York: Sparton Books).

[4] P. J. Denning, "The Working-Set Model for Program Behavior," *Comm. ACM*, 11, No. 5, 323–333 (May 1968).

[5] D. P. Gaver, "Probability Models for Multiprogramming Computer Systems," *J. ACM*, 14, No. 3, 422–438 (July 1967).

[6] J. W. Havender, "Avoiding Deadlocks in Multitasking Systems," *IBM Sys. J.*, 7, No. 2, 74–84 (1968).

[7] J. D. C. Little, "A Proof of the Queueing Formula: $L = \lambda W$," *Oper. Res.* 9, 383–387 (1961).

[8] J. M. McKinney, "A Survey of Analytical Time-Sharing Models," *Comput. Surv.*, 1, No. 2, 105–116 (June 1969).

[9] P. M. Morse, *Queues, Inventory, and Maintenance* (New York: Wiley, 1961).

[10] K. D. Ryder, "A Heuristic Approach to Task Dispatching," *IBM Sys. J.*, 9, No. 2, 189–198 (1970).

[11] M. Sakata, S. Noguchi, and J. Oizumi, "Optimal Scheduling in Single-Processor Systems," *Proc. 3rd Hawaii International Conf. on System Sciences*, 708–711 (Hawaii: University of Hawaii, 1970).

SCHEDULING OF REAL-TIME COMPUTER SYSTEMS

Donald L. Epley
Department of Computer Science, University of Iowa, Iowa City, IA

Several algorithms for scheduling real-time jobs on processors in computer systems are presented. These algorithms provide a basis for the implementation of a real-time job scheduler to be used in conjunction with the task scheduler or dispatcher of a computer operating system. The algorithms provide centralized control and scheduling of the overall real-time system, a clear interrelationship between system operation and scheduling parameters and valid system-overload detection. Real-time constraints and properties of jobs such as response time and periodicity properties are treated as design parameters.

I. INTRODUCTION

Because of the wide variety of real-time computer applications [1], the particular class of interest should be defined at the beginning. This class can loosely be defined as those applications in which response times or service requirements of inputs are defined by hard specifications. Examples include hybrid computer systems [2], real-time process control [3], and real-time space or avionics systems [4]. Time-shared systems [5], having apparent response time requirements in Aron's terminology [1], or soft specifications, are deliberately excluded. Processor scheduling in time-shared systems supporting conversational-mode terminals is an important problem which has received considerable attention. Because of the interaction of processor scheduling with the allocation of other resources in these general-purpose multiprogramming systems, there is a lack of understanding of the total resource allocation/scheduling problem. By limiting our discussion to a restricted class of special-purpose real-time systems, our attention can be focused on the processor-scheduling problem. The relationship between the scheduling algorithm and the resulting system behavior then becomes more apparent.

The fundamental aspects of the scheduling problem can be discussed in terms of a simple system model: a single-processor system with all active, i.e., schedulable, jobs in main memory and a nonpreemptive, execution-to-completion scheduling mode. Modifications required by multiple processors, nonresident jobs, and multiprogramming operation are discussed after presentation of the basic ideas. In Section II, the methodology which presently dominates the design of schedulers is critiqued, and the wide variety of possible scheduling rules are noted within a general framework. In Section III, a new approach to the processor-scheduling problem is presented, along with an outline of three scheduler algorithms.

To clarify the overall nature of the problem of scheduling real-time jobs on a

Contributed to the Proceedings of the Symposium on Computers and Automata Polytechnic Institute of Brooklyn, April 13–15, 1971.

processor, a description of jobs and the global operation of a real-time system is needed. A "real-time job" is a unit of work implying that an identified program processes certain identified data; this processing takes a certain amount of processor time. It is assumed that this job-processing time is approximately known in the form of maximum or mean-time estimates. The accuracy of these estimates is not crucial as will become evident. The hard specifications on job processing referred to earlier take two forms. For nonperiodic jobs, a *deadline time* is specified in terms of the maximum time delay allowable between a job-enablement event and the time at which processing of the job in response to this event must be started. A job-enablement event may be the receipt of new data from an external sensor or some other device. Note the validity of this data is time sensitive as reflected by the specification of the deadline time on the job. Other examples of job-enablement events are calls from other programs, and passage of certain specified real-time values. For periodic real-time jobs, the rate or the inverse, the period, is specified. Note that the specification of a period can be viewed as equivalent to specifying a job enablement time and a deadline time. If t_j is the completion time of the jth processing of a periodic job with period τ_j, then t_j can be used as an enablement time for the $(j+1)^{\text{th}}$ processing and $t_j + \tau_j$ as the deadline time for the $(j+1)^{\text{th}}$ processing.

Whether a particular job is viewed as nonperiodic or periodic is often arbitrary and can be left to the discretion of the system programmer or the real-time system designer. The scheduler design selected as well as the particular function of the job determines this choice. Another important aspect of job modeling is the interpretation of rate specifications.

This latter point is fundamental to later considerations and therefore three separate interpretations are identified and labeled. Jobs with *tight* rates are to be scheduled at the specified rate as precisely as possible. Jobs with *bounded* rates are to be scheduled within an interval $(t_j + \tau_{\max}, t_j + \tau_{\min})$, where: t_j is completion time of the last processing; and $\tau_{\max} (\tau_{\min})$ is the reciprocal of maximum (minimum) rate. Jobs with *relative* rates are to be scheduled as often as possible consistent with the various specified rates among the collection of all periodic jobs. Which interpretation is to be used is of course dependent upon the particular application and the nature of the job in question. In the majority of the applications with which the writer is familiar, either the tight or the relative interpretation is the more appropriate. Bounded rates tend to result from either redundant specifications or concern over a system operation which is inherently impossible to achieve. It is rather clear that from a scheduling viewpoint, jobs with tight rates can be treated as "nonperiodic" jobs with self-generating, *equal*-enablement and deadline times. For jobs with this characteristic, the notion of a time-driven system with almost continuous scheduling via interrupts is quite appropriate. The situation is radically different for systems with relative-rate specifications on periodic jobs. Scheduling methods for these systems are discussed in Section III.

II. CRITIQUE OF PRESENT SCHEDULING METHODS

The interrupt concept has become an exceedingly pervasive one in the design of operating systems since its evolution in early real-time and multiprogramming systems [6]. Together with the notion of priority, the interrupt concept is now used as the basis of the design of schedulers in general-purpose operating systems and real-time supervisors. Our goal here is to show that this approach has severe limitations, and to make some suggestions on how to go beyond these concepts to achieve better scheduler designs.

Our proposal is not to discard the interrupt concept entirely, of course. Interrupts are clearly needed in the two fundamental situations in which the idea originally arose. First, external signals arising from external devices, such as sensors, with limited data-storage capability must be recognized and serviced promptly. Thus, the notion of external interrupts should be retained. Secondly, the use of internal interrupts to handle unexpected program behavior, such as overflow, is also needed. Finally, the use of hardware priority-interrupt implementations to rank or order external signals is also attractive. If one now adds the notion of priorities to jobs, a direct solution to the scheduling problem results: schedule highest-priority active job first.

It is this last step in the progression which must be examined carefully. Also, as has been observed by others [7], there are two separate mechanisms at work: a hardware-interrupt system and a software priority-scheduling system. "Priority" is an inherently appealing idea. For one thing, it is a nice-sounding word. More importantly, almost any, or perhaps even all, scheduling rules can be cast into the framework of priorities if the priority values are allowed to change dynamically. Unfortunately, the question of priority assignment, whether by a fixed static rule or by an algorithm used dynamically to compute priority values, is seldom answered except by ad hoc schemes. In order to indicate some of the diversity in priority-scheduling rules, Table I is presented.

In any priority-scheduling scheme, the scheduler program examines all active or schedulable programs and selects the one of highest priority for immediate execution on the processor. The rules in Table I are simply different ways of specifying priority values of programs. The complexity of the rule increases as one moves down the table. The first is a uniform priority case in which the priority of the program which processes the data from an external interrupt is identical to the priority of the interrupt itself. In relatively small-scale real-time applications in which there is a one-to-one correspondence between real-time programs and external interrupts, this is a simple, workable scheme. The second case is the common one in which each real-time program is assigned a priority value by

TABLE I. Some priority-scheduling systems.

EXTERNAL PRIORITY ASSIGNMENT	JOB OR TASK PRIORITY	NAME
fixed p_e	fixed; $p_j = p_e$	data driven
fixed p_e	fixed p_j	task driven
fixed p_e	$p_j = t_e$ or t_d	time driven
fixed p_e	dynamic: $p_j = k_j \max(0, t - t_e)$ or $k_j \max(0, t_d - t)$	dynamic, time driven
fixed p_e	precedent dependent: assigned by calling program	dynamic, task driven

Here t_e: enablement time of job; t_d: deadline time of job; and t: value of real time for which priority value is computed.

the system programmer or designer. This program priority may not be directly related to the external-interrupt priorities although some degree of consistency in the separate assignments is necessary. The third case identifies priority with a time value associated with a program, the enablement or deadline time. This is not consistent with the usual implementation of a discrete number of priority values or levels but is meant to be a conceptual description. That is, the scheduler would order the active programs by the t_e's or t_d's to determine a scheduling priority. Note that this priority value is determined at the time of a job-enablement event and remains fixed at this value. In the next case, the fourth, a similar determination is made but the priority value is made dynamic by making it dependent upon real-time t. The priority of a task increases linearly with time since enablement time $t - t_e$, or the lateness $t_d - t$. Note that additional flexibility is possible by assigning jobs different k_j's. This method requires the scheduler to compute the priorities of all active programs at the real-time value t during each scheduling operation. Of course, any explicit function $f(k_j, t, t_d, t_e)$ could be used to compute p_j. The linear one is a simple, easily-interpretable example. The fifth and final case is an extension achieved by making the priority value dependent upon the source of job enablement, a precedent task or calling program [2]. For the moment, the term "task" is left undefined. The difference between this case and the others is the capability of allowing a program's priority to depend upon the past sequence of processing. For example, Program A can be called by Program B with priority $p_A(B)$ and by Program C with priority $p_A(C)$. Moreover, $p_A(B)$ and $p_A(C)$ can be determined by a function of time as used in the fourth case. The combination of cases four and five leads to a scheduling scheme of such complexity over time that its performance can only be determined by actual system observations or detailed simulation.

The definition of the term "task" brings up another aspect of program modeling. Up to this point, the real-time job has been our basic unit for work and perhaps a one-to-one correspondence between real-time jobs and real-time programs has been implied. Such need not be the case. There exist applications in which it is more natural to organize the total real-time software into job programs partitioned into subprograms, i.e., callable, closed subroutines [3,8]. Different job programs may have identical subroutines—this situation is indeed part of the motivation for this approach since it avoids duplicate coding. Each job program is then viewed as a precedence or computation graph with subroutines as elements [8]. Subroutines are called by precedence subroutines and thus subroutines are the basic unit of processing work scheduled. If one defines task as a program together with the data set(s) upon which the program operates, the term can be applied to either job programs or subroutines. If the total system software is organized around job programs structured or partitioned into callable subroutines, then these subroutines are the scheduled tasks. And the ability of one task to call another task and define a priority of the called task appears to be an attractive one.

To complete our description of scheduling via interrupts and priorities, the scheduling of the scheduler must be specified. This is an inherent part of the interrupt-driven philosophy. Within the priority structure, system or supervisor routines are given highest priority. Given that no supervisor routines need to be executed, then the scheduler of the real-time jobs is then executed to determine the next real-time program to be run. Thus, the scheduler itself fits into the overall priority structure. For clarity, it might be helpful to think of the overall system scheduling in two levels; the scheduler which decides which real-time jobs are to be executed and the "dispatcher" which actually transfers control from program to program. Thus, the scheduler assists the dispatcher only in the scheduling of real-time programs. Other programs such as interrupt handlers and service routines which are system routines are scheduled by the interrupt and system-priority logic within the dispatcher. This two-level scheduling approach is fundamental to the schedulers presented in the following section. Those schedulers are intended to be used with typical dispatcher designs within the overall operating-system structure.

Our criticism thus is focused on the priority-scheduler concept. There are four fundamental weaknesses in priority schedulers when used to schedule real-time jobs:

(1) Local decision making
(2) Distributed or decentralized-scheduling control
(3) No effective overload-detection mechanism
(4) Too simple *or* too complex.

Since the scheduler only inspects priorities of currently-active jobs, it has no information except the current job load, i.e., local time information. Yet, information about periodic jobs can be built into the scheduler as shown in the next section. Such information does allow the scheduler to keep a record of the past job load and more importantly to have some predictive capability.

Decentralized scheduling control is a property of systems in which programs call other programs with a specified priority. Through this mechanism of calling, especially, in the dynamic, task-driven case, the scheduling is determined by the entire set of currently-active programs. Since there is no way of knowing all the multitude of programs which could be simultaneously active, it is impossible to really pinpoint the scheduling algorithm. Note also that each program makes its calls from complete ignorance of what other calls are being made. This has the additional disadvantage of having the scheduling control buried in detailed code; thus making changes in the scheduling algorithm quite difficult.

Overload detection, an essential feature in any real-time system which is going to be fully utilized, must be based on a priority measurement. Thus, some rule to the effect that *overload is present if programs of priority p are suffering delay greater than D* is used. Since priority values only reflect instantaneous load, this is not an accurate characterization. In order to have an accurate indication of load, a more global or average-over-time measurement is needed.

Simplicity and complexity are opposite extremes as reflected in Table I. The first entries are too simple, the last too complex. The schedules produced by the former are easily understood and their limitations obvious. The schedules produced by the latter are not predictable. One would hope that there is a middle ground.

III. OUTLINE OF SCHEDULER DESIGN

Our goal is to suggest an approach to the design of a scheduler for real-time jobs which satisfies the following objectives and thus avoids the limitations discussed above:

- Centralized scheduling control
- Effective scheduling achieved by taking the total real-time job load into account
- Conceptual simplicity so that variation of scheduling performance with changes in real-time job load is apparent
- Accurate overload detection.

The scheduler uses two task lists, a periodic-task list (PTL) and a nonperiodic-task list (NTL). The information in these lists needed by the scheduler depends upon the scheduling algorithm. For the first illustrative scheduler design, enablement time t_e and processing time p of all tasks are used. In addition, for periodic tasks, the period τ is needed. For task i, these quantities are denoted by t_{ei}, p_i, and τ_i, respectively. The first scheduler uses the earliest-enablement-time (EET) algorithm:

(1) Entry: T = real-time clock
(2) t_{ee} = EET in NTL;
If $t_{ee} > T$ go to 3), otherwise save $T - t_{ee} = T_N$ and schedule all time-enabled tasks in NTL;
Compute $p_N = \Sigma p$ for all tasks scheduled
(3) $T = T + p_N$;
t_{ej} = EET in PTL;
Save $T - t_{ej} = T_p$;
(Optional) If $T < t_{ej}$ set scheduler interrupt time = min (t_{ee}, t_{ej}) and exit;
Schedule k tasks from PTL in order of enablement times;
Update enablement times of scheduled tasks; $t'_{ej} = t_{ej} + \tau_j$;
Exit.

The above algorithm is written somewhat informally to suppress unnecessary detail. Hopefully, the nucleus of the algorithm is clear. The output of the scheduler is an ordered list, or schedule, of tasks which is used by the dispatcher.

The important characteristics of this algorithm are the following. Nonperiodic tasks are scheduled as they become time enabled. The maximum delay between enablement of a nonperiodic task and its scheduling is thus Δ_{max}, the maximum length of a schedule or the maximum time interval between successive scheduler executions. Note that Δ_{max}, which can at best be bounded for the actual length of Δ, is unknown because of the unknown delays caused by the unpredictable interrupts occurring during the actual processing of a schedule. Further, the maximum response time, defined as the time interval between the enablement and the completion of processing of a task, is clearly $< 2\,\Delta_{max}$. Without the optional test in Step (3), periodic tasks are scheduled as fast as possible. That is, a periodic task is scheduled *early* since t_{ej} may be less than T in Step (3). In some applications this is extremely effective since the system will never become unnecessarily idle and will execute the set of periodic tasks at the maximum possible rate. This makes the system self regulating and automatically adjusting to load variations. If this is not desirable, then the optional test can be included. Normally, nonreal-time background work will then be scheduled until the scheduler interrupt time. Alternately, an individual test for those periodic tasks which cannot be executed faster than their specified rate could be included.

The value of T_N and T_p saved are for overall load measurements. T_N measures the amount of delay between enablement and scheduling of a nonperiodic task. Similarly, T_p is a measurement of the periodic task load: if $T_p < 0$, the system is underloaded and as T_p becomes increasingly >0, the system becomes more overloaded. Hence, a value or a sequence of values of T_p can be specified to call special load-adjustment routine(s). Finally, values of Δ could be saved and recorded by simply saving the value of T upon each entry and computing $T(\text{new}) - T(\text{old}) = \Delta$. A value of Δ_{avg}, computed over several scheduling cycles, is also an excellent measure of load.

The number of periodic tasks scheduled, k in Step (3), is a parameter of the scheduler. For $k = 1$, scheduling is almost continuous, and in this case, the scheduler algorithm could perhaps be combined with the dispatcher and interrupt-control logic. However, in most real-time systems, a larger k and a separation of scheduler and dispatcher is worthwhile. Indeed, if possible, the schedulers now to be discussed which schedule over longer intervals should be used.

If the specified rates of periodic tasks are arbitrary or the set of distinct rates specified is large, then an upper bound on the length of the scheduling interval is determined by the following argument. Let $r_{\max}$ be the maximum possible rate in executions/sec. A maximum-rate task must then be scheduled every $\tau_{\min} = 1/r_{\max}$ sec. Let Δ_d be the scheduling interval expressed as a design parameter. $\Delta_d \leq \tau_{\min}$ if the maximum-rate tasks are scheduled only once in the interval Δ_d. A second constraint on the length of Δ_d may be imposed by the nonperiodic tasks. Enablements of nonperiodic tasks are reflections of demands for the execution of that task. (It is assumed that these demands are not queued as is sometimes done for demands upon interrupt service programs.) The minimum separation time $\delta_{\min}$, for successive demands on the same nonperiodic task is a constraint on Δ_d: $\Delta_d < \delta_{\min}$. Otherwise, a second request closely following an original request for a task would be lost.

Using $\Delta_d < \min(\tau_{\min}, \delta_{\min})$, a general bound on the scheduling interval is obtained. This bound could be used to determine an appropriate value for k in Step (3) of the EET algorithm.

If the number of distinct rates is small, the rate structure of the periodic tasks allows a more precise determination of scheduling intervals. The actual set of rates is important of course. It is easy to show that an arbitrary set of periodic tasks cannot be simultaneously scheduled so that all rates are met exactly. In this situation, one approach is to give preference to higher rate tasks and use task preemption as done by Wyle and Burnett [4]. This has the disadvantage of scheduling lower-rate tasks with unpredictable variations in rates. The method suggested here is to restrict the set of rates to a schedulable set. Without using preemption, the set of tasks can then be scheduled at predictable, deterministic rates.

If all rates are of the form $2^k r_0$, where r_0 is the minimum allowable rate, then the set is schedulable under nonoverloaded conditions. To show this fact, let the set of N periodic tasks be $\{(r_i, p_i)\}$ $(i = 1, 2, 3, \cdots, N)$. The total periodic-task load expressed in terms of fraction of real time required for their processing is then

$$\sum_{i=1}^{N} p_i r_i = L \quad . \tag{1}$$

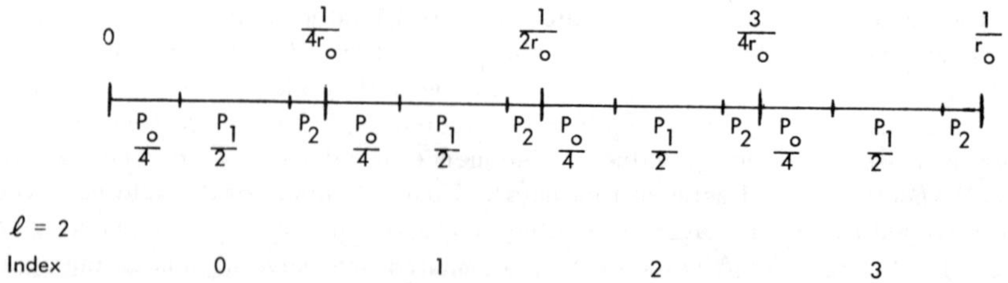

Fig. 1. Task arrangement in fully-loaded system.

Clearly, L must be ≤ 1 and $L = 1$ indicates that the periodic-task load uses all of the system capacity. However, the set may not be schedulable even if $L < 1$. In the special case $r_i = 2^k r_0$ for $k = 1, 2, 3, \cdots, \ell$, let P_k be the sum of the processing times of all tasks with rate $2^k r_0$. Then

$$\sum_{i=1}^{N} p_i r_i = \sum_{k-1}^{\ell} P_k (2^k r_0) = L \quad , \tag{2}$$

or

$$\sum_{k=1}^{\ell} P_k 2^k = L/r_0 \quad . \tag{3}$$

Figure 1 indicates the arrangement of tasks in a schedule for the fully loaded case of $L = 1$. The schedulability condition on the processing times is thus

$$\sum_{k=0}^{\ell} p_k 2^{-(\ell-k)} \leq 1/(2^{\ell} r_0) \quad . \tag{4}$$

These simple results indicate that a scheduler can be designed with a major and minor interval structure. $\tau_0 = 1/r_0$ is the length of the major interval and $\tau_{min} = 1/(2^{\ell} r_0)$ is the length of the minor interval. Figure 1 and Eq. (4) imply that the most efficient scheduling will result if the minor intervals are indexed and the periodic tasks distributed uniformly over the indexed minor intervals. This results in the periodic-task load being distributed uniformly over time. This shall be called the Indexed Interval Scheduler.

If knowledge sufficient to assign indices to periodic tasks is unavailable at the design stage, then an Interval Scheduler without indexing may be used. The basic interval can be either $\Delta_d = \tau_{min}$, or $\Delta_d = \tau_0$. The case $\Delta_d = \tau_{min}$ will be illustrated in the following algorithm. The definition of an algorithm for the other case is omitted but should be fairly self evident.

Minor-Interval Algorithm

(1) Entry: T = real-time clock

(2) Schedule enabled nonperiodic tasks as in EET algorithm with total processing time P_N

(3) Initialize $P = P_N$
Schedule enabled tasks from PTL in order of nonincreasing rates; for each task i scheduled, update P and t_{ei}: $P = P_N + p_i$;
If $P < \Delta_d$, $t_{ei} = t_{ei} + \tau_i$, otherwise $t'_{ei} = t_{ei} + \tau_i + \Delta_d$;
Exit.

The important feature of this algorithm is the rule for defining the new or next-enablement time of a periodic task t'_{ei}. The scheduler always schedules all enabled tasks. If the scheduled tasks can all be done in the next interval $P < \Delta_d$, then t_{ei} is updated as usual by adding τ_i. If $P > \Delta_d$, then the next execution of task is delayed by an additional amount Δ_d. This is equivalent to increasing the minor-interval index of the task as shown in Figure 1. By scheduling tasks in order of nonincreasing rates, the reverse of the order shown in Fig. 1, only the lower-rate tasks will be affected. Thus, as the load increases, lower-rate tasks will tend to be distributed over the minor intervals. Interval with index 0 will become filled first, then index 1, etc.

The Minor-Interval Algorithm as stated does not attempt to schedule periodic tasks early, i.e., at rates higher than those specified. To do so would eliminate the capability of distributing the load over time through the just-described self-regulation mechanism. Note the average value of Δ, as measured from actual real-time values at successive entries into scheduler, remains a valid measurement of overall load.

The two algorithms discussed thus far both schedule nonperiodic tasks as soon as possible. The response to a request for a nonperiodic task execution is thus $< 2\,\Delta_d$. This arrangement is satisfactory if the bulk of the real-time load is in periodic tasks or if requests for nonperiodic tasks are distributed fairly uniformly over time. A local peak in the requests for nonperiodic tasks would cause temporary slippage in time of periodic tasks however. If fast response to some or all nonperiodic task requests is not needed, then the nonperiodic task load can be distributed over time by use of a Major-Interval Scheduler.

A specific Major-Interval Algorithm will not be given since it is a relatively simple extension to the ideas already presented. Rather, several approaches to the definition of a Major-Interval Algorithm will be suggested.

Indexing of minor intervals is used to allow assignment of periodic *and* nonperiodic tasks to specific minor intervals. It has already been shown that this leads to a uniform distribution of the periodic-task load over time. To distribute the nonperiodic tasks over minor intervals, the scheduler must look at the entire set of nonperiodic tasks which are enabled at time T, the beginning of a major interval, or will become enabled during the next major interval. That is, the nonperiodic tasks with t_{ei} in interval $(T, T + \tau_0)$ should be considered for scheduling. Given this set of nonperiodic tasks, the scheduler can assign them to indexed minor intervals consistent with their processing and enablement times. This assignment allows the scheduler to schedule over a complete major interval by scheduling several executions of the higher-rate tasks. The scheduler itself only needs to be run once per major interval. A second implementation runs the scheduler each minor interval. The nonperiodic tasks to be scheduled are specified by the index assignment made at the beginning of a major interval. The scheduler only needs to keep track of the index of the minor interval and can use the Minor-Interval Algorithm or a suitable modification.

IV. ADDITIONAL CONSIDERATIONS

Since a scheduler will be executed very often in any real-time system, and must be considered an overhead operation, the computational complexity of the scheduler is an important factor. A comparison of the three scheduling algorithms suggested in the previous section using complexity as the criterion is in order. There is one significant difference. Observe that the EET algorithm selects the task with *earliest* enablement time. Thus, the NTL and PTL must be maintained as an ordered list or an ordering of the list by the scheduler would be necessary. If these lists are fairly large, this adds considerable complexity. The other two algorithms do not require an ordered list; however, they do require that the PTL be partitioned into sublists of equal rate tasks. Also, the Major-Interval Algorithm requires an internal indexing on each task in the list. Neither of these requirements are severe. In addition, the Major-Interval Algorithm contains an index-assignment subalgorithm. If the number of minor intervals within a major interval 2^{ℓ} becomes too large, this index assignment is a nontrivial computation. A tradeoff between its complexity and the benefits of distribution of load over the major interval would be necessary to choose between the last two schedulers.

The concept of scheduling real-time tasks for some interval in the future has certain implications to the allocation and scheduling of other resources. In systems for which some tasks are nonresident in core, the processing schedule generated can be used to schedule I/O operations in bringing in tasks or data required by tasks from secondary memory. Similarly the memory allocation algorithm could use this processor schedule information to create additional main-memory space.

Although normally in real-time systems, real-time tasks are not allowed to issue I/O instructions, this is primarily a result of how real-time software is modeled. Conceptually, it would be valid to model real-time programs at a higher level and allow a real-time task schedule to be executed in a multiprogramming mode by the dispatcher. That is, all tasks need not execute to completion on the processor. This will influence the variation in Δ observed by the scheduler, but does not weaken the principles of the schedulers discussed.

Multiprocessor-system organizations have often been motivated by the stringent requirements of large real-time problems [8]. In contrast to systems such as Illiac IV, for which programs and data are structured to match the machine architecture, the system may contain separate, independent processors so that any task may be scheduled and executed completely on any processor. This approach has been another rationale for decomposing real-time programs into the subroutines (tasks) discussed earlier.

Our scheduler philosophy readily applies to multiprocessor systems in which there exist a special control processor which controls and schedules the other processors. A very sophisticated scheduler could be implemented and executed by the control processor in such a system. Unfortunately, the problem of distributing tasks among the other processors in an optimal manner is largely unsolved [8]. In systems consisting of identical, democratic processors, our schedulers could be used by allowing any processor to execute the scheduler routine.

However, the timing of this execution is an unexplored problem. One does not want to wait until all processors are idle before generating a new schedule. On the other hand, planning a new schedule, while any real-time task which may enable other tasks is in execution, is not an attractive alternative.

V. CONCLUSIONS

The problem of scheduling of real-time jobs on computer systems has been treated from the viewpoint of the real-time system designer as opposed to the more general view of the operating-system designer. A general approach to designing a scheduler which supplies scheduling information to the operating system and takes into account the constraints on real-time jobs, such as response times and periodicity properties, has been formulated. In addition, outlines of the design of three distinct schedulers were presented. These schedulers are fairly simple and have the distinct advantage of allowing accurate overload detection, an important requirement in real-time applications.

Important open problems include the investigation in more detail of the interaction between the scheduler and operating-system dispatcher, the application of this philosophy to multiprocessor systems and study of efficient implementations. Lampson [7] has made a reasonably strong case for combining the interrupt and scheduling mechanisms and implementing these in hardware. Such an operating system design would be most attractive in real-time applications because of the reduction in overhead due to task switching. Hardware implementations, which provide for the specification of parameters by the real-time system designer, of the schedulers discussed in this paper would also be of interest and importance.

REFERENCES

[1] J. D. Aron, "Real-Time Systems in Perspective," *IBM Sys. J.*, **6**, 49–67 (1967).

[2] K. Ramsay and J. C. Strauss, "A Real Time Priority Scheduler," *Proc. ACM 21st National Meeting*, 161–166 (1966).

[3] C. L. Smith, "Digital Control of Industrial Processes," *ACM Comput. Surv.*, **2**, 211–241 (September 1970).

[4] H. Wyle and G. J. Burnett, "Management of Periodic Operations in a Real-Time Computation System," *Proc. AFIPS*, **31**, 201–203 (1967).

[5] H. Hellerman, "Some Principles of Time-Sharing Scheduler Strategies," *IBM Sys. J.*, **8**, 94–117 (1969).

[6] R. F. Rosin, "Supervisory and Monitor Systems," *ACM Comput. Surv.*, **1**, 37–54 (March 1969).

[7] B. Lampson, "A Scheduling Philosophy for Multiprocessing Systems," *Comm. ACM*, **11**, 347–360 (May 1968).

[8] G. K. Manacher, "Production and Stabilization of Real-Time Task Schedules," *J. ACM*, **14**, 439–465 (July 1967).

THE COMPLEXITY OF COMBINATORIAL COMPUTATIONS: A SURVEY

E. L. Lawler
Department of Electrical Engineering and Computer Sciences, University of California, Berkeley, CA

A survey is made of certain recently-obtained results concerning the complexity of more-or-less practical computations, where the complexity measures are themselves more-or-less practical in nature. Various models for the evaluation of complexity are discussed, and a number of algorithms are cited which have been shown to be optimal, optimal to within a linear scale factor, and possibly, but not necessarily, optimal. Most of the cited problems and algorithms are combinatorial in nature, many of them involving sorting or searching a list of numbers.

I. INTRODUCTION

The purpose of this paper is to call attention to a number of recent results concerning the complexity of more-or-less practical types of computations, where the measures of complexity are more-or-less practical in nature. The problems we review are primarily combinatorial in character. That is, they involve the ordering, selection, or arrangement of a finite set of objects. Examples include the selection of the largest number from among a given set of N numbers, or the ordering (sorting) of the numbers according to numerical value.

No attempt has been made to make this a comprehensive survey. In fact, the author is aware of several results which possibly should have been included. However, it is thought that the work which is reported here is fairly representative of ongoing research, and this survey may serve as a worthwhile introduction for persons unfamiliar with the area.

II. COMPLEXITY MEASURES

Much of the recent research on algorithmic complexity has been directed toward the minimization of one particular type of arithmetic or logical operation or subroutine. For example, the minimization of numerical-magnitude comparisons in sorting algorithms, or of scalar multiplications in matrix multiplications, or of the evaluation of linear forms in a variety of algorithms. Sometimes these particularized measures of complexity are adopted because they seem most appropriate for the given problem type, and at other times because they are the only measures that are susceptible to analysis.

However, even in the case where a particularized complexity measure is in

Presented at the Symposium on Computers and Automata
Polytechnic Institute of Brooklyn, April 13–15, 1971.

question, analysis is usually carried out in terms of a more-generalized computational model. Among the more significant of these are: (1) The computation tree; (2) The combinational-switching circuit; and (3) The idealized-programming model.

The concept of the computation tree is relatively simple. Each node of a rooted tree is identified with a specific computer instruction or subroutine. Ordinary arithmetic instructions, e.g., addition, multiplication, result in nodes with only one successor. Conditional-branch instructions result in nodes with two or more successors, corresponding to the possible conditions. Computation begins at the root node of the tree and proceeds from node to node until a node with no successor (a "leaf") is reached. A specified output or answer is identified with each such leaf. The length of the longest root-leaf path (in terms of the total of the complexities of the nodes along it), indicates the worst case or minimax length of the computation in question. The average root-leaf path length indicates the average length of the computation.

A few observations about the computation-tree model seem in order. For one thing, computer programs are generally not structured at all like computation trees, and it is sometimes hard to evaluate storage requirements and operational complexity in terms of such a model. For another, it is sometimes possible to establish the existence of a computation tree of a given complexity without having much of a notion of how to construct an algorithm of that complexity. For example, it is clear that for any given value of N, there exists a tree with complexity $\mathcal{O}(N^2)$ which will determine any desired property of an N-node graph. E.g., to determine whether or not a given graph is Hamiltonian, one can imagine constructing a computation tree in which each node is identified with a conditional branch instruction on a given element of the adjacency matrix of the graph. Each root-leaf path in the tree has length N^2 nodes and is identified with a different N-node graph. The leaves can be partitioned according to whether or not the corresponding graphs are Hamiltonian. It follows that it is possible to compute whether a graph is Hamiltonian, or possesses any other given property, with a computation that is $\mathcal{O}(N^2)$ in length.

The switching-circuit model assumes that the computation is to be carried out by a network of "elementary" logical components, where each of these components can be thought of, more or less, as performing the function of a single computer instruction or subroutine. The input data, e.g., the bits defining the adjacency matrix of a graph, serve as the primary inputs of the network, and the results of the computation, suitably encoded as switching signals, are the outputs of the network.

The switching-circuit model is interesting because it permits a well-established complexity theory of circuits, dating to Shannon's work of 1949, to be applied to the study of the complexity of algorithms. However, the limitations of this model include most of the limitations of the computation-tree model, and some others, besides. For example, the effect of a conditional-branch instruction can be reflected in the switching-circuit model. However, if one is concerned with counting the total complexity of the switching network, the effect of doing so is roughly equivalent to counting the total number of instructions that would be executed as a result of taking both sides of the branch. (It is also possible to count the number of levels of components in the network, which to some extent, at least, overcomes this objection.) Put another way, the switching circuit model is effective only for modeling "straight-line" computer programs, i.e., programs without branch instructions.

In many investigations, an attempt is made to overcome some of the limitations of the other models by considering a somewhat-idealized computer for which programs are to be written. Often, the details of this model are only implicit in the particular investigation. Some of the assumptions that are commonly made are that there exists an unboundedly-large random-access (core) memory, possibly with variable and unbounded word length, and symbolic addressing with unboundedly-long symbolic addresses. Input data are assumed to be resident in core memory at the beginning of the computation and results are left in core at the conclusion. Executable instructions include either more-or-less-conventional machine-language instructions or statements in a more-or-less-conventional algebraic-compiler language. Appropriate assumptions, often taking into account the length of operands, are made as to the amount of time required for the execution of various instructions. Complexity is measured both in terms of the maximum (or average) length of execution and of the maximum (or average) memory-storage requirement.

As we shall see, it is not always obvious how to interpret the various complexity measures, and there are pitfalls for the unwary.

III. LOWER BOUNDS ON COMPLEXITY

There is a distinct lack of techniques for producing good lower bounds on the complexity of various types of computations. Among those which do exist are the "look-at" argument and the "possible-outcomes" argument.

The "look-at" argument is roughly as follows. If a problem is specified by N nonredundant data items, and each elementary computational instruction can act on only k data items at a time, then at least N/k instructions must be executed to simply "look at" all the input data. Thus, one concludes that if a graphical computation is specified by the N^2 entries of an adjacency matrix, any graphical computation must have a complexity which is at least $\mathcal{O}(N^2)$.

The "possible-outcomes" argument is possibly best exemplified by the problem of sorting N numbers. There are $N!$ possible orderings which may result from the application of a sorting algorithm. Suppose each of these possible outcomes is identified with a leaf of a computation tree, and each node of the tree is identified with a conditional-branch instruction based on the comparison of the magnitudes of two of the numbers. It is easily seen that any such computation tree must have a root-leaf path length equal to $\log_2 N! \approx N \log_2 N$ comparison operations, and this is the generally-accepted lower bound on the length of sorting algorithms.

Other types of lower bounds are obtained from theorems on switching-circuit complexity, the geometry of convex polyhedra, and various ad-hoc arguments (sometimes quite elegant) which are made to fit the specific problem at hand.

IV. OPTIMAL ALGORITHMS

A sampling of computations which can be said to be optimal, in one sense or another, includes the following:

(a) Finding the Maximum of N Numbers. The obvious technique for performing this task requires exactly $N - 1$ numerical comparisons, which is easily shown to be optimal

(b) Finding the Maximum and Second Largest of N Numbers. It is possible to accomplish this task with $N - 2 + \lceil \log_2 N \rceil$ comparisons, which has been shown to be optimal [1]. However, relatively little is known about the optimality of algorithms for finding the maximum, 2nd largest, 3rd largest numbers

(c) Finding the Maximum and Minimum of N Numbers. This task can be accomplished with $\lceil \frac{3}{2} N \rceil - 2$ numerical comparisons. Pohl [2] has shown this to be optimal

(d) Merging Two Strings of N Numbers. Karp and Graham have independently shown that an algorithm involving $2N - 1$ numerical comparisons is optimal [4]

(e) Maximization of Unimodal Function. The well-known Fibonacci-search technique involves a minimum number of evaluations of the given unimodal function [5].

Optimality of other algorithms, and a sizable bibliography, can be found in Reingold [6].

V. ALGORITHMS OPTIMAL TO WITHIN A LINEAR-SCALE FACTOR

A. Shortest-path, Spanning-tree Computations

The algorithms of Dijkstra [7] and of Prim [8] for computing shortest paths and shortest-spanning trees in complete networks on N nodes are $\mathcal{O}(N^2)$ in complexity, and are therefore optimal to within a linear scale factor, inasmuch as each of the N^2 arcs must be "looked at." Moreover, it seems that these algorithms are strictly optimal, in other senses.

The Dijkstra shortest-path algorithm is, however, applicable only to networks in which all arc lengths are positive. The best algorithms for the more general case are all $\mathcal{O}(N^3)$ in complexity, but it has not been established that this complexity is optimal.

B. Planarity Testing of Graphs

Hopcroft and Tarjan [9, 21] have devised a method for testing the planarity of graphs which is $\mathcal{O}(N)$ in complexity.

This remarkable achievement would appear to violate a lower bound of $\mathcal{O}(N^2)$ which would be established by the "look-at" argument. The apparent paradox is explained by the fact that, first, no planar graph can have more than $3N - 2$ arcs, and Hopcroft and Tarjan propose to apply their algorithm only to graphs which satisfy this necessary condition for planarity. Second, they assume that the (no more than) $3N - 2$ arcs of the graph are appropriately arranged in a list as input data. (If the algorithm were to be applied to the adjacency matrix of the graph, the look-at argument would indeed dictate an $\mathcal{O}(N^2)$ complexity.) The algorithm itself makes use of relatively-sophisticated data structures and data-processing techniques.

C. Computing the Median of *N* Numbers

Floyd [3] has developed a computation to find the median of N numbers with $\frac{3}{2}N + \mathcal{O}(N)$ numerical comparisons, on the average, and has established $\frac{5}{4}N$ as a lower bound. Very recently Blum, et al. [22] have developed a median computation which requires about $5.43N$ comparisons in the worst case. A minimax lower bound of $\frac{3}{2}N$ has been established.

VI. GOOD, BUT NOT NECESSARILY OPTIMAL ALGORITHMS

A number of algorithms have been proposed which are surprisingly efficient, and which are possibly optimal, but optimality has not been demonstrated.

A. Sorting Algorithms

A number of sorting algorithms exceed by only a very small number of comparisons the lower bound of $\log_2 N! \approx N \log_2 N$. For all "practical" purposes these algorithms are optimal; they may even be optimal in the strictest sense, but it has not been possible to establish this [4].

B. Bipartite Matching

A "matching" is a subset of arcs in a graph, no two of which meet at the same node. The bipartite matching or "marriage" problem is to find the largest-possible matching in a bipartite graph with N nodes.

Many $\mathcal{O}(N^3)$ algorithms have been developed for this problem. Recently Hopcroft and Karp [10] developed an algorithm which is $\mathcal{O}(N^{2.5})$ in complexity.

It is noteworthy that this impressive result is in opposition to a result of Harper and Savage [11] to the effect that the bipartite matching problem is at least $\mathcal{O}(N^3)$ in complexity. However, the Harper-Savage lower bound was obtained with respect to a combinational-switching network, and thus establishes a lower bound on "straight-line" computer programs.

C. State Minimization of Finite-State Machines

As a by-product of their research on graph planarity, Hopcroft and Tarjan developed an $\mathcal{O}(N \log N)$ algorithm for obtaining the reduced form of an N-state finite-state machine. Previous algorithms for this problem were $\mathcal{O}(N^2)$ or greater in complexity.

D. Alphabetic Coding

Hu and Tucker [12] have developed an $\mathcal{O}(N^2)$ algorithm for obtaining optimal "alphabetic" codes, i.e., Huffman codes in which the lexical ordering of the variable-length code words is consistent with a given ordering of the N-encoded messages. Previous algorithms for this problem were $\mathcal{O}(N^3)$. These results may help suggest improved parsing algorithms for formal languages.

E. *K* Shortest Paths

Sometimes it is of interest to find not only the shortest path between two nodes of a network, but also the 2nd, 3rd, 4th, $\cdots$, K^{th} shortest paths. Various versions of this problem have been solved by Dreyfus [13], Yen [14], and Lawler [15]. These show that after the shortest path is obtained, each successive shortest path can be obtained by an amount of computation which is either $\mathcal{O}(N^2)$ or $\mathcal{O}(N^3)$, depending upon the nature of the problem.

F. Nonbipartite Matching

The matching problem for nonbipartite graphs can be solved by a computation that is $\mathcal{O}(N^3)$, rather than $\mathcal{O}(N^4)$ as had generally been supposed [16]. It is not immediately apparent how the techniques of Hopcroft and Karp used for the bipartite problem can be applied in this more-general case, but this may be possible.

G. Matrix Multiplication

Strassen [17] has shown that N^3 scalar multiplications are not necessary to multiply two $N \times N$ matrices; instead, approximately $N^{2.7}$ such multiplications are sufficient. It is not known whether this result is optimal, except for a few special cases, e.g., 2×2 real matrices. Hopcroft and Kerr [18] have been able to generalize Strassen's result somewhat.

VII. CONCLUSION

One must conclude that this area of research is just beginning to develop. Much remains to be done, particularly in the development of systematic techniques for establishing complexity bounds.

Possibly the ultimate theoretical achievement would be to establish a lower bound of exponential complexity for the "traveling-salesman problem." (See [19, 20] for a line of research which offers a clue as to how to proceed in this direction.)

REFERENCES

[1] S. S. Kislicyn, "On the Selection of the kth Element of an Ordered Set By Pairwise Comparisons," *Sibirsk, Mat. Z.*, **5**, 557–564 (1964) (in Russian; see: *Math Rev.*, **29**, No. 2198 (1965)).

[2] I. Pohl, "A Sorting Problem and Its Complexity," University of California, Santa Cruz (March 1970) (unpublished paper).

[3] R. Floyd (to be published).

[4] D. E. Knuth, "Sorting and Searching," *The Art of Computer Programming*, **3** (to be published by Addison Wesley).

[5] D. J. Wilde, *Optimum Seeking Methods* (Prentice Hall, 1964).

[6] E. M. Reingold, "On Some Optimal Algorithms," PhD. dissertation, Cornell University (1971); available as Report No. 428, Department of Computer Science, University of Illinois, Urbana-Champaign.

[7] E. Dijkstra, "A Note on Two Problems in Connection With Graphs," *Numer. Math.*, **1**, 269–271 (1959).

[8] R. C. Prim, "Shortest Interconnection Networks and Some Generalizations," *Bell Sys. Tech. J.*, **36**, 1389–1401 (1957).

[9] J. Hopcroft and R. Tarjan, "Planarity Testing in $V \log V$ Steps: Extended abstract," SAN-CS-71-201, Computer Science Department, Stanford University (February 1971).

[10] R. M. Karp (1971) (private communication).

[11] L. Harper and J. E. Savage, "On the Complexity of the Marriage Problem," Jet Propulsion Lab., Pasadena, California (1971) (to be published).

[12] T. C. Hu and A. Tucker, Technical Report, Mathematics Research Center, University of Wisconsin, Madison (1970).

[13] S. E. Dreyfus, "An Appraisal of Some Shortest-Path Algorithms," *Operations Res.*, **17**, 395–412 (1969).

[14] J. Y. Yen, "Finding the K Shortest Loopless Paths in a Network" (to be published in *Management Sci.*).

[15] E. L. Lawler, "A Procedure for Computing the K Best Solutions to Discrete-Optimization Problems and Its Application to the Shortest-Path Problem" (to be published in *Management Sci.*).

[16] E. L. Lawler, "Networks and Matroids," *Combinatorial-Optimization Theory*, **1**, (to be published by Holt, Rinehart, and Winston).

[17] V. Strassen, "Gaussian Elimination is Not Optimal," *Numer. Math.*, **13**, 354–356 (1969).

[18] J. E. Hopcroft and L. R. Kerr, "Some Techniques for Proving Certain Simple Programs Optimal," *IEEE Conf. Record 1969 Tenth Annual Symp. Switching and Automata Theory* (1969).

[19] P. M. Spira, "Complete Linear Proofs of Systems of Linear Inequalities," (to be published).

[20] M. O. Rabin, "Proving Simultaneous Positivity of Linear Forms," *Proc. Third Annual ACM Symp. Theory of Computing*, Shaker Heights, Ohio (May 1971).

[21] R. Tarjan, PhD. Thesis, Computer Science Department, Stanford University (to be published).

[22] M. Blum, R. Floyd, V. Pratt, R. Rivest, and R. Tarjan, "Linear Bounds for Quantile Computations," University of California, Berkeley, and Stanford University (to be published).

MINIMAL-GROWTH-RATE MERGE SORT

M. Erol Arkun
Polytechnic Institute of Brooklyn, Brooklyn, NY

An exact, theoretical lower bound for the total number of unit-string transfers required to merge S unit strings employing K-way merges is derived by simulating the merge sort by the minimal external-path-length K-ary tree with S unity-weight external nodes. A merge-sort method with read-backward capability tapes as external storage is designed to attain the lower bound within an additive constant less than S and compared with the presently-available methods.

I. INTRODUCTION

In data-processing applications one often needs to sort the records constituting a file into an ordered sequence. For files that can not be fit in the core memory, a portion at a time is internally sorted, usually by replacement selection [1], and the resulting ordered sequence of blocked records, called unit strings, are outputted onto magnetic tapes for subsequent merging by methods such as balanced [2], cascade [3], polyphase [4–6], or oscillating sort [7]. Unit strings are properly transferred from tape to tape during merging; the total number of such transfers $T(S, K)$, being taken as a measure of cost [1] in merging S unit strings employing K-way merges on $K + 1$ tapes. $T(S, K)$ grows faster than $S \log_K S$ for the methods mentioned [8] and the problem of finding a merging method that optimizes it is unsolved [1].

This paper establishes an exact, theoretical lower bound on $T(S, K)$ and presents a new merging method for read-backward-capability tapes to attain it within an additive constant bounded by S.

II. TREE REPRESENTATION OF MERGING

Merging K unit strings by a K-way merge produces a string of relative length K. If K is the maximum order of the merge and there are $S > K$ unit strings to be merged, then several steps of K-way (and possibly some partial) merges are required to obtain a single string of relative length S. The merging process can always be represented by a weighted K-ary tree with S unity-weight external nodes as follows:

(1) An external node represents a unit string and an internal node with weight W an intermediate string of relative length W
(2) K internal nodes with weights $W_1, W_2, W_3, \cdots, W_K$ and their parent

Presented at the Symposium on Computers and Automata
Polytechnic Institute of Brooklyn, April 13–15, 1971.

node with weight $W = \sum_{i=1}^{K} W_i$, represent K-way merging of intermediate strings with lengths $W_1, W_2, W_3, \cdots, W_K$

(3) The root of the tree with weight S represents the final string.

Figure 1 shows three of the many possible ternary trees representing three different methods of 3-way merging of 9-unit strings. It can be readily verified that oscillating sort simulates Fig. 1(a) with 5 tapes, and Figs. 1(b) and 1(c) are simulated with 4 tapes by polyphase and modified cascade respectively.

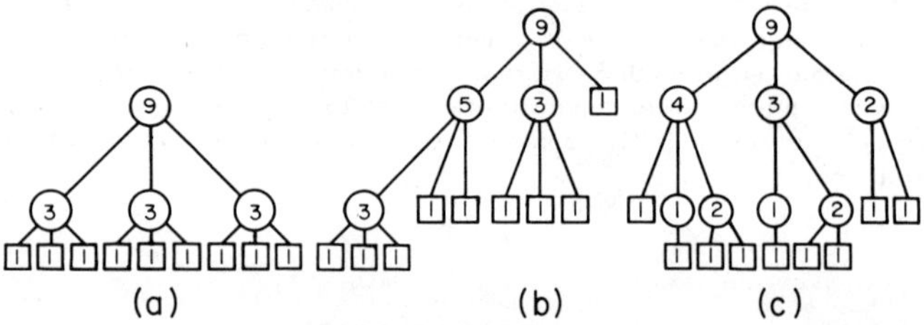

Fig. 1. Ternary merging trees.

III. MINIMAL-GROWTH-RATE TREES AND THEIR PROPERTIES

DEFINITION 1. *The external path length, denoted $E(S, K)$, of a K-ary tree with S unity-weight external nodes is the sum, taken over all external nodes, of the lengths of the paths from the root to each external node* [9].

DEFINITION 2. *A weight is said to be perfect if it is an integral power of K; nonperfect otherwise.*

Huffman [10] and Schwartz [11] gave algorithms for constructing the K-ary tree with S external nodes that minimizes the external-path length and the length of the maximum path. Such a tree has minimal growth rate. To construct it, form a sequence of S 1s representing unit weights preceded by Z $(0 \leq Z < K - 1)$ 0s where Z satisfies $\text{mod}_{K-1}(S + Z) = 1$. Obtain new weights by repeatedly merging consecutive groups of K weights in pass 1 until the sequence is exhausted or less than K unity weights are left. Pass 2 is preformed similarly on the sequence containing the left over 1s followed by the new weights obtained in pass 1. After a sufficient number of passes the process terminates when a single weight S is obtained. The tree can now be constructed by assigning S to the root, and the weights that yield S to the successors of the root, and so on. Figure 2 illustrates the case for $S = 18$ and $K = 3$.

It should be noted that pass 1 generates a single nonperfect weight iff $\text{mod}_{K-1} S \neq 1$; and any intermediate pass may also generate a single nonperfect weight even if $\text{mod}_{K-1} S = 1$. Once a nonperfect weight is generated it is perpetuated by the first merge of each subsequent pass. Clearly, the minimal (growth-rate) tree induces a K-part partition on any nonperfect weight W_i given by

$$W_i = \alpha_{i-1} K^{p-1} + \beta_{i-1} K^p + W_{i-1} \quad , \tag{1}$$

where

$$\alpha_{i-1} + \beta_{i-1} = K - 1 \qquad (\alpha_{i-1}, \beta_{i-1} \geq 0) \quad , \tag{2}$$

$$K^{p-1} < W_{i-1} < K^p \ , \tag{3}$$

for some p and K^{p-1}, K^p, and W_{i-1} are the weights of successors of the node with weight W_i.

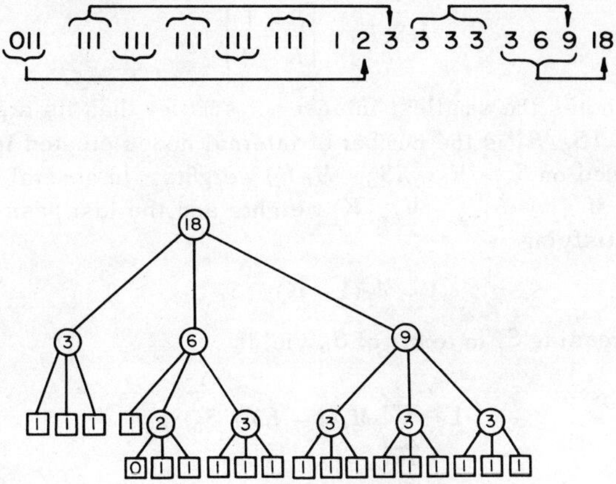

Fig. 2. Construction of a minimal-growth-rate ternary tree for $S = 18$.

THEOREM 1. *Let*

$$S = \sum_{i=0}^{p} a_i K^i \ ,$$

be the representation of the weight S in base K number system and

$$S = \alpha_1 K^{p-1} + \beta_1 K^p + S_1 \ , \tag{5}$$

its K-part partition. Then

$$\alpha_1 = (K-1) - a_p \ ,$$

$$\beta_1 = a_p \ ,$$

$$S_1 = \left[a_p + a_{p-1} - (K-1)\right] K^{p-1} + \sum_{i=0}^{p-2} a_i K^i \ ,$$

if $a_p + a_{p-1} > K - 1$, *and*

$$\alpha_1 = K - a_p \ ,$$

$$\beta_1 = a_p - 1 \ ,$$

$$S_1 = (a_p + a_{p-1}) K^{p-1} + \sum_{i=0}^{p-2} a_i K^i \ ,$$

if $a_p + a_{p-1} \leq K - 1$.

Proof: In both cases $\alpha_1 + \beta_1 = K - 1$, and $K^{p-1} \leq S_1 \leq K^p$ with Eq. (5) being satisfied. Q.E.D.

COROLLARY 1 [11]. *The external nodes of a minimal-growth-rate tree can lie at most on the two-highest levels.*

LEMMA 1. *The total number of merges and hence the number of internal nodes of a minimal K-ary tree with S external nodes is given by*

$$I(S,K) = \left\lceil \frac{S-1}{K-1} \right\rceil . \tag{6}$$

Proof. $\lceil\ \rceil$ denotes the smallest integer not smaller than its argument. Let $S_0 = S + Z$. $M_0 = \lfloor S_0/K \rfloor$ is the number of internal nodes created in pass 1, and pass 2 is performed on $S_1 = M_0 + (S_0 - M_0 K)$ weights. In general, pass i is performed on $S_{i-1} = M_{i-2} + (S_{i-2} - M_{i-2} K)$ weights and the last pass produces a single weight satisfying

$$1 = M_j (1 - K) + S_j \ ,$$

for some j. Expressing S_j in terms of S_0 yields

$$1 = \sum_{i=0}^{j} M_i (1 - K) + S_0 \ ,$$

and

$$I(S,K) = \sum_{i=0}^{j} M_i = \left\lceil \frac{S_0 - 1}{K-1} \right\rceil = \left\lceil \frac{S-1}{K-1} \right\rceil . \quad \text{Q.E.D.}$$

LEMMA 2. *The number of external nodes at the next-to-the-highest level is given by*

$$E_1(S,K) = \left\lfloor \frac{K^{\lceil \log_K S \rceil} - S}{K-1} \right\rfloor . \tag{7}$$

Proof. All the preceding levels contain internal nodes only. The next-to-the-highest level contains both internal and external nodes. At level i there are K^i nodes. The total number of nodes on levels 0 up to and including the next-to-the-highest level is given by

$$I(S,K) + E_1(S,K) = \sum_{i=0}^{p} K^i \ , \tag{8}$$

where $p = \lceil \log_K S \rceil - 1 = \lfloor \log_K S \rfloor$. Transposing and substituting for $I(S,K)$ yields

$$E_1(S,K) = \frac{K^{p+1} - (S+Z)}{K-1} = \left\lfloor \frac{K^{p+1} - S}{K-1} \right\rfloor . \quad \text{Q.E.D.} \tag{9}$$

COROLLARY 2. *The number of external nodes at the highest level is given by*

$$E_2(S,K) = S - E_1(S,K) \ , \tag{10}$$

THEOREM 2. *The external-path length of a minimal K-ary tree with S external nodes is given by*

$$E(S,K) = S \lceil \log_K S \rceil - \left\lfloor \frac{K^{\lceil \log_K S \rceil} - S}{K-1} \right\rfloor . \tag{11}$$

Proof. By Definition 1

$$E(S,K) = E_1(S,K)\lfloor \log_K S \rfloor + E_2(S,K)\lceil \log_K S \rceil \ ,$$

and substituting for $E_1(S,K)$, $E_2(S,K)$ and p yields Equation (11). Q.E.D.

LEMMA 3. *The sum of the weights of the internal nodes of a minimal tree equals* $E(S,K)$.

Proof. Level zero consists of only the root with weight S. The weights of the internal nodes at level 1 are parts of the K-part partition on S and their sum is also S. Inductively, the sum of the weights of the set of internal nodes at any level i ($i < \lfloor \log_K S \rfloor$), is S. Hence $S \lfloor \log_K S \rfloor$ is the sum of the weights of all the internal nodes excluding those on level $\lfloor \log_K S \rfloor$ whose sum is given by Equation (10). Hence

$$S\lfloor \log_K S \rfloor + S - E_1(S,K) = E(S,K) \ . \ \text{Q.E.D.}$$

Since the total number of unit-string transfers required is also given by the sum of the weights of the internal nodes as a consequence of our representation of merging, we have Corollary 3.

COROLLARY 3. *The minimal external path length of a K-ary tree with S unity-weight external nodes represents the K-way merging of S unit strings that require the minimum total number of unit-string transfers* $T(S,K) = E(S,K)$.

IV. SIMULATION OF THE MINIMAL TREE ON TAPES

This section presents a method of merge sort which simulates the minimal tree on read-backward-capability tape units. Replacement selection is assumed capable of producing ascending as well as descending unit strings. An ascending (descending) string of relative length i is denoted by $A_i(D_i)$. Strings are always written forwards, but reading may be done in both directions. Merging of ascending strings by reading forwards produces an ascending string; while reading backwards produces a descending string. Strings of opposite order can be merged only by reading them in opposite directions. The $K + 1$ tapes available for a K-way merge sort are denoted by $T_0, T_1, T_2, \cdots, T_K$, with T_K containing the unsorted input file initially.

A. Distribution

Count the number of unit strings generated by replacement selection in base-K number system by employing a K-ary counter initially set to 1. Output all unit strings on T_0 in ascending (descending) order except when the count indicates an odd number of trailing zeros in which case output the next string in descending (ascending) order.

The sequence of unit strings having such a pattern of ordering is said to be an image-pair sequence in which the ith string generated forms a p-image pair with the $(K^p - i)^{\text{th}}$ string.

LEMMA 4. *p-image pair strings have the same order.*

Proof. Let $i = \sum_{j=0}^{q} a_j K^j$. Then

$$K^p - i = \sum_{m=q+1}^{p-1} (K-1)K^m + \sum_{n=1}^{q} (K-1-a_n)K^n + K - a_0 \quad .$$

Now the ith string is D_1 iff

$$a_j = a_{j-1} = a_{j-2} = \cdots = a_0 = 0 \quad ,$$

for j even, and $K^p - i$ becomes

$$K^p - i = \sum_{m=q+1}^{p} (K-1)K^m + \sum_{n=j+2}^{q} (K-1-a_n)K^n + K - a_{j+1} \quad ,$$

with $j+1$ trailing zeros. Hence the $(K^p - i)^{\text{th}}$ string is also D_1. Otherwise both are A_1. Q.E.D.

Let S_K^p denote the image-pair sequence with K^p strings. Clearly, the terminal string of S_K^p is $A_1(D_1)$ when p is even (odd).

COROLLARY 4. *Let $S_K^p(t)$ denote S_K^p with its terminal string truncated. Then: $S_K^p(t)$ has the same pattern of ordering of its unit strings in either direction.*

Example 1. An image-pair sequence for $K = 3$ is exhibited below. Ternary and decimal-position numbers are also shown. (1, 2) is a 1-image pair; (1, 26), (2, 25), (3, 24), $\cdots$, (26, 1), are 3-image pairs.

A_1	A_1	D_1	A_1	A_1	D_1	A_1	A_1	A_1	A_1	A_1	D_1	$\cdots$	A_1	A_1	A_1	A_1	$\cdots$	A_1	D_1	A_1	$\cdots$
1	2	3	4	5	6	7	8	9	10	11	12		16	17	18	19	$\cdots$	26	27	28	$\cdots$
1	2	10	11	12	20	21	22	100	$\cdots$		110		$\cdots$		200		$\cdots$			1,000	$\cdots$

Note that S_K^p has K subsequences S_K^{p-1}; all identical except for the order of the terminal string in the Kth subsequence S_K^{p-1} which will be called an improperly-terminated subsequence.

The number of D_1 strings in S_K^p is given by

$$N(D_1) = \frac{K^p}{K} - \frac{K^p}{K^2} + \frac{K^p}{K^3} - \cdots \pm 1 \quad ,$$

$$N(D_1) = \sum_{i=1}^{p} (-1)^{i-1} K^{p-i} \quad . \tag{12}$$

B. Merging

It is convenient to consider the special case of merging $S = K^p$ unit strings first. The general case for an arbitrary S will be treated subsequently.

1. Special Case

All internal nodes of the corresponding minimal tree have perfect weights and to simulate it strings of relative lengths $K, K^2, K^3, \cdots, K^p$ must be obtained in proper numbers on tapes employing K-way merges. The particular pattern of ordering of the unit strings on T_0 allows one to generate strings of such specific lengths on any desired target tape T_t. For instance, to obtain a D_K string on T_K disperse the first $(K-1)$ A_1 strings from T_0 onto T_1 through T_{K-1}, then K-way merge onto T_K by reading the Kth string (D_1) on T_0 forwards and the dispersed strings (A_1's) backwards. ($K - 1$) such steps followed by a final dispersion pass process ($K^2 - 1$) of the unit strings on T_0 and lead to the configuration of tapes

	T_0	T_1	T_2	$\cdots$	T_K
$\cdots$	$\underset{\uparrow}{}A_1$	$\underset{\uparrow}{\text{—}}$	$D_K A_{1\uparrow}$		$D_K A_{1\uparrow}$

where arrows indicate the positions of the read-write heads. Now transfer the next A_1 from T_0 onto T_1, K-way merge onto T_0 writing backwards and once more merge onto T_1 to obtain A_{K^2}. Any perfect-length string can be built up by iterating this process.*

In view of Corollary 4 we can perform the same steps by reading backwards and writing forwards on T_0 if we first transfer onto T_1 the $(K^2)^{\text{th}}$ string generated in anticipation. The result will be a D_{K^2} string.

Two algorithms are now presented to K-way merge K^p unit strings for even and odd values of p. T_0 is initially ready for reading backwards, the remaining tapes are at load point for writing forwards. In a sequence of tapes starting with T_i, T_1 follows T_K. C_D and C_U are K-ary counters. Anticipating the requirements of the general case we incorporate provisions for designating any tape, including T_0, as a target in addition to handling improperly-terminated image-pair sequences. F holds the index of the designated-target tape.

Algorithm A: S_K^p, p even.

Step 1. $C_D \leftarrow K^p - 1$, $C_U \leftarrow 1$, $F \leftarrow f$. If $C_D \neq 0$ go to 3

Step 2. S_K^p properly terminated. If $F \neq 0$ transfer a string from T_0 onto T_f; otherwise transfer a string from T_0 onto T_{K-1}, rewind T_{K-1} and transfer from it onto T_0 again. Go to 12. S_K^p improperly terminated. If $F \neq 0$ transfer a string from T_0 onto T_i, $i \neq F$, then from T_i onto T_f; otherwise no operation. Go to 12

Step 3. If $F = 0$, $f \leftarrow K - 1$. Transfer a string from T_0 onto T_f

Step 4. Disperse one unit string onto each of the sequence of tapes starting with T_f and decrement C_D, increment C_U for each unit string dispersed until C_U indicates a sequence of trailing zeros. Let the last string dispersed be on T_i and N be the number of trailing zeros

Step 5. If N is odd, perform N K-way merges onto T_{i+1} and T_0 by alternating. $C_D \leftarrow C_D - 1$, $C_U \leftarrow C_U + 1$, $f \leftarrow i + 1$. Go to 4

Step 6. If $C_D = 0$ go to 7; otherwise transfer a unit string from T_0 onto T_{i+1}, perform N K-way merges onto T_0 and T_{i+1} by alternating. $C_D \leftarrow C_D - 1$, $C_U \leftarrow C_U + 1$, $f \leftarrow i + 2$. Go to 4

Step 7. If $F = 0$ go to 10

Step 8. If S_K^p is properly terminated, perform N K-way merges onto T_0 and T_{i+1} by alternating. $f \leftarrow i + 1$. Go to 12

Step 9. Rewind T_{i+1}, K-way merge onto T_0 once, rewind T_{i+1} again and perform ($N - 1$) K-way merges onto T_{i+1} and T_0 by alternating. $f \leftarrow i + 1$. Go to 12

*Oscillating sort proceeds likewise, but T_0 contains the unsorted-input file, ($K - 1$)-way merges are done using ($K + 1$) tapes, and the distribution pass is not required.

Step 10. If S_K^p is properly terminated rewind T_{K-1}, transfer onto T_0, rewind T_{K-1} again. Perform N K-way merges onto T_{K-1} and T_0 by alternating. $f \leftarrow 0$. Go to 12

Step 11. Transfer a string from T_{K-1} onto T_0. Perform N K-way merges onto T_{K-1} and T_0 by alternating. $f \leftarrow 0$

Step 12. Stop. Final string on T_f is D_{KP}.

Example 2. Figure 3 shows the steps of 3-way merging of properly-terminated S_3^2 with T_1 as target.

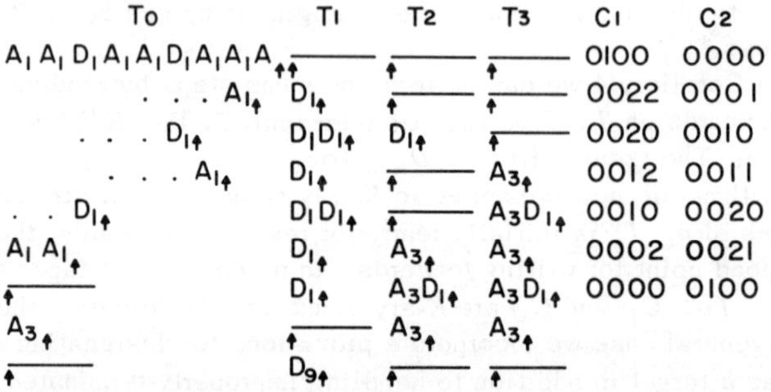

Fig. 3. Merging of 9-unit strings by Algorithm A.

Algorithm B: S_K^p, p odd.

Step 1. $C_D \leftarrow K^p - 1$, $C_U \leftarrow 1$, $F \leftarrow f$

Step 2. If $F = 0$, $f \leftarrow K - 1$. Transfer a string onto T_f

Step 3. Disperse one unit string onto each of the sequence of tapes starting with T_{f+1} and decrement C_D, increment C_U for each string dispersed until C_U indicates a sequence of trailing zeros. Let the last string dispersed be on T_i and N be the number of trailing zeros

Step 4. If N is even, transfer a string on T_{i+1}, perform N K-way merges onto T_0 and T_{i+1} by alternating. $C_D \leftarrow C_D - 1$. $C_U \leftarrow C_U + 1$, $f \leftarrow i + 1$. Go to 3

Step 5. If $C_D \neq 0$, perform N K-way merges onto T_{i+1} and T_0 by alternating. $C_D \leftarrow C_D - 1$, $C_U + 1$, $f \leftarrow i$. Go to 3

Step 6. If $F \neq 0$ go to 9

Step 7. If S_K^p is improperly terminated, perform N K-way merges onto T_0 and T_{K-1} by alternating. $f \leftarrow 0$. Go to 11

Step 8. Rewind T_{K-1}, perform a K-way merge onto T_0, rewind T_{K-1}, again perform $(N - 1)$ K-way merges onto T_{K-1} and T_0 by alternating. $f \leftarrow 0$. Go to 11

Step 9. If S_K^p is improperly terminated, rewind T_{i+1}, transfer onto T_0, rewind T_{i+1} again, perform N K-way merges onto T_{i+1} and T_0 by alternating. $f \leftarrow i + 1$. Go to 11

Step 10. Transfer a string from T_{i+1} onto T_0, perform N K-way merges onto T_{i+1} and T_0 by alternating. $f \leftarrow i + 1$

Step 11. Stop. Final string on T_f is $A_{K}p$.

2. General Case

The merge-sort algorithm simulating the minimal tree for arbitrary S is based on a *merging table* constructed recursively as follows:

(1) S is the entry in Row 0 and Column T_K. The parts of the K-part partition on S form the entries of the first row of the table where $\alpha_1 K^{p-1}$ are placed under columns T_1 through T_{α_1} and part S_1 is placed under T_K

(2) If S_i occupies the entry (i, T_K), then the parts of the K-part partition on S_i form row $i + 1$

(3) The last row is reached either when $S_r = 0$ or when $S_r = K^r$ for some r.

Let the two consecutive rows of a merging table be

$$\begin{matrix} K^q & K^q & K^q & \cdots K^q & K^{q+1} & K^{q+1} \cdots K^{q+1} & S_{i-1} \\ K^{q-1} & K^{q-1} & K^{q-1} \cdots & K^{q-1} & K^{q-1} & K^{q-1} \cdots K^q & S_i \end{matrix},$$

where $i = p - q + 1$. Let

$$\begin{matrix} \cdots & T_0 & T_1 & T_2 \cdots & T_{\alpha_i} & T_{\alpha_{i+1}} & T_{\alpha_{i+2}} \cdots & T_{K-1} & T_K \\ \cdots & K^0\, K^0 & \text{—} & \text{—} \cdots & \text{—} & \text{—} & \text{—} \quad \cdots & \text{—} & S_i \\ & \uparrow\ \uparrow & \uparrow & \uparrow & \uparrow & \uparrow & \uparrow & \uparrow & \uparrow \end{matrix}, \qquad \text{(C1)}$$

be the configuration of tapes after processing S_i unit strings to obtain a string of length S_i on T_K. Using Algorithms A and B, obtain α_i strings of length K^{q-1} on tapes T_1 through T_{α_i} and $(\beta_i - 1)$ strings of length K^q on tapes $T_{\alpha_{i+1}}$ through T_{K-2}. Obtain a string of length K^q on T_0. Rewind tapes T_1 through T_{α_i} (and T_K if S_i has the same order as the length K^{q-1} strings) to reach configuration (C2).

$$\begin{matrix} & T_0 & T_1 & T_2 \cdots & T_{\alpha_{i+1}} \cdots & T_{K-1} & T_K \\ \cdots & K^0\, K^0\, K^q & K^{q-1} & K^{q-1} \cdots & K^{q-1}\, K^q \cdots & \text{—} & S_i \\ & \uparrow\ \uparrow & & \uparrow & \uparrow \quad \uparrow & \uparrow & \uparrow \end{matrix}. \qquad \text{(C2)}$$

A K-way merge can now be performed on T_{K-1} to obtain a string of length S_{i-1}. Rewinding T_1 through T_{α_i} (and T_K) and interchanging the roles of T_{K-1} and T_K leads to configuration (C1) again where S_{i-1} replaces S_i. This process can be iterated to consecutively implement the rows of the merging table ending up with a string of length S on T_K. $S_{r-1} < K$ and can be generated on T_K by a partial merge. Note that all length K^{q-1} strings are generated before a length K^q string.

Distribution produces properly terminated subsequences $S_K^p, S_K^{p-1}, S_K^{p-2}, \cdots,$ S_K^1, S_K^0 and juxtaposes them on T_0 in decreasing order of their superscripts so that in a read reverse, between 0 and up to at most $K - 1$, properly terminated S_K^i $(i = 0, 1, 2, \cdots, p)$ are encountered. A string of length K^i is generated from S_K^i and the number of length K^i strings required by the merging table is not necessarily equal to the number of S_K^i subsequences on T_0, hence the additional S_K^i must be obtained from the next-available longer subsequence S_K^j where $j \geq i + 1$. If $(j - i)$ is odd (even) the first S_K^i obtained from S_K^j is improperly (properly) terminated while the remaining $(K - 1)$ subsequences are properly (improperly) terminated. Setting a K-ary counter to S initially and decrementing it by K^i for every S_K^i processed provides information as to the termination of the subsequence to be processed next. In any case, Algorithms A and B can be successfully used to implement any perfect-weight entry of the merging table.

Example 3. Let $S = 271$ and $K = 5$. Distribution produces properly terminated subsequences on T_0 such that

$$S = S_5^3 \quad S_5^3 \quad S_5^1 \quad S_5^1 \quad S_5^1 \quad S_5^1 \quad S_5^0 \ . \tag{13}$$

The merging table is given by

	T_1	T_2	T_3	T_4	T_5
0	—	—	—	—	271
1	5^2	5^2	5^2	5^3	71
2	5	5	5^2	5^2	11
3	1	1	1	5	3
$r = 4$	0	1	1	1	0

The simulation requires the subsequences

$$S_5^0 \quad \underline{S_5^0} \quad \underbrace{S_5^0 \quad S_5^0 \quad S_5^0 \quad S_5^0}_{S_5^1} \quad S_5^1 \quad S_5^1 \quad S_5^1 \quad \underline{S_5^2} \quad \underbrace{S_5^2 \quad S_5^2 \quad S_5^2 \quad S_5^2}_{S_5^3} \quad S_5^3 \ ,$$

in that order which is just the reverse of Eq. (13) when interpreted properly as indicated. The improperly-terminated subsequences are underlined. Implementation of the merging table by repeated application of Algorithms A and B interlaced with K-way merges to generate the strings with lengths 3, 11, 71, and 271 is obvious.

We now establish an upper bound on the total number of unit strings rewound during the implementation of a merging table. Let R_i denote the number of unit strings rewound in implementing row i. Then clearly, R_i is $2.K^{q-1}$ $(2.S_i)$ if S_i and K^{q-1} are in the opposite (same) order and there is at least one K^q; it is $0\,(2.S_i)$ if S_i and K^{q-1} are in the same (opposite) order and K^q is absent. In any case $R_i \leq 2.S_i$. Assume T_K is rewound at every row for the longest-possible strings of lengths corresponding to nonperfect weights so that $\Sigma\, R_i$ is maximum. It can be shown that the merging table in this case has the form

T_1	T_2	$\cdots$	T_{K-1}	T_K
—	—	$\cdots$	—	S
K^{2p}	K^{2p}	$\cdots$	K^{2p}	S_1
K^{2p}	K^{2p}	$\cdots$	K^{2p}	S_2
.	.	.	.	.
.	.	.	.	.
.	.	.	.	.
K^0	K^0	$\cdots$	K^0	S_{2p+1}
K^0	K^0	$\cdots$	K^0	S_{2p+2}

with

$$S = \sum_{j=0}^{p} 2(K-1)K^{2j} = 2(K-1)\,\frac{K^{2p+2}-1}{K^2-1}\ , \tag{14}$$

$$S_{2i} = \sum_{j=0}^{p-1} 2(K-1)K^{2j}\ , \tag{15}$$

$$S_{2i+1} = \sum_{j=0}^{p-i} 2(K-1)K^{2j} - (K-1)K^{2(p-i)}\ , \tag{16}$$

$$S_0 = S, \quad S_{2p+2} = 0, \quad S_{2p+1} = K-1 \qquad (S_1 > K^{2p})\ ,$$

and

$$S_{2i+1} + S_{2i+2} < K^{2(p-i)+1} \qquad (i = 0, 1, 2, \cdots, p)\ . \tag{17}$$

Then

$$\sum R_i = 2\left[\sum_{i=2}^{2p+2} S_i + K^{2p}\right],$$

$$= 2\left[\sum_{i=1}^{p} (S_{2i+1} + S_{2i+2}) + S_2 + K^{2p}\right]. \tag{18}$$

Using Eqs. (17) and (15) with $i = 2$ in Eq. (18) we have

$$\sum R_i = R(S,K) < 2\left[(3K-2)\,\frac{K^{2p}-1}{K^2-1} + K^{2p}\right]. \tag{19}$$

Expressing Eq. (19) in terms of S as given by Eq. (14)

$$R(K,S) < \delta(K)S\ , \tag{20}$$

where

$$\delta(K) \doteq \frac{K^2+3K-3}{K^2(K-1)}\ , \tag{21}$$

to a good approximation. $\delta(K)$ decreases with increasing K, and $\delta(2) = 1.75$, $\delta(5) = 0.37$.

V. COST OF THE SIMILATION

Let $T(S,K)$, $D(S,K)$, and $R(S,K)$ denote respectively the total number of unit strings transferred, dispersed, and rewound. The total cost of the simulation is then

$$C(S,K) = T(S,K) + D(S,K) + \rho R(S,K)\ , \tag{22}$$

where $T(S,K)$ is given by Eq. (11), ρ is the read-write to rewind-speed ratio of the tapes, $R(S,K)$ is given by Eq. (20), and

$$D(S,K) = \sum_{j=1}^{p} a_j \left[K^j \sum_{i=1}^{j} (-1)^{i-1} K^{j-i} \right] + a_0 < S, \tag{23}$$

by Eqs. (4) and (12), and the fact that D_1 strings are not dispersed.

For $\rho \leq 0.25$

$$D(S,K) + \rho R(S,K) \leq S \quad , \tag{24}$$

is insured for all $K \geq 2$, consequently

$$C(S,K) \leq S \lceil \log_K S \rceil - \left\lfloor \frac{K^{\lceil \log_K S \rceil} - S}{K-1} \right\rfloor + S \quad . \tag{25}$$

Equality can be attained very infrequently.

VI. COMPARISONS

The merge-sort method reported here requires more unit-string transfers than the presently-available methods for small values of S because of the dispersion. However, with increasing S the number of passes $\lceil \log_K S \rceil$ does not increase as fast as in the other methods and eventually considerable savings are realized as shown in Tables I through III. Comparisons are made for various pairs of two

TABLE I. Cascade vs minimal-growth-rate merge sort.

$K = 3$				$K = 5$			
S	LOWER BOUND $T(S,K)$	CASCADE (exact)	NEW METHOD (Upper Bound)	S	LOWER BOUND $T(S,K)$	CASCADE	NEW METHOD (Upper Bound)
70	275	350	345	190	652	760	842
71	279	426	350	191	656	955	847
157	742	982	899	671	2,742	3,355	3,413
158	747	1,106	905	672	2,747	4,032	3,419
793	4,854	6,344	5,647	2,353	11,572	14,118	13,925
794	4,862	7,146	5,656	2,354	11,578	16,478	13,932

TABLE II. Polyphase vs minimal-growth-rate merge sort.

$K = 3$				$K = 5$			
S	LOWER BOUND $T(S,K)$	POLY-PHASE (exact)	NEW METHOD (exact)	S	LOWER BOUND $T(S,K)$	POLY-PHASE (exact)	NEW METHOD (exact)
105	456	492	558	129	392	480	515
106	462	541	564	130	397	514	521
355	1,943	2,103	2,260	497	1,956	2,388	2,376
356	1,950	2,403	2,269	498	1,961	2,513	2,383
653	3,880	4,272	4,400	977	4,348	5,220	5,212
654	3,887	4,553	4,408	978	4,354	5,461	5,220
2,209	15,496	17,184	17,205				
2,210	15,505	18,118	17,215				

TABLE III. Oscillating sort vs minimal-growth-rate merge sort.

K = 3				K = 5			
S	LOWER BOUND T(S, K)	OSCIL-LATING SORT	NEW METHOD (Upper Bound)	S	LOWER BOUND T(S, K)	OSCIL-LATING SORT	NEW METHOD (Upper Bound)
32	104	160	136	256	932	1,024	1,188
33	108	198	141	257	936	1,285	1,193
64	248	384	312	1,024	4,594	5,120	5,619
65	252	455	317	1,025	4,600	6,150	5,625
256	1,300	2,048	1,556	4^7	99,253	114,688	115,637
257	1,306	2,313	1,563	$4^7 + 1$	99,260	131,080	115,644
				4^8	455,605	524,288	521,141

successive values of S, the first value corresponding to an ideal-distribution level where the compared method is at its best. The method reported here is competitive with any other method up to a value of S depending on K and the method compared, and becomes more-and-more efficient thereafter.

To analytically compare the present method with the oscillating sort, assume $S = (K-1)^p$ for which the latter is most effective and requires $p(K-1)^p$ unit-string transfers. Since

$$C(S,K) < (K-1)^p \lceil p \log_K (K-1) \rceil + (K-1)^p \ , \tag{26}$$

the present method is always faster if

$$\lceil p \log (K-1) \rceil = p - 1 \ ,$$

i.e., if p satisfies

$$p \geq \frac{1}{1 - \log_K (K-1)} \ . \tag{27}$$

The minimum p satisfying Eq. (27) is 4 for $K = 3$, 5 for $K = 4$, and 8 for $K = 5$. Actually, the present method is always faster than the oscillating sort for all $S \geq (K-1)^{p-1} + 1$ as shown in Table III, where p is given by Eq. (27).

VII. CONCLUSIONS

An exact, theoretical lower bound for the total number of unit-string transfers required in merge sorting S unit strings is established and a new method is presented that attains the lower bound within an additive constant less than S. Comparison of its performance with the presently-available methods indicates that it is preferable especially when the core memory is limited, the file to be sorted is large, and consequently a large number of unit strings are produced by replacement selection.

ACKNOWLEDGEMENTS

The author is grateful to Dr. E. J. Smith for his guidance and to Dr. A. C. McKellar, who introduced the problem, for his valuable suggestions and criticisms.

Research supported by the Air Force Office of Scientific Research, Contract No. F44620-69-C-0047, and by the Scientific and Technical Research Council of Turkey.

This paper was taken in part from the dissertation to be submitted to the Faculty of the Polytechnic Institute of Brooklyn in partial fulfillment of the requirements for the degree of Doctor of Philosophy (Electrical Engineering) in 1972.

REFERENCES

[1] D. E. Knuth, "Sorting and Searching," *The Art of Computer Programming*, **3** (Massachusetts: Addison-Wesley) (to be published).

[2] H. H. Goldstein and J. Von Neumann, "Planning and Coding of Problems for an Electronic Computing Instrument," **II**, Part II, Institute for Advanced Study, Princeton, New Jersey (1948).

[3] B. K. Betz and W. C. Carter, "New Merge-Sorting Techniques," *Proc. 14th National Meeting ACM*, Cambridge, Massachusetts (1959).

[4] R. L. Gilstad, "Polyphase Merge Sorting—An Advanced Technique," *Proc. Eastern Joint Computer Conf.* (1960).

[5] S. W. Reynolds, "A Generalized Polyphase Merge Algorithm," *Comm. ACM*, **4**, 347–349 (August 1961).

[6] A. G. Mendoza, "A Dispersion-Pass Algorithm for the Polyphase Merge," *Comm. ACM*, **5**, 502–04 (1962).

[7] S. Sobel, "Oscillating Sort—A New Merge-Sorting Technique," *J. ACM*, **9**, 372–74 (1962).

[8] R. M. Karp, "On the Complexity of Sorting Using Tapes," *Proc. 3rd Annual Princeton Conf.*, 297 (1969).

[9] D. E. Knuth, "Fundamental Algorithms," *The Art of Computer Programming*, **1** (Massachusetts: Addison-Wesley, 1968).

[10] D. A. Hoffman, "A Method for the Construction of Minimum-Redundancy Codes," *Proc. IRE*, 1088–1101 (September 1952).

[11] E. S. Schwartz, "An Optimum Encoding With Minimum Longest Code and Total Number of Digits," *Information & Control*, **7**, 37–44 (1964).

ARE HUMANLY-RECOGNIZABLE PATTERNS EFFECTIVE?

R. J. Nelson

Department of Philosophy, Case Western Reserve University, Cleveland, OH

This paper argues that any pattern recognizable by a human being is, in principle, recognizable by a digital computer. The paper does not propose yet another scheme for pattern recognition, but only gives plausibility arguments against those critics of pattern recognition who have argued from Gestalt psychology and from phenomenology and existentialist philosophy.

A basic thesis is that questions of the effectiveness of nondigital patterns can always be reduced to the questions of digital patterns. Another thesis is that the properties of patterns on which recognition depends are preserved under the reduction. Given these theses, the paper goes on to show that Turing machines exist for recognizing all the hard cases of patterns presented by the Gestaltists. For example, computers can represent the realizations of two distinct patterns in one set of objects and conversely, can find one pattern in two disjoint sets of objects. Likewise, it is possible for a computer (Turing machine) to have "expectations about wholes"; that is to say, to fill in underdetermined parts on the basis of a grasp of the whole. This is based on a simple variation of the idea of a machine which knows its own structure.

In this paper I will consider the question: "Are humanly recognizable patterns effective?" or "Can a computer recognize anything a human being can?" After introducing some needed basic technical material, I will consider this question in the light of certain negative points raised by H. Dreyfus [1], and conclude that humanly-recognizable patterns are *effective*. The conclusion results from a *plausibility argument*, certainly not from anything like a proof.

I. INTRODUCTION

A recognizer is a 5-tuple $\langle \mathbf{I}, \mathbf{Q}, \mathbf{f}, \mathbf{f}', \mathbf{Q}' \rangle$. $\mathbf{I}$ is a nonempty set of *individuals* or *objects*. Each individual is a whole of parts.

Example 1. A *sentence* is a whole of parts. In such a case a collection of individuals (sentences) $\mathbf{I}$ is a subset of $\mathbf{A}^*$ where $\mathbf{A}$ is the set of parts. In automata theory, $\mathbf{A}$ is the terminal alphabet.

Example 2. The individual inscription △◯, which for some perceivers is a whole of parts A′, and for others a whole of parts △ and ◯.

In Example 1 the parts are arranged by concatenation, and in Example 2, for one perceiver, by a kind of two-dimensional concatenation, and for the other perceiver by a kind of insertion.

Presented at the Symposium on Computers and Automata
Polytechnic Institute of Brooklyn, April 13–15, 1971.

An individual $\mathbf{x}$ and an individual $\mathbf{y}$ are *epistemically* the same iff whatever is true of one is true of the other, a form of the Principle of Leibnitz. In recognition theory a different criterion of identity is needed. Let $\mathbf{A}$ be the union of all sets $\mathbf{A}_i$ of parts belonging to perceivers $\mathbf{Z}_i$. Partition $\mathbf{A}$ into equivalence classes of parts (presumably by such "natural" properties as "thin, pink, circular disk about 1 in. in diameter"). Then two parts are the same iff they come from the same class. Two individuals are *perceptually the same* iff they are made up of the same parts arranged in the same way. In automata and language theory two individuals are perceptually the same if there is a pairing of same parts such that each element of each pair occurs in the same place in two instances of a concatenation. This can easily be made precise. However for more complicated wholes where the principle of organization is not so simple as concatenation, the idea must remain on a more-or-less-intuitive level until there is a mathematical theory of wholes and parts. In this paper "same individual" will always mean "perceptually the same individual."

A *pattern* is an observable physical property of individuals. Patterns $\mathbf{P}$ and $\mathbf{P}'$ are *epistemically* the same iff anything which is an instance of $\mathbf{P}$ is an instance of $\mathbf{P}'$ and vice versa. Assuming a clear meaning of "perceive the same way" (which we can partially obtain later for automata), $\mathbf{P}$ and $\mathbf{P}'$ are *perceptually the same* iff they are perceived in the same way. In this paper "same pattern" will always mean "perceptually the same pattern."

Using these distinctions one can talk about two different individuals being instances (tokens) of the same pattern (the same melody played in two different keys); and also about one and the same individual being an instance of two patterns (types) (an acoustical sequence perceived as one sound pattern by one perceiver and another by another).

$\mathbf{Q}$ is a nonempty set of perceiver *states*. $\mathbf{f}$ is the *perception function*. A perceiver perceives an individual $\mathbf{x} \in \mathbf{I}_p$ iff there is a $\mathbf{q} \in \mathbf{Q}$ such that $\mathbf{f}(\mathbf{x}) = \mathbf{q}$.

$\mathbf{Q}' \subseteq \mathbf{Q}$ is the set of recognizing states. $\mathbf{f}'$ is $\mathbf{f}$ restricted to $\mathbf{I}_p'$, a subdomain of $\mathbf{I}_p$ determined by some pattern type. A perceiver *recognizes* $\mathbf{x} \in \mathbf{I}_p'$ iff $\mathbf{f}'(\mathbf{x}) \in \mathbf{Q}'$. A pattern is *recognizable* iff there is a perceiver $\mathbf{Z}$ such that every instance (token) of the pattern (type) is recognized by $\mathbf{Z}$.

It should be noted that a perceiver can perceive without recognition, and that he can be *sensorially aware* of individuals $\mathbf{x} \in \mathbf{I}$ without $\mathbf{x}$ also being in $\mathbf{I}_p$; that is to say, perception is not necessarily defined for all $\mathbf{x} \in \mathbf{I}$. In automata theory this corresponds to the case where $\mathbf{I}$ is recursively enumerable rather than recursive; in the case of human perception it means that the human perceiver may *sense* without perceiving.

We make the assumptions that a perceiver can recognize at most one pattern, that it never errs, and that if it is a learning machine or organism we question its perceptual capabilities after it has learned and not before.

A recognizer as just defined is a generalization of a Turing machine recognizer. A *Turing machine recognizer* (TMR) is a recognizer such that the base alphabet $\mathbf{A}$ of $\mathbf{I}$ and the state sets are finite. The individuals of $\mathbf{I}$ are concatenations of the parts of $\mathbf{A}$. Moreover for TMR an object to be perceived is inscribed on $\mathbf{n}$ tapes, each one corresponding to a sense realm, from which the TMR reads input (an $\mathbf{n}$-tuple at a time) and on which it prints. We suppose, as usual, that the TMR can move each tape independently one square at a time, right or left.

The perception function of a TMR is determined by its *computations*. A *computation* is a finite sequence of TMR steps beginning in an initial instantaneous description (in perception theory, an *individual*), and by following quadruple rules either ending in a state or computing forever. The collection of such sequences as end in a state determines the perception function **f**. Its domain is the set of all objects **x** such that **qx** (**q** the initial state and **x** the input word or object to be perceived) goes into a terminal word $\cdots$ **q** $\cdots$, and its range **Q** is the set of such **q**'s.

The recognition function **f′** is **f** restricted to the subdomain of objects **x** such that **qx** goes under quadruple action into one of the recognizing states **q′** of **Q′**. A TMR **Z** *recognizes* x iff $f'(x) \in Q'$. A pattern **P** is TMR *recognizable* iff there is a TMR **Z** such that every token **x** of the pattern type **P** is such that **Z** recognizes **x**.

Equivalently a pattern is *effective* (or effectively recognizable) iff there is a TMR that recognizes it.

II. EFFECTIVENESS

In mathematics *effective* is explicated by Church's thesis which says that a function (set, or property) of integers is effective iff it is partially recursive. Functions (sets, properties (patterns)) of other objects such as physical individuals are effective iff their Gödel numbers form rec. en. sets. Since Gödel functions are defined only for concatenated wholes of parts just such (sets of) individuals are, properly speaking, effective. We will call such sets, sets of pairs (functions), etc., effective$_1$.

A pattern may be "noneffective$_1$" in two senses: first, its instances are digital words (concatenations), but there is no recognizing TMR; second, its individual instances are not words but more complicated configurations such as in Example 2. In the latter case it would be meaningless to talk about digital-computer recognition without some kind of scheme for transforming patterns into digital form or equivalently into automaton words.†

Engineers count many other kinds of objects or processes as mechanical or "effective", e.g., analog-to-digital conversion, which is effective since it can be accomplished by various kinds of physical devices. The domains of such transformations may be digital or continuous wholes or very complicated structures of discrete parts. We will call processes such as conversion or digitizing transduction "effective$_2$". The domains of such transformations are effective$_2$. Every effective$_1$ pattern is effective$_2$ but not conversely.

Example 3. A device for "digitizing" the set of patterns whose type is $\mathbb{A}$ would be an effective$_2$ transformation, and the set of tokens would be an effective$_2$ set.

In order to talk about TMR pattern recognition for arbitrary, not necessarily automaton-word patterns, we will need a pair of reduction assumptions which are

† Perceptron-like recognizers are functions with digital ranges and nondigital domains. They are compositions, in effect, of our effective$_2$ transformations to be introduced below and our TMR recognizers.

suggested by engineering practice (also by Gödel numbering) which enable one to cast questions about effectiveness$_2$ into ones about effectiveness$_1$.

Reduction Thesis I

Let **O** be an arbitrary set of individuals (determined by some pattern). **O** is effective$_2$ if there is a TMR **Z** with alphabet **A** and an effective$_2$ function **T** whose domain includes **O** and whose codomain is the set of all words on **A** such that the direct image **T**(**O**) of **T** is the subset of **A** recognized by **Z**, i.e., is effective$_1$.

Note that **T** is not necessarily one-one, in dysanalogy to Gödel functions, as we have to allow for the possibility that **O** be nondenumerable. This simply means, however, that to keep things straight a Turing machine (or a computer) need only keep track of what pattern instance $\mathbf{o} \in \mathbf{O}$ $\mathbf{T}(\mathbf{o})$ is an image of.

Reduction Thesis II

The function **T** preserves the properties of patterns on which recognition depends; furthermore it preserves degradations, distortions, displacements, etc. of various kinds occurring in the patterns to be recognized.†

III. GESTALT PATTERNS

I will now argue that certain hard properties of patterns, held by some to render the patterns noneffective$_2$ yet humanly recognizable, are all manageable by TMR in the sense that the latter can recognize digital surrogates of the patterns in which such properties are preserved (Thesis II). Since TMR can recognize such hard patterns, so can digital computers, because digital computers (provided they can be equipped with any amount of tape) are behaviorally equivalent to Turing machines.

The following is a list of properties of patterns which allegedly preclude computer recognition [1]. These properties are of the kind often emphasized by Gestalt psychologists in their treatments of perception.

(a) Human beings can recognize family resemblances where no two individuals have exactly the same traits in common
(b) For some patterns there exist other, different, patterns made up of the same parts
(c) The whole of a pattern instance may be discernible even if made up of entirely different parts in one token than in another
(d) A pattern token whole may determine the parts rather than the parts the whole
(e) Salient properties of tokens on which recognition depends are pre-

†I am aware of the difficulties involved in making any precise sense at all out to the notion of transformations which preserve, for example, the property of curving to the left in a range constituted of digital objects, that is to say of linearly-concatenated wholes. Yet practitioners of artificial intelligence do invent such transformations, and therefore it seems acceptable to assume the techniques could be formally regimented for our purposes.

served under various deformations such as dilations and compressions and under transformations such as rotation and displacement. I omit discussion of this case as there already is considerable literature on the topic. See for example [2] and further literature cited there.

(a) Human beings can recognize family resemblances where no two individuals have exactly the same traits in common.

According to Dreyfus we can "recognize such similarities by picking out a typical case and introducing intermediate cases." A computer, however, can only recognize by use of a specific list of traits, not by the use of paradigms and context [1, p. 19].

Let us assume (falsely) that **x** resembles **y** is transitive. If the family is infinite there must be members (token instances of the pattern determining the family) which are unrecognizable since the observer certainly could not introduce an infinite number of intermediate cases. So the family must be finite if it is humanly recognizable. But every finite set is recursive. So there is a TMR that can recognize any such pattern.

(b) For some patterns there exist other, different patterns made up of the same parts. As worded this is trivial. Suppose **Z** recognizes patterns 010101 ··· and **Z′** 100100100 ··· . Both have the same alphabet (parts).

However (b) may mean that one and the same individual could be perceived by two perceivers differently: the individual could be a token in two respects. More strongly, (b) could be interpreted to mean that one and the same *set* of objects may constitute the tokens of a certain type for one perceiver and the tokens of a different type for a second.

As an example of the second interpretation take "the same physical constellation of sound waves is heard as quite different phonemes depending on the expected meaning" [1, p. 17]. Here again the situation is trivial, since one and the same thing can be an element of two sets. More relevantly, the word 010 might be a token of the pattern for **Z**: having one occurrence of 1; or of the different pattern for **Z′**: $0^n 10^n$. In the case of sound waves provided there is an appropriate transformation **T** (Thesis I), the digital image of the waves could be interpreted as two different pattern tokens; one and the same constellation could be "heard" by TMR as perceptually-different phonemes.

In the stronger (third) interpretation, we seem to have a more complicated case than Gestalters have in mind. Identically the *same set* of individuals may be recognized by one perceiver as one type and by another as a different type. There are two cases, one rather simple.

(b.1) One perceiver might identify a whole by concentrating on one cluster of parts while another identify the same whole by a different one. In a degenerate sense there are two patterns involved. Van Gogh's paintings of the Arles period could all be identified by one perceiver as embodying a certain very distinctive, rather gross brush stroke; and by another as embodying a certain very distinctive hue of yellow. As a model let **Z** and **Z′** share the alphabet {**a**, **b**, **c**, **d**}, and let the pattern be: having an occurrence of an **a** and a **b**. Let the perceptual objects be the subset of {**a**, **b**, **c**, **d**}*, including all of this set less those words having single occurrences of **a** and no **b**'s or conversely. **Z** recognizes by finding **a**'s and **Z′** by finding **b**'s.

(b.2) Now let us consider the case wherein the individuals of a set are taken as instances of two entirely-different patterns. For the first time we need to heed our distinction between epistemic and perceptual sameness of patterns. The pattern types $(01)^n$ and $(100)^n$ are epistemically different, and by construction of two recognizing machines one can see that they perceive in different ways, by almost any conceivable criterion, and hence the patterns are also perceptually different.

However, cases of the opposite kind present a problem. If a set is determined by a pattern and yet is recognized in two different ways (recognized as a set of instances of two patterns), then we need some criterion of "difference" other than a given epistemic difference since there is no epistemic difference in the case. (The two pattern types have the same set of tokens in common). We must supply, now, an adequate definition of "perceive in the same way," as promised.

It is tempting to try to capture this case by specifying that two TMRs perceive differently if one is not the homomorphic image of the other. Two such TMRs could of course be equivalent in the sense of defining the same sets of words. This attack would solve the problem, as it would afford a natural way of saying that the two TMRs perceive the same things differently. However there is no received, useful concept of homomorphism in general for TMRs (there is, of course, for such automata as finite automata). This is so (at least for recognizers) for the following reason. If one defines "homomorphism" for TMRs in the usual mathematical way then it is easy to find two nonhomomorphic machines which are exactly the same in their modes of computation except possibly for small, irrelevant, computational excursions. Take, for example, a TMR which recognizes $0^n 10^n$ but which when in state **q** scanning an end marker goes to the right on tape, writes the first line of its favorite poem, erases it, moves back past the end marker and goes back to work. No one would say that this machine recognizes instances any differently than a certain standard TMR which does not indulge itself in such recreations. Yet the machines are not homomorphic.

A more promising attack on an analysis of "perceive in the same way" is based on the observation that two or more partially-computable functions defined on the same domain are computed in different ways. From this observation there in fact follows a procedure for constructing two computationally different TMRs for recognizing a common set. Unfortunately two quite different machines can be designed to compute one function, so it is not reasonable to *define* "perceive in the same way" as "compute in the same way." However "compute in a different way" is a *necessary* condition for "perceive in a different way." It follows that just as there may be several functions on a common domain, so there are different ways of perceiving a common pattern. Thus in principle there is nothing to bar construction of two TMRs that hear the instances of the same set of acoustical sequences as quite different sets of phonemic sequences.

(c) A pattern whole may be discernible even if made up of entirely different parts in one token than in another.

There are two interpretations here, both trivial to handle. The tokens 1, 010, 0100, · · · all differ perceptually and have different parts (e.g., neither of the first two have a part 100) yet they are all tokens of the same pattern $0^n 10^n$. A slightly more interesting interpretation of (c) is that the *alphabetic parts* be different. But two TMRs can be exactly the same to within alphabets.

Here the notion of TMR isomorphism is useful (although mathematically barren) for we can always construct, for a given TMR, another isomorphic one with a different alphabet, which perceives the same pattern because it *computes the same*. Assuming one could overcome the difficulty of correctly defining a transformation to reduce sound patterns to digital words (reduction Thesis I) a computer could recognize a melody (pattern) in one key as well as another in principle.

(d) A pattern-token whole may determine the parts rather than the parts the whole.

Our discussion about (d) will lead to an analysis of expectations in terms of TMRs. Before turning to this main task, however, I wish to point out two mistakes made by Gestalters. Since it may have characteristics independent of the specific nature of the parts, it is sometimes claimed that the whole determines all of the parts, or better, how all of the parts shall be taken by a perceiver. A classic statement of this view as follows:

> There are wholes, the behavior of which is not determined by that of their individual elements, but where the part-processes are themselves determined by the intrinsic nature of the whole [3].

Dreyfus extends this from a relatively modest "there are" to a universal thesis:

> In recognizing a melody, the notes get the values they have by being recognized as part of the melody, rather than the melody's being built up out of independently-recognized notes. (Likewise in perception of objects there are *no* (ital. mine) neutral traits. The same hazy layer which I would see as dust if I thought I was confronting a wax apple might appear as moisture if I thought I was seeing a fresh apple. The significance of the details and indeed their very look is determined by my perception of the whole [1, p. 17].

If this means merely that one can recognize a melody independently of the specific character of the notes (e.g., the key), then as we have already seen, computers are in Case (c), above. If, on the other hand, it means that whenever notes or other parts are missing during a listening the human listener can supply them or hear them, then the statement is simply mistaken. Many musical people can recognize a Bach four-voice fugue and yet can not reproduce a part (say, a voice, or even a measure or two) in its entirety in their heads. There are other people who are so gifted as to be able to identify such parts from a grasp of the whole, but surely this involves a special aptitude, not shared by all people, which goes considerably beyond the modest skill of recognizing the fugue transposed to another key or of expecting immediately later sections of the performance.

Gestalters may mean that the whole, being more than the sum of the parts, has certain emergent traits which are missed by an examination of the constituent parts alone, traits by which the pattern as a whole is recognized, and which when perceived determine the parts as perceived by the perceiver. Apparently some such traits of the whole as such constitute what Wertheimer termed in the above passage "the intrinsic whole." I maintain that such traits are either "the way way the pattern is organized" or are themselves observable physical parts that emerge from the bringing together of basic parts (e.g., the fourth triangular part of a figure formed by connecting the vertices at the bases of three congruent, equilateral triangles). If the first is the case our answer to Case (c) will also suffice here; if the second, the emergent part is simply another key to recognition: even though emergence be something of a mystery (which I deny) a trait once emerged is as good as any other as a basis for recognition. I recognize water by properties of water as such, some of which, presumably, are not predictable from my knowledge of the properties of hydrogen and oxygen; but these water properties are nonetheless physically observable and the possible bases for the recognition of water.

I conclude that generally not all perceivers can in every case supply missing parts from a grasp of the whole, and that recognition based on emergent properties is already accounted for in our machine theory.

Perceivers do, however, have expectations about objects they perceive. They do sometimes perceive wholes with missing parts and are able to fill in such parts. We do give "global meanings" to perceptual objects on the basis of which we have certain expectations. If the expectations are fulfilled, then the "global meaning" and the parts do become more determinate.

We proceed with an analysis of "expectation" in terms, to begin, of finite automata. A finite automaton, in accepting an input, is always either in a state such that further input segments could lead to a recognizing state or not. If the state could transit to a recognizing state then the state is a *winner*. An automaton *expects* a part **x** of a whole **xy** iff it is in a winning state **q** such that there is a computation from **qx** to **q**′ and **q**′ is a winner. By this definition an automaton could expect a class of sequences, and its expectations could be fulfilled by any member of the class.

Example 4. Suppose an automaton recognizes sequences having exactly one occurrence of a 1 (all other symbols are 0's). If presented with a sequence of 0's, it would be in a winning state. It would expect any sequence having at most one member 1.

Without going into the details here, let us suppose we have extended this definition of "winner" to the class of all Turing machines.

In the machines to be described shortly we require the ability to *pick a winner,* an ability on the part of a machine to tell whether or not one of its own states can be driven to a recognizing state. Now if a Turing machine could determine this about its own states, it could solve its own halting problem. However, since the halting problem is recursively unsolvable, our machines can not, in general, pick winners. This allows us two alternatives: (i) Restrict the theory to machines for which there is an effective procedure for picking winners; or (ii) Make the assumption that human beings could so detect such states, and mark them accordingly in the machine design, providing in this way capability for a machine to operate in the manner presently to be described. We choose Case (i) since to adopt Case (ii) is to beg an abstract version of the question with which this very paper is concerned. The machines on which we focus the discussion now are TMRs which are equivalent to (can recognize the same pattern as) some push-down automaton. The reason for this choice is that the push-down machines are the strongest machines (in the sense of the Chomsky hierarchy) for which the winner-decision problem is solvable.†

†This assertion follows directly from the well-known solvability results for context-free grammars.

Let **Z** be a Turing machine including (in its quadruples) a TMR $\mathbf{Z}_p$ which latter is equivalent to a pushdown automaton. A *special blank* β is a member of **Z**'s alphabet, but not of $\mathbf{Z}_p$'s. This symbol may be interpreted as the transform under a transformation **T** (Reduction Thesis II) of degenerate or degraded parts of patterns. Occurrences of β may be regarded as the not-fully-perceivable (to $\mathbf{Z}_p$) indeterminate parts which can occur in pattern Gestalten. Let the quadruples of $\mathbf{Z}_p$ be coded on **Z**'s tape—in a special section reserved for such storage, and not to be used in the perception computations.

Z begins computation in the initial state and follows the rules $\mathbf{Z}_p$ until a special blank occurs. If **Z** encounters a special blank, it then determines whether its present state **q** (a state of $\mathbf{Z}_p$) is a winner. If not, **Z** halts, and since **q** is not a winner it is not a recognizing state—**Z** halts without recognition. If **q** is a winner, **Z** goes into a routine which determines it to survey the quadruple list of $\mathbf{Z}_p$ on tape, locating all of those quadruples having **q** as the first component. It then chooses either at random or by a preplanned policy any one of the alphabetic symbols occurring in the second-component position of this selected set of quadruples which would take the machine into another (perhaps the same) winning state. The symbol selected is then printed by **Z** over the special blank and returns to state **q** to resume normal $\mathbf{Z}_p$ computation.†

I maintain, even on the basis of this rough sketch, that such a machine can "use underdetermined expectations of the whole in order to determine the elements of a whole" *in principle* as well as human perceivers. For nontemporal patterns, such as geometrical shapes, much more elaborate means such as repeated scans over the token could be introduced to render determinate degraded parts. Certainly such a TMR would not always "fill in wholes" the way a human being would. A computer might on occasion fill in a degraded individual whole so as to end up recognizing it as a token, while a human perceiver might not, and vice versa. But I question whether there are any grounds for selecting a human rather than a computer perceiver as a standard of what is or is not a token in such circumstances of degraded recognition unless one knows the intentions of the designer.

REFERENCES

[1] H. L. Dreyfus, "Why Computers Must Have Bodies in Order to Be Intelligent," *Rev. Metaphys.*, **21**, 13–32 (1967).

[2] M. Minsky and S. Papert, *Perceptrons: An Introduction to Computational Geometry* (Massachusetts: MIT Press, 1969).

[3] M. Wertheimer, "Gestalt Theory," *Social Res.*, **11**, 93 (1944).

†Of course Z can be designed so that it "knows" when it is in a winning state, if it is simple enough for the designer to make such a determination. Also, the quadruple-list search can be built into Z without the prior encoding on tape unless Z contains the sum of *many* recognizers Z_p—that is to say, unless Z recognizes many patterns. We do not deal with such machines here.

SIMILARITIES IN GAMES AND THEIR USE IN STRATEGY CONSTRUCTION

Ranan B. Banerji
Case Western Reserve University, Cleveland, OH

It is well-known that the ease with which a problem can be solved depends on the representation of the problem. If automatic changes of representation can be expected to yield an easier solution method, the method of change must be based on a precise understanding of how change of representation changes one game to another. The present paper is an attempt towards such an understanding.

A game is defined as a mathematical structure satisfying certain axioms. Most board games of pure skill satisfy these axioms. The major components of this structure are a set of "game states" and a binary relation on it called "moves". A "strategy" is defined to be a function which indicates a move choice.

A relation between two games is called an "s_0-morphism" if whenever two states reachable from a state s_0 are connected by a move, then any state homomorphically related to the first is connected to some state homomorphically related to the second. It has been shown that if a winning strategy exists for a reachable state of the first game, then one exists for each state in the second game homomorphically related to it.

If a game has no "draw" states and possesses certain symmetries, then one can obtain a graph which is a kind of "folded version" of the original move-graph which is sufficient to define the game. In these cases a winning strategy can be easily constructed from the Grundy function of this folded graph. In this case one can define a map between two games (the "D-morphism") which preserve the Grundy function. The relation between D-morphisms and s_0-morphisms is not that of one being a special case of the other but rather of being two generalizations of a certain mapping in two different ways. The D-morphism is a map, while the s_0-morphism is a relation. But the way moves are preserved by the two are entirely different.

Two classes of games have been isolated: the "graph-interpretable decomposable" and the "positional". Any game in either of the two classes have easy winning strategies. Hence it is of interest to know when a given game is related to some positional or decomposable game by either of the two previous homomorphisms. Conditions for a game to have such homomorphisms have been introduced. That is, it has been proven that if a game has certain congruence-like structures on them, then they have decomposable and positional homomorphic images according to the rules for wins.

On this basis, existence of homomorphisms between games has been suggested as a definition of similarity. It has been shown that defining similarity by similarity of rules may not lead to any useful strategy construction.

I. INTRODUCTION

It is becoming increasingly clear among workers in Artificial Intelligence that the ease with which a problem can be solved depends heavily on the way in which it is represented. People are beginning to contemplate the possibility of mechanically transforming the representation of a problem and thereby making it more amenable to solution.

Presented at the Symposium on Computers and Automata
Polytechnic Institute of Brooklyn, April 13-15, 1971.

What is called "change of representation" in the field has various theoretical interpretations [1]: In this paper we shall be concerned mainly with that interpretation where the structures of a problem are actually different in two representations. Amarel [2] has shown how the two structures can often have a homomorphism-like relationship between them. Newell [3] has shown how certain games, represented properly, can be considered isomorphic to tic-tac-toe. Such isomorphisms are often special cases of what is a rather general relational homomorphism; one of Newell's examples can quite readily give rise to a relation rather than a one-one map as in isomorphic structures. However, in some cases this relational homomorphism takes the form of a function or even a one-one map. In these cases the other aspect of representation becomes important, i.e., the aspect of a change in the language which describes the game space. We shall have further occasion to comment on this.

The phenomenon where a homomorphism (a change of representation) exists between two "similar" games should not be confused with the phenomenon where the same solution strategy is applicable to a class of games having certain properties. Very often it is advantageous to detect the existence of homomorphisms from a given game to any member of such a class of ("similar") games rather than to a specific game. The detection of such homomorphisms often can be done in terms of the above second interpretation of representation change, i.e., the isolation of a proper set of predicates in the language describing the game.

Starting from the next section we shall endeavor to give precise meanings to various kinds of homomorphisms and show how these can help in constructing strategies for games. In Section II we shall indicate two kinds of homomorphisms between games which help us to build strategies. To do this, we shall, of course, have to make the idea of games and strategies precise.

In Section III we shall introduce two rather-wide classes of games for which winning strategies are known and show that games which have homomorphisms with any members of these classes of games exhibit certain structural properties which, when recognized, indicate the existence of these homomorphisms.

Since many people in the field believe that precision of this kind defeats the kind of generality that the field of Artificial Intelligence aspires to, we shall have occasion to indicate, in Section IV, how the techniques of simplification which are available to one of the classes of games are completely useless (even after drastic modifications) for games which are very similar to this class. Without a precise theory, one might be tempted to apply the class-specific strategy to these latter games with no results. Minsky and Papert [11] have recently shown how precise analysis of certain problems in the pattern recognition field might have saved lots of wasted effort. Hence our effort at precision.

Our claim here is not that the results of this paper are in any way of lasting use to the general area of Artificial Intelligence. But we do believe that significant progress can not be made in the area merely on the basis of brilliant new ideas. The painstaking examinations and follow-ups of these ideas as they occur are equally important.

II. GAMES, STRATEGIES, AND HOMOMORPHISMS

We shall adopt the following abstract model for a two-person board game G. We are given a set S of "game states" and a binary relation R of "valid moves" on S. In addition, a subset of P of S is given, designated "player's moves" (the completement of P are the "opponents' moves"). W and L are the winning and losing states (for the player); for the opponent the roles are reversed, but we shall always take the "player's" point of view.

The axioms below express the fact that there is no legal move from winning or losing states (even though they will still be said to be either the players or the opponents move.) The players play alternately and either the player or the opponent can win only if he had been the last one to make a move. Thus the 5-tuple $\langle S, R, P, W, L \rangle = G$ satisfies the following axioms:

(G1) $(W \cup L) \cap R^{-1}(S) = \phi$
(G2) $L \subseteq P$
(G3) $W \cap P = \phi$
(G4) $sRt \longrightarrow s \in P \equiv t \notin P$.

Any such abstract structure is called a *game*. It can be readily seen that most two-person board games of pure skill fulfill these axioms.

We now proceed to give a definition of the word "strategy". In the field of Artificial Intelligence this word is used in various, albeit similar, senses. The definition below will be unlike most of them in that it will not model any search process. It may be looked upon as an indicator of the move that would be chosen by an A.I.-type search heuristic endowed with a perfect evaluation function. Our justification in doing this lies in our belief that approximate evaluation functions will be easier to analyze only if one can understand perfect strategies. It is to be recalled that the theory of approximate numerical solutions of equations is based heavily on the exact theory of equations.

DEFINITION. *A* Strategy *Q is a partial function on P which obeys the two following axioms*:

(S1) $Q(s) = t \longrightarrow sRt$
(S2) $Q(s) = t$, *tRu, and $u \in R^{-1}(S) \longrightarrow Q(s)$ is defined.*

The two axioms say that the strategy always predicts real moves and if it is defined for a state, then it is defined for every "non-dead-end" state which can be reached from that state on application of the strategy.

It will be noticed that we do not insist on a strategy being useful for winning. This, of course, is in keeping with game-theory literature [12]; also this allows us, for future purposes, to have a strategy space over which searches and optimization may be possible. But that is for some coveted later date.

Meanwhile, let us define a strategy as "winning" when anytime a win is possible, the strategy yields a win in the long run. To do this, we need an auxiliary definition.

DEFINITION. *Given $s \in P$ and a strategy Q, a sequence of states* $\{s_1, s_2, s_3, \cdots\}$ *is called a Q*-sequence *for s if $s_1 = s$, for each odd i, $Q(s_i) = s_{i+1}$ and for all i, $s_i R s_{i+1}$.*

A Q-sequence represents a possible play which could result if one applied the strategy.

DEFINITION. *A strategy Q is called* winning *for s if for every Q sequence for s there is an n such that $s_n \in W$. Clearly such a Q-sequence would be finite.*

It can also be seen on the basis of (G3) and (G4) above that n is even.

We are now in a position to indicate what it would mean to have a relationship between two games such that a winning strategy for one can be transferred to the other. What we shall say is that given such a relation between the two sets of game states, if there is a winning strategy for a state in one game, there will be one for any related state in the other game. Instead of doing this formally here, we shall introduce a specific relation which preserves strategies and the proof of the strategy preservation will indicate how the strategy for one can actually be constructed if the strategy for the other is known. In the construction of this homomorphism, we have been influenced by the fact that the similarity between two games often depends heavily on the state at which they are supposed to start. That is, if one of the games starts at some state other than this given specific state, it might take a course of play over a part of the state space which has very little similarity with the other game. We shall therefore include the set of states reachable from a specific starting state an important part of our definition.

DEFINITION. *Given a game* $G = \langle S, R, P, W, L \rangle$ *and* $s_0 \in S$, *the set of states reachable from it will be denoted by* $\hat{R}(s_0)$, *where* $\hat{R}$ *is the transitive closure of the move relation* R.

DEFINITION. *Given two games* $G = \langle S, R, P, W, L \rangle$ *and* $G = \langle S', R', P', W', L' \rangle$ *and* $s_0 \in S$, *a relation* $h \subseteq S \times S'$ *will be called an* s_0-morphism *from G to G iff*:

$$\text{(H1)}\quad s \in \hat{R}(s_0)\ \&\ s' \in h(s)\ \&\ s'R't' \longrightarrow (\exists t)\,(sRt\ \&\ t' \in h(t))$$
$$\text{(H2)}\quad s \in \hat{R}(s_0)\ \&\ sRt\ \&\ s' \in h(s) \longrightarrow (\exists t')\,(s'R't'\ \&\ t' \in h(t))$$
$$\text{(H3)}\quad s \in \hat{R}(s_0)\ \&\ s' \in h(s) \longrightarrow ((s \in W \equiv s' \in W')\ \&\ (s \in L \equiv s' \in L'))$$
$$\text{(H4)}\quad s \in \hat{R}(s_0)\ \&\ s' \in h(s) \longrightarrow (s \in P \equiv s' \in P').$$

Figure 1 shows two games which have an s_0-morphism between them (a more

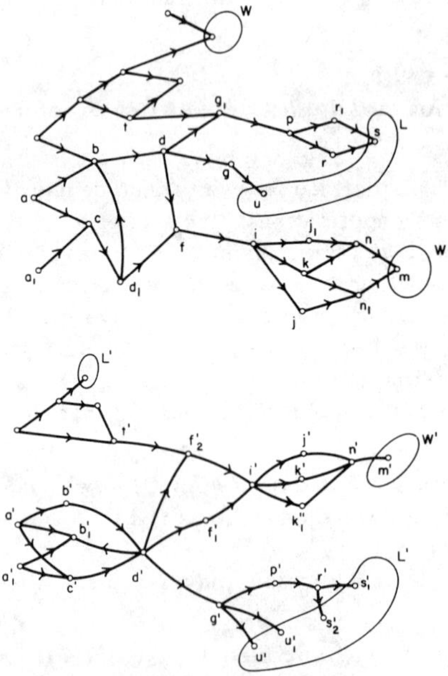

Fig. 1. Example of an *a*-morphism.

realistic example will be given later). The games are shown as two graphs. The set P has not been shown in either. The states in the range and domain of the homorphism have been labeled by letters. States labeled by the same letters (albeit with subscripts and primes) in the two graphs show the related nodes. It will be noted that although t is connected to g_1, t' is not connected to any node related to g_1. This is because Figure 1 portrays an a-morphism and t is not a member of $\hat{R}(a)$. It will also be noted in various places that the two games do not satisfy sRt & $s' \in h(s)$ & $t' \in t(s) \longrightarrow s'R't'$, but the weaker condition (H1); similarly for (H2).

Before proving the first theorem in this paper it will be necessary to introduce one more concept.

Given any strategy Q one can define a partial order $\leq_Q$ on P as follows: $s \leq_Q t$ if and only if either $s = t$ or there exists an $s_0 \in S$ such that Q is a winning strategy for s_0, and for some odd i and $j(i > j)$ in some winning sequence $\{s_1, s_2, s_3, \cdots\}$ for s_0, $s = s_i$ and $t = s_j$, i.e., t occurs "before" s in some winning sequence. It can be readily seen that $\leq_Q$ is a partial order which obeys the minimality conditions.

THEOREM 1. *If there is an s_0-morphism h from game $G = \langle S, R, P, W, L \rangle$ to game $G' = \langle S', R', P', W', L' \rangle$ and there is a winning strategy Q for $s \in \hat{R}(s_0)$, then there is a strategy Q' which is winning for each $s' \in h(s)$. Conversely, if Q' is a winning strategy for $s' \in S'$ then there is a winning strategy Q for every s such that $s \in \hat{R}(s_0)$ and $s' \in h(s)$.*

Proof. First we shall prove that Q is winning for s implies the existence of Q'. The proof will be by induction over the partial order $\leq_Q$ defined above. If s is a minimal element of this ordering, then, since Q is winning for s, $Q(s)$ is defined. Also, if there is t such that $Q(s)Rt$, then $t \leq_Q s$. Hence, there is no such t and $Q(s) \in W$, since otherwise, s, $Q(s)$ would be a Q-sequence which is not winning.

Now let $s' \in h(s)$; then by (H2), there is a t' such that $t' \in h(Q(s))$ and $s'R't'$. Define any Q' on P' such that $Q'(s') = t'$. By (H3) and $Q(s) \in W$, $t' \in W'$ and Q' is winning for s'.

Assume that if there is a strategy Q, which is winning for each $t <_Q s$, then there is a strategy Q', which is winning for every $t' \in h(t)$ such that $t <_Q s$. Now since Q is winning for s, Q is winning for each t such that $t <_Q s$.

Since $sRQ(s)$, and $s \in \hat{R}(s_0)$ there is by (H2) a $t' \in h(Q(s))$ such that $s'R't'$. Let $t'R'u'$. By the induction hypothesis we have that there is a Q' which is winning for u'. From this Q' we can construct, as follows, a strategy Q^*, which is winning for s': If $s' <_Q u'$ then $Q^*(s') = Q'(s')$; otherwise $Q^*(s') = t'$. This completes the first part of the proof.

To prove the second part of the theorem, suppose that $s' \in h(s)$ and $s \in \hat{R}(s_0)$. In addition suppose that Q' is winning for s'. The proof proceeds by induction on the ordering $<_{Q'}$.

Suppose that s' is a minimal element of $<_{Q'}$. Then $Q'(s') \in W'$ because Q' is winning for s'. By (H1) there exists a t such that $Q'(s') \in h(t)$ and sRt. Therefore, t must be in W by (H3). Thus, if we define $Q(s)$ to be t, Q is winning for s.

Assume that s' is not a minimal element of $<_{Q'}$, and that Q is a winning strategy for all u such that $u' <_{Q'} s'$ for some $u' \in h(u)$. Then by (H1) there is a t such that sRt and $Q'(s') \in h(t)$. Consider a u such that tRu. Then by (H2) there is a $u' \in h(u)$ such that $Q'(s')R'u'$. Since $u' <_{Q'} s'$ and $u' \in h(u)$, Q is winning for u. From this Q we can construct a winning strategy for s as follows: If $s <_Q u$ then Q is already winning for s; otherwise we define $Q(s)$ to be t. This new Q is winning for s. Q.E.D.

We shall give a somewhat trivial example of this homomorphism here, reserving for a later time a discussion of the full implications of the theorem.

Consider the following game, played on a chessboard with pawns only. Initially, the pawns are on their respective first row (where the major pieces are in the usual game). Either player in his turn can advance a pawn by one or two steps, irrespective of its present position. Captures are not allowed and no pawn can land on or jump over an opponent's pawn. The game ends when no further moves are possible and the last player to play wins.

One can now consider the following variant of the game of Nim. There are eight piles of sticks on the table. Each player, in his turn can remove one or two sticks from exactly one of the piles. The player who picks the last stick on the table wins the game.

One can define a homomorphism between these two games. For ease of description we shall assume that a state in the "Pawn" game is represented by an 8-tuple of pairs of integers $((x_1, y_1), (x_2, y_2), (x_3, y_3), \cdots, (x_8, y_8))$, the x's representing the position of the player's pawn and the y's that of the opponents pawn on each column (measured from the same edge of the board in both cases). In the Nim game each state is represented by an 8-tuple $(z_1, z_2, z_3, \cdots, z_8)$. If we map each pawn state into the nim-state $(x_1 - y_1, x_2 - y_2, x_3 - y_3, \cdots, x_8 - y_8)$ one can verify that this map is an s_0-morphism for any state s_0 for which $x_i \geq y_i$ for all i.

This case of s_0-morphisms (a more general example will be considered later) is very special in a number of senses. Since it is an s_0-morphism for all legal states, the conditions involving s_0 in the definitions of homomorphism is unnecessary. Also, it will be noticed that the set P played a very small part in the construction of the homomorphism. This is because of an inherent symmetry in the game which we shall discuss presently. Also, because of the fact that there were no "draw" positions in the game, (G1) could be strengthened to $\overline{W \cup L} = R^{-1}(S)$, i.e., all "terminal" positions are either a win or a loss. Let us consider these formally.

Given a game $\langle S, R, P, W, L \rangle$ and $s_0 \in S$, one can restrict the game to $\hat{R}(s_0)$ quite readily and if one does so, any s_0-homomorphism between this game and another will be an s-morphism for any $s \in R(s_0)$, as one can readily prove. Moreover, if there are no draw positions in the game then (G2), (G3), and (G4) would indicate that (H1), (H2), and (H3), imply (H4). We shall leave this as an exercise for the interested reader.

Another interesting specialization occurs for the case where a special kind of symmetry holds for the game. Elsewhere [10], we have called the existence of such a symmetry "graph interpretability". Translated into our present formalism, we may say that a game is *graph interpretable* iff there exists a graph $\langle \Omega, \rho \rangle$ such that:

(B1) $S = \Omega \times \{0, 1\}$
(B2) $(w, k) \in P$ iff $k = 1$
(B3) $(w_1, k_1) R (w_2, k_2)$ iff $w_1 \rho w_2$.

Given two graph-interpretable games given by $\langle \Omega, \rho \rangle$ and $\langle \Omega', \rho' \rangle$ one may consider a relation $h \subseteq \Omega \times \Omega'$ such that

$$(\text{h}'\text{i})\ w_1 \rho w_2 \ \&\ w_1' \in h(w_1) \longrightarrow (\exists w_2')(w_1' \rho' w_2' \ \&\ w_2' \in h(w_2))$$
$$(\text{h}'\text{ii})\ w_1' \rho' w_2' \ \&\ w_1' \in h(w_1) \longrightarrow (\exists w_2)(w_1 \rho w_2 \ \&\ w_2' \in h(w_2)),$$

and construct a homomorphism $h \subseteq S \times S'$ such that $(w, k) h (w', k')$ iff whw' and $k = k'$. (H3) would be automatically satisfied and (h′i), (h′ii) above would ensure (H1) and (H2). In what follows, we shall be considering a generalized albeit functional, form of such a homomorphism. However, before we discuss that generalization, it may be worthwhile to discuss our previous example of Nim.

It can be readily seen that the game of Nim is graph interpretable. In such games, a winning strategy can be calculated from the structure of the graph $\langle \Omega, \rho \rangle$ by calculating the Grundy function on the nodes Ω. A Grundy function $g : \Omega \longrightarrow N$ (where N is the set of non-negative integers) has the two properties:

$$\text{(a)}\ w_1 \rho w_2 \longrightarrow g(w_1) \neq g(w_2)$$
$$\text{(b)}\ m < g(w_1) \longrightarrow (\exists w_2)((w_1 \rho w_2) \ \&\ g(w_2) = m).$$

Any progressively-finite graph has an unique Grundy function. Also, it is known [4] that in any progressively-finite graph-interpretable game a winning strategy exists for a state $(w, 1)$ iff $g(w) \neq 0$. In all such cases, there is a node w_2 such that $w \rho w_2$ and $g(w_2) = 0$. In any winning strategy for $(w_1, 1)$, $Q((w_1, 1)) = (w_2, 0)$.

It is the existence of this strategy (and some easy ways of calculating the Grundy function) that makes the homomorphism between pawn and Nim interesting. In what follows we shall show that one can define a general functional homomorphism between graphs which preserve Grundy functions. The application of the theorem will be clearer as we go to the later considerations.

THEOREM 2 [10]. *Let $\langle \Omega, \rho \rangle$ and $\langle \Omega', \rho' \rangle$ be two graphs and $h : \Omega \longrightarrow \Omega'$ have the properties:*

$$\text{(i)}\ w_1 \rho w_2 \longrightarrow h(w_1) \rho' h(w_2) \vee h(w_2) \rho h(w_1)$$
$$\text{(ii)}\ h(w_1) \rho w_2' \longrightarrow (\exists w_2)(w_1 \rho w_2 \ \&\ h(w_2) = w_2').$$

If now $g' : \Omega' \longrightarrow N$ is a Grundy function then the Gunction $g : \Omega \longrightarrow N$ defined by $g(w) = g'(h(w))$ is also a Grundy function.

Proof. Let $w_1 \rho w_2$. Then by (i) above either $h(w_1) \rho' h(w_2)$ or $h(w_2) \rho h(w_1)$. In either case, since g' is a Grundy function $g'(h(w_1)) \neq g'(h(w_2))$. This shows that g obeys law (a) above for Grundy functions.

Let now $m < g(h(w_1))$. Then there exists an w_2' such that $h(w_1) \rho' w_2'$ and $g'(w_2') = m$, since g' is a Grundy function. By (ii) above there exists an w_2 such that $w_1 \rho w_2$ and $w_2' = h(w_2)$, i.e., $g'(h(w_2)) = m$. This proves how g obeys (b) above. Q.E.D.

At this point it would be worthwhile to notice that (ii) as given in this theorem is a specialization of (h′ii) above in that h is now a function rather than a relation. However, (i) is not just a specialization of (h′i); only the first disjunction of the consequent of (i) is a specialization of the first disjunct in the consequent of (h′i). The second disjunct of (i) above points towards a rather novel phenomenon.

The matter may be illustrated clearly by invoking the game of Staircase Nim. In this game there are piles of sticks on the steps of a staircase. A move consists of removing one or two sticks from a pile to the next lower pile. Players play alternately. The game ends with all the sticks in the bottom pile and the last player to move wins.

If one defines a state of Staircase Nim by an m-tuple $(x_0, x_1, x_2, \cdots, x_m)$ then one can define a map from the states of Staircase Nim to the states of Nim as follows

$$h((x_0, x_1, x_2, \cdots)) = (x_1, x_3, x_5, \cdots) .$$

It will be noticed that this map does not define a homomorphism in our initial sense. Notice that $(0, 0, 1, 0, 0, 0, \cdots) \rho (0, 1, 0, 0, 0, 0, \cdots)$ in Staircase Nim and $h((0, 0, 1, 0, 0, 0, \cdots)) = (0, 0, 0, \cdots)$. Thus there are nodes w_1 and w_2 such that $w_1 \rho w_2$ while there is no node w_2' such that $h(w_1) \rho' w_2'$, contrary to (h′i). However, (i) of Theorem 2 is still satisfied, since $(1, 0, 0, \cdots) \rho' (0, 0, 0, \cdots)$ and $(1, 0, 0, \cdots) = h(0, 1, 0, 0, 0, 0, \cdots)$.

Theorem 2 gives us a method for calculating the Grundy function for Staircase Nim in terms of the Grundy function of Nim. There exists a well-known method for the calculation of the Grundy function of Nim. We shall have occasion to discuss that method in the course of our discussion in the next section.

III. DECOMPOSABLE AND POSITIONAL GAMES

In the previous section we have exhibited two homomorphisms. The applicability of either of the two homomorphisms in a game however, depends heavily upon the availability of a winning strategy for a game to which the games under study is homomorphic. Also, given any game, a method should be available for testing for the existence of a homomorphism between it and other games. In this section we shall introduce two classes of games for which winning strategies are known. We shall then proceed to discuss necessary and sufficient conditions for the existence of homomorphisms between any game and games in these two classes.

Instead of going immediately to the class to which Nim belongs, let us relegate that for later discussion and introduce the class of games to which Tic-Tac-Toe belongs (we shall soon see that this is not a trivial exercise). The following things characterize Tic-Tac-Toe as belonging to this class, called the *positional* class [5]. First, we have a set of cells on the board on any one of which one of two marks can be made. Once these marks are made, they are never erased and marks can only be made on an empty cell. There are certain sets of cells (the lines or paths) such that if they are all filled by players marks, the player wins. Also, there are certain sets of cells (which may or may not be identical with the previous sets) which, when fulfilled by the opponents' marks, leads to a loss of the game. It will be noticed that many games like the Shannon network games [6], Go-Moku [7], Qubic and Bridg-it [6] all belong to this class. It is, therefore, worthwhile to give games of this class a formal definition.

A game $\langle S, R, P, W, L \rangle$ is called positional if there exists a set N and two subsets A and B of 2^N such that:

(P0) $S = \{((X, Y, \lambda), m) \mid m \in (0, 1) \text{ and } (X, Y, \lambda) \text{ is a partition on } N\}$
(P1) $((X, Y, \lambda), m) \in W$ iff $m = 0$ and $(\exists a)(a \in A \;\&\; a \subseteq X)$
(P2) $((X, Y, \lambda), m) \in L$ iff $m = 1$ and $(\exists b)(b \in B \;\&\; b \subseteq Y)$
(P3) $((X, Y, \lambda), m) \in P$ iff $m = 1$
(P4) $((X_1, Y_1, \lambda_1), m_1) R ((X_2, Y_2, \lambda_2), m_2)$ iff $((X_1, Y_1, \lambda_1), m_1) \notin W \cup L$ and either:

(i) $(\exists n)(n \in \lambda \;\&\; X_2 = X_1 \cup \{n\} \text{ and } \lambda_2 = \lambda_1 - \{n\}) \text{ and } m_1 = 1 \neq m_2$

or

(ii) $(\exists n)(n \in \lambda \;\&\; Y_2 = Y_1 \cup \{n\} \text{ and } \lambda_2 = \lambda_1 - \{n\}) \text{ and } m_1 \neq 1 = m_2.$

A major reason for our interest in positional games is that some very-efficient methods [5, 8, 9] are available for playing games in this class. It is therefore of interest to look for conditions in the structure of a game which enables one to construct a homomorphism between it and some positional game. The following definition and theorem introduces such a condition.

A game $\langle S, R, P, W, L \rangle$ is s_0-reducible for $s \in S$ iff the following axioms are true about n functions (properties) $f_i : S \longrightarrow \{0, 1, 2, 3\}$ and two classes, A and B, of subsets of $\{1, 2, 3, \cdots, n\}$:

(R1) $s \in \hat{R}(s_0) \longrightarrow \left[s \in W \equiv s \notin P \text{ and } (\exists a)\left(a \in A \text{ and } \bigwedge_{i \in a} (f_i(s) = 1)\right)\right]$

(R2) $s \in \hat{R}(s_0) \longrightarrow \left[s \in L \equiv s \in P \text{ and } (\exists b)\left(b \in B \text{ and } \bigwedge_{i \in b} (f_i(s) = 2)\right)\right]$.

Before introducing the remaining two axioms several definitions are needed. Given a situation s and a set $U \subseteq S$ in a reducible game, we define the following sets

$$\mathrm{XP}(s) = \{i \mid f_i(s) = 0 \text{ or } f_i(s) = 1\} \;,$$
$$\mathrm{YP}(s) = \{i \mid f_i(s) = 0 \text{ or } f_i(s) = 2\} \;,$$
$$\mathrm{XE}(U) = \{i \mid (\exists a)\,(a \in A,\ i \in a, \text{ and } a \subseteq U\} \;,$$
$$\mathrm{YE}(U) = \{i \mid (\exists b)\,(b \in B,\ i \in b, \text{ and } b \subseteq U\} \;.$$

These definitions all correspond to simple informal concepts which will be described below; first we shall finish stating the axioms of a reducible game.

(R3) $s \in \hat{R}(s_0)$, $s \in W \cup L$, and $f_i(s) = 0$ implies that there is a t such that:

(i) sRt

(ii) $$(\forall j)\Big[i \neq j \longrightarrow \Big(f_j(s) = f_j(t) \vee \Big(f_j(t) = 3,\ f_j(s) \neq 0, \text{ and } \Big[(s \in P \text{ and } j \notin \mathrm{XE}(\mathrm{XP}(s)) \cup (\mathrm{YE}\ \mathrm{YP}(s) - \{i\})) \vee (s \notin P \text{ and } j \notin \mathrm{YE}(\mathrm{YP}(s)) \cup \mathrm{XE}(\mathrm{XP}(s) - \{i\}))\Big]\Big)\Big)\Big]$$

(iii) $$\Big[s \in P \text{ and } \Big(f_i(t) = 1 \vee \Big(f_i(t) = 3 \text{ and } i \notin \mathrm{XE}(\mathrm{XP}(s))\Big)\Big)\Big] \vee \Big[s \notin P \text{ and } \Big(f_i(t) = 2 \vee \Big(f_i(t) = 3 \text{ and } i \notin \mathrm{YE}(\mathrm{YP}(s))\Big)\Big)\Big] .$$

(R4) $s \in \hat{R}(s_0)$ and sRt imply that there is an i such that:

$$
\begin{aligned}
&\text{(i)}\ f_i(s) = 0\\
&\text{(ii)}\ (\forall j)\ \Big[i \neq j \longrightarrow \Big(f_j(s) = f_j(t) \vee \Big(f_j(t) = 3,\ f_j(s) \neq 0 \text{ and}\\
&\qquad \Big[\big(s \in P,\ j \notin \mathrm{XE}(\mathrm{XP}(s)) \cup \mathrm{YE}(\mathrm{YP}(s) - \{i\})\big)\\
&\qquad \vee \big(s \notin P,\ j \notin \mathrm{YE}(\mathrm{YP}(s)) \cup \mathrm{XE}(\mathrm{XP}(s) - \{i\})\big)\Big]\Big)\Big)\Big]\\
&\text{(iii)}\ \Big[s \in P,\ \big(f_i(t) = 1 \vee (f_i(t) = 3 \text{ and } i \notin \mathrm{XE}(\mathrm{XP})(s))\big)\Big]\\
&\qquad \vee \Big[s \in P,\ \big(f_i(t) = 2 \vee (f_i(t) = 3 \text{ and } i \notin \mathrm{YE}(\mathrm{YP})(s))\big)\Big] .
\end{aligned}
$$

Each element of A corresponds to a winning set of properties. (R1) indicates that every position which is a win has the value of 1 for every property in a winning set of properties. Similarly, (R2) relates a loss to the value of 2 for every property in some losing set of properties.

XP (s) is the set of potentially-winning properties of situation s. (The X in XP denote player X.) A potentially-winning property has a value of 0 or 1 because a value of 2 or 3 is never changed into a 1 (according to (R3) and (R4)). Similarly, the potentially-losing properties YP (s), have 0's or 2's as their values.

Not every potentially-winning property is essential to the play of the game. For example, if every winning set contains a property whose value is 2, then the first player cannot possibly win. But, in such a position many properties may have the value of 0, and thus be potentially winning. XE $(\mathrm{XP}(s))$ is the set of essential properties that are potentially winning in s. Similarly, YE $(\mathrm{YP}(s))$ are the essential properties that are potentially losing in s.

The analogous set for a positional game defined by the same (N, A, B), can also be specified in terms of XE and YE. XE $(X \cup \lambda)$ are the essential cells that are potentially winning in position $((X, Y, \lambda), m)$ while YE $(Y \cup \lambda)$ are the essential potentially losing cells. The reason for defining the essential cells of a positional game is that the s_0-morphism from a reducible game to a positional game, defined below, involves this concept, mainly because (R3) and (R4) make use of the essential properties of a reducible game.

(R3) states that if position s has a property with the value of 0, then there is at least one legal move from it to some new position t, unless s is a win or a loss. In addition, all of the essential properties remain unchanged, except for the ith property whose new value is a 1 if the first player made the move, and 2 otherwise. However, any of the inessential properties in t may be assigned the value of 3. According to (R4), any position t which is a legal move from position s has all of its properties related to the properties of s as given by (R3).

The rules of a reducible game are quite complicated, as the reader can see. However, an example will help to clarify the axioms of a reducible game.

We shall now define a relation h between positional and reducible games. Theorem 2 proves that this relation is an s_0-morphism.

Given a s_0-reducible game G, i.e., given n functions f_i for $1 \leq i \leq n$ and the subsets A and B construct a positional game G defined by the triple (N, A, B) where $N = \{1, 2, 3, \cdots, n\}$. Now construct $h \subseteq S \times S'$ as follows: For each $s \in S$, the element $s' = ((X, Y, \lambda), m)$ will be related to s (i.e., $s' \in h(s)$) iff:

(1) $m = 1$ if $s \in P$; else $m = 0$
(2) Every j such that $f_j(s) = 1$ is in X

(3) Every j such that $f_j(s) = 2$ is in Y
(4) $j \in \lambda$ if and only if $f_j(s) = 0$
(5) $f_j(s) = 3 \longrightarrow j \notin \mathrm{XE}(X \cup \lambda) \cup \mathrm{YE}(Y \cup \lambda)$.

The following lemma about the reducible game (N, A, B), is needed for the proof of Theorem 3.

LEMMA 1. If $((X, Y, \lambda), m) \in h(s)$, then $\mathrm{XE}(\mathrm{XP}(s)) = \mathrm{XE}(X \cup \lambda)$ and $\mathrm{YE}(\mathrm{YP}(s)) = \mathrm{YE}(Y \cup \lambda)$.

Proof. Let $s' = ((X, Y, \lambda), m)$ and suppose $i \in \mathrm{XE}(\mathrm{XP}(s))$. Then there is an $a \in A$ such that $i \in a$ and $a \subseteq \mathrm{XP}(s)$. For every $j \in a$, $f_j(s)$ is 0 or 1. If $f_j(s) = 0$ then $i \in \lambda$ by (4). If $f_j(s) = 1$, then $i \in X$ by (2). Hence $a \subseteq X \cup \lambda$. Hence $i \in \mathrm{XE}(X \cup \lambda)$. Thus, $\mathrm{XE}(\mathrm{XP}(s)) \subseteq \mathrm{XE}(X \cup \lambda)$. Similarly, $\mathrm{YE}(\mathrm{YP}(s)) \subseteq \mathrm{YE}(Y \cup \lambda)$.

To prove the reverse inequality, let $i \in \mathrm{XE}(X \cup \lambda)$. Again there is an $a \in A$ such that $i \in a$ and $a \subseteq X \cup \lambda$. For any $j \in a$, if $j \in \lambda$, then $f_j(s) = 0$ by (4). If $j \in X$, then $f_j(s) \neq 2$ by (3) and by (5) $f_j(s) \neq 3$. Hence, $f_j(s) = 1$ because (4) insures that it is not 0. Therefore, $a \subseteq \mathrm{XP}(s)$ and $i \in \mathrm{XE}(\mathrm{XP}(s))$. Similarly, $\mathrm{YE}(Y \cup \lambda) \subseteq \mathrm{YE}(\mathrm{YP}(s))$ which completes the proof.

THEOREM 3 [13]. *Given a s_0-reducible game G, a positional game G', defined by (N, A, B) and a relation h that satisfies (1)–(5), h is a s_0-morphism from G to G'.*

Proof: The proof will be in four parts proving (H1)–(H4). Since the proof of (H1) and (H2) depends upon (H3) and (H4), we will prove the latter first.

Proof of (H3). Let $s \in W \cap \hat{R}(s_0)$ and let $s' = ((X, Y, \lambda), m) \in h(s)$. By (R1) there exists an $a \in A$ such that $f_i(s) = 1$ for each $i \in a$. Hence by clause (2), $a \subseteq X$. Also, $m = 0$ because of (1) and the fact that $s \notin P$ by (R1). Hence by (P1), $s' \in W'$.

Let $s' = ((X, Y, \lambda), m) \in W'$. Now, consider an s such that $s' \in h(s)$. Then, there is an $a \in A$ such that $a \subseteq X$. Hence, $a \subseteq \mathrm{XE}(X \cup \lambda)$, and thus $a \subseteq \mathrm{XE}(\mathrm{XP}(s))$ by lemma 1. By (5), if $j \in a$, then $f_j(s) \neq 3$. In addition, $f_j(s) \neq 0$ and $f_j(s) \neq 2$ by (3) and (4). Therefore $f_j(s) = 1$ for each j in a. By (R1) it follows that $s \in W$.

The second part of (H3) can be proved in a similar manner.

Proof of (H4). (H4) follows immediately from (P3) and (1).

Proof of (H1). Let $s \in \hat{R}(s_0) \cap \overline{W} \cap \overline{L}$, $s' = ((X, Y, \lambda), m) \in h(s)$ and $s' R' t'$. There are two cases: $s \in P$ and $s \notin P$. In the first case, $m = 1$ by (1). (P4) implies that there is a $k \in \lambda$ such that $t' = ((X \cup \{k\}), Y, \lambda - \{k\}), 0)$. By (4) $f_k(s) = 0$ because $k \in \lambda$. Since $s' R' t'$, $s' \notin W' \cup L'$ by (P4). Hence by (H3), $s \notin W \cup L$. By (R3) there is a t such that sRt, and for each $j \neq k$, $f_j(t) = f_j(s)$ or $f_j(t) = 3$. Also, $f_k(t)$ is 1 or 3 by (iii) of (R3).

It can now be seen that $t' \in h(t)$. By (G4) $t \notin P$ and by (P3), (1) in the definition of h is satisfied. To see that (2) is satisfied, consider any $j \in N$ such that $f_j(t) = 1$. If $j \neq k$, then $f_j(s) = f_j(t) \neq 3$, in which case $j \in X$, and hence $j \in X \cup \{k\}$. If $j = k$, clearly $j \in X \cup \{k\}$.

To see that (3) in the definition of h is satisfied, consider a j such that $f_j(t) = 2$. The only way that this can happen is if $f_j(s) = f_j(t) = 2$ so that $j \in Y$ since $s' \in h(s)$. Condition (4) is satisfied because, for any j such that $f_j(t) = 0$, $f_j(s) = 0$ and $j \neq k$, and thus $j \in \lambda - \{k\}$ since $s' \in h(s)$.

To see that Condition (5) is satisfied, suppose that $f_j(t) = 3$. There are two cases: $f_j(s) = 0$ and $f_j(s) \neq 0$. To consider the latter, assume (5) to be false; i.e., assume $j \in \mathrm{XE}(X \cup \lambda) \cup \mathrm{YE}(Y \cup \lambda - \{k\})$. If j were in $\mathrm{XE}(X \cup \lambda)$, then $j \in \mathrm{XE}(\mathrm{XP}(s))$ by Lemma 1, and thus $f_j(t) \neq 3$ by (ii) of (R3). Consequently, j must be in $\mathrm{YE}(Y \cup \lambda - \{k\})$. However, by the definition of YE, there is a b such that $j \in b \subseteq Y \cup \lambda - \{k\}$. Therefore, $b \subseteq \mathrm{YE}(Y \cup \lambda) = \mathrm{YE}(\mathrm{YP}(s))$ by Lemma 1. But since $k \notin b$, $b \subseteq \mathrm{YE}(\mathrm{YP}(s) - \{k\})$, in which case $f_j(t) \neq 3$ by (ii) of (R3). This is a contradiction, and hence (5) is satisfied when $f_j(s) = 0$.

In the case where $f_j(s) = 0$, $j \notin \mathrm{XE}(\mathrm{XP}(s))$ by (iii) of (R3). Therefore, by Lemma 1, $j \notin \mathrm{XE}(X \cup \lambda)$. But, by (4) we know that $j \in \lambda$ and that $j \notin \lambda - \{k\}$; thus $j = k$. This implies that $j \notin Y \cup \lambda - \{k\} = \mathrm{YP}(t')$. Hence, by the definition of YE, $j \notin \mathrm{YE}(Y \cup \lambda - \{k\})$ which concludes the proof that Condition (5) is satisfied.

In the case where $s \notin P$, $m = 0$ and the proof is similar to the above using (P4) instead of (P3).

Proof of (H2). Let $s \in \hat{R}(s_0)$, sRt, and $s' \in h(s)$. In addition, let $s' = ((X, Y, \lambda), 0)$, (assume $s \notin P$; the case, $s \in P$ is treated similarly). By (R4) there is a $k \in \lambda$ such that $f_k(s) = 0$, $f_k(t)$ is 2 or 3 and for all $j \neq k$, either $f_j(s) = f_j(t)$ or $f_j(t) = 3$. Since $f_k(s) = 0$, $k \in \lambda$ by Condition (4). Construct t' as $((X, Y \cup \{k\}, \lambda - \{k\}), 1)$. (P4) implies that $s'R't'$ because by (G1) and sRt, $s \notin W \cup L$ whence $s' \notin W' \cup L'$ by (H3).

To see $t' \in h(t)$, Conditions (1) and (4) in the definition of h follow immediately, as before. To prove (2), let $f_j(t) = 1$; by (R4) this implies $j \neq k$ (since $s \notin P$ and thus $f_k(t)$ is 2 or 3). Hence, $f_j(s) = f_j(t) = 1$, since $f_j(t) \neq 3$, and thus $j \in X$ because $s' \in h(s)$. Condition (3) can be proven in a way similar to the proof of (2) for the (H1) case.

Condition (5) is satisfied, as can be proven in a manner similar to the (H1) case. Q.E.D.

As an example of the application of this theorem, let us consider the following game which I shall call "Race" after Newell [3].

The game is played with eight fictitious horses running a race on a 3-step-long course. The object of the game is to buy some horses and to advance one of them to the winning post before the opponent does the same with his horses. To enable the owning and moving of horses, nine "tickets" are available for sale, each ticket, being marked with the names of two or more horses (See Figure 2(a)). Initially all horses are unowned and are stationed at the gate. The tickets are bought alternately by the two players. When the name of a horse appears on the purchased ticket, one of three things may happen, depending on circumstances:

(i) If the horse is unowned, it is owned by the purchaser of the ticket and advances one step from the gate

(ii) If the horse is previously owned by the purchaser of the ticket, it advances a step from its present position

(iii) If the horse is owned by the opponent of the purchaser of the ticket, the horse is disqualified and removed from the race.

Let us follow through a play of the "Race" game. Player A starts the game

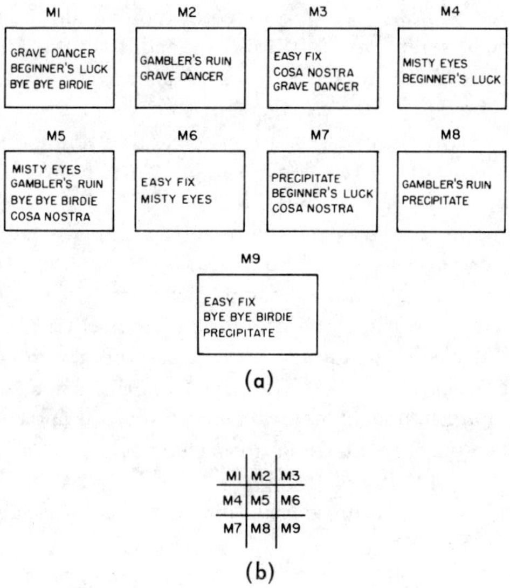

Fig. 2. The games of Race and Tic-Tac-Toe.

by buying Ticket 5, owning and advancing "Misty Eyes", "Gambler's Ruin", "Bye Bye Birdie" and "Cosa Nostra". Player B buys Ticket 2, disqualifying "Gambler's Ruin" and owning "Grave Dancer". Player A buys Ticket 9, owning and advancing "Easy Fix" and "Precipitate" while advancing "Bye Bye Birdie" to the second step. Since one more ticket makes "Bye Bye Birdie" win, Player B buys Ticket 1, disqualifying that horse and on his side owning and advancing "Beginner's Luck" and advancing "Grave Dancer" to the second step. A prevents immediate defeat by buying Ticket 3, thereby disqualifying "Grave Dancer" and preventing its advance to the 3rd step. However at this time Player A also owns "Precipitate", "Misty Eyes", "Cosa Nostra", and "Easy Fix" and the last two horses are sitting on the second step. B disqualifies "Cosa Nostra" by buying Ticket 7 (also disqualifying "Precipitate" in the process and advancing "Beginner's Luck" to a hairbreadth of victory)—but A buys Ticket 6 so that "Easy Fix" wins the race.

From the above discussion the reader can probably glean that the Race Game is really Tic-Tac-Toe, played on a board shown in Fig. 2(b) where buying ticket $Mi (i = 1, 2, 3, \cdots, 9)$ corresponds to placing an X or an O in the cell marked with Mi. To see how this follows from an application of Theorem 2 let us now look at the Race game somewhat more formally. Although there are several different ways to formulate Race, each must contain at least a minimal amount of information which must be known to the players if they have to make legal moves and be cognizant of the effects of such moves on subsequent wins or losses. One of the ways of doing this is to tell the players as to who is on move, what tickets are still available for purchase, and how the horses stand, i.e., to whom, if any, each horse belongs and where it stands on the track, which horses are disqualified and which are unowned.

Each situation, then, has three components, and we shall designate a situation by a triple (t, b, m) where m, the third component, is the usual move indicator, 0 or 1. The first component t is the set of unbought tickets. The second component b is the board, i.e., an assignment to each horse of K1, K2, K3, E1, E2, E3, UO or DQ. These values stand for "owned by the first player and in position 1, 2 or 3," "owned by the second player and in position 1, 2, or 3," "unowned" and "disqualified," respectively.

We may, at this point, make various conventions about whether any combination of these three components would be allowed. Should we, for instance, accept a situation where no tickets are bought, two horses (one owned by each player) have already won, while three others are disqualified? The answer, we believe, is a matter of taste. In any case, it makes no difference in the final analysis, because as long as we take the proper initial situation s_0 as one where all the tickets are unbought and all the horses are unowned, then the move rules restrict $\hat{R}(s_0)$ to exclude all such nonsense states, since such states can not be reached by any sequence of legal moves. This exemplifies the strong influence of the set $\hat{R}(s_0)$ on all our discussions and explains why it plays such an important role in our definitions.

Continuing with the example, let position (t_2, b_2, m_2) be a legal move from position (t_1, b_1, m_1). Then t_2 contains all the tickets in t_1 except some specific ticket Mi. Also $m_2 = 0$ if $m_1 = 1$ and vice versa, b_2 is obtained from b_1 as follows: the ownership and the position of all the horses are the same in b_2 and b_1 except for those whose name appears on the ticket Mi. For these horses, their values are advanced one step if they are unowned or belong to the player on move. That is, if $m_1 = 1$, then a value of K1 becomes K2, K2 becomes K3 and UO becomes K1. If $m_1 = 0$ then E1 becomes E2 etc. and UO becomes E1. If the horse belongs to the opponent of the player on move, it is disqualified, i.e., if $m_1 = 1$ then values of E1 and E2 become DQ and if $m_1 = 0$ then K1 and K2 become DQ. Disqualified horses on the Mi list remain disqualified.

A situation (t, b, m) is winning iff there is some horse h with a value K3 in b and $m = 1$. Similarly $(t, b, m) \in L$ iff $m = 0$ and there is a horse whose value is E3.

To see that this game is reducible, one sets up one function f_i for each ticket Mi as follows. The value of $f_i (1 \leq i \leq 9)$ for a situation is 0 iff Mi is unbought, i.e., if M$i \in t$. If Mi is not in t, the value of f_i has to be surmised from the values of the horse as given in b. If at least one horse appearing on the ticket Mi has a value K1, K2, or K3, the value of f_i is 1. If at least one horse on Mi has a value E1, E2, or E3, the value of f_i is 2. (If the game is played legally from a starting state where all the tickets are on the table and all the horses are unowned, then these two rules will never contradict one another). If all horses on Mi are disqualified, then f_i has the value 3 for the state.

It is clear that if any winning situation is reached from the usual starting situation, then the table shows that there should be exactly three tickets belonging to the winning player which has the winning horses name on it. So there is a set of f_i such that all their values are 1 at that situation. Thus, one can isolate a class of sets of the f_i such that a situation is a win if and only if all the members of some set in this class has the value 1. This shows that (R1) is true and the truth of (R2) can be seen similarly.

To see how this game obeys (R3), let the value of f_i be 0 for some situation. From what has gone above it is clear that in this case M*i* will be an unbought ticket. If this is a legal situation which is neither a win or a loss, then the player on move can buy this ticket. The resulting situation will satisfy (i) of (R3). Also, if all the horses on this ticket are either disqualified or belong to the opponent, then after buying this ticket all the horses on it will be disqualified and the value of the ticket for the new state will be 3. Otherwise the value of f_i will be determined by the name of the player (1 or 0). Thus (iii) will be satisfied. As far as all the other tickets are concerned, the unbought ones will remain unbought, and the others will either retain their values (since horses do not change hands, nor do the tickets bearing the horses names) or some tickets take on the value 3 if their horses get disqualified by the purchase. Thus (ii) in (R3) is also satisfied. (R4) can be verified similarly.

We shall now return to an application of Theorem 2, by considering necessary and sufficient conditions for the existence of a D-morphism from a game into any game of the Nim class. This class of games is interesting because their Grundy functions are very easy to calculate.

The basic idea behind this calculation would be to consider a Nim game where there is only one pile of sticks left. It is not hard to see that the Grundy function of the graph of this game is given by the number of sticks mod 3. If two nodes z and z' are connected, they cannot differ by more than 2 and hence are unequal mod 3. Also, if $m < z$ mod 3, then there is some node z' which differs from z by less than 3 and $z' = m$ (mod 3).

Now one can consider the actual Nim game as a composite of eight games of the above kind such that a move in this composite game consists in a move in any one component game. The following definitions and theorem will then show that the Grundy function of any node can be obtained as follows. Express the Grundy functions of each component node in the binary notation. Arrange the resulting strings in a column (as in addition of binary numbers). Add each column (mod 2 without carry). The resulting string is the binary representation of the Grundy function of the composite node.

This result need not be proved here but for the sake of future discussions, they are formally presented below.

Given n graphs $\langle \Omega_i, \rho_i \rangle$ $(1 \leq i \leq n)$ a graph $\langle \Omega, \rho \rangle$ will be called their *sum* iff:

$$\text{(S1)}\ \Omega = \Omega_1 \times \Omega_2 \times \Omega_3 \times \cdots \times \Omega_n$$
$$\text{(S2)}\ (\omega_1, \omega_2, \omega_3, \cdots, \omega_n)\, \rho\, (\omega'_1, \omega'_2, \omega'_3, \cdots, \omega'_n)$$

iff for some i, $\omega_i \rho_i \omega'_i$ and for all $j \neq i$ $\omega_j = \omega'_j$.

Let now a and b be integers and let

$$a = a_0 + 2a_1 + 2^2 a_2 + \cdots + 2^n a_k \quad ,$$

$$b = b_0 + 2b_1 + 2^2 b_2 + \cdots + 2^n a_k \quad ,$$

where a_i and b_i are either 0 or 1.

Define operator $\oplus$ on integers as follows

$$a \oplus b = c_0 \oplus 2c_1 \oplus 2^2 c_2 \oplus \cdots \oplus 2^k c_k \quad ,$$

where $c_i = 0$ if $a_i = b_i$ and 1 otherwise. It can be shown that if $\langle \Omega, \rho \rangle$ is the sum of $\langle \Omega_i, \rho_i \rangle (1 \le i \le n)$ then the Grundy function g for $\langle \Omega, p \rangle$ is given by

$$g((\omega_1, \omega_2, \omega_3 \cdots \omega_n)) = g_1(\omega_1) \oplus g_2(\omega_2) \oplus \cdots \oplus g_n(\omega_n) ,$$

where g_i is the Grundy function of $\langle \Omega_i, \rho_i \rangle$.

We shall call a game *decomposable* iff it is graph interpretable and if its graph is the sum of n graphs. The following theorem gives us an important method for calculating the Grundy functions of games which are not obviously decomposable in this sense.

THEOREM 4. *Let $\langle \Omega, \rho \rangle$ be a graph. Then there exist n graphs $\{\langle \Omega_i, \rho_i \rangle\}$ and a D-morphism for $\langle \Omega, \rho \rangle$ onto the sum of $\{\langle \Omega_i, \rho_i \rangle\}$ iff there exists a set of n equivalence relations $E_i (1 \le i \le n)$ on Ω such that*:

(D1) *Given $\omega_1, \omega_2, \omega_3, \cdots, \omega_n \in \Omega$ there exists an $\omega \in \Omega$ such that $\omega E_i \omega_i$ for each i*

(D2) *$\omega_1 \rho \omega_2$ implies there exists an i such that $\omega_1 E_j \omega_2$ for each $j \neq i$ and either*:

(i) *For all ω such that $\omega E_i \omega_1$ there exists an ω' such that $\omega' E_j \omega$ for all $j \neq i$, $\omega \rho \omega'$ and $\omega' E_i \omega_2$*

or

(ii) *For all ω such that $\omega E_i \omega_2$, there exists an ω' such that $\omega' E_j \omega$ for all $j \neq i$, $\omega \rho \omega'$ and $\omega' E_i \omega_1$.*

Proof of sufficiency. Construct n graphs $\langle \Omega_i, \rho_i \rangle$ as follows

$$\Omega_i = \{[\omega]^{E_i} \mid \omega \in \Omega\} ,$$

where $[\omega]^{E_i}$ is the equivalence class of E_i containing ω. Let

$$[\omega]^{E_i} \rho_i [\omega']^{E_i}$$

iff for all $\omega'' \in [\omega]^{E_i}$ there exists an $\omega''' \in [\omega']^{E_i}$ such that $\omega'' \rho \omega'''$ and $\omega'' E_j \omega'''$ for all $j \neq i$. Also define a relation

$$h \subseteq \Omega \times (\Omega_1 \times \Omega_2 \times \Omega_3 \times \cdots \times \Omega_n) ,$$

as follows

$$(\omega, ([\omega_1]^{E_1}, [\omega_2]^{E_2}, \cdots, [\omega_n]^{E_n})) \in h$$

iff $\omega E_i \omega_i$ for each i. It can be readily shown that h is a single-valued function of Ω onto $\Omega_1 \times \Omega_2 \times \Omega_3 \times \cdots \times \Omega_n$. Hence in future we shall write

$$h(\omega) = ([\omega]^{E_1}, [\omega]^{E_2}, \cdots, [\omega]^{E_n}) .$$

Let now $\langle \Omega', \rho' \rangle$ be the sum of the n graphs $\langle \Omega_i, \rho_i \rangle$. We shall now show that h is a D-morphism.

Let $\omega \rho \omega'$. By (D2) there exists an i such that $[\omega]^{E_j} = [\omega']^{E_j}$ for all $j \neq i$. Let now condition (ii) of (D2) hold so that all $\omega'' \in [\omega']^{E_i}$, there exists a ω''' such that $\omega''' \in [\omega]^{E_i}$, $\omega'' \rho \omega'''$ and $[\omega'']^{E_j} = [\omega''']^{E_j}$ for all $j \neq i$. But this is precisely the condition for $[\omega']^{E_i} \rho_i [\omega]^{E_i}$ and hence for

$$([\omega']^{E_1}, [\omega']^{E_2}, \cdots, [\omega']^{E_n}) \rho' ([\omega]^{E_1}, [\omega]^{E_2}, \cdots, [\omega]^{E_n}) ,$$

or

$$h(\omega')\rho' h(\omega) \ ,$$

fulfilling the second disjunct of the consequent of (i) in the definition of D-morphisms. The first disjunct holds if (i) in (D2) holds. Hence h fulfills the condition (i) for D-morphisms.

To prove condition (ii) for D-morphism, let $h(\omega)\rho'([\omega_1']^{E_1}, [\omega_2']^{E_2}, \cdots, [\omega_n']^{E_n})$, i.e., $([\omega]^{E_1}, [\omega]^{E_2}, \cdots, [\omega]^{E_n})\rho'([\omega']^{E_1}, [\omega']^{E_2}, \cdots, [\omega_n']^{E_n})$ then since $\langle \Omega', \rho' \rangle$ is the sum of $\{\langle \Omega_i, \rho_i \rangle\}$ there exists an i such that $[\omega]^{E_i}\rho_i[\omega_i]^{E_i}$ and for all $j \neq i$, $\omega E_j \omega_j'$. We have to show that there exists a ω' such that $\omega R \omega'$ and $h(\omega') = ([\omega_1']^{E_1}, [\omega_2']^{E_2}, \cdots, [\omega_n']^{E_n})$, i.e., that $\omega' E_j \omega_j'$ for all j. By definition of ρ_i, and since $\omega \in [\omega_i]^{E_i}$ there is an element ω' such that $\omega' \in [\omega_i']^{E_i}$, i.e., $\omega' E_i \omega_i'$ and $\omega' E_j \omega_j'$ for all $j \neq i$. Hence the existence is proved.

Proof of necessity. Let there be a D-morphism h from $\langle \Omega, \rho \rangle$ onto the sum $\langle \Omega', \rho' \rangle$ of $\{\langle \Omega_i, \rho_i \rangle \mid 1 \leq i \leq n\}$. Define the following sets of relations on Ω. If $h(\omega) = (\omega_1, \omega_2, \omega_3, \cdots, \omega_n)$ and $h(\omega') = (\omega_1', \omega_2', \omega_3', \cdots, \omega_n')$ then for each i, $\omega E_i \omega'$ iff $\omega_i = \omega_i'$. Evidently all these relations E_i are equivalence relations. To show that these have property (D1) let $\omega_1, \omega_2, \omega_3, \cdots, \omega_n$ be arbitrary points in Ω. Let for each $i (1 \leq i \leq \eta)$

$$h(\omega_i) = (\omega_{i1}, \omega_{i2}, \omega_{i3}, \cdots, \omega_{in}) \ .$$

Since h is onto, there exists an $\omega \in \Omega$ such that $h(\omega) = (\omega_{11}, \omega_{22}, \omega_{33}, \cdots, \omega_{nn})$. By definition of the equivalences, $\omega E_i \omega_i$ for each i.

To prove (D2) let $\omega \rho \omega'$. Let $h(\omega) = (\omega_1, \omega_2, \omega_3, \cdots, \omega_n)$ and $h(\omega') = (\omega_1', \omega_2', \omega_3', \cdots, \omega_n')$. Since h is a D-morphism onto the sum of the $\langle \Omega_i, \rho_i \rangle$, we have from Condition (i) of the hypothesis of Theorem 2 (i.e., definition of D-morphism) that there is i such that for all $j \neq i$ $\omega_j = \omega_j'$ and hence by the definition of E_j, $\omega E_j \omega'$. Also, either $\omega_i \rho_i \omega_i'$ or $\omega_i' \rho_i \omega_i$. Instead of dealing with both these cases in clearly-analogous manners, we shall only consider the case where $\omega_i \rho_i \omega_i'$. Let now $\omega'' E_i \omega$, and $h(\omega'') = (\omega_1'', \omega_2'', \omega_3'', \cdots, \omega_n'')$, so that $\omega_i'' = \omega_i$. Consider the n tuple $(\omega_1'', \omega_2'', \omega_3'', \cdots \omega_{i-1}'', \omega_i', \omega_{i+1}'', \cdots, \omega_n'')$. By definition of sum, this n-tuple is related by ρ' to $h(\omega'')$. Hence by Condition (ii) for D-homomorphisms, there is an ω''' such that $\omega'' \rho \omega'''$ and $h(\omega''') = (\omega_1'', \omega_2'', \omega_3'', \cdots, \omega_{i-1}'', \omega_i', \omega_{i+1}'', \cdots, \omega_n'')$. Then $\omega''' E_j \omega''$ for all $j \neq i$ and $\omega''' E_i \omega'$ and $\omega'' \rho \omega'''$ showing that (D2) is true. Q.E.D.

The following game can be quoted as a ready application of this theorem. One has a one-dimensional semi-infinite "mat" divided into consecutively numbered cells. 99 pennies and a dollar are placed in different cells of the mat, the dollar being in a higher coordinate then the pennies (i.e., "at the extreme right"). Each player moves any coin as many steps "to the left" as he wishes without crossing or landing on any other coin. Every time a player moves a coin to cell zero, he "captures" it. The player who captures the dollar (i.e., makes the last move) wins.

Each node on the graph of this game may be characterized by a 100-tuple $(x_1, x_2, x_3, \cdots, x_{100})$, the coordinates of the coins. Two nodes $(x_1, x_2, x_3, \cdots, x_{100})$ and $(y_1, y_2, y_3, \cdots, y_{100})$ are connected iff there is an i such that

$x_j = y_j$ for all $j \neq i$ and if $x_{i-1} > 0$ then

$$x_{i-1} < y_i < x_i \quad ,$$

and

$$0 \leq y_i < x_i \text{, otherwise} \quad ,$$

The game ends when $x_i = 0$ for all i, that is, when there is no outgoing arc from the node—according to conventional graph-interpretable games.

We define 50 equivalence relations on the nodes as follows: We define $(x_1, x_2, x_3, \cdots, x_n) E_i (y_1, y_2, y_3, \cdots, y_n)$ iff

$$y_{n-2i+2} - y_{n-2i+1} = x_{n-2i+2} - x_{n-2i+1} \quad ,$$

with the convention that $x_0 = y_0 = 0$. It is left to the reader to verify that (D1) and (D2) of Theorem 4 are satisfied by these equivalences. As an example, one can say that in a typical game of this kind, the node (5, 9, 12, 15, 21, 23) has the node (3, 2, 1) of Nim as a homomorphic image and hence is a losing node.

IV. A WARNING ABOUT SIMILARITIES

The discussions leading up to Theorem 4 have shown that the idea of decomposability of graphs allow us to play many games other than Nim in a way similar to the way one plays Nim. Let us now move to some other "similar" games in the Nim class.

So far we have talked only about the specific kind of Nim game where there are eight piles of sticks and one can only remove up to 2 sticks from exactly one pile. Our discussions above have shown that nothing essentially changes if the number of piles is changed from 8 to n. However, only one pile has to be changed if the definition of *sum* is to be maintained. For the time being let us consider that the upper limit for the number of sticks is still 2, giving us the class of game we shall call the $(2\text{-Nim})_1$ class. The number 2 is of significance in only so far as Grundy functions of the component graphs are given by the number of sticks mod 3. One can talk also about the essentially similar class $(k\text{-Nim})_1$ where the Grundy functions are numbers of sticks mod $(k + 1)$ and in the case of no upper bound, $(\infty\text{-Nim})_1$ where the Grundy functions are equal to the numbers of sticks.

As another variant of the game, we may consider $(\infty\text{-Nim})_p$, where any number of sticks can be picked from a pile and one can pick simultaneously from up to p piles. The winning strategy for this game is not identical to that for $(\infty\text{-Nim})_1$, but similar. Here the binary numbers representing the Grundy functions are added by columns mod $(p + 1)$. If the resulting sequence is nonzero, a move exists which reduces it to zero and this is the optimum move (4).

One is tempted to say that both $(\infty\text{-Nim})_p$ and $(k\text{-Nim})_1$ are games similar to $(\infty\text{-Nim})_1$ and this is supported by the fact that the winning strategies of these games are somewhat similar. However, the existence of the strategy for $(\infty\text{-Nim})_p$ is very heavily dependent on the fact that in each component pile, the empty pile is the only node with its Grundy function zero. Hence the similarity of strategies can not be extended to the case of $(k\text{-Nim})_p$, i. e., where one can draw only up to k sticks from up to p piles. One might be tempted to conjecture that this game, being similar to both $(\infty\text{-Nim})_p$ and $(k\text{-Nim})_1$, could have a related strategy. This is not so because in the components a pile of k sticks also has Grundy function zero.

One could perhaps save the situation as follows. The composition theorems regarding Grundy functions are useful because they give us ways of calculating the strategy of the composite game from the Grundy function of the components. The role of the Grundy function and the $\oplus$ operator is really incidental. One might set oneself the following more general task: "Construct two functions f and f' on nodes of a graph such that it is true for both of these that its value for a node is 0 iff it is not possible to win from that node. Construct an n-ary function F on integers such that in the $(k\text{-Nim})_p$ game if $f(\omega_1), f(\omega_2), f(\omega_3), \cdots, f(\omega_n)$ be the value of one of these "loss-indicating functions" for the components of the node $(\omega_1, \omega_2, \omega_3, \cdots, \omega_n)$ then $f'(\omega_1, \omega_2, \omega_3, \cdots, \omega_n) = F(f(\omega_1), f(\omega_2), f(\omega_3), \cdots, f(\omega_n))$."

We have already seen that such construction is possible for $p = 1$ if f and f' are the Grundy function and F is $\oplus$. Such construction is also known to be possible if $p = n - 1$ or n [10] or if each component graph is such that the "loss indicating function" is zero only at terminal nodes as in the case of $(\infty\text{-Nim})_p$ However, the following corollary of a previous theorem by C. A. Dunning [10] shows that except for these special cases, no further construction is possible.

THEOREM 5. *Let f and f' be any loss-indicating functions on graphs and let F by any n-ary operator on integers. There exists a node $(\omega_1, \omega_2, \omega_3, \cdots, \omega_n)$ in a $(k\text{-Nim})_p$ $(1 < p < n - 1)$ game such that*

$$F(f(\omega_1), f(\omega_2), f(\omega_3), \cdots, f(\omega_n) \neq f'(\omega_1, \omega_2, \omega_3, \cdots, \omega_n)) \ .$$

Proof. Consider the node $\omega = (k + 1, 1, 1, \cdots, 1, 0, \cdots, 0)$ where there are exactly $p + 1$ occurrences of 1's (since $p < n - 1$ this many components are available). Now the player on move at this node can easily win by picking k sticks from the first pile and 1 from the second pile reducing the state to $\omega' = (1, 0, 1, \cdots, 1, 0, \cdots, 0)$. There are still $p + 1$ piles with one stick in each of which the opponent must remove at least one but can not remove all. After this the first player can empty all piles and win.

We thus see that since it is not possible to win from ω' and possible to win from ω, $f'(\omega') = 0$ and $f'(\omega) \neq 0$. If a function F existed such that the conclusion of the theorem was not true, then we would have

$$F(f(k + 1), f(1), f(1), \cdots, f(1), f(0), f(0), \cdots, f(0)) = f'(\omega) = 0 \ ,$$

and

$$F(f(1), f(0), f(1), \cdots, f(1), f(0), f(0), \cdots, f(0)) = f'(\omega') \neq 0 \ .$$

However, in the component games, since it is not possible to win from a single pile of $k + 1$ sticks and an empty pile is terminal we have $f(k + 1) = f(0) = 0$. Thus

$$F(0, f(1), f(1), \cdots, f(1), 0, 0, \cdots, 0) = f'(\omega') = 0 ,$$
$$F(f(1), 0, f(1), \cdots, f(1), 0, 0, \cdots, 0) = f'(\omega) \neq 0 .$$

Since the game of $(\infty\text{-Nim})_p$ does not depend for its outcome on the orderings of the piles, but merely on the number and size of the piles and since both ω and ω' have the same number of 0's and 1's in them, it follows from symenetry that $f'(\omega') = f'(\omega)$ which contradicts the hypothesis that f' is a loss indicating function. Q.E.D.

V. CONCLUDING REMARKS

We took the following basis of discussion for this paper: that it would be desirable to have techniques whereby a machine (or a human—if the search space is too large for the machine) could find similarities between a problem and other problems whose solutions are known. To enable this, some precise definitions of similarity are needed (these definitions could well be in the form of computer programs: that would not make them any less precise and the need for assessing their effectiveness would still remain). One of the possible ways of doing this might be through a comparison of the statements (in some computer-interpretable and therefore formal language) about the two games. The games may be considered similar if all but some inessential statements about them are the same. However, our discussion in Section IV seems to indicate that what is essential and what is not is not always easily discernable. We therefore, feel obliged to leave this mode of consideration of similarity in human hands for a while.

Although it is too early to say yet, our belief is that somewhat more immediate returns may be had if a different definition of similarity is invoked, more in line with the direction of the previous work of Amarel and Newell. We call two games similar if there is a relation between them which preserves certain specific parts of the structure. We have called these the s_0-morphism and the D-morphism. We discuss in this paper two different ways in which the structures of two games can be related in both cases it being shown how they allow one to use a winning strategy in one to construct the winning strategy in the other.

We have also isolated two classes of games—the positional and the decomposable class. For any game in either of these two classes, a winning strategy can easily be constructed. It is therefore of interest to know how one can discover whether a certain game has either an s_0-morphism or a D-morphism with a positional or a decomposable game.

We have investigated this discovery procedure and find that it would involve the isolation of certain properties which are related to the rules of the game in given ways, like *if two game states are connected, then they differ in only one essential property* or *if two related states differ in a property then any other state sharing the property to the first state is connected to some state sharing the property with the second state.* This introduces an aspect of representation closely related to the transformation to similar games, i.e., that of the language of description used for the game. It will be noted that the isolation of properties referred to above would be highly facilitated if the language in which the game is described allows simple descriptions of the properties involved. For instance in the representation of the Pawn game we have given so far none of the 16 evident properties (i.e., those generated by the positions $x_1, x_2, x_3, \cdots, x_8, y_1, y_2, y_3, \cdots, y_8$ of the pawns) will be seen to have the characteristics required by the equivalences in Theorem 4. It would be a clever machine indeed (an excellent "feature extractor" or "representation changer") which could discover that $x_i - y_i$ would form excellent generators for the equivalences required in Theorem 4. If on the other hand the game was described by saying that a move consists of reducing the distance between the two pawns in any column and the game ends when all the distances are zero, then a mere search through all the properties mentioned in the rules would indicate that the hypotheses of Theorem 4 are fulfilled by the properties generated by the distances.

ACKNOWLEDGEMENTS

The work reported in this paper was supported by the U. S. Air Force Office of Scientific Research under Grant AFOSR-125-67 and by the National Science Foundation under Grants GK4115 and GJ-1135.

REFERENCES

[1] G. W. Ernst, Comments in Case Western Reserve University Symposium on Artificial Intelligence, *Proc. 1st Int. Joint Conf. on Artificial Intelligence*, Washington, D. C. (May 1969).

[2] S. Amarel, "On the Representation of Problems and Goal-Directed Procedures for Computers," *Theoretical Approaches to Non-Numerical Problem Solving* (Banerji and Mesarovic', Eds., New York: Springer-Verlag, 1970).

[3] A. Newell, "On the Representation of Problems," *Comput. Sci. Res. Rev.*, Carnegie Mellon University (1966).

[4] C. Berge, "The Theory of Graphs and its Applications" (John Wiley, 1962).

[5] E. B. Koffman, "Learning Games Through Pattern Recognition," *IEEE Trans. Sys. Sci. Cybern.*, SSC4-12 (March 1968).

[6] R. G. Busacker and T. L. Saaty, "Finite Graphs and Networks" (New York: McGraw Hill, 1968).

[7] E. Lasker, "The Game of Go and Go-Moku" (Dover Publications).

[8] P. F. King, "A Computer Program for Playing Positional Games," MSc. Thesis, Case Western Reserve University (1970).

[9] R. L. Citrenbaum, "Efficient Representation of Optimal Solutions for a Class of Games," Report No. SRC-69-5, Systems Research Center, Case Western Reserve University (1969).

[10] C. Dunning, H. M. Ko, and R. B. Banerji, "Some Results on Graph-Interpretable Games" (communicated).

[11] M. Minsky and S. Papert, "Perceptrons" (MIT Press, 1969).

[12] J. Von Newman and O. Morgenstern, "Theory of Games and Economic Behavior" (Princeton University Press, 1947).

[13] R. B. Banerji and G. W. Ernst, "Homomorphisms Which Preserve Strategies in Games," *Proc. 2nd Int. Joint Conf. on Artificial Intelligence*, Lnd (1971).

AN AUTOMATON-THEORETIC APPROACH TO THE FAST FOURIER TRANSFORM

M. Depeyrot, J. P. Marmorat, and J. Mondelli
Centre d'Automatique de l'Ecole Nationale Supérieure des Mines de Paris, Fontainebleau, France

The Fast Fourier Transform (discrete, finite) has been discovered at least four times in areas as diverse as:

- The statistics of factorial experiments (Yates-Good)
- The study of X-ray diffraction (Danielson-Lanczos)
- The design of multidirectional antennas (Butler-Lowe)
- The classification of logic functions (Blackwell-Rudolph).

An algebraic approach is required to gather these techniques within a consistent theory. Automata representations provide a hierarchy of tools for the elaboration of FFT algorithms. In particular: (i) For the computation of coefficients of the transforms (microscopic level); and (ii) The macroscopic representations of procedures and their acceleration.

A new class of semigroup extension is presented as the pseudodirect product which facilitates the study of the underlying number systems of the FFT. A new representation (nodal) can thus be developed, which is used when the series length is factorizable as a product of prime numbers (i).

A matrix (bimorphism) characterizing every type of Fourier Transform is exhibited with allows compact formulation and evaluation of the respective properties of each algorithm (ii).

Three new FFT algorithms are presented:

(1) The nodal diagonalized method eliminates the difficulty connected with permutations in previous methods [4, 5]
(2) The combination of hierarchical decomposition and the nodal diagonalized method, so as to permit permutation-free transforms of length 10^6 on an IBM 360/40
(3) The distributed method favors the elimination of permutations even when the series-length factors are not primes.

This approach makes feasible the efficient application of abstract-automata theory to signal analysis and image processing.

I. INTRODUCTION

Interest in algebraic methods has been significantly increased by the use of digital computers, since their discrete structure induces the use of finite-state models, and their programming requires dynamical models of algorithms.

Contributed to the Proceedings of the Symposium on Computers and Automata Polytechnic Institute of Brooklyn, April 13-15, 1971.

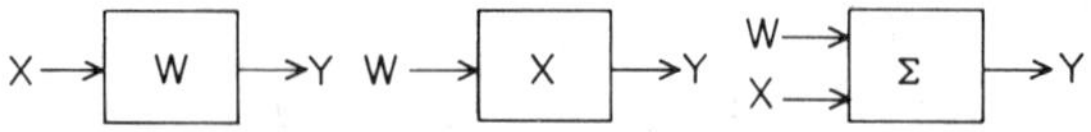

Fig. 1. The three automata of a transform algorithm W.

In this paper we make use of finite-automata theory at three levels:

(i) For the perception of the role of spectral analysis in time-series analysis (theoretical level) (Section II)
(ii) For the elaboration of coefficients w_N^{ij} entering the computations of the FFT (microscopic level) (Section III.B)
(iii) For the macroscopic representation of transform procedures and their acceleration (algorithmic level) (Section III.C).

DEFINITION. *A finite automaton is a quintuple* $\Sigma = \{U, Q, Y, \tau, \beta\}$ *where* U, Q, *and* Y, *respectively are input, state, and output spaces,* τ *is the transition function yielding the target state for any input u over an initial state* $\tau\colon Q \times U \longrightarrow Q\colon (q, u) \longrightarrow \tau(q, u) = q'$; *and where* β *is the output function* $Q \longrightarrow Y\colon q \longrightarrow \beta(q) = y$.

The advantage of automata over abstract algebra in computer science results from the not only functional but dynamical nature of the representations they provide for the mathematical phenomena they help exhibit: in that sense they more closely resemble procedures to be operated on a computer. An automaton could truly be considered as an abstract pair (U^*, β), i.e., an output function over the free semigroup generated by the input elements. But it is useful to make explicit a state space Q.

There actually are three ways to consider a transform algorithm W as an automaton: the first one consists of assimilating the time-series X to the input sequence U, and the transform W is the function $\beta[\tau(q_0, N)]$ such that $\beta[\tau(q_0, X)] = Y$, where q_0 is the rest state of the algorithm; the second way consists of assimilating the time-series X to the initial state q_0, and the transform W is defined by the input sequence $\bar{u}$ so that $\beta[\tau(X, \bar{u})] = Y$; and the third way consists of coding the input elements so that all data X and the algorithm W are sequentially fed into the automaton. We essentially make use of the former two ways.

Historically, the first authors who insisted that transforms W of the Fourier class should be considered as a "black box" with N inputs, and N outputs are Butler and Lowe [3].

II. AN AUTOMATON-THEORETIC GENERALIZATION OF THE FOURIER TRANSFORM

Linking Fourier-Transform acceleration and automata decomposition requires linking spectral analysis and automata algebra by means of conjugacy-class theory.

We first recall some results of algebra: the representation of groups, the classes and sums of conjugacy and the fundamental transform.

A. Matrix Representation

A representation of a semigroup $(T, \circ)$ is an endomorphism $m\colon T \longrightarrow \mathcal{T}(V)$ where $\mathcal{T}(V)$ is the full transformation semigroup over a set V which is called its representation space, such that: $m(t' \circ t'') = m(t')m(t'')$ for all t' and t'' in T. The regular representation of a group G is the morphism

$$r: G \longrightarrow \text{PERM}(G) \ , \tag{1}$$

where PERM(G) is the subgroup of $|G| \times |G|$ permutation matrices. There is a bijection between the representation space V and the group G. It is readily generalized to the semigroup case with row-monomial matrices over $\{0, 1\}$.

The diagonal representation $d(G)$ of a group which exists in the Abelian (commutative) case is obtained through the simultaneous diagonalization of all matrices $r(g_k)$ of the regular tensor $r(G)$. Elements of the representation space are represented as row vectors

$$(0,0,0, \cdots, 1,0,0, \cdots, 0) = \delta_{ij} \ . \tag{2}$$

B. Conjugacy Classes: the Class Automaton

The conjugacy class of an element g of a group G is the set

$$C_g \triangleq \{g_i g g_i^{-1} \mid g_i \in G\} \ , \tag{3}$$

the relation $g' = g_i g g_i^{-1}$ is an equivalence relation which defines a partition $\mathcal{C} = \{C_g\}$ on G. We can then consider the pair $(G, \mathcal{C})$ as an automaton

$$\Sigma_c = \{G, G, \mathcal{C}, (\cdot), A\} \ , \tag{4}$$

with: input space G; state space G; output space $\mathcal{C}$; transition function $(\cdot)$ the composition law on G; and output function A that associates to an element g of G its class C_g in $\mathcal{C}$.

The states of the automaton are represented as row vectors

$$q_g = (0,0,0, \cdots, 1,0,0, \cdots, 0) = \delta_{ig} \ , \tag{5}$$

so that actions over them are represented as permutation matrices $r(g)$ and their outputs are also noted as $|\mathcal{C}|$ row vectors

$$C_g = (0,0,0, \cdots, 1,0,0, \cdots, 0) \ , \tag{6}$$

related to the state representations through an aggregation matrix A such that $q_g A = C_g$. The sequential (or behavior [9]) function of Σ_c is written in the regular representation r

$$f_{g_0}(g_{i_1}, g_{i_2}, g_{i_3}, \cdots, g_{i_n}) = q_{g_0}[r(g_{i_1}) r(g_{i_2}) r(g_{i_3}) \cdots r(g_{i_n}) A] \ , \tag{7}$$

and gives the output, an element of $\mathcal{C}$, of Σ_c in the initial state q_{g_0} under the actions $g_{i_1}, g_{i_2}, g_{i_3}, \cdots, g_{i_n}$.

C. Class Sums

We consider the space $L_1(G)$ of formal sums [2]

$$X = \sum_{i=1}^{|G|} x_i g_i \ , \tag{8}$$

where the g_i's are elements of G and the x_i's are elements of a field K. $L_1(G)$ is a vector space on K. If C_g is a class on G which can be written

$$C_g = \{g_{i*} \mid i* \in I_g\} \ , \tag{9}$$

where I_g is a set of subscripts such that $|I_g| = \nu_g$. Then the formal sum

$$S_g = \sum_{i* \in I_g} \frac{1}{\nu_g} g_{i*} \ , \tag{10}$$

is an element of $L_1(G)$ which is called a class sum. The set $\{S_g\}$ of all the class sums generates a subvector space $\mathcal{S}$ of $L_1(G)$.

From the definition of C_g and S_g we have

$$g' S_g g'^{-1} = S_g \ , \tag{11}$$

for all g and g' in G, and then

$$g' S_g = S_g g' \ , \tag{12}$$

or

$$S'_g S_g = S_g S'_g \ . \tag{13}$$

If g_1 is the unity element of G, C_{g_1} has a unique element g_1, and $S_{g_1} = g_1$ is the unity element of $\mathcal{S}$.

It is easy to prove that $S_g S'_g$ is an element of $\mathcal{S}$.

ASSERTION. *$\mathcal{S}$ is a commutative algebra on K. We can now consider the dual automaton Σ_S* [9]

$$\sum_S = \{G, \mathcal{S}, \mathcal{S}, (\cdot), I_S\} \ , \tag{14}$$

with: input space G; state space $\mathcal{S}$; output space $\mathcal{S}$; transition function $(\cdot)$ the composition law on $\mathcal{S}$; and output function I_S which is the identity on $\mathcal{S}$.

ASSERTION. *The representation of $\mathcal{S}$ induced by the regular representation of G is*

$$S_g \longrightarrow s(g) = A^L \, r(g) A \quad \text{with} \quad C_g = q_g A \ ,$$

where the affine inverse A^L is a $|\mathcal{C}| \times |G|$ matrix [11] *such that $A^L A = I$ with entries*

$$A^L_{C_g, g'} = \begin{cases} 0 \ , & \text{if } g' \notin C_g \ , \\ \dfrac{1}{\nu_g} \ , & \text{if } g' \in C_g \ . \end{cases} \tag{15}$$

Notice the property that $s(C_g) = s(g_k) = A^L \, r(g_k) A \ \forall \ g_k \in C_g$ is a Markov matrix.

ASSERTION. *Let $M(Z)$ be the multiplication table of a monoid (semigroup) Z with entries $z_{ij} = z_i \cdot z_j$ and let $M(\mathcal{S})$ be the composition table of class sums:*

(a) $M(\mathcal{S})$ is symmetrical

(b) We now have a fast procedure to compute a semigroup character table since

$$M(\mathcal{S}) = A^L M(Z)(A^L)^T \ . \tag{16}$$

The scalar product on the Abelian algebra $\mathcal{S}$ is defined through

$$\langle S_i, S_j \rangle = \text{component of } S_{g_1} \text{ in the product } S_i S_j \ .$$

For each class S_g there is a unique class $S_{\bar{g}}$ which is the class of g^{-1} such that [7]

$$\langle S_g, S_{\bar{g}} \rangle \neq 0 \ .$$

More precisely

$$\langle S_g, S_{\bar{g}} \rangle = 1/\nu_g \ . \tag{17}$$

We now define the tensor γ_{ijk} by the relation

$$S_j S_i = \sum \nu_k \gamma_{ijk} S_{\bar{k}} \ , \tag{18}$$

the coefficients $\{\nu_k \gamma_{ijk}\}$ are the components of $S_j S_i \in \mathcal{S}$ on the basis of the $S_{\bar{k}}$'s.

Multiplying by $S_{\bar{i}} S_{\bar{k}}$ and because the product is commutative we see that γ_{ijk} is symmetrical

$$\gamma_{ijk} = \gamma_{\sigma(ijk)} \ , \tag{19}$$

for all permutations σ of i, j, and k.
We then have

$$\langle S_t, S_i S_j \rangle = \gamma_{ij\bar{t}} \ , \tag{20}$$

and

$$\langle S_i, S_j \rangle = \gamma_{1ij} \ . \tag{21}$$

Hence the concatenation for the automaton Σ_c gives place to the convolution in the algebra $\mathcal{S}$ for

$$\begin{aligned} \langle S_t, S_i S_j S_k \rangle &= \sum \nu_u \langle S_t, S_i S_u \rangle \langle S_u, S_j S_k \rangle \ , \\ &= \sum \nu_u \gamma_{\bar{t}iu} \gamma_{\bar{u}jk} \ , \end{aligned} \tag{22}$$

D. Group Characters

The commutative product on $\mathcal{S}$ leads us to look for a representation of the class sums by diagonal matrices. First we define the eigenvalues of the algebra $\mathcal{S}$.

DEFINITION. *A class eigenvalue λ_{gj} is a scalar such that*

$$S_g D_j = \lambda_{gj} D_j \ , \tag{23}$$

where: S_g is the class sum of C_g; and D_j is an element of $\mathcal{S}$

$$D_j = \sum_t \alpha_t^j S_t = \sum_u \nu_u w_{ju} S_{\bar{u}} \ . \tag{24}$$

By means of the tensor γ we write

$$S_g D_j = S_g \left(\sum \nu_t w_{jt} S_{\bar{t}}\right) = \sum \nu_t w_{jt} S_{\bar{t}} S_g \ ,$$
$$= \sum_t \nu_t w_{jt} \sum_u \nu_u \gamma_{g\bar{t}u} S_{\bar{u}} \ ,$$
$$= \lambda_{gj} \sum \nu_u w_{ju} S_{\bar{u}} \ . \tag{25}$$

We have to solve for λ_{gj} and the w's in

$$\sum_t \nu_t \gamma_{g\bar{t}u} w_{jt} = \lambda_{gj} w_{ju} \ . \tag{26}$$

There are $|\mathcal{C}|$ eigenvectors $\chi_j = (w_{1j}, w_{2j}, w_{3j}, \cdots, w_{|\mathcal{C}|j})$ such that

$$s(C_g)\chi_j^T = \lambda_j \chi_j^T \quad \text{for all } C_g \ . \tag{27}$$

The λ_j's are called the characters of the group.

THEOREM. *The character morphism formula is*

$$\chi_i(g_j) = C_i \overline{W}^T [A^L r(g_j) A] W^T C_i^T = C_i d(g_j) C_i^T \ , \tag{28}$$

and

$$\chi_i(C_j) \longrightarrow K \quad with \quad \chi_i[s(g_j)] \longrightarrow K \ ,$$
$$\chi_i(S_j)\chi_i(S_k) = \chi_i(S_j S_k) \ . \tag{29}$$

E. The Fundamental Transform

DEFINITION. *The fundamental transform $\mathfrak{F}$ of a monoid Z is the change of basis from the regular to the diagonal form of the tensor representation of its conjugacy series*

$$Z \xrightarrow{\ j^*\ } \mathcal{S} \xrightarrow{\ \mathfrak{R}\ } s(C), \qquad \mathcal{S} \xrightarrow{\ \mathfrak{D}\ } d(C) = \overline{W} s(C) W, \qquad s(C) \xrightarrow{\ \mathfrak{F}\ } d(C) \tag{30}$$

where: j^* is the antimorphism associated with the monoid Z the generator of its dual module $\mathcal{S}(\mathcal{S})$ of conjugacy series; and where the morphisms $\mathfrak{R}$ and $\mathfrak{D}$ provide

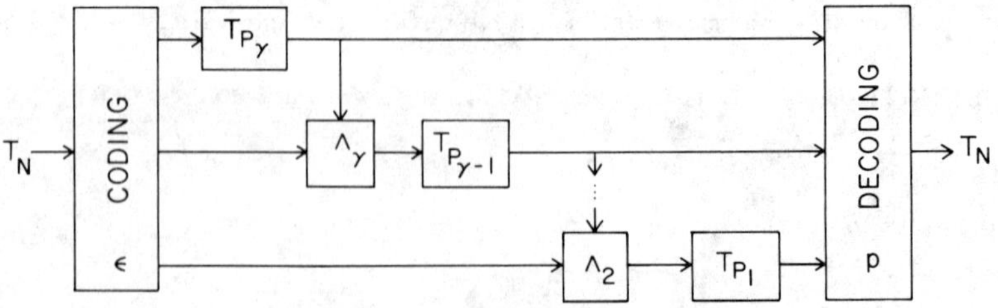

Fig. 2. Cascade decomposition of the class automaton.

the representations s(C) regular and d(C) diagonal of the conjugacy series, respectively.

The fundamental transform of Fig. 2 is represented by the matrix W of elements w_{ij} called the character table of the group G

$$d(C_i) = Ws(C_i)^T \overline{W} \quad \text{with} \quad \overline{W} = W^{-1} \quad . \tag{31}$$

The basic property of the fundamental transform of being a reversible change of basis can be applied to *spectral pattern recognition* on semigroups.

DEFINITION. *A group series X(G) in a set of data subscripted by the elements of a group G the associated matrix is a formal sum*

$$s(X) = \sum_{i=1}^{|G|} x_i r(g_i) \quad . \tag{32}$$

The aggregated matrix $\$* = A^L s(X)A = \Sigma_{i=1}^{|\mathcal{C}|} y_i s(C_i)$ defines the harmonic series Y. The fundamental transform yields

$$\$ = \sum_{i=1}^{|\mathcal{C}|} y_i d(C_i) = W \$* \overline{W} \quad , \tag{33}$$

the spectrum σ of X is the main diagonal of the representation $\$$

$$\sigma(X(G)) = \sigma(Y(\mathcal{C})) = \$ e_{|\mathcal{C}|} \quad , \tag{34}$$

with $e_{|\mathcal{C}|} = (1, 1, 1, \cdots, 1)$.

Since $|\mathcal{C}| \leq |G|$ there no longer is a bijection between group series and their spectra. More precisely, the spectral series space induces a partition of the group series space $L_1(G)$ through the pattern equivalence relation

$$X \equiv_F X' \longleftrightarrow Y = Y' \quad . \tag{35}$$

Each equivalence class admits a representative $\hat{X} = XAA^L$ where each element of a given class is given the same weight.

THEOREM. *Let $\hat{X}$ and $\hat{X}'$ be two representative series over a given group G. The series $\hat{V}$ resulting from the convolution of $\hat{X}$ and $\hat{X}'$ admits the representative regular representation $r(\hat{V}) = r(\hat{X})r(\hat{X}') \triangleq r(\hat{X} * \hat{X}')$.*

Proof. Since $r(\hat{V}) = A^L s(\hat{V})A$ and $s(\hat{V}) = \overline{W}^T s(\hat{V}) W^T$ with $s(\hat{V}) = s(\hat{X})s(\hat{X}')$ $\longleftrightarrow d(\hat{V}) = d(\hat{X})\, d(\hat{X}') \longleftrightarrow \sigma(\hat{V}) = \sigma(\hat{X}) \cdot \sigma(\hat{X}')$, where "·" denotes the term-by-term product of the spectrum. Q.E.D.

The fundamental transform thus permits the replacement of the convolution by the term-by-term product of the spectral series.

III. ACCELERATION OF THE FOURIER TRANSFORM IN THE COMMUTATIVE CASE

We now consider the previous results in the simpler case where G is a finite Abelian group, we then recall some known results on the decomposition of finite Abelian groups: we introduce a new class of semigroup extension and we consider the effect of these decompositions on character tables and fundamental transforms. This allows us to introduce a bimorphism matrix which characterizes each FFT algorithm.

A. Structure of Finite Abelian Groups

When G is a finite Abelian group the results of Section II become simpler. There is a unique element in each conjugacy class, hence a bijection between G and $\mathcal{S}$, and the modulus of each eigenvalue is one. Denoting by Z an Abelian group, and by T a cyclic Abelian group (time) we first recall some basic results.

1. The Finite Abelian Transform

The fundamental transform on a cyclic Abelian group T_N of degree N is represented by the character matrix

$$W_N = (W_{ij}) = (e^{-2\pi\sqrt{-1}\,(j-1)(i-1)/N}) \quad , \tag{36}$$

and is called the finite Abelian Transform. An harmonic series Y on an Abelian group T is equal to its spectrum.

Computing the spectrum of a series X on a group T just requires the change of basis $Y = XW$, there is a bijection between series X and its harmonic series Y. The fundamental transform is also invertible. The set of characters of a group G forms an isomorphic multiplicative group.

2. Decomposition of Groups

For any finite Abelian group Z_N there exists a unique set of integers $N_1, N_2, N_3, \cdots, N_\beta$ such that

$$N_i \text{ divides } N_{i-1}, \quad N = \prod N_i \quad , \tag{37}$$

and

$$Z_N = T_{N_1} \times T_{N_2} \times T_{N_3} \times \cdots \times T_{N\beta} \quad , \tag{38}$$

where N_1 is the smallest integer such that

$$Z_N^{N_1} = z_1 \quad \text{(unity element of the group)} \ . \tag{39}$$

A finite Abelian group cannot be written as the direct product

$$Z_N = T_{N_1} \times T_{N_2} \times T_{N_3} \times \cdots \times T_{N_\gamma} \quad , \tag{40}$$

iff it is cyclic and of order $N = p^\alpha$ where p is a prime. If Z_N is not cyclic, the T_i's are undecomposable by a direct product and their orders are $p_i^{\alpha_i}$. The collection of orders $(p_i^{\alpha_i})_{i=1}^{\gamma}$ is the decomposition list of N into elementary divisors. Thus the class automaton is decomposable into γ subautomata that operate in parallel (see Section IV).

3. Pseudodirect Product and Automaton Cascade

In order to consider more refined decompositions we need to introduce the following extension of groups.

DEFINITION. *The pseudodirect product of two cyclic groups H and K (generalizable to semigroups) is the group* [11, 13]

$$G = K \times_\Lambda H \tag{41}$$

with correction function Λ k_Λ ,

$$\Lambda: G \times K \longrightarrow H \text{ PERM}(H): (g', k) \longrightarrow \varepsilon(g')k_\Lambda \ ,$$

interlacing the image of g' *in* H *by the coding function* ε *with a permutation* k_Λ *of* H.

The groups H *and* K *form a cascade* $G = H \times_\Lambda K$ *iff the inputs of* H *are defined by a function*

$$\Lambda: (H \times K) \times K \longrightarrow H: ((h, k), k') \longrightarrow h' \ . \tag{42}$$

Theorem of the Cascade

THEOREM. *Three conditions permit cascade decomposition:*

(i) *For any group* G *with subgroups* H *and* K *such that* H *is a normal subgroup of* G, $K \cap H = g_1$ *(unity of* G*), and* $\{K \cup H\} \cong G$, G *is a semi-direct product* [12]. *If* G *is an Abelian group the product is direct*

(ii) *The class automaton* Σ_{T_N} *of a cyclic Abelian group with order* $N = \prod_{i=1}^{\gamma} p_i$, *where the* p_i*'s are prime with respect to each other, admits a direct and pseudodirect decomposition in* γ *subautomata* $\Sigma_{T_{p_i}}$

(iii) *The class automaton* $\Sigma_{T_{p^\alpha}}$ *of a cyclic Abelian group with order* $N = p^\alpha$ *where* p *is a prime admits the pseudodirect decomposition in* α *subautomata* $\Sigma_{T_{p_j}} = \Sigma_{T_p} j \in (1, 2, 3, \cdots, \alpha)$.

Refer to Fig. 3 for an example of cascade decomposition.

4. The Positional Representation

We now explicit a pseudodirect decomposition of an Abelian group.

DEFINITION. *The positional decomposition of an element* t *of an Abelian group is the list* $(\bar{p}_1, \bar{p}_2, \bar{p}_3, \cdots, \bar{p}_\gamma)$ *associated with the sequence* $\{T_{p_i}\}_{i=1}^{\gamma}$ *of* γ*-quotient subgroups with the conversion formula*

$$t \longrightarrow (\bar{p}_1, \bar{p}_2, \bar{p}_3, \cdots, \bar{p}_\gamma) = \bar{t} \ , \tag{43}$$

$$t = \sum_{i=1}^{\gamma} \bar{p}_i \left(\prod_{k=1}^{i-1} p_k \right) \quad \text{or} \quad t = (\bar{t}, \bar{p}) \ ,$$

with $\bar{p} = (1, p_1, p_1 p_2, \cdots, p_1 p_2 \cdots p_{\gamma-1})$.

B. Synthesis of the Character Table Through Factorization

1. The Bimorphism Operator

We have seen that the class automaton induces a fundamental transform $\mathcal{F}$ represented by its character table. We now observe the effect of the decomposition of groups (coding) on the associated fundamental transform: Characters are bimorphisms of two additive groups T_N and S_N in the multiplicative group $\{e^{2\pi\sqrt{-1}\,st/N}\}$ and the computation of the characters is the result of a bimorphism operator (Figure 4).

The cascade decomposition of Σ_S and Σ_T is the most general, so we now look for its effect on the computation of W_N.

2. The Bimorphism Matrix

Recall the formula

$$t = \sum_{i=1}^{\gamma} \bar{p}_i \left(\prod_{k=1}^{i-1} p_k \right) = (\bar{p}, \bar{t}) \ .$$

Dually for $s \in S_N$

$$s = \sum_{i=1}^{\gamma} \hat{p}_i \left(\prod_{k=i+1}^{\gamma} p_k \right) = (\hat{s}, \hat{p}) \ .$$

with: $\hat{p} = (p_\gamma p_{\gamma-1} p_{\gamma-2} \cdots p_2, p_\gamma p_{\gamma-1} p_{\gamma-2} \cdots p_3, \cdots, p_\gamma, 1)$; and $\hat{s} = (\hat{p}_1, \hat{p}_2, \cdots, \hat{p}_\gamma)$. Then

$$ts = \bar{t}\bar{p}^T \hat{p}\hat{s}^T = \bar{t} B_S \hat{s}^T \ ,$$

with $B_{\hat{S}}$ given in Fig. 2(a), from Eq. (45) with $N = \prod_{i=1}^{\gamma} p_i$ we obtain

$$B_S \bmod N = \begin{pmatrix} N/p_1 & N/p_1 p_2 & N/p_1 p_2 p_3 & \cdots & 1 \\ 0 & N/p_2 & N/p_2 p_3 & \cdots & p_1 \\ 0 & 0 & N/p_3 & \cdots & p_1 p_2 \\ 0 & 0 & 0 & \cdots & p_1 p_2 p_3 \\ \cdot & \cdot & \cdot & \cdot & \cdot \\ \cdot & \cdot & \cdot & \cdot & \cdot \\ \cdot & \cdot & \cdot & \cdot & \cdot \\ 0 & 0 & 0 & 0 & N/P_\gamma \end{pmatrix} . \tag{45}$$

This triangular matrix is independent of t and s and characterizes the decomposition. It is called the bimorphism matrix.

C. Triangularized Methods

Once the computation of the group characters is decomposed we must investigate the effect of this decomposition on the transform itself [10].

Theorem of Acceleration

THEOREM. *If $N = p \times q$ where p and q are integers, the matrix of the fundamental transform can be factorized in two ways. The first corresponds to the Gentleman-Sande algorithm, the second to the Cooley-Tukey algorithm. The formulae are respectively*

$$\begin{aligned} W_N^S &= (W_q \times I_p) D^{(p)} (I_q \times W_p) P^S \ , \\ W_N^T &= P^T (I_q \times W_p) D^{(p)} (W_q \times I_p) \ , \end{aligned} \tag{46}$$

where: "$\times$" is the Kronecker product of matrices; I_n is the identity matrix of order n; and P^S and P^T are permutation matrices such that

$$(P^S)^{-1} = \mathrm{Tr}[P^S] = P^T \ , \tag{47}$$

$$B_S = \begin{pmatrix} (p_\gamma p_{\gamma-1} p_{\gamma-2} \cdots p_2)1 & (p_\gamma p_{\gamma-1} p_{\gamma-2} \cdots p_3)1 & \cdots & p_\gamma & 1 \\ (p_\gamma p_{\gamma-1} p_{\gamma-2} \cdots p_2)p_1 & (p_\gamma p_{\gamma-1} p_{\gamma-2} \cdots p_3)p_1 & \cdots & p_\gamma p_1 & p_1 \\ (p_\gamma p_{\gamma-1} p_{\gamma-2} \cdots p_2)p_2 & (p_\gamma p_{\gamma-1} p_{\gamma-2} \cdots p_3)p_2 & \cdots & p_\gamma p_1 p_2 & p_1 p_2 \\ \vdots & \vdots & \vdots & \vdots & \vdots \\ (p_\gamma p_{\gamma-1} p_{\gamma-2} \cdots p_2)(p_1 p_2 p_3 \cdots p_{\gamma-1}) & (p_\gamma p_{\gamma-1} p_{\gamma-2} \cdots p_3)(p_1 p_2 p_3 \cdots p_{\gamma-1}) & \cdots & p_\gamma(p_1 p_2 p_3 \cdots p_{\gamma-1}) & (p_1 p_2 p_3 \cdots p_{\gamma-1}) \end{pmatrix}, \quad (44)$$

Figure 2(a).

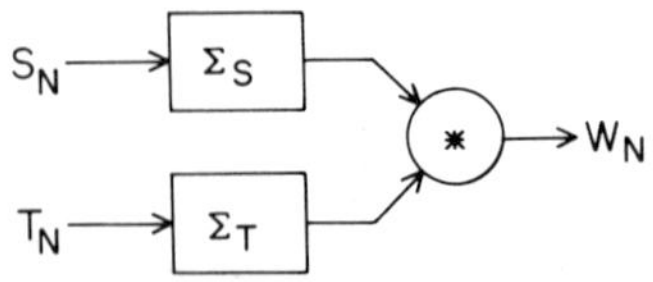

Fig. 3. The bimorphism operator.

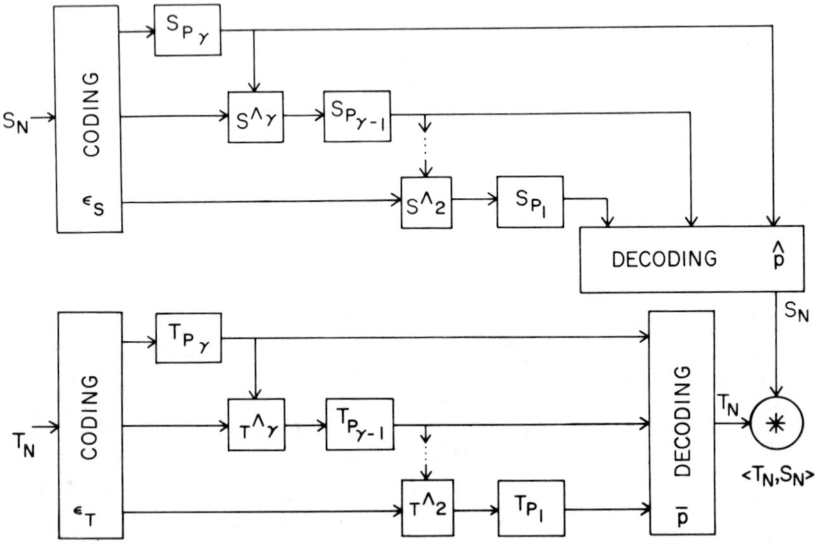

Fig. 4. Bimorphism operator before decomposition.

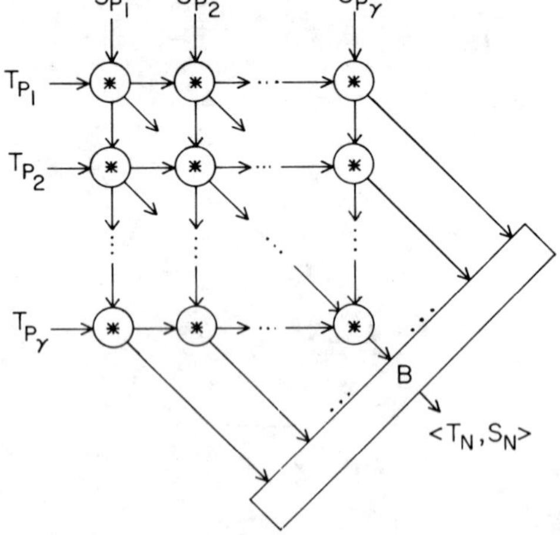

Fig. 5. Decomposed bimorphism.

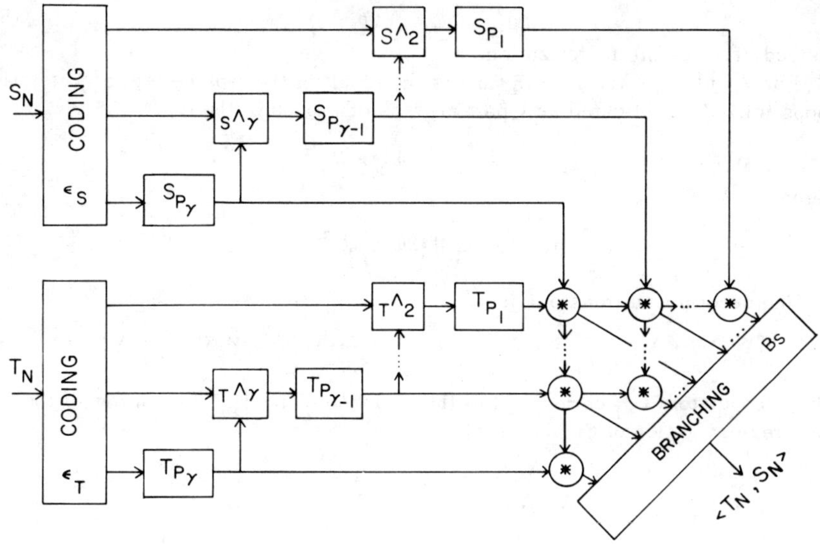

Fig. 6. Minimization of the decomposed bimorphism.

where $\mathrm{Tr}[P^S]$ *is the transpose of* P^S. $D^{(p)}$ *is a diagonal matrix with entries*

$$d_i^{(p)} = w_N^{[i/p]\,[i]_p} \qquad (i = 0, 1, 2, \cdots, N-1) \ , \tag{48}$$

with: $w_N = e^{-2\pi\sqrt{-1}/N}$, *and* $[i/p]$ *and* $[i]_p$ *are the quotient and the remainder of the division of* i *by* p, *respectively.*

The matrix P^S can be defined by the formulae

$$P^S\colon\ i = [i]_p + p[i/p], \quad j = [i]_p q + [i/p] \ , \tag{49}$$

or

$$P^S\colon\ s = (\hat{p}, \hat{s}) \longrightarrow s^P = (\bar{p}, \hat{s}) \ , \tag{50}$$

and

$$P^T\colon\ t = (\bar{t}, \bar{p}) \longrightarrow t^P = (\bar{t}, \hat{p}) \ . \tag{51}$$

Proof. [13] We have $\bar{t} = ([t]_q, [t/q])$ and $\hat{s} = ([s/p], [s]_p)$. Then P^S makes the permutation required by the difference between the composition sequences dually chosen for T_N and S_N.

To compute $Y = XW_N$ we generate all the characters $\langle t, s\rangle$, which can be done for a fixed s using the decomposed automaton Σ_{T_N}. By means of matrix B_S

$$y(s) = \sum_{\bar{p}_e} w_N^{(0,\bar{p}_2)B_S \mathrm{Tr}[\hat{s}]} \sum_{\bar{p}_1} x(\bar{t}\,\bar{p}^{\,T})\, w_N^{(\bar{p}_1 0)B_S \mathrm{Tr}[\hat{s}]} \ , \tag{52}$$

with

$$\bar{t} = (\bar{p}_1, \bar{p}_2) \ .$$

The matrices $W_q \times I_p$ and $W_q \times W_p$ contain many zeros and the computation requires a number of operations proportional to

$$pq^2 + qp^2 = N(p+q) \;, \tag{53}$$

instead of N^2 before factorization.

For $N = \prod_{i=1}^{\gamma} p_i$ the gain in time is the result of the replacement of γ iteration loops initially umbricated by γ partial-transform loops of the type

$$C_{p_i} = I_{p_\gamma p_{\gamma-1} p_{\gamma-2} \cdots p_{i+1}} \times W_{p_i} \times D^{(p_{i-1} p_{i-2} p_{i-3} \cdots p_1)} \;, \tag{54}$$

here

$$W_N = \left(\prod_{i=1}^{\gamma} C_{p_i} \right) P^S \;. \tag{55}$$

The decomposed transform is

$$X_\gamma \xrightarrow[C_{p_\gamma}]{} X_{\gamma-1} \xrightarrow[C_{p_{\gamma-1}}]{} X_{\gamma-2} \longrightarrow \cdots \xrightarrow[C_{p_1}]{} X_0(s) = Y(S^P) \xrightarrow[P^S]{} Y(s) \;. \tag{56}$$

The suboperators C_{p_i} correspond to the N/p_i transform W_{p_i} of each row of the toric representation of the data [13]

$$X_i \longrightarrow \begin{pmatrix} X_i(0) & X_i(N/p_i) & \cdots X_i(N - N/p_i) \\ X_i(1) & X_i((N/p_i)+1) & \cdots X_i(N - (N/p_i)+1) \\ \cdot & \cdot & \cdot \\ \cdot & \cdot & \cdot \\ \cdot & \cdot & \cdot \\ X_i((N/p_i)-1) & X_i((2N/p_i)-1) & \cdots X_i(N-1) \end{pmatrix} = \mathcal{T}_i(X_i) \;. \tag{57}$$

The diagram of a suboperator C_{p_i} is

$$\begin{array}{ccc} X_i(\cdot) & \xrightarrow{\quad C_{p_i} \quad} & X_{i-1}(\cdot) \\ \mathcal{T}_i \searrow & & \uparrow \mathcal{T}_i^{-1} \\ \mathcal{T}_i(X_i) & \xrightarrow[W_{p_i}]{} & \mathcal{T}_i(X_i) W_{p_i} \end{array} \tag{58}$$

The use of matrix formulations is to clarify the computation procedures of new algorithms and to permit a priori investigation and evaluation of their advantages for spectral analysis. Communication between analyst and programmer becomes easier. A new representation of numbers (nodal) and the compact formulation of the bimorphism matrix leads to a new diagonalized algorithm to be presented next.

IV. DIAGONALIZED METHODS

In the case where the p_i's are prime to each other, we can deduce from the decomposition of the group automaton, diagonalized methods for the factorization of the transform. They have the advantage over the triangularized methods of being permutation free and requiring less trigonometric computation of the characters.

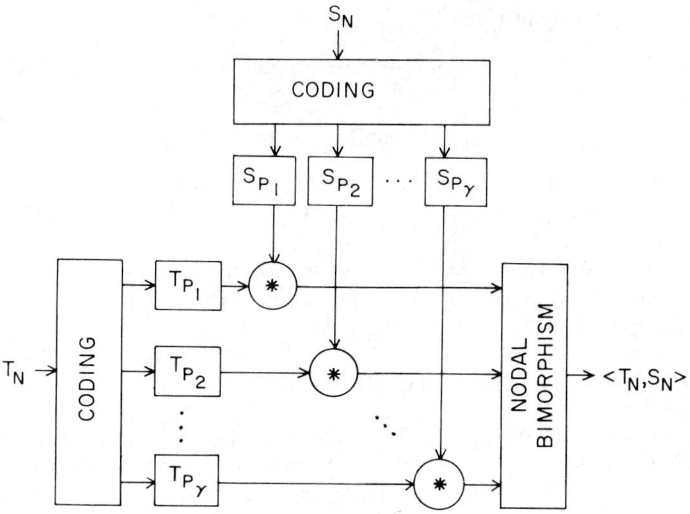

Fig. 7. Parallel decomposition of the bimorphism.

A. Modular and Nodal Representation

The bijection between Z_N and the direct product $\prod_{i=1}^{\gamma} T_i$ is built by means of the Chinese remainder theorem. For all integers $(p_1, p_2, p_3, \cdots, p_\gamma)$ that are prime to each other and for all integers $(\tilde{p}_1, \tilde{p}_2, \tilde{p}_3, \cdots, \tilde{p}_\gamma)$ the congruence list

$$t \bmod p_i = \tilde{p}_i \quad (i = 1, 2, 3, \cdots, \gamma) ,$$

admits a unique solution mod $N = \prod_{i=1}^{\gamma} p_i$, which is given by

$$t \bmod N = \sum_{i=1}^{\gamma} \delta_i N/p_i \tilde{p}_i ,$$

where $\delta_i \bmod p_i = (N/p_i)^{-1}$.

The list $(\tilde{p}_1, \tilde{p}_2, \tilde{p}_3, \cdots, \tilde{p}_\gamma)$ is the modular representation of t. While it is easy to compute the modular representation of $t \in Z_N$, the computation of the δ_i's makes it uneasy to compute t from the $\tilde{p}_i$'s. We thus introduce the *nodal representation*

$$t \in Z_N \longrightarrow (p_1^\dagger, p_2^\dagger, p_3^\dagger, \cdots, p_\gamma^\dagger) ,$$

with

$$p_i^\dagger \bmod p_i = \delta_i \tilde{p}_i ,$$

such that

$$t \bmod N = \sum_{i=1}^{\gamma} (N/p_i) p_i^\dagger .$$

B. The Bimorphism Matrices

THEOREM. *The modular and the nodal representation permit the building of three diagonal matrices*

$$B_{\text{mod}} \triangleq \text{Tr}[\tilde{p}]\tilde{p} \qquad \text{where} \quad \tilde{p} \triangleq (\delta_i N/p_i) \ ,$$

$$B_{\text{nod}} \triangleq \text{Tr}[p^\dagger]p^\dagger \quad \text{where} \quad p^\dagger \triangleq (N/p_i) \ ,$$

$$B_{\text{mix}} \triangleq \text{Tr}[\tilde{p}]p^\dagger = \text{Tr}[p^\dagger]\tilde{p} \ ,$$

these matrices are diagonal mod N. *The Good algorithm makes use of the matrix* B_{mix}. *It can be seen that the nodal representation avoiding the calculus of the* δ_i*'s is more efficient.*

C. Parallel Decomposition of the Bimorphism

The decomposition of Z_N in a direct product $Z_N = T_{p_1} \times T_{p_2} \times T_{p_3} \times \cdots \times T_{p_\gamma}$ induces a parallel decomposition of the bimorphism operator which generates the characters W_N. The automaton is then the product of γ subautomata that operate in parallel.

D. The Theorem of Nodal Acceleration [13]

We define the nodal transform W_p^D relative to N, of a p vector such that $(N/p, p) = 1$, where (p, q) means that the greatest common divisor of p and q is 1, by replacing the terms $w_p^{s^\ddagger t^\dagger}$ by $w_p^{s^\ddagger t^\dagger N/p}$, in the formula of the fundamental transform W_p, that is each entry of W_p is exponentiated to the power N/p.

THEOREM. The conditions are:

(i) *If* $N = p \times q$ *with* $(p,q) = 1$ *the matrix of the Fourier transform* W_N *can be factorized in*

$$W_N = Q^{-1}(W_q^D \times W_p^D)Q = Q^{-1}(W_q^D \times W_p^D)Q \ .$$

We must know the exponentials $w_p^{s^\ddagger t^\dagger}$ *and* $w_q^{s^\ddagger t^\dagger}$, *that means we have to compute* $p + q$ *instead of* pq *exponentials. The matrix* Q *is a permutation matrix*

$$Q\colon\ t = \langle(\bar{t}_1, \bar{t}_2, \bar{t}_3, \cdots, \bar{t}_\gamma), \bar{p}\ \rangle \longrightarrow \tilde{t} = \langle(\bar{t}_1, \bar{t}_2, \bar{t}_3, \cdots, \bar{t}_\gamma), p^\dagger\rangle$$

with

$$\bar{p} = (1, p_1, p_1 p_2, \cdots, p_1 p_2 p_3 \ldots p_{\gamma-1}) \ ,$$

$$p^\dagger = (N/p_1, N/p_2, N/p_3, \cdots, N/p_\gamma) \ .$$

(ii) *The Fourier transform can be accelerated by the nodal method without doing the permutation* Q *explicitly.*

Proof. Recall the formulae

$$t = \sum_{i=1}^{\gamma} (N/p_i)p_i^\dagger \ , \qquad s = \sum_{i=1}^{\gamma} (N/p_i)p_i^\ddagger \ ,$$

$$ts \bmod N = \sum_{i=1}^{\gamma} (N/p_i)^2 \, p_i^{\dagger} \, p_i^{\ddagger} \quad ,$$

and

$$w_N^{ts} = \prod_{i=1}^{\gamma} w_N^{(N/p_i)^2 p_i^{\dagger} p_i^{\ddagger}} = \prod_{i=1}^{\gamma} w_{p_i}^{(N/p_i) p_i^{\dagger} p_i^{\ddagger}} \quad ,$$

then

$$W_N = \prod_{i=1}^{\gamma} C_{p_i} \quad ,$$

with

$$C_{p_i} = Q^{-1}(I_{p_1 p_2 p_3 \cdots p_{i-1}} \times W_{p_i}^D \times I_{p_{i+1} p_{i+2} p_{i+3} \cdots p_\gamma}) Q \quad .$$

Let

$$X_\nu = X(I_\mu \times W_\nu) \quad ,$$

the μ first components of X_ν depend only on the μ first components of X and so on, so that a suboperator $Q^{-1}(I_\mu \times W_\nu)Q$ need only an auxiliary μ vector to process the transform and the permutations are implicitly done in the addressing.

So, when N is a product of γ factor prime with each other the gain in memory space for the exponentials, and their calculus and the gain in time by avoiding the permutation make the nodal method very efficient. Q.E.D.

V. SOME BASIC EXTENSIONS

A. Hierarchical Method for Large Series [14]

An advantage of the fact that no permutations must be done in the nodal transform is to permit transformations of long length series which cannot be stored in a computer memory.

If $N = p \times q$, with $(p, q) = 1$, and such that a transformation of order p or q can be performed in the computer. The hierarchical method of order N consists of q transforms of order p and q transforms of order q. To perform the transforms of order p and q, triangular or diagonal methods can be used.

Such a method allows 10^6 data transforms, for transforms of order 1,000 can easily be performed in conventional computers. The data must be stored in an external memory and the block of data to be transformed is stored in the computer memory only during its treatment. Another advantage in that we have to compute $(p + q)$ instead of pq values of a complex exponential, avoiding a loss of precision. For example the value of $\sin 2\pi \times 10^{-6}$ is always represented by zero in a finite-length word.

B. Distributed Methods and Parallel Computation [13]

The formula of the triangular methods can be iterated in the case where N is a product of more than two factors, $N = pqr$. Then

$$W_N^S = (W_r \times I_{pq}) D_N^{pq} (I_r \times W_{pq}) P_{r,pq}^S \quad ,$$

and

$$W_{pq}^S = (W_q \times I_p) D_{pq}^p (I_q \times W_p) P_{q,p}^S \quad ,$$

$$\longrightarrow W_N^S = \left[(W_r \times I_{pq}) D_N^{pq}\right] \left[I_r \times W_q \times I_p)(I_r \times D_{pq}^p)\right] (I_{rq} \times W_p)(I_r \times P_{q,p}^S) P_{r,pq}^S \quad ,$$

which can be written

$$W_N^S = C_r^S C_q^S C_p^S P_N^S \quad .$$

In the same way

$$W_N^P = (W_{rq} \times I_p) D_N^p (I_{rq} \times W_p) P_{rq,p}^S \quad ,$$

$$W_{rq}^P = (W_r \times I_q) D_{rq}^q (I_r \times W_q) P_{rq}^S \quad ,$$

$$\begin{aligned} \longrightarrow W_N^P &= \{[(W_r \times I_q) D_{rq}^q (I_r \times W_q) P_{r,q}^S] \times I_p\} D_N^p (I_{rq} \times W_p^S) P_{rq,p}^S \quad , \\ &= [W_r \times I_{qp}] \left[(D_{rq}^q \times I_p)(I_r \times W_q)(P_{rq}^S \times I_p)\right] \left[D_N^p (I_{rq} \times W_p^S) P_{rq,p}^S\right] \quad , \\ &= Z_r^S Z_q^S Z_p^S \quad . \end{aligned}$$

Thus we have included the permutation in the partial transform Z_{p_i} which allows parallel computation (of long length series in particular) on a multiprocessor computer, each processor performing a subtransform Z_{p_i}.

ACKNOWLEDGEMENTS

This work would not have been possible without the support of the I.R.I.A. (Institut de Recherche en Informatique et Automatique) and the E.D.F. (Direction des Etudes et Recherches de l'Electricité de France).

The contribution of Mark H. Schlam in the preparation of this paper for publication in this Proceedings is gratefully acknowledged.

REFERENCES

[1] I. J. Good, "The Interaction Algorithm and Practical Fourier Analysis," *J. Stat. Soc. B*, **20**, 361–372 (1958). Also **22**, 372–375 (1960).

[2] W. Rudin, "Fourier Analysis on Groups," No. 12 (Wiley, Interscience, 1960).

[3] J. Butler and R. Lowe, "Beam-Forming Matrix Simplifies Design of Electronically-Scanned Antennas," *Electron. Des.*, **9**, 170–173 (April 12, 1961).

[4] J, W. Cooley and J. W. Tukey, "An Algorithm for the Machine Calculation of Complex Fourier Series," *Math. Comput.*, **19**, No. 90, 297–301 (April 1965).

[5] W. M. Gentleman, G. Sande, "Fast Fourier Transforms—For Fun and Profit," *AFIPS*, **29**, 563–578 (Spartan, FJCC, 1966).

[6] J. W. Cooley, P. A. W. Lewis, and P. D. Welch, "Historical Notes on the Fast Fourier Transform," *Proc. IEEE*, **55**, No. 10, 1675–1677 (October 1967).

[7] G. G. Hall, "Applied Group Theory," *Mathematical Physics Series* (Longmans, 1967).

[8] M. C. Pease, "An Adaptation of the Fast Fourier Transform for Parallel Processing," *J. ACM*, **15**, No. 2, 252–264 (April 1968).

[9] M. Depeyrot, "Operand Investigation of Stochastic Systems," PhD. Thesis, Stanford (May 1968).

[10] P. K. Blackwell, II, "The Classification of Logic Functions," PhD. Thesis, Syracuse (June 1968).

[11] M. Depeyrot, "Un Algorithme Rapide de Décomposition," *Proc. Colloque International Systèmes Logiques-Conception et Applications* (Brussels, September 15–20, 1969).

[12] M. A. Arbib, "Theories of Abstract Automata," (Prentice-Hall, 1969).

[13] M. Depeyrot, "Fondements Algébriques de la Transformée de Fourier Rapide," *Cahier de l'IRIA*, No. 3 (November 1970).

[14] M. Depeyrot and J. Mondelli, "Organisation Hiérarchique de la Transformation de Fourier Rapide," *Automatisme* (April 1971).

[15] J. Mondelli, "Notice d'Emploi du Programme de T.F.R. Hiérarchisée," *Centre d'Automatique*, 16 (July 1970).

[16] J. P. Marmorat, "Notice d'Emploi du Programme de Transformation de Fourier Bidimensionnelle," *Centre d'Automatique*, 20 (April 1971).

AN INTERACTIVE SYSTEM FOR PROGRAM VERIFICATION

T. Lyons and J. Bruno
Department of Electrical Engineering, Princeton University, Princeton, NJ

In this paper we report our work on an interactive programming system which allows a programmer to verify certain properties of a program. The language used to express algorithms is based on *D*-charts and is restricted to the data types integer and "node." Semantic statements (statements about the algorithm) are made in the first-order predicate calculus and verification is achieved using "verification conditions" and mechanical theorem-proving techniques such as "resolution." It has been our goal to develop a system which is interactive and one which includes facilities for complex data structures.

The use of a GOTO-less programming language has proved to be beneficial in a number of ways. For example, it greatly eased the problem of assigning semantic statements (predicates) and enabled us to exhibit the dependence of "strongest verifiable conditions" at specific points in the program on the inductive hypothesis of every "while" clause and the entrance assertion.

In order to accommodate a top-down programming style, the notion of semantics has been posed so as to include the use of macrostatements which allow one to extend the basic language. The problem of recursively-defined predicates has been surfaced and a solution given which involves a further extension of the notion of semantics to include a description of these varying predicates.

INTRODUCTION

The logical validation of programs, based on the concepts advanced in Robert Floyd's paper "Assigning Meanings to Programs" [1], has attracted increasing attention. James King, for example, has demonstrated [2] that an interpretation-oriented theorem prover can establish the validity of a number of elementary algorithms in integer arithmetic. For the purpose of studying the problems peculiar to programs which primarily manipulate data structures, and the formal-proof techniques which are especially applicable to the validation process, we have designed an interactive system called VERIFIER, on which we report in this paper.

In its present form, VERIFIER accepts programs written in a skeletal structured language based on *D*-charts [3] and annotated with sentences of the first-order predicate calculus. Thru a liberal definition of the semantics which may be assigned to a program statement, VERIFIER accommodates the segmentation of the tasks of constructing and validating a program. And rules of inference have been discovered which allow annotation using recursively-defined predicate symbols which exhibit changes of state. The manual direction of mechanical-

Presented at the Symposium on Computers and Automata
Polytechnic Institute of Brooklyn, April 13–15, 1971.

refutation techniques has indicated which tasks VERIFIER must yet subsume autonomously before the process of verification becomes a convenient means of debugging programs.

ALGORITHM SPECIFICATION

The expression of algorithms in VERIFIER is done in a GOTO-less programming language. Flow of control is accomplished by using *if-then-else, while-do,* and *begin-end* constructions. Well-known algorithms, based on the introduction of Boolean flags, suffice to embed an arbitrary iterative program into a GOTO-less program. This transformation is possibly purchased, of course, at the price of merciless obfuscation. We advocate writing in the above style initially because it demands a mental discipline which facilitates annotation and verification.

D-charts provide a graphical representation for GOTO-less programs, which we shall use for expressing algorithms. The correspondence between syntax and *D*-chart elements is displayed in Figure 1. *D*-charts of programs can be obtained from VERIFIER.

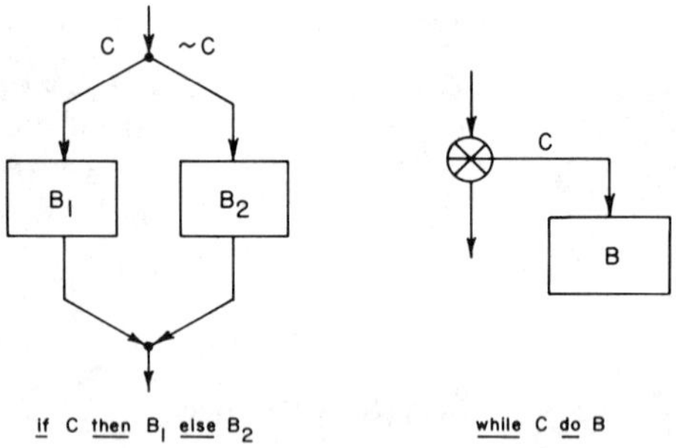

Fig. 1. The correspondence between GOTO-less syntax and *D*-chart elements.

In all respects we have sought to retain a simplicity in syntax consistent with the provision of material with which to experiment. All identifiers are globally declared and a macrodefinition facility (with no passing of parameters) is available. The two data types are integer and "node." Identifiers can denote integer or pointer variables, fields, or multidimensional arrays. The minimal arithmetic operations are defined. And nodes comprise an intrinsically unconstrained set wherein links find their domain and range. Within this framework, however, even such constructions as recursive-procedure calls can be imitated.

PROGRAM SEMANTICS

The semantics of a program P are determined by the semantic predicates which express the effect of passing control thru a node of the associated *D*-chart. The semantics of traversing a path is given, in general, by a sentence $S(\xi, \xi')$ of the predicate calculus, which relates ξ', the final-state vector of function and variable symbols, to ξ, the initial-state vector. However, we observe the convention of suppressing all declarations, such as $x' = x$, that the value of a variable remains unchanged. The semantic predicate of the statement $i \longleftarrow i + 1$, for example, is expressed as $i' = i + 1$. The decision node *if* $A(i) > A(j)$ *then* $\cdots$ contributes the semantics $A(i) > A(j)$ to its "true" branch and $\sim A(i) > A(j)$ to its "false" branch.

The calculation of the semantics (called a *path predicate*) of moving from a point p_1 in the *D*-chart of *P* to another point p_2 along a specified path is straightforward. Let $S_1, S_2, S_3, \cdots, S_n$ be a sequence of statements, where in the case of a decision node the "true" or "false" branch is specified. Then $S_{12}(\xi, \xi')$, the semantics of passing from S_1 to S_n in sequence, is given by

$$S_{12}(\xi,\xi') = \exists\, \xi^1, \exists\, \xi^2, \exists\, \xi^3 \cdots \exists\, \xi^{n-1}$$
$$S_1(\xi,\xi^1) \wedge S_2(\xi^1,\xi^2) \wedge S_3(\xi^1,\xi^2) \wedge \cdots \wedge S_n(\xi^{n-1},\xi') \ , \quad (1)$$

where $S_i(\cdot\,,\cdot)$ is the semantic predicate for statement S_i for $i = 1, 2, 3, \cdots, n$.

A path predicate $S(\xi, \xi')$ may incorporate temporaries, in the form of existentially bound variables, which cannot be removed during the process of forward substitution. For example, we prefer to defer expanding the description of an array to which multiple assignments have been made by introducing new symbols for its intermediate states. Further, the semantics which we shall allow to be assigned to the invocation of a macro will frequently be complex formulas.

PROGRAM ANNOTATION

The annotation of *P* consists in attaching to the edges of its *D*-chart (or equivalently at points in the text of *P*) assertions $A(\xi)$ which purport to characterize the state vector at the particular point of the program. The verification of properties of *P* is attempted in terms of the assertions and semantics associated with *P*. For example, if $A_1(\xi)$ is an assertion at point p_1 of *P*, $S_{12}(\xi, \xi')$ is a path predicate from p_1 to p_2, and $A_2(\xi)$ is an assertion at point p_2, then the validity of

$$A_1(\xi) \wedge S_{12}(\xi,\xi') \longrightarrow A_2(\xi') \ , \quad (2)$$

implies that if $A_1(\xi)$ is true at p_1, and the execution of *P* follows the path associated with $S_{12}(\xi, \xi')$, then $A_2(\xi')$ will be true at p_2.

A program may be said to be sufficiently annotated when it has been endowed with an *input assertion* $A_0(\xi)$ and *inductive assertions* $A_i(\xi)$, for $i = 1, 2, 3, \cdots, m$, numerous enough to interdict all of the loops of the program. Under these circumstances there are but a finite number of (simple) paths along which control can flow from one assertion to another, hence, a finite number of formulas of the form

$$A_i(\xi) \wedge S_{ij}(\xi,\xi') \longrightarrow A_j(\xi') \ . \quad (3)$$

Suppose that each form of Eq. (3) is valid and that the input assertion $A_0(\xi)$

is true for an input state ξ_0. It follows that at any future time during the execution of P, if ξ' is the current state at the point p_j to which the jth inductive assertion is attached, then $A_j(\xi')$ must be true.

More generally, consider an arbitrary point p, and let $S_{ip}^{(k)}(\xi, \xi')$ range over the semantic predicates associated with simple paths from an inductive assertion or input condition to p. Then one of the following sentences is true of the current state ξ' at p

$$\exists \xi \left[A_i(\xi) \wedge S_{ip}^{(k)}(\xi, \xi')\right] , \tag{4}$$

namely, the one associated with the path along which control most recently flowed to p.

THE VALIDATION TASK

Due to the limitations placed on branching in GOTO-less programs, one obtains a sufficiently annotated program by attaching inductive assertions to the "true" branch of each "while" clause. Henceforth, we assume P to be endowed with precisely this set of *inductive assertions*. Let $A_i(\xi)$ adorn the ith while clause for $i = 1, 2, 3, \cdots, m$, and for a point p in P, let C_{ip} denote the collection of simple control paths from the right branch of the ith while clause to p. If $\gamma \in C_{ip}$, then let $S_\gamma(\xi, \xi')$ be the associated path predicate. Given the annotation, the strongest possible consequence which can be derived at the point p is

$$\bigvee_{\gamma \in C_{ip}} \exists \xi_0 [A_i(\xi_0) \wedge S_\gamma(\xi_0, \xi)] \qquad (\text{for } i = 0, 1, 2, \cdots, m) . \tag{5}$$

An assertion $B(\xi)$ at p can be inferred from the annotation if it is not stronger than this strongest possible consequence, or equivalently if

$$\bigwedge_{\gamma \in C_{ip}} \{A_i(\xi) \wedge S_\gamma(\xi, \xi') \longrightarrow B(\xi')\} \qquad (\text{for } i = 0, 1, 2, \cdots, m) , \tag{6}$$

is valid.

The *output assertion* $B(\xi)$ at the exit point p of the program should, in particular, satisfy Equation (6). This requirement along with the validity of Eq. (3), may be incorporated into the following statement: *The problem of proving a program correct consists of verifying that the annotation by inductive assertions is consistent and potent, that is, that each inductive assertion and the output assertion follows from the strongest possible consequence at its respective location.*

As it stands, of course, the validation of Eq. (6) is too demanding a task for either man or machine. Rather, recognizing that the validity of the formula $\vee C_i \longrightarrow \wedge D_j$ is equivalent to the concurrent validity of the formulas $C_i \longrightarrow D_j$, one casts the consistency of an annotation as the problem of proving that the individual conjuncts of an inductive assertion are implied by the strongest-possible consequence obtained along each of the several control paths which flow from another inductive assertion or the initial condition. To have a machine merely handle the bookkeeping required to propagate forward the semantic path predicates and define the theorems which must be proved is a great convenience.

THE SEMANTICS OF MACROSTATEMENTS

The construction of an algorithm of moderate complexity can often be facilitated by generating it from the top down, in the manner proposed by Dijkstra [4] and recently demonstrated by Hoare [5], proceeding to a more detailed specification of its components only after they have been properly coordinated at a higher level of abstraction. To accommodate this style of programming in a system for verification requires the ability, firstly, to define the meaning of higher-level operations and, secondly, to confirm this meaning in more detailed specifications. In practice, VERIFIER permits the unconstrained assignment of semantic predicates $S(\xi, \xi')$ to the macrostatements within a program and expects the annotator to justify his assignments thru validation of the macrotext. Foregoing this incidental validation is equivalent to extending the basic language. New symbolic statements, posed as dummy macros, may be defined by their effect on the environment.

But to insure that the semantics declared during the top-down generation of an algorithm are, indeed, realizable requires the validation of macros. Let a macrotext be prefixed by the copying of its initial program state ξ into a static vector ξ_0; in fact, only those components need be copied to which comparison will be made upon exit and which will be rewritten before exit. Annotation of the text may then be made in terms of the new state vector (ξ_0, ξ), as in the example of Figure 2. *If $P(\xi)$ is the input assertion and $Q(\xi_0, \xi)$ is the output assertion of*

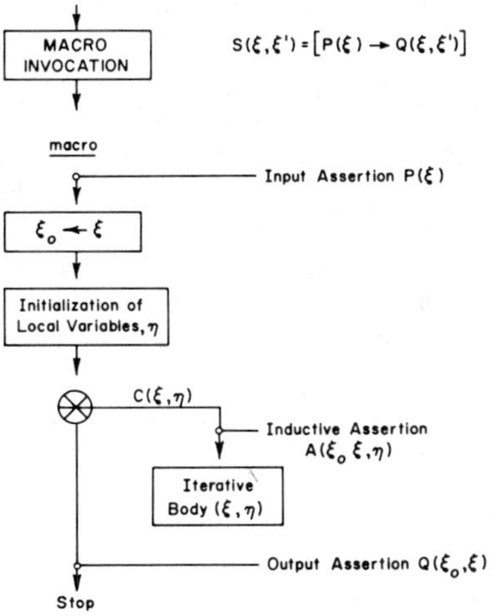

Fig. 2. The replacement of an iterative routine by a macroinvocation. Semantics no stronger than those indicated may be attached to the invocation.

the validated text, then semantics as strong as $P(\xi) \longrightarrow Q(\xi, \xi')$ may be attached to its invocations. Conversely, $S(\xi, \xi')$ constitutes a valid semantic predicate, if it can be inferred as a valid output assertion from the input assertion "True."

The judicious replacement of complicated *D*-chart segments by appropriately-semanticized macros mitigates the validation task, because the number of formulas (Eq. (3)) to be established is the number of simple paths between inductive assertions. Isolating a deeply nested iterative routine from the major inductive assertions removes an annoying source of control paths.

PREDICATE SYMBOLS

The discussion until this point has tacitly assumed that the semantics $S(\xi, \xi')$ and inductive assertions $A(\xi)$ can be compounded from the primitive predicates which control program execution. In fact, we observe the need to introduce to the annotation, predicate symbols whose meaning *cannot* be expressed in terms of the symbols which are known to the program. Many predicates which are characteristically recursive cannot otherwise be accommodated. The extended-successor relations in a complex data structure are a case in point. Symbolic predicates are useful also for subsuming functionals like the summation operator. Writing sigma(sum, m, n, a) in place of sum $= \sum_{i=m}^{n} a(i)$, is equally useful and more convenient; both notations require the support of several inference rules. One can distinguish sets of integers or nodes by introducing predicates which denote membership, or predicate symbols can quite simply be used as a shorthand for cumbersome formulas.

Each predicate symbol which is introduced must be accompanied by a set of inference rules which delimit its *meaning*. Sometimes the rules will define templates or schema which can be considered universally valid, available to the theorem prover as axioms at all points of the program, e.g., rules for inequalities. At other times the predicates will be recursively defined in terms of variable and function symbols belonging to the program. Then the predicate symbol itself exhibits changes of state which must be recorded during the process of forward substitution.

As the terms which enter into the description of a recursively-defined predicate are rewritten, the predicate itself undergoes a possibly violent change. Consider, for example, a recursive-predicate symbol D defined by the formula Defn(ξ, D). Suppose $A_1(\xi, D)$ and $A_2(\xi, D)$ are assertions at points p_1 and p_2 in P, respectively, and that $S_{12}(\xi, \xi')$ is the path predicate associated with a simple path from p_1 to p_2, then the validity of

$$A_1(\xi, D) \wedge S_{12}(\xi, \xi') \longrightarrow A_2(\xi', D') \quad , \tag{7}$$

implies that if $A_1(\xi, D)$ is true at p_1 and execution of P follows the path associated with $S_{12}(\xi, \xi')$, then $A_2(\xi', D')$ will be true at p_2. The axioms Defn(ξ, D) and Defn(ξ', D') can, of course, be used in a refutation. The important feature to notice about Eq. (7) is that there is no term which directly relates D' to D and, moreover, the change in D cannot, in general, be mechanically deduced. Indeed, the inference rules which describe the predicate do not, in general, secure it unambiguously.

Our remedy for this difficulty is to insist on a description of these recursive-predicate symbols in terms of their previous states, which means in terms of Eq. (7) that one must include in the path-predicate terms which relate D' and D.

In the general case, let Ψ be the vector of recursive-predicate symbols used in annotating P, the semantics of traversing a path is given by a sentence $S(\xi, \xi', \Psi, \Psi')$ in the predicate calculus and the general form for Eq. (1) is

$$S_{12}(\xi, \xi', \Psi, \Psi') = \exists \xi^1, \exists \xi^2, \exists \xi^3 \cdots \exists \xi^{n-1}\, S_1(\xi, \xi^1, \Psi, \Psi^1) \wedge S_2(\xi^1, \xi^2, \Psi^1, \Psi^2) \wedge S_3(\xi^2, \xi^3, \Psi^2, \Psi^3) \wedge \cdots \wedge S_n(\xi^{n-1}, \xi', \Psi^{n-1}, \Psi') \;. \quad (8)$$

Verification of the *asserted* changes, to the extent that it is possible, will be done by the theorem prover as a separate problem.

The transitive closure of a relation appears to us to be a sufficiently-useful and prevalent construction as warrants some ability to manipulate it mechanically. Accordingly, we interpret the equation $D(x, y) = {}^*A(x, y)$ as meaning that D is the least predicate which satisfies the formula

$$D(x, y) \longleftrightarrow x = y \vee A(x, y) \vee \exists z \left[D(x, z) \wedge D(z, y)\right] \;. \quad (9)$$

Elementary inferences like Eqs. (10) and (11) follow from the definition of D. Beyond this, resolution of two conflicting transitive closures proceeds on the basis of rules like Eq. (12) and its reflection

$$\left[A(x, y) \longrightarrow A'(x, y)\right] \longrightarrow \left[D(x, y) \longrightarrow D'(x, y)\right] \;, \quad (10)$$

$$D(x, y) \wedge x \neq y \longrightarrow A(x, y) \vee \exists z \left[z \neq x \wedge A(x, z) \wedge D(z, y)\right] \;, \quad (11)$$

$$D(x, y) \wedge \sim D'(x, y) \longrightarrow \exists z_1 \exists z_2 \left[D(x, z_1) \wedge A(z_1\, z_2) \wedge D(z_2, y) \wedge D'(x, z_1) \wedge \sim A'(z_1, z_2)\right] \;. \quad (12)$$

The validation of programs which have been annotated with the limits of theorem proving in mind can be supported by just such inference rules. Indeed, these rules prove adequate to deduce the perturbation to D which results from such an expansion of A as occurs during the course of elementary algorithms.

One explanation for the difficulties frequently encountered in drawing deductions from formulas which involve recursive-predicate symbols is that those predicates which exhibit changes of state embody a great deal of information which is not being recorded in program variables and functions. One does, in fact, encounter instances in which augmenting the program by an explicit temporal variable and a vector of periodic snapshots allows the substitution of explicit comparisons with past states, grounded on elementary literals, for a more intractable recursive predicate. One cannot hope, however, to replace conveniently the extended-successor relations in complex-data structures, which are instances of the transitive closure. The need to manipulate diverse predicate symbols, externally imposed upon a program, requires techniques of formal theorem proving beyond whatever interpretation-oriented mechanisms may have been adapted to the programming language itself.

EXAMPLE: TREESORT

An example of an annotated program which illustrates many of the points made above, albeit gratuitously, is the TREESORT Algorithm of Figure 3. A binary tree is grown by successively inserting the elements of an array $a(1), a(2), a(3)$,

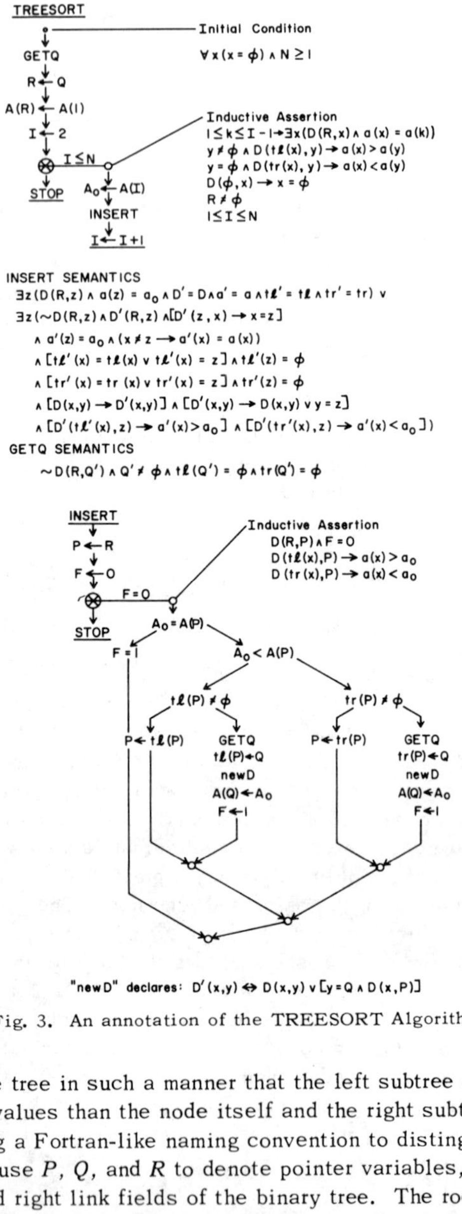

Fig. 3. An annotation of the TREESORT Algorithm.

. . . , $a(n)$, into the tree in such a manner that the left subtree of any node contains only lesser values than the node itself and the right subtree only greater values. Following a Fortran-like naming convention to distinguish pointer from integer types, we use P, Q, and R to denote pointer variables, and $t\ell$ and tr to denote the left and right link fields of the binary tree. The root of the tree we constantly denote by R, and ϕ denotes a distinguished node which will mimic a null link.

The main routine of TREESORT iterates the macro "INSERT." INSERT strikes a path into the tree from the root, looking for the proper place to deposit a_0. The semantics of INSERT are involved, (1) Because they reflect two alternative outcomes: the discovery that a_0 is already in the tree or that it is necessary to create a new node to accommodate it; and, (2) Because the second outcome demands a description of how the data structure has changed. INSERT itself calls on the macro GETQ to allocate a node which is not already in the tree. The existence of such a node can be asserted by merely attaching the indicated semantics to GETQ. It becomes unnecessary to write down a specific routine for generating new nodes. Finally, the dummy macro newD provides an avenue for describing the change to the descendant relation D which occurs when a new node is attached as a leaf to the tree. The system does not prompt dynamically for such information.

The descendant relation D is conveniently described as the transitive closure

$$D(x, y) = * \ [y = t\ell(x) \vee y = tr(x)] \wedge y \neq \phi \quad , \tag{13}$$

of the son relationship. The left subtree of x can then be characterized as the set of all y such that $D(t\ell(x), y)$ is true, the right subtree similarly. The set of nodes in the tree consists of just those x such that $D(R, x)$ is true. The three major clauses of the inductive assertion of TREESORT assert that the first $(i - 1)$ values have found a place in the tree and that the values are properly sorted. We cannot envision how the assertion of "being sorted" could be more cogently expressed. Certainly some complex predicate must be introduced, for simple assertions like $a(t\ell(x)) < a(x) < a(tr(x))$ are inadequate.

The axioms required to manipulate D and to prove the theorems which validate the annotation are six in number

$$\begin{aligned}
&D(x, y) \wedge D(y, z) \longrightarrow D(x, z) \ , \\
&y \neq \phi \wedge [y = t\ell(x) \vee y = tr(x)] \longrightarrow D(x, y) \ , \\
&D(x, y) \wedge x \neq y \longrightarrow \exists z \, [z \neq \phi \wedge (z = t\ell(x) \vee z = tr(x))] \ , \\
&D(x, t\ell(y)) \longrightarrow x = t\ell(y) \vee D(x, y) \ , \\
&D(x, tr(y)) \longrightarrow x = tr(y) \vee D(x, y) \ , \\
&\sim D(t\ell(x), R) \wedge \sim D(tr(x), R) \ .
\end{aligned} \tag{14}$$

The first three are consequences of D's definition. The latter three require the special knowledge that D describes descent in a tree. Given the description of a tree below, one can derive these further axioms and can validate the annotation at newD on the basis of such inferences from the transitive closure as were described above.

Specifically, one postulates in the special case of a tree, that

$$\begin{aligned}
&tr(x) = t\ell(y) \longrightarrow tr(x) = \phi \wedge t\ell(y) = \phi \ , \\
&x \neq y \wedge t\ell(x) = t\ell(y) \longrightarrow t\ell(x) = \phi \wedge t\ell(y) = \phi \ , \\
&x \neq y \wedge tr(x) = tr(y) \longrightarrow tr(x) = \phi \wedge tr(y) = \phi \ , \\
&D(t\ell(x), x) \vee D(tr(x), x) \longrightarrow x = \phi \ , \\
&x \neq \phi \longleftrightarrow D(R, x) \ , \\
&t\ell(\phi) = \phi \wedge tr(\phi) = \phi \ .
\end{aligned} \tag{15}$$

Should one insist on a more-thorough validation of TREESORT, it becomes necessary to assert the formulas of Eq. (15) inductively and to strengthen the semantics of INSERT. The semantics of GETQ must also be expanded into a more explicit allocation scheme; the semantics as they stand contradict the fifth clause. The complexity of the annotation, thus, increases to the point where the essential mechanism of the algorithm is obscured. The validation task also grows to encompass, in effect, the establishment as lemmas of what were listed in Eq. (14) as reasonable axioms. For an algorithm as easily comprehended as TREESORT it would be folly to pursue the annotation beyond what we have given.

The more complex programs which we aspire to validate will be granted access to a library of formulas, which characterize such data structures as binary tree, list, and queue, and a library of transformations which render them invariant. For example, Tree $(D, R, t\ell, \mathrm{tr})$ might serve as an abbreviation for the formulas

$$\begin{aligned}
&D(x, y) = *\left[(y = t\ell(x) \vee y = \mathrm{tr}(x)) \wedge y \neq \phi\right] \ , \\
&D(R, x) \wedge D(R, y) \wedge \mathrm{tr}(x) = t\ell(y) \longrightarrow \mathrm{tr}(x) = \phi \wedge t\ell(y) = \phi \ , \\
&D(R, x) \wedge D(R, y) \wedge x \neq y \wedge t\ell(x) = t\ell(y) \longrightarrow t\ell(x) = \phi \wedge t\ell(y) = \phi \ , \\
&D(R, x) \wedge D(R, y) \wedge x \neq y \wedge \mathrm{tr}(x) = \mathrm{tr}(y) \longrightarrow \mathrm{tr}(x) = \phi \wedge \mathrm{tr}(y) = \phi \ , \\
&D(R, x) \longrightarrow \sim D(t\ell(x), x) \wedge \sim D(\mathrm{tr}(x), x) \ , \\
&R \neq \phi \ .
\end{aligned} \tag{16}$$

It then need be verified only once that Tree $(D', R, t\ell', \mathrm{tr})$ is the consequence of Tree $(D, R, t\ell, \mathrm{tr})$ and the following semantic transformation

$$\begin{aligned}
&D(R,P) \ , \qquad t\ell(P) = \phi \ , \\
&D(x, Q) \vee D(Q, x) \longrightarrow x = Q \qquad (Q \neq \phi) \ , \\
&t\ell'(P) = Q \ , \qquad x \neq P \longrightarrow t\ell'(x) = t\ell(x) \ , \\
&D'(x, y) \longleftrightarrow D(x, y) \vee (y = Q \wedge D(x, P)) \ .
\end{aligned} \tag{17}$$

These semantics can be assigned to a macro named "insert Q as the left leaf of P."

Note that as one admits to consideration nodes external to the tree being observed, one must explicitly restrict quantifications to the range $\{x: D(R, x)\}$. Sets of nodes can somewhat more easily be distinguished by explicitly maintaining their characteristic functions as additional fields in every node. Nonetheless, the complexity of the theorems which must be proved creates an awesome task for one who attempts to manage data structures on the elementary level of assigning links.

To return to our example, however, it might be of interest to witness a deduction which is a small part of the validation of TREESORT. We choose to show that

$$y \neq \phi \wedge D(t\ell(x), y) \longrightarrow a(x) > a(y) \ , \tag{18}$$

remains true throughout an iteration of the primary loop. We shall assume that a node has been added to the tree during Insert, that is, we shall consider only the following alternative of the path predicate

$$
\begin{array}{lll}
a_0' = a(i) \ , & i' = i + 1 \ , & \\
D(r, z_0) \ , & D'(r, z_0) \ , & D'(z_0, x) \longrightarrow x = z_0 \ , \\
a'(z_0) = a_0' \ , & x \neq z_0 \longrightarrow a'(x) = a(x) \ , & \\
\multicolumn{3}{l}{t\ell'(x) = t\ell(x) \vee t\ell'(x) = z_0 \ ,} \\
\multicolumn{3}{l}{tr'(x) = tr(x) \vee tr'(x) = z_0 \ ,} \\
t\ell'(z_0) = \phi \ , & tr'(z_0) = \phi \ , & \\
\multicolumn{3}{l}{D(x, y) \longrightarrow D'(x, y) \ ,} \\
\multicolumn{3}{l}{D'(x, y) \longrightarrow D(x, y) \vee y = z_0 \ ,} \\
\multicolumn{3}{l}{D'(t\ell'(x), z_0) \longrightarrow a'(x) > a_0' \ ,} \\
\multicolumn{3}{l}{D'(tr'(x), z_0) \longrightarrow a'(x) < a_0' \ .}
\end{array}
\tag{19}
$$

We wish to show that these formulas imply

$$y \neq \phi \wedge D'(t\ell'(x), y) \longrightarrow a'(x) > a'(y) \ . \tag{20}$$

We proceed via refutation, as a machine would, but we do not attempt to mimic any machine-level strategy. The detailed argument appears in the Appendix. Hopefully, it is clear from the context that x and y denote free variables and that z_0, x_0, and y_0 denote constants generated through the introduction of Skolem functions.

This argument is typical of what we have seen so far, in that it proceeds most easily through the mechanisms of positing in turn the alternatives of a distinguished disjunction, of instantiating free variables to derive a ground clause, and of inferring from two ground clauses a third. Direction is provided by the heuristic of seeking to eliminate primed symbols. We have discovered that resolution directed entirely by a person at the console is unfeasible because of a frequent multiplication and recombination of literals, upon passing to conjunctive-normal form, which obscures the import of a supposedly-unsatisfiable formula. Where resolution can easily be steered to the goal of a refutation, one finds that it is so because a preference for unit ground clauses provides sufficient guidance.

THE SCOPE OF MECHANICAL ASSISTANCE

The present design of VERIFIER accommodates a number of modules which permit refutations from conjunctive-normal form to be derived manually. The assistance which they provide is primarily in the field of bookkeeping; they prevent the oversight of details which confounds pencil and paper simulations of mechanical procedures. Resolution, instantiation, substitution, the manipulation of inequalities, and the positing of the alternative disjuncts of a clause are techniques which appear adequate to the task of validating annotations from which the perturbations of recursive predicates can be excised or deferred. Sophisticated resolution strategies and unification in its general form seem to be required only for the automatic verification of the state changes of predicates. Otherwise path predicates embody enough specific terms and ground clauses to provide a refutation. Indeed, if no inductive assertion or macrosemantic is existentially quantified, then set-of-support theorems demonstrate that the validation of a consistent annotation can be based on resolution with pairs of clauses at least one of which is a ground clause. In any case, simplifications can be made upon such systems as that of Allen and Luckham [6] merely because the reconstruction of proofs has no interest for us.

Our current interest is in the attempt to exploit interaction to a greater degree by allowing the computer to generate all the resolvents of whatever ground clauses lie in the theorem-proving buffer, in coordination with useful instantiations of other clauses selected by the annotator. In the event that a refutation is not discovered, the response of the machine will be to offer up a small number of the more-concise new consequences which it may have discovered. The selection of alternative disjuncts and the preference for eliminating certain terms thru substitution will be determined by the annotator. Failing a refutation, the response of the machine can be expected to indicate either that more detailed guidance will approach a refutation, or that the current annotation requires greater strengthening and precision. This aid will be all the more appreciated to the extent that the response can be prefaced by a deconversion from conjunctive normal form to the parlance of human logic.

One of the problems which confronts us is the inherent complexity of descriptions of data structures from the primitive level of nodes and link fields. The verification of real programs would seem to suggest the desirability of investigating the problems of annotating in such detail, which is what encouraged us to choose the elementary programming language which we did. Better methods for defining predicates over a set of nodes, whose structure is constantly changing, are sorely needed. Many compromises were made in our annotation of TREESORT to cut down to reasonable size the allocation routine GETQ and the axiomatization of the descendant relation D. Currently it is merely a hope that by operating with recursive predicates on a macroscopic level and by defining acceptable semantics for common transformation of data structures, and other large scale operations, we can establish properties of programs which are more complex than the sorting algorithms which have thus far received attention.

APPENDIX: AN EXAMPLE OF A REFUTATION FROM TREESORT

1	$y_0 \neq \phi$	denial of conclusion
2	$D'(\mathrm{t}\ell'(x_0), y_0)$	denial of conclusion
3	$a'(x_0) \leq a'(y_0)$	denial of conclusion
4	$\mathrm{t}\ell'(x) = \mathrm{t}\ell(x) \vee \mathrm{t}\ell'(x) = z_0$	path predicate
5	$\mathrm{t}\ell'(x_0) = \mathrm{t}\ell(x_0) \vee \mathrm{t}\ell'(x_0) = z_0$	4
6	*assume* $\mathrm{t}\ell'(x_0) = z_0$	
7	$D'(z_0, y_0)$	2, 6
8	$D'(z_0, x) \longrightarrow x = z_0$	path predicate
9	$y_0 = z_0$	7, 8

10	$D'(t\ell'(x_0), z_0)$	2, 9
11	$D'(t\ell'(x), z_0) \longrightarrow a'(x) > a_{0'}$	path predicate
12	$a'(x_0) > a_{0'}$	10, 11
13	$a'(z_0) = a_{0'}$	path predicate
14	$a'(y_0) = a_{0'}$	9, 13
15	$a'(x_0) \leq a_{0'}$	3, 14
16	*contradiction*	12, 15
6	*otherwise* $t\ell'(x_0) \neq z_0$	
7	$t\ell'(x_0) = t\ell(x_0)$	5, 6
8	$D'(t\ell(x_0), y_0)$	2, 7
9	$D'(x, y) \longrightarrow D(x, y) \vee y = z_0$	path predicate
10	$D'(t\ell(x_0), y_0) \longrightarrow D(t\ell(x_0), y_0) \vee y_0 = z_0$	9
11	$D(t\ell(x_0), y_0) \vee y_0 = z_0$	8, 10
12	*assume* $y_0 = z_0$	
13	$D'(t\ell'(x_0), z_0)$	2, 12
14	$D'(t\ell'(x), z_0) \longrightarrow a'(x) > a_{0'}$	path predicate
15	$a'(x_0) > a_{0'}$	13, 14
16	$a'(z_0) = a_{0'}$	path predicate
17	$a'(y_0) = a_{0'}$	12, 16
18	$a'(x_0) \leq a_{0'}$	3, 17
19	*contradiction*	15, 18
12	*otherwise* $y_0 \neq z_0$	
13	$D(t\ell(x_0), y_0)$	11, 12
14	$D(t\ell(x), y) \longrightarrow a(x) > a(y)$	inductive assertion
15	$a(x_0) > a(y_0)$	13, 14
16	$x = z_0 \vee a'(x) = a(x)$	path predicate
17	$y_0 = z_0 \vee a'(y_0) = a(y_0)$	16
18	$a'(y_0) = a(y_0)$	12, 17
19	$x_0 = z_0 \vee a'(x_0) = a(x_0)$	16
20	*assume* $x_0 = z_0$	
21	$t\ell'(z_0) = \phi$	path predicate
22	$t\ell'(x_0) = \phi$	20, 21
23	$t\ell(x_0) = \phi$	7, 22
24	$D(\phi, y_0)$	13, 23
25	$D(\phi, x) \longrightarrow x = \phi$	inductive assertion
26	$y_0 = \phi$	24, 25
27	*contradiction*	1, 26
20	*otherwise* $x_0 \neq z_0$	
21	$a'(x_0) = a(x_0)$	19, 20
22	$a(x_0) \leq a(y_0)$	3, 18, 21
23	*contradiction*	15, 22

ACKNOWLEDGEMENTS

This work was partially supported by the National Science Foundation under grant number GK-5535.

REFERENCES

[1] R. W. Floyd, "Assigning Meanings to Programs," *Proc. Symp. in Applied Mathematics*, **19**, 19–32 (American Mathematical Society, 1967).

[2] J. King, "A Program Verifier," Ph.D. Thesis, Carnegie-Mellon U., Pittsburgh, Pa. (1969).

[3] J. Bruno and K. Stieglitz, "The Expression of Algorithms by Charts" (submitted for publication).

[4] E. W. Dijkstra, "Structured Programming" (privately circulated).

[5] C. A. R. Hoare, "Proof of a Program; FIND," *Corr. CACM*, **14**, No. 1, 39–45 (January 1971).

[6] J. R. Allen and D. Luckham, "An Interactive Theorem-Proving Program," *Machine Intelligence*, **5**, 321–336 (Edinburgh University Press, 1970).

SUBRECURSIVE-PROGRAMMING LANGUAGES III, THE MULTIPLE-RECURSIVE FUNCTIONS $\mathcal{R}^n$

Robert L. Constable
Cornell University, Ithaca, NY

The characterization of program structure is an elusive aspect of the theory of programming languages. Contingent on such a characterization is an interesting study of the trade-off relationships between program structure and efficiency, between structure and intelligibility, between structure and size, and so forth.

One promising definition of program structure is suggested by the studies of the structure of recursion schemata pursued by logicians in the 1930s. In this paper we carry over some of these ideas to programming and present new computer-oriented definitions of certain well-known classes of recursive functions, namely the multiple-recursive functions $\mathcal{R}^n$ of Péter. The treatment will facilitate discussions of ultracomplex functions when the need arises. Surprisingly, the need to discuss them does arise frequently at least for doubly-recursive functions when teaching results about primitive-recursive functions and the various languages for computing them. Students want examples of nonprimitive-recursive functions and computations. Theoreticians also want simple examples of functions which have high-structural as well as computational complexity. $\mathcal{R}^2$ functions and the languages given here serve these purposes.

I. INTRODUCTION

In the past ten years, computer scientists investigating computational complexity have turned their attention to classes of recursive functions such as the primitive-recursive and elementary functions, which were well known in recursive-function theory. They have found elegant new definitions for these previously difficult-to-motivate classes [3, 15, 16]. They have discovered new and significant results about them [3, 14, 15] and they have applied these classes in developing a theory of computation which in some instances may be useful to the applied-computer scientist [5, 15].

This paper will present new computer-oriented definitions of certain well-known classes of recursive functions, namely the multiple-recursive functions $\mathcal{R}^n$ of Péter. Hopefully this will make these classes more accessible to various theoreticians in computer science. At least it will facilitate the discussion of ultracomplex functions when the need arises. Surprisingly, the need to discuss them does arise frequently at least for $\mathcal{R}^2$ functions when teaching results about $\mathcal{R}^1$ functions and the various languages for computing them. Students want examples of non-$\mathcal{R}^1$ functions and computations. Researchers also need simple examples of

Presented at the Symposium on Computers and Automata
Polytechnic Institute of Brooklyn, April 13–15, 1971.

functions which have very high structural as well as computational complexity because certain phenomena show up only at such levels. $\mathcal{R}^2$ functions and the language given here serve these purposes.

II. PRELIMINARIES

A Model for Program-Language Semantics

In the next subsection certain theoretical "programming languages" will be defined. It is well known that an abstract machine model is convenient for describing the semantics of such languages. The following machine model is presented for this purpose. The model is an instance of Elgot & Robinson's [8] RASP (Random Access Stored Program machine), which in the way used here, is a very natural model whose characteristics will be familiar even to the computer scientist unacquainted with the model.

Let the machine have as *contents* $B = \mathbb{N}$, and as *addresses* $A = \mathbb{N}$ for $\mathbb{N} = \{0, 1, 2, \cdots\}$.

The addresses identify computer *words* (or registers) which are (memory) locations holding elements of B. The contents of word a is denoted by $k(a)$ or $k(\ ): A \longrightarrow B$. A *memory configuration* of the RASP is simply a content function $k(\ )$. The set of all possible memory configurations is the set $B^A = K$ of all functions from A into B. The subset of functions of finite support is denoted K_0.

The operation of a RASP is determined by defining the effect of an instruction on the memory configuration, $k(\ ) \in K$, and on the location of the next instruction which will control the computation. For the reader familiar with digital computers, this definition is quite natural. A specific RASP is determined below by presenting the instructions which generate its change of memory and change of control mappings.

DEFINITION 2.1.

MNEMONIC FORM	MACHINE FORM	MEANING
TRN(v, n)	$2^0 \cdot 3^v \cdot 5^n$	*T*ransfer the *n*umber n to the location having address v
TRV(v, w)	$2^1 \cdot 3^v \cdot 5^w$	*T*ransfer the *v*alue in location w to the location having address v
AN(v, w)	$2^2 \cdot 3^v \cdot 5^w$	*A*dd one to the value in location w and place the result in location v (leaving w unchanged)
SN(v, w)	$2^3 \cdot 3^v \cdot 5^w$	If the contents of w are positive then subtract one and place the result in location v, otherwise place 0 in v; in either case leave the value of w unchanged
TRI(v, w)	$2^4 \cdot 3^v \cdot 5^w$	*T*ransfer *i*ndirectly by using the value of w, $k(w)$ as the address, i.e., execute TRV($v, k(w)$)

The above table describes the effect of the instructions on memory. A complete description of the instruction includes specification of where to find the next instruction. This depends on how the instructions are stored in memory. For simplicity it is assumed here that all instructions are stored sequentially in *even* locations. The *odd*-numbered locations hold data. Intuitively this means that memory is divided into two banks: program bank and data bank.

For each of the above instructions, if it is located at address a (even), then the next instruction is found at location $a + 2$. The conditional branch allows interruption of this fixed flow of control.

$c(v, b)$	$2^5 \cdot 3^w \cdot 5^b$	If the value of w is nonzero (positive) then the next instruction is taken from address b otherwise from address $a + 2$

These instructions will generate the transition functions H_1 and H_2 of the RASP. Thus by the terminology of [8] the abstract machine is $<\mathbb{N}, \mathbb{N}, 0, K_0, H_1, H_2>$ where K_0 is the set of functions of finite support in $\mathbb{N}^{\mathbb{N}}$.

The language based on these instructions is intuitively clear enough for the purposes of this paper that no difficulties should result from following this intuition. However, the formal-RASP model in [8] or [24] is available to the reader if difficulties arise.

A Higher-Level Universal Language

The RASP machine language provides a formal semantic basis for all further programming languages considered here. But in order to use the language for that purpose, it is convenient to introduce a simple higher-level language (e.g., an assembly language) as an intermediate step.

The language, called G, is characteristic of the core of many numerical-programming languages. It is based on assignment statements and conditionals which test predicates and reference a linearly-ordered set of statement labels.

DEFINITION 2.2. *Syntax for* G-*type languages. Variables over integers are denoted by subscripted capital letters,* $A, B, C, \cdots, X, Y, Z, A_1, B_1, C_1, \cdots$. *Operations on integers are denoted by* f_i *so that* assignments *have the form* $w \leftarrow f(v_1, v_2, v_3, \cdots, v_n)$, *where* w *and* v_i *denote variables. The usual operators will be* $+1$, $\dot{-}1$, $+$ *and* $\cdot$.

The relations are denoted p_i and predicates are denoted $p(v_1, v_2, v_3, \cdots, v_n)$. The positive integers are used as labels and are denoted ℓ_i. A conditional has the form "if $p(v_1, v_2, v_3, \cdots, v_n)$ then ℓ_i." The usual relations are $=0$, $\neq 0$, $=$, and $\neq$.

The language also uses go to statements: go to $+\ell_i$, go to $-\ell_i$. The semantics for a specific G-type language are given below.

This high-level-type language is interpreted on a RASP by assigning variables to data locations, statements to machine-language instructions and machine instructions to locations. The details are as follows: Let $\pi = s_1; s_2; s_3; \cdots; s_n$ be any G program and let $\text{Var}(\pi) = <V_1, V_2, V_3, \cdots, V_p>$ be the list of distinct variables (in order of occurrence). A *1* – 1 function addr: $\text{Var}(\pi) \longrightarrow$ Odd addr: $\{s_1, s_2, s_3, \cdots, s_n\} \longrightarrow$ Even where $\text{addr}(s_i) = 2(i-1)$ is called a *loader table* for π. The table determines an even address corresponding to each label L or π. Let this address be denoted L^1. With respect to this table the statements of π are interpreted on the RASP as follows.

DEFINITION 2.3. *Semantics for* G.

LOCATION IN π	G STATEMENT	MACHINE-LANGUAGE STATEMENT
s_i	$v \leftarrow n$	TRN (addr (v), n)
s_i	$v \leftarrow w$	TRV (addr (v), addr (w))
s_i	$v \leftarrow w + 1$	AN (addr (v), addr (w))
s_i	$v \leftarrow w \dot{-} 1$	SN (addr (v), addr (w))
s_i	go to $+n$	$C\,(p_1, a_i + 2n)$, where: p_1 is the address of a constant 0; and a_i is the address of s_i, i.e., addr $(s_i) = a_i$. Also n must be positive
s_i	go to $-n$	$C\,(p_1, a_i - 2n)$ and n must be positive
s_i	if $v \neq 0$ then b	C (addr (v), b'), where b' is the address of the statement of π labeled b

The Loop Language

A very elegant language for expressing primitive-recursive functions has been defined independently by Minsky [16] & Ritchie [15]. Following Ritchie, the language is called the "Loop Language." The syntax for a version of Loop is presented below using a context-free grammar.

DEFINITION 2.4. *Loop Syntax.*

<letter> : : = $A \mid B \mid C \mid \cdots \mid X \mid Y \mid Z$

<label> : : = 1 | 2 | 3 | ···

<variable> : : = <letter> | <letter><label>

<term> : : = 0 | <variable> | <variable> + 1

<assignment> = <variable> ⟵ <term>

<iterative> : : = DO <variable> ; <program> ; END

<program> : : = <assignment> | <iterative> | <program> ; <program>

DEFINITION 2.5. *Loop Semantics. The Loop language is easily interpreted in terms of* G, *which in turn has been interpreted in the* RASP-*machine language. Let* v *and* w *be any variable.*

LOOP STATEMENT OR PROGRAM		INTERPRETATION IN G
$v \leftarrow 0$		$v \leftarrow 0$
$v \leftarrow w + 1$		$v \leftarrow w + 1$
if π, α, β, are programs		
α		$\overline{\alpha}$
DO v		$\overline{v} \leftarrow v$
π	1	if $\overline{v} = 0$ then 2
END		$\overline{\pi}$
β		$\overline{v} \leftarrow \overline{v} \dot{-} 1$
		go to 1
	2	$\overline{\beta}$
		where 2 labels the first statement of $\overline{\beta}$, and where $\overline{v}$ does not occur in $\overline{\pi}$, $\overline{\alpha}$, or $\overline{\beta}$, the translations of π, α, or β, respectively

Note: The variable $\overline{v}$ is called the *loop control* variable of the DO loop.

The Loop language was originally defined using the more-restricted syntax of $v \longleftarrow v + 1$, but the languages have the same computational power. In fact, one can easily define the Loop programs which will carry out the following G instructions,* for v, w_i any variables, $n \in \mathbb{N}$

$$v \longleftarrow n; \quad v \longleftarrow w; \quad v \longleftarrow w - 1; \quad v \longleftarrow w_1 + w_2; \quad v \longleftarrow w_1 \cdot w_2; \quad v \longleftarrow w_1 \div w_2 \;.$$

For example, $x \longleftarrow n$ is accomplished by the $n + 1$ statement: $X \longleftarrow 0$; $X \longleftarrow X + 1$; $X \longleftarrow X + 1$; $\cdots$; $X \longleftarrow X + 1$. The instruction $X \longleftarrow X \dot{-} 1$ is defined by the program: $S \longleftarrow 0$; DO X; $X \longleftarrow S$; $S \longleftarrow S + 1$; END.

It is shown in Meyer & Ritchie [15] and in [16] that the Loop language as defined by Ritchie, hence by the above remarks this version of the Loop language, expresses algorithms for all and only primitive-recursive functions. That is, the class $\mathcal{R}^1$ of primitive-recursive functions characterizes Loop.

The class $\mathcal{R}^1$ is the initial class of the earliest subrecursive hierarchy. $\mathcal{R}^1 \subset \mathcal{R}^2 \subset \mathcal{R}^3 \subset \cdots \subset \mathcal{R}^n$, called the Péter hierarchy [18]. The class $\mathcal{R}^n$ is called the class of (nested) *n-fold recursive functions*. A language called Loopstack will be defined. It is characterized by $\mathcal{R}^2$. The language is then generalized to define $\mathcal{R}^n$ for all n.

The critical idea in defining $\mathcal{R}^2$ is to use a push-down *stack* along with the DO-statement to define a deeper type of recursion than can be defined without the stack. A push-down stack is a "first-on-last-off" memory device. The formal semantics for it can be defined on the RASP model. The operations wanted are:

DEFINITION 2.6. *(a)* $\text{STACK}_i \longleftarrow X$ *and (b)* $X \longleftarrow \text{STACK}_i$, *where* STACK_i *is the* i^{th} *stack which has been defined and (a) means put the value of X on top of the stack (i.e., push it down) and (b) means load the top element of the stack into X ("pop" the stack, thus releasing the top element).*

In the RASP model, the stack is defined by allocating an infinite subset of $\mathbb{N}$ as the possible-memory region of the stack and using "pointers" to indicate its top element. The pointer is a memory location, named STACK_i, which contains the address of the top of the stack. Each computer word in the region allocated to STACK_i has the form <data, address>. This form is achieved by using pairing functions to store and retrieve data.

The instruction (a) $\text{STACK}_i \longleftarrow X$ has the effect of:

(1) Pair the contents of X and contents of the pointer, STACK_i
(2) Place the pair in the next (free) location in the region allocated to STACK_i after first "zeroing out" the new location (this is accomplished by applying a function "$\text{next}_i(\;)$" to STACK_i)
(3) Replace the contents of STACK_i by "$\text{next}_i(\text{STACK}_i)$".

The instruction (b) $X \longleftarrow \text{STACK}_i$ has the effect of:

(1) "Unpair" the contents of the word whose address is in STACK_i, and put the first component of the pair in X
(2) Replace the contents of STACK_i with second component of the above pair.

*Assign to v the integer part of w_1/w_2.

These informal instructions can be directly translated into the RASP instruction set once the *region function* $\text{next}_i(\ )$, and the pairing functions $P_2(\ )$, $s_2^2(\ )$ are specified. The following suffice:

$$\text{next}_i(x) = 3^i \cdot 5^x, \quad p_2(x, y) = [2^x \cdot (2y + 1) - 1]$$

$$s_1^2(z) = \text{largest } u \text{ which divides } z + 1$$

$$s_2^2(z) = [(z + 1/2^{s_1^2(z)}) - 1]/2.$$

The $\text{next}_i(\ )$ function allows for the specification of ω-many stacks, and it leaves all of even-addressed memory available for storage of programs.

III. THE LOOPSTACK LANGUAGE

The new language is obtained from the loop language by augmenting it with the instruction whose syntax is

LOOPSTACK X
π
END

where π is any program of the new language.

The semantics of the instruction will appear involved but the idea is actually quite simple. The instruction as given is intended to execute the program

$$\left.\begin{array}{l} \text{DO } X \\ \text{DO } X \\ \text{DO } X \\ \cdot \\ \cdot \\ \cdot \\ \text{DO } X \end{array}\right\} X \text{ times },$$

$$\pi \tag{3.1}$$

$$\left.\begin{array}{l} \text{END} \\ \text{END} \\ \text{END} \\ \cdot \\ \cdot \\ \cdot \\ \text{END} \end{array}\right\} X \text{ times } .$$

This is carried out by means of the following program in the language G augmented by the stack instructions as defined above.

DEFINITION 3.1.

```
     CODE                              COMMENTS

     W ← 1
     if X = 0 then go to 1
     N ← 1
     CLEAR STACK_1                     See remarks following program
     DO X        }
     STACK_1 ← X }                     Load stack
     END         }
 1   W ← STACK_1
 *   DO W  }
     π     }                           Perform the inner loop (* refers to a key location
     END   }                              described later)
 2   if STACK EMPTY then exit          See remarks following program
     Z ← STACK_1  }
     Z ← Z ∸ 1    }                    Decrease first nonzero stack element
     STACK_1 ← Z  }
     if STACK_1 ≠ 0 then 3             Look for a nonzero entry in stack
     N ← N + 1                         Keep track of depth of search for 0
     P ← STACK_1                       "Pop stack" to remove 0 item
     go to 2
 3   DO N
     STACK_1 ← X
     END
     N ← 1
     go to 1
```

Remarks: A simple stack is "cleared" by setting the *base variable* to [0, 0], i.e., contents 0 and next address 0, and setting the pointer (located at $3^i \cdot 5^0$) to have the base address $3^i \cdot 5$. The fact that the address portion of the base is 0 allows easy recognition of the end of the stack. A similar technique works for multiple stacks.

Succintly written, the language Loopstack or "LS" for short, consists of [$v \leftarrow w$; $v \leftarrow w + 1$; $v \leftarrow n$; DO; END; LOOPSTACK; END]. Each use of the pair DO; END results in the allocation of a new *loop control register* (the $\overline{v}$ in DEFINITION 2.5). Similarly, each use of the LOOPSTACK, END pair results in the allocation of a new stack.

DEFINITION 3.2. *The precise definition of the LS language involves*

<stack iterative> : : = LOOPSTACK <variable> ; <program> ; END

and the program clause of Loop is replaced by

<program> : : = <assignment> | <iterative> | <stack iterative> | <program> ; <program> .

Computing Functions

The programs of G, Loop, or LS can be regarded as function-computing programs if inputs and outputs are specified. Details of doing this vary (see [5, 8]).

We adopt the convention of Constable & Borodin [5] which follows the usual standards. This involves selecting a set IN, of input variables and a set (here a unit set) OUT, of output variables. These sets constitute the I/O (input/output) of the program. Say that the function program π *with I/O computes* f: $\mathbb{N}^n \longrightarrow \mathbb{N}$ iff when each X_i of $\{X_1, X_2, X_3, \cdots, X_n\} = I$ has initial value x_i the program π terminates with $f(x_1, x_2, x_3, \cdots, x_n) = y$ in Y, $\{Y\} = 0$. A function f is *LS computable* iff there exists a $\pi \in$ LS such that π with I/O computes f.

The simplest use of the LOOPSTACK instruction computes an enormous function. To understand what LOOPSTACK X; $X \leftarrow X + 1$; END computes requires examining a sequence of Loop programs.*

Consider the sequence f_0 is $X \leftarrow X + 1$ and f_{n+1} is DO X; f_n; END.

These programs compute an interesting sequence of functions (written $f_n(\ )$ to distinguish them from their canonical programs, f_n): $f_0(x) = x + 1$, $f_1(x) = 2x$, $f_2(x) = 2^x \cdot x$, $\cdots$. The general rule for an algebraic definition of $f_n(\ )$ involves *iterates*. Given any f: $\mathbb{N} \longrightarrow \mathbb{N}$, the iterates of f are defined by $f^{(0)}(x) = x$, $f^{(n+1)}(x) = f(f^{(n)}(x))$, which is called the $(n + 1)^{st}$ iterate of f.

The LOOPSTACK program: LOOPSTACK X; $X \leftarrow X + 1$; END, will be denoted f_ω. The function it computes is defined from the sequence $\{f_n(\ )\}$ by *diagonalization*. That is, $f_\omega(x) = f_x(x)$, and $f_\omega(x)$ is simply

```
DO X  ⎫
DO X  ⎪
DO X  ⎪
 .    ⎬ X times ,
 .    ⎪
 .    ⎪
DO X  ⎭
X ← X + 1
END   ⎫
END   ⎪
END   ⎪
 .    ⎬ X times .
 .    ⎪
 .    ⎪
END   ⎭
```

Proving this statement requires a careful analysis of the semantic definitions of LOOPSTACK X. The general theorem is given by defining DO_X X; π; END to be the program

```
DO X  ⎫
DO X  ⎪
DO X  ⎪
 .    ⎬ X times
 .    ⎪
 .    ⎪
DO X  ⎭
```

*If Var$(\pi) = V$ then the I/O is assumed to be $I = \{V\} = 0$ for the purpose of discussing function programs.

$$\begin{array}{l} \pi \\ \left.\begin{array}{l} \text{END} \\ \text{END} \\ \text{END} \\ \cdot \\ \cdot \\ \cdot \\ \text{END} \end{array}\right\} X \text{ times} \end{array}$$

for π any program.*

THEOREM (Interpretation) 3.1. LOOPSTACK X; π; END *and* DO_X X; π; END *with* IN $= X$, OUT $= X$ *compute the same function.*

To facilitate understanding the theorem, an example of DO_X X; π; END translated into the base language is provided below.

Example. For $X = 3$

```
                 X1 ← X
            1    if X1 = 0 then END1
                 X2 ← X
            2    if X2 = 0 then END2
                 X3 ← X
            3    if X3 = 0 then END3
                 π
                 X3 ← X3 ∸ 1
                 go to 3
        END3     X2 ← X2 ∸ 1
                 go to 2
        END2     X1 ← X1 ∸ 1
                 go to 1
        END1     ________
```

The translation of LOOPSTACK X in Eq. (3.1) should be handy for comparison with the preceding example.

Proof. The two programs can be proved equivalent by defining a type of *isomorphism* between their computations. This constitutes a rather strong statement of equivalence. A computation for a RASP-like machine is defined in [8]. Of particular concern in this case are: the registers of π as they appear in each computation, (say $V_1, V_2, V_3, \cdots, V_n$ in LOOPSTACK and $\overline{V}_1, \overline{V}_2, \overline{V}_3, \cdots, \overline{V}_n$ in DO_X) the loop control registers X_i, of the DO_X program and the locations on the stack which are loaded during the load stack operation, denoted by $S_1, S_2, S_3, \cdots, S_x$ (reading from top down so that S_1 is the first location loaded). Consider two key locations in the control of LOOPSTACK, the instruction after the one labelled 1 (DO W) and the one labelled 3 (DO N) (see "*" in Definition 3.1).

*In Constable [4], where program modification is used as the basis for computing functions like $f_\omega(x)$, this type of program is precisely defined in RASP environment. Here the interpretation is left informal.

Call these locations a and b respectively. Other important locations are $N \leftarrow N+1$ and the END_i of DO_X.

The first type of correspondence which holds is this: The V_i correspond to $\overline{V}_i$, S_i correspond to X_i, and W to X_3. Then two facts are important: (1) At location a of one program the *configuration* $< V_1, V_2, V_3, \cdots, V_n, S_1, S_2, S_3, \cdots, S_{x_1}, W>$ has the same value as its image in the other program at the "if $X_n = 0$ then END_i" instruction of the inner most DO loop (call this location a'); and (2) Also at location b the configuration has the same value that its image in the DO_X program has when it reaches the outer-most END_i instruction before control transfers to an $X_i \leftarrow X$ after leaving the inner Loop (call this location b', b'_j would be clearer notation since b' is a function of the number of steps; but b' will be adequate). Figure 1 depicts the situation.

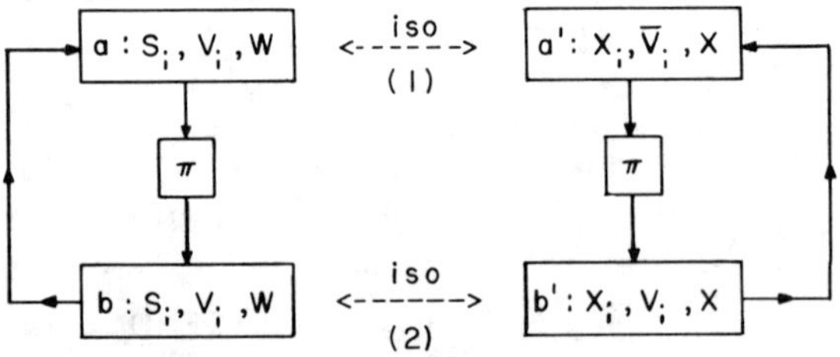

Figure 1.

The programs each execute π between a, b and a', b'. The LOOPSTACK program will recycle from point b only if not all $S_i = 0$. Likewise DO_X will recycle from b' only if not all X_i are 0.

If either halts at point b, i.e., does not recycle in the above diagram, then either changes the registers of π. So given that facts (1) and (2) above are true, the programs are equivalent.

To conclude the proof of the theorem, facts (1) and (2) must be verified. A careful inspection of the programs will quickly reveal this, and the proof is omitted here. Q.E.D.

PROPERTY 3.2. $f_\omega = [\text{LOOPSTACK } X;\ X \leftarrow X+1;\ \text{END}]$.

Proof. By definition $f_\omega(x) = f_x(x)$, and by the Interpretation Theorem the program computes $f_x(x)$. Q.E.D.

The programs $f_{\omega+m}$ are defined for $n = 1, 2, 3, \cdots$, by DO X; $f_{\omega+n-1}$; END. Clearly the function $f_{\omega+n}(\ )$ is defined by

$$f_{\omega+n}(x) = f_{\omega+n-1}^{(x)}(x) \qquad (\text{for } n = 1, 2, 3, \cdots) .$$

The LOOPSTACK instructions can be nested to define yet-faster-growing functions.

IV: USING ORDINAL NOTATIONS TO DESCRIBE PROGRAM STRUCTURE

A more refined set of functions can be used in place of the $f_n(\ )$ to yield sharper results. Let $h_1(x) = x+1$ and $h_n(x) = x+n$. The canonical program h_n will be

$$h_n \quad \left.\begin{array}{l} X \leftarrow X + 1 \\ X \leftarrow X + 1 \\ X \leftarrow X + 1 \\ \cdot \\ \cdot \\ \cdot \\ X \leftarrow X + 1 \end{array}\right\} n \text{ times}$$

Then $h_\omega(x) = h_x(x) = x + x = 2x = f_1(x)$. The canonical program for $h_\omega(\ )$ is: DO X; $X \leftarrow X + 1$; END.

Considering h_ω as a "limit" program suggests that the DO block be represented in some way by the ordinal notation ω. Following this suggestion leads to a useful *assignment of ordinal notations to programs.*

The statement <variable> $\leftarrow$ <variable> + 1 is assigned the numeral 1. Each pair (LOOPSTACK, END) (DO, END) determines a *block,* namely all statements in their scope. Every LS program π has the *outer structure* b_1; b_2; b_3; . . . ; b_n where each b_i is an assignment statement or a block. An ordinal notation β_i is assigned to each block b_i, and the notation $\beta_1 + \beta_2 + \beta_3 + \cdots + \beta_n$ is assigned to π. To assign a notation to a block, assume that the program π_i which is the scope of the block b_i has been assigned notation γ_i, then notation $(\gamma_i)\cdot\omega$ is assigned to DO <variable>; π_i; END. An assignment to LOOPSTACK <variable>; π_i; END is considered below.

For example: $X \leftarrow X + 1$; $X \leftarrow X + 1$; DO $X \leftarrow X + 1$; END; DO X; $X \leftarrow X + 1$, $X \leftarrow X + 1$; END; END is assigned the ordinal notation $(1 + 1) + 1\cdot\omega + (2\cdot\omega)\cdot\omega$.

The notation $(1 + 1) + (1)\cdot\omega + (2\cdot\omega)\cdot\omega$ simplifies to $2 + \omega + 2\cdot\omega^2$, and the ordinal it names is the same as that named by ω^2, therefore in terms of meaning $2 + \omega + 2\cdot\omega^2 = \omega^2$ (just as in arithmetic $(1 + 1)\cdot 3 = 6$). In this paper, the notation will be the main object of interest as opposed to the ordinal itself. This is indicated by writing "the notation $2\cdot\omega^2$" (just as in arithmetic one writes "the expression $(1 + 1)\cdot 3$").

An ordinal notation $<\omega^\omega$ will be in Cantor-normal form (CNF) iff it appears as

$$\omega^{n_1}\cdot a_1 + \omega^{n_2}\cdot a_2 + \omega^{n_3}\cdot a_3 + \cdots + \omega^{n_p}\cdot a_p + a_{p+1} \ ,$$

where $n_i > n_{i+1}$ and $n_i, a_i \in \mathbb{N}$. As is well known, every ordinal has a unique CNF (see [25] for a proof).

THEOREM 4.1. *If* $\pi \in$ Loop *and* $\alpha(\pi)$ *is the ordinal notation associated with* π, *then the maximum exponent of* ω *in the* CNF *of* $\pi(\alpha)$ *is the maximum depth of nesting of the* DO *blocks (loop complexity).*

Proof. The only way that ω^n can appear in the CNF is if $c_1\cdot\omega\cdot c_2\cdot\omega\cdot c_3\cdot\omega \cdots c_n\cdot\omega$, appears in $\pi(\alpha)$ which means that DO-END pairs are nested n deep. Q.E.D.

The ordinal notation assigned to a LOOPSTACK-block, LOOPSTACK <variable>; π_i; END is $(\gamma_i)\cdot\omega^\omega$ where γ_i is the notation assigned to π_i. With this rule, ordinals can be assigned to all $\pi \in$ LS.

The ordinals denoted by $\alpha(\pi)$ for $\pi \in$ LS are less than ω^{ω^2}. The CNF for these ordinals is

$$\omega^{\beta_1} \cdot a_1 + \omega^{\beta_2} \cdot a_2 + \omega^{\beta_3} \cdot a_3 + \cdots + \omega^{\beta_n} \cdot a_n + a_{n+1} \quad ,$$

where: $a_i \in \mathbb{N}$; $\beta_i > \beta_{i+1}$; and $\beta_i < \omega^2$ is in CNF. From $\alpha(\pi)$ the structural complexity of π can be determined.

DEFINITION. *The* stack complexity *of an* LS π *is n iff the deepest nesting of* LOOPSTACK *instructions is n. The* pure (0) loop *complexity of* π is *n iff the deepest nesting of* DO *statements around a program* α *not containing a* LOOPSTACK *statement is n. The m-loop complexity of* π *is the maximum depth of nesting around programs of stack complexity m.*

PROPOSITION 4.1. *The stack and m-loop complexity of a Loopstack program can be effectively determined from the program.*

PROPOSITION 4.2. *The stack complexity of* $\pi \in$ LS *is the maximum n such that* $\omega \cdot n + m$ *occurs as an exponent of* ω *in* $\alpha(\pi)$. *The n-loop complexity of* π *is the maximum m such that* $\omega \cdot n + m$ *occurs as an exponent of* ω *in* $\alpha(\pi)$.

The ordinal $\alpha(\pi)$ is a measure of the structural complexity of π. In the next section we examine its relationship to computational complexity.

V. CHARACTERIZATION OF LOOPSTACK

The Loopstack language can express only terminating programs.

THEOREM 5.1. *If* $\pi \in$ LS, *then* $\pi(x)\downarrow$ *for all* x, *i.e.,* $\pi(x)$ *halts.*

Proof. Clear from THEOREM 3.1. Q.E.D.

As in the Loop language, the run time of Loopstack programs can be estimated from the syntax of the program.

DEFINITION 5.1. *Given Loopstack program* π, *the run time of* π *on input* x *is denoted by* $t\pi(x)$ *and is defined using the run time of the* RASP-*program image of* π.

THEOREM 5.2. *If* $\pi \in$ LS *and its stack complexity is m and the m-loopstack complexity is n, then there is a* p *such that*

$$t\pi(x) < f^{(p)}_{\omega\cdot m+n}(x) \qquad \text{(for all x)} \ .$$

The proof of this theorem is best broken down into simple lemmata. Essential to the analysis are the following properties of the functions $f_{\omega\cdot n+m}(\ )$, called *spine functions* after the terminology of [6].

LEMMA 5.1. *If* $\alpha < \beta < \omega^2$ *and* α, β *are in* CNF, *then:*

(i) $f_\alpha(\ )$ is strictly increasing in x

(ii) $f_\alpha(x) < f_\beta(x)$ efs* (therefore $\exists p$, $f_\alpha(x) < f^{(p)}_\beta(x)$ (for all x))

(iii) $\exists q, p$, where $f_\alpha(f_\beta(x)) < f^{(q)}_\beta(x)$ and $f_\beta(f_\alpha(x)) < f^{(p)}_\beta(x)$ (for all x).

Proof. Elementary. Q.E.D.

The next two lemmata are not required for this proof, but they show that $\{f_\alpha\}$ forms a spine in the sense of [6].

*The abbreviation efs means except on a finite set.

DEFINITION 5.2. *Let* $t_1 f_\alpha(x)$ *for* α *in* CNF *denote the number of times the* "$X \longleftarrow X + 1$" *statement is executed in* f_α.

PROPOSITION 5.3. *For all* f_α, $0 \leq \alpha < \omega^2$, *and* α *in* CNF,

$$t_1 f_\alpha(x) + x = f_\alpha(x) \quad .$$

PROPOSITION 5.4. *For* α *as above,* $\exists c_\alpha \in \mathbb{N}$ *such that* $tf_\alpha(x) \leq c_\alpha \cdot t_1 f_\alpha(x)$.

It is easily verified that depending on the form of α, the "overhead" instructions executed in getting to the inner loop are bounded by a constant times the value of x.

To assist further with Theorem 5.2:

DEFINITION 5.3. *The instruction pair* LOOPSTACK, END *can be regarded as an operator,* $O_{\omega\omega}[f(\ )]$, *on one-argument functions* $f(\ )$. *Using a program* f *with input* X *and output* X, $O_{\omega\omega}[f(\ )](x)$ *is the output of* LOOPSTACK *X*; *f*; END *for X having initial value* x. *The* iteration operator *is denoted* O_ω *and defined as* $O_\omega[f(\ )](x)$ *output of* DO *X*; *f*; END *when X starts at* x.

LEMMA 5.2. *If* $f(x) < g(x)$ *for all* x, *and* $g(\ )$ *is monotone increasing then*

(i) $O_\omega[f](x) < O_\omega[g](x)$ (for all x)

(ii) $O_{\omega\omega}[f](x) < O_{\omega\omega}[g](x)$ (for all x)

Proof. Elementary. Q.E.D.

With these lemmata Theorem 5.2 is easily proved by induction. For similar-type proofs in detail see [4, 5, or 22]. Q.E.D.

Characterization of the Language

The Loopstack language can easily be characterized using the class $\mathcal{R}^2$ of doubly-recursive functions. From Robbin [22] two critical facts are known:

THEOREM 5.5. $\mathcal{R}^2 = \bigcup_{\alpha < \omega^2} \mathcal{E}(f_\alpha)$.

THEOREM 5.6. $\phi_i \in \mathcal{R}^2$ *iff* $t\phi_i(x) \leq f_\alpha(x)$ *efs for* $\alpha < \omega^2$.

From these two theorems we get:

THEOREM 5.7. $f(\ ) \in \mathcal{R}$ *is* LS *computable iff* $f(\ ) \in \mathcal{R}^2$.

Proof.

(1) Show $\mathcal{R}^2 \subseteq$ LS: It is known by definition that $f_\alpha \in$ LS for all $\alpha < \omega^2$. It is also known that $\mathcal{E}(f_\alpha) \subset \mathcal{R}^1(f_\alpha)$, thus since $\mathcal{R}^1(f_\alpha) \subseteq$ LS for all $\alpha < \omega^2$, it follows by Theorem 5.6 that $\mathcal{R}^2 = \bigcup_{\alpha < \omega^2} \mathcal{E}(f_\alpha) \subseteq$ LS

(2) Show that LS $\subseteq \mathcal{R}^2$: Note that any Loopstack program π is a RASP-program of a special sort. By Theorem 5.2 on estimating run times it is known that $t\pi(x) < f_\alpha(x)$ for all x, and some $\alpha < \omega^2$. Thus by Theorem 5.6, $\pi(\ ) \in \mathcal{R}^2$. Q.E.D.

Efficiency of the Language

According to the last theorem, Loopstack can be interpreted as a language for $\mathcal{R}^2$. A general programming language, like G used earlier to define Loopstack, can also compute $\mathcal{R}^2$ and more. The added flexibility of G may make it possible to compute elements of $\mathcal{R}^2$ more efficiently. But, there is a limit to the possible added efficiency as the following theorem shows.

THEOREM 5.8. *Let* $g(x) = x^x$, *then for all* $f(\ ) \in \mathcal{R}^2$ and for all $\phi_i(\ ) = f(\ )$ *such that* $t\phi_i(\ ) < k(\ ) \in \mathcal{R}^2$, *there is an* LS *program* $\alpha_j(\ ) = f(\ )$ *such that*

$$t\alpha_j(x) \le c \cdot g\,(t\phi_i(x))\ .$$

The theorem says that LS programs need not be more than exponentially inefficient. Granted that for practical purposes this is terrible; but things could be worse. For instance, it might be that for any $h \in \mathcal{R}^2$ there is $f \in \mathcal{R}^2$ such that $\phi_i(\ ) = f(\ )$ and for *all* $\alpha_j(\ ) = f(\ )$

$$h\,(t\phi_i(x)) < t\alpha_j(x) \qquad \text{(for all x).}$$

That situation would be really terrible.

Proof. The theorem is proved by simulating ϕ_i in Loop and using f_α, $\alpha < \omega^2$ as a clock to shut off the simulation. The clock can be computed in parallel and turned off when the simulation stops. The g cost enters in estimating the "over run" on the clock. This is the time it requires for the clock to run down once the simulation program has sent the signal to stop (has stopped the clocks "feedback"). The details of such a procedure are given in Constable & Borodin [5].

The basic idea is represented by the following diagram. Let $\bar{\phi}_i$ be the program simulating ϕ_i and suppose for illustration that $t\phi_i(x) < f_{\omega+2}(x)$ for all x. LOOPSTACK X; DO X; DO X; $\bar{\phi}_i$; $Z \leftarrow Z + 1$; END; *; END; *; END, where * is the translation of the following line into LOOP * if $S = 0$ then $X \leftarrow Z$ else $X \leftarrow 0$.

The variable S will remain 0 until the simulation, of $\bar{\phi}_i$, stops; then S is increased to 1 signaling the clock to stop (i.e., stopping the feedback of Z into X which is what allows computation of $f_{\omega+2}$).

When the clock receives the signal to stop, the largest value in the stack will be Z, a value equal to the number of steps of ϕ_i simulated (close to $t\phi_i(x)$). Once $S = \phi$, LOOPSTACK runs until all stack elements are 0. Since there is no feedback, the process requires $c \cdot Z^Z$ steps because

```
DO Z  ┐
DO Z  │
DO Z  │
.     ├ Z times (requires Z^Z steps)
.     │
.     │
DO Z  ┘
K ← K + 1
END   ┐
END   │
END   │
.     ├ Z times
.     │
.     │
END   ┘
```

Q.E.D.

The cost of using LS programs can be reduced to a simple constant factor of the cost in G by having an instruction which allows immediate exit from any loop.

A sufficient instruction would be a "go to" of the form "go to + c" which means go to the instruction located c instructions below this one. With such an instruction the program of Theorem 5.8 would be modified to use for * the following

$$* \ \text{if } S = 0 \text{ then } X \leftarrow Z \text{ else go to } + c \ ,$$

where c causes a branch beyond the end of the program (causing a halt).

The language could also be made more flexible by breaking LOOPSTACK into two separate instructions:

(1) STACK ← X, load stack
(2) DO STACK X, regard the stack as described in lines 8 through 24 of the definition of LOOPSTACK.

Then LOOPSTACK X is equivalent to: DO X; $\text{STACK}_1 \leftarrow X$; END; DO $\text{STACK}_1 \leftarrow X$; π; END.

VI. CONCLUSION

Generalizations to *n*-fold Recursion

The LOOPSTACK type of instructions can be generalized to "multidimensional" stack-like lists. A two-dimensional stack can be regarded as a stack of stacks.

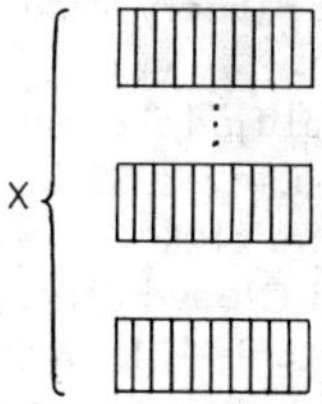

The command to

```
LOOPSTACK² X
π
END
```

would cause a two dimensional stack to be loaded as

$$X \text{ times} \left\{ \begin{array}{l} \overbrace{X, X, X, \cdots, X}^{X \text{ times}} \\ X, X, X, \cdots, X \\ X, X, X, \cdots, X \\ \cdot \\ \cdot \\ \cdot \\ X, X, X, \cdots, X \end{array} \right.$$

Then the top level stack would execute LOOPSTACK^2 X. When it finished, the top-most element on the next stack would be decreased and the top stack would be loaded again by the current value of X. Then the top stack would execute LOOPSTACK X again. The effect of continuing this is to compute a function $f_{\omega^2}(x) = f_{\omega \cdot x}(x)$.

Clearly the whole process can be carried over to LOOPSTACK^n X where LOOPSTACK^n X; $X \longleftarrow X + 1$; END; computes $f_{\omega^n}(x) = f_{\omega^{n-1} \cdot x_n}(x)$. Using the results of [25] it is easily shown as in §5 that LS^n is characterized by $\mathfrak{R}^n$. The structural complexity can be characterized by an ordinal of the form

$$\alpha = \omega^{\beta_1} \cdot a_1 + \omega^{\beta_2} \cdot a_2 + \omega^{\beta_3} \cdot a_3 + \cdots + \omega^{\beta_n} \cdot a_n + a_{n+1} < \omega^{\omega^{\omega}},$$

where $\omega^{\omega^{n_i}}$ describes the maximum depth of nesting of LOOPSTACK^{n_i} instructions. The details of this are similar enough to the case ω^2 that they can be left to the interested reader. The case of $\mathfrak{R}^2$ is general enough to illustrate the ideas, yet simple enough to provide an easily-intelligible presentation. The case $\mathfrak{R}^2$ is also the most needed for pedagogical purposes.

Historical Note

It is interesting to note the long line of research leading to a computational approach to $\mathfrak{R}^1$ and $\mathfrak{R}^n$ for $n > 1$. The primitive-recursive functions appeared as early as 1888 in the work of Dedekind [27]. In 1925 (published 1928) Ackerman [27] produced the first known nonprimitive recursive function. Both Péter and Kleene studied primitive-recursive functions extensively in the mid-1930s. They were useful in logic (Kleene [11]) and number theory (Péter [18]) but there was no natural reason known for studying them.

In 1947, Robinson [23] considerably simplified the methods of dealing with primitive recursion by reducing it to iteration. In 1953 Grzegorczyk [9] contributed rather-deep insights into the structure of $\mathfrak{R}^1$ by defining the Grzegorczyk hierarchy. This work stimulated Axt [1] and Cleave [3] to investigate $\mathfrak{R}^1$ still further. Cleave motivated by the work of Ritchie [21] in relating function classes ($\mathcal{E}$) to computational complexity gave the first computational account of $\mathfrak{R}^1$. Building on the work of Robinson & Axt, Ritchie and Minsky offered an elegant, syntactial definition of $\mathfrak{R}^1$ in terms of programming languages. Finally, McCreight & Meyer [14] established a relationship between $\mathfrak{R}^1$ and a wide class of computational-complexity measures Φ and their complexity classes $\mathfrak{R}_t^{\Phi}$.

At this point a good deal of deep knowledge has been accumulated about $\mathfrak{R}^1$. It appears to be a natural and fundamental class, but there is as yet no satisfactory account of why this is so. Can one say that its importance is due to more than convenience and historical chance?

The investigation of $\mathfrak{R}^n$ for $n > 2$ has been more-or-less "academic." These classes have been interesting examples, but they have not been extensively "used" in logic, number theory, or computing theory. Only a few workers have studied them in the literature. They appeared First in Péter's work, 1936. Robinson examined double recursion in 1948. A deep analysis of their structure (in relation to ordinal recursion) appeared by Tait [26] in 1961. This work inspired Robbin [22] in 1965 to analyze their structure systematically in terms of

Grzegorczyk's work on $\mathcal{R}^1$ and in terms of the Hartmanis & Stearns [10] approach to computational complexity. Building on the spade work of Robbin, Ritchie first extended the Loop-type approach to $\mathcal{R}^n$. Likewise using Robbin's results, Constable, using program modification on a RASP, extended the Cleave approach to $\mathcal{R}^n$ and beyond to define a hierarchy up to ε_0. The work of McCreight & Meyer in 1969, is also applicable to an analysis of $\mathcal{R}^n$. Again for these classes one is curious about their apparent naturalness.

ACKNOWLEDGEMENTS

Many of the results reported here were discovered in 1966 by D. Ritchie while engaged in research under the direction of P. Fischer at Harvard. They were written down but not published, and then rediscovered by this author in 1968 and circulated in technical-report form. From the reaction to these reports the author was made aware of Ritchie's work.

Since there is little prospect that Ritchie's work will be available, and since these ideas are a logical sequel to "Subrecursive Programming Languages I," by Constable & Borodin, a number of people felt that this version should be published with appropriate historical commentary.

Part of this work was supported by NSF Contract GJ-579.

REFERENCES

[1] P. Axt, "Enumeration and the Grzegorczyk Hierarchy," *Z. Math Logik Grund. Math,* 9, 53–65 (1963).

[2] L. J. Bass and P. R. Young, "Hierarchies Based on Computational Complexity and Irregularities of Class-Determined Measured Sets," *Proc. ACM Symp. on the Theory of Computing,* 37–39 (Northampton, 1970).

[3] J. P. Cleave, "A Hierarchy of Primitive Recursive Functions," *Z. Math Logik Grund. Math,* 9, 331–345 (1963).

[4] R. L. Constable, "Extending and Refining Hierarchies of Computable Functions," Computer Science Technical Report No. 25. University of Wisconsin (1968).

[5] R. L. Constable and A. Borodin, "On the Efficiency of Programs in Subrecursive Formalisms," *IEEE Conf. Rec. of the 10th Annual Symposium of Switching and Automata Theory* (to appear in *J. ACM* as "Subrecursive Programming Languages, I").

[6] R. L. Constable, "Subrecursive Programming Language II, On Program Size" (to appear in Special of *J. CSS,* 1971).

[7] M. Davis, *The Undecidable* (Raven Press, 1965).

[8] C. C. Elgot & A. Robinson, "Random-Access Stored-Program Machines, An Approach to Programming Languages," *J. ACM,* 11, 365–399 (1964).

[9] A. Grzegorczyk, "Some Classes of Recursive Functions," *Rozprawy Mathematcyzne,* 1–45 (1953).

[10] J. Hartmanis and R. E. Stearns, "On the Computational Complexity of Algorithms," *Trans. AMC* 5, No. 117, 285–306 (1965).

[11] S. C. Kleene, *Introduction to Metamathematics* (Princeton, 1952).

[12] S. C. Kleene, "Extension of an Effectively-Generated Class of Functions by Enumeration," *Colloq. Math G*, 67–78 (1958).

[13] A. H. Lachlan, "Multiple Recursion," *Z. Math Logik Grund. Math*, **8**, 81–107 (1962).

[14] E. M. McCreight and A. R. Meyer, "Classes of Computable Functions Defined by Bounds on Computations," *Proc. ACM Symp. on Theory of Comput.*, 79–88 (1969).

[15] A. R. Meyer and D. M. Ritchie, "The Complexity of Loop Programs," *Proc. 22nd National ACM Conference*, 465–470 (1967).

[16] M. Minksy, *Computation: Finite and Infinite* (Prentice-Hall, 1967).

[17] C. Parsons, "Hierarchies of Primitive-Recursive Functions," *Z. Math. Logik Grund. Math*, **14**, 357–376 (1968).

[18] R. Péter, *Recursive Functions*, 3rd ed. (New York: Academic Press, 1967).

[19] D. M. Ritchie, "Program Structure and Computational Complexity," PhD. Thesis, Harvard University (1966).

[20] R. W. Ritchie, "Classes of Recursive Functions Based on Ackermann's Function," *Pacific J. Math*, **15**, 1027–44 (1965).

[21] R. W. Ritchie, "Classes of Predictably-Computable Functions," *Trans. AMS*, **106**, 139–173 (1963).

[22] J. Robbin, "Subrecursive Hierarchies," PhD. Dissertation, Princeton (1965).

[23] R. M. Robinson, "Primitive Recursive Functions," *Bull. AMS*, **53**, 915–942 (1947).

[24] J. C. Shepherdson and H. E. Sturgis, "Computability of Recursive Functions," *J. ACM*, **10**, 217–255 (1963).

[25] W. Sierpinski, *Cardinal and Ordinal Numbers* (Warsaw, 1965).

[26] W. W. Tait, "Nested Recursion," *Math. Ann.*, **143**, 236–250 (1961).

[27] J. van Heijenoort, *From Frege to Gödel* (Cambridge, 1967).

RING-SUM EXPANSIONS OF BOOLEAN FUNCTIONS

M. Davio
MBLE Research Lab., Brussels, Belgium

INTRODUCTION

Ring-sum of product expansions of Boolean functions are well known, and their study goes back to Muller [1]. They may be classified into canonical expansions, in which every variable appears with a single polarity (i.e., complemented or not) and noncanonical expansions in which every variable is allowed to appear with both polarities. Akers [2] has shown that the canonical expansions may be interpreted as Taylor expansions of Boolean functions: indeed, the coefficients of such expansions are the values at some point of the Boolean derivatives of the given function. In a recent paper [3], Mukhopadhyay and Schmitz give a precise formulation of the minimization problems in ring-sum expansions.

Problem 1. Among all the ring-sum expansions of a Boolean function (canonical or not) find the expansions having a minimum number of summed terms.

Problem 2. Among all the canonical ring-sum expansions of a Boolean function, find the expansions having a minimum number of summed terms. They propose a solution to the second problem and point out the relationship of ring-sum expansions with cellular logic.

In the present paper, Mukhopadhyay and Schmitz's approach is related to Boolean differential calculus: this enlightens some of the properties of their polarity functions and brings quite a saving in proofs. A parallel saving in computation and memory requirement is achieved by introducing a Kronecker-product structure of the transformation matrices. This property has been obtained by Lechner [4].

This paper also describes an algorithm that provides noncanonical ring-sum expansions: these expansions called pseudocanonical expansions enjoy the property of having at most as many terms as the best canonical ones. Further, their comparatively-low computational complexity makes them a useful tool in the obtention of reasonable ring-sum expansions.

NOTATIONS:

$\oplus$; $\sum$: ring sum, modulo-2 sum ,

x_i: binary variable.

Boolean Exponentiation

$$x^{(e)} = \overline{x} \text{ iff } e = 0 \quad ,$$

Presented at the Symposium on Computers and Automata
Polytechnic Institute of Brooklyn, April 13–15, 1971.

$$x^{(e)} = x \text{ iff } e = 1 \ .$$

With this definition $x^{(e)} = \overline{(x \oplus e)}$.

Ring Exponentiation

$$x^e = 1 \quad \text{iff} \quad e = 0 \ ,$$
$$x^e = 0 \quad \text{iff} \quad e = 1 \ .$$

Vectors and Products of Literals

$$\mathbf{X} = (x_0, x_1, x_2, \cdots, x_{n-1})\text{: vector of variables} \ ,$$
$$\mathbf{H} = (h_0, h_1, h_2, \cdots, h_{n-1})\text{: vector of constants} \ ,$$
$$\mathbf{X} \oplus \mathbf{H} = \text{componentwise ring sum of vectors} \ ,$$
$$\mathbf{X}^{(\mathbf{E})} = \text{componentwise Boolean exponentiation of vectors} \ ,$$
$$\mathbf{X}^{\mathbf{E}} = \{x_i \mid e_i = 1\} \ .$$

The same notations are also used to denote products of literals; thus $\mathbf{X}$ may also mean $\prod_{i=0}^{n-1} x_i$. The appropriate meaning is always clear from the context.

Matrices

Matrix products (dot or no symbol) are computed over modulo-2 field. The Kronecker matrix product is denoted by "$\times$".

I. TAYLOR EXPANSIONS OF BOOLEAN FUNCTIONS

Any Boolean function may be expressed as a modulo-2 sum of products of literals in which each of the n variables x_i appears with a single polarity.

One is readily convinced of the existence of such an expansion by the elementary properties of the modulo-2 sum applied, e.g., to the canonical-disjunctive expansion of the function.

Akers [2] has shown that the coefficients of such an expansion may be interpreted as the values at some point $\mathbf{X} = \mathbf{H}$ of the domain of the Boolean derivatives of $f(\mathbf{X})$ with respect to the subsets of $\{\mathbf{X}\}$. The 2^n possible Taylor expansions of a Boolean function $f(\mathbf{X})$ are given by

$$f(\mathbf{X}) = \sum_{\mathbf{E}} (\partial f / \partial \mathbf{X}^{\mathbf{E} \oplus \mathbf{H}})_{\mathbf{X}=\mathbf{H}} (\mathbf{X} \oplus \mathbf{H})^{\mathbf{E} \oplus \mathbf{H}}, \qquad (\mathbf{E} = 0, 1, 2, \cdots, 2^n - 1) \ . \tag{1}$$

The Taylor expansion of $f(\mathbf{X})$ for $\mathbf{H} = \mathbf{0}$ is also called the Maclaurin expansion of this function.

The purpose of this section is to provide a computation method of the coefficients $(\partial f / \partial \mathbf{X}^{\mathbf{E} \oplus \mathbf{H}})_{\mathbf{X}=\mathbf{H}}$ of Eq. (1); the proposed method enlightens an early statement of Lechner [4].

The set of minterms $\{X^{(E)}\}$ and the set of products $\{(X \oplus H)^{E \oplus H} \mid E = 0, 1, 2, \cdots, 2^n - 1\}$ are two bases of the linear algebra of Boolean functions. The expansion coefficients $(\partial f / \partial X^{E \oplus H})_{X=H}$ will easily result from the knowledge of the linear transformation matrix $A(H)$ relating the two bases. Now, if the enumeration order of the vectors in the two aforementioned bases are appropriately chosen, the transformation matrix $A(E)$ receives a Kronecker product structure, with a corresponding saving both in computation time and in storage requirements [4].

Consider first a Boolean function $f(x)$ of a single variable. It may be expressed as a ring sum expansion in three different ways

$$f = [a_0\ a_1] \begin{bmatrix} \bar{x} \\ x \end{bmatrix}, \tag{2}$$

$$f = [b_0\ b_1] \begin{bmatrix} 1 \\ x \end{bmatrix}, \tag{3}$$

$$f = [c_0\ c_1] \begin{bmatrix} \bar{x} \\ 1 \end{bmatrix}, \tag{4}$$

where

$$[b_0\ b_1] = [a_0\ a_1] \begin{bmatrix} 1 & 1 \\ 0 & 1 \end{bmatrix}, \tag{5}$$

and

$$[c_0\ c_1] = [a_0\ a_1] \begin{bmatrix} 1 & 0 \\ 1 & 1 \end{bmatrix}. \tag{6}$$

The matrix

$$\begin{bmatrix} 1 & 1 \\ 0 & 1 \end{bmatrix},$$

will be denoted by A. Its transpose is A^T. We further use the following notation

$$x^h = \begin{bmatrix} 1 \\ x \end{bmatrix}, \text{ iff } h = 1 \ ,$$

$$x = \begin{bmatrix} \bar{x} \\ 1 \end{bmatrix}, \text{ iff } h = 0 \ .$$

Consider next a Boolean function of n variables $f(x_0, x_1, x_2, \cdots, x_{n-1})$. The minterm basis is expressed as the Kronecker-matrix product

$$[X^{(E)}] = \begin{bmatrix} \bar{x}_{n-1} \\ x_{n-1} \end{bmatrix} \times \begin{bmatrix} \bar{x}_{n-2} \\ x_{n-2} \end{bmatrix} \times \cdots \times \begin{bmatrix} \bar{x}_0 \\ x_0 \end{bmatrix} . \tag{7}$$

Similarly, the Taylor-expansion basis is expressed as the Kronecker product

$$[(X \oplus H)^{E \oplus H}] = x_{n-1}^{h_{n-1}} \times x_{n-2}^{h_{n-2}} \times \cdots \times x_0^{h_0} . \tag{8}$$

Elementary properties of the Kronecker product lead to the following.

THEOREM 1. *The transformation matrix from the minterm basis (Eq. (7)) to the Taylor basis (Eq. (8)) is the Kronecker product*

$$\mathbf{A}^{T^{h_{n-1}}} \times \mathbf{A}^{T^{h_{n-2}}} \times \cdots \times \mathbf{A}^{T^{h_0}} \quad ,$$

where: $\mathbf{A}^{\mathbf{T}^{h_i}} = \mathbf{A}$, iff $h_i = 1$; and $\mathbf{A}^{\mathbf{T}^{h_i}} = \mathbf{A}^{\mathbf{T}}$, iff $h_i = 0$.

Proof. From Eqs. (4) and (5) it is clear that

$$\begin{bmatrix} \overline{x} \\ x \end{bmatrix} = \mathbf{A}^{\mathbf{T}^{h}} \cdot \mathbf{x}^{h} \quad .$$

Hence, by a known property of the Kronecker product [6]

$$[\mathbf{X}^{(\mathbf{E})}] = \mathop{\times}_{i=n-1}^{0} \begin{bmatrix} \overline{x}_1 \\ x_i \end{bmatrix} = \mathop{\times}_{i=n-1}^{0} (\mathbf{A}^{\mathbf{T}^{h_i}} \cdot \mathbf{x}_i^{h_i}) = \left(\mathop{\times}_{i=n-1}^{0} \mathbf{A}^{\mathbf{T}^{h_i}} \right) \cdot \left(\mathop{\times}_{i=n-1}^{0} \mathbf{x}_i^{h_i} \right)$$

$$= \left(\mathop{\times}_{i=n-1} \mathbf{A}^{\mathbf{T}^{h_i}} \right) \cdot [(\mathbf{X} \oplus \mathbf{H})^{\mathbf{E} \oplus \mathbf{H}}] \quad . \quad \text{Q.E.D.}$$

This theorem leads to a recurrent algorithm of computation of the expansion coefficients $(\partial f/\partial \mathbf{X}^{\mathbf{E}\oplus\mathbf{H}})_{\mathbf{X}=\mathbf{H}}$ from the truthtable $[a_0, a_1, a_2, \cdots, a_{2^n-1}]$ of the function f; the truth vector $[a_{\mathbf{E}}]$ is first transformed by the matrix $\mathbf{A}^{\mathbf{T}h_{n-1}}$: this operation merely reduces to the modulo-2 addition of two vectors of length 2^{n-1}. Once this is performed, one is left with two similar and independent problems in $(n - 1)$ variables and the procedure may be carried out.

Example.

$$f = \overline{x}_2\overline{x}_1\overline{x}_0 + \overline{x}_2\overline{x}_1 x_0 + x_2\overline{x}_1 x_0 + x_2 x_1 \overline{x}_0$$

$[a_{\mathbf{E}}] = [1 \quad 1 \quad 0 \quad 0 \quad 0 \quad 1 \quad 1 \quad 0]$

[H]				[1 0 0]									[0 1 0]			
$\mathbf{A}^{\mathbf{T}^{h_2}}$	1	1	0	0	0	1	1	0	1	1	0	0	0	1	1	0
					1	1	0	0	0	1	1	0				
	1	1	0	0	1	0	1	0	1	0	1	0	0	1	1	0
$\mathbf{A}^{\mathbf{T}^{h_1}}$	0	0			1	0					1	0			0	1
	1	1	0	0	0	0	1	0	1	0	0	0	0	1	1	1
$\mathbf{A}^{\mathbf{T}^{h_0}}$	1		0		0		0		0		0		1		1	
	0	1	0	0	0	0	1	0	1	0	0	0	1	1	0	1
f	$\overline{x}_1 \oplus x_2\overline{x}_0$								$\overline{x}_2\overline{x}_0 \oplus \overline{x}_0 \oplus 1 \oplus x_1$							

II. RESEARCH OF MINIMAL TAYLOR EXPANSIONS OF BOOLEAN FUNCTIONS.

The minimal Taylor expansions of a Boolean function are, by definition, these expansions, among the 2^n possible ones, that have a minimum number of summed products. A brute-force approach to the solution of this problem is thus to compute according to Section I the 2^n possible expansions and their number of terms.

In a recent paper, Mukhopadhyay and Schmitz [3] introduced a different method to achieve the same result. This method is based on the computation of the so-called "polarity functions". However, a reinterpretation of these functions as Boolean derivatives* leads to a simpler and more natural computation. The underlying idea is actually a very simple one: If one knows the set $\{\partial f/\partial \mathrm{X}^{\mathrm{E}} \mid \mathrm{E} = 0, 1, 2, \cdots, 2^n - 1\}$ of derivatives of the given function f, one has only to determine a point $\mathrm{X} = \mathrm{H}$ where a maximum number of derivatives vanish. Further, the computation of the derivatives is straightforward as the following theorem shows.

THEOREM 2.

$$[\partial f/\partial \mathrm{X}^{\mathrm{E}}] = \left(\begin{bmatrix} \overline{x}_{n-1} & x_{n-1} \\ 1 & 1 \end{bmatrix} \times \begin{bmatrix} \overline{x}_{n-2} & x_{n-2} \\ 1 & 1 \end{bmatrix} \times \cdots \times \begin{bmatrix} \overline{x}_0 & x_0 \\ 1 & 1 \end{bmatrix}\right) [a_H] \ . \tag{9}$$

Proof. The first row of Eq. (9) is nothing but the canonical-disjunctive expansion of f expressed as a modulo-2 sum of minterms. The $(\mathrm{E}+1)^{\mathrm{th}}$ row, corresponding to $\partial f/\partial \mathrm{X}^{\mathrm{E}}$ is simply deduced from the former by replacing in the former the minterm $\mathrm{X}^{(\mathrm{H})}$ or $(\mathrm{X} \oplus \overline{\mathrm{H}})$ by $(\mathrm{X} \oplus \overline{\mathrm{H}})^{\mathrm{E}}$: this is an obvious consequence of the linearity of the derivation operator over modulo-2 field. Q.E.D.

Note by the way that the various theorems and rules derived in [3] are mostly straightforward consequences of the properties of Boolean derivatives. At this stage, one is left with the problem of determining the point (or points) where a maximum number of derivatives vanish. This problem amounts for instance to find, in the set of multiple-output prime implicants of the set of derivatives those belonging to a maximum number of derivatives. However, this is merely a restatement of Mukhopadhyay's [3] Step 4 since the research of prime implicates and that of maximal cliques are algebraically equivalent [5]. We use here a different approach that consists in a direct generation of the truth tables of the derivatives from the truth table of the given function.

THEOREM 3.

$$[\partial f/\partial \mathrm{X}^{\mathrm{E}}] = \sum_{\mathrm{H}} \left\{ a_{\mathrm{H}} \left(\bigtimes_{i=n-1}^{0} \mathbf{B}_{h_i} \right) \right\} [\mathrm{X}^{(\mathrm{H})}] \ , \tag{10}$$

where

$$\mathbf{B}_0 = \begin{bmatrix} 1 & 0 \\ 1 & 1 \end{bmatrix} = \mathrm{A}^{\mathrm{T}} \text{ and } \mathbf{B}_1 = \begin{bmatrix} 0 & 1 \\ 1 & 1 \end{bmatrix} .$$

Proof. The proof is achieved by perfect induction on the number of variables. The initial step is immediate since obviously

$$\begin{bmatrix} f \\ \partial f/\partial x_0 \end{bmatrix} = \left\{ a_0 \begin{bmatrix} 1 & 0 \\ 1 & 1 \end{bmatrix} \oplus a_1 \begin{bmatrix} 0 & 1 \\ 1 & 1 \end{bmatrix} \right\} \begin{bmatrix} \overline{x}_0 \\ x_0 \end{bmatrix} .$$

Assuming then as induction hypothesis that Eq. (10) holds true for any function of at most k variables, and using the fact that $f(x_0, x_1, x_2, \cdots, x_k) = f(x_0, x_1, x_2, \cdots, 0)\, \overline{x}_k \oplus f(x_0, x_1, x_2, \cdots, 1)\, x_k$, one achieves the proof by a routine computation. Q.E.D.

An algorithm for the computation of the truth tables of the derivatives is now

*Up to a complementation of variables.

at hand. Indeed, using the $(2^k + 1)^{\text{th}}$ row of Eq. (10), it turns out that $(\partial f/\partial x_k)$ assumes the value $a_i \oplus a_{i+2^k}$ at the two points $X^{(i)}$ and $X^{(i+2^k)}$. Hence, from f, $\partial f/\partial x_0$ is readily computed and, from the couple $(f, \partial f/\partial x_0)$ on, the new couple $\partial f/\partial x_1, \partial(\partial f/\partial x_0)/\partial x_1)$ is found, etc. This algorithm is illustrated by means of Mukhopadhyay's [3] Example 1

$$\begin{bmatrix} f \\ \\ \partial f/\partial x_3 \\ \\ \partial f/\partial x_2 \\ \partial f/\partial x_3 x_2 \\ \\ \partial f/\partial x_1 \\ \partial f/\partial x_3 x_1 \\ \partial f/\partial x_2 x_1 \\ \partial f/\partial x_3 x_2 x_1 \end{bmatrix} = \left[\begin{array}{cccccccc} 1 & 0 & 1 & 0 & 0 & 0 & 1 & 1 \\ \hline \\ \hline 1 & 1 & 1 & 1 & 0 & 0 & 0 & 0 \\ \hline \\ \hline 0 & 0 & 0 & 0 & 1 & 1 & 1 & 1 \\ 0 & 0 & 0 & 0 & 0 & 0 & 0 & 0 \\ \hline \\ \hline 1 & 0 & 0 & 1 & 1 & 0 & 0 & 1 \\ 1 & 1 & 1 & 1 & 1 & 1 & 1 & 1 \\ 1 & 1 & 1 & 1 & 1 & 1 & 1 & 1 \\ 0 & 0 & 0 & 0 & 0 & 0 & 0 & 0 \end{array}\right] \begin{bmatrix} \overline{x}_1\overline{x}_2\overline{x}_3 \\ \\ \overline{x}_1\overline{x}_2 x_3 \\ \\ \overline{x}_1 x_2\overline{x}_3 \\ \overline{x}_1 x_2 x_3 \\ \\ x_1\overline{x}_2\overline{x}_3 \\ x_1\overline{x}_2 x_3 \\ x_1 x_2\overline{x}_3 \\ x_1 x_2 x_3 \end{bmatrix} .$$

$$\begin{array}{cccccccc} 5 & 3 & 4 & 4 & 4 & 3 & 4 & 5 \end{array}$$

In the obtained matrix, each column contains the coefficients of a Taylor expansion and the minimal expansions are accordingly selected from the column weights. In the example, columns 1 (001) and 5 (101) have minimum weight 3 giving two minimal Taylor expansions at the points (110) and (010). The corresponding expansions are $\overline{x}_3 \oplus \overline{x}_3 x_1 \oplus x_2 x_1$ and $x_2 \oplus \overline{x}_3 \overline{x}_1 \oplus x_2 \overline{x}_1$.

III. PSEUDO CANONICAL EXPANSIONS OF BOOLEAN FUNCTIONS.

A ring expansion of a Boolean function stops being canonical if, for some variable x_i, the three possible types of terms (i.e., terms containing x_1, $\overline{x}_i$, and no occurence of x_i) are present.

Consider the explicit expressions of Eqs. (2) to (4)

$$f = a_0 \overline{x}_{n-1} \oplus a_1 x_{n-1} \quad ,$$

$$f = a_0 \oplus (a_0 \oplus a_1)\, x_{n-1} \quad ,$$

$$f = a_1 \oplus (a_0 \oplus a_1)\, \overline{x}_{n-1} \quad .$$

Any choice between these three expansions results in a choice of a couple of functions of $(n - 1)$ variables among the triple

$$a_0, a_1, a_0 \oplus a_1 \quad .$$

The number of variables upon which the three functions depend has been lowered by one unit and the process may thus be iterated: namely the first part of the construction will amount to build a binary vector of 3^n components; in this vector:

(a) Each triple of components represents a function of the single variable x_0; after selection of an appropriate couple of binary components such a function will require 0 or 1 term
(b) Each 9-tuple represents a function of two variables; for its synthesis, one selects two triples requiring together a minimum number of terms
(c) The process is carried on for the functions of $3, 4, 5, \cdots, n$ variables selecting at each step the couple of subfunctions leading to the minimum number of required terms.

Example. We come back to Mukhopadhyay's example. The initial vector

$$[1 \ 0 \ 1 \ 0, 0 \ 0 \ 1 \ 1] ,$$

is first completed with the modulo-2 sum of its two halves

$$[1 \ 0 \ 1 \ 0, 0 \ 0 \ 1 \ 1, 1 \ 0 \ 0 \ 1] .$$

The same operation is performed over the three obtained 4-tuples

$$[1 \ 0, \ 1 \ 0, \ 0 \ 0; \ 0 \ 0, \ 1 \ 1, \ 1 \ 1; \ 1 \ 0, \ 0 \ 1, \ 1 \ 1] ,$$

and, finally, over the nine pairs

$$[1 0 1, 1 0 1, 0 0 0; 0 0 0, 1 1 0, 1 1 0; 1 0 1, 0 1 1, 1 1 0] .$$

The selection process is now carried on; the eliminated subvectors are replaced by dashes:

(a) At the triples level, one selects, e.g.

$$[- 0 1, - 0 1, 0 0 0; 0 0 0, 1 - 0, 1 - 0; - 0 1, 0 - 1, 1 - 0]$$

(b) At the 9-tuples level, one selects

$$[- 0 1, \text{———}, 0 0 0; 0 0 0, \text{———}, 1 - 0; - 0 1, \text{———}, 1 - 0]$$

(c) Finally, at the function level

$$[- 0 1, \text{———}, 0 0 0; 0 0 0, \text{———}, 1 - 0; \text{—————————}].$$

One obtains an expansion having only two terms

$$f = \bar{x}_2 \bar{x}_0 \oplus x_2 x_1 ,$$

while the best Taylor expansions computed in Section II had three terms.

The expansions obtained in the above described way are called *pseudocanonical*. It is clear that any Taylor expansion may be obtained by the preceding algorithm. Hence, the resulting expansion has at most as many terms as the best Taylor expansion. Further, an upper bound for the number of terms in a pseudocanonical expansion is clearly 2^{n-1}.

It should finally be pointed out that pseudocanonical ring expansions are not always optimal. The simplest example of this fact is the function

$$[1 \ 0 \ 0 \ 1 \ 0 \ 1 \ 1 \ 1] .$$

The best Taylor expansions of this function have 5 terms. There are five such expansions among which

$$\bar{x}_0 \oplus x_1 \oplus x_2 \oplus x_1 x_2 \oplus \bar{x}_0 x_1 x_2 .$$

The best pseudocanonical expansions have 4 terms. An example of such an expansion is

$$\overline{x}_0 \oplus x_1 \oplus x_2 \oplus x_0 x_1 x_2 \quad .$$

Finally, the function has three expansions with 3 terms, e.g.

$$x_0 \oplus \overline{x}_1 \overline{x}_2 \oplus \overline{x}_0 x_1 x_2 \quad .$$

It is thought however that pseudocanonical expansions have their own interest, in view of the simplicity of their obtention.

ACKNOWLEDGEMENTS

The author is most indebted to his colleagues G. Bioul, who first stated Theorem 2, and J. M. Goethals, for fruitful discussions.

REFERENCES

[1] D. E. Muller, "Application of Boolean Algebra to Switching-Circuit Design and to Error Detection," *IRE Trans. Electr. Comput.*, EC-3, 6–12 (September, 1954).

[2] Sh. B. Akers, "On a Theory of Boolean Functions," *J. SIAM*, 7, No. 4, 487–498 (December 1959).

[3] A. Mukhopadhyay and G. Schmitz, "Minimization of Exclusive or and Logical Equivalence Switching Circuits," *IEEE Trans. Comput.* C-19, No. 2, 132–140 (February 1970).

[4] R. J. Lechner, "Transformations Among Switching-Function Canonical Forms," *IEEE Trans. Electr. Comput.* EC-12, (Corr.), No. 2, 129–130 (April 1963).

[5] M. Davio and G. Bioul, "Representation of Lattice Functions," *Philips Research Rep.*, 25, 370–388 (October 1970).

[6] C. C. Mc Duffee, "The Theory of Matrices (New York: Chelsea, 1964) (Reprint of first edition).

THE LATTICE STRUCTURE OF GRAPH PARTITIONS

E. Schroeppel
Polytechnic Institute of Brooklyn, Brooklyn, NY
and
A. C. McKellar
IBM Thomas J. Watson Research Center, Yorktown Heights, NY

Various problems in the packaging of digital circuits and in the design of paged-memory computers have been approached as problems in partitioning the nodes of a linear graph into clusters that satisfy some optimization criteria. This paper examines the set of all such partitions of a graph, particularly those (called "clusterings") for which each cluster is a connected subgraph. It is shown that these clusterings form a lattice. The types of lattices, their properties, and their construction are examined. The question of the realization of a graph from its cluster lattice is investigated and it is shown that the set of clusterings provides sufficient information to realize the graph.

I. INTRODUCTION

In recent years several authors have reported results associated with the problem of partitioning the nodes of a linear graph into clusters satisfying various optimization criteria [4, 5, 6]. Such work finds application in the partitioning of digital networks to minimize propagation delay, the number of modules, etc. It also applies to the optimal segmentation of computer programs in paging environments.

This paper does not seek to present methods for selecting any particular "optimum" partitions but rather it examines the relationships among all possible partitions of a graph. This relationship is shown to constitute a lattice whose properties depend on the graph to which it corresponds. The properties of these lattices and their construction as well as the problem of constructing a graph from a lattice are considered.

II. PARTITIONS AND LATTICES

A *partition* π on a set V is a collection of nonempty disjoint subsets of V whose set union is V, that is

$$\pi = \{N_i\} ,$$

such that

$$N_i \cap N_j = \phi \qquad (\text{for } i \neq j) ,$$

Presented at the Symposium on Computers and Automata
Polytechnic Institute of Brooklyn, April 13–15, 1971.

and

$$\cup\{N_i\} = V \quad .$$

In particular we will consider partitions of the form

$$\pi = \{N_1; N_2; N_3; \cdots ; N_k\} \quad ,$$

where N_i is called a *block* of π and is of the form

$$N_i = \{v_1, v_2, v_3, \cdots , v_p\} \quad ,$$

where v_j is a vertex of graph G. Throughout this paper we will be concerned with a more interesting form of partition which we call a clustering. A *clustering* is a partition such that for any block the set of vertices N_i and their corresponding edges form a *connected* subgraph of G.

Thus, for a given undirected graph G, we may define a set of clusterings of the nodes of G. For example, for the graph G_1 of Fig. 6, $\pi_1 = \{a, b, e; c, d\}$ is a clustering whereas $\pi_2 = \{a, e; b, c, d\}$ is a partition but not a clustering.

The *product* of two partitions, written $\pi_1 \cdot \pi_2$, is defined as follows: v_i and v_j are contained in the same block of $\pi_1 \cdot \pi_2$ iff v_i and v_j are contained in the same block of π_1 and in the same block of π_2. $\pi_1 \cdot \pi_2$ can be computed by intersecting blocks of π_1 and π_2. That is, for each v_i in π_1, the block in which it is contained is intersected with the block of π_2 to which it belongs. The resulting set of intersections are the blocks of $\pi_1 \cdot \pi_2$.

We say that two sets A and B are connected if $A \cap B \neq \phi$. Any two sets of a collection, say A and C, are chain connected if there exists a sequence of sets $A = A_1, A_2, A_3, \cdots , A_n = C$ such that A_i is connected to A_{i+1} for $i = 1, 2, 3, \cdots , n-1$. The *sum* $\pi_1 + \pi_2$, of two partitions consists of the set union of all the blocks of π_1 and π_2 that are chain connected.

We say that $\pi_2 \leq \pi_1$ iff every block of π_2 is contained in a block of π_1, that is, $\pi_1 \cdot \pi_2 = \pi_2$ and $\pi_1 + \pi_2 = \pi_1$. The smallest partition corresponds to the partition in which each block consists of a single element. The largest partition consists of a single block. The *least-upper bound*, lub (π_1, π_2), of π_1 and π_2 is the smallest partition π_3 such that $\pi_1 \leq \pi_3$ and $\pi_2 \leq \pi_3$. The *greatest-lower bound*, glb (π_1, π_2), is the largest partition π_4 such that $\pi_4 \leq \pi_1$ and $\pi_4 \leq \pi_2$. We shall see later that in the case of clusterings, although lub $(\pi_1, \pi_2) = \pi_1 + \pi_2$, glb (π_1, π_2) is not always $\pi_1 \cdot \pi_2$ as defined above. This *partial ordering* leads us to the concept of a lattice.

A lattice is a partially-ordered set $L = (S, \leq)$, which has a least-upper bound and a greatest-lower bound for every pair of elements. The partially-ordered set of all clusterings of a graph is a lattice. We shall see that in some cases the sum and product of two clusterings must be redefined in terms of the graph itself. By a *cluster lattice* we shall mean a lattice formed by the set of clusterings of a graph.

LEMMA 1. *Defining the sum and product of two clusterings as above, the sum of two clusterings of an arbitrary graph is a clustering but the product of two clusterings is not necessarily a clustering.*

Proof. If π_1 and π_2 are two clusterings of graph G having blocks $a_1, a_2, a_3, \cdots , a_n, b_1, b_2, b_3, \cdots , b_m$ and $c_1, c_2, c_3, \cdots , c_p, b_1, b_2, b_3, \cdots , b_m$, respectively, then $\pi_1 + \pi_2$ has a block $a_1, a_2, a_3, \cdots , a_n, c_1, c_2, c_3, \cdots , c_p,$

$b_1, b_2, b_3, \cdots, b_m$. Since there was at least one a_i connected to a node b_j and at least one c_i connected to a node b_k, the block formed above is a legitimate block in a clustering of G. Since this is true for all blocks $\pi_1 + \pi_2$ is a clustering of G. Consider the graph of Figure 1. Let $\pi_2 = \{a, b, c; d\}$ and $\pi_6 = \{a, c, d; b\}$. Then $\pi_2 \cdot \pi_6 = \{a, c; b; d\}$ is not a legitimate clustering since the blocks do not form connected subgraphs. Q.E.D.

The example of Fig. 1 raises some interesting questions: In what cases is the product of two clusterings as defined earlier in this section a clustering? Do the clusterings of all graphs form lattices? What is the structure of these lattices?

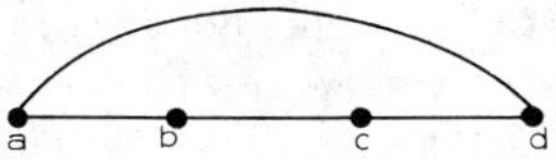

Figure 1.

THEOREM 2. *The set of all clusterings of an arbitrary graph forms a lattice.*

Proof. By Lemma 1 we may define lub (π_i, π_j) as $\pi_i + \pi_j$ for any two clusterings π_i and π_j. $\pi_i + \pi_j$ will exist and be unique. For those graphs for which $\pi_i \cdot \pi_j$ is a clustering for two clusterings π_i and π_j we may define glb (π_i, π_j) as $\pi_i \cdot \pi_j$. The product will thus exist and be unique. Suppose that for two clusterings the product $\pi_i \cdot \pi_j$ as defined previously is not a clustering. Then the product represents the glb of the partitions π_i and π_j and is a partition. Suppose that we refine this partition in the minimum number of steps necessary to make it a clustering. This clustering exists, is unique, and is the glb of clusterings π_i and π_j. Hence, the set of all clusterings of a graph forms a lattice. Q.E.D.

Thus, for any graph there is a partial ordering of clusterings and, as we showed above, a lattice. In general, if the product of two clusterings is to be a clustering the operation of product must depend on the graph. For the example of Fig. 1 we may define the product of π_2 and π_6 as $\{a; b; c; d\}$ and thus obtain the cluster lattice of Figure 2. For any graph the cluster lattice may be formed

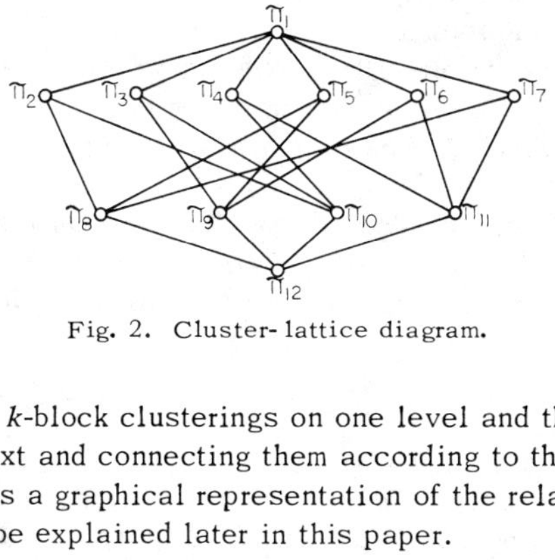

Fig. 2. Cluster-lattice diagram.

merely by listing the k-block clusterings on one level and the $(k + 1)$-block clusterings on the next and connecting them according to the ordering "$\leq$." The lattice diagram is a graphical representation of the relationships among clusterings and will be explained later in this paper.

A lattice is *complemented* if for every element π_i there exists an element π_j such that $\pi_i + \pi_j$ is the largest partition and $\pi_i \cdot \pi_j$ is the smallest partition. A lattice is *distributive* if the complement of every element is uniquely determined. A Boolean lattice is both complemented and distributive.

THEOREM 3. *The set of all clusterings of a tree forms a Boolean lattice.*

Proof. Every subset of the set of edges of a tree defines a unique clustering, namely that which has these edges as its breakpoints. Thus this set (and the clusterings defined by it) is isomorphic to the set of all subsets of a set. Since the set of all subsets of a set forms a Boolean lattice the set of all clusterings of a tree forms a Boolean lattice. Q.E.D.

The complement of a clustering π_i having a set of intercluster edges $\{e_i\}$ is that clustering π_j whose set of intracluster edges is $\{e_i\}$. Thus π_i has breaks wherever π_j does not, and vice versa.

In the case of trees the product of two clusterings can be taken independently of the graph. There is a wider class of graphs than trees in which the product can be found independently of the shape of the graph. It is, of course, understood that the last phrase means that the product of two clusterings can be taken according to the rule given at the beginning of this section and it is not necessary to check if the result is a legitimate clustering.

THEOREM 4. *The product of two clusterings of a graph, where "product" is defined independently of the graph, is a legitimate clustering in every case iff there are no two nodes which are nonadjacent (not connected by a path of length 1) but which are connected by at least two nonintersecting paths of length greater than 1.*

Proof. Sufficiency: Let a and b be two nodes connected by two nonintersecting paths of length greater than 1 as shown in Figure 4. a and b are not connected by a path of length 1. Then there exists a clustering π_1 having a block $a, d_1, d_2, d_3, \cdots, d_m, b$, and a clustering π_2 having a block $a, c_1, c_2, c_3, \cdots c_n, b$, all other nodes belonging to blocks of size 1 in each clustering. Then $\pi_1 \cdot \pi_2$ has a block a, b. Since a and b are not directly connected the partition is not a clustering. Necessity: Under what conditions will $\pi_1 \cdot \pi_2$ not be a clustering? When two or more disjoint sets of nodes are connected in π_1 and π_2 by some pair of disjoint sets of intermediate nodes. This is the only way that two disjoint nodes can be linked within a block of a product. Q.E.D.

Thus, in constructing a lattice one must be careful about taking the product of clusterings. In the example of Fig. 1, Nodes a and c are connected by two nonintersecti ng paths, one through b and the other through d.

LEMMA 5. *The cluster lattice of a graph that is not a tree is complemented but not distributive.*

Proof. For all edges not belonging to a loop the complement of clustering π_i has break points where π_i has none, and vice versa. If an edge belongs to a loop (of three or more nodes of course) we have the situation shown in Figure 3. If π_1 contains a block $a, c_1, c_2, c_3, \cdots, c_n, b$, then π_1' contains $a; c_1; c_2; c_3; \cdots; c_n; b$. If π_2' contains a block $a, c_1, c_2, c_3, \cdots, c_i$ and/or $c_{i+1}, c_{i+2}, c_{i+3}, \cdots, c_n, b$, then π_2 contains $a; c_1; c_2; c_3; \cdots; c_i$ and/or $c_{i+1}; c_{i+2}; c_{i+3}; \cdots; c_n; b$, respectively. If π_3 contains a block $c_i, c_{i-1}, c_{i-2}, \cdots, a, b, c, \cdots, c_{j+1}, c_j$ then π_3' contains blocks $c_i; c_{i-1}; c_{i-2}; \cdots; a; b; c; \cdots; c_{j+1}; c_j$, where these blocks in each case are properly modified to take care of nodes outside the loop. Thus a

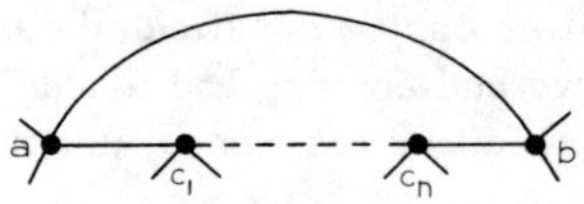

Fig. 3. Cluster-lattice diagram where an edge belongs to a loop.

clustering will always have a complement. Let $b, a; c_1; c_2; c_3; \cdots; c_n$ be a set of blocks of a clustering π_4. Then π_4' has blocks $a; b, c_n; c_1; c_2; \cdots; c_{n-1}$ but there is also another complement $b; a, c_1; c_2; c_3; \cdots; c_n$. Hence, if there is a loop there is at least one clustering with two complements. Thus the lattice is not distributive. Q.E.D.

THEOREM 6. *The cluster lattice of a graph is a Boolean lattice iff the graph is a tree.*

Proof. The *if* part follows from Theorem 3 and the *only if* follows from Lemma 5 as a consequence of the nondistributivity of the lattice of a graph which is not a tree. Q.E.D.

It has been shown that graphs can be classified according to their cluster lattices. The smallest class is that of a tree having a Boolean lattice under the operations $\cdot$ and $+$. A larger class is that of a graph with loops and having a nonBoolean lattice under the operations $\cdot$ and $+$. The most general class of graphs has a lattice in which the operation $\cdot$ must depend on the graph itself.

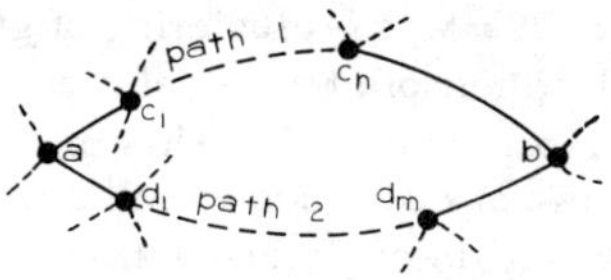

Figure 4.

III. LATTICE CONSTRUCTION

A cluster lattice may always be constructed by the following algorithm:

(1) Form levels 0 and 1 of the cluster lattice. (Note that there are N levels, where N is the number of nodes in the graph. The levels are labeled from 0 to $N-1$. The smallest partition is on level 0)

(2) Let $i = 2$

(3) Form level i by forming the sums of all pairs of elements on level $i-1$

(4) Is $i = N - 1$? If so, the procedure ends. If not, let $i = i + 1$ and go to Step (3).

Because of the exhaustive nature of this technique it is of interest to have a simpler method for constructing a cluster-lattice diagram from a graph.

First, let us consider the structure of the cluster lattice of a tree with k edges. There are 2^k clusterings in all. The ith level has $\binom{k}{i}$ clusterings. This regular structure is due to the fact that the lattice is Boolean.

The cluster lattice of a tree can be constructed easily. Let L be the cluster lattice of tree T. Suppose we add an edge and a node x' to the tree T at node x and thus obtain tree T'. The lattice diagram L' is constructed as follows:

(1) Draw lattice L
(2) Redraw lattice L to its right and raised up one level
(3) Connect the corresponding points in each lattice to one another.

The result is lattice L'. The clusterings are found as follows:

(1) If π was a clustering in L then $\{\pi; x'\}$ is the corresponding clustering in L'. This labels the part of L' drawn in Step (1) above
(2) The part of the lattice drawn in Step (2) above is labeled $\{\pi x'\}$ where this notation means that x' is within the same block as x.

The cluster lattice of a tree can be formed by starting with the cluster lattice of any subtree and adding edges until the tree is formed, constructing the lattice as each edge is added.

The construction procedure above applies to more general graphs than trees.

THEOREM 7. *Let G be a graph whose set of clusterings form a lattice diagram L. Suppose that to any node in G we append a leaf thereby forming graph G′. The lattice diagram L′ of graph G′ can be constructed by the technique given above.*

Proof. Let the appended node be node x' and let the node to which it is directly connected be node x. If π was a clustering of graph G then $\{\pi; x'\}$ must be a clustering of graph G′. Furthermore the set of clusterings of this form must form a lattice diagram L_1 isomorphic to L. This represents all the clusterings of G′ in which edge $x - x'$ is not contained within a cluster. The set of clusterings of G′ for which edge $x - x'$ is contained within a cluster is the set of clusterings of G with x and x' always within the same block. This set of clusterings also has a lattice L_2 isomorphic to L. To each clustering π_2 in lattice L_2 there belongs the clustering π_1 in L_1 in which x' is in a block apart from x but the blocks retain the same form otherwise. Thus each node of lattice diagram L_2 is connected to one node of L_1 on the level just below in order to form L'. These nodes are the corresponding nodes of L_2 and L_1. The construction procedure accomplishes this and thus results in L'. Q.E.D.

From the fact that the lattices are Boolean, it follows that if tree T_1 has N nodes and tree T_2 has N nodes then the cluster lattice of T_1 is isomorphic to that of T_2. Theorem 7 shows that there is an even larger class of graphs that can have isomorphic lattices. For example, the graphs of Fig. 6 have isomorphic lattices. Theorem 7 showed the effect of adding a leaf to a graph. One may ask

Fig. 5. Are the cluster lattices isomorphic?

about the effect of adding an edge as a bridge. For example, are the cluster lattices of the two graphs in Fig. 5 isomorphic? Theorem 8 answers this question.

THEOREM 8. *Let G be the graph with articulation point* N_1

G:

Let G' be the graph formed by creating a bridge and adding a node N_2

G':

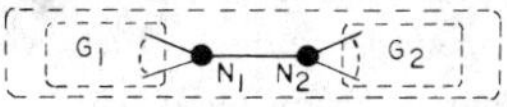

Let G'' be the graph formed by adding a leaf to G.

G'':

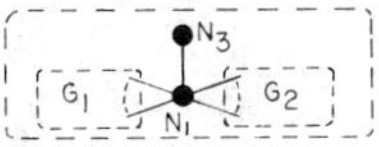

Then G' and G'' have isomorphic cluster lattices.

Proof. It has been shown that the cluster lattice of graph G'' is a graph which is constructed using two copies of the lattice of G, one a level higher than the other and with corresponding elements connected. Consider the effect of splitting a node N_1 in graph G into two nodes, N_1 and N_2, as we did to form G'. G' will have a set of clusterings in which N_2 will be joined to N_1 in each block containing N_1. This set of clusterings is formed by taking the cluster lattice of G and, wherever N_1 appears, N_2 is placed within the same block as N_1. The resulting lattice will be called L_1. The set of clusterings in which N_1 and N_2 belong to separate blocks is obtained by taking the cluster lattice L_1 and splitting the blocks in which N_1 appears into two blocks such that N_1 and all those nodes of the block of L_1 which are chain connected to it are in one block and N_2 and all those nodes of the block of L_1 which are chain connected to it are in the other block. Call the resulting lattice L_2. The elements of L_2 are related in the same way that they were related in L_1 and each element of L_2 on level k belongs to one element of L_1 on level $k+1$, namely that element which was split to form the corresponding element of L_2. Thus, the cluster lattice of G' is formed the same way that the cluster lattice of G'' is formed. Hence, the lattices are isomorphic. Q.E.D.

Theorem 8 has important implications for the construction of graphs from lattices. In particular, the only edges of real concern are those that belong to loops. One of the reasons that the Theorem only holds if N_1 and N_2 do not belong to a loop is that one or more nodes chain connected to N_1 would also be chain connected to N_2, thus complicating the splitting of the block of lattice L_1. The theorem may be repeatedly applied to a graph to form graphs with isomorphic lattices. For example, those below have isomorphic lattices.

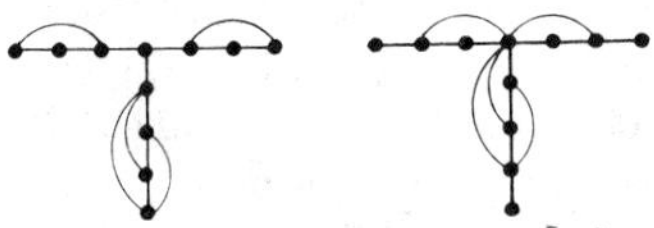

The type of graph formed by the construction procedure above is called a *permutation graph* [3]. A permutation graph consists of two disjoint identically-labeled copies of a graph G, say G and G', along with additional edges which connect corresponding nodes of G and G'. Hence it can be said that if a graph has one or more leaves (and/or bridges) then its lattice is a permutation graph. It is also possible to say that, given two nonisomorphic graphs G_1 and G_2, if one prunes each graph, a leaf (or a bridge) at a time, if after k prunings of each the resulting graphs are isomorphic then the original graphs had isomorphic cluster lattices.

Another result that applies in a particular case is, nonetheless, interesting. Let G be a graph consisting of N nodes arranged in a straight line. To G there corresponds lattice L. Add an edge spanning all N nodes, thus forming a circle of nodes. The lattice is drawn by drawing lattice L, redrawing levels $0, 1, 2, \cdots, N-3$ to the right and up one level, connecting the corresponding nodes in the two graphs, and connecting all nodes on level $N-2$ to the node on level $N-1$.

As an example utilizing the construction procedure above the construction of the lattice for graph G_1 is shown in Figure 6. Notice that the cluster lattice for graph G_2 is isomorphic to that of G_1.

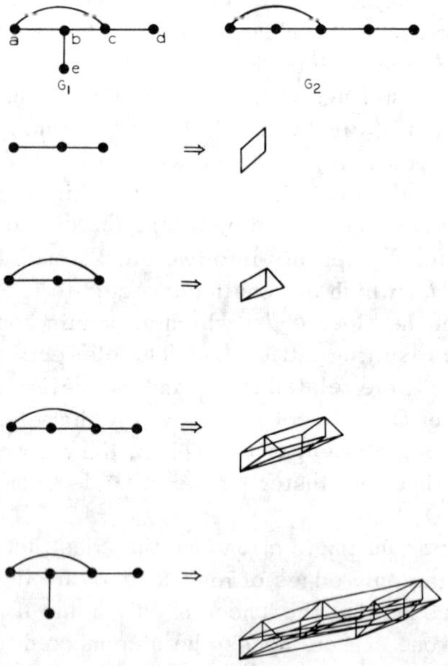

Fig. 6. Example of lattice construction for graph G_1.

The problem of construction of cluster lattices would be solved if the effect of forming a loop by adding an edge could be explained in general. To see the difficulties more clearly consider the graph below. We compare the effect of adding node 5 and edge 3–5 to that of adding edge 3–1.

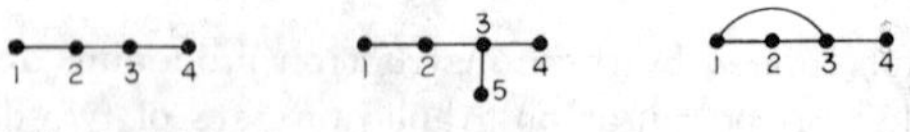

Originally we had clusterings

$\{1, 2, 3, 4\}$

$\{1, 2, 3; 4\}$ $\{1, 2; 3, 4\}$ $\{1; 2, 3, 4\}$

$\{1, 2; 3; 4\}$ $\{1; 2, 3; 4\}$ $\{1; 2; 3, 4\}$

$\{1; 2; 3; 4\}$

Adding node 5 gives {the above; 5} and also

{1,2,3,4,5}
{1,2,3,5;4} {1,2;3,4,5} {1;2,3,5,4}
{1,2;3,5;4} {1;2,3,5;4} {1;2;3,4,5}
{1;2;3,5;4}

Adding edge 3–1 gives the original clusterings plus

{1,3,4;2}
{1,3;2;4} .

If we let 5 equal 1, the result does not reduce to the above because the result is duplications of clusterings, i.e., 1, 2, 3 is the same as 2, 3, 5. Thus we could form the lattice as we do for a tree if we had a mechanism for eliminating duplications on levels $2,3,4,\cdots,N-2$. Notice that no duplications (if we do not add any elements above level $N-2$) occur on levels $0,1,N-1$ and these are no problem. It is asserted that when one adds an edge to a graph to form a loop of m nodes (the smallest loop of those formed) then the procedure for constructing the lattice for a tree holds from level 0 to level $m-2$ regardless of the rest of the graph. This is true since there are no blocks of size m until level $m-1$. This is why the procedure on the previous page worked for a graph of N nodes and a loop of N nodes. The tree procedure worked to level $N-2$ and then level $N-1$ obviously has only one element.

IV. CONSTRUCTION OF GRAPHS FROM LATTICES

In addition to the questions already considered there exist two others to be answered. The first asks, "Given a lattice, is it a cluster lattice corresponding to some graph?" The second, which will be treated later, asks if we can construct the corresponding graph. The first approach we will take in attempting to answer question one involves an attempt to list the necessary and sufficient conditions which a lattice must display in order for it to be a cluster lattice. Theorem 9 will be found useful in this endeavor.

THEOREM 9. *Let G_1 and G_2 be two graphs with N nodes and let G_1 be a proper subgraph of G_2. Then the cluster lattice of G_1 is a proper sublattice of the cluster lattice of G_2.*

Proof. Let the cluster lattice of G_1 be L_1 and let G_{11} be a graph formed by adding an edge to G_1 directly connecting node i and node j. The cluster lattice L_{11} corresponding to G_{11} contains all clusterings of L_1 since these correspond to the clusterings of G_{11} in which edge $i-j$ is broken. In addition to this there is at least one clustering not belonging to G_1, namely that in which $i-j$ belongs to a single block and all other nodes belong to separate blocks. Hence L_1 is a proper sublattice of L_{11}. Repeating this procedure one edge at a time to form $G_{1,i+1}$ from G_{11} we eventually arrive at G_2. L_1 is therefore a proper sublattice of L_2. Q.E.D.

It follows from the proof above that removal of edges from a graph results in removal of clusterings. Since a tree corresponds to the graph from which no edges can be removed without creating an unconnected graph and since all trees have isomorphic cluster lattices the cluster lattice of the tree with N nodes is a sublattice of the cluster lattice of any graph having N nodes. Since the complete graph with N nodes can have no edges added to it its lattice must have as a sublattice the cluster lattice of any graph with N nodes. Hence, the cluster lattices of the tree and of the complete graph represent extremes with respect to the cluster lattices of all graphs having the same number of nodes.

Necessary conditions for a lattice to be a cluster lattice are:

(1) A lattice with N levels $(0, 1, 2, \cdots, N-1)$ corresponds to a graph with N nodes if it corresponds to any graph. The number of elements on level 1 gives the number of edges in the graph. By Theorem 9 every lattice having N levels and corresponding to a graph must have as a sublattice the cluster lattice of a tree with N nodes and must itself be a sublattice of the cluster lattice of the complete graph with N nodes

(2) Because of the condition above, level i must contain at least $\binom{N-1}{i}$ elements, as previously shown. The problem of partitioning the complete graph with N nodes in every possible way is equivalent to the problem of partitioning a set of N objects in all possible ways. This is a well-known combinatorial problem. The number of ways of partitioning a set of N objects into m blocks is given by the Stirling number of the second kind $S(N, m)$. Hence the ith level contains at most $S(N, N-i)$ elements. We also mention that because every element on level i is directly connected to elements only on levels $i-1$ and $i+1$ the lattice is a bipartite graph, that is, its nodes can be partitioned into two sets such that every edge has an end point in each set. A property of bipartite graphs is that they contain no odd cycles (where the lattice diagram is considered undirected). Hence there are only even cycles in a cluster-lattice diagram

(3) Some other necessary conditions are concerned with the degrees of the elements of the lattice. We define the outdegree (OD) of an element on level k as the number of edges incident with elements on level $k+1$ and the indegree (ID) as the number of edges incident with elements on level $k-1$. The degree of an element is the sum of the OD and ID. In the cluster lattice of the tree with N nodes every element has degree $N-1$. An element on level k has ID $= k$ and OD $= N-k-1$. This is a general property of Boolean lattices. It follows from Theorem 9 as a corollary that the ID and OD of a level for a tree are lower bounds on those of any graph with the same number of nodes. For the complete graph we may state the following theorems. (For proofs see [8].)

THEOREM 10. *In the cluster lattice of the complete graph with N nodes every element on the kth level has outdegree* $\binom{N-k}{2} = (N-k)(N-k-1)/2$.

THEOREM 11. *Let $P(N, m) = k_1 + k_2 + k_3 + \cdots + k_m$ be a partition into exactly m parts of the integer N. Then there exists a corresponding partition of the set of N objects having blocks of size $k_1, k_2, k_3, \cdots, k_m$ and indegree given by*

$$\mathrm{ID} = \sum_{j=1}^{m} q_j \ ,$$

where

$$q_j = \begin{cases} 0, & k_j = 1 \ , \\ \displaystyle\sum_{i=1}^{(k_j-1)/2} \binom{k_j}{i}, & k_j \ odd, \neq 1 \ , \\ \displaystyle\sum_{i=1}^{(k_j/2)-1} \binom{k_j}{i} + \frac{1}{2}\binom{k_j}{k_j/2}, & k_j \ even \ . \end{cases}$$

Thus a single level can have a variation of indegrees. These indegrees display some unusual patterns as shown in Table I (extrapolated for $N = 11$ and $N = 12$). A discussion of this behavior appears in [8].

The necessary conditions given above do not tell us exactly how many elements are on each level of the lattice diagram for a given graph nor do they tell us how the elements are interconnected. Hence, they are not sufficient conditions. The following paragraphs lead to a procedure for determining the realizability of a given cluster lattice.

What does the lattice diagram tell us about the corresponding graph? The number of levels tells us the number of nodes. The number of elements on level 1 tells us the number of edges. Hence the number of fundamental loops is number of edges-number of nodes + 1. The realization problem is one of identifying edges. There are three kinds of edges: (A) Edges belonging to cycles; (B) Edges forming bridges between cycles but not themselves belonging to cycles; and (C) Edges on trees connected to loops. The second and third types of edges have been shown to give rise to permutation graphs. Since this is true it would seem to be desirable to be able to decompose a cluster lattice into the component parts of its permutation graph. This would have the effect of pruning leaves from the corresponding graph. When no further decomposition is possible the graph corresponding to the resulting lattice diagram would contain only edges of Type (A). After constructing the graph with edges of Type (A) the remaining leaves may be appended in a quite arbitrary manner (not forming any cycles, of course). An algorithm for performing this decomposition is given in [8]. This step is really not necessary but it may simplify some of the steps to be described later.

The ($N - 2^{\text{th}}$) level of the lattice gives the 2-block clusterings of the graph. For any element on level $N - 2$ the edges which are not contained within the clusters can be determined by tracing all paths from the given element to level 1. Any elements on level 1 which are not intersected by such a path represent the edges not contained within the clusters. These edges are a proper cutset of the graph. The set of all cutsets can be determined by this procedure and thus the cutset matrix can be formed. The cutset matrix is then tested for realizability by any of the methods given in the literature. If it is not realizable then the lattice is not a cluster lattice. If it is realizable then the matrix must be expanded to a full cutset matrix (if it isn't one already), a lattice constructed from this matrix, and the two lattices compared for isomorphism. If isomorphic, the original

TABLE I.

		TREE			COMPLETE GRAPH											
N	Level	#	OD	ID	#	OD	ID									
2	0	1	1	0	1	1	0									
	1	1	0	1	1	0	1									
3	0	1	2	0	1	3	0									
	1	2	1	1	3	1	1									
	2	1	0	2	1	0	1									
4	0	1	3	0	1	6	0									
	1	3	2	1	6	3	1									
	2	3	1	2	7	1	3	2								
	3	1	0	3	1	0	7									
5	0	1	4	0	1	10	0									
	1	4	3	1	10	6	1									
	2	6	2	2	25	3	3	2								
	3	4	1	3	15	1	7	4								
	4	1	0	4	1	0	15									
6	0	1	5	0	1	15	0									
	1	5	4	1	15	10	1									
	2	10	3	2	65	6	3	2								
	3	10	2	3	90	3	7	4	3							
	4	5	1	4	31	1	15	8	6							
	5	1	0	5	1	0	31									
7	0	1	6	0	1	21	0									
	1	6	5	1	21	15	1									
	2	15	4	2	140	10	3	2								
	3	20	3	3	350	6	7	4	3							
	4	15	2	4	301	3	15	8	6	5						
	5	6	1	5	63	1	31	16	10							
	6	1	0	6	1	0	63									
8	0	1	7	0	1	28	0									
	1	7	6	1	28	21	1									
	2	21	5	2	266	15	3	2								
	3	35	4	3	1050	10	7	4	3							
	4	35	3	4	1701	6	15	8	6	5	4					
	5	21	2	5	966	3	31	16	10	9	7					
	6	7	1	6	127	1	63	32	18	14						
	7	1	0	7	1	0	127									
9	0	1	8	0	1	36	0									
	1	8	7	1	36	28	1									
	2	28	6	2	462	21	3	2								
	3	56	5	3	2646	15	7	4	3							
	4	70	4	4	6951	10	15	8	6	5	4					
	5	56	3	5	7770	6	31	16	10	9	7	6				
	6	28	2	6	3025	3	63	32	18	17	14	11	9			
	7	8	1	7	255	1	127	64	34	22						
	8	1	0	8	1	0	255									
10	0	1	9	0	1	45	0									
	1	9	8	1	45	36	1									
	2	36	7	2	750	28	3	2								
	3	84	6	3	5880	21	7	4	3							
	4	126	5	4	22827	15	15	8	6	5	4					
	5	126	4	5	42525	10	31	16	10	9	7	6	5			
	6	84	3	6	34105	6	63	32	18	17	14	11	10	9	8	
	7	36	2	7	9330	3	127	64	34	33	22	20	15	13		
	8	9	1	8	511	1	255	128	66	32	30					
	9	1	0	9	1	0	511									
11	0						0									
	1						1									
	2							2								
	3								3		4					
	4												5			
	5															
	6															
	7															
	8															
	9															
	10															
12	0						0									
	1						1									
	2							2								
	3								3		4					
	4												5			
	5															- 6
	6															
	7															
	8															
	9															
	10															
	11															

N: number of nodes in graph
Levels go from 0 to N-1.
#: number of nodes on level
ID : number of edges of lattice incident with an element on level from below.
OD : number of edges of lattice incident with an element on level from above.

lattice was a cluster lattice. If not isomorphic, the lattice was not a cluster lattice. Theorem 12 shows that one can construct a unique (to an isomorphism) cluster lattice from a given cut-set matrix.

THEOREM 12. *All elements of the cluster lattice can be found by taking the union of proper cutsets.*

Proof. Let π_{jk} be an element j on level k. There is a path from π_{jk} to elements $\pi_1, \pi_2, \pi_3, \cdots, \pi_\ell$ $(\ell \geq 2)$ on level $N-2$. Let $\{K_1\}, \{K_2\}, \{K_3\}, \cdots, \{K_\ell\}$ be the proper cutsets implied by $\pi_1, \pi_2, \pi_3, \cdots, \pi_\ell$. Then since $\pi_{jk} < \pi_i (i = 1, 2, 3, \cdots, \ell)$ the set $\{e_{jk}\}$ of intercluster edges of π_{jk} must contain $\bigcup_{i=1}^{\ell} \{K_i\}$, that is, $\bigcup_{i=1}^{\ell} \{K_i\} \subseteq \{e_{jk}\}$. Then, $\{e_{jk}\} - \bigcup_{i=1}^{\ell} \{K_i\}$ must be a set of intercluster edges of π_{jk} not contained in $\bigcup_{i=1}^{\ell} \{K_i\}$. Since every edge of a graph must belong to at least one cutset, $\{e_{jk}\} - \bigcup_{i=1}^{\ell} \{K_i\} = \phi$, the null set. Hence π_{jk} is determined by the union of all cutsets having a direct path to π_{jk}. Q.E.D.

It follows from this that, given all proper cutsets in the form of a cutset matrix, taking the union of all pairs, all sets of 3, 4, etc. will generate all elements of the cluster lattice, the partial ordering of which is evident. If it is desired to construct the graph corresponding to the given cluster lattice this can be done by realizing the cutset matrix. The graph obtained will be unique to a 2-isomorphism [11].

In addition to the cutset matrix it is possible to obtain a circuit-basis matrix from the cluster lattice. This follows from the following Theorem (proven in [8]).

THEOREM 13. *Let $1, 2, 3, \cdots, k$ be a loop of nodes such that no subset is a loop. Then there corresponds an element in the cluster lattice on level $k-1$ with indegree $\binom{k}{2}$. Conversely an element on level $k-1$ with indegree $\binom{k}{2}$ and no predecessor elements on level p with indegree $\binom{p+1}{2}$ implies the existence of such a loop.*

The algorithm for constructing the circuit basis matrix is the following. Given lattice L, check all elements on level $k-1$ with indegree exactly $\binom{k}{2}$. Compute the number of fundamental loops, f. Label the checked elements $1, 2, 3, \cdots, m$ starting with the lowest level and proceeding to the next after all have been labeled on any level. Then:

(1) Let $i = 1$, $j = 1$

(2) Examine all downward paths from element i. If a checked element is intersected by a path go to Step (5). If not form an entry in the circuit matrix where edges (elements on level 1) intersected by these paths are given 1s and 0 otherwise. Call this entry C_j

(3) Is $j = f$? If so go to Step (6). If not go to Step (4)

(4) Let $i = i + 1$, $j = j + 1$. Go to Step (2)
(5) Let $i = i + 1$. Go to Step (2)
(6) Stop, the matrix is completed.

No method has been developed for constructing a cluster lattice from its circuit matrix so the algorithm above is not useful for testing a given lattice to determine if it is a cluster lattice. However, it can be used to realize a graph (to a 2-isomorphism) from a known cluster lattice. The problem of realizing a graph from a circuit or cutset matrix has been covered in the literature [1, 2, 7, 9, 10]. Since it has not been proven that a circuit matrix implies a unique cluster lattice it is possible that there is only one graph which has the given cluster lattice and circuit matrix. That is, it has not been shown that 2-isomorphic graphs have isomorphic cluster lattices. Hence, there are two alternatives. The first is to realize the graph from the cutset matrix. The second is to realize a graph from the circuit matrix, draw its cluster lattice and compare with the given lattice. If they are not isomorphic, another graph will have to be realized and the procedure repeated until the desired graph is obtained.

From the discussion above it is evident that a clear statement of the relationship between 2-isomorphic graphs and isomorphic cluster lattices would be desirable. On one hand, if two graphs are 2-isomorphic they have the same circuit matrix but it is not known if this implies a unique cluster lattice. On the other hand, if two graphs have the same cutset matrix they have the same cluster lattice to an isomorphism. However, the cutset matrices of 2-isomorphic graphs differ by a nonsingular transformation. This question has not yet been resolved.

Several of the algorithms above have the disadvantage of requiring a great deal of computation. In some cases this may be decreased. For example, in constructing a cluster lattice from its cutset matrix, all possible unions of cutsets needn't be formed since redundant terms can be eliminated during the computation. The construction of cluster lattices from graphs can be simplified by the techniques presented in this paper. The task of comparison of two lattices L and L' to determine isomorphism may be aided if L is decomposed as mentioned earlier. As L is decomposed the isomorphism of its components is checked at each step. When L can be decomposed no further the corresponding graph has edges of Type (A) alone. Its lattice need only be compared to the decomposed lattice to determine isomorphism. Thus the comparison of two large lattices is reduced to comparisons of smaller ones. Of course this is not possible if G has only edges of Type (A).

V. CONCLUSIONS

This paper has examined the structure of the set of clusterings of a graph. It has investigated the properties of the lattices formed by these clusterings and has presented some rules for their construction. It has also shown that a cluster lattice contains sufficient information to characterize the graph it represents to a 2-isomorphism.

At least two questions remain unanswered:

(1) If graph G has cluster lattice L, what is the effect on L of appending an edge between arbitrary nodes of G?

(2) How can one relate 2-isomorphism in graphs to isomorphism of cluster lattices?

These do not appear to be extremely difficult questions to answer.

ACKNOWLEDGEMENT

Taken from the dissertation submitted to the Faculty of the Polytechnic Institute of Brooklyn in partial fulfillment of the requirements for the degree of Doctor of Philosophy (E.E.), 1971.

REFERENCES

[1] R. B. Ash and W. H. Kim, "On Realizability of a Circuit Matrix," *IRE Trans. Cir. Theory*, CT-6, 219–223 (June 1959).

[2] S. G. Chan and J. F. Nale, "On Realization of a Circuit Matrix," *Proc. of the 7th Annual Allerton Conf. on Circuit and System Theory*, 477–486 (1969).

[3] G. Chartrand and F. Harary, "Planar Permutation Graphs," *Les Annales de L'Institute Henri Poincare*, III, No. 4, Sec. B, 433–438 (1967).

[[4] L. L. Gorinshteyn, "The Partitioning of Graphs," *Eng. Cybernetics*, No. 1, 76–82 (1969).

[5] B. W. Kernighan, "Some Graph Partitioning Problems Related to Program Segmentation," PhD. Dissertation, Princeton University (1969).

[6] E. L. Lawler, K. N. Levitt, and J. Turner, "Module Clustering to Minimize Delay in Digital Networks," *IEEE Trans. Comput.*, C-18, No. 1, 47–57 (January 1969).

[7] W. Mayeda, "Necessary and Sufficient Conditions for Realizability of Cutset Matrices," *IRE Trans. Cir. Theory*, CT-7, 79–81 (March 1960).

[8] E. A. Schroeppel, "Graph Partitioning," PhD. Dissertation, Polytechnic Institute of Brooklyn (1971).

[9] W. J. Tutte, "A Homotopy Theorem for Matroids I, II," *Trans. Am. Math. Soc.*, 88, 144–174 (1958).

[10] W. J. Tutte, "Matroids and Graphs," *Trans. Am. Math. Soc.*, 90, 527–552 (1959).

[11] H. Whitney, "2-Isomorphic Graphs," *Am. J. Math.*, 55, 245–254 (1933).

METHODS FOR REALIZING SEQUENTIAL MACHINES ON IDENTICAL INTEGRATED CIRCUITS

Svetlana P. Kartashev
Department of Computer Science, The Johns Hopkins University, Baltimore, MD

The development of integrated circuits has revised traditional views of switching theory. The problem of minimization of the number of memory or logical elements has yielded to the problem of optimal realization of a given sequential machine with integrated circuits.

In this report, assignment techniques are developed for realization from identical integrated units.

In contrast to the majority of minimization methods, the given methods do not require exploring many combinations, an important factor in their possible implementation.

In the sequel we introduce some definitions. Given a sequential machine $A(U, \chi, \delta)$, where: U is the set of states; χ is the set of input symbols; and δ is the translation function. We presume that the outputs are unspecified. We are interested in the state assignment problem. Let $\overline{U}$ be the set of assigned states, $\overline{\chi}$ the set of assigned inputs. Each state is assumed to be coded into an n-bit number, and each input into a p-bit number.

Let $F = (F_1, F_2, F_3, \cdots, F_n)$ be the set of excitation functions which define the corresponding logical network. Each F_i $(i = 1, 2, 3, \cdots, n)$ is the input to the ith storage element and is a function of $(p + n)$ arguments. Functions F_i and F_j are said to be *similar* if a mapping u exists such that

$$F_i(y_1, y_2, y_3, \cdots, y_p; \quad x_1, x_2, x_3, \cdots, x_n) = F_j(y_1, y_2, y_3, \cdots, y_p; \\ u(x_1'), u(x_2'), u(x_3'), \cdots, u(x_n'))$$

for any vector $y = (y_1, y_2, y_3, \cdots, y_p)$ from the input set $\overline{\chi}$ and for any vectors $x = (x_1, x_2, x_3, \cdots, x_n)$, $x' = (x_1', x_2', x_3', \cdots, x_n')$ from the state set $\overline{U}$.

Clearly, similarity is an equivalence relation. If the set F is contained in one equivalence class then the realization is said to be normal, and the $F_1, F_2, F_3, \cdots, F_n$ can be realized using n identical integrated units which are different from each other only in the interconnections of the transmitted variables. The internal structure of the unit is presumed to be invariant.

Using the above definitions, the following topics are investigated. First we investigate for the necessary and sufficient conditions of normal realization for arbitrary sequential machines: A sequential machine for which a normal realization exists is defined to be a regular—others are called irregular.

In the article, the following conditions are shown necessary and sufficient for an arbitrary sequential machine to be regular. Let there be a set of s cyclic registers $R_1, R_2, R_3, \cdots, R_s$, where each register has n positions. At any instant the state of the sequential machine is defined by the state of one of the registers* $R_1, R_2, R_3, \cdots, R_s$ in such a way that n sets Δ_i $(i = 1, 2, 3, \cdots, n)$ of n periods of regularity can be built. These sets have the following features:

*The state of the register R_i is defined as an arbitrary position in which the register R_i happens to be before or after the shift.

Presented at the Symposium on Computers and Automata
Polytechnic Institute of Brooklyn, April 13–15, 1971.

(a) Each period Δ_i ($i = 1, 2, 3, \cdots, n$) contains s states $A_1^{(i)}, A_2^{(i)}, A_3^{(i)}, \cdots, A_s^{(i)}$, where $A_1^{(i)} \in R_1, A_2^{(i)} \in R_2, \cdots, A_s^{(i)} \in R_s$
(b) If $A_j^{(s)} \in \Delta_i$ then a state $A_m^{(i)} \in \Delta_i$ and an input vector $x \in \chi$ can be found such that

$$\delta(A_j^{(i)}, x) = A_m^{(i)} ,$$

or

$$\delta(A_m^{(i)}, x) = A_j^{(i)}$$

(c) Let $A_j^{(1)}, A_j^{(2)}, A_j^{(3)}, \cdots, A_j^{(n)} \in R_j$ be the states of the register R_j distributed through the periods $\Delta_1, \Delta_2, \Delta_3, \cdots, \Delta_n$ in the following way

$$A_j^{(1)} \in \Delta_1, A_j^{(2)} \in \Delta_2, \cdots, A_j^{(n)} \in \Delta_n .$$

The states $A_j^{(1)}, A_j^{(2)}, A_j^{(3)}, \cdots, A_j^{(n)}$ will be said to have an equivalency relationship "$\sim$" such that if $A_j^{(i)} \sim A_j^{(m)}$ where $A_j^{(i)} \in \Delta_i, A_j^{(m)} \in \Delta_m$ ($i, m = 1, 2, 3,, \cdots, n$; $j = 1, 2, 3, \cdots, a$) then for any input vector $x \in \chi$ for which $\delta(A_j^{(i)}, x)$ is defined, the state $\delta(A_j^{(m)}, x)$ is defined and

$$\delta(A_j^{(i)}, x) \sim \delta(A_j^{(m)}, x)$$

(d) Let $A_j^{(i)}$ be an arbitrary state from the period Δ_i ($i = 1, 2, 3, \cdots, n$). Then

$$\pi A_j^{(i)} \in \pi \Delta_i ,$$

where π is the shift operation which shifts every one of the state $A_j^{(i)}$ from the rth position to the $(r+1)^{th}$ position. Since the register has a cyclic nature then the one previously in the highest position appears in the lowest position. $\pi \Delta_i$ denotes the set of the states Δ_i which have been subjected to the shift operation π.

Second, techniques for putting irregular sequential machines into regular form are investigated. These techniques are called regularization.

Third, assignment algorithms for regularized sequential machines are developed.

The methods of regularization as well as assignment are direct in that they do not require backtracking, a significant factor when we are dealing with large sequential machines.

It is also shown that for any sequential machine of k states, the code length n for a state assignment satisfies the relation

$$\lceil \log_2 k \rceil \leq n \leq \lceil \log_2 k \rceil + \lfloor \log_2 n \rfloor + 1 , \tag{A.1}$$

where $\lceil i \rceil$ denotes the least integer greater than or equal to i, and $\lfloor i \rfloor$ denotes the greatest integer less than or equal to i. The lower limit is valid for the regular sequential machine, while the upper limit is necessary for some irregular sequential machine.

It follows from (A.1) that the assignment length n of the sequential machine, subjected to the regularization process, increases by the value $\tau = \lfloor \log_2 n \rfloor + 1$, which for $n < 16$ is no more than 4.

INTRODUCTION

The development of integrated circuits has revised traditional views of switching theory. The problem of minimization of the number of memory or logical elements has yielded to the problem of optimal realization of a given sequential machine with integrated circuits.

In the report assignment techniques are developed for realization from identical integrated units.

In contrast to the majority of minimization methods, the given methods do not require exploring many combinations, an important factor in their possible implementation.

In the sequel we introduce some definitions. Define a sequential machine $A(\mathfrak{U}, \mathfrak{X}, \delta)$, where $\mathfrak{U}$ is the set of states, $\mathfrak{X}$ is the set of input symbols, and δ is the transition function; we presume that the outputs are unspecified. Here we are interested in the state assignment problem. Let $\overline{\mathfrak{U}}$ be the set of assigned states, $\overline{\mathfrak{X}}$ the set of assigned inputs. Each state is assumed to be coded into an n-bit number, and each input into a p-bit number.

Let $\mathbf{F} = (F_1, F_2, F_3, \cdots, F_n)$ be the set of excitation functions which define the corresponding logical network. Each F_i $(i = 1, 2, 3, \cdots, n)$ is the input to the ith storage element and is a function of $(p + n)$ arguments. Functions F_i and F_j are said to be *similar* if a mapping u exists such that

$$F_i(y_1, y_2, y_3, \cdots, y_p;\quad x_1, x_2, x_3, \cdots, x_n)$$
$$= F_j(y_1, y_2, y_3, \cdots, y_p;\quad u(x_1'), u(x_2'), u(x_3'), \cdots, u(x_n')) \quad ,$$

for any vector $y = (y_1, y_2, y_3, \cdots, y_p)$ from the input set $\overline{\mathfrak{X}}$ and for $\underline{\text{any}}$ vectors $x = (x_1, x_2, x_3, \cdots, x_n)$ $x' = (x_1', x_2', x_3', \cdots, x_n')$ from the state set $\overline{\mathfrak{U}}$.

Clearly, similarity is an equivalence relation. If the set F is contained in one equivalence class then the realization is said to be normal, and the $F_1, F_2, F_3, \cdots, F_n$ can be realized using n identical integrated units which are different from each other only in the interconnections of the transmitted variables. The internal structure of the unit is presumed to be invariant.

Using the above definitions, the following topics are investigated. First we investigate for the necessary and sufficient conditions of normal realization for arbitrary sequential machines. A sequential machine for which a normal realization exists is defined to be a regular—others are called irregular.

Second, techniques for putting an arbitrary irregular sequential machine into regular form are investigated. These techniques are called regularization.

Third, a state assignment algorithm for regularized sequential machines is developed.

The methods of regularization, as well as assignment, are direct in that they do not require backtracking, a significant factor when we are dealing with large sequential machines.

It is also shown that for any sequential machine of k states, the code length n for a state assignment satisfies the relation

$$\lceil \log_2 k \rceil \leq n \leq \lceil \log_2 k \rceil + \lfloor \log_2 n \rfloor + 1 \quad , \qquad \text{(I.1)}$$

where $\lceil i \rceil$ denotes the least integer greater than or equal to i, and $\lfloor i \rfloor$ denotes the greatest integer less than or equal to i. The lower limit is valid for the regular sequential machine, while the upper limit is necessary for some irregular sequential machines.

It follows from Eq. (I.1) that the assignment length n of the sequential machine, subjected to the regularization process, increases by the value $T = \lfloor \log_2 n \rfloor + 1$, which for $n < 16$ is no more than 4.

I. REGULAR SEQUENTIAL MACHINES

Given sequential machines $A(\mathfrak{U}, \mathfrak{X}, \delta)$, where $\mathfrak{U}$ is the set of internal states, $\mathfrak{X}$ is the set of inputs, δ is the transition function; the set $R = (R_1, R_2, R_3, \cdots, R_s)$

consists of s n-bit binary cyclic registers, where $R_i \in R$ is the set of shifts of an n-bit number. Cyclic means that the one in the highest position after a shift goes to the lowest position.

Suppose that the internal states from the set $\mathfrak{U}$ are identified with the states* of the registers $R_1, R_2, R_3, \cdots, R_s$ in such a way that at any instant $t > 0$ the state of sequential machine $A(\mathfrak{U}, \mathfrak{X}, \delta)$ is equal to the state of some register

$$R_j \in R \quad .$$

Clearly this process is identical to the assignment process. We assume that the assignment is subjected to the following restrictions:

(T1) The assigned states can be distributed through n sets which *further called periods of regularity* Δ_i $(i = 1, 2, 3, \cdots, n)$, each set consists of s elements

$$\Delta_i = (A_1^{(i)}, A_2^{(i)}, A_3^{(i)}, \cdots, A_s^{(i)}) \quad ,$$

where

$$A_1^{(i)} \in R_1, A_2^{(i)} \in R_2, A_3^{(i)} \in R_3, \cdots, A_s^{(i)} \in R_s$$

(T2) $\pi\Delta_i = \Delta_{i+1} \pmod n$ where π is a shift operation on 1 bit, applied to all of the elements from the set Δ_i $(i = 1, 2, 3, \cdots, n)$

(T3) If $A \in \Delta_i$, then we can find $B \in \Delta_i$ and input $x \in \mathfrak{X}$ such that either $\delta(A, x) = B$ or $\delta(B, x) = A$

(T4) If $\delta(C, x) = D$, for $C \in R_i$, $D \in R_j$, then

$$\delta(R_i, x) = R_j, \quad \text{and} \quad \delta^{-1}(R_j, x) = R_i \quad ,$$

which means that the domain of transition function δ is all of the states of the register R_i and the range of all the states of the register R_j. On the other hand, inverse function δ^{-1} has the domain defined by all of the states of the register R_j and the range by all of of the states of the register R_i.

The sequential machine $A(\mathfrak{U}, \mathfrak{X}, \delta)$ for which the assignment possessing by the properties (T1)–(T4), exists is called *s-regular* where s is the number of registers which take part in the construction. All others are called irregular.

Sometimes we will omit the number s, calling s-regular sequential machine simply regular. We presume that the sequential machines under consideration satisfy the following two axioms:

AXIOM 1 (*Uniqueness*). *For any state $A \in \mathfrak{U}$ no more than one state B exists, which satisfies*

$$\delta(A, x) = B \quad ,$$

where $x \in X$.

AXIOM 2 (*Incomplete—Complete Specification*). *For any state $A \in \mathfrak{U}$ the transition function δ is specified at least for one $x \in X$, i.e. $\delta(A, x) \neq \phi$.*

As follows from Property (T1) that each state of the s-regular sequential machine is the element of a period of regularity Δ_j $(j = 1, 2, 3, \cdots, n)$ and on the other hand is the element of a register R_i $(i = 1, 2, 3, \cdots, s)$, i.e., the distribution of the states through the periods and registers is easily described with the

*A *state* of the register $R_i \in R$ is any n-bit number in R_i.

matrix of the states of the dimension $n \times s$, where the rows of the matrix are identified as periods and the columns as registers. The state $A \in R_i$, Δ_j is the element of the ith column and the jth row.

Example.

	R_1	R_2
Δ_1	100	110
Δ_2	010	011
Δ_3	001	101

Assume that $\delta(R_1, x) = R_2$, $\delta(R_2, y) = R_2$. Then the given matrix can describe, for example, the following regular sequential machine.

INPUTS \ STATES	100	010	001	110	011	101
x	110	011	101	—	—	—
y	—	—	—	011	101	110

II. THE PROPERTIES OF THE CYCLIC REGISTERS

Introduce several aspects concerning the properties of the cyclic registers. Let $A \in R_i$ and $\pi_k A = A$ where $\pi_k = \pi(\pi_{k-1})$ and $k \geq 1$ is the minimal number which possesses the given property. The register R_i is said to be k-adic.

LEMMA 2.1. *A k-adic register has k states (obvious).*

Let $\mathfrak{B}_n$ be the set of all the divisors of the number n.

LEMMA 2.2. *p-adic n-bit registers exist iff $p \in \mathfrak{B}_n$.*

Proof. The existence of at least one p-adic p-bit register R_0 is obvious: for example, the p-bit register which contains a single one. Find $n/p = t$. Build the sequence of t; p-adic n-bit registers R_0. The result is the register R which has the form

$$R = \underbrace{R_0\, R_0\, R_0 \cdots R_0}_{t} \ .$$

The register R has n digits and is p-adic. Indeed, let A_0 be an arbitrary state of the register R_0. Using the definition of p-adic register we obtain

$$\pi_p A_0 = A_0 \ .$$

Then $A = \underbrace{A_0\, A_0\, A_0 \cdots A_0}_{t \text{ times}}$ is the state of the register R. Find

$$\pi_p A = \pi_p \underbrace{(A_0\, A_0\, A_0 \cdots A_0)}_{t \text{ times}} = \underbrace{\pi_p A_0\, \pi_p A_0\, \pi_p A_0 \cdots \pi_p A_0}_{t \text{ times}} = \underbrace{A_0\, A_0\, A_0 \cdots A_0}_{t \text{ times}} \ .$$

Since p is the minimal number of bits for any p-adic register, then any length n should contain t times a number p, where $t \geq 1$. Q.E.D.

COROLLARY 1. *Let $p \in \mathcal{B}_n, \mathcal{B}_c$. Then the number of p-adic n-bit registers is equal to the number of p-adic c-bit registers.*

Example 1.1. Build a 2-adic 8-bit register R.

$$\tfrac{8}{2} = 4, \quad R_0 = (10,01), \quad R = R_0 R_0 R_0 R_0 = (10101010, 01010101) \ .$$

The theorem which follows proposes a very convenient recursive formula for the calculation of the whole number of p-adic n-bit registers. Let D_p be the number of p-adic registers.

THEOREM 2.1. *For any $p \in \mathcal{B}_n$*

$$D_p = \frac{2^p - \sum\limits_{b \in \mathcal{B}_p - p} bD}{p} \ .$$

Proof. Consider a 1-dimensional cube, which has 2 states: 0 and 1, evoking two 1-adic registers R_1 and R_2

$$R_1 = \{0\}, \quad R_2 = \{1\}^* \ ,$$

i.e., $D_1^{(1)} = 2$, where the index in the upper brackets denotes the dimension of the cube, in which the calculation is under way. Let c be an arbitrary prime number and

$$\mathcal{B}_c = (c, 1) \ .$$

The registers $R_1' = \underbrace{R_1 R_1 R_1 \cdots R_1}_{\text{c times}}$ and $R_2' = \underbrace{R_2 R_2 R_2 \cdots R_2}_{\text{c times}}$. The registers R_1' and R_2' are 1-adic and c-bit. Using Corollary 1 of Lemma 2.2, we obtain

$$D_1^{(c)} = D_1^{(1)} = D_1 \ .$$

On the other hand, in a c-dimensional cube only c-adic and 1-adic registers exist (Lemma 2.2) as $D_1 = 2$, then

$$D_c^{(c)} = \frac{2^c - D_1^{(c)}}{c} \ , \tag{2.1}$$

since each c-adic register has c states.

Let $r = c \cdot t$, where $\mathcal{B}_c = (c, 1)$, $\mathcal{B}_t = (t, 1)$; i.e., $\mathcal{B}_r = (r, c, t, 1)$. Using Lemma 2.2 in an r-dimensional cube, r-adic, c-adic, t-adic, and 1-adic registers can be built. Using Corollary 1

$$D_1^{(1)} = D_1^{(r)}, \quad D_c^{(c)} = D_c^{(r)} \ ,$$

where it follows that $D_1^{(r)} = 2$.

$$D_t^{(r)} = \frac{2^t - D_1^{(r)}}{t} \ ,$$

*The iterational brackets mean that all other states of the register are produced by successive shifts of the state in brackets.

$$D_c^{(r)} = \frac{2^c - D_1^{(r)}}{c} .$$

Hence $D_1^{(r)} + tD_t^{(r)} + cD_c^{(r)} + rD_r^{(r)} = 2^r$ and

$$D_r^{(r)} = \frac{2^r - \sum\limits_{b \in \mathcal{B}_r - r} bD_b^{(r)}}{r} .$$

Considering Corollary 1 to (lemma 2.2) index (r) can be omitted and

$$D_r = \frac{2^r - \sum\limits_{b \in \mathcal{B}_r - r} bD_b}{r} , \tag{2.2}$$

i.e., we come to the arbitrary number p, for all of factors of which Eq. (2.2) is valid. It follows from the way of D_r construction, that for D_p a similar expression is satisfied

$$D_p = \frac{2^p - \sum\limits_{b \in \mathcal{B}_p - p} bD_b}{p} . \quad \text{Q.E.D.}$$

Table 2.1 presented below will be referred to often in the rest of this article. In the table the following relations are enumerated: n, D_n, $\lceil \log_2 D_n \rceil$ where $\lceil \log_2 D_n \rceil$ is the minimal assignment length, necessary for sequential machine with D_n states

TABLE II.1.

n	1	2	3	4	5	6	7	8	9	10	11	12	13	14	15	16
D_n	2	1	2	3	6	9	18	30	56	99	186	335	630	1161	2182	4080
$\log_2 D_n$	1	1	1	2	3	4	5	5	6	7	8	9	10	11	12	12
$n - \log_2 D_n$	0	1	2	2	2	2	2	3	3	3	3	3	3	3	3	4

III. SOME PROPERTIES OF THE REGULAR SEQUENTIAL MACHINES

Given a regular sequential machine $A(\mathcal{U}, \mathcal{X}, \delta)$ assigned by the n-bit registers $R_1, R_2, R_3, \cdots, R_s$.

THEOREM 3.1. *Let registers R_i and R_j be related by*

$$\delta(R_i, x) = R_j ,$$

where $x \in \mathcal{X}$. *If R_i is a k-adic register, then R_j is an m-adic register where*

$$m \in \mathcal{B}_k .$$

Proof. Each state $A \in R_i$ is an element of $p = n/k$ periods of regularity

$\Delta_{i_1}, \Delta_{i_2}, \Delta_{i_3}, \cdots, \Delta_{i_p}$, where the indices $i_1, i_2, i_3, \cdots, i_p$ are related by

$$\pi_k i_1 = i_2, \cdots, \pi_k i_p = i_1 \text{ (Property (T2))} \quad . \tag{3.1}$$

On the other hand, each state B of the m-adic register R_j is an element of $r = n/m$ periods of regularity $\Delta_{j_1}, \Delta_{j_2}, \Delta_{j_3}, \cdots, \Delta_{j_r}$, where

$$\pi_m j_1 = j_2, \cdots, \pi_m j_2 = j_1 \quad .$$

According to (T1) at least one period Δ_t exists, for which $A, B \in \Delta_t$. By condition

$$\delta(A, x) = B \quad .$$

Show that $B \in \Delta_{i_1}, \Delta_{i_2}, \Delta_{i_3}, \cdots, \Delta_{i_p}$. Suppose that at least one period Δ_{i_ℓ} exists, for which

$$A \in \Delta_{i_\ell}, \quad B \,\overline{\in}\, \Delta_{i_\ell} \quad .$$

According to (T1)

$$\Delta_{i_\ell} \cap R_j = (C) \quad .$$

Using (T4), $\delta(A, x) = C$, which contradicts Axiom 1 (uniqueness). Hence

$$(i_1, i_2, i_3, \cdots, i_p) \cap (j_1, j_2, j_3, \cdots, j_r) = (i_1, i_2, i_3, \cdots, i_p) \quad . \tag{3.2}$$

From this it follows that if

$$\pi_k i_1 = i_2, \cdots, \pi_k i_p = i_1 \quad ,$$

then

$$\pi_{m \cdot t} i_1 = i_2, \cdots, \pi_{m \cdot t} i_p = i_1 \quad ,$$

that is

$$k = m \cdot t, \quad \text{and} \quad m \in \mathcal{B}_k \quad . \quad \text{Q.E.D.}$$

COROLLARY 1. *If $\delta(R_i, x) = R_j$ and $\delta(R_j, y) = R_i$, then registers R_j and R_i have an equal number of states.*

We will call the registers $R_1, R_2, R_3, \cdots, R_k$, related to each other by

$$\delta(R_1, y_1) = R_2, \quad \delta(R_2, y_2) = R_3, \cdots, \delta(R_k, y_k) = R_1 \quad , \tag{3.3}$$

as registers which define k-reversive neighboring relation over inputs $y_1, y_2, y_3, \cdots, y_n$, not necessarily all distinct.

COROLLARY 2. *Registers $R_1, R_2, R_3, \cdots, R_k$ identifying k-reversive neighboring relation have an equal number of states.*

Let $R_1, R_2, R_3, \cdots, R_k$ be a sequence of n-bit registers, setting up k-reversive neighboring relation. We presume that $\pi_i R_j$ is the shift operation of degree i, undertaken over the states of the register R_j. Suppose that the register R_1 is turned up to the initial state A_0: $R_1 = \{A_0\}$. Then if $\delta(R_k, y_k) = \pi_0 R_1$, then registers $R_1, R_2, R_3, \cdots, R_k$ produce n components of connectivity, each containing k states (having length k). In this case the k-reversive neighboring relation is said to be unconnected.

If $\delta(R_k, y_k) = \pi R_1$, then registers $R_1, R_2, R_3, \cdots, R_k$ produce one component of connectivity, consisting of $k \cdot n$ states, (of length $k \cdot n$) and the k-reversive neighboring relation is said to be connected.

The sequential machine $A(\mathcal{U}, \mathcal{X}, \delta)$, generating connected (unconnected) k-reversive neighboring relations, is said to be k-regular string connected (unconnected) of length $k \cdot n$ (connected or unconnected) over the input $y_1, y_2, y_3, \cdots, y_k$, which are not tied to be distinct.

Example 3.1. Build a connected 2-regular string over the input x, y using $n = 3$. In this case that sequential machine is described by the state matrix of the dimension 3×2 and can be built with the registers R_1, R_2 generating a connected 2-reversive neighboring relation over the input x, y

$$\delta(R_1, x) = R_2 \ ,$$

$$\delta(R_2, y) = \pi R_1 \ ,$$

	R_1	R_2
Δ_1	100	110
Δ_2	010	011
Δ_3	001	101

The state diagram of the connected 2-regular string is shown in Fig. 3.1 (the pe-

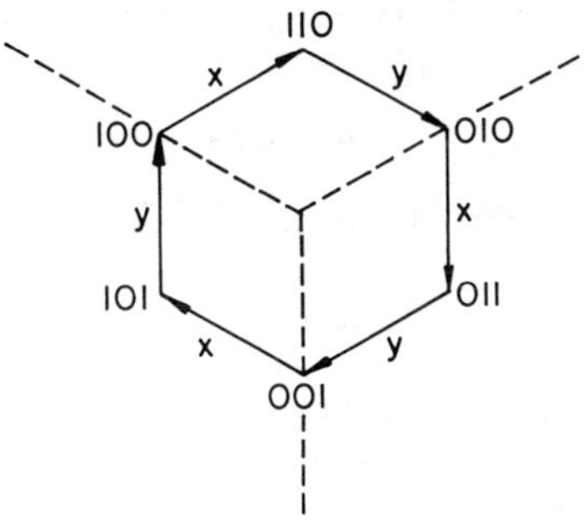

Fig. 3.1. Connected 2-regular string.

riods are separated by dashed lines). The regular sequential machine which is not identical to the regular string is said to be a regular tree.

THEOREM 3.2. *In an arbitrary s-regular tree it is always possible to pick out a k-regular string (connected or unconnected) where $k < s$, over the inputs $y_1, y_2, y_3, \cdots, y_n$, which are not bound to be different in pairs.*

Proof. The proof is obvious and follows from (T4) and Axiom 2 of incomplete specification. Q.E.D.

The regular sequential machine $A(\mathcal{U}, \mathcal{X}, \delta)$, built by means of n-bit registers $R_1, R_2, R_3, \cdots, R_s$, is said to be nondegenerate, if each of the registers $R_1, R_2, R_3, \cdots, R_s$ is n-adic. Otherwise a sequential machine $A(\mathcal{U}, \mathcal{X}, \delta)$ is called degenerate.

THEOREM 3.3. *In a nondegenerate sequential machine each string of the length r (connected or unconnected) is p-regular, where $p = r/n$.*

Proof. Obvious. Q.E.D.

And now, consider a degenerate sequential machine realized by means of the set of registers $R = (R_1, R_2, R_3, \cdots, R_s)$. Put into correspondence the number

m_i to each m_i-adic register $R_i \in R$. The number m_i is further called the mark of the register R_i $(i = 1, 2, 3, \cdots, s)$. Let

$$m^* = \min(m_1, m_2, m_3, \cdots, m_s) \ . \tag{3.4}$$

THEOREM 3.4. *In a degenerate regular sequential machine a t-regular string always exists (connected or unconnected) where* $t \geq 1$ *with length* $t \cdot m^*$ *(connected or unconnected).*

Proof. Let $\mathbf{R}_0^*$ be the subset of all of the m^*-adic registers, containing k elements. Suppose that

$$\mathbf{R}_0^* = (R_1^*, R_2^*, R_3^*, \cdots, R_k^*) \ ,$$

each of the registers $R_i^* \in \mathbf{R}_0^*$ is put into correspondence with the register $\lambda(R_i^*)$, neighboring to the register R_i^* at least over one of the inputs $x \in \mathcal{X}$

$$\lambda(R_i^*) = \delta(R_i^*, x) \ . \tag{3.5}$$

The choice of $\lambda(R_i^*)$ is made arbitrarily. In view of the axiom of incomplete specification, all of the registers $\lambda(R_i^*)$ are specified, where $i = 1, 2, 3, \cdots, k$. Applying Theorem 3.1 and considering Eq. (3.4), obtain that the set

$$\lambda(\mathbf{R}_0^*) = (\lambda(R_1^*), \lambda(R_2^*), \lambda(R_3^*), \cdots, \lambda(R_k^*)) \ ,$$

is the set of m^*-adic registers. Hence

$$\lambda(\mathbf{R}_0^*) \subseteq \mathbf{R}_0^* \ .$$

Find $\mathbf{R}_0^*/\lambda(\mathbf{R}_0^*)$. Then the following cases can be exhibited:

(a) $\mathbf{R}_0^*/\lambda(\mathbf{R}_0^*) \neq \phi$
(b) $\mathbf{R}_0^*/\lambda(\mathbf{R}_0^*) = \phi$.

In Case (a) we find $\mathbf{R}_1^* = \lambda(\mathbf{R}_0^*)$. Build $\lambda(\mathbf{R}_1^*) \subset \lambda(\mathbf{R}_0^*)$. Find $\mathbf{R}_1^*/\lambda(\mathbf{R}_1^*)$. If this set is not empty, build $\mathbf{R}_2^* = \lambda(\mathbf{R}_1^*)$, find $\lambda(\mathbf{R}_2^*)$ and $\mathbf{R}_2^*/\lambda(\mathbf{R}_2^*)$. In the common case find

$$\mathbf{R}_i^* = \lambda(\mathbf{R}_{i-1}^*) \ ,$$

and

$$\lambda(\mathbf{R}_i^*) \subset \lambda(\mathbf{R}_0^*) \ .$$

Build $\mathbf{R}_i^*/\lambda(\mathbf{R}_i^*)$. Clearly for any numbers i, j $(i > j)$ which

$$\mathbf{R}_i^*/\lambda(\mathbf{R}_i^*) \ ,$$

and

$$\mathbf{R}_j^*/\lambda(\mathbf{R}_j^*) \ ,$$

are not equal to empty sets

$$\mathbf{R}_i^*/\lambda(\mathbf{R}_i^*) \subset \mathbf{R}_j^*/\lambda(\mathbf{R}_j^*) \ .$$

Hence we can find the number ℓ, for which

$$\mathbf{R}_\ell^*/\lambda(\mathbf{R}_\ell^*) = \phi \ ,$$

where $R_\ell^* \neq \phi$. Therefore the above procedure leads sooner or later to Case (b).

In Case (b) $\mathbf{R}_i^*/\lambda(\mathbf{R}_i^*) = \phi$, where $i \geq 0$. This means that the registers from set $\mathbf{R}_i^*$ produce a series of reversive neighboring relations. Hence in the set $\mathbf{R}_i^*$ it is always possible to find t $(t \geq 1)$ m^*-adic registers $R_1^*, R_2^*, R_3^*, \cdots, R_t^*$, which produce

$$\delta(R_1^*, x_1) = R_2^*, \cdots, \delta(R_i^*, x_t) = R_1^* ,$$

where the inputs $x_1, x_2, x_3, \cdots, x_i$ are not bound to be different in pairs. Therefore the registers $R_1^*, R_2^*, R_3^*, \cdots, R_t^*$, produce a t-regular string (connected or unconnected) with length $m^* \cdot t$ (connected or unconnected). Q.E.D.

IV. REGISTER FLOW TABLE

It follows from Property (T4) that an arbitrary s-regular sequential machine can be specified by data of a transition function on the set of registers $\mathbf{R} = (R_1, R_2, R_3, \cdots, R_s)$. It is easy to perform by means of register flow table. The columns of the table are identified as elements of the set $\mathbf{R}$; the rows are identified as input symbols from the set $\mathfrak{X}$. The entry of xth row and $R_j{}^{\text{th}}$ column is specified as the register $\delta(R_j, x)$. We presume that the registers $R_1, R_2, R_3, \cdots, R_s$ are in fixed initial states $A_1, A_2, A_3, \cdots, A_s$. Then $\pi_i R_j$ is the register in shifted state $\pi_i A_j$. From the point of view of the given definitions, the registers in the initial and shifted states can be given as the entries in the flow table.

If the sequential machine is nondegenerate (degenerate) then the corresponding register flow table is said to be nondegenerate (degenerate). The difference between those two tables consists of the introduction of a special row of marks to a degenerate flow table, marking each register R_i by the corresponding mark m_i.

If an arbitrary nondegenerate register flow table specifies some nondegenerate regular sequential machine, then the row of marks of a degenerate register table has to satisfy certain restrictions to be able to specify a degenerate sequential machine. These restrictions are listed in the following theorem.

THEOREM 4.1. *An arbitrary degenerate register table specifies a degenerate regular sequential machine, assigned by the code length n, iff:*

(1) *Each mark m_j of the register R_j is a divisor of the number n: $m_j \in \mathfrak{B}_n$*
(2) *If $\delta(R_i, x) = R_j$, then $m_j \in \mathfrak{B}_{m_i}$, where m_i, m_j are the marks of the registers R_i and R_j*
(3) *The number t of the registers with the marks $m_{j_1}, m_{j_2}, m_{j_3}, \cdots, m_{j_t}$ equal to the number $c \in \mathfrak{B}_n$ is no more than D_c of Table II.1.*

It follows that not every register flow-table can serve as degenerate register table. The essential restriction is Condition (2) which is not always satisfied. But if in the given register table a row of marks can be built then the process of specification of this table to a degenerate regular sequential machine is more preferable since the resulting code length is reduced.

Example 4.1. Given an arbitrary register table with 6 registers

REGISTERS / INPUT	1	2	3	4	5	6
x	1	2	2	5	6	3
y	—	1	3	4	1	2

The given 6 registers can be built as 5-bit, since $D_5 = 6$ (see Table II.1). That is, the resulting 6-regular sequential machine is assigned by the code length $n = 5$. On the other hand we shall try to select the row of marks to convert the given register table to a degenerate one. Let us try to take $n = 4$. For $n = 4$, three 4-adic, one 2-adic, and two 1-adic registers can be built. The whole number of registers is also equal to 6.

Under Condition (2) of Theorem 4.1 only registers 1 and 2 can serve as 1-adic. Mark them with the marks $m_1 = 1$, $m_2 = 1$. Then the only register which can be built as 2-adic is register 3, i.e., $m_3 = 3$. Since $\delta(3, x) = 2$, then $m_2 \in \mathcal{B}_{m_3}$. Registers 4, 5, and 6 can serve as 4-adic since they have all the registers as entries in the flow table. Hence the degenerate register table has the following form

MARKS	1	1	2	4	4	4
REGISTERS / INPUTS	1	2	3	4	5	6
x	1	2	2	5	6	3
y	—	1	3	4	1	2

Therefore the degenerate 6-regular sequential machine can be assigned by the assignment length $n = 4$, while the nondegenerate modification of the machine needs $n = 5$.

So we can come to the following conclusions:

(1) The flow table of an arbitrary sequential machine, containing s states, is equivalent to a nondegenerate register table, which has s registers

(2) In order for a flow table of a sequential machine containing s states to be equivalent to a degenerate register table it is necessary and sufficient:

(a) For the existence of a row of marks, marking every state A by some mark m_A, which is a divisor of the number n

(b) That the number n is identified through the relation

$$s \leq \sum_{b \in \mathcal{B}_n} D_b ,$$

where each of the numbers D_b is found in Table II.1

(c) If the states A and B with the marks m_A and m_B are related by

$$\delta(A, x) = B ,$$

where $x \in X$, then the mark m_B is a divisor of the mark m_A

(d) That the number t of the states of a sequential machine, having marks equal to C is no more than D_C from Table II.1.

(3) Identification of a flow table with a degenerate register flow table is preferable since we economize in the length n of an assignment.

V. THE CONSTRUCTION OF REGULAR SEQUENTIAL MACHINE THROUGH THE REGISTER FLOW TABLE

Since a nondegenerate register table is a particular case of a degenerate one, an algorithm can be formulated only in the case of degenerate register tables. At the same time, a given algorithm provides a means for supplementation of any irregular sequential machine to a regular one, and can serve as regularization algorithm in connection with the equivalency relation between a flow table of sequential machine and a register flow table (degenerate or nondegenerate). Hence the regular machine construction algorithm will be further called a regularization algorithm.

Regularization Algorithm

Given a degenerate register table T_1, containing s elements and the row of marks W, find the least common multiple n of all the marks of the set W. Then n is the length of the assignment. Build the matrix M of the dimension $n \times s$, where the rows of the matrix are denoted by periods and the columns by registers.

The first row of the matrix is produced by the states of the register flow table. The next rows are supplemented by additional states which are introduced into each of the registers in accordance with its mark.

The states of an arbitrary m_j-adic register R_j are distributed through n periods in such a way, that each state of the register gets into n/m_j periods of regularity shifted with respect to each other on m_j binary digits.

Denote the transition function δ for the additional states involved. Let $A, B \in R_j$, and the state B is additional and A is involved in Table T_1. Then for any $x \in X$ we presume that $\delta(B, x)$ belongs to the same column (register) as $\delta(A, x)$. On the other hand, by construction A, $\delta(A, x) \in \Delta_1$. Let $B \in \Delta_i$, then $\delta(B, x) \in \Delta_i$. Hence with the aid of the matrix M the position of $\delta(B, x)$ which is sought is completely specified.

Example 5.1. Build the matrix M using the degenerate register table from Example 4.1.

	1	1	2	4	4	4
	R_1	R_2	R_3	R_4	R_5	R_6
Δ_1	1	2	3	4	5	6
Δ_2	1	2	7	8	11	14
Δ_3	1	2	3	9	12	15
Δ_4	1	2	7	10	13	16

Define the transition function for additional states which have been introduced

$$\delta(3, x) \in R_2, \quad \text{hence} \quad \delta(7, x) = 2 \ ,$$

$$\delta(3, y) \in R_3, \quad \text{hence} \quad \delta(7, y) = 7 \ .$$

$\delta(8, x)$ is located on the intersection of the row Δ_2 and the column R_5, since $\delta(4, x) \in R_5$. Hence $\delta(8, x) = 11$. $\delta(8, y)$ is located in the row Δ_2 and in the column R_4, i.e., $\delta(8, y) = 8$. $\delta(9, x)$ is located in the row Δ_3 and in the column R_5, since $\delta(4, x) \in R_5$ and so forth. The resulting flow table has the following form:

	1	2	3	4	5	6	7	8	9	10	11	12	13	14	15	16
x	1	2	2	5	6	3	2	11	12	13	14	15	16	7	3	7
y	—	1	3	4	1	2	7	8	9	10	1	1	1	2	2	2

Using the matrix M it is easy to assign the resulting regular sequential machine. Let

$$R_1' = \{1\} \ , \quad R_2' = \{0\} \ . \qquad \text{(1-adic, 1-digit registers)} \ .$$

Then

$$R_1 = R_1' R_1' R_1' R_1' = \{1111\} \ ,$$

$$R_2 = R_2' R_2' R_2' R_2' = \{0000\} \ ,$$

Let

$$R_3' = \{10\} \qquad \text{(2-adic, 2-digit register)} \ .$$

Then

$$R_3 = R_3' R_3' = \{1010\} \ ,$$

$$R_4 = \{1000\}, \quad R_5 = \{1100\}, \quad R_6 = \{1110\} \ ,$$

where iterational braces mean that all other states are produced by applying a shift operation to the state, concluded in the braces.

The element A_{ij}, found in i^{th} row and j^{th} column can be obtained by applying shift operation π_{i-1} to the element $A_{1j} \in R_j$. Hence

$$1 = 1111, \quad 2 = 0000, \quad 3 = 1010, \quad 4 = 1000, \quad 5 = 1100, \quad 6 = 1110 \ ,$$

$$7 = \pi_1\, 1010 = 0101 \ ,$$

$$8 = \pi_1\, 1000 = 0100 \ ,$$

$$9 = \pi_2\, 1000 = 0010 \ ,$$

$$10 = \pi_3\, 1000 = 0001 \ ,$$

$$11 = \pi_1\, 1100 = 0110 \ ,$$

$$12 = \pi_2\, 1100 = 0011 \ ,$$

$$13 = \pi_3\, 1100 = 1001 \ ,$$

$$14 = \pi_1\, 1110 = 0111 \ ,$$

$$15 = \pi_2\, 1110 = 1011 \ ,$$

$$16 = \pi_3\, 1110 = 1101 \ .$$

VI. ASYMPTOTIC ESTIMATIONS OF THE LENGTH OF THE ASSIGNMENT *n* FOR ANY SEQUENTIAL MACHINE SUBJECTED TO REGULARIZATION ALGORITHM (OR REGULARIZED SEQUENTIAL MACHINE)

The estimations will be produced for nondegenerate regularized sequential machines, since this is the more general case in its application which has a larger length n than degenerate machines. Given an irregular machine $A(\mathfrak{U},\mathfrak{X},\delta)$, containing S states, using Table II.1, find the least D_n, which satisfies

$$S \leq D_n \ .$$

In this connection we can be confronted with the following cases:

Case (1) $2^{n'} < S \leq D_n < 2^{n'+1}$

Case (2) $D_{n-1} < S \leq 2^{n'} < D_n$,

where n' is the largest integer which satisfies (1) and (2).

In Case (1) $\lceil \log_2 S \rceil = \lceil \log_2 D_n \rceil$. In Case (2) $\lceil \log_2 S \rceil = n'$, $\lceil \log_2 D_n \rceil = n' + 1$. Hence $\lceil \log_2 S \rceil = \lceil \log_2 D_n \rceil - 1$. Evidently if the given sequential machine were regular it could have been assigned by the $n_{\min}$ which is equal to:

(1) $n_{\min} = \lceil \log_2 D_n \rceil$ for Case (1)

(2) $n_{\min} = \lceil \log_2 D_n \rceil - 1$ for Case (2).

But since it is not regular, then the required number D_n of n-bit n-adic registers can be provided by the number n which relates to D_n in the following way

$$D_n \cdot n = 2^n - \sum_{b \in \mathcal{B}_n - n} bD_b \ ,$$

$$\lceil \log_2 D_n \rceil = \left\lceil \log_2 \left(2^n - \sum_{b \in \mathcal{B}_n - n} bD_b\right)\right\rceil - \lfloor \log_2 n \rfloor \ , \tag{6.1}$$

That is

$$n_{\min} = \left\lceil \log_2 \left(2^n - \sum_{b \in \mathcal{B}_n - n} bD_b\right)\right\rceil - \lfloor \log_2 n \rfloor \ , \tag{6.2}$$

for Case (1) and

$$n_{\min} = \left\lceil \log_2 \left(2^n - \sum_{b \in \mathcal{B}_n - n} bD_b\right)\right\rceil - \lfloor \log_2 n \rfloor - 1 \tag{6.2a}$$

for Case (2). Show that

$$\left\lceil \log_2 \left(2^n - \sum_{b \in \mathcal{B}_n - n} bD_b\right)\right\rceil = n \ . \tag{6.3}$$

For the purpose it is necessary to show that

$$\sum_{b \in \mathcal{B}_n - n} bD_b < 2^{n-1} \ .$$

Then $2^n - \sum_{b \in \mathcal{B}_n - n} bD_b > 2^{n-1}$, which proves Equation (6.3).

Let $\overline{\mathcal{B}}_n = (\alpha_1, \alpha_2, \alpha_3, \cdots, \alpha_k)$, i.e., the set of all the prime nontrivial factors of the number† n. Then it is easy to see that

$$\sum_{b \in \mathcal{B}_n - n} bD_b = \sum_{\alpha_i \in \overline{\mathcal{B}}_n} 2^{n/\alpha_k} - \sum_{\alpha_i = 1}^{k} \sum_{\alpha_j = 1}^{k} 2^{(n/\alpha_i, n/\alpha_j)} , \tag{6.4}$$

where $(n/\alpha_i, n/\alpha_j)$ is the greatest common divisor of the numbers n/α_i and n/α_j. Taking into consideration that the least nontrivial prime factor is the number 2, we find that

$$2^{n/\alpha_i} \leq 2^{n/2} .$$

That is

$$\sum_{b \in \mathcal{B}_n - n} bD_b \leq k \cdot 2^{n/2} ,$$

where k is the number of prime nontrivial factors of the number n. Estimate k for all of the single digit, two-digit and three-digit n, which covers all our practical necessities.

In order for $\sum_{b \in \mathcal{B}_n - n} bD_b$ to be less than 2^{n-1} it is necessary that k be less than $\frac{2^{n-1}}{2^{n/2}} = 2^{n-2/2}$. The least one-digit number which has $k = 1$ is $n = 2$. For $n = 2$, $k = 2^{2-2/2} = 1$. Hence for all of the other one-digit n, which have $k = 1$, $k < 2^{n-2/2}$. The least one-digit number, which has $k = 2$ is $n = 2 \cdot 3 = 6$. For $n = 6$, $k < 2^{6-2/2} = 2^2$. Hence for all of the other n having $k = 2$, $k < 2^{n-2/2}$. The least n for which $k = 3$ is equal $2 \cdot 3 \cdot 5 = 30$. But for it $2^{n-2/2} = 2^{14}$, i.e., $n \ll 2^{14}$. The least n for which $k = 4$ is equal to

$$2 \cdot 3 \cdot 5 \cdot 7 = 210 .$$

But for it $2^{n-2/2} = 2^{104}$, hence $k \ll 2^{104}$. Therefore in the limits of practical values of n apart from the point $n = 2$ in which $k = 2^{n-2/2} = 1$

$$k < 2^{n-2/2} .$$

That is

$$\sum_{b \in \mathcal{B}_n - n} bD_b < 2^{n-2/2} \cdot 2^{n/2} = 2^{n-1} ,$$

and

$$\left\lceil \log_2 \left(2^n - \sum_{b \in \mathcal{B}_n - n} bD_b \right) \right\rceil = \lceil \log_2 2^n \rceil = n .$$

That is

$$n_{\min} = n - \lfloor \log_2 n \rfloor$$

†The single prime trivial factor of any number m is 1.

for Case (1) and

$$n_{\min} = n - \lfloor \log_2 n \rfloor - 1 \ ,$$

for Case (2).

From this it follows that assignment length n for a regularized sequential machine increases by the quantity $\tau = \lfloor \log_2 n \rfloor$ for Case (1) and $\tau = \lfloor \log_2 n \rfloor + 1$ for Case (2), which for $n < 16$ is no more than 3 for Case (1), and 4 for Case (2).

VII. NECESSARY AND SUFFICIENT CONDITIONS FOR NORMAL REALIZATION EXISTENCE

Below the basic theorem of the given work will be formulated and proven, specifying necessary and sufficient conditions for normal realization existence. Given sequential machine $A(\mathfrak{U}, \mathfrak{X}, \delta)$, $\mathbf{F} = (F_1, F_2, F_3, \cdots, F_n)$ is the set of excitation functions, defining its logical realization.

THEOREM 7.1. *In order for a normal logical realization to exist it is necessary and sufficient that $A(\mathfrak{U}, \mathfrak{X}, \delta)$ be regular.*

Proof. Necessity. Show that for regular sequential machines a proper assignment can be found which defines normal realization $\mathbf{F} = (F_1, F_2, F_3, \cdots, F_n)$. If the sequential machine is regular then such an assignment exists that internal states can be distributed through the registers $R_1, R_2, R_3, \cdots, R_s$ and periods $\Delta_1, \Delta_2, \Delta_3, \cdots, \Delta_n$. Let Δ_i be defined as an arbitrary i^{th} period of regularity. Suppose that

$$\Delta_i = (A_i, B_i, C_i, \cdots, K_i) \ , \tag{7.1}$$

where: $A_i \in R_1, B_i \in R_2, C_i \in R_3, \cdots, K_i \in R_s$. Let A_i contain $\mathbf{a}$ unit positions occupying the digits $a_1, a_2, a_3, \cdots, a_{\mathbf{a}}$. The state B_i contains $\mathbf{b}$ unit positions occupying the digits $b_1, b_2, b_3, \cdots, b_{\mathbf{b}}$, the state K_i contains $\mathbf{k}$ unit positions occupying the digits $k_1, k_2, k_3, \cdots, k_{\mathbf{k}}$.

Assume that $[j, i]$ is the distance between positions j and i, defining how many left shifts of the 1st order one must pass to make a transition from the position i to position j. Then $\pi_{[\ell, a_1]}, \pi_{[\ell, a_2]}, \pi_{[\ell, a_3]}, \cdots, \pi_{[\ell, a_{\mathbf{a}}]}$ is a sequence of shifts transferring the ones from the positions $a_1, a_2, a_3, \cdots, a_{\mathbf{a}}$ to the position ℓ. Hence each of the states $\pi_{[\ell, a_1]}A_i, \pi_{[\ell, a_2]}A_i, \pi_{[\ell, a_3]}A_i, \cdots, \pi_{[\ell, a_{\mathbf{a}}]}A_i$ contains a one in the ℓth position. On the other hand, $A_i, \pi_{[\ell, a_1]}A_i, \pi_{[\ell, a_2]}A_i, \cdots, \pi_{[\ell, a_{\mathbf{a}}]}A_i$ are the states of register R_1.

Since for each digit only one left shift exists which transfers this digit to the position ℓ, then the following and only the following states of the register R_1 contain an ℓth unit position

$$\pi_{[\ell, a_1]}A_i, \pi_{[\ell, a_2]}A_i, \pi_{[\ell, a_3]}A_i, \cdots, \pi_{[\ell, a_{\mathbf{a}}]}A_i \ . \tag{7.2}$$

Similarly, find the sequence of the states of the register R_2, containing an ℓth unit digit

$$\pi_{[\ell, b_1]}B_i, \pi_{[\ell, b_2]}B_i, \pi_{[\ell, b_3]}B_i, \cdots, \pi_{[\ell, b_{\mathbf{b}}]}B_i \ , \tag{7.3}$$

and so on, and the sequence of the states of the register R_s, containing an ℓth unit digit

$$\pi_{[\ell,k_1]}K_i, \pi_{[\ell,k_2]}K_i, \pi_{[\ell,k_3]}K_i, \cdots, \pi_{[\ell,k_{\mathbf{k}}]}K_i \ .$$

Hence in the sequential machine $A(\mathfrak{U},\mathfrak{X},\delta)$ the following and only the following states contain an ℓth unit's digit

$$\begin{bmatrix} \pi_{[\ell,a_1]}A_i, \pi_{[\ell,a_2]}A_i, \cdots, \pi_{[\ell,a_{\mathbf{a}}]}A_i \\ \pi_{[\ell,b_1]}B_i, \pi_{[\ell,b_2]}B_i, \cdots, \pi_{[\ell,b_{\mathbf{b}}]}A_i \\ \cdot \quad \cdot \quad \cdot \quad \cdot \\ \cdot \quad \cdot \quad \cdot \quad \cdot \\ \cdot \quad \cdot \quad \cdot \quad \cdot \\ \pi_{[\ell,k_1]}K_i, \pi_{[\ell,k_2]}K_i, \cdots, \pi_{[\ell,k_{\mathbf{k}}]}K_i \end{bmatrix} . \quad (7.4)$$

In all other states of the sequential machine $A(\mathfrak{U},\mathfrak{X},\delta)$ $\ell = 0$. The states from the Eq. (7.4) will be called unity over ℓ. Let B be an arbitrary unit state over ℓ. Find all the states C such that

$$\delta(C, x) = B,$$

where $x \in X$. Let $T_B(\ell) = (xC\colon \delta(C, x) = B, x \in X)$, where B is unit state over ℓ. xC is the complete state of a sequential machine, obtained by left attaching of the input state x to the internal state C. Clearly for any element of the set $T_B(\ell)$ the excitation function F_ℓ of the ℓth memory element assumes the value of one. $T_B(\ell)$ is called unit set over ℓ. For all the unit states over ℓ build the unit sets over ℓ.

We obtain the following matrix of unit sets over ℓ; listing all the unit sets over ℓ of the sequential machine $A(\mathfrak{U},\mathfrak{X},\delta)$.

$$\begin{bmatrix} T_{a_1}(\ell), T_{a_2}(\ell), \cdots, T_{a_{\mathbf{a}}}(\ell) \\ T_{b_1}(\ell), T_{b_2}(\ell), \cdots, T_{b_{\mathbf{b}}}(\ell) \\ \cdot \quad \cdot \quad \cdot \quad \cdot \\ \cdot \quad \cdot \quad \cdot \quad \cdot \\ \cdot \quad \cdot \quad \cdot \quad \cdot \\ T_{k_1}(\ell), T_{k_2}(\ell), \cdots, T_{k_{\mathbf{k}}}(\ell) \end{bmatrix} . \quad (7.5)$$

(Here for simplification of the notation, the lower index of each unit set over ℓ is the characteristic lower index of the corresponding unit state over ℓ. Hence the excitation function F_ℓ assumes the value of 1 only for all of the complete states of the unit sets over ℓ producing the matrix of Equation (7.5)). For all of the complete states which are not included in the unit sets over ℓ $F_\ell = 0$. Fulfill similar constructions for the excitation function F_m of the mth memory element. First of all build the matrix of unit states over m

$$\begin{bmatrix} \pi_{[m,a_1]}A_i, \pi_{[m,a_2]}A_i, \cdots, \pi_{[m,a_{\mathbf{a}}]}A_i \\ \pi_{[m,b_1]}B_i, \pi_{[m,b_2]}B_i, \cdots, \pi_{[m,b_{\mathbf{b}}]}B_i \\ \cdot \quad \cdot \quad \cdot \quad \cdot \\ \cdot \quad \cdot \quad \cdot \quad \cdot \\ \cdot \quad \cdot \quad \cdot \quad \cdot \\ \pi_{[m,k_1]}K_i, \pi_{[m,k_2]}K_i, \cdots, \pi_{[m,k_{\mathbf{k}}]}K_i \end{bmatrix} \quad (7.6)$$

and the matrix of unit sets over m

$$\begin{bmatrix} T_{a_1}(m), T_{a_2}(m), \cdots, T_{a_a}(m) \\ T_{b_1}(m), T_{b_2}(m), \cdots, T_{b_b}(m) \\ \cdot \quad \cdot \quad \cdot \quad \cdot \\ \cdot \quad \cdot \quad \cdot \quad \cdot \\ \cdot \quad \cdot \quad \cdot \quad \cdot \\ T_{k_1}(m), T_{k_2}(m), \cdots, T_{k_k}(m) \end{bmatrix} \quad . \tag{7.7}$$

It follows from the constructions of Eqs. (7.5) and (7.7) that a shift $\pi_{[m,\ell]}$ exists which transfers an arbitrary element $T_i(m)$ of matrix Eq. (7.7) to the corresponding element of matrix Equation (7.5). Here a shift over a set means a shift over all of the elements of a set, and the shift over a complete state $x \cdot A$ is understood as a shift only over its internal part A, that is, $\pi x \cdot A = x \cdot \pi A$. From this it follows that

$$F_\ell = \pi_{[m,\ell]} \cdot F_m \quad ,$$

where F_ℓ, $F_m \in \mathbf{F}$ which proves the necessity.

Sufficiency. The set of functions $\mathbf{F} = (F_1, F_2, F_3, \cdots, F_n)$ is available, containing n similar excitation functions. This means that for any $F_i, F_j, F_s \in \mathbf{F}$ such permutations π_{m_1} and π_{m_2} exist that

$$\begin{aligned} F_j &= \pi_{m_1} F_i \quad , \\ F_s &= \pi_{m_2} F_i \quad . \end{aligned} \tag{7.8}$$

Each of the functions F_i is given by some set of its complete states of the length $p + n$, where p is assigned for inputs, and n for internal states. In this connection if

$$\underbrace{x}_{p}\ \underbrace{A}_{n} \quad ,$$

a complete state of a function F_i, then $\pi_m xA = x\pi_m A$ and $x\pi_m A \in \pi_m F_i$, where π_m is the shift of the mth order. That is, the shift is undertaken only under the internal part of state, whereas the input state remains invariant to the shift operation.

But if A is an internal state represented by an n-digit binary number then no more n shifts exist which transfer the complete state $x \cdot A$ from the function F_i to the complete state $x \cdot \pi A \in \pi F_i$, to the complete state $x \cdot \pi_2 A \in \pi_2 F_i, \cdots$, to the complete state

$$x\pi_{n-1} A \in \pi_{n-1} F_i \quad .$$

Evidently the functions $F_i, \pi_1 F_i, \pi_2 F_i, \cdots, \pi_{n-1} F_i$ are not equal to each other in pairs. Hence the set of functions $F_i, \pi_1 F_i, \pi_2 F_i, \cdots, \pi_{n-1} F_i$ coincides with the set $\mathbf{F} = (F_1, F_2, F_3, \cdots, F_n)$. It follows from the above reasoning that the set $\mathbf{F} = (F_1, F_2, F_3, \cdots, F_n)$ possesses the property of completeness consisting of the following: if $x \cdot A$ is a complete state of a function $F_i \in \mathbf{F}$, then for any complete state $x \cdot \pi_j A$ it is possible to find such a function $F_m = \pi_j F_i$, that

$$x \cdot \pi_j A \in F_m \quad ,$$

where $j = 0, 1, 2, \cdots, n-1$. Hence internal states

$$R_1 = (A, \pi_1 A, \pi_2 A, \cdots, \pi_{n-1} A) \quad , \tag{7.9}$$

producing the set R_1, are the internal states of given sequential machine. By a construction it follows that R_1 is n-digit cyclic binary register

$$R = \{A\} \quad . \tag{7.10}$$

Find

$$\delta(A, y) = B \quad , \tag{7.11}$$

where $y \in X$, $A \in R_1$, $B \notin R_1$. Suppose that the internal state B has ones in the numbers $(j_1, j_2, j_3, \cdots, j_k)$. This means that complete state $y \cdot A \in F_{j_1}, F_{j_2}, F_{j_3}, \cdots, F_{j_k}$, where $F_{j_1}, F_{j_2}, F_{j_3}, \cdots, F_{j_k} \in \mathbf{F}$. We have shown above that for any $y \in X$ $y \pi_i A \in \pi_i F_{j_1}, \pi_i F_{j_2}, \pi_i F_{j_3}, \cdots, \pi_i F_{j_k}$ where $i = 0, 1, 2, \cdots, n-1$. Hence it is possible to find such a state C, which contains ones in the positions

$$\pi_i j_1, \pi_i j_2, \pi_i j_3, \cdots, \pi_i j_k \quad .$$

Whence it follows that $C = \pi_i B$ and that if $\delta(A, y) = B$, then for any shift π_i $(i = 0, 1, 2, \cdots, n-1)$ $\delta(\pi_i A, y) = \pi_i B$. Therefore, the sequential machine contains the set of internal states

$$R_2 = (B, \pi_1 B, \pi_2 B, \cdots, \pi_{n-1} B) \quad ,$$

producing an n-digit binary register R_2 and for any $x \in X$, such that $\delta(A, x) = B$, where $x \in X$, $A \in R_1$, it follows that

$$\delta(R_1, x) = R_2 \quad \text{and} \quad \delta^{-1}(R_2, x) = R_1 \quad . \tag{7.12}$$

Equation (7.12) means that if the transition function δ is specified for at least one element of the set R_1 in the domain of definition of the set R_2 then it is specified for all elements of the set R_1 in the domain of the set R_2. Continuing the similar process we can come to the following conclusion: The set of the states $\mathfrak{U}$ of sequential machine $A(\mathfrak{U}, \mathfrak{X}, \delta)$, which has the normal realization, in a view of its finiteness is decomposed to s pairwise, disjoint subsets

$$R_1, R_2, R_3, \cdots, R_s \qquad \text{(follows from Equation (7.9))} \quad .$$

The sets $R_1, R_2, R_3, \cdots, R_s$ are equivalent to n-digit shift registers. The data of transition function δ at least for one element of the set R_i is equivalent to the data of δ for all elements of the set R_i. That is, if $A \in R_i$ and $\delta(A, x) = B$, where $B \in R_j$, then

$$\delta(R_i, x) = R_j \quad ,$$

and

$$\delta^{-1}(R_j, x) = R_i \quad .$$

Select one representative A_i from each of the registers R_i $(i = 1, 2, 3, \cdots, s)$, satisfying the following condition: For any $A_i \in R_i$ at least one $A_j \in R_j$ and one $x \in X$ exist such that either

$$\delta(A_i, x) = A_j \quad ,$$

or

$$\delta(A_j, x) = A_i \quad .$$

Considering Eq. (7.12) and the concept of strong connectivity of the initial sequential machine, this restriction is not essential. We obtain

$$\Delta_1 = (A_1, A_2, A_3, \cdots, A_s) \ .$$

Now we want to show that

$$\pi_j \Delta_i = (\pi_j A_1, \pi_j A_2, \pi_j A_3, \cdots, \pi_j A_s) \quad (j = 0, 1, 2, \cdots, n-1) \ ,$$

is a subset of the internal states of the given sequential machine. Indeed, it has been shown above that for any

$$A_i \in R_i, \Delta_1 \qquad (i = 1, 2, 3, \cdots, s) \ ,$$

a state $\pi_j A_i$ exists, which belongs to R_i also $(j = 0, 1, 2, \cdots, n-1)$. Hence it is possible to construct

$$\pi_j \Delta_1 = (\pi_j A_1, \pi_j A_2, \pi_j A_3, \cdots, \pi_j A_s) \ ,$$

and

$$\Delta_1, \Delta_2 = \pi_1 \Delta_1, \Delta_3 = \pi_2 \Delta_1, \cdots, \Delta_n = \pi_{n-1} \Delta_1 \ ,$$

are different subsets, belonging to $\mathfrak{U}$, which are pairwise disjoint. According to the above construction these subsets satisfy the following conditions:

(1) $\Delta_i = (A_1^{(i)}, A_2^{(i)}, A_3^{(i)}, \cdots, A_s^{(i)})$, where $A_1^{(i)} = \pi_{i-1} A_1$, $A_2^{(i)} = \pi_{i-1} A_2$, $A_3^{(i)} = \pi_{i-1} A_3, \cdots, A_s^{(i)} = \pi_{i-1} A_s$; $A_1, A_2, A_3, \cdots, A_s \in \Delta_1$, and $A_1^{(i)} \in R_1, A_2^{(i)} \in R_2, A_3^{(i)} \in R_3, \cdots, A_s^{(i)} \in R_s$

(2) $\pi \Delta_i = \Delta_{i+1} \bmod n$.

Hence a sequential machine $A(\mathfrak{U}, \mathfrak{X}, \delta)$ which has a normal realization is equivalent to a certain s-regular sequential machine built over the shift registers $R_1, R_2, R_3, \cdots, R_s$. Q.E.D.

VIII. ASSIGNMENT ALGORITHMS

The assignment algorithms consist of three stages.

(1) Verification of whether the given sequential machine is regular or not
  (a) If regular go to Stage (3)
  (b) If irregular go to Stage (2)
(2) Regularization
(3) Assignment.

Consider each of the stages mentioned above.

Stage 1

This consists of two algorithms:

(a) Algorithm 1.1—specification of the assignment length
(b) Algorithm 1.2—construction of the state matrix.

ALGORITHM 1.1. Given sequential machine $A(\mathfrak{A}, \mathfrak{X}, \delta)$:

(1) Pick out all of the closed paths G_i of the length a_i. If any pair of the paths G_i, G_j has a number of common vertices:

(a) Less than the length of at least one of the paths, then the sequential machine is irregular

(b) Equal to the length of at least one of the paths, then the path with a greater number of vertexes is picked out, and a path with a lesser number of vertexes is absorbed

The resulting set is $N = (a_1, a_2, a_3, \cdots, a_p)$ which contains all isolated, unabsorbable paths

(2) Build the set of numbers Z, each element η of which possesses the following properties: N is decomposed in no more than 2 subsets N' and N'' such that:

(a) For each $a_i \in N'$ and $a_i > 1$

$$(\eta, a_i) \neq 1 \quad ,$$

where (η, a_i) = the greatest common divisor of the numbers η and a_i

(b) $\eta \in \mathfrak{B}_{\nu(a_\ell)}$, where $a_\ell \in N''$ and $\nu(a_\ell)$ = the number of paths with the length a_ℓ. $\mathfrak{B}_{\nu(a_\ell)}$ = the set of all factors of the number $\nu(a_\ell)$.

(3) For each $c = (\eta, a_i)$, where $a_i \in N'$ construct

$$W_c = (a_i: (\eta, a_i) = c) \quad .$$

Find $D'_c = \sum_{a_i \in W_c} a_i/c$ and compare this value with that of D_c from Table II.1. If $D'_c > D_c$ then delete the corresponding element η from the set. Pick out other element $\eta' \in Z$ and 2 – a. If $D'_c \leq D_c$, then go to (4).

(4) Determine whether the divisor $\eta = (\eta, a_i)$, where $a_i \in N'$ exists:

(a) If it does then find $D_\eta - D'_\eta = D''_\eta$ and go to (5)

(b) If it does not, then suppose $D_\eta = D''_\eta$ where D'_η is looked for in the (3) and D_η in Table II.1

(5) Find $D'''_\eta = \dfrac{\nu(a_\ell)}{\eta} \cdot a_\ell$, where $a_\ell \in N''$

(6) Find $D''_\eta - D'''_\eta = \gamma$. If $\gamma \geq 0$, then leave the corresponding number η in the set Z, otherwise delete

(7) Find $\eta_{\min} = \min Z$

(8) Find $\lceil \log_2 s \rceil$ where s is the number of states. What is the area of location of s:

(a) $2^{n'} < s \leq D_{n''}$

(b) $D_{n''-1} < s \leq 2^{n'} < D_{n''}$

where subsequent meanings of D_n are sought on Table II.1. If s satisfies (a) mark it with one star. If it satisfies (b) mark it with two stars.

(9) Find $\eta_{min} - \log_2 s^* = \varphi^*$ or $\eta_{min} - \log_2 s^{**} = \varphi^{**}$. If $\varphi^* \leq \log_2 \log_2 s^*$ choose the assignment length n be equal to η_{min}, otherwise go to (2). If $\varphi^{**} \leq \log_2 \log_2 s^* + 1$, choose the assignment length n be equal to η_{min}, otherwise go to (2).

Example 8.1. $N = (4, 6, 2, 3, 1_{14})$, where the lower index 14 indicates the number of entries of element 1 in the set N. In this connection $N' = (4, 6, 2, 3, 1, 1)$, $N'' - (1_{12})$, and $Z = (6, 12)$. Find the *GCD* (greatest common divisor) of the number $\eta = 6$ with each of the numbers of the set N'

$$(6,4) = 2; \quad (6,6) = 6, \quad (6,2) = 2, \quad (6,3) = 3, \quad (6,1) = 1 \ ,$$

$$W_2 = (4,2), \quad W_6 = (6), \quad W_3 = (3), \quad W_1 = (1,1) \ ,$$

$$D_2' = \tfrac{4}{2} + \tfrac{2}{2} = 3, \quad D_6' = 1, \quad D_3' = 1, \quad D_1' = \tfrac{1}{1} + \tfrac{1}{1} = 2 \ .$$

Using Table II.1, we can find that

$$D_2 = 1, \quad D_6 = 9, \quad D_3 = 2, \quad D_1 = 2 \ .$$

That is $\eta = 6$ is deleted from the set. Consider $\eta = 12$ for $12 \in Z$.

$$N' = (4, 6, 2, 3, 1, 1), \quad N'' = (1_{12}) \ .$$

The *GCD* of 12 with each of the numbers from N' are

$$(12,4) = 4, \quad (12,6) = 6, \quad (12,2) = 2, \quad (12,3) = 3, \quad (12,1) = 1 \ ,$$

$$D_4' = 1, \quad D_6' = 1, \quad D_2' = 1, \quad D_3' = 1, \quad D_1' = 1 \ ,$$

$$D_4 = 3, \quad D_6 = 9, \quad D_2 = 1, \quad D_3 = 2, \quad D_1 = 2 \ .$$

Find $D_{12} = 335$ and $D_{12}''' = \dfrac{\nu(\ell)}{12} \cdot 1 = 1$

$$D_{12} - D_{12}''' = 334 \ .$$

Hence $\eta = 12$ can be left in the set Z, $\eta_{min} = 12$. Let the number of states be 100. Find that

$$D_{10} < 100 < 2^7 < D_{11} \ ,$$

where $D_{10} = 99$, $D_{11} = 186$. Hence 100 satisfies condition (8b) and subjects itself to be marked with two stars. Find $\log_2 100^{**} = 7^{**}$. Find $\varphi^{**} = 12 - 7^{**} = 5^{**}$. Find $\log_2 5^{**} = 3$. Hence $\varphi^{**} > 3 + 1$ and it is profitable to consider this machine irregular and make it to be regularized. Otherwise we lose in the length of assignment.

ALGORITHM 1.2. Construction of the state matrix. Given the set of unabsorbable paths $N = (a_1, a_2, a_3, \cdots, a_p)$, length of assignment n. Define the *GCD* between n and each of the numbers a_i

$$t_1 = (n, a_1), \ t_2 = (n, a_2), \ t_3 = (n, a_3), \ \cdots, \ t_p = (n, a_p) \ .$$

Then periods of regularity of each of the paths are

$$s_1' = \frac{a_1}{t_1}, \ s_2' = \frac{a_2}{t_2}, \ s_3' = \frac{a_3}{t_3}, \ \cdots, \ s_p' = \frac{a_p}{t_p} \ .$$

In each of the paths a_i specify the periods s_i'' of alternation of input signals. We presume that the real period of regularity in any closed path be equal: $s_i = \max(s_i', s_i'')$. If it is not possible to pick any period of input alternation, then sequential machine is irregular.

Verification of the input alternations in all closed paths of the set N gives us the right to call them regular strings (connected or disconnected). This means that each string of the length a_i ($i = 1, 2, 3, \cdots, p$) is realized through $s_i = \dfrac{a_i}{t_i}$ t_i-adic n-bit registers. Distribute the states of each string through s_i t_i-adic registers. For this purpose each string is supposed to be decomposed into t_i equal parts with s_i elements in each. In any period Δ_j, s_i elements of this part are put down and two such parts from the strings a_m and a_t are brought to tho same period Δ_j, if at least for one state A of the string a_m such state B of the string a_m such state B of the string a_m exists that

$$\delta(A, x) = B \quad ,$$

where $x \in X$. Let the string a_i be realized over registers from $\mathbf{R}_{a_i} = (R_1, R_2, R_3, \cdots, R_{s_i})$. In each register $R_j \in \mathbf{R}_{a_i}$ those and only those states from the string are brought to which have the distance on the string equal to s_i.

To similar procedure all strings from the set N are subjected. The result of this technique appears in distribution of internal states through s_1 of t_1-adic registers, s_2 of t_2-adic registers, $\cdots$, s_p of t_p-adic registers and through n periods. After this distribution it is easy to build the state matrix of the dimension $n \times s$ where $s = s_1 + s_2 + s_3 + \cdots + s_p$, the columns of each are marked by registers and the rows by periods.

Any state $A \in R_i$, where R_i is t_i-adic register, appears in n/t_i periods with the distance from each other in t_i digits.

Next is the process of matrix expansion, consisting of its specification with new states which have not yet been distributed. Let R_j be a t_j-adic register and let $B \in R_j$ be an arbitrary state of this register which satisfies the condition: At least one $x \in X$ exists that $\delta(B, x) = C$, or $\delta(C, x) = B$, where C is the state which was not distributed over registers and periods. Then if $B \in \Delta_i$, let $C \in \Delta_i$. Pick a new register R_{s+1} for the state C and make it be an element of the column $s + 1$ and of the row Δ_i.

Find the state

$$D \in R_j \cap \pi \Delta_{i+1} \quad .$$

Find $\delta(D, x) = E$, if $\delta(B, x) = C$, or $\delta(E, x) = D$, if $\delta(C, x) = B$. The state E is the second state of the register R_{s+1}. On the other hand, $E, D \in \pi\Delta_i$. By this the position of the state E in the state matrix is completely specified and so the expansion results in the construction of a new register R_{s+1}, containing the number of states t_{s+1}, which is either a multiple or a divisor of the number t_j of the register R_j and relating to the register R_j in of the following expressions

$$R_{s+1} = \delta(R_j, x), \quad \text{if } C = \delta(B, x) \quad , \tag{8.1}$$

or

$$R_j = \delta(R_{s=1}, x), \quad \text{if } \delta(C, x) = B \quad . \tag{8.2}$$

In Eq. (8.1) $t_{s+1} \in \mathfrak{B}_{t_j}$. In Eq. (8.2) $t_j \in \mathfrak{B}_{t_{s+1}}$. Verify whether all states of the register R_{s+1} are new or it contains at least one old state already distributed in the state matrix.

If all states are new then continue with the expansion, otherwise, go to Stage (2).

Expansion expires after distribution of all the states over periods and registers.

Example 8.2. Given sequential machine.

STATES / INPUTS	1	2	3	4	5	6	7	8	9	10	11	12	13	14	15	16	17
x	2	—	4	—	6	—	7	8	1	3	5	1	3	5	2	17	4
y	3	3	5	5	1	1	8	7	10	11	12	13	14	9	16	7	18

STATES / INPUTS	18	19	20	21	22	23	24	25	26
x	19	6	21	2	23	4	25	6	15
y	8	20	7	22	8	24	7	26	8

By simple consideration of the state diagram we obtain the following unabsorbable closed paths

$$G_1 = (1x, 2y, 3x, 4y, 5x, 6y), \quad a_1 = 6 \quad ,$$

$$G_2 = (7y, 8y), \quad a_2 = 2 \quad ,$$

$$G_3 = (9y, 10y, 11y, 12y, 13y, 14y), \quad a_3 = 6 \quad ,$$

$$G_4 = (15y, 16x, 17y, 18x, 19y, 20x, 21y, 22x, 23y, 24x, 25y, 26x), \quad a_4 = 12 \quad .$$

Thereby $N = (6, 2, 6, 12)$. Build the set Z, $Z = (4, 6, 8, 12)$, since for each element $b \in Z$ the GCD of this number with any $a_j \in N$ is not trivial. Verify $\eta = 4$. For $\eta = 4$, N is decomposed into the following N' and N''

$$N' = N, \quad N'' = \phi \ .$$

$$(4,6) = 2, \quad (4,2) = 2, \quad (4,6) = 2, \quad (4,12) = 4 \ .$$

$$W_2 = (6,2,6), \quad W_4 = (12) \quad ,$$

$$D_2' = \tfrac{6}{2} + \tfrac{2}{2} + \tfrac{6}{2} = 3 + 1 + 3 = 7, \quad D_4' = \tfrac{12}{4} = 3 \ .$$

Using Table II.1, we find that

$$D_2 = 1, \qquad D_4 = 3 \ .$$

Therefore delete 4 from the set Z, choose $\eta = 6$.

$$N' = N, \quad N'' = \phi \quad ,$$

$$(6,6) = 6, \quad (6,2) = 2, \quad (6,6) = 6, \quad (6,12) = 6 \quad ,$$

$$W_2 = (2), \quad D_2' = 2/2 = 1, \quad D_2 = 1 \quad ,$$

$$W_6 = (6, 6, 12), \quad D_6' = 6/6 + 6/6 + 12/6 = 4, \quad D_6 = 9 \ .$$

Since $6 = \min Z/(4)$, then $\eta_{\min} = 6$. We find that $2^4 < 26 < D_s = 30$, 26 is marked with one star and we find that $6 - (\log_2 26^*) = 1^*$, since $1^* < \lceil \log_2 \log_2 26 \rceil = 3$, then the length of the assignment is supposed to be $n = \eta_{\min} = 6$.

Example 8.3. Apply to a given sequential machine Algorithm 1.2. Given $N = (6, 2, 6, 12)$, $n = 6$. Find the *GCD* for n and each $a_j \in N$

$$t_1 = (6,6) = 6, \quad t_2 = (6,2) = 2, \quad t_3 = (6,6) = 6, \quad t_4 = (6,12) = 6 \ .$$

$$s_1' = 6/6 = 1, \quad s_2' = 2/2 = 1, \quad s_3' = 6/6 = 1, \quad s_4' = 12/6 = 2 \ .$$

Find the periods of input alternations in each of the closed paths

$$s_1'' = 2, \quad s_2'' = 1, \quad s_3'' = 1, \quad s_4'' = 2 \ .$$

The periods of regularity of each string are

$$s_1 = \max(s_1', s_1'') = 2, \quad s_2 = \max(1,1) = 1, \quad s_3 = 1, \quad s_4 = 2 \ .$$

Bring to the point the number t_i of each register R_i

$$t_i = 6/2 = 3, \quad t_2 = 2, \quad t_3 = 6, \quad t_4 = 6 \ .$$

Distribute the states of each string over registers and periods. Decompose the string G_1 into $t_1 = 3$ equal parts with $s_1 = 2$ elements in each

$$1x\,2y \mid 3x\,4y \mid 5x\,6y \mid \ .$$

Then 3-adic registers R_1 and R_2 are specified as follows

$$R_1 = (1,3,5), \quad R_2 = (2,4,6) \ .$$

At the same time

$$\Delta_1 = (1,2), \quad \Delta_2 = (3,4), \quad \Delta_3 = (5,6), \quad \Delta_4 = (1,2), \quad \Delta_5 = (3,4),$$
$$\Delta_6 = (5,6) \ .$$

The same procedure is applied to all of the other strings

$$G_2 = 7y \mid 8y \mid \ .$$

Since $s_2 = 1$, then the string is built over one 2-adic register $R_3 = (7,8)$. The string G_3 is decomposed into $t_3 = 6$ equal parts and realized over one register R_4

$$9y \mid 10y \mid 11y \mid 12y \mid 13y \mid 14y \ .$$

$R_4 = (9, 10, 11, 12, 13, 14)$. Since $\delta(9, x) = 1$, then let $9 \in \Delta_1$, $10 \in \Delta_2$, $11 \in \Delta_3$, $12 \in \Delta_4$, $13 \in \Delta_5$, $14 \in \Delta_6$.

The expanded periods are

$$\Delta_1 = (1,2,9), \quad \Delta_2 = (3,4,10), \quad \Delta_3 = (5,6,11), \quad \Delta_4 = (1,2,12),$$
$$\Delta_5 = (3,4,13), \quad \Delta_6 = (5,6,14) \ .$$

The string G_4 is decomposed into $t_4 = 6$ equal parts and since $s_4 = 2$ it is realized over two 6-adic registers R_5 and R_6.

$$G_4 = |\,15y, 16x\,|\,17y, 18x\,|\,19y, 20x\,|\,21y, 22x\,|\,23y, 24x\,|\,25y, 26x\,| \ ,$$

$$R_5 = (15, 17, 19, 21, 23, 25) \ ,$$

$$R_6 = (16, 18, 20, 22, 24, 26) \ .$$

Since $\delta(15, x) = 2$ and $\delta(15, y) = 16$, then we presume that

$$15, 16 \in \Delta_1; \ \ 17, 18 \in \Delta_2; \ \ 19, 20 \in \Delta_3; \ \ 21, 22 \in \Delta_4; \ \ 23, 24 \in \Delta_5; \ \ 25, 26 \in \Delta_6 \ .$$

The expanded periods have the form

$$\Delta_1 = (1, 2, 9, 15, 16), \quad \Delta_2 = (3, 4, 10, 17, 18), \quad \Delta_3 = (5, 6, 11, 19, 20),$$
$$\Delta_4 = (1, 2, 12, 21, 22), \quad \Delta_5 = (3, 4, 13, 23, 24), \quad \Delta_6 = (5, 6, 14, 25, 26) \ .$$

We can find that $\delta(16, y) = 7$, $\delta(18, y) = 8$, $\delta(20, y) = 7$, $\delta(22, y) = 8$, $\delta(24, y) = 7$, $\delta(26, y) = 8$; hence $7 \in \Delta_1, \Delta_3, \Delta_5$ and $8 \in \Delta_2, \Delta_4, \Delta_6$. The expanded matrix of states has the following form

	R_1	R_2	R_3	R_4	R_5	R_6
Δ_1	1	2	7	9	15	16
Δ_2	3	4	8	10	17	18
Δ_3	5	6	7	11	19	20
Δ_4	1	2	8	12	21	22
Δ_5	3	4	7	13	23	24
Δ_6	5	6	8	14	25	26

The given matrix embraces all states of the sequential machine. Hence, it is regular.

Complement to Algorithm 1.2. It can happen that the set N contains only trivial strings (of the length 1) which do not provide any information about state distribution over registers and periods. In this case the state diagram of the given sequential machine has the form of a tree with one or several root points, producing the strings of the length 1.

In this connection if the root points $A_1, A_2, A_3, \cdots, A_n$ belong to the k-adic register R, where $k \in \mathcal{B}_n$, then the sequential machine can be easily decomposed into k-isomorphic subtrees with the root points $A_1, A_2, A_3, \cdots, A_n$ producing 1-cycles. If such an isomorphism does not exist then the root points belong to the register with the lesser number of states and again for all subtrees with root points, belonging to one register, the isomorphic relation is valid. Otherwise the sequential machine is irregular and subject to regularization.

Example 8.4. Examine over regularity the sequential machine from Example 5.1. For this sequential machine the set N contains only trivial strings. On the other hand, the state diagram has the form of a tree with root point $1 \in R_1$. All other states producing 1-cycles (for example, 2, 7, 8, 9, 10) have the transitions to other states and only 1 is closed on itself. But $2 \notin R_1$, because the subgraph with the root point 2 is not isomorphic to the subgraph with the root point 1. Hence, $2 \in R_2$ and R_1, R_2 are 1-adic registers. Then the expansion technique begins. $\delta(7, x) = 2$, $\delta(3, x) = 2$, $\delta(7, y) = 7$, $\delta(3, y) = 3$. Hence, $7, 3 \in R_3$ and R_3 is a 2-adic register. Indeed, $\delta(R_3, x) = R_2$, $\delta(R_3, y) = R_3$. The states 6, 15, 14, $16 \in R_4$, since

$$\delta(R_4, x) = R_3, \quad \delta(R_4, y) = R_2, \; \delta^{-1}(R_3, x) = R_4, \quad \delta^{-1}(R_2, y) = R_4 \; .$$

The states $4, 9, 8, 10 \in R_6$, since

$$\delta(R_6, x) = R_5, \quad \delta^{-1}(R_5, x) = R_6, \quad \delta(R_6, y) = R_6, \quad \delta^{-1}(R_6, y) = R_6 \; .$$

The matrix of states is described in Example 5.1. Then it follows that given sequential machine is regular.

Stage 2. Regularization

This was established in Section V.

Stage 3. Assignment

Given a state matrix of dimension $n \times s$, where n is the number of rows and s is the number of columns. The columns are marked by registers $R_1, R_2, R_3, \cdots, R_s$, and rows by periods $\Delta_1, \Delta_2, \Delta_3, \cdots, \Delta_n$. First of all, assign registers $R_1, R_2, R_3, \cdots, R_s$. This results in s registers appearing, each of which is represented in the form $\{A_i\}$, where A_i is an arbitrary state of the register R_i $(i = 1, 2, 3, \cdots, s)$. Iterative braces mean that all other states are obtained by successive shifts of the state A_i. The first row of the matrix is assigned by the states, shown in iterative braces. An arbitrary matrix element, belonging to the jth row and i^{th} column is assigned by the code $\pi_{j-1} A_i$.

Example 8.5. Use the state matrix from Example 8.3. Assign its states. First of all assign the registers.

Since

R_1 is a 3-adic register, then $R_1 = \{100100\}$,
R_2 is also 3-adic register, hence $R_2 = \{110110\}$,
R_3 is 2-adic register, then $R_3 = \{101010\}$,
R_4 is 6-adic register and $R_4 = \{100000\}$,
R_5 is 6-adic register and $R_5 = \{110000\}$,
R_6 is 6-adic register: $R_6 = \{111000\}$.

Assign the states of the first row by the states of registers indicated in iterative braces.

$$1 = 100100, \; 2 = 110110, \; 7 = 101010, \; 9 = 100000, \; 15 = 110000, \; 16 = 111000 \; .$$

The states of the next rows are obtained by applying shift operation to the states of the first row

3 = 010010, 4 = 011011, 8 = 010101, 10 = 100000, 17 = 011000, 18 = 011100,
5 = 001001, 6 = 101101, 11 = 001000, 19 = 001100, 20 = 001110, 12 = 000100,
21 = 000110, 22 = 000111, 13 = 000010, 23 = 000011, 24 = 100011,
14 = 000001, 25 = 100001, 26 = 110001 .

TABLE I. Excitation functions.

INPUTS \ FUNCTION (given by its table of states)	F_1	F_2	F_3	F_4	F_5	F_6
when $x = 1$	x100100	x010010	x001001	x100100	x010010	x001001
	x001001	x100100	x010010	x001001	x100100	x010010
	x101010	x010101	x101010	x010101	x101010	x010101
	x100000	x010000	x001000	x000100	x000010	x000001
	x000100	x000010	x000001	x100000	x010000	x001000
	x110000	x011000	x001100	x000110	x000011	x100001
	x001100	x000110	x000011	x100001	x110000	x011000
	x000110	x000011	x100001	x110000	x011000	x001100
	x100011	x110001	x111000	x011100	x001110	x000111
	x100001	x110000	x011000	x001100	x000110	x000011
	x110001	x111000	x011100	x001110	x000111	x100011
when $x = 0$	$\bar{x}$001001	$\bar{x}$100100	$\bar{x}$010010	$\bar{x}$001001	$\bar{x}$100100	$\bar{x}$010110
	$\bar{x}$101101	$\bar{x}$110110	$\bar{x}$011011	$\bar{x}$101101	$\bar{x}$110110	$\bar{x}$011011
	$\bar{x}$010101	$\bar{x}$101010	$\bar{x}$010101	$\bar{x}$101010	$\bar{x}$010101	$\bar{x}$101010
	$\bar{x}$000001	$\bar{x}$100000	$\bar{x}$010000	$\bar{x}$001000	$\bar{x}$000100	$\bar{x}$000010
	$\bar{x}$110000	$\bar{x}$011000	$\bar{x}$001100	$\bar{x}$000110	$\bar{x}$000011	$\bar{x}$100001
	$\bar{x}$111000	$\bar{x}$011100	$\bar{x}$001110	$\bar{x}$000111	$\bar{x}$100011	$\bar{x}$110001
	$\bar{x}$001110	$\bar{x}$000111	$\bar{x}$100011	$\bar{x}$110001	$\bar{x}$111000	$\bar{x}$011100
	$\bar{x}$100011	$\bar{x}$110001	$\bar{x}$111000	$\bar{x}$011100	$\bar{x}$001110	$\bar{x}$000111
	$\bar{x}$100001	$\bar{x}$110000	$\bar{x}$011000	$\bar{x}$001100	$\bar{x}$000110	$\bar{x}$000011
	$\bar{x}$000011	$\bar{x}$100001	$\bar{x}$110000	$\bar{x}$011000	$\bar{x}$001100	$\bar{x}$000110

ACKNOWLEDGEMENT

*Work supported in full by the United States Atomic Energy Commission under Contract AT(30-1)-4209.

IMPLEMENTATION OF CHECKABLE, ACYCLIC AUTOMATA BY MORPHIC BOOLEAN FUNCTIONS

W. C. Carter, A. B. Wadia, and D. C. Jessep

IBM Thomas J. Watson Research Center, Yorktown Heights, NY

Data contamination is the greatest problem in recovery for an ultrareliable computer. The use of self-checking and self-testing circuitry can reduce data contamination if the checker, syndrome, and exceptional condition output lines can be controlled by self-checking and self-testing logic circuits. These output lines in usual design are single lines which take a constant value which changes only when an error occurs. Thus these lines cannot be tested during normal operation. As with self-checking checkers, replace each such line by a pair of lines that take on values $\{(e_1, e_2)$ or $(e_1', e_2')\}$ corresponding to a 1 on the single line and values $\{(e_1, e_2')$ or $(e_1', e_2)\}$ corresponding to a 0 on the single line, where e_1, $e_2 \in \{0, 1\}$. Each line of the new pair can now take on both values 0 and 1, during normal operation so can be tested and the logic value on the single line replaced corresponds to the parity of the pair. For successful recovery, complex self-testing and self-checking logic functions must be realized with such a pair of lines as inputs. To provide such realizations, this paper provides an algebraic basis for the treatment of circuits utilizing these line pairs by formulating a new two-element morphic Boolean algebra. This two-element Boolean algebra is defined by the use of a morphism which relates the variables and logic operations of the new algebra to the variables and logic operations used in the original circuit. Next, the paper defines a correspondence between ordinary Boolean functions and morphic Boolean functions. For self-checking and self-testing function implementation the paper gives a universal set of self-testing morphic operator blocks and an algorithm for interconnecting these blocks to implement a self-testing replacement for any given logic circuit. By following straightforward rules, error-handling circuitry can be designed to facilitate computer recovery.

I. INTRODUCTION

The importance of careful treatment of error and other exception signals in the design of self-repairing computers was expressed by von Neumann [1], "Such a system ... is (so) ... well organized that as soon as an error shows up the system automatically senses whether this error matters or not." In this paper, it will be assumed that only one component fault will occur in one small time interval (computer cycle), but such single-circuit faults can cause zero, one, or more errors, where an error is the mutation of a single-line logic state. A circuit line normally takes on both values 0 and 1, and this is normally assumed to fail as stuck at 0 or stuck at 1. In order for a line to be testable it clearly must change

Presented at the Symposium on Computers and Automata
Polytechnic Institute of Brooklyn, April 13–15, 1971.

state during normal computer operation. However, there are several situations within a computer where lines usually assume constant values during normal operation. For example, let some computer signals be encoded at an interface so the presence of an error can be detected by a checking circuit. A single-output checker will have its output line take on a constant value, either 0 or 1, during normal operation, the other being required to indicate the error event. Such a line cannot be tested during normal operation. In [2] it was proved that a computer could be designed so that all such errors could be detected during normal operation. The principal results of this paper embodied in the concepts of self-checking checking circuits, which have two output lines instead of the usual one, and of reduction circuits for checker outputs which reduced the number of checker output lines while simultaneously testing themselves. These checking and testing ideas can be formalized by the following definitions. A self-checking logic circuit is one in which an erroneous result induced by a single gate failure does not go undetected. A self-testing logic circuit is one in which every single gate failure is detected during normal operation.

Recent papers [3, 4] have pointed out that computers can be fault-tolerant only if errors can be detected and their effect overcome. As shown in [5], lines which in normal operation have a single value (called semipassive lines in this paper) occur frequently in the error and exception handling portions of a computer. Examples are key code lines in memory-protection circuitry, switching lines for subunit replacement on detection of failure, intra-computer control-signal lines, ALU-overflow condition lines, and I/O over-run lines. Becoming more important recently are the syndrome lines of an error-correcting decoder where during code-space operation the syndrome lines are all zero or (exclusively) one, depending on the even or odd parity convention of the encoded words. A set of semipassive lines have little useful application as individual lines but are normally interconnected by logic operators to result in semipassive Boolean functions; e.g., the OR function that takes the outputs of several checkers and produces one output as an error signal, the AND function that realizes the correction conjunct of the syndromes in the error-correcting decoder, or the function which detects and signals a double error in a Hamming SEC/DED code. In these logic functions, all input, internal and output lines are semipassive and thus susceptible to undetected failure. Such failures can mask errors, allowing them to go undetected with resulting data contamination and lack of fault-tolerance for the computer system. It should be clear that in the design of fault-tolerant computers the semipassive lines and semipassive logic functions must be made self-checking and self-testing.

In this paper, it will be shown that semipassive lines can be replaced by a pair of lines testable in normal operation. This paper also demonstrates how semipassive logic functions can be designed to be self-testing beginning from an initial point of defining the desired Boolean function in the conventional sense, using an algebraic morphism to relate the original variables to self-testing variables, combining these variables by use of a new universal set of self-testing operators, and interconnecting these operators according to an algorithm which will insure that the resultant circuit will be a self-testing, checkable, acyclic automata.

II. MORPHIC BOOLEAN FUNCTIONS

The necessary condition for self-testability requires the passive lines to be replaced by a pair of lines both of which during normal operation take on both values 0 and 1. There exist two natural correspondences between the values taken by the new pair and the value taken by the single passive line, viz.

$$M: ((e_1, e_2), (e_1', e_2')) \longmapsto 1 \ ,$$
$$((e_1, e_2'), (e_1', e_2)) \longmapsto 0 \ ,$$

where e_1, $e_2 \in \{0, 1\}$. Note that each line of the new pair can take on both values 0 and 1, no matter which constant value is associated with the single line and the single-line value corresponding to the new-pair value can be easily determined by the parity of the two-tuple on the new pair. This mapping allowed a theory of self-checking checkers to be developed, in [2, 4, 5]. However, if more-complicated logic structures, such as the translator from Hamming SEC/DED code to byte parity code are to be checked, logic functions of such line pairs must be performed [6]. Because, as shown in [5], there are many more complicated logic functions to be implemented, this problem must be stated and solved in general for the efficient handling of error conditions in ultrareliable computers [7].

The problem is, given an ordinary function $g(a_1, a_2, a_3, \cdots, a_n)$ in the usual Boolean Algebra $B_1 = \{0, 1, \{*\}\}$, where $\{*\}$ is the set of usual logic operations, to set up a correspondence between g and a logic function G whose inputs and output are line pairs satisfying the mapping M; Fig. 1 shows the problem graphically.

To solve this problem, define Boolean operators over the status space $\{e_1, e_2\}$ of the pair of lines replacing the semipassive line. These operators can be defined by extending the previous mapping M to be a morphism between $\{0, 1, \{*\}\}$ and

$$\{\{(e_1, e_2), (e_1', e_2')\}, \{(e_1, e_2'), (e_1', e_2)\}, \{*_M\}\} \ ,$$

where: $*_M$ is defined by the commuting property of the morphism and the operations $*_M$ and $*$, viz., if

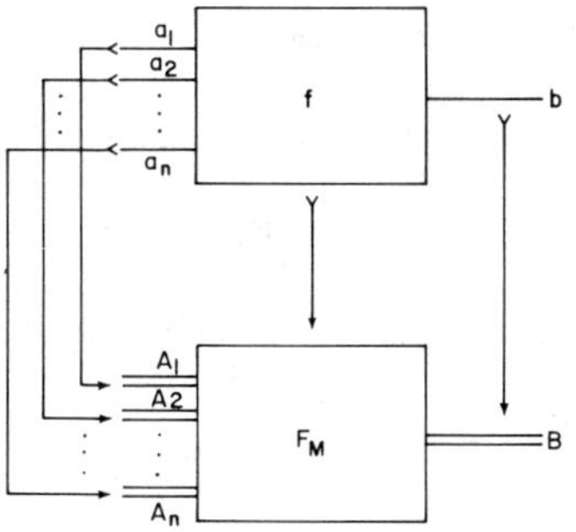

Fig. 1. Correspondence between semipassive function f and its morphic replacement F_M.

$$s_i,\ s_j \in \{(0,0),\ (0,1),\ (1,0),\ (1,1)\} \equiv S\ ,$$

following [8]

$$M(s_i *_M s_j) = M(s_i) * M(s_j)\ . \qquad (1)$$

Equation (1) defines morphic Boolean operators $\{*_M\}$.

Just as an ordinary Boolean variable is associated with each of the semipassive lines, a morphic Boolean variable can be associated with its pair replacement. The morphic variable is said to have a "value" T when, and only when, the pair of lines have the value $M^{-1}(1)$ and the morphic variable is said to have a "value" F when and only when the pair of lines have the values $M^{-1}(0)$. The values $M^{-1}(1)$ will be called the intrinsic status space and the values $M^{-1}(0)$ will be called the extrinsic status space of the input lines which correspond to the morphic variables.

The following theorem follows from the definition.

THEOREM 1. *The status space and operators* $*_M$

$$B_M = \{\{(e_1, e_2),\ (e_1', e_2')\},\ \{(e_1, e_2'),\ (e_1', e_2)\},\ \{*_M\}\}\ ,$$

form a Boolean algebra by definition of the morphism M.

This will be referred to as a morphic Boolean algebra. In the following, capital letters with single subscripts (e.g., A_i) will be used to denote morphic variables, i.e., the variable associated with the new pair of lines. As a variable over B_1 can also be associated with each of the lines of the new pair, they will be denoted by lower case letters with double subscripts. For example, the pair of variables that are associated with the two lines implementing A_i are (a_{i1}, a_{i2}). The symbol :: will be read as "is implemented by." Thus, $A_i :: (a_{i1}, a_{i2})$.

In addition, the following may be proven.

THEOREM 2. *There is a natural correspondence between functions* $g(a_1, a_2, a_3, \cdots, a_n)$ *in the ordinary Boolean algebra* $B_1 = \{0, 1, \{*\}\}$, *and functions* $G(A_1, A_2, \cdots, A_n)$ *in the morphic Boolean algebra* $B_M = \{\{(e_1, e_2), (e_1', e_2')\}, \{(e_1, e_2), (e_1, e_2')\}, \{*_M\}\}$.

Now that it has been shown how morphic Boolean functions originate, it is clear that their most-interesting properties are those following from their implementation, and their self-checking and self-testing features should be examined.

Any implementation of a morphic Boolean function derives properties from its relation to the semipassive parent circuit. During normal operation, its inputs will be a set of patterns that correspond to a single pattern $A_1, A_2, A_3, \cdots, A_n$ where $A_i = \mathrm{F}$ for $i \in \{i_1, i_2, i_3, \cdots, i_k\}$ $(0 \leq k \leq n)$, and $A_i = \mathrm{T}$ for $i \notin \{i_1, i_2, i_3, \cdots, i_k\}$. The values taken on by the 2^n lines implementing the n morphic variables for a single morphic pattern $\alpha_1 \alpha_2 \alpha_3 \cdots \alpha_n$, $\alpha_i \in \{\mathrm{T}, \mathrm{F}\}$ will be called the semipassive pattern space. For example, in case of two input variables, the semipassive pattern spaces will be either $\begin{Bmatrix}01\\10\end{Bmatrix} \times \begin{Bmatrix}01\\10\end{Bmatrix}$, $\begin{Bmatrix}00\\11\end{Bmatrix} \times \begin{Bmatrix}01\\10\end{Bmatrix}$, $\begin{Bmatrix}01\\10\end{Bmatrix} \times \begin{Bmatrix}00\\11\end{Bmatrix}$, or $\begin{Bmatrix}00\\11\end{Bmatrix} \times \begin{Bmatrix}00\\11\end{Bmatrix}$.

The Boolean functions which were defined with the constant-value lines as inputs can now be replaced by implementation of their morphic Boolean counterparts, with double-line inputs and outputs as shown symbolically in Figure 1. For example, a morphic NOT (MNOT) function can be implemented by adding an inverter to one of the lines (a_{11}, a_{12}). A morphic AND (MAND) function can be implemented by

$$A_1 \wedge A_2 = G :: (a_{12}\, a_{22} \vee a'_{12}\, a_{21},\ a_{11}\, a_{22} \vee a'_{11}\, a_{21}) \equiv (g_1, g_2) \ .$$

These functions have been studied and their properties are reported in [7]. It can be shown that as usual the testability of the inputs of a circuit implementing a morphic Boolean function depends only on the functional specification and the semipassive input pattern space considered and not on the functional implementation nor the particular morphism used. Formally, let any semipassive input pattern space P correspond to $A_i = \mathrm{F}$ for $i \in \{i_1, i_2, i_3, \cdots, i_k\}$ $(0 \leq k \leq n)$ and $A_i = \mathrm{T}$ for $i \notin \{i_1, i_2, i_3, \cdots, i_k\}$. The following can be stated regarding input testability.

THEOREM 3. *An input A_j is testable at the output G of a morphic Boolean Function $G(A_1, A_2, A_3, \cdots, A_n)$ in the input space P iff the number of terms containing A_j and not containing A_i, $i \neq j$ and $i \in \{i_1, i_2, i_3, \cdots, i_k\}$, in the Boolean polynomial equivalent to* F *is odd.*

A self-testing and self-checking implementation of a morphic Boolean function is an implementation such that every single failure causes the output to change from T to F or vice versa, for the input patterns that correspond to a semipassive pattern space.

A fundamental point regarding self-checkability follows from morphic Boolean function implementation. A self-checking circuit as explained above is one in which a single failure does not produce an erroneous result that goes undetected. Correct morphic Boolean function outputs are identically T (or F). Thus, detection in case of morphic Boolean function is determination whether the value of the output variable does change from T to F or vice versa in the presence of a failure. Hence a failure that causes the output to go from one representation of T to the other is not detected but neither is this an error. This proves:

THEOREM 4. *Any implementation of a morphic Boolean function is self-checking.*

Hence, the property of nontrivial importance is the self-testability of the internal lines of a functional implementation of a morphic Boolean function. The following theorem [7] shows the numerous implementations available.

THEOREM 5. *The morphic Boolean function G of n variables has 2^{2^n} specifications in terms of the underlying Boolean functions (g_1, g_2) over the Boolean algebra $\{1, 0, \{*\}\}$ (with associated possible hardware/implementation). However, not all are self-testable!*

The basic problem attacked in this paper is that of obtaining a self-testing implementation of any given morphic Boolean function; i.e., given a morphic Boolean function and a semipassive input pattern, an implementation is to be specified such that every single internal line failure causes, during normal operation, the output to change from T to F, or vice versa.

III. SELF-TESTING IMPLEMENTATION BY UNIVERSAL MORPHIC OPERATOR BLOCKS

It is known that any Boolean function can be expressed as an interconnection of a universal set of operator blocks e.g., {NOT, AND, OR}, {NAND} or {NOR}. It is also true, moreover, that any morphic Boolean function can be implemented by an interconnection of a universal set of morphic operator blocks. However, such an implementation need not be self-testing. Simulator studies have emphasized that caution must be exercised when combining morphic Boolean variables in logic circuitry to prevent the loss of the self-testability property at the circuit outputs. The problem is that the restricted set of semipassive input patterns is further restricted several levels down in the tree-structure implementation of a circuit.

These sections will show that there exists a set of universal blocks, called a "universal self-testing set," and there is an algorithm for interconnecting these blocks which gives a self-testing implementation for any morphic Boolean function.

The morphism used for the input is $\{(0,1), (1,0)\} \longmapsto$ T and $\{(0,0), (1,1)\} \longmapsto$ F and it is first assumed that the space P of semipassive input patterns corresponds to $A_i = \mathrm{T}$ ($i = 1, 2, 3, \cdots, n$). The implementation structure for the case in which a mixed input morphism is used and for the case in which any arbitrary semipassive input pattern space is used is discussed in Sections V and VI, respectively.

A. The Universal Self-Testing Set of Morphic Operator Blocks

The universal self-testing set of morphic blocks consists of the following blocks:

(1) A morphic inverter testable for all semipassive input spaces

(2) a) A morphic AND block for two variables A_1, A_2 which is testable in each of the three semipassive input spaces $\{A_1 = A_2 = \mathrm{T}\}$, $\{A_1 = \mathrm{T}, A_2 = \mathrm{F}\}$, and $\{A_1 = \mathrm{F}, A_2 = \mathrm{T}\}$

b) A Morphic AND block for ℓ variables $A_1, A_2, A_3, \cdots, A_\ell$, which takes less circuitry than a corresponding tree formed from the two variable morphic AND block described above, and which is testable in the semipassive space $A_1 = A_2 = A_3 = \cdots = A_\ell = \mathrm{T}$.

(3) A morphic XOR block for two variables, which is testable in all four semipassive input spaces.

Figure 2 shows the morphic inverter (MNOT). The block consists of a single gate. The testability in all semipassive input spaces is obvious.

Figure 3 shows the implementation of the morphic AND (MAND) block with two variables. The MAND requires eight conventional logic gates as shown for a two-variable input. The block was designed by techniques given in [9]. The tables headed DETECT are outputs of a diagnostic program testdetect [10] implemented on the APL/360 [11]. Each row gives the testability of the line indicated at the head of the column for the input pattern that appears as the initial segment of that row. A 1(0) entry means that the line is testable for the stuck-at-1(0)

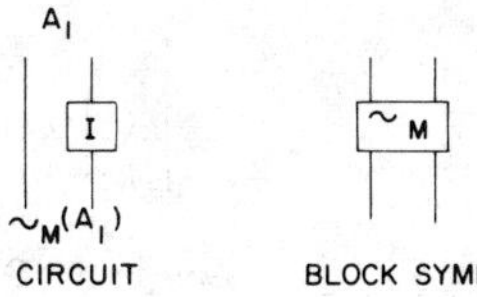

Fig. 2. The Morphic-inverter block.

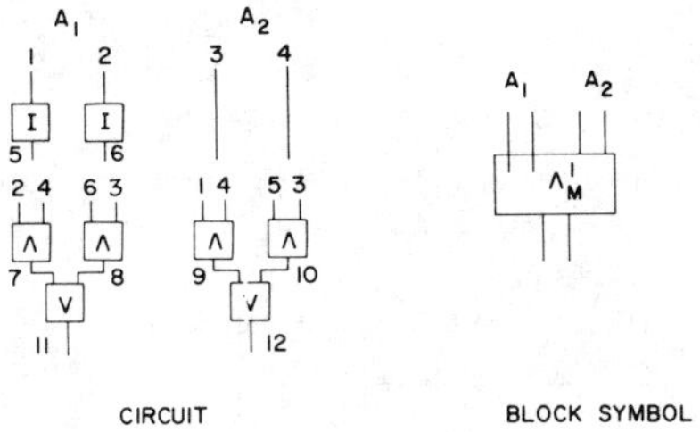

TESTDETECT RESULTS:

1234	111 123456789012	1234	111 123456789012	1234	111 123456789012
0101	1010 0 1101	0001	11 111111	0100	11 111111
0110	10010111 010	0010	11 00 0 000	0111	000 0 000
1001	0110 110 10	1101	00 0 0 00	1000	11 111111
1010	010110 01101	1110	00 11111111	1011	00 0 00 00

Fig. 3. The two variable morphic AND block.

failure. A blank means that that line is not tested by the input pattern corresponding to the row. From the DETECT runs in Fig. 3, it can be seen that the MAND implementation given there is self-testing in either of the spaces $\{A_1 = \mathrm{T}, A_2 = \mathrm{T}\}$ and $\{A_1 = \mathrm{F}, A_2 = \mathrm{T}\}$. However, in the space $\{A_1 = \mathrm{T}, A_2 = \mathrm{F}\}$, the inverters 5 and 6 are not tested for a stuck-at-1 failure. Hence, whenever two variables A_i and A_j with $A_i = \mathrm{T}$ and $A_j = \mathrm{F}$ have to be MANDed, care should be taken to apply A_j to the input lines of the MAND block that has the inverters, viz. lines 1 and 2. In the figure of the block symbol, the lines having the inverters are indicated by extension into the block, to distinguish them from the input lines which do not have the inverters.

In order to realize a conjunct of ℓ variables such as $A_1 A_2 A_3 \cdots A_\ell$ a tree of the two variable MAND gate would give a testable implementation for the semi-passive spaces $\{A_i = \mathrm{T}\ (i = 1, 2, 3, \cdots, \ell)\}$ and $\{A_I = \mathrm{F}, A_{i \neq I} = \mathrm{T}\}$. A technique for minimizing the gate count in a tree structure of blocks, each of which is a two-level AND/OR structure, is to alternate the block structure from AND/OR to OR/AND at each block-tree level and merge the AND(OR) gate of one level with the AND(OR) gates of the next. Partial merging may be accomplished for a MAND-tree structure as shown in Fig. 4; other ways of merging are prevented by the inverters on one pair of input lines. This circuit is only testable in the space $A_1 = A_2 = A_3 = \cdots = A_\ell = \mathrm{T}$, because if there exists an $A_I = \mathrm{F}$, then the MAND block into which that A_I is an input has an output corresponding to F which feeds into the lines not having the inverters of the succeeding MAND

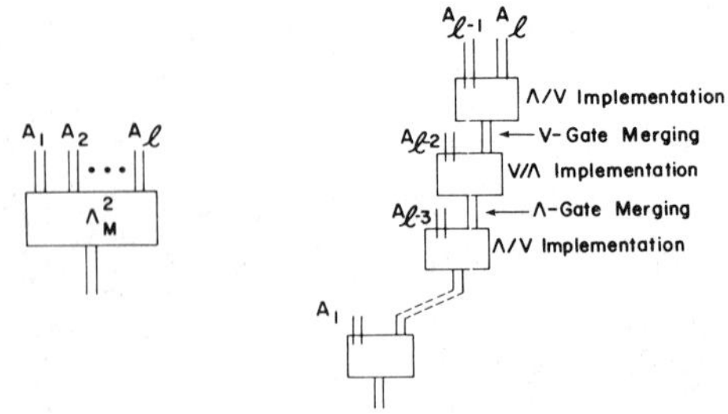

BLOCK SYMBOL CIRCUIT IMPLEMENTATION

Fig. 4. Implementation of ℓ-variable, level-merged, morphic AND block.

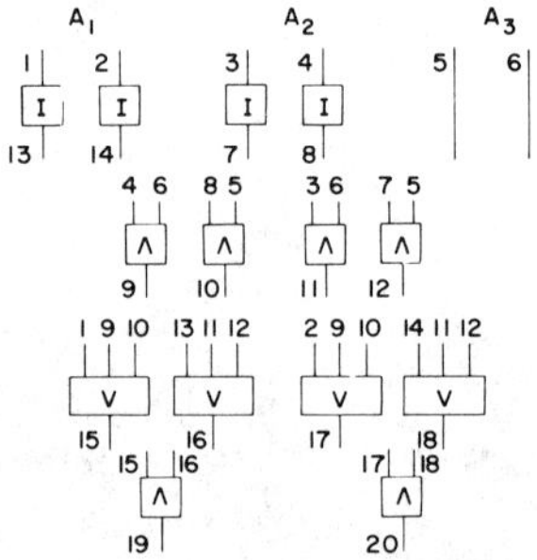

CIRCUIT

TESTDETECT RESULTS:

123456	11111111112 12345678901234567890
010101	101010 0 110100 101
010110	1010010111 0 1 0010
011001	100110 110 1 0010
011010	10010110 0110100 101
100101	011010 0 1110 10010
100110	0110010111 0 001 01
101001	010110 110 001 01
101010	01010110 01110 10010

Fig. 5. The three variables, level-merged, morphic AND block.

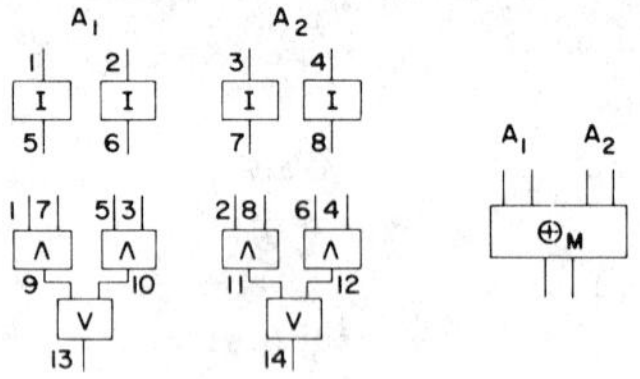

CIRCUIT BLOCK SYMBOL

TESTDETECT RESULTS:

1234	11111 12345678901234	1234	11111 12345678901234	1234	11111 12345678901234
0000	1111 111111	0100	1011 0110 10	0101	1010 1 1111111
0011	110000 0 000	0111	100001 1 01101	0110	10010 0 00 00
1100	0011 000 0 00	1000	0111 0 0 1101	1001	0110 00 0 000
1111	00001111111111	1011	0100101 11 010	1010	01011 1 111111

Fig. 6. The morphic XOR block.

block, causing the inverters in the succeeding block, and blocks in succeeding levels, to be untested. Figure 5 shows a 3-variable merged MAND block testable in the space $A_1 = A_2 = A_3 = \mathrm{T}$. The total number of gates required for an ℓ variable merged structure is $6(\ell - 1) + 2$, whereas that for the unmerged case is $8(\ell - 1)$.

Figure 6 shows an implementation of the morphic XOR (MXOR) structure. The number of gates required is 10. The implementation is testable in all semipassive spaces. The inverters on the input lines prevent any kind of level merging technique from being applied to an ℓ-variable MXOR tree.

B. Algorithm of Interconnection

This subsection describes an algorithm for reducing a morphic Boolean function into a "parenthesized form" which can be made to correspond to a testable structure in the space in which all input variables have value T and which uses a minimum number of the blocks described in Section III.A.

The Interconnection Algorithm starts with the morphic Boolean function in the equivalent Boolean polynomial form and consists of applying recursively three main steps which will be called:

(1) The factorization step
(2) The parenthesis removal step
(3) The complementation step.

1. Factorization Step

Take the subpolynomial S consisting of the largest number of terms containing a common variable, say A_{i_1}, and replace it by $A_{i_1}(P_1)$, where P_1 is a Boolean polynomial such that $A_{i_1}(P_1) \equiv S$.

Apply the above step recursively to the remaining terms of the polynomial G until the remaining polynomial has no terms with variables in common.

At the end of the factorization step, the resulting expression will be of the form $A_{i_1}(P_1) + A_{i_2}(P_2) + \cdots + A_{i_k}(P_k) + P_{k+1}$, where: P_1 is a Boolean polynomial not containing A_{i_1}; P_2 is a Boolean polynomial not containing A_{i_1} and A_{i_2}; P_k is a Boolean polynomial not containing $A_{i_1}, A_{i_2}, A_{i_3}, \cdots, A_{i_k}$; and P_{k+1} is a Boolean polynomial not containing $A_{i_1}, A_{i_2}, A_{i_3}, \cdots, A_{i_k}$ and has no terms with variables in common.

2. Parenthesis-Removal Step

If any Boolean polynomial within the innermost parenthesis has an odd number of terms and is immediately followed by two right parentheses that match with two left parentheses without a "+" between the two parentheses, then delete the outer parentheses.

Apply Steps (1) and (2) alternately until no more factorization or parenthesis removal is possible.

3. Complementation Step

In the form which cannot be subjected to further factorization or parenthesis removal, replace the substructure $1 + P$ by P'.

A self-testing structure implementing the morphic Boolean function is obtained as follows from the final parenthesized form resulting from the above algorithm. The complementation is implemented by the MNOT Block. The + is implemented by the MXOR Block. The AND structure that appears in the final expression as the subexpression $A_{i_1} A_{i_2} A_{i_3} \cdots A_{i_{\ell-1}}(P)$ is implemented using the ℓ variable MAND block with level merging. The AND structure that appears in the final expression as the subexpression $A_{i_1}\left(A_{i_2}\left(\cdots\left(A_{i_{\ell-1}}(P)\right)\cdots\right)\right)$ is implemented as an $(\ell - 1)$ morphic-level tree structure of the two-variable MAND block with P applied to the input lines of the top-most AND block that carry the inverters.

An example showing use of the algorithm to obtain a testable structure using the morphic operator blocks discussed above follows. Let

$$G = A_7 + A_1 A_2 + A_7 A_8 A_9 + A_7 A_8 A_9 A_{10} + A_7 A_8 A_9 A_{11} + A_1 A_2 A_3 A_4 A_5 + A_1 A_2 A_4 A_5 A_6 \; .$$

Step 1. $A_7(1 + A_8 A_9 + A_8 A_9 A_{10} + A_8 A_9 A_{11}) + A_1(A_2 + A_2 A_3 A_4 A_5 + A_2 A_4 A_5 A_6)$
Step 2. No change in expression
Step 1. $A_7(1 + A_8(A_9 + A_9 A_{10} + A_9 A_{11})) + A_1(A_2(1 + A_3 A_4 A_5 + A_4 A_5 A_6))$
Step 2. $A_7(1 + A_8(A_9 + A_9 A_{10} + A_9 A_{11})) + A_1 A_2(1 + A_3 A_4 A_5 + A_4 A_5 A_6)$
Step 1. $A_7\big(1 + A_8(A_9(1 + A_{10} + A_{11}))\big) + A_1 A_2(1 + A_4(A_3 A_5 + A_5 A_6))$
Step 2. $A_7(1 + A_8 A_9(1 + A_{10} + A_{11})) + A_1 A_2(1 + A_4(A_3 A_5 + A_5 A_6)))$
Step 1. $A_7(1 + A_8 A_9(1 + A_{10} + A_{11})) + A_1 A_2\big(1 + A_4(A_5(A_3 + A_6))\big)$
Step 2. $A_7(1 + A_8 A_9(1 + A_{10} + A_{11})) + A_1 A_2\big(1 + A_4(A_5(A_3 + A_6))\big)$
Step 3. $A_7(A_8 A_9(A_{10}' + A_{11}))' + A_1 A_2\big(A_4(A_5(A_3 + A_6))\big)' \, .$

The implementation corresponding to the above parenthesized expression is shown in Figure 7.

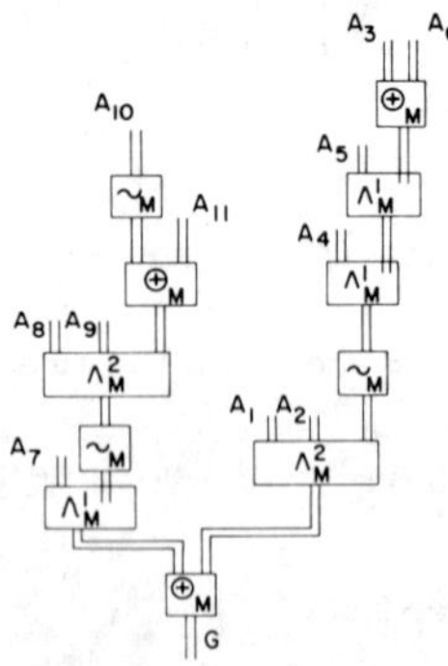

Fig. 7. The morphic Boolean structure corresponding to $A_7(A_8A_9(A_{10}' + A_{11}))' + A_1A_2\left(A_4(A_5(A_3 + A_3))\right)'$.

IV. PROOF OF SELF-TESTABILITY OF THE IMPLEMENTATION OF SECTION III.B

THEOREM 6. *The logic circuit implementing the final parenthesized form obtained from the Interconnection Algorithm is self-testing in the space* $A_1 = A_2 = A_3 = \cdots = A_n = \mathrm{T}$.

The above algorithm puts the morphic Boolean function into a parenthesized form in which four distinct substructures corresponding to the morphic blocks of Section III.A can be identified. It need, hence, only be shown that these substructures as implemented by the morphic blocks are testable in the input space $A_1 = A_2 = A_3 = \cdots = A_n = \mathrm{T}$. In order to prove this, it has to be shown that the input to each of the morphic blocks takes on all the input patterns required to test that block.

For example, the input to:

(1) The morphic NOT block should take on either the values $\begin{Bmatrix}01\\10\end{Bmatrix}$ or $\begin{Bmatrix}00\\11\end{Bmatrix}$

(2) The two-variable MAND blocks should take on the values

$$\begin{Bmatrix}01\\10\end{Bmatrix} \times \begin{Bmatrix}01\\10\end{Bmatrix}, \quad \begin{Bmatrix}00\\11\end{Bmatrix} \times \begin{Bmatrix}01\\10\end{Bmatrix}, \quad \text{or} \quad \begin{Bmatrix}01\\10\end{Bmatrix} \times \begin{Bmatrix}00\\11\end{Bmatrix}$$

(3) The ℓ-variable merged MAND block should take on the values $\begin{Bmatrix}01\\10\end{Bmatrix}^{\ell}$

(4) The two-variable MXOR blocks should take on the values

$$\begin{Bmatrix}01\\10\end{Bmatrix} \times \begin{Bmatrix}01\\10\end{Bmatrix}, \begin{Bmatrix}00\\11\end{Bmatrix} \times \begin{Bmatrix}01\\10\end{Bmatrix}, \begin{Bmatrix}01\\10\end{Bmatrix} \times \begin{Bmatrix}00\\11\end{Bmatrix}, \text{ or } \begin{Bmatrix}00\\11\end{Bmatrix} \times \begin{Bmatrix}00\\11\end{Bmatrix}.$$

In order to prove testability of a complex circuit, we will adopt the following technique. The complexity of the parenthesized form obtained as a result of applying the Interconnection Algorithm will be defined recursively and testability of the structure will be proved by induction on the complexity of the structure. A parenthesized expression has complexity 1 if it is of the form

$$A_{i_1} A_{i_2} A_{i_3} \cdots A_{i_k} \ .$$

A parenthesized form has complexity n if it is of the following types.

Type 1. $(P^1)'$

Type 2. $A_{i_1} A_{i_2} A_{i_3} \cdots A_{i_\ell} (P^2)$

Type 3. $A_{i_1}(A_{i_2}(A_{i_3} \ \cdots (A_{i_\ell}(P^3)) \cdots)$

Type 4. $P_1^4 + P_2^4 + P_3^4 + \cdots + P_\ell^4$,

where: P^1 is a parenthesized form of type 2, 3, or 4 and complexity $(n-1)$; P^2 is a parenthesized form of type 1, 3, or 4 of complexity $(n-1)$, is independent of all of $A_{i_1}, A_{i_2}, A_{i_3}, \cdots, A_{i_\ell}$ and such that the Boolean polynomial equivalent to P^2 has odd number of terms; P^3 is a parenthesized form of Type 1, 2, or 4 of complexity $(n-1)$, is independent of all of $A_{i_1}, A_{i_2}, A_{i_3}, \cdots, A_{i_\ell}$ and such that the

Boolean polynomial equivalent to P^3 has even number of terms; $P_1^4, P_2^4, P_3^4, \cdots,$ P_ℓ^4 are of Type 2, 3, or 4 and at most one of Type 1 with the complexity of the most complex of these being $(n-1)$ and P_i^4 contains at least one variable that is not in any of $P_{i+1}^4, P_{i+2}^4, P_{i+3}^4, \cdots, P_\ell^4$.

It is clear that the parenthesized form resulting from the application of the Interconnection Algorithm is one of the four types stated above.

Following the above definition of complexity, a unique complexity number can be associated with each parenthesized form obtained by the algorithm given. For example, the complexity number for the parenthesized form $A_7(A_8 A_9(A_{10}' + A_{11}))' + A_1 A_2 (A_4(A_5(A_3 + A_6)))'$ is 6.

To prove the self testability of the circuit corresponding to the final parenthesized form use induction on n, the complexity of the parenthesized form.

Consider the case of $n = 1$. Every parenthesized form of complexity 1 is of the form $A_{i_1} A_{i_2} A_{i_3} \cdots A_{i_k}$ and the k-variable level-merged morphic AND block gives a testable implementation in the space $A_{i_1} = A_{i_2} = A_{i_3} = \cdots = A_{i_k} = \mathrm{T}$, as the input pattern is $\begin{Bmatrix} 01 \\ 10 \end{Bmatrix}^k$ since all A_{i_j}'s are distinct.

Assume all parenthesized form of complexity $(n-1)$ have testable implementation and consider the parenthesized form of complexity n, which must be of Type 1, Type 2, Type 3, or Type 4.

Type 1. $(P^1)'$

As a testable implementation for P^1 exists by assumption, consider an implementation which consists of the testable implementation of P^1 followed by a morphic inverter. As the implementation of P^1 is testable, the lines realizing P will take on either both values 01 and 10 or both values 00 and 11; hence the following inverter is testable and thus the implementation of $(P^1)'$ is testable.

Type 2. $A_{i_1} A_{i_2} A_{i_3} \cdots A_{i_\ell}(P^2)$

P^2 has a testable implementation by assumption. Since the Boolean polynomial equivalent to P^2 has an odd number of terms its output is T. Thus the P^2 output lines take on both the values 01 and 10. Also, as P^2 is independent of $A_{i_1}, A_{i_2}, A_{i_3}, \cdots, A_{i_\ell}$ the space of $(A_{i_1}, A_{i_2}, A_{i_3}, \cdots, A_{i_\ell}, P^2) = \begin{Bmatrix} 01 \\ 10 \end{Bmatrix}^{\ell+1}$ and hence an $(\ell + 1)$-variable merged MAND block following the implementation of P^2 will be testable. Hence, the implementation of $A_{i_1} A_{i_2} A_{i_3} \cdots A_{i_\ell}(P^2)$ is testable.

Type 3. $A_{i_1}\left(A_{i_2}\left(A_{i_3} \cdots (A_{i_\ell}(P^3)) \cdots\right)\right)$

P^3 has a testable implementation by assumption. Since the Boolean polynomial equivalent to P^3 has an even number of terms, the P^3 output lines take on both values 00 and 11. Also, as P^3 is independent $A_{i_1}, A_{i_2}, A_{i_3}, \cdots, A_{i_\ell}$ the space of $(A_{i_\ell}, P^3) = \begin{Bmatrix} 01 \\ 10 \end{Bmatrix} \times \begin{Bmatrix} 00 \\ 11 \end{Bmatrix}$ and hence a two variable MAND block realizing $A_{i_\ell}(P^3)$ is testable and hence $A_{i_\ell}(P^3)$ if P^3 is applied to the lines containing the inverters. As $A_{i_\ell}(P^3)$ is shown to have a testable implementation, the lines realizing it will take on both values 00 and 11. As $A_{i_\ell}(P^3)$ is independent of $A_{i_{\ell-1}}$, $A_{i_{\ell-1}}(A_{i_\ell}(P^3))$ can be similarly implemented by another two variable MAND block. Proceeding similarly, $A_{i_1}\left(A_{i_2}\left(A_{i_3}\left(\cdots\left(A_{i_\ell}(P^3)\right)\cdots\right)\right)\right)$ can be implemented in a testable form by following the testable implementation of P^3 by a two variable MAND tree of ℓ levels with $A_{i_1}, A_{i_2}, A_{i_3}, \cdots, A_{i_\ell}$ being applied to the input lines that do not have the inverters of the MAND block at each level.

Type 4. $P_1^4 + P_2^4 + P_3^4 + \cdots + P_\ell^4$

By assumption, P_i^4 $(i = 1, 2, 3, \cdots, \ell)$ has a testable implementation. The lines realizing P_i^4 take on either both values 01 and 10 or both values 00 and 11. P_1^4 contains a variable A_{i_1} not present in P_2^4. It can be seen from the implementation of the MNOT block, the MAND blocks, and the MXOR block, that a change of the values on lines realizing a single input variable form 01(10) to 10(01) or from 00(11) to 11(00) cause a change in the values of the lines realizing their output from 01(10) to 10(01) or from 00(11) to 11(00). As P_1^4 is an interconnection of such blocks, a change in values of lines realizing A_{i_1} would cause the values on lines realizing P_1^4 to also change. However as P_2^4 does not contain A_{i_1} the values of lines realizing P_2^4 will remain fixed at either 01 or 10, or, 00 or 11. Then, by changing the value on the lines realizing P_2^4 to change to either 10 or 01, or, 11 or 00 respectively (and this is possible as implementation of P_2^4 is assumed testable), changing A_{i_1} would cause all the four patterns of either $\begin{Bmatrix} 01 \\ 10 \end{Bmatrix} \times \begin{Bmatrix} 01 \\ 10 \end{Bmatrix}$, $\begin{Bmatrix} 01 \\ 10 \end{Bmatrix} \times \begin{Bmatrix} 00 \\ 11 \end{Bmatrix}$, $\begin{Bmatrix} 00 \\ 11 \end{Bmatrix} \times \begin{Bmatrix} 01 \\ 10 \end{Bmatrix}$, or $\begin{Bmatrix} 00 \\ 11 \end{Bmatrix} \times \begin{Bmatrix} 00 \\ 11 \end{Bmatrix}$ to appear across lines realizing P_1^4 and P_2^4. Thus the MXOR realizing $P_1^4 + P_2^4$ is testable. Now $P_1^4 + P_2^4$ is a parenthesized from which has a testable implementation and has a variable A_{i_1} not present in P_3^4. Thus, by an argument similar to the one above, the second MXOR that operates on $P_1^4 + P_2^4$ and P_3^4 is also testable, giving a testable realization for $P_1^4 + P_2^4 + P_3^4$. Proceeding similarly, it can be shown that $P_1^4 + P_2^4 + P_3^4 + \cdots + P_\ell^4$ is testable if realized as a $(\ell - 1)$-level MXOR tree. It can also be proved that any MXOR tree realization is testable. This completes the proof.

As an example, consider the implementation of the Morphic OR function using the above technique, for testability in the space $A_1 = \mathrm{T}$, $A_2 = \mathrm{T}$.

$$
\begin{aligned}
G &= A_1 \vee A_2 \\
&= A_1 + A_2 + A_1 A_2 \cdots \text{(which is the Boolean polynomial equivalent to G)} \\
&= A_1 + A_2(1 + A_1) \\
&= A_1 + A_2 A_1' \ .
\end{aligned}
$$

From Theorem 3 it is seen that none of the input variables are testable. Figure 8 shows the circuit as an interconnection of Morphic blocks of Section 3.1. The DETECT results for the circuit show that it is completely testable in the space $A_1 = A_2 = T$.

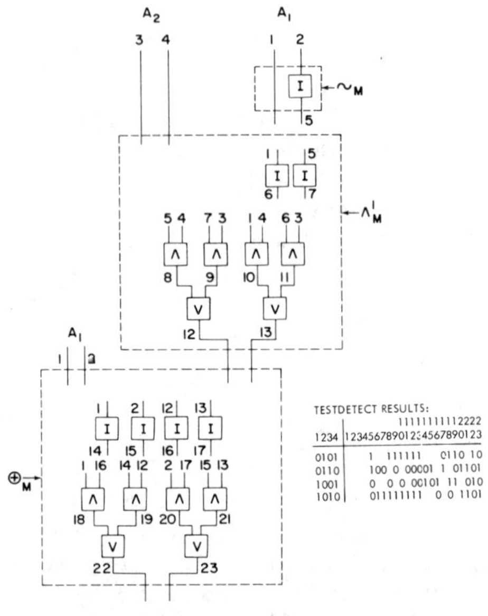

Fig. 8. Implementation of the morphic OR function for the input space and morphism

$$A_1 = T \longleftrightarrow \begin{Bmatrix} 01 \\ 10 \end{Bmatrix}, \quad A_2 = T \longleftrightarrow \begin{Bmatrix} 01 \\ 10 \end{Bmatrix}.$$

V. AN IMPLEMENTATION FOR MIXED INPUT MORPHISMS

In the Interconnection Algorithm it was assumed that the intrinsic status space for all input variables was $\begin{Bmatrix} 01 \\ 10 \end{Bmatrix}$. In a general situation, this may not be the case, as some input variables may have $\begin{Bmatrix} 00 \\ 11 \end{Bmatrix}$ as the intrinsic status space.

A way of extending the previously described method to such a general situation is to place a MNOT block on each variable with intrinsic status space $\begin{Bmatrix} 00 \\ 11 \end{Bmatrix}$. The interface so obtained has $\begin{Bmatrix} 01 \\ 10 \end{Bmatrix}$ for intrinsic status space for all variables, and the previously described Interconnection Algorithm is used to obtain the testable implementation. It should be noted that if A_i has intrinsic space $\begin{Bmatrix} 00 \\ 11 \end{Bmatrix}$ and appears in an even number of terms in the Boolean polynomial equivalent to the function, then the MNOT on A_i required in order to change the intrinsic space to $\begin{Bmatrix} 01 \\ 10 \end{Bmatrix}$ will be untestable, a result of Theorem 3 (the input is not testable). The easiest way of overcoming this difficulty is to replace all variables A_i, with intrinsic status space $\begin{Bmatrix}00\\11\end{Bmatrix}$, that appear in even number of terms in the Boolean polynomial, by two variables A_i^1 and A_i^2, both of which appear in an odd number of terms in the Boolean polynomial. The intrinsic status spaces of A_i^1 and A_i^2 are changed to $\begin{Bmatrix}01\\10\end{Bmatrix}$ by two distince MNOTs. As A_i^1 and A_i^2 each now appear in an odd number of terms, according to Theorem 3 they are testable and hence the MNOTs producing them will be testable. A certain minimization can be achieved by replacing $(A_i^1)'$ and $(A_i^2)'$ in the final parenthesized from by A_i.

Example. Consider the implementation of the morphic Boolean function $A_1 \vee A_2$ with intrinsic space of A_1 being $\begin{Bmatrix}00\\11\end{Bmatrix}$, and that of A_2 being $\begin{Bmatrix}01\\10\end{Bmatrix}$, and the semipassive space being $A_1 = T$ and $A_2 = T$.

$$G = A_1 + A_2 + A_1 A_2 \quad .$$

Replace

$$A_1 \text{ by } A_1^1 \text{ and } A_1^2 \;,$$

$$\begin{aligned} G &= A_1^1 + A_2 + A_1^2 A_2 \\ &= A_1^1 + A_2(1 + A_1^2) \\ &= A_1^1 + A_2(A_1^2)' = A_1^1 + A_2 A_1 \quad . \end{aligned}$$

The complete circuit, using the morphic operator blocks discussed earlier, is shown in Fig. 9 along with the DETECT results that show all internal lines to be testable.

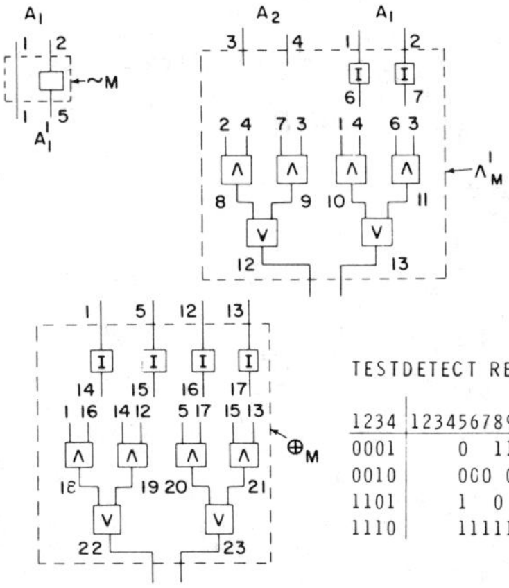

TESTDETECT RESULTS:

1234	1	2	3	4	5	6	7	8	9	10	11	12	13	14	15	16	17	18	19	20	21	22	23
0001					0			1	1	1	1	1	1				0	1	1	0		1	0
0010					0	0	0		0		0	0	0	0	1		1		0	1	1	0	1
1101					1			0		0		0	0	1	0	1		1	1		0	1	0
1110					1	1	1	1	1	1	1	1	1			0		0		1	1	0	1

Fig. 9. Implementation of the morphic OR function for the input space and morphism

$$A_1 = T \longleftrightarrow \begin{Bmatrix}00\\11\end{Bmatrix} \;,\quad A_2 = T \longleftrightarrow \begin{Bmatrix}01\\10\end{Bmatrix} \;.$$

VI. IMPLEMENTATION FOR AN ARBITRARY SEMIPASSIVE INPUT PATTERN

Consider next the case in which the semipassive pattern space is $A_i = F$ for $i \in \{i_1, i_2, i_3, \cdots, i_k\}$ $(0 \le k \le n)$ and $A_i = T$ for $i \notin \{i_1, i_2, i_3, \cdots, i_k\}$. The self-testing morphic Boolean structure is obtained as follows. Attach an MNOT at each A_i, $i \in \{i_1, i_2, i_3, \cdots, i_k\}$, and let the variable associated with the outputs of these inverters be B_i, $i \in \{i_1, i_2, i_3, \cdots, i_k\}$. Obtain the morphic Boolean function $H(B_{i_1}, B_{i_2}, B_{i_3}, \cdots, B_{i_k}, A_{i_{k+1}}, A_{i_{k+2}}, A_{i_{k+3}}, \cdots, A_{i_n})$, which is identically equal to the function $G(A_{i_1}, A_{i_2}, A_{i_3}, \cdots, A_{i_n})$ to be implemented. The problem now reduces to implementing H to be testable for the semipassive pattern in which all variables of H have the value T. This does not, however, prove the testability of the inverters hanging from A_i $i \in \{i_1, i_2, i_3, \cdots, i_k\}$. The problem is overcome as follows. Take the B_i's that occur an even number of times in the Boolean polynomial equivalent to H and split them up into two sets, each containing an odd number of elements. Treat the elements of the two sets as separate variables B_i^1 and B_i^2 and proceed to design as before with the separate variables coming from independent inverters of the same variable. After the final parenthesization replace $(B_i^1)'$ and $(B_i^2)'$ by A_i. These facts can be collected in a final theorem.

THEOREM 7. *The logic circuit implementing the final parenthesized form obtained from the modified Interconnection Algorithm is self-testing for mixed input morphisms or arbitrary semipassive input patterns.*

Example. Implementation of the function $G = A_1 A_2$ for the semipassive space $A_1 = F$, $A_2 = F$.

Let

$$B_1 = A_1' \text{ and } B_2 = A_2'.$$

Then

$$H(B_1, B_2) \equiv (B_1 \vee B_2)' \equiv A_1 A_2 \equiv G(A_1, A_2) \ ,$$

$$H = B_1 + B_2 + B_1 B_2 + 1 \ .$$

Split B_1 into B_1^1 and B_1^2 and B_2 into B_2^1 and B_2^2.

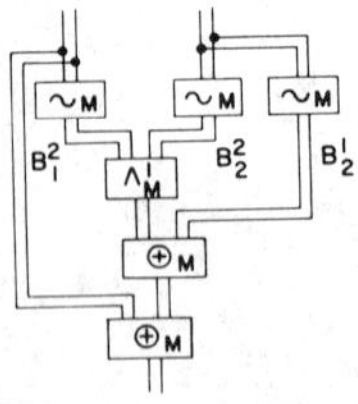

Fig. 10. Implementation of the morphic AND function for the input space and morphism

$$A_1 = F \longleftrightarrow \begin{Bmatrix} 00 \\ 11 \end{Bmatrix}, \quad A_2 = F \longleftrightarrow \begin{Bmatrix} 00 \\ 11 \end{Bmatrix}.$$

Then

$$\begin{aligned} H &= B_1^1 + B_2^1 + B_1^2 B_2^2 + 1 \\ &= (B_1^1)' + B_2^1 + B_1^2 B_2^2 \ . \\ &= A_1 + B_2^1 + B_1^2 B_2^2 \ . \end{aligned}$$

As A_1, B_2^1, B_1^2, and B_2^2 are treated as different variables, no further reduction is possible. The testable morphic Boolean structure is shown in Figure 10.

VII. CONCLUSIONS

It is important to know, in the initiation of recovery processes for an ultra-reliable computer, whether a unit being checked has failed functionally, and this has been detected, or if the circuits being used to monitor the self-testing checker outputs have failed and the functional capabilities of the checked unit are unimpaired. This paper has shown how the additional circuitry used to monitor self-testing checker outputs may, itself, be realized in self-testing form. The outputs of such circuitry are then directly interpretable by the computer recovery software to initiate the recovery process. This paper has shown how self-testing acyclic circuitry may be designed by initially defining the desired Boolean function in the conventional sense then using a morphism to relate the original variables to self-testing variables and generalized morphic operators to define a morphic function. This function is implemented by using a new universal set of self-testing operators blocks and interconnecting these blocks according to an Interconnection Algorithm which will insure that the resultant circuit will be self-testing and self-checking. The universal set of blocks defined were shown to be self-testing and implementable by modest amounts of ordinary logic gates. The algorithm, by its utilization in several examples, is seen to be easily applied. Hence, it is important to note that the results of this paper provide techniques for the use of self-testing dynamic checker outputs in an ultra-reliable computer in a simple, economic fashion, easily interfacing with normal recovery processes.

REFERENCES

[1] J. von Neumann, *Theory of Self-Reproducing Automata*, University of Illinois Press, Urbana and London (1960).

[2] W. C. Carter and P. R. Schneider, "Design of Dynamically-Checked Computers," *Proc. IFIPS Conf.*, Edinburgh, Scotland, 878–883 (August 1968).

[3] A. Avizienis, "Design of Fault-Tolerant Computers," *Proc. AFIPS Conf.*, FJCC, 733–743 (1967).

[4] W. C. Carter et al., "A Theory of Design of Fault-Tolerant Computers Using Standby Sparing," *Proc. Int. Symp. Fault-Tolerant Computing*, Pasadena, California (March 1–3, 1971).

[5] W. C. Carter et al., "Logic Design for Dynamic and Interactive Recovery," *Proc. Int. Symp. Fault-Tolerant Computing*, Pasadena, California (March 1–3, 1971).

[6] W. C. Carter, D. C. Jessep, and A. B. Wadia, "Error-Free Decoding for Failure-Tolerant Memories," *Proc. IEEE Int. Computer Group Conf.*, 229–239 (June 1970).

[7] W. C. Carter, A. B. Wadia, and D. C. Jessep, "Computer Error Control By Testable Morphic Boolean Functions," IBM Research Report RC-3099 (to be published).

[8] S. MacLane and G. Birkhoff, *Algebra* (New York: MacMillan, 1967).

[9] A. B. Wadia, W. C. Carter, and P. R. Schneider, "Design of Modules with High Failure Detection Ability for a Self-Repairing Environment," IBM Research Report RC-3100 (November 12, 1970).

[10] J. P. Roth, W. G. Bouricius, and P. R. Schneider, "Programmed Algorithm to Computer Tests to Detect and Distinguish Between Failures in Logic Circuits," *IEEE Trans. Electr. Comput.*, **16**, No. 5, 567–580 (October 1967).

[11] A. D. Falkoff and K. E. Iverson, "APL/360: User's Manual," IBM Research Center, Yorktown Heights, New York (1968).

FAULT EQUIVALENCE IN SEQUENTIAL MACHINES

R. Boute and E. J. McCluskey

Digital Systems Laboratory, Departments of Computer Science and Electrical Engineering, Stanford University, Stanford, CA

This paper is concerned with the relationships among faults as they affect sequential machine behavior. Of particular interest are equivalence and dominance relations.

It is shown that for output faults (i.e., faults that do not affect state behavior), fault equivalence is related to the existence of an automorphism of the state table. For the same class of faults, the relation between dominance and equivalence is considered and some properties are pointed out. Another class of possible faults is also considered, namely, memory faults (i.e., faults in the logic feedback lines). These clearly affect the state behavior of the machine, and their influence on machine properties, such as being strongly connected, is discussed. It is proven that there exist classes of machines for which this property of being strongly connected is destroyed by every possible single fault. Further results on both memory and output faults are also presented.

I. INTRODUCTION

The increasing complexity of digital systems has necessitated a more systematic approach in designing adequate test procedures than the heuristic or intuitive methods that prevailed in the early days of computer technology.

For sequential machines, the first "testing" was done by Moore [1] although his primary interest was in analyzing the state behavior of a machine rather than in looking for possible faults. Seshu and Freeman [2, 13] designed test sequences to detect faults, while looking at the possible ways in which a given circuit can be affected by a fault. Hennie [3] also developed fault detecting methods, but the test sequences were designed without the extra information obtainable from an investigation of the influence of faults from a given fault set on the machine: The sequences verify whether or not the machine performs its given task. Thus this method links up with Moore's approach.

A systematic procedure, guaranteeing optimal test sequences for sequential machines, is given by Poage and McCluskey [4]. In this paper, all the information concerning the faults that is available is used, as in the Seshu and Freeman method, but the procedure used does not suffer from the disadvantages of local optimization. It is also in the work of Poage and McCluskey that the idea of "dominance" for faults in sequential circuits is introduced, in analogy with dominance of rows and columns in prime implicant tables [5].

Presented at the Symposium on Computers and Automata
Polytechnic Institute of Brooklyn, April 13–15, 1971.

While studying the behavior of combinational circuits, it was soon realized that relations existed between faults. Investigations on equivalence relations have been done by Clegg and McCluskey [6, 7] and Schertz [8, 9]. Roughly speaking, two faults are said to be equivalent iff they have the same effect on the circuit according to some suitable criterion, different criteria giving rise to different equivalence relations. Perhaps the most basic type of equivalence is *functional equivalence*: Two faults are functionally equivalent if they give rise to the same set of circuit output functions. For most of the definitions used, equivalence always implies functional equivalence. This means that the corresponding partitions are refinements of the partition induced by functional equivalence, and thus all faults in the same equivalence class yield the same input/output behavior. The importance of this observation becomes clear from the fact that fault detecting sets have to be designed only for as many faults as there are equivalence classes, instead of for each element of the specified fault set separately.

Another kind of relation exists in combinational circuits, namely dominance. A fault F_1 dominates a fault F_2 iff it can be detected by every test for F_2. This also will reduce the number of faults that have to be examined separately. Mei [10] has shown that dominance gives rise to drastic reductions in the number of faults which must be considered when the circuit satisfies some general conditions.

Similar phenomena also exist in sequential machines, and it is the main objective of this paper to point out those similarities. Further, some specific aspects of faults in sequential machines that have no counterpart in combinational circuits are also examined, such as the properties of output faults and the influence of memory faults on the strong-connectedness of the machine. This last aspect might seem rather loosely related to equivalence and dominance, but the results derived will show the desirability of having reset circuitry in case we want to compare faulty machines with each other.

The considerations on dominance and equivalence in this paper have a dual purpose: First, the simplification of the task of designing test sequences by reducing the number of faults that need to be considered separately; and second, the gaining of a better understanding of the phenomena that affect the behavior of a machine in the presence of faults.

In what follows, we first introduce the notation used throughout this paper. Subsequently, the concepts of equivalence and dominance in sequential and combinational circuits are clearly defined and their significance explained. Also, the concept of "reset" is introduced in order to pin down these ideas more closely. Then we consider a particular class of faults, namely, output faults (i.e., those that do not affect the state behavior) and the existence of an equivalence relation is shown to depend on the existence of a state-table automorphism.

The relationships between dominance and equivalence are explored for combinational circuits and then for sequential circuits, thus enabling us to point out some similarities between the two cases. It will become clear at this point that the presence of reset circuitry makes the setting up of a basis for comparing sequential machines much easier.

Finally, the problem of memory faults will be considered and we will show that there exist classes of strongly connected machines for which every single fault destroys this property. The main result of this section implies in fact that reset circuitry is important if we want to compare two faulty machines for all possible initial states. We conclude then with some suggestions on future research.

II. NOTATION

A. Combinational Circuits

Let C be a combinational circuit realizing a mapping $\Phi\colon \sigma^n \longrightarrow \sigma^m$, where σ is a finite nonempty set of symbols. In most applications, $\sigma = \{0, 1\}$ and Φ is then a Boolean function.

The number of input leads is n and the number of output leads is m. Input leads are denoted by x_i; output leads by y_i; see for example Figure 1(a).

$$\Phi(x_1, x_2, x_3, \cdots, x_n) = \langle y_1, y_2, y_3, \cdots, y_n \rangle \quad .$$

Here we write ( ) instead of (⟨ ⟩) for simplicity, but otherwise we will always use angle brackets ⟨ ⟩ to denote ordered n-tuples.

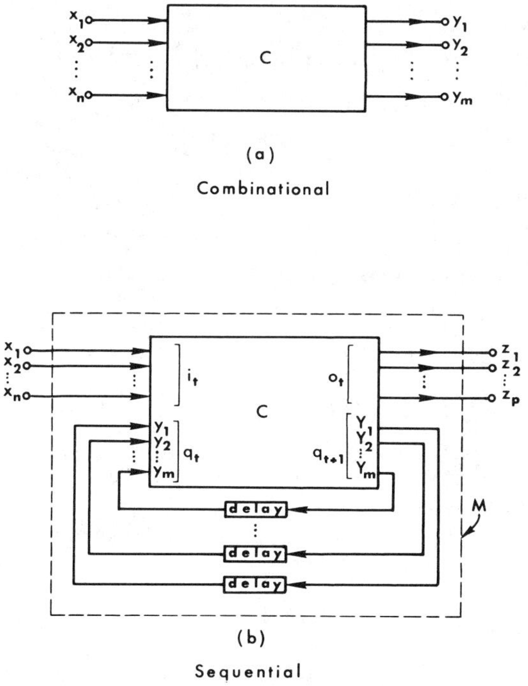

Fig. 1. Representation of a combinational circuit C and a sequential machine M.

B. Sequential Machines

A sequential machine M is a 5-tuple

$$M = \langle I, O, Q, \delta, \lambda \rangle , \tag{1}$$

where: I = a finite nonempty set of inputs,
O = a finite nonempty set of outputs,
Q = a finite nonempty set of states,
δ = the next-state function: $\delta: Q \times I \longrightarrow Q$, defined by $\delta: \langle q_t, i_t \rangle \longmapsto q_{t+1}$, the subscript t standing for "at time t,"
λ = the output function:

(a) For a Moore machine, $\lambda: Q \longrightarrow O$, defined by $\lambda: q_t \longmapsto o_t$
(b) For a Mealy machine, $\lambda: Q \times I \longrightarrow O$, defined by $\lambda: \langle q_t, i_t \rangle \longmapsto o_t$.

Following Hartmanis and Stearns [11], we define now

I^+ = the set of all finite input sequences of nonzero length consisting of symbols from I,

$I^* = I^+ \cup \{\Lambda\}$ where Λ is the empty sequence.

Elements of I^+ or I^* will be denoted by $\bar{x}$. We extend δ to $Q \times I^*$ in the following recursive way:

(1) $\delta(q, \Lambda) = q \;\; \forall q \in Q$
(2) $\delta(q, \bar{x}x) = \delta[\delta(q, \bar{x}), x]$, where $q \in Q$, $x \in I$, $\bar{x} \in I^*$.

We also define $\bar{\lambda}$ as follows. Let $q \in Q$, $x \in I$, $\bar{x} \in I^*$ (or I^+), then:

(a) For a Moore machine, $\bar{\lambda}: Q \times I^* \longrightarrow I^+$, defined by $\bar{\lambda}(q, \Lambda) = \lambda(q)$, and $\bar{\lambda}(q, \bar{x}x) = \bar{\lambda}(q, \bar{x}) \cdot \lambda[\delta(q, \bar{x}x)]$
(b) For a Mealy machine, $\bar{\lambda}: Q \times I^+ \longrightarrow I^+$, defined by $\bar{\lambda}(q, x) = \lambda(q, x)$, and $\bar{\lambda}(q, \bar{x}x) = \bar{\lambda}(q, \bar{x}) \cdot \lambda[\delta(q, \bar{x}), x]$.

One of the possible realizations is shown in Figure 1(b).

$$Q = \sigma^m = \{q \mid q = \langle y_1, y_2, y_3, \cdots, y_m \rangle, \; y_i \in \sigma\} , \tag{2a}$$

$$I = \sigma_I^n = \{i \mid i = \langle x_1, x_2, x_3, \cdots, x_n \rangle, \; x_j \in \sigma_I\} , \tag{2b}$$

$$O = \sigma_O^p = \{o \mid o = \langle z_1, z_2, z_3, \cdots, z_p \rangle, \; z_k \in \sigma_O\} . \tag{2c}$$

Usually one has: $\sigma_I = \sigma = \sigma_O = \{0, 1\}$, but in general $\sigma_{..}$ can be any set of symbols (finite and nonempty). Except when explicitly mentioned, such as will be the case for the section on memory faults, we will think about the machine as the abstract device specified by Eq. (1), without referring to the representation of Figure 1(b).

C. Faults

In what follows we will only consider permanent faults. By this we mean that their effect on machine behavior does not change during or in between tests. It will also be assumed that a fault in a combinational network does not transform the network into a sequential circuit. No other restrictions on the faults are assumed unless they are explicitly stated.

We will use the notation $F(C)$ for the combinational circuit C affected by a fault F, and similarly $F(M)$ for a sequential machine M with fault F. The use of the notation for F as if it were a function can be justified as follows. If we consider interconnections between circuit elements also as "components," then the domain of F is the set of all machines that have a specified subset of their components in common. The mapping F is then defined by describing the way in which F affects the components of that common subset. Note that this applies to a wide variety of faults, including bridging faults. However, we will only use this approach for the case of memory faults, where the subset mentioned above will be clearly specified. Another point of view can be that the domain contains only a single machine (C or M).

The absence of a fault is denoted by e, called the "empty fault." So, for example, $e(C) = C$ and $e(M) = M$.

If Φ is the function realized by C, then Φ_F is the one realized by $F(C)$. The same convention is used for sequential machines,

$$\text{if } M = \langle I, O, Q, \delta, \lambda \rangle ,$$

then

$$F(M) = \langle I, O, Q_F, \delta_F, \lambda_F \rangle .$$

There is no advantage gained by letting F affect I and O, but for Q it will become conceptually useful.

Finally, the set of all faults that will be considered for a given machine or class of machines (circuits) will be denoted by $\mathcal{F}$. $\mathcal{F}$ includes e, by convention.

D. Classes of Faults

In general, a fault F in a sequential machine can affect the next-state function δ as well as the output function λ. For many realizations, however, it is reasonable to consider subclasses of faults that affect either δ or λ, but not both. This is especially true for cases in which δ and λ are realized by separate circuits. Thus, we can consider as special subclasses:

Output Faults

A fault F is said to be an "output fault" for a machine M iff $Q_F = Q$ and $\delta_F = \delta$. The set of all output faults for a machine M will be denoted by $\mathcal{F}_\lambda$.

Next-State Faults

A fault F is a next-state fault for a machine M iff $\delta_F \neq \delta$, while the output circuitry is unaffected. The set of all next-state faults for a given machine is denoted by $\mathcal{F}_\delta$. A further subclass of next-state faults are the memory faults described next.

Memory Faults

We consider the set $\mathcal{M}_m$ of all machines with m delay elements and a given alphabet σ (see Figure 1(b)). For the set of feedback lines $L_m = \{\ell_i \mid i = 1, 2, 3, \cdots, m\}$ we define a *stuck-at fault* F as a map

$$F: L_m \longrightarrow \sigma \cup \{N\} \ , \tag{3}$$

assigning to each line a stuck-at value or the status N ("normal"). We denote by $\mathcal{F}_Q$ the set of all such faults.

$[|\mathcal{F}_Q| = (|\sigma| + 1)^m]$. It will become clear at a later stage how this definition is made compatible with the notation $F(M)$. We will also define $T_F = \{k \mid F(\ell_k) \neq N\}$.

III. DEFINITIONS

A. Combinational Circuits

A *detection set* for a fault F is a subset of the set of inputs defined by

$$S_F = \{ \langle x_1, x_2, x_3, \cdots, x_n \rangle \mid \Phi_F(x_i, x_j, x_k, \cdots, x_n) \neq \Phi_e(x_1, x_2, x_3, \cdots, x_n)\} \ (S_F \subseteq \{0,1\}^n) \ .$$

A combinational circuit is *nonredundant* iff $S_F \neq \phi \ \forall \ F \in \mathcal{F} - \{e\}$. This refers to a well-specified class of faults $\mathcal{F}$.

A fault F_1 *dominates* a fault F_2 iff $S_{F_1} \supseteq S_{F_2}$. Thus every test detecting F_2 also detects F_1. Notation used: $F_1 \geq F_2$.

Two faults F_1 and F_2 are *functionally equivalent,* written $F_1 \sim F_2$, or briefly *equivalent* iff

$$\Phi_{F_1}(x) = \Phi_{F_2}(x) \ \forall \ x \in \{0,1\}^n \ .$$

Two faults F_1 and F_2 are *detection equivalent,* written $F_1 \simeq F_2$, iff $S_{F_1} = S_{F_2}$.

B. Sequential Machines

Two machines M_1 and M_2 are *equivalent* iff

$$\forall \, q_1 \in Q_1 \ (\text{state set of } M_1) \ \exists \ q_2 \in Q_2$$

such that

$$\bar{\lambda}_1(q_1, \bar{x}) = \bar{\lambda}_2(q_2, \bar{x}) \ \forall \ \bar{x} \in I^* \ \text{or} \ I^+ \ ,$$

and vice versa.

Two faults F_1 and F_2 in a sequential machine M are *equivalent* iff $F_1(M)$ and $F_2(M)$ are equivalent.

C. Resets

Let $M = \langle I, O, Q, \delta, \lambda \rangle$ be a sequential machine with a reset circuit. By this we mean an extra set of input terminals on which we can apply inputs from a given set J. The circuit is constructed in such a way that for some subset of J, denoted by I_R (the "*reset inputs*"), there exists a map ρ: $I_R \longrightarrow Q$ with the following property: If any $i \in I_R$ is applied to the reset terminals, the machine goes to state $\rho(i)$, no matter what the state was before. For practical reasons we require that I_R be a proper subset of J and that all $i \in J - I_R$ remain without effect on the machine. Indeed, the machine should be able to distinguish resets from normal operation mode. One can also use the elements of $J - I_R$ to put the machine in other modes ("partial resets," for example, where only some of the y_i in $q = \langle y_1, y_2, y_3, \cdots, y_m \rangle$ are reset), but we will not exploit this possibility at this point, although it can result in more flexible test sequence design.

Note that this approach, where we consider resets as an extra feature, is only taken for convenience. Indeed, these extra circuits can be incorporated in the usual model for a sequential machine by redefining the machine $M = \langle I, O, Q, \delta, \lambda \rangle$ as $M = \langle I', O, Q, \delta', \lambda' \rangle$ where $I' = I \times J$ (cartesian product)

$$\delta'(q, \langle i, j \rangle) = \begin{cases} \delta(q, i), & \text{if } j \notin I_R \ , \\ \rho(j), & \text{if } j \in I_R \ , \end{cases}$$

$$\lambda'(q, \langle i, j \rangle) = \begin{cases} \lambda(q, i), & \text{if } j \notin I_R \ , \\ \text{undefined}, & \text{if } j \in I_R \ . \end{cases}$$

Conversely, if a machine M has already inputs i such that $\delta(q, i) = \delta(q', i) \ \forall \ q, q' \in Q$, then we can define the set I_R as being the set of elements with this property. In this case $I - I_R$ is the set of "normal" machine inputs.

This way the two points of view can be considered as equivalent.

Example. Figure 2 represents a sequential machine with a reset circuit con-

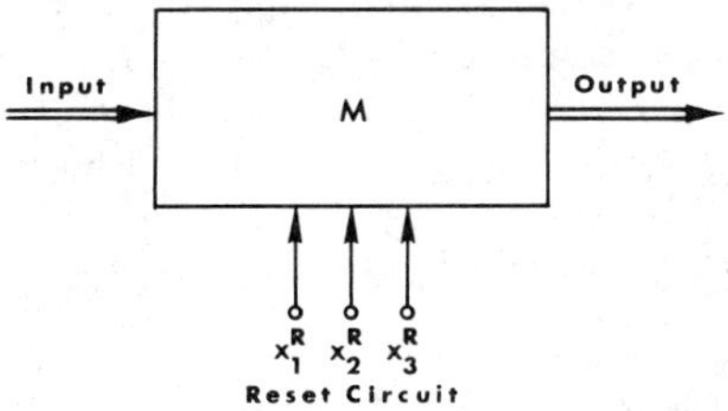

Fig. 2. A sequential machine with a reset circuit.

sisting of three extra inputs: x_1^R, x_2^R, x_3^R, where $x_i^R \in \{0, 1\}$. Thus $J = \{0, 1\}^3$. We define I_R arbitrarily as the set

$$I_R = \{ \langle x_1^R, x_2^R, 1 \rangle \mid x_i^R \in \{0, 1\} \} \subset J \ .$$

Physically, this means that we consider x_3^R as the enable/disable line for the reset circuitry.

We now can specify ρ, for example, as follows

$$\forall \ \langle x_1^R, x_2^R, 1 \rangle = i \in I_R \ ,$$
$$\rho(i) = \langle x_1^R + x_2^R, \ x_2^R, \ x_1^R \rangle \in Q \ .$$

This results in Table I

TABLE I.

RESET INPUT	RESET STATE
0 0 1	0 0 0
0 1 1	1 1 0
1 0 1	1 0 1
1 1 1	1 1 1

If the elements of I are of the form $\langle x_1, x_2, x_3, \cdots, x_n \rangle$, we can denote those of I' by $\langle x_1, x_2, x_3, \cdots, x_n, x_1^R, x_2^R, x_3^R \rangle$ and define

$$\delta'(q, \langle x_1, x_2, x_3, \cdots, x_n, x_1^R, x_2^R, x_3^R \rangle) = \begin{cases} \delta(q, \langle x_1, x_2, x_3, \cdots, x_n \rangle), & \text{if } x_3^R = 0 , \\ \rho(x_1^R, x_2^R, x_3^R), & \text{if } x_3^R = 1 . \end{cases}$$

D. Faults and the Reset Circuitry

Suppose we have a machine with reset as described above, but with a fault F.

This fault F may act in such a way that upon application of $i \in I_R$, the new state also depends on the previous one. For simplicity, we will assume such faults do not occur;* i.e., in the faulty machine M_F we still have a map ρ_F: $I_R \longrightarrow Q_F$ that determines $\rho_F(i)$ as the state after the application of an input $i \in I_R$.

Although possibly ρ_F differs from ρ, we will say that, in such cases, the reset is *unaffected* by the fault F. This simply means that, if we know the fault, we also know the state of the machine after applying any $i \in I_R$.

This becomes important in the following definition: A *reset test sequence* for a fault F is a sequence $\bar{x} \in I^+$ or I^* preceded by a reset input $i \in I_R$, such that

$$\bar{\lambda}[\rho(i), \bar{x}] \neq \bar{\lambda}_F[\rho_F(i), \bar{x}] .$$

A fault F_1 *dominates* a fault F_2 iff every reset test sequence for F_2 is also a reset test sequence for F_1 (i.e., $S_{F_1} \supseteq S_{F_2}$ where $S_F = \{\bar{x} \mid \bar{x}$ is a reset test sequence for $F\}$).

Single reset machines are machines where $|I_R| = 1$.

A machine M_1 is *reset equivalent* to M_2 (both same type) iff:

(1) $I_{R_1} = I_{R_2}$, $I_1 = I_2$
(2) For all $i \in I_R$ and $\bar{x} \in I^+$ or I^*, we have

$$\bar{\lambda}_1[\rho_1(i), \bar{x}] = \bar{\lambda}_2[\rho_2(i), \bar{x}] .$$

A fault F_1 is *reset equivalent* to F_2 ($F_1 \sim F_2$) iff M_{F_1} is reset equivalent to M_{F_2}.

A fault F_1 is *detection equivalent* to F_2 iff $S_{F_1} = S_{F_2}$.

*In the case of stuck-at faults, this assumption is very reasonable, except for such cases as x_3^R stuck at 0 in the example just discussed.

IV. EQUIVALENCE OF OUTPUT FAULTS IN SEQUENTIAL MACHINES

DEFINITION. *An output function* λ *is nontrivial iff* $\exists\, q_1, q_2 \in Q$ *and* $i_1, i_2 \in I$ such that $\lambda(q_1, i_1) \neq \lambda(q_2, i_2)$, *or if* $|Q \times I| = 1$ *(i.e., don't blame* λ *if* M *is trivial).*

LEMMA. *Given* λ_1 *and* λ_2, *both defined on* $Q \times I$, *and* $\lambda_1 \neq \lambda_2$. *Then, in case* $\exists\, q_1, i_1$ *and* q_2, i_2 *such that* $\lambda_1(q_1, i_1) = \lambda_2(q_2, i_2)$, *at least one of them is nontrivial.*

Proof. Suppose $\lambda_1(q_1, i_1) = \lambda_1(q, i)\ \forall\, q, i$ (i.e. , λ_1 trivial). Since $\lambda_1 \neq \lambda_2\ \exists\, q_3, i_3 \ni \lambda_1(q_3, i_3) \neq \lambda_2(q_3, i_3)$. So $\lambda_2(q_2, i_2) = \lambda_1(q_1, i_1) = \lambda_1(q_3, i_3) \neq \lambda_2(q_3, i_3)$; i.e., $\lambda_2(q_2, i_2) \neq \lambda_2(q_3, i_3)$, and λ_2 is nontrivial. Q.E.D.

For the remainder of this section, let F_1 and F_2 be output faults for a machine M, and in the interest of simplicity, let λ_{F_1} and λ_{F_2} be denoted by λ_1 and λ_2, respectively.

THEOREM. *If* $F_1(M)$ *and* $F_2(M)$ *are equivalent and* $\lambda_{F_1} \neq \lambda_{F_2}$, *then both* λ_{F_1} *and* λ_{F_2} *are nontrivial.*

Proof. Let $q_1, q_2, q_3, q_4 \in Q$. Since $F_1(M)$ and $F_2(M)$ are equivalent, $\forall\, q_1\ \exists\, q_2$ (and $\forall\, q_2\ \exists\, q_1$), such that $\bar{\lambda}_1(q_1, \bar{x}) = \bar{\lambda}_2(q_2, \bar{x})\ \forall\, \bar{x} \in I^*$ (or I^+). Thus, $\exists\, q_1$ and q_2 such that $\lambda_1(q_1, i) = \lambda_2(q_2, i)\ \forall\, i \in I$ and $\exists\, q_1$ and q_2, and $\exists\, i_1$, $i_2 \in I$ such that $\lambda_1(q_1, i_1) = \lambda_2(q_2, i_2)$ (take simply $i_1 = i_2 = i$).

According to the previous lemma, one or both output functions is nontrivial, say, $\lambda_1(q_3, i_3) \neq \lambda_1(q_4, i_4)$. But since $F_1(M)$ and $F_2(M)$ are equivalent: $\exists\, q_3', q_4'$ such that $\lambda_2(q_3', i_3) = \lambda_1(q_3, i_3)$ and $\lambda_2(q_4', i_4) = \lambda_1(q_4, i_4)$. So $\lambda_2(q_3', i_3) \neq \lambda_2(q_4', i_4)$ and λ_2 is also nontrivial. Q.E.D.

Trivial λ_i are uninteresting since they make all states of $F_i(M)$ equivalent and don't reveal anything about the state transitions in the machine. Therefore, the above theorem is interesting because it assures us that no trivial λ_i exist in the conditions specified.

A. State Table Automorphisms and Output Faults

DEFINITION. *A state table automorphism for a machine* M *is a bijective map* φ: $Q \longrightarrow Q$ *such that* $\delta[\varphi(q), i] = \varphi[\delta(q, i)]$ *for all* $q \in Q$, $i \in I$.

More general definitions such as Φ: $Q \times I \longrightarrow Q \times I$, etc., are possible, but we will not consider them here. See also [14–18].

The trivial automorphism ($\varphi = 1$) always exists.

THEOREM. *Let* F_1 *and* F_2 *be equivalent. Then* $F_1(M)$ *and* $F_2(M)$ *are equivalent (by definition), and if* $F_1(M)$ *is reduced then*:

(1) $F_2(M)$ *is reduced*
(2) $\exists$ *is a uniquely defined state table automorphism* φ
(3) φ *is nontrivial if* $\lambda_1 \neq \lambda_2$.

Remark. By "uniquely defined" we mean "uniquely specified" by λ_1 and λ_2, not necessarily that the automorphism itself is unique for the given M.

Proof. Define a relation

$$q R q' \text{ iff } [\bar{\lambda}_1(q, \bar{x}) = \lambda_2(q', \bar{x})\ \forall\, \bar{x} \in I^+ \text{ or } I^*] \ , \tag{4}$$

Now define $S(q)$ as the set $\{q' \in Q \mid qRq'\}$:

(a) Because of machine equivalence: $\forall q \in Q \ \exists \ q' \in Q$ such that qRq', i.e., $S(q) \neq \phi \ \forall q$

(b) Further, suppose $q' \in S(q_i) \cap S(q_j)$, i.e., $q_i Rq'$, $q_j Rq'$, then $\bar{\lambda}_1(q_i, \bar{x}) = \bar{\lambda}_2(q', \bar{x}) = \bar{\lambda}_1(q_j, \bar{x}) \ \forall \ \bar{x} \in I^+$ or I^*. But this implies, since $F_1(M)$ is reduced, $q_i = q_j$. So $q_i \neq q_j \Longrightarrow S(q_i) \cap S(q_j) = \phi$.

This implies, for an N-state machine $\left| \bigcup_{i=1}^{N} S(q_i) \right| = \sum_{i=1}^{N} |S(q_i)|$ with $|S(q_i)| \geq 1$

because of (a). Since $\bigcup_{l=1}^{N} S(q_1) \subseteq Q$ we obtain $\sum_{l=1}^{N} |S(q_1)| \leq N$ and conclude

$|S(q_i)| = 1$. Therefore R is a function which we denote by $\varphi: Q \longrightarrow Q$. Further

$\left| \bigcup_{i=1}^{N} S(q_i) \right| = N$ implies that φ is surjective, and since the range and the domain

are the same set, bijective. Thus $\forall q \in Q$ one can write $qR\varphi(q)$.

(1) Take $q_1' \neq q_2'$ then $\varphi^{-1}(q_1') \neq \varphi^{-1}(q_2')$ (bijective φ) and $\bar{\lambda}_1[\varphi^{-1}(q_1'), \bar{x}] \neq \bar{\lambda}_1[\varphi^{-1}(q_2'), \bar{x}]$ for some $\bar{x}$ because $F_1(M)$ is reduced. This implies also $\bar{\lambda}_2(q_1', \bar{x}) \neq \bar{\lambda}_2(q_2', \bar{x})$ by definition of φ. So $F_2(M)$ is reduced

(2) The relation R and thus φ is uniquely defined. We have only to prove now φ is an automorphism. Take any $q \in Q$, then the definition of φ implies

$$\bar{\lambda}_1(q, x\bar{x}) = \bar{\lambda}_2[\varphi(q), x\bar{x}) \ \forall x \in I \text{ and } \bar{x} \in I^+ \text{ or } I^* ,$$

$$\bar{\lambda}_1[\delta(q, x), \bar{x}] = \bar{\lambda}_2\{\delta[\varphi(q), x], \bar{x}\} \ \forall x \in I \text{ and } \bar{x} \in I^+ \text{ or } I^* ,$$

i.e., $\delta(q, x) R \delta[\varphi(q), x] \ \forall x \in I$, and since R defines φ uniquely (i.e., $\forall q \in Q \ \exists$ only one $q' \in Q$ such that qRq', namely $q' = \varphi(q)$), we get $\delta[\varphi(q), x] = \varphi[\delta(q, x)] = \varphi[\delta(q, x)] \ \forall x \in I$, and since q was arbitrarily chosen, also $\forall q \in Q$

(3) If $\lambda_1 \neq \lambda_2$, then $\exists \ q, i \in Q, I$ such that $\lambda_1(q, i) \neq \lambda_2(q, i)$ i.e., $\varphi(q) \neq q$. is nontrivial. Note that $\lambda_1 \neq \lambda_2 \Longrightarrow \begin{cases} \lambda_1 \text{ and } \lambda_2 \text{ nontrivial} , \\ \varphi \text{ nontrivial} . \end{cases}$ Q.E.D.

Application of the Theorem

As will become clear from the considerations below, most machines do *not* have a nontrivial state-table automorphism. For such a machine M without nontrivial state-table automorphisms, every fault $F \in \mathfrak{F}_\lambda$ with the property that $F(M)$ is reduced will fall in a separate equivalence class of its own. In most cases, this will necessitate separate testing for each of these faults, especially when no dominance relations exist.

B. The Automorphisms of a State Table

The general problem of finding all automorphisms of a given state table is as yet unsolved. The same holds for the equivalent task of finding the automorphisms of a graph, which is an important problem in organic chemistry and many other areas.

Nevertheless, several heuristic approaches are possible. In particular, for state tables that are not too large, inspection "by eye" usually reveals very quickly the nonexistence of a nontrivial automorphism, if such is the case.

A study of the properties of state table automorphisms may simplify the heuristic approach considerably, since they show what one should look for first, while searching for automorphisms.

Weeg, Fleck, and Barnes have done a considerable amount of work in the area of automorphisms of machines [14–17].

Let us point out some of the facts that are relevant to this problem.

Since a state-table automorphism φ implies a bijective mapping from the state set Q onto itself, it is in fact a permutation on Q.

LEMMA. *The set A_M of all state-table automorphisms for a machine M with N states forms a subgroup of S_N (under composition).*

Proof. Closure, identity, inverses are easily verified, and the remark above implies that $A \subseteq S_N$. Q.E.D.

LEMMA. *If M is strongly connected, then A_M is a group of regular permutations. By this we mean: the cycles of every permutation have equal length.*

Proof. Let q and q' be two arbitrary elements of Q, and φ a state-table automorphism. Then we can find an input sequence $\bar{x} \in I^*$ such that $q' = \bar{\delta}(q, \bar{x})$. Suppose k is the length of the cycle of φ that contains q where φ is considered as a permutation on Q written in cycle notation. Then $\varphi^k(q) = q$ and $\varphi^k(q') = \varphi^k[\delta(q, \bar{x})] = \delta[\varphi^k(q), \bar{x}] = \delta(q, \bar{x}) = q'$, as can be easily seen from the definition of δ. Therefore, the length k' of the cycle containing q' satisfies $k' \leq k$. Similarly, one shows $k \leq k'$ and thus $k' = k$. Q.E.D.

LEMMA. *If M is strongly connected and $\tau \in A_M$, then giving $\tau(q_0)$ for any $q_0 \in Q$ specifies τ completely.*

Proof. By assumption, any $q \in Q$ can be written as $q = \delta(q_0, \bar{x})$ for some $\bar{x} \in I^*$. Therefore $\tau(q) = \tau[\delta(q_0, \bar{x})] = \delta[\tau(q_0), \bar{x}]$. Q.E.D.

The above lemmas can be found, under a slightly different form, in the references mentioned. Let us now introduce some lemmas that can be used in the heuristic approach for finding state table automorphisms.

LEMMA. *Consider a state machine $M = \langle I, Q, \delta \rangle$ and let $I = I_1 \cup I_2 \cup I_3 \cup \cdots \cup I_k$. If we define $M_j = \langle I_j, Q, \delta \mid Q \times I_j \rangle$, then the automorphism group A_M is given by $A_M = A_{M_1} \cap A_{M_2} \cap A_{M_3} \cap \cdots \cap A_{M_k}$.*

Proof. Obvious. Q.E.D.

This last lemma is very important, since it allows us to consider separate columns of the state table ($I_j = \{i_j\}$) and thus reduces the problem of finding the automorphism group of the state table to finding the group for each single column separately, and then taking the intersection.

LEMMA. *If $i \in I$ is a permutation input, i.e., the map π_i: $Q \longrightarrow Q$, defined by $\pi_i(q) = \delta(q, i)$ is bijective, then π is an automorphism for the ith column of the state table which represents the state machine $\langle \{i\}, Q, \delta|_{Q\times \{i\}} \rangle$.*

Proof. $\delta(q, i) = \pi_i(q)$ for all q in Q. Thus, $\delta[\pi_i(q), i] = \pi_i[\pi_i(q)] = \pi_i[\delta(q, i)]$ for all q in Q. Q.E.D.

COROLLARY. *If the permutation π_i in the above lemma has a single cycle, then the automorphism group for the ith column is the cyclic group generated by π.*

Proof. For any q_0, $q \in Q$ we can write $q = \pi^k(q_0)$ for some $k \in N$ (non-negative numbers). Thus, the machine is strongly connected by $q = \delta(q_0, i^k)$, and any arbitrary τ of the state table is then completely specified by $\tau(q_0)$. Now the powers π^k of π assign to q_0 successively all elements q of Q if k ranges over $0, 1, 2, \cdots, |Q| - 1$. Therefore τ must be one of these powers. Q.E.D.

Remark. In case π is not a single cycle, the situation is more complicated. Let us only note here that elements of a given cycle can be mapped to elements of another cycle only in case the cycles have the same length.

LEMMA. *If, in a given column of the state table, an element q_k occurs with multiplicity m_k, and there exists an automorphism that maps q_k into q_ℓ, we must have $m_k = m_\ell$.*

Proof. Obvious. Q.E.D.

Application to Heuristics

The two main cases considered are mutually exclusive: either an input i is a permutation input, or in the corresponding column some q_k must occur with multiplicity $m_k > 1$. Note further the duality between length of a cycle and multiplicity of a state.

The lemmas above aid very much in a fast visual check for automorphisms. Needless to say, they can also be incorporated in algorithms,

Finally, it is clear that state tables with automorphisms are the exception rather than the rule.

C. Examples of Output Equivalent Faults

(1) Consider a machine M with output faults F_1 and F_2 yielding the machines $F_1(M)$ and $F_2(M)$ shown below.

$F_1(M)$ — $\delta(q, i), \lambda_1(q, i)$

q	0	1
A	D, 0	J, 0
B	D, 0	K, 1
C	A, 1	L, 1
D	L, 1	H, 0
E	C, 0	D, 0
F	E, 0	B, 1
G	E, 1	A, 1
H	I, 1	E, 0
I	G, 1	C, 0
J	H, 0	G, 0
K	H, 1	F, 0
L	J, 0	I, 1

$F_2(M)$ — $\delta(q, i), \lambda_2(q, i)$

q	0	1
A	D, 0	J, 0
B	D, 1	K, 0
C	A, 0	L, 1
D	L, 1	H, 0
E	C, 1	D, 0
F	E, 0	B, 1
G	E, 0	A, 0
H	I, 0	E, 0
I	G, 1	C, 1
J	H, 1	G, 1
K	H, 0	F, 1
L	J, 1	I, 0

$F_1(M)$ is reduced as can be seen as follows. Consider the equivalence relation defined by

$$q_1 \equiv q_2 (\pi'), \text{ iff } \lambda_1(q_1, x) = \lambda_1(q_2, x) \; \forall x \in I = \{0, 1\} ,$$

then

$$\pi' = \overline{AJE}, \overline{FLB}, \overline{CG}, \overline{HKDI} ,$$

under input

$$\left.\begin{array}{ll} 0 & \overline{DHC}, \overline{EJD}, \overline{AE}, \overline{IHLG} \\ 1 & \overline{JGD}, \overline{BIK}, \overline{LA}, \overline{EFHC} \end{array}\right\} \text{shows next states, grouped as parts of blocks of } \pi'$$

$F_1(M)$ and $F_2(M)$ are equivalent, as can be seen from direct product [19, p. 25]: denote states of $F_2(M)$ with a prime and consider a 24-state machine*

$$\pi = \overline{AG'\,JA'\,EH'}, \overline{FK'\,LC'\,BF'}, \overline{CI'\,GJ'}, \overline{HD'\,KB'\,DE'\,IL'} ,$$

$$\text{input} \begin{cases} 0 & \overline{DE'\,HD'\,CI'}, \overline{EH'\,JA'\,DE'}, \overline{AG'\,EH'}, \overline{IL'\,HD'\,LC'\,GJ'} \\ 1 & \overline{JA'\,GJ'\,DE'}, \overline{BF'\,IL'\,KB'}, \overline{LC'\,AG'}, \overline{EH'\,FK'\,HD'\,GI'} \end{cases}$$

We obtain

$$\{\overline{AG'}\,\overline{JA'}\,\overline{EH'}\,\overline{FK'}\,\overline{LC'}\,\overline{BF'}\,\overline{CI'}\,\overline{GJ'}\,\overline{HD'}\,\overline{KB'}\,\overline{DE'}\,\overline{IL'}\} = \pi_R \,^\dagger$$

This represents the relation R, giving directly the automorphism φ

q	A	B	C	D	E	F	G	H	I	J	K	L
$\varphi(q)$	G	F	I	E	H	K	J	D	L	A	B	C

This is, of course, not the only one, since

$$\delta[\varphi^n(q), i] = \varphi\,\delta[\varphi^{n-1}(q), i] = \cdots = \varphi^n \delta(q, i) ,$$

$\forall q \in Q$, $i \in I$, $n \in Z^+$, but it is uniquely specified by λ_1 and λ_2 as obtained by the above procedure.

(2) Consider the machine M such that

$M_q =$

	0	1
A	A	B
B	A	B

Clearly, there exists no nontrivial automorphisms. According to the theorem, for no reduced $F_i(M)$ does there exist a $F_j(M)$ such that $F_i(M) \equiv F_j(M)$. Consider all reduced $F_i(M)$ possible (write only λ_i):

	0	1
A	0	0
B	0	1_1

	0	1
A	0	1
B	0	0_4

	0	1
A	1	1
B	0	0_7

	0	1
A	1	0
B	0	0_{10}

	0	1
A	0	0
B	1	0_2

	0	1
A	0	1
B	1	0_5

	0	1
A	1	1
B	0	1_8

	0	1
A	1	0
B	0	1_{11}

*The states are ordered in such a way that the partitions with substitution property can be easily recognized.

$^\dagger\pi_R$: see [12, pp. 55–56].

	0	1		0	1		0	1		0	1
A	0	0	A	0	1	A	1	1	A	1	0
B	1	1_3	B	1	1_5	B	1	0_9	B	1	1_{12}

We then obtain for the product machine

$$\pi = \frac{\overline{A_1A_2A_3B_4B_7B_{10}},\ \overline{A_4A_5A_6B_1B_8B_{11}},}{\overline{A_7A_8A_9B_3B_6B_{12}},\ \overline{A_{10}A_{11}A_{12}B_2B_5B_9}},$$

$$\text{input}\begin{cases} 0 & \overline{A_1A_2A_3}\,\overline{A_4}\,\overline{A_7}\,\overline{A_{10}},\ \overline{A_4A_5A_6}\,\overline{A_1}\,\overline{A_8}\,\overline{A_{11}}, \\ & \overline{A_7A_8A_9}\,\overline{A_3}\,\overline{A_6}\,\overline{A_{12}},\ \overline{A_{10}A_{11}A_{12}}\,\overline{A_2}\,\overline{A_5}\,\overline{A_9} \\ 1 & \overline{B_1}\,\overline{B_2}\,\overline{B_3}\,\overline{B_4B_7B_{10}},\ \overline{B_4}\,\overline{B_5}\,\overline{B_6}\,\overline{B_1B_8B_{11}}, \\ & \overline{B_7}\,\overline{B_8}\,\overline{B_9}\,\overline{B_3B_6B_{12}},\ \overline{B_{10}}\,\overline{B_{11}}\,\overline{B_{12}}\,\overline{B_2B_5B_9} \end{cases}$$

$\pi_R = \{\overline{A_1}, \overline{A_2}, \overline{A_3}, \cdots, \overline{B_{12}}\}$. So no two machines are equivalent; there exist not even two equivalent states in product machine.

This last remark illustrates the following.

THEOREM [20]. *If M_1 and M_2 are strongly connected and nonequivalent, then no state in M_1 is equivalent to any state in M_2.*

Proof. Trivial. Q.E.D.

Observe the fact that M is strongly connected in this example.

D. Case where the Faulty Machines Are Not Reduced

ANTITHEOREM. *The theorem does not hold in case $F_1(M)$ is not reduced.*

Proof. The theorem breaks down in part (3). (It is not interesting to consider $\lambda_1 = \lambda_2$ = trivial case, since then state transitions do not influence output.) A nontrivial case is ($\lambda_1 \neq \lambda_2$)

	0	1
A	C, 0	A, 1
B	C, 0	A, 1
C	A, 1	C, 1

$F_1(M)$

	0	1
A	C, 1	A, 1
B	C, 1	A, 1
C	A, 0	C, 1

$F_2(M)$

The machines $F_1(M)$ and $F_2(M)$ are equivalent. This can be seen from the equivalences described by the following pairs of states denoted by $\langle q_1, q_2\rangle$ where q_1 is a state of $F_1(M)$ and q_2 is a state of $F_2(M)$: $\langle A, C\rangle$, $\langle B, C\rangle$, $\langle C, A\rangle$, and $\langle C, B\rangle$. There is no nontrivial automorphism for this machine M. Before we investigate what happens in the case where $F_1(M)$ is not reduced (therefore, $F_2(M)$ is not reduced either), we recall [12]: A partition π on Q has substitution property iff $q_1 \equiv q_2\ (\pi)$ implies that $\delta(q_1, i) \equiv \delta(q_2, i)$ for all i in I. We denote the set of partition blocks by Q_π.

If π is a partition with substitution property, then the *π-image* of M is the state machine $M_\pi = \langle I, Q_\pi, \delta_\pi\rangle$, where, for all $B_\pi \in Q_\pi$

$$\delta_\pi(B_\pi, i) = B'_\pi ,$$

iff

$$\delta(B_\pi, i) \subseteq B'_\pi \quad . \text{ Q.E.D.}$$

THEOREM. *In case a machine M has no two partitions* π_1 and π_2 *with substitution property such that* $\pi_1 \neq \pi_2$ *but* M_{π_1} *is isomorphic to* M_{π_2}, *then the equivalence of two faults* F_1 *and* F_2 *implies the existence of a unique (in the same sense as before) automorphism for the state table of the reduced machine of* $F_1(M)$. *The automorphism is nontrivial in case* $\lambda_{F_1} \neq \lambda_{F_2}$.

Proof. The equivalence between $F_1(M)$ and $F_2(M)$ implies the equivalence of the corresponding reduced machines, denoted by M_1 and M_2, which are, therefore, isomorphic.

The states of the reduced machines are blocks of some partitions π_1 and π_2, both with substitution property. From the assumption, it follows that $\pi_1 = \pi_2 = \pi$ and therefore, M_1 and M_2 must have the same state set Q_π.

Further, $\lambda_{F_1} \neq \lambda_{F_2}$ implies also that the reduced machines have different output functions since they have the same state set Q_π and, for all $q_1, q_2 \in B_\pi \in Q_\pi$, $\delta(q_1, i) = \delta(q_2, i)$. Q.E.D.

Thus we are reduced to the situation of the previous theorems.

Strongly-Connected Machines

(1) For a long time we conjectured that there exists no strongly-connected machine with two different substitution-property partitions, π_1 and π_2, such that $M_{\pi_1} \approx M_{\pi_2}$. In case M_{π_1} (thus also M_{π_2}) has only two states, this conjecture holds, according to a private communication from J. Ullman. In general, however, it is false, as can be illustrated by the example of Table I.

TABLE I.

M	0	1
1	6	3
2	8	4
3	4	8
4	5	7
5	4	8
6	1	2
7	1	2
8	2	1

M_{π_j}	0	1
B_1^*	B_3^*	B_2^*
B_2^*	B_2^*	B_3^*
B_3^*	B_1^*	B_1^*

$$\pi_1 = \{\overline{12}, \overline{345}, \overline{678}\} = \{B_1, B_2, B_3\} ,$$
$$\pi_2 = \{\overline{3567}, \overline{28}, \overline{14}\} = \{B'_1, B'_2, B'_3\} ,$$

(2) Note that M_{π_1} does *not* have a nontrivial automorphism in the above example. However, it seems to be true that the existence of two different substitution-property partitions π_1 and π_2 with $M_{\pi_1} \approx M_{\pi_2}$ implies the existence of a nontrivial automorphism for M_π (where $\pi = \pi_1 \cdot \pi_2$) that can be found according to the following procedure:

Assume, without loss of generality, that the blocks $\{B_i\}$ of π_1 and $\{B'_i\}$ of π_2 are indexed in such a manner that B'_i corresponds to B_i in the isomorphism $M_{\pi_1} \approx M_{\pi_2}$. Since $\pi_1 \neq \pi_2$, there exists at least one pair of blocks B_j and B'_j such that $B_j \neq B'_j$. Therefore one of these two blocks contains a state q_0 that does not belong to the other one*; without loss of generality we can assume $q_0 \in B_j'$ but $q_0 \notin B_j$. Further, $q_0 \in B_k$ for some $k \neq j$.

Now define a map φ on the state set Q_π of M_π as follows: Let D be a block of Q_π such that $D \subseteq B_j$ and define $\varphi(D) = B_\pi(q_0)$. Since M, and thus M_π, is strongly connected, for every $D' \in Q_\pi$ there exists a sequence $\bar{x} \in I^*$ such that $D' = \delta_\pi(D, \bar{x})$. Thus we define

$$\varphi(D') = \delta_\pi[\varphi(D), \bar{x}] \;.$$

Our conjecture is now that φ is well defined, i.e., if $\bar{x}_1$ and $\bar{x}_2$ are two sequences satisfying $\delta_\pi(D, \bar{x}_1) = \delta_\pi(D, \bar{x}_2)$, then we have $\delta_\pi[B_\pi(q_0), \bar{x}_1] = \delta_\pi[B_\pi(q_0), \bar{x}_2]$. Once this fact is established, it is easily shown that φ is an automorphism: let indeed D' be any element of Q_π; then we have for all $\bar{x}' \in I^*$

$$\begin{aligned} \varphi[\delta_\pi(D', \bar{x}')] &= \varphi[\delta_\pi(D, \overline{xx'})] \\ &= \delta_\pi[\varphi(D), \overline{xx'}] \quad \text{(definition of } \varphi \text{ and conjecture)} \\ &= \delta_\pi\{\delta_\pi[\varphi(D), \bar{x}], \bar{x}'\} \\ &= \delta_\pi[\varphi(D'), \bar{x}'] \;, \end{aligned}$$

where $\bar{x}$ is the sequence leading from D to D'. Note here that φ is necessarily nontrivial because $q_0 \notin D$ and thus $\varphi(D) = B_\pi(q_0) \neq D$. Further, φ is not always unique, since it depends on the choice of D and q_0.

(3) *Example.* Using the machine described by Table I, where

$$\pi = \pi_1 \cdot \pi_2 = \{\bar{1}, \bar{2}, \overline{35}, \bar{4}, \overline{67}, \bar{8}\} = \{D_1, D_2, D_3, \cdots, D_6\} \;,$$

we obtain the following automorphisms for M_π

B_j	D	q_0	$\varphi(D_1)$	$\varphi(D_2)$	$\varphi(D_3)$	$\varphi(D_4)$	$\varphi(D_5)$	$\varphi(D_6)$
B_1	D_1	3	D_3	D_5	D_6	D_2	D_4	D_1
B_1	D_1	6	D_5	D_3	D_2	D_6	D_1	D_4
B_1'	D_3	1	D_6	D_4	D_1	D_5	D_2	D_3

There are, in fact, two more nontrivial automorphisms for M_π, namely $\varphi(D_1) = D_2$ and $\varphi(D_1) = D_4$, but these cannot be obtained from the above procedure since 1 and 2 appear in the same block of B_1, and 1 and 4 in the same block of B_3'.

$\pi = \pi_1 \cdot \pi_2$

M_π	0	1
D_1	D_5	D_3
D_2	D_6	D_4
D_3	D_4	D_6
D_4	D_3	D_5
D_5	D_1	D_2
D_6	D_2	D_1

(4) *Conclusion.* If the conjecture stated above holds, then we can conclude that, for strongly connected machines, equivalence of two output faults, F_1 and

*In fact, one can show that $B_j \cap B_j' \neq \phi$ implies $\pi_1 = \pi_2$.

F_2, with $\lambda_{F_1} \neq \lambda_{F_2}$ always implies a nontrivial automorphism for the state table of M_π for some substitution-property partition π. Here π may be the trivial partition $\pi = 0$ where the blocks are the states of M.

V. EQUIVALENCE AND DOMINANCE

A. Combinational Circuits

LEMMA 1. *Dominance induces partial ordering on the equivalence classes with respect to detection equivalence.*

Proof. The proof follows from the correspondence between faults and detection sets

$$F_1 \geq F_2 \Longleftrightarrow S_{F_1} \supseteq S_{F_2} \quad . \text{ Q.E.D.}$$

LEMMA 2. *For single-output, irredundant networks, $F_1 \sim F_2$ iff $F_1 \approx F_2$.*

Proof. Assume $F_1 \sim F_2$ and let $x \in S_{F_1}$; then, $\Phi_{F_1}(x) = \Phi_{F_2}(x) \neq \Phi_\lambda(x)$ so $x \in S_{F_2}$ and $S_{F_1} \subseteq S_{F_2}$. Similarly, $S_{F_2} \subseteq S_{F_1}$, so $S_{F_1} = S_{F_2}$ and $F_1 \simeq F_2$. Next assume $F_1 \approx F_2$ and consider $x \in \{0, 1\}^n$ (any x), either

$$x \notin S_{F_1} = S_{F_2} \quad ,$$

then

$$\Phi_{F_1}(x) = \Phi_\lambda(x) = \Phi_{F_2}(x) \quad ,$$

or

$$x \in S_{F_1} = S_{F_2} \quad ,$$

then

$$\Phi_{F_1}(x) \neq \Phi_\lambda(x) \quad ,$$
$$\Phi_{F_2}(x) \neq \Phi_\lambda(x) \quad .$$

But, for single output, $\Phi_F(x) \in \{0, 1\}$ which forces $\Phi_{F_1}(x) = \Phi_{F_2}(x)$. Q.E.D.

LEMMA 3. *The above does not hold, in general, for multiple-output networks.*

Proof. The circuit in Fig. 3 realizes

$$y_1 = x_1 \cdot x_2 \quad ,$$
$$y_2 = x_1 \oplus x_2 \quad .$$

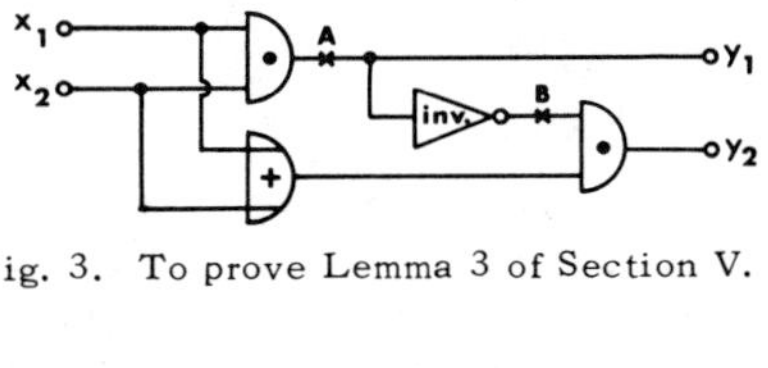

Fig. 3. To prove Lemma 3 of Section V.

Referring to this figure, let

$$F_1 = \text{“}A \text{ stuck at } 0\text{”}$$
$$F_2 = \text{“}B \text{ stuck at } 1\text{”} \quad .$$

Then the only test for F_1, as well as for F_2, is $x_1 = x_2 = 1$. In the case of

$$\begin{cases} F_1 \text{ we get } \begin{cases} y_1 = 0 , \\ y_2 = x_1 + x_2 , \end{cases} \\ F_2 \text{ we get } \begin{cases} y_1 = x_1 \cdot x_2 , \\ y_2 = x_1 + x_2 , \end{cases} \end{cases}$$

i.e., $\Phi_{F_1} \neq \Phi_{F_2}$. So in this case

$$\begin{cases} S_{F_1} = S_{F_2} = \{ \langle 1, 1 \rangle \} \Longrightarrow F_1 \approx F_2 , \\ \Phi_{F_1} \neq \Phi_{F_2} \Longrightarrow F_1 \not\simeq F_2 . \end{cases} \quad \text{Q. E. D.}$$

Remarks.

(1) Clearly $F_1 \sim F_2 \Longrightarrow F_1 \simeq F_2$ (in proving sufficiency of Lemma 2, a single-fault assumption was not used)

(2) Conjectures (multiple output)
  (a) If reconvergent fanout, every circuit has faults exhibiting Lemma 3
  (b) If no reconvergent fanout, Lemma 2 holds always.

B. Sequential Circuits

LEMMA 1′. *Dominance induces partial ordering on the set of equivalence classes with respect to detection equivalence.*

LEMMA 2′. *If two faults are reset equivalent, they are also detection equivalent.*

Proof. Proofs are analogous to the combinational case. Q.E.D.

LEMMA 3′. *Detection equivalence does not always imply reset equivalence.*

There are necessary and sufficient conditions for detection equivalence to imply reset equivalence, but they will not be discussed here.

Proof. Consider the machine M and its fault versions as described below. Let

$$|I_R| = 1 \text{ and } \rho(i) = A \qquad (i \in I_R) ,$$
$$\rho_{F_1}(i) = B ,$$
$$\rho_{F_2}(i) = A .$$

Consider

M

	0	1
A	B, 0	C, 1
B	A, 1	C, 0
C	D, 1	E, 1
D	A, 0	C, 1
E	D, 0	E, 0

$F_1(M)$

	0	1
A	B, 1	C, 0
B	A, 0	C, 1
C	D, 0	E, 0
D	B, 1	B, 1
E	D, 0	A, 1

$F_2(M)$

	0	1
A	D, 0	E, 1
B	A, 0	C, 1
C	D, 1	C, 0
D	A, 1	E, 0
E	D, 0	C, 0

Using the method described by Poage and McCluskey [4], we obtain

	0	1
$A\ B\ A$	$B\ A\ D$ 0 0 0	$C\ C\ E$ 1 1 1
$B\ A\ D$	$A\ B\ A$ 1 1 1	$C\ C\ E$ 0 0 0
$C\ C\ E$	D x x 1 – –	E x x 1 – –
D x x	A x x 0 – –	C x x 1 – –
E x x	D x x 0 – –	E x x 0 – –

From this table it is clear that $S_{F_1} = S_{F_2}$. Nevertheless, if we apply the input sequence

$$\langle\text{reset}\rangle\ ,\ 0,\ 1,\ 1,\ 0,\ 1\ ,$$

we get as outputs

$$F_1(M)\text{: } 0\ 0\ 0\ 0\ 0\ ,$$

$$F_2(M)\text{: } 0\ 0\ 0\ 1\ 0\ ,$$

so clearly $F_1(M)$ and $F_2(M)$ are *not* reset equivalent. So $F_1 \simeq F_2$ but $F_1 \not\approx F_2$. Q.E.D.

VI. REMARKS ON MEMORY FAULTS

In this section we discuss the influence of stuck-at faults in the feedback lines of a sequential circuit on the behavior of the machine. In particular, it will be shown that, for some machines, the fundamental properties can be very drastically changed, thus adding extra complexity to the problem.

Consider now the fault F as defined in Section III under "memory faults." On the set $\mathfrak{M}_m$ the fault F defines a map which we denote by the same symbol as the map defined by Equation (3) .

$$F\text{: } \mathfrak{M}_m \longrightarrow \mathfrak{M}_h \ (h = m - |\, T_F \,|)\ ,$$

$$M = \langle I, O, Q, \delta, \lambda \rangle \longmapsto \langle I, O, Q_F, \delta_F, \lambda_F \rangle = F(M)\ ,$$

where $F(M)$ is defined as the result of the following transformation on the model of M (Fig. 1b):

(a) Delete all $\ell_i \ni F(\ell_i) \neq N$ and corresponding memory elements delays)

(b) For each of these ℓ_i, the corresponding input to the combinational logic is fixed at the value $F(\ell_i)$ and the combinational function is redefined on the remaining variables only.

The set Q_F is obtained from Q by deleting in each $q = \langle y_1, y_2, y_3, \cdots, y_m \rangle \in Q$ those y_i that correspond to $F(\ell_i) \neq N$. The corresponding map $c_F: Q \longrightarrow Q_F$ will be called "fault projection function."

We also define a map $r_F: Q \longrightarrow Q$

$$r_F: \langle y_1, y_2, y_3, \cdots, y_m \rangle \longmapsto \langle y'_1, y'_2, y'_3, \cdots, y'_m \rangle ,$$

as follows

$$y'_i = \begin{cases} y_i, & \text{if } F(\ell_i) = N , \\ F(\ell_i), & \text{otherwise} . \end{cases}$$

From this it is possible to find a bijective map

$$b_F: Q_F \longrightarrow r_F(Q) \subseteq Q , \tag{5}$$

such that the diagram of Fig. 4(a) commutes. The reader can consult Arbib [11] for the concept, "commuting diagram."

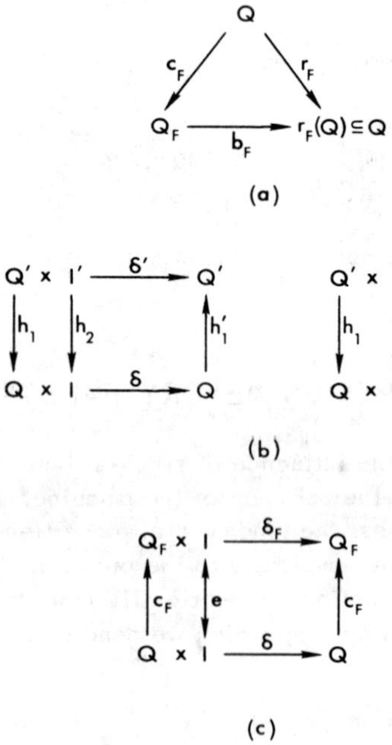

Fig. 4. (a) To define b_F. (b) A machine M describing M'. (c) To illustrate when $F(M)$ is the homomorphic image of M.

It is also easy to verify that b_F is unique. In fact, b_F does nothing else than insert the "defective" y_i with the corresponding values of $F(\ell_i) \neq N$ in the representation of $q = \langle \cdots \rangle \in Q_F$.

The maps b_F and c_F will be used throughout this section.

DEFINITION. *A machine* $M = \langle I, O, Q, \delta, \lambda \rangle$ *describes a machine* $M' =$ $I', O', Q', \delta', \lambda'$ *iff there exist maps*

$$h_1: Q' \longrightarrow Q \ ,$$
$$h'_1: Q \longrightarrow Q' \ ,$$
$$h_2: I' \longrightarrow I \ ,$$
$$h'_3: O \longrightarrow O' \ ,$$

such that

$$\delta'(q', i') = h'_1\{\delta[h_1(q'), h_2(i')]\} \ ,$$
$$\lambda'(q', i') = h_3\{\lambda[h_1(q'), h_2(i')]\} \ ,$$

i.e., the diagrams of Fig. 4(b) commute.

THEOREM 1. *M describes F(M).*

Proof. If the machine $F(M)$ is in state q', then the machine M in presence of the fault F is in the state q_B defined by $q_B = b_F(q')$ according to the definition (Eq. (5)) of b. The next state of M is then $\delta[b_F(q'), i]$ and for $F(M)$ this is thus $c_F\{\delta[b_F(q'), i]\}$. We obtain

$$\delta_F(q', i) = c_F\{\delta[b_F(q'), i]\} \ . \tag{6a}$$

Similarly

$$\lambda_F(q', i) = \lambda[b_F(q'), i] \ . \tag{6b}$$

Taking now

$$h_1 = b_F \ ,$$
$$h'_1 = c_F \ ,$$
$$h_2 = \text{identity map on } I \ ,$$
$$h'_3 = \text{identity map on } O \ ,$$

we see that M describes $F(M)$ in the sense defined above. Q.E.D.

Remark. The relationship between M and $F(M)$ is not, in general, a homomorphism since the diagram of Fig. 4(c) does not, in general, commute. It can be shown that the diagram commutes in case the "fault partition" π_F, defined by $q_1 \equiv q_2 (\pi_F)$ iff $c_F(q_1) = c_F(q_2)$, has substitution property.

Example. $F(\ell_3) = 0$, $F(\ell_1) = F(\ell_2) = N$ ($\sigma = \{0, 1\}$, $m = 3$).

q $\langle y_1 y_2 y_3 \rangle$	$\delta(q, i_0)$ $\langle y_1, y_2, y_3 \rangle$	$c_F(q)$ q'	$b_F(q')$ q_B
0 0 0	1 0 0	00	000
0 0 1	1 1 0		
0 1 1	1 0 1	01	010
0 1 0	0 1 0		
1 1 0	0 1 0	11	110
1 1 1	1 1 0		
1 0 1	0 0 1	10	100
1 0 0	1 1 1		

This table yields, using Eq. (6a), the state table for $F(M)$

q'	$\delta'(q', i_0)$
00	10
01	01
11	01
10	11

Let us now consider the influence of memory faults on the strongly connectedness of machines. The following point will be useful in proving a theorem on this subject.

For all m and all finite sets of the form $\sigma = \{0, 1, 2, \cdots, |\sigma| - 1\}$ there exists a single cycle permutation ψ on $Q = \sigma^m$, with the property that q and $\psi(q)$ differ only in a single component y_i for any $q \in Q$.

We will not provide a proof for this. It is, in fact, a consequence of a stronger result, where ψ has to satisfy the extra requirement that the difference between the y_i that are unequal in q and $\psi(q)$ is always 1 mod $|\sigma|$. See also the related material about "unit distance codes" in [5].

The following example shows, for $m = 3$, one of the permutations ψ that satisfy this stronger requirement.

Example. We describe ψ by arbitrarily taking $q_0 = \langle 0\ 0\ 0 \rangle$ and listing all $\psi^j(q_0)$ as j ranges over $0, 1, 2, \cdots, |Q| - 1$. $|\sigma| = 2$ yields the table

$j =$	0	1	2	3	4	5	6	7
y_3	0	0	0	0	1	1	1	1
y_2	0	0	1	1	1	1	0	0
y_1	0	1	1	0	0	1	1	0

while $|\sigma| = 3$ yields

$j =$	0	1	2	3	4	5	6	7	8	9	.	.	.	.	.	.	.	.	.	.	.	.	.	.	.	.	26
y_3	0	1	2	2	1	0	0	1	2	2	1	0	0	0	1	2	2	1	1	1	2	2	2	1	0	0	0
y_2	0	0	0	1	1	1	2	2	2	2	2	2	1	0	0	0	1	1	1	0	0	1	2	2	2	1	0
y_1	0	0	0	0	0	0	0	0	0	1	1	1	1	1	1	1	1	1	2	2	2	2	2	2	2	2	2

It is useful to look at the paths $q_0, \psi(q_0), \cdots$ in 3-dimensional space, since it shows how these sequences are formed and how the fact stated above can be proven in general.

THEOREM 2.

(1) *For all m there exist a large class of strongly-connected machines such that every single fault* $F \in \mathfrak{F}_Q$ *destroys the strongly connectedness*

(2) *For all m there exist strongly connected machines M such that* $F(M)$ *is strongly connected for all* $F \in \mathfrak{F}_Q$.

Proof. Part 1. Let δ be defined as follows

$$\delta(q, i) = \begin{cases} \psi(q), & \text{for some } i_q \in I \ , \\ q, & \text{for all other } i \neq i_q \ . \end{cases}$$

This corresponds to a very wide class of strongly-connected (ψ has a single cycle) machines. Let F be an arbitrary single fault defined by $F(\ell_k) = \alpha \in \sigma$.

The definition of ψ implies the existence of a state

$$q = \langle y_1, y_2, y_3, \cdots, y_k = \alpha, \cdots, y_n \rangle \ ,$$

such that

$$\psi(q) = \langle y_1, y_2, y_3, \cdots, y_k' \neq \alpha, \cdots, y_n \rangle \ .$$

For $F(M)$ this implies that $c_F(q) = c_F \psi(q) = q' \in Q_F$ and $b_F(q') = q$.

The next-state function for the faulty machine gives, for q';

$$\delta_F(q', i) = c_F \delta[b_F(q'), i] \qquad \{\text{from (6a)}\}$$

$$= c_F \delta(q, i)$$

$$= \begin{cases} c_F(q), & \text{in case } i \neq i_q \ , \\ c_F \psi(q), & \text{in case } i = i_q \ . \end{cases}$$

Therefore, the only state reachable from $q' \in Q_F$ is q' itself, and therefore, $F(M)$ is not strongly connected. This process is illustrated in Fig. 5 for $|\sigma| = 2$, $m = 2$, and y_2 stuck at zero.

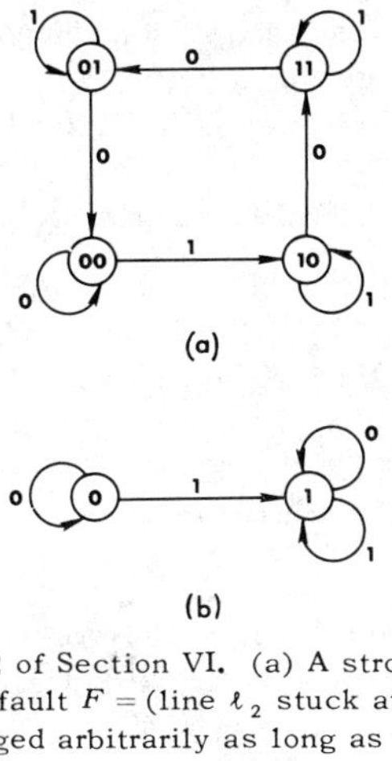

Fig. 5. To illustrate Theorem 2 of Section VI. (a) A strongly-connected machine M. (b) The machine $F(M)$ after the fault F = (line ℓ_2 stuck at 0) occurred. Note that the input labeling in M can be changed arbitrarily as long as the graph remains deterministic.

Part 2. Consider a machine M with $Q = I$ and $\delta(q, i) = i$ for all q and i in I. It is easily verified that M is strongly connected and also that, in $F(M)$, any $q' \in Q_F$ can be reached from any other state of Q_F by applying an input satisfying $c_F(i) = q'$.

Of course, many less trivial machines with this property can be found easily. Q.E.D.

Consequences for the study of equivalence and dominance. This theorem clearly illustrates the need for having several reset states available in order to have a sound basis for comparing faulty machines. It would be inaccurate to say that two faulty machines are (reset) equivalent based on only one single reset state from which only a small portion of the actual states can be reached.

VII. CONCLUSION

From this paper, three main ideas have become clear. First, the possibility that output faults are equivalent, without being functionally equivalent for the output function, can be investigated directly from the structure of the state table only. This gives certain information on the equivalence classes.

Second, it has been shown for both combinational (mainly to demonstrate the parallel) and sequential networks that reset equivalence and detection equivalence are not always the same thing.

Finally, the invalidity of the assumption that a strongly-connected machine is still strongly connected after a fault occurs has been demonstrated by exhibiting some large class of machines for which it is clearly false. Another consequence is the need to have a reset circuitry in order to be able to compare such machines in a meaningful way.

It has also become apparent that extreme caution is needed when comparing machines, i.e., the basis for comparison must be specified very precisely, and as insensitive to faults as possible.

Further research is being done to find conditions under which faulty machines are equivalent under faults of a certain class. Also, the relationship between reset and detection equivalence is being further investigated.

ACKNOWLEDGEMENTS

Research reported in this paper was supported by the National Science Foundation under Grant GJ 27527, by the Joint Services Electronics Program under Contract N-00014-67-A-0112-0044, and while Mr. Boute was partially supported by the National Fonds voor Wetenschappelijk Onderzoek of Belgium.

REFERENCES

[1] E. F. Moore, "Gedanken Experiments on Sequential Machines," *Automata Studies*, No. 34, 129–133 (New Jersey: Princeton University Press, 1956).

[2] S. Seshu and D. N. Freeman, "The Diagnosis of Asynchronous Sequential Switching Systems," *IRE Trans. Electron. Comput.*, EC-11, No. 4, 459–465 (August 1962).

[3] F. C. Hennie, "Fault Detecting Experiments for Sequential Circuits," *Proc. 5th Ann. Symp. Switching Theory and Logical Design*, 95–110 (New Jersey: November 1964).

[4] J. F. Poage and E. J. McCluskey, "Derivation of Optimum Test Sequences for Sequential Machines," *Proc. 5th Ann. Symp. Switching Theory and Logical Design*, 121–132 (New Jersey: 1964).

[5] E. J. McCluskey, *Introduction to the Theory of Switching Circuits* (New York: McGraw-Hill, 1965).

[6] F. W. Clegg and E. J. McCluskey, "Algebraic Properties of Faults in Logic

Networks," Technical Report No. 4, Digital Systems Laboratory, Stanford Electronics Labs, Stanford, California (March 1970).

[7] F. W. Clegg and E. J. McCluskey, "The Algebraic Approach to Faulty Logic Networks," *Proc. IEEE 1971 International Symposium on Fault-Tolerant Computing*, 44-45, Pasadena, California (March 1971).

[8] D. R. Schertz, "On the Representation of Faults," Report R-418, Coordinated Science Laboratory, University of Illinois (1969).

[9] D. R. Schertz and G. Metze, "On the Indistinguishability of Faults in Digital Systems," *Proc. 6th Ann. Allerton Conf. Circuit and System Theory*, 572-760 (1968).

[10] K. C. Y. Mei, "Fault Dominance in Combinational Circuits," Technical Note No. 2, Digital Systems Laboratory, Stanford Electronics Labs, Stanford University, California (August 1970).

[11] M. A. Arbib, *Theories of Abstract Automata* (Prentice-Hall, 1969).

[12] J. Hartmanis, R. E. Stearns, *Algebraic Structure Theory of Sequential Machines* (Prentice-Hall, 1966).

[13] H. X. Chang, E. G. Manning, G. Metze, *Fault Diagnosis of Digital Systems* (Wiley, 1970).

[14] G. P. Weeg, "The Structure of an Automaton and its Operation-Preserving Transformation Group," *J. ACM*, **9**, No. 3, p. 345 (1962).

[15] A. C. Fleck, "Isomorphism Groups of Automata," J. ACM, **9**, No. 4, 469 (1962).

[16] A. C. Fleck, "On the Automorphism Group of an Automaton," *J. ACM*, **12**, No. 4, 566 (1965).

[17] B. Barnes, "Groups of Automorphisms and Sets of Equivalence Classes of Input for Automata," *J. ACM*, **12**, No. 4, 561 (1965).

[18] H. O. Rabin and D. Scott, "Finite Automata and Their Decision Problems," *IBM J. Res. Dev.*, No. 3, 114-125 (1959).

[19] F. C. Hennie, *Finite-State Models for Logical Machines* (Wiley, 1968).

[20] A. Gill, *Introduction to the Theory of Finite-State Machines* (New York: McGraw-Hill, 1962).

DIGITAL COMPUTER ARITHMETIC: A UNIFIED ALGORITHMIC SPECIFICATION

Algirdas Avižienis

UCLA Computer Science Department, University of California, Los Angeles, CA

The paper presents a method for the description of digital-computer arithmetic in terms of a set of primitive *digit algorithms*. Digit algorithms are specified as arithmetic operations on the values of individual digits of *digit vectors* which represent numerical values in the computer. Complete arithmetic operations in digital processors are described as *vector algorithms* which are composed from digit algorithms.

I. INTRODUCTION

A. Objectives of the Specification

The field of digital-computer arithmetic has evolved as an aspect of the logic design and system architecture of digital computers. This heuristic development has been of practical rather than theoretical nature. Consequently, digital arithmetic has not been recognized as a separate aspect of the theory of computing. The principal difficulty in the presentation of digital arithmetic and in its evaluation has been the lack of a clear distinction between the arithmetic algorithm and its logic implementation. The numerous details of logic design which are included in the description of a given algorithm severely obscure its arithmetical properties. (For an illustration, see [1].) The assessment of the originality of an algorithm and the measurement of its relative efficiency (in terms of speed and cost) with respect to other algorithms for the same arithmetical operation become difficult tasks. The comparison is usually limited to only one class of logic elements.

More recently, initial steps have been taken in the theoretical evaluation of arithmetic algorithms [2, 3, 4]. The general properties of arithmetic algorithms are being identified, and there is a need to formulate digital-computer arithmetic in terms which will provide a unified viewpoint for both the theoretician and the system designer. The benefits of such an algorithmic formulation are expected to be:

(1) A simplification of the description of arithmetic processors
(2) A foundation for the comparison and evaluation of arithmetical algorithms
(3) The separation of a discipline of "arithmetic design" from logic design.

Presented at the Symposium on Computers and Automata
Polytechnic Institute of Brooklyn, April 13–15, 1971.

The objective of this paper is to formulate a methodology for the description of algorithms for digital arithmetic [5]. The goals listed above have been considered as objectives of the formulation. The contributions of Markov [6], Iverson [7], Patterson [8], Robertson [9], and Garner [10] have been important stimuli in this effort. Many aspects of Iverson's notation [7] are used in the subsequent sections.

B. The User's View of Arithmetic Processors

A digital arithmetic processor can be described from two different viewpoints: the viewpoint of the *user*, and the viewpoint of the *designer*. The user sees the arithmetic processor as a "black box" shown in Figure 1. It is described in terms of its inputs, outputs, and operation times.

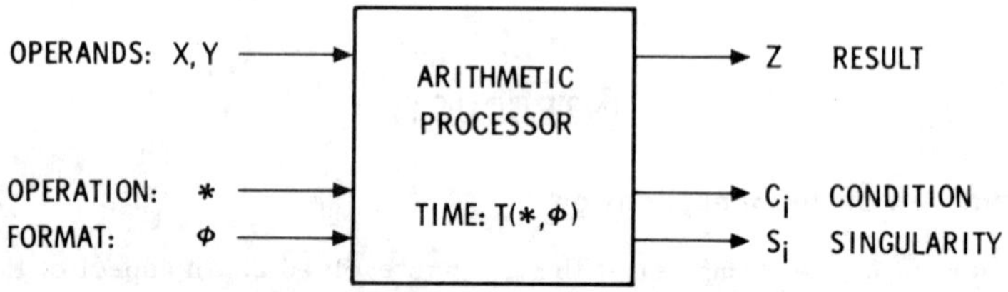

Fig. 1. User's specification of an arithmetic processor.

(1) *The inputs* to the processor are:
(a) One or more *numerical values* $X, Y, Z, \cdots$
(b) An *operation symbol* $*$
(c) A *format symbol* ϕ

The input numeric values (*operands*) are characterized by three properties:

(a.1) They are members of a *finite set* $\mathfrak{N}$ of numerical values with a specified *range*

$$N_{\min} \leq X \leq N_{\max} ,$$

(a.2) They are known within a specified *precision*

$$X - \Delta X_L \leq X \leq X + \Delta X_H ,$$

(a.3) They are stated by means of a defined *number representation,* consisting of an *n*-tuple of symbols

$$\mathbf{x}_{n-1}, \cdots, \mathbf{x}_i, \cdots, \mathbf{x}_0 ,$$

and a set of rules for the interpretation of this *n*-tuple as the numerical value X.

The *operation symbols* represent a set of defined arithmetic operations. The set $\{+, -, \times, \div\}$ is commonly available; however, both more extensive and more limited sets may be encountered. When more than one *format* (type of representation) is allowable for the input operands, the operation symbol is supplemented by a *format symbol* ϕ.

(2) *The outputs* of the processor are:
(a) One or more *numerical results* $Z, Y, X, \cdots$
(b) One or more condition symbols $C_0, C_1, C_2, \cdots$
(c) One or more *singularity symbols* $S_0, S_1, S_2, \cdots$
The *numerical output results* possess similar properties as the operands (range, precision, and representation); however, they may differ from those of the operands in details.

The *condition symbols* identify specific conditions associated with the value of the result, such as whether the result is negative, positive, zero, etc.

The *singularity symbols* are issued when the input operands and operation symbol do not yield a "legal" result. The singularity symbols may include:
(c.1) "Overflow," i.e., the result value is not representable in the range allowed for output values
(c.2) Excessive loss of precision (significant digits) in floating-point operations
(c.3) Error caused by a logic fault in the hardware of the processor.
A *pseudo-result* $Z(S_i)$ instead of the expected result Z appears at the output together with the singularity symbol S_i.

(3) An *operation time* $T(*)$ is specified for every allowable operation symbol of the processor. When more than one format is allowed, separate operation times $T(*, \phi)$ are specified for every format ϕ. Operation times may be either *fixed*, or *variable* over a specified range $T(*)_{\text{min}} \leq T(*) \leq T(*)_{\text{max}}$.

Here we note two key aspects of the user's viewpoint:

(1) The definition of an "arithmetic processor" includes a broad spectrum of "black boxes," from a simple counter with "add one" as the only operation, to a processor which computes trigonometric functions or the fast Fourier transform
(2) The internal structure of the arithmetic processor is specified only in terms of the execution time associated with the operation symbol $*$ and the format of the operands. It must be emphasized that while Fig. 1 is given in terms of two operands and one result, the variations of single-operand, multiple-operand, and multiple-result arithmetic operations are also possible and fit equally well within the given specification.

C. The Designer's View of Arithmetic Processors

The detailed specification of the internal structure of the processor is the responsibility of the designer. The designer's viewpoint must consider both the detailed arithmetic algorithms and the logic structure of the processor. At this point we establish a distinction between arithmetic design and logic design.

Arithmetic design begins with the overall system specifications of the processor (as given in the "user's viewpoint") and translates them into detailed specification of arithmetic operations at the level of individual digits of the number representation. These digit-level algorithms serve as a complete truth-table specification for the *logic design*. The logic designer specifies the logic nets using the currently preferred logic elements and design techniques, for example, medium-scale or large-scale integrated circuits.

The principal advantage of separating arithmetic design is that it makes the description of algorithms separate and independent of any given set of logic building blocks.

The designer's "black-box" specification of an arithmetic processor is obtained by making the following changes in the user's specification of Figure 1:

(1) *The inputs* are operand-digit vectors

$$\mathbf{x} \equiv \mathbf{x}_{n-1}, \cdots, \mathbf{x}_i, \cdots, \mathbf{x}_0 \qquad \text{(representing } X\text{)} ,$$

$$\mathbf{y} \equiv \mathbf{y}_{m-1}, \cdots, \mathbf{y}_i, \cdots, \mathbf{y}_0 \qquad \text{(representing } Y\text{)} ,$$

and an (operation-and-format) code, abbreviated as "o&f code," vector

$$\Omega \equiv \Omega_t, \cdots, \Omega_i, \cdots, \Omega_0 ,$$

representing the operation and format symbols $*$ and ϕ.

(2) *The outputs* are the result-digit vector

$$\mathbf{z} \equiv \mathbf{z}_{k-1}, \cdots, \mathbf{z}_i, \cdots, \mathbf{z}_0 \qquad \text{(representing } Z\text{)} ,$$

a condition-code vector

$$\varepsilon \equiv \varepsilon_q, \cdots, \varepsilon_i, \cdots, \varepsilon_0 \qquad \text{(representing } C_i\text{)} ,$$

and a singularity-code vector

$$\sigma \equiv \sigma_p, \cdots, \sigma_i, \cdots, \sigma_0 \qquad \text{(representing } S_i\text{)} .$$

(3) The *objective of arithmetic design* is to develop for every o&f-code vector Ω a *vector algorithm* A (Ω) which specifies the value of every result digit $\mathbf{z}_i$ by one of two methods:

(1) Directly

(2) As an arithmetic function of operand digits ($\mathbf{x}_j, \mathbf{y}_j$) from one or more positions j of the operand digit vectors $\mathbf{x}$ and $\mathbf{y}$.

The values of digits $\mathbf{z}_i$ must be such that the result numerical value $Z \equiv X * Y$ is represented by the digit vector $\mathbf{z}$ in the specified number representation system. If the representation is not possible due to range limits or other constraints, the corresponding singularity-code vector σ is to be generated, and the vector $\mathbf{z}$ must represent the corresponding pseudo-result $Z(S_i)$. Finally, the condition code vector ε must be specified in terms of the result digits $\mathbf{z}_i$ to represent the required condition symbol C_i of the result value Z.

II. DIGITAL REPRESENTATION OF NUMERICAL VALUES

A. Digit Vectors

Numerical values in a digital arithmetic processor are represented by an n-tuple $\mathbf{x}$ of symbols $\mathbf{x}_i$, called *digits*

$$\mathbf{x} \equiv \mathbf{x}_a, \cdots, \mathbf{x}_i, \cdots, \mathbf{x}_b .$$

The n-tuple $\mathbf{x}$ will be called a *digit vector* (abbreviated "*d vector*") in the subsequent discussion. The *length* n of the d vector is the count of its components, designated by $\rho\,\mathbf{x}$

$$\rho\,\mathbf{x} \equiv |a - b| + 1 \quad .$$

In addition to its length, a d vector has two other explicit properties: the indexing system and the range of values for each digit.

The first explicit property of a d vector is the indexing employed to identify its component digits

$$\mathbf{x} \equiv \mathbf{x}_a, \mathbf{x}_{a\pm 1}, \cdots, \mathbf{x}_i, \cdots, \mathbf{x}_{b\mp 1}, \mathbf{x}_b \quad .$$

The index set of $\mathbf{x}$ consists of consecutive integers

$$\{a, a \pm 1, \cdots, i, \cdots, b \mp 1, b\} \quad .$$

The index set is described by its *origin*, defined as the lesser of the two end values

$$\text{origin} \equiv \min(a, b) \quad ,$$

and by the direction (with respect to the origin) in which the indices increase: *leftward* or *rightward*. For example, $\{3, 2, 1, 0\}$ is zero-origin leftward indexing, while $\{1, 2, 3, 4\}$ is one-origin rightward, and $\{2, 1, 0, -1, -2, -3\}$ is minus-three-origin leftward indexing. Several index origins and both directions have been used in the practice of computer design and description, following the author's preference. The main need in indexing is consistency in adhering to one indexing system. Inconsistency in indexing still occurs in practice and leads to severe difficulties in understanding an algorithm or a design. Zero-origin leftward indexing $\{n - 1, \cdots, i, \cdots, 0\}$ will be used throughout this discussion unless explicitly otherwise specified.

The second explicit property of a d vector is the range of values of its digits. The digit $\mathbf{x}_i$ is a variable ranging over a set of allowed values $\Sigma_i \equiv \{a, b, c, \cdots, k\}$. In cases of practical interest this set consists of two or more consecutive integers, for example

$$\{0, 1\}; \quad \{\bar{1}, 0, 1\}; \quad \{0, 1, 2, \cdots, 9\} \quad , \text{etc.}$$

The *overbar* (e.g., $\bar{1}$, $\bar{9}$, $\overline{14}$) will be used to designate negative-digit values. Digit values greater than 9 will always be given in the conventional decimal (radix-10) notation. The distinction between canonical, noncanonical, and redundant sets of digit values is discussed in the next section.

B. Number-Representation Systems

A *number-representation system* is specified by a rule which associates one numerical value X with every "legal" d vector $\mathbf{x}$. (All digits of a "legal" d vector assume only allowed values.) When the value X is different for every allowed d vector $\mathbf{x}$, the number system is *nonredundant*. When two or more distinct d vectors represent the same value X, the number system is *redundant*. For example, the d vectors

$$\mathbf{x} \equiv 0, 1, 1, 1 \quad \text{and} \quad \mathbf{y} \equiv 1, 0, 0, \bar{1}$$

both represent the value "seven" in the radix-2 system with allowed digit values $\{\bar{1}, 0, 1\}$. Redundancy of representation has not been useful in manual arithmetic; however, redundant number systems have been found to possess desirable attributes in automatic digital-computer arithmetic.

First, we assume a zero-origin leftward indexing of the *d* vector $\mathbf{x}$ and consider the explicit representation of numerical values by digit vectors.

The most commonly-used number representation systems are *weighted* number systems in which an *explicit value* x is associated with the *d* vector $\mathbf{x}$ according to the rule

$$x \equiv \sum_{i \equiv 0}^{n-1} \mathbf{x}_i \times \mathbf{w}_i \;, \quad \text{or} \quad x \equiv +/\mathbf{x} \times \mathbf{w} \;,$$

where $\mathbf{w}$ is the *weight-vector* associated with the *d* vector $\mathbf{x}$. The weight vector is obtained from the *radix vector* $\mathbf{r}$, which specifies a radix $\mathbf{r}_i$ for every component $\mathbf{x}_i$ of the *d* vector $\mathbf{x}$. The components of the weight vector are defined as follows

$$\mathbf{w}_0 \equiv 1 \;,$$

$$\mathbf{w}_i \equiv \mathbf{w}_{i-1} \times \mathbf{r}_{i-1} \qquad (\text{for } 1 \leq i \leq n-1) \;.$$

The magnitude $|\mathbf{r}_i|$ of the ith radix in a nonredundant number system is an integer equal to the number of allowed values of the digit $\mathbf{x}_i$.

In a *fixed-radix* number system all components of the radix vector $\mathbf{r}$ have the same value, such as 10, 2, or $\bar{2}$. In a *mixed-radix* number system more than one radix value occurs in $\mathbf{r}$. Representation of elapsed-time values in terms of weeks, days, hours, minutes, and seconds is a system which employs the mixed-radix vector

$$\mathbf{r} \equiv 10, 10, 7, 24, 60, 60 \;,$$

when the range of 100 weeks is chosen for the system.

Conventional number systems are fixed-radix systems with the same positive integer radix $\mathbf{r}_i \geq 2$ for all digits $(0 \leq i \leq n-1)$, and with the *canonical* set of digit values

$$\Sigma_i \equiv \{0, 1, 2, \cdots, \mathbf{r}_i - 1\} \qquad (\text{for } 0 \leq i \leq n-1) \;,$$

In design practice attention has been focused on conventional systems with radices 10, 2, 4, 8, and 16. Practical applications have been found for *noncanonical* digit sets such as the *nonredundant* radix-10 set

$$\{\bar{4}, \bar{3}, \bar{2}, \bar{1}, 0, 1, 2, 3, 4, 5\} \;,$$

in decimal multiplier recoding, as well as the several *redundant* sets, such as the radix-2 sets

$$\{\bar{1}, 0, 1\} \quad \text{and} \quad \{0, 1, 2\} \;,$$

in fast binary arithmetic [10] and the radix-10 and radix-16 sets, respectively

$$\{\bar{6}, \cdots, 0, \cdots, 6\} \quad \text{and} \quad \{\bar{9}, \cdots, 0, \cdots, 9\} \;,$$

in signed-digit arithmetic [11].

Nonconventional weighted number systems with negative radices [12], and complex radices [13], have been postulated and investigated, but thus far they have not found wider acceptance by practicing designers.

Nonweighted number systems are those in which the relative position i of the digit $\mathbf{x}_i$ does not convey "weighting" information (other than the value of the radix $\mathbf{r}_i$) in the expression for the explicit value x being represented. The interchange of any two digits (together with their associated radices and sets of allowed values) will not change the value x. The best known example is the residue number systems (RNS) [14], in which the radices $\mathbf{r}_i$ are mutually pairwise-prime positive integers (7, 9, 11) and the digit values which represent the explicit value x are

$$\mathbf{x}_i \equiv \mathbf{r}_i \mid x \quad ,$$

where $\mathbf{r}_i \mid x$ means "the modulo $\mathbf{r}_i$ residue of x." The "most-significant digit" and "the least-significant digit" do not exist in a nonweighted representation. The rule for the explicit value x of a RNS d vector can be considered to be that of a weighted number representation under a generalization defined by Garner [10].

C. Implicit Values of Single *d* Vectors

The preceding discussion dealt exclusively with the *explicit value* x of the d vector $\mathbf{x}$. The explicit value x is a function of the digit values $\mathbf{x}_i$, radices $\mathbf{r}_i$, and indices i of the d vector under the assumption of *normal* (zero-origin leftward) indexing. The explicit values are either integers (assuming that fractional radices and digit values are excluded), or natural numbers when negative radices and digit values are not allowed (e.g., in conventional number systems). The explicit values cover a finite *explicit range* of the number system represented by the vectors $\mathbf{x}$, $\mathbf{r}$, and Σ.

Explicit values x provide the most direct interpretation of the d vector $\mathbf{x}$ with the associated vectors $\mathbf{r}$ and Σ. However, a further interpretation of x is frequently specified to describe the numerical value X (called the "*implicit value*" of $\mathbf{x}$) which the user wishes to represent by means of the d vector x.

The *implicit value* X of the d vector $\mathbf{x}$ is an arithmetic function of the explicit value x which is defined by further interpretations attached to the d vector $\mathbf{x}$. The major implied attributes of $\mathbf{x}$ which are used to define the implicit value X are:

(a) The location of the radix point
(b) The representation of negative values
(c) The presence of nonsignificant digits in $\mathbf{x}$ [15]
(d) Encoding in an error-detecting or error-correcting code [16].

The variety of possible implicit values of a radix-2 d vector is shown by examples in Table I.

Two key points are to be noted in the discussion of explicit and implicit values:

(1) The implicit value is the only value of interest to the *user* of the computer

(2) The *arithmetic designer* must devise algorithms which operate on operand digits representing the explicit values. These algorithms generate digits of the result such that the correct implicit value of the result is represented.

For an illustration of (2), consider a left shift (multiplication by two) of the operand $\mathbf{x} \equiv 11011$ ($x \equiv 27$) used in Table I, line 6 (fraction, "one's complement," with $X = -4/16$). The shift will yield $\mathbf{y} \equiv 10111$ as a result, since an "end-around" shift is the specified algorithm. The new explicit value is $y \equiv 23$, and the implicit value is $Y \equiv 2^{-4} \times (-2^5 + 1 + y) = -8/16$, which is the correct implicit value. The operation

$$y \equiv (x - 16) \times 2 + 1 \quad ,$$

on the explicit value x caused the operation

$$Y = 2 \times X \quad ,$$

on the implicit value X.

TABLE I. Some implicit values of radix-2 d-vector $\mathbf{x} \equiv 1\ 1\ 0\ 1\ 1$.

IMPLIED ATTRIBUTES: RADIX POINT, NEGATIVE NUMBER REPRESENTATION, OTHERS	EXPRESSION FOR IMPLICIT VALUE X AS A FUNCTION OF EXPLICIT VALUE x	NUMERICAL IMPLICIT VALUE X (IN DECIMAL)
Integer, Magnitude	$X = x$	27
Integer, "Two's Complement"	$X = -2^5 + x$	−5
Integer, "One's Complement"	$X = -(2^5 - 1) + x$	−4
Fraction, Magnitude	$X = 2^{-5} \times x$	27/32
Fraction, "Two's Complement"	$X = 2^{-4} \times (-2^5 + x)$	−5/16
Fraction, "One's Complement"	$X = 2^{-4} \times (-2^5 + 1 + x)$	−4/16
Integer, Magnitude, "AN" Error Detection Encoding with $A = 3$ [16]	$X = x \div 3$	9
Fraction, "Two's Complement," Floating-Point Coefficient in Significant-Digit Arithmetic [15]	$X = \left(2 \times (2^{-4} \times (-2^5 + x))\right) \times 2^{-1}$	$(-5/8) \times 2^{-1}$

D. Variable-Length and Multiple *d* Vectors

The most common format of d vectors in computers is the *fixed-length, single d vector* format which has been used in the discussion of implicit values of the preceding section. *Variable-length* d vectors are allowed in a number of computers as well, in which the number of digits may range from one to some maximum length n_{max}. The additional cost of such representation is the *length indicator* which must be provided for each d vector. The methods of length indication of d vectors are:

(1) Special symbols (flag bits, etc.) are used to identify the ends of the d vector

(2) A separate fixed-length d vector λ representing the length of the variable-length d vector is attached at one end (the *reference* end, usually the least significant end) of the d vector.

The method (2) above makes use of two separate *d* vectors $(\mathbf{x}, \lambda)$ to represent a numerical value X for the purposes of arithmetical processing. Other forms of *multiple d* vectors (double, triple, etc.) also have been used for the representation of numbers. The most common forms are:

(1) The use of a *sign tag* $\sigma\mathbf{x}$ (values 0, 1) with a *d* vector $\mathbf{x}$ representing a magnitude X to form a *sign-and-magnitude d* vector

$$\mathbf{y} \equiv (\sigma\mathbf{x}, \mathbf{x}) \quad \text{represents} \quad Y \equiv (-1)^{\sigma\mathbf{x}} \times X$$

(2) The use of an *exponent* $\mathbf{e}$ to form a *floating-point d* vector

$$\mathbf{y} \equiv (\mathbf{e}, \mathbf{x}) \quad \text{represents} \quad Y \equiv X \times R^E$$

where $R \equiv \mathbf{r}_i^k$, given a fixed radix $\mathbf{r}_i$ of $\mathbf{x}$ and an integer $k \geq 1$

(3) The use of a *significance tag* vector $\mathbf{s}$ with a floating-point *d* vector to give a *significant-digit d* vector

$$\mathbf{y} \equiv (\mathbf{e}, \mathbf{x}, \mathbf{s}) \quad \text{represents} \quad Y \equiv X \times R^E$$

where X is known to S significant digits (the length of $\mathbf{x}$ usually exceeds S)

(4) The use of two or more *d* vectors to give *multiple-precision* forms, which represent the implicit value to a higher precision than provided by a single *d* vector

$$\mathbf{y} \equiv (\mathbf{x}, \mathbf{x}') \quad \text{represents} \quad Y \equiv X \times r^n + X'$$

where n is the length of $\mathbf{x}'$ and r is the radix (fixed) of $\mathbf{x}$ and $\mathbf{x}'$.

(5) The use of two *d* vectors to represent an *interval number* for interval arithmetic

$$\mathbf{z} \equiv (\mathbf{x}, \mathbf{y}) \quad \text{represents} \quad X \leq Z \leq Y$$

(6) Error-detection encoding by a separate code using a *check vector* $\mathbf{c}$ to form the *residue-encoded d* vector

$$\mathbf{y} \equiv (\mathbf{x}, \mathbf{c}) \quad \text{represents} \quad X \text{ iff } \mathrm{c} \equiv A \mid \mathrm{x}$$

where: A is the check modulus, and $A \mid \mathrm{x}$ means "modulo-A residue of x."

In the use of multiple *d* vectors to represent one implicit value the expression for this implicit value involves the implicit values of all the component *d* vectors, which are processed separately when an arithmetical algorithm is carried out. It should be noted that these component *d* vectors themselves can be multiple; for example, sign-and-magnitude format may be used for floating-point *d* vectors $\mathbf{e}$ and $\mathbf{x}$ in (2) above, and floating-point *d* vectors may be used as the two interval-number representation *d* vectors in (5).

III. SPECIFICATION OF DIGITAL ARITHMETIC

A. The Digit-Algorithm Approach

The types of *d* vectors which are employed in digital computers and their interpretations in terms of implicit values have been presented in the preceding part of this paper. At this point we set out to provide a basis for arithmetic design by describing a set of primitive operations, called *digit algorithms,* which are carried out on the individual digits of one or more *d* vector *operands* and yield values for individual digits of intermediate or final *result d* vectors.

One digit is the least indivisible component of a *d* vector in the arithmetic processing of numerical information. Each digit $\mathbf{x}_i$ of the *d* vector $\mathbf{x}$ is identified by its index i, its associated radix $\mathbf{r}_i$, and its set of allowed values Σ_i. Algorithms for arithmetical processing of *d* vectors consist of rules for transforming the digits of the operands into the digits of the result. These rules for the handling of individual digits of the operands and for the generation of the digits of a result are called *digit algorithms.* The rules for the handling of entire-digit vectors are called *vector algorithms*; they are composed of combinations or sequences of digit algorithms.

Digit algorithms for various number systems and arithmetical operations differ in their complexity. Whenever the set Σ_i contains more than two allowed digit values, a single binary storage element is not sufficient to store the digit $\mathbf{x}_i$. In this case the digit values are specified in terms of an *encoding* which establishes the equivalences between the allowed values of $\mathbf{x}_i$ and combinations of the logic values 1 and 0. Each element of the *d* vector is represented by a logic vector. Examples are the various encodings which have been devised for digit values in radix-10 arithmetic processors (8-4-2-1, excess-three, etc.).

A digit algorithm may be implemented either as a *table-lookup* operation (implemented by a combinational-logic network) or as a sequence of *subalgorithms.* When a radix-*r* digit value is specified by a logic vector (the states of several Boolean variables), it may be convenient to consider the radix-*r* digit to be composed of radix-2 *subdigits.* At this microscopic level of processing each radix-*r* digit is one *d* vector in a radix-2 number system, and the radix-*r* digit algorithm can be further specified as a combination or sequence of radix-2 subalgorithms. Finally, at the level of logic design, every digit algorithm or subalgorithm is expressed in terms of combinational or sequential Boolean functions. The specific form of these Boolean functions reflects the constraints imposed by the characteristics of currently available building blocks (fan-out, fan-in, cascading, delays, etc.). An example of a digit algorithm implemented in terms of subalgorithms is the one-decimal-digit adder in binary coded decimal (8-4-2-1) or in "excess-three" arithmetic processor.

Digit algorithms are classified according to the number of digits with the same index i which enter as operands to form the ith result digit. For example

$$\mathbf{z}_i \longleftarrow 9 - \mathbf{x}_i \quad ; \quad \text{and} \quad \mathbf{z}_i \longleftarrow \mathbf{x}_{i-1} \quad ,$$

are *one-digit* algorithms, while

$$\mathbf{cg}_i \longleftarrow \lfloor (\mathbf{x}_i + \mathbf{y}_i) \div 10 \quad ,$$

is a *two-digit* algorithm for radix-10, conventional arithmetic, and

$$\mathbf{s}_i \longleftarrow \left(\sum_{j=1}^{11} \mathbf{x}_i^{(j)} \right) - 10 \times \mathbf{t}_{i+1} \quad ,$$

is an eleven-digit algorithm in a minimal-redundancy signed-digit radix-10 arithmetic [17].

Another important property of a digit algorithm for the ith position

$$\mathbf{z}_i \longleftarrow f(\mathbf{x}_j, \mathbf{y}_j) \quad ,$$

is the number of positions j which affect $\mathbf{z}_i$. When j has only *one* value, the digit algorithm is *local*. For examples, see the four preceding examples. When j has k different values, the digit algorithm is *k-dependent*. For example

$$\mathbf{z}_i \longleftarrow 10 \mid (\mathbf{x}_i + \mathbf{y}_i + \mathbf{c}_i) \quad ,$$

with

$$\mathbf{c}_i \longleftarrow \lfloor (\mathbf{x}_{i-1} + \mathbf{y}_{i-1} + \mathbf{c}_{i-1}) \div 10 \quad ,$$

is an $(i + 1)$-dependent digit algorithm in radix-10 conventional arithmetic.

B. Digit Algorithms for Three Classes of Number Systems

The concept of digit-algorithms is illustrated with the sets of digit-algorithms for three classes of number representation systems:

(1) *Conventional* (symbol CO) with a fixed positive radix $\mathbf{r}_i \geq 2$ and the canonical digit-value set $\{0, 1, 2, \cdots, \mathbf{r}_i - 1\}$
(2) *Signed-Digit* (symbol SD) with a fixed positive radix $\mathbf{r}_i \geq 3$ and the redundant digit-value set $\{-a, \cdots, -1, 0, 1, \cdots, a\}$ in which a is an integer satisfying $\mathbf{r}_i \div 2 < a < \mathbf{r}_i$ [11, 17]
(3) *Residue* (symbol RE) with a set of positive radices $\mathbf{r}_i$ such that $\mathrm{GCD}(\mathbf{r}_i, \mathbf{r}_j) \equiv 1$ for every pair of radices, and the digit-value sets $\{0, 1, 2, \cdots, \mathbf{r}_i - 1\}$ for every $\mathbf{r}_i$ [14].

The Iverson ("APL") [7] notation is used to state digit algorithms, and zero-origin leftward indexing is employed. The notation is summarized in Table II. Note that the order of execution of APL statements is from right to left except as indicated by parentheses.

Table III lists digit algorithms which use one or two operand digits $\mathbf{x}_i$, $\mathbf{y}_i$ (per position i) to form a single result-digit. The "SYMBOL" column contains a symbol used to identify the digit algorithm in vector algorithm specifications. The rightmost column "DEP.k" lists the dependency k of the digit algorithm as defined in the preceding section. Table IV lists the more complex digit algorithms which produce two result-digits (except for the RE number system) and may receive more than two operand-digits $(\mathbf{x}^1, \mathbf{x}^2, \mathbf{x}^3, \cdots, \mathbf{x}^m)$, or $(\mathbf{x}, \mathbf{y}, \mathbf{u}^1, \cdots, \mathbf{u}^q)$. All these digit algorithms are local. They are used to implement fast multiplication and multioperand summation vector algorithms, such as the "carry-save" addition for CO numbers.

TABLE II. Summary of notation.

SYMBOL	NAME	EXPLANATION
$\mathbf{x}$	d vector	n-tuple of digits
$\mathbf{x}_i$	digit	i^{th} component of $\mathbf{x}$
x	explicit value of $\mathbf{x}$	an integer, function of $\mathbf{x}$ and $\mathbf{r}$, defined by number system spec.
X	implicit value of $\mathbf{x}$	arithmetic function of x, defined by implied properties of $\mathbf{x}$
$\mathbf{r}_i$	radix of ith digit	integer (except: $0, 1, -1$)
$\mathbf{w}_i$	weight of ith digit	$\mathbf{w}_0 \equiv 1$; $\mathbf{w}_i \equiv \mathbf{r}_{i-1} \times \mathbf{w}_{i-1}$
Σ_i	value set of ith digit	set of $\mathbf{r}_i$ or more consecutive integers, including 0
$\rho\mathbf{x}$	size (length) of $\mathbf{x}$	count of digits in $\mathbf{x}$
$X @ Y$	relational operator $@ \equiv \{< \leqslant = \geqslant > \neq\}$	result is 1 if the relation @ holds, and 0 otherwise
$\mid X$	magnitude of X	
$Y \mid X$	residue	modulo Y residue of X
$\lfloor X$	floor	integer such that $\lfloor X \leqslant X < 1 + \lfloor X$ holds
$\times X$	signum	$\times X \equiv (X > 0) - (X < 0)$ values are $+1, 0, -1$
$X * Y$	power	X to the Yth power
$\equiv$	identity	$X \equiv Y$ asserts identity; not to be confused with operator $=$

TABLE III. One-digit and two-digit algorithms with one-digit results.

ALGORITHM NAME	NO. SYSTEM "NS"	SYMBOL: D_{xx}/NS	DIGIT ALGORITHM: ARITHMETIC SPECIFICATION	DEP. k
TRANSFER	All	$\longleftarrow$	$\mathbf{z}_i \longleftarrow \mathbf{x}_i$	1
LEFT SHIFT (m positions)	CO, SD	DLm/NS	$\mathbf{z}_{i+m} \longleftarrow \mathbf{x}_i$	1
	RE		not defined	
RIGHT SHIFT (m positions)	CO, SD	DRm/NS	$\mathbf{z}_{i-m} \longleftarrow \mathbf{x}_i$	1
	RE		not defined	
INVERSE	CO, RE	DI/NS	$\mathbf{z}_i \longleftarrow (\mathbf{r}_i - 1) - \mathbf{x}_i$	1
	SD	DI/SD	$\mathbf{z}_i \longleftarrow 0 - \mathbf{x}_i$	1
CARRY (2 digits)	CO	DC/CO	$\mathbf{c}_{i+1} \longleftarrow (\mathbf{x}_i + \mathbf{y}_i + \mathbf{c}_i) \geqslant \mathbf{r}_i$	$i + 1$
	SD	DC/SD	$\mathbf{t}_{i+1} = (\times \mathbf{x}_i + \mathbf{y}_i) \times (a \leqslant \mid (\mathbf{x}_i + \mathbf{y}_i))$	1
	RE		not defined	
SUM (2 digits)	CO	D+/CO	$\mathbf{s}_i \longleftarrow \mathbf{r}_i \mid (\mathbf{x}_i + \mathbf{y}_i + \mathbf{c}_i)$	$i + 1$
	SD	D+/SD	$\mathbf{s}_i \longleftarrow \mathbf{x}_i + \mathbf{y}_i + \mathbf{t}_i - \mathbf{t}_{i+1} \times \mathbf{r}_i$	2
	RE	D+/RE	$\mathbf{s}_i \longleftarrow \mathbf{r}_i \mid (\mathbf{x}_i + \mathbf{y}_i)$	1
BORROW (2 digits)	CO	DB/CO	$\mathbf{b}_{i+1} \longleftarrow ((\mathbf{x}_i - \mathbf{y}_i) - \mathbf{b}_i) < 0$	$i + 1$
	SD	DB/SD	$\mathbf{t}_{i+1} \longleftarrow (\times \mathbf{x}_i - \mathbf{y}_i) \times (a \leqslant \mid (\mathbf{x}_i - \mathbf{y}_i))$	1
	RE		not defined	
DIFFERENCE (2 digits)	CO	D−/CO	$\mathbf{d}_i \longleftarrow \mathbf{r}_i \mid (\mathbf{x}_i - \mathbf{y}_i) - \mathbf{b}_i$	$i + 1$
	SD	D−/SD	$\mathbf{d}_i \longleftarrow (\mathbf{x}_i - \mathbf{y}_i) + \mathbf{t}_i - \mathbf{t}_{i+1} \times \mathbf{r}_i$	2
	RE	D−/RE	$\mathbf{d}_i \longleftarrow \mathbf{r}_i \mid (\mathbf{x}_i - \mathbf{y}_i)$	1

TABLE IV. Local-digit algorithms with multidigit inputs and/or two-digit results.

ALGORITHM NAME; NOTES	NO. SYSTEM "NS"	SYMBOL: Dxx/NS	DIGIT ALGORITHM: ARITHMETIC SPECIFICATION
PRODUCT	CO	D×/CO	$\mathbf{ps}_i \longleftarrow \mathbf{r}_i \vert (\mathbf{x}_i \times \mathbf{y}_i)$
(2 digits)			$\mathbf{pc}_{i+1} \longleftarrow \lfloor (\mathbf{x}_i \times \mathbf{y}_i) \div \mathbf{r}_i$
	SD	D×/SD	$\mathbf{ps}_i \longleftarrow (\mathbf{x}_i \times \mathbf{y}_i) - \mathbf{pc}_{i+1} \times \mathbf{r}_i$
			$\mathbf{pc}_{i+1} \longleftarrow (\times \mathbf{x}_i \times \mathbf{y}_i) \times \lfloor (((\mathbf{r}_i - 1) - a) + \vert (\mathbf{x}_i \times \mathbf{y}_i)) \div \mathbf{r}_i$
	RE	D×/RE	$\mathbf{z}_i \longleftarrow \mathbf{r}_i \vert (\mathbf{x}_i \times \mathbf{y}_i)$
SUM	CO[1]	D+m/CO	$\mathbf{ms}_i \longleftarrow \mathbf{r}_i \vert (\mathbf{x}_i^1 + \cdots + \mathbf{x}_i^m)$
(m digits)			$\mathbf{mc}_{i+1} \longleftarrow \lfloor (\mathbf{x}_i^1 + \cdots + \mathbf{x}_i^m) \div \mathbf{r}_i$
[1]for CO, SD:	SD[1]	D+m/SD	$\mathbf{ms}_i \longleftarrow (\mathbf{x}_i^1 + \cdots + \mathbf{x}_i^m) - \mathbf{mc}_{i+1} \times \mathbf{r}_i$
$m \leqslant \mathbf{r}_i + 1$			$\mathbf{mc}_{i+1} \longleftarrow \mathbf{sn}_i \times \lfloor (((\mathbf{r}_i - a) - 1) + \vert (\mathbf{x}_i^1 + \cdots + \mathbf{x}_i^m)) \div \mathbf{r}_i$
[2]for RE:			where: $\mathbf{sn}_i \longleftarrow \times (\mathbf{x}_i^1 + \cdots + \mathbf{x}_i^m)$
m, q are arbitrary	RE[2]	D+m/RE	$\mathbf{z}_i \longleftarrow \mathbf{r}_i \vert (\mathbf{x}_i^1 + \cdots + \mathbf{x}_i^m)$
PRODUCT-AND-SUM	CO[3]	D×+q/CO	$\mathbf{ns}_i \longleftarrow \mathbf{r}_i \vert (\mathbf{u}_i^1 + \mathbf{u}_i^2 + \mathbf{x}_i \times \mathbf{y}_i)$
(2 and q digits)			$\mathbf{nc}_{i+1} \longleftarrow \lfloor (\mathbf{u}_i^1 + \mathbf{u}_i^2 + \mathbf{x}_i \times \mathbf{y}_i) \div \mathbf{r}_i$
	SD[4]	D×+q/SD	$\mathbf{ns}_i \longleftarrow (\mathbf{u}_i^1 + \cdots + \mathbf{u}_i^q + \mathbf{x}_i \times \mathbf{y}_i) - \mathbf{nc}_{i+1} \times \mathbf{r}_i$
[3]for CO:			$\mathbf{nc}_{i+1} \longleftarrow \mathbf{sn}_i \times \lfloor (((\mathbf{r}_i - a) - 1) + \vert (\mathbf{u}_i^1 + \cdots + \mathbf{u}_i^q + \mathbf{x}_i \times \mathbf{y}_i)) \div \mathbf{r}_i$
$q \leqslant 2$ [4]for SD:			where: $\mathbf{sn}_i \longleftarrow \times (\mathbf{u}_i^1 + \cdots + \mathbf{u}_i^q + \mathbf{x}_i \times \mathbf{y}_i)$
$q \leqslant \mathbf{r}_i - a + 1$	RE[2]	D×+q/RE	$\mathbf{z}_i \longleftarrow \mathbf{r}_i \vert (\mathbf{u}_i^1 + \cdots + \mathbf{u}_i^q + \mathbf{x}_i \times \mathbf{y}_i)$

C. Vector Algorithms for Conventional Number Systems

In order to perform arithmetic, the digit algorithms are organized into *vector algorithms*. A vector algorithm is a prescription for generating the result(s) from the given operand(s). The *operands* are *d* vectors (**x**, **y**, etc.), employing zero-origin leftward indexing and characterized by their length n, the radix vector $\mathbf{r}$ and the sets of allowed digit values Σ_i for $0 \leq i \leq n-1$. In the conventional number systems the fixed radix $\mathbf{r}_i > 1$ and the canonical set of digit values are employed for every position. The weight $\mathbf{r}_i^i$ is associated with the digit $\mathbf{x}_i$.

The *result* may be either a digit vector (**z**, **p**, **q**, etc.), or a condition-code vector ε. A *d* vector will be generated when an arithmetic operation (for example: addition, subtraction, multiplication, division) is specified by the operation code. A two-valued logic variable ε_i (1 for true and 0 for false) will be the result for magnitude comparison, zero detection, overflow detection, range estimate, and similar algorithms.

The vector algorithms describe the digits of the result(s) in terms of the operand digits. Some digits of the result(s) may be specified directly as a function of the particular number system (for instance, the right-end digit in a left shift, etc.). If the result is a condition-code logic variable, its value is specified in terms of all or some digits of the operand(s).

The arithmetic algorithms usually specified by the set of operation codes are: transfer, additive inverse (sign change), absolute value, addition, subtraction, multiplication, roundoff, arithmetic shifts (for normalization, overflow correction, alignment in floating point) and division. Occasionally inter-radix conversions, square root, exponentiation, trigonometric functions and other more-elaborate algorithms may be specified, as well as intersystem or interformat conversions (residue to binary, etc.). The extension and contraction of range, although not explicitly stated, are implied in the above list. The preceding algorithms all yield numeric results; besides them logic results are obtained from the sign test, zero test, comparison and range-estimate algorithms.

Table V lists a typical set of vector algorithms with one or two operands. This is the "user's viewpoint" in which only the implicit values and the lengths of the results are specified. The "Statement" column uses APL function notation to describe the vector algorithms. The dollar sign $ represents a number-system identifier which uniquely identifies the details (both explicit and implied) of the number representation system. In addition to operand length, radix vector, indexing system, it also describes the implied properties, such as those listed in Table I. A program specifying the result-digits by means of digit algorithms exists for every identifier.

Tables VI and VII illustrate vector algorithm descriptions for some of the

TABLE V. Common one-vector and two-vector algorithms: symbols and "user's" specifications.

VECTOR ALGORITHM	STATEMENT[1]	LENGTH ρz[2]	IMPLICIT VALUE Z
TRANSFER	z ← x	n	$Z \leftarrow X$
RANGE EXTENSION[3]			
m positions	z ← m REX$ x	$n+m$	$Z \leftarrow X$
RANGE CONTRACTION			
m positions	z ← m RCN$ x	$n-m$	$Z \leftarrow X$
LEFT ARITH. SHIFT[4]			
m positions	z ← m LSH$ x	n	$Z \leftarrow X \times \mathbf{r}_i * m$
RIGHT ARITH. SHIFT[4]			
m positions	z ← m RSH$ x	n	$Z \leftarrow X \times \mathbf{r}_i * (-m)$
ADDITIVE INVERSE	z ← INV$ x	n	$Z \leftarrow 0 - X$
ROUNDOFF[5]			
m positions	z ← m RND$ x	$n-m$	$Z \leftarrow (X - D)$
SUM	z ← x SUM$ y	n	$Z \leftarrow X + Y$
DIFFERENCE	z ← x DIF$ y	n	$Z \leftarrow X - Y$
PRODUCT	z ← x PRD$ y	$n+n$	$Z \leftarrow X \times Y$
QUOTIENT[6]	q ← x QNT$ y	n	$Q \leftarrow (X - W) \div Y$
REMAINDER[6]	w ← x REM$ y	n	$W \leftarrow X - Q \times Y$
ZERO TEST[7]	ε_0 ← ZRO$ x		$\varepsilon_0 \leftarrow X = 0$
POSITIVE TEST[7]	ε_1 ← POS$ x		$\varepsilon_1 \leftarrow X > 0$
NEGATIVE TEST[7]	ε_2 ← NEG$ x		$\varepsilon_2 \leftarrow X < 0$
RANGE TEST (A, B)[7]	ε_3 ← A, B RTS$ x		$\varepsilon_3 \leftarrow (X < A) \vee (X > B)$

[1]The symbol $ represents the number system identifier for the algorithm.

[2]Operands **x**, y have the length n unless explicitly noted otherwise.

[3]If radix of **x** is not fixed, replace m by a vector listing the m new radices to be used.

[4]Applicable to fixed-radix ($\mathbf{r}_i \geqslant 2$) operands only.

[5]The range of D is $D_{min} < D < D_{max}$; the range is a function of the m deleted digits and their radices.

[6]Length of operand **x** is $n + n$ digits. The remainder W has the same sign as the dividend X and satisfies $(|W) < (|Y)$.

[7]The tests yield two-valued results ε_i, which form the condition-code vector $\boldsymbol{\varepsilon}$.

algorithms listed in Table V. The CO (conventional) number system with n-digit operands and an even fixed radix $\mathbf{r}_i$ has been selected. Two methods to represent negative numbers are employed:

(1) The symbol RC stands for Range Complement (often called two's or ten's complement when $\mathbf{r}_i$ is 2 or 10, respectively) in which negative numbers are represented as complements with respect to $(\mathbf{r}_i)^n$

(2) The symbol DC stands for Digit Complement (colloquially: one's, or nine's complement when $\mathbf{r}_i$ is 2 or 10, respectively) in which negative numbers are represented as complements with respect to $(\mathbf{r}_i)^n - 1$.

Table VI specifies vector algorithms which generate a digit vector as the result. The rightmost column identifies and labels the singularities which may occur with the given algorithm. Three common variants of the roundoff algorithm are specified. The "exact round" singularity for method 2 identifies the case in

TABLE VI. Vector algorithm specifications.

VECTOR ALGORITHM	NUMBER SYSTEM ID. "\$"	DIGIT POSITIONS IN z	DIGIT ALGORITHMS FOR SPECIFIED POSITIONS OF z	NAME OF SINGULARITY (SEE TABLE VII)
$\mathbf{z} \leftarrow m$ REX\$ $\mathbf{x}$	RC, DC	$0, \cdots, n-1$	$\mathbf{z}_i \leftarrow \mathbf{x}_i$	None
	RC, DC	$n, \cdots, n+m-1$	$\mathbf{z}_i \leftarrow (\mathbf{r}_i - 1) \times (\mathbf{x}_{n-1} \geqslant \mathbf{r}_i \div 2)$	
$\mathbf{z} \leftarrow m$ RCN\$ $\mathbf{x}$	RC, DC	$0, \cdots, n-m-1$	$\mathbf{z}_i \leftarrow \mathbf{x}_i$	Overflow OF/RCN\$
	RC, DC	$n-m, \cdots, n-1$	$\mathbf{z}_i \leftarrow \iota 0$ (null)	
$\mathbf{z} \leftarrow m$ LSH\$ $\mathbf{x}$	RC, DC	$m, \cdots, n-1$	DLm/CO	Overflow OF/LSH\$
	RC	$0, \cdots, m-1$	$\mathbf{z}_i \leftarrow 0$	
	DC	$0, \cdots, m-1$	$\mathbf{z}_i \leftarrow (\mathbf{r}_i - 1) \times (\mathbf{x}_{n-1} \geqslant \mathbf{r}_i \div 2)$	
$\mathbf{z} \leftarrow m$ RSH\$	RC, DC	$0, \cdots, n-m-1$	DRm/CO	Truncation TR/RSH\$
	RC, DC	$n-m, \cdots, n-1$	$\mathbf{z}_i \leftarrow (\mathbf{r}_i - 1) \times (\mathbf{x}_{n-1} \geqslant \mathbf{r}_i \div 2)$	
$\mathbf{z} \leftarrow$ INV\$ $\mathbf{x}$	DC	$0, \cdots, n-1$	DI/CO	Inverse Anomaly AN/INV\$
	RC	$0, \cdots, n-1$	D+/CO with: $\mathbf{x}_i \leftarrow 0$, $\mathbf{y}_i \leftarrow (\mathbf{r}_i - 1) - \mathbf{x}_i$	
	RC	0	$\mathbf{c}_0 \leftarrow 1$	
$\mathbf{z} \leftarrow \mathbf{x}$ SUM\$ $\mathbf{y}$	RC, DC	$0, \cdots, n-1$	D+/CO or D−/CO	Overflow OF SUM\$ or OF/DIF\$
or	RC	0	$\mathbf{c}_0 \leftarrow 0$ or $\mathbf{b}_0 \leftarrow 0$	
$\mathbf{z} \leftarrow \mathbf{x}$ DIF\$ $\mathbf{y}$	DC	0	$\mathbf{c}_0 \leftarrow \mathbf{c}_n$ or $\mathbf{b}_0 \leftarrow \mathbf{b}_n$	
$\mathbf{z} \leftarrow m$ RND\$ $\mathbf{x}$	RC, DC	$0, \cdots, m-1$	$\mathbf{z}_i \leftarrow \iota 0$ (null)	
(1) Truncation	RC, DC	$m, \cdots, n-1$	$\mathbf{z}_i \leftarrow \mathbf{x}_i$	None
(2) Local Adjust.	RC, DC	m	$\mathbf{z}_m \leftarrow \mathbf{x}_m + (\mathbf{x}_m < \mathbf{r}_i \div 2)$	Exact Round EX/RND2\$
		$m+1, \cdots, n-1$	$\mathbf{z}_i \leftarrow \mathbf{x}_i$	
(3) Sum Adjust.	RC, DC	m	D+/CO with: $\mathbf{c}_m \leftarrow 0$, $\mathbf{y}_m \leftarrow (\mathbf{x}_{m+1} \geqslant \mathbf{r}_i \div 2)$	Overflow OF/RND3\$
		$m+1, \cdots, n-1$	D+/CO with: $\mathbf{y}_i \leftarrow 0$	

TABLE VII. Vector algorithms for tests and singularities.

VECTOR ALGORITHM	NUMBER SYSTEM	ALGORITHM SPECIFICATION
TESTS:		
$\varepsilon_0 \longleftarrow$ ZRO$ **x**	RC	$\varepsilon_0 \longleftarrow (0 = +/\mathbf{x})$
	DC	$\varepsilon_0 \longleftarrow (0 = +/\mathbf{x}) \vee ((+/\mathbf{x}) = (\mathbf{r}_i - 1) \times \rho\mathbf{x})$
$\varepsilon_1 \longleftarrow$ POS$ **x**	RC, DC	$\varepsilon_1 \longleftarrow (\mathbf{x}_{n-1} < \mathbf{r}_i \div 2)$
$\varepsilon_2 \longleftarrow$ NEG$ **x**	RC, DC	$\varepsilon_2 \longleftarrow (\mathbf{x}_{n-1} \geqslant \mathbf{r}_i \div 2)$
SINGULARITIES:		
$\sigma_0 \longleftarrow$ OF/*m*RCN$ **x** $\sigma_0 \longleftarrow$ OF/*m*LSH$ **x**	RC, DC	$\sigma_0 \longleftarrow ((\mathbf{x}_{n-m-1} < \mathbf{r}_i \div 2) \wedge (0 \neq +/(m \uparrow \mathbf{x})) \vee$ $(\mathbf{x}_{n-m-1} \geqslant \mathbf{r}_i \div 2) \wedge (\rho\mathbf{x} \times (\mathbf{r}_i - 1)) \neq +/(m \uparrow \mathbf{x})$
$\sigma_1 \longleftarrow$ TR/*m*RSH$ **x**	RC	$\sigma_1 \longleftarrow (0 \neq +/(-m \uparrow \mathbf{x}))$
$\sigma_1 \longleftarrow$ EX/RND2$ **x**	DC	$\sigma_1 \longleftarrow (0 \neq +/(-m \uparrow \mathbf{x})) \vee (\rho\mathbf{x} \times (\mathbf{r}_i - 1)) \neq +/(-m \uparrow \mathbf{x})$
$\sigma_2 \longleftarrow$ AN/INV$ **x**	RC	$\sigma_2 \longleftarrow (\mathbf{x}_{n-1} = \mathbf{r}_i \div 2) \wedge ((+/\mathbf{x}) = (\mathbf{r}_i \div 2))$
	DC	$\sigma_2 \longleftarrow (0 = +/\mathbf{x})$
$\sigma_3 \longleftarrow$ OF/SUM$ **x**, **y** $\sigma_3 \longleftarrow$ OF/DIF$ **x**, **y**	RC, DC	$\sigma_3 \longleftarrow ((\mathbf{x}_{n-1} < \mathbf{r}_i \div 2) \wedge (\mathbf{y}_{n-1} < \mathbf{r}_i \div 2) \wedge (\mathbf{z}_{n-1} \geqslant \mathbf{r}_i \div 2)) \vee$ $((\mathbf{x}_{n-1} \geqslant \mathbf{r}_i \div 2) \wedge (\mathbf{y}_{n-1} \geqslant \mathbf{r}_i \div 2) \wedge (\mathbf{z}_{n-1} < \mathbf{r}_i \div 2))$
$\sigma_4 \longleftarrow$ OF/RND3$ **x**	RC, DC	$\sigma_4 \longleftarrow ((\mathbf{x}_{n-1} < \mathbf{r}_i \div 2) \wedge (\mathbf{z}_{n-1} \geqslant \mathbf{r}_i \div 2)) \vee$ $((\mathbf{x}_{n-1} \geqslant \mathbf{r}_i \div 2) \wedge (\mathbf{z}_{n-1} < \mathbf{r}_i \div 2))$

which truncation should take place regardless of the value of $\mathbf{x}_m$. The sum and difference algorithms represent the "ripple" carry or borrow implementation. The methods of fast addition (lookahead, conditional sum, etc.) can also be specified in a similar fashion. The specifications of fast addition, multiplication, and division will appear together with their comparative evaluations in a subsequent paper.

Table VII specifies the algorithms which generate test results ε_i and singularity indicators σ_i. Two new operator symbols appear in this table. The sum reduction operator $+/\mathbf{x}$ forms the sum $\mathbf{x}_0 + \mathbf{x}_1 + \mathbf{x}_2 + \cdots + \mathbf{x}_{n-1}$ of all digits of $\mathbf{x}$. The "take" operator $k \uparrow \mathbf{x}$ takes the leftmost k digits of $\mathbf{x}$ if k is positive, and the rightmost k digits of $\mathbf{x}$ if k is negative.

In the singularity list, σ_0 indicates that a left shift or range contraction cannot be done without losing an "overflow" part of the result. The signal σ_1 indicates that a right shift will result in an imprecise (truncated) result. The signal σ_2 indicates an anomaly in the inverse—for RC, it results in an overflow, and for DC the "minus zero" is generated. Signals σ_3 and σ_4 detect overflow after add, subtract and round (with addition) operations.

The main conclusion which can be drawn from Tables III–VII is that a purely arithmetical specification of digital computer processors offers a compact and technology-independent method of describing the operations which are needed. The logic designer takes over at this point and chooses the algorithms which are most effective for his present set of logic circuitry.

ACKNOWLEDGEMENT

This research was supported in part by the U. S. Atomic Energy Commission, Contract No. AT(11-1) Gen 10, Project 14.

Thanks are due to the many graduate students in the UCLA Computer Science Department Course 225A "Computer System Design: Arithmetic Processors" whose comments and constructive criticism on the description of computer arithmetic have stimulated the evolution of this paper.

REFERENCES

[1] D. L. MacSorley, "High Speed Arithmetic in Digital Computers," *Proc. IRE*, **49**, No. 1, 67–91 (January 1961).

[2] S. Winograd, "On the Time Required to Perform Addition," *J. ACM*, **12**, No. 2, 277–285 (1965).

[3] S. Winograd, "On the Time Required to Perform Multiplication," *J. ACM*, **14**, No. 4, 793–802 (1967).

[4] A. Avižienis, "On the Problem of Computational Time and Complexity of Arithmetic Functions," *Proc. ACM Symp. Theory of Computing*, Los Angeles, California, 255–258 (May 5–6, 1969).

[5] A. Avižienis, "Theory of Digital-Computer Arithmetic," Notes for UCLA Course Engineering 225A, Ch. 1–3 (to be published).

[6] A. A. Markov, *Theory of Algorithms*, USSR Academy of Sciences: MOSCOW, 1954. English translation published by the Israel Program for Scientific Translations, PST Catalog No. 219, Jerusalem (1961).

[7] K. E. Iverson, *A Programming Language* (New York: Wiley, 1962).

[8] G. W. Patterson, "Algebraic Foundations of Number-Representation Systems," Univ. of Pennsylvania, The Moore School of Electrical Engineering, Report No. 59-00 (September 1, 1958).

[9] J. E. Robertson, "Redundant Number Systems for Digital-Computer Arithmetic," Notes for the University of Michigan Eng. Summer Conf., "Topics in the Design of Digital Computing Machines," Ann Arbor, Mich. (July 6–10, 1959).

[10] H. L. Garner, "Number Systems and Arithmetic," *Advances in Computers*, **6**, 131–194 (Academic Press, 1965).

[11] A. Avižienis, "Signed-Digit Number Representations for Fast Parallel Arithmetic," *IRE Trans. Electr. Comput.*, **EC-10**, No. 3, 389–400 (September 1961).

[12] G. F. Songster, "Negative-Base Number Representation Systems," *IEEE Trans. Comput.*, **EC-12**, No. 3, 274–277 (June 1963).

[13] D. E. Knuth, "An Imaginary Number System," *Comm. ACM*, **3**, 245–247 (April 1960).

[14] A. Svoboda, "The Numerical System of Residual Classes," *Digital Information Processors*, 543–574 (W. Hoffman, Ed., New York: Interscience Publishers, 1962).

[15] N. Metropolis and R. L. Ashenhurst, "Significant-Digit Computer Arithmetic," *IRE Trans. Elec. Comput.*, **EC-7**, No. 4, 265-267 (December 1958).

[16] W. W. Peterson, *Error-Correcting Codes*, 236–244 (Massachusetts: The MIT Press, 1961).

[17] A. Avižienis and C. Tung, "A Universal Arithmetic Building Element (ABE) and Design Methods for Arithmetic Processors," *IEEE Trans. Comput.*, **C-19**, No. 8, 733–745 (August 1970).

CELLULAR ARRAYS AND ARITHMETIC UNITS: A SYNTHESIS PROCEDURE

R. G. Cornell and H. C. Torng
School of Electrical Engineering, Cornell University, Ithaca, NY

This paper presents: (1) A synthesis procedure for cellular arrays by which the typical cell is derived from a set of predetermined array specifications; and (2) Its application in the design and evaluation of a parallel arithmetic unit.

The concept of modified dominoes and their corresponding total states are introduced. A set of total states is specified for each of the array's operational requirements. The collection of all the sets thus specified characterizes the typical cell, which is used iteratively to form an array. The resulting array is capable of performing *all* of the desired operations.

The arithmetic unit cell obtained contains no identifiable computing circuits such as full adders, accumulators, etc. Its implementation meets the constraints imposed by current LSI technology.

I. INTRODUCTION

With the advent of large-scale integration (LSI), the focus of computer design is turning toward systems compatible with the special attributes and constraints of the new technology. LSI will allow for the fabrication of highly complex logic circuits on subminiature substrates. As the bulk of the cost of these chips will be devoted to the design and layout of the circuit, mask design, and debugging, it is economically sensible to design circuits which will perform many functions, rather than to design individual circuits for each function. This consideration brings about the study of iterative arrays. The building block of such arrays would be a single-cell type into which is incorporated the hardware necessary to allow the total array to perform all of its required functions.

In the majority of the work reported in the field of cellular computing devices [1, 3, 4], the designer prespecifies the cell structure and then investigates the resulting array properties. This approach may result in a cell which is composed of an excessive amount of hardware.

In this paper, the authors propose a systematic procedure by which the desired performance of the total computing array is used to specify a set of cell *total states*. These total states completely describe the necessary input-output-memory behavior of the basic cell. In order to describe these total states, a modification of the domino method is proposed. We will describe the design of a cellular arithmetic unit as an illustrative example of the procedure proposed. The procedure is not limited to arithmetic processors but could be easily used to

---

Presented at the Symposium on Computers and Automata
Polytechnic Institute of Brooklyn, April 13–15, 1971.

design associative memory arrays, control logic arrays, I/O devices, and other cellular-computing devices.

II. CONSTRAINTS IMPOSED BY LSI

A major concern in the design procedure presented is to keep the amount of logic per cell within the bounds of what can be produced on a single LSI chip. Currently, LSI chips feature between 200 and 500 gates [5].

Another limitation of LSI which must be considered in circuit design is that of external connections. We assume that LSI chips allow a maximum of 10 connective leads per edge and 40 leads per chip.

A final limitation of note is that of loading. No multicell information busses are used. The result is that all intercell communication must be on a nearest-neighbor basis.

III. SYNTHESIS PROCEDURE

Communication between the array and external devices takes place only at its four boundaries. There are two forms of communication between the array and external devices, those of data transfer and of array control. Input data to be processed by the array, the *primary input,* appear along its top boundary. The array's data output may appear at either the array's top or bottom boundaries and is termed its *primary output.*

External control of the array is performed at the array's side boundaries; control signals directing the operation of individual rows of the array appear at the left boundary and are termed the *row-function initiation* (RFI) inputs; control signals supplying information to the array concerning its size and contents appear at the right boundary and are termed the *row-end* (RE) inputs. The array format appears as Figure 1.

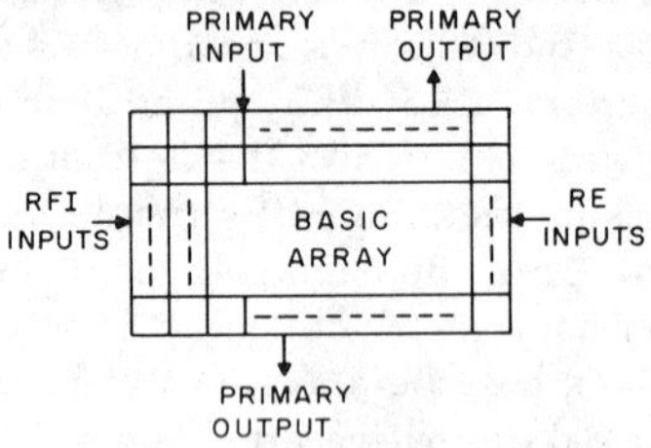

Fig. 1. Array format.

The *cell,* which is the building block of the array, is itself two dimensional, with all communication occurring at the cell edges. Intercell communication in the array occurs along the array axes, *horizontal intercell signals* parallel to the array's rows and *vertical signals* parallel to the array's columns. This suggests a cell having four edges at which intercell communication is possible (Figure 2).

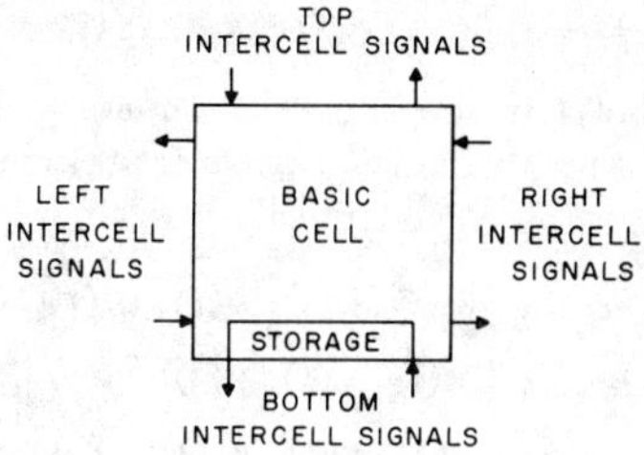

Fig. 2. Cell format.

The use of a two-dimensional network lends itself perfectly to the processing of data in the parallel mode. The array is thus a stack of rows, each row containing a word and acting as a unit when given an instruction. Each cell in the row acts on one bit of the word contained. By this scheme, the primary input to the array appears in parallel, one bit per column. The number of columns is determined by the size of words and the number of rows by the complexity of computation of array operations ordered by an external control unit. The actual specification of array size will be discussed in Section VI.

IV. CELL ANALYSIS UTILIZING THE CONCEPT OF CELL TOTAL STATE

Intercell signals will be represented by lower-case letters when they are incoming communications or *cell inputs*. Conversely, intercell signals representing *cell outputs* are denoted by upper-case letters.

Time is represented in cell analysis by integers. Each cell (Fig. 3) is an automaton with a finite set of internal states. The cell *internal state* at instant $t+1$, $s_i(t+1)$, is uniquely determined at instant t by the internal state function f_I

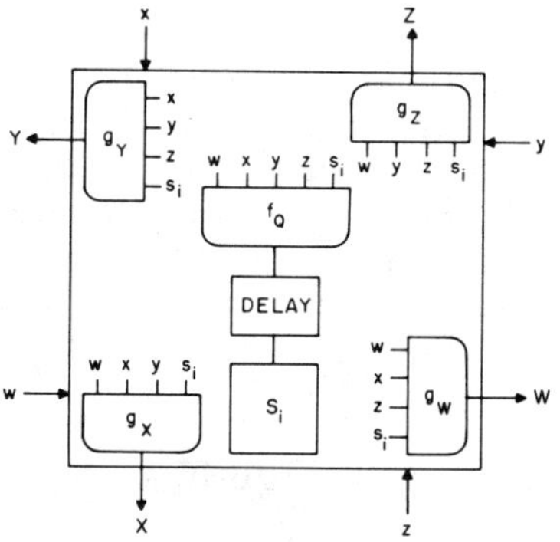

Fig. 3. Cell internal structure.

$$s_i(t+1) = f_I\left[w(t),\ x(t),\ y(t),\ z(t),\ s_i(t)\right] ,$$

where $\{w(t),\ x(t),\ y(t),\ z(t)\}$ is the set of all inputs to the cell at t. The cell responds to its inputs at t by producing four outputs which are specified by their respective output functions, as follows

$$W(t) = g_W\left[w(t),\ x(t),\ z(t),\ s_i(t)\right] ,$$
$$X(t) = g_X\left[w(t),\ x(t),\ y(t),\ s_i(t)\right] ,$$
$$Y(t) = g_Y\left[x(t),\ y(t),\ z(t),\ s_i(t)\right] ,$$
$$Z(t) = g_z\left[w(t),\ y(t),\ z(t),\ s_i(t)\right] .$$

At t, each edge of a cell receives an input from the adjacent cell (or array boundary) and sends an output to it. This input-output pair is termed an *intercell state*. For our two-dimensional cell, $s_a \equiv \{x, Z\}$, $s_r \equiv \{y, W\}$, $s_b \equiv \{z, X\}$, and $s_\ell \equiv \{w, Y\}$ denote the top-, right-, bottom-, and left-intercell states respectively. A cell specified completely by the 4-tuple $[s_a,\ s_r,\ s_b,\ s_\ell]$ is called a "domino" [2]

The general cell previously specified includes an internal state, hence the domino method of cell evaluation is not applicable. We define a *modified domino* (MD) which is endowed with an *internal state* s_i. With the introduction of an internal state, the MD describes a sequential circuit.

A cell's *total state* at t, $S(t)$, is represented by the 6-tuple $\left[s_t(t), s_r(t), s_b(t),\ s_\ell(t),\ s_i(t),\ s_j(t)\right]$ where $s_j(t) = s_i(t+1)$. In essence, $s_j(t)$ is the next internal state. The MD describing a cell total state has each edge marked by a symbol which represents an intercell state and an internal and next-internal states indicated in the center (Figure 4).

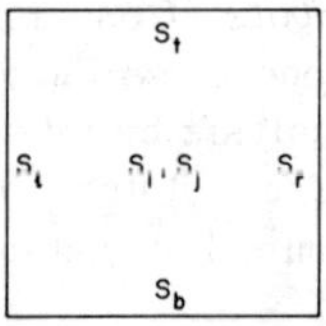

Fig. 4. The modified domino.

Each *type* of MD (one MD type per cell total state) has a specific orientation; no MD may be rotated or flipped over. MDs may be placed side-by-side, provided the markings on adjacent edges match exactly. There is no restriction on the number of times a specific MD type may be used in an array. In addition, the internal state of the MD to be inserted at t in an array location must match the next internal state of the MD to occupy that array location at $t - 1$. The domino model for cell representation is thus a special case of MD, one for which the internal state remains unchanged.

V. CELL SYNTHESIS PROCEDURE—AN ARITHMETIC UNIT

The mechanics of translating an array description into an MD set and the subsequent specification of the corresponding typical cell is best presented by an example. We will describe the construction of a parallel arithmetic unit (AU) whose array format is represented in Fig. 1, with any individual row being capable of performing any of the following *row functions* (arbitrarily specified) upon the proper RFI command (a symbol representing the RFI command follows each function in parentheses):

1. Idle (Z)
2. Accumulate (S)
3. Enter Row Above (C)
4. Exclusive-OR (bitwise with primary input) (D)
5. (Two's) Complement (T)
6. Logical Left Shift (G)
7. Logical Right Shift (J)
8. Load Row as Array Top Primary Output (L)
9. Arithmetic Right Shift (M)
10. Arithmetic Left Shift (N)
11. Logical OR (bitwise with primary input) (P)
12. Logical AND (bitwise with primary input) (Q)

The general procedure of cell specification is as follows:

(1) A set of MDs is generated corresponding to each function desired. The collection of these sets describes the behavior of the typical cell

(2) A tabular representation of the MDs is utilized to determine the five basic switching functions f_I, g_W, g_X, g_Y, and g_Z

(3) The switching functions are implemented with prescribed gates.

A. Modified Domino Assignment

For the arithmetic unit proposed, bilateral communication occurs along both axes. The basic cell structure is independent of the size of the array, hence the cell may be derived from the array specifications as applied to an array of any size. In the AU, each row must act as a unit upon the word contained. We will study at this point the $1 \times n$ array (Figure 5). The array boundary inputs consist

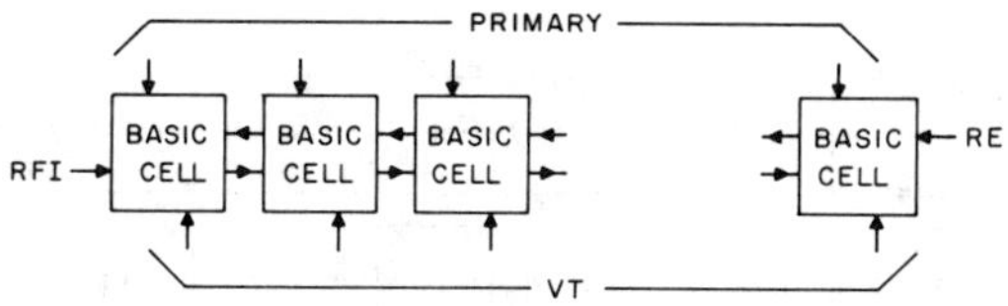

Fig. 5. Single-row array: boundary inputs.

of RFI (left) signal, RE (right) signal, a primary-input (top) signal and a vertical-transfer (VT) signal (bottom).

For an AU designed to operate on words of constant size, only one RE signal is needed. It will be a constant for all row operations. Each row operation is defined and initiated by some RFI signal. The vertical inputs are independent of the row function at t. A set of MDs may be determined for each of the RFI signals, and the set of all such MDs will completely describe the array's basic cell.

1. Specification of "Accumulate" MDs

As an example of MD specification, the MD set corresponding to the RFI command "*S*" ("Accumulate") will be presented.

The RFI command "*S*" initiates a unilateral right-going intercell signal containing the information "perform an accumulation." This signal must reach all cells in the row, and is not altered by the contents or other inputs to a row, hence we may assign the symbol "*S*" to the **w** input and **W** output of all cells. The RE input (defined to be "*R*") must convey the information "lowest-order bit, no carry." It initiates a left-going unilateral intercell signal which contains the information "carry absent/present" and is altered by the primary input and internal state of each cell it passes through. The left-going signal between adjacent cells may therefore take on two values, denoted "*A*" ("carry absent") and "*B*" ("carry present"). It follows that the cell's **y** input may assume the values "*R*", "*A*", or "*B*", while the **Y** output may assume the values "*A*" and "*B*". The primary input to each cell consists of a single digit of the primary input word, hence may assume the values {0, 1}. We shall specify that the cell primary output **X** is the same as the cell present state (s_i) and may therefore assume the values {0, 1}. The cell's VT input **z** does not affect an accumulation, and is regarded as a don't-care literal (similarly **Z**). In summary, each cell receives three inputs: *y*, *w*, and *x*. These inputs, together with the internal state s_i, generate three outputs, *Y*, *W*, and *X*, and a next internal state s_j.

The set of intercell states, which denote horizontal communications, consists of two elements, namely (*S*, *A*) and (*S*, *B*). The set of intercell states, which denote vertical communications, consists of two elements, namely (0, *z*) and (1, *z*). The set of all internal states is {0, 1}.

The twenty resulting MDs for accumulation are shown in Figure 6.

The use of these MDs in describing an accumulation is shown in the following example: accumulate 5 into 3 (binary). It is assumed that the row in question (Fig. 7) has the number 0011 in the cell storage devices of the four-cell row. At

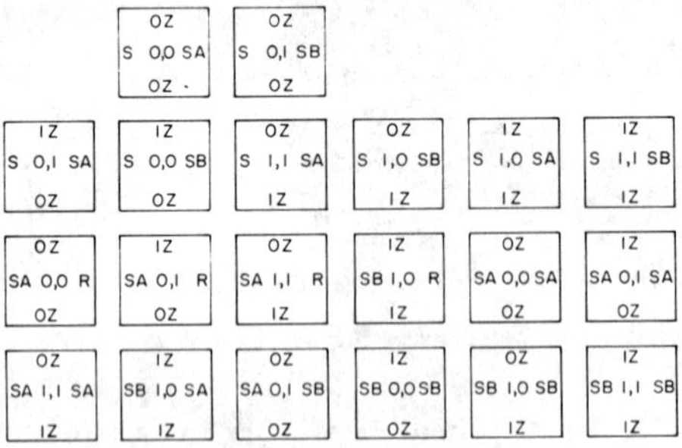

Fig. 6. "Accumulate" MDs.

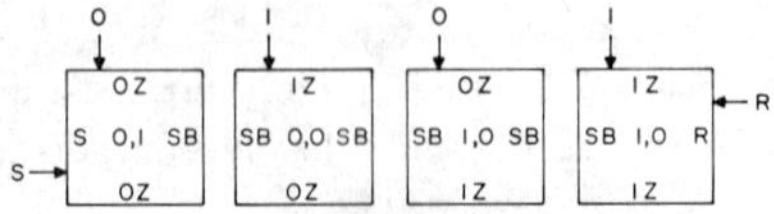

Fig. 7. "Accumulate" MD example.

t, these values appear as the cells' present internal states. The binary number 0101 appears as the primary input. "*S*" appears as the RFI input and "*R*" the RE input.

2. Specification of MDs to Complete the Arithmetic Unit

The same procedure is followed to specify dominoes for the remaining eleven row functions. Each is handled as though it was to be the sole function of the eventual cell. The MDs representing the remaining functions appear as Figure 8.

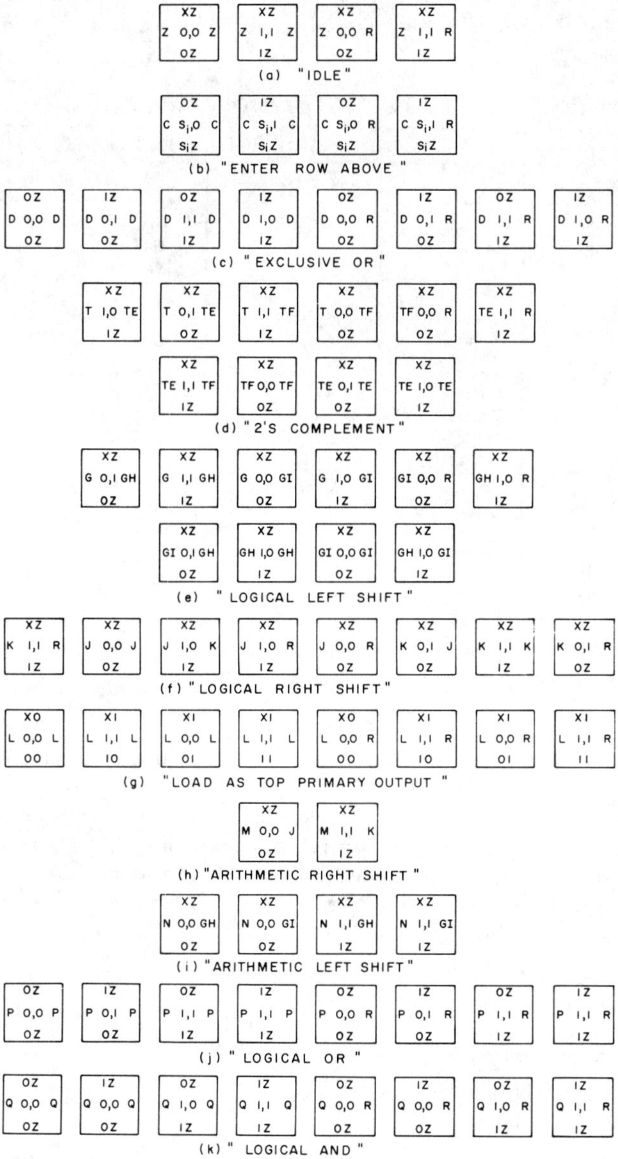

Fig. 8. Remaining MDs describing the arithmetic unit's basic cell.

B. Tabular Representation of MDs

An intercell state successor table [2] is constructed to represent the cell's unilateral signal behavior in each of the four possible directions.

1. *Table Representing Right-Going Signals*

If the set of MDs defined are considered to describe right-going (horizontal) signal behavior, we can produce an intercell state (IS) successor table, featuring $\{s_\ell\}$ as the table's predecessor states, $\{s_i, s_t\}$ as the table's independent parameters, and $\{s_r\}$ as the set of IS successors. The table (Table I) is filled by inspection of the MDs.

TABLE I. Unreduced IS successor table for right-going signals.

LEFT-EDGE PREDECESSOR	INDEPENDENT PARAMETERS (s_i, s_t)			
	00	01	10	11
S	*SA, SB*	*SA, SB*	*SA, SB*	*SA, SB*
SA	*SA, SB, R*	*SA, R*	*SA, R*	—
SB	—	*SB*	*SB*	*SA, SB, R*
Z	*Z, R*	*Z, R*	*Z, R*	*Z, R*
C	*C, R*	*C, R*	*C, R*	*C, R*
D	*D, R*	*D, R*	*D, R*	*D, R*
T	*TE, TF*	*TE, TF*	*TE, TF*	*TE, TF*
TE	*TE*	*TE*	*TE, TF, R*	*TE, TF, R*
TF	*TF, R*	*TF, R*	—	—
G	*GH, GI*	*GH, GI*	*GH, GI*	*GH, GI*
GH	—	—	*GH, GI, R*	*GH, GI, R*
GI	*GH, GI, R*	*GH, GI, R*	—	—
J	*J, R*	*J, R*	*K, R*	*K, R*
K	*J, R*	*J, R*	*K, R*	*K, R*
L	*L, R*	*L, R*	*L, R*	*L, R*
M	*J*	*J*	*K*	*K*
N	*G*	*G*	*G*	*G*
P	*P, R*	*P, R*	*P, R*	*P, R*
Q	*Q, R*	*Q, R*	*Q, R*	*Q, R*

This table may be "reduced" by applying three criteria:

(1) Each successor state in a table must also appear as a predecessor state

(2) A right (left) array-boundary state may not appear as a left (right) predecessor in an IS successor table, hence those literals may be dropped from any term which is used to form new predecessors

(3) Predecessor states which are neither RFI (or RE) inputs nor sucessors of *other* predecessors are removed (these states are never called for).

Applying the criteria in the order presented yields the following *reduced* IS successor table (Table II).

2. *Table Representing Right-Going Signals*

The same methods and criteria are applied to yield the reduced left-going IS successor table (Table III).

TABLE II. Reduced IS successor table for right-going signals.

LEFT-EDGE PREDECESSOR	INDEPENDENT PARAMETERS (s_i, s_t)			
	00	01	10	11
S	SA, SB	SA, SB	SA, SB	SA, SB
SA, SB	SA, SB	SA, SB	SA, SB	SA, SB
Z	Z	Z	Z	Z
C	C	C	C	C
D	D	D	D	D
T	TE, TF	TE, TF	TE, TF	TE, TF
TE, TF	TE, TF	TE, TF	TE, TF	TE, TF
G	GH, GI	GH, GI	GH, GI	GH, GI
GH, GI	GH, GI	GH, GI	GH, GI	GH, GI
J	J	J	K	K
K	J	J	K	K
L	L	L	L	L
M	J	J	K	K
N	G	G	G	G
P	P	P	P	P
Q	Q	Q	Q	Q

TABLE III. Reduced IS successor table for left-going signals.

RIGHT-EDGE PREDECESSOR	INDEPENDENT PARAMETERS (s_i, s_t)			
	00	01	10	11
R	SA, TF, GI, K	SA, TF, GI, K	SA, TF, GH, K	SB, TE, GH, K
SA, TF, GI, K	SA, TF, GI	SA, TF, GI	SA, TE, GH, K	SB, TE, GH, K
SA, TE, GH, K	SA, TE, GI	SA, TE, GI	SA, TE, GH, K	SB, TE, GH, K
SB, TE, GH, K	SA, TE, GI	SB, TE, GI	SB, TE, GH, K	SB, TE, GH, K
SA, TE, GI	SA, TE, GI	SA, TE, GI	SA, TE, GH	SB, TE, GH
SB, TE, GI	SA, TE, GI	SB, TE, GI	SB, TE, GH	SB, TE, GH
SA, TE, GH	SA, TE, GI	SA, TE, GI	SA, TE, GH	SB, TE, GH
SB, TE, GH	SA, TE, GI	SB, TE, GI	SB, TE, GH	SB, TE, GH
SA, TF, GH	SA, TF, GI	SA, TF, GI	SA, TE, GH	SB, TE, GH

TABLE IV. Reduced IS successor table for upward-going signals.

BOTTOM-EDGE PREDECESSOR	INDEPENDENT PARAMETERS (s_ℓ)					
	L	S	SA	SB	...	Z
00	x0	x0	x0	x0	...	x0
01	x1	x1	x1	x1	...	x1
10	x1	x0	x0	x0	...	x0
11	x1	x1	x1	x1	...	x1

3. *Table Representing Vertical Signals Downward*

The cell bottom-edge output is identical to s_i, hence no gate is needed: the uncomplemented output of the storage flip-flop is used directly.

4. *Table Representing Vertical Signals Upward*

Following the methods and criteria of Section V.B.1 the reduced table representing signals travelling vertically upward is constructed (Table IV).

5. Table Representing the Cell Next State

The methods detailed above yield four sets of intercell signals appearing as the sets of IS predecessors for each table (actually the g_X table is degenerate in this example). These predecessors may be given binary secondary assignments to be used as the values taken on by intercell signals. The cell next state, $s_j = f_I(w, x, y, z, s_i)$, may be expressed as a successor table featuring the 4-tuple $[w, x, y, z]$ as the table's independent parameters and the present state s_i, as the predecessor. In our example the table is already in its reduced state. The actual table will be omitted.

C. Implementation of the Tables as Boolean Functions

Using the established methods of circuit implementation and minimization, the tables may be expressed as Boolean expressions, and subsequently as logical circuits. Four literals are needed to describe each mode of horizontal communication while one literal describes each of the vertical directions of communication. The four unilateral signal switching functions have been identified, and consist of a total of 48 products. Similarly, the switching function generating the next internal state has been found to contain 61 products. Without applying further minimization we have realized these functions, and hence the cell, with 140 NAND gates.

VI. ARRAY SPECIFICATION AND ANALYSIS

The general arithmetic unit is composed of an iteration of the typical cell to form an $m \times n$ array, where n is equal to the word size and m is dependent upon the complexity of multifunctional operations to be performed by the unit.

Each operation to be performed by the array, such as multiplication, division, mask-and-test, etc., must be described by an algorithm utilizing a set of q single-row arrays. The arithmetic unit must contain at least enough rows to perform the operation requiring the greatest number of rows, i.e., $m = \max(q_{\text{op}1}, q_{\text{op}2}, q_{\text{op}3}, \ldots)$. Additional rows may be required by the control unit to act as index registers, counters, mask words, etc.

As an illustrative example, the familiar "shift-and-add" algorithm for multiplication will be adapted to our array. It will be assumed that the mask word "-2" in two's complement form is available and that the control unit can detect the "all-ones" word.

An array of four rows is available, labled from the top row: $R1$, $R2$, $R3$, and $R4$. Initially the rows contain (respectively) the mask word, multiplier, multiplicand, and "all zeros." The basic cycle repeated n times is:

(1) $R2$ loaded into control unit and subsequently OR'ed into $R1$
(2) $R1$ loaded into control where it is examined for "all ones." If false, Step (3) is skipped
(3) If test in Step 2 is true, $R3$ accumulated (nondestructively) into $R4$
(4) $R3$ shifted left once arithmetically, $R2$ shifted right once arithmetically, mask word entered into $R1$.

At the end of the cycle the product is contained in $R4$.

VII. SPEED AND STABILITY OF ARRAYS BASED ON TOTAL-STATE CELLS

The cycle time of an array based on total-state cells is independent of the function being performed. As seen in Fig. 3, the cell introduces approximately equal signal delays in any of the four intercell directions. For bilateral communications, the cycle time limit will be the time necessary for a unilateral signal to propagate once in each direction. If the delay introduced by a cell is t_g, then the minimum array cycle time must be

$$(\text{array cycle time})_{\min} = \max \quad (2mt_g, 2nt_g) \quad ,$$

assuming bilateral communication on each array axis.

The stability of the array may be assured by establishing the stability of the general cell. The only source of feedback occurs between the internal state and the next internal state, s_i and s_j, respectively. Any problems are eliminated through the delay properties of a flip-flop, which is assumed to be the storage element employed. Array synchronization may be achieved by "clocking" certain boundary inputs. In our Arithmetic Unit example, the RFI inputs may be clocked to the array in parallel on clock times such that

$$\text{clock rate} < 1/\text{min array cycle time} = 1/\max\,(mt_g, 2nt_g) \quad .$$

The all-zero RFI input is defined as the "idle" instruction, permitting the above convention. (It should be noted that the array primary input must appear at least nt_g before the RFI inputs are clocked.) The use of other well-known synchronization techniques is available as well.

VIII. SUMMARY

The typical cell for a multifunctional arithmetic unit described requires only 20 peripheral leads (neglecting power, ground, and clock) and features approximately 140 gates. Both values fall within the constraints of today's LSI technology. In addition, transit-time delays through the cell in any direction need be at most equal to the delay introduced by three gates. For an array designed to process words of 32 bits, the minimum cycle time would be $64t_g$, or approximately 1.1 μsec assuming an average NAND gate delay of 6 nsec.

In general, this synthesis procedure is not limited to the design of arithmetic units, but may be applied to the design of associative memory arrays, control arrays (ROMs etc.), or general cells capable of performing all of the above, given the proper array boundary constraints.

An important advantage of this procedure lies with the set of MDs generated. An array's performance may be described and/or evaluated simply by manipulating the complete set of MDs describing that array.

REFERENCES

[1] J. O. Campeau, "The Block-Oriented Computer," *IEEE Trans. Comput.*, C-18, No. 8, 706–718 (August 1969).

[2] F. C. Hennie, *Finite State Models for Logical Machines* (New York: John Wiley, 1968).

[3] R. C. Minnick, "Survey of Microcellular Research," *J. ACM,* **14**, 203–241 (1967).

[4] W. H. Kautz, "Cellular Logic-In-Memory Arrays," *IEEE Trans. Comput.*, **C-18**, 719–727 (August 1969).

[5] R. L. Petritz, "Current Status of LSI," *IEEE J. Solid State Circuits,* **SC-2**, No. 4, 130–147 (December 1967).

A MODEL OF THE DIGITAL COMPUTER

Serafino Amoroso
U.S. Army Electronics Command, Ft. Monmouth, NJ and
Stevens Institute of Technology, Hoboken, NJ
and
Stephen Bloom
Stevens Institute of Technology, Hoboken, NJ

Many questions can be formulated concerning digital computer structure and programming languages that would appear to have considerable potential interest to certain theoretically inclined computer scientists and mathematicians. Unfortunately, it is usually not apparent how to formulate such questions with mathematical precision. This situation has been recognized for some time, and there have been many attempts to construct formal frameworks in which such questions can be stated and studied with mathematical precision. None of these attempts, however, stimulated any widespread lasting enthusiasm for various reasons.

In this paper we report some of our initial experiences working with a mathematical model where certain questions natural to real digital computers appear to be capable of being treated in a natural and manageable way.

We begin by defining the *unrestricted internally-driven machine*, the concepts of *machine-language instruction*, *instruction-type*, and *computations* on such machines. The notion of function computed by such machines leads to that of program. We show that by varying instruction-type sets there exist machines incapable of computing certain computable partial functions except with infinite programs, and that there exist machines capable of computing arbitrary computable partial functions with finite instruction-type sets, and with sets which include no conditional instructions.

INTRODUCTION

A great many questions can be formulated concerning digital computer structure and programming languages that would appear to have considerable potential interest to certain theoretically inclined mathematicians or computer scientists. Unfortunately, it is usually not apparent how to formulate such questions with mathematical precision. For example: "In what sense does a digital computer need a conditional instruction in its basic machine language instruction set?" "For any higher-level language, is it always possible to organize a computer to accept the language as its machine language?" "What exactly does a common storage for programs and data imply?" "Can any mechanizable process be mathematically formalized?"

There have been many attempts to formulate mathematical models of the digital computer. Some were directly motivated by the desire to study questions such as the above with mathematical precision. For example: "The primary objective

Presented at the Symposium on Computers and Automata
Polytechnic Institute of Brooklyn, April 13–15, 1971.

of this article is to give a formal description of the notion of a computation carried out on a computer and do this in such a way that certain practical problems of central importance that arise in computing activity can be stated and studied rigorously within this formalism [4]." "In this paper we set up a framework which permits a rational discussion of such languages [i.e., problem-oriented and machine languages], . . . [2]" None of these projects, however, stimulated any widespread lasting enthusiasm for various reasons. Some were mathematically too tedious to work with, and others seemed unnatural. Since we feel that a natural and manageable model of the digital computer to be still a worthwhile goal, we should like to report here on a model that seems to be a modest improvement over what has been formulated up until now. Some of our initial experiences in trying to extract some meaningful and natural results from the model will also be reported.

THE INTERNALLY-DRIVEN MACHINE

Let M, B, and A be sets such that $M \cap B \supseteq A \neq \phi$, $M \neq A$. We shall call the elements of M, *memory locations* (or more properly, memory location *names*), the elements of B, *information units*, and the elements of A, *addressable memory locations*. Distinct elements m_h and m_0 in $M - A$, called the *ON-OFF flip-flop* and the *instruction counter*, respectively, will play a special role.

With each $m \in M$ we associate a subset of B as follows: for any $m \in M$

$$R(m) = \begin{cases} A, & \text{if } m = m_0 \ , \\ \{\text{ON, OFF}\}, & \text{if } m = m_h \ , \\ B, & \text{otherwise.} \end{cases}$$

$R(m)$ can be visualized as the set of possible "contents" of memory location m. Elements of the set $\mathcal{S} = \prod_{m \in M} R(m)$ will be called *machine states.*

Let F be a set of (total) functions each one of which has the form

$$B^k \times A \longrightarrow B^r \times A \ ,$$

for some $k, r \geq 0$. The elements of F are called *instruction types.*

Let Q be the set of all ordered pairs (s_1, s_2) where each component s_i is a finite sequence of distinct elements from $M - \{m_0\}$.

Let

$$\mathfrak{M}_1 \colon B \longrightarrow F \ ,$$

and

$$\mathfrak{M}_2 \colon B \longrightarrow Q \ ,$$

be compatible functions in the sense that for any $b \in B$, if $\mathfrak{M}_1(b)\colon B^k \times A \longrightarrow B^r \times A$, then $\mathfrak{M}_2(b) = ((m_1, m_2, m_3, \cdots, m_k), (\bar{m}_1, \bar{m}_2, \bar{m}_3, \cdots, \bar{m}_r))$, i.e., the sequence "lengths" equal the respective exponents on B.

DEFINITION. *For any $b \in B$, the pair $(\mathfrak{M}_1(b), \mathfrak{M}_2(b))$ is called an* instruction *(for $\mathfrak{M}$) (the instruction* "determined *by b*").

We sometimes speak of "the instruction b" meaning the instruction determined by b.

DEFINITION. *A partial function* $\mathcal{M}: \mathcal{S} \longrightarrow \mathcal{S}$, *called an* (unrestricted, internally-driven) machine, *is defined as follows: the domain of definition for* $\mathcal{M}$, *denoted by* $\mathcal{S}_{ON}$, *is* $\{S \in \mathcal{S}: S(m_h) = ON\}$.

Given $S \in \mathcal{S}_{ON}$, let $a = S(m_0) \in A$, $b = S^2(m_0) \in B$, $\mathcal{M}_2(b) = ((m_1, m_2, m_3, \cdots, m_k), (\bar{m}_1, \bar{m}_2, \bar{m}_3, \cdots, \bar{m}_r))$, $\mathcal{M}_1(b): B^k \times A \longrightarrow B^r \times A$ such that $\mathcal{M}_1(b)(S(m_1), S(m_2), \cdots, S(m_k), S(m_0)) = (\bar{b}_1, \bar{b}_2, \cdots, \bar{b}_r, \bar{a})$, then for any $m \in M$

$$\mathcal{M}(S)(m) = \begin{cases} \bar{a}, & \text{if } m = m_0, \\ \bar{b}_j, & \text{if } m = \bar{m}_j \quad (1 \leq j \leq r) \\ S(m), & \text{otherwise.} \end{cases}$$

Note that if machine $\mathcal{M}$ "switches" state S to $\bar{S}$, it does so by extracting the contents of the addressable memory location "pointed" to by the instruction counter, i.e., $S^2(m_0)$, and then treating this symbol as an instruction.

THE COMPUTATION OF FUNCTIONS

A *computation* (by $\mathcal{M}$) is a finite or infinite sequence

$$S_0, S_1, S_2, \cdots ,$$

of machine states such that $S_0 \in \mathcal{S}_{ON}$, and $S_{i+1} = \mathcal{M}(S_i)$ for all $i = 0, 1, 2, \cdots$, if the sequence is infinite.

(Note that no term S_i in an infinite computation is such that $S_i(m_h) = OFF$.) If a computation

$$S_0, S_1, S_2, \cdots, S_n ,$$

is finite (again $S_0 \in \mathcal{S}_{ON}$ and $S_{i+1} = \mathcal{M}(S_i)$, $0 \leq i < n$) then $S_n(m_h) = OFF$. Such computations will be called *successful*. Successful computations, therefore, *terminate* in the first state for which $\mathcal{M}$ is undefined.

DEFINITION. *Given* $S \in \mathcal{S}_{ON}$, *and finite subsets* IR $= \{m_1, m_2, m_3, \cdots, m_q\}$ *and* OR $= \{\bar{m}_1, \bar{m}_2, \bar{m}_3, \cdots, \bar{m}_t\}$ *of* A (*called the* input region *and* output region *respectively*), *we define the partial function*

$$\mathcal{M}_{S,IR,OR}: B^q \longrightarrow B^t ,$$

as follows: for $(b_1, b_2, b_3, \cdots, b_q) \in B^q$, *let* $S(m_i/b_i) = S_0$, $1 \leq i \leq q$. *If the computation* $S_0, S_1, S_2, \cdots$, *is unsuccessful, then* $\mathcal{M}_{S,IR,OR}((b_1, b_2, b_3, \cdots, b_q))$ *is undefined. If the computation is successful terminating in* S_n, *then* $\mathcal{M}_{S,IR,OR}((b_1, b_2, b_3, \cdots, b_q)) = (S_n(\bar{m}_1), S_n(\bar{m}_2), S_n(\bar{m}_3), \cdots, S_n(\bar{m}_t))$.

Such functions (as $\mathcal{M}_{S,IR,OR}$) will be called $\mathcal{M}$-*computable*.

COMPUTATION OF PARTIAL RECURSIVE FUNCTIONS

In this section we present a detailed example of a particular machine and show it can be "programmed" to compute an arbitrary partial recursive function.

It is intended mainly to illustrate the concepts introduced so far, and to motivate some of the definitions to follow.

Let $\mathfrak{M}$ be such that $A = B = N = \{0, 1, 2, \cdots\}$ and let $M = N \cup \{m_0, m_h\}$. $\mathfrak{M}$ will be capable of interpreting the following instructions. (We shall refer to the instructions by using more suggestive names than numerals. There will be no need to give the correspondence between the names used and the elements of B.)

Increment the contents of location x

$$\mathfrak{M}_1(\text{INC x}) \colon B \times A \longrightarrow B \times A \;,$$
$$(b, a) \longmapsto (b + 1, a + 1) \;,$$
$$\mathfrak{M}_2(\text{INC x}) = (\text{x}, \text{x}) \;\; (\text{x} \in A) \;.$$

Note that for each $\text{x} \in A$ there is an instruction INC x, but all these are defined from one and the same element of F.

Store the contents of location x into location y

$$\mathfrak{M}_1(\text{STO x}, y) \colon B \times A \longrightarrow B \times A \;,$$
$$(b, a) \longmapsto (b, a + 1) \;,$$
$$\mathfrak{M}_2(\text{STO}, \text{x}, y) = (\text{x}, y) \;\; (\text{x}, y \in A) \;.$$

Halt

$$\mathfrak{M}_1(\text{HLT}) \colon B^0 \times A \longrightarrow B \times A \;,$$
$$(-, a) \longmapsto (\text{OFF}, a) \;,$$
$$\mathfrak{M}_2(\text{HLT}) = (-, m_h) \;.$$

Again all the STO x, y instructions (for each x, y) are defined from only one element of F. Note also that all instructions introduced so far would be called "unconditioned" instructions, i.e., the location of the "next instruction" to be interpreted is dependent only on the location of the present instruction being interpreted. This will not be the case for the final class of instructions which we now present.

Jump to z if the contents of location x differs from the contents of location y

$$\mathfrak{M}_1(\text{JMP x}, y, z) \colon B^2 \times A \longrightarrow B^0 \times A \;,$$
$$(u, v, a) \longmapsto \begin{cases} (-, a + 1), & \text{if } u = v \;, \\ (-, z), & \text{if } u \neq v \;, \end{cases}$$
$$\mathfrak{M}_2(\text{JMP}, \text{x}, y, z) = ((\text{x}, y), -) \;\; (\text{x}, y, z \in A) \;.$$

Unlike the previous instructions, the JMP instructions (as defined) require a different element of F for each $z \in A$. Hence, this instruction set requires that F be an infinite set of functions.

These are the only instructions that $\mathfrak{M}$ will be capable of interpreting (they are the ones used in [2]).

Let $f \colon N^{n+1} \longrightarrow N$, $n \geq 0$, be a total function. The function $g \colon N^n \longrightarrow N$ defined from f by

$$g(\text{x}_1, \text{x}_2, \text{x}_3, \cdots, \text{x}_n) = y$$

iff y is the smallest natural number such that $f(y, \text{x}_1, \text{x}_2, \text{x}_3, \cdots, \text{x}_n) = 0$.

$g(x_1, x_2, x_3, \cdots, x_n)$ will be undefined if no such y exists. Partial function g is said to arise from f by minimalization.

The class of *partial recursive functions* is the smallest class of functions closed under composition and minimalization containing the following functions:

(1) The *successor function*

$$S(x) = x + 1, \qquad \text{for each } x \in N$$

(2) The *constant function*

$$C(x) = 0, \qquad \text{for each } x \in N$$

(3) The *projection functions*, for each $n \geq 1$ and each i $(0 \leq i < n)$

$$\bigcup_i^n (x_0, x_1, x_2, \cdots, x_{n-1}) = x_i$$

(4) The *addition function*

$$A(x_1, x_2) = x_1 + x_2$$

(5) The *proper subtraction* function

$$D(x_1, x_2) = \begin{cases} x_1 - x_2, & \text{if } x_1 \geq x_2 , \\ 0, & \text{if } x_1 < x_2 \end{cases}$$

(6) The *multiplication function*

$$M(x_1, x_2) = x_1 \cdot x_2 .$$

THEOREM 1. *$\mathfrak{M}$ can compute any partial recursive function.*

Proof. (a) *$\mathfrak{M}$ can compute the constant function.* Let IR = $\{a\}$, OR = $\{b\}$, and let $S \in \mathcal{S}_{ON}$ be such that $S(c) = 0$, $S(c+1) =$ STO c, b, and $S(c+2) =$ HLT. $\mathfrak{M}_{S,IR,OR}$ is then the constant function if the entrance to the program is $c + 1$. We can say that the program "contains a 0 in location c, a STO instruction in location c + 1, and a HLT instruction in location c + 2." We abbreviate all this by writing:

IR = $\{a\}$
OR = $\{b\}$
[c] 0
→ [c + 1] STO c, b
[c + 2] HLT

The lines of the *program* are written below the IR and OR, and the arrow specifies the program *entrance*. We shall usually assume the obvious disjointness between the IR, OR, and program, when different letters (as above) are used. Although the above program can be improved by identifying locations b and c, we would rather emphasize the fact that IR, OR, and the program can be situated independently and arbitrarily in the addressable memory. In this case we say *the program is relocatable*. It will be noted that each program to be presented below will be relocatable in this sense. Also, each program will be *finite* in the sense that only finitely many locations are needed for all computations for any function we shall be concerned with.

(b) $\mathfrak{M}$ *can compute any projection function.* We shall use the abbreviated notation introduced above.

$$\mathrm{IR} = \{a, a+1, a+2, \cdots, a+n-1\}$$

$$\mathrm{OR} = \{b\}$$

$\longrightarrow$[c] STO $a+i, b$

[c + 1] HLT

(c) $\mathfrak{M}$ *can compute the successor function*

$$\mathrm{IR} = \{a\}$$

$$\mathrm{OR} = \{b\}$$

$\longrightarrow$ [c] INC a

[c + 1] STO a, b

[c + 2] HLT

(d) $\mathfrak{M}$ *can compute the addition function.*

$$\mathrm{IR} = \{a, a+1\}, \quad \mathrm{OR} = \{b\}$$

[c] 0

$\longrightarrow$ [c + 1] STO c, b

[c + 2] STO c, c + 13

[c + 3] JMP c + 13, a, c + 7

[c + 4] INC b

[c + 5] INC c + 13

[c + 6] JMP c, c, c + 13

[c + 7] STO c, c + 13

[c + 8] JMP c + 13, $a + 1$, c + 12

[c + 9] INC b

[c + 10] INC c + 13

[c + 11] JMP c, c, c + 8

[c + 12] HLT

(e) $\mathfrak{M}$ *can compute the proper subtraction function.*

$$\mathrm{IR} = \{a, a+1\}, \quad \mathrm{OR} = \{b\}$$

[c] 0

$\longrightarrow$ [c + 1] STO c, b

[c + 2] JMP $a, a + 1$, c + 12

[c + 3] STO a, c + 13

[c + 4] STO $a + 1$, c + 14

[c + 5] INC c + 13

[c + 6] JMP c + 13, a + 1, c + 11

[c + 7] INC c + 14

[c + 8] INC b

[c + 9] JMP c + 14, a, c + 12

[c + 10] JMP c, c, c + 5

[c + 11] STO c, b

[c + 12] HLT

(f) *$\mathfrak{M}$ can compute the multiplication function.*

IR = $\{a, a + 1\}$

OR = $\{b\}$

[c] 0

→ [c + 1] STO c, b

[c + 2] STO c, c + 13

[c + 3] STO a + 1, c + 14

[c + 4] JMP c, a, c + 12

[c + 5] JMP c, b, c + 12

[c + 6] STO c + 14, u

[c + 7] STO b, v

[c + 8] JMP c, c, [ADD]

[c + 9] INC c + 13

[c + 10] JMP c + 13, a, c + 12

[c + 11] JMP c, c, c + 6

[c + 12] HLT

In line [c + 8], [ADD] means the entrance to an addition program with IR = $\{u, v\}$, OR = $\{b\}$, and all HLT instructions replaced by JMP c, c, c + 9. (The ADD program is thus being used as a "subroutine" and this will transfer control back to the MULTIPLY program.) All locations used by the ADD program, except b, are of course disjoint from those above.

(g) *The $\mathfrak{M}$-computable functions are closed under composition.*

This follows easily from the fact that each program computing a function will involve only finitely many locations and all programs are relocatable. If IR_1 and OR_1 are input regions for a program P_1 computing a function f_1, then let OR_1 = IR_2, i.e., the input region for a program P_2 computing a function f_2. If one replaces all HLT instructions in P_1 by JMP c, c, e where c is arbitrary and e is the entrance to P_2, then by relocating P_2 so that it is disjoint from the locations used in P_1, the combined programs will clearly compute the composition of f_1 and f_2. Note that the resulting program will again be finite and relocatable.

(h) $\mathfrak{M}$-*computable functions are closed under minimalization.*

Let f be any total ($\mathfrak{M}$-computable) function computed by a program P with IR = $\{y, x_1, x_2, x_3, \cdots, x_n\}$, OR = $\{z\}$, and altered so that each HLT instruction is replaced by JMP c, c, c + 4. Let the entrance to P be α. For the program below, let IR = $\{x_1, x_2, x_3, \cdots, x_n\}$, OR = $\{w\}$.

[c] 0
→[c] STO c, y
[c + 1] JMP c, c, α
[c + 3] JMP c, z, c + 6
[c + 4] INC y
[c + 5] JMP c, c, α
[c + 6] STO y, w
[c + 7] HLT .

This completes our verification that $\mathfrak{M}$ can compute any partial recursive function. Q.E.D.

Excepting the IR, note that certain locations had their contents specified in advance for any program. If for any computation the contents of *these* locations are never altered, and if every interpreted instruction for any computation is taken from one of these locations, then we say the program is *fixed.* Note that all the programs above were fixed, hence we have:

COROLLARY 1.1. *Any partial recursive function can be computed by* $\mathfrak{M}$ *by some fixed program.*

It should be emphasized that the concept of an (unrestricted) machine is extremely general. For example, no restrictions exist for the set F. We have not even ruled out a noncomputable function in F. As we proceed, we shall be making many (hopefully) meaningful restrictions on our model. We begin with one that seems to us natural and will prove convenient. With the HLT instruction defined as above, we have

THEOREM 2. *For any machine* $\mathfrak{M}$ *there is a machine* $\mathfrak{M}'$ *that computes all the functions of* $\mathfrak{M}$ *and terminates computations only by interpreting* HLT *instructions.*

Proof. (Outline). For each instruction b of $\mathfrak{M}$ capable of terminating computations, let b' be defined for $\mathfrak{M}'$ where b' acts exactly like b except when b would place "OFF" in m_h, b' transfers unconditionally to a fixed location containing the HLT instruction. Q.E.D.

From now on we require for any machine $\mathfrak{M}$, if $S(m_h)$ = ON and $\mathfrak{M}(S)(m_h)$ = OFF, then $S^2(m_0)$ = HLT, i.e., computations will be terminated from now on only by the HLT instruction. We also require that any machine have the HLT instruction, i.e., for any $\mathfrak{M}$ there is some $b \in B$ interpreted by $\mathfrak{M}$ as the HLT instruction.

We have seen that each S, IR, and OR for any machine defines a partial function $\mathfrak{M}_{S,\mathrm{IR},\mathrm{OR}}$. It seems intuitively clear that some "part" of the initial state S should be considered the "program" computing this function. We now offer a definition of the concept of a *program computing an* $\mathfrak{M}$-*computable function.*

Programs for Computing Functions

$m \in M - \text{IR}$ is called *irrelevant* to $\mathfrak{M}_{S,\text{IR},\text{OR}}$ if for any $b \in B$

$$\mathfrak{M}_{S(m/b),\text{IR},\text{OR}} = \mathfrak{M}_{S,\text{IR},\text{OR}} \; .$$

Let

$$\text{REL}\,(\mathfrak{M}_{S,\text{IR},\text{OR}}) = M - (\text{IR} \cup \{m_h\} \cup \{m\colon m \text{ is irrelevant to } \mathfrak{M}_{S,\text{IR},\text{OR}}\}) \; .$$

Define

$$A\colon \mathcal{S}_{\text{ON}} \longrightarrow \mathcal{P}(M) \; ,$$

by $A(S) = \{S(m_0), m_1, m_2, m_3, \cdots, m_k\} - \text{IR}$, where

$$\mathfrak{M}_2(S^2(m_0)) = ((m_1, m_2, m_3, \cdots, m_k), (\bar{m}_1, \bar{m}_2, \bar{m}_3, \cdots, \bar{m}_r)) \; .$$

Define

$$A(k, S)\colon N \times \mathcal{S}_{\text{ON}} \longrightarrow \mathcal{P}(M) \; ,$$

by $A(0, S) = A(S) \cup \{m_0\}$. Assume $A(k-1, S)$ is defined, and let $\mathfrak{M}(S) = S_1$, $\mathfrak{M}(S_1) = S_2, \cdots, \mathfrak{M}(S_k) = S_{k+1}$. Then

$$A(k, S) = A(k-1, S) \cup \{m \in A(S_k)\colon S_k(m) = S(m)\} \; .$$

If the computation $S, \mathfrak{M}(S), \mathfrak{M}(S_1), \cdots, \mathfrak{M}(S_{n-1}) = S_n$, is successful, terminating in S_n, then $A(S_n)$ is undefined, hence, $A(n, S)$ is as yet undefined. For this case, we define $A(k, S) = A(n-1, S)$ for all $k \geq n$.

Having defined $A(k, S)$ for any $S \in \mathcal{S}_{\text{ON}}$ and any $k = 0, 1, 2, \cdots$, we define

$$A_\infty(S) = \bigcup_k A(k, S) \; .$$

Intuitively, this set contains all locations, except m_h and those in IR, whose contents in S could possibly have influenced the computation determined by S.

Note that if $S_1 = \mathfrak{M}(S)$, then $a = S_1(m_0)$ is in $A(1, S)$ if $S(S_1(m_0)) = S^2(m_0)$. It may be the case that $a \in A(1, S)$ and $S(S_1(m_0)) \neq S^2(m_0)$ since a may be a component of $\pi_1 \mathfrak{M}_2 S^2(m_0)$.

If $S^2(m_0)$ is the halt instruction, then $\pi_1 \mathfrak{M}_2 S^2(m_0) = S(m_0)$, so $A_\infty(S) = \{S(m_0), m_0\}$. Define

$$C\colon \mathcal{S}_{\text{ON}} \longrightarrow \mathcal{P}(M) \; ,$$

by $C(S) = \{\bar{m}_1, \bar{m}_2, \bar{m}_3, \cdots, \bar{m}_r\}$, where

$$\mathfrak{M}_2(S^2(m_0)) = ((m_1, m_2, m_3, \cdots, m_k), (\bar{m}_1, \bar{m}_2, \bar{m}_3, \cdots, \bar{m}_r)) \; .$$

Define

$$C\colon N \times \mathcal{S}_{\text{ON}} \longrightarrow \mathcal{P}(M) \; ,$$

by $C\colon (0, S) = C(S)$. Assume $C(k-1, S)$ is defined, and let $\mathfrak{M}(S) = S_1, \mathfrak{M}(S_1) = S_2, \cdots, \mathfrak{M}(S_k) = S_{k+1}$. Define

$$C(k, S) = C(k-1, S) \cup C(S_k).$$

If $\mathfrak{M}^n(S) = S_n$ is terminal, let $C(k, S) = C(n-1, S)$ for all $k \geq n$. Finally let

$$C_\infty(S) = \bigcup_k C(k, S) \quad .$$

Given $S \in S_{ON}$, IR, and OR, let D be the domain of definition of $\mathfrak{M}_{S,IR,OR}$, we define $\mathrm{PROG}(\mathfrak{M}_{S,IR,OR}) \subseteq M$ as

$$\bigcup_{\beta \in B^k} A_\infty \;(S(\mathrm{IR}/\beta)) \cup [\,\mathrm{OR} - \bigcup_{\beta \in D} C_\infty(S(\mathrm{IR}/\beta))] \quad .$$

Finally, the *program* computing $\mathfrak{M}_{S,IR,OR}$ is defined to be

$$S \mid \mathrm{PROG}(\mathfrak{M}_{S,IR,OR}) - \{m_0\} \quad ,$$

in which case we sometimes say that the program is *held* in state S. $S(m_0)$ will be called the *entrance* to the program. $\#(\mathrm{PROG}(\mathfrak{M}_{S,IR,OR}) - \{m_0\})$ will be called the *length* of the program. (This may be infinite).

$C_\infty(S)$ was introduced for the following reason. Suppose $m_i \in$ OR and at no time during any computation in the calculation of some $\mathfrak{M}_{S,IR,OR}$ is the contents of m_i ever changed or even examined. In this case, the value of m_i in S must be specified in advance by the programmer, hence, it should be considered "part of the program."

Note that by definition, if $m \in$ IR, then for any $\mathfrak{M}_{S,IR,OR}$, $m \notin \mathrm{PROG}(\mathfrak{M}_{S,IR,OR})$. This does not mean, however, that the contents of m cannot be called upon to be interpreted as an instruction. I.e., for some k and β, it is possible that $\mathfrak{M}^k(S(\mathrm{IR}/\beta))(m_0) = m$.

Let M be ordered, and suppose $\mathrm{PROG}(\mathfrak{M}_{S,IR,OR}) = \{m_1, m_2, m_3, \cdots, m_j\}$, where $S(m_i) = b_i$ $(1 \leq i \leq j)$, m_{i+1} is a descendent of m_i in the ordering on M, $1 \leq i < j$, and finally $S^2(m_0) = m_k$ for some k $(1 \leq k \leq j)$. We shall abbreviate this situation by writing

$$\begin{array}{ll} [m_1] & b_1 \\ \cdot & \\ \cdot & \\ \cdot & \\ \longrightarrow [m_k] & b_k \\ \cdot & \\ \cdot & \\ \cdot & \\ [m_j] & b_j \end{array}$$

Note that we already used this convention informally in our earlier examples.

THEOREM 3. *For any $\mathfrak{M}$-computable function $\mathfrak{M}_{S,IR,OR}$,*

$$\mathrm{REL}(\mathfrak{M}_{S,IR,OR}) \subseteq \mathrm{PROG}(\mathfrak{M}_{S,IR,OR}) \quad .$$

Proof. For $m \in M$ to be relevant to the computation of $\mathfrak{M}_{S,IR,OR}$ (i.e., for m to be in $\mathrm{REL}(\mathfrak{M}_{S,IR,OR})$) means $\mathfrak{M}$ "uses" $S(m)$ at some time in the calculation of $\mathfrak{M}_{S,IR,OR}$. Clearly, the only way the contents of $m \in M$ in S can affect some computation determined by some $S(\mathrm{IR}/\beta)$, $\beta \in B^k$, is for m to be a component of $\pi_1 \mathfrak{M}_2 S_i^2(m_0)$ for some S_i in a computation, where $S_i(m) = S(m)$, or for m to be the value of m_0 at some time, but these cases would place m in PROG$(\mathfrak{M}_{S,IR,OR})$. Q.E.D.

It is trivial to show that the containment symbol in Theorem 3 cannot be changed to equality. It might be noted that if PROG$(\mathfrak{M}_{S,IR,OR})$ is a restriction of some $S' \neq S$, then $\mathfrak{M}_{S',IR,OR} = \mathfrak{M}_{S,IR,OR}$, provided $S'(m_0) = S(m_0)$.

COMPOSITION OF $\mathfrak{M}$-COMPUTABLE FUNCTIONS

For an arbitrary machine $\mathfrak{M}$, can any two $\mathfrak{M}$-computable functions be composed? It is easy to show that the answer is no.

First, M may be *finite* and there may not be enough memory space for certain compositions.

Example.

$$M = \{m_0, m_h, 0, 1, 2\} \quad ,$$

$$B = \{b_h(=0), b_1(=1), b_2(=2), 3, 4, \cdots ,\} = N \text{ (the natural numbers)},$$

$$A = \{0, 1, 2\} \quad .$$

Let

$$\mathfrak{M}_1(b_i)\colon B \times A \longrightarrow B \times A \quad ,$$

$$(x, a) \longmapsto (x + i, a + 1) \quad ,$$

$$\mathfrak{M}_2(b_i) = ((0), (0)) \quad (i = 1, 2) \quad ,$$

and let all $b \in B - \{b_1, b_2, b_h\}$ be passive in the sense

$$\mathfrak{M}_1(b)\colon B^0 \times A \longrightarrow B^0 \times A \quad ,$$

$$(-, a) \longmapsto (-, a) \quad .$$

$\mathfrak{M}$ can clearly compute $f_1(x) = x + 1$, and $f_2(x) = x + 2$, but cannot compute $f_3(x) = f_2(f_1(x)) = x + 3$. One location in A must be the input region, another must hold b_h, leaving only one location for the composition which is impossible.

Even if $\mathfrak{M}$ is such that A is denumerably infinite, it is still easy to see that $\mathfrak{M}$ may not be able to compose all of its $\mathfrak{M}$-computable functions.

Example. Let $\mathfrak{M}$, besides the halt instruction, have only two *active* (nonpassive) instructions, b_1 and b_2 defined by

$$\mathfrak{M}_1(b_1)\colon B \times A \longrightarrow B \times A, \quad ,$$

$$(0, a) \longmapsto (1, a + 1) \quad ,$$

$$(x, a) \longmapsto (x, a + 1) \quad (\text{for any } a \in A, x \neq 0) \quad ,$$

$$\mathfrak{M}_2(b_1) = ((a_1, m_0), a_1) \quad ,$$

and

$$\mathfrak{M}_1(b_2)\colon B \times A \longrightarrow B \times A \quad ,$$

$$(1, a) \longmapsto (2, a + 1) \quad ,$$

$$(x, a) \longmapsto (x, a + 1) \quad (\text{for any } a \in A, \text{ and } x \neq 1) \quad ,$$

$$\mathfrak{M}_2(b_2) = ((a_2, m_0), a_2) \quad (a_2 \neq a_1) \quad .$$

Clearly, $\mathfrak{M}$ can compute

$$f_1(x) = \begin{cases} 1, & \text{if } x = 0 \ , \\ x, & \text{if } x \neq 0 \ , \end{cases}$$

and

$$f_2(x) = \begin{cases} 2, & \text{if } x = 1 \ , \\ x, & \text{if } x \neq 1 \ , \end{cases}$$

but $\mathfrak{M}$ cannot compute

$$f(x) = f_2(f_1(x))$$

(intuitively, because $\mathfrak{M}$ cannot "line up" the range of f_1 and the domain of f_2).

A program computing a function $\mathfrak{M}_{S,IR,OR}$: $B^k \longrightarrow B^r$ is said to be *relocatable* if there exist subsets IR′, OR′ of A, # OR = # OR′, and # IR = # IR′, and for any finite subset $G \subseteq A$, there exists a program (held in S') computing $\mathfrak{M}_{S',IR',OR'} = \mathfrak{M}_{S,IR,OR}$, such that

$$(\text{IR}' \cup \text{OR}' \cup \text{PROG}(\mathfrak{M}_{S',IR',OR'})) \cap G = \phi \ .$$

The *range of influence of a program P* computing a function $\mathfrak{M}_{S,IR,OR}$: $B^k \longrightarrow B^r$, denoted RI(P), is the set of all locations whose contents are changed at some time during any computation of the function. More precisely, RI(P) is the set of all $m \in M$ such that for some $\beta \in B^k$, and some n

$$\mathfrak{M}^n(S(\text{IR}/\beta))(m) \neq \mathfrak{M}^{n+1}(S(\text{IR}/\beta))(m) \ .$$

Let P_1 and P_2 be arbitrary finite programs held in states S_1 and S_2, respectively, computing $\mathfrak{M}_{S_1,IR_1,OR_1}$: $B^{k_1} \longrightarrow B^{r_1}$, and $\mathfrak{M}_{S_2,IR_2,OR_2}$: $B^{k_2} \longrightarrow B^{r_2}$, such that RI$(P_1) \cap$ RI$(P_2) = \phi$. We say that $\mathfrak{M}$ has the ability to "link" P_2 to P_1 if there is some program P that for all IR_1-states "acts exactly like" P_1 until P_1 would have halted at which time P begins to act like P_2 with IR_2 containing what it found when P_1 finished. More precisely, $\mathfrak{M}$ *can link* P_2 *to* P_1 if there exists an $S \in \mathcal{S}_{ON}$ such that for any $\beta \in B^{k_1}$, (1)-(4) below hold:

(1) If the computation beginning with $S_1(\text{IR}_1/\beta)$ is unsuccessful, so is the computation beginning with $S(\text{IR}_1/\beta)$ unsuccessful

(2) If the computation beginning with $S_1(\text{IR}_1/\beta)$ is successful terminating in $\mathfrak{M}^n(S_1(\text{IR}_1/\beta))$, then $\mathfrak{M}^{n+1}(S(\text{IR}_1/\beta))$ is defined

(3) If IR_2 in state $\mathfrak{M}^n(S(\text{IR}_1/\beta))$ contains $\gamma \in B^{k_2}$, then if the computation beginning with $S_2(\text{IR}_2/\gamma)$ is unsuccessful, so is the computation beginning with $S(\text{IR}_1/\beta)$

(4) If the computation beginning with $S_2(\text{IR}_2/\gamma)$ is successful terminating in $\mathfrak{M}^p(S_2(\text{IR}_2/\gamma))$, then the computation beginning with $S(\text{IR}_1/\beta)$ is also successful terminating in $\mathfrak{M}^{n+p}(S(\text{IR}_1/\beta))$ and $\mathfrak{M}^{n+p}(S(\text{IR}_1/\beta)) \mid \text{OR}_2 = \mathfrak{M}^p(S_2(\text{IR}_2/\gamma)) \mid \text{OR}_2$.

It should be obvious that certain machines may not have instructions sufficient to ensure program linking in the above sense.

THEOREM 4. *Suppose a machine $\mathfrak{M}$ has the following properties:*

(a) *Each $\mathfrak{M}$-computable function can be computed by some program with a finite range of influence*

(b) *For any two finite programs with disjoint ranges of influence, $\mathfrak{M}$ can link either to the other*

(c) *Any finite program is relocatable.*

Then the class of $\mathfrak{M}$-computable functions is closed under composition.

Proof. Obvious. Q.E.D.

Let $\mathfrak{M}$ be such that $B = N$, and for any $b \in B$, if

$$\mathfrak{M}_1(b): B^k \times A \longrightarrow B^r \times A \ ,$$

and $\mathfrak{M}_2(b) = ((m_1, m_2, m_3, \cdots, m_k), (\bar{m}_1, \bar{m}_2, \bar{m}_3, \cdots, \bar{m}_r))$, then for any $\beta_1' \in (M - \{m_0\})^k$ and $\beta_2' \in (M - \{m_0\})^r$, there exists a $b' \in B$ such that $\mathfrak{M}_1(b) = \mathfrak{M}_1(b')$ and $\mathfrak{M}_2(b') = ((\beta_1'), (\beta'_2))$. Informally, $\mathfrak{M}$ is such that any of its instructions can take its values from "arbitrary locations" and can place its results in arbitrary locations. The reader may be tempted to conjecture that any program P for such a machine, computing, say $\mathfrak{M}_{S,\mathrm{IR},\mathrm{OR}}$, can be relocated as follows: For an appropriate $a \in N$, let $\mathrm{IR}' = \{x + a \mid x \in \mathrm{IR}\}$, $\mathrm{OR}' = \{y + a \mid y \in \mathrm{OR}\}$, and for each $b = S(m)$ for some $m \in \mathrm{PROG}(\mathfrak{M}_{S,\mathrm{IR},\mathrm{OR}})$ where b is interpreted as an instruction, change b to b' where $\mathfrak{M}_1(b) = \mathfrak{M}_1(b')$ and if $\mathfrak{M}_2(b) = ((m_1, m_2, m_3, \cdots, m_k), (\bar{m}_1, \bar{m}_2, \bar{m}_3, \cdots, \bar{m}_r))$ then $\mathfrak{M}_2(b') = ((m_1 + a, m_2 + a, \cdots, m_k + a), (\bar{m}_1 + a, \bar{m}_2 + a, \bar{m}_r + a))$. Then S modified in this way would compute the same function. This conjecture, however, is false.

Example. Let $\mathfrak{M}$ have the instructions b_1, b_2, and b_3 interpreted as follows

$$\mathfrak{M}_1(b_1): B \times A \longrightarrow B^0 \times A$$

$$(x, a) \longmapsto \begin{cases} (-, a + 1), & \text{if } x \geq 0 \ , \\ (-, a_4), & \text{if } x < 0 \ , \end{cases}$$

$$\mathfrak{M}_2(b_1): ((a_0), (-)) \ ,$$

$$\mathfrak{M}_1(b_2): B^0 \times A \longrightarrow B \times A \ ,$$

$$(-, a) \longmapsto (b_3, a + 1) \ ,$$

$$\mathfrak{M}_2(b_2) = ((-), (a_3)) \ ,$$

$$\mathfrak{M}_1(b_3): B^0 \times A \longrightarrow B^0 \times A \ ,$$

$$(-, a) \longmapsto (-, a_4) \ .$$

If $\mathrm{IR} = \{a_0\}$ and $\mathrm{OR} = \{a_3\}$, then program

$\longrightarrow [a_1]$ b_1 (Transfer to a_4 if $\mathrm{IR} < 0$)

$[a_2]$ b_2 (Place an unconditional transfer to a_4 in a_3)

$[a_3]$ 0

$[a_4]$ b_h (HALT)

will compute the function

$$f(x) = \begin{cases} 0, & \text{if } x < 0 \ , \\ b_3, & \text{if } x \geq 0 \ . \end{cases}$$

Notice that our relocating this program as suggested above will not work. The reason is that the function $\mathfrak{M}_1(b_2)$ must be altered, i.e., in the relocated program we no longer want to transfer to location a_4. Note that the relocation scheme conjectured above cannot be salvaged for this example by simply changing the interpretation of b_2 so that the correct transfer instruction (no longer b_3) is placed in the required place. The reason is that b_3 is what the function being computed requires, hence, a more extensive revision of the program would be required for relocation.

A symbol $b \in B$ is said to be *interpreted* by $\mathfrak{M}$ in the computation of $\mathfrak{M}_{S,\text{IR},\text{OR}}$: $B^q \longrightarrow B^t$ if for some $\beta \in B^q$ and some k, $\mathfrak{M}(\mathfrak{M}^k(S(\text{IR}/\beta)))$ is defined and $[\mathfrak{M}^k S(\text{IR}/\beta)]^2(m_0) = b$. In this case we say b is *interpreted at location* $[\mathfrak{M}^k S(\text{IR}/\beta)](m_0)$.

A program computing a function $\mathfrak{M}_{S,\text{IR},\text{OR}}$: $B^q \longrightarrow B^t$ is said to be *fixed* if for any $m \in \text{PROG}(\mathfrak{M}_{S,\text{IR},\text{OR}}) - \{m_0\}$, any $\beta \in B^q$, and any k such that $\mathfrak{M}^k(S(\text{IR}/\beta))$ is defined

$$\mathfrak{M}^k(S(\text{IR}/\beta))(m) = S(\text{IR}/\beta)(m) \ ,$$

and

$$[\mathfrak{M}^k(S(\text{IR}/\beta))]^2(m_0) \in \text{PROG}(\mathfrak{M}_{S,\text{IR},\text{OR}}) \ .$$

Intuitively, a program is fixed if no part of the program is ever changed during a computation, and every interpreted instruction is read from a location holding part of the original program.

A program that places a symbol into a location $m \notin \text{PROG}$ and subsequently interprets the symbol at m as an instruction, is an example of a nonfixed program. This type of nonfixed program is said to be *generating code*.

THEOREM 5. *There exist machines and functions that can be computed by these machines only with infinite programs.*

Proof. Let $\mathfrak{M}$ be a machine with $A = B = N$ capable of interpreting besides HLT only the following instructions

ADD 1, [3]:

$$\mathfrak{M}_1(\text{ADD } 1,[3]): B \times A \longrightarrow B \times A \ ,$$
$$(b, a) \longmapsto (b + 1, a + 1) \ ,$$
$$\mathfrak{M}_2(\text{ADD } 1,[3]) = ((3),(3)) \ .$$

STI [0], [2]:

$$\mathfrak{M}_1(\text{STI } [0],[2]): B \times A \longrightarrow B \times A \ ,$$
$$(b, a) \longmapsto (b + 3, a + 1) \ ,$$
$$\mathfrak{M}_2(\text{STI } [0],[2]): ((0),(2)) \ .$$

TRA m_i:

For each $i \in N - \{0, 1, 2\}$, $\mathfrak{M}$ interprets i as an instruction TRA m_i, where the

$m_i \in A$ are defined by

$$m_i = \begin{cases} m_3 = 4, & \text{if } i = 3 \ , \\ m_i = m_{i-1} + 2\,(i \dot{-} 4) + 1, & \text{otherwise} \ , \end{cases}$$

and

$$\mathfrak{M}_1(\text{TRA } m_i)\colon B^0 \times A \longrightarrow B^0 \times A \ ,$$
$$(-, a) \longmapsto (-, m_i) \ .$$

Let

0 be interpreted as HLT ,

1 be interpreted as ADD 1, [3] ,

2 be interpreted as STI [0], [2] .

The following infinite program computes the function $f\colon N \longrightarrow N$ where $f(n) = 2n$.
IR = {0}, OR = {3}

```
→ [1]            STI [0], [2]
  [2]
  [3]            0
  [4]            HLT
  [5]            ADD 1, [3] ⎫
  [6]            ADD 1, [3] ⎭ 2 times
  [7]            HLT
  [8]            ADD 1, [3] ⎫
  [9]            ADD 1, [3] ⎪
  [10]           ADD 1, [3] ⎬ 4 times
  [11]           ADD 1, [3] ⎭
  [12]           HLT
  [13]           ADD 1, [3] ⎫
   .                        ⎪
   .                        ⎬ 8 times
   .                        ⎪
  [20]           ADD 1, [3] ⎭
  [21]           HLT
   .
   .
   .
  [m_i - 1]      HLT
  [m_i]          ADD 1, [3] ⎫
   .                        ⎪
   .                        ⎬ 2^(i-3) times
   .                        ⎪
  [m_i + 2^(i-3) - 1]  ADD 1, [3] ⎭
                 HLT
```

Suppose f can be computed by $\mathfrak{M}$ with some finite program. Since only [2] and [3] can be affected by $\mathfrak{M}$'s instructions, it is impossible to construct a program that can grow arbitrarily long (by code generation). Starting with n in some IR, any program would have to eventually halt with $2n$ in some OR. The values $2n$ for all n cannot have been stored in advance since the program is finite and they would have to be considered part of the program. Hence, the values $2n$ for any n have to be built up by the program. Only ADD 1, [3] can be used to build up these values and as n increases an arbitrarily large number of these ADD instructions must be interpreted. This implies that the program must be "looping," i.e., some location must be having its contents interpreted an unbounded number of times depending on the given value in the IR. This location cannot be [3] since only this location can be used to form the value of the function. If [3] is interpreted repeatedly, the program would eventually have to transfer control to an unbounded number of locations. The instruction STI can modify the contents of a location, but only once in any program computation. All this implies that the program must be cycling, i.e., repeating a given sequence of location contents none of which can be altered. Hence, the program could not always halt.

CONDITIONAL INSTRUCTIONS

An instruction b is said to be *unconditional* or *unconditioned* if there exists a mapping $f\colon A \longrightarrow A$ such that the diagram

$$\begin{array}{ccc} B^k \times A & \xrightarrow{\mathfrak{M}_1(b)} & B^r \times A \\ \downarrow{\scriptstyle \pi_{k+1}} & & \downarrow{\scriptstyle \pi_{r+1}} \\ A & \xrightarrow{f} & A \end{array}$$

commutes, where $\pi_i(x_1, x_2, x_3, \cdots, x_n) = x_i$. An unconditioned instruction is therefore one where the next value of the instruction counter is a function only of the previous instruction counter value.

THEOREM 6. *Suppose* $\mathfrak{M}_{S,\mathrm{IR},\mathrm{OR}}\colon B^q \longrightarrow B^t$ *is such that for some* $\beta, \gamma \in B^q$, $\mathfrak{M}_{S,\mathrm{IR},\mathrm{OR}}(\beta)$ *is defined, and* $\mathfrak{M}_{S,\mathrm{IR},\mathrm{OR}}(\gamma)$ *is undefined. If* $\mathfrak{M}_{S,\mathrm{IR},\mathrm{OR}}$ *is being computed by a fixed program, then the program must contain some conditional instruction interpreted by* $\mathfrak{M}$ *in the computation of* $\mathfrak{M}_{S,\mathrm{IR},\mathrm{OR}}$.

Proof. Both of the computations

$$S(\mathrm{IR}/\beta), S_1, S_2, \cdots$$

and

$$S(\mathrm{IR}/\gamma), S_1', S_2', \cdots$$

begin by interpreting $b = [S(\mathrm{IR}/\beta)]^2(m_0) = [S(\mathrm{IR}/\gamma)]^2(m_0)$. Since the first computation converges and the second does not, there is a smallest i such that $S_i(m_0) \neq S_i'(m_0)$. $S_{i-1}(m_0) = S_{i-1}'(m_0) = a$ must contain a conditional, and from the fact that the program is fixed it must be in $\mathrm{PROG}(\mathfrak{M}_{S,\mathrm{IR},\mathrm{OR}})$. Q.E.D.

The condition that the program be fixed was necessary as can be seen by the following example.

Example. A properly partial function computed without a conditional by a nonfixed program (generating code).

Let $f: B \longrightarrow B$ be defined by

$$f(x) = \begin{cases} b_1, & \text{if } x = b_1 \ , \\ \text{diverges}, & \text{if } x \neq b_1 \ . \end{cases}$$

Let $b_T \in B$ be such that

$$\mathfrak{M}_1(b_T): B \times A \longrightarrow B \times A \ ,$$
$$(b_1, a) \longmapsto (b_h, a+1) \ ,$$
$$(y, a) \longmapsto (b_c, a+1) \ (y \neq b_1)$$
$$\mathfrak{M}_2(b_T) = ((a_0), (a_1 + 1))$$

and let

$$\mathfrak{M}_1(b_c): B^0 \times A \longrightarrow B^0 \times A \ ,$$
$$(-, a) \longmapsto (-, a) \ .$$

b_h is the halt instruction. With IR = OR = $\{a_0\}$, f is computed by the program: $\longrightarrow [a_1]\, b_T$. Note that the program is not fixed and is generating code.

It should be noted that Theorem 6 depends on our requiring that computations be terminated only by the HLT instruction. However, an instruction that either terminates a computation or continues it, depending on the state of the machine at the moment, and which advances the instruction counter independently of the machine state, is intuitively a "conditioned" instruction even though it would not be according to our definition. Hence, for the unrestricted case (of machines with "halting" nonHLT instructions) our definition of conditioned instruction would have to be broadened, thus preserving Theorem 6.

COROLLARY 6.1. *If $\mathfrak{M}_{S,\mathrm{IR},\mathrm{OR}}: B^q \longrightarrow B^t$ is computed by a fixed program that never interprets a conditional, then either $\mathfrak{M}_{S,\mathrm{IR},\mathrm{OR}}$ is always undefined, or is total. In that latter case, if the program is finite, then each computation will halt in not more than k steps, k being the program length.*

Proof. Most of this is a rewording of the previous theorem. The last part follows from the fact that under the given assumptions, if the contents of m_0 cycles, the computation must diverge. Q.E.D.

The reader might have conjectured at this point that if, for any converging computation, a machine $\mathfrak{M}$ has interpreted no conditional instructions, then the length of the computation must be bounded by the length of the program at hand. This can be seen to be false by the following example which shows that such computations may not be bounded at all.

Example. Let $B = \{0, 1, 2, \cdots\}$ and let

$$\mathfrak{M}_1(0): B \times A \longrightarrow B \times A \ ,$$
$$(x, a) \longmapsto (x, a+1) \ ,$$
$$\mathfrak{M}_2(0) = ((a_1), (a_1 + 2)) \ ,$$

1 is interpreted by $\mathfrak{M}$ as the HALT instruction, and for each $i > 1$

$$\mathfrak{M}_1(i)\colon B \times A \longrightarrow B \times A \ ,$$
$$\begin{cases} (x, a) \longmapsto (x-1, a) & (x \neq 0) \ , \\ (0, a) \longmapsto (0, a) \ , \end{cases}$$
$$\mathfrak{M}_2(i) = ((a_1+2), (a_1+2)) \ .$$

Consider the program

$$\longrightarrow [a_1 + 1]\, 0$$

with IR $= \{a_1\}$. Note that for any $k > 1$ there is a successful computation of length k, yet no conditioned instructions exist.

Note that this example also refutes the following conjecture: "If $\mathfrak{M}$ has no conditioned instructions, then for any finite program, if a computation is such that the contents of the instruction counter repeats, i.e., $\mathfrak{M}^k(S)(m_0) = \mathfrak{M}^j(S)(m_0)$, $k \neq j$, then the computation cannot end."

Using nonfixed programs, it becomes possible to compute any partial recursive function without using conditional instructions. Let $\mathfrak{M}^*$ be capable of interpreting exactly

HLT
INC x
STO x, y
TRA x
SIM x, y, z, w (for any $x, y, z, w, \in A$) ,

where INC x, STO x, y are as defined earlier, TRA x is coded by $b_x \in B$, and

$$\mathfrak{M}_1(\text{TRA x})\colon B^0 \times A \longrightarrow B^0 \times A \ ,$$
$$(-, a) \longmapsto (-, x) \ ,$$

and

$$\mathfrak{M}_1(\text{SIM } x, y, z, w)\colon B^2 \times A \longrightarrow B \times A \ ,$$
$$\begin{cases} (b_1, b_2, a) \longmapsto (b_z, a), & \text{if } b_1 = b_2 \ , \\ (b_1, b_2, a) \longmapsto (b_{a+1}, a), & \text{if } b_1 \neq b_2 \ , \end{cases}$$
$$\mathfrak{M}_2(\text{SIM } x, y, z, w) = ((x, y), w) \ .$$

THEOREM 7. *There exists a machine that interprets no conditioned instructions, that can compute any partial recursive function.*

Proof. We saw earlier that a machine $\mathfrak{M}$ capable of interpreting INC x, STO x, y, JMP x, y, z, and HLT could be programmed to compute any partial recursive function. $\mathfrak{M}^*$ interprets no conditioned instructions yet

[a] JMP x, y, z ,

is equivalent to

[a] SIM x, y, z, a.

Taking advantage of the lack of restrictions on F, Theorem 7 can be proven in a more direct, but far less "realistic" way as follows.

Let $\mathfrak{M}$ be a machine with $A = B = N$ having a HLT instruction, a "cycle" instruction defined by

$$\mathfrak{M}_1(\text{CYCLE}): B^0 \times A \longrightarrow B^0 \times A \ ,$$
$$(-, a) \longmapsto (-, a) \ ,$$

and for each partial recursive function $f: N^k \longrightarrow N^r$, a symbol $b_f \in B$ interpreted by $\mathfrak{M}$ as follows

$$\mathfrak{M}_1(b_f): B^k \times A \longrightarrow B^r \times A \ ,$$
$$(b_1, b_2, b_3, \cdots, b_k, a) \longmapsto (f(b_1, b_2, b_3, \cdots, b_k), a + 1) \ ,$$

if f is defined for $b_1, b_2, b_3, \cdots, b_k$

$$(b_1, b_2, b_3, \cdots, b_k, a) \longmapsto (b_1, b_2, b_3, \cdots, b_{r-1}, \text{CYCLE}, a + 1) \ ,$$

if f is undefined for $b_1, b_2, b_3, \cdots, b_k$, where CYCLE is the symbol interpreted as the "cycle" instruction.

$$\mathfrak{M}_2(b_f) = ((m_1, m_2, m_3, \cdots, m_k), (\bar{m}_1, \bar{m}_2, \bar{m}_3, \cdots, \bar{m}_r)) \ .$$

For any partial recursive function f, $\mathfrak{M}$ computes f with no conditioned instructions by the following program where IR $= \{m_1, m_2, m_3, \cdots, m_k\}$, and OR $= \{\bar{m}_1, \bar{m}_2, \bar{m}_3, \cdots, \bar{m}_r\}$.

$$\longrightarrow \ [\bar{m}_r - 1] \quad b_f$$
$$[\bar{m}_r] \quad b_h \quad \text{Q.E.D.}$$

The reader can note that in each proof of Theorem 7 given, F was not finite. In the first proof, for each $x \in N$, TRA x gave a distinct element of F. Also, SIM x, y, z, w gave a distinct element of F for each $z \in N$. These infinitely many SIM instructions can be replaced by another infinite set of slightly different instructions where the entire set contributes only one element to the set F. For each $x, y, u, v, w \in A$, let

$$\mathfrak{M}_1(\text{SIM } x, y, u, v, w): B^4 \times A \longrightarrow B \times A \ ,$$
$$\begin{cases} (b_1, b_2, b_3, b_4, a) \longmapsto (b_3, a), & \text{if } b_1 = b_2 \ , \\ (b_1, b_2, b_3, b_4, a) \longmapsto (b_4, a), & \text{if } b_1 \neq b_2 \ , \end{cases}$$
$$\mathfrak{M}_2(\text{SIM } x, y, u, v, w) = ((x, y, u, v), w) \ .$$

Note that each $x, y, u, v, w \in A$ gives rise to the same element of F. We saw earlier that any partial recursive function can be computed by some program using a fixed number of SIM x, y, z, w instructions. Each SIM x, y, z, a can be replaced by SIM x, y, u, v, a where u and v are locations used only to store b_z (i.e., TRA z) and b_{a+1} (i.e., TRA $a + 1$), respectively. In summary, we have established:

COROLLARY 7.1. *There exists a machine that interprets no conditioned instructions, that has a set F which is infinite only because of unconditioned transfers (i.e.,* TRA x *instructions), that can compute any partial recursive function.*

The infinitely many TRA x instructions can be replaced by another infinite set of ("indirectly addressed") transfer instructions defined for each $m \in A$ by

$$\mathfrak{M}_1(\text{TRA}\ \langle m \rangle)\colon B \times A \longrightarrow B^0 \times A \ ,$$
$$(\text{x}, a) \longmapsto (-, \text{x}) \ ,$$
$$\mathfrak{M}_2(\text{TRA}\ \langle m \rangle) = ((m), -) \ .$$

Note that TRA x is simulated by TRA $\langle m \rangle$ provided m contains x. Also, TRA $\langle m \rangle$ yields the same element of F for each $m \in A$. These transfer instructions, however, are conditioned, according to our definition. These remarks prove:

THEOREM 8. *There exists a machine with a finite set F that can be finitely programmed to compute any partial recursive function.*

CONCLUDING REMARKS

Probably the two most important open questions are: "Does there exist a machine with a finite set F of instruction types that can be finitely programmed to compute any recursive partial function with: (1) Only *fixed* programs? and (2) Without using conditional instructions?"

No topic introduced has to our knowledge been thoroughly studied and as a result open questions are easy to find. For example, the existence of an $\mathfrak{M}$-computable function that can be computed by $\mathfrak{M}$ only with a program of infinite length suggests many questions: "Is there a machine that can compute any recursive partial function but not if limited to finite programs?" "What are some conditions on a machine's instructions that necessitate programs of infinite length for the computation of some functions?"

Looking upon a machine's instructions as generators of its $\mathfrak{M}$-computable functions suggests the concept of two instructions being "computationally independent" which seems worthy of some thought.

The topic of *functional composition* suggests not only the problem of finding tighter conditions ensuring closure on the composition of a machine's $\mathfrak{M}$-computable functions, but also conditions on a machine's instruction set allowing program relocation.

Many results and questions concerning decision problems could have been formulated, but since results of this type usually have minor relevance to the concerns of those involved with the "real world" of computers, we chose to play down this topic.

Due to the importance of programming and programming languages, it would appear that future efforts might consider developing a good definition of the concept of a "machine language" for an internally-driven machine. Intuitively, a machine language would be a "programming language" whose "atomic sentences" would have a close relation to the instructions of some internally-driven machine. Such a definition might eventually suggest a way of studing with some rigor the question of whether or not any programming language can be a machine language for some machine organization.

REFERENCES

[1] H. Wang, "A Variant to Turing's Theory of Computing Machines," *J. ACM*, 4 (1957).

[2] C. C. Elgot and A. Robinson, "Random-Access Stored-Program Machines, An Approach to the Theory of Programming Languages," *J. ACM* (October 1964).

[3] W. W. Maurer, "A Theory of Computer Instructions," *J. ACM*, **13** (1966).

[4] R. Narashimhan, "Programming Languages and Computers: A Unified Metatheory," *Advances in Computers*, **8** (Academic Press, 1967).

[5] E. G. Wagner, "Bounded-Action Machines: Toward an Abstract Theory of Computer Structure," *J. Comput. Sys. Sci.*, **2** (1968).

[6] Z. Pawlak, "On the Notion of a Computer," *Logic, Methodology and Philosophy of Science*, **III** (B. Van Rootselaat and J. F. Staal, Eds., North-Holland, 1968).

MODELING AND SIMULATION: STRUCTURE PRESERVING RELATIONS FOR CONTINUOUS AND DISCRETE TIME SYSTEMS

Bernard P. Zeigler
Logic of Computers Group, Department of Computer and Communication Sciences, University of Michigan, Ann Arbor, MI

This paper has established a basis for the formal treatment of modeling and simulation when continuous time systems occur as elements of the basic simulation triad (i.e., either the system to be simulated, the model or the computer doing the simulating is a continuous time system). The key idea is that of constructively specifying a system in a way analogous to the use of the one step transition and output functions of the usual sequential machine formulation. This enables one to develop useful criteria for determining when one constructively specified system simulates or models another.

I. INTRODUCTION

Recently, there have been a number of efforts toward a framework in which system models commonly distinguished along a digital-analog axis could be given unified treatment. Mesarovic [1], Windeknecht [2], Zodeh and Desoer [3] have considered abstract formulations of systems theory. Kalman, Falb, and Arbib [4] work with a more structured formulation which specializes more readily into the sequential machine and optimal control formalisms commonly employed. Wymore [5] has taken the first steps in considering the new applications areas made possible by a unified systems theory. These areas relate to systems containing components of both the digital and analog variety in which an adequate understanding of overall system operation can be better gained by treating such components and their interaction in a unified way.

The utility of such a systems approach is most readily apparent in the consideration of hybrid computing systems but there are other important areas of applications such as in the digital simulation of continuous state models and the design of asynchronous processors.

In this paper, I shall be concerned with the formalization of a relation existing between two systems whereby the first might be said to be a "simulation" or "realization" of the second or the second might be said to be a "model" of the first. The basis for such a development has been laid in Zeigler and Weinberg [6] and Zeigler [7]. The former paper showed how the system theoretic concepts of homomorphism and coordinate aggregation could be usefully applied in actual

Presented at the Symposium on Computers and Automata
Polytechnic Institute of Brooklyn, April 13-15, 1971.

computer simulation of biological systems. Zeigler [7] showed how a simulation could be regarded as a triple (*system to be simulated, model, computer*) in which a preservation relation holds between model and system (determining what properties of the system are to be preserved in the model) at the same time that another preservation holds between model and computer (which governs the manner in which the model is implemented on the computer). The relations in question were formalized as *structure preserving morphisms* (with varying degrees of strength) and shown to be inclusive of existent notions of modeling and simulation. Complexity measures relevant to usage of time and space resources of a simulation were defined and their behavior under structure preserving morphisms studied with a view toward the construction of models with reduced complexity.

The entities in a simulation (simulated system, model, computer) however, were taken to be automata—essentially discrete time systems, though continuous state spaces were allowed. The theory developed in this way presupposes a discretization of time which would be unnatural when applications to continuous time models and hybrid or analog computers are considered. Thus by extending the notions of "system" and the class of structure preserving morphisms which can relate systems, a more adequate and applicable simulation theory can be developed.

The plan of this paper is as follows:

(1) A concept of system is developed which allows both continuous and discrete time operation. This is essentially based on Arbib's definition [4] which I feel to be much less clumsy than Wymore's [5]

(2) Behavior and function preserving morphisms are defined and studied for these systems. Behavior and function preserving morphisms are weaker than the structure preserving morphisms of [7] but are necessary prior elements in dealing with these stronger preservation concepts. There is not space in this paper to complete the connection

(3) A notion of *constructive specification* of systems is developed. This is a generalization of the usual sequential machine *one-step transition structure* formulation for discrete time systems. The great advantage afforded by such a specification is that it makes possible a practical procedure for constructing a system which will simulate or model another. This is analogous to the case of sequential machines where judgements concerning the *behavioral* relations of machines (involving extended operation) can be determined by examination of the single step transition and output functions.

Constructive specification of continuous time systems involves difficulties which do not arise in the discrete time case. Much of the paper is devoted to providing reasonable solutions to these problems

(4) Examples are provided which give evidence for the applicability of the theoretical development. It is shown, for example, how Wymore's [5] results on the realization of discrete time systems by continuous time systems and simulation of continuous time systems by discrete time systems are more easily formulated in this framework.

II. SYSTEMS

2.0 System Definition

A *time invariant mathematical system* (hereafter called a system when the context is clear) is a structure

$$S = \langle \Omega, Q, Y, \delta, \lambda \rangle ,$$

where: Ω is a set of *input segments*; Q a nonempty set of *states*; Y a set of *outputs*; and

$$\delta : Q \times \Omega \longrightarrow Q ,$$
$$\lambda : Q \times \Omega \longrightarrow Y ,$$

are the state *transition function* and *output function*, respectively.

The objects above must satisfy the following axioms:

AXIOM A.1. *Structure of* Ω. *T denotes the underlying* time *set where T is either the reals R or the integers I. X denotes the* input value *set.*

AXIOM A.1.1. *ω is a function on a finite closed interval.* $\omega \in \Omega \Longrightarrow$ *there are* $t_0, t_1 \in T$, $t_0 \leq t_1$ *and ω is a map* ω: $[t_0, t_1] \longrightarrow X$.

AXIOM A.1.2. *Closure under translation.* $\omega \in \Omega \Longrightarrow$ *for every* $\tau \in T$ *there is an* $\omega' \in \Omega$ *such that*

$$\omega' : [t_0 + \tau, t_1 + \tau] \longrightarrow X ,$$

and

$$\omega'(t) = \omega(t - \tau) ,$$

for all $t \in [t_0 + \tau, t_1 + \tau]$. *$\omega'$ is said to be a* translate *of* ω.

Remark. From here on we do not distinguish between an input segment and any of its translates. More formally we define the equivalence relation "$\equiv$" on Ω where

$$\omega \equiv \omega' \Longleftrightarrow \omega' \text{ is a translate of } \omega .$$

An equivalence class $[\omega]$ will be represented by any one of its members as is appropriate. For example, if we are interested in segments starting at some time t_0 and write ω we mean that segment in $[\omega]$ we defined on an interval $[t_0, -]$.

AXIOM A.1.3. *Closure under concatenation.* $\omega \in \Omega$ *and* $\omega' \in \Omega \Longrightarrow$ *there is a segment* $\omega\omega' \in \Omega$, *where if*

$$\omega : [t_0, t_1] \longrightarrow X ,$$

and

$$\omega' : [t_1, t_2] \longrightarrow X ,$$

then

$$\omega\omega' : [t_0, t_2] \longrightarrow X ,$$

and is given by

$$\omega\omega'(t) = \begin{cases} \omega(t), & \text{for } t \in [t_0, t_1] \ , \\ \omega'(t), & \text{for } t \in (t_1, t_2] \ , \end{cases}$$

and $T = R$. *For* $T = I$ *the usual concatenation operation is assumed.*

Remark. With this condition Ω becomes a semigroup since as can readily be verified concatenation is associative.

AXIOM A.2. *Time invariance. For all* $\omega, \omega' \in \Omega$, $q \in Q$

$$\omega \equiv \omega' \Longrightarrow \delta(q, \omega) = \delta(q, \omega') \text{ and } \lambda(q, \omega) = \lambda(q, \omega') \ .$$

Remark. This means that $\delta(q, \omega)$ and $\lambda(q, \omega)$ are uniquely determined once the state q and any representative ω of the equivalence class $[\omega]$ are given. As a consequence we adopt the same convention as in A.1.2, i.e., we let the context determine the particular translate of ω which is of interest.

This convention makes possible an enormous gain in notational manipulation; c.f., Wymore [5] and Kalman et al. [4] who do not make use of this convention. Of course, it relies on a time invariant system formulation, but this is always possible to achieve by considering T as a state space component.

AXIOM A.3. *Composition or semigroup property. For all* $\omega, \omega' \in \Omega$, $q \in Q$

$$\delta(q, \omega\omega') = \delta(\delta(q, \omega), \omega') \ ,$$

and

$$\lambda(q, \omega\omega') = \lambda(\delta(q, \omega), \omega') \ .$$

With $\omega \in \Omega$ *represented by* $\omega : [0, \tau] \longrightarrow X$ *we associate two segments* $\omega_{t]}$ *and* $\omega_{[t}$ *for every* $t \in [0, \tau]$. *The* left segment $\omega_{t]} = \omega \mid [0, t]$, *i. e., the function* ω *restricted to the subdomain* $[0, t]$. *The* right segment $\omega_{[t} = \omega \mid [t, \tau]$.

A system $S = \langle \Omega, Q, Y, \delta, \lambda \rangle$ is called *input decomposable* if in addition to Axioms A.1–A.3 it satisfies:

AXIOM A.4. *Restriction closure.* $\omega \in \Omega$ *and* $\omega : [0, \tau] \longrightarrow X \Longrightarrow \omega \mid [t, t'] \in \Omega$ *for all* $0 \leq t \leq t' \leq \tau$.

AXIOM A.5. *Consistency. For all* $q \in Q$, $\delta(q, \Lambda) = q$, *where* Λ *is any translate of* $\omega_{[0,0]}$, *the zero length input segment.*

2.1 Time Discrete Systems

A *discrete time sequential system* is a structure $M = \langle X, Q, Y, \delta_M, \lambda_M \rangle$ where X, Q, Y are nonempty sets of *inputs, states,* and *outputs,* respectively and $\delta_M : Q \times X \longrightarrow Q$, $\lambda_M : Q \longrightarrow Y$ are the *one step transition* and *output functions,* respectively.

This is the usual Moore machine except that no finiteness restriction is placed on X, Q, Y.

We may associate with a discrete time system M a general system S_M as follows

$$S_M = \langle \Omega, Q, Y, \tilde{\delta}, \tilde{\lambda} \rangle \ ,$$

where Ω is the translation closure of X^+,

$$\tilde{\delta} : Q \times X^+ \longrightarrow Q \text{ and } \tilde{\lambda} : Q \times X^+ \longrightarrow Y \ ,$$

are the *extended* transition and output function, respectively, defined by

$$\tilde{\delta}(q, s) = \delta(q, s) \quad (\text{for } s \in X) \ ,$$

$$\tilde{\delta}(q, xs) = \delta(\tilde{\delta}(q, x), s) \quad (\text{for } x \in X^+) \ ,$$

and

$$\tilde{\lambda}(q, x) = \lambda_M(\tilde{\delta}(q, x)) \ .$$

Here $X^+ = \{\omega \mid \omega : \{1, 2, 3, \cdots, n\} \longrightarrow X, n = 1, 2, 3, \cdots\}$, i.e., the set of all finite sequences of elements of X. The underlying time set has been assumed to be the integers I. Note that by the translation closure assumption each sequence $x_1 x_2 x_3 \cdots x_n \in X^+$ represents any of its possible translates in Ω.

The reader may verify that S_M satisfies the axioms for a time invariant system.

2.2 Time Continuous Systems

Before exemplifying a class of continuous time systems we need the following concepts:

A system $S = (\Omega, Q, Y, \delta, \lambda)$ defines *trajectories* through the state and output sets as follows:

With each $q \in Q$, $\omega \in \Omega$ there are associated segments $\text{STRAJ}_{(q,\omega)}$, $\text{OTRAJ}_{(q,\omega)}$. Choosing the representative $\omega : [0, \tau] \longrightarrow X$ we have

$$\text{STRAJ}_{(q,\omega)} : [0, \tau] \longrightarrow Q \ ,$$

given by

$$\text{STRAJ}_{(q,\omega)}(t) = \delta(q, \omega_{t]}) \quad (\text{for } t \in [0, \tau]) \ ,$$

$\text{STRAJ}_{(q,\omega)}$ is *state trajectory* associated with initial state q and input segment ω. Similarly

$$\text{OTRAJ}_{(q,\omega)} : [0, \tau] \longrightarrow Y \ ,$$

is the *output trajectory* associated with initial state q and input segment ω, where

$$\text{OTRAJ}_{(q,\omega)}(t) = \lambda(q, \omega_{t]}) \quad (\text{for } t \in [0, \tau]) \ .$$

Remark. It is easy to see that in the same way that ω represents its translates in $[\omega]$, $\text{STRAJ}_{(q,\omega)}$, and $\text{OTRAJ}_{(q,\omega)}$ also represents translation equivalence classes.

A *Differential Equation Specified System*, DESS is a structure

$$D = (\Omega, Q, Y, f, N) \ ,$$

where: Ω is a set of input segments satisfying A.1 and A.4 with $T = R$ and $X \subseteq R^m$ for some $m \geq 1$; $Q \subseteq R^n$ for some $n \geq 1$; $Y \subseteq R^p$ for some $p \geq 1$; and f, N are maps

$$f : Q \times X \longrightarrow Q \ ,$$

$$N : Q \longrightarrow Y \ .$$

Remark. Often D is presented in the form

$$\frac{dq}{dt} = f(q, x) \quad ,$$

$$y(t) = N\,(q(t)) \quad .$$

A time segment $\Phi: [0, \tau] \longrightarrow Q$ is a *state trajectory* of D if there is an input segment $\omega \in \Omega$ and a (starting) state $q \in Q$ such that

$$\text{(i)} \qquad \Phi(0) = q \quad ,$$

and

$$\text{(ii)} \qquad \frac{d\Phi}{dt}(t) = f\,(\Phi(t), \omega(t)) \quad ,$$

for all $t \in [0, \tau]$.

A segment $\Psi: [0, \tau] \longrightarrow Y$ is an *output trajectory* of D if there is a state trajectory $\Phi: [0, \tau] \longrightarrow Q$ such that

$$\Psi(t) = N\,(\Phi(t)) \text{ for } t \in [0, \tau] \quad .$$

A DESS will be said to have *unique solutions* if given any $q \in Q$, $\omega \in \Omega$ there is a *unique* state trajectory satisfying (i) and (ii), call it $\Phi_{(q,\omega)}$. Uniqueness of $\Phi_{(q,\omega)}$ clearly implies uniqueness of output trajectory $\Psi_{(q,\omega)}$.

The following is well known from other approaches:

THEOREM 2.2.1. *Given a* DESS *with unique solutions* $D = (\Omega, Q, Y, f, N)$ *we may associate with* D *an input decomposable system* S_D *as follows.*

$$S_D = (\Omega, Q, Y, \delta, \lambda) \quad ,$$

where for $q \in Q$, $\omega \in \Omega$, $t \in T$

$$\delta(q, \omega_{t]}) = \Phi_{(q,\omega)}(t) \quad ,$$

$$\lambda(q, \omega_{t]}) = \Psi_{(q,\omega)}(t) \quad .$$

Moreover S_D represents D in the sense that it generates exactly the same set of trajectories, i.e., for all $q \in Q$, $\omega \in \Omega$

$$\text{STRAJ}_{(q,\omega)} = \Phi_{(q,\omega)} \quad ,$$

and

$$\text{OTRAJ}_{(q,\omega)} = \Psi_{(q,\omega)} \quad .$$

An interesting subclass of the differential equation systems are the linear (time invariant) systems. DESS $D = (\Omega, Q, Y, f, N)$ is *linear* if X, Q, Y are vector spaces and f, N are linear transformations given by

$$f(q, x) = Aq + Bx \quad ,$$

$$N(q) = Cq \quad .$$

The underlying differential equation takes the usual form

$$\dot{q} = Aq + Bx \quad .$$

The corresponding system $S_D = (\Omega, Q, Y, \delta, \lambda)$ has

$$\delta(q, \omega_{t]}) = e^{At} q + \int_0^t e^{A(t-t')} B\omega(t')\, dt' ,$$

and

$$\lambda(q, \omega_{t]}) = C\delta(q, \omega_{t]}) .$$

III. MODELING AND SIMULATION RELATIONS

3.0 The Essential Difference Between Discrete and Continuous Time Systems

It is important to note the essential differences between the two general classes of systems just mentioned.

In the sequential machine case, the transition function $\tilde{\delta}$ is determined by extending the given one-step transition function δ_M. Thus given an input string $s_1 s_2 s_3 \cdots s_n$ and a state q we can compute the trajectory $q_1, q_2, q_3, \cdots, q_n$ where $q_1 = q$ and for $i = 1, 2, 3, \cdots, n-1$, $q_{i+1} = \delta_M(q_i, s_i)$.

This step by step iteration is precisely the idea underlying digital computer simulation of systems.

More explicitly, given two sequential machine derived systems S_M and $S_{M'}$ there are a number of criteria available for determining whether S_M simulates $S_{M'}$ or whether $S_{M'}$ is a model of S_M. This is done essentially by examining the one-step transition and output functions (δ_M, λ_M) given in by the M, M' specifications.

In the continuous time case very few such criteria are known. We are reduced to having to compare the total system descriptions S and S' to determine whether S can simulate S'.

To see the import of this, consider the case where we have two DESS's D and D' and wish to determine whether S_D can simulate $S_{D'}$. Since D, D' are known we can program an analog computer to simulate S_D and $S_{D'}$ just as knowing M and M' we can program a digital computer to simulate each. In contrast to the discrete time case however, it is *generally unknown how to use the structure of these programs (or equivalently the functions f, N) to determine whether S_D can simulate $S_{D'}$. This must be done by an exhaustive generation and comparison of their trajectories.* (The only exception to this I know of, concerns linear systems where one can determine behavioral equivalence from the similarity of the matrices A, B, and C.)

The following sections present an approach to this problem within the system theoretic framework given above. The essential idea is consider continuous time systems which have enough of the properties of discrete time systems to enable the application structure preserving criteria already known in the latter area.

3.1 Basic Preservation Relations

We begin by reviewing and generalizing known behavior and function preserving relations for systems.

The input-output behavior of a system $S = \langle \Omega, Q, Y, \delta, \lambda \rangle$ is the collection of functions $\{\beta_q \mid q \in Q\}$ where for $q \in Q$

$$\beta_q : \Omega \longrightarrow Y \quad ,$$

and is given by

$$\beta_q(\omega) = \lambda(q, \omega) \quad ,$$

for all $\omega \in \Omega$.

A *behavior preserving morphism* from S to S' is a triple (h_1, h_2, h_3) where

$$h_1 : \Omega' \longrightarrow \Omega \quad ,$$
$$h_2 : Q' \longrightarrow Q \quad ,$$
$$h_3 : Y \longrightarrow Y' \quad ,$$

such that for all $q' \in Q'$

$$\beta'_{q'} = h_3 \circ \beta_{h_2(q')} \circ h_1 \quad .$$

Remark. More expansively, let us say that $\beta'_{q'} \mid \beta_q$ ($\beta'_{q'}$ *divides* β_q) using an input encoding map h_1 and an output decoding map h_3 if $\beta'_{q'} = h_3 \circ \beta_q \circ h_1$. Then the existence of a behavior morphism (h_1, h_2, h_3) means that for each state $q' \in Q'$ there is a state $q \in Q$ (namely $h_2(q')$) such that $\beta'_{q'} \mid \beta_q$ using (h_1, h_3).

A *function preserving morphism* (homomorphism) from S to S' is a triple (g, h, k) where

$$g : \Omega' \longrightarrow \Omega \quad ,$$
$$h : Q_1 \longrightarrow Q' \quad \text{(onto)} \quad ,$$
$$k : Y \longrightarrow Y' \quad ,$$

where:

(i) $Q_1 \subseteq Q$ is closed under $g(\Omega')$

$$\omega' \in \Omega', \; q \in Q_1 \Longrightarrow \delta(q, g(\omega')) \in Q_1$$

(ii) For all $q \in Q_1$, $\omega' \in \Omega'$

$$h(\delta(q, g(\omega'))) = \delta'(h(q), \omega')$$

and

$$\beta'_{h(q)} = k \circ \beta_q \circ g \quad .$$

A behavior morphism will be said to *time local* if $h_1 : \Omega' \longrightarrow \Omega$ is a semigroup homomorphism, i.e., for all $\omega_1, \omega_2 \in \Omega'$, $h_1(\omega_1 \omega_2) = h_1(\omega_1) h_1(\omega_2)$. A function morphism is similarly designated if $g : \Omega' \longrightarrow \Omega$ is a semigroup homomorphism.

Remark. Time local morphisms are desirable since they enable input segments to be encoded by concatenating encoded subsegments. Their existence comes much easier for discrete time systems than for continuous time systems, as we shall see.

THEOREM 3.1.1. *The existence of a function morphism from S to S′ implies the existence of a behavior morphism from S to S′.*

Proof. Let (g, h, k) be a function morphism from S to S'. Construct a behavior morphism (h_1, h_2, h_3) as follows: Set

$$h_1 = g \ ,$$
$$h_3 = k \ ,$$

and define $h_2 : Q' \longrightarrow Q$ by $h_2(q')$ is a designated representative of the inverse image $h^{-1}(q') = \{q \mid h(q) = q'\}$.

Then $h(h_2(q')) = q'$ implies

$$\beta'_{q'} = k \circ \beta_{h_2(q')} \circ g \quad \text{((ii) of function morphism condition)} \ ,$$
$$= h_3 \circ \beta_{h_2(q')} \circ h_1 \ . \quad \text{Q.E.D.}$$

A system $S = \langle \Omega, Q, Y, \delta, \lambda \rangle$ is *reduced* if for all $q_1, q_2 \in Q$, $\beta_{q_1} = \beta_{q_2} \Longrightarrow q_1 = q_2$.

THEOREM 3.1.2. *The existence of a time local behavior morphism from S to S′ implies the existence of a time local function morphism from S to S′ if S′ is reduced.*

Proof. Let (h_1, h_2, h_3) be a time local behavior morphism from S to S'. Construct a function morphism (g, h, k) as follows: Set

$$g = h_1 \ ,$$
$$k = h_3 \ ,$$

and define $h : Q_1 \longrightarrow Q'$ by

(a) $Q_1 = \{q \in Q \mid \text{there is a } q' \in Q' \text{ such that } \beta'_{q'} \mid \beta_q \text{ using } h_1, h_3\}$

(b) For $q \in Q_1$, $h(q) = q' \Longleftrightarrow \beta'_{q'} \mid \beta_q$.

LEMMA. $\beta'_{q'} \mid \beta_q \Longrightarrow \beta'_{\delta'(q',\omega')} \mid \beta_{\delta(q, g(\omega'))}$.

Proof. For all $\omega_1, \omega_2, \in \Omega'$

$$\beta'_{q'} \mid \beta_q \Longrightarrow \beta'_{q'}(\omega_1 \omega_2) = h_3 \circ \beta_q \circ h_1(\omega_1 \omega_2)$$
$$\Longrightarrow \beta'_{q'}(\omega_1 \omega_2) = h_3 \circ \beta_q (h_1(\omega_1) h_1(\omega_2))$$
$$(h_1 \text{ is a homomorphism})$$
$$\Longrightarrow \lambda'(q', \omega_1 \omega_2) = h_3 \circ \lambda(q, h_1(\omega_1) h_1(\omega_2))$$
$$\Longrightarrow \lambda'(\delta'(q', \omega_1), \omega_2) = h_3 \circ \lambda(\delta(q, h_1(\omega_1)), h_1(\omega_2))$$
$$\text{(composition property)}$$
$$\Longrightarrow \beta'_{\delta'(q',\omega_1)}(\omega_2) = h_3 \circ \beta_{\delta(q, h_1(\omega_1))} \circ h_1(\omega_2)$$
$$\Longrightarrow \beta'_{\delta'(q',\omega_1)} \mid \beta_{\delta(q, h_1(\omega_1))} . \quad \text{Q.E.D.}$$

Using the Lemma we see readily that Q_1 is closed undet $g(\Omega')$ as required.

To show that h is well defined by (b), note that if $\beta_{q'} \mid \beta_q$ and $\beta_{q''} \mid \beta_q$ we have $\beta_{q'} = h_3 \circ \beta_q \circ h_1 = \beta_{q''}$. Since S' is reduced $q' = q''$ as is required.

Next we show that (g, h, k) as defined above have the requisite commutative properties. From definition (b) of h, $h(q) = q \Longrightarrow \beta'_{q'} \mid \beta_q \Longrightarrow \beta'_{h(q)} \mid \beta_q$ as required.

Also by the lemma,

$$\beta'_{\delta'(q',\omega')} \mid \beta_{\delta(q,g(\omega'))}$$

So from definition (b) of h

$$\begin{aligned} h\left(\delta\left(q, g(\omega')\right)\right) &= \delta'(q', \omega') \\ &= \delta'\left(h(q), \omega'\right) , \end{aligned}$$

as required. Q.E.D.

Remark. That the homomorphisms of topological dynamics (e.g., Ura [9]) are special cases of the behavior morphism can be seen as follows: Let S be an autonomous input decomposable continuous time system, i.e., X is a singleton set. Since Ω now consists of all constant value segments, these segments are uniquely identified by the length of their associated interval. Thus we may set $\Omega = R$; $\omega + \omega'$ then represents the segment $\omega\omega'$. $\delta: Q \times \Omega \longrightarrow Q$ now satisfies the composition law: $\delta(q, \omega + \omega') = \delta\left(\delta(q, \omega), \omega'\right)$ and the consistency law $\delta(q, 0) = q$. Given two such systems, for time local function morphism (g, h, k) to exist, g must be a homomorphism of the real additive group R into itself. This result is the usual homomorphism of topological dynamics except that the topological structure of the state space may also be preserved.

3.2 Constructive Nature of Discrete Simulation

For time discrete systems the ability to go back and forth between transition function descriptions and behavior descriptions can be significantly strengthened.

Consider time discrete systems $M = \langle X, Q, Y, \delta, \lambda \rangle$. A *function preserving morphism* from M to M' is a triple (g, h, k) where

$$\begin{aligned} &g: X' \longrightarrow X^+ \ , \\ &h: Q_1 \longrightarrow Q' \quad \text{(onto)} \ , \\ &k: Y \longrightarrow Y' \ , \end{aligned}$$

where $Q_1 \subseteq Q$ is closed under $g(X')$ and for all $s \in X'$, $q \in Q_1$, (g, h, k) satisfy

$$h\left(\tilde{\delta}\left(q, g(s)\right)\right) = \delta'\left(h(q), s\right) ,$$

and

$$k\left(\lambda(q)\right) = \lambda'\left(h(q)\right) .$$

THEOREM 3.2.1. *Let $S_M, S_{M'}$ be systems derived from discrete time systems M and M'. There is a function preserving morphism from M to M' iff there is a local time function morphism from S_M to $S_{M'}$.*

Proof. Necessity. Let (g_M, h_M, k_M) be a function morphism from M to M'. We construct a function morphism (g, h, k) from S_M to S_M, as follows: Set

$$\begin{aligned} h &= h_M \ , \\ k &= k_M \ , \end{aligned}$$

and define $g: (X')^+ \longrightarrow X^+$ by

$$g(s'_1 s'_2 s'_3 \cdots s'_n) = g_M(s'_1)\, g_M(s'_2)\, g_M(s'_3) \cdots g_M(s'_n) ,$$

for all strings $s'_1 s'_2 s'_3 \cdots s'_n$ in $(X')^+$. g is the extension to homomorphism of semigroups of the function g_M defined on the generators. Since $(X')^+$ is a free semigroup this extension is well-defined ($s'_1 s'_2 s'_3 \cdots s'_n = s''_1 s''_2 s''_3 \cdots s''_n$ implies $n = m$ and $s'_i = s''_i$ for all $i = 1, 2, 3, \cdots n$).

Since g is a homomorphism as required (g, h, k) will be a time local function morphism if

$$h\left(\tilde{\delta}\,(q, g(x'))\right) = \tilde{\delta}'\,(h(q), x')\ ,$$

and

$$\beta'_{h(q)} \mid \beta_q\ ,$$

using g, k for all $q \in Q_1$, $x' \in (X')^+$.

Using induction on $\ell(x')$ (the length of x') we can readily show that $h\left(\delta\,(q, g_M(s))\right) = \delta'(h(q), s)$ for all $s \in X'$, $q \in Q_1$ implies

$$h\left(\tilde{\delta}\,(q, g(x'))\right) = \tilde{\delta}'(h(q), x')\ ,$$

for all $x' \in (X')^+$, $q \in Q_1$ as required.

Also the closure of Q_1 with respect to $g(X')$ readily implies the closure of Q_1 with respect to $g(X')^+$.

Finally, for all $x' \in (X')^+$, $q \in Q_1$,

$$\begin{aligned}
k \circ \beta_q \circ g(x') &= k\left(\tilde{\lambda}\,(q, g(x'))\right) && \text{(definition of } \beta_q\text{)}\\
&= k\left(\lambda\left(\tilde{\delta}\,(q, g(x'))\right)\right) && \text{(definition of } \tilde{\lambda}\text{)}\\
&= \lambda'\left(h\left(\tilde{\delta}\,(q, g(x'))\right)\right) && \text{(definition of function morphism)}\\
&= \lambda'\left(\tilde{\delta}'(h(q), x')\right) && \text{(definition of function morphism)}\\
&= \tilde{\lambda}'(h(q), x') && \text{(definition of } \tilde{\lambda}'\text{)}\\
&= \beta'_{h(q)}(x') && \text{as required .}
\end{aligned}$$

Sufficiency. Let (g, h, k) be a function morphism from S_M to $S_{M'}$. We construct a function morphism (g_M, h_M, k_M) from M to M' as follows: Set

$$h = h_M\ ,$$

$$k = k_M\ ,$$

and let $g_M : X' \longrightarrow X^+$ be the restriction of $g : (X')^+ \longrightarrow X^+$ to X', i.e.

$$g(s') = g_M(s') \quad \text{(for all } s' \in X'\text{)}\ .$$

The requisite properties now follow immediately. Q.E.D.

IV. CONSTRUCTIVE SPECIFICATION OF CONTINUOUS SYSTEMS

4.0 Introduction

We see from the Theorems of Section 3 that the ability to determine whether one system simulates or models another by examining their one-step transition structures depends crucially upon the existence of certain properties of the input encoding map $g : \Omega' \longrightarrow \Omega$. Namely: (1) g is a semigroup homomorphism; and

(2) Ω' is generated by a smaller subset such that g need only be defined on this subset. In the case of discrete time systems these conditions are readily satisfiable. However, corresponding constructs for continuous time systems have been lacking. Thus the task now is to give a constructive specification for classes of continuous time systems analogous to that available for discrete time systems.

From here on we restrict attention to state transition system $S = \langle \Omega, Q, \delta \rangle$ since we shall be interested in function rather than behavior morphisms as appropriate for modeling and simulation.

4.1 Maximal Length Segmentation

Analogous to the case of discrete time systems we seek a generating set Ω_G for Ω with certain useful properties.

Given a subset $\Upsilon \subseteq \Omega$ where $\Lambda \notin \Upsilon$ we designate by Υ^+ the least set of segments containing Υ and closed under concatenation. It is easy to see that $\Upsilon^+ = \bigcup_{i=1}^{\infty} \Upsilon^i$ where $\Upsilon^i = \{\omega_1 \omega_2 \omega_3 \cdots \omega_i \mid \omega_j \in \Upsilon,\ j = 1, 2, 3, \cdots, i\}$.

Υ *generates* Ω (Υ is a generating set for Ω) if $\Upsilon^+ = \Omega$. Members of Υ are called generators or generating elements.

We shall say that $\omega_1, \omega_2, \omega_3, \cdots, \omega_n$ is a *decomposition* of $\omega \in \Omega$ by Υ if $\omega = \omega_1 \omega_2 \omega_3 \cdots \omega_n$.

A set Ω_G is an *admissible* set of generators if for all $\omega \in \Omega_G^+$, if $t^* = \max\{t \mid \omega_{t\rangle} \in \Omega_G\}$ exists and $\omega_{\langle t^*} \in \Omega_G^+$.

Explanation. Refer to Figure 4.1.1 where $\omega_{t^*\rangle}$ is the longest generator which is also a left segment of ω. The condition for admissibility is that the

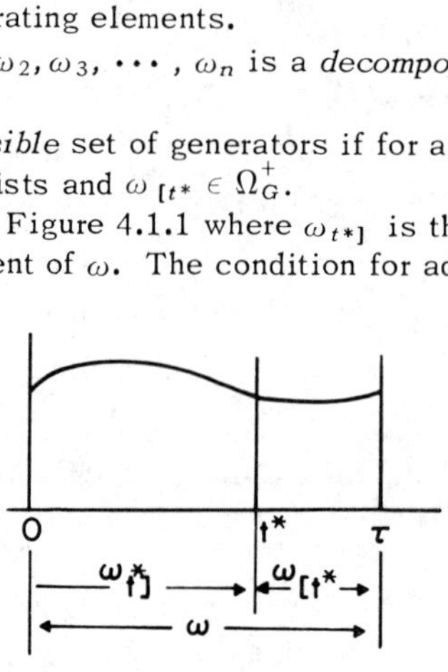

Fig. 4.1.1. Maximal length segmentation.

remaining right segment $\omega_{\langle t^*}$ must be generated by Ω_G. Examples of admissible sets are given in Section 4.2.

Suppose now that $\Omega_G^+ = \Omega$. This means that for every element in Ω, Ω_G can be obtained by concatenating a finite number of generators. However, there may be more than one way to do this. That is, in contrast to the discrete time case Ω_G^+ is not necessarily a free semigroup. To remedy this situation we do not try to force uniqueness of compositions but seek conditions guaranteeing a unique *cannonical* decomposition of elements of Ω in terms of generators Ω_G. The requirement of admissibility is just such a condition as we now show:

A decomposition $\omega_1, \omega_2, \omega_3, \cdots, \omega_n$ of ω by Ω_G is said to be a *maximal length segment* (mls) decomposition if for each $i \in \{1, 2, 3, \cdots, n\}$ whenever there is an $\omega' \in \Omega_G$ such that ω' is a left segment of $\omega_i \omega_{i+1} \omega_{i+2}, \cdots, \omega_n$ then ω' is a left segment of ω_i.

In other words for each i, ω_i is the longest generator which is also a left segment of $\omega_i \omega_{i+1}, \cdots, \omega_n$.

ASSERTION 4.1.1. *If ω has a* mls *decomposition by Ω_G it is unique.*

Proof. Let $\omega_1, \omega_2, \omega_3, \cdots, \omega_n$ and $\omega_1', \omega_2', \omega_3', \cdots \omega_n'$ be mls decompositions of ω. Then ω_1 is a left segment of ω_1' (since ω_1' is the longest generator which is also a left segment of ω), and vice versa ω_1' is a left segment of ω_1; so $\omega_1 = \omega_1'$. This establishes the basis for an induction hypothesis: $\omega_i = \omega_i'$ for $i \le j \Longrightarrow \omega_{j+1} = \omega_{j+1}'$, the proof of which is straightforward. Q.E.D.

THEOREM 4.1.2. *If Ω_G is an admissible set of generators for Ω then every $\omega \in \Omega$ has a unique* mls *decomposition by Ω_G.*

Proof. Refer to Figure 4.1.2. Let $\omega \in \Omega$. Since Ω_G generates Ω, $\omega = \omega_1 \omega_2 \omega_3 \cdots \omega_n$ for some $\omega_i \in \Omega_G$, $i = 1, 2, 3, \cdots, n$.

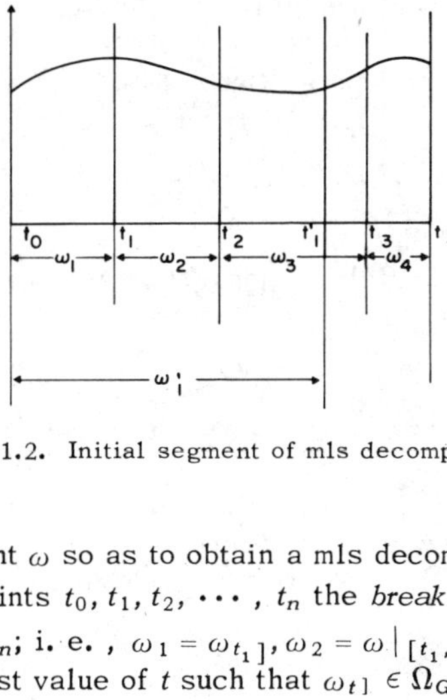

Fig. 4.1.2. Initial segment of mls decomposition.

We wish to resegment ω so as to obtain a mls decomposition $\omega_1', \omega_2', \omega_3', \cdots, \omega_m'$. Let us call the points $t_0, t_1, t_2, \cdots, t_n$ the *break points* of the decomposition $\omega_1, \omega_2, \omega_3, \cdots, \omega_n$; i. e., $\omega_1 = \omega_{t_1]}, \omega_2 = \omega|_{[t_1, t_2]}$, etc.

Let t_1' be the greatest value of t such that $\omega_{t]} \in \Omega_G$.

Then t_1' is the first break point of the mls decomposition and $\omega_1' = \omega_{t_1']}$. Since Ω_G is admissible, $\omega_{[t_1'} \in \Omega_G^+$.

Note that $t_1' \ge t_1 > 0$ since $\omega_{t_1]} = \omega_1$ and $\omega_1 \ne \Lambda$. Let k be the integer such that $t_k \le t_1' < t_{k+1}$. ($k = 2$ in Figure 4.1.2.)

Now $\omega_{[t_1'}$ is a proper right segment of ω and we proceed to find the break point t_2' and a maximal length segment ω_2' of $\omega_{[t_1'}$. Continuing in this way we generate a sequence $t_1', t_2', t_3', \cdots$ which must terminate since if $t_\ell \le t_2' < t_{\ell+1}$ then $t_\ell > t_k$, etc.

Thus, there is an integer $m \le n$ such that $\omega_1', \omega_2', \omega_3', \cdots, \omega_m'$ is a mls decomposition of ω. By Assertion 4.1.1 it is unique. Q. E.D.

4.2 Admissible Generators

There are more transparent but also more stringent conditions that guarantee admissibility.

PROPOSITION 4.2.1. *Consider the following conditions:*

(1) *(Prefix property)* $\omega_1 \in \Omega_G$ *and* $\omega_1\omega_2 \in \Omega_G \Longrightarrow \omega_2 = \Lambda$ *(no generator is a proper left segment of another generator)*

(2) *No generator is a proper left* or *right segment of any other*

(3) Ω_G *is closed under right segmentation and* t^* *of the definition always exists*

(4) Ω_G *is closed under* both *left and right segmentation*, etc.

Then (2) $\Longrightarrow$ (1) $\Longrightarrow$ Ω_G *is admissible and* (4) $\Longrightarrow$ (3) $\Longrightarrow$ Ω_G *is admissible.*

Proof. Left as an exercise for the reader. Q.E.D.

COROLLARY 4.2.1. *For discrete time systems* $M = \langle X, Q, \delta \rangle$, *the input symbols* S *are admissible generators.*

Proof. $\{\omega \mid \omega : \{1\} \longrightarrow X\}$ satisfies Proposition 4.2.1(1). Q.E.D.

COROLLARY 4.2.2. *If Proposition 4.2.1*(1) (*the prefix property*) *holds then if* $\omega_1, \omega_2, \omega_3, \cdots, \omega_n$ *is a decomposition of* ω *by* Ω_G *it is the* mls *decomposition.*

We now give some examples of admissible sets.

Example 1. *Step Function Inputs.* Let a_t denote a *constant real valued function on a segment of length t*, i.e.,

$$a_t : [0, t] \longrightarrow R \ ,$$

where $a_t(t') = a$ for all $t' \in [0, t]$.

Then $\Omega_G = \{a_t \mid t \in R,\ a \in R\}$ is an admissible set of generators and generates the set

$$\Omega_G^+ = \{a_{t_1}\, a'_{t_2 - t_1}\, a''_{t_3 - t_1} \cdots a^{(n)}_{t_n - t_{n-1}} \mid n = 1, 2, 3, \cdots\} \ .$$

Note that the segments a_t can have arbitrary length hence that essential use is being made of the continuous time base.

That Ω_G is admissible follows from Proposition 4.2.1(4).

Figure 4.2.1 shows three distinct decompositions of the same segment. The decomposition in (a) is the mls decomposition. Note that there are infinitely

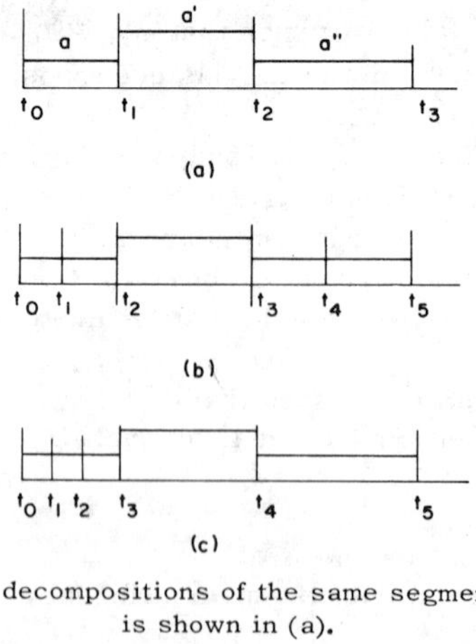

Fig. 4.2.1. Three distinct decompositions of the same segment. The mls decomposition is shown in (a).

many decompositions but only one mls decomposition. For this case of step functions the break points of the mls decomposition are just the points at which step changes occur.

Example 2. *Pulse inputs.* The set $\Omega_G = \{a_{t_2} 0_{t_2-t_1} \mid a \neq 0,\ t_1 \neq 0\}$ is admissible. This can be determined directly from the definition and does not follow from Proposition 4.2.1. See Figure 4.2.2.

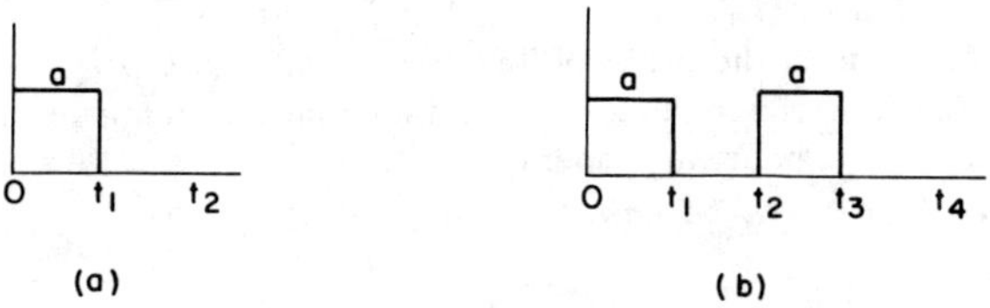

Fig. 4.2.2. Generator shown in (a) and generated segment shown in (b).

Counterexample 3. The set $\Omega_G = \{a_{t_1}\ 0_{t_2-t_1} \mid a \neq 0,\ t_1 \neq 0\} \cup \{a_{t_1} 0_{t_2-t_1} b_{t_3-t_2} \mid a,\ b \neq 0\}$ is not admissible since $a_{t_1} 0_{t_2-t_1} b_{t_3-t_2}$ is the mls of $a_{t_1} 0_{t_2-t_1} b_{t_3-t_2} 0_{t_4-t_3}$ but $0_{t_4-t_3} \notin \Omega_G$. See Figure 4.2.3.

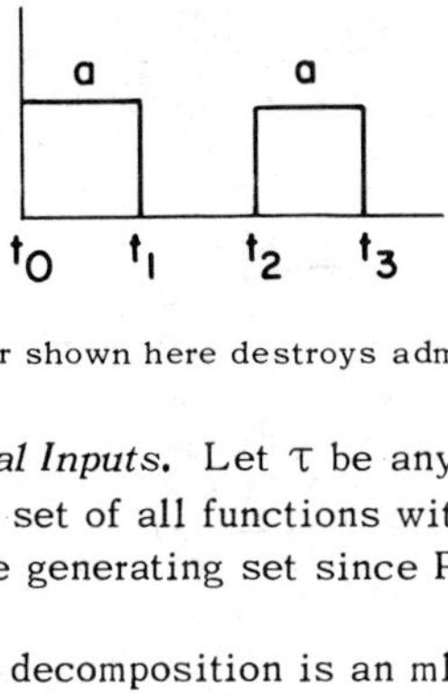

Fig. 4.2.3. Adding generator shown here destroys admissibility of generating set.

Example 3. *Fixed Interval Inputs.* Let τ be any interval and let $\Omega_G \subseteq R^\tau$; i.e., Ω_G is any subset of the set of all functions with domain τ.

Then Ω_G is an admissible generating set since Proposition 4.2.1(1) is satisfied.

By Corollary 4.2.2, every decomposition is an mls decomposition.

A well known special case is where Ω_G consists of a single segment ω; then Ω_G^+ consists of finite length periodic functions. See Figure 4.2.4.

Example 4. *Piecewise Continuous Functions.* Let $\Omega_G = \{\omega \mid \omega : [0, \tau] \rightarrow R$ is a continuous function$\}$. Then $\Omega_G^+ = \{\omega \mid \omega$ is a piecewise continuous function with a finite number of discontinuities$\}$. That Ω_G is admissible follows from Proposition 4.2.1(4).

Note Example 1 is a special case of Example 4. Many other subsets of the continuous functions lead to admissible generators.

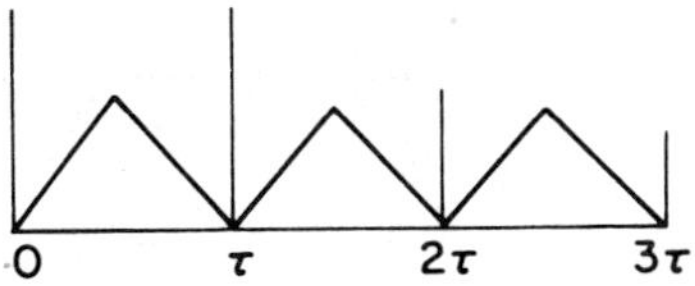

Fig. 4.2.4. Periodic input segments.

4.3 Some Properties of Admissible Sets

We shall need the following results later on. For any decomposition $\omega_1, \omega_2, \omega_3, \cdots, \omega_n$ of ω by Ω_G let $\#(\omega) = n$, the number of generators used.

Let $size(\omega) = n$, where n is the number of generators used in the mls *decomposition* of ω by Ω_G.

ASSERTION 4.3.1. size$(\omega) = \min\{\#(\omega)\}$ *where the minimization is over all decompositions of* ω *by* Ω_G.

Proof. Follows from the proof of Theorem 4.1.2. Q.E.D.

The following is a consequence of the fact that segmentation by maximal length sequences is a "causal" operation.

LEMMA 4.3.2. *Let* Ω_G *be an admissible set.*

(a) *If* $\omega_1', \omega_2', \omega_3', \cdots, \omega_n'$ *is a* mls *decomposition for* $\omega' \in \Omega_G^+$ *then for any* $\omega'' \in \Omega_G^+$, $\omega_1', \omega_2', \omega_3', \cdots, \omega_{n-1}'$ *is the first part of a* mls *decomposition for* $\omega'\omega''$

(b) *Conversely, let* $\omega_1, \omega_2, \omega_3, \cdots, \omega_n$ *be a* mls *decomposition for* $\omega \in \Omega_G^+$. *For any left segment* $\omega_{t]} \in \Omega_G^+$ *the* mls *decomposition of* $\omega_{t]}$ *is* $\omega_1', \omega_2', \omega_3', \cdots, \omega_m'$. *where* $t_m \leq t < t_{m+1}$ *and* $\omega_m' = \omega\,|_{[t_m, t]}$.

Proof. (a) Refer to Figure 4.3.1. Clearly the maximal length segmentation of $\omega_{t_{n-1}]}$ does not depend on ω''. ($n = 3$ in the figure.)

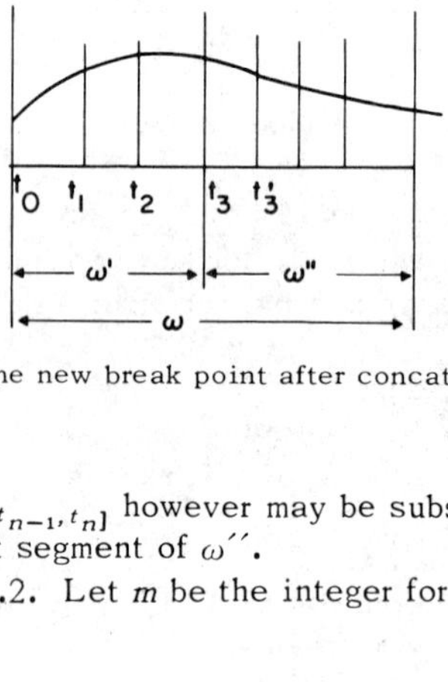

Fig. 4.3.1. t_3' is the new break point after concatenating ω' with ω''.

The segment $\omega_n = \omega_{1\,[t_{n-1}, t_n]}$ however may be subsumed by a new mls segment when adjoining a left segment of ω''.

(b) Refer to Figure 4.3.2. Let m be the integer for which $t_m \leq t < t_{m+1}$. The

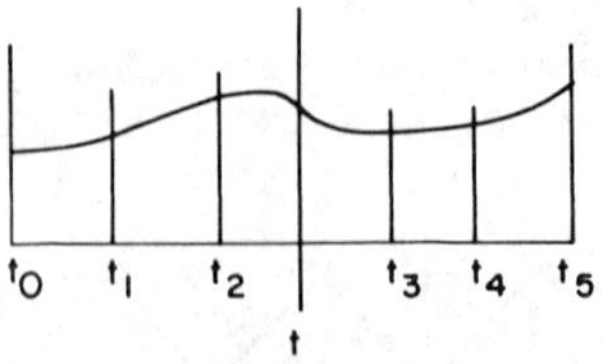

Fig. 4.3.2. Since $t_2 < t < t_3$, the mls decomposition process does not alter the break points t_1 and t_2.

segmentation of $\omega_{t_{m-1}]}$ does not depend on $\omega_{[t}$. This gives $\omega_{t]} = \omega_1 \omega_2 \cdots \omega_{m-1} \omega'_m$ where $\omega'_m = \omega \mid_{[t_m, t]}$. Q.E.D.

PROPOSITION 4.3.3. *Let Ω_G be admissible and* $\omega \in \Omega_G^+$:

(a) $\text{size}(\omega) \geq 1$
(b) $\text{size}(\omega) = 1 \Longleftrightarrow \omega \in \Omega_G$
(c) $\omega = \omega'\omega''$ *for* $\omega', \omega'' \in \Omega_G^+ \Longrightarrow \text{size}(\omega) \leq \text{size}(\omega') + \text{size}(\omega'')$
(d) $\omega = \omega'\omega''$ *for* $\omega', \omega'' \in \Omega_G^+ \Longrightarrow \text{size}(\omega') \leq \text{size}(\omega)$.

Proof.

(a) $\Lambda \notin \Omega_G \Longrightarrow \text{size}(\omega) \geq 1$

(b) For $\omega \in \Omega_G$ such that $\omega: [0, \tau] \longrightarrow X$, $\max_t \{\omega_t \mid \omega_t \in \Omega_G\} = \tau$

(c) Refer to Figure 4.3.3. Let $\omega'_1, \omega'_2, \omega'_3, \cdots, \omega'_p$ and $\omega''_1, \omega''_2, \omega''_3, \cdots, \omega''_q$ be mls decompositions of ω' and ω'' respectively; then $\omega =$

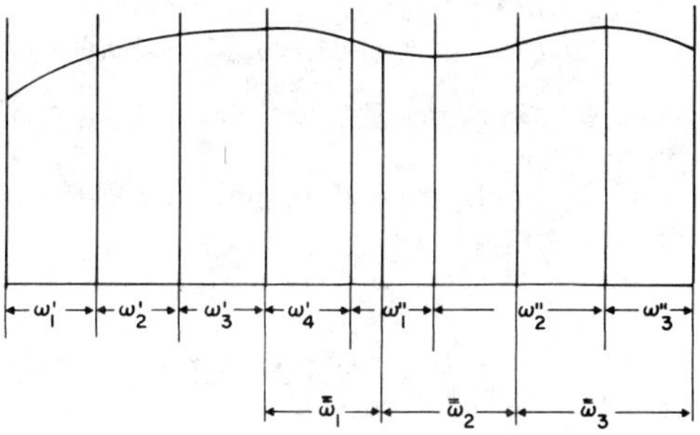

Fig. 4.3.3. $\text{size}(\omega) < \text{size}(\omega') + \text{size}(\omega'')$.

$\omega'_1, \omega'_2, \omega'_3, \cdots, \omega'_p, \omega''_1, \omega''_2, \omega''_3, \cdots, \omega''_q$; ($p = 4$, $q = 3$ in the Figure). Lemma 4.3.2 (a) tells us that $\omega'_1, \omega'_2, \omega'_3, \cdots, \omega'_{p-1}$ begins the mls decomposition of ω. Since $\omega'_p \in \Omega_G$ and $\omega'' \in \Omega_G^+$, $\omega'_p \omega''_1 \cdots \omega''_q \in \Omega_G^+$. Let $\bar{\bar{\omega}}_1, \bar{\bar{\omega}}_2, \bar{\bar{\omega}}_3, \cdots, \bar{\bar{\omega}}_r$ be the mls decomposition for $\omega'_p \omega''_1 \cdots \omega''_q$. Then $\omega'_1, \omega'_2, \omega'_3, \cdots, \omega'_{p-1}, \bar{\bar{\omega}}_1, \bar{\bar{\omega}}_2, \bar{\bar{\omega}}_3, \cdots, \bar{\bar{\omega}}_r$ is the mls decomposition of ω.

Thus $\text{size}(\omega) = p - 1 + r$. But by Assertion 4.3.1, $r = \text{size}(\omega'_p \omega''_1 \cdots \omega''_q) \leq 1 + q$. So $\text{size}(\omega) \leq p - 1 + 1 + q = p + q = \text{size}(\omega') + \text{size}(\omega'')$. Thus part (c) is proved.

(d) Note that $\text{size}(\omega') = p = \text{size}(\omega) + 1 - r$. Now by (a) $r = \text{size}(\omega'_p \omega'') \geq 1$. Q.E.D.

PROPOSITION 4.3.4. *Suppose Proposition* 4.2.1(1), *the prefix property holds. Then if* $\omega'_1, \omega'_2, \omega'_3, \cdots, \omega'_n$ *is a* mls *decomposition for* ω' *and* $\omega''_1, \omega''_2, \omega''_3, \cdots, \omega''_n$ *is a* mls *decomposition for* ω'' *then* $\omega'_1, \omega'_2, \omega'_3, \cdots, \omega'_n, \omega''_1, \omega''_2, \omega''_3, \cdots, \omega''_n$ *is a* mls *decomposition for* $\omega'\omega''$.

Proof. Immediate from the discussion of Proposition 4.3.3. Q.E.D.

4.4 Constructive Specification

We shall want to define a *one-segment transition function* $\delta_G : Q \times \Omega_G \longrightarrow Q$ in such a way that it can consistently be extended to Ω_G^+. We proceed as follows:

Given a set Ω of segments, a segment μ (not necessarily in Ω) is a *right remnant* if for some $\omega \in \Omega$, $\omega\mu \in \Omega$.

A *constructive specification* is a structure $G = \langle \Omega_G, Q, \delta_G \rangle$ where

Ω_G is a set of generators ,

Q is a nonempty set (of states) ,

$\delta_G : Q \times \Omega_G \longrightarrow Q$ is the *one-segment transition function* .

Ω_G must satisfy the axioms:

AXIOM C.1. *Admissibility. Ω_G is an admissible set of generators.*

AXIOM C.2. *Closure with respect to right remnants.* μ a right remnant with respect to $\Omega_G \Longrightarrow \mu \in \Omega_G$; δ_G must satisfy the axiom:

AXIOM C.3. *Internal composition. For all $\omega, \omega' \in \Omega_G$*

$$\omega\omega' \in \Omega_G \Longrightarrow \delta_G(q, \omega\omega') = \delta_G(\delta_G(q, \omega), \omega') \text{ for all } q \in Q \ .$$

Remark. If Ω_G has the prefix property then Axiom C.2 is vacuously satisfied since there are no right remnants.

On the other hand, if Ω_G is closed with respect to right segmentation than Axiom C.2 is (more than) satisfied.

Remark. Although they look similar, Axioms C.1 and C.2 are independent axioms. In fact one can show

PROPOSITION 4.4.1. *Let Ω_G be closed under right remnants. Ω_G is admissible iff Ω_G^+ is closed under right remnants.*

Proof. Left for the reader. Q.E.D.

Remark. Given a system $S = \langle \Omega, Q, \delta \rangle$ we can generate constructive specifications as follows. Let Ω_G be any subset of Ω which satisfies Axioms C.1 and C.2. Let δ_G be δ restricted to Ω_G, i.e., set $\delta_G(q, \omega) = \delta(q, \omega)$ for all $q \in Q$, $\omega \in \Omega_G$. Since δ satisfies the composition Axiom A.3, δ_G will automatically satisfy Axiom C.3. Actually, if S is derived from a DESS with unique solutions we need only solve the differential equation for the segments in Ω_G to obtain δ_G satisfying Axiom C.3.

Example. Step responses of linear first-order lag system. Consider

$$G = \langle \Omega_G, Q, \delta_G \rangle \ ,$$

where

$$\Omega_G = \{a_t \mid t \in R,\ a \in R\} \ ,$$
$$Q = R \ ,$$

and

$$\delta_G : Q \times \Omega_G \longrightarrow Q \ ,$$

is given by

$$\delta_G(q, a_t) = qe^{-t/T} + a - ae^{-t/T} \ .$$

Since Ω_G is closed under right segmentation it is both admissible and closed under right remnants. Since δ_G is derived from a DESS with unique solutions it is internally decomposable. Thus G is a constructive specification.

THEOREM 4.4.2. *Given a constructive specification* $G = \langle \Omega_G, Q, \delta_G \rangle$ *we can associate with it a system* $S_G = \langle \Omega_G^+, Q, \delta \rangle$ *where* $\delta: Q \times \Omega_G^+ \longrightarrow Q$ *is defined as follows:*

$$\delta(q, \omega) = \begin{cases} \delta_G(q, \omega), & \text{for } \omega \in \Omega_G,\ q \in Q\ , \\ \delta\left(\delta_G(q, \omega_1),\ \omega_2\omega_3 \cdots, \omega_n\right), & \text{for } \omega \in \Omega_G^+,\ q \in Q\ , \end{cases}$$

where $\omega_1, \omega_2, \omega_3, \cdots, \omega_n$ *is the* mls *decomposition of* ω *by* Ω_G.

Note that $\omega_2, \omega_3, \omega_4, \cdots, \omega_n$ *is the* mls *decomposition for* $\omega_2\omega_3\omega_4 \cdots \omega_n$.

Proof. Since δ_G is assumed to be time invariant, δ will be time invariant. That δ_G is well-defined follows from the uniqueness of the mls decomposition. Thus we need only show that the composition property obtains, i.e., we must show that $\delta(q, \omega'\omega'') = \delta(\delta(q, \omega')\omega'')$ for all $\omega', \omega'' \in \Omega_G^+$. We proceed by induction on $\max\{\text{size}(\omega'), \text{size}(\omega'')\}$.

Basis. $\text{Max}\{\text{size}(\omega'), \text{size}(\omega'')\} = 1$. By Proposition 4.3.2(a), (b) $\text{size}(\omega') = \text{size}(\omega'') = 1$ and $\omega', \omega'' \in \Omega_G$. Now by 4.3.2(c)

$$\begin{aligned} \text{size}(\omega'\omega'') &\le \text{size}(\omega') + \text{size}(\omega'') \\ &\le 2\ . \end{aligned}$$

If $\text{size}(\omega'\omega'') = 1$ then $\omega'\omega'' \in \Omega_G$ (by 4.3.2(a)) and by the internal composition of δ_G we have

$$\begin{aligned} \delta(q, \omega'\omega'') &= \delta_G(q, \omega'\omega'') \\ &= \delta_G(\delta_G(q, \omega'), \omega'') \\ &= \delta(\delta(q, \omega'), \omega'')\ . \end{aligned}$$

If $\text{size}(\omega'\omega'') = 2$, refer to Figure 4.4.1.

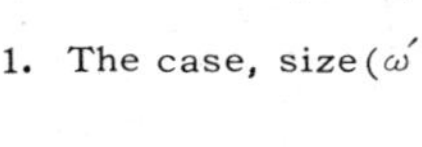

Fig. 4.4.1. The case, $\text{size}(\omega'\omega'') = 2$.

Let $\bar{\omega}, \bar{\bar{\omega}}$ be the mls decomposition for $\omega'\omega''$ and let $\bar{\omega} = \omega'\mu$, so that $\mu\bar{\bar{\omega}} = \omega''$. Since $\omega'\mu \in \Omega_G$ and $\omega' \in \Omega_G$, μ is a right remnant and by Axiom C.1, $\mu \in \Omega_G$. Now

$$\begin{aligned} \delta(\delta(q, \omega'), \omega'') &= \delta_G(\delta_G(q, \omega'), \omega'') && (\omega', \omega'' \in \Omega_G) \\ &= \delta_G(\delta_G(q, \omega'), \mu\bar{\bar{\omega}}) && (\omega'' = \mu\bar{\bar{\omega}}) \\ &= \delta_G\left(\delta_G(\delta_G(q, \omega'), \mu), \bar{\bar{\omega}}\right) && (\mu\bar{\bar{\omega}} \in \Omega_G) \end{aligned}$$

$$\begin{aligned}
&= \delta_G\left(\delta_G(q, \omega'\mu), \overline{\overline{\omega}}\right) && (\omega'\mu \in \Omega_G)\\
&= \delta_G\left(\delta_G(q, \overline{\omega}), \overline{\overline{\omega}}\right) && (\omega'\mu = \overline{\omega})\\
&= \delta_G(q, \overline{\omega}\overline{\overline{\omega}}) && (\overline{\omega}, \overline{\overline{\omega}} \in \Omega_G)\\
&= \delta_G(q, \omega'\omega'') \;.
\end{aligned}$$

For the induction step, assume $\delta(q, \omega'\omega'') = \delta\left(\delta(q, \omega', \omega'')\right)$ for $\max\{\text{size}(\omega'), \text{size}(\omega'')\} \le n$. Let $\omega = \omega'\omega''$ where $\max\{\text{size}(\omega'), \text{size}(\omega'')\} = n + 1$. Refer to Figure 4.4.2.

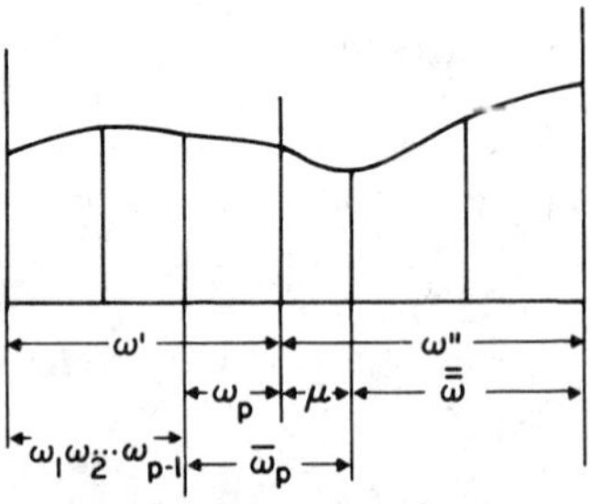

Fig. 4.4.2. The case, $\max\{\text{size}(\omega'), \text{size}(\omega'')\} = n + 1$.

Let $\omega_1, \omega_2, \omega_3, \cdots, \omega_p$ be the mls decomposition for ω' where $p \le n + 1$. Let $\overline{\omega}_p$ begin the mls decomposition for $\omega_p\omega''$ and let $\overline{\overline{\omega}}$ be the associated right segment, i.e., $\omega_p\omega'' = \overline{\omega}_p\overline{\overline{\omega}}$.

Let $\overline{\omega}_p = \omega_p\mu$; then since μ is a right remnant $\mu \in \Omega_G$.

$$\delta\left(\delta(q, \omega'), \omega''\right) =$$

$$\begin{aligned}
&= \delta\left(\delta(q, \omega_1\omega_2\cdots\omega_{p-1}\omega_p), \omega''\right) && (\omega' = \omega_1\omega_2\cdots\omega_{p-1}\omega_p)\\
&= \delta\left(\delta\left(\delta(q, \omega_1\omega_2\cdots\omega_{p-1}), \omega_p\right), \omega''\right) && (\text{size}(\omega_1\omega_2\omega_3\cdots\omega_{p-1}) \le n \text{ and size}(\omega_p) = 1)\\
&= \delta\left(\delta\left(\delta(q, \omega_1\omega_2\cdots\omega_{p-1}), \omega_p\right), \mu\overline{\overline{\omega}}\right) && (\mu\overline{\overline{\omega}} = \omega'')\\
&= \delta\left(\delta\left(\delta(q, \omega_1\omega_2\cdots\omega_{p-1}), \omega_p\mu\right), \overline{\overline{\omega}}\right) && (\omega_p\mu \in \Omega_G)\\
&= \delta\left(\delta\left(\delta(q, \omega_1\omega_2\cdots\omega_{p-1}), \overline{\omega}_p\right), \overline{\overline{\omega}}\right) && (\overline{\omega}_p = \omega_p\mu)\\
&= \delta\left(\delta(q, \omega_1\omega_2\cdots\omega_{p-1}\overline{\omega}_p), \overline{\overline{\omega}}\right) && (\text{size}(\omega_1\omega_2\omega_3\cdots\omega_{p-1}) \le n \text{ and size}(\overline{\omega}_p) = 1)\\
&= \delta(q, \omega_1\omega_2\cdots\omega_{p-1}\overline{\omega}_p\overline{\overline{\omega}})\\
&= \delta(q, \omega'\omega'') \;.
\end{aligned}$$

The next to the last line relies on the easily proved Lemma: If $\omega_1, \omega_2, \omega_3, \cdots, \omega_n$ is the mls decomposition for ω then for $i \in \{1, 2, 3, \cdots, n-1\}$

$$\delta\left(\delta(q, \omega_1\omega_2\cdots\omega_i), \omega_{i+1}\cdots\omega_n\right) = \delta(q, \omega). \quad \text{Q.E.D.}$$

V. MORPHISMS FOR CONSTRUCTIVELY SPECIFIED SYSTEMS

5.0 Definitions

With the foregoing definition of constructively specified systems, we are ready to formulate a notion of simulation which retains the essential character of the discrete time idea.

A *function morphism* from $G = \langle \Omega_G, Q, \delta_G \rangle$ to $G' = \langle \Omega'_G, Q', \delta'_G \rangle$ is a pair (g, h) where

$$g: \Omega'_G \longrightarrow \Omega^+_G \ ,$$
$$h: Q_1 \longrightarrow Q' \quad \text{(onto)} \ ,$$

and:

(i) $Q_1 \subseteq Q$ is closed under $g(\Omega'_G)$
(ii) $h\big(\tilde{\delta}_G(q, g(\omega'))\big) = \delta'_G\,(h(q), \omega'),$

for all $\omega' \in \Omega'_G$, $q \in Q_1$.

Remark. $\tilde{\delta}_G : Q \times \Omega^+_G \longrightarrow Q$ is δ_G extended to Ω^+_G by the mls definition of Theorem 4.42. Actually, to determine whether (ii) holds we need only extend δ_G to segments in $g(\Omega'_G)$. If g is "size preserving," i.e., $g(\Omega'_G) \subseteq \Omega_G$ then δ_G need not be extended at all.

A *function morphism* from S_G to S'_G is a pair $(\bar{g}, \bar{h})$ such that

$$\bar{g}: (\Omega'_G)^+ \longrightarrow \Omega^+_G \ ,$$
$$\bar{h}: Q_1 \longrightarrow Q' \quad \text{(onto)} \ ,$$

where:

(i) $Q_1 \subseteq Q$ is closed under $\bar{g}\,((\Omega'_G)^+)$
(ii) $\bar{h}\,\big(\delta\,(q, \bar{g}(\omega'))\big) = \delta'\,(\bar{h}(q), \omega'),$

for all $q \in Q_1$, $\omega' \in (\Omega'_G)^+$.

Generalizing Theorem 3.2.1 we have:

THEOREM 5.0.1. *There is a function morphism from G to G′ iff there is a function morphism from S_G to $S_{G'}$.*

Proof. Necessity. Let (g, h) be a function morphism from G to G′. We construct a function morphism $(\bar{g}, \bar{h})$ from S_G to S'_G as follows

$$\text{Set } \bar{h} = h \ ,$$

and define

$$\bar{g}: (\Omega'_G)^+ \longrightarrow \Omega^+_G$$

by

$$\bar{g}(\omega) = g(\omega_1)\, g(\omega_2)\, g(\omega_3) \cdots g(\omega_n) \ ,$$

where $\omega_1, \omega_2, \omega_3, \cdots, \omega_n$ is the mls decomposition of $\omega \in \Omega^+_G$.

First note that $\bar{g}$ is well defined because of the uniqueness of the mls decomposition.

We use induction on size(ω') to show that for all $q \in Q_1$

$$\bar{h}\left(\delta\left(q, \bar{g}(\omega')\right)\right) = \delta'\left(\bar{h}(q), \omega'\right) \ .$$

Basis. size$(\omega') = 1$ $\quad \omega' \in \Omega'_G$. Thus $\bar{g}(\omega') = g(\omega)$ and the equality is just that given.

Assume the equality holds for all ω' such that size$(\omega') = n$.

Let size$(\omega') = n + 1$, and let $\omega'_1, \omega'_2, \cdots, \omega'_{n+1}$ be the mls decomposition for ω'.

$$\bar{h}\ \delta\left(q, \bar{g}(\omega'_1\omega'_2\omega'_3 \cdots \omega'_{n+1})\right)$$
$$= \bar{h}\left(\delta\left(q, \bar{g}(\omega'_1\omega'_2\omega'_3 \cdots \omega'_n)\, g(\omega'_{n+1})\right)\right) \qquad \text{(definition of } \bar{g})$$
$$= h\left(\delta\left(\delta\left(q, g(\omega'_1\omega'_2\omega'_3 \cdots \omega'_n), g(\omega'_{n+1})\right)\right)\right) \qquad \text{(composition of } \delta)$$
$$= \delta'\left(\bar{h}\left(\delta\left(q, \bar{g}(\omega'_1\omega'_2\omega'_3 \cdots \omega'_n)\right), \omega'_{n+1}\right)\right) \qquad (\text{size}(\omega'_{n+1}) = 1)$$
$$= \delta'\left(\delta\left(\bar{h}(q), \omega'_1\omega'_2, \omega'_3 \cdots \omega'_n\right), \omega_{n+1}\right) \qquad (\text{size}(\omega'_1\omega'_2\omega'_3 \cdots \omega'_n) = n)$$
$$= \delta'\left(\bar{h}(q), \omega'_1\omega'_2, \omega'_3 \cdots \omega'_n\omega'_{n+1}\right) \ . \qquad \text{(composition of } \delta')$$

That Q_1 is closed under $g(\Omega')^+$ now follows readily from its assumed closure under $g(\Omega'_G)$.

This establishes the forward direction. The reverse direction is immediate. Q.E.D.

Remark. In the foregoing theorem $\bar{g}$ is not necessarily a semigroup homomorphism of $(\Omega'_G)^+$ to Ω^+_G. In general, we cannot expect $\bar{g}(\omega\omega') = \bar{g}(\omega)\,\bar{g}(\omega')$ since the mls decomposition for $\omega\omega'$ is not simply the concatenation of those of ω and ω'.

For example, let $\Omega_G = \{a_t \mid t \in R,\ a \in R\}$ and let $g: \Omega_G \longrightarrow \Omega_G$ be defined for some $a, b, c \in R$ where $b \neq c$ by

$$g(a_t) = \begin{cases} b_t, & \text{for } t \in [0, 1] \ , \\ c_t, & \text{for } t > 1 \ . \end{cases}$$

Then

$$\bar{g}(a_{0.5}, a_{0.6}) = \bar{g}(a_{1.1}) = g(a_{1.1}) = c_{1.1} \ ,$$

while

$$\bar{g}(a_{0.5})\,\bar{g}(a_{0.6}) = g(a_{0.5})\,g(a_{0.6}) = b_{0.5}\,b_{0.6} = b_{1.1} \ .$$

PROPOSITION 5.0.1. $\bar{g}: (\Omega'_G)^+ \longrightarrow \Omega^+_G$ *is a homomorphism* $\Longleftrightarrow \bar{g}(\omega\omega') = \bar{g}(\omega)\,\bar{g}(\omega')$ *for all* $\omega, \omega' \in (\Omega'_G)^+$ *such that* $\omega\omega' \in \Omega'_G$.

Proof. Entirely analogous to that of Theorem 4.4.2. Q.E.D.

COROLLARY 5.0.1. *If Prefix Property holds for* Ω'_G, $\bar{g}$ *is a homomorphism.*

COROLLARY 5.0.2. *If the right and left segmentation closure holds then* $\bar{g}$ *is a homomorphism* $\Longleftrightarrow g(\omega\omega') = g(\omega)\,g(\omega')$ *for all* $\omega, \omega' \in \Omega'_G$ *such that* $\omega\omega' \in \Omega'_G$.

We shall now give evidence of the applicability of these concepts by considering some illustrative problems arising in modeling and simulation.

5.1 Time and Amplitude Scaling for Continuous Time Systems

(A) Time scale change

Let $G = \langle \Omega_G, Q, \delta_G \rangle$ be specified as follows: $\Omega_G = \{\omega \mid \omega$ is a real valued continuous function defined on a finite closed interval$\}$

$$Q = R \ ,$$

$$\delta_G : Q \times \Omega_G \longrightarrow Q \ ,$$

is given by

$$\delta_G (q, \omega_{\tau]}) = \Phi_{(q,\omega)}(\tau) \ ,$$

for all $\omega_{\tau]} \in \Omega_G$.

Here

$$\Phi_{(q,\omega)}(0) = q \ ,$$

and

$$\frac{d}{dt} \Phi_{(q,\omega)}(t) = f(\Phi_{(q,\omega)}(t), \omega(t)) \ \text{(for } t \in \text{dom } \omega) \ .$$

The underlying DESS, $D = (\Omega_G, Q, f)$ is assumed to have unique solutions.

Since Ω_G is closed under right segmentation Axioms C.1 and C.2 are satisfied. Also, since the underlying DESS has unique solutions we have Axiom C.3 satisfied (see the Remark following Proposition 4.4.1) thus G is a constructive specification.

Let $G' = \langle \Omega'_G, Q, \delta'_G \rangle$ be specified by

$$\Omega'_G = \Omega_G \ ,$$

$$Q' = R \ ,$$

$$\delta'_G : Q' \times \Omega'_G \longrightarrow Q' \ ,$$

is given by

$$\delta'_G (q, \omega_{\tau]}) = \Phi'_{(q,\omega)}(\tau) \ \text{(for all } \omega_{\tau]} \in \Omega_G) \ .$$

Here

$$\Phi'_{(q,\omega)}(0) = q \ ,$$

and

$$\frac{1}{\sigma} \frac{d}{dt} \Phi'_{(q,\omega)}(t) = f(\Phi'_{(q,\omega)}(t), \omega(t)) \ \text{(for } t \in [0, \tau]) \ .$$

By the same argument, $S_{G'}$ is a system. Its rate of operation, however, is σ times that of S_G where σ is a positive real number.

THEOREM 5.1.1. *(g, h) is a time local function morphism from G to G' where*

$$h : Q \longrightarrow Q' \ ,$$

is the identity map and

$$g : \Omega'_G \longrightarrow \Omega_G \ ,$$

is given by

$$g(\omega_{[0,\tau]}) = \bar{\omega}_{[0,\sigma\tau]} ,$$

where

$$\bar{\omega}_{[0,\sigma\tau]}(t) = \omega_{[0,\tau]}(t/\sigma) \quad \big(\text{for } t \in [0, \sigma\tau]\big) .$$

Proof. Since in this case $Q_1 = Q$ it is closed under $g(\Omega'_G)$. And since h is the identity map we need only show that for all $q \in Q$, $\omega_{[0,\tau]} \in \Omega'_G$

$$\delta(q, g(\omega_{[0,\tau]})) = \delta'(q, \omega_{[0,\tau]}) .$$

Equivalently for all $\tau \in R$

$$\delta(q, \bar{\omega}_{[0,\sigma\tau]}) = \delta'(q, \omega_{[0,\tau]}) ,$$
$$\Phi_{(q,\bar{\omega})}(\sigma\tau) = \Phi'_{(q,\omega)}(\tau) ,$$
$$\Phi \circ T_\sigma = \Phi' ,$$

where $T_\sigma(t) = \sigma t$ for all $t \in R$, and $\Phi_{(q,\bar{\omega})} = \Phi$, $\Phi'_{(q,\omega)} = \Phi'$.

To show this we prove that $\Phi \circ T_\sigma$ satisfies the differential equation for Φ'.

$$\frac{1}{\sigma}\frac{d}{dt}(\Phi \circ T_\sigma)(t) = \frac{1}{\sigma}\frac{d}{d(\sigma t)}\Phi(\sigma t)\frac{d(\sigma t)}{dt} .$$

Integrating the differential equation satisfied by Φ yields

$$\Phi(t) = q + \int_0^t f(\Phi(t'), \bar{\omega}(t'))\, dt' .$$

Thus

$$\frac{d\Phi(\sigma t)}{d(\sigma t)} = \frac{d}{d(\sigma t)}\left(q + \int_0^{\sigma t} f(\Phi(t'), \bar{\omega}(t'))\, dt'\right)$$
$$= f(\Phi(\sigma t), \bar{\omega}(\sigma t))$$
$$= f(\Phi \circ T_\sigma(t), \bar{\omega}(t)) ,$$

so

$$\frac{1}{\sigma}\frac{d}{dt}(\Phi \circ T_\sigma)(t) = f(\Phi \circ T_\sigma(t), \omega(t)) .$$

Also,

$$\Phi \circ T_\sigma(0) = \Phi(0) = q ,$$

so

$$\Phi \circ T_\sigma = \Phi' ,$$

by uniqueness of solutions.

Finally, since Ω_G is closed under right and left segmentation it is enough to show that $g(\omega\omega') = g(\omega)g(\omega')$ for all $\omega, \omega' \in \Omega_G$ such that $\omega\omega' \in \Omega_G$. But it is easily seen that $\overline{\omega\omega'} = \bar{\omega}\,\bar{\omega}'$ as required. Q.E.D.

(B) Amplitude Scale Change

THEOREM 5.1.2. *Let G, G′ above be such that $f'(q, x) = af_2(q/a, b)$ for fixed $a, b \in R$. Then (g, h) is a time local function morphism from G to G′ where $h: Q \longrightarrow Q'$ and $g: \Omega'_G \longrightarrow \Omega_G$ are given by*

$$h(q) = aq \ ,$$
$$g(\omega) = \omega/b \ ,$$

where $\omega/b(t) = \omega(t)/b$ *for all* $t \in \text{dom}\ \omega$.

Proof. An exercise for the reader. Q. E. D.

5.2 Simulation of Continuous Time Systems by Discrete Time Systems

Let $G = \langle \Omega_G, Q, \delta_G \rangle$, $G' = \langle \Omega'_G, Q', \delta'_G \rangle$ be discrete and continuous time constructive specifications respectively. Let (g, h) be a function morphism from G to G′. Then $g: \Omega'_G \longrightarrow \Omega^+_G$.

Thus g is a mapping from functions with *real* domains into functions with *integer* domains; i.e., g must encode a continuous wave into a discrete one. Let $\Omega'_G = \{\omega' \mid \omega': [0, \tau] \longrightarrow R\}$; then in general Ω_G must have the cardinalitility of Ω'_G if a function preserving relation is to hold.

Clearly this is impractical and it is interesting to examine cases where Ω_G need be no more numerous than the real numbers.

Example 1. Sampled equispaced step functions (Figure 5.3.1).

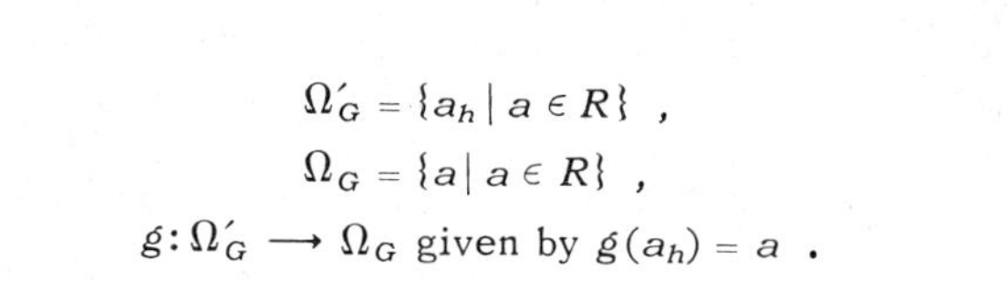

Fig. 5.3.1. Sampled equispaced step functions.

$$\Omega'_G = \{a_h \mid a \in R\} \ ,$$
$$\Omega_G = \{a \mid a \in R\} \ ,$$
$$g: \Omega'_G \longrightarrow \Omega_G \text{ given by } g(a_h) = a \ .$$

Example 2. Sampled arbitrarily spaced step functions (Figure 5.3.2).

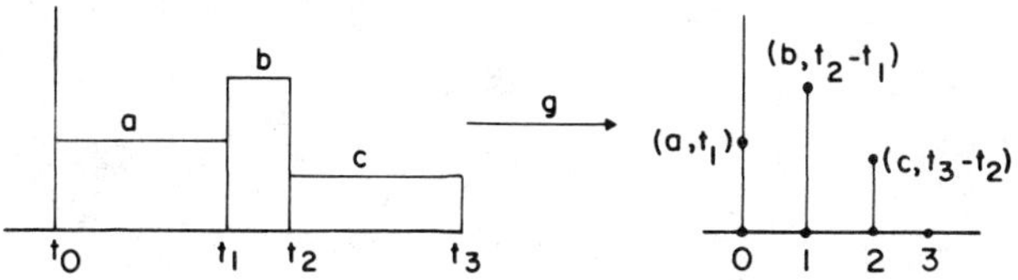

Fig. 5.3.2. Sampled variable spaced step functions.

$$\Omega'_G = \{a_t \mid t \in R,\ a \in R\} \ ,$$
$$\Omega_G = \{(a, t) \mid t \in R,\ a \in R\} \ ,$$
$$g: \Omega'_a \longrightarrow \Omega_G \text{ given by } g(a_t) = (a, t) \ .$$

Example 3. Band and time limited waves. Let $\{e_i \mid i = 1, 2, 3, \cdots, n\}$ be a finite set of functions $e_i : T \longrightarrow R$. For example $\{e_i\}$ might be a truncated Fourier series, Tchebychev polynomials, etc. Then

$$\Omega'_G = \ \omega \mid \omega = \sum_{i=1}^{n} c_i\, e_i \ \ (\text{for some } c_i \in R,\ i = 1, 2, \cdots, n) \ ,$$

$$\Omega_G = R \ ,$$

and

$$g: \Omega'_G \longrightarrow \Omega_G^+$$

is given by

$$g(\omega) = c_1\, c_2\, c_3 \cdots c_n \ ,$$

if

$$\omega = \sum_{i=1}^{n} c_i\, e_i \ .$$

This describes a common situation in speech generation where discrete sequences of parameters characterizing a speech wave form are fed to a speech production device.

5.4 Realization of Discrete Time Systems by Continuous Time Systems

With the formalism developed it is possible to characterize explicitly and simply the realization of discrete time systems by continuous time systems. The following shows how a two-state, two-input sequential machine may be realized by a set-reset flip-flop with instantaneous feedback. The example may be readily extended to arbitrary finite state sequential machines and is presented as only one possible model for such realizations.

The flip-flop will be modelled as a DESS $D = (\Omega, Q, f)$ where

$$\Omega = \{a_t \mid a \in R,\ t \in R\}^+ \ ,$$
$$Q = R \times R \ ,$$

and

$$f: Q \times R \longrightarrow Q \ ,$$

is given by

$$f\left(\begin{bmatrix} q_1 \\ q_2 \end{bmatrix}, x\right) = \frac{1}{\tau}\begin{bmatrix} -q_1 - \operatorname{sgn}(q_2) + Z(\operatorname{sgn}(q_1), x) \\ -q_2 - \operatorname{sgn}(q_1) - Z(\operatorname{sgn}(q_1), x) \end{bmatrix} .$$

Here

$$\operatorname{sgn}(q) = \begin{cases} 1, & \text{if } q \geq 0 \ , \\ -1, & \text{if } q < 0 \ , \end{cases}$$

and $Z: \{1, -1\} \times R \longrightarrow \{1, -1, 0\}$ is such that $Z(\mathrm{x}, 0) = 0$ for $\mathrm{x} \in \{1, -1\}$. Figure 5.4.1 displays an analog model of this network.

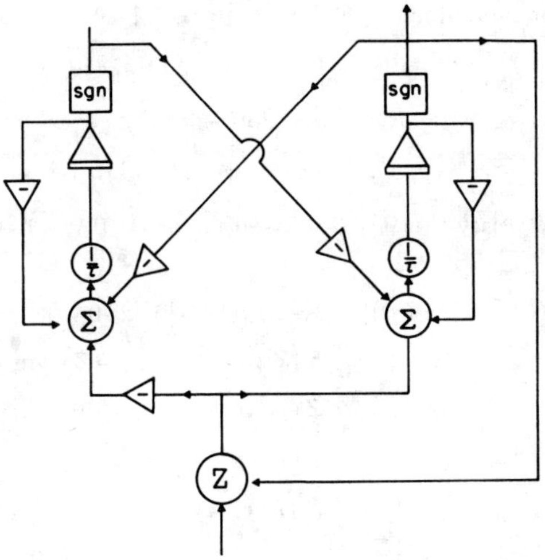

Fig. 5.4.1. A set-reset flip-flop realization of a two-state sequential machine.

It can be readily shown that D has unique solutions. Moreover, there are positive numbers σ and ρ (related to the system time constant τ) such that for any input of the form $\mathrm{x}_\sigma 0_\rho$

$$\begin{aligned} \delta(q_1, q_2, \mathrm{x}_\sigma 0_\rho) &= \Phi_{(q_1, q_2, \mathrm{x}_\sigma 0_\rho)}(\sigma + \rho) \\ &= \big(Z(\operatorname{sgn}(q_1), \mathrm{x}), -Z(\operatorname{sgn}(q_1), \mathrm{x})\big) \ . \end{aligned}$$

Here $\mathrm{x} \in \{1, -1\}$. In other words, the final state of the flip-flop after a pulse of width σ followed by a ρ-length quiescence is completely determined by the polarities of the initial state and pulse.

THEOREM 5.4.1. *Let* $G' = \langle\{1, -1\}, \{1, -1\}, \delta'\rangle$ *be a discrete time sequential machine. There is a continuous time constructive specification* G *such that* G' *is a time local function morphic image of* G *(i.e.,* G *realizes* G'*).*

Proof. Let $G = \langle \Omega_G, Q, \delta_G \rangle$ be obtained by extraction from the flip-flop DESS above. Specifically, let

$$\Omega_G = \{1_\sigma 0_\rho, -1_\sigma 0_\rho\} \ ,$$
$$Q = R \times R \ ,$$

and let

$$\delta_G : Q \times \Omega_G \longrightarrow Q \ ,$$

be defined by

$$\delta_G\left((q_1, q_2), x_\sigma 0_\rho\right) = \left(Z(\mathrm{sgn}(q_1), x), -Z(\mathrm{sgn}(q_1), x)\right) ,$$

where

$$Z(y, x) = \delta'(y, x) \quad (\text{for all } y, x \in \{1, -1\}) .$$

Since Ω_G has the prefix property Axioms C.1 and C.2 are satisfied and Axiom C.3 is vacuously satisfied.

For the function morphism (g, h) from G to G' let

$$g: \{1, -1\} \longrightarrow \{1_\sigma 0_\rho, -1_\sigma 0_\rho\} \text{ be given by } g(x) = x_\sigma 0_\rho .$$

Let $Q_1 = \{(1, -1), (-1, 1)\} \subseteq R \times R$ and define $h: Q_1 \longrightarrow Q'$-by

$$h(y, -y) = y \quad (\text{for } y \in \{1, -1\}) .$$

The reader may verify that Q_1 is closed under $\{1_\sigma 0_\rho, -1_\sigma 0_\rho\}$. Next for $(y, -y) \in Q_1$

$$\begin{aligned} h\left(\delta_G((y, -y), g(x))\right) &= h\left(\delta_G((y, -y), x_\sigma 0_\rho)\right) \\ &= h\left(Z(\mathrm{sgn}(y), x), -Z(\mathrm{sgn}(y), x)\right) \\ &= Z(y, x) \\ &= \delta'(y, x) \\ &= \delta'(h(y, -y), x) . \end{aligned}$$

Finally, since G' is a discrete time system g is extendable to a semigroup homomorphism of $\{1, -1\}^+$ to $\{1_\sigma 0_\rho, -1_\sigma 0_\rho\}^+$. Q.E.D.

Remark. By expanding Ω_G to the set $\Omega_G = \{x_{t_1} 0_{t_2 - t_1} \mid x \in \{1, -1\}, t_1, t_2 \in R\}$ one can study the degradation of the sequential machine realization when badly timed pulses are used.

ACKNOWLEDGEMENTS

*This work was supported by the National Science Foundation, Grant No. GJ-519 and the National Institutes of Health, Grant No. GM-12236.

REFERENCES

[1] M. Mesarovic, "Auxiliary Functions and Constructive Specification of General Systems," *Math. Sys. The.*, 2, 203–222 (1968).

[2] T. G. Windeknecht, "Mathematical Systems Theory: Causality," *Math. Sys. The.*, 1, No. 4 (1967).

[3] L. A. Zadeh and C. A. Desoer, *Linear Systems Theory* (McGraw-Hill, 1963).

[4] R. E. Kalman; P. L. Falb; M. A. Arbib; *Topics in Mathematical Systems Theory*, Ch. 1, 6 (McGraw-Hill, 1969).

[5] A. W. Wymore, "Discrete Systems and Continuous Systems," *Advances in Mathematical Systems Theory* (P. Hammer, Ed., 1969). Also: *A Mathematical Theory of Systems Engineering: The Elements* (Wiley, 1967).

[6] B. P. Zeigler and R. Weinberg, "System Theoretic Analysis of Models: Computer Simulation of a Living Cell," *J. The. Biol.*, **29**, 35-56 (1970).

[7] B. P. Zeigler, "Towards a Formal Theory of Modeling and Simulation, I," University of Michigan Technical Report 03296-5-T. Submitted to *J.ACM* (1970).

[8] T. Ura, "Local Isomorphisms and Local Parallizability in Dynamical Systems Theory," *Math. Sys. The.*, **3**, No. 1 (1968).

GENERAL PURPOSE CELLULAR COMPUTERS

Arthur E. Laemmel
Polytechnic Institute of Brooklyn, Farmingdale, NY

The cellular computer considered here is a linear array of finite state machines. Such a computer can simulate a Turing machine if each cell has as few as two states and with connections only to the two immediate neighbors. However, the computation would proceed very slowly and the programming would be very tedious. Several methods for making universal cellular computers of more practical value will be discussed. Generally the object is to exploit the homogeneity of the array by having as many operations going on simultaneously as possible. Cellular computers of simple structure might be realized with molecular components, and thus offer a possible mechanism for memory and thought processes.

I. INTRODUCTION

This paper presents several new ways to design arrays of finite state machines, and then suggests applications to the design of parallel computers. Interest in cellular arrays has increased recently because of the rapid advances in integrated circuit technology which makes their fabrication economically attractive. However, a more fundamental reason for studying radically different computer architectures is that there are types of problems (such as pattern recognition, weather prediction, etc.) for which present computer types seem totally unsuited. While there is no firm reason to believe that an economical weather predicting computer ever can be made, there is definite reason to believe that many of the important problems in pattern recognition and other aspects of artificial intelligence can be solved by a parallel computer. The reason is that the human biological computer does solve them in real time with elements which have speeds measured in milliseconds instead of nanoseconds. It seems almost certain that the biological computer must have a high degree of parallelism, i.e., many operations going on simultaneously, in order to achieve reaction times which are reasonable. If comparable parallel computers are to be built in the future their design might properly be classified under "computer architecture," but this term is often used in a much narrower sense involving only such details as how many accumulators of what size to provide to a programmer. There is at present no inkling of how existing biological computers are structured or how comparable electronic computers might be designed. Nevertheless, it is believed that cellular computers already show sufficient promise for efficient solution of some problems to encourage further study.

The arrays and computers which are to be discussed will usually have very

---

Presented at the Symposium on Computers and Automata
Polytechnic Institute of Brooklyn, April 13–15, 1971.

many simple cells, and the individual cell will not be a computer in itself, as in the Illiac IV, or anything close to a computer. This simple cell is desired for several reasons:

(1) To provide a bound on how far one can go in the direction of cell simplicity,
(2) To allow some speculation on how a cell might be a unit in a long macromolecule,
(3) To contribute to a basic theory of optimal array synthesis, etc.

It does not seem that the simplest cell will result in the most efficient or economical computer in many cases, but neither is it as inefficient as the smallest state-symbol product Turing machine.

II. ARRAYS

A linear array of finite state machines, "array" for short, is characterized by 4 parameters: S stable memory states; c different types of cells or finite state machines; ϕ different control signals; and dependence on neighbors d cells away on each side. Upon receipt of a clock signal the next state of a cell is a function of its previous state and the previous state of its $2d$ closest neighbors.* The c types of cells occur in cyclic order along the array, and the ϕ control signals are fed to all cells simultaneously and in an order which is independent of the states of the cells. That is, signals are permitted from a central control to a cell, but not from a cell to a central control. Since the c cell types occur periodically along the array, the parameter c might also be called a block length.

The state of a cell represents its memory of its previous states and the previous states of its neighbors. Note that since S is fixed and fairly small, everything about the previous states is not remembered, the storage state merely corresponds to a memory of something about previous states including the starting states. For example, an n-stage binary counter remembers the number of pulses fed to it only modulo 2^n. It is often convenient to partition the memory or factor the state into several parts. Thus, if each cell has m registers having $S_1, S_2, S_3, \cdots, S_m$ stable states, the whole cell has $S_1 S_2 S_3 \cdots S_m = S$ stable states. The whole key to analyzing and designing any complicated device is to avoid talking about its total state. Descriptions are vastly simplified by talking of one register changing state at a time, usually depending on very few other registers in how it changes.

An array will usually be used to perform some computation in the following sense: the cells are set initially to states which represent the input data and program, the array is allowed to operate for a time T under the control of the clock, and the answers are then read from the final states of some or all of the cells. The action of the array will be called a "computation" in spite of the fact that the behavior of some simple arrays might not ordinarily be called by that name. An array $\mathbf{A}$ will be said to perform the same computation as an array A, $\mathbf{A}$

*Terminology is not yet standardized, some writers consider the cell itself as a neighbor, some do not. Thus, $d = 1$ can be called either the 2-neighbor case or the 3-neighbor case.

said to simulate A, if the initial states of $\mathbf{A}$ are simple functions of the initial states of A, and if the final states of A are simple functions of the final state of $\mathbf{A}$. As in discussing simple Turing machines, the definition of "simple function" in the above will not be too precise (see [1, p. 277]). The principal results to be obtained here concern the various exchanges which are possible among the parameters of the array. Suppose the total length of the array performing a computation such as that above is L cells. The parameters L and T are different from the parameters S, c, ϕ, and d in that the former depend on the problem being solved. Since varying S, c, ϕ, and d usually requires changing L and T, it is desirable to introduce scaling factors to describe such changes. If one array of length L_0 solves a problem in time T_0, and if a second array of length $L_1 = \lambda L_0$ solves the same problem in time $T_1 = \tau T_0$, then the factors λ and τ can often be made to depend only on the cell structure and to be independent of the problem. If the L_0 array is a standard, then λ and τ are parameters of the L_1 array. Otherwise, λ and τ are not parameters of an array, but rather parameters of an array change.

III. ELEMENTARY EXCHANGES

Several elementary exchanges can be made between the array parameters. These will later be combined with other exchanges. The first concerns reduction of cell states at the expense of cell types and array length.

Splitting

Given an array A of S state cells with neighbor dependency d, number of cell types c, and ϕ control signals; there exists an array $\mathbf{A}$ which simulates A; the array $\mathbf{A}$ having $\langle S^{1/n}\rangle$ states, neighbor dependency $n(d+1)-1$, nc cell types, and ϕ control signals. Here $\langle x\rangle$ is the smallest integer not exceeded by x. The number of states of $\mathbf{A}$ could also have been taken as $S_1, S_2, S_3, \cdots, S_n$ where $S_1, S_2, S_3, \cdots, S_n \le S$. The array length is increased by a factor of n, $\lambda = n$, but the operation time is not changed, $\tau = 1$.

This exchange follows directly from the fact that a digital signal which can take on one of n values can be replaced by n digital signals, each of which can take on one of $\langle S^{1/n}\rangle$ values. Therefore, the logic circuits (circles in Fig. 1(a)) which form the next state can be single with $2d+1$ inputs, or else in n parts with $n(2d+1)$ inputs. There are now n different logic units for each cell group, so that the most distant cell which influences a particular cell is at a distance $nd + (n-1)$.

Bunching

The inverse of the splitting process can be used to reduce neighbor dependency and cell types at the expense of the number of cell states. In Fig. 1(b) an array of cells of two types is reduced to an array with cells of only one type by simply bunching the cells in pairs and calling a pair a new single-type cell. Generally, an array of c types with S states is reduced to an array of one type

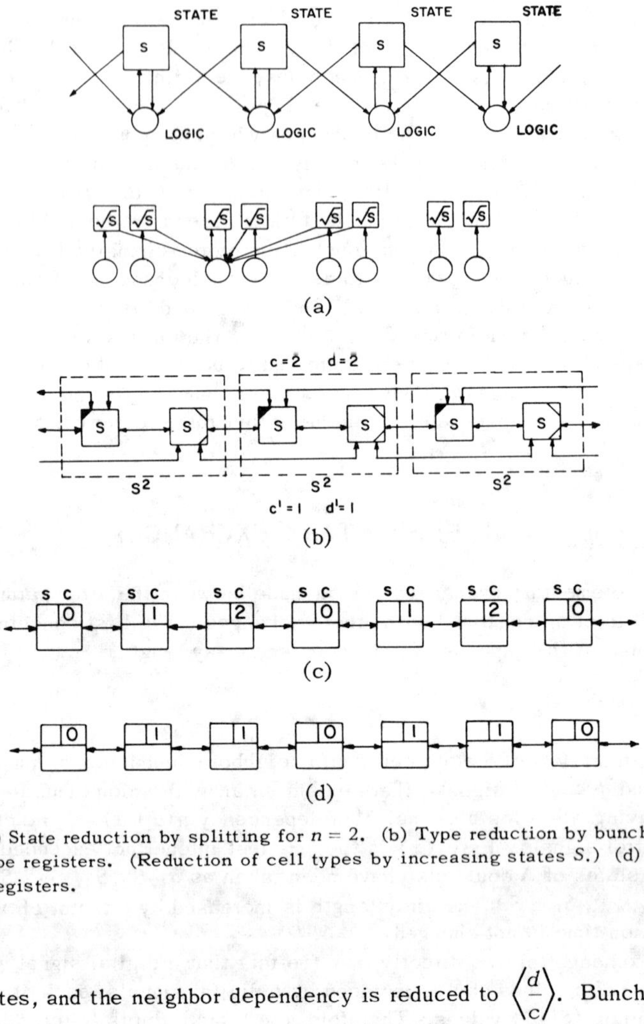

Fig. 1. (a) State reduction by splitting for $n = 2$. (b) Type reduction by bunching. (c) Cell-type registers. (Reduction of cell types by increasing states S.) (d) Distributed cell-type registers.

and S^c states, and the neighbor dependency is reduced to $\left\langle \frac{d}{c} \right\rangle$. Bunching could also be used to reduce the number of cell types to a number between c and 1. If the number of cell types is one initially, bunching n cells together increases the number of states to S^n, while making a (possible) reduction of neighbor dependency to $\left\langle \frac{d}{n} \right\rangle$. The number of control signals ϕ is not affected by splitting or bunching, nor is the time factor τ. If the number of cell types is reduced from c to 1, the length of the array is decreased by a factor $\lambda = 1/c$, but this is merely a matter of definition and obviously not a simplification. In fact, neither splitting nor bunching change the total array complexity or efficiency to any extent, and they are essentially redefinitions of what constitutes a cell.

Cell-type Registers

An array of S state cells of c types can be simulated by an array of Sc state cells all of the same type. Any set of c different logic circuits can be replaced by a single type by providing fixed storage elements whose contents are fed to the single larger logic circuit, thus replacing wired-in differences. Similarly, an array of S state cells of c different types and with ϕ different control signals could be simulated by an array of kSc state cells of a single type and with no control signals except for one periodic timing signal. Here k is a function of the pattern in which the ϕ signals occur, $k = \phi$ if the signals occur cyclically, $k > \phi$ if the signals occur in some pattern of period k. The factor k could be reduced by distributing the signal counter over several cells; but this would increase d except in special cases, the value of k becomes very large if the cascade reduction described below is utilized.

The number of cell states can be realistically reduced below the value Sc just given if the cell-type information is distributed over several adjacent cells. This is possible because the cell types occur periodically and not at random. For example, if $c = 3$ and $d = 1$ as in Fig. 1(c), the cell-type information could be extracted from the binary sequence 011011 ··· instead of the ternary sequence 012012 ··· as shown in Figure 1(d). The decoding is done according to 101 $\longrightarrow$ 0, 011 $\longrightarrow$ 1, 110 $\longrightarrow$ 2. Generally, an array of S state cells of c types with $d = 1$ can be simulated by an array of $\langle c^{1/3} \rangle S$ state cells of a single type with $d = 1$.

The different cell types often arise from the splitting process described above. Starting with an array with $d = 1$ and a single cell type of S states, if an n-way split is made, an array results with $\langle S^{1/n} \rangle$ states, $d = 2n - 1$, and n types. Then, if the cell-type register is distributed over $4n - 2$ states to agree with the neighbor dependency of the state registers, there results a number of states

$$\langle n^{1/4n-1} \rangle \langle S^{1/n} \rangle .$$

By making n sufficiently large, this can be reduced to 4, since the first term is always 2 for $n \geq 2$. Thus, any S-state array can be simulated by a 4-state array, both with single-cell types. The 4-state array usually has very large neighbor dependency so that the total complexity is not reduced and may be increased.

The exchange of fewer cell types for more cell states could be very valuable in spite of a probable increase in total circuit complexity. Any wired-in differences reduce the versatility of the array. With the cell type determined by the contents of a storage register, the entire array operation can be changed either to suit a new problem or because of experience gained in its use.

IV. FRAMING

The number of cell types can be reduced, or number of cell states can be reduced without increasing the number of cell types, by several more complicated methods of encoding a cell state into a block of cell states. For simplicity assume that there is only one cell type and immediate neighbor dependency initially, i.e., $c = 1$, $d = 1$, and also that each cell state of the array A is encoded into a block of n 2-state cells of the array **A**. If each cell of **A** is to be identical, each cell must be able to look at $4n - 2$ of its neighbors and tell what the states of A are in the same and two neighboring cells. This means that the cell of **A** must be able to tell where it is in the block of n cells, i.e., where the word divisions are. This synchronization or word framing problem is frequently encountered in designing communication systems, and can be solved by using comma-free codes. A comma-free set of words $\mathbf{x}, \mathbf{x}, \mathbf{z}, \cdots$ is defined as one such that if $x_1 x_2 x_3 \cdots x_n$ and $y_1 y_2 y_3, \cdots y_n$ are words of the set, possibly identical, then none of $x_2 x_3 x_4 \cdots x_n y_1$, $x_3 x_4 x_5 \cdots x_n y_1 y_2, \cdots, x_n y_1 y_2 \cdots y_{n-1}$ is a word of the set. Since none of these overlap sequences is a word, the word divisions are established if any $2n - 2$ successive digits are known. An upper bound on the number of words in a comma-free set, and therefore on the number of states of A is this encoding as used in [13].

$$S \leq \frac{1}{n} \sum_{i \mid n} \mu(i)\, 2^{n/i} ,$$

where $\mu(i)$ is the Möbius function and $i \mid n$ means i divides n. This bound can actually be attained if n is odd [14], and can be attained for even n provided that more than the usual (for comma-free codes) $2n - 2$ digits are examined [15, 16]. An upper bound on the number of digits which need be examined in the even n case is $\frac{n}{2}\, 2^{n/2}$, but in the present application only $4n - 1$ digits would ordinarily be examined to get the state information. As pointed out by Stiffler [20], codes with commas are sometimes more efficient than comma-free codes. In this application a comma would be a block of cells with a unique state pattern to divide the blocks containing state information.

Another method for establishing framing has been described by Smith [17, 19]. He uses alternate cells in **A** to store a fixed sequence of synchronizing digits.

TABLE I. Comparison of using separate sync cells with using comma-free code.

BLOCK LENGTH IN **A**: n	COMMA-FREE CODE		SEPARATE SYNC CELLS	
	STATES IN *A* CELL	CELLS IN NEIGHBORHOOD	STATES IN *A* CELL	CELLS IN NEIGHBORHOOD
1	2	3	—	—
2	1	7	1	2
3	2	11	—	—
4	3	15	2	7
5	6	19	—	—
6	9	23	5	11
7	18	27	—	—
8	30	31	12	16
9	56	35	—	—
10	99	39	27	20
11	186	44	—	—
12	335	47	58	24

This uses more cells, but fewer cells $\left(\xi, \text{ where } \xi \text{ is the smallest integer for which } \frac{n}{2} < 2^{\xi}\right)$ need be examined to establish synchronization. Table I compares using a separate sync sequence of alternate cells with using a comma-free code.

The second method can simulate more states with a given neighborhood size, but the fact that the cells of the neighborhood are not contiguous could be a disadvantage (requiring connections to more distant cells, larger d). Although the various methods of framing decrease the number of cell types, the total complexity and size of the array is increased. In some cases this greater complexity will be justified by greater versatility, i.e., lack of specialization.

V. SEQUENTIAL SYNTHESIS

The complexity of a cell is measured both by the number of its storage states and by the size of its logic circuit. The latter depends largely on the number of variables determining the new state, i.e., on distance of the neighbors which help determine the new state. Dependence on distant neighbors also requires direct paths to distant cells which in turn increases the difficulty of integrated circuit fabrication. Fortunately, a design method which has been devised for memoryless cascades provides a way to arbitrarily reduce neighbor dependency at the expense of a fixed increase in the number of storage states, computation time, and control complexity. These disadvantages may not be as serious as they appear at first glance, and there will also be a gain in versatility and possibly reliability.

THEOREM 1. *An array of 2-state cells with neighbor dependency d can be simulated by an array of 8-state cells with neighbor dependency* 1.

Proof. The proof of the theorem and resulting design method are very easy if the minterm method of Short [2] is used. Pick out one cell in the original array, call its old state x_{d+1}, call the states of its d neighbors on its left $x_1, x_2, x_3, \cdots x_d$ and on its right $x_{d+1}, x_{d+2}, x_{d+3}, \cdots, x_{2d+1}$, and call its new state $f(x_1, x_2, x_3, \cdots, x_{2d+1})$. Expand f as a sum of minterms, for example

$$f(x_1, x_2, x_3) = a_0\, x_1\, x_2\, x_3 + a_1\, x_1\, x_2\, x_3' + a_2\, x_1\, x_2'\, x_3 + \cdots + a_7\, x_1'\, x_2'\, x_3' \ .$$

Now refer to the 2-rail cascade of Fig. 2(a) where the bottom rail is used to form the minterm products and the top rail is used to collect the sum of the appropriate minterms. Obviously f will appear on the top rail after at most $n\,2^n + 1$ cells. Next, instead of using a cascade of memoryless cells connected by 2 rails, use a single cell whose function is changed by control signals and whose rail inputs are stored values of its previous rail outputs. Figure 2(b) shows such a circuit. Specifically, if the variables are presented to the cells of Fig. 2(a) in a fixed order, six cell types suffice: $(r_1, x_i r_2)$, $(r_1, x_i' r_2)$, $(r_1 + r_2, x_i)$, $(r_1 + r_2, x_i')$, (r_1, x_i) and (r_1, x_i'). This number can be reduced. The point here is, a single cell type suffices if $\phi = 6$, since the control then just chooses the desired logic function. The desired new state function for a particular cell is shown in Figure 2(b).

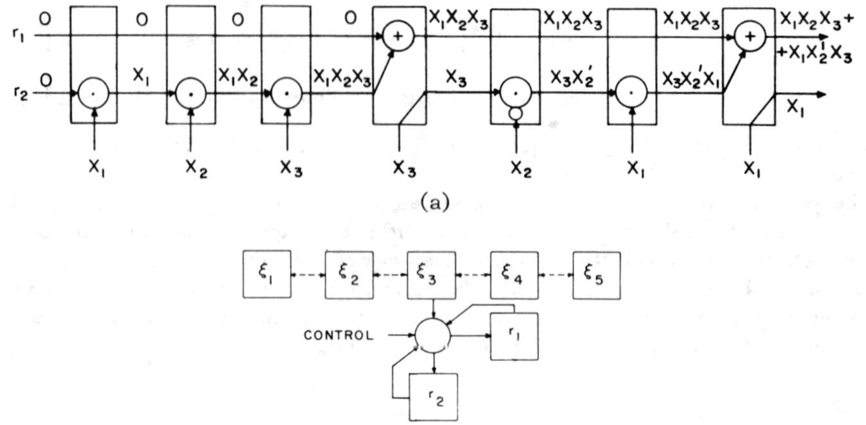

Fig. 2. (a) Realization of $f = x_1\, x_2\, x_3 + x_1\, x_2'\, x_3 + x_1'\, x_2\, x_3 + \cdots$ as a Short cascade. (b) Sequential form for above circuit. (c) Same as (b), except for an array of similar cells. (d) Reduction of states at expense of neighbor dependency.

Since each cell is to have the same new state function, although with different values for its arguments, the shift register of Fig. 2(b) can be replaced by the whole array's original state variables being shifted as in Figure 2(c). The minterm expansion can be replaced by a sum-of-products expansion with a loss of regularity but a gain in operating speed. Q.E.D.

COROLLARY 1. *An array of 2-state cells with neighbor dependency d can be simulated by an array of 2-state cells with neighbor dependency* 3.

This follows from Theorem 2 by the simple expedient of arranging the 3 1-bit registers in a single line, as in Figure 2(d). Note that except for a simple shift of ξ by 3 cells, the neighbor dependency is really only 1.

It has been shown by Yoeli and others [3–6] that a 2-rail memoryless cascade can realize 2 independent Boolean functions, in fact if the intercell rails can carry an M-valued signal the cascade can realize any function of $x_1 x_2 x_3 \cdots x_n$ to $1, 2, 3, \cdots, M$. In the present context, this can be stated as:

THEOREM 2. *An array of S state cells* ($S \geq 3$) *with neighbor dependency d can be simulated by an array of* S^2 *state cells with neighbor dependency* 1.

Proof. The proof of this theorem and the corresponding method of design is more difficult than in the case of the first theorem, and the cell functions are not as closely related to ordinary switching theory. As before, consider first a cascade of memoryless cells as shown in Figure 3(a). The x's are fed to the cells

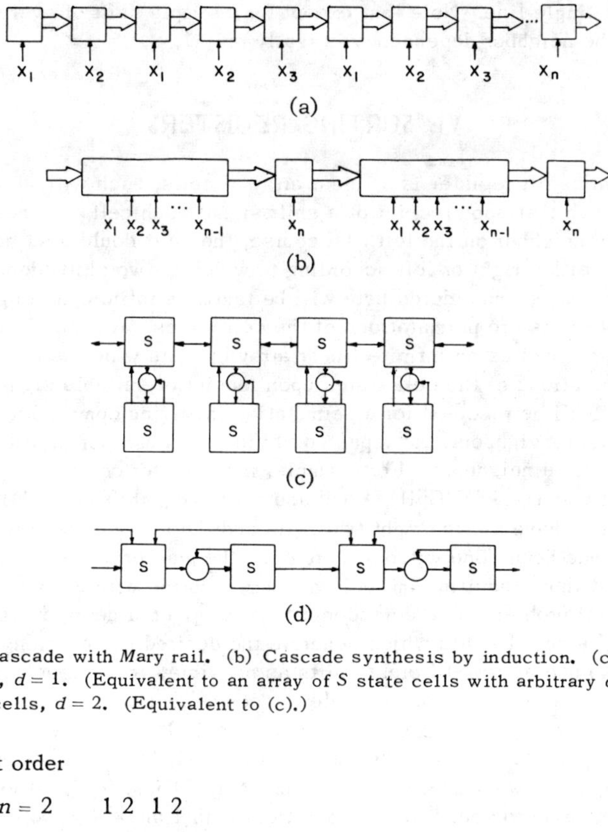

Fig. 3. (a) Cascade with Mary rail. (b) Cascade synthesis by induction. (c) Array with S^2 state cells, $d = 1$. (Equivalent to an array of S state cells with arbitrary d.) (d) Array with S state cells, $d = 2$. (Equivalent to (c).)

in a different order

$n = 2$ 1 2 1 2

$n = 3$ 1 2 1 2 3 1 2 1 2 3

$n = 4$ 1 2 1 2 3 1 2 1 2 3 4 1 2 1 2 3 1 2 1 2 3 4

The length of the cascade is thus $3 \cdot 2^{n-1} - 2$. The order in which the variables are fed fits the pattern

$$x_1 x_2 x_3 \cdots x_{n-1} x_n x_1 x_2 \cdots x_{n-1} x_n ,$$

as shown in Figure 3(b). The proof that an arbitrary function $F(x_1 x_2 x_3 \cdots x_n)$ can be realized in the form shown is by induction, but the key step in the whole process might be regarded as proving a little more than is necessary [3–6]: A cell or a cascade of cells can be regarded either as providing a function F at the output rail which ranges over $\{1, 2, 3, \cdots, M\}$ when the input rail is suitably fixed, or they can be regarded as mapping the input rail set into the output rail set. The latter describes the cascade connection much more nicely, in fact if the mapping is 1 : 1 the cell corresponds to a group element and the cascade connection corresponds to group multiplication.

COROLLARY 2. *An array of S state cells* ($S \geq 3$) *with arbitrarily d can be simulated by an array of S state cells with neighbor dependency* 2.

Proof. The proof parallels that of Corollary 2, i.e., just by drawing the cell diagram in a single line. Note that except for a simple shift of every second cell by 2 cells, the neighbor dependency is really only 1.

VI. SORTING REGISTERS

An ordinary shift register is a linear array of cells, each with m stable memory states, such that upon receipt of a shift signal each cell assumes the state of its immediate neighbor on the left. Of course, the shift could also be from the right, or from either right or left according to which of two shift signals is received. The arrays considered here will be taken as infinite in length, so that left and right shifts are permutations of the cell states. A generalized shift register will be defined as an infinite linear array of cells which is capable of more general permutations of the cell states upon receipt of suitable signals. The term "shift" will be reserved for a permutation involving communication only between immediate neighbors, but repeated shifts can cause permutations not involving immediate neighbors. For example, if a register contains $\cdots$F3G4H5$\cdots$ a shift might cause $\cdots$3F4G5H$\cdots$ and another (right) shift $\cdots$E3F4G5$\cdots$. Here the letters have shifted right two cells and the numbers have remained fixed. This has been done without increasing the number of cell states (say $m = 36$) and without requiring immediate communication with distant neighbors.

The central problem to be considered here is, given a desired set of permutations, to find a set of shifts which generate the desired permutations. It is advantageous to use as few different shifts as possible, and to reach each desired permutation in as few steps as possible. A convenient notation for permutations is $(x_0\, x_1\, x_2 \cdots x_{n-1})$ meaning that the state of cell 0 goes to cell x_0, the state of cell 1 goes to cell x_1, etc. Also, the state of cell $i + n$ ($-\infty \leq i \leq \infty$) goes to cell $x_i + n$, and no two states go to the same cell. Thus, (4, 0) is not allowed since it does not correspond to a permutation (both 1 and -4 go to 0, etc.). If ψ is the smallest value of n which so describes a permutation, the permutation will be said to have length ψ. Only permutations of finite length will be considered here. The simple right and left shifts are respectively (1) and (-1) and have length 1. The null shift, no change, will be denoted by θ and will be defined to have length 0.

There are simple rules which allow any permutation to be expressed as a sequence of shifts:

Rule 1. Interchange the states of even-odd pairs of cells if they are in the wrong order, then repeat with the odd-even pairs, then repeat for the first set, etc. To illustrate, suppose (3 1 2 0) is desired. First, two interchanges result

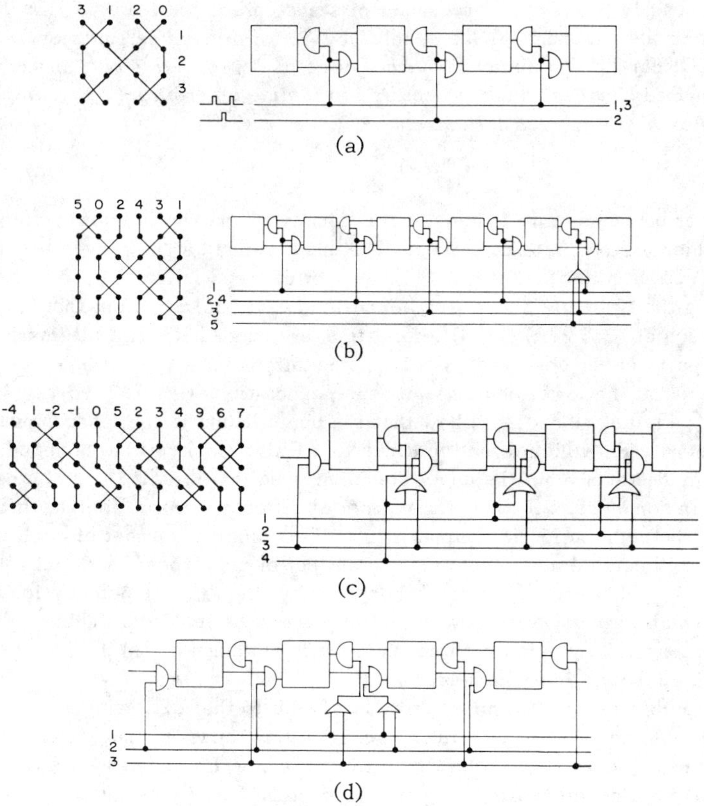

Fig. 4. (a) Permutation by interchanging adjacent elements. (b) Same as (a). (c) Permutation on an infinite array, with some transfers out of block. (d) Same as (c), with only one pair interchanged. Permutation realized by 1222 1313.

in $(\overparen{1\ 3}\ \overparen{0\ 2})$, then an interchange results in $(1\ \overparen{0\ 3}\ 2)$, finally the first interchanges are repeated to result in the desired order $(\overparen{0\ 1}\ \overparen{2\ 3})$. These are illustrated in Figure 4(a). Another example is shown in Figure 4(b).

So far, all examples have involved only permutations of the finite set of ψ cells. The circuits shown on the right repeat periodically, with no transfers between blocks. Now consider the permutation (0 5 2 3). Three cells retain their former state, and the state of the remaining cell is transferred to the corresponding cell in the next block on the right. The rule given above can be augmented as follows to handle permutations which are not confined to a block.

Rule 2. Proceed as in Rule 1 above except that no transfers are to be made between blocks unless the two states are both to go to different blocks. If, as in Fig. 4(c), the rightmost state of the left block is to be transferred to the right, but the leftmost state of the right block is not to be transferred out of the block, then all states are to be transferred to the right.

The number of steps required to realize a given permutation as a sequence of shifts is easily bounded. The number of steps can be viewed as a time scale factor, and the minimum will be denoted by τ_0 for a given permutation.

THEOREM 3. *The minimum number of steps* τ_0 *involving only immediate neighbor interchanges which is required to realize an arbitrary permutation of* ψ *cell states is bounded as follows*

$$\max_i |x_i - i| \leq \tau_0 \leq \psi .$$

The lower bound is quite evident, being simply the maximum distance along the array which a state is to be moved. The upper bound can be proved by induction, refer to [12, Figure 3]. Note that the number of steps is usually minimized by following the first rule above (the bound is always realized), but that in certain cases such as (3 1 2 0 7 5 6 4) fewer steps are needed if strict alternation of shifted pairs is not observed. Cyclic permutations $(\psi - 1, 0, 1, 2, \cdots, \psi - 2)$ can be realized at the lower bound, while the permutations $(\xi + 2, \xi + 3, \xi + 4, \cdots, 2\xi + 1, \xi + 1, 0, 1, 2, \cdots, \xi)$ show that the upper bound is the least upper bound.

A permutation which is not confined to a finite block is also bounded from below as in Theorem 3 but the upper bound must be increased. It may be more important in some cases to limit the number of different control signals than to achieve the permutation in minimum time. Reducing the number of control signals here is equivalent to reducing the number of cell types. With only three shifts: all right, all left, and interchange every *i*th pair, any permutation with a period which is equal to *n* or which divides *n* can be realized. This is illustrated in Figure 4(c). Any pair which needs to be interchanged is shifted to the pair of cells which can be interchanged.

The problem of sorting in an array is similar to that of sorting numbers in a computer [9], and also to generating permutation groups [8], but these are restricted to finite sets. Only in the former case is efficiency important, but the conditions are different from the present problem if a sequential computer is assumed. Therefore, these fields offer little help in optimizing the sorting process in the array case.

VII. COMBINED EXCHANGES

The various exchanges between array parameters described above can be combined to simultaneously reduce cell states and neighbor dependency. In Fig. 5 the reduction of a 16-state array to a 4-state array is shown with immediate neighbor dependency. The original array could have had any neighbor dependency without increasing the neighbor dependency of the final array. The steps in the reduction are splitting, cascade synthesis, and generalized shifting. The final array could have been reduced even more to only 3 states by the same process, but not to 2 states since single rail (i.e., 2-state) cascades cannot realize all functions. Two-state arrays can be reached by the slight modification of using 2-rail cells for every variable cell. The example shown in Fig. 5 has 4 different types of cells; these could have been reduced by using one of the framing techniques in connection with the splitting process. However, the minimum number of cell types for immediate neighbor dependency in the final array will be 2 types for 3 or more states, 3 types for 2 states.

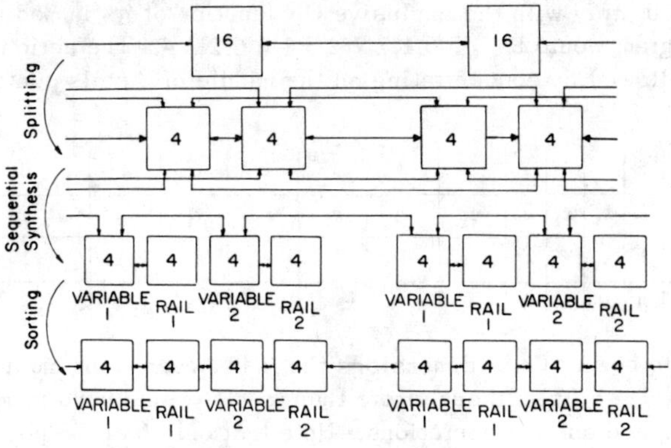

Fig. 5. Combined exchanges.

VIII. CELL OF MINIMUM COMPLEXITY

A particularly simple cell will now be described which is capable of forming an array which can simulate any given array. An array of these cells can be seen to be computation universal directly, not thru the usual route of its simulating a universal Turing machine. Since it can directly simulate a given specific Turing machine in cellular form, or in fact any array of finite state machines, it is much easier to use than the usual universal machine. Also, since no wiring in the cell need be changed if the particular machine being simulated is changed, the cell and its arrays have the advantage of versatility. The price to be paid for the simplicity of the cell is the possible complexity of the control unit, the multiplicity of the control leads to the cells, and the possible increase in computation time.

The cell to be described will be based on the cascade shown in Figure 2. There will be 8 states realized by 3 binary bistable units $\mathcal{X}$, $\mathcal{P}$, and $\mathcal{S}$, representing in turn the variable, the rail used to accumulate Boolean products, and the rail used to accumulate the Boolean sum. A convenient small number of operations, but not the minimum possible number, is listed below:

(1) Replace p by px
(2) Replace p by px'
(3) Replace s by $s + p$; set p to 1
(4) Replace x by s
(5) Set s to 0
(6) Replace x by x from the cell on the left
(7) Replace x by x from the cell on the right.

The first 3 operations are necessary to realize a Boolean function in minterm canonical form, or as a sum of products. The last 2 operations shift neighboring variables into view; and the remaining 2 operations are used to replace the simulated cells contents with the new state just calculated, and to reset to start the next state transition. Suppose it is desired to replace each state variable in a binary simulated array with the exclusive OR function of its immediate neighbors. A suitable program would be 3 5 6 1 7 7 2 3 1 6 6 2 3 4. The action of the program can be followed by concentrating on the middle of 3 cells containing $x_1\, x_2\, x_3$ initially.

		3	5	6	1	7	7	2	3	1	6	6	2	3	4
x	x_2	x_2	x_2	x_1	x_1	x_2	x_3	x_3	x_3	x_3	x_2	x_1	x_1	x_1	$x_1 x_3' + x_1' x_3$
p	p_0	1	1	1	x_1	x_1	x_1	$x_1 x_3'$	1	x_3	x_3	x_3	$x_1' x_3$	1	1
s	s_0	$s_0 + x_2$	0	0	0	0	0	0	$x_1 x_3'$	$x_1 x_3'$	$x_1 x_3'$	$x_1 x_3'$	$x_1 x_3'$	$x_1 x_3' + x_1' x_3$	$x_1 x_3' + x_1' x_3$

If the array is to be in $n(\geq 2)$ dimensions the last 2 operations must be replaced by at least $(n+1)$ shifts, although more than $(n+1)$ would usually make for easier programming and quicker operations. Note that only 6 of the possible 8 states are really needed, since, if $s = 1$, it is no longer necessary to keep track of whether $p = 0$ or $p = 1$. A diagram of the cell described is shown in Figure 6(a).

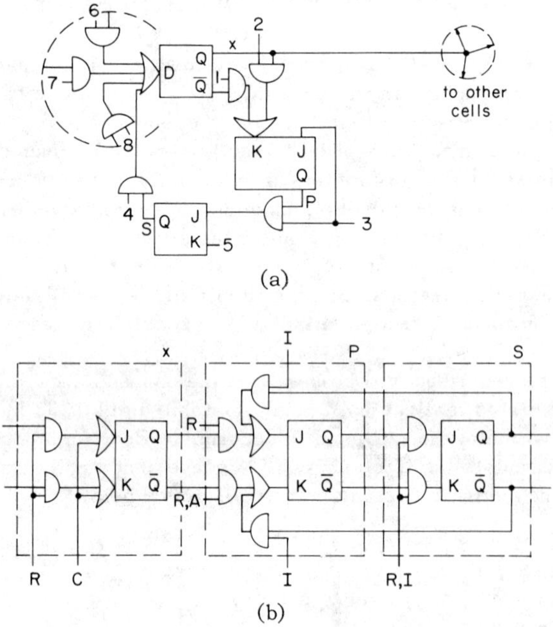

Fig. 6. (a) 6-state cell. (b) 2-state cell.

It is now very easy to derive from the 6-state cell an array of 2-state cells. Simply arrange the $\mathcal{X}\,\mathcal{P}\,\mathcal{S}$ in an array as in Figure 6(b). Since there is shifting possible among the $\mathcal{X}$ cells, the state transition calculation might as well be placed in the $\mathcal{X}$ cell to the right as it can always be shifted back if desired. If the array is to have communication only with immediate neighbors, the last two operations must be replaced, say by:

(8) Shift all cell contents to the right
(9) Shift all cell contents to the left

(10) Interchange the contents of $\mathcal{P}$ and $\mathcal{S}$

(11) Interchange the contents of $\mathcal{X}$ and $\mathcal{P}$.

Now a right shift of x's is accomplished by 11-10-8 and a left shift by 9-10-11.

The operation set 1 to 5 and 8 to 11 is certainly not minimal. As pointed out in Section VI above, only one interchange is necessary, thus -11- can be replaced by 8-10-9 in any program with identical results. If the entire computation is allowed to drift to the right, then 9 is superfluous. This can be seen by the fact that 888 can be inserted anywhere in any program if the array user remembers to look for the answer in its shifted position. By inserting 888 after every 9, the 9 is effectively replaced by 88. Since 5 is used to start a function calculation when the contents of p does not matter, it can be replaced by 128. Similarly, since 4 is used at the end of a function calculation, it can be replaced by 8. An alternative to having 1 and 2 is to have 1 and:

(13) Replace x by x'.

This allows 3 to be replaced by a subroutine which has the effect of replacing s by $(s'p')'$. To summarize, a universal array of 3 types of 2-state cells is possible with 4 control signals:

(A) Replace p by px

(C) Replace x by x'

(R) Shift all states to the right one cell

(I) Interchange the states of p and s.

IX. APPLICATIONS

As has been pointed out by Minsky [1], the quest for a universal Turing machine of minimum state-symbol product is a very intriguing puzzle of almost no mathematical importance. At first glance it would seem that this quest, and the equivalent quest for a computation-universal array with cells of minimum complexity, would have even less practical importance. It may be that arrays of the simple cells shown in Fig. 6 will turn out to be impractical for all applications, but there is reason to believe that cells of slightly larger than minimum size might be useful in several applications.

One of the first questions which comes up when considering applications is that of economy. The goal is usually to get the most computation per unit cost, but there are many exceptions: If the computer is to sit on a person's desk and used once in a while, the total cost is more important. If the computer is to be used for real-time computations, cost per computation may be secondary to working or not working. If the computer is to be sent to Jupiter, the cost is much less important than reliability and weight. If the computer is to be used on a succession of different problems, the computer hardware costs may be less important than ease of programming. Assume that the primary criterion is the number of computations per unit cost, e.g., that two black boxes that do a given computation in 1 minute and cost \$10 each are equivalent to one black box which does the same computation in 30 sec and costs \$46. How would the sequential synthesis process influence such costs? This apparently increases the computation time by an undue amount, yet the increase is roughly proportional to the number of variable occurrences in the sum-of-products expansion of the next-state function, a factor which also represents the number of gate-inputs to a two-level instantaneous logic circuit. The latter is a common criterion for the cost of a logic circuit, so that the slowing down due to sequential synthesis is not excessive, at least in the first approximation. Note also that the versatility of this means that simple functions take less time, whereas the instantaneous logic must carry along a complexity determined by the most complicated function at all times. Whether permutations by adjacent interchanges are economical depends more strongly on how important the reduction of distant connections are.

Several suggestions can be made as to how the ideas on sequential synthesis, sorting, and simple cell design might be applied to computers working on specific problems:

A. Optical Processors

A parallel computer consisting of a 2-dimensional array of cells with a central control seems much more naturally suited to problems of pattern recognition and picture processing than does a sequential computer. An early proposal along these lines was made by Ungar [21], and a later design by Golay [22] has already been put to practical use in counting and classifying blood cells [23, 24].

B. Lee Memories

An array of cells in which parallel operations can take place is very desirable if the memory is to be searched in some way, i.e., information obtained from the memory without knowing its exact address. An original paper by C. Y. Lee [25] has been followed by improvements [26, 27], applications to processing [28], and in fact by a complete computer [29]. A disadvantage of these memories and computers is that they have communications to the central control as well as from it. This prevents true parallel operations in different parts of the array. A solution is to feed in requests and to feed out information by shifting thru the cells in additional registers. The delay in getting the information will be increased, but the rate of getting a stream of information can be kept the same.

C. Multihead Turing Machines

The ordinary Turing machine is notoriously slow and difficult to use, all the more so if its structure is made very simple. When the Turing machine is realized in cellular form one of its chief virtues, its economical tape storage, is lost, making the prospects even bleaker. However, an all electronic cellular Turing machine need not be limited to one head, and this allows parallel operations which will possibly bring the Turing machine back into the realm of practicality. It is common knowledge that a multihead Turing machine can calculate nothing that a suitably designed single head Turing machine cannot also calculate. There are even ways of defining complexity classes of calculations so that the multihead machines do not enlarge the complexity class [30]. Arbib [31] does prove that "two heads are better than one," but the general tenor of the few papers which mention multiheads is that they gain little. Few, if any, papers on Turing machines are concerned with practical efficiency. A possibility which seems to have been ignored is that an electronic cellular Turing machine need not be bound to 1, 2, or *n* heads, but the number of heads can vary with time, i.e. heads can split, combine or disappear [32]. Since there is a continuous spectrum possible from one head to "heads" everywhere, cellular arrays as usually considered, it is believed that further study of Turing machine techniques may have practical importance.

D. Molecular Arrays

A very far-out possibility is that if the individual cell is made really simple, it can be realized by a molecular group of only a few atoms.

REFERENCES

[1] M. L. Minsky, *Computation: Finite and Infinite Machines* (New Jersey: Prentice-Hall, 1967).

[2] R. A. Short, "Two-Rail Cellular Arrays," *AFIPS Conf. Proc.*, **27**, Part 1, 355–369 (Washington, DC: Spartan Books, 1965).

[3] M. Yoeli, "A Group-Theoretical Approach to Two-Rail Cascades," *IEEE Trans.*, **EC-14**, 815–822 (December 1965).

[4] M. Yoeli and J. Turner, "Decompositions of Group Functions with Applications to Two-Rail Cascades," *Inf. & Control*, **10**, 565–571 (1967).

[5] B. Elspas and H. Stone, "Decomposition of Group Functions and the Synthesis of Multirail Cascades," *IEEE Conf. Rec. 8th Ann. Symp. on Switching and Automatic Theory*, 184–196 (October 1967).

[6] I. Shinahr and M. Yoeli, "Group Functions and Multivalued Cellular Cascades," *Inf. & Control*, **15**, 369–376 (1969).

[7] K. Krohn, W. D. Maurer, and J. Rhodes, "Realizing Complex Boolean Functions With Simple Groups," *Inf. & Control*, **9**, 190–195 (April 1966).

[8] H. J. Zassenhaus, *The Theory of Groups* (New York: Chelsea, 1958).

[9] R. S. Ledley, *Digital Computer and Control Engineering* (New York: McGraw Hill, 1960).

[10] C. E. Shannon, "A Universal Turing Machine with Two Internal States," *Automata Studies, Annals of Math Studies*, **34**, 157–165, Princeton Univ. Press (1956).

[11] M. D. Davis, "A Note on Universal Turing Machines," loc. cit., 167–175.

[12] W. H. Kantz, K. N. Levitt, and A. Waksman, "Cellular Interconnection Arrays," *IEEE Trans.*, **C-17**, 443–451 (May 1968).

[13] S. W. Golomb, B. Gordon, and L. R. Welch, "Comma-Free Codes," *Can. J. Math.*, **10**, 202–209 (1958).

[14] W. L. Eastman, "On the Construction of Comma-Free Codes," *IEEE Trans.*, **IT-11**, 263–267 (April 1965).

[15] W. L. Eastman and S. Evan, "On Synchronizable and PSK-Synchronizable Block Codes," *IEEE Trans.*, **IT-10**, 351–356 (October 1964).

[16] S. W. Golomb and B. Gordon, "Codes with Bounded Synchronization Delay," *Inf. & Control*, **8**, 355–372 (1965).

[17] A. R. Smith III, "Cellular Automata Theory," Technical Report No. 2, Stanford Electronics Labs (December 1969).

[18] A. R. Smith III, "Simple Computation-Universal Space," *J. ACM*, **18**, 339–353 (July 1971).

[19] A. R. Smith III, "Cellular Automata Complexity Trade-Offs," *Inf. & Control*, **18**, 466–482 (June 1971).

[20] J. J. Stiffler, "Comma Codes vs Comma-Free Codes," *Int. Symp. Information Theory*, Ellenville (January 1969). See abstract in *IEEE Trans.*, **IT-16**, 128 (January 1970).

[21] S. H. Ungar, "A Computer Oriented Toward Spatial Problems," *Proc. IRE*, **46**, 1744–1750 (October 1958).

[22] M. J. E. Golay, "Hexagonal Parallel Pattern Transformations," *IEEE Trans.*, **C-18**, 733–740 (August 1969).

[23] M. Ingram and K. Preston, Jr., "Automatic Analysis of Blood Cells," *Sci. Amer.*, **223**, 72–82 (November 1970).

[24] K. Preston, Jr., "Use of the Golay Logic Processor in Pattern-Recognition Studies Using Hexagonal Neighborhood Logic," *Proceedings of the Symposium on Computers and Automata* (New York: Polytechnic Press of the Polytechnic Institute of Brooklyn, 1971).

[25] C. Y. Lee, "Interconnecting Cells-Basis for a Distributed Logic Computer," *Proc. Fall Joint Computer Conf.*, 130–136 (December 1962).

[26] C. Y. Lee and M. C. Paull, "A Content Addressable Distributed Logic Memory with Applications to Information Retrieval," *Proc. IEEE*, **51**, 924–932 (June 1963).

[27] R. S. Gains and C. Y. Lee, "An Improved Cell Memory," *IEEE Trans.*, **EC-14**, 72–75 (February 1965).

[28] B. A. Crane and J. A. Githens, "Bulk Processing in Distributed Logic Memory," *IEEE Trans.*, **EC-14**, 186–196 (April 1965).

[29] J. N. Sturman, "An Iteratively Structured General-Purpose Digital Computer," *IEEE Trans.*, **C-17**, 2–9 (January 1968).

[30] J. Hartmanis and R. E. Stearns, "On the Computational Complexity of Algorithms," *Trans. AMS*, **17**, 285–306 (1965).

[31] M. A. Arbib, "Theories of Abstract Automata" (New Jersey: Prentice-Hall, 1969).

[32] L. Librizzi, "Cellular Multihead Turing Machine," MSc. Thesis, Polytechnic Inst. of Brooklyn (June 1970). Also: Technical Report RADC-TR-70-181 (September 1970).

USE OF THE GOLAY LOGIC PROCESSOR IN PATTERN-RECOGNITION STUDIES USING HEXAGONAL NEIGHBORHOOD LOGIC

K. Preston, Jr.
The Perkin-Elmer Corporation, Norwalk, CT

The Golay LOgic PRocessor, or "GLOPR," is a hard-wired digital logic unit which may be used to perform Golay hexagonal pattern transforms. GLOPR is constructed as peripheral firmware interfaced to a minicomputer. The minicomputer now in use is a Varian 620i with 16,000 words of core. The minicomputer enters one or more binary input images into the GLOPR logic unit along with instruction words which set up the hexagonal pattern transform desired, as well as specifying image size, selecting subfields, and giving the subfield order. The minicomputer extracts from GLOPR the resultant binary image which is calculated at a speed at least 2 orders of magnitude faster than achievable by software in the minicomputer itself.

GLOPR has been used in large-scale pattern recognition studies by the author which have been concerned with the automatic analysis of human white blood cell morphology. Recently a closer look has been taken on the quantitative value of Golay hexagonal pattern transforms in pattern recognition. Using a bimodal, real-world image set, measurements have been scored and evaluated sequentially during the performance of a sequence of hexagonal pattern transforms. By tabulating such statistical parameters as the *F*-test, the *U*-test, the Mahalanobis and the Bhattacharyya distances as the sequence proceeds, a quantitative evaluation of feature-enhancement by hexagonal pattern transforms has been obtained. This paper reports on results of the above investigations and shows how simple hexagonal pattern transforms can be used to produce a significant enhancement of the bimodality of the original image set.

Also discussed in this paper are the results of the pattern recognition game called "GLOPR Life." GLOPR Life is analogous to J. H. Conway's new solitaire game called "Life." The author, in cooperation with Golay, has investigated the results of this game for all of the hexagonal terminoes and has found that all terminoes either die or stabilize into cyclic patterns after a finite number of moves. Most interesting are the results obtained using GLOPR to analyze the equilateral termino. This termino was found to reach a stable, modulo-6 cyclic pattern after 321 moves. The remarkable result consists of 127 subpatterns, cycling modulo-2, and 9 other subpatterns cycling modulo-6.

More than a decade ago Golay [1] proposed a form of 2-dimensional picture logic for processing binary pictures, i.e., pictures whose elements are either black or white. Golay's picture logic is based to a certain extent upon the earlier work of Unger [2] in that it uses a 2-dimensional local operator which is position independent over the picture. By applying Golay's logic to a picture it is transformed into a new picture. The transformation is orientation independent

---

Presented at the Symposium on Computers and Automata
Polytechnic Institute of Brooklyn, April 13-15, 1971.

and is computed from a knowledge of the binary state of each picture element and the states of its immediate neighbors. Thus the computational speed may be very rapid.

Golay transformations may be iterated so that the original picture is modified many times. By counting the binary ones in the picture after the execution of each transformation, measurements may be generated which are useful in pattern recognition. Extensive use has been made of Golay's picture logic in the CELLSCAN^{TM} system picture processing experiments [3-5] which have been concerned with the problem of the automatic recognition of human white blood cells on microscope slides. Some specific results are given as illustrations below.

Recently Golay has generalized his logic so as to make it applicable to multilevel, i.e., grey-scale, pictures by representing these pictures as oriented stacks of binary picture planes. Golay has also transferred from a square to a hexagonal tessellation of picture elements and calls the resultant picture logic "hexagonal pattern transformations" [6]. These hexagonal pattern transformations are related to earlier work by McCormick [7] where they have been used in conjunction with the Illiac III Project as well as to operators discussed by both Deutsch [8] and Gray [9].

It is the purpose of this paper to describe the Golay LOgic PRocessor (GLOPR) which is a hard-wired digital logic unit for use in performing Golay's hexagonal pattern transformations. GLOPR is constructed as peripheral firmware which is interfaced to and controlled by a minicomputer. The minicomputer in turn interfaces with various image input scanners and other peripherals as shown in the overall block diagram (Figure 1.) The minicomputer now in use is a Varian

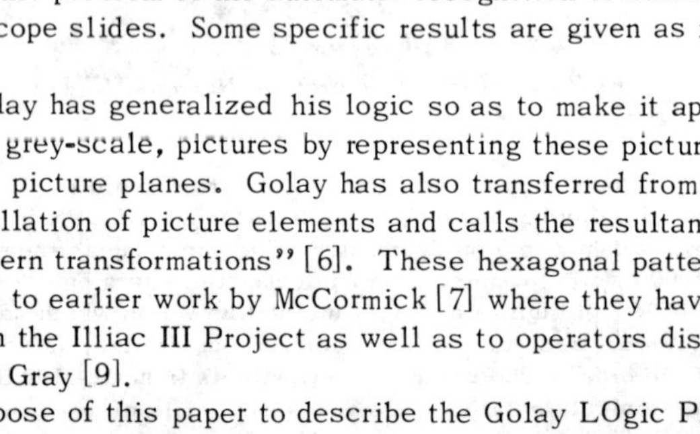

Fig. 1. Block diagram of GLOPR/Varian system.

620i with 16,000 words of core storage. This minicomputer enters one or more binary pictures into GLOPR accompanied by two 16-bit instruction words. One of these instruction words sets up the particular hexagonal pattern transformation desired while the other specifies such things as window size, subfield configuration, and subfield order (see below). GLOPR operates upon the binary input picture(s) in a sequential fashion examining one picture element at a time and its 6 nearest neighbors. It tests for the 14 orientation-independent binary hexagonal nearest neighbor configurations shown in Figure 2. These configurations are

```
 0 0      1 0      1 1      1 1      1 1      1 1      1 1
0 X 0    0 X 0    0 X 0    0 X 1    1 X 1    1 X 1    1 X 1
 0 0      0 0      0 0      0 0      0 0      1 0      1 1

ZERO     ONE      TWO      THREE    FOUR     FIVE     SIX


 1 0      1 1      1 1      1 1      1 0      0 0      1 1
0 X 1    0 X 0    0 X 0    0 X 1    0 X 1    1 X 1    0 X 0
 1 0      0 1      1 0      1 0      0 0      0 0      1 1

SEVEN    EIGHT    NINE     TEN      ELEVEN   TWELVE   THIRTEEN
```

Fig. 2. The 14 orientation-independent Golay surrounds in the hexagonal tessellation.

called the "Golay surrounds". During one pass over the image GLOPR may examine the picture elements in order, row by row, or GLOPR may make n examinations of the picture by processing $1/n$ elements each time in a specified order. This latter mode of operation is referred to by Golay as an "operation in subfields" which is necessary in performing certain pattern recognition tasks. Figure 3 illustrates the numbering of subfields for $n = 3$.

The software language which is used to program the GLOPR/Varian system is called GLOL (Golay LOgic Language). The command structure of GLOL is given in Table I. The first item in this table is the GLOL statement which is the basic command used for executing a Golay hexagonal pattern transformation. In addition to the GLOL statement there exist a series of other commands which permit the user to perform other picture processing operations such as Boolean logic between pairs of pictures, selection of certain picture constituents (PICK), and tabulation of the total number of binary ones in a picture (COUNT). In addition the user has at his disposal commands which permit him to acquire images from a scanner, to calculate and display photometric histograms, to select thresholding levels either manually of automatically, to read and write arrays onto or from magnetic tape, to output measurements, and, by weighting these measurements, to identify specific objects. Branching and looping operations are included in the GLOL command structure as well as commands which permit certain simple arithmetic operations to be performed.

The GLOL software system is basically an interpreter which permits the user to enter and execute GLOL commands on a line by line basis. The user may also name and store subroutines which are called "GLOL procedures" for future

```
  (1) (2) (3) (1) (2) (3)
(2) (3) (1) (2) (3) (1)
  (1) (2) (3) (1) (2) (3)
(2) (3) (1) (2) (3) (1)
  (1) (2) (3) (1) (2) (3)
(2) (3) (1) (2) (3) (1)
```

Fig. 3. Subfield map for subfields of 3.

TABLE I. GLOL Commands.

Golay Statement	
$D=[G(A)B+G'(A)C]N1\ldots N2,N3,N4/N5\ldots N6$	
Logical Operations	
$A=B+C$	Generates image plane A with contents equal to the union of planes B and C.
$A=B*C$	Generates image plane A with contents equal to the intersection of planes B and C.
$A=B-C$	Generates image plane A with contents equal to Exclusive OR of planes B and C.
$A=B$	Generates image plane A with contents identical to B.
$A=0$	Sets the contents of image plane A to ZERO.
Definitives	
DEFINE SYSTEM	Sets window size to 32×32, 64×64, or 128×128.
DEFINE ARRAY $V/N1$	Allocates $N1$ memory locations for a measurement array labeled "V".
DEFINE BUFFER	Allocates memory locations for an image plane labeled "A".
DEFINE PROCEDURE XYZ... END PROCEDURE XYZ	Permits the user to enter a series of GLOL commands which are then filed under the procedure name XYZ.
Tabulators	
COUNT $A, V(N1)$	Causes the sum of all binary ONE's to image plane A to be stored as the value of array element $V(N1)$.
CATALOGUE	Causes names of all previously defined procedures and arrays to be listed at the teletype.
Identifiers	
IDENTIFY NOW	Multiplies the measurement array with sets of preassigned weights, calculates the sums, compares with the appropriate constant, and outputs the resultant object identification. (This command may be used pair-wise for as many as 8 simultaneous object types.)
IDENTIFY TABULATE	Generates a table of the number of objects identified as a function of object type.
Deletives	
DELETE BUFFER A	Causes memory locations previously allocated for buffer A to be released.
DELETE PROCEDURE XYZ	Causes mamory locations previously allocated to procedure XYZ to be released.
DELETE ARRAY $V(N1)$	Causes memory locations previously allocated to array $V(N1)$ to be released.
Input/Output	
OUTPUT $N1, V(N2\text{-}N3)$	Causes values $N2$ through $N3$ stored in measurement array V to be printed on the teletype ($N1 = 1$), on paper tape ($N1 = 2$), on both the teletype and paper tape ($N1 = 3$), or on magnetic tape ($N1 = 4$).

TABLE I. GLOL Commands. (Continued)

PAPER TAPE	Used after DEFINE PROCEDURE *XYZ* to cause procedure to be loaded from paper tape reader.
END OUTPUT	Writes end of file mark on magnetic tape.
WRITE *A*	Stores the contents of one-bit image plane *A* on magnetic tape.
READ *A*,*N*1	Spools out magnetic tape to the *N*1th one-bit image and stores it in image plane *A*.
SEARCH *A*,*N*1...*N*2	Searches magnetic tape for the one-bit image specified and stores it in image plane *A*.
BACK *N*1	Back spaces *N*1 one-bit images.
BEGIN	Rewinds the tape.
END TAPE	Goes to last one-bit image on the tape.
FETCH	Searches magnetic tape for the multi-bit image specified.
Cathode Ray Tube	
DISPLAY *A*	Causes the contents of image plane *A* to be exhibited on the GLOPR display screen.
CLEAR	Stops the operation of the display.
Executives	
EXECUTE PROCEDURE *XYZ*	Causes the procedure *XYZ* to be carried out.
RUN *N*1	Causes a list of commands and/or procedures to be executed *N*1 times.
Automatic Microscope	
FIND	Causes the automatic microscope to locate an object of interest.
ACQUIRE *A*,*N*1	Causes a multilevel image to be thresholded at level *N*1 and stored in image plane *A*.
WAVELENGTH *N*1	Causes the wavelength of illumination used by the scanner to be shifted to a color having the preassigned number *N*1.
Histogramming	
HISTOGRAM *A*	Causes the photometric histogram of a multi-bit image to be computed and stored in image array *A*.
SMOOTH *A*,*N*1	Causes the histogram stored in array *A* to be smoothed by pair-wise averaging for *N*1 cycles.
GRAPH *A*	Causes the histogram stored in array *A* to be placed in an image buffer and displayed.
Selection	
PICK *A*,*N*1	Causes the *N*1th isolated ONE in image plane *A* to be retained and sets all other image elements to ZERO.
Arithmetic	
AR $V(n1)=V(N2)+V(N3)$	Causes the sum of $V(N2)$ and $V(N3)$ to be stored in location $V(N1)$.
AR $V(N1)=V(N2)-V(N3)$	Causes the difference of $V(N2)$ and $V(N3)$ to be stored in location $V(N1)$.
AR $V(N1)=V(N2)*V(N3)$	Causes the product of $V(N2)$ and $V(N3)$ to be stored in location $V(N1)$.

TABLE I. GLOL Commands. (Continued)

AR $V(N1)=V(N2)/V(N3)$	Causes the ratio of $V(N2)$ and $V(N3)$ to be stored in location $V(N1)$.
Loop	
DO $V(N1), V(N2), V(N3)$...STOP	Causes the commands listed to be executed with the loop index going from $V(N1)$ to $V(N2)$ in increments of $V(N3)$.
Branch	
IF...ELSE...STOP	Using an ALGOL-like IF, executes either the first or second list of GLOL commands depending upon the outcome.
Transfer	
AID	Causes transfer of control to the Varian 620i AID II system for housekeeping and test purposes.

recall and utilization. While either coding or executing GLOL procedures the user may monitor the progress of his work by observing the GLOPR binary image display. This display may be programmed by the user to operate using a picture size or "window" which is either 32×32, 64×64, or 128×128. The user may operate in subfields of 1, 3, or 7 and also may perform simultaneous logic in 1, 2, or 3 windows.

The minicomputer accesses the GLOPR firmware as it would access a fast subroutine. Pictures are passed from core into GLOPR 16 bits at a time. The transformed picture is calculated by GLOPR at a speed at least 2 orders to magnitude faster than that achievable by a subroutine executed internally by the minicomputer itself. This transformed picture is then passed back by GLOPR to the minicomputer. Execution time for 1 pass through a 128×128 image in subfields of 1 is approximately 50 msec; 12 msec for 64×64; and about 3 msec for 32×32. This makes possible the execution of a GLOL procedure consisting of several hundred picture transformations in a few seconds.

As mentioned above, the GLOPR/Varian system has been utilized in large-scale pattern-recognition studies by the author related to the automatic analysis of human white blood cell morphology [10]. The following paragraphs demonstrate the power of Golay hexagonal pattern transformations in extracting certain significant morphological features. Figure 3 shows a gray-scale image of a typical human white blood cell produced using illumination in the yellow-red (5700-6700 Å). The dark regions of the picture are the nucleus. Surrounding the nucleus is the cytoplasm which, at the illumination utilized, is of low contrast. In the neighborhood of the white blood cell it is possible to see several low-contrast circular objects which are red cells. By selecting a proper thresholding level it is possible to obtain the white cell nucleus alone. Such a picture (for a cell similar to but not identical to that shown in Fig. 4) is shown in Figure 5. This figure shows the portions of the white cell nucleus which are below threshold as binary ones (intensified points) against a background of binary zeros (dark points).

A simple but, as we shall see, efficacious method of performing the pattern recognition required to identify the type of white blood cell is to simply measure

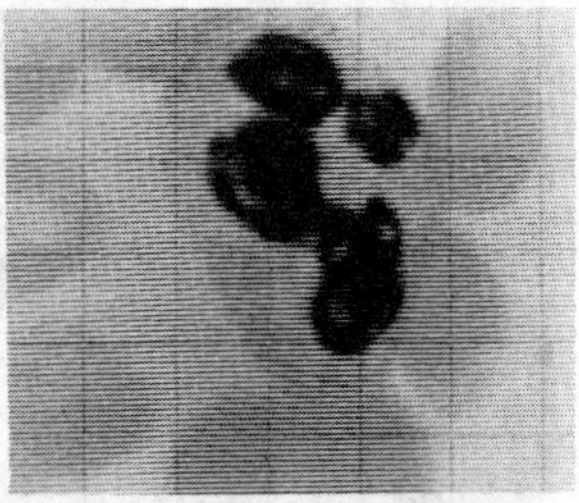

Fig. 4. Television image of a human peripheral blood neutrophil.

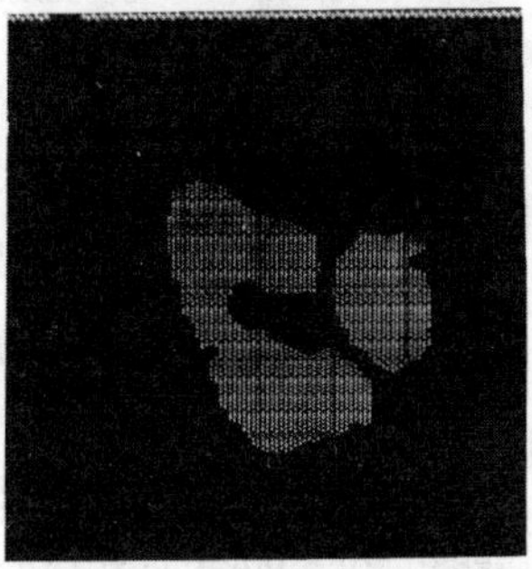

Fig. 5. Binary picture of white blood cell nucleus.

both the area and the perimeter of the nucleus. This operation may be carried out using the simple GLOL procedure given below.

```
COUNT A,X(1)
B=[G′(A)A]6,,
COUNT B,X(2)
```

Here the first comand simply counts the number of binary ones in the picture (named A) and records this as the first measurement (named X_1). The second command creates a new picture (named B) whose picture elements are binary ones wherever picture elements in picture A are not interior points (do not have the Golay surround 6). Thus B contains binary ones corresponding to the perimeter of the nucleus in A. The third command records the number of binary ones in B. After executing this procedure picture B is as shown in Figure 6. The execution time for this GLOL procedure is less than 0.2 sec for the 128×128 window used here.

It was discovered by the author and others some time ago [4] that picture processing by "shrinking" was an effective technique for distinguishing various types of white blood cells. A GLOL procedure for performing this type of picture processing is given below.

```
DO I=3,7,2
A=[G′(A)A] 1-4,5,3
COUNT A,X(I)
```

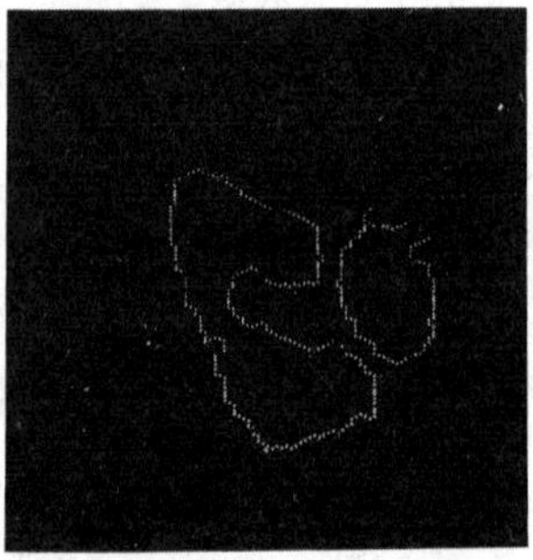

Fig. 6. Perimeter of white blood cell nucleus.

B=[$G'(A)A$]6,,
ARITHMETIC J=I+1
COUNT B,$X(J)$
END LOOP

After executing the first cycle of the loop the picture B is as shown in Figure 7. The corresponding count statements cause area and perimeter measurements to be recorded. The subsequent cycle of the loop continues the operation with the result shown in Figure 8. Area and perimeter counts are again recorded and the loop cycles once more with reasonably obvious results. Upon the completion of both of the procedures, which takes less than 3 sec in time, 8 measurements have

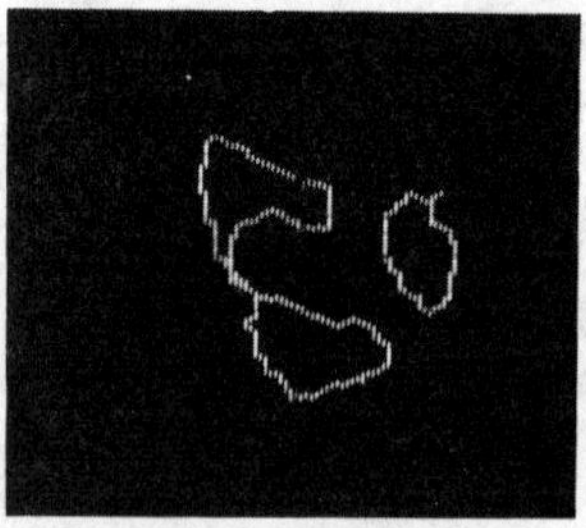

Fig. 7. Perimeter of white blood cell nucleus after one cycle of image contraction.

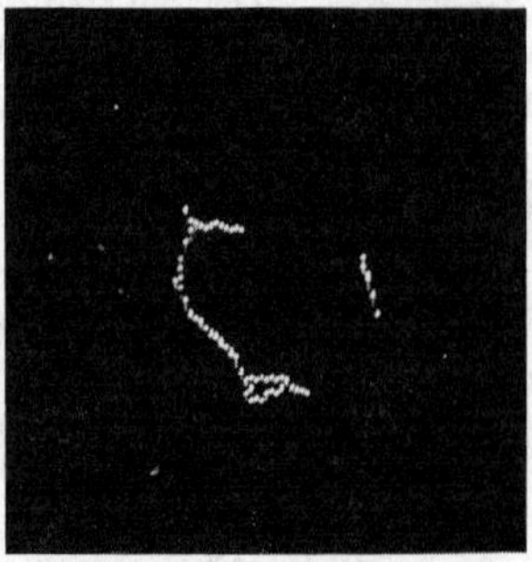

Fig. 8. Perimeter of white blood cell nucleus after two cycles of image contraction.

been scored as the measurement vector $X_1, X_2, X_3, \cdots, X_8$. As is illustrated below, this measurement vector may now be used in conjunction with one or more linear discriminant functions to assist in the identification of the white blood cell in question.

In order to provide quantitative information on the value of the above procedures an experiment was conducted on a large real-world sample of human white blood cells. The nuclear images of 185 of the cell type called "neutrophil" and 131 of the cell type called "lymphocyte" were recorded and stored on magnetic tape. One image at a time was then transferred from tape in a 128×128 format and the above picture processing procedures were applied. To evaluate the utility of these Golay hexagonal pattern transformations in detecting the inherent bimodality of the image set, 2-dimensional frequency of occurrence plots were made showing the distribution of measurements in X_1, X_2-space, X_3, X_4-space, X_5, X_6-space, and X_7, X_8-space. These plots are shown in Figure 9. They were made using a logarithmic scale in the X_i-plane while the scale in the z-direction (orthogonal to the X_i-plane) is linear. As can be seen, there is little or no hint of bimodality in the frequency of occurrence plot of initial area and initial perimeter although, upon a close examination of the data points, it can be said that neutrophils showed a significantly lower value of X_1 than did lymphocytes. However, the bimodality of the image set in the area/perimeter plane became more apparent after the first and second cycles of shrinking. The final cycle caused many nuclear images to collapse to the point where area and perimeter were essentially equal and the bimodality became less pronounced.

Besides the evident confirmation of bimodality enhancement by this particular Golay hexagonal transformation as demonstrated in Fig. 9, further confirmation was obtained by the application of several statistical tests. A modified Kolmogorov distance [10] was calculated as given by the equation

$$K' = \sum_{x} |p(L/\Delta x) - p(N/\Delta x)| \quad , \tag{1}$$

where $p(L/\Delta X)$ is the probability that measurements lying in the region ΔX correspond to the lymphocyte group; $p(N/\Delta X)$, the neutrophil group. This modified

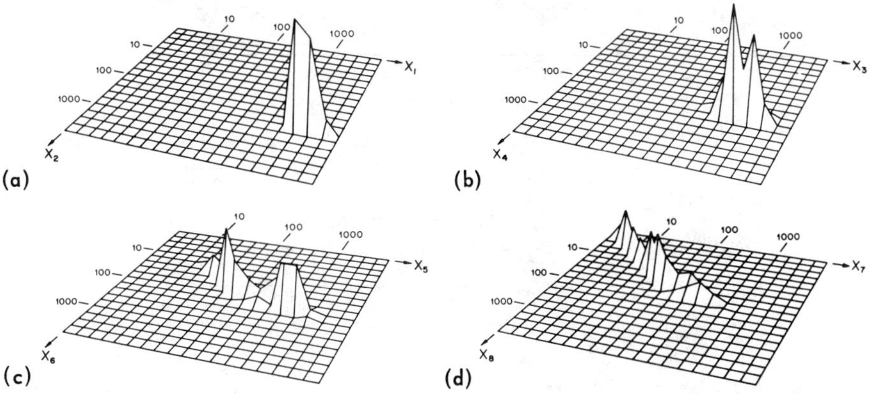

Fig. 9. Frequency of occurrence histograms for four area/perimeter measurement pairs.

Kolmogorov distance has a value of 2.0 then there is a complete separation between groups and a value of 0.0 when there is complete overlap. This distance is useful in that it is computed without any *a priori* assumption of the normality of the group frequency of occurrence distributions about their means.

The Mahalanobis distance was also computed. This distance is given by

$$M = (X_{ML} - X_{MN})' P_{LN}^{-1} (X_{ML} - X_{MN}) \quad , \tag{2}$$

where P_{LN} is the pooled covariance matrix; and X_{ML} and X_{MN} are the lymphocyte and neutrophil means, respectively. The validity of the Mahalonobis distance is not only based on the assumption of normality but also upon the assumption that both group frequency of occurrence distributions have identical covariance. Since these may be weak assumptions, still other commonly used statistical tests were computed for purposes of comparison. A test called the U'-test was calculated which is simply the inverse of the well known Fisher U-statistic and is given by

$$U' = |T|/|P| \quad , \tag{3}$$

where $|T|$ is the determinant of the total covariance matrix and $|P|$ is the determinant of the pooled covariance matrix. Two other tests, called U'' and U''', were also calculated as given by the equations

$$\begin{aligned} U'' &= |T|/(|W_L|^2 + |W_N|^2)^{1/2} \quad , \\ U''' &= |T|/(|W_L|\,|W_N|)^{1/2} \quad , \end{aligned} \tag{4}$$

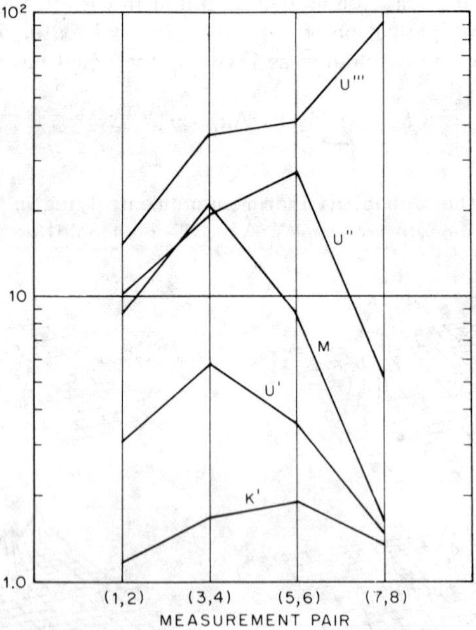

Fig. 10. Values of various statistical separability tests as a function of measurement pair.

where $|W_L|$ is the determinant of the lymphocyte covariance matrix and $|W_N|$ is the determinant of the neutrophil covariance matrix. The U''-test when compared with the U'-test is useful in comparing the effect of the inequality of the group covariance matrices. The U''-test is dominated by the group whose covariance matrix has the largest determinant. Conversely, the U'''-test is dominated by the group whose covariance matrix has the smallest determinant. Its value becomes infinite for a singular determinant.

Figure 10 plots the values of all these statistical tests for the 4 measurement pairs whose frequency of occurrence plots are shown in Figure 9. Disregarding the U'''-test, one would select the (3,4) measurement pair for best discrimination when relying on the Mahalanobis distance or on the Fisher U-statistic, whereas measurement pair (5,6) is preferred if one utilizes either the Kolmogorov distance or the U''-test. For both measurement pairs the neutrophil/lymphocyte separation is excellent for the sample size (316 cells) given and is far better than would be obtained from the initial area/perimeter measurements. This analysis thus validates in a quantitative manner the utility of the relatively simple Golay hexagonal pattern transformation which produces shrinking.

Other GLOL procedures have been devised for somewhat more sophisticated picture processing. Procedures have been designed for the purpose of counting and sizing nuclear inclusions, i.e., regions of relatively high transmission within the nucleus as well as for counting and sizing irregularities or "concavities" in

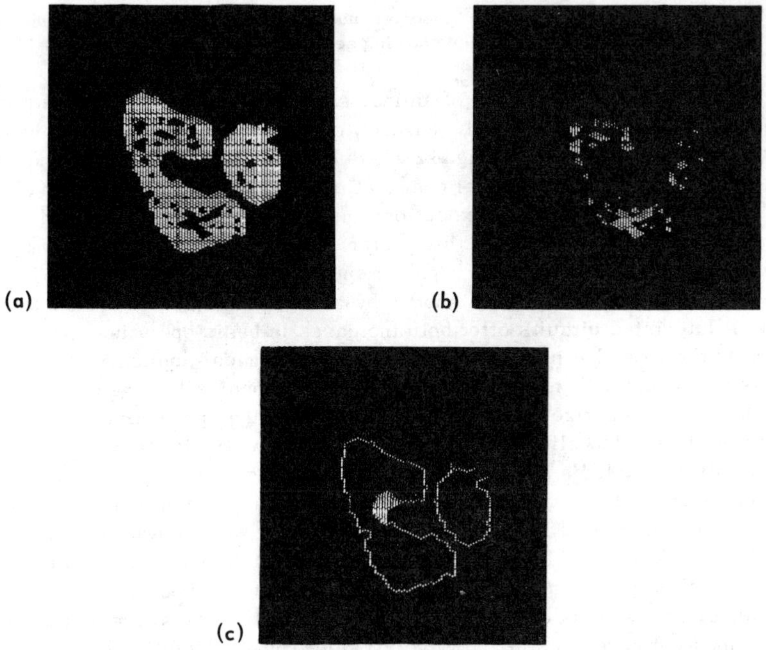

Fig. 11. (a) Binary image of white blood cell nucleus with threshold adjusted so that nuclear inclusions are evident. (b) Binary image of nuclear inclusions. (c) Image showing selection of a major nuclear concavity.

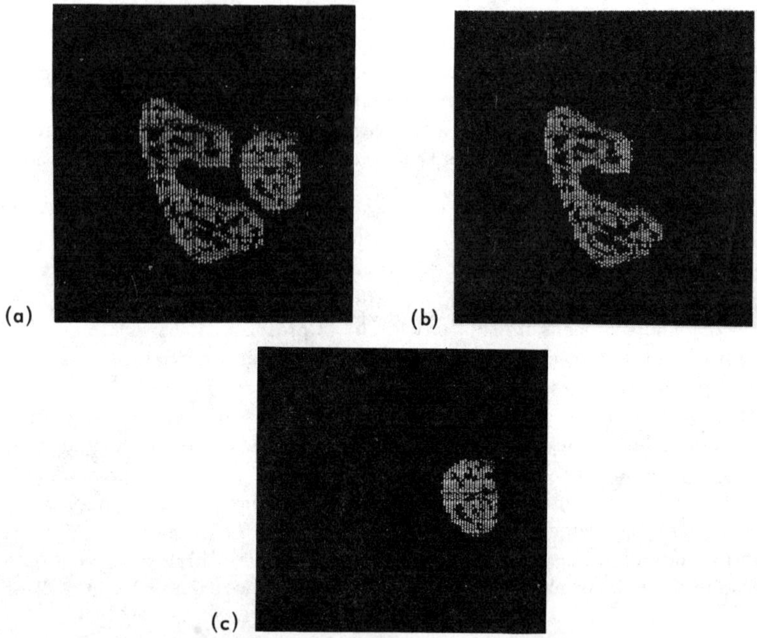

Fig. 12. (a) Binary image of white blood cell nucleus. (b) Image showing selection of left nuclear lobe. (c) Image showing selection of right nuclear lobe.

the nuclear outline. The results of an inclusion selecting and concavity marking procedure are shown in Figure 11. Finally, the result of utilizing the selection or PICK command is shown in Fig. 12 where each nuclear lobe and its inclusions have been extracted for individual examination. Again, due to the power of GLOL and the high speed of GLOPR, execution time is in fractions of a second using the present system. Also, since this system is now 3 or 4 years old, it may be predicted that still further speed improvements with resultant reductions in processing time may be achieved shortly by taking advantage of modern integrated circuits. Integrated circuits offer both increases in basic operating speed as well as further speed improvements due to the economical application of parallel processing. In fact, as regards the processing of blood cell images, it may soon be possible to categorize many thousands of cell images per hour thus outperforming the skilled clinician in carrying out this particular task.

Not only can Golay's hexagonal pattern transforms perform useful functions in the work-a-day world, but they can also provide fascinating enlightenment to those who are interested in cellular automata. As is well known to readers of the Scientific American [11] John Horton Conway has devised a solitaire called "Life" which is played using all the squares of a checkerboard. The rules of play cause the positions of the checkermen constantly to be altered until they are either wiped out or reach static (or cyclic) stability. Conway's rules of play relate to the square tessellation and run as follows:

(1) If an empty space exists whose immediate neighborhood contains 3 checkermen, it is filled with a new checkerman

(2) If a checkerman has in his immediate neighborhood 2 or 3 neighbors, he stays put

(3) If the immediate neighborhood of a checkerman contains less than 2 or more than 3 checkermen, he is removed.

All three rules are applied for each "move" in the solitaire.

The player commences by selecting an initial starting configuration of the checkermen on the board. Many interesting configurations have been obtained. Some die or stabilize in one or two moves; others after more than 1,000 moves. Certain starting configurations have been found which, after many moves, generate groups of "gliders" or "space-ships" each of which is a cyclically stable pattern whose center of gravity moves across the board. Gliders have been found to fly out from the center of the board in a manner somewhat like the exploding universe.

The hexagonal tessellation of GLOPR may also be used for playing a modification of Conway's solitaire. For example a generalized GLOL procedure instrumenting Conway's three rules is given below.

$$B=[G(A)A']N1...,,$$
$$C=[G(A)A]N2...,,$$
$$D=[G'(A)A]N3...,,$$
$$B=B+C$$
$$A=B+D$$

where: the numerics $N1...$ refer to the surrounds of elements which are to be filled; $N2...$, surrounds of elements to be retained; and $N3...$, to surrounds of elements to be removed.

Golay has extensively investigated the algorithm that both filling and retention occur for surrounds 2 and 11. To exercise Golay's algorithm for $N4$ cycles the GLOL procedure is given simply by a single statement, namely

$$A=[G(A)]2/11,N4,$$

Using the above statement the most interesting starting pattern has been found to be the equilateral termino which leads to the cyclically stable pattern shown in Fig. 13 when $N4=321$. The computation time required to reach this point using the GLOPR/Varian system is about 15 sec.

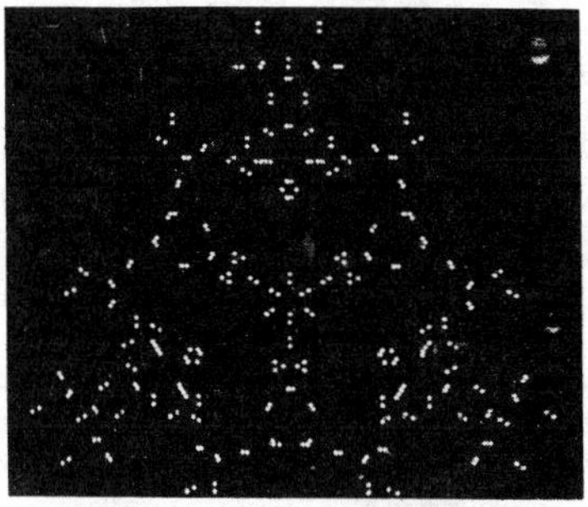

Fig. 13. Binary image of 321st move using equilateral termino as starting pattern and Golay's "GLOPR Life" algorithm.

(a)
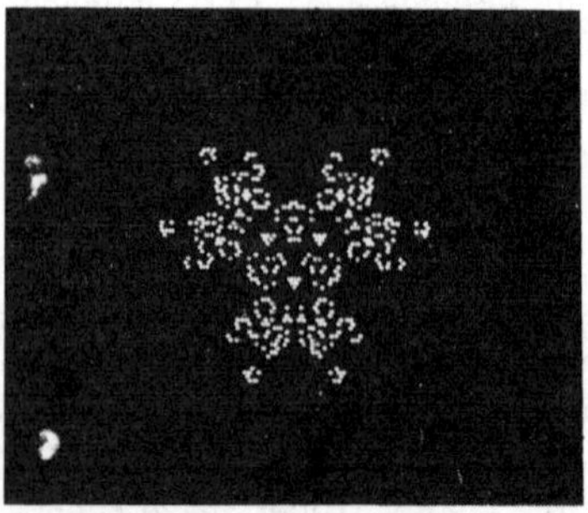
(b)

Fig. 14. (a) Binary images of pattern resulting when Preston's algorithm is applied to filled hexagon having edges alternately 3 and 4 points long after 116th move. (b) After 148th move.

Other procedures have been investigated recently by the author. One of the most interesting is

$$B=[G(A)A']2/11,,$$
$$A=[G(A)A]2/11/12,,$$
$$A=A+B$$

When this procedure is applied to a starting pattern consisting of a filled hexagon whose sides are alternately of length 4 and 3, 6 gliders are generated on the 116th move (Fig. 14(a)), propogate towards the edge of the GLOPR display screen (Fig. 14(b)), and vanish. Six more gliders are generated on move 406 that are immediately "gobbled up." Still six more gliders appear on the 470th move and succeed in escaping as did the original six. After this the growth of the pattern of binary ones exceeds the size of the display screen and exhausts GLOPR's memory capacity.

We find that in using GLOPR for the above investigations major advances in picture processing may be made in a short period of time. In an hour at the keyboard a study may be performed which would have consumed months with our previous equipment. Thus validity of a system architecture which pairs the versatile minicomputer with high speed special purpose firmware is more than justified.

REFERENCES

[1] R. M. Landsman, L. B. Scott, and M. J. E. Golay, "Apparatus for Counting Bi-Nucleate Lymphocytes in Blood," U.S. Patent #3,214,574 (Filed October 1959, Issued October 1965).

[2] S. H. Unger, "A Computer Oriented Toward Spatial Problems," *Proc. IRE*, **46**, 1744 (1958).

[3] K. Preston, Jr., "The CELLSCAN System—A Leukocyte Pattern Analyzer," *Proc. WJCC*, 173 (1961).

[4] N. F. Izzo, and W. Coles, "Blood Cell Scanner Identifies Rare Cells," *Electronics*, **35**, 52 (April 1962).

[5] M. Ingram, P. E. Norgren, and K. Preston, Jr., "Automatic Differentiation of White

Blood Cells," *Image Processing in Biological Science* (University of California Press, 1968).

[6] M. J. E. Golay, "Hexagonal Parallel Pattern Transformations," *IEEE Trans. Comput.*, **C-18**, 733 (1969).

[7] B. H. McCormick, "The Illinois Pattern Recognition Computer—ILLIAC III," *IEEE Trans. Electr. Comput.*, **EC-12**, 791 (1963).

[8] E. S. Deutsch, "On Some Preprocessing Techniques for Character Recognition," *Proc. Symp. Computer Processing in Communications*, 221 (New York: Polytechnic Press, 1969).

[9] S. B. Gray, "Local Properties of Binary Images in Two Dimensions," IEEE Computer Group Repository, Paper R-70-160 (1970).

[10] B. P. Adhikari, and D. D. Joshi, "Distance Discrimination et Resume Exhaustif," *Pubs. Inst. Stat.*, **5**, 57 (1956).

[11] M. Gardner, "Cellular Automata," *Sci. Amer.*, **224**, 122 (February 1971).

IMPLEMENTATION OF A COMPUTING-MEMORY CELL

E. Della Torre and F. K. W. Ho
Department of Electrical Engineering, McMaster University, Ontario, Canada

This paper describes the design of a cell with arithmetic and logic capabilities, which can be used as an element of an array computer. The design is based on a set of minimal parameters regarding the number of words per cell, the cell operations desired, and the type of arithmetic to be used.

INTRODUCTION

Cellular-array computers have been discussed in many papers [1–8]. In this paper, a cell which has array-processing capabilities and is designed to operate as a peripheral device for a minicomputer in such applications as process control is described. These cells are organized in a rectangular array. Each cell is capable, under central control, of arithmetic and logic functions between the various words stored in the cell and its neighbors.

In order to design a practical cell it is first necessary to decide upon the number of words per cell, the amount of local control, the nature of arithmetic and logic functions that can be performed in the cell, and the type of interconnection between cells. In this preliminary investigation of this problem, arbitrary decisions on these questions were made. In the resulting cell design it is now possible to gauge the complexity resulting from each of these decisions. Work currently in progress is directed to the optimization of these parameters using the data presented in this paper.

In the context of a minicomputer, it was felt that each cell should consist of few relatively small words, all arithmetic operations would be carried out in serial fashion, fixed-point arithmetic would be used and control bits stored in the word would inhibit central-processor commands in order to achieve local control.

DESIGN OBJECTIVES

In this paper, rather than discuss the applications of the array processor, the aim is to establish the minimum requirements of a useful and practical cell for an array processor. Each of the cells in this processor should be capable of a certain amount of arithmetic and logic and at least a single cell should be capable of being constructed on an LSI chip. Then they may be mass produced to make

Presented at the Symposium on Computers and Automata
Polytechnic Institute of Brooklyn, April 13–15, 1971.

relatively-large arrays feasible. The cells in the array are to be organized in a rectangular matrix where each cell can communicate with its 4 nearest neighbors, as well as a central buffer. In addition, in this organization each row of cells can communicate with a row of buffer cells external to the array and each column of cells can communicate with a column of buffer cells external to the array as shown in Figure 1. To be compatible with minicomputer word sizes, it was decided that the memory words in the cells would be 16 bits long. The cell design reported here is operating in conjunction with a PDP-8L which is a 12-bit device. However, this will be replaced by a 16-bit computer shortly.

A minimal, practical cell configuration consists of three words per cell. A cell with a larger number of words has the same basic design complexity and in order to minimize the cost of the prototype cell, it was decided to work with the minimal size, although it is evident that eventually a cell would consist of up to 15 or more words. Since this cell will be driven by a PDP-8L I/O cycle which lasts 4.25 μsec, serial arithmetic and logic operations are fast enough and certainly much cheaper.

The cell that was constructed is shown in the block diagram of Figure 2. It consists of a serial-processing unit, a memory bank, select logic which determines data-flow paths, some control logic, access lines to and from neighboring cells and also access lines to the external buffers and to the central buffer.

Data from the 3 memory words is selected by one data selector and channeled to the first-operand input of the processing unit. Data from either the word m_1 or an external source such as the central buffer or the external buffers or a neighboring cell can be selected by the other data selector as the second operand.

Each memory word is divided into 2 parts, 12 data bits, and 4 control bits. Since a control command is executed by all cells in unison, an inhibit structure is necessary to limit the operation to only certain desired cells. Control bit "0" is set by the control unit for this purpose. Control bits 1 and 2 are set

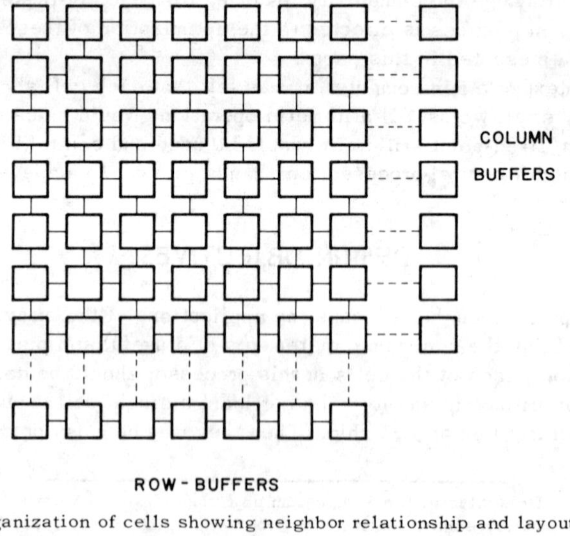

Fig. 1. Organization of cells showing neighbor relationship and layout of buffers.

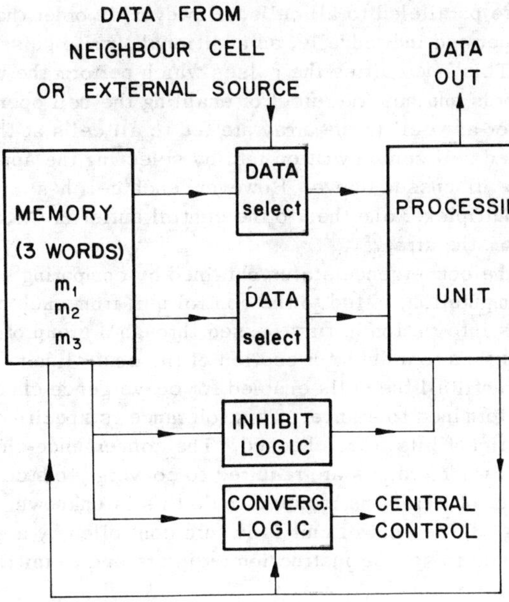

Fig. 2. Block diagram of a cell.

automatically in those cells in which an end-around transfer occurs during a vertical or horizontal transfer of data. Control bit 3 is used to store information on convergence and would be used to recycle an iteration in the array until all selected cells have converged sufficiently in an iteration calculation. The convergence logic is designed to compare stored and computed values of data in order to decide if iteration should be stopped. This comparison can be carried out to various accuracies by comparing a variable number of most-significant bits. For example, if the result of a previous calculation is stored in word m_3 and the processing unit is computing a new value, then the convergence circuit will produce an output when these data differ by more than a preset amount. This comparison is performed at the same time as the processing-unit output is being stored in word three. If any enabled-convergence circuit produces an output, this is detected in the control circuitry and could be used to start another cycle of iteration.

CONTROL UNIT

The control unit consists of two parts: The first part includes the clock and logic circuits which generate the serial-address code for sequentially selecting the individual bits of the memory words so that they may be accessed serially. This part also generates pulse trains to operate the various cell elements; The second part is the instruction register which controls various gates in the cells to determine the path of data flow and hence together with the pulse trains, determines the function to be performed.

Control lines are paralleled to all cells. However, in order that the cells of the array may be operated individually, an additional "write-pulses" line to each cell is provided. This line carries the pulses which perform the writing of data into the memory words and has the effect of enabling the cell operation.

Data destined for any cell in the array are fed to all cells at the same time, but only the selected cell can be written into by selecting the appropriate "write-pulses" line discussed above. However, each cell has an unique line connected to a demultiplexer and then to the central buffer in the control unit for reading data out from the array.

Information on the convergence status obtained by comparing stored m_3 data from the current computation, is fed to the control unit from each cell. In the present design, this information is first passed through a group of OR gates in the control unit and then to a detector section of the control unit which will recycle the iteration until all the cells enabled for convergence check have converged to the predetermined tolerance. This tolerance is specified by setting the number of significant bits to be checked. The convergence-check facility is useful in operations where values are required to converge to a desired tolerance, and the number of iterations required to do this is unknown.

As shown in Fig. 3, the control unit is in turn controlled by a general-purpose computer which serves to set the instruction registers and to initiate execution of array operations.

INSTRUCTION SET

In the present system, the commands which drive the cells are stored in the PDP-8L memory. The command for each cell operation consists of 31 bits of

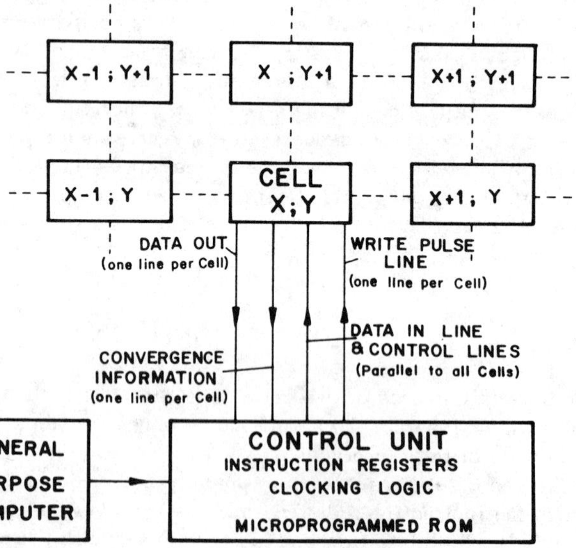

Fig. 3. General organization—communication with arbitrary cell X; Y.

control information which are used to generate appropriate pulse trains and to set the cell-control lines. In order to perform a cell operation, the appropriate command is first transferred to the instruction register in the control unit, then the operation cycle is initiated, both of these operations are performed by a subroutine.

In order to conveniently run the system, a set of subroutines was written and a low-level language was devised whose instructions serve to call the appropriate subroutine and to set operand parameters.

The instruction set used in conjunction with the array consists of a three- or four-letter operation code followed by several operands. These instructions, presented in Table I, were written so that they could be interpreted using PAL3. The operands i; j; k; l; where they appear, may represent a word address (address of a word in a cell), a cell address (address of a cell in the array) or the position of a neighbor cell. The operand "*" either sets the condition under which the operation is performed for arithmetic operations, or sets the variation of the function to be performed for the logical and complement functions, or sets the direction of the operation for the shift and transfer operations.

TABLE I. Instruction set for the array.

INSTRUCTION	FUNCTION
LOAD; i; j; k; ℓ	Loads the number ℓ into word i of cell j; k. If $j = k = 0$, loads ℓ into word i of all cells. If $j = k = \ell = 0$, loads data from allocated PDP-8L memory locations to word i
READ; i; j; k	Reads data from word i of cell j; k. If $j = k = 0$, reads word i of all cells into allocated PDP-8L memory locations
CLEAR; i; j; k	Clears word i of cell j; k. If $j = k = 0$, clears word i of all cells. If $i = 0$, clears all words of all cells
ADD; $*$; i; j; k; ℓ	Addition, $m_i + m_j = m_k$. m_i is obtained from the cell given by ℓ (0 = same cell, N = north, S = south, E = east, W = west, neighbors). Operation is subject to the condition $*$ (where $* =$, I = inhibit, C = convergence check, B = both inhibit and convergence, N = no conditions).
	Note: m_i is restricted to m_1
SUB; $*$; i; j; k; ℓ	As above for subtraction. $m_i - m_j = m_k$
MUL; $*$; i	Multiplication of word m_1 of the array by the external constant i. If $i = 0$, $m_1 \times m_2 = m_3$ is performed subject to condition $*$ (where $* =$, I = inhibit, N = no conditions)
DIV; $*$; i	Division of word m_1 of the array by constant i. Actual operation performed is $m_1 \times 1/i$ subject to condition $*$ (where $* =$, I = inhibit, N = no conditions)
SHF; $*$; i	Shift m_1 data by i bits. Subject to condition $*$ (where $* =$, R = right, L = left)
CMP; $*$; i	Complement word m_i. Subject to condition $*$ (where $* =$, T = two's complement, N = one's complement)
LGC; $*$; i; j; k	Logical operation $m_i * m_j = m_k$ (where $* =$, A = AND, O = OR, E = exclusive OR).
	NOTE: m_i is restricted to m_1 except for OR operation
INC; i; j; k; ℓ	Increment word i of cell j; k, by the value ℓ. If $j = k = 0$, increment all cells
TRN; $*$; i; j	Transfer array data from word i to word j of cell $*$ (where $* =$, N = north, S = south, E = east, W = west, 0 = same cell).

It is intended that a small memory will be included in the control unit in future for storing the microprogrammed instructions.

DESIGN OF THE CELL

The functions that can be performed between words in the cell are listed in Table II. In addition to them, it is also possible to operate on data from a neighboring cell without having first to transfer the data into a word of the cell in question.

The cell schematic is shown in Figure 4. The memories used in this design have the disadvantage of requiring separate pulses for writing logic 1 and logic 0. This means that the gates for "select write" (see Fig. 4) have to be

TABLE II. Cell functions.

ARITHMETIC FUNCTIONS	
$m_1 + m_1$ $m_1 + m_2$ $m_1 + m_3$ $m_1 - m_1$ $m_1 - m_2$ $m_1 - m_3$	Results of these operations can be stored in m_1, m_2, or m_3.
$m_1 \times m_2 = m_3$ $m_1 \times A = m_3$	A is set external to the array, and operates on the whole data plane.
$m_1 \div 2^n$	$n = 0, 1, 2, \cdots, 11$ This operation also operates on the whole data plane.
Shift data 1 bit left Shift data 1 bit right	Operates on m_1 only.
LOGIC FUNCTIONS	
$m_1 \cdot m_2$ $m_1 \cdot m_3$ $m_1 + m_2$ $m_1 + m_3$ $m_1 + m_2 + m_3$ $m_1 \oplus m_2$ $m_1 \oplus m_3$ Complement (m_1, m_2, m_3)	The results can be stored in m_1, m_2, or m_3.
Note: All the above functions can be inhibited in any selection of cells by setting control bits 0, 1, or 2.	
COMPARISON	
$m_3(t-1)$ vs $m_1(t)$ $m_3(t-1)$ vs $m_2(t)$ $m_3(t-1)$ vs $m_3(t)$	This means that current data in m_3 can be compared with results of computations being performed. If data are equal the output of the comparison is "0", if not, a sequence of ones.

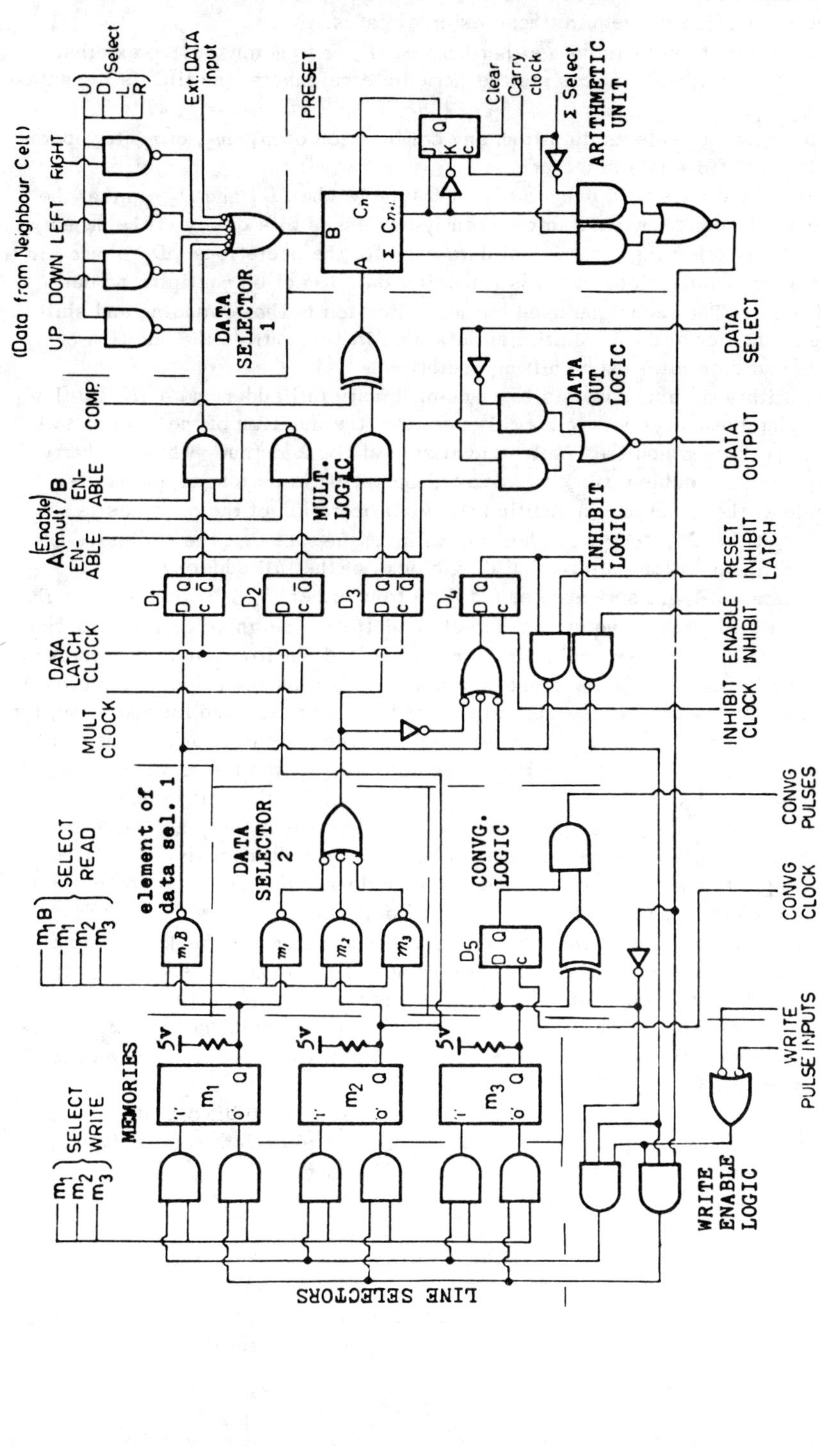

Fig. 4. Cell schematic.

duplicated, three for writing 1s and three for writing 0s. (Note: memories are available which do not require these external gates.)

Data selector$_1$ selects data either from $m_1(B)$ or from any of five external sources; four of these sources are the immediate neighbors, the fifth is the data input.

Data selector$_2$ selects data from any combination of m_1, m_2, or m_3 for operation with data from data selector$_1$.

Selected data are held temporarily in D-type latches D_1 and D_3, so that the resulting data can be written into currently-addressed bits of any of the memory words without affecting the original data used for the operations. D_2 is used in performing multiplication. It holds multiplier data to act on multiplicand data stored in m_1. The technique used for multiplication is that of adding and shifting the multiplicand data. Multiplier data held in D_2 controls the addition of multiplicand data after each shifting operation.

The arithmetic unit consists of a one-bit binary full adder and a JK flip-flop for delaying the carry-out. In normal operation, the addition of the Operands A and B is performed and the result is available at the Σ output. When the carry-out flip-flop is disabled, the exclusive-OR operation is performed and is also available at the Σ output; in addition the AND operation of the operands is available at the C_{n+1} output. This follows from the fact that the exclusive-OR and the AND operations are the building blocks of the full adder.

The data-out logic serves to select data from either D_1 or D_3. Data from D_1 are selected when it is required to direct m_1 data to a neighbor cell for processing. Data from D_3 are selected for normal data read-out from any of the words.

D_4 and its associated logic gates perform the inhibit operation. This circuit is designed to interrogate the control bits of the word, selected for operation, for inhibit information. If a logic 1 is detected in either bits 0, 1, or 2 of the word, the inhibit circuit will disable writing new information into the memory words, and in effect is equivalent to inhibiting an operation for the cell in question.

Two sets of write pulses are presented to the write-enable logic. One set is common to all cells and thus operates on all cells simultaneously. The other set is unique to each cell, being selected by a demultiplexer in the control unit, and thus performs operations in the selected cell only.

D_5 and its associated circuitry performs the convergence-check operation. Data stored in m_3, say from the previous computation, is compared with incoming data from the current computation by the exclusive-OR gate. If these data differ, a pulse is generated which is used to inform the control unit that convergence is not yet attained. D_5 serves to interrogate bit 3 of m_3 to see if a convergence check is required.

In this cell, the cumulative-propagation times limit a 16-bit operation (e.g., addition) to not less than 3 μsec. A twelve-bit multiplication requires twenty four 16-bit operations and takes not less than 72 μsec.

DISCUSSION

The present design was implemented using 17 IC packages per cell, drawing a total of 1.5 W per cell. Four cells are mounted on a single PC board. The overall system consisting of five such boards can be expanded by simply wiring in more such boards. The control unit and interface circuits are contained on two other PC boards.

At this point, it must be emphasized that the cell described in this paper is only a preliminary study for the design of a practical cell for general applications.

The parameters such as the number of words per cell, the arithmetic and logic operations required in a cell, the degree of local control in a cell, and the intercommunication required in an array, originally selected arbitrarily have now resulted in a cell where they may be better understood. It is now possible to gauge how each section of the cell has to be varied if it is required to expand the cell.

If the number of words in a cell is to be increased, this is done by increasing both the memory words and the data selectors accordingly. If floating-point arithmetic is required, a new section will have to be implemented to perform this. The arithmetic unit and the data latches can remain basically the same so long as serial arithmetic is acceptable. The inhibit logic and the convergence logic too can remain practically the same.

The accessibility to the cell for data input and output can be varied to meet specific requirements. However, it is felt that the present arrangement of common-data input and unique-data output is desirable. This characteristic is made possible by allowing the write pulses to be either directable to all cells or to one cell. The system can be extended to allow operations on selected groups of cells for cases where different operations are required for two or more groups of cells in the array.

Although, it was not originally intended, it was found that "content addressability" could be implemented by just adding one more flip-flop per cell. This flip-flop could be located either on each cell or in the control unit.

Say, for example, that the cell is to be addressable by some or all bits in m_3, then the first step to be taken is to load the data for which a match is to be found in the central buffer. Then all cells are commanded to perform a convergence check between m_3 data and data from the control buffer (which is fed to all cells simultaneously). The cells in which these data do not match will generate a pulse (or pulses) which can be detected at the flip-flop. Data can then be read out from those cells in which a match occurred (i.e., in which a "no-match" condition did not occur). Compared to the associative memories discussed in [9, 10] and to those currently available, this cell will be considered extremely slow for this application. However, content addressability is only a secondary characteristic of this cell and could still prove relatively fast where large arrays are involved.

CONCLUSION

It is felt that, in order to solve a practical problem, a somewhat-larger number of words per cell is required so that trigonometric functions and floating-point arithmetic, which would require additional circuitry, can be performed in the cell.

For applications as a peripheral device to a minicomputer, it is felt that the cells of the array should be rather simple, contrasted to the cells of the ILLIAC IV [3] for example, where each cell has 2048 words. If the cost of this cell is reasonable, a fairly-large array would then be feasible. The cell described is supposed to be for general applications, but an optimum structure will be determined by the specific application.

ACKNOWLEDGEMENTS

The authors wish to acknowledge Dr. R. Kitai and D. Lawrence for making available their work [11]. The authors wish to thank J. Majithia, K. Siemens, J. Roitman, and J. Wolkowsky for helpful discussions.

This work was supported by the National Research Council of Canada. It is based on a M. Eng. Thesis submitted by F. Ho to the Department of Electrical Engineering, McMaster University.

REFERENCES

[1] D. L. Slotnick, W. C. Brock, and R. C. McReynolds, "The Solomon Computer," *Proc. AFIPS Fall Joint Computer Conf.*, 97–107 (1962).

[2] W. Y. Dere and D. J. Sakrison, "Berkeley Array Processor," *IEEE Trans. Comput.*, C-19, 444–447 (May 1970).

[3] G. H. Barnes et al., "The ILLIAC IV Computer," *IEEE Trans. Comput.*, C-17, 746–757 (August 1968).

[4] K. J. Thurber and J. W. Myrna, "System Design of A Cellular APL Computer," *IEEE Trans. Comput.*, C-19, 291–303 (April 1970).

[5] S. H. Unger, "A Computer Oriented Towards Spatial Problems," *Proc. IRE*, 46, 1744–1750 (October 1958).

[6] B. A. Cranes and J. A. Githens, "Bulk Processing in Distributed-Logic Memory," *IEEE Trans. Electr. Comput.*, EC-14, 186–196 (April 1965).

[7] W. H. Kautz, "Cellular Logic in Memory Arrays," *IEEE Trans. Comput.*, C-18, 719–727 (August 1969).

[8] N. R. Scott, *Electronic Computer Technology* (New York: McGraw-Hill, 1970).

[9] C. Y. Lee and M. C. Paull, "A Content-Addressible Distributed-Logic Memory with Applications to Information Retrieval," *Proc. IEEE*, 51, 924–932 (June 1963).

[10] C. C. Yang and S. S. Yau, "A Cutpoint Cellular-Associative Memory," *IEEE Trans. Electron. Comput.*, EC-15, 522–529 (August 1966).

[11] D. A. Lawrence, "A Computing Memory: Design and Applications With Special Reference to Correlation," M. Eng. Thesis, McMaster University (1970).

[12] F. K. W. Ho, "Implementation of a Cellular Computing-Memory Array," M. Eng. Thesis, McMaster University (1971).

A COMPUTER MODELED AFTER AN AUTOMATON

Mario R. Schaffner
Smithsonian Astrophysical Observatory, Cambridge, MA
and
Massachusetts Institute of Technology, Cambridge, MA

Among the several results of automata theory, it appears that the McCullock-Pitts correspondence between logical descriptions and logical networks could be more fully exploited. This paper describes an experiment in that direction.

An automaton composed of a programmable black box and a memory capable of storing pages of data is outlined. In this automaton, several Finite-State Machines (FSM) can perform their processing while they share the same black box in time sequence. Each FSM has all the pertinent data, along with the related program for the black box, in a page; when a page enters the black box, the specialized configuration demanded is implemented and a cycle is executed for that FSM; as a result, new data and the next state are produced and stored in the page, ready for a next cycle. Features are provided for which the several FSMs may perform independent jobs or different parts of a complex job. The relation between this automaton and a Turing machine is discussed. It is shown that such an automaton possesses capabilities and flexibilities similar to those of conventional general-purpose computers, but with higher efficiency.

With this automaton as a model, an actual computer has been constructed and used for the processing of radar signals in real time and for a variety of different computations. The most interesting characteristic of the system is that the program in machine language consists of the description of the process modeled as an abstract FSM. Assuming the FSM model forms a convenient user language, no compiler is needed. Other significant characteristics are also described. The organization in autonomous pages provides a natural capability for time sharing. The close correspondence between machine language and process model, and the functional complexity of each cycle make real-time processing practical. The memory capacity required is reduced as a result of the large reduction in internal addresses and the conciseness of the programs. As the computer structure adapts itself to each problem, overhead is extremely small. Program debugging and execution check are facilitated by the one-to-one correspondence between machine steps and elements of the process model.

I. INTRODUCTION

The power of a computer increases with the speed of the operating elements and the available memory capacity. For this reason, in recent decades digital circuits of increased speed, as well as very large memories, have been developed.

With a given speed of the logical elements and a given memory capacity, the

---

Presented at the Symposium on Computers and Automata
Polytechnic Institute of Brooklyn, April 13–15, 1971.

power of a computer varies further in accordance with the way the problems are modeled, and thus the way they are executed by the computer. In turn, the way a problem can be modeled in order to be executed by a computer depends on the characteristics of the computer, which are a consequence of the techniques available. The first computers were made with electromagnetic relays and then with electronic tubes, thus it was mandatory to minimize the hardware. The consequent modeling was to express the problems in the form of a long sequence of elementary steps. The introduction of automatic translation of the problems expressed in high-level languages into programs in machine language has relieved the user from the burden of those long sequences, and the original approach used in computers was consolidated.

The development of high speed and large memories produced also higher reliability, a drastically higher function density and made the cost of logical components negligible. In this new environment different characteristics are possible to computers, therefore it is now sensible to explore possible advantages of different modeling of the problems to be given to a computer.

This paper presents an experiment in this direction. The problems are not described in terms of the steps available to a given computer but are modeled as an abstract machine of a form suitable for the user. Then the computer is structured to approach closely that abstract machine.

II. THE McCULLOCH-PITTS CORRESPONDENCE

In 1943, McCulloch and Pitts [1] published a set of theorems demonstrating the correspondence, valid under broad conditions, between a logical description of a process and a network of logical neurons (axiomatic models of the biological neurons). This correspondence was fundamental in neurophysiology because it gave a possible model of the nervous systems—even that of the highest complexity, the human brain. The correspondence could not be of any practical importance in the field of computers, which were at that time just emerging as automatic calculating machines.

In 1948, von Neumann [2], in comparing the different processing complexity achievable by computing machines and by living organisms (in particular, by the human central nervous system), was pointing out three causes of that difference:

(1) The size of the components. This difference was caused essentially by the ratio between the interelectrode space depth (~ 1 mm) of the vacuum tubes and the membrane thickness ($\sim 1\ \mu$) of the neurons
(2) The reliability of the components. This difference was dramatically expressed by comparing the irreversible tendency of the artificial components to break down with the natural tendency of the living organisms to restore themselves when injured
(3) The lack of a logical theory of automata. Von Neumann pointed out three needs: theories for minimizing the effect of errors; theories for self-reproduction; and exploitation of the McCulloch-Pitts correspondence between logical descriptions and logical networks.

All these differences caused the Eniac (the largest computer of that time) to weigh 30 tons and to dissipate 150 kW, while the human central nervous system, functionally several orders of magnitude larger, weighs about 1 lb and is supplied by a small fraction of the body metabolism.

Today's technology produces logical elements where the control space depth is of the order of microns, and need a power in the region of microwatts. These elements exhibit a typical reliability several orders of magnitude larger than that of the electromagnetic relays of von Neumann's time.

As a consequence, the importance of points (1) and (2) has decreased drastically. Point (3) appears now to be of first importance. Theories for minimizing the effect of errors have been developed to the extent that is needed. Properties of self-reproduction are being explored theoretically in cellular automata. The McCulloch-Pitts correspondence, on the other hand, has not received much attention. Its potential importance has probably been best presented by von Neumann [2].

> The McCulloch-Pitts result ... proves that anything that can be exhaustively and unambiguously described, anything that can be completely and unambiguously put into words, is ipso-facto realizable by a suitable, finite neural network. Since the converse statement is obvious, we can therefore say that there is no difference between the possibility of describing a real or imagined mode of behavior completely and unambiguously in words, and the possibility of realizing it by a finite, formal neural network. The two concepts are coextensive. A difficulty of principle embodying any mode of behavior in such a network can exist only if we are also unable to describe that behavior completely.

Furthermore, von Neumann argued that for very-complex processes, it is quite possible that the description of a logical network might be simpler than a logical description of the process itself. As an example, he refers to the general concept of analogy that dominates our interpretation of vision; a verbal description of the visual analogy may lead to an extremely large number of volumes (if even possible), while it is known that a finite number of connections in the visual brain does the job. The implications for computers are obvious.

There is no question but that a specifically designed logical network (a special-purpose computer, in engineering terms) can be particularly efficient in performing a given job. But such an approach would require a new machine for each new job. Therefore, it would be of particular interest to have a machine in which different networks, in response to different jobs, could be implemented at the will of the user.

Analog computers are of this type, but they have three main limitations:

(1) Specific analog devices that simulate some analytical functions are the operational components of analog computers. Therefore, the user has to model the problems in terms of these functions, rather than in terms of arbitrary functions appropriate for each problem

(2) High precision in analog devices is increasingly difficult to achieve

(3) Analog computers have to be set up, with more-or-less cumbersome techniques, before each problem. Even hybrid computers present a large overhead for setting up the analog parts.

In the machine presented in this paper, specific logical networks as required in each cycle of each problem are implemented automatically by the program. In other words, the programs are made up of logical networks rather than of logical statements. From the McCulloch-Pitts correspondence, we know that this approach has the same generality as the conventional approach. In accordance with von Neumann's observation, we can expect, at least for complex processes, that programs might be simpler.

III. THE FINITE-STATE MACHINE MODEL

As discussed in the previous section, the McCulloch-Pitts correspondence suggests that the programs for a computing machine could be made in the form of a description of a logical network rather than as a logical description of the process. But if for each problem we had to design a special logical machine to perform our process efficiently, we would need a team of engineers to program such a hypothetical computer. Such a need would nullify any advantage that the network approach might offer. Clearly, the network approach can be of practical interest only if an easy, standard procedure can be found for designing these networks. This paper shows that the use of a finite-state machine model for describing the processes to be performed makes feasible the network approach.

Finite-state machine models were initially introduced for the analysis of unknown devices [3] and for the synthesis of sequential circuits [4]. Today, they are widely used in mathematics [5], logical design [6], and neurological research [7]. Such a variety of applications already promises general applicability of the model. The attractive features of a finite-state machine model can be listed as follows:

(1) It constitutes a general and standard procedure for modeling a process. The model is so abstract that it can be considered as an essential representation of the process with a minimum influence by actual machines or specialized languages

(2) The model is indeed simple. In each phase of a process, the mechanism is always the same: new values for the variables are obtained as a given function of the present values of the variables and of the state; the next state is obtained as another given function of the same variables

(3) It provides a way of automatic memorization. A great deal of memorization of past events can be obtained, without any further effort, during the construction of the model in terms of states and transitions between them. When this way is adopted, the user has the impression that the finite-state machine carries only the information that is relevant for the future and automatically drops all other information. At each moment of a process, all the past history that is relevant for the process is automatically summarized and memorized by the present state. If the process at a certain moment is in one state, it is because of the occurrence of certain events in the past. If the history had been different, the process would probably have been in a different state.

The finite-state machine model appears in the literature typically for modeling simple processes where the characterizing functions can be expressed in tabular form. But the notion of a finite-state machine is not limited to these cases. A finite-state machine can be formulated with any type of function, provided that the output values belong to the alphabet of the machine. Allowing the characterizing functions to be of the form appropriate for each process, we obtain a user-suitable general procedure for modeling processes. In the use of a finite-state machine as a general model for processes, it is convenient to introduce the two following formal features:

(1) The definition of the states and their number are key points in making a finite-state machine a suitable model for the user. For this reason, considerable use will be made of the interchangeability shown by Shannon [8] between symbols and states of a machine. In each process to be modeled, the most appropriate choice will be made of what is to be represented as a state and what is to be represented as a numerical variable

(2) Given the variety of functions appearing in practical processes (as opposed to the sole tabular functions in the usual applications of the finite-state machines), it would be difficult to express the different operations to be performed, in the different states, by means of a unique pair of characterizing functions. Therefore, the characterizing functions will be broken into simpler pairs unique for each state.

In our formulation, a finite-state machine is composed of a black box (Fig. 1) containing a finite set of internal variables $[y] = \mathbf{y}$, a finite number of input lines connected to a finite set of input variables $[x] = \mathbf{x}$ available in the environment, and a finite number of output lines bringing a subset $[y]'$ of $[y]$ to the environment. The time is defined in discrete intervals i (Fig. 2) in each of which the black box assumes one of a finite number of internal configurations, called states and indicated with the symbol s. A state s_j (a configuration of the black box) is

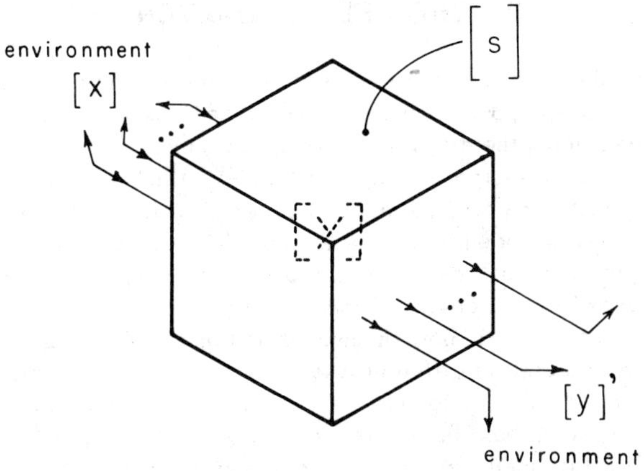

Fig. 1. A visualisation of a finite-state machine.

defined by two functions, F_j and T_j, characterizing the performance of the state throughout the following expressions

$$\begin{aligned} \mathbf{y}(i+1) &= F_j[\mathbf{x}(i), \mathbf{y}(i)] \quad , \qquad (a) \\ s(i+1) &= T_j[\mathbf{x}(i), \mathbf{y}(i+1)] \quad . \qquad (b) \end{aligned} \qquad (1)$$

The black box produces, in each time interval i, a new value $\mathbf{y}(i+1)$ of the vector $\mathbf{y}$ as a function of the present values of $\mathbf{x}$ and $\mathbf{y}$ in accordance with Eq. (1a) of the present state, and produces the next state $s(i+1)$ as a function of $\mathbf{x}$ and of the new values of $\mathbf{y}$ in accordance with Eq. (1b) of the present state. The next state assigns the function that will be performed by the black box in the next time interval. The vector $\mathbf{y}$ is supposed at zero at the beginning of each process. The McCulloch-Pitts correspondence ensures the equivalence between the functions of Eq. (1) and the states (internal configurations) of the black box.

In this formulation, a finite-state machine with n states is described by n doublets $[F, T]$. The characterizing functions are broken in n pairs of functions describing each state; therefore, the state does not appear as argument in the functions. These functions are also defining the internal variables $[y]$.

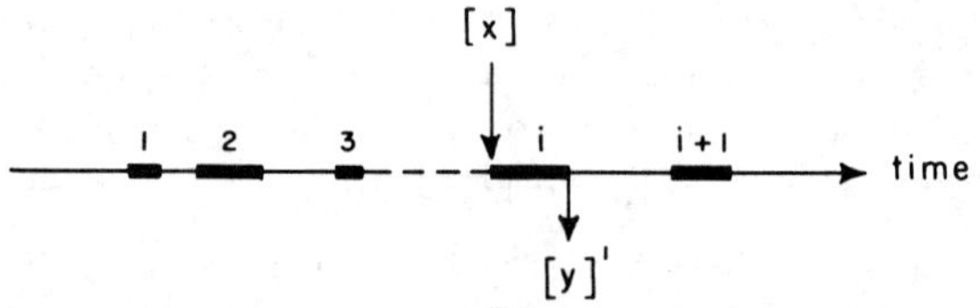

Fig. 2. Discreteness of time in a finite-state machine.

The time intervals of Fig. 2 will be called the cycles of the machine. The letters FSM will be used in the sequel to indicate a finite-state machine formulated in this form.

IV. THE CPL AUTOMATON

The FSM formulated in the previous section is a machine performing a specific task—a special-purpose computer. We are seeking a machine that can organize itself to perform all the different tasks we demand.

Conventional general-purpose computers achieve this capability by means of programs that describe the desired process in terms of logic statements. For the McCulloch-Pitts correspondence, the same capability can be achieved with a machine that accepts programs describing a process in terms of logic networks. The FSM just described can easily become such a machine.

The black box of Fig. 1 is now thought of as composed of logical elements that can be interconnected in different ways to form special networks that perform the functions F and T of Equation (1). We imply a language that allows the user to prescribe to the black box the desired networks. In this case, the black box will not have a well-defined structure that can switch to any of n given states. But it will be a loose ensemble of logical elements that becomes a specific FSM when a program consisting of the description of n specific states, doublets $[F, T]$, arrives from the environment through the input lines.

Now we can see the advantage of the use of the McCulloch-Pitts correspondence with the FSM modeling. Any nontrivial process will be modeled in a number of states; therefore, the user is not required to design a special logical machine to perform his process—he has to design logical networks to perform the functions F and T into which his process is broken down. These networks are much simpler than a single one representing the entire process. A complete machine, on the other hand, results from the work of modeling the process in the FSM form. As the FSM is an abstract machine, the user does not do the work of an engineer, but simply describes the process in abstract form.

The logical networks performing the functions F and T also do not require engineering knowledge. The McCulloch-Pitts correspondence is not limited to biological neurons or to digital circuits but is deeply imbedded in the notion of function. McCulloch and Pitts proved the correspondence for particular axiomatic logical elements called neurons; but all the functions that we use in describing practical processes can be obtained with networks made up of those neurons; these networks in turn can be considered as new logic elements of higher level. Therefore, we can think of logical networks as made up of these new logical elements, and yet the correspondence between logical statements and logical networks still obtains. For each function F and T conceived in modeling a process, we can envision an abstract structure we think of as the function made up of these logical elements. In this way, we produce a description of the functions F and T valid for our FSM, without concern for any sort of mechanical or electrical technique.

Now there is the question of finiteness. A process may require more variables than are initially implied in the black box. A function may need more logical elements than are supposed available. In these cases, the process model could be broken down into more states, each needing no more variables and logical elements than are available. But the number of states may exceed the capacity implied for the program in the black box. There is also another affair: Complex processes are advantageously modeled in the form of many FSMs, all contributing to the accomplishment of the task. To solve these different problems, an automaton is here introduced, composed of a programable black box as described, and a memory (Fig. 3) with some of the input and output lines of the black box connected to the output and input lines, respectively, of the memory. The automaton has a control that, at the end of each cycle of the black box, removes all the data inside the box and stores them in the memory in the form of a page. A page here is the ensemble of data referring to a state of a process modeled as an FSM. Every time the black box is empty, the same control transfers a page from the memory into the box in such a way that all the data of the page take the same locations they had when previously removed from the box.

The characteristics of the memory are as follows:

(1) At a command from the control, the memory acquires in parallel a page through its input lines

(2) At a command from the control, the memory delivers a page in parallel through its output lines

(3) The pages are produced at the output lines in the same order in which they were acquired at the input lines.

Because the pages move as in a queue line, this type of memory will hereafter be called a Q memory. The defining characteristics of the Q memory do not imply any specific storage structure. One can think of a loose storage medium where pages are packed and are waiting to come out. The pages are supposed to have a loose organization by which they assume the configuration of the information they hold and preserve the data allocation in the black box.

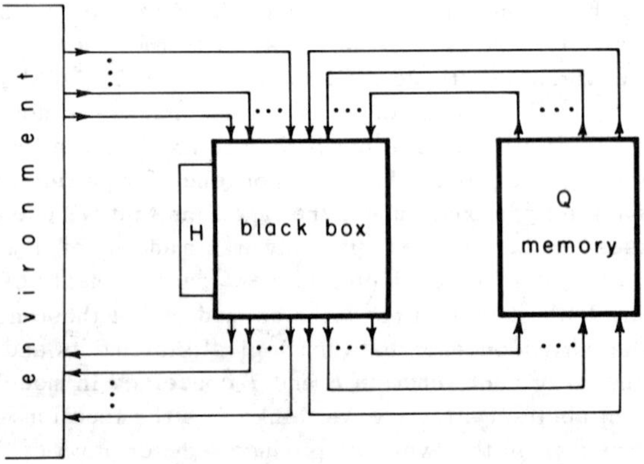

Fig. 3. The CPL automaton.

In this automaton, a plurality of FSMs can perform their processes sharing the same black box, with the related data stored in a page circulating in the loop formed by the black box and the Q memory. Figure 4 gives an example of how the cycles of different FSMs may succeed each other in the black box. Because we are dealing with a theoretical machine, there is no limitation of generality in supposing that the environment is giving and taking the proper data, at the right times, to and from the several FSMs, through some of the input and output lines of the black box. An auxiliary storage H, capable of holding a page, is available to the black box in order to allow transfer of data between different pages, i.e., different FSMs.

Now, if an FSM requires more variables, more logical elements, or larger programs than are possible in the black box, that FSM can be decomposed into several sub-FSMs that interact through the storage H. If the number and complexity of sub-FSMs exceed the capacity of the Q memory, we invoke auxiliary page storages in the environment, and the process can be executed by the automaton in in teraction with those outside auxiliary storages.

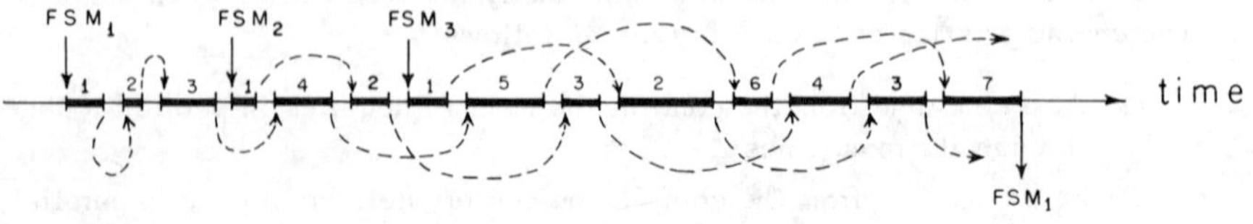

Fig. 4. Several FSMs in time sharing.

Since the peculiar features of the automaton are its organization into autonomous pages, their automatic circulation, and the loose structure of the black box, it will be called hereafter the Circulating-Page Loose (CPL) automaton.

In the CPL automaton, processing can be programed in several directions:

(1) Designing logical arrays inside the black box
(2) Designing sequential networks inside the black box
(3) Organizing arrays of pages in the circulation
(4) Describing a sequential pattern for each circulating page.

For each type of process, the modeling, i.e., the programing, will develop according to an appropriate mix of these directions. Depending on the configuration prescribed in the black box, some pages can play the role of segments of a program, segments of sequentially ordered data, or segments of addressable data. As the description of the FSM is in the page, some functions of the FSM may change or may complete the description itself, in accordance with the course of the process or of the data from outside. This feature of course does not change the finiteness of the machine but allows simplification in the modeling of certain processes. As an example, a portion of an FSM can serve several parts of the process, if that portion can be modified, adapted, or updated. An FSM, with proper configurations of the black box, can develop itself further, or it can generate other FSMs inside the automaton. Clearly, this automaton exhibits the flexibilities and the features known in general-purpose computers.

If the environment is used to simulate an extension of the Q memory when needed, the automaton is equivalent to a Turing machine. The page may be viewed as a unique symbol belonging to an extremely large alphabet or as a cell of a multidimensional tape. The tape has a circular form and can have additional cells every time new storage is required [9]. The state descriptions that are the doublets $[F, T]$ play a role equivalent to that of the quintuplets $[X_i S_i X_j S_j M]$ (symbol read on the tape, present state, symbol written on the tape, next state, movement of the head) that describe a Turing machine.

On the other hand, we can see a different approach in the simulation. The simulation of a specific Turing machine producing a desired function is obtained by means of a string of symbols that teach a universal Turing machine all the steps it has to do to simulate the same operations as the specific Turing machine. In a CPL automaton, the simulation of a specific machine is done by means of a string of symbols (representing items F and T) that, rather than indicating the steps for the simulation, teach the black box to assume the structures of the FSM that produces the desired function. This fact ensures efficiency of the automaton.

V. THE CPL SYSTEM

Given the interesting characteristics of the automaton described in the previous section, let us examine how closely it can be approached by real machines. A realizable system developed according to the principles of the CPL automaton is outlined here.

In the real world, it is not sensible to expect that the environment is at our

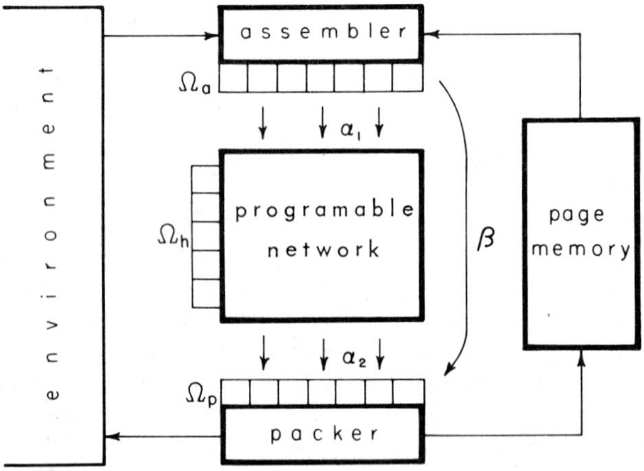

Fig. 5. The CPL system.

beck and call. In fact, it will be composed of peripheral devices, usually with low speed, with their own timing, and without any knowledge of what is going on inside the black box. Therefore, buffers and means for selecting and controlling the peripherals will be necessary. Accordingly, let us introduce two auxiliary units: An "assembler" between the output of the memory and the input of the black box, which we will now call the programable unit (NP) and a "packer" between the output of the NP and the memory (Figure 5). At the same time, let us introduce two new items in the state descriptions: a prescription I of the new input data $[x]$ for that state, and the routing R of some internal variables $[y]'$ to some outside output devices. Now the states of an FSM will be described by quadruplets $[I, F, T, R]$.

Every time the assembler receives a page from the memory, it calls for specific new input data $[x]$ from the environment, responsive to the information in I of the present state. It assembles the page into an array of registers Ω_a, called the page array, in a form suitable for execution of the functions of the present state. At the proper time, the page is transferred into the programable network. Note that if the outside storages are not yet ready to give the new data, the page can follow path β, leaving the operating unit available to other pages; at some future circulation, that page will acquire the new data and follow path α.

When the packer receives a page into its page array Ω_p from the programable network, it calls for outside peripherals into which some data are transferred, responsive to information in R of the present state. If a peripheral is not yet available, the data can be kept in the page and transferred during some future circulation. Note that R can be used not only for prescribing transfers to the environment, but also for prescribing movement of data in the page without the involvement of the operating unit.

For each FSM, there will be an initial state in which the page will circulate through path β in order to acquire all the data necessary to start the processing, and an output state in which the page again will circulate through path β in order to deliver all the results to the environment. When the FSM description exceeds the storage capacity of the page, that description can be stored outside and the assembler calls for only the portion of program that is relevant to the present state. The assembler, programable network, and packer perform their functions simultaneously, and page buffers allow the different durations that their operations might have to be matched. It is apparent that the structure outlined in Fig. 5 has a pipeline architecture and provides the functions that are performed by peripheral processors in conventional computers.

The programable network has h registers for holding the values y and x and k functional elements interconnectable with those registers. The possible operating configurations (not all of practical interest) are an exponential function of h and k. For prescribing specific configurations, several methods can be analyzed:

(1) Assigning an independent bit for each controllable trait (a controllable connection, function, operational characteristic) of the programable network. This method is not practical because of the large number of bits that would result and the complicated work to prescribe them correctly

(2) Listing all the interesting configurations and assigning them a code. Correspondingly, decoders are wired in the programable network for controlling the necessary traits. This method also is not practical because the user would have to look in a dictionary of thousands of specialized operating configurations

(3) Coding functions and connections with an inflected language at the level in which the user conceives operating the abstract machines [10]. This method has proved to be practical.

The page organization is the key point to reduce to a minimum the overhead of the machine. There is obviously also an interest in minimizing the size of the pages. The solution developed over the centuries for storing information on a printed page is adopted here. Given an alphabet, a sequence of words articulated by auxiliary symbols (such as space, comma, period, etc.) is packed into a storage medium (paper for the printed pages or, in this case, storage-cell arrays or channels for waves). The content of the words, their relative positions, and the sequence of the auxiliary symbols are all relevant to the information carried by the page.

To minimize redundancy in the FSM description, hierarchical distribution of the prescriptions is used. An initial code word carries all the information that remains unchanged in the entire FSM. Successive code words hold the information that is common to all the prescriptions in each state. Each configuration description is coded in a word in which the interpretation of each group of digits is dependent on the content of the previous group of digits.

Several means of implementation are possible for the Q memory. Given the presence of the assembler and packer, the function of control, buffering and serial parallel conversion can be assigned to these units, and the memory is reduced to a First-Input/First-Output (FIFO) storage. A FIFO memory can be implemented with static or dynamic techniques.

The system outlined in Fig. 5 maintains the philosophy of the CPL automaton and is suitable for practical implementation with today's digital techniques. Accordingly, it has been named the Circulating Page Loose (CPL) system.

VI. A FIRST IMPLEMENTATION

An actual machine following the principles of the CPL system has been designed and constructed. This work originated in 1964 from the necessity of processing in real-time radar signals at the Radio Meteor Project of the Harvard College Observatory. Several fixed-program processors were designed and installed. Subsequently a programable system was developed [10] and installed at the Meteor Radar Station of the Smithsonian Astrophysical Observatory. Since then, the system has been used for processing weather radar signals at the Massachusetts Institute of Technology [11, 12]. A new version of the system is at present under construction at M.I.T.

In the first machine, called CPL 1, the operating unit has 4 registers for the [x], 4 registers for the [y], a set of registers for the configuration descriptions, 1 storage page array, and 117 controllable traits for the configurations. The circulating pages do not carry the FSM description but have a key word containing the present-state label and other auxiliary information; when a page arrives into the assembler, the description of the present state is acquired from outside storage in response to the key word. A state description is composed of a code word of 12 bits, an input prescription I up to 16 bits, a function F prescription up to 36 bits, a function T prescription up to 16 bits, and a routing R of 4 bits. These bits, representing I, F, T, and R, are interpreted in different ways according to the content of the 12-bit code word.

A supervisor program schedules different FSMs in time and in sequences of pages, performing independent or concurrent jobs. Possible inputs are analog signals, digital signals, and numbers set on dials. Output peripherals are a magnetic tape recorder, a fast printer, and oscilloscopes for analog signals.

VII. THE PROGRAMING

There are two basic steps in programing a CPL System:

(1) Modeling the process in the form of an FSM. The essential features of the process should be well defined, then an abstract machine should be invented to produce them. The best results are obtained when the user ignores any connection with real machines. The FSM model per se is so abstract that it pushes the user inevitably to discover the really essential features of the process. The ingenuity of a program, its effectiveness and efficiency, are established at this point by the way the problem is modeled. In conventional computers, strategies may be used to exploit to the full the structure of a particular computer or of a particular compiler language. In this case, the user is forced to investigate these structures, even though he is not interested in them. In programing the CPL system, strategy has to be used in describing the problem, that is to say, the structure of the problem itself. Therefore, we may expect the user to be interested in expending effort in this direction. Furthermore, he will not later feel himself to be a slave to the computer because, in preparing the model of his process, unconsciously he designed the computer he is going to use.

During the modeling, a continuous choice is made among the different possible definitions of states and variables y's. In each case, different criteria may

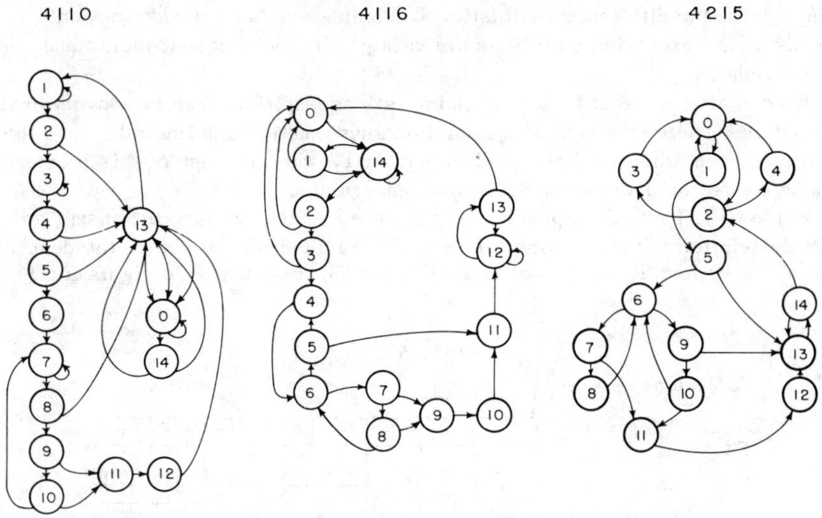

Fig. 6. State diagrams of actual programs.

guide these choices. The end product of this step is a state diagram. Figure 6 gives some examples of structure. Several features can be used for helping the conciseness of the state diagram, such as tagged states and stopover transitions. As an example, the transition between state 12 and state 0 in Program 4110 of Fig. 6 stops over state 13.

(2) Description of the configurations. The model obtained in Step (1) consists of a number of states, each of which contains functions F and T. Now these functions should be expressed as abstract networks that are possible for the machine at hand. In this step, the requirements of the problem and the characteristics of the machine have to be considered simultaneously. As previously stated, these networks are purely symbolic and are prescribed with a language whose elements are those we normally use for describing our functions. Sometimes it may be necessary to introduce into the model new states to break down the functions into simpler parts. States can be added to or borrowed from other FSMs, and no problems of addresses or compatibility arise, since a state is an independent quadruplet $[I, F, T, R]$.

There will then be a third clerical step of writing in a proper medium, with the machine codes, all the items describing the FSM, in the proper coded sequence.

It is interesting to note that in making a machine program for conventional computers, a programmer or a compiler starts from a set of machine instructions and builds up a quite cumbersome description of the process. In making a machine program for CPL systems, he starts from a concise description of the process and builds up machine configurations to match that concise description. If the process is of a type that can be modeled efficiently as a machine with the structure of a conventional computer, its conventional program and its program in FSM form will be comparable. Otherwise, the FSM program is more concise. In many cases, the difference is drastic. Designing special networks not only speeds up the execution but eliminates a large number of dependencies and computer overhead.

We can also say that here programing is less empirical than in conventional computers. There is a kind of standard and systematic guideline related to the problem. From what has been said in Section IV, the language of this programing can be viewed as user oriented and problem oriented.

In the CPL 1 machine, punch cards are used as the medium to transmit an FSM description to the machine. The card is divided into fields for the description of the various items of the states (Figure 7). Because a configuration F

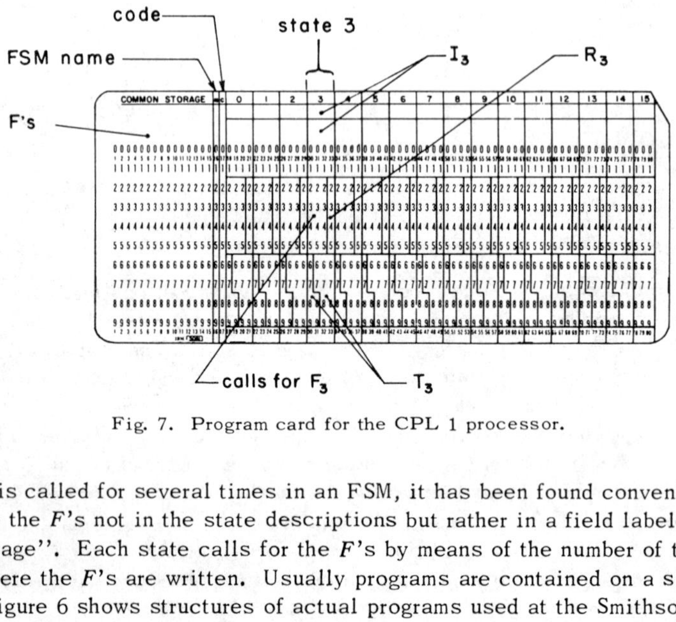

Fig. 7. Program card for the CPL 1 processor.

usually is called for several times in an FSM, it has been found convenient to describe the F's not in the state descriptions but rather in a field labeled "common storage". Each state calls for the F's by means of the number of the columns where the F's are written. Usually programs are contained on a single card. Figure 6 shows structures of actual programs used at the Smithsonian Meteor Radar Station for recording meteor echoes of intensity below the noise in the form of three dimensional matrices (integrated echo intensity, echo duration, and range). Each of these programs, including the supervisor section and other auxiliary FSMs for noise measurements, test, and messages, are contained in three cards.

VIII. DISCUSSION

The system described introduces the modeling in the form of abstract machines as a language for programing a general-purpose computer. The mathematical basis for this approach is the McCulloch-Pitts correspondence. The general procedure to make it practical is the FSM model.

From the viewpoint of automata theory, the following comments can be made. Automata have generally been used as mathematical tools, typically for demonstrating properties and for classifying processes or languages. The most outstanding case is the Turing machine used for defining the computability of a function. In this context, the simplicity of the machine has been of high interest, while the efficiency of its performance is completely irrelevant. As a consequence, there has not been as great an influence of automata theory on computer design as might be expected. Here instead, the purpose has been precisely to guide the design of real machines by taking advantage of already known properties of automata. The result is an automaton of high complexity in its description, but of high efficiency in its performance. The automaton can also be viewed as a universal finite-state machine.

From the viewpoint of an actual computer, the following characteristics can be outlined.

The program describes specialized processors rather than specialized sequences of given instructions. In other words, software is used to implement specialized hardware executing the desired process with simple, standard sequences rather than to command specialized sequences for executing the desired process with a simple, standard hardware. As a consequence, the CPL system shares the generality of the general-purpose computer with the efficiency of the special-purpose computer.

In conventional computers, the approach is to minimize the complexity of the machine (hardware) at the expense of the complexity of the problem description (software). Here the complexity of the software is minimized at the expense of the complexity of the hardware. The fact that a computer is designed only once and by specialized people, while programs are written many times by a variety of people, suggests that a trade-off might favor the second approach. Further analysis and experience are necessary to evaluate the possible advantages of FSM modeling over a plurality of specialized high-level languages.

An indication of the rationality of this approach is the following. In the conventional approach, the more complex the machine and the more extended the parallelism are (in order to increase the throughput), the lower the overall efficiency and the higher the complexity of the programing are. Here the higher the complexity of the machine, the larger is the overall efficiency of the machine and the simpler is the programing, as a consequence of the closer similarity between the FSM model of the process and the actual structure of the computer. The rationale of network programing lies in the fact that the number and the complexity of the functions that can be implemented directly increase very rapidly with little increase in the complexity of the loose network.

The suitability for real-time processing is readily apparent from the fast execution resulting from specialized networks. The circulation of the pages, each representing an independent process, makes the system easily suited for time-sharing uses.

One of the main causes of the small overhead in the CPL system is the negligible need of addresses. One can visualize the system (as far as each program is concerned) as a box that permanently contains the data of the problem; from time to time some old data disappear and some new data enter the box. Through these data, operating networks are passing in succession. These networks are called for by means of the present-state label. There is only one state label per page, and the range of this label is of the order of a few tens.

From experience, it is already clear that debugging a program in a CPL system is a deterministic task and can be easily executed by persons not familiar with the computer. This is a result of the fact that the user's model of the problem and the actual machine program are the same.

Given the complexity of the hardware, one might suspect that troubleshooting would constitute a serious problem. It turns out, on the contrary, that it is eased by the different paths of data flow that can be produced by routine programing.

As a conclusion, we can delineate the basic question relevant to the applicability of this system: whether the programing in the form of abstract machines will be felt by the majority of users as a too demanding task or, on the contrary, as a natural way of describing problems concisely and unambiguously.

ACKNOWLEDGEMENT

This work was supported in part by Grants NASr-158 and NSR-09-015-033 from the National Aeronautics and Space Administration.

REFERENCES

[1] W. S. McCulloch and W. Pitts, "A Logical Calculus of the Ideas Immanent in Nervous Activity," *Bull. Math. Biophys.*, **5**, 115–133 (1943).

[2] J. Von Neumann, "The General and Logical Theory of Automata," *Proc. Hixon Symp.* (California, September 1948). Reprinted in: A. H. Taub, "John Von Neumann Collected Works," V, 288–328 (Pergamon Press, 1963).

[3] E. F. Moore, "Gedanken-Experiments on Sequential Machines," *Automata Theory* (Annals of Mathematics Studies No. 34), 129–153 (Princeton University, 1956).

[4] D. A. Huffman, "The Synthesis of Sequential Switching Circuits," *J. Franklin Inst.*, **257**, 161–190, 275–303 (March, April 1954).

[5] M. L. Minsky, *Computation: Finite and Infinite Machines* (New Jersey: Prentice-Hall, 1967).

[6] F. C. Hennie, *Finite-State Models for Logical Machines* (New York: John Wiley, 1968).

[7] *Information Processing in the Nervous System* (K. N. Leibovic, Ed., New York: Springer-Verlag, 1969).

[8] C. E. Shannon, "A Universal Turing Machine with Two Internal States," *Automata Studies* (Annals of Mathematics Studies No. 34), 157–165 (Princeton University, 1956).

[9] M. A. Arbib, *Theories of Abstract Automata* (New Jersey: Prentice-Hall, 1969).

[10] M. R. Schaffner, "The Circulating Page Loose System, a New Solution for Data Processing," Research Rep. No. 15, Radio Meteor Project, Smithsonian Astrophysical Observatory, Cambridge, Mass. (1966).

[11] M. R. Schaffner, "CPL Processor for Weather Radar," *Proc. 13th Weather Conf.*, 328–331 (Massachusetts: Amer. Meteor. Soc., 1968).

[12] P. M. Austin and M. R. Schaffner, "Computations and Experiments Relevant to Digital Processing of Weather-Radar Echoes," *Prepr. 14th Weather Radar Conf.*, 375–380 (Massachusetts: Amer. Meteor. Soc., 1970).

INDEX TO CONTRIBUTORS